Paul and Tracey
AAA Members,
Bargain Hunters

At Days Inns our money gets the best mileage.

AAA Members: Save 10% - 30%* at 22 Days Inn® hotels in Western Canada and Alaska.

Just book and save at the AAA-approved Days Inn® locations listed in this Tourbook.® You'll get a free continental breakfast and a free national newspaper at most properties**. When you join TripRewards,® you can earn points that are good for an amazing selection of rewards. Not to mention special bonus offers for AAA Members all year long!

Show Your Card & Save

DAYS INN
The Best Value Under The Sun

For specific locations and reservations, call
1-800-432-9755 or
daysinn.com

Western Canada & Alaska

Are we meeting your travel needs?

Send written comments to:

AAA Member Comments
1000 AAA Drive, Box 61
Heathrow, FL 32746-5063

Published by:
AAA Publishing
1000 AAA Drive
Heathrow, FL 32746-5063
Copyright AAA 2005

**Advertising Rate and Circulation
Information**
Call: (407) 444-8280

Printed in the USA by Quebecor
World, Buffalo, NY

Photo Credit: (Cover & Title Page)
Yukon Territory, north of Whitehorse
© George Hunter / Robertstock

Western Canada & Alaska

■ Manitoba

■ Northwest Territories and Nunavut

■ Saskatchewan

■ Yukon Territory

■ Alaska

Featured Information

4

ALL I WANT IS...

Getting away just got better.

Want to plan a fun and affordable trip quickly and easily? Visit **aaa.com** to get exclusive travel information, find ways to save money and access easy-to-use travel planning tools.

Searchable TourBook®guides. Find AAA's famous TourBook travel information including: Approved hotels (get Diamond ratings, member discounts on room rates, plus online reservations), Approved restaurants, recommended attractions, local events, and detailed destination descriptions.

AAA TripTiks®. Create your own customized TripTik: get door-to-door driving directions and maps, find AAA Approved hotels and reserve a room, locate AAA recommended restaurants, and discover things to do and see at your destination and along the way.

AAA Drive Trips*. Review AAA recommended drive trips.

Vacation Getaways. Take to the skies, hit the high seas or select a tour and receive exclusive benefits from AAA's Preferred Travel Partners.

Travel Guides. Get a 5% discount on AAA's famed travel guides at aaa.com/barnesandnoble.

Disney® Vacations. Get exclusive benefits and savings on AAA Vacations® Disney vacation packages.

Hertz Rental. Save up to 20% on car rental.

Show Your Card & Save. Search for savings on lodging, travel, entertainment, retail, and e-merchants.

AAA Travel Money. Get no-fee travelers cheques, foreign currency and prepaid cards.

AAA Map Gallery*. Know the best way to go wherever you travel.

Cash Back. Get up to a 5% rebate every time you use your AAA credit card to gas up.

AAA Approved Auto Repair. Find your nearest AAR shop to get your car ready for the road.

Travel to aaa.com to do all your vacation planning!

aaa.com

Travel With Someone You Trust®

*Products and Services available through participating AAA and CAA Clubs.

Smithsonian
National Museum of American History
Behring Center

See how we got here.

Immerse yourself in a new museum experience and explore how transportation has changed America. National Museum of American History, Washington, D.C. americanhistory.si.edu/onthemove.

AMERICA
ON THE MOVE

Trust
the AAA TourBook® guide for objective travel information. Follow the pages of the TourBook Navigator to thoroughly understand this unique member benefit.

Making Your Way Through the AAA Listings

Attractions, lodgings and restaurants are listed on the basis of merit alone after careful evaluation, approval and rating by one of our full-time, professionally trained Tourism Editors. Annual evaluations are unannounced to ensure that our Tourism Editors see an establishment just as our members would see it.

Those lodgings and restaurants listed with an **fyi** icon have not gone through the same evaluation process as other rated properties. Individual listings will typically denote the reason why this icon appears. Bulleted recreational activity listings are not inspected but are included for member information.

An establishment's decision to advertise in the TourBook guide has no bearing on its evaluation or rating. Advertising for services or products does not imply AAA endorsement.

How the TourBook is
Organized

Geographic listing is used for accuracy and consistency. This means attractions, lodgings and restaurants are listed under the city in which they physically are located—or in some cases under the nearest recognized city. The Comprehensive City Index located in the back of the book contains an A-to-Z list of cities. Most listings are alphabetically organized by state, province, region or island; city; and establishment name. A color is assigned to each state or province so that you can match the color bars at the top of the page to switch from ❶ Points of Interest to ❷ Lodgings and Restaurants.

Destination Cities and Destination Areas

The TourBook guide also groups information by destination city and destination area. If a city is grouped in a destination vicinity section, the city name will appear at its alphabetical location in the book, and a handy cross reference will give the exact page on which listings for that city begin. Maps are placed at the beginning of these sections to orient you to the destinations.

❸ **Destination cities**, established based on government models and local expertise, are comprised of metropolitan areas plus nearby vicinity cities.

Destination areas are regions with broad tourist appeal. Several cities will comprise the area.

All information in this TourBook guide was reviewed for accuracy before publication. However, since changes inevitably occur between annual editions, we suggest you contact establishments directly to confirm prices and schedules.

Points of Interest Section

Orientation maps

near the start of each Attractions section show only those places we call points of interest. Coordinates included with the city listings depict the locations of those cities on the map. A GEM symbol (⬇) accents towns with "must see" points of interest which offer a *Great Experience for Members*®. And the black ovals with white numerals (**22** for example) locate items listed in the nearby Recreation Areas chart.

Destination area maps

illustrate key travel areas defined by local travel experts. Communities shown have listings for AAA approved attractions.

National park maps

represent the area in and around the park. Some campground sites and lodges spotted on the maps do not meet AAA/CAA criteria, but are shown for members who nevertheless wish to stay close to the park area.

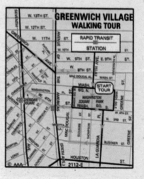

Walking or self-guiding tour maps

correspond to specific routes described in TourBook guide text.

City maps

show areas where numerous points of interest are concentrated and indicate their location in relation to major roads, parks, airports and other landmarks.

Lodgings & Restaurants Section

Destination area maps
illustrate key travel areas defined by local travel experts. Communities shown have listings for AAA-RATED® lodgings and/or restaurants.

Spotting maps
show the location of lodgings and restaurants. Lodgings are spotted with a black background (**22** for example); restaurants are spotted with a white background (**23** for example). Spotting map indexes have been placed immediately after each map to provide the user with a convenient method to identify what an area has to offer at a glance. The index references the map page number where the property is spotted, indicates if a property is an Official Appointment and contains an advertising reference if applicable. It also lists the property's diamond rating, high season rate range and listing page number.

Downtown/city spotting maps
are provided when spotted facilities are very concentrated. GEM points of interest also appear on these maps.

Vicinity spotting maps
spot those properties that are outside the downtown or city area. Major roads, landmarks, airports and GEM points of interest are shown on vicinity spotting maps as well. The names of suburban communities that have AAA-RATED® accommodations are shown in magenta type.

Featured Information Section

Driving distance maps
are intended to be used only for trip-distance and driving-time planning.

Sample Attraction Listing

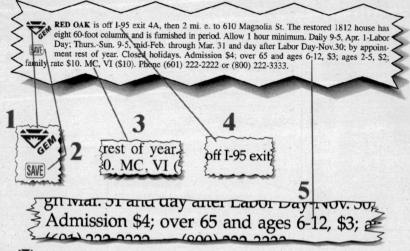

RED OAK is off I-95 exit 4A, then 2 mi. e. to 610 Magnolia St. The restored 1812 house has eight 60-foot columns and is furnished in period. Allow 1 hour minimum. Daily 9-5, Apr. 1-Labor Day; Thurs.-Sun. 9-5, mid-Feb. through Mar. 31 and day after Labor Day-Nov.30; by appointment rest of year. Closed holidays. Admission $4; over 65 and ages 6-12, $3; ages 2-5, $2; family rate $10. MC, VI ($10). Phone (601) 222-2222 or (800) 222-3333.

1   **3**   **4**

2

rest of year. 0. MC, VI (

off I-95 exit

5

gh Mar. 31 and day after Labor Day-Nov. 30;

Admission $4; over 65 and ages 6-12, $3; a

(601) 222-2222 (800) 222-2222

1   This attraction is of exceptional interest and quality and therefore has been designated a AAA GEM—offering a *Great Experience for Members*®.

2   SAVE Participating attractions offer AAA/CAA, AAA MasterCard or AAA Visa cardholders a discount off the attraction's standard admission; members should inquire in advance concerning the validity of the discount for special rates. Present your card at the admission desk. A list of participating points of interest appears in the Indexes section of the book. The SAVE discount may not be used in conjunction with other discounts. Attractions that already provide a reduced senior or child rate may not honor the SAVE discount for those age groups. All offers are subject to change and may not apply during special events, particular days or seasons or for the entire validity period of the TourBook. Shopping establishments preceded by a SAVE icon also provide discounts and/or gift with purchase to AAA/CAA members; present your card at the mall's customer service center to receive your benefit.

3
AX=American Express	DS=Discover	MC=MasterCard
CB=Carte Blanche	JC=Japan Credit Bureau	VI=VISA
DC=Diners Club		

4   Unless otherwise specified, directions are given from the center of town, using the following highway designations: I (interstate highway), US (federal highway), Hwy. (Canadian or Caribbean highway), SR (state route), CR (county road), FM (farm to market road), FR (forest road), MM (mile marker), Mex. (Mexican highway).

5   Admission prices are quoted without sales tax. Children under the lowest age specified are admitted free when accompanied by an adult. Days, months and age groups written with a hyphen are inclusive. Prices pertaining to points of interest in the United States are quoted in U.S. dollars; prices for Canadian province and territory points of interest are quoted in Canadian dollars; prices for points of interest in Mexico and the Caribbean are quoted as an approximate U.S. dollar equivalent.

Bulleted Listings: Casino gambling establishments are visited by AAA personnel to ensure safety; casinos within hotels are presented for member information regardless of whether the lodging is AAA approved. Recreational activities of a participatory nature (requiring physical exertion or special skills) are not inspected. Wineries are inspected by AAA Tourism Editors to ensure they meet listing requirements and offer tours. All are presented in a bulleted format for informational purposes.

These Show Your Card & Save® partners provide the listed member benefits. Admission tickets that offer greater discounts may be available for purchase at the local AAA/CAA club. The discount applies to the cardholder; the attraction, at its discretion, may also offer the discount to up to five family members.

Attraction Partners

SeaWorld/Busch Gardens (aaa.com/seaworld)

SAVE Save $5 on general admission at the gate at SeaWorld and Busch Gardens

SAVE Save $3 on general admission at the gate at Sesame Place, Water Country USA and Adventure Island

SAVE Save 10% on select up-close dining. Reservations are required; visit Guest Relations for details

Six Flags Theme Parks

SAVE Save $4 on general admission at the gate

SAVE Save $12 on general admission at the gate each Wednesday

SAVE Save 10% on selected souvenirs and dining (check at main gate for details)

Universal Orlando (aaa.com/universal)

SAVE Save $4 on a 2-day/2-park pass or $5 on a 3-day/2-park pass at Universal Orlando's theme parks (savings apply to tickets purchased at the gate)

SAVE Save 10% on select dining and souvenirs at both Universal Orlando theme parks and at select Universal CityWalk Orlando restaurants (except Emeril's)

Universal Studios Hollywood (aaa.com/universal)

SAVE Save $3 on a 1-day Universal Studios pass (savings applies to tickets purchased at the gate)

SAVE Save 10% on select dining and souvenirs at Universal Studios Hollywood and Universal CityWalk

Gray Line (aaa.com/grayline)

SAVE Save 10% on sightseeing tours of 1 day or less

Restaurant Partners

Landry's Seafood House, The Crab House, Chart House, Muer Seafood Restaurants, Joe's Crab Shack

SAVE Save 10% on food and non-alcoholic beverages at Landry's Seafood House, The Crab House, Chart House, Muer Seafood Restaurants and Joe's Crab Shack and 10% on merchandise at Joe's Crab Shack. Savings applicable to AAA/CAA member and up to five additional people

Hard Rock Cafe

SAVE Save 10% on food, non-alcoholic beverages and merchandise at all U.S. and select Canadian and international locations. Savings applicable to AAA/CAA member and up to five additional people.

Visit aaa.com to discover all the great Show Your Card & Save® discounts in your area.

Sample Lodging Listing

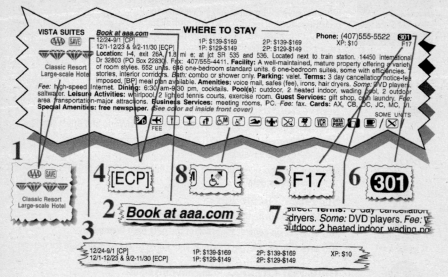

1 ⒶⒶⒶ or ⒶⒶ indicates our Official Appointment (OA) lodgings. The OA program permits properties to display and advertise the ⒶⒶⒶ or ⒶⒶ emblem. We highlight these properties with red diamonds and classification. Some OA listings include special amenities such as free continental breakfast; expanded continental breakfast or full breakfast; early check-in/late check-out; free room upgrade or preferred room, such as ocean view or poolside (subject to availability); free local phone calls; and free daily newspaper. This does not imply that only these properties offer these amenities. The ⒶⒶⒶ or ⒶⒶ sign helps traveling members find accommodations that want member business.

▼▼▼ ▼▼▼ or ▼▼▼▼▼ The number of diamonds—not the color—informs you of the overall level of quality in a lodging's amenities and service. More diamond details appear on page 16.

Classic Resort Large-scale Hotel or Classic Resort Large-scale Hotel: All diamond rated lodgings are classified using three key elements: style of operation, overall concept and service level. See pages 22-23 for details about our Lodging Classifications and Subclassifications.

Member Values

⟨SAVE⟩ Official Appointment properties guarantee members a minimum 10% discount off the standard room rates published in TourBook guides or the lowest public rate available at the time of booking for the dates of stay, for standard rooms.

⟨S/D⟩ Establishments offer a minimum senior discount of 10% off the listed rates. This discount is available to members 60 or older.

⟨ASK⟩ Many properties offer discounts to members even though the lodgings do not participate in a formal discount program. The ⟨ASK⟩ is another reminder to inquire about available discounts when making your reservations or at check-in.

Discounts normally offered at some lodgings may not apply during special events or holiday periods. Special rates and discounts may not apply to all room types. Some Member Values may not apply in Mexico or the Caribbean.

To obtain published rates or discounts, you must identify yourself as a AAA or CAA member, request AAA rates when making reservations and have written confirmation sent to you. The SAVE or senior discount may not be used in conjunction with other discounts. At registration, show your membership card and verify the room rate.

Discounts normally offered at some lodgings may not apply during special events or holiday periods. Special rates and discounts may not apply to all room types. Some Member Values may not apply in Mexico or the Caribbean.

The rates listed for approved properties are provided to AAA by each lodging and represent the regular (rack) rate for a standard room. Printed rates, based on rack rates and last room availability, are rounded to the nearest dollar. Rates do not include taxes and discounts. U.S., Mexican and Caribbean rates are in U.S. dollars; rates for Canadian lodgings are in Canadian dollars.

2 Book at aaa.com - Internet Reservations
Indicates AAA/CAA members can conveniently check room availability and make reservations in a secure online environment at aaa.com.

3 Rate Lines
Shown from left to right: dates the rates are effective; meal plan provided with rates (see Meal Plan Indicators-if no plan noted, rate includes room only); rates for 1 person or 2 persons; extra person charge (XP); and any applicable family plan indicator.

Rates Guaranteed
AAA/CAA members are guaranteed that they will not be charged more than the maximum regular rate printed in each rate range for a standard room. Rates may vary within the range depending on season and room type. Listed rates are based on last standard room availability. Rates for properties operating as concessionaires for the U.S. National Park Service are not guaranteed due to governing regulations. Rates in the Mexico TourBook are not guaranteed and may fluctuate based on the exchange rate of the peso.

Exceptions
Lodgings may temporarily increase room rates, not recognize discounts or modify pricing policies during special events. Examples of special events range from Mardi Gras and Kentucky Derby (including pre-Derby events) to college football games, holidays, holiday periods and state fairs. Although some special events are listed in AAA/CAA TourBook guides, it is always wise to check, in advance, with AAA travel professionals for specific dates.

Discounts
Member discounts will apply to rates quoted, within the rate range, applicable at the time of booking. Special rates used in advertising, and special short-term, promotional rates lower than the lowest listed rate in the range, are not subject to additional member discounts.

4 Meal Plan Indicators
The following types of meal plans may be available in the listed room rate:
AP = American Plan of three meals daily
BP = Breakfast Plan of full hot breakfast
CP = Continental Plan of pastry, juice and another beverage
ECP = Expanded Continental Plan, which offers a wider variety of breakfast items
MAP = Modified American Plan of two meals daily
See individual listing "Terms" section for additional meal plans that are not included in the room rate.

> Check-in times are shown in the listing only if they are after 3 p.m.; check-out times are shown only if they are before 10 a.m.

5 Family Plan Indicators
F = Children stay free
D = Discounts for children
F17 = Children 17 and under stay free (age displayed will reflect property's policy)
D17 = Discount for children 17 and under

6 Lodging Locators
Black ovals with white numbers are used to locate, or "spot," lodgings on maps we provide for larger cities.

7 Unit Types
Unit types, amenities and room features preceded by the word "Some" indicate the item is available on a limited basis, potentially within only one unit.

8 Lodging Icons
A row of icons is included with each lodging listing. These icons represent the member values, member services, and facilities offered by that lodging. See page 19 for an explanation of each icon.

The Lodging Diamond Ratings

AAA Tourism Editors evaluate and rate each lodging based on the overall quality, the range of facilities and the level of services offered by a property. The size, age and overall appeal of an establishment are considered as well as regional architectural style and design.

While guest services are an important part of all diamond ratings, they are particularly critical at the four and five diamond levels. A property must provide a high level of service, on a consistent basis, to obtain and support the four and five diamond rating.

These establishments typically appeal to the budget-minded traveler. They provide essential, no-frills accommodations. They meet the basic requirements pertaining to comfort, cleanliness, and hospitality.

These establishments appeal to the traveler seeking more than the basic accommodations. There are modest enhancements to the overall physical attributes, design elements, and amenities of the facility typically at a modest price.

These establishments appeal to the traveler with comprehensive needs. Properties are multifaceted with a distinguished style, including marked upgrades in the quality of physical attributes, amenities and level of comfort provided.

These establishments are upscale in all areas. Accommodations are progressively more refined and stylish. The physical attributes reflect an obvious enhanced level of quality throughout. The fundamental hallmarks at this level include an extensive array of amenities combined with a high degree of hospitality, service, and attention to detail.

These establishments reflect the characteristics of the ultimate in luxury and sophistication. Accommodations are first-class. The physical attributes are extraordinary in every manner. The fundamental hallmarks at this level are to meticulously serve and exceed all guest expectations while maintaining an impeccable standard of excellence. Many personalized services and amenities enhance an unmatched level of comfort.

The lodging listings with fyi in place of diamonds are included as an "information only" service for members. The icon indicates that a property has not been rated for one or more of the following reasons: too new to rate; under construction; under major renovation; not evaluated; or may not meet all AAA requirements. Those properties not meeting all AAA requirements are included for either their member value or because it may be the only accommodation available in the area. Listing prose will give insight as to why the fyi designation was assigned.

Guest Safety

Room Security

In order to be approved for listing in AAA/CAA TourBook guides for the United States and Canada, all lodgings must comply with AAA's guest room security requirements.

In response to AAA/CAA members' concern about their safety at properties, AAA-RATED® accommodations must have dead-bolt locks on all guest room entry doors and connecting room doors.

If the area outside the guest room door is not visible from inside the room through a window or door panel, viewports must be installed on all guest room entry doors. Bed and breakfast properties and country inns are not required to have viewports. Ground floor and easily accessible sliding doors must be equipped with some other type of secondary security locks.

Tourism Editors view a percentage of rooms at each property since it is not feasible to evaluate every room in every lodging establishment. Therefore, AAA cannot guarantee that there are working locks on all doors and windows in all guest rooms.

Fire Safety

Because of the highly specialized skills needed to conduct professional fire safety inspections, AAA/CAA Tourism Editors cannot assess fire safety.

Properties must meet all federal, state and local fire codes. Each guest unit in all U.S. and Canadian lodging properties must be equipped with an operational, single-station smoke detector. A AAA/CAA Tourism Editor has evaluated a sampling of the rooms to verify this equipment is in place.

For additional fire safety information, read the page posted on the back of your guest room door, or write:

National Fire Protection Association
1 Batterymarch Park
P.O. Box 9101
Quincy, MA 02269-9101

Requirements for some features, such as door locks and smoke detectors/sprinkler systems, differ in Mexico and the Caribbean. If a property met AAA's security requirements at the time of the evaluation, the phrase "Meets AAA guest room security requirements" appears in the listing.

Access for Mature Travelers and Travelers with Disabilities

Qualified properties listed in this guide are shown with symbols indicating they meet the needs of the hearing-impaired or offer some accessible features for mature travelers or travelers with disabilities.

Hearing Impaired

Indicates a property has the following equipment available for hearing-impaired travelers: TDD at front desk or switchboard; visual notification of fire alarm, incoming telephone calls, door knock or bell; closed caption decoder; text telephone or TDD for guest room use; telephone amplification device, with shelf or electric outlet next to guest room telephone.

Accessible Features

Indicates a property has some accessible features meeting the needs of mature travelers and travelers with disabilities. Lodging establishments will provide at least one guest room meeting the designated criteria as well as accessible restrooms and parking facilities. Restaurants provide accessible parking, dining rooms and restrooms.

AAA/CAA strongly urges members to call the property directly to fully understand the property's exact accessibility features. Some properties do not fully comply with AAA/CAA's exacting accessibility standards but may offer some design standards that meet the needs of some guests with disabilities.

AAA/CAA does not evaluate recreational facilities, banquet rooms, or convention or meeting facilities for accessibility.

Service Animals

No fees or deposits, even those normally charged for pets, may be charged for service animals. Service animals fulfill a critical need for their owners—they are *not* pets.

The Americans With Disabilities Act (ADA) prohibits U.S. businesses that serve the public from discriminating against persons with disabilities. Some businesses have mistakenly denied access to persons who use service animals. ADA, a federal mandate, has priority over all state and local laws, as well as a business owner's standard of business, which might bar animals from the premises. Businesses must permit entry to guests and their service animals, as well as allow service animals to accompany guests to all public areas of a property. A property is permitted to ask whether the animal is a service animal or a pet, and whether the guest has a disability. The property may not, however, ask questions about the nature of the disability, the service provided by the animal or require proof of a disability or certification that the animal is a service animal.

Note: These regulations may not apply in Canada, Mexico or the Caribbean.

What The Lodging Icons Mean

NAVIGATOR • Lodgings

Member Values
(see p. 14)

AAA or **AA** Official Appointment

SAVE Offers minimum 10% discount or lowest public rate *(see p. 14)*

ASK May offer discount

S/D Offers senior discount

fyi Informational listing only

Member Services

➕ Airport transportation

🐾 Pets allowed

🍽 Restaurant on premises

🍽→ Restaurant off premises (walking distance)

24 24-hour room service

🍸 Cocktail lounge

👶 Child care

Accessibility Feature
(see p. 18)

&M Accessible features

♿ Roll-in showers

👂 Hearing impaired

Safety Features
(Mexico and Caribbean only)

S Sprinklers

D Smoke detectors

Leisure Activities

🎲 Full service casino

🏊 Pool

💪 Health club on premises

💪→ Health club off premises

✖ Recreational activities

In-Room Amenities

✖ Designated non-smoking rooms

AC No air conditioning

TV No TV

CTV No cable TV

VCR VCR

🎬 Movies

DATA PORT Data port/modem line

✆ No telephones

🍱 Refrigerator

🍱 Microwave

☕ Coffee maker

Availability and Additional Fees

If an in-room amenity is available only on a limited basis (in one or more rooms), the term "SOME UNITS" will appear above those icons. Fees may be charged for some of the services represented by the icons listed here. The word "FEE" will appear below each icon when an extra charge applies.

SOME UNITS

&M 👂 **VCR** 🎬 ☕ / ✖ **DATA PORT** 🍱 /
FEE FEE   FEE

Preferred Lodging Partners

AAA. Every Day.

SAVINGS. SELECTION. SATISFACTION. — When contacting one of the partners listed, you will be given AAA's best rates for your dates of stay. Your valid membership card must be presented at check-in.

SATISFACTION GUARANTEE — If you are not satisfied with any part of your stay, you must provide the property the opportunity to correct the situation during your stay. If the matter cannot be resolved, you will be entitled to recompense for a portion of, or your entire, stay. Satisfaction guarantee varies by chain.

Select the chain you want and have your membership card available when making a reservation and checking in.

Making Reservations

When making reservations, you must identify yourself as a AAA or CAA member. Give all pertinent information about your planned stay. Ask about the lodging's pet policy, or the availability of any other special feature that is important to your stay. Request written confirmation to guarantee: type of room, rate, dates of stay, and cancellation and refund policies. At registration, show your membership card. Note: Age restrictions may apply.

Confirm Deposit, Refund and Cancellation Policies

Most establishments give full deposit refunds if they have been notified at least 48 hours before the normal check-in time. Listing prose will note if more than 48 hours notice is required for cancellation. However, when making reservations, confirm the property's deposit, cancellation and refund policies. Some properties may charge a cancellation or handling fee.

When this applies, "cancellation fee imposed" will appear in the listing. If you cancel too late, you have little recourse if a refund is denied.

When an establishment requires a full or partial payment in advance, and your trip is cut short, a refund may not be given.

When canceling reservations, phone the lodging immediately. Make a note of the date and time you called, the cancellation number if there is one, and the name of the person who handled the cancellation. If your AAA/CAA club made your reservation, allow them to make the cancellation for you as well so you will have proof of cancellation.

Review Charges for Appropriate Rates

When you are charged more than the maximum rate listed in the TourBook guide for a standard room, question the additional charge. If management refuses to adhere to the published rate, pay for the room and submit your receipt and membership number to AAA/CAA within 30 days. Include all pertinent information: dates of stay, rate paid, itemized paid receipts, number of persons in your party, the room number you occupied, and list any extra room equipment used. A refund of the amount paid in excess of the stated maximum will be made if our investigation indicates that unjustified charging has occurred.

Get the Room You Reserved

When you find your room is not as specified, and you have written confirmation of reservations for a certain type of accommodation, you should be given the option of choosing a different room or finding one elsewhere. Should you choose to go elsewhere and a refund is refused or resisted, submit the matter to AAA/CAA within 30 days along with complete documentation, including your reasons for refusing the room and copies of your written confirmation and any receipts or canceled checks associated with this problem.

How to Get the Best Room Rates

You'll find the best room rate if you book your reservation in advance with the help of a travel professional or agent at your local AAA/CAA office.

If you're not yet ready to make firm vacation plans or if you prefer a more spontaneous trip, take advantage of the partnerships that preferred hotel chains have arranged with AAA. Phone the toll-free number 866-AAA-SAVE that has been set up exclusively for members for the purpose of reserving with these Show Your Card & Save® chain partners.

Even if you were unable to make a reservation, be sure to show your membership card at the desk and ask if you're being offered the lowest rate available for that time. Many lodgings offer reduced rates to members.

Lodging Classifications

To ensure that your lodging needs/preferences are met, we recommend that you consider an establishment's classification when making your travel choices.

While the quality and comfort at properties with the same diamond rating should be consistent (regardless of the classification), there are differences in typical décor/theme elements, range of facilities and service levels. Please see the descriptions below.

Hotel Royal Plaza, Lake Buena Vista, FL

Large-scale Hotel

A multistory establishment with interior room entrances. A variety of guest unit styles is offered. Public areas are spacious and include a variety of facilities such as a restaurant, shops, fitness center, spa, business center, or meeting rooms.

Small-scale Hotel

A multistory establishment typically with interior room entrances. A variety of guest unit styles is offered. Public areas are limited in size and/or the variety of facilities available.

Baymont Inn, Dallas/Ft. Worth-Airport North, TX

Best Western Deltona Inn, Deltona, FL

Motel

A one- to three-story establishment typically with exterior room entrances facilitating convenient access to parking. The standard guest units have one bedroom with a bathroom and are typically similar in décor and design throughout. Public areas are limited in size and/or the variety of facilities available.

Country Inn

Similar in definition to a bed and breakfast, but usually larger in scale with spacious public areas and offers a dining facility that serves at least breakfast and dinner.

Greenville Inn, Greenville, ME

1884 Paxton House Inn, Thomasville, GA

Bed & Breakfast

Small-scale properties emphasizing a high degree of personal touches that provide guests an "at home" feeling. Guest units tend to be individually decorated. Rooms may not include some modern amenities such as televisions and telephones, and may have a shared bathroom. Usually owner-operated with a common room or parlor separate from the innkeeper's living quarters, where guests and operators can interact during evening and breakfast hours. Evening office closures are normal. A continental or full, hot breakfast is served and is included in the room rate.

Condominium

Vacation-oriented or extended-stay, apartment-style accommodations that are routinely available for rent through a management company. Units vary in design and décor and often contain one or more bedrooms, living room, full kitchen, and an eating area. Studio-type models combine the sleeping and living areas into one room. Typically, basic cleaning supplies, kitchen utensils and complete bed and bath linens are supplied. The guest registration area may be located off-site.

Sands of Kahana, Kahana, Maui, HI

Cabin/Cottage

Vacation-oriented, small-scale, freestanding houses or cabins. Units vary in design and décor and often contain one or more bedrooms, living room, kitchen, dining area, and bathroom. Studio-type models combine the sleeping and living areas into one room. Typically, basic cleaning supplies, kitchen utensils, and complete bed and bath linens are supplied. The guest registration area may be located off-site.

Desert Rose Inn, Bluff, UT

Ranch

Typically a working ranch with an obvious rustic, Western theme. In general, equestrian-related activities are featured, but ranches may include other animals and activities as well. A variety of guest unit styles is offered in a family-oriented atmosphere.

Lost Valley Ranch, Deckers, CO

Vacation Home

Vacation-oriented or extended-stay, large-scale, freestanding houses that are routinely available for rent through a management company. Houses vary in design and décor and often contain two or more bedrooms, living room, full kitchen, dining room, and multiple bathrooms. Typically, basic cleaning supplies, kitchen utensils, and complete bed and bath linens are supplied. The guest registration area may be located off-site.

ResortQuest, Hilton Head Island, SC

Lodging Subclassifications

The following are subclassifications that may appear along with the classifications listed above to provide a more specific description of the lodging.

Casino

Extensive gambling facilities are available such as blackjack, craps, keno, and slot machines. **Note:** This subclassification will not appear beneath its diamond rating in the listing. It will be indicated by a dice icon and will be included in the row of icons immediately below the lodging listing.

Classic

Renowned and landmark properties, older than 50 years, well-known for their unique style and ambience.

Historic

These properties are typically over 75 years of age and exhibit many features of a historic nature with respect to architecture, design, furnishings, public record, or acclaim. Properties must meet one of the following criteria:
- Maintained the integrity of the historical nature
- Listed on the U.S. National Register of Historic Places
- Designated a U.S. National Historic Landmark
- Located in a U.S. National Register Historic District

Separate criteria designate historic properties in Canada, Mexico and the Caribbean.

Resort

Recreation-oriented, geared to vacation travelers seeking a specific destination experience. Travel packages, meal plans, theme entertainment, and social and recreational programs are typically available. Recreational facilities are extensive and may include spa treatments, golf, tennis, skiing, fishing, or water sports, etc. Larger resorts may offer a variety of guest accommodations.

Sample Restaurant Listing

WHERE TO DINE

THE SEASONS RESTAURANT *Menu on aaa.com* **Dinner:** $16-$36 **Phone:** 336/555-5555 ⑤
Location: On I-459, exit 13 (US 31); 0.3 mi n of jct SR 892. 1000 Ocean Blvd 35244. **Hours:** 6 pm-10 pm. Closed Mon, also Tues 5/1-11/15. **Reservations:** suggested. **Features:** Guests are in for a treat at this top-notch establishment. Dining is an all-around pleasurable experience—from the wait staff's casually elegant service approach to the tranquil, oceanfront setting to the striking grounds views from the cozy dining area. The chef transforms ingredients, based on what is seasonally and regionally available, into mouthwatering dishes. Decadent desserts put an exclamation mark on the meal. Dressy casual attire; cocktails; entertainment. **Parking:** valet. **Cards:** AX, CB, DC, DS, MC, VI. **Classic**

Regional American

2 **Dinner: $16-$36** **5** **Classic** **6** ⑤

1 Regional American

3 **Cards:** AX, DC, DS, MC, VI.

Menu on aaa.com

4

---

1 🔺🔺🔺 or 🔺🔺🔺 indicates our Official Appointment (OA) restaurants. The OA program permits properties to display and advertise the 🔺🔺🔺 or 🔺🔺🔺 emblem. We highlight these properties with red diamonds and cuisine type. The 🔺🔺🔺 or 🔺🔺🔺 sign helps traveling members find restaurants that want member business.

▽▽▽ or ▽▽▽▽ The number of diamonds—not the color—informs you of the overall level of quality for food and presentation, service and ambience. Menus for red Diamond restaurants can be viewed on <u>aaa.com.</u>

A cuisine type is assigned for each restaurant listing. AAA currently recognizes more than 90 different cuisine types.

2 Prices represent the minimum and maximum entree cost per person. Exceptions may include one-of-a-kind or special market priced items.

3 AX = American Express
CB = Carte Blanche
DC = Diners Club
DS = Discover
JC = Japan Credit Bureau
MC = MasterCard
VI = VISA

4 These three icons are used in restaurant listings. When present, they indicate: the presence of a cocktail lounge, the lack of air conditioning, and/or that the restaurant has a designated non-smoking section or is entirely smoke-free.

5 If applicable, restaurants may be further defined as:

Classic—renowned and landmark restaurant operations in business longer than 25 years, known for unique style and ambience.

Historic—properties must meet one of the following criteria:
- Listed on the U.S. National Register of Historic Places
- Designated a U.S. National Historic Landmark
- Located in a U.S. National Register Historic District

Separate criteria designate historic properties in Canada, Mexico and the Caribbean.

6 These white ovals with black numbers serve as restaurant locators and are used to locate, or "spot," restaurants on maps we provide for larger cities.

The Restaurant Diamond Ratings

AAA Tourism Editors are responsible for determining a restaurant's diamond rating based on established criteria.

These criteria were established with input from AAA trained professionals, members and restaurant industry experts. They are purposely broad to capture what is typically seen throughout the restaurant industry at each diamond rating level.

A one diamond restaurant must meet basic requirements pertaining to management, cleanliness and overall quality. The primary focus is on providing wholesome, straightforward and familiar food at an economical price. Generally, the menu selection is limited to a restaurant's specialty, such as hamburgers, fried chicken, pizza or tacos. Service is limited, in many instances self service, and the surroundings are often utilitarian.

A two diamond restaurant displays noticeable enhancements to food presentation such as the use of common garnishes in combination with the dishware. Typically, the menu offers a wide selection featuring familiar favorites or home-style foods often cooked to order and reasonably priced. The service, while often limited, is plain-speaking and relaxed. The surroundings, while limited in scope, typically reflect a clear theme. All elements combine to provide a familiar, often family-oriented experience.

A three diamond restaurant often employs a professional chef and a supporting staff of highly trained cooks. The menu is skillfully prepared and often reflects interpretations of the latest trends or a mastering of traditional cuisine. Typically, there are expanded offerings of beverages in compliment to the menu such as, international/regional wines, specialty beers, cocktails and soft drinks. The front of the house is headed by a professional dining room manager with a compliment of efficient service staff. The service reflects some degree of refinement such as reservations accepted, personal assistance or the ability to adapt to a guests's specific needs. The decor reflects the use of well-coordinated design mediums that provide a distinct theme and good comfort. Restaurants at this level convey an entry into fine dining and are often positioned as an adult-oriented experience.

A four diamond restaurant is geared to individuals in search of a distinctive fine-dining experience. Often orchestrated by an executive chef and an accomplished staff, menus reflect a high degree of creativity and complexity using imaginative presentations to enhance high quality, market fresh ingredients. The equally proficient service staff demonstrates a strong desire to meet or exceed guest expectations. A wine steward is typically available to provide menu-specific knowledge on wine selection. The ambiance is highly refined, comfortable and well coordinated incorporating quality materials and a variety of upscale design enhancements that give a first-class impression. The overall dining experience is typically expensive.

A five diamond restaurant is renowned and consistently provides a world-class experience. This is *haute cuisine* at its best. Menus are cutting edge, using only the finest ingredients available. Food is prepared in a manner that is highly imaginative and unique. The combination of technique and ingredients is extraordinary reflecting the impeccable artistry and awareness of highly acclaimed chefs. A maitre d' heads an expert service staff that exceeds guest expectations by attending to every detail in an effortless and unobtrusive manner.

The restaurants with fyi in place of diamonds are included as an "information only" service for members. These establishments provide additional dining choices but have not yet been evaluated.

YOU'RE READY...

NOW YOU'RE READY FOR ANYTHING.

Travellers Cheques

Available in Canadian
Dollars, US Dollars, Euros,
and Pounds Sterling; CAA
VISA® Travellers Cheques
are accepted worldwide.

Cash Passport Card

With CAA Cash Passport
you can withdraw cash
in the local currency
from any VISA ATM in
the world.

Foreign Currency

We supply over 100
different currencies
and can advise which
is the best for your
destination.

CAA TRAVEL MONEY
Know Before You Go.

Visit Participating CAA offices   **Click** caa.ca and go to Travel   **Call** 866-339-3378

Savings for all Seasons

Hertz rents Fords and other fine cars, ® REG. U.S. PAT. OFF. © HERTZ SYSTEM INC., 1999/2006-99

No matter the season, Hertz offers CAA members exclusive discounts and benefits.

Operating in 150 countries at over 7,000 locations, Hertz makes traveling more convenient and efficient wherever and whenever you go. Hertz offers CAA members discounts up to 20% on car rentals worldwide.

To receive your exclusive CAA member discounts and benefits, mention your CAA membership card at time of reservation and present it at time of rental. **In addition**, to receive a free one car class upgrade, in the United States mention PC# 929714, in Canada mention PC# 929725 and in Puerto Rico mention PC# 929736 at the time of reservation. Offer available through 12/15/05.

For reservations and program details, call your CAA Travel office or the Hertz/CAA Desk at **1-800-263-0600; Toronto (416) 620-9620.**

28

Get More for Your Money

Get more for your money at any of the following merchants:

Stay
Call 866-AAA-SAVE
Best Western
Comfort Inn
Comfort Suites
Quality Inn
Clarion
Sleep Inn
Mainstay Suites
Econo Lodge
Rodeway Inn
Days Inn
Hampton Inn
Hampton Inn & Suites
Hyatt Hotels
La Quinta Inn
La Quinta Inn & Suites
Marriott Hotels, Resorts, Suites
Renaissance Hotels
Courtyard by Marriott
Fairfield Inn
Residence Inn
SpringHill Suites
TownePlace Suites

Play
Busch Gardens®
SeaWorld®
Sesame Place®
Water Country USA®
Adventure Island®
Hard Rock Cafe®
Hard Rock Vault®
Chart House®
Muer Seafood Restaurants®
Joe's Crab Shack®
The Crab House®
Landry's Seafood House®
Six Flags
Universal Orlando
Universal CityWalk Orlando
Universal Studios Hollywood
Universal CityWalk Hollywood

Go
Hertz Car Rental
  800-654-3080
Aloha Airlines
AAA Visa® Traveler's Cheques
AAA Cash Passport Card
Travelex Foreign Currency
Amtrak®
Gray Line Tours
  www.aaa.com/grayline

Shop
AAA Visa® Gift Cards
Casual Corner®
Petite Sophisticate®
August Max Woman®
Greg Norman Outlet Stores
Hertz Car Sales
LensCrafters
NAPA
Penske Truck Rental
Prime Outlets
Ralph Lauren Footwear Outlet Stores
Reebok Outlet Stores
Rockport Outlet Stores

Shop America VIP
Sunglass Hut
Tanger Outlets
Wal-Mart Pharmacy
Watch Station
Watch World

Click
www.ftd.com/aaa
www.aaa.com/hickoryfarms
www.aaa.com/inmotionpictures

Your AAA/CAA membership card also saves you money when you travel outside the USA and Canada.

Visit caa.ca or aaa.com/save for thousands of additional merchants near you and around the world.

Alberta

Camping
Doesn't get better than in Alberta

Shop 'til You Drop
In a mall so large it has a hotel and a water park

The Old West is Alive and Well
For 10 days in the Canadian Rockies during the Calgary Stampede

Variety Unsurpassed
Placid lakes, prairies, red rock canyons, lush forests, and soaring mountains

Lake Louise
Ski it in winter, hike it in summer, admire it all year

Maligne Lake,
Jasper National Park
© SuperStock

seasons
in the sun

Ukrainian Cultural Heritage Village, Edmonton
© Richard Cummins / SuperStock

Alberta is a *happening* place.

In any season you're bound to find Albertans commemorating some aspect of their multifaceted province. And with the Canadian Rockies blocking eastbound Pacific moisture, odds are great that whatever the event, it will take place in sunshine.

Winter festivals in Jasper and Banff showcase snowy weather sports like skiing, sledding and ice skating against a backdrop of postcard-beautiful alpine scenery.

As spring and summer heat things up, Edmonton earns its reputation as "Canada's Festival City," with events celebrating local ethnic diversity. First Nations films, singing and dancing are highlights of The Dreamspeakers Festival, while food lovers can take a gastronomic trip around the world as they sample from a spectrum of cuisines during Edmonton's Heritage Festival.

The bronc-buckin' Calgary Stampede all but steals the spotlight. Much more than a big-time rodeo, this Wild West exhibition turns into a huge outdoor party with parades and a carnival midway.

In autumn, the Calgary Zoo—distinguished by its painting elephant and an array of artificial dinosaurs—gets into the Halloween spirit with Boo at the Zoo, when ghosts and witches haunt the grounds.

Of course, you don't have to trick or treat or rope a steer if you travel to Alberta. Just visiting Canada's sunniest province is a special event.

Mirror images of mountain peaks reflected in calm, clear lakes. The twinkling, shimmering dance of lights known as "aurora borealis." Blankets of golden wheat and vivid canola pulled up snugly over the rolling countryside.

Typical visions of the Wild West? Hardly.

But Alberta urges you to stretch the definition of what the Canadian West is all about.

Plenty in the province fits neatly into the Western mold. Take Calgary, for instance. The former cow town's very roots are in ranching and meatpacking. Thousands of folks in denim and 10-gallon hats gather to watch the rough-and-tumble rodeo and chuck wagon races of the 10-day Calgary Stampede. Even the roof of the Saddledome, home of the National Hockey League's Calgary Flames, is in the shape of—you guessed it—a saddle.

But although Calgary is decidedly Western in many ways, it prides itself on having cultured a personality that's much more well-rounded.

A Multifaceted Identity

In 1988 the world's best athletes united in the city for the Olympic Winter Games. From grizzly bears to wood bison, the renowned Calgary Zoo offers the best chance to see native wildlife. It also is home to more than 10,000 plants and 20 life-size replicas of dinosaurs in a simulated Mesozoic landscape. Futuristic elevated "pedways" link nearly half of the buildings downtown.

And so it goes with the rest of the province, where such dichotomies are commonplace.

The faintly sweet aroma of 18 varieties of orchids in Cypress Hills Interprovincial Park lends to an air of tranquility and peace. But just a scant hop and skip to the northwest, volatile Medicine Hat harnesses an extensive reserve of natural gas that prompted Rudyard Kipling to describe the city as having "all hell for a basement."

Rafters steel themselves against the raging rapids of the Elbow, Highwood and Kananaskis rivers in Kananaskis Country. Turbulent rushes of water sweeping over rock at Athabasca and Sunwapta falls become imposing towers of irresistible ice to climbers who chink away at them in winter. Amid the chaos, however, canoeists ply the placid,

The Hudson's Bay Co. gets fur-trading rights in a portion of what is now Alberta.
1670

Anthony Henday is the first European to visit the area.
1754

Robert Rundle, the first missionary, arrives.
1840

1795
Edmonton is founded as a Hudson's Bay trading fort.

Alberta Historical Timeline

1875
Calgary is established as a North West Mounted Police fort.

Library of Congress

emerald waters of Banff National Park's Moraine Lake and gaze upon the 10 glaciated summits that rise around it to provide a serene habitat for elk, deer and bighorn sheep.

The ground in Fort McMurray holds a significant reserve of lucrative oil sands deposits, but most people visit the town for its treasure in the sky: a spectacular view of the northern lights.

A Canadian Melting Pot

Alberta's diversity also stems from the many ethnic currents that run through it.

A strong Ukrainian heritage marks the area east of Edmonton. At the Ukrainian Cultural Heritage Village costumed interpreters demonstrate what life was like for settlers from the 1890s to 1930. The design of Vegreville's famed bronze, gold and silver pysanka, or Ukrainian Easter egg, depicts the people's faith and commemorates the protection provided to them by the Royal Canadian Mounted Police. A museum in Mundare holds a collection of cultural items.

West of Edmonton, English-, French- and German-speaking emigrants from central Europe established villages. A living-history museum in Stony Plain tells their story.

The history of native cultures is evident at the Head-Smashed-In Buffalo Jump Interpretive Centre near Fort Macleod and in the petroglyphs and pictographs at Writing-on-Stone Provincial Park, near Milk River. Indian Battle Park in Lethbridge details a significant battle between the Cree and Blackfoot Indians.

Traditions of the aboriginal people are remembered in Edmonton's Provincial Museum of Alberta. The territory around Cypress Hills Interprovincial Park—now home to ruminants, beavers and coyotes—nurtured a community of aborigines more than 7,000 years ago.

Prehistoric denizens of the Red Deer Valley, the dinosaurs, left their mark on the region by way of the fossils left behind in walls of sediment. Drumheller best captures the age along the Dinosaur Trail and through displays in its museums. To the southeast, a fertile fossil bed at Dinosaur Provincial Park contains the remains of 35 species of dinosaurs.

Alberta weaves a rich, vibrant tapestry of cultures, geography and a wealth of experiences. Westward ho.

The Canadian Pacific Railway reaches Calgary.
1883

© Hulton-Deutsch Collection/Corbis

The first plant to extract synthetic crude oil from oil sands is built in Fort McMurray.
1967

West Edmonton Mall's fourth and last phase of construction is completed; the world's largest mall has more than 800 shops and seven attractions.
1998

1905
The province of Alberta is formed.

© Wally McNamee/Corbis

1988
Calgary hosts the Winter Olympic Games.

2005
Alberta celebrates its 100th year as a Canadian province.

1914
Oil is discovered in the Turner Valley.

Recreation

Alberta is a nature lover's paradise. A place where unspoiled landscapes lend themselves to exploration in any season. A place where midnight summer sunsets in the north cap off long days of rest and relaxation. A place where towering mountains in the west beckon to all who appreciate unrestrained beauty.

Outdoor enthusiasts often look to Alberta's five national parks. Hikers, golfers, boaters, bicyclists, horseback riders, anglers and skiers are among the people who trek to them: Banff, Canada's first national park; Elk Island, an oasis for rare and endangered species; Jasper, a land of glaciers; Waterton Lakes, where the Rockies and prairie meet; and Wood Buffalo, which reaches north into Northwest Territories.

And although the national parks are arguably the most popular spots for recreational escape, sites throughout the grand expanse of untamed Alberta are equally as irresistible.

Experienced guides lead half-day to multiweek **trail riding** expeditions through the Elbow and Sheep valleys in the Kananaskis high country, west of Calgary; Ram Falls, southwest of Rocky Mountain House National Historic Site; and Cooking Lake-Blackfoot Provincial Recreational Area, east of Edmonton.

Only your imagination limits what you can do in the challenging Rockies. **Hiking, mountain climbing** and **mountain biking** are among the ways to get to know the peaks.

High-Octane Excitement

Pulse-pounding thrills await adventurists who take on raging rivers for a **white-water rafting** diversion. Beginners and veterans alike appreciate the draw of the Athabasca, Elbow, Highwood, Kananaskis, Kicking Horse, Red Deer and Sunwapta rivers.

The Blackstone River, a hot spot for **kayaking** in inflatable boats, cuts through the foothills of the Rockies. Slip into the North Saskatchewan River for a memorable **canoeing** experience.

When a blanket of snow covers the majestic Rockies, bundle up and head for the mountains. **Snowshoeing, tobogganing, cross-country skiing** and **sledding,** which can be done nearly anywhere there's snow, are mainstays of Canadian family fun.

To up the exhilaration factor, take advantage of one of North America's longest ski seasons, which can range from early November to late May in places. Some of the best

downhill skiing and **snowboarding** the province has to offer is at Ski Marmot Basin, 19 kilometres (12 miles) south of Jasper; Lake Louise, 57 kilometres (35 miles) northwest of Banff; Sunshine Village and Banff Mount Norquay, both within 15 minutes of Banff; Fortress Mountain, in Kananaskis Country; and Nakiska, at 90 kilometres (55 miles) west the closest mountain ski area to Calgary. The boldest of the bold tackle waterfall **ice climbing** or **heli-skiing,** in which a helicopter takes skiers to untouched powder.

Leaving a Wake of Powder

Wide, open expanses of windswept grasslands, rolling hills and heavily dusted valleys make for lots of good **snowmobiling,** too. For cheek-reddening mirth, zip through the region around Grande Prairie.

One of Alberta's most popular winter adventures is a trip to Fort McMurray to catch the best view of the awe-inspiring aurora borealis, or "northern lights."

Nearly anywhere you go in the province, you'll find opportunities galore for **fishing.** Alberta's numerous trophy lakes, so designated because of the huge fish that inhabit them, brim with pike, whitefish, perch and walleye. Some notable fly-in trophy lakes are Gardiner and Namur, northwest of Fort McMurray, and Winefred, northeast of Lac La Biche. Head to the Bow River for exceptional trout fly-fishing. Phone (780) 944-0313 for information about regulations and licensing.

For an unforgettable **camping** experience, charter a plane out of Cold Lake, Fort McMurray, Fort Smith, Fort Vermilion, High Level or Lac La Biche and fly to a lodge or camp in the northern lakes.

Recreational Activities

Throughout the TourBook, you may notice a Recreational Activities heading with bulleted listings of recreation-oriented establishments listed underneath. Similar operations also may be mentioned in Destination City recreation sections. Since normal AAA inspection criteria cannot be applied, these establishments are presented only for information. Age, height and weight restrictions may apply. Reservations often are recommended and sometimes are required. Addresses and/or phone numbers are provided so visitors can contact the attraction for additional information.

Fast Facts

POPULATION: 2,974,807.

AREA: 661,848 sq km (255,539 sq mi); ranks 6th.

CAPITAL: Edmonton.

HIGHEST POINT: 3,747 m/12,293 ft., Mount Columbia.

LOWEST POINT: 183 m/600 ft., Salt River at border with the Northwest Territories.

TIME ZONE(S): Mountain. DST.

MINIMUM AGE FOR UNRESTRICTED DRIVER'S LICENSE: 16.

MINIMUM AGE FOR GAMBLING: 18.

SEAT BELT/CHILD RESTRAINT LAWS: Seat belts required for driver and all passengers. Child safety seats are required for children under age 6 or those weighing less than 18 kilograms (40 lbs.).

HELMETS FOR MOTORCYCLISTS: Required for driver and passenger.

RADAR DETECTORS: Permitted.

FIREARMS LAWS: By federal law, all nonresidents entering Canada with a firearm must declare their weapon in writing and pay a fee of $50 (Canadian). Contact the Canadian Firearms Centre at (800) 731-4000 to receive a declaration form or for additional information.

HOLIDAYS: Jan. 1; Good Friday; Easter Monday; Victoria Day, May 24 or the closest prior Mon.; Canada Day, July 1; Heritage Day, Aug. (1st Mon.); Labour Day, Sept. (1st Mon.); Thanksgiving, Oct. (2nd Mon.); Remembrance Day, Nov. 11; Dec. 25 and 26.

TAXES: Alberta has no provincial sales tax. However, there is a 5 percent provincial rooms tax in addition to the 7 percent national GST.

INFORMATION CENTERS: Travel Alberta Visitor Centres provide information about accommodations and campgrounds as well as maps. They are located at Canmore on Hwy. 1; Crowsnest Pass on Hwy. 3; Field, British Columbia, on Hwy. 1; Grande Prairie on 106th St.; Hinton on Hwy. 16; Lloydminster on Hwy. 16; Milk River on Hwy. 4; Oyen on Hwy. 9; Walsh on Hwy. 1; and West Glacier, Mont. Most centers are open daily 9-6, mid-May through Labour Day. A tourism office is open year-round in Canmore.

FURTHER INFORMATION FOR VISITORS:

Travel Alberta
P.O. Box 2500
Edmonton, AB, Canada T5J 2Z4
(780) 427-4321
(800) 252-3782

RECREATION INFORMATION:

Alberta Community Development
Parks & Protected Areas
9820 106th St., 2nd Floor
Edmonton, AB, Canada T5K 2J6
(780) 427-3582
(866) 427-3582

FISHING AND HUNTING REGULATIONS:

Alberta Environmental Information Centre
9945 108th St., Main Floor
Edmonton, AB, Canada T5K 2G6
(780) 944-0313

ALCOHOL CONSUMPTION: Legal age 18.

Alberta Temperature Averages Maximum / Minimum (Celsius)

From the records of the National Weather Service

	JAN	FEB	MAR	APR	MAY	JUNE	JULY	AUG	SEPT	OCT	NOV	DEC
Banff	-6 / -16	-2 / -14	3 / -10	10 / -4	15 / 1	18 / 4	23 / 6	22 / 5	16 / 5	10 / -2	1 / -8	-4 / -13
Calgary	-3 / -15	-2 / -14	3 / -9	11 / -3	17 / 3	20 / 7	25 / 10	24 / 8	18 / 4	12 / -1	3 / -8	-2 / -13
Edmonton	-8 / -18	-6 / -17	1 / -10	11 / -2	18 / 4	21 / 8	24 / 11	22 / 8	17 / 4	11 / -1	1 / -9	-7 / -16
Jasper	-6 / -16	-1 / -13	4 / -8	11 / -3	16 / 1	20 / 5	24 / 7	22 / 6	17 / 3	11 / -1	2 / -8	-4 / -13

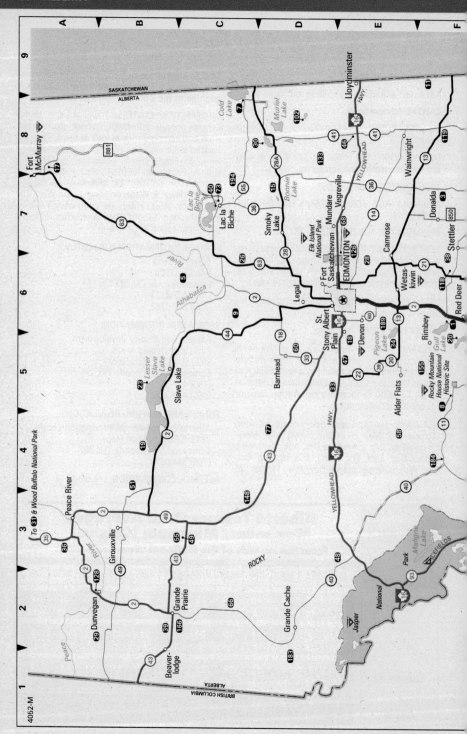

4052-M

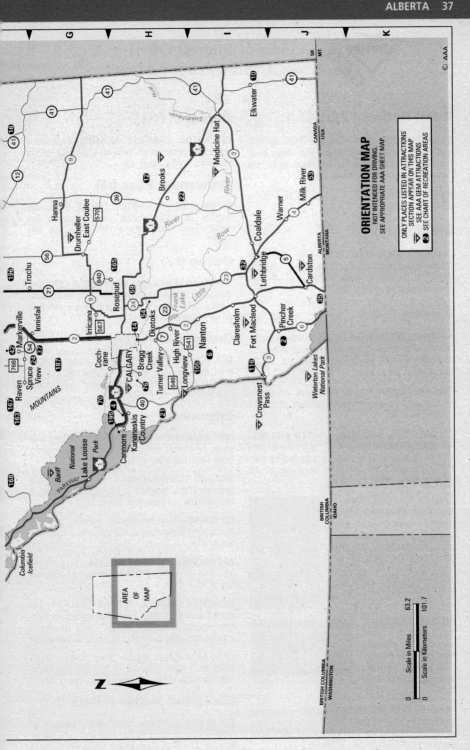

ORIENTATION MAP
NOT INTENDED FOR DRIVING.
SEE APPROPRIATE AAA SHEET MAP.

ONLY PLACES LISTED IN ATTRACTIONS
SECTION APPEAR ON THIS MAP
▽ SEE AAA GEM ATTRACTIONS
🔲 SEE CHART OF RECREATION AREAS

AREA
OF
MAP

N

Scale in Miles
0   63.2

Scale in Kilometers
0   101.7

Columbia
Icefield

Banff
National
Park

Lake Louise

PARKWAY

Bow

MOUNTAINS

Canmore

Kananaskis
Country

Spruce
View

Raven

Markerville

Innisfail

Trochu

Hanna

Drumheller
East Coulee

Rosebud

Irricana

Cochrane

CALGARY

Bragg Creek

Turner Valley

High River

Longview

Okotoks

Nanton

Claresholm

Fort Macleod

Pincher Creek

Crowsnest Pass

Waterton Lakes
National Park

Lethbridge

Cardston

Coaldale

Warner

Milk River

Brooks

Medicine Hat

Elkwater

Bow   River

Saskatchewan   River

Little   Bow   River

Frank Lake

SK
MT

CANADA
USA

ALBERTA
MONTANA

BRITISH COLUMBIA
IDAHO

BRITISH COLUMBIA
WASHINGTON

G   H   I   J   K

Points of Interest Offering A
Great Experience for Members®

Banff National Park (G-4)

BANFF NATIONAL PARK—This awe-inspiring wildlife refuge is spectacular in autumn when four-footed residents seem to be reveling in the riotous display of color. See p. 43.

ICEFIELDS PARKWAY—This is a really cool scenic drive. See p. 48.

Brooks (H-7)

DINOSAUR PROVINCIAL PARK—Visit the spectacular grasslands and badlands of this UNESCO World Heritage Site, where dinosaurs played millions of years ago. See p. 49.

Calgary (H-5)

BUTTERFIELD ACRES CHILDRENS FARM—Kids, including kids at heart, get to meet and play with newborn animals at this whimsical and educational farm. See p. 54.

CALGARY TOWER—"As far as the eye can see" is all the way to the Rocky Mountains atop this tower. See p. 55.

CALGARY ZOO, BOTANICAL GARDEN AND PREHISTORIC PARK—Whoop it up with the cranes and more than 900 animals in this facility partially supported by paintings done by an elephant. See p. 55.

CANADA OLYMPIC PARK—Test your strength, intelligence, accuracy, speed and endurance in simulated athletic competitions in the park's museum. See p. 55.

GLENBOW MUSEUM—You'll find out how cowboys removed their boots when you view early settlement everyday objects. See p. 56.

WHERE THE WORLD MEETS THE WEST

HERITAGE PARK HISTORICAL VILLAGE—Return to the Spartan days of the fur trade, the stark days of settlement and the comforts of the early 20th century at this village. See p. 56.

Cardston (J-6)

REMINGTON CARRIAGE MUSEUM—Experience the transportation of yesterday without being taken for a ride. See p. 63.

Crowsnest Pass (I-5)

FRANK SLIDE INTERPRETIVE CENTRE—Walkways outside the center provide amazing views of the devastation caused by the 1903 rock slide. See p. 63.

Devon (E-6)

CANADIAN PETROLEUM INTERPRETIVE CENTRE—This attraction is hard to miss; a 53-metre (174-ft.) replica derrick marks the spot of the area's first oil well. See p. 75.

Drumheller (G-7)

THE ROYAL TYRRELL MUSEUM—Take a high-tech, hands-on journey to the Mesozoic Era and see skeletons of the dinosaurs that lived in the Red Deer River Valley. See p. 65.

Edmonton (E-6)

FORT EDMONTON PARK—This living-history museum re-creates periods in Edmonton's history from 1846-1920. See p. 71.

MUTTART CONSERVATORY—The plants in these four pyramids received a two-green-thumbs-up review from our inspector. See p. 71.

ODYSSIUM—This ultra-modern building is nearly as thought provoking as the exhibits it contains. See p. 71.

PROVINCIAL MUSEUM OF ALBERTA—Gain insight into the natural and cultural history of Alberta. See p. 71.

UKRAINIAN CULTURAL HERITAGE VILLAGE—Restored buildings and living-history demonstrations depict the story of the area's Ukrainian immigrants, who arrived prior to 1930. See p. 72.

WEST EDMONTON MALL—"Shop 'til you drop" takes on a new meaning in this 800-plus store mall that also offers a bungee jump. See p. 72.

Elk Island National Park (D-7)

ELK ISLAND NATIONAL PARK—Enjoy all sorts of recreational pursuits at the park, which is home to a large herd of plains bison. See p. 77.

Fort Macleod (I-6)

HEAD-SMASHED-IN BUFFALO JUMP INTERPRETIVE CENTRE—For more than 10,000 years this site was crucial to the survival of the Plains Indians. See p. 78.

Fort McMurray (A-8)

OIL SANDS DISCOVERY CENTRE—A stop here will tell you everything you always wanted to know about mining oil sands. See p. 79.

Jasper National Park (E-2,3)

JASPER NATIONAL PARK—Craggy mountain peaks, lush valleys and mirror-smooth lakes make this park a photographer's dream. See p. 80.

JASPER TRAMWAY—Take in spectacular views from atop 2,277-metre (7,470-ft.) Whistler's Mountain. See p. 83.

Lethbridge (I-6)

NIKKA YUKO JAPANESE GARDEN—Discover the beauty and serenity engendered by minimalism in this spot where East meets West. See p. 85.

Longview (H-5)

BAR U RANCH NATIONAL HISTORIC SITE—Formerly one of the country's largest ranching operations, the site commemorates the importance of ranching played in the development of Canada. See p. 85.

Medicine Hat (I-8)

MEDICINE HAT CLAY INDUSTRIES NATIONAL HISTORIC SITE—Peek inside beehive kilns and learn about the pottery industry that thrived here in the late 19th century. See p. 86.

Rocky Mountain House National Historic Site (F-5)

ROCKY MOUNTAIN HOUSE NATIONAL HISTORIC SITE—See the ruins of four failed fur-trading posts at this formerly forested frontier. See p. 89.

Waterton Lakes National Park (J-5)

WATERTON LAKES NATIONAL PARK—The prairies meet the mountains in this popular summer vacation site. See p. 91.

Wetaskiwin (E-6)

REYNOLDS-ALBERTA MUSEUM—In the summer you can ride in a vintage automobile or airplane at this museum, which presents the history of agriculture, industry and transportation in the province. See p. 92.

RECREATION AREAS

	MAP LOCATION	CAMPING	PICNICKING	HIKING TRAILS	BOATING	BOAT RAMP	BOAT RENTAL	FISHING	SWIMMING	PETS ON LEASH	BICYCLE TRAILS	WINTER SPORTS	VISITOR CENTER	LODGE/CABINS	FOOD SERVICE
NATIONAL PARKS *(See place listings)*															
Banff (G-4) 6,641 square kilometres. Horse rental.		•	•	•	•	•	•	•	•	•			•	•	•
Elk Island (D-7) 194 square kilometres.		•	•	•	•	•			•	•			•		
Jasper (E-2,3) 10,878 square kilometres. Horse rental.		•	•	•	•	•	•	•	•	•	•	•	•	•	•
Waterton Lakes (J-5) 525 square kilometres. Golf; horse rental.		•	•	•	•	•	•	•	•	•			•	•	•
PROVINCIAL															
Aspen Beach (F-6) 214 hectares on Gull Lake, 17 km w. of Lacombe on Hwy. 12. *(See Red Deer p. 88)*	❶	•	•	•	•	•		•	•	•		•			•
Beauvais Lake (J-5) 1,160 hectares 11 km w. and 8 km s. of Pincher Creek off Hwy. 507.	❷	•	•	•	•			•		•	•	•			
Big Knife (F-7) 295 hectares 8 km w. and 13 km s. of Forestburg on Hwy. 855.	❸	•	•		•	•		•	•	•					
Calling Lake (C-6) 738 hectares 55 km n. of Athabasca on Hwy. 813.	❺	•	•		•	•		•	•	•					
Carson-Pegasus (D-4) 1,209 hectares 6 km w. of Whitecourt on Hwy. 43, 11 km n. on Hwy. 32, then 5 km e. on access road.	⓱	•	•	•	•	•	•	•	•	•	•	•			•
Chain Lakes (I-5) 409 hectares 38 km s.w. of Nanton on Hwy. 533.	❻	•	•		•	•		•		•					•

RECREATION AREAS

	MAP LOCATION	CAMPING	PICNICKING	HIKING TRAILS	BOATING	BOAT RAMP	BOAT RENTAL	FISHING	SWIMMING	PETS ON LEASH	BICYCLE TRAILS	WINTER SPORTS	VISITOR CENTER	LODGE/CABINS	FOOD SERVICE
Cold Lake (C-8) 5,855 hectares 3 km n.e. of Cold Lake off Hwy. 28.	7	•	•	•	•	•		•	•	•			•		
Cooking Lake-Blackfoot (E-7) 9,700 hectares 24 km e. of Sherwood Park s. of Hwy. 16. Canoeing.	68		•	•						•	•	•			
Crimson Lake (F-5) 3,209 hectares 14 km w. and 6 km n. of Rocky Mountain House on Hwy. 756. Interpretive programs.	8	•	•	•	•	•		•	•	•		•			•
Cross Lake (C-6) 2,076 hectares 8 km n. and 19 km n.e. of Jarvie off Hwy. 663.	9	•	•	•	•	•	•	•	•	•	•				•
Cypress Hills (I-9) 20,451 hectares 35 km s.e. of Medicine Hat on Hwy. 1, then 35 km s. on Hwy. 41. Interpretive programs. *(See Elkwater p. 77)*	10	•	•	•	•	•	•	•	•	•	•		•	•	•
Dickson Dam-North Valley (G-5) 6 km s. of Spruce View off Hwy. 54. *(See Spruce View p. 89)*	24	•	•	•	•	•		•	•	•	•				
Dillberry Lake (F-9) 1,205 hectares 15 km s. of Chauvin on Hwy. 17.	11	•	•	•	•			•	•	•					
Dinosaur (H-8) 7,332 hectares 48 km n.e. of Brooks via Hwys. 873, 544 and 876. Historic. Canoeing; interpretive programs. *(See Brooks p. 49)*	12	•	•	•						•			•		
Dry Island Buffalo Jump (F-6) 1,598 hectares 15 km e. of Huxley off Hwy. 21 on an access road.	196	•	•					•	•	•					
Dunvegan (B-2) 9 hectares off Hwy. 2 on the n. side of the Peace River beside Dunvegan Suspension Bridge. Interpretive programs. *(See Dunvegan p. 65)*	128		•					•		•			•		
Fish Creek (H-6) 1,189 hectares in Calgary off 37th St. S.W. Interpretive programs; horse rental.	14		•	•				•	•	•	•		•		
Garner Lake (D-7) 74 hectares 5 km n. of Spedden off Hwy. 28.	15	•	•	•	•			•	•	•					
Ghost Reservoir (G-5) 24 hectares 22 km w. of Cochrane on Hwy. 1A. Sailing, windsurfing.	70	•	•		•	•	•	•		•					
Gooseberry Lake (F-8) 52 hectares 12 km n. of Consort on Hwy. 41, then 2 km e. on access road.	16	•	•					•	•	•					
Gregoire Lake (A-8) 696 hectares 19 km s. of Fort McMurray on Hwy. 63, then 10 km e. on Hwy. 881.	17	•	•	•	•	•		•	•	•			•		•
Hilliard's Bay (B-4) 2,323 hectares 10 km e. of Grouard off Hwy. 750.	19	•	•	•	•	•		•	•	•					
Kananaskis Country (H-4) *(See place listing p. 83)*															
Bow Valley (H-5) 3,129 hectares 25 km e. of Canmore on Hwy. 1 and .5 km n. on Hwy. 1X. Canoeing; interpretive programs.	4	•	•	•				•		•	•	•	•		•
Bragg Creek (H-5) 128 hectares 2 km s.w. of Bragg Creek on Hwy. 758.	76		•	•					•	•		•			
Canmore Nordic Centre (H-5) 435 hectares 3 km s. of Canmore on Spray Lakes Rd.	195		•	•						•	•	•		•	•
Peter Lougheed (H-5) 50,142 hectares 43 km s.e. of Canmore off Hwy. 40. Interpretive programs.	21	•	•	•	•	•		•		•	•	•	•	•	
Sheep River (H-5) 25 km w. of Turner Valley on SR 546. Equestrian trails.	105	•	•	•				•		•					
Kinbrook Island (H-7) 540 hectares 13 km s. of Brooks off Hwy. 873.	22	•	•	•	•	•		•	•	•	•				•
Lakeland (C-8) 59,030 hectares 40 km n.e. of Lac La Biche on Hwy. 36. Canoeing. *(See Lac La Biche p. 84)*	194	•	•	•	•	•		•	•	•	•				

RECREATION AREAS

	MAP LOCATION	CAMPING	PICNICKING	HIKING TRAILS	BOATING	BOAT RAMP	BOAT RENTAL	FISHING	SWIMMING	PETS ON LEASH	BICYCLE TRAILS	WINTER SPORTS	VISITOR CENTER	LODGE/CABINS	FOOD SERVICE
Lesser Slave Lake (B-5) 7,566 hectares 32 km n. of Slave Lake off Hwy. 88. Interpretive programs, water sports. *(See Slave Lake p. 89)*	23	•	•	•	•			•	•	•	•	•			
Long Lake (C-6) 769 hectares 20 km s. of Boyle off Hwy. 831, then 2 km n.e. on access road.	26	•	•	•	•	•	•	•	•	•	•	•			•
Medicine Lake (F-5) 24 hectares 47 km n. of Rocky Mtn. House on Hwy. 22, then 8 km s.e. on access road.	155	•	•		•	•		•	•	•					
Miquelon Lake (E-6) 835 hectares 3 km s. of New Sarepta on Hwy. 21, then 20 km e. on Hwy. 623. Interpretive programs.	28	•	•	•				•	•	•	•	•			•
Moonshine Lake (B-2) 1,103 hectares 27 km w. of Spirit River on Hwy. 49, then 7 km n. on Hwy. 725.	29	•	•	•	•	•		•	•	•		•			•
Moose Lake (C-8) 736 hectares 5 km n. of Bonnyville on Hwy. 41, 10 km w. on Hwy. 660, then 2 km s.	30	•	•	•	•	•		•	•	•		•			
Notikewin (A-3) 9,697 hectares 37 km n. of Manning via Hwy. 35, then 30 km e. on Hwy. 692.	31	•	•	•	•			•		•					
Park Lake (I-6) 224 hectares 22 km n.w. of Lethbridge on Hwy. 25, then w. and n. on Hwy. 101.	32	•	•	•	•	•	•	•	•	•	•	•	•		•
Pembina River (D-5) 167 hectares 3 km n.e. of Evansburg on Hwy. 16A. Canoeing.	33	•	•	•				•	•	•		•			
Peppers Lake (F-4) 18 hectares 84 km s.e. of Nordegg on Hwy. 734.	163	•		•		•		•		•					
Police Outpost (J-6) 223 hectares 10 km s. and 23 km w. of Cardston on Hwy. 2.	35	•	•	•				•	•	•		•			
Prairie Creek (F-5) 42 hectares 41 km s.w. of Rocky Mountain House on Hwy. 752.	167	•	•	•				•		•		•			
Queen Elizabeth (A-3) 86 hectares 3 km n. and 5 km w. of Grimshaw off Hwy. 35.	36	•	•	•	•	•				•		•			
Ram Falls (F-4) 116 hectares 64 km s. of Nordegg on Hwy. 734.	168	•	•	•				•		•		•			•
Red Lodge (G-5) 129 hectares 15 km w. of Bowden on Hwy. 587. Canoeing.	37	•	•	•				•	•	•					
Rochon Sands (F-6) 119 hectares 14.5 km n. of Erskine off Hwy. 835.	38	•	•			•		•	•	•		•			
Saskatoon Island (B-2) 101 hectares 21 km w. of Grande Prairie on Hwy. 43, then 4 km n. on an access road. Water sports.	39	•	•	•	•			•		•		•	•		•
Sir Winston Churchill (C-7) 239 hectares 13 km n.e. of Lac La Biche on Hwy. 881. *(See Lac La Biche p. 84)*	40	•	•	•	•	•		•	•	•	•	•			
Sylvan Lake (F-5) 85 hectares 18 km n.w. of Red Deer on Hwy. 11 in town of Sylvan Lake. *(See Red Deer p. 88)*	42		•					•	•	•		•			•
Two Lakes (D-1) 1,554 hectares 130 km s.w. of Grande Prairie.	183	•		•		•		•		•					
Upper Shunda Creek (F-4) 47 hectares 3 km w. of Nordegg off Hwy. 11.	184	•		•				•		•	•	•	•		
Vermilion (E-8) 759 hectares 1.5 km n. of Vermilion on Hwy. 41 from jct. Hwy. 16, then w. on 50th Ave. Canoeing.	46	•	•	•		•		•	•	•	•	•			
Wabamun Lake (E-5) 231 hectares 3 km e. and 1 km s. of Wabamun off Hwy. 16A.	47	•	•	•	•	•		•	•	•	•	•			•
Whitney Lakes (D-8) 1,489 hectares 24 km e. of Elk Point off Hwy. 646. Interpretive programs.	102	•	•	•	•	•		•	•	•	•	•	•		

RECREATION AREAS

Recreation Area	MAP LOCATION	CAMPING	PICNICKING	HIKING TRAILS	BOATING	BOAT RAMP	BOAT RENTAL	FISHING	SWIMMING	PETS ON LEASH	BICYCLE TRAILS	WINTER SPORTS	VISITOR CENTER	LODGE/CABINS	FOOD SERVICE
William A. Switzer (E-3) 6,268 hectares 3 km w. of Hinton on Hwy. 16, then 19 km n. on Hwy. 40. Interpretive programs.	48	•	•	•	•	•	•	•	•	•	•	•		•	
Williamson (C-3) 17 hectares 17 km w. of Valleyview on Hwy. 43, then 2 km n. on an access road.	49	•	•		•			•	•	•					
Winagami Lake (B-4) 6,542 hectares 20 km n. of High Prairie on SR 749, 10 km w. on SR 679, then 7 km n. on access road.	51	•	•	•	•	•		•		•			•		
Writing-on-Stone (J-8) 1,718 hectares 32 km e. of Milk River on Sec. Hwy. 501 and 10 km s. on an access road. Historic. Canoeing; interpretive program. *(See Milk River p. 87)*	53	•	•	•				•	•	•	•				•
Young's Point (B-3) 3,072 hectares 26 km w. of Valleyview on Hwy. 43, then 10 km n.e. on an access road. Water sports.	55	•	•	•	•	•		•		•	•		•		
OTHER															
Beaver Lake (C-7) 15 hectares 6 km s.e. of Lac La Biche off Hwy. 36 to Hwy. 663, on the n.e. shore of Beaver Lake.	73	•	•		•	•		•	•	•	•				•
Brazeau Reservoir (E-4) 46 hectares 25 km s.w. of Lodgepole along SR 620.	58	•	•	•	•	•		•	•	•					
Chinook (I-5) 48 hectares 12 km n.w. of Coleman. Canoeing.	116	•	•	•	•	•		•	•	•			•		
Content Bridge (F-6) 12 hectares 6 km s. of Nevis off Hwy. 21.	118	•	•					•	•	•					•
Eagle Lake Park (H-6) 7 km e. and 6 km s. of Strathmore via Hwy. 1.	59	•	•		•	•		•		•					
Elks Beach (D-5) 14 km s. of Barrhead, e. off Hwy. 33.	60	•	•		•			•	•	•					•
Half Moon Lake (E-7) 4 hectares 3 km e. of Sherwood Park on Hwy. 630. Horse rental.	126	•	•	•	•			•	•	•					•
Hasse Lake (E-5) 81 hectares 5 km w. and 10 km s. of Stony Plain on Hwy. 16.	18		•	•	•			•	•						
Iosegun Lake (C-3) 257 hectares 11 km n. of Fox Creek off Hwy. 43.	148	•	•	•		•	•		•	•	•			•	
Jarvis Bay (F-5) 86 hectares 4 km n. of Sylvan Lake townsite off Hwy. 20.	20	•								•	•	•			•
Musreau Lake (C-2) 72 km s. of Grande Prairie on Hwy. 40, then 6 km e. on an access road.	66	•	•	•	•	•	•	•	•	•					
Pigeon Lake (E-5) 443 hectares 5 km w. and 10 km n. of Westerose off Hwy. 771.	34	•	•	•	•	•		•	•	•	•	•			
Pipestone Creek (C-2) 15 km s. of Wembley.	166	•	•	•	•	•	•								
Shorncliff Lake (F-8) 2 hectares 3 km w. of Czar.	119	•	•		•					•	•				•
Stony Lake (D-8) 158 hectares on Stony Lake, 16 km s.w. of Elk Point off Hwy. 646.	133	•	•		•	•		•		•					
Westward Ho Park (G-5) 8 km e. of Sundre off Hwy. 27.	187	•	•					•	•	•					
Wizard Lake (E-6) 20 km s.w. of Calmar.	189	•	•	•	•	•		•	•	•					•
Wyndham-Carseland (H-6) 178 hectares 4 km e. and 2 km s. of Carseland on Hwy. 24. Canoeing.	54	•	•	•					•		•	•			

Points of Interest

ALDER FLATS (E-5)
pop. 133, elev. 953 m/3,125′

EM-TE TOWN is 3 km (1.9 mi.) s. of jct. Hwys. 13 and 22, then 10 km (6.2 mi.) w. on a gravel road following signs. This replica of a Western ghost town includes a saloon, gazebo, church, blacksmith shop, school, emporium and jail. Trail rides, cabins, camping and teepee rentals are offered. Food is available. Allow 1 hour minimum. Daily 9-6. Admission $7; ages 6-17, $5; over 64, $4. One-hour trail ride $25. MC, VI. Phone (780) 388-2166.

GEM BANFF NATIONAL PARK (G-4)

Elevations in the park range from 1,326 metres (4,350 ft.) around the Bow River to 3,625 metres (11,900 ft.) at Mount Forbes. Refer to CAA/AAA maps for additional elevation information.

Banff National Park is approached from the southeast via the Trans-Canada Highway (Hwy. 1) west of Canmore, from the northeast via Hwy. 11 southwest of Abraham Lake, or from the north via Hwy. 93 from Jasper. The park's majestic beauty is

BANFF NATIONAL PARK

Discover our true nature.

Offering a range of activities as vast and diverse as the landscape itself, Alberta is an easy choice for your next vacation. Come explore our true nature and discover your true self. Alberta, Canada's Rocky Mountain Playground.

AIR CANADA
The most non-stops between
the U.S. and Canada

TravelAlberta.com
1.800.ALBERTA

Canada
Discover our true nature

inescapable. These routes lead to a region where mountains and the forces of nature inspire awe and command respect.

This is Canada's oldest national park: Evidence suggests that prehistoric habitation dates back 11,000 years. Remnants of the more recent Assiniboine, Blackfoot, Cree, Kootenay and Stoney settlements also have been found in the park. European explorers did not arrive until the early 1800s, and when they did, they argued over the land's resources, prompting the government to establish the park in 1885.

In this 6,641-square-kilometre (2,564-sq.-mi.) section of the Canadian Rockies there are only two main centers of activity: Banff and Lake Louise. The glacial-green Bow River flows through the mountain-ringed valley that is the setting for Banff. The dry, bracing climate, alpine grandeur and mineral hot spring pools enhance Banff's attractiveness.

The town of Banff, granted autonomy from federal jurisdiction Jan. 1, 1990, is within the park. Development within the town is strictly controlled; residents do not own their land but lease it from the park.

Situated 58 kilometres (36 mi.) west of Banff at an elevation of 1,731 metres (5,680 ft.) is icy, blue-green Lake Louise. About 2 kilometres (1.2 mi.) long, .6 kilometres (.4 mi.) wide and 69 metres (225 ft.) deep, it was discovered in 1882. Lake Louise springs from Victoria Glacier, whose meltwater carries the silt and rock flour that give the lake the opaque turquoise color common to most of the area's waters. The upper portion of the glacier is 61 to 91 metres (200 to 300 ft.) thick; the lower part ranges from 122 to 152 metres (400 to 500 ft.).

The park's well-known peaks include Rundle, Cascade, Victoria, Lefroy, Temple, Castle, Forbes, Chephren, Hector and the Ten Peaks, all ranging from 2,752 to 3,618 metres (9,030 to 11,870 ft.)

above sea level. The upper slopes of the ranges are either bare and rugged or glacier crowned, while the lower slopes are forested. Many mountains are mirrored in Moraine, Peyto and other lakes.

Banff National Park is a wildlife refuge. Animals are especially visible in the fall; elk, deer and bighorn sheep are most common, while sightings of mountain goats and moose often require binoculars. Bears, wolves, coyotes, lynxes and other predators are seen occasionally. Black magpies and other members of the crow family, including the gray jay, Clark's nutcracker and raven, dart through the trees.

Although most of the park's lakes and rivers—particularly the Bow River—sustain healthy fish populations, some lakes cannot due to the "winter kill." This phenomenon occurs when a lake freezes to such a great depth that oxygen is depleted at the bottom of the lake, thereby killing all fish.

Note: Night travelers should be alert for animals on the highways. It is not only dangerous but also against park regulations to feed, molest, touch or tease the animals.

General Information and Activities

The park, which is open all year, has about 354 kilometres (219 mi.) of scenic roads. Hwy. 1 to Vancouver and Hwy. 93 (Banff-Windermere Highway) are open year-round, as is the northern end of Hwy. 93 (Icefields Parkway) from Lake Louise to Jasper; check locally for road conditions. One- or multiple-day bus tours of the park's major points of interest also are available.

More than 1,300 kilometres (800 mi.) of trails traverse the park. All activities involving an overnight stay in the back country require a park use permit offered at information centers and park warden offices in the Banff and Lake Louise townsites. The many public campgrounds in the park are

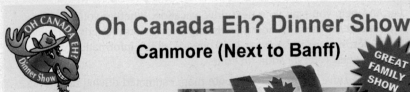

available on a first-come, first-served basis; no reservations are accepted.

If such potentially risky activities as mountain climbing or hiking away from designated trails are planned, visitors should register their trips in person at a park warden office or information center. Upon return, notify the warden office or information center in person or by phone. Phone (403) 762-1550 for back-country trail information, including weather and avalanche bulletins.

Lake Louise's waters, about 6 C (43 F), are too cold for swimming but are ideal for boating. Motors are not permitted; motorboats may be used only on Lake Minnewanka. Cruises on Lake Minnewanka are offered during the summer. Skating, skiing, curling and hockey are available in the park in winter.

Park naturalists conduct interpretive film and slide programs at major campgrounds most evenings. Bankhead, a once-booming mining town 4.8 kilometres (3 mi.) northeast of Banff, has a self-guiding trail with explanatory signs and a mining exhibit. The trail is open daily 24 hours.

Throughout the summer guides and outfitters offer fishing, hiking and float trips. Saddle horses are available for trips through the mountains to glacier-fed lakes, and helicopter tours can be arranged outside the park boundaries in Canmore and in Golden, British Columbia.

Information, interpretive program schedules and back-country trail tips are available at Banff Information Centre, (403) 762-1550, 224 Banff Ave., and Lake Louise Information Centre, (403) 522-3833, on Village Road; topographical maps and trail guides are sold at both locations. The Banff center is open daily 8-8, late June to mid-Sept.; 9-5, rest of year. The Lake Louise center is open daily 9-7, late June to mid-Sept.; 9-4, rest of year. Audiotape tours by CCInc. Auto Tape Tours are available at the Banff Information Centre at the Friends of Banff outlet; phone (403) 762-8918.

Fishing is permitted; national park fishing permits are sold at park information, administration and warden offices as well as at some boat concessionaires and tackle shops. Check at the information centers in Banff or Lake Louise for a summary of park fishing regulations.

Hunting is strictly prohibited; visitors entering the area must have firearms dismantled. *See Recreation Chart and the AAA/CAA Western Canada & Alaska CampBook.*

ADMISSION to the park for 1 day is $8 per person; over 65, $6. Admission for two to seven people in a private vehicle for 1 day is $16. An annual pass, valid at all Canadian national parks, is available. AX, MC, VI.

PETS are allowed in the park but must be leashed, crated or physically restrained.

ADDRESS inquiries to the Superintendent, Banff National Park, P.O. Box 900, Banff, AB, Canada T1L 1K2; phone (403) 762-1550.

Points of Interest

Natural points of interest within the park include hoodoos—mushroom-shaped pillars of glacial silt and clay—east of Banff; Vermilion Lakes and Johnston Canyon to the west; Bow Falls to the south; Mount Norquay, Lake Louise, Moraine Lake and Valley of the Ten Peaks to the northwest via the Trans-Canada Highway; and Hector, Bow and Peyto lakes and Bow Summit to the northwest on the Icefields Parkway.

BANFF PARK MUSEUM NATIONAL HISTORIC SITE is at 91 Banff Ave. Established in 1895, the collection moved to its present building in 1903. The museum depicts the way natural history exhibits were presented and interpreted at the beginning of the 20th century. Exhibits include mounted animals and mineral specimens.

Allow 30 minutes minimum. Daily 10-6, mid-June to mid-Sept.; 1-5, rest of year. Closed Jan. 1 and Dec. 25-26. Guided tours are given daily at 3, Victoria Day-Labour Day. Admission $4; over 64, $3.50; ages 6-18, $3; family rate $10. Phone (403) 762-1558.

BANFF SULPHUR MOUNTAIN GONDOLA LIFT is 3.2 km (2 mi.) s. of Banff on Mountain Ave. (lower terminal next to the Upper Hot Springs). The lift rises 701 metres (2,300 ft.) from the 1,585-metre (5,200-ft.) level to the 2,451-metre (8,040-ft.) peak in 8 minutes.

An open-air observation deck affords spectacular views of Banff and the surrounding mountains.

Food is available. Daily 7:30 a.m.-9 p.m., June 1-Sept. 1; otherwise varies. Closed Jan. 8-19. Fare $22.50; ages 6-15, $11.25. AX, MC, VI. Phone (403) 762-2523, or (403) 762-5438 for recorded information.

[SAVE] **BANFF UPPER HOT SPRINGS** is 4 km (2.5 mi.) s. of Banff via Mountain Ave. Natural hot springs feed this bathing pool with temperatures ranging between 34 and 42 C (93 and 108 F). Swimsuit, towel and locker rentals are available. A day spa is on the premises.

Food is available. Allow 1 hour minimum. Daily 9 a.m.-11 p.m., early May to mid-Oct.; Sun.-Thurs. 10-10, Fri.-Sat. 10 a.m.-11 p.m., rest of year. Admission $7.50; over 64 and ages 3-17, $6.50; family rate (two adults and two children) $23.50, with each additional child $3.50. AX, MC, VI. Phone (403) 762-1515 or (800) 767-1611. *See color ad.*

[SAVE] **BUFFALO NATIONS MUSEUM** is just w. of Banff Ave. at 1 Birch Ave. This log-fort museum re-creates the era when Europeans first arrived on the Plains to find a culture rich in ceremonies, songs and legends. Arts, crafts, dioramas and displays showcase the historical journey of the Northern Plains Indians, their culture and the flora and fauna of the surrounding area.

Allow 30 minutes minimum. Daily 10-6, Victoria Day-Thanksgiving; 1-5, rest of year. Closed Dec. 25. Admission $7; over 65 and students with ID $5;

ages 6-12, $3; family rate $15. MC, VI. Phone (403) 762-2388.

THE CASCADE ROCK GARDENS encircle the park's administration building. These gardens are built in a series of rock terraces connected by small cascades that highlight flowers, plants and shrubs, rustic bridges, pavilions and flagged walks. Allow 30 minutes minimum. Free.

THE CAVE AND BASIN NATIONAL HISTORIC SITE is at 311 Cave Ave. A cave and hot springs were discovered in 1883 by three Canadian Pacific Railway workers. The site consists of naturally occurring warm mineral springs inside the cave and an emerald-colored basin outside. Exhibits, interpretive trails and a 30-minute videotape presentation explain the history of the springs and the development of the national park.

Allow 1 hour minimum. Daily 9-6, mid-May through Sept. 30; Mon.-Fri. 11-4, Sat.-Sun. 9:30-5, rest of year. Closed Jan. 1 and Dec. 25-26. Guided tours are given daily at 11, June-Sept. Admission $4; over 64, $3.50; ages 6-18, $3; family rate $10. Phone (403) 762-1566.

DISCOVER BANFF TOURS is at 215 Banff Ave. in the Sundance Mall and meets passengers at area hotels. Various year-round guided tours are offered, including ice walks, snowshoe treks, dogsled trips, sleigh rides, mountain hikes, evening safaris, horseback riding, white-water rafting and nature walks. Some tours include lunch. Inquire about cancellation policies. Allow 2-9 hours minimum, depending on tour. Daily (weather permitting) 8 a.m.-10 p.m. Tour times vary; phone ahead. Fees $59-$300. AX, MC, VI. Phone (403) 760-5007 or (877) 565-9372.

ICEFIELDS PARKWAY (HWY. 93) The drive connects the towns of Lake Louise and Jasper and crosses Banff and Jasper national parks. The 230-kilometre (143-mi.) route offers spectacular vistas of snowcapped mountains, waterfalls, lakes and rivers that drain the Columbia Icefields' glacial meltwater to the oceans. While the terrain is rugged, the road is well-engineered to provide a relatively easy drive.

Roadside signs explain the terrain. Long hikes through the wilderness are available, as are shorter trails leading to scenic Sunwapta Falls and Athabasca Falls.

Just inside Jasper National Park is the Athabasca Glacier. A tongue of the Columbia Icefield *(see Jasper National Park p. 82)*, it comes to within 1.5 kilometres (.9 mi.) of the parkway.

Note: Drivers should be alert for slow or stopped vehicles and animals. Snow tires and/or chains are recommended in winter; check for weather and road conditions. Parkway free; drivers must pay the national park entrance fee regardless of whether they stop inside the park. Phone (403) 762-2088 for weather information or (403) 762-1450 for road condition information.

LAKE LOUISE SIGHTSEEING LIFT AND GONDOLA is just n. of Hwy. 1 interchange. The lift offers an impressive aerial view of Lake Louise and

the mountains of the Continental Divide. Ride and dine packages also are offered. Food is available. Daily 8:30-6, June 1-Sept. 15. Fare $21; over 65 and ages 13-17, $19; ages 6-12, $9.95. AX, DC, MC, VI. Phone (403) 522-3555.

SAVE **LAKE MINNEWANKA BOAT TOURS** is on Lake Minnewanka, 8 km (5 mi.) n.e. of Banff on Hwy. 1, then n. 7 km (4 mi.) from the beginning of Lake Minnewanka Loop. The interpretive sightseeing cruises, in glass-enclosed, heated boats, last 1 hour, 30 minutes. Motorboats can be rented. Cruises depart daily at 10:30, 12:30, 3 and 5, mid-May through first weekend in Oct. (also at 7, mid-May through Labour Day). Fare $32; ages 5-11, $15. MC, VI. Phone (403) 762-3473.

NATURAL HISTORY MUSEUM is at 112 Banff Ave. in the Clock Tower Mall. Exhibits explain area geology, archeology and botany. Native art also is displayed. Daily noon-5, July-Sept. Free. Phone (403) 762-4652.

ROCKY MOUNTAIN RAFT TOURS tickets are available at Banff Springs Hotel and at the canoe rental dock at jct. Wolf and Bow sts. Bus transportation to the launching area departs from the Banff Park Lodge and from the Banff Springs Hotel. Scenic 1-hour float trips on the Bow River are offered. Canoe rentals also are available. One-hour raft trips depart daily (weather permitting) at 9:20, 11:20, 1:20 and 3:20, mid-May through Labour Day. Fare $28; under 12, $14. Phone (403) 762-3632.

WALTER PHILLIPS GALLERY is in Glyde Hall at The Banff Centre at jct. Mountain Dr. and St. Julien Rd. Exhibits contain international and Canadian contemporary art. Media include painting, sculpture, printmaking, textiles, ceramics, photography, videotape, performance and visual art. Works by established and emerging artists are featured. Tues.-Sun. noon-5; closed national holidays. Donations. Phone (403) 762-6281.

SAVE **WHYTE MUSEUM OF THE CANADIAN ROCKIES** is at 111 Bear St. The museum features the works of regional and national artists as well as displays that detail the story of Banff and the national park. Heritage homes are open in the summer; phone for schedule. Allow 30 minutes minimum. Daily 10-5; closed Jan. 1 and Dec. 25. Admission $6, over 64 and students with ID $3.50, under 6 free, family rate (up to four people) $15. Phone (403) 762-2291.

RECREATIONAL ACTIVITIES
Horseback Riding

- **Trail Riders of the Canadian Rockies** departs from Banff. Write P.O. Box 6742, Station D, Calgary, AB, Canada T2P 2E6. Three- and 6-day trips depart Sun. or Wed., July-Aug. Phone (403) 684-4086.

Skiing

- **Lake Louise Ski Area** is in Banff National Park, 60 km (36 mi.) w. of the town of Banff. Other activities are offered. Write 1505 17th Ave. S.W.,

Calgary, AB, Canada T2T 0E2. Daily, early Nov. to mid-May. Phone (403) 591-7777, (403) 256-8473 or (800) 258-7669.

- **Ski Banff Norquay** is 6 km (4 mi.) n. of the town of Banff on the Mount Norquay access road. Write P.O. Box 1520, Banff, AB, Canada T1L 1B4. Daily 9-4 (also Fri. 4-9, Jan.-Mar.), early Dec. to mid-Apr. Phone (403) 762-4421.
- **Sunshine Village Ski Resort** is 8 km (5 mi.) w. of the town of Banff on Hwy. 1. Write P.O. Box 1628, Banff, AB, Canada T1L 1B5. Daily 9-4, mid-Nov. to late May. Phone (403) 762-6500 or (877) 542-2633.

White-water Rafting

- **Wild Water Adventures** provides pick-up service at Banff and Lake Louise locations. Write P.O. Box 25, Lake Louise, AB, Canada T0L 1E0. Departures twice daily (weather permitting), mid-May to mid-Sept. Phone (403) 522-2211 or (888) 647-6444.

BARRHEAD (D-5)
pop. 4,213, elev. 648 m/2,125′

BARRHEAD CENTENNIAL MUSEUM is at 5629 49th St. Displays depict early area history. Exhibits include farm equipment, pioneer furniture, tools, woodcrafts, a wildlife display and Native artifacts. The museum also serves as a visitor information center. Allow 1 hour minimum. Mon.-Sat. and holidays 10-5, Sun. 1-5, May 1-Labour Day; by appointment rest of year. Donations. Phone (780) 674-5203.

BEAVERLODGE (B-1) pop. 2,110

First settled in 1908, Beaverlodge derives its name from the Beaver Indians who made their temporary home, or lodge, in the area. With the arrival of the railway in 1928, a new townsite was created about 1.6 kilometres (1 mi.) northwest of the original hamlet; many original buildings were moved. In the Beaverlodge Valley, the town serves as a gateway to Monkman Pass and is a large agricultural center.

Beaverlodge & District Chamber of Commerce: P.O. Box 303, Beaverlodge, AB, Canada T0H 0C0; phone (780) 354-8785.

SOUTH PEACE CENTENNIAL MUSEUM is 3 km (1.9 mi.) n.w. on Hwy. 43. Pioneer items, equipment and furnishings used in the early 1900s are on display. A 1928 pioneer house is furnished in period. Other exhibits include a trading post, general store, flour mill, antique steam engines, a schoolhouse, railway caboose, Anglican church and vintage cars and trucks. Daily 10-6, mid-May to early Sept. Admission $3, under 12 free. Phone (780) 354-8869.

BRAGG CREEK — see Calgary p. 61.

BROOKS (H-7) pop. 11,604

Brooks is surrounded by 105,222 hectares (260,000 acres) of irrigated farmland and more than 404,700 hectares (1 million acres) of rangeland used for cattle grazing. An aqueduct that was operational until 1977 has been preserved as a monument to the engineers and agriculturalists who developed the region. This semiarid short-grass section of the province is the setting for wildlife and horticultural research centers.

Brooks Chamber of Commerce Tourist Information Centre: 403 2nd Ave. W., Suite 6, P.O. Box 400, Brooks, AB, Canada T1R 1B4; phone (403) 362-7641.

BROOKS AND DISTRICT MUSEUM is .4 km (.2 mi.) w. of Trans-Canada Hwy. Exhibits about Indian culture, ranchers, homesteaders, the Royal Canadian Mounted Police, railroading and irrigation trace local history from the late 19th and early 20th centuries. Several restored buildings, including a log cabin, a schoolhouse and a church, are on the grounds. Allow 1 hour, 30 minutes minimum. Daily 8:30-7, May-Aug. Donations. Phone (403) 362-5073.

DINOSAUR PROVINCIAL PARK is 48 km (30 mi.) n.e. via Hwys. 873 and 544, following signs. The park, declared a UNESCO World Heritage Site in 1979, covers 7,332 hectares (18,116 acres) of badlands and prairie along the Red Deer River. One of the richest fossil beds in the world, it contains the remains of 37 species of dinosaurs from 75 million years ago as well as crocodile, fish, flying reptile, small mammal and turtle fossils.

Five self-guiding trails explore three habitats: prairie grassland, badlands and riverside. Each offers opportunities for bird-watching. The Field Station Visitor Centre contains exhibits, a theater and preparation lab.

Camping and picnicking are permitted. Food is available. Allow a full day. Park daily 24 hours. Field Station Visitor Centre daily 8:30 a.m.-9 p.m., Victoria Day-Aug. 31; 9-5, Sept. 1-second Mon. in Oct.; 9-4, May 1-16; Mon.-Fri. 9-4, rest of year. Interpretive programs are available Victoria Day-second Mon. in Oct.

Park admission free. Field Station Visitor Centre $3; over 64, $2.50; ages 7-17, $2; family rate $8. Interpretive programs $6.50; ages 7-17, $4.50. Preparation lab talks $2; ages 7-17, $1. Reservations are recommended for campsites and interpretive programs. Phone (403) 378-4342 for information, (403) 378-4344 for interpretive program bookings, or (403) 378-3700 May-Aug. for camping reservations. *See Recreation Chart and the AAA/CAA Western Canada & Alaska CampBook.*

The Royal Tyrrell Museum Field Station is within Dinosaur Provincial Park. The interpretive center and research facility contains dinosaur skeletons, interpretive displays depicting the park's geological and paleontological resources, a preparation lab and the park administration office. Daily 8:30 a.m.-9 p.m., Victoria Day-Aug. 31; 9-4, Sept. 1-second Mon. in Oct.; Mon.-Fri. 9-4, rest of year. Closed national winter holidays. Admission $3; over 64, $2.50; ages 7-17, $2; family rate $8. Phone (403) 378-4342.

Calgary

Calgary, once considered a cow town, now is a city of skyscrapers, light-rail transit, shopping complexes and contemporary houses. The city's economy began with—and still includes—ranching and the subsequent meat-packing industry, but the discovery of oil just south of the city in 1914 and just north in 1947 fueled a spurt of growth that turned an agricultural community into a metropolis.

Calgary today boasts a high concentration of head offices, the second largest in Canada. Energy, agriculture, tourism, manufacturing, research and development, and advanced technology comprise Calgary's industrial base.

The region's history of human habitation began almost 10,000 years before the first 19th-century fur and whiskey traders arrived. Indian tribes chose the confluence of the Bow and Elbow rivers as a campsite; emerging as the dominant tribe was the Blackfoot. Their acquisition of horses allowed them to hunt buffalo and fight almost every other prairie tribe with great success. As European settlement increased, so did the friction between the natives and the newcomers.

An 1877 treaty calmed the rough waters, and relative peace among all factions has existed since. Several reservations, including the Tsuu T'ina Reserve south of the city, are near Calgary. Native North Americans have sought to assimilate themselves into Canadian culture while retaining their native heritage.

Chinese were recruited abroad in the early 1900s to build the railroads; once the trains were running, however, Chinese immigration was restricted severely. Oil and money lured many American entrepreneurs who brought the technology and investment funds needed to get Calgary's petroleum industry started. But many of those who came for the money enjoyed the area and stayed, becoming Canadian citizens.

Calgary's modern sophistication is offset by a romantic perception of the past—a past in which the city was established as a North West Mounted Police fort in 1875. The Calgary Stampede, a 10-day Western winging, is attended by more than a million residents and visitors who relive the days of chuck wagons and lassos. Those days existed more than a century ago, after the North West Mounted Police—the forerunner of today's Royal Canadian Mounted Police—and the railroad brought law, order and homesteaders to a region previously settled by trappers, buffalo hunters and whiskey traders.

Although Calgary's growth has been rapid, it has been practical. The bustling downtown district was designed to accommodate a large amount of activity, even during winter when below-freezing temperatures normally would inhibit commerce. Enclosed walkways called "plus-15s" (they are 15 feet above street level) connect almost half

Calgary Stampede / © Gibson Stock Photography

Downtown / © Gibson Stock Photography

the downtown buildings, making it possible to eat, work, shop or visit neighbors without donning so much as a mitten.

The Stephen Avenue Walk, a pedestrian mall in the city center lined with trees, benches and fountains, is an urban refuge from traffic as well as a nice place to enjoy lunch or a stroll in warm weather.

All is not business in Calgary. Music, ballet, theater and plenty of outdoor recreation are readily available. In addition Calgary distinguished itself as host city of the 1988 Winter Olympic Games. Such educational institutions as Mount Royal College, Southern Alberta Institute of Technology and the University of Calgary prepare Canadians for the future. Natural resources and man-made technology will continue to drive Calgary in the 21st century.

Approaches

By Car

Two major highways pass through Calgary. Hwy. 2 runs north and south through the city; Trans-Canada Hwy. provides access from the east and west. Hwy. 1A, which connects Calgary and Cochrane, also serves as an alternate route between Calgary and the towns of Canmore and Banff. Hwy. 8 connects Calgary with Bragg Creek.

Getting Around

Street System

Calgary is divided into quadrants, with Centre Street separating the east and west sectors and the Bow River and Memorial Drive delineating north and south. Streets run north and south, avenues east and west. All are numbered from the intersection of Centre Street and Centre Avenue, just north of downtown. Roads in suburban areas are numbered where they form grids and named where they do not.

The speed limit is 50 kilometres per hour (30 mph) or as posted. A right turn on red after stopping is permitted unless otherwise posted; U-turns are not. Other restrictions apply during rush hours in certain areas; be aware of signs, especially in school and playground zones. Pedestrian crosswalks are designated by "X" signs, and motorists must yield to pedestrians.

Parking

Parking is not permitted on major roads in the downtown core during rush hours, between 6:30 and 9 a.m. and 3:30 and 6 p.m. Downtown metered street parking usually is limited to 2 hours at a maximum cost of $3.50 per hour. Pay parking for extended periods is available at numerous locations; rates average

(continued on p. 54)

The Informed Traveler

City Population: 878,866

Elevation: 1,048 m/3,440 ft.

Sales Tax: The federal Goods and Services Tax is 7 percent and applies to most goods, food/beverages and services, including lodgings. Alberta does not have a provincial sales tax but does impose a 5 percent tax on accommodations.

WHOM TO CALL

Emergency: 911

Police (non-emergency): (403) 266-1234

Fire: (403) 287-4299

Weather: (403) 299-7878

Road Conditions: (403) 246-5853

Hospitals: Alberta Children's Hospital, (403) 943-7211; Foothills Hospital, (403) 944-1110; Peter Lougheed Centre, (403) 943-4555; Rockyview General Hospital, (403) 943-3000.

WHERE TO LOOK

Newspapers

Calgary's daily newspapers are the *Calgary Herald* and the *Calgary Sun*, both morning papers. The national newspapers are *The Globe and Mail* and the *National Post*.

Radio

Calgary radio station CBC (1010 AM) is a member of Canadian Broadcasting Corporation.

Visitor Information

Tourism Calgary: 238 11th Ave. S.E., Room 200, Calgary, AB, Canada T2G 0X8; phone (403) 263-8510 or (800) 661-1678. Visitor information also is available at the Calgary International Airport on the arrivals level; and at Riley & McCormick Western Store at 200 Barclay Parade in the Eau Claire Festival Market.

TRANSPORTATION

Air Travel

Calgary International Airport is northeast of downtown. Cardinal Coach Lines is one of the companies providing transportation between the airport and downtown. Buses run between the airport and eight major hotels daily every half-hour 6:30 a.m.-11:30 p.m. Rates are $11 one-way, $17 round-trip; phone (403) 531-3909.

Rental Cars

Hertz, downtown or at the airport, offers discounts to CAA and AAA members. Phone (403) 233-8366 downtown, (403) 221-1676 at the airport, (800) 263-0600 in Canada or (800) 654-3131 out of Canada.

Rail Service

The nearest VIA Rail stations are in Jasper and Edmonton; phone (506) 857-9830, or (888) 842-7245 in western Canada.

Buses

Greyhound Lines Inc. operates from the depot at 850 16th St. S.W.; phone (403) 265-9111. Red Arrow Express operates luxury motor coaches between Calgary, Red Deer, Edmonton and Fort McMurray; phone (403) 531-0350.

Taxis

Taxi companies include Checker Cab, (403) 299-9999; Mayfair Taxi, (403) 255-6555; Prestige Limousine, (403) 730-6666; Red Top Taxi, (403) 974-4444; and Yellow Cab, (403) 974-1111. Rates begin at $2.50, plus 20c for each additional 162 metres (over 1/5 km) or 721 ft. (about 1/7 mi.). Cabs can be hailed on the street, but phoning ahead is recommended.

Public Transport

Calgary has both bus and light-rail rapid transit (LRT) service; the latter is free in the downtown core. Calgary Transit's office, 240 7th Ave. S.W., has schedules and maps and sells transit passes. Fares are $2 for adults and $1.25 for ages 6-14. Day passes are $5.60 for adults and $3.60 for ages 6-14; phone (403) 262-1000.

Handi-Bus provides transportation for the physically and mentally impaired (visitors and residents alike) within the city limits; registration is required. A day's notice is requested. The fare is $1.75; phone (403) 276-8028.

Destination Calgary

*A*lthough a thriving ranching industry and the discovery of oil helped put Calgary on the map, it was the 1988 Olympic Games that turned all eyes on the former cow town.

*T*oday visitors can travel to an observation terrace in the sky, peruse museums and historic sites and ski in the same park where the games were held.

Calgary Zoo

Calgary Zoo, Botanical Garden and Prehistoric Park.
Meet this sweet-faced tiger cub at Calgary's zoo, which features many rare and endangered species among its 900 residents. (See listing page 55)

Calgary Stampede.
This 10-day celebration of the Wild West, held in early July, comes complete with chuck wagon races, a rodeo, livestock shows, pancake breakfasts, parades and a midway. (See mention page 60)

Calgary Stampede

Travel Alberta

Canada Olympic Park, Calgary.
Although the ski jump tower brings back memories of the 1988 Winter Olympic Games held in Calgary, the park is now a site for year-round sports activities. (See listing page 55)

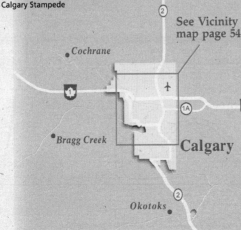

See Vicinity map page 54

Cochrane

Bragg Creek

Calgary

Okotoks

Heritage Park

Heritage Park Historical Village, Calgary.
You'll receive a warm welcome when you visit this living-history village, re-created to resemble a pre-1914 settlement in western Canada. (See listing page 56)

*P*laces included in this AAA Destination City:

around $1.50 per hour or portion thereof, to a maximum of $16 per day, Mon.-Sat. 6-6; free on Sun.

What To See

(SAVE) THE AERO SPACE MUSEUM OF CALGARY is at 4629 McCall Way N.E. In a former Royal Air Force drill hall, the museum contains exhibits about western Canada's aviation history. Aircraft are displayed, including an F86 Sabre jet, a Bell 476 helicopter and one of the few remaining World War I Sopwith Triplanes. Also featured are piston and jet aircraft engines, aviation artwork and a Martin Baker ejection seat.

Allow 30 minutes minimum. Daily 10-5; closed Jan. 1 and Dec. 24-26. Admission $6; over 59 and ages 12-17, $3.50; ages 6-11, $2; family rate $15. AX, MC, VI. Phone (403) 250-3752.

(GEM) BUTTERFIELD ACRES CHILDRENS FARM is 3 km (1.9 mi.) n. of Crowchild Tr. at 254077 Rocky Ridge Rd. Children and adults can meet and play with animals such as baby goats, rabbits, chicks, calves, sheep, llamas and a 450-pound pig named Scarlett at this whimsical, educational farm.

In addition to interactive displays, children also will enjoy milking demonstrations and pony rides. They can play on an old tractor or hammer nails. Hayrides are popular during the winter months; phone for information.

Picnicking is permitted. Food is available. Allow 2 hours minimum. Daily 10-4, July-Aug.; Mon.-Fri. 10-2, Sat.-Sun. 10-4, last weekend in Mar.-June 30 and in Sept. Admission $7.49; over 65 and ages 1-17, $5.49. MC, VI. Phone (403) 547-3595 or (403) 239-0638.

CALAWAY PARK is 10 km (6 mi.) w. on Hwy. 1 at the Springbank Rd. exit. The 28-hectare (69-acre) entertainment and amusement park has 28 rides, including a roller-coaster, log ride, Ferris wheel, bumper boats and skill games. Musical shows are presented daily. The landscaped grounds include waterfalls, a miniature golf course, a fishing pond and picnic areas.

Small kennels are available for pets. Food is available. Allow 4 hours minimum. Mon.-Thurs. 10-7, Fri.-Sun. 10-8, late June-early Sept.; Fri. 5-9, Sat.-Sun. 10-8, mid-May to late June; Sat.-Sun. 11-6, early Sept. to mid-Oct. Admission (inludes unlimited rides) $23; ages 3-6, $17; over 50, $15; family rate (up to four people) $65. AX, MC, VI. Phone (403) 240-3822.

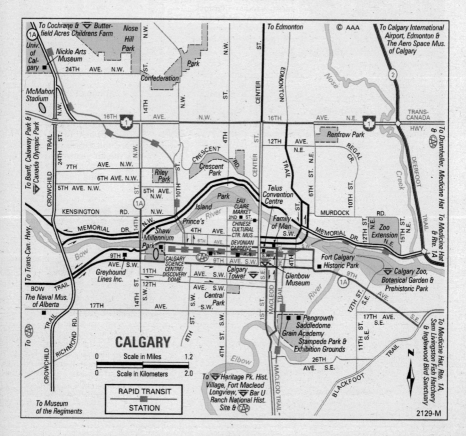

CALGARY SCIENCE CENTRE/DISCOVERY DOME is at 11th St. and 7th Ave. S.W. The center presents multimedia productions and large-format films in the Discovery Dome. Science is at the core of hands-on exhibits, demonstrations and live theater. Daily 9:30-5:30, late June to mid-Sept.; Mon.-Thurs. 9:45-4, Fri. 9:45-5; Sat.-Sun. 10-5, rest of year. Closed Dec. 25. Admission $11; over 64 and ages 13-18, $9; ages 3-12, $8; family rate (two adults and up to four children under 18) $39.95. Parking $4 (valid for 6 hours). MC, VI. Phone (403) 268-8300.

CALGARY TOWER is in Tower Centre at 101 9th Ave. S.W. at Centre St. S. The tower rises 191 metres (626 ft.) above the city. An observation terrace and revolving restaurant provide a panorama of the city and the nearby Rocky Mountains. The reception lobby offers a display from the World Federation of Great Towers, photographs and historical perspectives of the Calgary skyline.

A torch atop the tower burned nonstop during the 1988 Olympic Games; it is illuminated on special occasions. Daily 7 a.m.-10:30 p.m. Admission $9.95; over 64, $8; ages 5-17, $7. AX, MC, VI. Phone (403) 266-7171.

CALGARY ZOO, BOTANICAL GARDEN AND PREHISTORIC PARK is at 1300 Zoo Rd. N.E. at Memorial Dr. and 12th St. E. The zoo is dedicated to conservation, education, recreation and scientific study. Such rare and endangered species as the Siberian tiger and the whooping crane are among more than 900 animals in the zoo. Varied habitats simulate such ecosystems as the boreal forest and an African rainforest and savannah. An Asian elephant is noteworthy for her ability to paint; profits from the sale of her works benefit the environmental enrichment fund.

A tropical aviary and conservatory contains a butterfly garden and more than 10,000 plants. A prehistoric park contains more than 20 life-size replicas of dinosaurs in 2.6 hectares (6.5 acres) of re-created Mesozoic landscape. Allow 3 hours minimum. Daily 9-5. Admission $15; over 64, $13; ages 13-17, $9; ages 3-12, $7.50. AX, MC, VI. Phone (403) 232-9300.

CANADA OLYMPIC PARK is off Trans-Canada Hwy. Bowfort Rd. exit. The park, the host area for ski jumping, freestyle skiing, bobsled and luge events at the 1988 Winter Olympic Games, remains a site for year-round sports activities.

The 2-hour Olympic Odyssey guided bus tour includes visitor access to the Olympic Hall of Fame and Museum, the bobsleigh/luge track and the observation level of the 90-metre (295-ft.) ski-jump tower. Guests can see athletes training on ski jumps or in the sliding center, where bobsleigh, skeleton-sled and luge athletes practice. Self-guiding tours also are permitted; a tour booklet is available.

In winter visitors can learn to ski and snowboard. During summer guests can try the bobsleigh/luge track, at speeds up to 95 kilometres per hour (59 mph). Also on the premises is a mountain bike park with 25 kilometres (15 mi.) of trails.

Food is available. Allow 2 hours minimum. Guided tours are given daily on the hour 9-8, Victoria Day weekend-Labour Day weekend; hours vary rest of year. Self-guiding tour May 1-second Mon. in Oct. $10, family rate (two adults and their children) $35. Self-guiding tour rest of year $7, family rate $24. Guided bus tour $15, family rate $40. Activities and rides additional. AX, MC, VI. Phone (403) 247-5452.

Olympic Hall of Fame and Museum is in Canada Olympic Park. Two floors of exhibits include Winter Olympic Games memorabilia from 1924 to the present. An Olympic timeline, photographs, medals and interactive videotapes spotlight prominent Canadian Olympians. A bobsled simulator re-creates the twists of the Olympic bobsleigh/luge track at Canada Olympic Park. A ski jump simulator re-creates the tower.

Daily 8-6, Victoria Day weekend-Labour Day; 10-5, rest of year. Closed Dec. 25. Admission included in Canada Olympic Park admission. Phone (403) 247-5452.

CHINESE CULTURAL CENTRE MUSEUM is at 197 1st St. S.W. Exhibits represent Chinese culture and history and include sculptures, ceramics and other artifacts dating back thousands of years. Permanently displayed is a replica of the army of terra-cotta soldiers found during a 1974 excavation at Mount Li in China. The clay archers, bowmen, cavalry, chariots and saddled cavalry horses were found in battle-ready formation guarding the Tomb of Qin Shihuang; each figure is unique. Daily 11-5. Admission $4; over 64 and ages 6-12, $2. Phone (403) 262-5071.

DEVONIAN GARDENS is on the 4th level of Toronto Dominion Square, 317 7th Ave. S.W. These 1-hectare (2.5-acre) glassed-in, indoor gardens contain 15,700 subtropical trees and plants as well as waterfalls, fountains and a reflecting pool. Monthly exhibits display works by local artists. A 200-seat amphitheater occasionally hosts shows at noon. Daily 9-9. Free. Phone (403) 268-2489, or (403) 268-2300, ext. 9845 for recorded information.

FAMILY OF MAN is outside the Calgary Board of Education Building at 515 Macleod Tr. S.E. The grouping of sculpted metal figures stands 6.5 metres (21 ft.) tall. Originally commissioned as part of Great Britain's exhibit for Expo 67, the statues were created by Mario Armengol. Nude and lacking a discernible race, the figures extend their arms and hands in gestures of goodwill and friendship. Daily 24 hours. Free.

FIREFIGHTERS MUSEUM SOCIETY is off Macleod Tr. to 42nd Ave. then just n. on 11th St. S.E. Photographs, artifacts, uniforms and equipment depict the history of the city's firefighters. A large collection of restored fire engines also is featured. Allow 1 hour minimum. Thurs.-Mon. 10:30-4, mid-May to mid-Oct. Admission $3, senior citizens $2, under 12 free. Phone (403) 246-3322.

FORT CALGARY HISTORIC PARK is at 750 9th Ave. S.E. The 16-hectare (40-acre) riverside park is on the site of a North West Mounted Police fort. Interactive exhibits, costumed interpreters, hands-on activities and audiovisual presentations tell the story of the site, the settlement and the people of Calgary 1875-1940. In the park are the reconstructed 1875 fort; an interpretive center; and the Deane House Historic Site, the last remaining building from the site's days as a garrison.

Food is available. Daily 9-5. Admission $9; over 64, $7; ages 7-17, $5. AX, MC, VI. Phone (403) 290-1875.

GLENBOW MUSEUM is at 130 9th Ave. S.E., across from the Calgary Tower. The complex includes a museum, art gallery, library and archives. Colorful displays trace the history of the settlement of western Canada. From a Blackfoot tepee and the elegant quillwork of the Plains Cree to the hard-won comforts of a pioneer cabin, the museum celebrates Western heritage. Visitors also can explore interactive exhibits about warriors, gemstones and West Africa.

Art galleries showcase historical, modern and contemporary art from extensive collections. The Discovery Room offers hands-on activities. Food is available. Allow 2 hours minimum. Tues.-Sat. and Mon. holidays 9-5, Sun. noon-5; closed Jan. 1 and Dec. 25. Admission $12; over 65, $9; students with ID and ages 6-12, $8; family rate (two adults and up to four children) $37.50. AX, MC, VI. Phone (403) 268-4100.

GRAIN ACADEMY is at Stampede Park off 4th St. S.E. on the second floor of Round Up Centre. Visitors can learn about the process of bringing grain from the field to the table. Highlights include a miniature grain elevator and a working model train that depicts the transportation of grain from the prairie to the Pacific coast. A movie theater and displays describing the history of grain also are featured. Allow 1 hour minimum. Mon.-Fri. 10-4; closed holidays. Free. Parking $7. Phone (403) 263-4594.

HERITAGE PARK HISTORICAL VILLAGE is 2.5 km (1.5 mi.) w. off Hwy. 2 to 1900 Heritage Dr. S.W. The re-created pre-1914 village sits on 25 hectares (60 acres). The village reflects the fur trade of the 1860s, the pre-railway settlements of the 1880s and businesses and residences 1900-14.

Among the park's more than 150 exhibits are a general store, an antique midway, pioneer farm machinery and a Hudson's Bay Co. trading post. Most of the buildings are originals that have been moved to the park. An antique steam train circles the park, and a 200-passenger stern-wheeler boat cruises Glenmore Reservoir.

Daily 9-5, mid-May through Labour Day; Sat.-Sun. 9-5, day after Labour Day to mid-Oct. Admission with rides $22; ages 3-17, $17; family rate (two adults and children ages 3-17) $79. Village only $13; ages 3-17, $8; family rate $45. AX, MC, VI. Phone (403) 268-8500 to verify prices.

INGLEWOOD BIRD SANCTUARY is at 2425 9th Ave. S.E. on the Bow River. Self-guiding trails wind throughout the forest, where some 280 species of birds and various mammals have been sighted. Natural history programs and guided nature walks also are offered. Allow 1 hour minimum. Trails daily dawn-dusk. Visitor center daily 10-5, May-Sept.; Tues.-Sun. 10-4, rest of year. Closed Jan. 1, Easter, Nov. 11 and Dec. 24-26. Donations. Phone (403) 221-4500.

(SAVE) **MUSEUM OF THE REGIMENTS** is at 4520 Crowchild Tr. S.W., off Flanders Ave. exit. The museum depicts the history of Lord Strathcona's Horse (Royal Canadians) regiment, Princess Patricia's Canadian Light Infantry, The King's Own Calgary Regiment and The Calgary Highlanders.

The Alberta Gallery has displays about Alberta's military history since 1874, and the Imperial Oil Gallery features rotating exhibits about Canada's military history. Vintage tanks and carriers can be seen outside. Food is available. Allow 1 hour minimum. Daily 9:30-4; closed Jan. 1 and Dec. 25. Admission $6; senior citizens $4; ages 13-19, $3; active military with ID and their families free. Phone (403) 974-2850 for recorded information.

(SAVE) **THE NAVAL MUSEUM OF ALBERTA** is at 1820 24th St. S.W. Exhibits present the history of the Royal Canadian Navy and the Royal Canadian Naval Reserve, which existed 1910-68, together with Canada's Merchant Marine. A display commemorates Canadians who served in World Wars I and II and the Korean War. Housed in the building are the only three fighter aircraft flown by the Canadian Navy as well as exhibits and photographs documenting the history of the service.

Allow 30 minutes minimum. Daily 10-5, July-Aug.; Tues.-Fri. 1-5, Sat.-Sun. and holidays 10-5, rest of year. Closed Jan. 1 and Dec. 25. Admission $5; over 64 and students with ID $3; under 12, $2; family rate (five or more family members) $12. VI. Phone (403) 242-0002.

(SAVE) **THE NICKLE ARTS MUSEUM** is on the University of Calgary campus at 434 Collegiate Blvd. N.W. Four galleries present changing exhibits of contemporary and historical arts and numismatic collections. Lectures, gallery talks and other events are offered throughout the year. Allow 1 hour minimum. Mon.-Fri. 10-5 (also Thurs. 5-9), Sat. 1-5, Sept.-May; Mon.-Fri. 10-5, rest of year. Closed holidays. Admission $2; over 59 and ages 7-17, $1; college faculty and students with ID free; free to all Tues. Phone (403) 220-7234.

SAM LIVINGSTON FISH HATCHERY is at 1440 17A St. S.E. in Pearce Estate City Park. Exhibits tell about fisheries management and fish culture

programs in Alberta. Aquariums of trout and a film are featured. **Note:** The hatchery is closed for renovation until summer 2005; phone ahead for updates. Allow 30 minutes minimum. Mon.-Fri. 10-4, Sat.-Sun. and holidays 1-5, Apr.-Sept.; Mon.-Fri. 10-4, rest of year. Donations. Phone (403) 297-6561.

CASINOS

- **Cash Casino Place** is at 4040 Blackfoot Tr. S.E. Daily 10 a.m.-3 a.m.; closed Dec. 25. Phone (403) 287-1635.

- **Casino Calgary** is at 1420 Meridian Rd. N.E. Daily 10 a.m.-3 a.m.; closed Dec. 25. Phone (403) 248-9467.

- **Elbow River Casino** is at 1919 Macleod Tr. S.E. Table games daily 10 a.m.-3 a.m. Poker daily 24 hours. Closed Dec. 25. Phone (403) 266-4355.

- **Frank Sisson's Silver Dollar Casino** is at 1010 42nd Ave. S.E. Daily 10 a.m.-3 a.m.; closed Dec. 25. Phone (403) 287-1183.

- **Stampede Casino** is at 1801 Big Four Tr. S.E. Daily 10 a.m.-3 a.m.; closed June 29-July 2, July 14-18 and Dec. 25. Phone (403) 261-0422.

What To Do

Sightseeing

Bus, Train and Van Tours

Brewster Transportation and Tours offers a 4-hour bus tour of Calgary's attractions as well as trips to Banff, Lake Louise, Jasper and the Columbia Icefield; phone (403) 221-8242 for schedules and fares.

Rocky Mountaineer Vacations offers scenic, 2-day, all daylight, narrated rail tours between Banff, Calgary and Jasper in Alberta and Vancouver, British Columbia. Westbound and eastbound departures are offered mid-April to mid-October, with winter rail trips available in December. Onboard meals and snacks as well as overnight hotel accommodations in Kamloops, British Columbia, are included. Phone (604) 606-7245 or (800) 665-7245.

Walking Tours

Free pamphlets about a self-guiding tour of the Stephen Avenue Walk are available at the City of Calgary Municipal Building, 800 Macleod Tr. S.E., plaza level, second floor. This pedestrian mall, which extends from Macleod Trail west along 8th Avenue to 3rd Street S.W., is a showcase for historic buildings, many of which are restored. Other walking-tour and historical pamphlets also are available.

Sports and Recreation

Calgary was an appropriate choice as host of the 1988 Winter Olympic Games—opportunities for indoor and outdoor recreation abound. In winter public **skiing** facilities at Canada Olympic Park and in numerous areas nearby are available. Canada Olympic Park *(see attraction listing p. 55)* also is where to go for other **winter sports,** such as luge, bobsledding, ski jumping and snowboarding.

At Talisman Centre, 2225 Macleod Tr. S., **swimming, track events** and **weight lifting** are among the popular activities; phone (403) 233-8393. Similar facilities are offered at the following leisure centers: Eau Claire YMCA, 101 Third St. S.W.; YWCA, 320 Fifth Ave. S.E.; Southland Leisure Center, 19th Street and Southland Drive S.W.; and Village Square Leisure Center, 2623 56th St. N.E. The latter two offer wave pools.

Ice skating is featured during the winter at Olympic Plaza as well as year-round at more than two dozen other locations. The Olympic Oval, at 2500 University Dr. N.W., is the site of the 1988 Olympic speed-skating events; skate rentals are available.

Several parks are in the city, particularly along the Bow River. Fish Creek Provincial Park *(see Recreation Chart)* has a visitor center and a small lake providing swimming in summer and ice skating in winter. Joggers and bicyclists use the park's extensive trail system. Other recreation sites include Bowness, Edworthy and Riley parks in northwest Calgary and Prince's Island Park in the city center. The 145-hectare (360-acre) Glenmore Reservoir

provides ample space for **sailing** and **canoeing;** the Dragon Boat races are held in late July.

With spectacular natural areas nearby, many visitors to Calgary will be lured to the wilds to enjoy canoeing, **camping, rafting, hiking** and other outdoor pursuits. **Walking** and **bicycling** trails meander through these regions, as do **cross-country skiing** routes. **Tennis** and swimming enthusiasts will find courts and pools throughout Calgary; for details phone the parks and recreation office at (403) 268-3888.

Golf lovers can play at more than 40 local courses, including 18 holes at Maple Ridge, 1240 Mapleglade Dr. S.E.; McCall Lake, 1600 32nd Ave. N.E.; McKenzie Meadows, 17215 McKenzie Meadows Dr. S.E.; and Shaganappi Point, 1200 26th St. S.W. Nine-hole courses are at Confederation, 3204 Collingwood Dr. N.W.; Lakeview, 5840 19th St. S.W.; and Richmond Green, 2539 33rd Ave. S.W. Some private courses accept visiting golfers; check locally for greens fees and restrictions.

With names like Flames, Stampeders Roughnecks and Hitmen, Calgary's major sports teams cannot help but be exciting. The Flames play **ice hockey** at Pengrowth Saddledome in Stampede Park; phone (403) 777-2177.

The local Canadian **Football** League team, the Calgary Stampeders, pounds the turf at McMahon

Stadium on Crowchild Trail N.W., off 16th Avenue. Tickets can be obtained by phoning the box office at (403) 289-0258. Ticket prices are $27-$55; over 60 and under 18, $23-$47.

For those wishing to get behind the wheel, Kart World Family Fun Center, 5202 1st St. S.W., offers **go-carts**, which can be rented. Helmets, clothing and instructions are provided. Tamer tracks for children also are available; phone (403) 253-9555.

Horse racing, including Thoroughbred and harness varieties, is featured at Stampede Park. The park's entrances are at the intersection of 4th Street and 14th Avenue S.E., and on 25th Avenue off Macleod Trail. Phone (403) 261-0214 for race dates and (403) 261-0120 for clubhouse reservations. Legalized **gambling** casinos and "bingo barns" are available if you care to try your luck.

Note: Policies concerning admittance of children to pari-mutuel betting facilities vary. Phone for information.

Spruce Meadows, an outdoor equestrian center and show jumping venue 3 kilometres (2 mi.) west on Hwy. 22X (Spruce Meadows Trail) from Macleod Trail, has world-class programs, including international show jumping events. On days when no shows are scheduled the grounds are open free to the public, daily 9-5. Visitors are invited to wander the grounds, picnic and view horses in the stables. Phone (403) 974-4200 for a schedule of Spruce Meadows events.

Shopping

Stephen Avenue Walk, a downtown pedestrian mall, extends from Bankers Hall to the city municipal buildings. This popular spot for people-watching features shops, galleries and restaurants housed within historic buildings. Also downtown, a five-block shopping complex linked by an indoor walkway includes the more than 200 boutiques, department stores and retail chains of Calgary Eaton Centre/TD Square, Bankers Hall, Scotia Centre and Penny Lane Mall.

Unique specialty shops, kiosks and restaurants are the draw at Eau Claire Festival Market, adjacent to the Bow River and Prince's Island Park at 2nd Avenue and 2nd Street S.W.

The trendy Uptown 17th Avenue, a scenic neighborhood and upscale shopping district, features stylish fashion shops, antiques stores and eclectic craft boutiques. The avenue also is home to the exclusive shops at Mount Royal Village. The Kensington district features smaller stores in new and old buildings. Originally Atlantic Avenue, Ninth Avenue S.E. now is lined with antiques and home-furnishings stores, bookstores and cappuccino bars.

Major department stores and a wide variety of chain and specialty stores occupy the city's shopping centers: Chinook Centre at the corner of Macleod Trail and Glenmore Trail S.W., Deerfoot Outlet Mall at 901 64th Ave. N.E., Market Mall at 3625 Shaganappi Tr. N.W., North Hill Mall at 16th Avenue and 14th Street N.W., Northland Village Shoppes at Crowchild Trail N.W. and Shaganappi Trail N.W., Shawnessy Centre at 162nd Avenue and Macleod Trail, Southcentre Mall at Macleod Trail and Anderson Road S.E., Sunridge Mall at 2525 36th St. N.E., Westhills Towne Centre at Stewart Green S.W. off Richmond Road and Sarcee Trail S.W. and Willow Park Village on Macleod Trail S.

Theater and Concerts

Four of Calgary's most illustrious theater and music companies perform in the Epcor Centre for the Performing Arts at 205 8th Ave. S.E. The center is shared by Alberta Theatre Projects, Theatre Calgary, One Yellow Rabbit Theatre Company and Calgary Philharmonic Orchestra. In addition to four theaters and a concert hall, it contains shops, a restaurant and a coffee bar. For information about performance schedules and ticket sales phone Ticketmaster at (403) 777-0000 or (403) 299-8888.

Southern Alberta Jubilee Auditorium, just south of 14th Avenue and 14th Street N.W., stages a variety of performing arts, including touring companies of Broadway musicals and presentations by Calgary Opera; for details phone the opera company at (403) 262-7286 or the auditorium at (403) 297-8000. **Note:** The auditorium is closed for renovation until September 2005. Phone ahead for updates.

Loose Moose Theatre Company performs adult comedy and drama as well as children's theater; for information phone (403) 265-5682. Pumphouse Theatre, 2140 Pumphouse Ave. S.W., gets its name from the 1913 former pumphouse that the city converted into two theaters; phone (403) 263-0079 for schedule and ticket information. Midday performances take place in the aptly named Lunchbox Theatre on the second level in Bow Valley Square, 205 Fifth Ave. S.W.; phone (403) 265-4292.

A popular dinner theater that often showcases well-known performers in its productions is Stage West, 727 42nd Ave. S.E.; phone (403) 243-6642. Other theater, dance and music companies operate locally; check newspapers for performance schedules.

Special Events

To celebrate the season and showcase local arts, culture and sports, Calgary Winter Festival takes place for 11 days in February. The festival, which takes advantage of the venues from the 1988 Winter Olympics, features dog sledding, snowboarding and the Winter Village; phone (403) 543-5480.

Calgary International Children's Festival, which begins the third Wednesday in May and continues for 5 days, draws performers from such locales as Peru, Germany, Russia and Zimbabwe. The festival's many offerings include music, puppetry, dance and storytelling; phone (403) 294-7414.

Musicians from all corners of the globe gather in mid-June at the Calgary International Jazz Festival to celebrate jazz as well as world music, blues and gospel. Cabarets, dance parties and other outdoor festivities also are characteristic of the celebration; phone (403) 249-1119.

Despite a focus on the modern oil and gas industry, Calgary citizens recall their past starting the first Friday after Canada Day (July 1) with The Calgary Stampede *(see color ad)*. This 10-day Wild West exhibition features a rodeo, chuck wagon races, livestock shows, a turn-of-the-20th-century Western village, a Las Vegas-style revue, informative displays and a midway. Parades, fireworks, street dancing, pancake breakfasts and other activities create a carnival-like atmosphere; phone (403) 261-0101 or (800) 661-1767.

Calgary Folk Music Festival is held for 4 days in late July. In early September the Spruce Meadows outdoor equestrian center, off Hwy. 22X (Spruce Meadows Trail) and Macleod Trail, plays host to the Masters Tournament. Other racing and dressage events are held at the center throughout the year. Phone (403) 974-4200 for a schedule of Spruce Meadows events.

The Calgary Vicinity

BRAGG CREEK (H-5) pop. 678

Bragg Creek, 40 kilometres (25 mi.) southwest of Calgary on Hwy. 22, was named after Albert Bragg, a rancher who settled in the area in 1894. The town has been a popular weekend getaway and year-round recreation area since the 1920s. Known as the "Gateway to the Kananaskis" for its proximity to the Northern Rockies, the area has evolved as an artist's community with sculptors, potters, weavers, painters and other artisans practicing their crafts.

Bragg Creek offers picnic areas, hiking trails, cross-country skiing, campgrounds and scenic Elbow Falls.

Bragg Creek Chamber of Commerce: 23 White Ave., Bragg Creek, AB, Canada T0L 0K0; phone (403) 949-0004.

COCHRANE (G-5) pop. 11,798

Cochrane—named for Sen. Matthew Henry Cochrane, who initiated the first large-scale cattle ranch in the area in the 1880s—is known locally for its homemade ice cream, made by the same family since 1948; hang gliding; horseback riding; and canoe trips down the Bow River. Stoney Indian Reserve, 16 kilometres (10 mi.) west on Hwy. 1A, was the site of several movies, including Arthur Penn's "Legends of the Fall" and "Little Big Man," and of the television series "Lonesome Dove."

The downtown's Western-style architecture provides a backdrop for local arts and crafts and specialty shops. Of particular interest is Studio West, a foundry and art gallery where visitors can view the 3,000-year-old sculpting technique known as the "lost wax" process.

Cochrane & District Chamber of Commerce: Bay #5, 205 First St. E., Cochrane, AB, Canada T4C 1X6; phone (403) 932-6810.

COCHRANE RANCHE is near jct. hwys. 1A and 22. This 60-hectare (150-acre) provincial historic site and park is where Sen. Matthew Cochrane began his large-scale cattle operation in 1881. A visitor center, interpretive programs, walking trails and picnic grounds are available. The "Men of Vision" bronze statue overlooks the grounds. Allow 30 minutes minimum. Daily 9-5, mid-May through Labour Day. Donations. Phone (403) 932-1193.

OKOTOKS (H-6)
pop. 11,664, elev. 1,036 m/3,400'

Incorporated in 1904, Okotoks thrived on brick making, lumber and oil distribution in its early days. Today Okotoks is a commuter community of Calgary. The town gets its name from the Blackfoot name "okatoks," meaning "rocks." Big Rock, 7 kilometers (4 mi.) west, is the continent's largest known glacial boulder, having been carried here during an ice age.

A popular recreational retreat, Okotoks offers such leisure pursuits as fishing and hiking. Events include a parade and Youth Festival in mid-June and the Coors Pro Rodeo and Western Art Show on Labour Day weekend.

Okotoks Chamber of Commerce: The Station Cultural Centre, 53 N. Railway St., P.O. Box 149, Okotoks, AB, Canada T0L 1T0; phone (403) 938-2848.

Self-guiding tours: Heritage Walking Tour brochures are available from the information desk at The Station Cultural Centre.

This ends listings for the Calgary Vicinity.
The following page resumes the alphabetical listings
of cities in Alberta.

CAMROSE (E-7) pop. 14,854

Camrose, first settled around 1900 as a trading post, has a strong sense of its Norwegian heritage. Known originally as the Hamlet of Sparling, its name was changed to Camrose in 1906. Camrose salutes country music during Big Valley Jamboree, the first week in August.

Camrose Chamber of Commerce: 5402 48th Ave., Camrose, AB, Canada T4V 0J7; phone (780) 672-4217.

CAMROSE AND DISTRICT CENTENNIAL MU-SEUM is 2 blks. s. of Hwy. 13 at jct. 53rd St. and 46th Ave. The museum houses items from Camrose's pioneer days. Buildings include a country school, a fire hall and a restored log pioneer house and church, both furnished in period. A steam engine, a replica of the first newspaper building and a working model of an early threshing machine are displayed. Tues.-Sun. 9:30-5, Victoria Day-Labour Day; by appointment rest of year. Donations. Phone (780) 672-3298, or (780) 672-5373 for off-season appointments.

CANMORE (H-4)

pop. 10,792, elev. 1,341 m/4,400'

Established in 1883 as a coal-mining center, Canmore was the first Canadian Pacific Railroad divisional point west of Calgary. Recreational activities are abundant; the town was the site of the biathlon and cross-country ski events of the 1988 Winter Olympics. Hiking, mountain biking and cross-country skiing are popular along the area's numerous trails.

Canmore/Kananaskis Chamber of Commerce: #12, 801 8th St., Canmore, AB, Canada T1W 2B3; phone (403) 678-4094.

ALPINE HELICOPTERS LTD. is off Hwy. 1 Canmore exit, following signs to Canmore Municipal Heliport. Scenic flights over the Canadian Rockies are offered. Passengers can view alpine valleys, glaciers, ice fields, the Continental Divide, Banff National Park and towering Mount Assiniboine— the "Matterhorn of the Canadian Rockies." Helicopters carry four to six passengers.

Flights are offered daily (weather permitting) 8:30-4:30; closed Jan. 1 and Dec. 25-26. Fare $155 per passenger for a 25-minute tour or $75 for a 12-minute tour. Reservations are required. Phone (403) 678-4802.

CANMORE MUSEUM AND GEOSCIENCE CENTER is at 902B 7th Ave. Displays detail Canmore's past through photographs, coal-mining artifacts. The museum also houses a geology exhibit with fossils, rocks, photographs and movies. Historical walking tours are offered. Allow 30 minutes minimum. Wed.-Sun. 1-8, June 1-Labour Day; noon-4, rest of year. Walking tours Tues. and Thurs. Donations. Phone (403) 678-2462.

OH CANADA EH?! DINNER SHOW is at 125 Kananaskis Way. The show provides guests with a humorous take on Canadian culture and tradition. Singing Mounties, lumberjacks, a hockey player as well as other characters serve guests a family-style Canadian meal during the show.

Allow 2 hours, 30 minutes minimum. Shows are presented daily at 6:30, May-Oct.; otherwise varies. Admission $55; ages 13-17, $45; under 12, $27.50. Reservations are required. MC, VI. Phone (403) 609-0004 or (800) 773-0004. *See color ad p. 45.*

RECREATIONAL ACTIVITIES

Skiing

• **Nakiska Ski Resort** is just n. of Kananaskis Village on Hwy. 40. Write 1505 17th Ave. S.W., Calgary, AB T2T 0E2. Mon.-Fri. 9-4, early Dec. to mid-Apr. Phone (403) 591-7777, (403) 256-8473, or (800) 258-7669.

White-water Rafting

• **Mirage Adventure Tours Ltd.** departs from Canmore Rafting Centre. 20 Lincoln Park, Canmore, AB T1W 3E9. Other activities are offered. Departures daily at 10 and 1:30, May-Sept. Phone (403) 678-4919 or (888) 312-7238 in Canada.

CARDSTON (J-6)

pop. 3,475, elev. 1,185 m/3,888'

A son-in-law of Brigham Young, Charles Ora Card, led 10 Mormon families from Utah into Canada in 1887, hoping to find freedom from American anti-polygamy laws. Settling in Cardston, the immigrants founded the country's first Mormon settlement and named the town after their leader, who became its first mayor.

Alberta Temple of the Church of Jesus Christ of Latter-day Saints, 348 3rd St. W., is built on land donated by Card in 1887. It was completed and dedicated in 1923. The temple serves a large area of western Canada and Montana; approximately 80 percent of Cardston residents are Mormon. Non-Mormons are not permitted to enter the structure but can tour the grounds, where a visitor center offers information; phone (403) 653-1696.

Cardston & District Chamber of Commerce: P.O. Box 1212, Cardston, AB, Canada T0K 0K0; phone (403) 653-2798.

C. ORA CARD HOME is at 337 Main St. The log cabin of the Mormon leader has been restored and refurnished with hand-carved furniture. Allow 30 minutes minimum. Mon.-Sat. 1:30-5, June-Aug. Donations. Phone (403) 653-3366.

COURT HOUSE MUSEUM is at 89 3rd Ave. W. Displays include local pioneer memorabilia in a stone courthouse dating from 1907. Allow 1 hour minimum. Mon.-Sat. 9-12:30, June-Aug. Donations. Phone (403) 653-3366.

REMINGTON CARRIAGE MUSEUM is at 623 Main St. More than 250 19th- and early 20th-century horse-drawn vehicles are showcased. Interactive displays and exhibit galleries provide the feeling of riding in the horse-drawn transportation of that era, and an introductory multimedia presentation provides an overview of that time.

The exhibit galleries, which include a smithy and livery stable, carriage factory, carriage dealership, a working restoration shop, frontier settlement and racetrack, depict 19th-century society and its dependence on this mode of transportation. Sound effects, lighting and audiovisual presentations enhance many of the vignettes. A working stable shows horses being groomed and harnessed. In summer visitors may schedule rides on vintage and reproduction vehicles for a fee.

Guided tours are available. Picnicking is permitted. Food is available. Allow 1 hour, 30 minutes minimum. Daily 9-6, May 15-Sept. 14; 10-5, rest of year. Closed Jan. 1, Easter and Dec. 24-25. Admission $7.50; over 65, $6.50; ages 7-17, $4; family rate $17. Fifteen-minute carriage ride $4; ages 7-17, $2.50; family rate $12. MC, VI. Phone (403) 653-5139.

CLARESHOLM (I-5) pop. 3,622

CLARESHOLM MUSEUM is at 5126 1st St. W. Displays are housed in a historic sandstone Canadian Pacific Railway station. Early 20th-century items represent pioneer life. Town history is highlighted in railway, medical and educational displays. On the grounds are a one-room schoolhouse, a historic log cabin, a train and a playground. Daily 9:30-5:30, Victoria Day-Thanksgiving; by appointment rest of year. Donations. Phone (403) 625-3131.

COALDALE (I-7) pop. 6,008

THE ALBERTA BIRDS OF PREY CENTRE is 3 blks. n. of jct. hwys. 3 and 845, then w. on 16th Ave. The center rehabilitates injured and orphaned birds of prey and prepares them for release back to the wild. A captive breeding program returns threatened and endangered species to their native habitats. A self-guiding nature walk provides a close-up view of caged or tethered hawks, falcons, owls, eagles and vultures. Birds fly freely during daily demonstrations.

Guided tours are available. Picnicking is permitted. Allow 1 hour, 30 minutes minimum. Daily 9:30-5, early May-early Sept. Admission $8; over 59, $7; ages 6-17, $5; ages 3-5, $4; family rate $17. MC, VI. Phone (403) 345-4262.

COCHRANE—*see Calgary p. 61.*

COLUMBIA ICEFIELD—

see Jasper National Park p. 82.

CROWSNEST PASS (I-5) pop. 6,400

An area of wild beauty and haunting legends, the municipality of Crowsnest Pass is an amalgamation of the former coal-mining towns of Bellevue, Blairmore, Coleman, Frank and Hillcrest. Scenic Hwy. 3 through Crowsnest Pass connects Burmis to Fernie, British Columbia, via the Rocky Mountain Range and the Continental Divide.

The area provides visitors with recreational opportunities and stimulates the imagination with such stories as the curse of the Lost Lemon Gold Mine, rum-running and the shootout at Bellevue Cafe.

The town of Frank made national headlines April 29, 1903, when close to 70 residents were killed in the spectacular slide of Turtle Mountain on the east side of the pass. Ninety million tons of limestone swept over 1.5 kilometres (.9 mi.) of the valley before dawn, destroying part of the town and burying a mine plant and railway. The old town was at the western edge of the slide; many cellars still are visible.

BELLEVUE UNDERGROUND MINE TOUR is n. off Hwy. 3 Bellevue exit, following signs. Participants don a miner's helmet and lamp, strap on a battery pack and follow guides along the same path taken by coal miners 1903-61, when this was an active coal mine. The half-hour tour provides insights into the process of coal mining and the events that led to the mine's closing. The temperature in the mine can reach 7 C (45 F); dress in warm clothing and wear sturdy footwear.

Allow 30 minutes minimum. Tours depart daily every 30 minutes 10-5:30, May 15-Labour Day. Fee $6; over 65 and ages 6-17, $5; family rate $18. MC, VI. Phone (403) 564-4700.

FRANK SLIDE INTERPRETIVE CENTRE is 1.5 km (.9 mi.) n. off Hwy. 3 at w. edge of Frank Slide. The center overlooks the site of the 1903 rockslide. Displays and a 20-minute audiovisual program, "In the Mountain's Shadow," describe area history from early settlement to the decline and fall of the mining industry and the events surrounding the Frank Slide. A 47-minute documentary, "On the Edge of Destruction," also is featured. Walkways outside the center provide views of the devastation and the surrounding area. A 1.5-kilometre (.9-mi.) self-guiding trail over the slide allows visitors to view the debris. Interpretive programs are offered in summer.

Allow 1 hour, 30 minutes minimum. Daily 9-6, May 15-Sept. 14; 10-5, rest of year. Closed Jan. 1, Easter and Dec. 24-25. Admission $6.50; over 64, $5.50; ages 7-17, $3; family rate $15. AX, MC, VI. Phone (403) 562-7388.

LEITCH COLLIERIES PROVINCIAL HISTORIC SITE is 3 km (1.9 mi.) e. of Bellevue on Hwy. 3. Founded in 1907, this was the first wholly Canadian-owned mine. The area was the site of a sophisticated early colliery—a coal mine and the buildings and equipment connected with it. The remains of the power house, washery, mine manager's residence and coke ovens still stand. Interpretive signs explain the mining and processing methods.

Self-guiding tours are available year-round. Interpreters are on site daily 10-5, mid-May through Labour Day. Donations. Phone (403) 562-7388.

DEVON—see Edmonton p. 75.

DONALDA (F-7) pop. 230

Situated in the heart of Alberta, Donalda was established in 1911 and named after Donald A. Mann, an official with the Canadian National Railway. It overlooks the scenic Meeting Creek Coulee. The region's unusual Paskapoo sandstone rock formations attract sportsman, hikers, artists and photographers. Donalda also claims an unusual man-made distinction. A 12.8-meter (42-foot) lamp, said to be the world's largest, was built by townspeople. It glows each evening as dusk falls.

DONALDA AND DISTRICT MUSEUM is at Main St. and Railway Ave. More than 900 lamps ranging from the antique bicycle variety to colorful living room types are displayed. Some 40 tiny courting lamps, which hold only an hour's worth of fuel and were used in the 1800s to signal the end of a suitor's visit, also can be seen. An art gallery, a 1909 railway station and a creamery are included. Allow 30 minutes minimum. Mon.-Fri. 9-5, Sat.-Sun. 11-5, early May-second Mon. in Oct.; Mon.-Fri. 9-5 and by appointment, rest of year. Donations. Phone (403) 883-2100.

DRUMHELLER (G-7) pop. 7,785

About 65 million years before Sam Drumheller began promoting the 1910 townsite later named for him, the surrounding Red Deer Valley was the home of immense dinosaurs. Plant-eating hadrosaurs, flesh-eating tyrannosaurs and their formidable cousins stomped through the swampy lowlands and forests bordering the Mowry Sea, which once covered the North American plains. Fossils of prehistoric creatures often are discovered in the multilayered sedimentary walls of the valley; several life-size dinosaur replicas can be seen in town.

A larger-than-life version of one of these prehistoric beings, an 84-foot-tall facsimile of a tyrannosaurus rex, has been built over the top of the Drumheller Regional Chamber of Development and Tourism on First Avenue. Visitors can climb up to a viewing platform in the dinosaur's mouth.

Although the local coal industry founded in 1911 by American Jesse Gouge has declined, remnants of old mines still exist. In Midland Provincial Park off N. Dinosaur Trail (Hwy. 838), a self-guiding walking trail leads to the former site of Midland Mine.

Gas and oil wells sporadically dot the nearby rolling prairies, but the shortgrass country is occupied mostly by geese and antelopes.

Hoodoos—mushroom-shaped pillars of rock that have been carved into unusual formations by centuries of wind and rain—can be seen 18 km (11 mi.) southeast on Hwy. 10. Because of their fragile nature, climbing these formations is not permitted.

Another nearby remarkable natural site is Horseshoe Canyon, 17 kilometres (11 mi.) southwest on Hwy. 9. Deriving its name from its horseshoe shape, the canyon is in an area of badlands amidst the Alberta prairies. Viewpoints provide opportunities to survey multicolored canyon walls and unusual rock formations.

An outdoor natural amphitheater is the site in early July for six performances of the Canadian Badlands Passion Play. In a setting closely resembling the Holy Land, a cast of 150 and a 100-voice choir relate the life of Christ; phone (403) 823-2001.

Stretching over the Red Deer River, the Rosedale Suspension Bridge on Hwy. 10 originally was used to carry miners across the river to the now-abandoned Star Mine. In 1931 the swinging bridge replaced the original cable car system and was used until the mine closed in 1957. A park with picnic facilities is available.

Drumheller Regional Chamber of Development and Tourism: 60 First Ave. W., P.O. Box 999, Drumheller, AB, Canada T0J 0Y0; phone (403) 823-8100.

DINOSAUR TRAIL (HWY. 838) is a 50-km (30-mi.) circle tour, which winds w. from Drumheller through the Red Deer Valley, part of Alberta's Badlands. The trail is marked. The arid terrain is distinguished by hoodoos—mushroom-shaped rock pillars carved by thousands of years of wind and rain.

A short distance along the north trail is The Little Church, a meditation chapel that holds six visitors. The cable-run Bleriot Ferry crosses the Red Deer River. The ferry departs on demand, early May to late Oct.

Badlands Historical Centre is at 335 First St. E. Displays focus on pioneer history, the coal-mining boom and the region's ecology. A lapidary collection includes fossils, gems and minerals. Interactive exhibits are available. Daily 10-8, May-Oct. Admission $4; over 64 and ages 7-17, $3; family rate $12. AX, MC, VI. Phone (403) 823-2593.

HOMESTEAD ANTIQUE MUSEUM is .7 km (.5 mi.) n.w. via Hwy. 9 to 901 N. Dinosaur Tr. Pioneer and Indian items as well as clocks, gramophones, radios, early cars, fine china, jewelry,

tractors and farm implements are on display. There also are collections of military badges, medals and early 20th-century clothing.

Allow 1 hour, 30 minutes minimum. Daily 10-8, mid-June through Labour Day; 10-5, mid-May to mid-June and day after Labour Day-second Mon. in Oct. Admission $3; over 64 and ages 6-17, $2; family rate $10. Phone (403) 823-2600.

REPTILE WORLD is at 95 Third Ave. Home to more than 85 species of reptiles and amphibians, including snakes, frogs and turtles, the facility features Fred, a 700-pound alligator. Allow 1 hour minimum. Daily 9 a.m.-10 p.m., July-Aug.; Thurs.-Mon. 10-5, rest of year. Closed Jan. 1 and Dec. 25. Admission $4.50; over 64 and ages 5-17, $3.50. AX, MC, VI. Phone (403) 823-8623.

THE ROYAL TYRRELL MUSEUM is 6 km (4 mi.) n.w. on N. Dinosaur Tr. (Hwy. 838). The museum is in the badlands of the Red Deer River Valley, surrounded by one of the richest fossil deposits in the world. Dinosaurs that once roamed Alberta are now showcased in the museum's Dinosaur Hall, where more than 35 skeletons and lifelike models are displayed.

Fossils, models, computers, DVD centers, a preparation laboratory, hands-on exhibits and an indoor garden illustrate millions of years of geological and biological development. The garden contains plants that are virtually the same today as they were more than 65 million years ago. The museum also houses a research center and operates a field station near Brooks (*see place listing p. 49*).

Allow 3 hours minimum. Daily 9-9, Victoria Day weekend-Labour Day; 10-5, day after Labour Day-second Mon. in Oct.; Tues.-Sun. 10-5, rest of year. Closed Dec. 25. Admission $10; over 64, $8; ages 7-17, $6; family rate (two adults and children ages 7-17) $30. MC, VI. Phone (403) 823-7707, or (888) 440-4240 out of Alberta.

DUNVEGAN (A-2)

DUNVEGAN PROVINCIAL PARK is off Hwy. 2 on the n. side of the Peace River beside Dunvegan Suspension Bridge. The park was a fur-trading post and the site of one of the first Roman Catholic missions in Alberta. Three original buildings remain: the 1877-78 Factor's House, part of the Hudson's Bay Co.'s fort; the 1885 church of St. Charles Mission; and its 1889 rectory. Guided walks and educational programs explain the site's history. A visitor center offers a video about the history of Dunvegan.

Allow 1 hour minimum. Daily 10-6, May 15-Labour Day. Admission $3; over 64, $2; ages 6-17, $1.50; family rate $8. Phone (780) 835-7150. *See Recreation Chart.*

Edmonton

Few first-time visitors to Edmonton are prepared for what they discover when they arrive. From trading post to metropolis within some 200 years, this capital city continues to surprise visitors by its size, quality of life, sophistication and its beautiful river valley location.

Edmonton owes its existence to an abundant and varied supply of natural resources, which prompted each of its three major booms. In 1795 the Hudson's Bay Co. founded Fort Edmonton on the banks of the North Saskatchewan River. Traders bartered with Cree and Blackfoot Indians for luxuriant and sought-after pelts of otters, beavers, muskrats, minks and foxes. A trading settlement developed and became the main stopping point on routes to the north and to the Pacific.

This stopping point became a starting point for prospectors rushing to the Klondike for gold; they stocked up on supplies in Edmonton for the harsh trip northward. When gold failed to materialize and many prospectors realized they were not going to get rich, let alone get rich quick, they headed back to Edmonton to settle for a slower but surer way of life.

A bust for prospectors was a boom for Edmonton. The city grew to six times its previous size, making it a prime choice for the provincial capital when Alberta was formed in 1905.

In the years that followed, the capital city earned its nickname, "Gateway to the North," because of its status as a transportation hub and gateway to the regions beyond. In 1915 Edmonton became a major link in the Canadian Pacific Transcontinental Railroad, emerging as an important crossroads stop between east and west as well as north and south.

The city's reputation as a transportation center was reinforced during the 1930s as bush pilots transported vital medical supplies, food and mail to northern communities. And when construction began on the Alaska Highway in 1942, Edmonton found itself again in the role of a major distribution and supply center. Edmonton also is an important air travel link.

When the last big boom was fading from memory, the Leduc No. 1 Well gushed forth black crude oil only 40 kilometres (25 mi.) southwest of Edmonton. This discovery in February 1947 was just the beginning. Since then more than 2,250 wells within a 40-kilometre (25-mi.) radius of Edmonton have coaxed the precious natural resource to the surface. Enormous industrial growth resulted; the city's population quadrupled in the 25 years following the Leduc gusher. Today more than 450,000 barrels of crude oil are refined daily in Greater Edmonton.

"Canada's Festival City" is a city growing in both prosperity and beauty. With about 666,000 residents in

Fort Edmonton Park / © Gibson Stock Photography

North Saskatchewan River / © Richard Cummins / SuperStock

the greater metropolitan area, Edmonton has been careful not to sacrifice the natural resource that makes it livable—its green space. Edmonton's river valley parkland is reputed to be the largest stretch of urban parkland in North America, encompassing 7,340 hectares (18,348 acres). The city contains more than 11,000 hectares (27,181 acres) of parkland, playgrounds and open areas.

Stretches of parks along the North Saskatchewan River valley let residents spend long summer days enjoying the outdoors. The city park system provides a winter playground for such activities as cross-country skiing, ice skating, dog sledding and snowshoeing. For visitors who prefer the indoors, an extensive system of underground and overhead "pedways" in the downtown area makes it possible to travel in climate-controlled comfort regardless of the weather; Edmonton Tourism provides pedway maps.

Approaches

By Car

Two major highways run through Edmonton. The Trans-Canada Yellowhead Highway (Hwy. 16) provides access from the east and west; Hwy. 2 runs north and south.

Getting Around

Street System

Edmonton's street system is a grid with streets running north and south and avenues running east and west. Most streets and avenues are numbered starting from the southeast corner of the city; a few are named.

Edmonton's street plan includes several traffic circles. When approaching a traffic circle, make sure you are in the correct lane. Use the right lane if you plan to exit, the left lane if you are traveling around the circle. When in the circle, the vehicle on the outside must yield to the vehicle on the inside.

The city speed limit is 50 kilometres per hour (30 mph) or as posted. A right turn on red after stopping is permitted; U-turns are not. A sign that reads "Bus and Taxi Lane Only" means it is illegal to drive, park or stop any vehicle other than the above in that lane.

Parking

Street parking restrictions vary throughout the city; watch for and heed the signs. Parking is not permitted in the residential areas surrounding Northlands Park, Telus Field and Commonwealth Stadium during major events; cars parked there will be towed.

Rates for city-operated parking meters are $1.25 per hour. Most meters are free after 6 p.m. and on

(continued on p. 70)

The Informed Traveler

City Population: 666,104

Elevation: 670 m/2,198 ft.

Sales Tax: The federal Goods and Services Tax is 7 percent and applies to most goods, food/beverages and services, including lodgings. Alberta does not have a provincial sales tax but does impose a 5 percent tax on accommodations.

WHOM TO CALL

Emergency: 911 or (780) 426-3232

Police (non-emergency): (780) 423-4567

Fire: (780) 496-3900

Ambulance: 911 or (780) 426-3232

Distress Line: (780) 482-4357

Weather: (780) 468-4940

Road Reports: (780) 471-6056

Hospitals: Grey Nuns, (780) 450-7000; Misericordia, (780) 930-5611; Royal Alexandra, (780) 477-4111; University of Alberta, (780) 407-8822.

WHERE TO LOOK

Newspapers

Edmonton has two daily newspapers, the *Edmonton Journal* and the *Edmonton Sun,* both distributed in the morning. Canada's national newspapers, *The Globe and Mail* and the *National Post,* also are available at newsstands.

Radio

Radio station CBC (740 AM) is a member of Canadian Broadcasting Corp.

Visitor Information

Edmonton Tourism: 9990 Jasper Ave. N.W., Edmonton, AB, Canada T5J 1P7; phone (780) 496-8400 or (800) 463-4667.

Edmonton Tourism—Gateway Park Information Center: 2404 Gateway Blvd. S.W./Hwy. 2, Edmonton, AB, Canada T6W 1A1; phone (780) 496-8400 or (800) 463-4667.

Visitor information also is available at the Edmonton International Airport.

TRANSPORTATION

Air Travel

Edmonton International Airport is 29 kilometres (18 mi.) south of the city center; for information phone (780) 890-8382 or (800) 268-7134. Sky Shuttle scheduled service to downtown costs $13 one way and $20 round-trip; phone (780) 465-8515, or (888) 438-2342. Taxi service between the airport and downtown averages $40-$44; a limousine is $48. Many hotels offer free shuttle service for their guests.

Rental Cars

Hertz, downtown or at the airport, offers discounts to CAA and AAA members. Phone (780) 423-3431 downtown, (780) 890-4435 at the airport, (800) 263-0600 in Canada or (800) 654-3001 out of Canada.

Rail Service

The VIA Rail station is at 12360 121st St.; phone (780) 448-2575 for baggage information, (888) 842-7245 for arrival and departure information.

Buses

The downtown depot for Greyhound Lines Inc. is at 10324 103rd St.; phone (780) 413-8747 or (800) 661-8747. The south side depot is at 5723 104th St. Red Arrow Express offers luxury motor coach service between Edmonton, Calgary, Fort McMurray and Red Deer; phone (780) 424-3339 or (800) 232-1958.

Taxis

Taxi companies include Alberta Co-Op Taxi, (780) 425-2525; Prestige/Checker Cabs, (780) 484-8888 or (780) 462-4444; Skyline Cabs Ltd., (780) 468-4646; and Yellow Cab, (780) 462-3456. Taxi rates start at $2.80, plus $1.10 is charged for each additional kilometre. Taxis can be hailed, but phoning is recommended.

Public Transport

Edmonton Transit System's Churchill Station Information Centre, 99th Street and 102A Avenue, is open Mon.-Fri. 8:30-5:30; phone (780) 496-1611. Buses operate 6 a.m.-1 a.m., Mon.-Sat., 6:30 a.m.-12:30 a.m., Sun. and holidays. The Light-Rail Transit (LRT) operates 5:30 a.m. to 1 a.m. Fare is $2; over 64 and ages 6-16, $1.75. A 1-day pass is $6.

Disabled Adult Transit System (DATS) serves those who can't use other transit facilities. Visitors may request a temporary registration number by phoning (780) 496-4570. DATS takes reservations from 1 to 3 days in advance.

Destination Edmonton

Once a tiny settlement where traders sought to swap for furs with Cree and Blackfoot Indians, today's bustling Edmonton holds its heritage in high regard.

Reminders of the city's past can be found at museums, living-history demonstrations, historic sites and archives. But don't forget to step into the present for a visit to what may be the world's largest mall.

© Roth and Ramberg Photography, Inc. / West Edmonton Mall

West Edmonton Mall.
You can experience a little bit of New Orleans while browsing at this shopping and entertainment complex that claims to be the world's largest mall. (See listing page 72)

Travel Alberta

Edmonton International Street Performers Festival.
Magicians, clowns, jugglers, mime artists and musicians take to the street for 10 days in July—just one example of why Edmonton is known as "Canada's Festival City." (See mention page 75)

Provincial Museum of Alberta

Provincial Museum of Alberta, Edmonton.
Alberta's natural and human history are examined in galleries that explore the story of the province's aboriginal peoples as well as its gem and mineral resources, dinosaurs, insects, vegetation and birds. (See listing page 71)

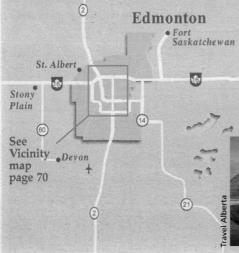

Edmonton

• Fort Saskatchewan

St. Albert

Stony Plain

See Vicinity map page 70

• Devon

Travel Alberta

Muttart Conservatory, Edmonton.
The conservatory's pyramid-shaped greenhouses form a frame for the city's skyline. (See listing page 71)

Places included in this AAA Destination City:

Sundays and holidays; however, there are some 24-hour meters.

Rates for downtown parking lots range $1.50-$3 per half-hour during the day. At lots participating in the city's Park in the Heart program, parking costs $2 from 6 p.m. to midnight Monday through Friday and for the first 3 hours on Saturdays and Sundays.

What To See

SAVE **ALBERTA AVIATION MUSEUM** is at The Hangar on Kingsway at 11410 Kingsway Ave. This double-long, double-wide hangar was a training facility for air crews during World War II. The museum displays 27 historic aircraft including a carefully restored Fairchild 71 and a fighter-bomber version of the De Havilland Mosquito as well as 1920s biplanes and jet fighters from the Cold War era. Other displays detail the history of aviation in Edmonton and Alberta.

Allow 1 hour minimum. Mon.-Fri. noon-8, Sat.-Sun. and holidays 10-4; closed Jan. 1 and Dec. 25. Hours may vary; phone ahead. Admission $5; over 59, $4; ages 13-17, $3; ages 6-12, $2; family rate (parents and up to four children under 17) $15. AX, MC, VI. Phone (780) 451-1175.

ALBERTA LEGISLATURE BUILDING is at 10800 97th Ave. Public-use parkland, monuments, pools and fountains surround the building, which was built with imported sandstone and marble and completed in 1912. Displays outline Alberta's history and parliamentary traditions. Guided 40-minute tours begin in the Legislature Interpretive Centre.

Allow 1 hour minimum. Tours are given daily at 9, 10 and 11 and then every half-hour 12:30-4, May 1-Oct. 15; Mon.-Fri. on the hour 9-3, Sat.-Sun. noon-4, rest of year. Closed Jan. 1, Good Friday and Dec. 25. Free. Phone (780) 427-7362 for tour reservations.

ALBERTA RAILWAY MUSEUM is 2 km (1.2 mi.) s. of Hwy. 37 at 24215 34th St. The museum resembles a railway terminal, with a train yard, locomotive and car shops, and a station. More than 50 pieces of rolling stock are displayed. There are

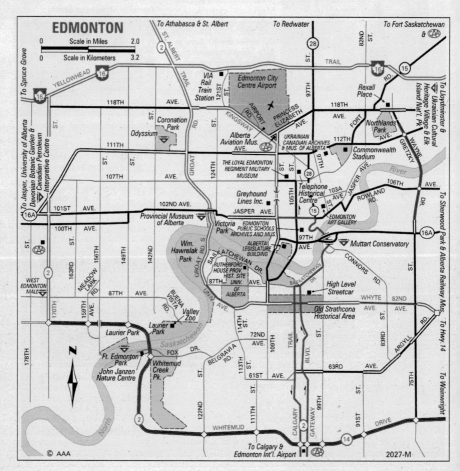

many exhibits about railway history, including telegraph systems and railway technology. A diesel train provides 20-minute excursions on Sundays during July and August.

Guided tours are available with a week's notice. Picnicking is permitted. Food is available. Allow 1 hour, 30 minutes minimum. Daily 10-5, Victoria Day weekend-Labour Day. Admission $4; senior citizens and students with ID $2.50; ages 3-12, $1.25. Train rides $3. VI. Phone (780) 472-6229.

EDMONTON ART GALLERY is at 2 Sir Winston Churchill Sq. The gallery exhibits fine and applied arts, with an emphasis on Canadian historical art and western Canadian contemporary art. Allow 1 hour minimum. Tues.-Fri. 10:30-5 (also Thurs. 5-8), Sat.-Sun. 11-5; closed major holidays. Admission $8; over 64 and students with ID $6; ages 6-12, $4; family rate (two adults and up to four children) $20. MC, VI. Phone (780) 422-6223.

EDMONTON PUBLIC SCHOOLS ARCHIVES AND MUSEUM is at 10425 99th Ave. This 1905 brick school is in the historic McKay Avenue School, site of the first session of the Alberta Legislature. The building has been carefully restored and features the 1906 legislative chamber, period classrooms and displays that trace the history of Edmonton public schools. Also on the grounds is the restored Edmonton 1881 Schoolhouse, the first public school in Alberta.

Allow 1 hour minimum. Tues.-Fri. 12:30-4 (also Wed. 4-9), Sun. 1-4, May-Sept.; Tues.-Fri. 12:30-4, rest of year. Closed holidays. Free. Phone (780) 422-1970.

FORT EDMONTON PARK is at the jct. of Fox and Whitemud drs. This park, reputed to be Canada's largest living-history museum, depicts Edmonton in four eras: as an 1846 Hudson's Bay Co. fur-trading fort and native encampment, as an 1885 settlement, as a developing capital in 1905 and as a 1920 business community.

Costumed interpreters give demonstrations and encourage visitor participation in such period activities as playing pool, horseshoes and pioneer children's games, driving in antique cars, firing a round in the shooting gallery, learning to bead and tasting bannock. Steam train and streetcar rides are included.

Food is available. Pets are not permitted. Allow 3 hours minimum. Daily 10-6, late June-Labour Day; Mon.-Fri. 10-4, Sat.-Sun. 10-6, Victoria Day-late June; otherwise varies. Admission $9; over 64 and ages 13-17, $6.75; ages 2-12, $4.50; family rate $28.50. MC, VI. Phone (780) 496-8787.

JOHN JANZEN NATURE CENTRE is at jct. Fox and Whitemud drs. Adjacent to Fort Edmonton Park, the center has exhibits, self-guiding nature trails through the river valley, small animals, hands-on exhibits for children and interpretive programs and events designed to promote awareness and appreciation of wildlife and the environment.

Allow 1 hour minimum. Mon.-Fri. 10-5, Sat.-Sun. 11-5, late June-Labour Day; Mon.-Fri. 9-4, Sat.-Sun. 1-4, rest of year. Closed Jan. 1 and Dec. 25-31. Admission $1.75; over 64 and ages 13-17, $1.50; ages 2-12, $1.25; family rate $4.75. Phone (780) 496-8787.

THE LOYAL EDMONTON REGIMENT MILITARY MUSEUM is 2 km (1.2 mi.) n. on 105th St., then just w. to 10440 108th Ave. in the Prince of Wales Armouries Heritage Centre. The museum's two galleries examine the history of The Loyal Edmonton Regiment, Alberta's oldest infantry unit, and explore military life. Displays include weapons, military equipment, uniforms, medals and badges, photographs and documents. Allow 1 hour minimum. Mon.-Fri. 10-4. Donations. Phone (780) 421-9943.

MUTTART CONSERVATORY is at 9626 96A St. at the e. end of the James MacDonald Bridge. Four pyramid-shaped glass greenhouses contain plants. Palm trees, orchids and hibiscus, typical of warm, moist climates, thrive in the rain forest atmosphere of the Tropical Pyramid, while the Arid Pyramid displays vegetation indigenous to North America as well as Africa and the Mediterranean area. The Temperate Pyramid shows seasonal changes, and the Show Pyramid features changing exhibits of colorful floral displays. The conservatory's outdoor grounds can be enjoyed on a stroll (weather permitting).

Food is available. Allow 1 hour minimum. Mon.-Fri. 9-5:30; Sat.-Sun. 11-5:30; closed Dec. 25. Admission $7; over 64, students with ID and ages 13-18, $6; ages 2-12, $4; family rate $22. Phone to confirm prices. MC, VI. Phone (780) 496-8787.

ODYSSIUM is at 142nd St. and 111th Ave. Exhibits, games, models, galleries and science demonstrations explain and explore unique phenomena. Films are offered in an IMAX theater. The Margaret Zeidler Star Theatre presents planetarium and laser shows on its 23-metre (75-ft.) domed ceiling.

Weekend visitors can explore the world of computers in the Dow Computer Lab. Food is available. Center daily 10-9, Victoria Day-Labour Day; Sun.-Thurs. 10-5, Fri.-Sat. 10-9, rest of year. Closed Dec. 25. Observatory open Fri.-Sun. (weather permitting) 1-5 and 6:30-10:30, with additional hours during peak times.

Exhibit galleries and planetarium or one IMAX film $9.95; over 64 and ages 13-17, $8.95; ages 3-12, $7.95; family rate (two adults and four children) $38.95. Combination admission to exhibit galleries, planetarium and one IMAX film $15.95; over 64 and ages 13-17, $13.50; ages 3-12, $11.95; family rate $59.95. MC, VI. Phone (780) 451-3344.

PROVINCIAL MUSEUM OF ALBERTA is at 12845 102nd Ave. Alberta's natural and human history museum is housed in a 1967 Canadian centennial project. The building is surrounded by a sculpture park overlooking the river valley.

The Natural History Gallery offers specimens of plants, animals, birds, live insects, fossils and minerals depicting the 1 billion-year odyssey from dinosaurs to rare minerals and gems. The Syncrude Gallery of Aboriginal Culture tells the story of 11,000 years of aboriginal history. The Wild Alberta exhibit encourages visitors to look at the environment from a different perspective. Changing displays and events are scheduled throughout the year.

Food is available. Allow 2 hours minimum. Daily 9-5; closed Dec. 24-25. Hours may vary during special exhibits. Admission $10; over 64 and students with ID $8; ages 7-17, $5; family rate $28. Admission half-price Sat.-Sun. 9-11. An additional fee may be charged during special exhibits. AX, MC, VI. Phone (780) 453-9100.

SAVE RUTHERFORD HOUSE PROVINCIAL HISTORIC SITE is at 11153 Saskatchewan Dr. on the University of Alberta campus. The structure was home to A.C. Rutherford, Alberta's first premier and a founder of the University of Alberta. Completed in 1911, the elegant Jacobethan (a blend of Jacobean and Elizabethan styles) Revival house established a new standard in domestic architecture and marked the end of the pioneer style in Alberta. Guides in period dress conduct house tours upon request. Events are scheduled throughout the year.

Food is available. Allow 1 hour minimum. Daily 9-5, May 15-Labour Day; Tues.-Sun. noon-5, rest of year. Closed Jan. 1, Good Friday and Dec. 25. Admission $3; over 65 and ages 7-17, $2; family rate $8. Phone (780) 427-3995.

TELEPHONE HISTORICAL CENTRE is at 108th Ave. and 104th St. in the Prince of Wales Armouries. The center presents the history of telecommunications in Edmonton dating from the introduction of telephone service in 1885. The facility features numerous interactive exhibits and a 30-minute theater presentation with Xeldon the Robot. Allow 1 hour minimum. Tues.-Fri. 10-4. Donations. Phone (780) 433-1010.

UKRAINIAN CANADIAN ARCHIVES & MUSEUM OF ALBERTA is at 9543 110th Ave. Exhibits trace the history of Alberta's Ukrainian pioneers. Displays include traditional apparel and musical instruments, costumes, Ukrainian currency, photographs, church artifacts and folk art. Allow 1 hour minimum. Tues.-Fri. 10-5, Sat. noon-5; closed national holidays. Donations. Phone (780) 424-7580.

UKRAINIAN CULTURAL HERITAGE VILLAGE is 50 km (31 mi.) e. on Hwy. 16. The lifestyle of the region's Ukrainian immigrant population is portrayed in a village re-created to resemble a typical east central Alberta settlement 1892-1930.

Living-history demonstrations center around 34 restored historic buildings, including houses, farm buildings, churches and stores. The site comprises four areas: a town, a farmstead, a rural community and an overview area. Costumed interpreters depicting a wide variety of characters from the turn of the 20th century re-create the lives of the people who lived in each of the buildings, demonstrating the settlers' daily routines. Special events are held throughout the summer.

Picnicking is permitted. Allow 2 hours minimum. Daily 10-6, Victoria Day weekend-Labour Day; Sat.-Sun. 10-6, day after Labour Day-second Mon. in Oct. Admission $8; over 64, $7; ages 7-17, $4; family rate (two adults and two children) $20. MC, VI. Phone (780) 662-3640.

SAVE UNIVERSITY OF ALBERTA DEVONIAN BOTANIC GARDEN is 14 km (9 mi.) s. on Hwy. 60 from jct. Hwy. 16W and the Devon Hwy. overpass. Comprising 32 hectares (80 acres) of cultivated gardens and 44.5 hectares (110 acres) of natural area, the garden features a Kurimoto Japanese Garden, tropical butterfly house, ecological reserves and collections of native and alpine plants.

Picnicking is permitted. Food is available. Allow 2 hours minimum. Daily 10-9, early June-early Sept.; daily 10-7, early Sept. to mid-Oct.; daily 10-4, early May to early June; Sat.-Sun. 11-4, mid-Oct. to early Dec. Admission $9; over 64 and ages 12-17, $7; ages 2-11, $5; family rate (2 adults and three children) $27. MC, VI. Phone (780) 987-3054 or (780) 987-3055.

VALLEY ZOO is at Buena Vista Rd. (87th Ave.) and 134th St. More than 300 domestic, endangered and exotic animals from around the world call the zoo home. Animal interpretive programs, a merry-go-round and paddle boats are featured. A miniature train and a children's zoo are available during summer.

Food is available. Allow 1 hour, 30 minutes minimum. Daily 9:30-8, late June-Labour Day; daily 9:30-6, early May-late June; Mon.-Fri. 9:30-4, Sat.-Sun. 9:30-6, day after Labour Day-second Mon. in Oct.; daily 9:30-4, rest of year. Closed Dec. 25. Admission $7; over 64 and ages 13-17, $5.25; ages 2-12, $3.75; family rate $21.50. Admission is reduced in winter. MC, VI. Phone (780) 496-8787.

WEST EDMONTON MALL is at jct. 87th Ave. and 170th St. The huge, two-level complex has more than 800 stores and services, 26 movie theaters, more than 100 eateries and six major theme attractions. It is listed in the *Guinness Book of World Records* as the world's largest shopping center.

Galaxyland features 32 rides and attractions. Deep Sea Adventure features submarine rides, one of the world's largest indoor lakes and a life-size replica of Christopher Columbus' *Santa Maria*. Sea Life Caverns contains more than 200 species of marine life. With more than 2 hectares (5 acres) under one roof, World Waterpark houses a giant indoor wave pool. The Ice Palace is an NHL-size ice rink in the center of the complex.

Allow a full day. Shops open Mon.-Fri. 10-9, Sat. and most holidays 10-6, Sun. noon-6. Attractions, theaters and restaurants are open later.

Galaxyland unlimited 1-day pass $29.95, under 48 inches tall and senior citizens $21.95, family rate (up to four members) $74.95. Individual ride ticket $1.20. Water park $29.95; senior citizens and ages 3-10, $21.95; family rate $74.95. Ice Palace $5.50; senior citizens and ages 3-10, $3; family rate $13.95. Deep Sea Adventure $12; senior citizens and ages 3-10, $5; family rate $29.95. Miniature golf $9; senior citizens and ages 3-10, $6. Sea Life Caverns $6. AX, MC, VI. Phone (780) 444-5300 or (800) 661-8890 for attraction hours of operation.

CASINOS

- **Baccarat Casino** is at 10128 104th Ave. N.W. Slots daily 10 a.m.-3 a.m. Table games daily noon-2 a.m. Poker daily 24 hours. Closed Dec. 25. Phone (780) 413-3178.

- **Casino Edmonton** is at 7055 Argyll Rd. Daily 10 a.m.-3 a.m. Poker daily 24 hours. Closed Dec. 25. Phone (780) 463-9467.

- **Casino Yellowhead** is at 12464 153rd St. N.W. Daily 10 a.m.-3 a.m. Poker daily 24 hours. Closed Dec. 25. Phone (780) 424-9467.

- **Palace Casino** is at 2710 West Edmonton Mall, 8882 170th St. N.W. Table games daily noon-2 a.m. Slots daily 10 a.m.-3 a.m. Poker daily 24 hours. Phone (780) 444-2112.

What To Do

Sightseeing

Bus, Streetcar and Van Tours

Nite Tours offers pub crawls and double-decker bus tours; phone (780) 454-0303 or (877) 600-6483.

HIGH LEVEL STREETCAR departs from Jasper Plaza between 109th and 110th sts., and from the Old Strathcona stop at the rear of the farmers' market at 103rd St. and 84th Ave. A vintage streetcar takes passengers along the old CPR rail line across the High Level Bridge built 1911-13 to link Old Strathcona and Edmonton. The 3-kilometre (1.9-mi.) trip offers excellent views of the city and the river valley.

Allow 30 minutes minimum. Daily 11-4, late May-Labour Day; Fri.-Sun. 11-4, day after Labour Day-early Oct. Phone to confirm schedule. Hours may be extended during the Fringe Festival in Aug. Fare $3; senior citizens and ages 6-18, $3; family rate $10 (maximum two people over 18). Phone (780) 437-7721.

SAVE **OUT AN' ABOUT TOURS** depart from local hotels. These 3-hour to full-day van excursions highlight area cultural and historical sites. Downtown Edmonton tours includes the Alberta Legislature Building and Fort Edmonton Park.

Other tours visit the Ukrainian Cultural Heritage Village, Elk Island National Park and the North Saskatchewan River; and the Royal Tyrrell Museum and the badlands at Drumheller.

Some departures require a minimum of two to three people. Daily May 1-second Mon. in Oct.; otherwise varies. Fare $40-$225, children $25-$175. Fares include all applicable admission charges. Reservations are recommended. Phone (780) 909-8687.

Driving Tours

The most scenic areas in Edmonton are along the North Saskatchewan River valley. On the south side, the drive north along Saskatchewan Drive from 76th Avenue and 120th Street to 99th Street offers a picturesque trip around the University of Alberta campus. The views from the Provincial Museum of Alberta, 102nd Avenue and 128th Street, and the residential district of Glenora are impressive.

Walking Tours

Heritage Trail leads from the Shaw Conference Center to the Alberta Legislature Building, a route that links government and industry by way of Edmonton's past. Old Strathcona, south of the North Saskatchewan River, offers a view of many original buildings and street scenes characteristic of an early 20th-century prairie town. Edmonton Gallery Walk joins seven private art galleries around Jasper Avenue and 124th Street.

Guided walking tours of the 30,000-student University of Alberta are available year-round; phone (780) 492-1648.

Sports and Recreation

Whatever the season, there are opportunities for both indoor and outdoor recreation. The North Saskatchewan River valley is an oasis of parkland, with 122 kilometres (76 mi.) of trails, four lake systems and 22 parks. Depending on the time of year, you can **golf, hike, jog, cycle, ride horseback, fish, ski (cross-country and downhill), skate** or even pan for gold in a park.

The largest park is Capital City Recreation Park, composed of many smaller areas in the center and on the east side of the city. Within the park are 30 kilometres (19 mi.) of paths for **bicycling** and **jogging**. For information about activities and facilities phone Community Services at (780) 496-7275 Monday through Friday.

Playing host to three major sporting events—the Commonwealth Games in 1978, the World University Games in 1983 and the World Championships in Athletics in 2001—has provided Edmonton with a legacy of world-class sporting facilities. Several multiple-purpose centers—including Commonwealth Stadium Sport & Fitness Centre, 11000 Stadium Rd. at 91st Street, (780) 944-7400; Kinsmen Sports Centre, 9100 Walterdale Hill, (780) 944-7400; and Mill Woods Recreation Centre, 7207 28th Ave., (780) 496-2900—offer such activities as **swimming, diving, racquetball, squash** and **track** events.

Bring your set of clubs and try out one of more than 70 **golf** courses scattered about the Edmonton area. Three courses in the city's river valley are Riverside, on Rowland Road (106th Avenue) on the south side of the Dawson Bridge; Rundle Park, in the east end of Edmonton off 118th Avenue and Victoria Trail; and Victoria, said to be the oldest municipal golf course in Canada, on River Valley Road, accessible from Groat Road or from either 109th Street via the Walterdale Bridge from the south, or from 101st Street from the north.

Spectator sports can be enjoyed throughout the year. Budweiser Motorsports Park, 2 kilometres (1.2 mi.) west of Hwy. 2 on Hwy. 19, offers motorsport racing May through September; phone (780) 461-5801 or (780) 955-5540. Northlands Park, 7300 116th Ave., offers a chance to watch **harness racing** from early March to mid-June and from October to mid-December; phone (780) 471-7379 to confirm the dates for the racing schedule. **Thoroughbred racing** takes place from June to October; phone (780) 471-7379.

Note: Policies concerning admittance of children to pari-mutuel betting facilities vary. Phone for information.

Home to four professional sports teams, Edmonton is referred to fondly as the City of Champions. The Edmonton Oilers, several-time Stanley Cup champions of the National **Hockey** League, play from September to April in Rexall Place at 118th Avenue and 74th Street; phone (780) 414-4625. The Edmonton Eskimos **football** team, many times the Grey Cup champions of the Canadian Football League, play at Commonwealth Stadium, 111th Avenue and Stadium Road, from June to November; phone (780) 448-3757.

Northern League **Baseball** is played from April to September at Telus Field, south of downtown at 96th Avenue and 102nd Street; phone (780) 414-4450. **Soccer** is presented by the Edmonton Aviators Soccer Club, which plays at Commonwealth Stadium, 111th Avenue and Stadium Road.

Shopping

For the intrepid shopper, there is nothing like West Edmonton Mall *(see attraction listing p. 72)*, which occupies a 44-hectare (110-acre) site at 87th Avenue and 170th Street. Inside are more than 800 stores and services.

For those who want shopping on a less imposing scale, other popular malls include Kingsway Garden Mall, 109th Street and Princess Elizabeth Avenue; Londonderry Mall, 137th Avenue and 66th Street; and Southgate Centre, 111th Street and 51st Avenue.

Downtown offers boutiques and restaurants as well as covered shopping areas joined by enclosed walkways or pedways. The Edmonton City Centre complex between 100th and 103rd streets on 102nd Avenue contains Hudson's Bay Co., 140 other shops and a nine-screen theater among its four glittering floors.

ManuLife Place, Jasper Avenue and 101st Street, contains designer boutiques and Holt Renfrew, an elegant retail store with a quaint in-store cafe. Connected to ManuLife Place is Commerce Place, which features several shops with signature fashions.

Rice Howard Way, an attractive outdoor pedestrian area lined with sidewalk seating and eateries, is downtown at 100th Street and 101A Avenue. It is particularly popular in summer.

Old Strathcona at Whyte Avenue (82nd Avenue from 99th to 109th streets), the main outdoor shopping street on the south side of the city, has the look of historic Edmonton and offers boutiques, specialty shops, restaurants, bistros and coffee bars.

Don't forget that the major museums have interesting shops with items sometimes impossible to find elsewhere. Of particular interest are the six period shops in Fort Edmonton Park and the shop in the interpretive center at the Alberta Legislature Building.

Theater and Concerts

Theater season runs from September through May. For live theater visit the Citadel Theatre complex, 99th Street and 101A Avenue, which consists of four theaters, an amphitheater and a beautiful atrium; phone (780) 425-1820. Family-themed theater, produced by Fringe Theatre Adventures, can be enjoyed by all ages in October, December and February at the Arts Barns in Old Strathcona at 103rd Street and 84th Avenue; phone (780) 448-9000.

Prominent Canadian and American performers take to the stage at Mayfield Dinner Theatre at Mayfield Inn & Suites, 166th Street and 109th Avenue; phone (780) 483-4051. Celebrations Musical Dinner Theatre, 13103 Fort Rd., provides an entertainment experience for all ages; phone (780) 448-9339. Jubilations Dinner Theatre, in the West Edmonton Mall at the intersection of 87th Avenue and 170th Street, features musical comedy; phone (780) 484-2424.

The Alberta Ballet Company, (780) 428-6839, and the Edmonton Opera, (780) 429-1000, perform in Northern Alberta Jubilee Auditorium on the University of Alberta campus at 87th Avenue and 114th Street; phone (780) 427-2760 for auditorium information. **Note:** The auditorium is closed for renovation until September 2005. Phone ahead for updates. The Edmonton Symphony Orchestra, (780) 428-1414, performs at Francis Winspear Centre, 4 Sir Winston Churchill Sq.; phone (780) 428-1414 for concert information. Shaw Conference Centre, Francis Winspear Centre, Northern Alberta Jubilee Auditorium and Rexall Place play host to a variety of concerts ranging from classical music to rock.

Billy's Guide, See Magazine and *Where Edmonton* give detailed, up-to-date information about arts and entertainment in Edmonton, and local newspapers provide current performance information. Ticketmaster outlets handle ticket sales for most sports, recreation, theater and concert events; phone (780) 451-8000.

Special Events

Edmonton offers a smorgasbord of events. Independent short and feature-length movies are celebrated in March at the week-long Local Heroes International Film Festival.

Concerts, workshops, club dates and outdoor events characterize the Jazz City International Music Festival, held from mid- to late June; phone (780) 432-7166. Also in June, The Works Art and Design Festival brings together artists and artisans; phone (780) 426-2122.

Edmonton Celebrate Canada is a 12-day celebration, beginning late June with National Aboriginal Day. On June 24 are Francophone festivities honoring St. Jean Baptiste. The celebration concludes on Canada Day (July 1), with a full day of events and the Fireworks Finale.

During late June to mid-July the River City Shakespeare Festival presents two shows on alternating nights in William Hawrelak Park. Edmonton International Street Performers Festival in early July offers 10 days of free performances by street acts including magicians, clowns, jugglers, mime artists, musicians and comics.

The city's biggest event is Klondike Days. Every July Edmontonians don their finest Gay '90s apparel for the event that commemorates Edmonton's early days as a frontier community and gateway to the Yukon during the gold rush. Parades, casinos, gold panning, a chuck wagon derby and various other forms of entertainment keep the city alive with activity for 10 days. The Sourdough River Festival, the Sunday Promenade and A Taste of Edmonton are highlights.

Colored lights illuminate Great Divide Waterfall on Sunday evenings of summer holiday weekends; the best view is northeast of the High Level Bridge at 109th Street and 97th Avenue.

August brings the world to Edmonton during the 4-day Heritage Festival, which offers more than 60 outdoor ethnic pavilions showcasing international music, dance, art and cuisine. Also in August are the Edmonton Folk Music Festival; the Cariwest Caribbean Arts Festival; the Labatt Blues Festival; the Dragon Boat Festival; and the International Fringe Theatre Festival, an 11-day extravaganza of plays, dance, music, mime and street performances.

In September is the Edmonton Symphony Orchestra's 5-day Symphony Under the Sky Festival at Hawrelak Park. Post-summer events include the Edmonton International Film Festival in October and the Canadian Finals Rodeo in early November, and New Year's Eve special events.

The Edmonton Vicinity

DEVON (E-6) pop. 4,969, elev. 680 m/2,230′

Canada's first planned community, Devon was created by Imperial Oil Resources Ltd. in 1948 to provide accommodations for the workers employed in the company's oilfields. Imperial Leduc No. 1, the area's first well, had just put the town of Devon on the map. The town's name was derived from the Devonian formation, the oil's source, a strata 5,000 feet underground.

Town of Devon: #1 Columbia Ave. W., Devon, AB, Canada T9G 1A1; phone (780) 987-8300.

CANADIAN PETROLEUM INTERPRETIVE CENTRE is 2 km (1.2 mi.) s. on Hwy. 60. The center not only provides insight into the workings of the oil industry but also looks at area history, the story behind Leduc No. 1 and how Canada became self-sufficient in oil production. A 15-minute video presentation, interactive energy displays, geological exhibits, equipment, artifacts, photographs, scale models, murals and an outdoor interpretive trail help explain how oil is produced and refined.

Oilfield veterans are on hand to share their experiences and answer questions. A 53-metre (174-ft.) replica of the original derrick has been erected on the discovery site. Allow 1 hour minimum. Daily 9-5, Apr. 15-Sept. 15. Admission $5; over 65, $4; ages 6-18, $3; family rate $13. VI. Phone (780) 987-4323.

FORT SASKATCHEWAN (D-6) pop. 13,121

SAVE FORT SASKATCHEWAN MUSEUM AND HISTORIC SITE is downtown at 10006 100th Ave. A 1909 courthouse contains clothing and documents pertaining to area history, exhibits about the North West Mounted Police, and the original courtroom. Also comprising the site are an early 20th-century pioneer house, schoolhouse, church and a blacksmith shop. Displays include a vintage fire truck, antique automobiles, carriages and farm equipment.

Allow 1 hour minimum. Daily 10-4, Victoria Day-Labour Day; Tues.-Fri. 10-4, rest of year. Closed holidays and Dec. 26-31. Admission $4; over 64, $3; under 6 free. Phone (780) 998-1783.

ST. ALBERT (D-6) pop. 53,081

Alberta's oldest nonfortified community, St. Albert was established in 1861. The city is the site of the first cathedral west of Winnipeg. Its founder—Father Albert Lacombe—devoted 62 years to acting as a peacemaker between the Crees and the Blackfoot and as a negotiator between the Blood Indians and the Canadian Pacific Railway.

St. Albert lays claim to western Canada's largest outdoor farmers' market, which operates every Saturday July through September as well as an interactive water play park and a vibrant arts community.

In late May performers in varied arts are offered a showcase for their theater, music, dance, storytelling and puppetry at the Northern Alberta International Children's Festival. The Kinsmen Rainmaker Rodeo also is in late May.

St. Albert Information Center: 71 St. Albert Rd., St. Albert, AB, Canada T8N 6L5; phone (780) 459-1724.

SAVE **FATHER LACOMBE CHAPEL** is just w. of Hwy. 2 at 7 St. Vital Ave. The log chapel, built under Lacombe's direction in 1861, is said to be Alberta's oldest building. Guided tours explain the importance of Lacombe to the French/Métis community and the priest's role as spiritual leader, peacemaker and negotiator in the 1860s. Tours are conducted in English and French.

Allow 30 minutes minimum. Tours are given by request daily 10-6, May 15-Labour Day. Admission $2; senior citizens and ages 7-17, $1.50; family rate $5. Phone (780) 459-7663.

MUSÉE HERITAGE MUSEUM is w. of Hwy. 2 at 5 St. Anne St. in St. Albert Place. Exhibits are dedicated to the heritage of St. Albert. Changing displays are featured. Allow 1 hour minimum. Mon.-Sat. 10-5, Sun. 1-5; closed legal holidays. Donations. Phone (780) 459-1528.

STONY PLAIN (E-6) pop. 9,589

Plentiful water and abundant fish and game attracted the first settlers to the region in 1881. By 1892 the name of the community itself was changed from Dogrump Creek or Dog Creek to Stony Plain. The Stony Plain of today is an agricultural community.

Murals depicting historical remembrances, events and pioneers prominent in the early settlement of Stony Plain have been painted by local artists on 22 buildings in town. Memories of an early 1900s Christmas from a child's point of view are the basis for one mural, while another shows the multiculturalism of the area's early residents. The Heritage Walk Murals can be seen on a walking tour.

Stony Plain & District Chamber of Commerce: Rotary Park, 4815-44 Ave., Stony Plain, AB, Canada T7Z 1V5; phone (780) 963-4545.

MULTICULTURAL HERITAGE CENTRE AND OPPERTSHAUSER HOUSE is at 5411-51 St. Restored buildings feature local history and art exhibits, programs and events. The center, built as the area's first high school in 1925, offers regional archives as well as a living-history museum, a demonstration farm, an art gallery and the 1910 Oppertshauser House. Food is available. Allow 30 minutes minimum. Mon.-Sat. 10-4, Sun. 10-6; closed Dec. 24-Jan. 2. A country market takes place Sat. 9-1, May-Oct. Donations. Phone (780) 963-2777.

This ends listings for the Edmonton Vicinity. The following page resumes the alphabetical listings of cities in Alberta.

EAST COULEE (G-7)
pop. 156, elev. 671 m/2201'

ATLAS COAL MINE NATIONAL HISTORIC SITE is just s. on Hwy. 10. The site explores the coal mining history of the Drumheller Valley. Visitors can take a tour of an eight-story wooden tipple, see restored mine offices, a lamp house and a miner's shack, hike on interpretive trails and climb on antique mining machines. Coal cars, pulled by a restored mine locomotive, provide rides through the site. Allow 1 hour, 30 minutes minimum. Mon.-Sat. (weather permitting) 9:30-8:30, Sun. 9:30-5:30, July-Aug.; daily 9:30-5:30, May-June. Admission $5, under 6 free, family rate $15. MC, VI. Phone (403) 822-2220.

ELK ISLAND NATIONAL PARK (D-7)

Elevations in the park range from 709 metres (2,326 ft.) at Goose Lake to 754 metres (2,475 ft.) at Tawayik Lake. Refer to CAA/AAA maps for additional elevation information.

About 45 kilometres (28 mi.) east of Edmonton, Elk Island National Park is reached by Hwy. 15 from the north and Hwy. 16 from the south. The park is small—only 194 square kilometres (75 sq. mi.)—but its lakes, ponds, forests and meadows provide a haven for many species of animals and plants.

The park occupies the Beaver Hills region, which first was settled by Sarcee and Plains Cree Indians. They trapped beavers and hunted bison and elk, as did the European fur traders who arrived between the late 18th and the mid-19th centuries. Soon the animals became nearly extinct, and the natives were forced to seek sustenance elsewhere.

In 1906 five local men asked that the government establish a wildlife refuge to preserve the remaining elk. A year later 400 plains bison were added, while another preserve near Wainwright was being established. Most of these animals later were transferred, but about 50 stayed and produced the plains bison herd of more than 600 that remains today north of Hwy. 16. A herd of several hundred wood bison, a threatened subspecies, is kept separate from this herd south of Hwy. 16.

As the wildlife populations grew, so did the park's area; more land was added to the refuge in 1922, 1947, 1957 and 1978. Many small lakes dot the landscape, but the major bodies are Tawayik and Astotin, the latter being the larger. The lakes and marshes support the more than 250 bird species, including ducks, gulls, terns, grebes and loons.

Marsh marigolds and several types of lilies are among several plants rarely seen outside the park. Song birds occupy the many aspen, spruce and birch forests, but few fish inhabit the waters due to low oxygen levels. The herd of elk for which the park was established flourish nicely among the meadows and forests, as do reintroduced colonies of beavers. Deer, minks, moose and coyotes also roam the park.

General Information and Activities

The park is open daily all year. Most recreation facilities center on Astotin Lake, which offers nonmotorized boating, wildlife observations, picnic facilities, a nine-hole golf course, camping, hiking and walking trails. A campground is on the east side of the lake; interpretive talks, events and displays explain the park's history and features.

A visitor information center is .8 kilometres (.5 mi.) north of Hwy. 16 before the park's south gate entrance. Staff members and displays describe Elk Island and other national parks. The center is open mid-May through Labour Day weekend; phone (780) 922-5790 to confirm schedule.

Camping and picnicking are popular in summer. The park's approximately 100 kilometres (60 mi.) of trails are popular with hikers and cross-country skiers. Hunting and fishing are prohibited. *See Recreation Chart and the AAA/CAA Western Canada & Alaska CampBook.*

ADMISSION to the park is $5; over 64, $4.25; ages 6-16, $2.50. Admission for three to seven people in a private vehicle is $12.50; over 64, $10.50. An annual pass, valid at all Canadian national parks, is available.

PETS must be kept on a leash at all times. Dogs are discouraged from using trails to prevent potential conflicts with free-ranging bison.

ADDRESS inquiries for additional information to Elk Island National Park, Site 4, R.R. 1, Fort Saskatchewan, AB, Canada T8L 2N7; phone (780) 992-2950.

ELKWATER (I-9) pop. 50

Before Europeans came to the Elkwater region, Assiniboine, Blackfoot, Cree and Sioux shared the land with grizzly bears, wolves, bison and a large number of elk. After settlers and trappers arrived, the wolves and elk were hunted to extinction; the elk population since has been reintroduced. An 1873 massacre of Assiniboine Indians by wolf hunters and whiskey traders prompted the formation of the North West Mounted Police and the establishment of Fort Walsh.

The Cypress Hills area, shared by Alberta and Saskatchewan, is noted for its lodgepole pine forests, water resources and wildlife. The hills, which rise to more than 1,466 metres (4,810 ft.), offer visitors a cool climate, scenic views and diverse flora and fauna. Elkwater serves as the area's hub.

CYPRESS HILLS INTERPROVINCIAL PARK is 70 km (43 mi.) n. of the U.S. border on Hwy. 41; it straddles the boundary between Alberta and Saskatchewan. Fossils of early mammals dating back 40 million years have been found in the hills. An aboriginal culture flourished in the area for more than 7,000 years. Ruminants, beavers, coyotes and varied birds and plants now live in the park. Park interpreters schedule programs May through September. The visitor center offers information, displays and audiovisual presentations.

Camping is permitted. Park daily 24 hours. Visitor center daily 9-5, mid-May through June 30; daily 9-8, July 1-Labour Day. Free. Phone (403) 893-3833 or (403) 893-3777 for the visitor center, or (403) 893-3835 for camping reservations May-Aug. *See Recreation Chart and Medicine Hat in the AAA/CAA Western Canada & Alaska CampBook.*

FORT MACLEOD (I-6)
pop. 2,990, elev. 955 m/3,133′

At the end of their 1,126-kilometre (700-mi.) march through the prairie wilderness to rid western Canada of whiskey traders, in 1874 the North West Mounted Police, now the Royal Canadian Mounted Police, chose the site of what is now Fort Macleod as their first headquarters.

A commanding view of the countryside and the natural protection afforded by the Oldman River made Fort Macleod an important outpost; a cairn at 2nd Avenue and 25th Street commemorates its founding. Guided walking tours of the historic district, ranging from 30 minutes to 1 hour, can be arranged in advance during the summer by contacting the Main Street Office; phone (403) 553-2500, or the Museum of the North West Mounted Police *(see attraction listing).*

The highland physical geography that made the Fort Macleod outpost successful also helped the Plains Indians survive long before the first traders appeared in the area. In order to kill the buffalo for food, the Plains hunters stampeded them over the high cliffs.

Fort Macleod & District Chamber of Commerce: 7th Ave., P.O. Box 178, Fort Macleod, AB, Canada T0L 0Z0; phone (403) 553-4955 Victoria Day weekend-Labour Day.

HEAD-SMASHED-IN BUFFALO JUMP INTERPRETIVE CENTRE is 3 km (1.9 mi.) n. on Hwy. 2, then 16 km (10 mi.) w. on Hwy. 785. For more than 10,000 years the Plains Indians stampeded herds of buffalo over sandstone cliffs to their deaths. The hunters then butchered the kill at their campsite below the cliffs. This is one of the oldest, best-preserved buffalo jump site. A 12-minute film re-enacts the hunts.

The site's name is derived from a young brave who stood under a ledge of the cliff to watch the buffalo as they fell past him. As the number of carcasses multiplied, his skull was crushed as he became trapped between the animals and the cliff.

Built into that cliff today is a seven-story interpretive center with displays. Exhibits focus on the geographical and climatic factors affecting these tribes as well as their lifestyle and history. The hunting site is preserved; short trails lead to the main areas.

Food is available. Allow 2 hours minimum. Daily 9-6, mid-May to mid-Sept.; 10-5, rest of year. Closed Jan. 1, Easter and Dec. 24-25. Admission mid-May to mid-Sept. $8.50; over 65, $7; ages 7-17, $4; family rate $19. Admission rest of year $6.50; over 65, $5.50; ages 7-17, $3; family rate $15. MC, VI. Phone (403) 553-2731.

MUSEUM OF THE NORTH WEST MOUNTED POLICE is at 25th St. and 3rd Ave. The site is a representation of the original Fort Macleod. Exhibits set among historic structures focus on pioneer settlers, southern Alberta Indians and the history of the fort and its mounted police. Of particular interest are the summer Mounted Patrol Musical Rides, eight people on horseback, in replicas of 1878 RCMP uniforms, who perform precision movements to music.

Allow 1 hour minimum. Daily 9-6, July 1-Labour Day; daily 9-5, May 16-June 30 and day after Labour Day-Oct. 15; Mon.-Fri. 9-5, Mar. 1-May 15 and Oct. 16-Dec. 23. Mounted Patrol Musical Rides are given daily (weather permitting) at 10, 11:30, 2 and 3:30, July 1-last Sun. in Sept. Admission July-Aug. $7.50; over 64, $7; ages 12-17, $5.50; ages 6-11, $4.50; family rate (two adults and four children) $22. Admission Mar.-June and day after Labour Day-Dec. 23 $6; over 64, $5.50; ages 12-17, $4; ages 6-11, $3; family rate $17. MC, VI. Phone (403) 553-4703.

FORT McMURRAY (A-8)

At the confluence of the Clearwater and Athabasca rivers in the fur country of northern Alberta, Fort McMurray began as the home of the Woodland Cree and Chipewyan Indians. In 1778 explorers led by Peter Pond opened the vast fur trade region of the Mackenzie River basin. In 1870 Henry John Moberly built a post and named it Fort McMurray after his chief factor, William McMurray of Hudson's Bay Co.

Soon after a steamboat terminus was established near Fort McMurray in 1884, the region's vast resources began to attract attention. Oil sands containing some 1.7 trillion barrels of oil were found around Lake Athabasca. The first commercially successful extractions, however, did not take place until the late 1960s. Since then Fort McMurray has boomed, serving oil recovery plants that now extract from the sands about 600,000 barrels of synthetic crude oil per day.

The city is the southern terminus of the vast water transportation system that navigates Great Slave Lake and the Mackenzie River en route to the Arctic. Logging and tourism further bolster the economy. Fort McMurray is a service center for surrounding areas and the oil sands plants.

Re-creating the city's past is Heritage Park, on the banks of the Hangingstone River just off King Street on Tolen Drive. A museum highlights the history of boat building, aviation, river travel, lumbering, fishing, salt production and fur trading. Phone (780) 791-7575.

Fort McMurray Tourism: 400 Sakitawaw Tr., Fort McMurray, AB, Canada T9H 4Z3; phone (780) 791-4336 or (800) 565-3947.

OIL SANDS DISCOVERY CENTRE is at jct. Hwy. 63 and MacKenzie Blvd. Exhibits relate the geology, history and technology of the Athabasca Oil Sands, said to be the world's single largest oil deposit. Oil sands mining, technology and new methods of exploration are explained through interpretive displays, demonstrations and the video presentation "Quest for Energy." Outside in the Industrial Garden are a seven-story bucket-wheel excavator and other pieces of massive mining equipment.

Seasonal bus tours to view the production facilities of Syncrude Canada Ltd. and Suncor depart from the discovery center; reservations for the 3.5-hour tours can be arranged through the Fort McMurray Visitors Bureau.

Allow 1 hour, 30 minutes minimum for the center. Daily 9-5, May 15-Labour Day; Tues.-Sun. 10-4, rest of year. Closed Jan. 1 and Dec. 24-26. Bus tours to the plants are given daily July-Aug.; Sat.-Sun., May-June; Fri., Sept.-Oct. Admission $6; over 64, $4; ages 7-17, $3; family rate $15. Bus tour $15 (includes center admission). Under 12 are not permitted on bus tour. Reservations are required for bus tour. VI, MC. Phone (780) 791-4336 or (800) 565-3947 for tour reservations.

FORT SASKATCHEWAN—
see Edmonton p. 75.

GIROUXVILLE (B-3) pop. 306

GIROUXVILLE MUSEUM is on Main St. (Hwy. 49). More than 6,000 artifacts tell the story of the indigenous people, devout missionaries and rugged pioneers who lived and settled here. Nature admirers will enjoy the displays of mounted birds and fur-bearing animals. Transportation Means of Yesterday includes sleighs, an antique snowmobile, a birch bark canoe and a 1927 Chevrolet truck.

Allow 1 hour minimum. Mon.-Fri. 10-5, May 1-last Fri. in Aug.; by appointment rest of year. Admission $3; ages 6-17, $1.50. Phone (780) 323-4252.

GRANDE CACHE (D-2)

Grande Cache was named after a large shipment of furs cached nearby in 1821 by Ignace Giasson, an Iroquois working for Hudson Bay Trading Company. The Grande Cache area historically served as a major trading area for marten, lynx and beaver pelts.

Grande Cache is known for the many recreational activities available nearby. The town is surrounded on three sides by Willmore Wilderness Park, which has the Continental Divide and Jasper National Park as its western and southern borders, respectively; the park can be accessed only by horseback, mountain bike or by hiking.

Lakes, rivers and mountains are favorites with outdoor enthusiasts, who come for white-water rafting, horseback riding, hiking, kayaking, fishing, canoeing and mountain biking. Pacific Western Helicopter Tours offers various sightseeing tours; phone (780) 827-3911.

Interpretive displays in the tourism center, on the south side of Grande Cache, feature dinosaur tracks, artifacts from the ice age and memorabilia from the fur trade era.

Grande Cache Tourism and Interpretive Centre: 9701 100th St., P.O. Box 300, Grande Cache, AB, Canada T0E 0Y0; phone (780) 827-3300 or (888) 827-3790.

RECREATIONAL ACTIVITIES
White-water Rafting

- **Wild Blue Yonder White Water Rafting** is w. off Hwy. 40 in Shopper's Park Mall, following signs. Write P.O. Box 1611, Grande Cache, AB, Canada T0E 0Y0. Trips are available daily May-Sept. Phone (780) 827-5450 or (877) 945-3786.

GRANDE PRAIRIE (C-2) pop. 36,983

Surrounded by a colorful checkerboard of rich farmland along the gateway to the Alaska Highway, Grande Prairie serves as the business and transportation center of Alberta's Peace River country.

Glimpses into the Peace River region's past are evident in the Kleskun Hills, just east via Hwy. 43. Erosion of the glacial drift of clay, sand, gravel and boulders has uncovered dinosaur tracks and aquatic fossils embedded in a prehistoric river delta formed more than 70 million years ago.

Local culture and artistry are displayed at Prairie Gallery, 10209 99th St.; phone (780) 532-8111. Muskoseepi Park has hiking and bicycling trails, picnicking areas and recreation facilities. Other area recreational pursuits include swimming, boating, bird-watching and fishing. A pioneer-oriented event is the Grande Prairie Stompede the first weekend in June. Other festivals celebrated throughout the summer highlight the region's diversity.

Grande Prairie Regional Tourism Association: 11330 106th St. #114, Grande Prairie, AB, Canada T8V 7X9; phone (780) 539-7688 or (866) 202-2202.

Shopping areas: Prairie Mall, 11801 100th St., features Shopper's and Zellers.

GRANDE PRAIRIE MUSEUM is at 102nd St. and 102nd Ave. in Muskoseepi Park. The 10-building village features a one-room schoolhouse, country store, church and a log homesteader's cabin. The main exhibit building houses artifacts depicting the life of Peace River area pioneers 1908-16. The gallery also features natural history items and aboriginal artifacts. Daily 10-6, May-Oct.; Mon.-Fri. 10-4, Sat.-Sun. 1-4, rest of year. Admission $3; ages 6-17, $2; family rate $10. Phone (780) 532-5482.

CASINOS

- **Great Northern Casino** is at 10910 107A Ave. Mon.-Sat. 10 a.m.-2 a.m., Sun. 10 a.m.-1 a.m. Phone (780) 539-4454.

HANNA (G-7) pop. 2,986

A 1912 roundhouse, a throwback to the town's beginning as a Canadian National Railway terminal, still graces Hanna's skyline.

HANNA PIONEER MUSEUM is at Pioneer Tr. and 4th Ave. E. Restored 19th-century buildings, arranged in a pioneer village setting, include a general store, school, four-room hospital, church, power windmill, Canadian National Railway station, telephone office, ranch house and smithy, and the Hanna archives. Among displays are antique automobiles and farm machinery.

Guided tours are available. Allow 1 hour, 30 minutes minimum. Daily 10-6, June-Aug.; by appointment in May and Sept. Last tour begins 1 hour, 30 minutes before closing. Admission $4; under 12, $1. Phone (403) 854-4244.

HIGH RIVER (H-6) pop. 9,345

A ranching and farming town, High River counts among its events Little Britches Rodeo and Parade, on Victoria Day weekend in late May, and the North American Chuckwagon Championship and the Guy Weadick Memorial Rodeo, both held in June.

High River Chamber of Commerce: 406 1st St. S.W., P.O. Box 5244, High River, AB, Canada T1V 1M4; phone (403) 652-3336.

HIGH RIVER HISTORICAL MURALS can be seen on guided or self-guiding tours that begin at the Museum of the Highwood *(see attraction listing)*. Area history unfolds on 18 colorful paintings that decorate the exteriors of many commercial buildings. The murals illustrate varied subjects, ranging from farming, chuck wagons and polo to famous residents, writer W.O. Mitchell and former Prime Minister Joe Clark.

Guided tours can be booked through the chamber of commerce May-Aug. Brochures for a self-guiding tour are available year-round. Free. Phone (403) 652-3336.

MUSEUM OF THE HIGHWOOD is at 406 1st St. S.W. The museum takes its name from the nearby Highwood River. Changing exhibits are housed in an 1893 sandstone building once used as a Canadian Pacific Railway station. Displays detail local history, primarily from the mid-19th century to the present. A family discovery room has interactive exhibits. Food is available. Allow 30 minutes minimum. Mon.-Sat. 10-5, Sun. 1-5, Victoria Day-Labour Day; Mon.-Fri. 10-5, rest of year. Closed Jan. 1 and Dec. 25. Admission $3; over 59, $2.50; under 16 free. Phone (403) 652-7156.

INNISFAIL (G-6) pop. 6,928, elev. 3,071'

BLUE HERRON ADVENTURES is off Hwy. 2 Innisfail exit, then w. on 50th St. Guided half-day and full-day nature tours and fishing trips are offered on the Red Deer and Bow rivers. Guides narrate the trips, which feature opportunities for photography and wildlife viewing. Lunch is served on full-day tours. The tours are given in drift boats, which accommodate two guests, or pontoon boats which carry one guest. Ice fishing is offered in winter. Tackle, equipment and a fishing license are required for fishing trips. Inquire about cancellation policies. Daily (weather permitting) 7-7, late May-late Oct. Fee $100-$300. Reservations are required. MC, VI. Phone (403) 227-5780 or (877) 220-5760.

IRRICANA (G-6) pop. 1,038

PIONEER ACRES MUSEUM is off Hwy. 9, 1 km n., then 1 km w. This living-history village depicts life in a pioneer farming community and features one of the largest collections of antique farm equipment in western Canada. The museum also displays furniture, tools, memorabilia and clothing. A collection of early buildings includes a family homestead, a school, a steam-engine shop and a blacksmith shop. Guided tours are available. Allow 1 hour, 30 minutes minimum. Daily 9-5, May 15-Sept. 30. Admission $5, under 12 free. Phone (403) 935-4357.

▼ JASPER NATIONAL PARK (E-2,3)

> Elevations in the park range from 1,000 metres (3,300 ft.) in the town of Jasper to 3,747 metres (12,293 ft.) at Mount Columbia. Refer to CAA/AAA maps for additional elevation information.

Reached from the east and west via the Yellowhead Highway (Hwy. 16) and from the south by the Icefields Parkway (Hwy. 93), Jasper National Park, Banff National Park's northern neighbor, was established in 1907. The park was named after Jasper Hawes, who was in charge of a Hudson's Bay Co. trading post in the early 1800s.

Less developed and less crowded than Banff National Park, its 10,878 square kilometres (4,200 sq. mi.) of majestic mountains, valleys and lakes offer equally spectacular views of the Rocky Mountain wilderness. The variety and beauty of its numerous lakes, of which Maligne Lake is the largest, are perhaps the area's chief attractions.

Nature's scenic sculpting process at work can be seen at Athabasca Falls and Sunwapta Falls, both just west of Icefields Parkway south of Jasper. To the east off Hwy. 16 is Miette Hot Springs, where mineral pools are open for bathing Victoria Day weekend through the second Monday in October. Northeast of Jasper 51-metre-deep (170-ft.) Maligne Canyon surrounds the river that carved it over the years.

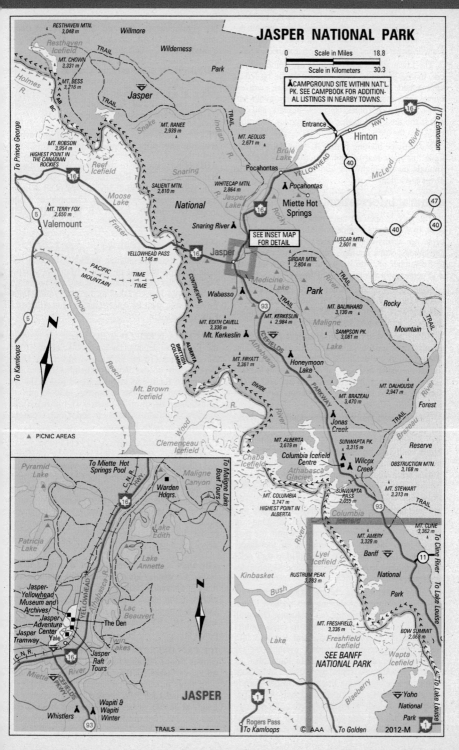

JASPER NATIONAL PARK

Scale in Miles 0 — 18.8
Scale in Kilometers 0 — 30.3

▲ CAMPGROUND SITE WITHIN NAT'L. PK. SEE CAMPBOOK FOR ADDITIONAL LISTINGS IN NEARBY TOWNS.

RESTHAVEN MTN. 3,048 m
Resthaven Icefield
MT. CHOWN 3,331 m
MT. BESS 3,216 m
Willmore
Wilderness
Park
Jasper
MT. ROBSON 3,954 m HIGHEST POINT IN THE CANADIAN ROCKIES
Reef Icefield
To Prince George
MT. RANEE 2,939 m
MT. AEOLUS 2,671 m
Entrance
Hinton
YELLOWHEAD HWY.
To Edmonton
40
McLeod River
Holmes R.
Snake R.
Indian R.
Brûlé Lake
Pocahontas
Pocahontas
Miette Hot Springs
Snaring
SALIENT MTN. 2,810 m
WHITECAP MTN. 2,864 m
Jasper Lake
National
Moose Lake
Fraser R.
MT. TERRY FOX 2,650 m
Valemount
5
To Kamloops
Canoe Reach
Wood R.
Mt. Brown Icefield
Clemenceau Icefield
PACIFIC MOUNTAIN TIME
TIME
Snaring River ▲
Jasper
SEE INSET MAP FOR DETAIL
YELLOWHEAD PASS 1,146 m
16
Wabasso
93
MT. EDITH CAVELL 3,336 m
Mt. Kerkeslin
MT. KERKESLIN 2,984 m
MT. FRYATT 3,361 m
CONTINENTAL
ALBERTA
BRITISH COLUMBIA
DIVIDE
Medicine Lake
Maligne Lake
Honeymoon Lake
SIRDAR MTN. 2,804 m
LUSCAR MTN. 2,601 m
MT. BALINHARD 3,130 m
SAMPSON PK. 3,081 m
Rocky
Mountain
Forest
Athabasca R.
ICEFIELDS PARKWAY
MT. BRAZEAU 3,470 m
MT. DALHOUSIE 2,947 m
Jonas Creek
MT. ALBERTA 3,619 m
SUNWAPTA PK. 3,315 m
Columbia Icefield Centre
Wilcox Creek
OBSTRUCTION MTN. 3,168 m
Reserve
Athabasca Glacier
Chaba Icefield
Columbia Icefield
MT. COLUMBIA 3,747 m HIGHEST POINT IN ALBERTA
SUNWAPTA PASS 2,035 m
MT. STEWART 3,313 m
93
Brazeau R.
TRAIL
Maligne River
▲ PICNIC AREAS
MT. CLINE 3,362 m
To Cline River
To Lake Louise
MT. AMERY 3,329 m
Banff
11
Lyel Icefield
National
RUSTRUM PEAK 3,283 m
Park
Kinbasket
Bush
MT. FRESHFIELD 3,336 m
Freshfield Icefield
BOW SUMMIT 2,068 m
Wapta Icefield
SEE BANFF NATIONAL PARK
Lake
1
Blaeberry R.
Rogers Pass
To Kamloops
To Golden
© AAA
2012-M
Yoho National Park
To Lake Louise
1

Inset Map (JASPER)

Pyramid Lake
To Miette Hot Springs Pool
C.N.R.
Maligne Canyon
16
Warden Hdqrs.
To Maligne Lake Boat Tours
Patricia Lake
Lake Edith
Lake Annette
YELLOWHEAD
Athabasca R.
Jasper-Yellowhead Museum and Archives
Jasper Adventure Center
Jasper Tramway
The Den
Yale
Lac Beauvert
Twin Lakes
C.N.R.
Jasper Raft Tours
16
Miette R.
ICEFIELDS PKWY.
Whistlers
93
Wapiti & Wapiti Winter
JASPER
TRAILS - - - - -

Park wildlife is as diverse as its peaks and valleys. Mountain goats and bighorn sheep inhabit the crags and highlands, although the sheep frequently wander down within good viewing distance.

The lower slopes and meadows are home to deer, elk, moose and bears, which never should be fed or approached. More elusive are coyotes, wolves, lynxes and other predators that usually avoid humans. Lodgepole pines, spruces, poplars and firs forest the area, and eagles, jays, magpies and other birds dot the skies.

Note: Since hunting is illegal, some animals may have lost their fear of human activity; be alert for animals on the highways both day and night, and never feed them.

General Information and Activities

The park is open all year, though weather conditions in winter make some portions inaccessible except to cross-country skiers and those on snowshoes. Some facilities are open only from May to September or October. A Parks Canada information center is in the townsite of Jasper.

Many hiking trails, including the 11.2-kilometre (7-mi.) trip to Valley of Five Lakes and the loop to Lac Beauvert, depart from Old Fort Point, 1.6 kilometres (1 mi.) east of Jasper on Hwy. 93.

Hikers and skiers staying overnight in the back country must have a valid back-country use permit. These permits are available at the Parks Canada information center in Jasper, at the Columbia Icefield Centre from early June to mid-October and at the Sunwapta (Poboktan) warden station during the winter.

Campgrounds are open varying durations: Whistler early May through the second Monday in October; Snaring River mid-May to late September; Wapiti mid-June to mid-September; and Wabasso late June through Labour Day. Limited camping facilities are available in winter at the Wapiti campgrounds. For campground information phone (780) 852-6176.

There are many ways to explore the park's features, either alone or with a guide. One- or multiple-day bus tours to attractions within the park depart from Jasper. Several stables in the Jasper area offer 1-hour and half- and full-day trail rides from mid-May to mid-September and sleigh rides in winter.

Winter sports include curling, skating, tobogganing, ice climbing, snowshoeing and hockey. Cross-country skiing tours operate out of Jasper. Downhill skiing is available at Marmot Basin; cross-country trails also traverse the Maligne and Pyramid lake areas. Interpretive guides conduct evening fireside gatherings and slide talks. Wildlife tours also are available. Audiotape tours by CCInc. Auto Tape Tours are available at the Friends of Jasper store in the Parks Canada information center, 415 Connaught Dr.; phone (780) 852-4767.

Fishing permits can be obtained at information centers, campgrounds and local sport fishing shops.

Boats with electric motors are allowed on lakes unless signs indicate otherwise. *See Recreation Chart and the AAA/CAA Western Canada & Alaska CampBook.*

ADMISSION to the park for 1 day is $7; over 64, $6; ages 6-16, $3.50. Admission for two to seven people in a private vehicle for 1 day is $12-$14. An annual pass, valid at Jasper and 10 other western Canada national parks, is available. MC, VI.

PETS are allowed in the park but must be leashed, crated or physically restrained at all times.

ADDRESS inquiries to the Superintendent, Jasper National Park, P.O. Box 10, Jasper, AB, Canada T0E 1E0; phone (780) 852-6176. For other area information contact Jasper Park Chamber of Commerce, P.O. Box 98, Jasper, AB, Canada T0E 1E0; phone (780) 852-3858.

Points of Interest

Natural points of interest include Edith and Annette lakes to the east of Jasper; Maligne Canyon, Maligne Lake and Medicine Lake to the northeast; Pyramid and Patricia lakes to the north; and Mount Edith Cavell, with its Angel Glacier, and Athabasca Falls to the south.

COLUMBIA ICEFIELD is the largest ice mass in the Rocky Mountains. Its main bulk, about 16 by 24 kilometres (10 by 15 mi.), straddles the Great Divide, part of the British Columbia border and portions of Banff and Jasper national parks. The ice covers about 325 square kilometres (130 sq. mi.) to an estimated depth of 350 metres (1,148 ft.). Three glaciers—Stutfield, Athabasca and Dome—can be seen from Icefields Parkway.

Columbia Icefield Centre is 105 km (64 mi.) s. of Jasper on Hwy. 93. The center overlooks Athabasca and Dome glaciers and offers views of major mountain peaks surrounding the Columbia Icefield. An interpretive center contains models of the ice field and an ice cave. The center offers maps, information and details about interpretive programs. Food is available. Allow 30 minutes minimum. Daily 9-6, May 1-Oct. 15. Free. Phone (877) 423-7433.

THE DEN is in the lower level of Whistler's Inn in Jasper. On display are more than 150 mounted animals in simulated habitats. All animals shown were native to the area. Allow 30 minutes minimum. Daily 8 a.m.-10 p.m. Admission $3; over 60 and ages 6-16, $2; family rate $6. Phone (780) 852-3361.

ICE EXPLORER ON THE ATHABASCA GLACIER departs from Columbia Icefield Centre, 105 km (64 mi.) s. of Jasper on Hwy. 93N *(see attraction listing).* Tours provide the opportunity to see and walk on a glaciated ice field formed by snow falling as long ago as 400 years. The bus driver provides anecdotes and information during this 80-minute excursion.

Allow 1 hour, 30 minutes minimum. Tours depart daily every 15 minutes (weather permitting) 9-5, mid-Apr. to mid-Oct. Fare $29.95; ages 6-15, $15; under 6 in lap free. AX, MC, VI. Phone (877) 423-7433.

 **ICEFIELDS PARKWAY—**
see Banff National Park p. 48.

SAVE **JASPER ADVENTURE CENTRE** is on Connaught Dr. in Jasper National Park. The company offers guided sightseeing van tours, wildlife tours and walking tours. Daily 8-8, June 15-Sept. 15; 8-6, rest of year. Closed Dec. 25. Fare $35-$99, half-price for ages 6-14. MC, VI. Phone (780) 852-5595 or (800) 565-7547.

GEM **JASPER TRAMWAY** is accessed 3 km (1.8 mi.) s. on Hwy. 93, then 4 km (2.5 mi.) w. at Whistler's Mountain Rd. Passengers take a short, narrated tram ride up 973 m (3,243 ft.) to the treeline of Whistler Mountain, where scenic views await. Six surrounding mountain ranges, glacial-fed lakes and the Jasper townsite are visible. Once at the top, visitors may hike to the summit. Interpretive panels describe natural features. Allow 1 hour minimum. Daily 8:30 a.m.-10 p.m., July 1 to mid-Aug.; 9:30-6:30, Apr.-June and mid-Aug. through Sept. 30; 9:30-4:30, in Oct. Fare $21; ages 5-14, $10; family rate (two adults, two children) $52. MC, VI. Phone (780) 852-3093.

JASPER-YELLOWHEAD MUSEUM AND ARCHIVES is at 400 Pyramid Lake Rd. An art gallery features the works of local artists, and exhibits depict Jasper history. Interpretive programs also are included. The archives has photographs, maps, documents and oral history tapes. Allow 30 minutes minimum. Daily 10-9, Victoria Day-Labour Day; daily 10-5, day after Labour Day-second Mon. in Oct.; Thurs.-Sun. 10-5, rest of year. Closed Jan. 1 and Dec. 25-26. Admission $3.50, over 64 and students with ID $2, under 6 free, family rate $8. Phone (780) 852-3013.

MALIGNE LAKE BOAT TOURS is 48 km (30 mi.) s.e. via Maligne Lake Rd.; shuttles are available from the town of Jasper. The 90-minute tours, which offer a brief stop at Spirit Island, also provide exceptional views of Maligne Narrows and insight into area geology and wildlife. White-water rafting, hiking and trout-fishing trips as well as boat, canoe and sea kayak rentals are available June to September.

Allow 1 hour, 30 minutes minimum. Boat tours depart daily on the hour (weather permitting) 10-5, May-Sept. Fare $35; over 64, $29.75; ages 6-12, $17.50. AX, MC, VI. Phone (780) 852-3370 for information and shuttle schedule and rates.

SAVE **MIETTE HOT SPRINGS POOL** is 61 km (37 mi.) n.e. of Jasper on Miette Rd., then 17 km (11 mi.) e. from the jct. with Hwy. 16. Two manmade pools are fed by sulfur hot springs. The water is a constant 39 C (103 F). One pool is about 1.5 metres (5 ft.) deep; the second pool averages .5 metres (2 ft.) deep. Wildlife viewing opportunities are available.

Changing rooms and bathing suit and towel rentals are available. Hiking trails are nearby. Picnicking is permitted. Allow 30 minutes minimum. Daily 8:30 a.m.-10:30 p.m., mid-June through Labour Day; 10:30-9, early May to mid-June and day after Labour Day to mid-Oct. Admission $6.25; over 64 and ages 3-17, $5.25; family rate (two adults and two children) $18.75, $3.50 each additional child. AX, MC, VI. Phone (780) 866-3939 or (800) 767-1611. *See color ad p. 47.*

RECREATIONAL ACTIVITIES

Horseback Riding

- **Pyramid Stables** is 4 km (2.5 mi.) n. on Pyramid Lake Rd. Write P.O. Box 1200, Jasper, AB, Canada T0E 1E0. Daily 8:30-4:30, mid-May to mid-Oct. Phone (780) 852-7433.

- **Skyline Trail Rides Ltd.** depart from The Fairmont Jasper Park Lodge. Write P.O. Box 207, Jasper, AB, Canada T0E 1E0. Daily 9:30-6:30, late Apr.-late Oct. Phone (780) 852-3301, ext. 6189.

White-water Rafting

- SAVE **Jasper Raft Tours** meet in the Brewster Bus Depot/Jasper Train Station at 607 Connaught Dr. Write P.O. Box 398, Jasper, AB, Canada T0E 1E0. Trips depart daily, May 15-Sept. 30. Phone (780) 852-2665, (780) 852-3332 or (888) 553-5628.

KANANASKIS COUNTRY (H-4)

Kananaskis Country is a four-season, multiuse recreation area that encompasses more than 4,000 square kilometres (1,544 sq. mi.) of mountains and foothills. West of Calgary, the area contains Blue Rock, Bow Valley, Bragg Creek, Canmore Nordic Centre and Peter Lougheed provincial parks as well as Bow Valley and Elbow-Sheep wildland parks. In addition, there are numerous provincial recreation areas with campgrounds, day use areas and trails *(see Recreation Chart)*.

Year-round recreational activities are offered, including hiking, horseback riding, snowmobiling, kayaking, mountain biking, fishing, snowshoeing and downhill and cross-country skiing. The area begins just south of Hwy. 1 and extends south on Hwy. 40 to the intersection of Hwys. 532 and 940. Animals, including elk, deer, bighorn sheep, lynxes, moose, mountain goats, bears and porcupines, can be observed in the area.

Two major visitor information centers within Kananaskis Country provide brochures, maps, displays and travel information. The Barrier Lake Visitor Information Centre is 6 kilometres (4 mi.) south of Hwy. 1 on Hwy. 40, and Peter Lougheed Visitor Information Center is 50 kilometres (31 mi.) south on Hwy. 40. Campground amphitheaters offer interpretive programs during July and August. The area is open daily. Hwy. 40 from Peter Lougheed Provincial Park to Hwy. 541 is closed from December 1 to June 15.

Kananaskis Country General Inquiries: Suite 201, Provincial Building, 800 Railway Ave., Canmore, AB, Canada T1W 1P1; phone (403) 678-5508 or (403) 673-3985.

PASSING OF THE LEGENDS MUSEUM is at Rafter 6 Ranch, 2 km (1.2 mi.) s. of Hwy. 1 overpass after the Seebe exit. Exhibits include Indian, North West Mounted Police and pioneer memorabilia; antique carriages; and artworks. Movies and television commercials have been filmed on the property.

Adventure programs, including trail riding, white-water rafting and hiking tours, can be organized at the ranch. Daily 9-5, Victoria Day-Labour Day. Admission $5; senior citizens and ages 5-12, $3. Phone (403) 673-3622, (403) 264-1251 or (888) 267-2624.

RECREATIONAL ACTIVITIES

White-water Rafting

• **SAVE** **Mirage Adventure Tours Ltd.** departs from the Delta Lodge. Write 20 Lincoln Park, Canmore, AB, Canada T1W 3E9. Other activities are offered. Trips depart daily at 10 and 1:30, May-Sept. Phone (403) 678-4919 or (888) 312-7238 in Canada.

LAC LA BICHE (C-7) pop. 2,776

South of town, Portage La Biche was discovered in 1798 by renowned geographer and explorer David Thompson of the North West Co. This area encompasses the land between the Churchill and Athabasca-Mackenzie basins. Soon after its discovery, the portage became a key link in Canada's main fur trade routes and a passageway to the Pacific Ocean.

The 1853 founding of Lac La Biche Mission played a vital role in the settlement of the area, which quickly developed into a major transportation center of the north.

Lakeland Provincial Park, 40 kilometres (25 mi.) northeast on Hwy. 36, provides such recreational opportunities as camping, cross-country skiing, hiking, biking, bird-watching, nature photography, fishing and swimming. The park also offers Alberta's only back-country canoe circuit. Sir Winston Churchill Provincial Park, 13 km (8 mi.) northeast on Hwy. 881, is the largest of the 12 islands on Lac La Biche. *See Recreation Chart and the AAA/CAA Western Canada & Alaska CampBook.*

In 1920 Lac La Biche and its islands were designated as a migratory bird sanctuary; today visitors can view more than 200 species. Historical, lake, industry and cultural tours are available in the area.

Lac La Biche Regional Community Development Corporation: 10106 102nd Ave., P.O. Box 2188, Lac La Biche, AB, Canada T0A 2C0; phone (780) 623-2662 or (877) 623-9696.

LAKE LOUISE—*see Banff National Park p. 45.*

LEGAL (D-6) pop. 1,058

Best known for its collection of building-sized historical murals, the small town of Legal lies 50 kilometres (31 mi.) north of Edmonton. The Francophone community is named after Father Emile Legal, a French bishop, missionary and architect.

The town takes pride in its Francophone pioneer history, as is depicted by its huge outdoor murals. Subject matter ranges from the Grey Nuns—who built the first educational center for rural children—to Alexandre Lavoie, whose court battle helped French-Canadians throughout the country obtain federal services in French.

ACFA and Centralta Community Centre: 5109-46 St., P.O. Box 328, Legal, AB, Canada T0G 1L0; phone (780) 961-3665.

LETHBRIDGE (I-6)
pop. 67,374, elev. 930 m/3,051'

Founded in the 1870s, abundant agricultural resources helped Lethbridge to become one of Alberta's major feedlot and grain distribution centers. The region reportedly receives more hours of sunshine annually than any other spot in Canada and therefore requires irrigation to counterbalance the semiarid climate; more than 400,000 hectares (988,000 acres) produce crops of grain and sugar beets. Livestock, oil and gas also support the economic base.

Numerous parks and green spaces complement the city's commercial enterprises. Two popular areas are Lethbridge Nature Preserve in Indian Battle Park at 3rd Avenue S. and Scenic Drive, and Henderson Park at S. Parkside Drive and Mayor Magrath. The park has a golf course, a 60-acre lake with tennis courts, a picnic area and a campground. Rose and Japanese gardens, a stadium and an ice-skating center are included.

Lethbridge holds Whoop-Up Days and International Airshow, both in August.

Chinook Country Tourist Association: 2805 Scenic Dr. S., Lethbridge, AB, Canada T1K 5B5; phone (403) 320-1222 or (800) 661-1222.

Shopping areas: Hudson's Bay Co. anchors Lethbridge Centre, off Hwy. 3 at 200 4th Ave. S. Park Place Mall, 1st Avenue S. on Scenic Drive, has more than 100 stores and features Sears.

BREWERY GARDENS is just w. off 1st Ave. S. at Brewery Hill on Scenic Dr. Developed by a former brewery, the gardens present eight floral displays May through the first frost as well as displays for Easter, Halloween, Remembrance Day and Christmas. The gardens are not walk-through gardens, but are a 1 hectare (2.5 acre) plot on the side of a coulee. Visitors view them across the coulee. Daily dawn-dusk. Free. Phone (403) 320-1223.

INDIAN BATTLE PARK is 1 km (.6 mi.) w. of jct. Scenic Dr. and 3rd Ave. S. under the High Level

Bridge. This is the site of the last intertribal battle in North America, between the Cree and Blackfoot Indians. Within the park are attractions, self-guiding trails and picnic and playground facilities. Daily 7 a.m.-10:30 p.m., May-Sept.; 7 a.m.-8:30 p.m., rest of year. Free.

Coal Banks Interpretive Sites are scattered throughout the city. Five informational signs explain the origin of coal mining in the area. Three of the signs are in or near the park at Helen Schuler Coulee Centre and Nature Reserve *(see attraction listing)*, by the Elks Recreation Centre and between the Lodge and the Sir Alexander Galt Museum and Archives *(see attraction listing p. 85)*. The others are at Brewery Gardens *(see attraction listing)* and on Hwy. 2 near Kipp. Daily 24 hours. For more information phone the Sir Alexander Galt Museum at (403) 320-3898.

SAVE **Fort Whoop-Up** is on the river in Indian Battle Park. This is a replica of a fort built in 1869 by American traders in Canadian territory. Trade in guns and illegal alcohol, in addition to reports of an American flag flying in Canada, led to the formation of the North West Mounted Police and their march west in 1874. An interpretive center offers presentations, exhibits, dioramas and replicas of period shops and houses. Guided tours are available by request.

Allow 30 minutes minimum. Mon.-Sat. 10-6, Sun. noon-5, May-Sept.; Tues.-Fri. and Sun. 1-4, rest of year. Closed Dec. 25. Admission $5, students with ID $3, family rate $10. MC, VI. Phone (403) 329-0444.

Helen Schuler Coulee Centre and Nature Reserve is n. of Indian Battle Park. Desertlike flora and fauna are found on the coulee slopes and in cottonwood forests along the Oldman River. The 79-hectare (196-acre) reserve is home to the great horned owl, porcupines and white-tailed deer. Most of the park is accessible via three self-guiding trails; pets, bicycles, inline skates and skateboards are not permitted. The center has seasonal exhibits.

Allow 30 minutes minimum. Reserve daily 7 a.m.-11 p.m. Center Sun.-Thurs. 10-8, Fri.-Sat. 10-6, June-Aug.; Tues.-Sat. 1-4, Sun. 1-6 in May and Sept.; Tues.-Sun. 1-4, rest of year. Closed Dec. 25. Free. Phone (403) 320-3064.

The High Level Bridge spans the Oldman River. This is one of the highest and longest steel viaduct railroad bridges in the world. Daily 24 hours. Free.

GEM **NIKKA YUKO JAPANESE GARDEN** is at 9th Ave. and Mayor Magrath Dr. in Henderson Park. Five basic types of traditional SAVE Japanese gardens are incorporated into the overall design, which is one of the most authentic of its kind in North America. A pavilion, bridges, a bell tower imported from Japan and cypress wood from Taiwan are featured; paths punctuated by footbridges over ponds and streams weave through the gardens.

Hostesses in traditional kimonos conduct half-hour tours as needed. Visitors can enjoy ongoing activities such as art exhibits, live theater, pruning and gardening techniques, and meditation. Traditional Japanese art, such as bonsai, flower arranging and calligraphy, are demonstrated Saturdays at 1. A tea ceremony is offered Sundays at 2. Allow 1 hour minimum. Daily 9-9, mid-June to early Sept.; 9-5, early May to mid-June and early Sept. to mid-Oct. Admission $5; over 64, $4; ages 6-17, $3. Phone (403) 328-3511.

ST. MARY'S RIVER DAM is 78 km (47 mi.) s. The earth-filled dam is one of the largest in Canada. Water sports and a campground are available. Phone (403) 653-5158.

SIR ALEXANDER GALT MUSEUM AND ARCHIVES is at the w. end of 5th Ave. S. The museum is named for the founder of North Western Coal and Navigation Co. Exhibits deal primarily with the growth of Lethbridge following the rise and fall of the coal industry in the 1870s and the development of dry farming and variation techniques suited to the area's semiarid climate. Allow 30 minutes minimum. Daily 10-6, July-Aug.; 10-4:30, rest of year. Closed winter holidays. Admission $5, senior citizens and students with ID $3, family rate (two adults and three children) $12. Phone (403) 320-3898.

SOUTHERN ALBERTA ART GALLERY is at 601 3rd Ave. S. Exhibits showcase works of Canadian and international artists with an emphasis on contemporary art. Allow 30 minutes minimum. Tues.-Sat. 10-5, Sun. 1-5; closed holidays except July 1. Free. Phone (403) 327-8770.

CASINOS

- **Casino Lethbridge** is at 3756 2nd Ave. S. Daily 9:30 a.m.-3 a.m.; closed Dec. 25. Phone (403) 381-9467.

LLOYDMINSTER—*see Saskatchewan p. 250.*

LONGVIEW (I-5) pop. 300

GEM **BAR U RANCH NATIONAL HISTORIC SITE** is 15 km (9 mi.) s. on Hwy. 22. The site focuses on the history of ranching in SAVE Canada and the role that occupation played in the country's development. Visitors learn the history of the Bar U Ranch, one of Canada's largest and most preeminent ranching operations, from the 1880s to 1950—from the days of open range ranching, through its prominence as a breeding center for cattle and Percheron horses to its position as part of a multiple-ranch cattle operation.

The visitor center has exhibits and a presentation about the ranch's history. Guests can tour the 148-hectare (367-acre) site on foot or via a hay wagon. Historic structures include the 1882-83 saddle horse barn, blacksmith shop, stud horse barn, wintering pens, 1910 cook house, storage sheds and a ranch office/post office. Ranch chores are demonstrated.

Food is available. Mon.-Fri. 10-6, Victoria Day-Thanksgiving. Admission $6.50; over 64, $5.50; ages 6-16, $3; family rate $15. MC, VI. Phone (403) 395-3044 or (800) 568-4996.

MARKERVILLE (F-6) pop. 50

On June 27, 1888, 50 Icelanders from the drought-plagued Dakota Territory crossed the Red Deer River to settle in Markerville, where they hoped to maintain their language and customs. For a time they produced woolen outerwear, pastries, sweets and smoked mutton in the traditional Icelandic manner.

During the 1920s, however, an increase in intermarriage with other ethnic groups and improved transportation diluted their cultural isolation. Less than 10 percent of the population is now of purely Icelandic descent, but many traditional customs are celebrated during heritage days.

HISTORIC MARKERVILLE CREAMERY MUSEUM is off Hwys. 781 and 592 on Creamery Way. Begun by 34 Icelandic farmers as a cooperative in 1899 and in operation until 1972, the creamery has been restored to depict the operation as it was in the 1930s. Costumed guides offer tours.

Picnicking is permitted. Food is available. Allow 30 minutes minimum. Mon.-Sat. 10-5:30, Sun. noon-5:30, May 15-Labour Day; by appointment rest of year. Admission $2; over 64 and ages 7-17, $1.50; family rate (two adults and two children) $5. MC, VI. Phone (403) 728-3006.

[SAVE] **STEPHANSSON HOUSE PROVINCIAL HISTORIC SITE** is 7 km (4 mi.) n., following signs. Historical displays highlight the Icelanders who founded Markerville, including Stephan G. Stephansson, a prominent poet and farmer. His restored home contains original furnishings from the early 1900s. Costumed guides give 15- to 30-minute tours.

Self-guiding tours are available. Allow 30 minutes minimum. Daily 10-6, May 15-Labour Day. Admission $2; over 64 and ages 7-17, $1.50; family rate $5. Phone (403) 728-3929, or (780) 427-1787 in the off season.

MEDICINE HAT (I-8)
pop. 51,249, elev. 715 m/2,346'

According to popular legend, the name Medicine Hat originated because of a battle between Cree and Blackfoot Indians on the banks of a southern Alberta river. The Cree fought bravely until their medicine man deserted them, losing his headdress in midstream. Believing this to be a bad omen, the Cree put down their weapons and were killed by the Blackfoot. This site became known as "Saamis," which translates as "medicine man's hat."

A buried prehistoric river, or aquifer, serves as a source of unlimited cool water. More than 20 billion cubic metres (26 billion cubic yards) of natural gas reserves inspired Rudyard Kipling in 1907 to describe Medicine Hat as possessing "all hell for a basement."

Outdoor opportunities include swimming, boating and fishing at Echo Dale Park. Riverside Waterslides & Amusement Park offers waterslides, miniature golf and go-carts. Circuit cowboys and spectators gather for 4 days in late July for the Medicine Hat Exhibition & Stampede.

Tourism Medicine Hat: 8 Gehring Rd. S.W., Medicine Hat, AB, Canada T1A 7G5; phone (403) 527-6422.

Shopping areas: Medicine Hat Mall, 3292 Dunmore Rd. S.E., features The Bay, Sears and Zellers among its more than 100 stores.

 MEDICINE HAT CLAY INDUSTRIES NATIONAL HISTORIC SITE is at 703 Wood St. S.E. The manufacture of brick, tile and pottery was a prominent industry in Medicine Hat in the late 19th century due to a supply of clay deposits, natural gas and the availability of railroad transportation. The city once boasted several potteries, such as Medicine Hat Potteries (now Hycroft China Ltd.). The Hycroft site now serves as an interpretive center with displays.

At the Medalta Potteries site, visitors can see beehive kilns constructed in the early 1920s. Artifacts and production machines are on display, and demonstrations of pottery making are given daily. Guided tours are available at both sites. Allow 2 hours minimum. Daily 10-5, May 15-Sept. 15; Mon.-Fri. 9-4, rest of year. Guided tours are offered daily on the hour 10-11 and 1-4, May 15-Sept. 15; by appointment rest of year. Admission to one site $5; over 65, students with ID and ages 7-16, $4. Admission to both sites $8; over 65, students with ID and ages 7-16, $6; family rate $20, MC, VI. Phone (403) 529-1070.

MEDICINE HAT MUSEUM AND ART GALLERY is at 1302 Bomford Crescent. Displays present the region's cultural heritage and include Indian artifacts, pioneer items and art exhibits. Allow 1 hour minimum. Mon.-Fri. 9-5, Sat.-Sun. and holidays 10-5, Victoria Day weekend-Labour Day weekend; Mon.-Fri. 9-5, Sat.-Sun. and holidays noon-5, rest of year. Closed Jan. 1, Good Friday and Dec. 25. Donations. Phone (403) 502-8580.

SAAMIS TEEPEE is at jct. Hwy. 1 and South Ridge Dr. Made of steel, the tepee stands approximately 20 stories high. Storyboards incorporated in the tepee stand 3.6 metres (12 ft.) high and depict Indian history. Used during the 1988 Olympics in Calgary, the tepee was moved to Medicine Hat where it now stands on Saamis Archaeological Site—the location of a 16th-century buffalo camp. Allow 1 hour minimum. Daily 8:30-6:30, Victoria Day weekend-Aug. 31. Donations. Phone (403) 527-6422.

CASINOS

- **Casino by Van Shaw** is at 1051 Ross Glen Dr. S.E. Daily 10 a.m.-3 a.m.; closed Dec. 25. Phone (403) 504-4584.

MILK RIVER (J-7) pop. 879

Milk River lies on the east side of Milk River Ridge, an area more than 1,200 metres (3,900 ft.) high, 39 kilometres (24 mi.) long and 29 kilometres (18 mi.) wide. Quartzite, granite and gneiss rock formations indicate prehistoric glacial action; meltwater carved the Milk River Valley 10,000 years ago. The river, formed from small streams and springs in southwest Alberta and northern Montana, joins the Missouri and Mississippi rivers to flow to the Gulf of Mexico.

Throughout the area and predominantly in Writing-on-Stone Provincial Park *(see attraction listing)* are mushroom-shaped sandstone hoodoos, odd rock formations that once led Indians to believe spirits inhabited the valley.

The Alberta Tourism Information and Interpretive Centre: General Delivery, Milk River, AB, Canada T0L 1M0; phone (403) 647-3938 or (403) 647-3938.

WRITING-ON-STONE PROVINCIAL PARK is 32 km (20 mi.) e. and 10 km (6 mi.) s. on Sec. Hwy. 501 to the jct. with Hwy. 500, following signs. The archeological preserve overlooks the Milk River. Massive sandstone outcrops display pictographs and petroglyphs created by nomadic Shoshoni and Blackfoot Indians. Fire-burned stones, broken bones and horn tools as well as other implements have been found at former campsites. Interpretive programs are presented mid-May through early September.

Note: Temperatures in excess of 40 C (104 F) are often recorded along the trail. Park daily 24 hours. Guided 90-minute tours depart daily during summer. Park free. Fee for tours $8; ages 6-17, $6; family rate $20. Phone (403) 647-2877. *See Recreation Chart and the AAA/CAA Western Canada & Alaska CampBook.*

MUNDARE (D-7) pop. 653

BASILIAN FATHERS MUSEUM is 1 km (.6 mi.) n. of Hwy. 16 on Hwy. 855. Operated by the Basilian Fathers, the museum houses exhibits about Ukrainian immigration and the religious order's work in east central Alberta and throughout Canada. Guided tours are available. Mon.-Fri. 10-4 (also Sat.-Sun. 1-5, July-Aug.); closed holidays Sept.-June. Donations. Phone (780) 764-3887.

NANTON (I-6) pop. 1,841

NANTON LANCASTER SOCIETY AIR MUSEUM is s. on Hwy. 2 following signs. Exhibits honor Royal Canadian Air Force and Royal Air Force members who waged bombing operations during World War II. Among displays are a Canadian-built Lancaster bomber, other bombers and training planes, simulators, gun turrets and instrumentation and photographs of training aircraft in action. Allow 1 hour minimum. Daily 9-5, May-Oct.; Sat.-Sun. 10-4, rest of year. Closed Jan. 1 and Dec. 25-26. Donations. Phone (403) 646-2270.

OKOTOKS—*see Calgary p. 61.*

PEACE RIVER (A-3) pop. 6,240

Formed by the confluence of the Smoky and Heart rivers, the Peace River flows north and east of the town of the same name to Lake Athabasca and to the west into British Columbia. The area was known as "The Forks" by trappers and traders in the 1700s and "Sagitawa" (meeting of the waters) by the Cree Indians. On his historic trek across the northern continent, Alexander Mackenzie explored the region and built a fort and wintered here 1792-93.

A wooden statue honors prospector and local legend Henry Fuller "Twelve-Foot" Davis. The Vermont native, known for his generosity and hospitality, achieved great social stature when he mined $15,000 worth of gold from a 3.5-metre (12-ft.) plot between two gold claims. Davis said on his deathbed that he was not afraid to die because "I never kilt nobody, I never stole from nobody and I kept open house for travelers all my life." His grave overlooks the confluence of the Peace, Heart and Smoky rivers.

Nearby forests, rivers and streams make Peace River a popular center for year-round recreation in northern Alberta. Golf courses, swimming, canoeing, downhill skiing and dogsledding are all options.

Peace River and District Chamber of Commerce: 9309 100th St., P.O. Box 6599, Peace River, AB, Canada T8S 1S4; phone (780) 624-4166.

PINCHER CREEK (J-6) pop. 3,666

Pincher Creek was established in 1878 by the North West Mounted Police as a horse farm to provide remounts for Fort Macleod *(see place listing p. 78).* The town was named for a pair of pincers that presumably were left behind by prospectors. After hearing that the area had ample grassland, other settlers soon arrived.

Pincher Creek & District Chamber of Economic Development and Information Centre: 1037 Beverly McLachlin Dr., P.O. Box 2287, Pincher Creek, AB, Canada T0K 1W0; phone (403) 627-5855 or (888) 298-5855.

KOOTENAI BROWN PIONEER VILLAGE is at 1037 Beverly McLachlin Dr. Displays include more than 14,000 local relics—including military uniforms, agricultural equipment, jewelry, clothing and books about local history—in 12 historical buildings. On the grounds is the restored log cabin of George "Kootenai" Brown, an Irish adventurer and one of the region's first settlers who helped establish Waterton Lakes National Park. Other period buildings are on the grounds.

Allow 2 hours minimum. Mon.-Fri. 8-8, Sat.-Sun. 10-8, mid-May to mid-Sept.; Mon.-Fri. 8-4:30, rest of year. Admission $6; over 64, $4; ages 10-17,

$3; under 10, $2; family rate $16. Phone (403) 627-3684.

RAVEN (F-5)

MEDICINE RIVER WILDLIFE CENTRE is 4 km (2.5 mi.) s. of Hwy. 54, then 2 km (1.2 mi.) e. The organization provides rehabilitation for injured and orphaned wildlife. It also serves as an environmental education center, offering a videotape presentation and displays about wildlife and natural history. A trail leads to an observation tower that provides views of wildlife and a 30-hectare (75-acre) marsh. Allow 1 hour minimum. Daily 10-5, May-Oct.; by appointment rest of year. Donations. Phone (403) 728-3467.

RED DEER (F-6)
pop. 67,707, elev. 905 m/2,969'

Red Deer's name comes from the Cree Indian word *was-ka-soo*, meaning "elk." Early Scottish settlers mistook the native elk for the red deer of their homeland and the name stuck. A creek and park running through Red Deer still bear the name Waskasoo.

The original settlement was several kilometres upstream on the Red Deer River where the water was shallow and easy to cross. Dr. Leonard Gaetz, a Methodist minister who arrived in 1884, persuaded the Calgary and Edmonton Railway to cross the river on his property by donating half of his land for use as a townsite. The trains came through, and the town took root at its current site. Agriculture and petroleum products are the major local industries.

City Hall Park, 48th Avenue and Ross Street, is a landscaped oasis known for its Christmas light and flower displays. West of town is Sylvan Lake, which accommodates Jarvis Bay and Sylvan Lake parks *(see Recreation Chart)*. A noteworthy lake resort north at Gull Lake is Aspen Beach Provincial Park *(see Recreation Chart and Lacombe in the AAA/CAA Western Canada & Alaska CampBook)*.

Lacombe, also north of the city, is the site of the Canadian Agriculture Department's experimental farm; visitors can tour the facility.

Events include the Silver Buckle Rodeo in spring; the Highland Games in June; International Folk Festival/Canada Day celebrations on July 1; Westerner Days in mid-July; and the International Air Show, held every other year in August.

Tourism Red Deer: 30A Riverview Park, Red Deer, AB, Canada T4N 1E3; phone (403) 346-0180 or (800) 215-8946.

Self-guiding tours: A brochure outlining a walking tour of historic downtown is available from The Red Deer and District Museum and from the visitor information center west of Heritage Ranch in Waskasoo Park *(see attraction listings)*.

Shopping areas: Bower Place, Gaetz Avenue and 28th Street, is anchored by The Bay and Zeller's.

Red Deer Centre, 67th Street and Gaetz Avenue, has Sears and 120 smaller shops.

ALBERTA SPORTS HALL OF FAME & MUSEUM is on Hwy. 2, n. of 32nd St. by Heritage Ranch. Alberta's sports history and heroes are celebrated through the display of 7,000 artifacts, archival material and interactive exhibits, including an Alpine ski racer game, a baseball pitching station, a 200-metre (656-ft.) wheelchair race and a hockey shoot-out.

Picnicking is permitted. Food is available. Allow 1 hour, 30 minutes minimum. Daily 9-6, Victoria Day weekend-second Mon. in Oct.; 10-5, rest of year. Closed Jan. 1, Good Friday, Easter and Dec. 25-26. Admission $3; over 55 and ages 6-17, $2; family rate (two adults and all children) $9. MC, VI. Phone (403) 341-8614.

THE RED DEER AND DISTRICT MUSEUM is at 4525 47A Ave. Galleries tell the story of diverse cultures who lived in the Red Deer River Valley from the days of the First Nations to the start of modern civilization. Changing art exhibits are featured. Mon.-Sat. 10-5 (also Wed.-Thurs. 5-9), Sun. and holidays 1-5, June-Aug.; Mon.-Fri. 10-5 (also Wed.-Thurs. 5-9), Sat.-Sun. and holidays 1-5, rest of year. Closed Jan. 1 and Dec. 25. Donations. Phone (403) 309-8405.

ST. MARY'S CHURCH is at 6 McMillan Ave. This ultramodern 1968 structure of unusual design is the work of architect Doug Cardinal. Local architect Graham Leadbeater designed the parish center addition. Alois Peter Marx of Germany created the sculpture displays. Mon.-Fri. 10-4; closed legal holidays. Free. Phone (403) 347-3114.

WASKASOO PARK borders the Red Deer River and runs throughout the city. The park has more than 70 kilometres (43 mi.) of trails. Included are Bower Ponds; the 1911 Victorian Cronquist House Multicultural Centre; Fort Normandeau, with an interpretive center; Heritage Ranch; Kerry Wood Nature Centre, which houses nature displays; and Gaetz Lake Sanctuary, a wildlife preserve. Many recreational pursuits are possible. Picnicking is permitted.

CASINOS

- **Cash Casino** is at 6350 67th St. Daily 10 a.m.-3 a.m.; closed Dec. 25. Phone (403) 346-3339.

- **Jackpot Casino Ltd.** is at 4950 47th Ave. Sun.-Thurs. 10 a.m.-2 a.m., Fri.-Sat. 10 a.m.-3 a.m. Phone (403) 342-5825.

RECREATIONAL ACTIVITIES
Recreational Complex

- **Collicutt Centre** is at 3031 30th Ave. Red Deer, AB, Canada T4R 2Z7. Mon.-Fri. 5:30 a.m.-10:30 p.m., Sat.-Sun. 6:30 a.m.-10:30 p.m., holidays 10-8 (1-4 on Dec. 25). Phone (403) 358-7529.

RIMBEY (F-6) pop. 2,118

PAS-KA-POO HISTORICAL PARK is 1 km (.6 mi.) n. at Hwy. 20 and 56th Ave. The park's Smithson International Truck Museum features 20 half-ton trucks dating 1934-74. A restored village includes a log schoolhouse, town office, train station, legion hall, trapper's cabin, homesteader's cabin, general store, church, barbershop and blacksmith shop. Each contains artifacts and memorabilia.

Guided tours are available. Truck museum daily 10-5; closed Jan. 1 and Dec. 25. Village daily 10-5, May 1-early Sept. Admission $5, under 12 free. Phone (403) 843-2004.

⬧ ROCKY MOUNTAIN HOUSE NATIONAL HISTORIC SITE (F-5)

In west central Alberta, about 80 kilometres (50 mi.) west of Red Deer on Hwy. 11 and 6 kilometres (4 mi.) west from the town of Rocky Mountain House via Hwy. 11A, following signs, Rocky Mountain House National Historic Site tells the story of the fur trade era that existed 1799-1875. The site, on the banks of the North Saskatchewan River, protects the remains of four fur-trading posts.

Both the North West Co. and Hudson's Bay Co. were expanding in an attempt to reach the area's native peoples. The two rivals arrived here within a week of each other in 1799, their goal being to stimulate trade with the Kootenai, who were on the western side of the Rocky Mountains. The Blackfoot people blocked the planned trade. Rocky Mountain House traded with nine different aboriginal groups in its 76 years of operation.

Well-known cartographer and fur trader David Thompson used Rocky Mountain House for a time as a base for exploring routes over the mountains. Thompson was the first person of European descent to cross Howse Pass, accomplishing this feat in 1807.

Trade competition remained intense between the two companies until their merger in 1821. The influx of illegal whiskey traders into southern Alberta in 1869 disrupted trade with the aboriginal people, and in 1875 the last of the four posts was abandoned.

Two walking trails along the North Saskatchewan River and through a scenic wooded area connect the remains of the four forts. Eight listening stations and illustrated interpretive panels are spaced along the trail system. A 30-minute walk leads past the two later forts, the reconstructed chimneys at the last fort site, a replica flat-bottom York boat, Red River cart and a fur press. A longer 90-minute walk travels to the first two forts built at Rocky Mountain House, passing tepees, the 1967 Centennial Canoe Race exhibit and a buffalo viewing area. Visitors often can see deer, coyotes, bluebirds and hawks along the trails.

The visitor center features exhibits containing trade items and aboriginal objects; a theater presents films and interpretive programs on a regular basis. Bicycle rentals are available.

The visitor center is open daily 10-5, Victoria Day-Labour Day; hours vary, day after Labour Day-Sept. 30. Admission $2.50; over 64, $2; ages 6-16, $1.50; family rate $5.50. MC, VI. Phone (403) 845-2412.

ROSEBUD (H-6) pop. 87

A pioneer ranching settlement founded in the 1880s, Rosebud has become a thriving cultural center. The community participates in the activities of Rosebud School of the Arts. Rosebud Theatre offers dinner and theater entertainment at matinees and evening performances Wednesday through Saturday from March through December; phone (403) 677-2001 or (800) 267-7553.

Among Rosebud's historic buildings is an early 20th-century Chinese laundry, which now is home to Centennial Museum. The museum displays local memorabilia and an array of western Canadiana. Works by Alberta artists are exhibited in Akokiniskway Art Gallery and other shops along the town's self-guiding historic walking tour.

ST. ALBERT—*see Edmonton p. 75.*

SLAVE LAKE (C-5) pop. 6,600

Slave Lake is on the southeast shore of Lesser Slave Lake, Alberta's largest auto-accessible lake. Lesser Slave Lake Provincial Park *(see Recreation Chart)*, which surrounds a golf course and hugs the lake's east shore, provides snowshoeing and cross-country skiing opportunities in winter and camping, hiking and bird-watching during the summer.

The Provincial Sandcastle Championship is held in July, and Riverboat Daze takes place in August.

SMOKY LAKE (D-7) pop. 1,011

VICTORIA SETTLEMENT PROVINCIAL HISTORIC SITE is 10 km (6 mi.) s. on Hwy. 855 and 6 km (3.6 mi.) e. on Victoria Tr. Settlement began in 1862 as a Methodist mission. A Hudson's Bay Co. fur-trading post soon followed, and by the beginning of the 20th century the village was known as Pakan. Guided tours are offered of a 1906 Methodist Church and the clerk's quarters, which is furnished with pioneer articles. A videotape presentation describes local history.

Allow 1 hour minimum. Daily 10-6, May 15-Labour Day. Admission $2; over 64 and ages 7-17, $1.50; family rate $5. Phone (780) 656-2333.

SPRUCE VIEW (F-5) pop. 100

Founded at the turn of the 20th century, Spruce View was named for its omnipresent spruce trees. Such recreational opportunities as boating, camping, fishing and picnicking are available at Dickson Dam-North Valley Provincial Recreation Area *(see Recreation Chart and Innisfail in the AAA/CAA Western Canada & Alaska CampBook).*

DICKSON DAM VISITOR CENTRE is 6 km (4 mi.) e. on Hwy. 54, following signs. Perched on a hillside, the center offers a bird's-eye view of Dickson

Dam. Exhibits and a short video focus on the dam's history and topography. Sat.-Sun. 8-4, June-Aug. Hours may vary; phone ahead. Donations. Phone (403) 227-1106.

DICKSON STORE MUSEUM is 3.2 km (2 mi.) s., following signs from Hwy. 54. This restored, family-owned general store, dating from the early 1900s, also served as the town post office and local gathering place. Renovated to a style typical of the 1930s, the museum features exhibits of dry goods, hardware and groceries common to that time. The second floor contains the family living quarters, furnished in period.

Allow 30 minutes minimum. Mon.-Sat. 10-5:30, Sun. 12:30-5:30, mid-May through Labour Day weekend; Sat. 10-5:30, Sun. 12:30-5:30, day after Labour Day-Sept. 30. Donations. Phone (403) 728-3355.

STETTLER (F-7) pop. 5,215

ALBERTA PRAIRIE RAILWAY EXCURSIONS depart the train station at 47th Ave. and 46th St. Steam- and diesel-powered rail excursions are offered through the Alberta countryside in vintage passenger coaches. Trips last 5 to 6 hours; all include a buffet-style meal at the destination in the summer or on-board dining during the winter. Theme trips also are scheduled.

Trains operate Sat.-Sun. and selected weekdays, May-Oct. Departure times vary. Fare $71-$125; ages 11-17, $55-$110; ages 4-10, $32-$110. Reservations are required. AX, MC, VI. Phone (403) 742-2811.

STONY PLAIN—*see Edmonton p. 76.*

TROCHU (G-6) pop. 1,033

ST. ANN RANCH TRADING CO. PROVINCIAL HISTORIC SITE is .5 km (.3 mi.) s. on King George Ave. The reconstructed 1905 French settlement contains restored historic houses and reproductions of period buildings. The site includes a small school, post office, hospital and chapel. An interpretive center contains displays recounting the

history of the settlement, which was founded by aristocratic officers from the French cavalry. Allow 30 minutes minimum. Daily 9-9. Admission $2. Phone (403) 442-3924, or (888) 442-3924 in Canada.

TURNER VALLEY (H-5)
pop. 1,608, elev. 1,219 m/4,000'

TURNER VALLEY GAS PLANT HISTORIC SITE is 1 km (.6 mi.) s.e. at 223 Main St. N.E. (Hwy. 22). Artifacts relate to the natural gas industry. A 20-minute videotape documents the discovery of gas in the area. Guided 1-hour tours, offered on request, educate visitors about the impact of the industry on the provincial economy. Plant visitation is only by guided tour. Allow 1 hour minimum. Daily 10-6, May 15-Labour Day. Last tour departs 1 hour before closing. Donations. Phone (403) 933-7738.

VEGREVILLE (E-7) pop. 5,376

The center of eastern Alberta's Ukrainian culture, Vegreville has the distinction of possessing the largest known *pysanka*, or Easter egg, in the world. The 9.4-metre-high (31-ft.) egg, decorated to reflect Ukrainian folk art, was erected in 1975 for the centennial of the formation of the Royal Canadian Mounted Police in Alberta.

The egg's bronze, gold and silver design, made from more than 3,500 pieces of aluminum, illustrates the local settlers' struggles and the protection the mounted police provided them. Queen Elizabeth and Prince Phillip unveiled the plaque next to the giant egg in Elks/Kinsmen Park during their visit in 1978. The Ukrainian Pysanka Festival is held in early July.

Town of Vegreville Parks, Recreation & Tourism: 4509-48 St., Vegreville, AB, Canada T9C 1K8; phone (780) 632-3100.

WAINWRIGHT (E-8) pop. 5,117

WAINWRIGHT & DISTRICT MUSEUM is at 1001 1st Ave. Displays include items and memorabilia relating to family life in the town since its founding in 1908. The histories of Buffalo National Park and

a local prisoner of war camp also are presented. The museum is housed in an original Canadian National Railway station built in the early 1930s. Allow 30 minutes minimum. Mon.-Sat. 9-5, Sun. 1-5; closed Jan. 1, Good Friday and Dec. 25. Donations. Phone (780) 842-3115.

WARNER (J-7) pop. 379, elev. 1,017 m/3,336′

DEVIL'S COULEE DINOSAUR HERITAGE CENTRE is w. off Hwy. 4, following signs. Small fossil fragments found on the Milk River Ridge in 1987 were from a hadrosaur (a duck-billed dinosaur); the location was the first nesting site found in Canada. A 2-hour tour to the dinosaur egg site leaves from the center. A museum displays a hadrosaur nest, embryo, fossils and models of dinosaurs. Also included is an exhibit about early area settlement.

Note: The nesting site is in a primitive area not suitable for small children or those with mobility or medical problems. Allow 30 minutes minimum for the museum, 3 hours minimum for tour and museum. Museum daily 9-5, Victoria Day weekend-Labour Day weekend. Tours to the nesting site are given daily (weather permitting) at 10 and 1.

Museum admission $3, children $2, family rate (up to five people) $10. Tour to dig site (includes museum admission) $10, family rate $25. Reservations are recommended for the tour. AX, MC, VI. Phone (403) 642-2118.

▽ WATERTON LAKES NATIONAL PARK (J-5)

Elevations in the park range from 1,279 metres (4,200 ft.) in the town of Waterton Park to 2,920 metres (9,580 ft.) at Mount Blakiston. Refer to CAA/AAA maps for additional elevation information.

The most direct approach into the national park from the south is over Chief Mountain International Highway (SR 17/Hwy. 6) from Glacier National Park in Montana; the park also is accessible via Hwy. 5 from Cardston or Hwy. 6 from Pincher Creek. Covering 525 square kilometres (203 sq. mi.), Waterton Lakes National Park adjoins Glacier National Park. Together the two parks form Waterton-Glacier International Peace Park. The customs office is open daily 7 a.m.-10 p.m., June 1-Sept. 1; 9-6, Victoria Day weekend-May 31 and Sept. 2-30.

For thousands of years this was aboriginal territory, where the Kootenai and Blackfoot were the primary aboriginal tribes. In 1858 Lt. Thomas Blakiston became the first European on record to explore the area; he named the lakes for Charles Waterton, an 18th-century English naturalist.

Local rancher Fred Godsal, American journalist and naturalist George Bird Grinnell and others lobbied their respective governments in the late 19th century to set aside parts of this wilderness area for future generations. They succeeded, and Waterton Lakes and Glacier national parks were established in 1895 and 1910, respectively.

Waterton Lake is divided into three parts: Upper, Middle and Lower Waterton lakes. The townsite, the location of park headquarters, is on the north shore of Upper Waterton Lake, which juts 4.7 kilometres (3 mi.) into Glacier National Park. The mountains on either side tower 900 to 1,200 metres (3,000 to 4,000 ft.) above the lake. Mount Crandell rises to the north; Sofa Mountain and Vimy Peak are east across the lake.

Wildlife ranging from squirrels and marmots to deer and bears inhabits the park. A small herd of plains bison is in the buffalo paddocks on the northern boundary, 1.6 kilometres (1 mi.) north of the Waterton River Bridge on Hwy. 6. Thousands of waterfowl visit the lakes during spring and fall migrations. Hunting is prohibited.

Among the many rare wildflowers that grace prairie and mountain landscapes are bear grass, pygmy poppy and mountain lady-slipper. Evergreens blanket the slopes and peaks below mountain goat country at an altitude of about 2,286 metres (7,500 ft.).

General Information and Activities

The park is open all year, though most concessions operate only from Victoria Day weekend through the second Monday in October. Red Rock Canyon, 15 kilometres (11 mi.) northwest of Waterton, offers a .7-kilometre (.4-mi.) loop trail along the canyon and a 1-kilometre (.6-mi.) trail to Blakiston Falls. Riding stables are 2.5 kilometres (1.5 mi.) north of town near the main entrance road; horses can be rented.

Just north of the townsite is an 18-hole public golf course that is open daily, Victoria Day weekend through the second Monday in October. A free four-court tennis facility is on Cameron Falls Drive.

The park visitor center, at the junction of the entrance road and Prince of Wales Road, is open daily (weather permitting) 8-7, mid-June through Labour Day; 9-5, mid-May to mid-June and day after Labour Day-Sept. 30. Interpretive display centers at Cameron Lake and the Waterton townsite describe the park's subalpine forest and the history of the International Peace Park. All are open daily 24 hours.

Illustrated talks are given every evening at 8:30 at the park's indoor theaters. There also are guided walks and other interpretive programs; phone (403) 859-5133.

Those wishing to camp in Waterton's backcountry campsites must obtain a park use permit at the visitor center. You also can register your outing with the Park Warden Service.

Hunting is prohibited. Anglers need a fishing license, which can be obtained along with fishing regulations at the park offices, information center, campgrounds, from park wardens or at service stations in the townsite. Motorboats are permitted on both Upper and Middle Waterton lakes; water skiing, however, is permitted only on Middle Waterton

Lake. *See Recreation Chart and the AAA/CAA Western Canada & Alaska CampBook.*

ADMISSION to the park is $5; over 64, $4.25; ages 6-16, $2.50. Admission for up to seven people in a private vehicle is $12.50. An annual pass, valid at all Canadian national parks, is available.

PETS must be leashed at all times while in the park.

ADDRESS inquiries to the Superintendent, Waterton Lakes National Park, Waterton Park, AB, Canada T0K 2M0; phone (403) 859-2224.

WATERTON SHORELINE SIGHTSEEING CRUISES depart from Waterton Marina. Narrated trips cross Waterton Lake, with stops at the 49th parallel (passengers do not disembark); at Goat Haunt in Montana, where passengers may stay and return on a later boat; and at Crypt Landing, where hikers are picked up or dropped off.

Trips depart daily at 10, 1 and 4, mid- to late June and day after Labour Day to mid-Sept.; at 9 and 10, late June-Labour Day; at 10, early May to mid-June. Fare $26; ages 13-17, $13; ages 4-12, $9. Phone (403) 859-2362.

WETASKIWIN (E-6) pop. 11,154

Wetaskiwin is a Cree name meaning "the hills where peace was made." The Red Deer River was the dividing line between the Blackfoot in the south and the Cree in the north, but the Blackfoot often crossed the river to hunt buffalo in Cree territory, causing dissension between the tribes. It is believed that a peace agreement was made in the area during the 1860s to end the conflicts.

Wetaskiwin City Hall: 4904 51st St., Wetaskiwin, AB, Canada T9A 1L2; phone (780) 361-4400.

 REYNOLDS-ALBERTA MUSEUM is 2 km (1.2 mi.) w. on Hwy. 13. Displays interpret the history of ground and air transportation, agriculture and industry in Alberta. Audiovisual presentations, displays and demonstrations supplement the actual operation of vintage automobiles, bicycles, and farm and industrial machinery. One area features a reproduction of a small drive-in theater, complete with old films, metal speakers and seats shaped like the back end of 1950-era automobiles.

The museum also is home to Canada's Aviation Hall of Fame in a separate exhibit building. Vintage aircraft are displayed. Canadians who have contributed significantly to aviation history are recognized.

Food is available. Allow 2 hours minimum. Daily 10-6, July 1-Labour Day; Tues.-Sun. (and Mon. holidays) 10-5, rest of year. Closed Jan. 1 and Dec. 24-25. Admission $9; over 64, $7; ages 7-17, $5; family rate (two adults and children under 18) $25, May 14-Sept. 5. Admission $6.50; over 64, $5.50; ages 7-17, $3; family rate $15, rest of year. MC, VI. Phone (780) 361-1351 or (800) 661-4726.

WOOD BUFFALO NATIONAL PARK—

see Northwest Territories and Nunavut p. 233.

British Columbia

Tea Rooms & Totem Poles

British and Indian influences profile a cultural potpourri

Beautiful Victoria

English gardens and turreted buildings reflect a distinctive British essence

Splendid by Nature

The Canadian Rockies create a mountain playground amid glacial lakes and parks

Relaxing Hot Springs

Soak your stresses away and get an invigorating rush in warm mineral baths

A Land of Plenty

Orchards, vineyards and farms produce bountiful harvests

"a perfect
Eden"

Yoho National Park
© Natural Moments Photography
PictureQuest

S ailing along Vancouver Island's untamed coast in 1842, James Douglas visited the site of present-day Victoria and reported: "The place itself appears a perfect Eden. . . one might be pardoned for supposing it had been dropped from the clouds. . ."

Prophetic words considering that Douglas, who later became colonial governor of British Columbia, was describing the "Garden City" many years before its first flower beds were planted.

Today, Edenic gardens are the province's forte: From Victoria's renowned, blossom-loaded Butchart Gardens to lush Queen Elizabeth Park atop the city of Vancouver's tallest hill, horticultural delights are everywhere.

And if a single apple was enough to tempt Adam and Eve, then they would no doubt have found BC's fertile Okanagan Valley irresistible. Not only do orchards here produce more than a third of Canada's apples, the valley also lures vacationers with sunny weather, sandy lakefront beaches and picturesque rolling hills striped by orderly rows of grapevines. According to legend, Okanagan Lake even harbors a serpentlike monster called Ogopogo, although unlike the biblical serpent, this elusive beast seems quite shy.

If you were searching for the Garden of Eden on Earth, British Columbia wouldn't be a bad place to start.

"Once upon a time. . ."

For generations, parents have used these four words to introduce children to the fantastic, magic-filled realms of fairy tales. Say them, and a spell is cast, transforming restless young ones into an attentive audience eagerly awaiting a story. Maybe you remember feeling such anticipation yourself.

If not, then a trip to British Columbia might just help recapture that youthful expectation of adventure. Though far removed from the Old World settings popularized in the works of Hans Christian Andersen and the Brothers Grimm, this far western province—with its daunting, snowcapped mountains and mist-filled rain forests—seems to have sprung from the pages of a storybook.

Into the Woods

Walk among centuries-old Douglas firs in MacMillan Provincial Park's Cathedral Grove and it's easy to imagine bumping into Little Red Riding Hood on her way to grandmother's house. Not only will these giants make you feel child-size by comparison; the perpetual twilight created by their lofty, intertwining branches can play tricks on your eyes, too. Look up at the high, dim ceiling of needle-heavy boughs arching overhead, and you'll understand how this grove got its name. Logging may have taken its toll on British Columbia's old-growth forests, but many stands continue to thrive in such havens as Pacific Rim National Park Reserve and Strathcona Provincial Park, both on Vancouver Island.

Another of these sylvan sanctuaries is in the city of Vancouver's Stanley Park. This urban wilderness embraces an evergreen woodland so extensive that while wandering its paths you might forget you're in the heart of Canada's third largest city. A miniature railway, children's zoo and the Vancouver Aquarium make this park a great Sunday getaway for families—and a perfect backdrop for storytelling.

Some of the most interesting tales told in Stanley Park are silently portrayed by stylized figures carved into totem poles. A thicket of these cedar columns loom at the park's eastern edge, and each one communicates its own story, whether it be a family history, a notable event or an age-old myth. Travel along the mainland coast or among British Columbia's offshore islands and you'll find more outstanding examples carved by the Bella Coola,

The Queen Charlotte Islands are occupied by Haida Indians.

© Dewitt Jones/Corbis

1750

George Vancouver, an English explorer, surveys the British Columbian coast.

1792

Spanish explorers first sight the coast of Vancouver Island.

© Bettmann/Corbis

1774

Vancouver Island becomes a crown colony.

1849

1786

The British establish profitable fur trade with local Indians.

British Columbia Historical Timeline

1820

The powerful Hudson's Bay Co. controls fur trading in the Pacific Northwest.

Haida, Kwakwaka'wakw, Nootka, Salish, Tlingit and Tsimshian peoples.

Symbolizing strength and authority, the bears glaring down from totem poles may not be the only ones you see in British Columbia: Grizzlies are common within Mount Revelstoke and Glacier national parks. Part of the Columbia Mountains, the terrain here consists of narrow, steep-walled valleys that fill with snow in winter to create icebound Shangri-Las. And like the heart of Andersen's title character in "The Snow Queen," here the glaciers never thaw.

Not far away, in the Canadian Rockies, Kootenay National Park preserves land that seems equally imbued with magic. At the park's southern end are the Radium Hot Springs, which bubble forth hot, mineral-tinged water no matter what time of year it is.

Enchanted Gardens

On the other hand, changing seasons mean a world of difference at Victoria's flower-crowded Butchart Gardens. As some plants bloom, others fade, producing a dramatic shift in hues seemingly conjured by a wizard's wand. Meandering paths thread among blossoming trees and shrubs, past softly splashing fountains and around countless flower beds in this rainbow-saturated wonderland. Rhododendrons and azaleas enjoy the limelight in spring and early summer; roses steal the show in late June.

Across the Straits of Georgia, Vancouver's VanDusen Botanical Garden is similarly endowed with floral color. Careful tending has transfigured this former golf course into a city showplace of lakes, streams, hedge mazes and whimsical topiary figures.

And what childhood fantasy would be complete without a castle? Victoria boasts two. Turrets, columns and rough sandstone walls lend 19th-century Craigdarroch Castle a medieval air that greatly pleased its builder, Robert Dunsmuir, a wealthy Scottish immigrant and industrialist. Hatley Castle, on the Royal Roads University campus, looks even more like a genuine fortress from the Middle Ages. Topped by battlements, this imposing mansion would be at home in a European fable.

To anyone who has ever been mesmerized by fanciful storybook illustrations, British Columbia should seem delightfully familiar.

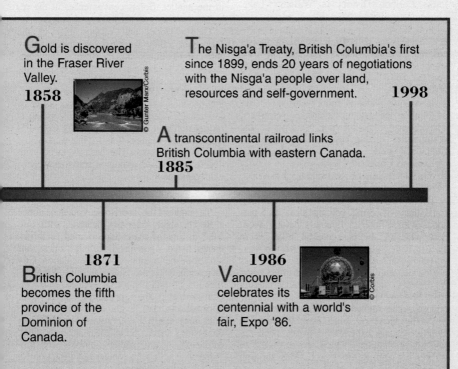

Gold is discovered in the Fraser River Valley.
1858

© Gunter Marx/Corbis

The Nisga'a Treaty, British Columbia's first since 1899, ends 20 years of negotiations with the Nisga'a people over land, resources and self-government.
1998

A transcontinental railroad links British Columbia with eastern Canada.
1885

1871
British Columbia becomes the fifth province of the Dominion of Canada.

1986
Vancouver celebrates its centennial with a world's fair, Expo '86.

© Corbis

Recreation

The Rocky Mountain and Cascade ranges, a lush valley, and a system of rivers, lakes and protected ocean waterways are the hallmarks of British Columbia's natural beauty and the sources of unlimited recreational possibilities.

Summer Sojourns

Extended **canoeing** trips await you on the Outside Trail, a chain of lakes in the Kootenay region's Champion Lakes Provincial Park. The coastal area's 57-kilometre (35-mi.) Powell Forest Canoe Route, eight lakes connected by portage routes, begins on Lois Lake and ends at the marina on Powell Lake.

The 116-kilometre (72-mi.) canoeing and **kayaking** circuit (plus portage routes) in Bowron Lake Provincial Park is so popular that reservations are required and daily access is limited to 25 boats. Paddling through this unspoiled wildlife sanctuary could take up to 7 days, depending on the weather or how much time you spend gawking at bears, deer, moose, mountain goats or the beautiful Cariboo Mountains. Approach the park from Wells, which is just north of Barkerville Historic Town. For more information contact BC Parks Cariboo District in Williams Lake; phone (250) 398-4414.

In addition to spectacular mountain scenery, canoeists will find calm, turquoise-colored glacial lakes nestled in the snowcapped Rockies; two of these—O'Hara and the aptly named Emerald—are in Yoho National Park.

If rushing water is more your speed, try negotiating the Thompson and Fraser rivers. They converge near Lytton, said to be the white-water rafting capital of Canada; outfitters and guide services are plentiful. The Chilko and Chilcotin tributaries of the Fraser River, which lie west of Williams Lake, also have a reputation for adventure.

Every region has a network of **hiking** trails that will bring you up close and personal with British Columbia's natural wonders. One of the best coastal hikes is in Pacific Rim National Park Reserve, on Vancouver Island. The Long Beach Unit, accessed off Hwy. 4 near Ucluelet, offers eight moderately challenging hiking venues ranging from beaches to rain forests. The park's pride and joy—the rugged West Coast Trail—follows the shoreline from Port Renfrew to Bamfield. Only experienced hikers need apply for reservations, which are restricted to 50 per day during the season, May through September.

But that's just the tip of the iceberg when it comes to trekking around the province. Five national and nearly 650 provincial parks and recreation areas are your gateways to discovery.

Take the family **swimming, water skiing** or **windsurfing** inland at one of seven provincial beach parks on Okanagan Lake, or to Osoyoos Lake, the warmest in the province; both are in the desertlike Okanagan Valley.

The valley's climate and terrain invite other types of activities. The Kettle Valley Railway bed, west of Penticton, provides easy **mountain biking**, while tougher trails cross nearby Campbell Mountain and Ellis Ridge.

World-class Wintering

The **skiing** amenities at Whistler and Blackcomb mountains, north of Vancouver, are world renowned. Some 32 high-speed lifts, 200 trails and 12 alpine bowls—all on more than 2,800 hectares (7,000 acres)—make up one of the largest ski resorts in North America. **Snowboarding** and skiing lessons keep the children happy. Off the slopes, adults have unlimited après ski options in Whistler Village's eclectic mix of pubs, dance clubs and culinary nightspots; shops, spas and art galleries also are tucked in the hamlet. Bonus conveniences at the resort include several ski-in/ski-out lodgings.

Gentle slopes and rolling hills in the Okanagan Valley are ideal for snowboarding and **cross-country skiing.** Resorts and community ski areas near the towns of Osoyoos, Oliver, Penticton, Westbank and Kelowna, along the Hwy. 97 corridor, have quite a following; most offer night skiing, too. Some of western Canada's best cross-country skiing is farther north on Hwy. 97, stretching from 100 Mile House to Quesnel and lying west of the Cariboo Mountains. The area is laced with dozens of marked, groomed trails as well as wilderness paths.

Recreational Activities

Throughout the TourBook, you may notice a Recreational Activities heading with bulleted listings of recreation-oriented establishments listed underneath. Similar operations also may be mentioned in Destination City recreation sections. Since normal AAA inspection criteria cannot be applied, these establishments are presented only for information. Age, height and weight restrictions may apply. Reservations often are recommended and sometimes are required. Addresses and/or phone numbers are provided so visitors can contact the attraction for additional information.

Fast Facts

POPULATION: 3,907,738.

AREA: 944,735 sq km (364,762 sq mi); ranks 5th.

CAPITAL: Victoria.

HIGHEST POINT: 4,663 m/15,295 ft., Mount Fairweather.

LOWEST POINT: Sea level, Pacific Ocean.

TIME ZONE(S): Mountain/Pacific. DST in portions of the province.

MINIMUM AGE FOR UNRESTRICTED DRIVER'S LICENSE: 16 years, 3 months.

SEAT BELT/CHILD RESTRAINT LAWS: Seat belts required for driver and all passengers; child restraints and safety seats required for under age 9 and up to 18 kg (40 pounds). Children under 12 must be seated in the rear seat of the vehicle, if available.

HELMETS FOR MOTORCYCLISTS: Required for rider and passenger.

RADAR DETECTORS: Permitted.

FIREARMS LAWS: By federal law, all nonresidents entering Canada with a firearm must declare their weapon in writing and pay a fee of $50 (Canadian). Contact the Canadian Firearms Centre at (800) 731-4000 to receive a declaration form or for additional information.

HOLIDAYS: Jan. 1; Easter Monday; Victoria Day, May 24 (if a Mon.) or closest prior Mon.; Canada Day, July 1; British Columbia Day, Aug. (1st Mon.); Labour Day, Sept. (1st Mon.); Thanksgiving, Oct. (2nd Mon.); Remembrance Day, Nov. 11; Dec. 25 and 26.

TAXES: British Columbia's provincial sales tax is 7.5 percent. There also is a provincial room tax of 8 percent to 10 percent on lodgings. A 7 percent Goods and Services Tax (GST) also is levied.

INFORMATION CENTERS: British Columbia has more than 110 visitor information centers throughout the province. Of these more than 80 are open all year and can be found in all major cities including Victoria and Vancouver. The smaller community travel information centers are open June through August. For further information phone Hello BC at (800) 435-5622.

FURTHER INFORMATION FOR VISITORS:
1-800-HELLOBC
P.O. Box 9830, Stn.
Prov. Govt.
Victoria, BC, Canada
V8W 9W5
(250) 387-1642
(604) 435-5622
(in Greater Vancouver)
(800) 435-5622

RECREATION INFORMATION:
BC Parks
800 Johnson St.
Victoria, BC, Canada V8V 1N3
(604) 689-9025 (camping reservations in Greater Vancouver)
(800) 689-9025 (camping reservations)

FISHING AND HUNTING REGULATIONS:
BC Fish and Wildlife Recreation and Allocation Branch
P.O. Box 9374
Victoria, BC, Canada V8W 9M1
(250) 387-9717

ALCOHOL CONSUMPTION: Legal age 19.

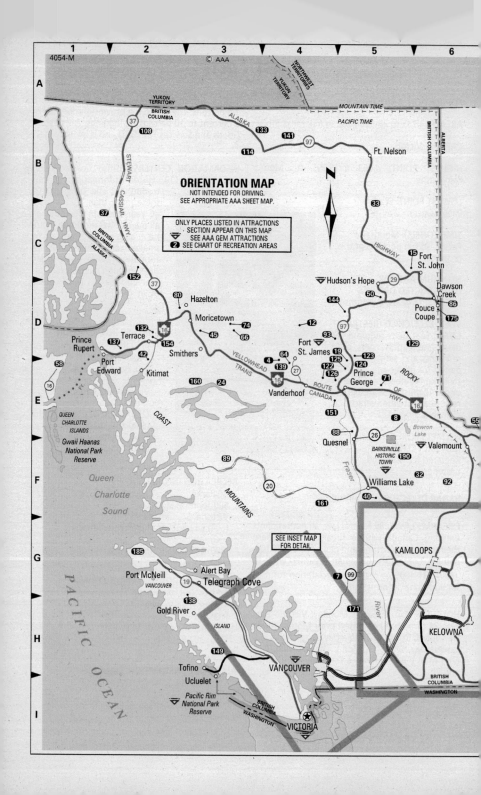

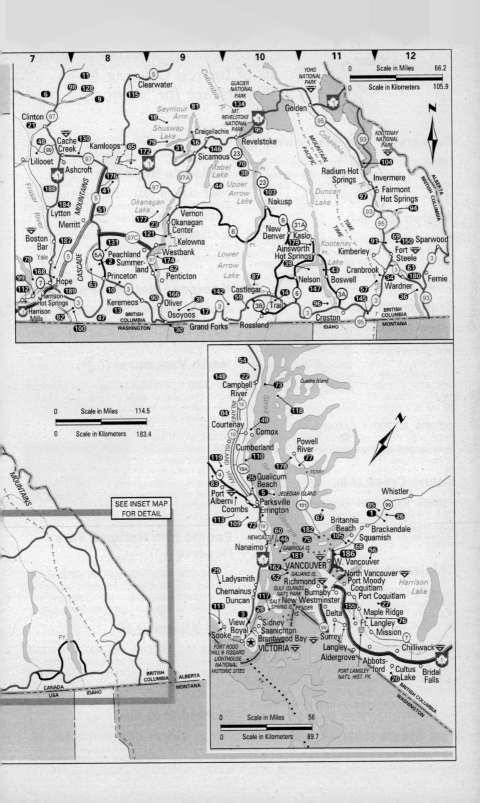

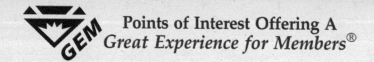
Barkerville Historic Town (F-5)

BARKERVILLE HISTORIC TOWN—The restored 1870s gold rush town features 125 original and reconstructed buildings, such as the Barkerville Hotel and the Wake Up Jake Cafe. See p. 112.

Boston Bar (C-7)

HELL'S GATE AIRTRAM—Descending into the narrowest part of Fraser Canyon, the tram travels a route that lets visitors view fishways, a suspension footbridge and a film about salmon. See p. 112.

Brentwood Bay (H-10)

BUTCHART GARDENS—Among the gardens' most interesting features are a show greenhouse, fountains and a sunken garden created on the site of a depleted limestone quarry. See p. 179.

VICTORIA BUTTERFLY GARDENS—Visitors learn about and interact with up to 2,000 exotic free-flying butterflies in this tropical rain forest environment. See p. 179.

Cache Creek (B-8)

HISTORIC HAT CREEK RANCH—Established in 1861, the roadhouse provided food, lodging and supplies to thousands of miners and settlers headed north on the Cariboo Waggon Road. See p. 113.

Chilliwack (H-12)

MINTER GARDENS—At the base of the Coastal Mountain Range, the 11 thematic gardens of the 11-hectare (27-acre) site bloom in bursts of seasonal color. See p. 115.

Fort St. James (D-4)

FORT ST. JAMES NATIONAL HISTORIC SITE OF CANADA—Reconstructed and restored buildings—including the officers' dwelling, fish cache and chicken yard—comprise the former Hudson's Bay Co. trading post. See p. 120.

Fort Steele (C-12)

FORT STEELE HERITAGE TOWN—A bakery, photography studio, restaurant and newspaper office are among the buildings in this representation of a typical 1890-1905 East Kootenay town. See p. 120.

Hudson's Hope (C-4)

PEACE CANYON DAM—At the outlet of Peace River Canyon, the dam uses water that generated electricity at a dam upstream. See p. 125.

W.A.C. BENNETT DAM—Built to produce electrical power for British Columbia, the dam produces a backup that forms the province's largest lake. See p. 125.

Kootenay National Park (B-12)

KOOTENAY NATIONAL PARK—Extensive faults are responsible for two of the park's significant features: Radium Hot Springs and the Paint Pots. See p. 129.

North Vancouver (G-11)

CAPILANO SUSPENSION BRIDGE—Fear of heights won't keep visitors away from the park's perennial gardens, rain forest, totem park and First Nations carvers and dancers. See p. 162.

GROUSE MOUNTAIN—Look down on the town from this recreationally rich gathering spot where activities range from sleigh riding to paragliding. See p. 163.

Pacific Rim National Park Reserve (I-3)

PACIFIC RIM NATIONAL PARK RESERVE—Sandy beaches, rocky headlands, temperate rain forests and an island archipelago make up this spectacular park on Vancouver's west coast. See p. 134.

Port Alberni (F-9)

McLEAN MILL NATIONAL HISTORIC SITE—A 1929 steam locomotive transports visitors to this 13-hectare (32-acre) site, which commemorates the early days of British Columbia's logging industry. See p. 137.

Richmond (G-10)

GULF OF GEORGIA CANNERY NATIONAL HISTORIC SITE—Canada's West Coast fishing industry is documented through films, equipment demonstrations and interactive exhibits. See p. 164.

Valemount (F-6)

MOUNT ROBSON PROVINCIAL PARK—Home to the highest peak in the Canadian Rockies, the 224,866-hectare (555,656-acre) park features an abundance of wildlife, scenic views and outdoor activities. See p. 145.

Vancouver (H-4)

H.R. MacMILLAN SPACE CENTRE—Children have fun learning about everything that's space-related. See p. 152

SCIENCE WORLD—Scientific phenomena can be explained here. See p. 153.

STANLEY PARK—Among the park's highlights are a miniature steam railway, a farmyard for children and totem pole displays. See p. 153.

STORYEUM—Visitors descend into a subterranean theater and journey through Canada's past. The presentation also recounts the stories of the First Nations people, European explorers and the gold rush era. See p. 153.

VANCOUVER AQUARIUM MARINE SCIENCE CENTRE—Aquarium exhibits let visitors learn about endangered species, frogs, beluga whales, sea lions and sea otters. See p. 154.

VANDUSEN BOTANICAL GARDEN—From inside the intricate gardens—set amid lakes, lawns and rock displays—visitors can gaze out upon the mountains and the city. See p. 155.

Victoria (I-4)

CRAIGDARROCH CASTLE—Built 1887-89, this coal baron's 39-room castle contains fine Victorian appointments; a turret leads to a panoramic view of Victoria, the Strait and the Olympic Mountains. See p. 173.

MINIATURE WORLD—Animation, lights and sound bring to life highly detailed miniature scenes that reflect fairy tales, nursery rhymes, historic battles and classic novels. See p. 174.

ROYAL BC MUSEUM—Two floors of displays let visitors explore a frontier town, a coastal rain forest, the First Peoples Gallery and Haida argillite carvings. See p. 175.

ROYAL LONDON WAX MUSEUM—Featured are some 300 wax figures ranging from political and religious leaders to royalty and movie stars. See p. 176.

Yoho National Park (A-11)

YOHO NATIONAL PARK—Takakkaw Falls, one of the highest falls in Canada, is but one natural wonder that explains how the park got the name *yoho,* an exclamation of astonishment in the Cree Indian language. See p. 182.

British Columbia Temperature Averages Maximum / Minimum (Celcius)
From the records of the National Weather Service

	JAN	FEB	MAR	APR	MAY	JUNE	JULY	AUG	SEPT	OCT	NOV	DEC
Fort St. John	-11 / -19	-7 / -17	-1 / -10	8 / -2	17 / 4	20 / 8	22 / 11	20 / 10	16 / 5	9 / 0	-2 / -10	-9 / -17
Kamloops	-2 / -10	4 / -5	10 / -1	16 / 3	22 / 7	26 / 11	29 / 13	28 / 12	23 / 8	14 / 3	6 / -1	1 / -6
Prince George	-7 / -17	-1 / -12	3 / -8	10 / -2	17 / 2	20 / 6	22 / 8	21 / 7	17 / 3	10 / 0	1 / -7	-4 / -12
Prince Rupert	4 / -1	5 / -1	7 / 1	10 / 3	13 / 6	16 / 8	17 / 10	17 / 11	16 / 9	12 / 6	8 / 3	5 / 1
Vancouver	6 / 1	8 / 1	11 / 3	15 / 6	18 / 8	21 / 11	24 / 13	24 / 12	20 / 10	15 / 7	10 / 4	7 / 2
Victoria	6 / 2	8 / 3	10 / 4	13 / 6	16 / 7	18 / 10	20 / 11	20 / 11	18 / 10	14 / 8	10 / 5	7 / 3

RECREATION AREAS

Recreation Area	MAP LOCATION	CAMPING	PICNICKING	HIKING TRAILS	BOATING	BOAT RAMP	BOAT RENTAL	FISHING	SWIMMING	PETS ON LEASH	BICYCLE TRAILS	WINTER SPORTS	VISITOR CENTER	LODGE/CABINS	FOOD SERVICE
NATIONAL PARKS *(See place listings)*															
Glacier (A-10) 1,350 square kilometres.		•	•	•				•		•		•	•	•	•
Gulf Islands (H-10) 33 square kilometres. Golf, kayaking, scuba diving. Recreational activities vary on each island.		•	•	•	•		•		•	•					
Gwaii Haanas (F-1) 1,495 square kilometres. Kayaking.		•			•			•					•		
Kootenay (B-12) 1,406 square kilometres.		•	•	•	•			•	•	•	•	•	•		•
Mount Revelstoke (A-10) 260 square kilometres.		•	•					•		•	•	•	•		
Pacific Rim (I-3) 510 square kilometres.		•	•	•	•	•		•	•	•					
Yoho (A-11) 1,313 square kilometres. Cross-country skiing; horse rental.		•	•	•	•		•	•		•	•	•	•	•	•
PROVINCIAL															
Adams Lake (A-9) 56 hectares 15 km n. of Chase off Hwy. 1. Archeological sites. Canoeing, horseback riding, scuba diving, water skiing, windsurfing.	18	•		•	•	•		•	•						
Alice Lake (G-12) 396 hectares 13 km n. of Squamish on Hwy. 99. Canoeing.	1	•	•	•	•		•	•	•	•	•				
Allison Lake (C-8) 23 hectares 28 km n. of Princeton on Hwy. 5A.	2	•	•		•			•	•						
Andy Bailey (C-5) 174 hectares 11 km s.e. of Hwy. 97 near Fort Nelson.	33	•	•		•	•		•	•						
Arrow Lakes (Shelter Bay) (B-10) 93 hectares on Hwy. 23. *(See Castlegar p. 114)*	38	•	•		•	•		•	•	•					
Babine Lake-Pendleton Bay Marine (D-3) 37 hectares 35 km n. of Burns Lake off Hwy. 16.	66	•			•	•			•						
Bamberton (H-10) 28 hectares 32 km n. of Victoria off Hwy. 1.	3	•	•	•				•	•	•					
Bear Creek (C-9) 178 hectares 8 km n. of Hwy. 97 near Kelowna.	121	•	•					•	•	•					
Beaumont (E-4) 191 hectares on Fraser Lake, 129 km w. of Prince George off Hwy. 16. Water skiing, windsurfing.	4	•	•	•	•	•		•	•	•					
Big Bar Lake (A-7) 332 hectares 40 km n. of Clinton off Hwy. 97.	6	•	•		•	•		•	•	•					
Birkenhead Lake (G-4) 9,955 hectares 55 km n.e. of Pemberton off Hwy. 99. Cross-country skiing, windsurfing.	7	•	•	•	•	•		•	•	•		•	•		
Blanket Creek (B-10) 318 hectares 30 km s. of Revelstoke on Hwy. 23.	70	•	•	•				•	•	•					
Bowron Lake (E-5) 149,207 hectares 112.5 km e. of Quesnel via a gravel access road off Hwy. 26. Water circuit of connecting lakes.	8	•		•	•	•		•	•	•				•	
Boya Lake (B-2) 4,597 hectares 40 km n.e. of Cassiar off Hwy. 37. Canoeing, kayaking.	108	•			•	•		•	•						
Brandywine Falls (F-11) 143 hectares 25 km s. of Whistler on Hwy. 99.	85	•	•	•						•		•	•		
Bridge Lake (A-8) 6 hectares 51 km e. of 93 Mile House off Hwy. 24. Water skiing.	9	•	•		•	•		•	•	•					
Bromley Rock (D-8) 149 hectares 19 km e. of Princeton off Hwy. 3.	10	•	•					•	•	•					
Bull Canyon (F-4) 369 hectares 10 km w. of Alexis Creek on Hwy. 20.	161	•	•	•				•		•					
Canim Beach (A-8) 6 hectares on Canim Lake, 43 km e. of 100 Mile House off Hwy. 97. Canoeing, kayaking.	11		•	•	•	•		•	•	•					
Cape Scott (G-2) 22,566 hectares 64 km w. of Port Hardy. Canoeing, hunting, kayaking.	185	•		•	•	•		•		•					

RECREATION AREAS

	MAP LOCATION	CAMPING	PICNICKING	HIKING TRAILS	BOATING	BOAT RAMP	BOAT RENTAL	FISHING	SWIMMING	PETS ON LEASH	BICYCLE TRAILS	WINTER SPORTS	VISITOR CENTER	LODGE/CABINS	FOOD SERVICE
Carp Lake (D-4) 38,612 hectares 32 km s.w. of McLeod Lake off Hwy. 97. Canoeing, hunting, ice fishing, kayaking.	12	•	•	•	•	•		•	•	•		•			
Cathedral (D-8) 33,272 hectares 24 km s.w. of Keremeos off Hwy. 3. Hunting, mountaineering.	13	•		•	•			•	•						
Cedar Point (E-5) 8 hectares 45 km n.e. of Williams Lake off Hwy. 97 on Quesnel Lake. Water skiing; mining displays.	190	•	•			•	•	•							•
Champion Lakes (D-10) 1,426 hectares 10 km s. of Castlegar off Hwy. 3B. Cross-country skiing. Power boats prohibited.	14	•	•	•	•	•		•	•	•	•	•			
Charlie Lake (C-5) 92 hectares 13 km n.w. of Fort St. John off Hwy. 97.	15	•	•	•	•	•		•		•	•				
Chilliwack Lake (D-8) 9,121 hectares 84 km s.e. of Chilliwack via an access road off Hwy. 1. Hunting, water skiing.	100	•	•	•	•	•		•	•						
Cinnemousun Narrows (B-9) 176 hectares 22.5 km n. of Sicamous via boat. Scuba diving, water skiing, windsurfing.	16	•	•	•	•	•		•	•	•				•	
Conkle Lake (D-9) 587 hectares 28 km n.e. of Osoyoos via Hwy. 3, then 26 km to entrance. Windsurfing.	17	•	•	•	•			•	•	•					
Crooked River (D-5) 970 hectares 72 km n. of Prince George on Hwy. 97. Cross-country skiing, ice fishing, windsurfing. Power boats prohibited.	19	•	•	•	•			•	•	•	•	•			
Cultus Lake (H-12) 656 hectares 11 km s.w. of Chilliwack off Hwy. 1. Water skiing. *(See Cultus Lake p. 117)*	20	•	•	•	•	•		•	•	•					
Cypress (G-11) 3,000 hectares n. of Vancouver off hwys. 1 and 99. Cross-country and downhill skiing, primitive camping. *(See West Vancouver p. 165)*	186	•	•	•								•	•		
Dionisio Point (G-10) 142 hectares 64 km n. of Victoria on Galiano Island via car ferry. Scuba diving. *(See Galiano Island p. 123)*	162	•	•	•				•	•	•	•				
Downing (A-7) 100 hectares 16 km s.w. of Clinton off Hwy. 97.	21	•	•		•	•			•						
E.C. Manning (D-8) 70,844 hectares on Hwy. 3 between Hope and Princeton. Scenic. Cross-country and downhill skiing, mountain biking, snowshoeing; canoe, kayak and horse rentals. *(See Hope p. 125)*	47	•	•	•	•	•	•	•	•	•	•	•	•	•	•
Elk Falls (E-10) 1,087 hectares 10 km n.w. of Campbell River off Hwy. 28. *(See Campbell River p. 113)*	22	•	•	•				•	•	•					
Ellison (C-9) 200 hectares on Okanagan Lake, 16 km s.w. of Vernon off Hwy. 97. Rock climbing.	23	•	•	•				•	•	•					
Emory Creek (C-7) 15 hectares 18 km n. of Hope on Hwy 1.	187	•						•	•	•					
Englishman River Falls (G-10) 97 hectares 13 km s.w. of Parksville off Hwy. 4.	109	•	•	•				•	•	•					
Fillongley (F-10) 23 hectares on Denman Island via ferry from Buckley Bay. Canoeing, kayaking.	110	•	•	•	•			•	•	•					
Fintry (C-9) 360 hectares 32 km n. of Kelowna off Hwy. 97. Hunting, scuba diving, water skiing.	177	•	•	•				•	•	•					
French Beach (H-9) 59 hectares 5 km e. of Jordan River off Hwy. 14. Windsurfing.	111	•	•	•					•	•					
Garibaldi (G-12) 194,650 hectares accessible by trail from Hwy. 99 or the British Columbia Railway. Cross-country skiing. *(See Squamish p. 142)*	26	•			•			•	•					•	
Gladstone (D-9) 39,322 hectares 5 km n. of Christina Lake on Hwy. 3. Hunting, scuba diving, water skiing.	142	•		•	•	•		•	•	•	•				
Golden Ears (H-12) 55,590 hectares 11 km n.w. of Maple Ridge off Hwy. 7. Water skiing, windsurfing. Horse rental.	27	•	•		•	•		•	•	•					
Goldpan (B-7) 5 hectares 10 km s. of Spences Bridge between the Thompson River and Hwy. 1. Canoeing, kayaking.	188	•	•	•	•			•		•					

RECREATION AREAS

Recreation Area	MAP LOCATION	CAMPING	PICNICKING	HIKING TRAILS	BOATING	BOAT RAMP	BOAT RENTAL	FISHING	SWIMMING	PETS ON LEASH	BICYCLE TRAILS	WINTER SPORTS	VISITOR CENTER	LODGE/CABINS	FOOD SERVICE
Goldstream (H-10) 388 hectares 19.3 km n.w. of Victoria via Hwy. 1. Salmon spawning in fall.	28	•	•	•				•	•	•				•	•
Gordon Bay (G-9) 51 hectares 14 km w. of Lake Cowichan off Hwy. 18. Freshwater diving, water skiing, windsurfing.	29	•	•	•	•	•		•	•	•					
Green Lake (A-8) 347 hectares 16 km e. of Hwy. 97 at 70 Mile House.	128	•	•	•	•	•		•	•	•	•				
Gwillim Lake (D-5) 32,326 hectares 40 km. n.w. of Tumbler Ridge on Hwy. 29. Canoeing, kayaking, rock climbing, scuba diving, water skiing, windsurfing.	129	•	•	•	•	•		•	•	•			•		
Haynes Point (D-9) 38 hectares 2 km s. of Osoyoos on Hwy. 97. Water skiing.	30	•	•	•	•	•	•	•	•	•	•				
Herald (B-9) 79 hectares 12.8 km n.e. of Tappen off Hwy. 1. Scuba diving, water skiing, windsurfing.	31	•	•	•	•	•		•	•	•	•				
Horsefly Lake (F-6) 148 hectares 68 km e. of 150 Mile House off Hwy. 97. Water skiing.	32	•	•	•	•	•	•	•	•	•	•				
Inkaneep (D-9) 21 hectares 5 km n. of Oliver on Hwy. 97.	166	•								•	•				
Inland Lake (E-11) 2,000 hectares 12 km n. of Powell River on Inland Lake Rd. Canoeing, kayaking. *(See Powell River p. 138)*	178	•	•	•	•	•		•	•	•	•				
Jedediah Island Marine (F-10) 240 hectares between Lasqueti and Texada islands in the Sabine Channel of the Strait of Georgia. Accessible only via boat from Lasqueti Island. Kayaking, primitive camping; sandy bays.	5	•		•				•	•	•					
Jimsmith Lake (C-12) 14 hectares 2 km s.w. of Cranbrook off Hwy. 3.	34	•	•	•				•	•	•					
Juniper Beach (B-8) 260 hectares 20 km e. of Cache Creek on Hwy. 1.	130	•	•	•	•			•	•	•					
Kentucky Alleyne (C-8) 144 hectares 30 km s. of Merritt on Hwy. 5A.	131	•		•	•	•		•	•	•					
Kettle River (D-9) 179 hectares 5 km n. of Rock Creek on Hwy. 33. Cross-country skiing, snowshoeing.	35	•	•	•				•	•	•		•			
Kikomun Creek (D-12) 682 hectares 64 km s.e. of Cranbrook via Hwy. 3, then 11 km s. to entrance. Canoeing.	36	•	•	•	•	•		•	•	•				•	
Kilby (D-7) 3 hectares 2 km e. of Harrison Mills on Hwy. 7. Historic. Water skiing.	112	•	•		•	•		•	•	•					
Kinaskan Lake (C-1) 1,800 hectares on Hwy. 37 at Kinaskan Lake.	37	•	•	•	•	•		•	•	•					
Kleanza Creek (D-2) 269 hectares 20 km e. of Terrace on Hwy. 16. Snowshoeing.	132	•	•	•				•		•		•			
Kokanee Creek (C-11) 260 hectares 19 km n.e. of Nelson on Hwy. 3A. Cross-country skiing, snowshoeing, water skiing, windsurfing.	39	•	•	•	•			•	•	•		•			
Kokanee Glacier (C-10) 32,035 hectares 19 km n.e. of Nelson on Hwy. 3A. Back- and cross-country skiing, snowshoeing.	179	•	•	•	•	•		•		•		•			
Kootenay Lake (Davis Creek/Lost Ledge) (C-11) 343 hectares near Kaslo on Hwy. 31. Water skiing, windsurfing.	147	•			•	•		•	•	•					
Lac La Hache (F-5) 24 hectares 13 km n. of Lac la Hache on Hwy. 97. Water skiing.	40	•	•		•	•		•	•	•					
Lac Le Jeune (B-8) 213 hectares 28 km s.w. of Kamloops off Hwy. 5. Nature programs. Cross-country skiing, ice fishing, snowshoeing; canoe rental, playground.	41	•	•	•	•	•	•	•	•	•	•	•	•		
Lakelse Lake (D-2) 354 hectares 26 km s. of Terrace on Hwy. 37. Canoeing, water skiing, windsurfing.	42	•	•	•	•	•		•	•	•		•			
Liard River Hot Springs (B-3) 1,082 hectares at Liard River on Hwy. 97. Playground.	133	•	•	•					•	•					

RECREATION AREAS

	MAP LOCATION	CAMPING	PICNICKING	HIKING TRAILS	BOATING	BOAT RAMP	BOAT RENTAL	FISHING	SWIMMING	PETS ON LEASH	BICYCLE TRAILS	WINTER SPORTS	VISITOR CENTER	LODGE/CABINS	FOOD SERVICE
Little Andrews Bay (E-3) 45 hectares 60 km w. of Hwy. 35, s. of Burns Lake on Oosta Lake.	160	•	•		•	•		•	•	•					
Little Qualicum Falls (F-10) 440 hectares 13 km s.w. of Parksville off Hwy. 4. Canoeing, kayaking, scuba diving, water skiing, windsurfing.	113	•	•	•					•	•	•				
Lockhart Beach (C-11) 3 hectares 53 km n. of Creston on Hwy. 3A.	43	•	•	•	•	•			•	•	•				
Loveland Bay (E-9) 30 hectares 18 km w. of Campbell River off Hwy. 28.	148	•			•	•			•	•	•				
Mabel Lake (B-9) 187 hectares 76 km n.e. of Vernon via an access road off Hwy. 6.	44	•	•	•	•	•		•	•	•	•				
Marble Canyon (B-7) 550 hectares 40 km n.w. of Cache Creek off Hwy. 12. Rock climbing.	48	•	•	•	•			•	•	•	•				
Martha Creek (A-10) 71 hectares 20 km n. of Revelstoke on Hwy. 23.	134	•	•	•	•	•			•	•	•				
McConnell Lake (B-8) 189 hectares 23 km s.w. of Kamloops off Hwy. 5. Canoeing, cross-country skiing, kayaking, ice fishing, snowshoeing.	176		•	•	•		•		•		•		•	•	•
Meziadin Lake (C-2) 335 hectares 50 km e. of Stewart off Hwy. 37.	152	•	•					•	•	•	•				
Miracle Beach (E-10) 137 hectares 22.5 km n. of Courtenay off Hwy. 19.	49	•	•	•				•	•	•			•		
Moberly Lake (D-5) 98 hectares 24 km n.w. of Chetwynd on Hwy. 29.	50	•	•	•	•	•		•	•	•	•				
Monck (B-8) 87 hectares 22 km n.e. of Merritt off Hwy. 5A. Water skiing, windsurfing.	51	•	•	•	•	•		•	•	•	•	•			
Montague Harbour Marine (G-10) 97 hectares 48 km n. of Victoria on Galiano Island via car ferry. *(See Galiano Island p. 123)*	52	•	•	•	•	•		•	•	•	•				
Morton Lake (E-10) 67 hectares 32 km n.w. of Campbell River on Hwy. 19.	54	•	•	•	•			•	•	•	•				
Mount Fernie (C-12) 259 hectares 3 km w. of Fernie on Hwy. 3. *(See Fernie p. 118)*	180	•	•	•				•		•	•				
Mount Robson (E-6) 224,866 hectares bordering Jasper National Park on Hwy. 16. Spelunking; horse rental. *(See Valemount p. 145)*	55	•	•	•	•	•		•	•	•	•	•	•	•	
Mount Seymour (G-11) 3,508 hectares 24 km n.e. of Vancouver off Hwy. 1. Cross-country skiing. *(See Vancouver p. 163)*	56	•	•	•					•	•	•	•	•		•
Moyie Lake (D-11) 91 hectares 19 km s. of Cranbrook on Hwy. 3. Canoeing, ice fishing, kayaking, windsurfing; playground.	57	•	•	•	•	•		•	•	•	•				
Muncho Lake (B-3) 88,420 hectares on Hwy. 97 at Muncho Lake. Canoeing, kayaking, scuba diving, water skiing.	114	•	•	•	•	•		•	•	•	•	•		•	
Naikoon (E-1) 72,640 hectares on n. tip of Graham Island in the Queen Charlotte Islands. *(See Queen Charlotte Islands p. 140)*	58	•	•	•				•	•	•	•				
Nairn Falls (H-5) 171 hectares 4 km s. of Pemberton on Hwy. 99.	171	•	•	•				•		•					
Nancy Greene (D-10) 203 hectares 26 km n.w. of Rossland via Hwy. 3B. Cross-country skiing, snowshoeing.	59	•	•	•	•			•	•	•	•	•	•		
Newcastle Island Marine (G-10) 336 hectares on an island e. of Nanaimo via passenger ferry. *(See Nanaimo p. 132)*	60	•	•	•	•	•		•	•	•					•
Nicolum River (C-7) 24 hectares 8 km e. of Hope on Hwy. 3.	189	•	•					•		•					
Niskonlith Lake (B-8) 238 hectares 8 km n.w. of Chase off Hwy. 1. Cross-country skiing, ice fishing, scuba diving, snowshoeing, windsurfing.	172	•			•	•		•		•		•	•		

RECREATION AREAS

RECREATION AREAS	MAP LOCATION	CAMPING	PICNICKING	HIKING TRAILS	BOATING	BOAT RAMP	BOAT RENTAL	FISHING	SWIMMING	PETS ON LEASH	BICYCLE TRAILS	WINTER SPORTS	VISITOR CENTER	LODGE/CABINS	FOOD SERVICE
Norbury Lake (C-12) 97 hectares s.e. of jct. hwys. 93 and 95 at Fort Steele.	61	•	•	•	•	•		•	•	•					
North Thompson River (A-8) 126 hectares 5 km s. of Clearwater off Hwy. 5.	115	•	•	•				•	•	•					
Okanagan Lake (C-9) 98 hectares 28 km n.w. of Penticton off Hwy. 97. Water skiing, windsurfing.	62	•	•	•	•	•	•	•	•	•					•
Okanagan Mountain (C-9) 10,542 hectares 40 km n. of Penticton off Hwy. 97. Canoeing, kayaking, horseback riding, hunting, mountain biking, water skiing.	174	•	•	•	•	•		•	•	•	•			•	
One Island Lake (D-6) 61 hectares 30 km s. of Tupper off Hwy. 2. Canoeing, backcountry skiing, kayaking, scuba diving, snow-shoeing, water skiing, windsurfing; playground.	175	•	•	•				•	•	•		•			
Otter Lake (C-8) 51 hectares on Otter Lake, 25 km w. of Princeton off Hwy. 5A.	63	•	•	•	•	•	•	•	•	•					
Paarens Beach (D-4) 43 hectares 10 km s.w. of Fort St. James off Hwy. 27. Water skiing, windsurfing.	64	•	•	•	•	•		•	•	•					
Paul Lake (B-8) 670 hectares 25 km n.e. of Kamloops off Hwy. 5.	65	•	•	•	•	•		•	•	•					
Pirates Cove Marine (G-10) 31 hectares 16 km s.e. of Nanaimo on DeCourcy Island via boat.	181	•	•	•				•	•	•					
Plumper Cove Marine (G-11) 57 hectares on Keats Island. Boat and ferry access only.	182	•	•	•	•			•	•	•					
Porpoise Bay (F-11) 61 hectares 4 km n.e. of Sechelt on East Porpoise Bay Rd.	67	•	•	•				•	•	•					
Porteau Cove (G-11) 50 hectares 30 km n. of Vancouver on Hwy. 99. Scuba diving.	68	•	•	•	•	•			•	•					
Premier Lake (C-12) 662 hectares 16 km e. of Skookumchuck via Hwy. 95.	69	•	•	•	•			•	•	•					
Prudhomme Lake (D-2) 7 hectares 20 km e. of Prince Rupert on Hwy. 16.	137	•		•				•		•					
Purden Lake (E-5) 2,521 hectares 64 km e. of Prince George off Hwy. 16. Water skiing.	71	•	•	•	•	•		•	•	•					
Rathtrevor Beach (G-10) 347 hectares 3 km s. of Parksville on Hwy. 19. Nature programs. Windsurfing; playground.	72	•	•	•				•	•	•					
Rebecca Spit Marine (E-10) 177 hectares on Quadra Island via ferry from Campbell River, then 5 km e. on Heriot Bay Rd. Scuba diving, windsurfing.	73		•	•	•	•		•	•	•					
Red Bluff (D-3) 148 hectares 48 km n. of Topley via an access road.	74	•	•	•	•			•	•	•					
Roberts Creek (G-11) 14 hectares 10 km w. of Gibsons Landing on Hwy. 101.	75	•	•					•	•	•					
Rolley Lake (H-11) 115 hectares 13 km n.w. of Mission off Hwy. 7.	76	•	•	•	•				•	•					
Ruckle (H-10) 486 hectares at Beaver Point on Salt Spring Island via ferry from Swartz Bay. Scuba diving, windsurfing. *(See Salt Spring Island p. 123)*	117	•	•	•				•		•					
Saltery Bay (F-11) 69 hectares at Saltery Bay w. of ferry landing on Hwy. 101. Scuba diving.	77	•	•	•				•	•	•					
Sasquatch (C-7) 1,220 hectares 6.4 km n. of Harrison Hot Springs via an access road off Hwy. 7. Canoeing, water skiing, windsurfing; playground.	78	•	•	•	•	•		•	•	•					
Schoen Lake (H-3) 8,430 hectares 20 km n. of Sayward, 12 km s. of Hwy. 19.	138	•	•		•			•	•	•					
Seeley Lake (D-2) 24 hectares 6 km w. of Hazelton on Hwy. 16.	80	•	•	•	•			•	•	•					

RECREATION AREAS

	MAP LOCATION	CAMPING	PICNICKING	HIKING TRAILS	BOATING	BOAT RAMP	BOAT RENTAL	FISHING	SWIMMING	PETS ON LEASH	BICYCLE TRAILS	WINTER SPORTS	VISITOR CENTER	LODGE/CABINS	FOOD SERVICE
Shuswap Lake (B-9) 149 hectares 19.25 km n. of Squilax. Nature programs. Canoeing, kayaking, snorkeling, water skiing, windsurfing; playground.	79	●	●	●	●	●	●	●	●	●			●		
Silver Beach (A-9) 130 hectares at n. end of Shuswap Lake at Seymour Arm.	81	●		●	●	●		●	●	●					
Skagit Valley (D-7) 32,577 hectares 8 km w. of Hope via Hwy. 1, then 43 km s. on Second Rd. Interpretive programs. Hunting; horse trails, playground.	82	●	●	●	●	●		●	●	●					
Skihist (C-7) 33 hectares 6 km e. of Lytton on Hwy. 1.	184	●	●	●	●			●		●					
Smelt Bay (E-10) 16 hectares on Cortes Island via ferry from Campbell River. Canoeing, kayaking.	118	●	●		●			●	●	●					
Sowchea Bay (E-4) 13 hectares on Stuart Lake, 13 km w. of Fort St. James off Hwy. 27.	139		●		●	●		●	●	●					
Sproat Lake (F-9) 39 hectares 13 km n.w. of Port Alberni on Sproat Lake Rd. Water skiing. *(See Port Alberni p. 136)*	83	●	●	●	●	●		●	●	●			●		
Stamp River (F-9) 327 hectares 14 km w. of Port Alberni on Stamp River Rd.	119	●	●	●				●		●					
Stone Mountain (B-4) 25,690 hectares 125 km w. of Fort Nelson on Hwy. 97. Canoeing, kayaking.	141	●	●	●	●	●		●		●		●		●	
Strathcona (E-10) 250,000 hectares 48.25 km w. of Campbell River via Hwy. 28. Cross-country and downhill skiing, mountain biking, rock climbing, snowshoeing, water skiing, windsurfing.	84	●	●	●	●	●	●	●	●	●	●	●	●	●	●
Swan Lake (D-6) 67 hectares at Tupper, 38 km s. of Dawson Creek via Hwy. 2. Canoeing, kayaking, scuba diving, water skiing, windsurfing; playground.	86	●	●	●	●	●		●	●	●					
Syringa (C-10) 4,417 hectares 17 km n. of Robson off Hwy. 3. Canoeing, kayaking, water skiing, windsurfing; playground. *(See Castlegar p. 114)*	87	●	●	●	●	●		●	●	●					
Taylor Arm (H-3) 791 hectares 15 km w. of Port Alberni on Hwy. 4.	149	●	●	●				●	●	●					
Ten Mile Lake (E-4) 260 hectares 10 km n. of Quesnel on Hwy. 97. Cross-country and water skiing.	88	●	●	●	●	●		●	●	●	●	●	●		
Top of the World (C-12) 8,790 hectares 95 km e. of Kimberley off Hwy. 93, then 54 km e. on a gravel access road. Cross-country skiing, mountain biking, snowshoeing; horse trails.	150	●	●	●				●		●	●	●		●	
Tudyah Lake (D-4) 56 hectares on Hwy. 97 at Mackenzie.	144	●	●		●	●		●	●	●					
Tweedsmuir South (F-3) 506,000 hectares 349 km n.w. of Williams Lake on Hwy. 20. Canoeing circuit, cross-country and downhill skiing; horse rental.	89	●	●	●	●	●		●	●	●		●		●	●
Tyhee Lake (D-3) 33 hectares 8 km w. of Telkwa on Hwy. 16. Canoeing, cross-country skiing, kayaking.	45	●	●	●	●	●		●	●	●		●			
Vaseux Lake (D-9) 12 hectares at Vaseux Lake on Hwy. 97. Canoeing, ice fishing, kayaking.	90	●	●	●	●			●	●	●		●			
Wasa Lake (C-11) 144 hectares 21 km n. of Fort Steele off Hwy. 93/95. Canoeing, water skiing, windsurfing; playground.	91	●	●	●	●	●		●	●	●	●			●	
Wells Gray (F-6) 540,000 hectares 30 km n. of Clearwater via an access road off Hwy. 5. Interpretive programs. Canoeing, cross-country skiing, horseback riding, kayaking, snowshoeing; horse rental. *(See Clearwater p. 115)*	92	●	●	●	●	●		●	●	●		●	●	●	
West Lake (E-5) 256 hectares 29 km s.w. of Prince George off Hwy. 16.	151		●	●	●			●	●	●		●			
Whiskers Point (D-4) 50 hectares 127 km n. of Prince George off Hwy. 97. Canoeing, kayaking, water skiing, windsurfing; nature trail, playground.	93	●	●	●	●	●		●	●	●					
Whiteswan Lake (C-12) 1,994 hectares 25 km s. of Canal Flats off Hwy. 93/95. Canoeing, ice fishing, kayaking.	94	●	●	●	●	●		●	●	●					

RECREATION AREAS

	MAP LOCATION	CAMPING	PICNICKING	HIKING TRAILS	BOATING	BOAT RAMP	BOAT RENTAL	FISHING	SWIMMING	PETS ON LEASH	BICYCLE TRAILS	WINTER SPORTS	VISITOR CENTER	LODGE/CABINS	FOOD SERVICE
Wistaria (E-3) 40 hectares 40 km w. of Hwy. 35, s. of Burns Lake on Ootsa Lake.	24		•		•	•		•	•						
Yahk (D-11) 9 hectares on Hwy. 3/93 at Yahk.	145	•	•					•	•						
Yard Creek (B-9) 61 hectares 20 km n. of Sicamous on Hwy. 1.	146	•	•	•				•	•	•					
OTHER															
Berman Lake Park (E-4) 38 hectares 45 km w. of Prince George. Canoeing.	122		•	•				•	•						
Canyon Hot Springs (B-10) Hot mineral springs 35.5 km e. of Revelstoke. *(See Revelstoke p. 141)*	95	•	•	•				•	•	•				•	•
Creston Valley (D-11) 7,000 hectares 9.5 km w. of Creston on Hwy. 3. Birdwatching, canoeing, cross-country skiing, hunting. *(See Creston p. 117)*	96	•	•	•				•		•	•	•	•		•
Descanso Bay Regional Park (G-10) 16 hectares 1 km e. of Nanaimo on Gabriola Island via ferry. Kayaking.	46	•	•	•				•	•	•	•				
Fairmont Hot Springs (B-11) Hot mineral springs on Hwy. 95 in Fairmont Hot Springs. Downhill skiing; horse rental. *(See place listing p. 118)*	97	•	•	•					•	•		•	•	•	•
Ferry Island (D-2) 61 hectares 1 km e. of Terrace off Hwy. 16. Cross-country skiing.	154	•	•	•				•		•		•			
Giscome Portage (D-5) 22 hectares 50 km n. of Prince George. Historic. Cross-country skiing.	123		•	•						•		•			
Green Lake Area (A-7) 347 hectares 10 km e. of 70 Mile House on Green Lake Rd. Hunting, snowmobiling, water skiing; horse rental.	98	•	•	•	•	•	•	•	•	•		•		•	•
Harold Mann (D-5) 13 hectares 50 km n.e. of Prince George. Canoeing; nature trail.	124	•						•	•	•					
Harrison Hot Springs (C-7) Hot mineral springs on Harrison Lake, 5 km n. of Hwy. 7 on Hwy. 9. Canoeing, golf, hunting, rock hunting; horse rental. *(See place listing p. 124)*	99	•	•	•	•	•	•	•	•	•		•	•	•	•
Horne Lake Regional Park (F-10) 105 hectares 35 km n.w. of Qualicum Beach on Hwy. 19 to exit 75 (Horne Lake Rd.), then 13 km w. on a gravel road, following signs. Nature programs. Canoeing; water skiing.	25	•	•	•	•	•		•	•	•					
Kanaka Creek (H-11) 400 hectares 2 km e. of Haney. Canoeing; fish hatchery, horse trails. *(See Maple Ridge p. 161)*	155		•	•	•			•		•	•				
Kawkawa Lake (C-7) 7 hectares 5 km e. of Hope off Hwy. 5.	168	•	•	•	•	•		•	•						
Nakusp Hot Springs (B-10) Hot mineral springs 3 km n. of Nakusp on Hwy. 23, then e. on Hot Springs Rd. Cross-country skiing. *(See Nakusp p. 132)*	103	•	•	•				•		•		•	•	•	•
Ness Lake (E-5) 14 hectares 32 km n.w. of Prince George. Canoeing, cross-country skiing.	125		•	•				•	•	•		•			
Radium Hot Springs (B-12) Hot mineral springs near the w. entrance of Kootenay National Park. Horse rental. *(See place listing and Kootenay National Park p. 129)*	104	•	•	•				•	•	•		•	•	•	•
Whytecliff Park (G-11) 40 acres 22.5 km n.e. of Vancouver on the North Shore. Scuba diving.	105		•	•				•	•	•					
Wilkins Park (E-4) 57 hectares 14 km w. of Prince George. Cross-country skiing; nature trail.	126	•	•	•	•			•		•		•	•		•

Points of Interest

ABBOTSFORD (H-11)
pop. 115,463, elev. 58 m/190'

Abbotsford is the regional shopping center as well as the center of trade and industry for the fruit, livestock, poultry and dairy farms of the surrounding Fraser Valley. Several area industries and farms offer tours, including Clayburn Industries Ltd., at Railway and Pine streets. Castle Park Golf and Games Amusement Park, 36165 N. Parallel Rd., provides a range of family entertainment.

Tourism Abbotsford Visitor InfoCentre: 2478 McCallum Rd., Abbotsford, BC, Canada V2S 3P9; phone (604) 859-1721 or (888) 332-2229.

TRETHEWEY HOUSE HERITAGE SITE ON MILL LAKE is at 1B-32320 Dahlstrom Ave., next to John Mahoney Park. Restored and furnished to its 1925 appearance, this Arts and Crafts-style house features reconstructions of a playhouse and a carriage house as well as period gardens and an archives library.

Guided tours are offered. Allow 30 minutes minimum. House open Thurs.-Sun. 11-1, Mon.-Wed. and holidays 1-5, July-Aug.; Tues.-Fri. 1-5, rest of year. Archives by appointment Tues. 9-noon and Wed.-Thurs. 1-5. Closed Jan. 1 and Dec. 25-31. House $2, over 64 and students with ID $1. Archives fee $4.25; over 64, $2.80; students with ID $2.65; children $2.25. Phone (604) 853-0313 for the house or (604) 853-3722 for the archives.

AINSWORTH HOT SPRINGS (C-11)
elev. 538 m/1766'

AINSWORTH HOT SPRINGS RESORT is on Hwy. 31. Overlooking Kootenay Lake, the springs feature a natural, odorless mineral cave pool with an average temperature of 40-44 C (104-111 F), and a main pool averaging 35 C (97 F). The cold plunge pool, fed by a natural spring, has an average temperature of 4 C (40 F). Towels can be rented. Food

is available. Daily 10-9:30. Last admission 30 minutes before closing. Admission $7; over 59, $6.50; ages 3-12, $5. AX, MC, VI. Phone (250) 229-4212 or (800) 668-1171.

ALDERGROVE—see Vancouver p. 160.

ALERT BAY (G-3) pop. 583, elev. 15 m/49'

On crescent-shaped Cormorant Island off Vancouver Island's northeast coast, Alert Bay is a fishing village reached by ferry from Port McNeill (see place listing p. 137). The influence of native cultures is evident in the many totem poles, including a memorial pole for totem carver Chief Mungo Martin.

Alert Bay Travel InfoCentre: 118 Fir St., P.O. Box 2800, Alert Bay, BC, Canada V0N 1A0; phone (250) 974-5024.

ALERT BAY PUBLIC LIBRARY AND MUSEUM is at 118 Fir St. This small museum houses Kwakwaka'wakw artifacts and items depicting local history. Its archives include Alert Bay newspapers and more than 6,000 photographs. Allow 30 minutes minimum. Mon.-Sat. 1-4, July-Aug.; Mon., Wed. and Fri.-Sat. 1-4, rest of year. Closed holidays. Donations. Phone (250) 974-5721.

CHRIST CHURCH is on Front St. The 1881 cedar church with stained-glass windows reflects the blending of Indian and European cultures. Guided tours are available. Allow 30 minutes minimum. Mon.-Sat. 11-5, late June-early Sept. Donations. Phone (250) 974-5024 for information from the Travel InfoCentre.

TOTEM POLE is near the corner of Park and Wood sts. Erected in 1973, the 53-metre (173-ft.) pole is considered to be the world's tallest. It features 22 figures, including a sun at the top. Binoculars are recommended for viewing. The totem pole stands

near the 'Namgis Big House, a Kwakwaka'wakw ceremonial center not open to the public. Allow 30 minutes minimum. Daily dawn-dusk. Free.

SAVE **U'MISTA CULTURAL CENTRE** is 2 km (1.2 mi.) n. of the ferry on Front St. The collection includes elaborately carved masks, traditional and historical carvings, woven cedar pieces, ceremonial regalia, paintings and other artifacts from Indian potlatches—the gift-giving ceremonies that mark such important occasions as birth, marriage and death. There also are films and small galleries with short-term exhibits.

Daily 9-5, Victoria Day-Labour Day; Mon.-Fri. 9-5, rest of year. Closed holidays. Admission $5.35; over 59 and students with ID $4.28; under 12, $1.07. MC, VI. Phone (250) 974-5403 or (800) 690-8222

ASHCROFT (B-7)
pop. 1,788, elev. 305 m/1,000'

Ashcroft Manor, a roadside house on Cariboo Wagon Road, was named for the English home of its settlers, Clement and Henry Cornwall. The Cornwalls established themselves as cattlemen in 1862 and lived the pioneer life in the style of gentlemen, practicing such rituals as afternoon tea and riding to hounds through sagebrush and scrub in pursuit of coyotes. The manor is south of town on Hwy. 1.

ASHCROFT MUSEUM is at 404 Brink St. Exhibits recount the history of the southern Cariboo, the Indian tribes that first settled Ashcroft. Artifacts and photographs are displayed in the windows of old shops, churches and houses along a board sidewalk, depicting life as it was in Ashcroft's glory days between the first settlement in 1884 and the great fire in 1916. A re-creation of the Hat Creek Mine also is displayed. Daily 9-5, July-Aug.; Thurs.-Mon. 9-5, Apr.-June and Sept.-Oct.; otherwise varies. Closed holidays. Donations. Phone (250) 453-9232.

▼GEM BARKERVILLE HISTORIC TOWN (F-5)

Barkerville is approximately 80 kilometres (50 mi.) east of Quesnel via Hwy. 26. The restored 1870s gold rush town once had the largest population north of San Francisco and west of Chicago. In those days when more than $50 million of gold—at $16 per ounce—had been mined from the area, soap cost $1 a bar and a dance with a hurdy-gurdy girl cost $1 a whirl.

The town was named for Billy Barker, a Cornish miner who first found gold in large quantities in the early 1860s. Barkerville became a virtual ghost town a few years later when the gold ran out.

The town contains 125 original and reconstructed buildings, including the Barkerville Hotel, St. Saviours Church, the Mason and Daly General Store and the Wake Up Jake Cafe; many are manned by attendants in period dress. Board sidewalks and dirt streets help preserve the essence of the original site.

Theatre Royale presents period melodrama, dance and music Victoria Day-September 30. Treasure seekers can pan for gold at Eldorado Mine. A visitor center presents videos and exhibits about the history of Barkerville. Guided town, Chinatown and cemetery tours as well as living-history programs are offered.

The townsite is open daily 8-dusk. Full visitor services operate daily, mid-June through Sept. 30. Pets are not permitted. Admission mid-June through Sept. 30, $12.50; over 64, $11.25; ages 13-17, $7.25; ages 6-12, $3.50; family rate $28.50. Free rest of year. Phone (250) 994-3332.

BARKERVILLE PROVINCIAL PARK is on Hwy. 26. Hiking trails are offered at the provincial park, which includes three campgrounds. Daily 8-dusk, May-Oct. Camping $14-$17. Phone (800) 435-5622. *See the AAA/CAA Western Canada & Alaska CampBook.*

BOSTON BAR (C-7)
pop. 233, elev. 309 m/1,013'

Boston Bar, which began as a gold mining town, was named for a Dutchman who came from Boston to prospect in the 1860s. Because Boston was the home port to many of the ships bringing prospectors, local Indians called the newcomers Boston men. Boston Bar is a logging and trade center, with the Canadian National Railway passing through town. The Canadian Pacific Railway parallels the National on the other side of Fraser River Canyon and passes through the village of North Bend.

Boston Bar is the access point for the Nahatlach Valley, which features the Nahatlach River and a chain of lakes. Recreation includes camping, fishing and white-water rafting.

▼GEM **HELL'S GATE AIRTRAM** is 11 km (7 mi.) s. on Hwy. 1 to 43111 Trans-Canada Hwy. SAVE in Fraser River Canyon. The tram descends 153 metres (502 ft.) across the river to the narrowest part of Fraser Canyon and across Hell's Gate Fishways, where millions of salmon annually swim upstream to their spawning grounds. Visitors can see eight fishways from observation decks or a suspension bridge. A film about the life cycle of the salmon is shown at the education center.

Food is available. Allow 1 hour minimum. Daily 9:30-5:30, mid-May through Labour Day; 10-4, mid-Apr. to mid-May and day after Labour Day through mid-Oct. Fare $12.15; over 64, $10.28; ages 6-18, $8.41. MC, VI. Phone (604) 867-9277.

RECREATIONAL ACTIVITIES
White-water Rafting

• **REO Rafting Adventure Resort** is 18 km (11 mi.) n.w. on Hwy. 1 in Fraser Canyon. Write 845 Spence Way, Anmore, BC, Canada V3H 4Y7. Nahatlach River trips operate Apr.-Sept. Phone (604) 461-7238, or (604) 867-9500 Sat.-Sun., or (800) 736-7238.

BOSWELL (C-11) pop. 100, elev. 533 m/1,748'

THE GLASS HOUSE is on Hwy. 3A (Southern Trans-Canada Hwy.). This six-room, castlelike house is made of empty 16-ounce embalming fluid bottles. A funeral director built the house, archway and several terraces on the landscaped lakefront grounds. Allow 30 minutes minimum. Daily 8-8, July-Aug.; 9-5, May-June and Sept. 1 through mid-Oct. Admission $6; ages 13-19, $5; ages 6-12, $4. VI. Phone (250) 223-8372.

BRACKENDALE (G-11)

RECREATIONAL ACTIVITIES
White-water Rafting
- **Sunwolf Outdoor Centre—Bald Eagle Rafting** is at 70002 Squamish Valley Rd. Write P.O. Box 244, Brackendale, BC, Canada V0N 1H0. Other activities are available. Daily 8-8, June-Sept. Phone (604) 898-1537 or (877) 806-8046.

BRENTWOOD BAY—*see Victoria p. 179.*

BRIDAL FALLS (H-12) elev. 61 m/200'

SAVE **DINOTOWN** is off Hwy. 1 exit 135 following signs. Geared for ages 2-12, this 5-hectare (12-acre) amusement park features live shows, a train, paddleboats, bumper cars, miniature golf, a parade and a water park. Picnicking is permitted. Food is available. Allow 3 hours minimum. Daily 10-7, July-Aug.; daily 10-5, day after Father's Day-Labour Day; Sat.-Sun. 10-5, Mother's Day weekend-Father's Day and in Sept. Admission $12.15; over 64, $8.88. MC, VI. Phone (604) 794-7410 or (604) 794-3733.

TRANS-CANADA WATERSLIDES is at jct. hwys. 1 and 9 on Bridal Falls Rd. The park features 10 waterslides, a giant hot pool, miniature golf course, river ride, and picnic and barbecue facilities. Food is available. Allow 2 hours minimum. Daily 10-8, mid-June through Labour Day; Sat.-Sun. 10-6, late May to mid-June. Hours may vary; phone ahead. Admission $11.21, under 4 free. Admission after 5 p.m. $6.54. Admission may vary; phone ahead. MC, VI. Phone (604) 794-7455 or (888) 883-8852 to verify schedule or rates.

BRITANNIA BEACH (G-11)
pop. 300, elev. 6 m/20'

From 1930 to 1935 the Britannia Mine at Britannia Beach was the largest producer of copper in the British Empire. No longer in operation, the mine is now part of the British Columbia Museum of Mining.

BRITISH COLUMBIA MUSEUM OF MINING is on Hwy. 99. An underground mine tunnel ride is a highlight of the museum, which chronicles mining history through hands-on demonstrations and exhibits. On site is a 1921 concentrator mill and a 235-ton super mine truck. Gold panning is included with admission.

The tunnel temperature is a constant 12 C (54 F); warm clothing and comfortable walking shoes are recommended. Hard hats are provided. Allow 1 hour, 30 minutes minimum. Daily 9-4:30, first Sun. in May-second Mon. in Oct.; Mon.-Fri. 9-4:30, rest of year. Admission $12.95, over 64 and students with ID $10.95, family rate (two adults and two students) $48. MC, VI. Phone (604) 896-2233 or (800) 896-4044

BURNABY—*see Vancouver p. 160.*

CACHE CREEK (B-8)
pop. 1,056, elev. 450 m/1,500'

GEM SAVE **HISTORIC HAT CREEK RANCH** is 11 km (7 mi.) n. on Hwy. 97 at jct. hwys. 97 and 99. The 130-hectare (320-acre) ranch, on one of the few sections of the Cariboo Waggon Road still accessible to the public, consists of more than 20 historic buildings constructed 1863-1915 when the ranch served as a roadhouse for the horse-drawn stagecoaches and freight wagons of the B.C. Express line (known as the B.X.).

Guided tours are offered of the 1860 roadhouse, and visitors can explore a heritage apple orchard, a Shuswap village, a blacksmith shop and a collection of pioneer agricultural machinery. Camping is available. Food is available. Daily 9-5, May 1 through mid-Oct. Admission $8; over 54, $7; ages 6-12, $5; family rate $20. Camping $10-$15 per night. MC, VI. Phone (250) 457-9722 or (800) 782-0922.

CAMPBELL RIVER (E-10)
pop. 28,456, elev. 18 m/59'

An important lumber, mining and commercial fishing center, Campbell River is near a noted Vancouver Island timber stand. The Elk Falls Pulp and Paper Mill offers tours in the summer. Campbell River is headquarters of the Tyee Club, whose members must catch a salmon of 30 pounds or more while fishing from a rowboat in the raging waters of Discovery Passage.

Provincial parks preserve the area's natural beauty, typified by waterfalls and mountainous wilderness. At Elk Falls Provincial Park the Campbell River drops 27 metres (90 ft.) into a deep canyon. Strathcona Provincial Park contains Mount Golden Hinde, at 2,200 metres (7,218 ft.) the highest mountain on Vancouver Island, and 440-metre (1,445-ft.) Della Falls, the highest waterfall in Canada. Scuba diving is popular during the winter when the waters are particularly clear. *See Recreation Chart and the AAA/CAA Western Canada & Alaska CampBook.*

The 183-metre-long (600-ft.) Campbell River Fishing Pier, 655 Island Hwy., is available for fishing, strolling or watching the cruise ships pass through the Strait of Georgia.

Campbell River Visitor InfoCentre: 1235 Shoppers Row, P.O. Box 400, Campbell River, BC, Canada V9W 5B6; phone (250) 287-4636 or (866) 830-1113.

SAVE **MUSEUM AT CAMPBELL RIVER** is at 470 Island Hwy. with an entrance off 5th Ave. The museum displays artifacts crafted by First Nations people of northern Vancouver Island. Exhibits also follow the island's pioneer and industrial history, including vintage logging and fishing equipment and replicas of a pioneer cabin and a float house. The outdoor historical interpretation park includes indigenous plant gardens, a cod fishing boat and a logging steam donkey.

Allow 1 hour minimum. Mon.-Sat. 10-5, Sun. noon-5, May-Aug.; Mon.-Fri. 9-5, Sat. 10-4, Jan.-Apr.; daily 10-4, rest of year. Closed second Mon. in Oct., Nov. 11, and Dec. 25 and 31. Admission $5, over 64 and students with ID $3.75, under 6 free, family rate $12. Phone (250) 287-3103.

QUINSAM RIVER HATCHERY is .5 km (.3 mi.) w. on Hwy. 28, then 2.4 km (1.5 mi.) s. on Quinsam Rd. to 4217 Argonaut Rd. The salmon enhancement project produces pink, coho and chinook salmon and steelhead trout. A display room chronicles the life cycle of a salmon. Facilities range from an incubation unit to adult holding ponds. Adult salmon viewing is best from mid-September to mid-November. Daily 8-4. Free. Phone (250) 287-9564.

RECREATIONAL ACTIVITIES
Scuba Diving

• **Abyssal Dive Charters** departs from Quadra Island. Write P.O. Box 747, Quathiaski Cove, BC, Canada V0P 1N0. Other activities are available. Daily 7:30 a.m.-10:30 p.m. Phone (250) 285-2420 or (800) 499-2297.

CASTLEGAR (D-10)
pop. 7,002, elev. 494 m/1,620'

At the junction of hwys. 3 and 3A, Castlegar is considered the crossroads of the Kootenays. Just north is the 51-metre-high (167-ft.) Hugh Keenleyside Dam. The upper and lower Arrow Lakes, created by the dam, offer popular summer recreation areas including Arrow Lakes Provincial Park (Shelter Bay) and Syringa Creek Provincial Park. *See Recreation Chart and the AAA/CAA Western Canada & Alaska CampBook.*

Castlegar Chamber of Commerce: 1995 Sixth Ave., Castlegar, BC, Canada V1N 4B7; phone (250) 365-6313.

SAVE **DOUKHOBOR VILLAGE MUSEUM** is opposite the airport just off Hwy. 3A to 112 Heritage Way. The site is a seven-building replica of the communal settlement of the Doukhobors, a pacifist group of Russian immigrants who settled in the area 1908-13. There were about 90 such villages. Highlights include artifacts reflecting the settlement and an art gallery depicting Doukhobor life. Spinning and weaving demonstrations occur July through September. Allow 30 minutes minimum. Daily 10-6, May-Sept. Admission $7, students with ID $5. Phone (250) 365-6622.

KOOTENAY GALLERY OF ART, HISTORY AND SCIENCE is opposite the airport just off Hwy. 3A at 120 Heritage Way, next to Doukhobor Village Museum. Two galleries feature rotating historical, scientific and artistic exhibitions of local, national and international origin. Workshops and musical events are held throughout the year. Allow 30 minutes minimum. Daily 10-5, July-Aug.; Wed.-Sat. 10-5, Sun. noon-5, Sept.-Dec. and Mar.-June. Closed Easter and Dec. 25. Schedule may change; phone ahead. Admission $2, students with ID $1, under 12 free, family rate $10. Phone (250) 365-3337.

ZUCKERBERG ISLAND HERITAGE PARK is at 7th Ave. and 9th St. A suspension bridge leads to the island at the confluence of the Columbia and Kootenay rivers. Walking tours offers such sights as an Indian Kekuli or pit house, a cemetery, a log house, a sculpture of a seated woman carved from a tree stump and the Chapel House with its Russian Orthodox onion dome.

Picnicking is permitted. Allow 30 minutes minimum. Park open daily dawn-dusk. Chapel House open 10-6, July-Aug. Donations. Phone (250) 365-6440.

CHEMAINUS (G-10) pop. 2,706, elev. 6 m/20'

A lumber and manufacturing town, Chemainus added tourism to its economy with the creation of murals. More than 30 professional paintings on the walls of buildings portray the history of the Chemainus Valley. Subjects range from North American Indians to dramatic depictions of the logging industry.

Begun by local artists, the series of murals has attracted artists from around the world. Walking tour maps can be bought at the kiosk in the central parking area. Prearranged guided tours and horse-drawn carriage tours also are available for a fee; phone (250) 246-5055 or (250) 246-5279.

Chemainus Theatre offers dramas, comedies and musical productions; phone (250) 246-9820 or (800) 565-7738.

Chemainus Chamber of Commerce: 9796 Willow St., P.O. Box 575, Chemainus, BC, Canada V0R 1K0; phone (250) 246-3944.

CHILLIWACK (H-11) pop. 62,927, elev. 10 m/33'

In the heart of the upper Fraser River Valley, Chilliwack is the center of a prosperous farming and dairy region. The surrounding lakes, rivers, mountains and nearby provincial parks offer such varied recreation as skiing, hiking, fishing, rock hunting and white-water rafting. Scenic views and picnic facilities are available at Bridal Falls Provincial Park, 17 kilometres (11 mi.) east on Hwy. 1, Chilliwack Lake Provincial Park, 84 kilometres (54 mi.) southeast off Hwy. 1 (see Recreation Chart), and Cultus Lake Provincial Park, 11 kilometres southwest off Hwy. 1 (see Recreation Chart).

Tourism Chilliwack Visitor Information Centre: 44150 Luckakuck Way, Chilliwack, BC, Canada V2R 4A7; phone (604) 858-8121 or (800) 567-9535.

MINTER GARDENS is 19 km (12 mi.) e. on Hwy. 1 to exit 135 (Hwy. 9) at 52892 Bunker Rd. Covering nearly 11 hectares (27 acres), 11 thematic gardens display seasonal colors and plants from around the world. Highlights include an evergreen living maze, topiary sculptures, a Penjing rock collection and two Victorian-style conservatories.

Food is available. Allow 1 hour minimum. Daily 8:30-7, July-Aug.; 9-6, in June; 9-5:30 in May and Sept.; 10-5 in Apr. and Oct. Admission $11.21; over 64, $9.81; ages 6-18, $6.07; family rate $29.91. AX, MC, VI. Phone (604) 794-7191 or (888) 646-8377.

CLEARWATER (A-8) pop. 3,500

Clearwater gets its name from the clear waters of the nearby Clearwater River. Opportunities for riding, hiking, canoeing, skiing and fishing abound in the surrounding North Thompson Valley.

Wells Gray Provincial Park, north off Hwy. 5, offers a variety of scenery, particularly with regard to water. Scattered throughout its boundaries are five large lakes, two river systems, many streams and waterways and a multitude of waterfalls. Helmcken Falls, which drops 141 metres (465 ft.), is said to be the fourth highest in Canada. At Bailey's Chute Loop in late summer, visitors can view salmon jumping upstream to spawn. Extinct volcanoes and lava beds recall the region's fiery past. *See Recreation Chart and the AAA/CAA Western Canada & Alaska CampBook.*

Clearwater Chamber of Commerce: 425 E. Yellowhead Hwy., P.O. Box 1988, Clearwater, BC, Canada V0E 1N0; phone (250) 674-2646.

RECREATIONAL ACTIVITIES
White-water Rafting

- **Interior Whitewater Expeditions** is w. of Hwy. 5 at Old N. Thompson Hwy. Write P.O. Box 393, Clearwater, BC, Canada V0E 1N0. Daily 8-8, May-Sept., depending on water level. Phone (250) 674-3727 or (800) 661-7238.

CLINTON (A-7) pop. 621, elev. 274 m/898'

During the gold rush of the late 1850s and early 1860s Clinton was the junction of several wagon roads leading to northern goldfields. In 1863 Queen Victoria changed the town's name from Junction to Clinton. Retaining much of its frontier look, Clinton is a supply center for surrounding resorts, fishing camps and ranches. Summer activities include boating, fishing and camping at area lakes, which also attract various wildlife.

Clinton Chamber of Commerce: 1600 Cariboo Hwy., P.O. Box 256, Clinton, BC, Canada V0K 1K0; phone (250) 459-2640.

SOUTH CARIBOO HISTORICAL MUSEUM is at 1419 Cariboo Hwy. Built in 1892, this building has served as the town's schoolhouse and courthouse. Displays include photographs and pioneer artifacts. Allow 30 minutes minimum. Mon.-Fri. 8-8, June-Oct. Donations. Phone (250) 459-2442.

COMOX (E-10) pop. 11,172

Comox was founded in the mid-1800s, taking its name from the Salish word *Koumuckthay*, meaning "land of plenty." Once an important port for ships of the Royal Navy, the east coast village became the home of a Royal Air Force base in 1942. CFB Comox maintains search-and-rescue operations, maritime patrols and support of naval and air force defense.

COMOX AIR FORCE MUSEUM is e. on Ryan Rd. following signs to CFB Comox main entrance. Museum displays outline the history of the base and West Coast aviation. Two squadrons continue to fly Cormorant helicopters and Buffalo and Aurora aircraft. Nearby, a heritage aircraft park displays vintage aircraft. Canada's flight pioneers are recognized in a videotape presentation. On weekends visitors may view a Spitfire that is being restored. A comprehensive aviation library also is on site. Allow 30 minutes minimum. Museum daily 10-4. Heritage aircraft park daily 10-4, May-Sept. Closed Jan. 1 and Dec. 25. Museum admission by donations. Heritage aircraft park free. Phone (250) 339-8162.

FILBERG HERITAGE LODGE AND PARK is at 61 Filberg Rd. The 1929 Heritage Lodge and outbuildings stand on 4 hectares (9 acres) of landscaped grounds on Comox Bay. The timber lodge is restored and furnished in period. Rare and exotic trees, rhododendrons and herb gardens adorn the park, which offers 1-hour concerts most Sundays at 2 in July and August. A petting farm is available from mid-June to mid-August.

Food is available. Pets are not permitted. Allow 1 hour minimum. Park open daily 8-dusk. Lodge open daily 11-5, June 1-Labour Day; Fri.-Sun. 11-5, Easter weekend-May 31 and day after Labour Day-Sept. 30. Petting zoo daily 10-4. Closed Jan. 1, second Mon. in Oct. and Dec. 25-26. Lodge admission $2; ages 6-12, 50c. Petting farm $2, under 5 free. Park admission is charged during special events. Phone (250) 339-2715.

COOMBS (F-10) pop. 1,372

Coombs retains the atmosphere of a quaint village settled around 1910. The Coombs General Store, which has operated continuously since the settlement days, and the Old Country Market, which is unusual for the goats that are kept on the roof in summer, are two landmarks.

The town is on Vancouver Island, midway between Little Qualicum River Falls Provincial Park *(see Recreation Chart)* and Englishman River Falls Provincial Park *(see Recreation Chart)*, where there are many recreational opportunities.

SAVE **BUTTERFLY WORLD & GARDENS** is 1 km (.6 mi.) w. on Hwy. 4A at 1080 Winchester Rd. A walk-through tropical garden contains more than 30 species of free-flying butterflies. The insect's life cycle is portrayed through displays. Other exhibits include birds in an outdoor aviary, a Japanese water garden with exotic fish, a petting zoo in the summer and Big Bug Jungle—an insectary housing large live jungle insects. Allow 30 minutes minimum. Daily 10-5, May-Sept.; 10-4 in Apr. and Oct. Admission $8.75; over 64, $7.75; ages 13-18, $4.75; ages 3-12, $3.75. MC, VI. Phone (250) 248-7026.

COQUITLAM—*see Vancouver p. 160.*

COURTENAY (E-10)
pop. 18,304, elev. 25 m/82'

Courtenay was established in the late 1860s when settlers began a major farming community near the Comox Valley. Known for a garden called the Mile of Flowers, the town is now a year-round recreation area with good skiing and sailing nearby.

The 1989 Puntledge River discovery of the fossilized intact skull of a 14-metre-long (46-ft.) elasmosaur, a long-necked Cretaceous marine reptile 80 million years old, brought Courtenay to the attention of the world of paleontology.

Courtenay is the terminus of the Powell River Ferry, which makes round-trip excursions to the mainland.

Comox Valley Travel InfoCentre: 2040 Cliffe Ave., Courtenay, BC, Canada V9N 2L3; phone (250) 334-3234 or (888) 357-4471.

COURTENAY AND DISTRICT MUSEUM AND PALAEONTOLOGY CENTRE is at 207 Fourth St., downtown at jct. Fourth St. and Cliffe Ave. Permanent exhibits, enhanced by audiovisuals, focus on native history, exploration, agriculture, logging and pioneer life. A reconstruction of an elasmosaur is displayed along with locally excavated fossil evidence from the age of dinosaurs. The museum has archival material pertaining to the nearby Comox Valley. Guided fossil discovery tours are available.

Allow 1 hour minimum. Mon.-Sat. 10-5, Sun. noon-4, Victoria Day-Labour Day; Tues.-Sat. 10-5, Sun. noon-4, rest of year. Closed Jan. 1, Good Friday and Dec. 25. Admission $3; over 65 and ages 13-18, $2.50; ages 2-12, $1. Phone (250) 334-0686.

PUNTLEDGE HATCHERY is 3 km (1.9 mi.) w. on Lake Trail Rd., then 2 km (1.2 mi.) n. on Powerhouse Rd. following signs. The hatchery nurtures and releases several varieties of salmon and steelhead trout into the Puntledge River. Photographic displays outline the species' various stages of development. Daily 8-4; closed Jan. 1 and Dec. 25. Free. Phone (250) 703-0907.

RECREATIONAL ACTIVITIES
Skiing
• **Mt. Washington Alpine Resort** is 31 km (19 mi.) n.w. on the Strathcona Pkwy. Write P.O. Box

3069, Courtenay, BC, Canada V9N 5N3. Other activities are available. Daily 9-3:30. Phone (250) 338-1386 or (888) 231-1499.

CRAIGELLACHIE (B-9) pop. 100
SAVE **BEARDALE CASTLE MINIATURELAND** is at 5549 Hwy. 1. Miniature reproductions complete with working trains include a 1950s prairie town, a Swiss mountain village, a medieval German town and an English Tudor village. Also featured are a Canadian railroad heritage exhibit, animated fairy tale characters and an area devoted to Mother Goose nursery rhymes. The 6-hectare (15-acre) site includes a nature trail along the Perry River. Allow 30 minutes minimum. Daily 9-6, May-Sept. Admission $6.25; ages 3-14, $4. MC, VI. Phone (250) 836-2268.

CRANBROOK (C-11)
pop. 18,476, elev. 940 m/3,083'

Cranbrook is the key city of the eastern Kootenays and the center of many circle tours. Nearby lakes, rivers and mountains provide such recreational opportunities as swimming, fishing, hiking, hunting and skiing. A scenic portion of Hwy. 93 runs north from Cranbrook into Alberta to the junction with Hwy. 16 in Jasper.

Cranbrook Chamber of Commerce: 2279 Cranbrook St. (Hwy. 3/95), P.O. Box 84, Cranbrook, BC, Canada V1C 4H6; phone (250) 426-5914 or (800) 222-6174.

Self-guiding tours: Information about driving and walking tours is available from the chamber of commerce.

SAVE **CANADIAN MUSEUM OF RAIL TRAVEL** is at 57 Van Horne St. (Hwy. 3/95). The museum restores and preserves vintage Canadian Pacific Railway passenger train sets, including cars from the luxury Trans-Canada Limited. The lifestyle of rail travel is reflected in trains from 1880 to 1955, including cars of state, business and royalty. On the grounds is the original three-story café from the Canadian Pacific Railway's Royal Alexandra Hotel of Winnipeg.

Note: The museum is undergoing major renovations, but remains open to the public. A completion date is uncertain and renovations are anticipated to continue for a few years; phone ahead to confirm tour times. Allow 1 hour, 30 minutes minimum. Museum open daily 10-6, Easter-second Mon. in Oct.; Tues.-Sat. noon-5, rest of year. Guided tours are given daily every 45 minutes. Last tour begins 45 minutes before closing. Guided tours $7.75; over 64, $6.75; students with ID $3.50; family rate $18.95. Phone (250) 489-3918 to verify schedule and rates.

CASINOS
• **Casino of the Rockies** is at 7777 Mission Rd. Daily 10 a.m.-2 a.m. Phone (250) 861-5457.

CRESTON (D-11)
pop. 4,795, elev. 636 m/2,086'

The unusual Kutenai canoe, which has a bow and stern that both meet the waterline, was used by

Indians in the area around Creston in pre-pioneer days. The only other place such a canoe has been found is the Amur River region in southeastern Russia. The canoe's use in this area supports the theory that Asians migrated to North America over a frozen Bering Strait.

In the 1930s about 8,100 hectares (20,000 acres) of land were reclaimed from the Kootenay Delta for agriculture. The Creston Valley floor is now quilted with a variety of seed and root crops, grains and fruit orchards. Other Creston industries include forestry, dairying and brewing.

The Columbia Brewing Co., 6 blocks south on 16th Avenue, offers free narrated tours of its facilities mid-May to mid-October. Complimentary beer is available at the end of the tour. Free guided tours of a candlemaking factory are offered year-round at Kootenay Candles, 1511 Northwest Blvd.

Summit Creek Park, 9 kilometres (6 mi.) west, offers camping, natural history programs and hiking along the old Dewdney Trail, which carried gold seekers from Hope to the Wild Horse goldfields in the 1860s. Mountain Stream Trout Farm and Recreation Area, 7 kilometres (4 mi.) north, features nature trails and ponds stocked with fish for catching and barbecuing on the premises.

Creston Chamber of Commerce: 1711 Canyon St., P.O. Box 268, Creston, BC, Canada V0B 1G0; phone (250) 428-4342.

[SAVE] **CRESTON AND DISTRICT MUSEUM** is at 219 Devon St. via Hwy. 3A N. The 1957 Stone House, which has four stone fireplaces and walls more than one-third metre (1 ft.) thick, contains more than 5,000 pioneer and Indian artifacts, including a replica of a Kutenai Indian canoe and early agricultural tools. A schoolroom exhibit can be seen in the restored Kingsgate Schoolhouse on the museum grounds. Allow 1 hour minimum. Daily 10-3:30, May-Sept.; by appointment rest of year. Admission $3; ages 6-16, $2; family rate $5. Phone (250) 428-9262.

CRESTON VALLEY WILDLIFE MANAGEMENT AREA AND INTERPRETATION CENTRE is 9.5 km (6 mi.) w. on Hwy. 3. The 7,000-hectare (17,297-acre) area permits hiking, seasonal camping, bicycling, hunting, canoeing and picnicking in a managed waterfowl habitat. A variety of programs and canoe trips originate at the Interpretation Centre, which houses natural history displays and a theater.

Center open daily 9-5, mid-May through Labour Day; Wed.-Sun. 9-4, day after Labour Day-Oct. 31. Closed Thanksgiving. The recreation area is open year-round. Admission $3; ages 2-18, $2; family rate $9 (two adults and two children). Phone (250) 402-6900 or (250) 402-6908. *See Recreation Chart.*

CULTUS LAKE (H-12)
pop. 637, elev. 45 m/150′

Cultus Lake Provincial Park, 11 kilometres (7 miles) southwest of Chilliwack, off Hwy. 1, is a popular recreational area and offers camping, boating, fishing, horseback riding and hiking. *See Recreation Chart.* Cultus Lake Waterpark, Hwy. 1 exit 119A, has giant waterslides, twisting tunnels, pools and inner tube rides; phone (604) 858-7241 for more information.

CUMBERLAND (F-10) pop. 2,618

Cumberland's origins are rooted in the rigors of coal mining. From 1888 until the last of its nine mines closed in 1966, the village produced some 25 million tons of high-grade coal. The lucrative enterprise solidified Cumberland's economy and contributed to its multi-ethnic mix, drawing miners from locations as diverse as England, Scotland, Italy, China and Japan. The village and many of its streets were named for the mining region in England known as Cumbria.

Nestled in the foothills of the Beaufort Mountains and a stone's throw from Comox Lake, Cumberland offers ample snow skiing, hiking, fishing and boating opportunities.

Cumberland Chamber of Commerce and Tourism Information Centre: 2755 Dunsmuir, P.O. Box 250, Cumberland, BC, Canada V0R 1S0; phone (250) 336-8313 or (866) 301-4636.

CUMBERLAND MUSEUM & ARCHIVES is off Hwy. 19 Cumberland exit, 2 km (1.2 mi.) w. on Cumberland Rd./4th St., then just w. to jct. 1st St. and Dunsmuir Ave. Visitors can walk through a replica of a coal mine and view exhibits about Cumberland's mining history. Outdoor heritage tours are offered. Allow 30 minutes minimum. Daily 9-5, May-Sept.; Mon.-Sat. 9-5, rest of year. Admission $3; senior citizens $2; ages 13-18, $1. Tours $2. Phone (250) 336-2445.

DAWSON CREEK (D-6)
pop. 10,754, elev. 655 m/2,148′

Named for George Mercer Dawson of the Geological Survey of Canada, Dawson Creek was settled in 1912. Growth accelerated during World War II, as this was the southern terminus of the Alaska Hwy. The highway was then called the Alcan Military Hwy., and it served as a supply road to bases in Alaska. The Mile Zero Cairn, which marks the start of the Alaska Hwy., and the Zero Milepost are in the center of town. Alpine skiing, camping, hiking and fishing are popular recreational activities.

Dawson Creek & District Chamber of Commerce: 10201 10th St., Dawson Creek, BC, Canada V1G 3T5; phone (250) 782-4868.

DAWSON CREEK STATION MUSEUM AND VISITORS' INFORMATION CENTRE is at 900 Alaska Ave. Artifacts, fossils and mounted animals and birds from the Peace River region are displayed. Highlights include an early 1900s railway caboose and a 1930s grain elevator as well as an art gallery and a video presentation about construction of the

Alaska Highway. Daily 8:30-7, May 15-Labour Day; Tues.-Sat. 10-noon, rest of year. Closed Jan. 1, Good Friday, Nov. 11 and Dec. 25-26. Donations. Phone (250) 782-9595 for the Visitors' Information Centre.

WALTER WRIGHT PIONEER VILLAGE is just w. of jct. Hwy. 97N (Alaska Hwy.) and Hwy. 97S (Hart Hwy.). The complex of pioneer buildings includes a log schoolhouse, log cabin, general store, smithy and two churches. All contain period furnishings. An extensive collection of farm machinery and implements also is featured as well as nine flower gardens, a memorial rose garden and a lake for swimming. Food is available. Allow 1 hour minimum. Daily 9-9, June 1-Sept. 1. Donations. Phone (250) 782-7144.

DELTA—*see Vancouver p. 160.*

DUNCAN (G-10) pop. 4,699, elev. 15 m/49′

Founded in 1887 as Alderlea, Duncan was renamed in 1912 in honor of farmer William Duncan, who gave his land for the original townsite. Settlers were attracted by the promise of copper and coal on nearby Mount Sicker, where abandoned mines and original homesteads still can be seen. The growth of the logging and farming industries brought increasing numbers to Duncan and the Cowichan Valley.

The area around Duncan is known for the handspun woolen sweaters produced by the Cowichan Indians. West on Hwy. 18 is the Cowichan Valley Demonstration Forest with scenic viewpoints and signs describing forest management practices and ecology. More than 80 totem poles dot the town of Duncan.

Duncan-Cowichan Chamber of Commerce: 381 Trans-Canada Hwy., Duncan, BC, Canada V9L 3R5; phone (250) 748-1111.

Shopping areas: Whippletree Junction, a group of shops and boutiques with late 1800s storefronts, is 5 kilometres (3 mi.) south on the Trans-Canada Hwy.

SAVE **BC FOREST DISCOVERY CENTRE** is 1.5 km (1 mi.) n. off Hwy. 1 to 2892 Drinkwater Rd. The site has more than 40 hectares (99 acres) of forest and interactive displays and videotapes depicting British Columbia's forestry heritage, management practices and renewal efforts. In addition to a logging museum there are Douglas fir trees, a smithy, a sawmill and an old-time logging camp. A nature trail and a ride in a steam-powered logging train are available.

Daily 10-6, Victoria Day-Labour Day; 10-4, mid-Apr. through day before Victoria Day and day after Labour Day through mid-Oct. Admission $9; over 65 and ages 13-18, $8; ages 5-12, $5. MC, VI. Phone (250) 715-1113.

SAVE **QUW'UTSUN' CULTURAL AND CONFERENCE CENTRE** is 1 blk. w. of Hwy. 1 at 200 Cowichan Way. The 6-acre site consists of a living-history museum and a gallery dedicated to the preservation and dissemination of the culture of the Northwest Coast Indians. Exhibits include numerous totem poles and historical artifacts as well as the Comeakin longhouse and Khenipsen Carving House. Interpretive tours, craft demonstrations and a film presentation also are featured.

Food is available. Allow 1 hour minimum. Daily 9-7:30, June 15-Sept. 15; May-Sept. Daily 10-5, rest of year. Closed Jan. 1 and Dec. 25-26. Guided tours are offered on the hour; multimedia presentations begin on the half-hour. Admission $13; over 55 and ages 12-18, $11; ages 4-11, $2. Phone (250) 746-8119 or (877) 746-8119.

ERRINGTON (F-10) pop. 2,122

NORTH ISLAND WILDLIFE RECOVERY ASSOCIATION is .7 km (.4 mi.) e. on Grafton Ave., then .4 km (.25 mi.) n. to 1240 Leffler Rd. Bald eagles, owls, hawks, swans and black bears are among the animals that can be viewed at this 8-acre rehabilitation facility. An eagle flight cage houses eagles waiting to be released into the wild.

A nature museum, wildlife learning center, nature trails and a release pond are on the grounds. Picnicking is permitted. Allow 30 minutes minimum. Daily 10-4, Apr.-Oct. Admission $4.50; ages 3-12, $2; family rate (two adults and two children) $12. MC, VI. Phone (250) 248-8534.

FAIRMONT HOT SPRINGS (B-12) pop. 400, elev. 810 m/2,657′

At the north end of Columbia Lake, Fairmont Hot Springs were discovered about 1840. This popular resort area offers four hot mineral springs with temperatures averaging 35 to 45 C (95 to 113 F). Water sports and alpine and cross-country skiing also are available. *See Recreation Chart and the AAA/CAA Western Canada & Alaska CampBook.*

RECREATIONAL ACTIVITIES
Skiing
- **Fairmont Hot Springs Resort** is on Hwy. 93/95. Write P.O. Box 10, Fairmont Hot Springs, BC, Canada V0B 1L0. Daily 9:30-4, mid-Dec. to early Apr. Phone (250) 345-6311.

FERNIE (C-12) pop. 4,611, elev. 1,005 m/3,297′

At the foot of Trinity Mountain in the British Columbia Rockies, Fernie is a year-round recreation center. The many surrounding lakes and mountains provide opportunities for boating, fishing, hiking, camping and skiing. Mount Fernie Provincial Park is 4.8 kilometres (3 mi.) east *(see Recreation Chart and the AAA/CAA Western Canada & Alaska CampBook).* Prentice and Rotary parks are downtown.

Fernie Chamber of Commerce: 102 Commerce Rd., Fernie, BC, Canada V0B 1M5; phone (250) 423-6868 or (877) 433-7643.

RECREATIONAL ACTIVITIES
Skiing
- **Fernie Alpine Resort** is 5 km (3 mi.) s.w. off Hwy. 3 at 5339 Fernie Ski Hill Rd., Fernie, BC,

Canada V0B 1M6. Other activities are offered. Daily 9-4, early Dec. to mid-Apr. Phone (250) 423-4655 or (800) 258-7669.

White-water rafting

- **Mountain High River Adventures Inc.** collects passengers at Riverside Mountain Lodge at 100 Riverside Way. Write P.O. Box 221, Fernie, BC, Canada V0B 1M0. Other activities are offered. Daily 9-5, May-Sept. Reservations are required. Phone (250) 423-5008 or (877) 423-4555.

FORT LANGLEY (H-11)
pop. 2,641, elev. 12 m/39'

SAVE **BRITISH COLUMBIA FARM MACHINERY AND AGRICULTURAL MUSEUM** is at 9131 King St. This complex of buildings features artifacts and exhibits devoted to the development of farm machinery in British Columbia. Included are a handwrought plow, a threshing machine, carriages and buckboards, and a Tiger-Moth airplane used for crop dusting. Allow 30 minutes minimum. Daily 10-4:30, Apr. 1-second Mon. in Oct. Admission $4; over 60 and ages 13-18, $2; ages 6-12, $1. Phone (604) 888-2273.

LANGLEY CENTENNIAL MUSEUM AND NATIONAL EXHIBITION CENTRE is at 9135 King St. Regional artifacts reflect the lifestyle of early explorers, fur traders and First Nations peoples. Recreated period rooms include a parlor, a kitchen and a general store. Displays also feature wood carvings, stone artifacts and baskets from the Coast Salish culture. Changing exhibits focus on art, science and Canadian and world history. Mon.-Sat. 10-4:45, Sun. 1-4:45; closed Good Friday, Easter Monday, Nov. 11 and Dec. 25-Jan. 1. Donations. Phone (604) 888-3922.

FORT LANGLEY NATIONAL HISTORIC SITE OF CANADA (H-11)

Fort Langley National Historic Site of Canada is 6.5 kilometres (4 mi.) north of Langley off Hwy. 1 at 23433 Mavis Ave. The park occupies the Fraser River site of the 19th-century Hudson's Bay Company trading post, an important supply link in the company's network of fur trading forts west of the Rockies. British Columbia was proclaimed a colony from the site in 1858.

The site preserves an original 1840 storehouse and reconstructed Red River-style wooden buildings, including a cooperage and blacksmith's shop and a log palisade. From March to October interpreters in period costumes demonstrate fur-trading activities. A visitor center displays contemporary exhibits and an orientation videotape. Special events are presented throughout the year.

Picnicking is permitted. Allow 1 hour minimum. Daily 10-5, Mar.-Oct.; by appointment rest of year. Admission $6.50; over 64, $5.50; ages 6-16, $3.25; family rate $14. Phone (604) 513-4777.

FORT NELSON (B-5)
pop. 4,188, elev. 405 m/1,350'

Originally a fur-trading post, Fort Nelson thrived with the building of the Alaska Hwy. during World War II. Nearby mountains, lakes, parks, forests and diverse wildlife populations make Fort Nelson a destination for adventurous tourists, anglers and hunters.

Fort Nelson Visitor InfoCentre: 5500 Simpson Tr., Box 196, Fort Nelson, BC, Canada V0C 1R0; phone (250) 774-6400.

SAVE **FORT NELSON HERITAGE MUSEUM** is w. on Hwy. 97. An albino moose is among the stuffed animals displayed at the museum, which chronicles the history of Fort Nelson. Exhibits include vintage cars, photographs of the construction of the Alaska Hwy. and a trapper's log cabin. Allow 30 minutes minimum. Daily 8:30-7:30, May 1 through mid-Sept. Admission $3; senior citizens and ages 5-15, $2; family rate $6. MC, VI. Phone (250) 774-3536.

FORT RODD HILL AND FISGARD LIGHTHOUSE NATIONAL HISTORIC SITES—see Victoria p. 179.

FORT ST. JAMES (D-4)
pop. 1,927, elev. 680 m/2,230'

Established in 1806 by Simon Fraser and John Stuart, the fur-trading post of Fort St. James became the capital of New Caledonia in 1821. Furs from outlying New Caledonia posts were brought overland to Fort St. James by dog sled and then shipped south during the spring thaw to the coast by canoe and horse.

During this time George Simpson, governor of the Hudson's Bay Co.'s vast empire, visited the fort. Determined to impress the Carrier Indians, Simpson organized a flamboyant procession complete with flute, bugle and bagpipe players in Highland dress, accompanied by a dog with a music box around its neck. Thereafter, the awe-struck Indians reverently referred to Simpson as the "great chief whose dog sings."

A Roman Catholic mission was founded at the fort in 1843. Services continue to be held in Our Lady of Good Hope Church, which was built in 1873 and is one of the oldest churches in British Columbia.

Mining activity supplemented the capital's trapping enterprises after the discovery of gold in the Omineca region in 1869. Interest in mining rekindled during World War II when the Pinchi Mine a few kilometres north yielded more mercury than any other mine in the British Commonwealth.

A lack of highways and railways prompted Fort St. James to pioneer bush flying as a means of transportation; it has served as an air base since the earliest days of charter flight.

The north shore of Stuart Lake, 16 kilometres (10 mi.) west, features some of the earliest signs of habitation in the form of prehistoric rock paintings just above the high-water mark. Although Fort St. James has emerged from relative wilderness, its surrounding evergreen forests continue to be among the best big-game hunting areas in the province. Alpine skiing is available nearby.

Fort St. James Chamber of Commerce: 115 Douglas Ave., P.O. Box 1164, Fort St. James, BC, Canada V0J 1P0; phone (250) 996-7023.

FORT ST. JAMES NATIONAL HISTORIC SITE OF CANADA is 2 blks. w. of Hwy. 27. Established on the southern shore of Stuart Lake by the North West Co. in 1806, Fort St. James contains one of the largest groups of original wooden buildings from Canada's fur trade. A massive fur warehouse is a noted example of Red River framing. The fully restored Hudson's Bay Co. post on the site served as a hub of commerce between fur traders and the First Nations peoples—and as the capital of New Caledonia, now central British Columbia.

The visitor center provides pictorial displays, artifacts and an audiovisual presentation. Changing exhibits also are offered seasonally. Interpreters in period costume provide living-history demonstrations throughout the day. Food is available. Allow 2 hours minimum. Daily 9-5, mid-May through Sept. 30; by appointment rest of year. Admission $5.75; over 65, $5; ages 6-18, $3; family rate $14.50. Prices may vary; phone to confirm. Phone (250) 996-7191.

FORT ST. JOHN (C-6)
pop. 16,034, elev. 695 m/2,280′

One of the oldest European settlements in the province, Fort St. John was established in 1793 as a fur-trading outpost called Rocky Mountain Fort. Residents engage in gas and oil exploration as well as the lumber industry and cattle ranching. There are coalfields to the south and west.

Recreational activities include fishing for Arctic grayling and gray trout in nearby Charlie Lake *(see Recreation Chart and the AAA/CAA Western Canada & Alaska CampBook)*, canoeing the rapids of the Peace River, skiing, and hunting for mountain caribou, mountain goats and black bears in the Rocky Mountain foothills. Floatplanes operating out of Charlie Lake provide access to the wilderness surrounding Fort St. John, and Hwy. 29 provides scenic driving to Chetwynd.

Fort St. John Visitor InfoCentre: 9523-100th St., Fort St. John, BC, Canada V1J 4N4; phone (250) 785-3033 or (877) 785-6037.

FORT STEELE (C-12)
pop. 600, elev. 771 m/2,529′

Founded during the 1864 Kootenay gold rush, Fort Steele, then known as Galbraith's Ferry, became the site of the first North West Mounted Police west of the Rockies. In 1888 the settlement's name was changed to honor police superintendent

Samuel Steele, who peacefully settled tensions between European settlers and the Ktunaxa people.

As a result of the mining boom of the 1890s the town became a thriving center of trade, transportation, communication and social activity, with a population of more than 2,000. In 1898 the British Columbia Southern Railroad bypassed Fort Steele in favor of Cranbrook, 16 kilometres (10 mi.) southwest, and the town began its decline. At the end of World War II Fort Steele had fewer than 50 residents.

FORT STEELE HERITAGE TOWN is 3 km (1.9 mi.) s.w. on Hwy. 93/95. The 11-hectare (27-acre) site preserves an 1890s boomtown. More than 60 restored, reconstructed or original buildings include an operating bakery, restaurant, tinsmith shop, blacksmith shop and newspaper office. Street dramas and demonstrations such as quilting, horse farming and ice cream making help re-create life in the era.

Fort Steele's Clydesdales give wagon rides daily mid-June through Labour Day and perform a six-horse hitch show on July 1. Live entertainment is presented in the Wild Horse Theatre, late June through Labour Day. Steam train rides are available during this time. A visitor reception center contains exhibits about the town's history.

Grounds open daily 9:30-6, late June-Labour Day; 9:30-5, first Sat. in May-late June and day after Labour Day through mid-Oct. Programs, including street skits depicting daily life of the late 1890s, are presented daily 9:30-5:30, late June-Labour Day. The Wild Horse Theatre show is presented daily at 2, late June-Labour Day.

Admission late June-Labour Day $10.50; over 64, $9.50; ages 13-18, $4; ages 6-12, $2. Admission first Sat. in May-late June and day after Labour Day through mid-Oct., $8; over 64, $7.50; ages 13-18, $4; ages 6-12, $2. Train rides $6; over 64, $5; ages 13-18, $3; ages 6-12, $2. Phone (250) 417-6000 or (250) 426-7352.

GALIANO ISLAND—
see Gulf Islands National Park Reserve p. 123.

GLACIER NATIONAL PARK (A-10)

Elevations in the park range from 500 metres (1,640 ft.) at Revelstoke to 3,390 metres (11,121 ft.) at Mount Dawson. Refer to CAA/AAA maps for additional elevation information.

West of the Rockies in the southeast, Glacier National Park and its smaller counterpart Mount Revelstoke National Park *(see place listing p. 131)* encompass portions of the rugged Columbia Mountains. The 1,350 square kilometres (521 sq. mi.) of hard rock terrain present a jagged profile of angular mountains with narrow steep-walled valleys. The steep mountain slopes and enormous snowfall make this region susceptible to avalanches.

Rogers Pass in the heart of the park became the scene of a pitched 19th-century battle between the railroad engineers and these mountains. Sheer walls, numerous slide areas and severe weather proved almost insurmountable obstacles to the completion of Canada's first transcontinental railroad. Some of the largest railroad trestles then known were built to carry the line across raging streams to the summit of this pass across the Selkirks.

From there the tracks crossed to the southern wall of the valley on several loops to avoid the numerous avalanche slopes and the steep downgrade. Despite the ingenuity of its engineers, the new railroad had to be abandoned to the devastating winter forces that closed the pass the first year of construction. Avalanches attaining speeds of up to 325 kilometres (202 mi.) per hour tore up sections of the new track and left other sections buried under tons of snow.

Thirty-one snowsheds were built to shield the track, but even this was not enough. In 1910, 58 men were killed by an avalanche as they were clearing snow from an earlier slide. This incident, mounting costs and the dangerous grades of this section convinced the railroad to tunnel under Mount MacDonald.

The Trans-Canada Hwy. met similar obstacles as it crossed the pass, but the use of mobile howitzers to dislodge potential slides and other methods of controlling avalanches have held the road's position in the pass. Evidence of the struggle to build the railroad is visible from the road and the park's various campgrounds.

Several short trails follow the railroad's progress, winding past the ruins of Glacier House, a 19th-century resort hotel, remains of former snow sheds and the stone pillars that once supported the railroad trestles.

History is only part of the park's attractions. Twelve percent of the park is covered perpetually by snow and ice; more than 400 glaciers are scattered throughout the park. The contrast of the deep green forests and meadows with the glacial whites of these crags makes the park especially scenic.

Towering above the richly wooded valleys, the 3,297-metre (10,817-ft.) Mount Sir Donald rises to the east of the campgrounds, with Eagle and Uto peaks to the north. Day-hiking trails lead toward the Illecillewaet and Asulkan glaciers.

General Information and Activities

The park is open all year, but winter conditions are rigorous. Illecillewaet campground, the center of the park's best ski touring area, and Beaver River picnic area offer limited winter skiing. During the summer some of the popular activities are camping, hiking and mountaineering.

From Illecillewaet campground interpreters lead evening strolls and campfire talks as well as summer hikes that pass through the different life zones of the park's flora and fauna.

In addition, an extensive network of challenging day-hiking trails leads to such attractions as the Illecillewaet and Asulkan glaciers; Mount Abbott,

with several fine viewpoints; Mount Tupper; and the Rogers group of peaks.

Grizzly and black bears are common in Glacier National Park; be cautious and make noise frequently as you hike. Climbers and overnight hikers may register at Rogers Pass Centre before and after every trip. Topographical maps and a hiker's guide also are available. Park use permits can be purchased at the welcome stations and the Rogers Pass Centre. *See Recreation Chart and the AAA/CAA Western Canada & Alaska CampBook.*

ADMISSION to the park is $7; over 64, $6; ages 6-16, $3.50; all occupants of a private vehicle (up to seven people) $14. AX, MC, VI.

PETS are permitted in the park provided they are on a leash at all times.

ADDRESS inquiries to the Superintendent, Glacier and Mount Revelstoke National Parks, P.O. Box 350, Revelstoke, BC, Canada V0E 2S0; phone (250) 837-7500.

ROGERS PASS CENTRE is 1.3 km (.8 mi.) e. of the Rogers Pass summit. Modeled after the snowsheds that once protected the railroad from avalanches, the visitor center includes a theater, an exhibit hall with railway models and displays about natural history. Allow 30 minutes minimum. Daily 7:30-4:30, mid-June through Labour Day; daily 8-4, day after Labour Day-Oct. 31 and Dec. 1 through mid-June; Thurs.-Mon. 8-4, in Nov. Schedule may vary; phone ahead. Free. Phone (250) 814-5232.

GOLDEN (A-10) pop. 4,020, elev. 785 m/2,575′

On the Trans-Canada Hwy. at the confluence of the Columbia and Kicking Horse rivers, Golden is near Glacier *(see place listing p. 120)* and Yoho national parks *(see place listing p. 182)* as well as Banff National Park *(see place listing in Alberta p. 43).* The community also is an outfitting point for sports enthusiasts.

The Golden and District Museum is at 11th Avenue and 13th Street. The museum is housed in a restored one-room schoolhouse and contains local historical items.

Golden & District Chamber of Commerce: 500 10th Ave. N., P.O. Box 1320, Golden, BC, Canada V0A 1H0; phone (250) 344-7125 or (800) 622-4653.

RECREATIONAL ACTIVITIES

White-water Rafting

- SAVE **Alpine Rafting Co.** is at 1416 Goldenview Rd. Write P.O. Box 1272, Golden, BC, Canada V0A 1H0. Trips depart daily 8 a.m.-9 p.m., mid-May through Sept. 30. Phone (250) 344-6778 or (888) 599-5299.

- SAVE **Glacier Raft Company** is at 612 N. 7th St. Write P.O. Box 428, Golden, BC, Canada V0A 1H0. Trips depart daily at 10 and 1, mid-May to mid-Sept. Phone (250) 344-6521.

GOLD RIVER (H-2)
pop. 1,359, elev. 122 m/400'

At the joining of the Gold and Heber rivers, the town of Gold River was built in 6 months in 1965 for employees of a pulp mill. The town, with its beautiful untamed countryside, has become popular with fishermen, photographers, hikers and campers.

Full-day and overnight cruises aboard the MV *Uchuck III* depart from the dock on Hwy. 28. The trips explore Tahsis, Nootka Sound and Friendly Cove, where Capt. James Cook met Chief Maquinna and the Nootka Indians when he landed on Vancouver Island in 1778; phone (250) 283-2418 for the tourist information center or (250) 283-2207 for the municipal office during off-season.

GRAND FORKS (D-10) pop. 4,054

Settlement at the confluence of the Kettle and Granby rivers began in the late 1800s when copper, gold and silver were discovered in the area. After 20 years of prosperity Grand Forks suffered reverses when the local copper smelter, said to be the largest in the British Empire, closed due to faltering copper prices. The logging industry and seed growing operations later restored stability to the community.

The downtown Boundary District contains preserved historic homes, stores and civic buildings from the settlement period. It is flanked on the south and east by rivers, on the west by 5th Avenue and on the north by 75th Avenue. A walking tour map is available at the Boundary Museum *(see attraction listing)*.

Chamber of Commerce of the City of Grand Forks: 7362 Fifth St., P.O. Box 1086, Grand Forks, BC, Canada V0H 1H0; phone (250) 442-2833 or (866) 442-2833.

BOUNDARY MUSEUM is at 7370 Fifth St. The museum depicts the area's history from the late 1800s. Artifacts, maps and photographs show the lifestyles of the Doukhobor and First Nations cultures. Other exhibits include a scale model and display of Grand Forks' Chinatown in the 1900s, a wildlife exhibit and a 1929 fire truck. Mon.-Thurs. 9:30-5, Fri. 10-6, Sat. 10-4:30, Sun. 10-4, July-Aug.; Mon.-Fri. 10-4, rest of year. Admission $4; senior citizens and ages 12-18, $2; under 12 free with paying adult; family rate $7. Phone (250) 442-3737.

GULF ISLANDS NATIONAL PARK RESERVE (H-10)

Separated from the San Juan Islands in Washington only by an international boundary, the almost 200 islands of various shapes and sizes that make up the Gulf Islands nestle against the southeast coast of Vancouver Island. Formed by a series of moving land masses beginning about 100 million years ago, today's Gulf Islands are the result of a mass collision of land that produced the long ridges of sandstone, conglomerate and shale that constitute the islands' geology.

The area was discovered by Capt. George Vancouver while on a quest to find a northwest passage to the Orient in 1792. Erroneously named Gulf of Georgia by Vancouver, the water separating Vancouver Island from the southwestern portion of British Columbia was later correctly termed the Strait of Georgia. The islands, however, retained the designation Gulf Islands.

The area features a climate that is sunnier and milder than that found on the nearby mainland. The quiet waters promote a much quieter lifestyle as well, and the islands are a haven from the frantic pace of nearby cities. Each island, though similar in many respects, has its own distinct identity. Easily reached from the mainland, they have become popular weekend retreats offering varying degrees of amenities and activities. Artists and professionals have joined the population of local fishermen who relish the peaceful lifestyle created by the sparkling waters, cliffs, winding roads and parks.

The islands are a haven for various wildlife, including such endangered species as the anatum peregrine falcon, the sharp-tailed snake, Townsend's big-eared bat and the western meadowlark. The southern Gulf Islands are home to the endangered Garry Oak ecosystem. Various shorebirds, waterfowl, great blue herons, seals and sea lions also inhabit the area.

The main components of the southern Gulf Islands are Galiano, Mayne, North and South Pender, Salt Spring and Saturna islands. Although they can be explored by automobile, the best way to experience the islands is by bicycle or foot. The Islands Trust, a governmental agency, is charged with preserving and protecting the islands and waters in the Strait of Georgia.

BC Ferries provides year-round service to the main islands from Tsawwassen, south of Vancouver, and Swartz Bay, near Victoria. Vehicle reservations are recommended for travel between the mainland and the islands, but are not available for travel between Vancouver Island and the Gulf Islands or for inter-island travel. It is advisable to make reservations as far in advance as possible for summer and holiday travel. For schedule information and reservations phone (250) 386-3431 from the Victoria area and outside British Columbia or (888) 223-3779 from elsewhere in the province. Air service also is available.

Established in 2003, Gulf Islands National Park Reserve protects an island landscape of rocky headlands, forested hills and shorelines studded with colorful tidepools. The park encompasses areas of lands scattered over fifteen larger islands and includes many smaller islets and reefs. Waters adjacent to park lands, extending 200 metres (650 ft.) seaward, also are under Parks Canada management.

The park shares the larger populated islands of Mayne, Saturna and the Penders with communities that offer a range of tourist amenities. Facilities and services inside the national park reserve are currently limited. The populated larger islands are accessible by vehicle, bicycle and BC Ferries from Vancouver and Victoria. The smaller islands are accessible by only boat or kayak. Water taxis also operate in several areas. Many local tour operators offer such recreational opportunities as cycling, kayaking, scuba diving, whale-watching or hiking. Comfortable, sturdy shoes and water are recommended for all hiking excursions.

For more information contact the Gulf Islands National Park InfoCentre, 2220 Harbour Rd., Sidney, BC, Canada V8L 2P6; phone (250) 654-4000. *See Recreation Chart.*

Galiano Island (G-10) pop. 1,071

Named after Spanish explorer Dionisio Alcala Galiano, Galiano Island is a long narrow island that is a haven for bird watchers and naturalists. Bicycling, horseback riding, kayaking, fishing, sailing, diving, swimming and hiking are popular recreational activities. The efforts of hikers and cyclists are rewarded with grand vistas and viewpoints. Mount Galiano provides climbers with eye-catching views of the southern Gulf Islands and the Olympic Mountains.

Montague Harbour Marine Provincial Park has 3,000-year-old Indian middens; camping facilities are available at the park as well as at Dionisio Point Provincial Park *(see Recreation Chart and the AAA/CAA Western Canada & Alaska CampBook).* The Descanso Bay Regional Park offers 30 camping sites *(see Recreation Chart).*

Galiano Island Chamber of Commerce: P.O. Box 73, Galiano Island, BC, Canada V0N 1P0; phone (250) 539-2233 or (866) 539-2233.

Mayne Island (H-10) pop. 547

Although visited by the Spanish in the 1790s, it was not until the 1850s that British Capt. George Richards surveyed and mapped the area. Capt. Richards named Mayne Island after his lieutenant, Richard Charles Mayne. During the gold rush of the mid-1800s the island, halfway between Victoria and the mouth of the Fraser River, was a stopping point for miners heading for the riches to be found at the gold fields along the river.

The island is known as a haven for artists and artisans. Small and sparsely settled, Mayne offers quiet beaches and hiking trails; wildflowers; a landscape heavy with trees; seals, sea lions, salmon and sole offshore; and a large variety of birds, from tiny hummingbirds to soaring bald eagles.

Mayne Island Community Chamber of Commerce: P.O. Box 2, Mayne Island, BC, Canada V0N 2J0; phone (250) 539-3167.

Pender Islands (H-10)

The Penders, consisting of North and South Pender islands, are connected by a one-lane wooden bridge that spans the canal linking Bedwell and Browning harbors. An archeological dig conducted at the time the bridge was built found evidence of island occupation dating back 4,000 years.

The island's 20 public ocean access points and many coves allow ample opportunities for swimming and picnicking. Hiking, boating, fishing, golfing, bicycling, kayaking and scuba diving are other available recreational activities. Roadside stands offer locally grown produce. The view from the summit of Mount Norman is worth the climb.

Tourism Association of Vancouver Island—Pender Islands: 335 Wesley St., Suite 203, Nanaimo, BC, Canada V9R 2T5; phone (250) 754-3500.

Quadra Island (E-10) pop. 2,548

Old totem poles are found within the Indian reservation on Quadra Island, which is reached by a 15-minute ferry ride from Campbell River *(see place listing p. 113).*

Salt Spring Island (H-10) pop. 9,381

Originally called Chuan Island, then Admiral Island, Salt Spring Island is the largest of the Gulf Island group and a popular spot for yachting, cycling, fishing and golfing. Bicycle and kayak rentals are available.

Although it is one of the most developed of the islands, it retains a rural feel. Mount Maxwell Park has a scenic drive leading to 610-metre (2,001-ft.) Baynes Peak. Ruckle Provincial Park *(see Recreation Chart)* offers 7 kilometres (4.3 mi.) of shoreline and has walking trails; bicycling, fishing, kayaking and picnicking are permitted.

The island also features popular Saturday farmers markets and arts and crafts, and is home to many fine artists such as Robert Bateman and Carol Evans. Ganges is the island's commercial hub.

Ferries operate daily from the island's three ferry terminals—between Swartz Bay and Fulford Harbour, between Crofton and Vesuvius Bay and between Long Harbour (the largest of the terminals) and Tsawwassen. For schedules and information phone BC Ferries, (250) 386-3431 from the Victoria area or outside British Columbia or (888) 223-3779 from elsewhere in the province.

Salt Spring Island Travel InfoCentre: 121 Lower Ganges Rd., Salt Spring Island, BC, Canada V8K 2T1; phone (250) 537-5252 or (866) 216-2936.

Saturna Island (H-10) pop. 319

Saturna Island—remote, rugged and sparsely populated—is probably the least visited of the Gulf Islands. Mountain biking is one of the best ways to see the island. Its bays, beaches and tidal pools offer glimpses of many varieties of marine life. The southernmost of the Gulf Islands, Saturna offers hiking, bicycling and boating opportunities. There is no camping available and lodging is limited.

GWAII HAANAS NATIONAL PARK RESERVE AND HAIDA HERITAGE SITE (F-1)

Elevations in the park range from sea level along Kunghit and Moresby islands to 1,123 metres (696 ft.) at Mount de la Touche. Refer to CAA/AAA maps for additional elevation information.

Off the British Columbia coast west of Prince Rupert, Gwaii Haanas National Park Reserve and Haida Heritage Site is in the southern part of the Queen Charlotte Islands *(see place listing p. 140)*, a remote island chain. The Queen Charlotte Islands also are known as the Haida Gwaii Islands. This protected area is jointly managed by the Government of Canada and the Council of the Haida Nation.

The 1,470 square kilometres (912 sq. mi.) of Gwaii Haanas National Park Reserve and Haida Heritage Site offer a rich and fascinating diversity of flora, sea creatures and wildlife. Remnants of native village sites on the 138 islands capture the history of the Haida. Haida Gwaii Watchmen basecamps have been established at major sites of cultural significance. Watchmen provide site security and protection of the cultural features.

Access to the park reserve is challenging: The only way to and around Gwaii Haanas is by air or sea. Solo travel is recommended only for the experienced outdoor traveler. Licensed tour operators provide a variety of excursions. Sea kayaking, sailboat and powerboat charters are the most popular ways to tour Gwaii Haanas. There are no maintained trails or designated campsites, and only limited visitor facilities are provided within the park reserve.

The Queen Charlotte Islands can be reached by air from Vancouver and Prince Rupert. BC Ferries also provides year-round service between the islands and Prince Rupert. Arrangements for ferry transportation should be made well in advance and reservations are highly recommended; phone (250) 386-3431 from the Victoria area and outside British Columbia or (888) 223-3779 from elsewhere in the province.

Single-day admission $10, under 17 free. There is an additional nightly fee for camping as well as a $15 reservation fee. Reservations are required to visit the reserve May through September. Regulations allow for no more than 12 people on shore in one place at one time.

Note: All visitors must participate in one 90-minute orientation session offered daily at visitor centers in Sandspit and Queen Charlotte; phone (250) 559-8818 to guarantee a place. For more information write to Gwaii Haanas National Park Reserve and Haida Heritage Site, P.O. Box 37, Queen Charlotte, BC, Canada V0T 1S0, or contact Tourism BC for an information package; phone (604) 435-5622 or (800) 435-5622.

HARRISON HOT SPRINGS (D-7)
pop. 1,343, elev. 11 m/36′

At the foot of Harrison Lake, Harrison Hot Springs *(see Recreation Chart)* is a well-known health and vacation resort with two mineral springs and a sandy beach on the lakeshore. Strong area winds make this a favorite spot for windsurfing. The surrounding mountains are known as Sasquatch country, where sightings of the legendary apelike creature twice the size of a man have been reported dozens of times.

More likely to be found in the mountains are mutton-fat jades, garnets, agates, fossils and gold; the area is renowned among rockhounds.

Harrison Hot Springs Visitor InfoCentre: 499 Hot Springs Rd., P.O. Box 255, Harrison Hot Springs, BC, Canada V0M 1K0; phone (604) 796-5581.

HARRISON MILLS (D-7)
pop. 141, elev. 11 m/36′

SAVE **KILBY STORE AND FARM** is 1.6 km (.9 mi.) s. of Hwy. 7 at 215 Kilby Rd. Costumed interpreters conduct tours of this 5-acre living-history site, once the heart of a thriving community of lumber mills. The 1906 General Store contains forgotten foodstuffs, a wood stove and the traditional checkerboard. Other highlights include the Heritage Post Office, the Manchester House Hotel and animals of the Waterloo Farm. Food is available. Daily 11-5, May-Aug. Hours vary rest of year; phone ahead. Admission $7; over 65, $6; ages 6-18, $5; family rate $20. Phone (604) 796-9576.

HAZELTON (D-3) pop. 345, elev. 306 m/1,004′

A showplace of Indian culture, Hazelton originally was called Git-an-maks, meaning "where people fish by torchlight." European settlers arriving in 1872 renamed the area Hazelton, after the profusion of hazelnut trees covering the fertile farmland.

Considered holy by the Gitxsan Indian community, the forest land within a 64.4-kilometre (40-mi.) radius of Hazelton has the province's greatest concentration of standing totem poles, many portrayed in paintings by British Columbia artist Emily Carr.

'KSAN HISTORICAL VILLAGE & MUSEUM is 5 km (3 mi.) s. on Hwy. 62. The Gitxsan Indian village consists of seven tribal houses. The 'Ksan Museum, the Frog House of the Stone Age, the Wolf House or Feast House, the Eagle House, the Fireweed House, the studio, the 'Ksan Shop, and the carving shed and workshop are decorated with paintings, carved interior poles and painted scenes in classic West Coast Indian style.

Guided tours are available. Daily 9-6, Apr.-Sept. Admission $2. Tour $10, over 65 and students with

ID $8.50. MC, VI. Phone (250) 842-5544 or (877) 842-5518.

HOPE (C-7) pop. 6,184, elev. 39 m/127'

At the entrance to the Fraser River Valley, Hope dates from 1848 when the Hudson's Bay Co. established a fort. The town developed rapidly, especially during the gold rush of 1858. The 1859 Anglican Christ Church is one of the province's oldest churches. Visitors also may walk through the Othello Quintette tunnels that once were used by the Kettle Valley Railway; the tunnels are in the Coquihalla Canyon Recreation Area.

From Hope the Trans-Canada Hwy. leads north to Fraser Canyon (*see Boston Bar p. 112*). Kawkawa Lake (*see Recreation Chart*), Lake of the Woods, Mount Hope, Mount Ogilvie and Skagit Valley (*see Recreation Chart*) are just some of the nearby places that offer year-round recreational opportunities.

The result of the 1965 Hope Slide is evident about 16 kilometres (10 mi.) east beside Hwy. 3. A plaque at the edge of the present roadway explains the collapse of the side of Johnson Peak, which buried the highway under 45 metres (148 ft.) of rubble.

The Hope Arts Gallery, 349 Fort St., features the work of more than 20 artists; phone (604) 869-2408. The Hope Museum, inside the Hope Visitor InfoCentre, portrays the town's history through native artifacts and historical settings; phone (604) 869-2021. Hope was the filming location of several films, including "Rambo: First Blood," "Shoot to Kill" with Sidney Poitier, and Disney's "Far From Home: The Adventures of Yellow Dog."

Hope Visitor InfoCentre: 919 Water Ave., P.O. Box 370, Hope, BC, Canada V0X 1L0; phone (604) 869-2021.

E.C. MANNING PROVINCIAL PARK is e. on Hwy. 3. The mountain park includes the Hope-Princeton Hwy. (Hwy. 3), a 134-kilometre (83-mi.) ride that climbs from near sea level at Hope to the 1,346-metre (4,416-ft.) summit of Allison Pass. Blackwall Road off Hwy. 3 leads to Cascade Lookout and offers access to a subalpine meadow. Recreational activities include hiking, camping, canoeing, birdwatching, cross-country skiing, mountain biking and horseback riding.

The park is open daily 24 hours. Campgrounds are open May-Oct. Park free. Camping $14-$22 per night. Phone (250) 840-8822. *See Recreation Chart and the AAA/CAA Western Canada & Alaska CampBook.*

 **HELL'S GATE AIRTRAM—** *see Boston Bar p. 112.*

HUDSON'S HOPE (C-4)
pop. 1,039, elev. 520 m/1,706'

Hudson's Hope is one of the oldest settlements in the province: Only two communities on Vancouver Island have been continuously occupied from earlier dates. First discovered in 1793 by Alexander Mackenzie, the area was the site of a small fur-trading post built in 1805. In 1900 the post was moved to the present site of Hudson's Hope on the north side of the Peace River, where it flourished as a center of trade for the Hudson's Bay Co.

Hudson's Hope is an important supplier of hydroelectricity; its two dams generate about 38 percent of the hydropower used in British Columbia. The dams also are major recreation centers for the area.

Hudson's Hope Travel InfoCentre: 9555 Beattie Dr., P.O. Box 330, Hudson's Hope, BC, Canada V0C 1V0; phone (250) 783-9154 mid-May through Aug. 31, or (250) 783-9901 rest of year.

HUDSON'S HOPE MUSEUM is at 9510 Beattie Dr. Housed in a 1942 Hudson's Bay Co. store, the museum contains local artifacts and a collection of prehistoric items including ichthyosaur fossils that were unearthed during construction of the W.A.C. Bennett dam. Outbuildings include an active log church built in 1938, a trapper's cabin, a fur cache and a pioneer house. A steamboiler and other antique machines are displayed on the grounds. Daily 9:30-5:30, mid-May to mid-Oct.; by appointment rest of year. Donations. Phone (250) 783-5735.

PEACE CANYON DAM is 4 km (2.5 mi.) s. on Hwy. 29. Completed in 1980, the dam is 50 metres (165 ft.) high and 533 metres (1,750 ft.) long. It reuses water that has generated electricity at the W.A.C. Bennett Dam, 23 kilometres (14 mi.) upstream on the Peace River. Nearby recreational facilities include a campground, picnic facilities and a boat launch to Dinosaur Lake, the dam's reservoir.

Peace Canyon Dam Visitor Centre is next to the powerhouse. Exhibits reflect the area's natural history, its pioneer past and the Peace Canyon Project. Highlights include a replica of the stern-wheeler SS *Peace River*, a large-scale model of a generating unit, displays about the damming of the Peace River, and mammoth tusks found during excavation. Visitors can view the project's central control system, walk across the dam or visit the observation area on the main floor.

Daily 8-4, Victoria Day-Labour Day; Mon.-Fri. 8-4, rest of year. Closed Jan. 1, Easter, second Mon. in Oct., Nov. 11 and Dec. 25-26. Free. Phone (250) 783-7418.

W.A.C. BENNETT DAM is 21 km (13 mi.) w. on Canyon Dr. following signs. A major hydroelectric project on the Peace River, the dam was completed in 1967 to produce electrical power for British Columbia. It is 183 metres (600 ft.) high, 2 kilometres (1.2 mi.) long and .8 kilometre (.5 mi.) thick at the base. Backup water from the dam forms 164,600-hectare (406,727-acre) Williston Lake, British Columbia's largest lake. Its shoreline stretches for 1,770 kilometres (1,100 mi.).

W.A.C. Bennett Dam Visitor Centre is about 1 km (.6 mi.) s.e. of the dam. Photographs and artifacts chronicle the history and geology of the region and the construction of the dam and powerhouse. A participatory exhibit demonstrates the generation of electricity and magnetism. Underground bus tours into the powerhouse and manifold chambers are available. A 40-minute multimedia presentation also is offered in the theater. Note: Cameras, purses and bags are not permitted on the tour. Food is available. Center daily 10-6, Victoria Day through mid-Sept. Bus tours are available 10:30-4:30. Multimedia presentation offered every hour 10:30-4:30. Last presentation begins at 4:30. Free. Reservations are required for the tour. Phone (250) 783-5048 or (888) 333-6667.

INVERMERE (B-12) pop. 2,858

In the summer Invermere offers recreational opportunities that include hiking and camping, and fishing, boating and sailboarding on Lake Windermere. Hang gliders often are seen launching off nearby Mount Swansea. Birds can be seen at Wilmer National Wildlife Area, about 5 kilometres (3 mi.) north.

Invermere Chamber of Commerce: 651 Hwy. 93/95, P.O. Box 1019, Invermere, BC, Canada V0A 1K0; phone (250) 342-2844.

WINDERMERE VALLEY MUSEUM is at 622 Third St. Pioneer artifacts and local archives are displayed in a complex in a small park. The six log outbuildings have thematic displays. Allow 1 hour minimum. Tues.-Sat. 10-4, July 1-early Sept.; 1-4, in June. Admission $2, under 17 free. Phone (250) 342-9769.

KAMLOOPS (B-8)
pop. 77,281, elev. 345 m/1,131'

Founded in 1812 as a North West Co. depot, Kamloops later was a Hudson's Bay Co. post. Developed where the north and south branches of the Thompson River converge to form Kamloops Lake, Kamloops was named after an Indian word, *cumcloups,* or "the meeting of the waters." During the gold rush of the 1860s the Overlanders reached the city by rafting down the North Thompson.

Since the Cariboo's gold supply disappeared in the 1860s, Kamloops has developed as a center of cattle and sheep ranching.

Lumber is an important natural resource in the area. Weyerhaeuser Canada Ltd., a pulp mill on Mission Flats Road, offers guided tours of its facility in July and August. Under 12 are not permitted; long pants and flat, closed shoes are required. For information or reservations phone (800) 824-4412.

Area lakes offer good fishing; Kamloops trout are known to jump a few feet in the air after being hooked.

Kamloops Visitor InfoCentre: 1290 W. Trans-Canada Hwy., Kamloops, BC, Canada V2C 6R3; phone (250) 374-3377 or (800) 662-1994. *See color ad.*

Self-guiding tours: Kamloops is the site of several historical attractions, including the provincial courthouse and several old houses and churches. Self-guiding tour brochures are available from Kamloops Museum and Archives.

SAVE **BRITISH COLUMBIA WILDLIFE PARK** is 17 km (10 mi.) e. on Hwy. 1 to 9077 Dallas Dr. Sixty-five species of local and endangered wildlife, including grizzly bears, Siberian tigers, timber wolves, cougars, moose and birds of prey live in natural habitats at this 48-hectare (120-acre) park. Highlights include a children's play area and splash park, a seasonal miniature train, a herpetarium, gardens and a nature trail. A holiday light display is offered in December.

Park open daily 8 a.m.-8:30 p.m., July-Aug.; 8-4:30, rest of year. Train hours vary throughout the year; phone ahead. Closed Dec. 25. Admission $8.95; over 65 and ages 13-16, $7.95; ages 3-12, $5.95. Train $1; under 12, 50c. Admission may vary; phone ahead. MC, VI. Phone (250) 573-3242.

SAVE **KAMLOOPS ART GALLERY** is at 465 Victoria St. Works by regional, national and international contemporary and First Nations artists are featured. Exhibits change monthly and include paintings, sculptures, prints, drawings, photographs

and video art. Allow 30 minutes minimum. Mon.-Wed. and Fri. 10-5, Thurs. 10-9, Sat.-Sun. noon-4, Oct.-May; Mon.-Wed. and Fri. 10-5, Thurs. 10-9, Sat. noon-4, rest of year. Closed holidays. Admission Oct.-May $3; couples over 61, $3; over 61 and students with ID $2. Admission rest of year $5; couples over 61, $5; over 61 and students with ID $3; donations accepted Thurs. after 5. Admission may vary for certain exhibits; phone ahead. MC, VI. Phone (250) 828-3543.

KAMLOOPS HERITAGE RAILWAY is at #6-510 Lorne St. *The Spirit of Kamloops,* the restored steam locomotive 2141 with its hayrack cars and heritage coach, departs the Canadian National Railway station and carries passengers on a sightseeing tour, passing St. Joseph's Church along the way. Allow 1 hour, 30 minutes minimum. Train departs Fri. and Mon. at 7:30 p.m.; Sat. at 11 and 7:30 p.m.; Sun. at 11 and 8 p.m., July 1 through mid-Sept. Hours may vary; phone ahead to confirm. Passengers should arrive 30 minutes prior to departure. Fare $13.50; over 60, $11.75; ages 6-18, $9. AX, MC, VI. Phone (250) 374-2141.

KAMLOOPS MUSEUM AND ARCHIVES is at 207 Seymour St. The area's history is portrayed in displays of Indian culture, fly-fishing, a reconstructed Hudson's Bay Co. fur-trading cabin, pioneer and Victorian artifacts and tableaux, transportation items and natural history specimens. The archives has collections of photographs and manuscripts.

Guided tours are available. Allow 1 hour minimum. Mon.-Fri. 9:30-4:30, Victoria Day weekend-Labour Day weekend; Tues.-Sat. 9:30-4:30 rest of year. Closed holidays. Guided walking tours are available July-Aug. Donations. Phone (250) 828-3576.

ST. JOSEPH'S CHURCH is n. on Mount Paul Way, then w. to end of Chilcotin St. Constructed by Roman Catholic missionaries and the Kamloops Indian Band in the late 19th century, the church has been meticulously renovated. The building's elaborate gilded altar and its many period religious artifacts also have been restored. Allow 30 minutes minimum. Wed.-Sat. 12:30-7:30, July 1-Labour Day. Donations. Phone (250) 374-7323.

SECWEPEMC MUSEUM AND HERITAGE PARK is at 311-355 Yellowhead Hwy. The 5-hectare (12-acre) park interprets the history and culture of the Secwepemc, or Shuswap, Nation. A walking trail leads through the archeological remains of a 2,000-year-old Shuswap winter village, pit house reconstructions and a summer village. The park also features a museum and ethnobotanical gardens.

Allow 1 hour minimum. Daily 8:30-4:30, June 15-Labour Day; Mon.-Fri. 8:30-4:30, rest of year. Closed Jan. 1 and the last week in Dec. Admission $6; over 59 and ages 7-17, $4; family rate $15. MC, VI. Phone (250) 828-9801.

WANDA SUE departs from Salmon Arm Dock. The 26-metre (85-ft.) stern-wheeler offers 2-hour narrated cruises on Shuswap Lake. Food is available.

Cruises depart daily at noon and 3, May-Sept. Fare $20; ages 2-11, $10. Phone (250) 374-7447.

CASINOS

- **Lake City Casino** is at 540 Victoria St. Daily 10 a.m.-2 a.m. Phone (250) 372-3336.

RECREATIONAL ACTIVITIES

Skiing

- **Sun Peaks Resort** is 54 km (32.4 mi.) n. on Hwy. 5. Write 3150 Creekside Way, Suite 50, Sun Peaks, BC, Canada V0E 1Z1. Other activities are available. Daily 8:30-3:30, mid-Nov. to mid-Apr. Phone (250) 578-7842 or (800) 807-3257.

KASLO (C-11) pop. 1,032, elev. 588 m/1,929′

Kaslo began as a mill site in 1888. Following large silver strikes in 1893 the town quickly expanded to city proportions. A village once again, Kaslo is a distribution center for the Lardeau Valley.

Duncan Dam, 42 kilometres (26 mi.) north, was the first of the three dams constructed by B.C. Hydro in accordance with the Columbia River Treaty, ratified by British Columbia and the United States in 1964. Southwest of the dam is the Kokanee Spawning Channel, built to compensate for the loss of natural spawning areas resulting from the dam's construction. The 3.2-kilometre (2-mi.) channel, one of the longest in the world, is said to be the first constructed for freshwater fish.

SS *MOYIE* NATIONAL HISTORIC SITE is 1 blk. n. off Hwy. 31 at 324 Front St., following signs. Considered the world's oldest intact passenger stern-wheeler, the *Moyie* operated on Kootenay Lake 1898-1957, hauling travelers and freight from Nelson to northern destinations along the shore. It is the last active commercial stern-wheeler in the province and contains artifacts, antiques, a model of Kaslo Harbor, a railway display and a photograph exhibit relating to the history of the vessel and its crew.

Allow 30 minutes minimum. Daily 9-5, mid-May to mid-Oct. Admission $5; over 64 and students with ID $4; ages 6-12, $2; family rate $15. MC, VI. Phone (250) 353-2525.

KELOWNA (C-9)
pop. 96,288, elev. 420 m/1,387′

Kelowna is the center of a fruit and vineyard region around Lake Okanagan, from which one-third of all apples harvested in Canada are shipped. The lake also is known for its legendary monster, the Ogopogo, a Loch Ness type beast reportedly 9 to 21 metres (30-69 ft.) long with a head resembling that of a horse, goat or sheep.

The Kelowna Community Theatre stages productions during fall and winter; phone (250) 763-9018. The Okanagan Symphony Orchestra is another prominent cultural feature; phone (250) 763-7544.

Recreation in the area includes water sports, fishing and golf. City Park on Lake Okanagan is the city's largest park, with a beach, tennis courts and a children's water park.

Tourism Kelowna: 544 Harvey Ave., Kelowna, BC, Canada V1Y 6C9; phone (250) 861-1515 or (800) 663-4345. *See color ad.*

B.C. ORCHARD INDUSTRY MUSEUM is at 1304 Ellis St. The museum traces the development of the orchard industry in the province. A 15-metre (50-ft.) model train layout is displayed. Other displays explain fruit production from planting to processing and preserving. The Apple Tree Activities Centre is available for children. Allow 30 minutes minimum. Tues.-Sat. 10-5; closed Dec. 25. Donations. Phone (250) 763-0433.

The Wine Museum & VQA Wine Shop is at 1304 Ellis St. Housed in a converted 1917 packing house, the museum displays machines used for pressing and bottling as well as exhibits featuring the history of wine production in the area. Wine tastings are offered. Guided tours are available by appointment. Open Mon.-Sat. 10-5, Sun. noon-5; closed Dec. 25. Donations. Phone (250) 868-0441.

GEERT MAAS SCULPTURE GARDENS, GALLERY AND STUDIO is 10 km (6.2 mi.) n. on Hwy. 97N, then 2 km (1.2 mi.) w. on Sexsmith Rd. to 250 Reynolds Rd. Maas' semi-abstract sculptures of bronze, aluminum, stainless steel, stoneware and mixed media are exhibited in the gallery and in the .4-hectare (1-acre) sculpture garden. The complex contains one of the largest collections of bronze sculptures in Canada.

Medallions, paintings, etchings and reliefs can be seen in the permanent collection; changing exhibits also are offered. Allow 1 hour minimum. Mon.-Sat. 10-5, May 1-Oct. 1; by appointment rest of year. Hours may vary; phone ahead. Donations. Phone (250) 860-7012.

KELOWNA LAND AND ORCHARD CO. is 3 km (1.9 mi.) s. on Gordon Rd., 4 km (2.5 mi.) e. on K.L.O. Rd., then 1 km (.6 mi.) n. on E. Kelowna Rd. to 3002 Dunster Rd. The working orchard offers visitors a chance to see techniques of the past as well as farm animals and current technologies used in growing apples. Self-guiding walking tours and guided covered hay-wagon tours of the orchard are available. Juice samples are included. A cider-making facility also is on site.

Food is available. Allow 30 minutes minimum for the walking tour, 1 hour minimum for the wagon tour. Grounds open daily 9-5, Apr.-Oct. Guided wagon tours depart daily at 11, 1 and 3, July-Sept.; at 11 and 1, Apr.-June and Sept.-Oct. Tours $6.50, students with ID $3, under 12 free if accompanied by a parent. MC, VI. Phone (250) 763-1091.

KELOWNA MUSEUM is at 470 Queensway Ave. Natural history displays include fossils, mammals and birds from the Okanagan region. Other permanent exhibits depict human history themes, including First Nations heritage, exploration and settlement, and the cultures of Africa, Asia, the Americas and the Pacific Islands. Tues.-Sat. 10-5. Donations. Phone (250) 763-2417.

CASINOS

- **Lake City Casino** is at 1300 Water St. Daily 10 a.m.-2 a.m. Phone (250) 860-9467.

RECREATIONAL ACTIVITIES

Skiing

- **Big White Ski Resort** is 54 km (34 mi.) e. on Hwy. 33. Write P.O. Box 2039, Station R, Kelowna, BC, Canada V1X 4K5. Daily 8:45-3:30, mid-Nov. to mid-Apr. (also Tues.-Sat. 3:30-8, Dec. 17 through mid-Apr.). Phone (250) 765-3101 or (800) 663-2772.

WINERIES

- **Calona Vineyards** is at 1125 Richter St. Daily 9-6; closed Jan. 1 and Dec. 25-26. Tours are given at 11, 1, 3 and 5, June-Aug.; at 10 and 2, rest of year. Phone (250) 762-9144 or (888) 246-4472.

- **CedarCreek Estate Winery** is 12 km (7 mi.) s. at 5445 Lakeshore Rd. following signs. Tastings are available daily 10-6, May-Oct.; daily 11-5, rest of year. Tours daily 11-2, May-Oct. Phone (250) 764-8866.

- **Quail's Gate Estate Winery** is at 3303 Boucherie Rd. Daily 9-7, May-Oct.; 10-5, rest of year. Closed Jan. 1 and Dec. 25-26. Tours on the hour daily 11-4, May-Oct. Phone (250) 769-4451 or (800) 420-9463.

- **Summerhill Pyramid Winery** is at 4870 Chute Rd. Daily 9-6, May-Oct. Tours are given on the hour. Phone (250) 764-8000 or (800) 667-3538.

KEREMEOS (D-8) pop. 1,197, elev. 1,356′

The rich soil and desert climate of the Similkameen Valley drew early settlers, who planted the first fruit trees there in 1880. Today Keremeos is considered one of the best fruit-growing regions in British Columbia. Cherries, apples, grapes, peaches and apricots are among the area's bounties.

THE GRIST MILL AT KEREMEOS is 1.5 km (.9 mi.) n.e. on Hwy. 3A, then .8 km (.5 mi.) e. on Upper Bench Rd. Demonstrations of the principles of milling and restoration are offered at this 1877 flour mill, which features a working waterwheel and flume. A visitor center provides a schedule of living-history presentations for the Apple House Theatre and the summer kitchen. On the grounds are Victorian-era gardens, an heirloom apple orchard and heritage wheat fields.

Food is available. Camping is available. Allow 1 hour minimum. Daily 9-5, Mother's Day-second Mon. in Oct. Admission $6.50; over 59, $5.50; ages 6-18, $4.50; ages 3-6, $2. Phone (250) 499-2888.

KIMBERLEY (C-11)
pop. 6,484, elev. 1,113 m/3,651′

Kimberley is a winter sports center with a Bavarian theme and a pedestrian mall—the Platzl—complete with wandering minstrels and a huge cuckoo clock. The Kimberley Community Gardens present colorful views June through October.

Built on the slopes of Sullivan and North Star hills, Kimberley is one of Canada's highest cities. It is perhaps best known as the site of the Sullivan Mine, one of the world's largest underground silver, lead and zinc mines. The mine closed in 2001 after 92 years of production, yielding more than $20 billion in ore.

Kimberley Bavarian Society Chamber of Commerce: 150 Spokane St., Kimberley, BC, Canada V1A 2E5; phone (250) 427-3666.

KIMBERLEY DISTRICT HERITAGE SOCIETY is in the Platzl at 105 Spokane St. Permanent and changing exhibits depict local history and the legacy of mining in the area. Archives are available for research. Mon.-Sat. 9-4:30, July-Aug.; Mon.-Fri. 1-4, rest of year. Closed holidays. Donations. Reservations are required for archives. Phone (250) 427-7510.

SULLIVAN MINE & RAILWAY HISTORICAL SOCIETY offers narrated 1-hour train rides departing the lower train station, 2 blks. n.w. of the Platzl. Passengers are transported through the Mark Creek Valley on a narrow-gauge mine track. Daily 11-5, July 1-Labour Day. Fare $7; over 60 and ages 13-18, $6; ages 6-12, $3; family rate $18. MC, VI. Phone (250) 427-3666.

RECREATIONAL ACTIVITIES
Skiing

- **Kimberley Alpine Resort** is above town via Gerry Sorenson Way to 301 North Star Blvd. Write P.O. Box 40, Kimberley, BC, Canada V1A 2Y5. Other activities are offered. Daily mid-Dec. to mid-Apr. Phone (250) 427-4881 or (877) 282-1200.

KITIMAT (E-2) pop. 10,285, elev. 130 m/426′

Kitimat is a planned city built in the early 1950s by Alcan Smelters and Chemicals Ltd. The company chose the wilderness site for a new plant because of the area's deepwater harbor, flat land and hydroelectric plant.

Kitimat Chamber of Commerce: 2109 Forest Ave., P.O. Box 214, Kitimat, BC, Canada V8C 2G7; phone (250) 632-6294 or (800) 664-6554.

ALCAN PRIMARY METAL is n. on Hwy. 37. The company offers a videotape presentation and guided 90-minute bus tour of its aluminum smelter, one of the world's largest. Tours depart Mon.-Fri. at 10:30 and 1:30, June-Aug.; closed holidays. Free. Reservations are recommended. Phone (250) 639-8259 June-Aug. or (250) 639-8000 rest of year.

▼ KOOTENAY NATIONAL PARK (B-12)

Elevations in the park range from 918 metres (3,011 ft.) at the park entrance to 3,424 metres (11,235 ft.) at Deltaform Mountain. Refer to CAA/AAA maps for additional elevation information.

Straddling the Banff-Windermere Hwy. (Hwy. 93) as it travels down the western slope of the Rocky Mountains, Kootenay National Park encompasses 1,406 square kilometres (543 sq. mi.). Following the Vermilion and Kootenay river valleys, this slender 94-kilometre-long (63-mi.) park embraces several significant geologic features; Kootenay National Park, a World Heritage Site, is representative of the Rocky Mountain landscape.

Extensive faults created two of the park's significant and different features. Radium Hot Springs at the park's southern end resulted from rainwater and runoff being vaporized deep underground. The steam then returned to the surface via the earth's fissures and condensed in these springs, which were popularized by health buffs at the turn of the 20th century.

At the other end of the park are the Paint Pots, cold springs with a spiritual significance rather than physical. The exit holes, formed by the deposits of the iron-laden water, resemble earthen pots; Blackfoot, Stoney and Kootenay Indians once used the bright bronze mud to stain their bodies, decorate their tepees and draw rock paintings once visible near Sinclair Canyon.

Less dramatic are the topographical differences in the park. The Brisco and Stanford ranges intercept much of the coastal moisture bound for the park's southern region, but to the north, beyond Kootenay Crossing, the climate becomes much damper.

The dry southern climate offers winter shelter for animals migrating from the north and provides good grazing conditions for herds of bighorn sheep. Bears, moose, mountain goats and elk are common. Trails ranging from short hikes to overnight treks explore the park's wealth of evergreen forests, alpine meadows, glaciers and lakes.

General Information and Activities

Although the park is open all year, its three main campgrounds are open only from early May to late September. Winter camping is available at Dolly Varden campground. Information about self-guiding walks, trails, features and facilities can be obtained from information centers in the village of Radium Hot Springs and at Vermilion Crossing from Victoria Day weekend through Labour Day and at the gateway or park headquarters during the rest of the year.

Nonmotorized watercraft are permitted on all lakes and rivers in the park. Climbers can register at the information centers, and back-country campers must obtain a wilderness pass. *See Recreation Chart and the AAA/CAA Western Canada & Alaska CampBook.*

ADMISSION to the park is $7; over 64, $6; ages 6-16, $3.50; all occupants of a private vehicle (up to seven people) $14. MC, VI.

PETS must be leashed at all times. Pets are permitted in the back-country overnight.

ADDRESS inquiries to the Superintendent, Kootenay National Park, Box 220, Radium Hot Springs, BC, Canada V0A 1M0; phone (250) 347-9615 or (800) 748-7275.

Points of Interest

MARBLE CANYON is n. of McLeod Meadows along the Vermilion River and 90 m (295 ft.) from the road. The walls of gray limestone and quartzite laced with a stratum of white and gray dolomite make this one of the most beautiful canyons in the park. Tokumm Creek has cut a sheer, narrow cleft to the depth of about 39 metres (128 ft.).

A self-guiding trail follows the top edge of the canyon and leads to a waterfall. Interpretive signs describe the power of water in shaping the canyon's features. Allow 30 minutes minimum.

[SAVE] **RADIUM HOT SPRINGS** is just n. of the w. entrance to Kootenay National Park. Water temperatures range from 35 to 47 C (95 to 117 F). There is a hot pool, a cool pool and a 372-square-meter (4,000-sq.-ft.) day spa. Iron oxide also colors the towering sandstone cliffs, giving a perpetual sunset quality.

Pools open daily 9 a.m.-11 p.m., mid-May to mid-Oct.; Sun.-Thurs. noon-9, Fri.-Sat. noon-10, rest of year. Admission $6.50; over 64 and ages 3-17, $5.50; family rate $20 (two adults and two children, $3.50 for each additional child). MC, VI. Phone (250) 347-9485 or (800) 767-1611. *See place listing p. 140 and Recreation Chart. See color ad p. 47.*

LADYSMITH (G-10)
pop. 6,587, elev. 40 m/131'

On the 49th parallel, Ladysmith is noted for its scenic position between mountain and sea. Founded during the Boer War, Ladysmith was named for a sister city in South Africa. Black Nugget Museum, 12 Gatacre St., is a former hotel now housing a collection of antiques and memorabilia from the late 19th and early 20th centuries. The museum is open by appointment only; phone (250) 245-2112. Transfer Beach Park offers a playground, picnic tables and a swimming area watched by lifeguards.

Ladysmith & District Chamber of Commerce: 132C Roberts St., P.O. Box 598, Ladysmith, BC, Canada V9G 1A4; phone (250) 245-2112.

LANGLEY—*see Vancouver p. 161.*

LILLOOET (B-7) pop. 2,741, elev. 290 m/951'

Lillooet, on the Fraser River, marked the first leg of the Cariboo Wagon Road and was therefore sometimes referred to as "Mile 0." The trail reached north to such destinations as 100 Mile House and 150 Mile House, named for their distances from the start of the trail. In 1859, during the Cariboo Gold Rush, the 15,000 inhabitants of Lillooet made it the most populous city north of San Francisco and west of Chicago. The surrounding area now is of particular interest to rockhounds.

Lillooet Chamber of Commerce: 989 Main St., P.O. Box 650, Lillooet, BC, Canada V0K 1V0; phone (800) 217-3847.

LILLOOET MUSEUM AND VISITOR CENTRE is at 790 Main St. Displays in the former Anglican church include local pioneer relics, farm equipment, Indian artifacts, Chinese utensils and late 19th-century rooms. The museum houses the newspaper equipment collection of Margaret "Ma" Murray, Lillooet's beloved publisher. Daily 9-5, July-Aug.; Tues.-Sat. 11-3, May-June and Sept.-Oct. Donations. Phone (250) 256-4308.

LYTTON (C-7) pop. 319, elev. 199 m/650'

At the junction of the Thompson and Fraser rivers, Lytton derives its livelihood from its location.

Indians harvested tons of salmon from this river junction. Their trail along the Fraser became a major route to the gold fields, with Lytton as a base of supplies. This community calls itself the Rafting Capital of Canada and claims some of the warmest weather in the country.

Lytton & District Chamber of Commerce: 400 Fraser St., P.O. Box 460, Lytton, BC, Canada V0K 1Z0; phone (250) 455-2523.

RECREATIONAL ACTIVITIES

White-water Rafting

- **Kumsheen Rafting Adventures** is 6 km (4 mi.) n.e. on Trans-Canada Hwy. Write P.O. Box 30, Lytton, BC, Canada V0K 1Z0. Other activities are offered. Trips operate May-Sept. Phone (250) 455-2296 or (800) 663-6667.

MAPLE RIDGE—*see Vancouver p. 161.*

MAYNE ISLAND—
see Gulf Islands National Park Reserve p. 123.

MERRITT (C-8) pop. 7,088, elev. 858 m/2,814′

Merritt is known for its many lakes. Of particular interest is Nicola Lake, a large warm-water lake 10 kilometres (6 mi.) north of town. Recreational activities include swimming, fishing, sailing, water skiing and windsurfing. Monck Provincial Park, on the west side of the lake, offers camping and picnic facilities.

Merritt Chamber of Commerce: 2185B Voght St., P.O. Box 1649, Merritt, BC, Canada V1K 1B8; phone (250) 378-5634 or (877) 330-3377.

NICOLA VALLEY MUSEUM ARCHIVES is at 2202 Jackson Ave. The history of the region is chronicled in exhibits about mining, logging and ranching. Indian and pioneer artifacts are displayed, along with photographs depicting the lives of early settlers. Allow 30 minutes minimum. Mon.-Fri. 9-4:30, July-Aug.; Mon.-Fri. 10-3, rest of year. Closed holidays and Dec. 20-Jan. 3. Donations. Phone (250) 378-4145.

MISSION—*see Vancouver p. 161.*

MORICETOWN (D-3)
pop. 700, elev. 411 m/1,348′

Moricetown is a Wet'suwet'en community that still practices the traditional hereditary system of governance. Originally known as Kyah Wiget, it was once the largest village of the Bulkley River Carrier tribe, a settlement built some 4,000 years ago. The town later took the name of Father A.G. Morice, a missionary who lived among the Carrier Indians in the late 19th century.

MORICETOWN CANYON is on Hwy. 16. The Bulkley River plunges through this narrow gorge in a series of waterfalls. The canyon was vital to First Nations tribes, whose diet depended on salmon.

Visitors can view fish ladders that help five species of salmon reach their annual spawning grounds. During the summer Wet'suwet'en Indians still can be seen gaffing salmon as the fish fight their way upstream. Allow 1 hour minimum.

MOUNT REVELSTOKE NATIONAL PARK (A-10)

Elevations in the park range from 760 metres (2,493 ft.) at the bottom of Mount Revelstoke to 1,920 metres (6,300 ft.) at the Mount Revelstoke summit at Balsam Lake. Refer to CAA/AAA maps for additional elevation information.

On the west edge of the Selkirk Range in southeastern British Columbia, Mount Revelstoke National Park is 260 square kilometres (100 sq. mi.) of sharp peaks, heavily timbered slopes and flowering meadows. The Selkirk Mountains, flanked on the east by the Purcell Range and on the west by the Monashee Range, are distinguished by their height and geologic complexity.

Erosion by glaciers and the heavy rainfall of the region have carved the rock of the Selkirks into jagged forms. Complementing the park's dense green forests and lush wildflower meadows are glacier-fed streams and lakes as well as the deep snows that blanket the slopes until late June.

Deer inhabit the lower slopes; black and grizzly bears and mountain caribou also may be seen in the park. Most mountain species of birds are represented, including fox sparrows, hermit thrushes and northern hawk owls.

The Trans-Canada Hwy. passes through the southeastern portion of the park for 13 kilometres (8 mi.) and parallels its southern boundary for 18 kilometres (11 mi.).

General Information and Activities

The park is open all year. Visitor facilities and accommodations are available in Revelstoke at the western entrance. A park pass must be purchased at the park gates.

From Hwy. 1, a 26-kilometre (16-mi.) hard surface road that is open only in summer leads to the summit of Mount Revelstoke, which provides an excellent panoramic view. Along its length are several viewpoints; many wildflowers bloom in August. Picnic areas are available at Monashee, the 8-kilometre (5-mi.) viewpoint on this road, and at Balsam Lake, 1 kilometre (.6 mi.) from the summit. Other picnic areas and nature trails are along the Trans-Canada Hwy.

Recreation includes subalpine hiking, mountain climbing and fishing. More than 44 kilometres (27 mi.) of hiking trails lead to such sites as Miller and Jade lakes. Climbers and hikers traveling off park trails may register with a park warden before and after each trip. Fishing is by permit, available at the park administrative office in Revelstoke. *See Recreation Chart.*

ADMISSION to the park is $5; over 64, $4.25; ages 6-16, $2.50; all occupants of a private vehicle (up to seven people) $12.50. AX, MC, VI.

PETS are permitted in the park provided they are on leashes at all times.

ADDRESS inquiries to the Superintendent, Mount Revelstoke and Glacier National Parks, P.O. Box 350, Revelstoke, BC, Canada V0E 2S0; phone (250) 837-7500.

NAKUSP (B-10) pop. 1,698, elev. 914 m/2,998'

Nakusp, on the shore of Upper Arrow Lake between the Selkirk and Monashee mountain ranges, is named for an Indian word meaning "bay of quiet waters." Arrow Lake, part of the Columbia River system, is a popular destination for trout and salmon fishing. Heli-skiing is among the many winter activities offered in the area.

Nakusp Chamber of Commerce: 92 N.W. Sixth Ave., P.O. Box 387, Nakusp, BC, Canada V0G 1R0; phone (250) 265-4234 or (800) 909-8819 within British Columbia.

NAKUSP HOT SPRINGS is 12 km (7 mi.) n. on Nakusp Hot Springs Rd. Several mineral baths are sheltered by an outdoor cedar structure. The temperature of the pools varies from 36 to 41 C (97-107 F). Picnicking is permitted. Food is available. Daily 9:30 a.m.-10 p.m., Friday after Victoria Day-Sept. 30; 10-9:30, rest of year. Admission $6.25; over 60 and ages 6-17, $5.25; family rate (two adults and two children) $20, each additional child $3.25. Day pass $9.25; over 60 and ages 6-17, $8.25; family rate (two adults and two children) $30, each additional child $4.25. MC, VI. Phone (250) 265-4528. *See Recreation Chart.*

NANAIMO (G-10) pop. 73,000, elev. 30 m/98'

Some 120 kilometres (75 mi.) north of Victoria, Nanaimo began as a Hudson's Bay Co. outpost called Colvilletown, established for miners brought from England and Scotland to mine coal.

A thriving forest products industry and important deep-sea fishing port have replaced coal's economic influence. Nanaimo has made tourism and recreation a part of the economy.

Offshore islands and nearby mountains and lakes provide a variety of recreational opportunities including hiking, swimming, camping and picnicking. During winter and early spring charter companies offer marine wildlife tours to view the bald eagles and sea lions that winter in the area.

Exotic trees provide a setting for picnicking at Harmac Arboretum, 11 kilometres (7 mi.) south at Harmac Pulp Mill and Duke Point roads. Newcastle Island *(see Recreation Chart and the AAA/CAA Western Canada & Alaska CampBook)* is a marine provincial park accessible by a 10-minute ferry ride from Maffeo-Sutton Park, behind the Civic Arena. Automobiles are not permitted; the ferry operates daily on the hour, May 1-second Mon. in Oct.

Salmon sport fishing, scuba diving, windsurfing and sailing are available from Nanaimo's natural harbor, regularly visited by the ferry from Vancouver. An intertidal lagoon park with three lighted water curtains and a 4-kilometre (2.5-mi.) walkway along the seawall graces Nanaimo's waterfront. St. Jean's Custom Cannery is one of three factories where fishing enthusiasts can have their catch canned or smoked.

On a landscaped hillside, Malaspina College offers a view of the city and harbor below and also is the site of Nanaimo Art Gallery. Visitors interested in prehistoric art can see Indian sandstone carvings at Petroglyph Park, 3.25 kilometres (2 mi.) south on scenic Hwy. 1.

Nanaimo is accessible from the mainland by BC Ferries, which sails from Horseshoe Bay to Departure Bay and from Tsawwassen to Duke Point, 8 kilometres (5 mi.) south. For more information phone (888) 223-3779.

Tourism Nanaimo: 2290 Bowen Rd., Nanaimo, BC, Canada V9T 3K7; phone (250) 756-0106 or (800) 663-7337. *See color ad.*

NANAIMO ART GALLERY is on the Malaspina University-College campus at 900 Fifth St. Two galleries display local, regional and national exhibits; the second gallery is downtown at 150 Commercial St. New exhibits are installed frequently.

Allow 1 hour minimum. Campus gallery Mon.-Fri. 10-5, Sun. noon-4. Downtown gallery Tues.-Sat. 11-5. Closed holidays. Donations. Phone (250) 740-6350.

NANAIMO DISTRICT MUSEUM is at 100 Cameron Rd. Exhibits depict local history, including coal mining in Nanaimo, First Nations and the Old Town district. One gallery hosts changing exhibits. Daily 10-5, Victoria Day weekend-Labour Day; Tues.-Sat. 10-5, rest of year. Closed winter holidays. Admission $2; over 55 and students with ID $1.75; under 12, 75c. MC, VI. Phone (250) 753-1821.

The Bastion is on Front St. across from Coast Bastion Hotel. The small fort was built in 1853 to protect early settlers. A display shows how the bastion was used in the 1860s. A noon ceremonial cannon firing is conducted by staff dressed in period costumes. Daily 10-4:30, Victoria Day weekend-Labour Day weekend. Admission $1, senior citizens and students with ID 50c, under 6 free.

RECREATIONAL ACTIVITIES
Bungee Jumping

- **Bungy Zone** is at 35 Nanaimo River Rd., Nanaimo, BC, Canada V9R 5K2. Daily 11:30-6. Phone (250) 753-5867 or (800) 668-7771.

Hiking

- **Tracks Outdoor Adventures** is at 2130 Akenhead Rd., Nanaimo, BC, Canada V9X 1T9. Other activities are available. Daily 7:30-7. Tours are given 9-dusk. Phone (250) 754-8732 or (877) 898-8732.

NELSON (C-11) pop. 9,298, elev. 535 m/1,755′

An old iron and silver mining town, Nelson was settled by prospectors in the late 1880s. With the depletion of its mines, the town turned to logging, sawmilling and area trade. However, the legacy of the bonanza days lives on in the more than 350 heritage sites. Most of Nelson's historic commercial buildings are open to the public, but homes are private and closed to visitors. Free guided tours of Nelson's heritage attractions are available from the chamber of commerce early July through Labour Day.

Nearby parks, lakes, streams and mountains offer all types of summer and winter recreation. Kokanee Creek and Kokanee Glacier provincial parks *(see Recreation Chart and the AAA/CAA Western Canada & Alaska CampBook)* are 19 kilometres (12 mi.) northeast on Hwy. 3A.

Nelson Chamber of Commerce: 225 Hall St., Nelson, BC, Canada V1L 5X4; phone (250) 352-3433.

Self-guiding tours: Maps detailing walking and driving tours are available from the chamber of commerce.

RECREATIONAL ACTIVITIES
Skiing

- **Whitewater Ski Resort** is 20 km (12 mi.) s. off Hwy. 6. Write P.O. Box 60, Nelson, BC, Canada V1L 5P7. Daily 9-3:30, mid-Dec. to early Apr. Phone (250) 354-4944 or (800) 666-9420.

NEW DENVER (C-10)
pop. 538, elev. 555 m/1,850′

NIKKEI INTERNMENT MEMORIAL CENTRE is at 306 Josephine St. Dedicated to remembering the Japanese internment experience during World War II, the center commemorates the 22,000 Nikkei (people of Japanese descent) removed from their British Columbia homes and relocated to camps. Exhibits include a typical two-family shack, an outhouse and a peace garden. Tribute also is paid to the first generation of Japanese who arrived in Canada in 1877.

Allow 30 minutes minimum. Daily 9:30-5, mid-May to mid-Sept. Admission $4; over 60 and ages 13-17, $3; ages 5-12, $2; family rate $10. Phone (250) 358-7288.

NEW WESTMINSTER—see Vancouver p. 161.

NORTH VANCOUVER—see Vancouver p. 162.

OLIVER (D-9) pop. 4,224, elev. 307 m/1,007′

The northern tip of the American Great Basin Desert, which extends to Mexico, begins at Oliver. Irrigation begun in the 1920s converted the once desertlike valley floor and arid hillsides surrounding the town into productive orchards and vineyards. Abundant sunshine and little rain provide ideal conditions for growing wine grapes.

The area's climate also promotes numerous recreational activities. An 18-kilometre (11-mi.) paved bicycle trail travels through Oliver's rolling hills and along the Okanagan River. The valley lakes and streams offer boating and fishing. Vaseux Lake and Inkaneep provincial parks *(see Recreation Chart)* are nearby, as are Bear and Madden lakes, known for excellent trout fishing.

The Fairview Townsite, 3 kilometres (1.9 mi.) west on Fairview Road, formerly was the site of an 1880s boomtown. The town disappeared along with the gold in 1906; plaques at the site provide historical information.

Oliver & District Chamber of Commerce: 36205-93 St., P.O. Box 460, Oliver, BC, Canada V0H 1T0; phone (250) 498-6321.

WINERIES

- **Inniskillin Okanagan Vineyards** is 5 km (3 mi.) s. on Hwy. 97 to Rd. 11. Daily 10-5, May-Oct.; Mon.-Fri. 10-3, rest of year. Tours are given daily at 11 and 3, May-Oct. Phone (250) 498-6663, or (800) 498-6211 within Canada.

OKANAGAN CENTRE (C-9)
pop. 1,200, elev. 344 m/1,129′

WINERIES

- **Gray Monk Estate Winery** is at 1055 Camp Rd. Tours on the hour daily 11-4, Apr.-Oct.; daily at 2 and by appointment, Nov.-Dec.; Mon.-Sat. at 2 and by appointment, rest of year. Closed Jan. 1 and Dec. 25. Phone (250) 766-3168, or (800) 663-4205 in British Columbia.

OSOYOOS (D-9)
pop. 4,295, elev. 335 m/1,099′

From Osoyoos on the east side of Osoyoos Lake, an area of desert sand extends 48 kilometres (30 mi.) north to Skaha Lake and 24 kilometres (15 mi.) west along the Similkameen River. The area's similarity to Spain in climate and terrain inspired the citizens to adopt an Iberian style in their buildings. Despite its arid surroundings, Osoyoos has 19 kilometres (12 mi.) of sandy beach lining one of Canada's warmest freshwater lakes.

Man-made recreational facilities include the Wild Rapids on East Lakeshore Drive, with three large waterslides, five giant hot tubs and two minislides. Skiing is available nearby.

A heavy concentration of minerals, including evaporated copper, silver, gold and sulfate and Epsom salts, can be found at Spotted Lake, west on Crowsnest Hwy. 3, which provides 446 kilometres (277 mi.) of scenic driving all the way to Hope.

Osoyoos & District Chamber of Commerce: P.O. Box 227, Osoyoos, BC, Canada V0H 1V0; phone (250) 495-7142.

DESERT CENTRE is 2.9 km (1.9 mi.) n. of jct. hwys. 3 and 97, then 1.2 km (.7 mi.) w. to 14580 146th Ave. The 26.8-hectare (66-acre) ecological, interpretive and education center stands in the Great Basin Desert, which extends from Mexico to Canada. Narrated 60-minute guided tours on the 1.5-kilometre (1-mi.) boardwalk trail allow visitors to learn about rare, threatened and endangered plant and animal species.

Pets are not permitted. Picnic facilities are available. Allow 1 hour, 30 minutes minimum. Open daily 9-5. Guided tours are given Apr.-Oct. Hours may vary; phone ahead to confirm and to inquire about summer evening tours. Admission $6; over 64 and students with ID $5; under 13, $3; family rate $15. MC, VI. Phone (250) 495-2470 or (877) 899-0897 within British Columbia.

NK'MIP DESERT AND HERITAGE CENTRE is at 1000 Rancher Creek Rd. Visitors will experience a desert ecosystem and the traditions of the Okanagan people through interactive exhibits, artifacts, a recreated Okanagan village and self-guiding walking trails. The Village Trail is 1.4 kilometres (.9 mi.) long and has interpretive signs, benches and ramadas; the Loop Trail is 2 kilometres (1.2 mi.) and includes several uphill segments.

Guided tours are available. Allow 1 hour minimum. Daily 9-7, May 15-Aug. 31; daily 9-5, in Sept.; Mon.-Fri. 9-5, Apr. 10-May 14; Mon.-Fri 9-4, in Oct. Admission $7; ages 6-18, $5; family rate (two adults and two or more children) $20. MC, VI. Phone (250) 495-7901 or (888) 495-8555.

OSOYOOS MUSEUM is in Community Park at 19 Park Pl. The museum houses children's art from the Inkameep Day School Art Collection—art and photographs created 1931-43 under the guidance of Anthony Walsh, the teacher and principal who based his teaching on the importance of art in education. Exhibits also include a butterfly collection and an 1892 log building that served as a customs house, jail, school, residence and government office over the years. Allow 1 hour minimum. Daily 10-4, July-Aug.; daily 1-4, mid-May through June 30; Thurs 11-3, rest of year. Last admission 30 minutes before closing. Admission $3; under 14, $1. Phone (250) 495-2582.

WINERIES

- **Nk'Mip Cellars** is at 1400 Rancher Creek Rd. Daily 9-5, May-Oct.; 10-4, rest of year. Tours daily at 11, 1 and 3. Phone (250) 495-2985.

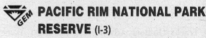 **PACIFIC RIM NATIONAL PARK RESERVE (I-3)**

Elevations in the park range from sea level along the Long Beach area to 140 metres (459 ft.) at Radar Hill. Refer to CAA/AAA maps for additional elevation information.

On the west coast of Vancouver Island, Pacific Rim National Park Reserve consists of three geographically distinct sections with different entry points: the Long Beach unit between Ucluelet and Tofino; the Broken Group Island unit, a cluster of islands in Barkley Sound; and the 75-kilometre-long (47-mi.) West Coast Trail unit between Bamfield and Port Renfrew.

Numerous contrasts exist in the 510-square-kilometre (197-sq.-mi.) reserve, which has sandy beaches, tranquil estuaries and lakes, rugged headlands, dense rain forests and rocky islands. Wildflowers nurtured by the area's moist and temperate climate thrive in an immense old-growth rain forest.

A stopping place for geese and ducks during their yearly migrations, the shoreline zone also accommodates colonies of sea birds and wildlife. Each spring some 20,000 gray whales migrate through the reserve's waters.

General Information and Activities

The reserve is open all year, although many facilities are seasonal. The Long Beach area, about 16 kilometres (10 mi.) west of the junction of Hwy. 4 and the Ucluelet highway, has 19 kilometres (12 mi.) of sandy beach and shoreline which are popular year-round with surfers and beachwalkers; wheelchair-accessible trails are available. Long Beach Information Centre, open mid-June to mid-September, is on Hwy. 4 inside the park boundary. There are self-guiding nature trails in the surrounding rain forest and other interpretive programs. The Wickaninnish Interpretive Centre features displays and films chronicling marine life of the Pacific.

The Broken Group Islands, accessible only by boat, offer pristine wilderness spread over a 100-island cluster in the center of Barkley Sound. Eagles and sea lions are abundant, while varied sea life and sunken ships create a diver's paradise. Camping is available in designated areas on eight islands.

The West Coast Trail, which had its beginnings as an avenue of rescue for shipwrecked sailors, follows the national park's rugged coastline between Port Renfrew and Bamfield. The trail is open to experienced hikers only and offers spectacular coastal scenery along its challenging path. Remnants of former settlements and shipwrecks can be seen along the shoreline.

The West Coast Trail Information and Registration Centres at Pachena Bay near Bamfield and at Port Renfrew are open May through September. Reservations to hike the trail may be made for June 15-Sept. 15; phone (800) 435-5622. *See Recreation Chart and the AAA/CAA Western Canada & Alaska CampBook.*

ADMISSION to the Long Beach area for private vehicles is $10 per day, Mar.-Oct. Camping fee at Long Beach is $14-$20 per person per night. Camping fee at other designated sites is $8 per person per night. West Coast Trail use permit is $90; reservation fee $25 (non-refundable). Ferry fee $14.

ADDRESS inquiries to the Superintendent, Pacific Rim National Park Reserve, P.O. Box 280, Ucluelet, BC, Canada V0R 3A0; phone (250) 726-7721, or (250) 726-4212 June 1 to mid-Sept.

PARKSVILLE (F-10)
pop. 10,323, elev. 80 m/262′

With its 1.6-kilometre-long (1-mi.) sandy beach on the Strait of Georgia, Parksville is a popular summer resort. Nearby Englishman and Little Qualicum rivers and parks, with scenic waterfalls, provide many opportunities for recreation, as do other area lakes, streams, mountains and parks. Rathtrevor Beach Provincial Park offers a beach, camping and picnicking. *See Recreation Chart and the AAA/CAA Western Canada & Alaska CampBook.*

Parksville & District Chamber of Commerce: 1275 E. Island Hwy., P.O. Box 99, Parksville, BC, Canada V9P 2G3; phone (250) 248-3613.

CRAIG HERITAGE PARK AND MUSEUM is 4 km (2.5 mi.) s. at 1245 E. Island Hwy. The collection

of historic buildings includes a church, a log house, a fire station, a turn-of-the-20th-century schoolhouse and two 19th-century post offices. Exhibits inside the buildings depict local history. Allow 30 minutes minimum. Daily 10-4, mid-May through Sept. 30. Admission $3; over 60 and ages 6-18, $2; family rate $6. Phone (250) 248-6966.

PEACHLAND (C-8)
pop. 4,654, elev. 366 m/1,200′

Peachland's rolling green countryside is a prosperous fruit growing, farming, lumber producing and mining area. The mining of molybdenum and copper from the Brenda Mines complex in the hills above Hwy. 97 drastically increased Peachland's population during the 1970s.

Nearby mountains, rivers and lakes, including Okanagan Lake *(see Recreation Chart),* offer abundant opportunities for skiing, hiking, fishing and water sports.

PENDER ISLANDS—
see Gulf Islands National Park Reserve p. 123.

PENTICTON (C-9)
pop. 30,985, elev. 345 m/1,131′

The first orchards in Okanagan Valley were planted by the Oblates at Okanagan Mission 1860-61, and the fruits, especially peaches, became a staple of the area. Tom Ellis established the first cattle ranch in 1865 and it was an empire when he sold it for a hefty sum in 1905; by 1909 orchards had replaced cattle in the agricultural economy. Today Penticton's fruit industry combines with tourism and lumber industries to keep the community strong.

Okanagan and Skaha lakes, at opposite ends of the city, offer ample expanses of shoreline for recreational pursuits. A popular summer activity is floating down the 8-kilometre (5-mi.) river channel from the mouth of Okanagan Lake *(see Recreation Chart and the AAA/CAA Western Canada & Alaska CampBook)* to Skaha Lake. The channel has rest and picnic areas and is paralleled by a bicycle path and a jogging trail.

Tourism Penticton: 888 Westminster Ave. W., Penticton, BC, Canada V2A 8S2; phone (250) 493-4055 or (800) 663-5052.

ART GALLERY OF THE SOUTH OKANAGAN is at 199 Marina Way. Four exhibition halls and an art loft comprise the facility on the shore of Okanagan Lake, where works by professional local, provincial and nationally known artists are displayed. Allow 30 minutes minimum. Tues.-Sat. 10-5; closed statutory holidays. Admission $2, under 19 free. MC, VI. Phone (250) 493-2928.

DOMINION RADIO ASTROPHYSICAL OBSERVATORY is 16 km (10 mi.) s.w. on Hwy. 97, then 7 km (4 mi.) s. on White Lake Rd. The site features radio telescopes used to study the universe. A self-guiding tour includes a 26-metre (85-ft.) parabolic antenna and an array of more sophisticated, computer-linked, 9-metre (30-ft.) antennae.

Since automobile ignitions cause radio interference, visitors are asked to leave their vehicles at the road and walk the 600 metres (.4 mi.) to the facility. Allow 30 minutes minimum. Visitor center daily 10-5, mid-Mar. through second Mon. in Oct.; Mon.-Fri. 10-5, rest of year. Guided tours are given Sun. 2-5, July-Aug. Free. Phone (250) 493-2277.

[SAVE] **OKANAGAN INLAND MARINE HERITAGE PARK & MUSEUMS** is on Okanagan Lake Beach at 1099 Lakeshore Dr. Featured on-site is the *Sicamous*, the last steam-powered stern-wheeler to operate on Okanagan Lake. Visitors can experience what once was a major means of transportation in the area. Allow 30 minutes minimum. Daily 9-9, June 26-Sept. 12; daily 9-6, May 1-June 25; daily 10-4, Sept. 13-Oct. 31; Mon.-Fri. 10-4, rest of year. Schedule may vary; phone ahead. Closed mid-Dec. to mid-Jan. Admission $5; senior citizens and students with ID $4; ages 5-12, $1; family rate $12. MC, VI. Phone (250) 492-0403.

PENTICTON (R.N. ATKINSON) MUSEUM is at 785 Main St. Displays describe the natural and social histories of the southern Okanagan Valley. A historic transportation exhibit about the Kettle Valley Railway is available along with an exhibit about the Canadian military. Summer programs include cemetery walks, heritage tours and children's activities. Allow 1 hour minimum. Mon.-Sat. 10-5, July-Aug.;

Tues.-Sat. 10-5, Sept.-Oct. and Apr.-June; Tues.-Sat. 10-4, rest of year. Closed holidays. Donations. Phone (250) 490-2451.

WONDERFUL WATERWORLD is at 225 Yorkton Ave. at Skaha Lake Rd. The water park includes seven large slides, five small slides, a hot pool, picnic area and miniature golf. Mon.-Sat. 10-9, Sun. 11-8, July 1-Labour Day. Admission $18.50, under 4 free. After 4:30 p.m., $13.50. Observer rates are available. Rates may vary; phone ahead. MC, VI. Phone (250) 493-8121.

CASINOS

• **Lake City Casino** is at 21 Lakeshore Dr. W. Daily 10 a.m.-2 a.m. Phone (250) 487-1280.

RECREATIONAL ACTIVITIES

Skiing

• **Apex Mountain Resort** is 32 km (20 mi.) w. on Green Mountain Rd. Write P.O. Box 1060, Penticton, BC, Canada V2A 6J9. Other activities are available. Daily 9-3:30, mid-Nov. to late Apr. Phone (877) 777-2739.

PORT ALBERNI (F-9)
pop. 17,743, elev. 60 m/197'

A deepwater port and important fishing and lumber shipping center, Port Alberni was discovered in 1791 by Don Pedro Alberni, a Spanish sea captain. Industry began in 1860 when nine workmen arriving on the schooner *Meg Merrilees* built a sawmill on the harbor's edge.

Port Alberni's harbor remains the city's focal point, enhanced by the Alberni Harbour Quay at the foot of Argyle Street. The facility includes shops, an arts and crafts outlet and the MV *Lady Rose* office. From the 1912 CPR Train Station, a logging locomotive takes visitors on a 35-minute journey along the waterfront to McLean Mill National Historic Site *(see attraction listing).*

Surrounded by mountains, lakes and forests, the city is a good base for naturalists and outdoors enthusiasts. Alpine and cross-country skiing are available nearby. Sproat Lake Provincial Park *(see Recreation Chart and the AAA/CAA Western Canada & Alaska CampBook)* features Indian carvings of mythological beasts. There are hundreds of giant Douglas firs, many that date from the late 12th century, at Cathedral Grove in MacMillan Provincial Park, 16 kilometres (10 mi.) east.

The region's natural wonders are protected by the Martin Mars Water Bombers based at Sproat Lake. Designed to combat forest fires, these huge aircraft carry 6,000 imperial gallons (7,206 U.S. gallons) of water.

Alberni Valley Chamber of Commerce: 2533 Redford St., R.R. #2, Site 215, C-1O, Port Alberni, BC, Canada V9Y 7L6; phone (250) 724-6535.

ALBERNI VALLEY MUSEUM is in Echo Centre at 4255 Wallace St. Collections relate to First Nations art, culture and community and Vancouver Island's domestic and industrial history. Highlights include an exhibit about the 1964 tidal wave, Nuu Chah Nulth basketry, Alberni Valley folk art, antique photographs and a display chronicling the history of the West Coast Trail. Traveling exhibits also are featured. Mon.-Sat. 10-5 (also Thurs. 5-8); closed statutory holidays. Donations. Phone (250) 723-2181.

McLEAN MILL NATIONAL HISTORIC SITE is 6 km (10 mi.) w. on Beaver Creek Rd., then 3 km (1.8 mi.) n. on Smith Rd., following signs. The 13-hectare (32-acre) site preserves a working 1926 steam sawmill that was operated by the R.B. McLean family until 1965. Thirty structures from the early days of British Columbia's forest industry include the camp where loggers and mill employees lived and worked. Interactive guided tours and stage shows and sawmill demonstrations are given Thursday through Monday.

Food is available. Allow 1 hour, 30 minutes minimum. Daily 10-4, mid-June through Labour Day. Hours may vary; phone ahead. Admission $8.50, senior citizens and students with ID $4.50, under 6 free, family rate $14. Rates may vary; phone ahead. MC, VI. Phone (250) 723-1376.

Alberni Pacific Railway departs from the CPR Station at Argyle and Kingsway sts. Passengers embark upon a 35-minute train ride along the original "steam donkey" route to McLean Mill National Historic Site. Trips depart Thurs.-Mon. at 10 and 1:45, mid-June through Labour Day. Last train leaves the mill at 4:45. Hours may vary; phone ahead. Round trip fare (includes mill admission) $24; senior citizens and students with ID $16; under 6, $5; family rate $55. Rates may vary; phone ahead. MC, VI. Phone (250) 723-1376.

SAVE MV *LADY ROSE* docks at the Argyle Pier in the Alberni Harbour Quay at the foot of Argyle St. The packet freighter takes visitors on an all-day cruise. The MV *Lady Rose* and her sister ship, the MV *Frances Barkley,* deliver mail and cargo to isolated villages, fishing resorts and camps. The freighters sail down the Alberni Inlet to Bamfield, Ucluelet and the Broken Group Islands.

Food is available. Sensible shoes and a sweater or light jacket are advisable. Departures to Bamfield Tues. and Thurs.-Sun. at 8 a.m.; July-Aug.; Tues., Thurs. and Sat. at 8 a.m., rest of year. Sailings to Ucluelet and Broken Group Islands Mon., Wed. and Fri. at 8 a.m., early June-late Sept. Hours may vary; phone ahead. Full-day, round-trip fares $48-$55; ages 8-15, $24-$28; under 7 free when accompanied by an adult. Reservations are recommended in summer. Fares may vary; phone ahead. AX, MC, VI. Phone (250) 723-8313, or (800) 663-7192 Apr.-Sept.

ROBERTSON CREEK FISH HATCHERY is 5 km (3 mi.) w. on Hwy. 4, then 7 km (4 mi.) n.w. on Great Central Lake Rd. The hatchery has an annual output of 8 million chinook and 800,000 coho salmon and 150,000 steelhead trout. Displays explain the fish breeding process from incubation through release. Facilities include outdoor rearing ponds and raceways. Daily 8-4. Free. Phone (250) 724-6521.

PORT COQUITLAM—*see Vancouver p. 163.*

PORT EDWARD (E-1) pop. 659

The river of mists, as the Indians called the Skeena River, bursts through the Coast Range and empties into the Pacific Ocean near Port Edward. The river provides the community's major commodity, fish, which is processed by local canneries. Salmon and steelhead trout, besides being economic staples, also offer a recreational challenge to anglers.

NORTH PACIFIC HISTORIC FISHING VILLAGE is 10 km (6 mi.) s. of Hwy. 16 at 1889 Skeena Dr. The restored 1889 cannery village includes the main cannery, reduction plant, staff housing and mess house. Artifacts of the fishing industry are displayed throughout the complex. Guided tours and live entertainment also are offered. Food is available. Daily 9:30-5, May-Sept.; 10-4, rest of year. Hours may vary; phone ahead. Admission $11.95; over 55, $9.95; ages 6-11, $7.95. Rates may vary; phone ahead. MC, VI. Phone (250) 628-3538.

PORT McNEILL (G-2)
pop. 2,821, elev. 15 m/49′

In the scenic, untamed wilderness of northern Vancouver Island, Port McNeill occupies a rich lumber and fishing region popular with adventurous hikers, campers, spelunkers, fishermen and other sports enthusiasts.

Of interest to rock collectors and geologists are several nearby natural phenomena, including the Vanishing River, which plunges underground into a maze of caves and tunnels; the Devil's Bath, a huge rock bowl continuously filled by an underground spring; and the Eternal Fountain, which gushes from a rock crevice and then disappears underground again. All are reached by logging roads that are accessible only in summer.

An inter-island ferry operates a shuttle service between Port McNeill, Sointula and Alert Bay *(see place listing p. 111).*

Port McNeill & District Chamber of Commerce: P.O. Box 129, Port McNeill, BC, Canada V0N 2R0; phone (250) 956-3131.

PORT MOODY—*see Vancouver p. 163.*

POUCE COUPE (D-6)
pop. 833, elev. 652 m/2,139′

The village of Pouce Coupe is referred to as the gateway to Peace country because it is one of the first communities travelers will see when entering British Columbia from Alberta.

POUCE COUPE MUSEUM is at 5006 49th Ave. Pioneer artifacts are housed in the former Northern Alberta Railway station. Live entertainment is offered on the grounds on weekends. Daily 8-5, May-Aug. Donations. Phone (250) 786-5555.

POWELL RIVER (E-11)
pop. 12,983, elev. 55 m/180'

Rich forests and abundant water brought the founders of the Powell River Company to the area in the early 1900s. The townsite is one of the oldest company-built communities in western Canada.

Separated from the mainland by Jervis Inlet, the area offers year-round recreation including freshwater and saltwater fishing, scuba diving, boating, kayaking, hiking and bicycling. The Powell Forest Canoe Route connects eight lakes around the Upper Sunshine Coast region with camping areas along the scenic circuit.

A panorama of the Strait of Malaspina unfolds from the Mount Valentine viewpoint, reached by a rock stairway in the heart of town. Bald eagles can be observed at any time of year, especially in late fall when they are attracted by salmon spawning in channels and small streams. Also of interest are Sliammon Fish Hatchery and Powell River Salmon Society Spawning Channel.

Guided 2-hour tours of the NorskeCanada Paper Mill are offered through the Visitor InfoCentre. Part of the tour is outdoors; appropriate dress and low-heeled, closed footwear are advised. Tours depart Mon.-Fri. at 9:30, June-Sept. Children under 12 are not permitted. For information and reservations phone (877) 817-8669.

Powell River Visitor InfoCentre: 4690 Marine Ave., Powell River, BC, Canada V8A 2L1; phone (877) 817-8669.

INLAND LAKE PROVINCIAL PARK is 12 km (7 mi.) n. on Inland Lake Rd. In a semi-remote area with abundant and varied wildlife, the park offers wheelchair-accessible facilities for camping, hiking and fishing. A 13-kilometre-long (8-mi.) circuit of crushed limestone with minimal grades has eight picnic and rest areas and six fishing wharves. Amenities include cabins exclusively for use by the physically impaired, and wheelchair-accessible outhouses.

Site open for day use daily 7 a.m.-10 p.m., Apr.-Oct. Hours may vary; phone ahead. Free. Phone (604) 487-4305. *See Recreation Chart.*

POWELL RIVER HISTORICAL MUSEUM AND ARCHIVES is on Marine Ave. across from Willingdon Beach. The museum houses artifacts, archival material and displays about the area's history. A children's treasure hunt is featured. Allow 30 minutes minimum. Daily 9-5, June 18-Aug. 31; Mon.-Fri. 9-4:30, rest of year. Closed holidays. Admission $2; ages 6-12, $1; family rate $5. Phone (604) 485-2222.

PRINCE GEORGE (E-5)
pop. 72,406, elev. 691 m/2,267'

At the confluence of the Nechako and Fraser rivers, the area was visited in 1793 by Alexander Mackenzie in his trek down the Fraser to the Pacific. In 1807 it became the site for Simon Fraser's North West Co. fort. Fraser's canoe brigades soon gave way to paddlewheelers and then railroads, which converged on this important northern crossroads. Prince George remains a major transportation and trade center, a role enhanced by a thriving forest industry.

Despite its urban transformation, the city has retained much of its natural heritage in its 116 parks. Of interest are Fort George Park, which contains a replica of Fraser's trading post; Connaught Park's manicured gardens and scenic views; and Cottonwood Island Park, which includes the Prince George Railway Museum and its collection of railroad artifacts and cars.

Prince George blends its pastoral features with such cultural centers as Studio 2880 and Vanier Hall. Studio 2880, home to six craft guilds, is the site of craft markets and special events throughout the year. Concerts by the Prince George Symphony and by visiting performers are held in Vanier Hall.

These cultural amenities coexist with the more rugged recreational opportunities available in the wilderness that surrounds the city. Nearby lakes, rivers and mountains present an array of activities ranging from rugged back-country hikes and fishing to skiing and ice skating.

Tourism Prince George: 101-1300 First Ave., Prince George, BC, Canada V2L 2Y3; phone (250) 562-3700 or (800) 668-7646.

EXPLORATION PLACE AT THE FRASER-FORT GEORGE REGIONAL MUSEUM is at the end of 20th Ave. at 333 Becott Pl. in Fort George Park. Fort George's history and development are explored through such topics as transportation, lumber and the First Nations culture. The Children's Gallery houses life-size dinosaur sculptures, skeletons and a dig pit. The Explorations Gallery features live animals and interactive computers. A SimEx virtual motion theater offers three rides daily. A steam locomotive ride is offered on weekends and holidays.

Allow 1 hour minimum. Daily 10-5, day after Victoria Day-day before second Mon. in Oct.; Wed.-Sun. 10-5, rest of year. Closed Jan. 1 and Dec. 25-26. Museum admission $8.95; over 59 and students with ID $6.95; ages 2-12, $5.95; family rate (two adults and up to four children under 19) $20.95. Combination ticket with movie ride $10.95; over 59 and students with ID $9.95; ages 2-12, $8.95; family rate (two adults and up to four children under 19) $29.95. Train rides $1. AX, MC, VI. Phone (250) 562-1612 or (866) 562-1612.

PRINCE RUPERT (D-1)
pop. 14,643, elev. 50 m/164'

At the turn of the 20th century Prince Rupert existed only in the imagination of Charles Hays, manager of the Grand Trunk Pacific Railway. Hays died with the sinking of the SS *Titanic*, but the Grand Trunk Pacific Railway carried out his intention to build a port to rival Vancouver on this rugged, un-inhabited island bordered by a natural harbor. The new site was expected to be successful because it was closer to the Far East than Vancouver and would provide an outlet for the untapped resources of Canada's far north.

Prince Rupert has fulfilled that potential and is now one of Canada's major seaports. It is the southernmost port of the Alaska Ferry System, the northern terminus of the British Columbia Ferry Corp. and the western terminus of the Canadian National Railway. Cruise ships en route to coastal glaciers and fjords also stop at Prince Rupert's harbor, said to be the world's third largest natural ice-free deep-sea harbor.

Before the coming of the railroad the northern coast was home to the Tsimpsean and Haida, cultures whose ancestors inhabited the area for almost 5,000 years. Both are renowned for their stylized artworks, the most familiar of which are totem poles. Many of these graceful monuments are shown in such city parks as Service Park, the colorful terraced Sunken Gardens, and Roosevelt Park with its sweeping views of the Pacific.

On the waterfront, Kwinitsa Railway Station is a relic of the modern era. Restored and moved from its original location, Kwinitsa is one of the last of the Grand Trunk Pacific Railway stations; inside are exhibits about the railroad's history.

Just beyond the city, climate and soil have stunted and twisted lodgepole pines into a natural bonsai garden at Oliver Lake Provincial Park. Another interesting phenomenon is Butze Rapids, a series of reversing rapids between Wainwright and Morse basins that rival the reversing falls at Saint John, New Brunswick. A dramatic view of the rapids occurs during a falling tide and can be seen from a viewing point on Hwy. 16, which offers scenic driving east to Terrace *(see place listing p. 144)*.

Guided tours are offered during the summer by Farwest Bus Lines Ltd., 225 Second Ave. W. Trans-Provincial Airlines and Northcoast Air Services offer flight tours of the region. Guided walking tours are available mid-May to mid-September from the visitor information center.

Prince Rupert Visitor Information Centre: 215 Cow Bay Rd., Suite 100, Box 100, Prince Rupert, BC, Canada V8J 1A2; phone (250) 624-5637 or (800) 667-1994.

Self-guiding tours: A walking tour that includes sunken gardens, the harbor, sections of the downtown area and various attractions is detailed on maps and brochures available from the visitor bureau at the Museum of Northern British Columbia *(see attraction listing).*

MUSEUM OF NORTHERN BRITISH COLUMBIA is at 100 First Ave. W. and McBride St. Models, maps, graphic displays and an ethnological collection explain pioneer history and the lifestyles of the coastal First Nations groups from prehistoric times through their contacts with Europeans. Changing exhibits are displayed in the art gallery. Of interest are an early 20th-century steamroller and a modern First Nations carving shed with local artists on site.

Mon.-Sat. 9-8, Sun. 9-5, June-Aug.; Mon.-Sat. 9-5, rest of year. Closed Jan. 1 and Dec. 25-26. Admission $5; students with ID $2; ages 6-12, $1; family rate $10. MC, VI. Phone (250) 624-3207.

PRINCETON (C-8) pop. 2,610

Named "Vermilion Forks" by fur traders in the early 1800s, Princeton developed as a ranching and mining outpost in the foothills of the Cascade Mountains. In 1860 the town was renamed to honor a visit by the Prince of Wales. Revitalized downtown storefronts boast murals and facades in keeping with Princeton's Western heritage.

Princeton & District Chamber of Commerce: Hwy. 3, P.O. Box 540, Princeton, BC, Canada V0X 1W0; phone (250) 295-3103.

Self-guiding tours: Maps detailing walking tours are available from the chamber of commerce.

PRINCETON AND DISTRICT MUSEUM AND ARCHIVES is at 167 Vermilion Ave. The collection includes fossils and minerals, aboriginal baskets, lace and textiles, antique cooking utensils, mining tools and equipment, a large butterfly collection and a stagecoach. Daily 10-7, June-Aug.; 10-5, Apr.-May and Sept.-Oct. Donations. Phone (250) 295-7588.

QUADRA ISLAND—
see Gulf Islands National Park Reserve p. 123.

QUALICUM BEACH (F-10)
pop. 6,921, elev. 9 m/30'

A popular resort and arts community, Qualicum Beach is known for its white sand beaches. Nearby Little Qualicum Falls and Englishman River Falls *(see Recreation Chart)* and Horne Lake Caves Provincial Park also present abundant recreational opportunities. Salmon and trout are raised at fish hatcheries on the Big and Little Qualicum rivers.

Qualicum Beach Visitor Information Centre: 2711 W. Island Hwy., Qualicum Beach, BC, Canada V9K 2C4; phone (250) 752-9532.

BIG QUALICUM RIVER HATCHERY is 12 km (7 mi.) n. on Hwy. 19A, then e. on Kenmuir Rd., following signs. Millions of chum, coho and chinook salmon are hatched here each year as part of the country's efforts to restore its salmon population. Steelhead and cutthroat trout also are raised. Visitors can see holding ponds, rearing channels and incubation units. Hiking trails are available. Allow 30 minutes minimum. Daily dawn-dusk. Donations. Phone (250) 757-8412.

MILNER GARDENS AND WOODLANDS, 2179 W. Island Hwy., comprises 24 hectares (60 acres) of Douglas fir woodland and 4 hectares (10 acres) of garden surrounding a gabled heritage house. Visitors may view the dining, sitting and drawing rooms as well as the library. Historical photos, artifacts and keepsakes of visits by members of the Royal family also are displayed. Allow 1 hour minimum. Daily 10-5, Mother's Day-Labour Day; Thurs.-Sun. and Mon. holidays 10-5, day after Labour Day through mid-Oct. Admission $9.35, students with ID $5.61, under 13 free when accompanied by an adult. Phone (250) 752-6153.

QUEEN CHARLOTTE ISLANDS (E-1)

The Queen Charlotte Islands were occupied by Haida Indians when Spanish sea captain Juan Pérez sighted the archipelago in 1774. A seafaring and artistic people, the Haida traded sea otter pelts with European traders during the early 1800s. By the late 19th century, however, the Haida had to vacate many of their ancestral villages to escape a devastating smallpox epidemic.

Only a fraction of their original number still inhabit the island—at Haida, near Masset, and Skidegate, near Queen Charlotte City. Continuing their cultural traditions, they carve elaborate works of art from argillite, a black slatelike stone found only in mountain deposits off the coast.

A group of about 150 islands forming an elongated triangle, the Queen Charlotte Islands stretch 250 kilometres (157 mi.) from north to south, 90 kilometres (56 mi.) off the coast of British Columbia. Characterized by fog and low clouds, these islands also are known as the Misty Islands. The towns are small and decidedly rural; the entire population of the Queen Charlotte Islands is about 5,000.

The largest of the islands is Graham. In the north on its broad and flat eastern side are most of the archipelago's communities—Masset, Old Masset, Port Clements, Queen Charlotte City, Skidegate, and Tlell—which are linked by a paved road. An airport is at Masset as well as at Sandspit, on the northeastern tip of Moresby Island.

A temperate marine climate supports dense coniferous forests, which, as the basis of the islands' economy, have been logged extensively. The fish and shellfish in the coastal waters supply the islands' important commercial fishing industry.

Visitors are attracted by the pristine wilderness, the hunting and fishing prospects, kayaking and hiking opportunities, and the handicrafts and art of the Haida. Wildlife is abundant; tiny Sitka deer and bald eagles frequent the shores, and seals, porpoises and whales often appear in the inlets. Bird-watching is a popular activity.

Points of interest include Naikoon Provincial Park (see Recreation Chart) on Graham Island, the remote Haida village sites, the Delkatla Wildlife Sanctuary in Masset, the Queen Charlotte Islands Museum in Skidegate and the various carving sheds in Skidegate and Old Masset.

Permission to visit Haida unoccupied village sites must be obtained from Band Council offices; phone (250) 559-8225.

The Queen Charlotte Islands can be reached by air from Prince Rupert and Vancouver and by ferry from Prince Rupert. Kayak rentals, fishing charters and various guided boat and land tours are available.

Queen Charlotte Visitor Information Centre: 3220 Wharf St., P.O. Box 819, Queen Charlotte, BC, Canada V0T 1S0; phone (250) 559-8316.

QUESNEL (F-4)
pop. 10,044, elev. 545 m/1,788'

Discovery of gold in the surrounding area in the 1860s contributed to Quesnel's growth. The city is the center of a popular hunting and fishing region at the junction of the Fraser and Quesnel rivers. Lumber, pulp and plywood manufacturing, tourism, cattle ranching and mining are the city's primary sources of income.

East of the city on Hwy. 26 is a historic remnant of the gold rush days, Barkerville Historic Town (see place listing p. 112), a restored boomtown of that era. Just beyond Barkerville is Bowron Lake Provincial Park (see Recreation Chart and the AAA/CAA Western Canada & Alaska CampBook), which has a 116-kilometre (72-mi.) canoe circuit of interconnecting lakes. Alpine skiing is available nearby.

Quesnel Visitor Information Centre: 703 Carson Ave., Quesnel, BC, Canada V2J 2B6; phone (250) 992-8716 or (800) 992-4922.

COTTONWOOD HOUSE HISTORIC SITE is 28 km (17 mi.) e. on Hwy. 26. Cottonwood was built 1864-65 as a roadhouse for travelers on the Cariboo Wagon Road en route to the gold fields. The reconstructed farm includes a double barn, stable, guesthouse, outbuildings and antique machinery. Costumed interpreters provide wagon rides and farming demonstrations. A walking trail winds along the river.

Daily 9-5:30, July-Aug.; daily 10-5, May-June; Sat.-Sun. 10-5, in Sept. Admission (includes wagon ride) $4.50; over 59 and ages 13-18, $2. MC, VI. Phone (250) 992-2071.

QUESNEL & DISTRICT MUSEUM AND ARCHIVES is .7 km (.5 mi.) s. on Hwy. 97 at 705 Carson Ave. Marking the area's history from the days of Alexander Mackenzie's explorations and the 1862 gold rush, the museum includes exhibits about pioneer life, a hands-on area for children, artifacts from the Titanic and an archives.

Allow 1 hour minimum. Daily 8-6, June-Aug.; daily 8:30-4:30, Apr.-May; Tues.-Sat. 8:30-4:30, rest of year. Closed statutory holidays. Admission $3; ages 13-17, $1.50. Phone (250) 992-9580.

RADIUM HOT SPRINGS (B-11)
pop. 583, elev. 805 m/2,641'

Renowned for its mineral hot springs (see Kootenay National Park p. 129 and Recreation

Chart), Radium Hot Springs also is a popular departure point for scenic and white-water river excursions. More than 10 golf courses are in the vicinity.

RECREATIONAL ACTIVITIES

Skiing

- **Panorama Mountain Village** is 12 km (7.5 mi.) w. on Hwy. 95. Write Panorama, BC, Canada V0A 1T0. Other activities are offered. Daily 8 a.m.-11 p.m., Dec.-Apr. Phone (800) 663-2929.

White-water Rafting

- **Kootenay River Runners** is at 4987 Hwy. 93. Daily at 9, early June to mid-Sept. Phone (250) 347-9210 or (800) 599-4399.

REVELSTOKE (B-10)

pop. 7,500, elev. 440 m/1,433′

Revelstoke is at the western end of Rogers Pass, the section of the Trans-Canada Hwy. that traverses Glacier National Park *(see place listing p. 120)*. Rogers Pass is one of the world's most scenic mountain roads. Downhill skiing is available nearby.

Revelstoke Chamber of Commerce: 204 Campbell Ave., P.O. Box 490, Revelstoke, BC, Canada V0E 2S0; phone (250) 837-5345 or (800) 487-1493.

CANYON HOT SPRINGS is 35.5 km (22 mi.) e. on Hwy. 1. Bathers can dip in a pool of 40 C (104 F) mineral waters or swim in a pool that is 30 C (86 F).

Camping is permitted. Food is available. Daily 9 a.m.-10 p.m., July-Aug.; 9-9, May-June and in Sept. Hours may vary; phone ahead. Day passes $8.50; over 59 and ages 5-14, $7; family pass (two adults and two children) $23. Single swim $6.50; over 59 and ages 5-14, $5.50; family rate (two adults and two children) $18. Rates may vary; phone ahead. Phone (250) 837-2420. *See Recreation Chart.*

SAVE **ENCHANTED FOREST** is 32 km (20 mi.) w. on Hwy. 1 to 7060 Trans-Canada Hwy. Some 300 handmade figurines include Old World fairy folk, dragons and dungeons in a natural forest setting with giant cedars, a stump house, a fish pond and a towering tree house. Swamp boat rides and a wetland boardwalk also are offered. Daily 8-8, June 21-Sept. 4; 10-5:30, May 15-June 20 and Sept. 5-Oct. 1. Admission $6.54; ages 3-15, $5.17. MC, VI. Phone (250) 837-9477 or (866) 944-9704.

SAVE **REVELSTOKE RAILWAY MUSEUM** is at 719 Track St. W. off Victoria Rd. The building of the Canadian Pacific Railway is traced with artifacts, photographs and original equipment. One of the company's largest steam locomotives is displayed beside a restored 1929 solarium car inside the museum, while the yard features such rolling stock as a caboose, a snow plow and a flange car. A diesel cabin simulator allows visitors to experience the feeling of driving a train.

Allow 30 minutes minimum. Daily 9-8, July-Aug.; daily 9-5, Apr.-June and Sept.-Nov.; Mon.-Fri. 1-5, rest of year. Closed Jan. 1, Good Friday, Easter, second Mon. in Oct. and Dec. 25-26. Admission $6; over 60, $5; ages 7-16, $3; family rate $13. MC, VI. Phone (250) 837-6060 or (877) 837-6060.

THREE VALLEY GAP HERITAGE GHOST TOWN is 19 km (12 mi.) w. on Hwy. 1. Near the original site of the 19th-century lumber and mining town of Three Valley are more than 40 relocated buildings including a hotel, a general store, a church, two schoolhouses, a saloon and many examples of handcrafted log buildings. An exhibit chronicles the history of steam, transportation and communication. Live performances of a musical stage show take place most nights May through September.

Guided 45-minute tours depart daily 9-4, mid-Apr. to mid-Oct. Admission $8.88; over 64, $7.01; ages 12-17, $6.54; ages 6-11, $4.67. An additional fee is charged for the stage show; reservations are required. AX, MC, VI. Phone (250) 837-2109 or (888) 667-2109.

RICHMOND—*see Vancouver p. 163.*

ROSSLAND (D-10)

pop. 3,646, elev. 1,039 m/3,408′

The 1890 gold rush on Red Mountain spurred the growth of Rossland from a prospectors' camp to a bustling town with 42 saloons, 17 law firms, four breweries and two distilleries. The area's vast mineral wealth, which supported a booming mining industry for 40 years, produced more than 6 million tons of ore valued at about $125 million.

Camping and picnicking are offered at King George VI Provincial Park, 9.6 kilometres (6 mi.) south near the U.S. border *(see the AAA/CAA Western Canada & Alaska CampBook)*; fishing, swimming and canoeing are available at Nancy Greene Provincial Park, 26 kilometres (16 mi.) northwest at hwys. 3 and 3B *(see Recreation Chart and the AAA/CAA Western Canada & Alaska CampBook)*.

Rossland Chamber of Commerce: 2185 Columbia Ave., P.O. Box 1385, Rossland, BC, Canada V0G 1Y0; phone (250) 362-5666.

ROSSLAND HISTORICAL MUSEUM AND LE ROI MINE is at jct. hwys. 3B and 22. Guided 45-minute tours enter a section of a hard-rock mine tunnel. The museum has mining artifacts and rock and mineral samples. There also are outdoor exhibits. Gold panning is offered.

Allow 2 hours minimum. Daily 9-5, mid-May to mid-Sept. Last mine tour departs 90 minutes before closing. Museum $4; over 59 and students with ID $3; ages 6-13, $1.50. Mine tours (museum included) $8; over 59 and students with ID $6; ages 6-13, $3; family rate $25. AX, MC, VI. Phone (250) 362-7722 or (888) 448-7444.

RECREATIONAL ACTIVITIES
Skiing

- **Red Mountain Ski Area** is 3 km (1.5 mi.) n. on Hwy. 3B. Write P.O. Box 670, Rossland, BC, Canada V0G 1Y0. Daily 9-3, mid-Dec. to early Apr. Phone (250) 362-7384 or (800) 663-0105.

SAANICHTON—see Victoria p. 179.

SALT SPRING ISLAND—
see Gulf Islands National Park Reserve p. 123.

SATURNA ISLAND—
see Gulf Islands National Park Reserve p. 123.

SICAMOUS (B-9)
pop. 2,720, elev. 352 m/1,155'

Flanked by Mara and Shuswap lakes, Sicamous has abundant recreational opportunities, including swimming, fishing, boating and other water sports. Full- and half-day cruises on Shuswap Lake *(see Recreation Chart)* and 2- and 3-hour evening excursions on Mara Lake depart from the public wharf at the foot of Finlayson Street. Houseboats, which can be rented, are a popular way of touring the arms of Shuswap Lake.

At nearby Adams River almost 10 million scarlet sockeye salmon bury their eggs each October; it is one of the largest spawning grounds in the country. Several spawning grounds can be seen at Roderick Haig-Brown Provincial Park.

Sicamous & District Chamber of Commerce: 110 Finlayson St., P.O. Box 346, Sicamous, BC, Canada V0E 2V0; phone (250) 836-3313.

SIDNEY—see Victoria p. 179.

SMITHERS (D-2)
pop. 5,414, elev. 520 m/1,706'

Named for A.W. Smithers, one-time chairman of the Grand Trunk Pacific Railway, Smithers owes its location to railway construction crews who in 1913 selected the scenic spot at the base of Hudson Bay Mountain. It became a village in 1921 and officially a town in 1967. Today it is a distribution and supply center for local farms, mills and mines. Murals adorn many buildings within its alpine-style Main Street district.

Smithers is popular as a year-round skiing center thanks to 2,652-metre (8,700-ft.) Hudson Bay Mountain. The town also is a convenient starting point for fossil hunting, fishing, mountain climbing and trail riding.

Smithers & District Chamber of Commerce: 1411 Court St., P.O. Box 2379, Smithers, BC, Canada V0J 2N0; phone (250) 847-5072 or (800) 542-6673.

Self-guiding tours: Information about driving and walking tours is available at the chamber of commerce.

SOOKE—see Victoria p. 180.

SPARWOOD (C-12)
pop. 3,812, elev. 1,143 m/3,750'

Once known as a mining town, Sparwood offers guided tours of the Elkview Coal Mine during summer. Popular area recreational activities include fly fishing, white-water rafting, hiking and mountain biking.

Sparwood Chamber of Commerce: 141 Aspen Dr., P.O. Box 1448, Sparwood, BC, Canada V0B 2G0; phone (250) 425-2423 or (877) 485-8185.

SQUAMISH (G-11) pop. 14,247, elev. 5 m/16'

Overshadowed by Stawamus Chief Mountain and other snowcapped peaks, Squamish was named for the Indian word meaning "mother of the wind." It is a popular stopover for tourists and recreation seekers. Rock climbing and windsurfing are popular activities.

Picnic facilities are available 3 kilometres (1.9 mi.) south at Shannon Falls, and camping facilities are available at Alice Lake Park *(see Recreation Chart and the AAA/CAA Western Canada & Alaska CampBook)* 13 kilometres (8 mi.) to the north.

Squamish & Howe Sound Chamber of Commerce: 37950 Cleveland Ave., P.O. Box 1009, Squamish, BC, Canada V0N 3G0; phone (604) 892-9244 or (866) 333-2010 within British Columbia.

GARIBALDI PROVINCIAL PARK is accessible by trail from Hwy. 99 or the British Columbia Railway. The 194,650-hectare (480,980-acre) park is a pristine wilderness of peaks, glaciers, meadows, lakes and streams.

Access to the Garibaldi Lake/Black Tusk Area is by a 7.25-kilometre (5-mi.) trail off Hwy. 99, about 37 kilometres (23 mi.) north of Squamish. A gravel road leads 16 kilometres (10 mi.) to the base camp parking lot, where a trail follows Paul Ridge 11.25 kilometres (7 mi.) to the Diamond Head Area. Glacier-fed Cheakamus Lake lies at an elevation of less than 914 metres (2,999 ft.). The park is open all year and is free. Phone (604) 582-5200 for more information. *See Recreation Chart.*

GLACIER AIR TOURS is at 46001 Government Rd. at Squamish Municipal Airport. Helicopter and airplane sightseeing flights and glacier-landing flights are offered. The latter may include dining on a glacier. Daily 9-7 (departure times vary), May-Oct.; on demand, rest of year. Fares for sightseeing flights start at $75. Reservations are recommended. MC, VI. Phone (604) 898-9016, or (800) 265-0088 within Canada.

WEST COAST RAILWAY HERITAGE PARK is 1 km (.6 mi.) w. off Hwy. 99 on Industrial Way, n. on Queensway Rd. to 39645 Government Rd. This outdoor museum features more than 60 railway heritage pieces dating to the early 1900s. Displays include steam and diesel locomotives, a sleeping car, caboose, bunk cars and a business car. A restoration exhibit demonstrates the process of restoring old railway cars. Visitors can ride a miniature train on a 7.5-gauge track around the property.

Food is available. Allow 30 minutes minimum. Daily 10-5. Miniature train operates daily 11-3. Admission $10; over 59 and ages 6-18, $8.50; family rate $32 (two adults and three children). Miniature railway rides $2. MC, VI. Phone (604) 898-9336.

RECREATIONAL ACTIVITIES
White-water Rafting

- SAVE **Elaho Adventures** is off Upper Squamish Valley Rd. to mile 16.5, following signs. Write P.O. Box 455, Brackendale, BC, Canada V0N 1H0. Daily May 1 through mid-Sept. and mid-Nov. to late Feb. Departure times vary with trip. Reservations are required. Phone (604) 898-4633 or (800) 713-7238.

SUMMERLAND (C-8)
pop. 10,713, elev. 454 m/1,489'

Surrounded by lush orchards and vineyards, Summerland depends on fruit cultivation as its main industry. Overlooking Okanagan Lake *(see Recreation Chart and the AAA/CAA Western Canada & Alaska CampBook)*, the first commercial orchard in the Okanagan Valley was planted in 1890.

Summerland also was the first town on the lake to employ electricity as an energy source; it was generated by a small hydroelectric plant built on the lakeshore in 1905. These and other historical landmarks are the focus of Summerland Museum on Wharton Street.

Fruit stands are the best way to sample the region's bountiful produce. The public can visit a fruit packing facility at B.C. Fruit Packers Co-op on Jubilee Road, depending on availability of fruit in season (usually June through October).

Giants Head Park on 910-metre (2,986-ft.) Giants Head Mountain offers picnic facilities and views of Summerland, the valley below and Okanagan Lake.

Many beaches, including Sunoka, Peach Orchard *(see the AAA/CAA Western Canada & Alaska CampBook)*, Powell and Rotary, line the shores of Okanagan Lake. Also of interest is the Summerland Trout Hatchery, Lakeshore Drive S., where rainbow, brook and Kokanee trout are raised.

Summerland Chamber of Commerce: 15600 Hwy. 97, P.O. Box 130, Summerland, BC, Canada V0H 1Z0; phone (250) 494-2686.

SAVE **KETTLE VALLEY STEAM RAILWAY** is 5 km (3 mi.) w. on Prairie Valley Rd. to 18404 Bathville Rd. Passengers take a 1-hour, 30-minute narrated tour on a portion of the original Kettle Valley Railway Line, which ran from Midway to Hope. The train departs from Prairie Valley Station Thurs.-Mon. at 10:30 and 1:30, July-Aug.; Sat.-Mon. at 10:30 and 1:30, mid-May through June 30

and Sept. 1-second Mon. in Oct. Fare $16; over 64, $15; ages 13-18, $14; ages 3-12, $10; family rate $53. Fares may vary; phone ahead. MC, VI. Phone (250) 494-8422 or (877) 494-8424.

SUMMERLAND ORNAMENTAL GARDENS is s. on Hwy. 97 to 4200 Hwy. 97 on the grounds of Pacific Agri-Foods Research Centre. Established in 1916, the 300-hectare (741-acre) site specializes in Xeriscape landscaping, the use of drought-tolerant plants. English gardens, roses, meadow plants and wetland plants also are cultivated. A butterfly and hummingbird garden is featured. Picnic facilities are available. Allow 1 hour minimum. Daily 8-dusk, Mar.-Nov.; otherwise varies. Admission $3. Phone (250) 494-6385.

SUMMERLAND SWEETS is at 6206 Canyon View Dr. The company offers tours of its factory, where fruit syrups, jams, jelly candies and fruit leather are made from fresh and frozen fruits. Tastings are available. Allow 30 minutes minimum. Tours depart every 30 minutes Mon.-Fri. 10-3:30, June-Aug. Free. Phone (250) 494-0377 or (800) 577-1277.

WINERIES

- **Scherzinger Vineyards Winery** is at 7311 Fiske St. Daily 10-5:30, Apr.-Oct. Hours vary rest of year; phone ahead. Phone (250) 494-8815.

- **Sumac Ridge Estate Winery** is 1 km (.6 mi.) n. at 17403 Hwy. 97. Daily 9-9, Mar.-Dec.; Mon.-Fri. 9-5, Sat.-Sun. 11-5, rest of year. Tours are given daily on the hour 10-4, May-Oct. Phone (250) 494-0451.

SUNSHINE COAST (H-4)

Lining the western edge of the British Columbia mainland, the Sunshine Coast offers a wide variety of marine and land habitats, from coastal rain forests and rocky beaches to an alpine wilderness with peaks reaching 2,500 metres (8,000 ft.).

Powell River *(see place listing p. 138)*, with more than 100 regional dive sites, exceptionally clear water and deep ocean currents, is called the "Dive Capital of Canada." Desolation Sound's warm, sheltered waters also contribute to the destination's popularity with scuba divers and kayakers. Sechelt is known for its rich artisan community, while Gibsons is home to up to 200 bird species throughout the year.

SURREY —*see Vancouver p. 164.*

TELEGRAPH COVE (G-3) pop. 1,600

The bay community served as the northern terminus of the telegraph line along the coast of Vancouver Island and later became a logging and salmon fishing area. Whale watching, fishing and camping are popular during the summer.

STUBBS ISLAND WHALE WATCHING departs from the end of the boardwalk. For excursions on the Johnstone Strait, vessels are equipped with underwater microphones for listening to whale vocalizations. Warm clothing is recommended. Allow 4 hours minimum. Daily departures early June to mid-Oct. Hours vary; phone ahead. Mid-day fare $70; over 64 and ages 1-12, $60. Morning and evening fare $59. Reservations are required. MC, VI. Phone (250) 928-3185 or (800) 665-3066.

TERRACE (D-2) pop. 12,109, elev. 215 m/705′

On the banks of the Skeena River, Terrace is a major producer of forest products. The area provides excellent recreational opportunities ranging from hiking on a variety of trails to fishing in nearby rivers and creeks. Among the region's wildlife is a rare species of black bear, the white Kermodei. Native to the area, it is the city's symbol.

Among the most popular recreation areas are Lakelse Lake (see Recreation Chart and the AAA/CAA Western Canada & Alaska CampBook); Lakelse River, a tributary of the Skeena River that harbors record-size salmon; and Williams Creek, which teems with spawning sockeye each August.

Several places of natural interest are nearby. At the eastern entrance to the city is Ferry Island, a park with hiking trails, swimming and camping (see Recreation Chart). About 20 kilometres (12 mi.) south of Terrace is Mount Layton Hot Springs Resort, which has waterslides and a pool filled with natural hot spring mineral water. Hwy. 16 offers a scenic drive west along the Skeena River to Prince Rupert.

Terrace Visitor InfoCentre: 4511 Keith Ave., Terrace, BC, Canada V8G 1K1; phone (250) 635-2063 or (800) 449-1637.

HERITAGE PARK MUSEUM is at 4702 Kerby Ave. Historic buildings depict the history of pioneers in the region. The structures contain more than 4,000 artifacts pertaining to the life of settlers to the area 1890-1950. Guided tours are available. Allow 1 hour minimum. Daily 10-6, late May-late Aug. Tours are given 10:30-4:30. Admission $4; over 60, students with ID and ages 4-18, $2; family rate $10. Phone (250) 635-4546.

NISGA'A MEMORIAL LAVA BED PROVINCIAL PARK is 4 km (2.5 mi.) w. on Hwy. 16, then 80 km (50 mi.) n. on Kalum Lake Dr. (Nisga'a Hwy.). Drivers should watch for logging trucks.

Miles of lava beds were formed by a volcanic eruption some 250 years ago that destroyed two Nisga'a tribal villages, causing 2,000 deaths. The valley floor resembles the moon's surface. Interpretive trails provide easy access through the park. The New Aiyansh Indian Village, 16 kilometres (10 mi.) north, features totem poles, a tribal council hall and a Nisga'a Lisims government building. Camping is available. Park daily dawn-dusk, May 1 through mid-Oct. Visitor center Wed.-Sun. and holidays 9-5, July-Aug. Guided hiking tours of the volcanic cone are offered on Sat. at 10, July-Aug. Visitor center $2, under 13 free. Park free. Guided hiking tour fee

$14; students with ID $12; under 12, $5. Phone (250) 798-2277.

TOFINO (H-3) pop. 1,466

A fishing and resort village with sandy beaches, Tofino is on the western side of Vancouver Island at the end of Hwy. 4. The area was the site of Fort Defiance, where Boston fur trader Robert Gray and his men spent the winter of 1791. The fort was stripped and abandoned the next spring, and all that remains are scattered bricks and ruins.

Near Clayoquot Sound and the northern end of Pacific Rim National Park Reserve, the town's shoreline and waters are popular with scuba divers and beachcombers. In the spring whales often can be seen migrating along the coast. The Whale Centre and Museum at 411 Campbell St. exhibits scientific and artistic displays, photographs and artifacts depicting past and present whale encounters.

Several companies, including Adventures Pacific, (250) 725-2811; Jamie's Whaling Station, (250) 725-3919; [SAVE] Remote Passages, (250) 725-3330; and Sea Trek Tours and Expeditions, (250) 725-4412, offer whale-watching excursions on Clayoquot Sound. Tours lasting up to 2.5 hours may afford sightings of sea lions, porpoises and eagles. Combination whale-watching and hot springs cruises that last approximately 6.5 hours also are available.

Tofino-Long Beach Chamber of Commerce: 1426 Pacific Rim Hwy., P.O. Box 249, Tofino, BC, Canada V0R 2Z0; phone (250) 725-3414.

TRAIL (D-10) pop. 7,575, elev. 430 m/1,410′

At City Hall a sculptured screen titled "City of Lead and Zinc" illustrates how Trail's mineral and industrial strength steadily developed since the discovery of gold and copper in the area about 1890. Hydroelectric dams along the Kootenay River power extensive mining and smelting operations, dominated by Teck Cominco Ltd.

Trail and District Chamber of Commerce and Visitor InfoCentre: 1199 Bay Ave., Suite 200, Trail, BC, Canada V1R 4A4; phone (250) 368-3144.

Self-guiding tours: Brochures for walking tours are available at the chamber of commerce.

TECK COMINCO LTD. tours depart from the Interpretive Centre downtown at 1199 Bay Ave., Suite 200. Guided tours are offered of one of the largest lead-zinc smelters in the world. Long pants, long-sleeved shirts and closed shoes are required; cameras and video equipment are prohibited. Individuals with pacemakers should not attend. Allow 2 hours minimum. Center open daily 9-5, July-Aug.; Mon.-Fri. 9-5, rest of year. Tours depart Mon.-Fri. at 10, June-Aug.; by appointment rest of year. Closed major holidays. Free. Under 12 are not permitted on tours. Phone (250) 368-3144.

UCLUELET (I-3) pop. 1,559

On Barkley Sound, Ucluelet was named for an Indian word meaning "safe harbor." Charter boats for salmon fishing, whale watching, skin diving and nature excursions are available; phone the chamber of commerce. The MV *Lady Rose* makes round trips between Port Alberni and Ucluelet June through September *(see attraction listing in Port Alberni p. 137)*. He Tin Kis Park allows visitors to experience a Canadian rain forest and follow a boardwalk trail that leads to the ocean. The 5-kilometre (3-mi.) Wild Pacific Trail passes a lighthouse en route to cliffside ocean views.

Ucluelet Chamber of Commerce: 100 Main St., P.O. Box 428, Ucluelet, BC, Canada V0R 3A0; phone (250) 726-4641.

VALEMOUNT (F-6)
pop. 1,195, elev. 792 m/2,600'

Valemount, the valley in the mountains, offers many activities for outdoor enthusiasts. The village, where the Rocky, Cariboo and Monashee mountain ranges meet, is popular for both summer and winter pursuits, including hiking, rafting, skiing and snowmobiling. The area is rich with birds and other wildlife. Off Hwy. 16 is Mount Terry Fox Provincial Park. A viewing area affords vistas of the peak named for the late athlete.

Village of Valemount Visitor Information Centre: 99 Gorse St., P.O. Box 168, Valemount, BC, Canada V0E 2Z0; phone (250) 566-4846, or (250) 566-9893 mid-June to mid-Sept.

GEORGE HICKS REGIONAL PARK is off Hwy. 5. The site offers a bird's-eye view of Chinook salmon as they near the end of a 1,280-kilometre (768-mi.)

upstream trip from mid-August to mid-September. Daily 24 hours. Donations. Phone (250) 566-9893.

 MOUNT ROBSON PROVINCIAL PARK is on Hwy. 16. Mount Robson, at 3,954 metres (12,972 ft.) is the highest peak in the Canadian Rockies. Other park highlights include glacier-fed lakes, valleys, canyons, waterfalls, rivers and streams. More than 180 species of birds reside here along with deer, moose, bears, elk, caribou, mountain goats and mountain sheep. Fishing, swimming, hiking, horseshoes, volleyball and a children's play area are just a few of the outdoor activities to be enjoyed.

Scenic views abound on the many walking and hiking trails. A visitor center is at the Mount Robson viewpoint. Picnicking and swimming are permitted. Park open daily 24 hours. Visitor center open May-Sept. Donations. Phone (250) 566-4325. *See Recreation Chart and the AAA/CAA Western Canada & Alaska CampBook.*

R.W. STARRATT WILDLIFE SANCTUARY is 1 km (.6 mi.) s. on Hwy. 5. The refuge is home to a variety of songbirds, waterfowl and other animals. Informational signs line a trail to two viewing platforms. Allow 30 minutes minimum. Daily 24 hours. Free. Phone (250) 566-9893.

RECREATIONAL ACTIVITIES
Winter Activities

- **Robson Helimagic Sightseeing Tours** is 5 km (3 mi.) n. on Hwy. 5 to 3010 Selwyn Rd. Write P.O. Box 18, Valemount, BC, Canada V0E 2Z0. Daily 8-dusk. Phone (250) 566-4700 or (877) 454-4700.

Vancouver

A great port, cultural center and tourist area, Vancouver is the crown jewel of western Canada. The city is dotted lavishly with greenery, posed against the rugged peaks of the perpetually blue Coast Range and ringed with sparkling Pacific waters. Although many think Vancouver occupies Vancouver Island, the city is on the mainland; Vancouver Island lies across the Strait of Georgia and on the island is the provincial capital of Victoria.

The first recorded exploration of the Strait of Georgia and English Bay was made by Don José Narváez in 1791. The second was by Capt. George Vancouver, who sailed into Burrard Inlet in 1792 while searching for the legendary Northwest Passage. At the time of his arrival, the area was a seasonal home for First Nations peoples. Fur traders followed Vancouver; in 1858 came the prospectors in the wake of a gold strike.

A wild community sprang up on the peninsula between the Fraser River and Burrard Inlet. Later that year Royal Engineers sent to keep law and order named the settlement Queensborough. Queensborough became New Westminster, now part of the Vancouver metropolitan area.

Settlers gradually drifted in to populate other parts of the peninsula, and in April 1886, Vancouver, with a population of 2,000, formally became a city. Two months later a fire destroyed the community and caused an estimated $1.3 million in damage. Undaunted by the disaster, residents began rebuilding, and by the year's end the reconstructed community housed approximately 2,500 people.

Two milestones marked Vancouver's rapid progress. On May 23, 1887, the first passenger train to cross the vast Canadian expanses from the East chugged into the city and belched soot and cinders onto an exuberant crowd. In 1891 the great white ships of the Canadian Pacific fleet sailed into Burrard Inlet to inaugurate transpacific shipping and to mark Vancouver as a major world port. The population mushroomed to 100,000 by 1900.

Vancouver has expanded to cover most of the peninsula between Fraser River and Burrard Inlet. Bordered by the Coastal Mountain Range, the downtown area occupies a tiny peninsula jutting into the inlet, with the magnificent harbor to the east and beautiful English Bay to the west. Broad beaches along English Bay enable office workers to join the bathers during lunch hours.

Behind the beaches rise pastel apartment buildings and fine old houses, some with a Tudor influence. Within walking distance is the busy waterfront, where ships of many nations discharge passengers, unload cargo or fill up for the return voyage. Vancouver also is the main terminal for cruise ships traveling to Alaska. Towering bridges link the downtown area with the city and suburbs.

© Gibson Stock Photography

Downtown / © Gibson Stock Photography

Atop suburban Burnaby Mountain is Simon Fraser University, British Columbia's instant university. Constructed in only 18 months, it is a bold concept of integrated design, with buildings executed in natural materials for a classic effect. One of the most beautifully located universities in North America is the University of British Columbia; from a forested campus its Gothic buildings overlook the Strait of Georgia while the North Shore Mountains form a distant backdrop.

Vancouver's character is West Coast with a liberal Oriental essence. The city's Chinatown is second only to San Francisco's in size in North America. Visitors to Vancouver can watch an engaging cricket match, celebrate Chinese New Year or enjoy a colorful Japanese summer festival—all without leaving town.

Vancouver is a big city—the financial, industrial, shipping and cultural center of Canada's west coast. Rapid growth has been tempered by the gentler influences of the arts and sciences. The city has much that is reminiscent of other parts of Canada and much of Europe as well as the Orient and the United States. The resulting blend is happy, carefree and relaxed.

Approaches

By Car

Hwy. 1 and hwys. 1A and 7 are the major east-west routes to Vancouver. To reach downtown on the Trans-Canada Hwy., use the First Avenue exit or continue to Hastings Street.

Hwy. 99 to S.W. Marine West becomes the major downtown artery, Granville Street. Before becoming a city street, Hwy. 99 begins its journey as I-5 at the Mexican border and crosses through California and the Pacific Northwest.

Aquabus Ltd., (604) 689-5858, provides ferry service between Granville Island, Hornby Street, Yaletown, Stamps Landing and Science World daily 7 a.m.-8 p.m. Times vary according to destination. Fare ranges from $2-$5. The Aquabus from Granville Island to Hornby Street is equipped to carry bicycles for an extra 50c.

Getting Around

Street System

All streets and avenues in Vancouver are named; many are one-way. Outside the business section, east-west avenues are numbered beginning with First Avenue, and north-south streets are named. Addresses begin at Ontario-Carrall streets for all east-west numbering and at Powell-Dundas streets for all north-south numbering.

The downtown peninsula is connected to western Vancouver by the Burrard, Granville and Cambie bridges and to North Vancouver and West Vancouver

(continued on p. 151)

The Informed Traveler

City Population: 545,671

Elevation: 3 m/10 ft.

Sales Tax: British Columbia's provincial sales tax is 7.5 percent. A room tax of 10 percent on lodgings also is levied in the Vancouver area.

WHOM TO CALL

Emergency: 911

Police (non-emergency): (604) 717-3321

Time and Temperature: (604) 664-9010

Hospitals: Mount Saint Joseph Hospital Site, (604) 874-1141; Vancouver Hospital and Health Sciences Centre, (604) 875-4111; Vancouver Hospital and Health Sciences Centre-UBC, (604) 822-7121.

WHERE TO LOOK

Newspapers

The two major daily newspapers, both published in the morning, are the *Province* and the *Vancouver Sun*.

Radio

Vancouver radio stations CBU-AM (690), CBU-FM (105.7), CHQM-FM (103.5), CKCL-FM (104.9), CKLG-FM (96.9) and CKWX-AM (1130) have news and weather reports.

Visitor Information

Vancouver Tourist InfoCentre: 200 Burrard St., Plaza Level, Vancouver, BC, Canada V6C 3L6; phone (604) 683-2000.

Maps, lodging reservations and literature about attractions as well as tickets for tours are available at the Vancouver Tourist Info-Centre which is open daily 8:30-6, Victoria Day weekend through mid-Sept.; Mon.-Sat. 8:30-5, rest of year.

TRANSPORTATION

Air Travel

Vancouver International Airport is reached via Granville St. and the Arthur Lang Bridge, then Sea Island Way, which leads into Grant McConachie Way. Vancouver Airporter buses run every 15 minutes 6 a.m.-midnight. One-way bus service departs most major downtown hotels every 30 minutes. The fare is $12, round trip $18; phone (604) 946-8866 or (800) 668-3141. Taxis average $26 one-way.

Rental Cars

Hertz, at 1128 Seymour St., offers discounts to AAA and CAA members; phone (604) 606-4711, (800) 263-0600 in Canada, or (800) 654-3080 out of Canada. Additional agencies are listed in the telephone directory.

Rail Service

The Via Rail passenger train terminal is at 1150 Station St.; phone (888) 842-7245 in Canada or in the United States.

Buses

The bus terminal is at 1150 Station St.; phone (604) 482-8747.

Taxis

Fares start at $2.56, plus $1.40 per kilometre (.6 mi.). Companies include Black Top, (604) 731-1111; MacLure's, (604) 731-9211; Yellow Cab, (604) 681-1111; and Vancouver Taxi, (604) 255-5111.

Public Transport

Translink offers bus service as well as SeaBus and SkyTrain service. *See Public Transportation for details.*

Boats

BC Ferries links Vancouver Island with the rest of the province. Nanaimo and Sunshine Coast ferries leave from Horseshoe Bay, 21 kilometres (13 mi.) west of the city in West Vancouver. From Tsawwassen south of Vancouver automobile/passenger ferries make frequent trips to the southern Gulf Islands, Nanaimo and Swartz Bay, north of Victoria; Vancouver-Victoria bus service is available on most sailings.

For schedules phone the British Columbia Automobile Association, (604) 268-5555, British Columbia Ferries Information Centre, (250) 386-3431 outside British Columbia, (888) 223-3779 in British Columbia, or Tourism Vancouver, (604) 683-2000.

Destination Vancouver

The nuances of cosmopolitan Vancouver's multiple cultures are revealed through the arts, in neighborhood preservation and by observing the lifestyle enjoyed by residents.

You'll find ambience in green spaces and historic places; at galleries and gardens; and on beaches, bays and gap-spanning bridges.

Vancouver Children's Festival.
Thousands of young people flock to this week-long celebration of the performing arts. (See mention page 159)

Grouse Mountain, North Vancouver.
An aerial tramway takes visitors to the summit, which offers a panoramic view of the city. (See listing page 163)

Vancouver Aquarium Marine Science Centre

Vancouver Aquarium Marine Science Centre.
Beluga whales are among the permanent residents here. (See listing page 154)

Science World, Vancouver.
Designed for Expo '86, this striking geodesic dome houses hands-on exhibits and a movie theater. (See listing page 153)

Places included in this AAA Destination City:

2122-M © AAA

by the Lions Gate and the Iron Workers Memorial (Second Narrows) bridges.

Rush hours are 6-9:30 a.m. and 3-6:30 p.m. Right turns on red are permitted after a stop, unless otherwise posted; drivers must yield to pedestrians and vehicles in the intersection and to city buses pulling into traffic.

Parking

On-street parking, controlled by meter, is restricted on many thoroughfares during rush hours; violators' cars will be towed. Off-street parking is available in lots and garages at rates ranging from $1.25 per half-hour to $11 or more per day. Parking in a school zone between 8 and 5 on any school day is strictly prohibited unless otherwise posted.

Public Transportation

Translink offers bus service to points throughout Vancouver and to all suburban areas; it also offers SeaBus and SkyTrain service as well as the West Coast Express commuter rail.

One-way bus fare within the city ranges from $2-$9.25. Exact change is required. Rush hour fares are higher. All-day passes, available from SkyTrain and SeaBus ticket machines, Safeway food stores and 7-11 stores, cost $8, senior citizens $6.

SeaBus service conveys commuters between North Vancouver and the city of Vancouver, connecting with the bus system at the foot of Granville Street; phone (604) 953-3333 daily 6:30 a.m.-11:30 p.m. for more information.

SkyTrain, Vancouver's rapid transit system, runs from Waterfront Station through downtown Vancouver to the suburbs of Burnaby and New Westminster and across the Fraser River to the suburb of Surrey. Trains operate every 5 minutes 5:30 a.m.-1:30 a.m. A 1-Zone fare (within Vancouver) is $2, 2-Zone fare is $3 and 3-Zone fare is $4. Fares are subject to change. Every SkyTrain station has information panels; phone (604) 953-3333.

What To See

B.C. SPORTS HALL OF FAME AND MUSEUM is at jct. Beatty and Robson sts., Gate A of the B.C. Place Stadium. The history of sports in British Columbia is traced from First Nations traditions to modern Olympic games. Honorees include amateur and professional teams, athletes, journalists and sports pioneers. Interactive galleries provide opportunities for running, climbing, throwing, riding and rowing. Rotating exhibits, a sports library and a stadium tour also are featured.

Daily 10-5. Admission $6, senior citizens and students $4, under 5 free, family rate $15. Half-price to B.C. Place Stadium or General Motors Place ticket-holders. Phone (604) 687-5520.

BLOEDEL CONSERVATORY— *see Queen Elizabeth Park p. 153.*

CHINATOWN—*see Shopping p. 159.*

CHRIST CHURCH CATHEDRAL is at 690 Burrard St. One of Vancouver's oldest stone churches, the cathedral is adorned with English and Canadian stained-glass windows. Mon.-Fri. 10-noon and 1-4. Donations. Phone (604) 682-3848.

SAVE **CN IMAX THEATRE AT CANADA PLACE** is at 201-999 Canada Pl. Various IMAX films are presented on a screen five stories tall. Three-dimensional movies are shown periodically. Food is available. Allow 1 hour minimum. Daily on the hour 11-10, July-Aug.; noon-9, rest of year. Admission $11; over 65, $10; ages 3-12, $9. AX, MC, VI. Phone (604) 682-4629 or (800) 582-4629.

SAVE **DR. SUN YAT-SEN CLASSICAL CHINESE GARDEN** is at 578 Carrall St. in the heart of Chinatown. The site is modeled after private classical gardens in the city of Suzhou during the 1368-1644 Ming Dynasty. Most of the garden's elements—from hand-fired roof tiles, carved woodwork and lattice windows to courtyard pebbles—are from China. Art and horticultural exhibits and demonstrations also are offered. Festivals and concerts are featured throughout the year.

Guided tours are available. Allow 30 minutes minimum. Daily 9:30-7, June 15-Aug. 31; daily 10-6, May 1-June 14 and in Sept.; Tues.-Sun. 10-4:30, rest of year. Closed Jan.1 and Dec. 25. Admission $8.75; over 65, $7; ages 5-17, $6; family

rate $18. Admission price includes a tour and tea. Phone (604) 662-3207.

HOLY ROSARY CATHEDRAL is at 646 Richards St. The church has stained-glass windows and eight bells hung in the rare English ringing style. Cathedral open Mon.-Sat. 6:15-6, Sun. 7 a.m.-9:30 p.m. Bell ringing Sun. at 10:30, Tues. at 7:30 p.m. Free. Phone (604) 682-6774.

H.R. MacMILLAN SPACE CENTRE is at 1100 Chestnut St. in Vanier Park. The Virtual Voyages motion simulator is among the interactive exhibits and games featured at the center. The Planetarium Star Theatre and GroundStation Canada present laser light shows and programs dealing with astronomy, solar history and space explorations.

Allow 1 hour, 30 minutes minimum. Daily 10-5, July-Aug.; Tues.-Sun. 10-5, rest of year. Laser shows Thurs.-Sat. at 9:30 p.m. (also Fri.-Sat. at 10:45 p.m.). Closed Dec. 25. Show times may vary; phone for schedule. Admission $13.50; over 64 and ages 11-18, $10.50; ages 5-10, $9.50. Laser light show $9.35. AX, MC, VI. Phone (604) 738-7827.

OLD HASTINGS MILL STORE MUSEUM is at 1575 Alma St. in Hastings Mill Park. The mill was the first industrial facility on the south shore of what is now Vancouver. One of the few buildings to withstand the ravages of the 1886 fire, it contains relics of early Vancouver. Guided tours are offered by appointment. Allow 30 minutes minimum. Tues.-Sun. 11-4, mid-June to mid-Sept.; Sat.-Sun. 1-4, rest of year. Donations. Phone (604) 734-1212.

PACIFIC NATIONAL EXHIBITION is on E. Hastings St. between Renfrew and Cassiar sts. The site occupies 58 hectares (144 acres) and is home to Pacific Coliseum, a tradeshow and entertainment complex, and a skateboard park. The Pacific National Exhibition Fair is held in late August. Various trade and hobby shows, rock concerts and sporting events are scheduled throughout the year. Food is available. Fair daily 11-11, mid-Aug. through Labour Day. Last admission 1 hour, 30 minutes before closing. Fair admission $10; ages 6-13, $8; over 64, $5. Phone (604) 253-2311.

Playland Amusement Park is on E. Hastings St. between Renfrew and Cassiar sts. The 4-hectare (10-acre) park features games, miniature golf and rides, including a large wooden roller coaster and three "extreme rides."

Daily 11 a.m.-midnight, late Aug.-Labour Day; daily 11-9, mid-June to late Aug.; Sat.-Sun. and holidays 11-7, mid-Apr. to mid-June and day after Labour Day-late Sept. (weather permitting). Park admission $24.95, under 122 centimetres (48 in.) tall $11.95, over 60 and under age 3 free. Parents $11.95 when accompanied by a paying child under 13. AX, MC, VI. Phone (604) 253-2311.

QUEEN ELIZABETH PARK is off Cambie St. and W. 33rd Ave. On 167-metre (548-ft.) Little Mountain, the highest point in Vancouver, the park offers magnificent views of the city, harbor and North Shore mountains. Other highlights include an arboretum; rose, sunken and quarry gardens; tennis courts; and pitch and putt greens. Daily 24 hours. Free.

SAVE **Bloedel Conservatory** is at 33rd Ave. and Cambie St. Climatically varied species of plants grow in a climate-controlled, illuminated triodetic dome 43 metres (141 ft.) in diameter and 21 metres (70 ft.) high. Tropical birds and a fish pond are other highlights. Allow 30 minutes minimum. Mon.-Fri. 9-8, Sat.-Sun. 10-9, Apr.-Sept.; Mon.-Fri. 10-5, rest of year. Closed Dec. 25. Admission $3.97; ages 13-18, $3.05; over 64, $2.80; ages 6-12, $1.96. MC, VI. Phone (604) 257-8570.

ST. ANDREW'S-WESLEY CHURCH is at 1012 Nelson St. The Gothic structure includes many stained-glass windows. Mon.-Fri. 10-4, July-Aug. Phone (604) 683-4574.

SCIENCE WORLD is at 1455 Quebec St. Hands-on exhibits and demonstrations explain scientific phenomena. The Eureka Gallery explores such themes as water, air, motion and invention. The Weyerhaeuser Science Theatre features a variety of high-definition video shows throughout the day. The Centre Stage presents science demonstrations daily. Human performance and nature are the subjects of additional galleries. The Kidspace Gallery features activities for children ages 2 through 6. Also of interest is the Alcan OMNIMAX theater that presents nature and science films.

Food is available. Allow 2 hours minimum. Daily 10-6, late June-Labour Day; Mon.-Fri. 10-5, Sat.-Sun. and holidays 10-6, rest of year. Exhibits and Science Theatre $13.95; over 64, students with ID and ages 4-18, $9.50. Exhibits, Science Theatre and one OMNIMAX film $17.75; over 64, students with ID and ages 4-18, $13.50. OMNIMAX only $11.25; over 64, students with ID and ages 4-18, $9. Parking $3-$7. Rates may vary; phone ahead. MC, VI. Phone (604) 443-7443.

STORYEUM is at 142 Water St. An elevator lowers visitors to a series of underground theaters. The 70-minute guided tour includes a multimedia presentation with a musical score and offers education and insight into British Columbia's past. Interactive displays and costumed actors convey key historical moments. Allow 2 hours, 30 minutes minimum. Tours are given daily on the half-hour 11-8, May-Oct.; daily on the hour 10-6, rest of year. Admission May-Oct. $22; over 64 and ages 13-18, $19; ages 6-12, $16. Admission rest of year $20; over 64 and ages 13-18, $18; ages 6-12, $15. AX, DC, DS, JC, MC, VI. Phone (604) 687-8142 or (800) 687-8142. *See color ad p. 152.*

STANLEY PARK is on the peninsula near the business district. Covering 405 hectares (1,000 acres) in downtown Vancouver, the urban oasis is considered one of the finest natural parks on the continent. Visitors can lawn bowl, watch a cricket match, swim, golf, play tennis or checkers, jog, or go bicycling over some of the 80 kilometres (50 mi.) of roads and trails.

Also featured are a children's farmyard, rose garden, miniature steam railway and totem pole displays. Shows are presented at the open-air theater at Malkin Bowl in July and August. An information booth is in the lower farmyard parking lot on Park Drive just off the Georgia Street entrance. A free shuttle travels between the park's most popular destinations in summer; the shuttles depart from the miniature railway parking lot.

Park open daily 24 hours. Information booth open 10-5, June 15-Sept. 15; 10-4, May 1-June 14 and Sept. 16-second Mon. in Oct. Booth hours may vary; phone ahead. Children's farmyard and railway daily 11-4, June 1-early Sept. and during the holiday season; Sat.-Sun. 11-4, Mar.-May (weather permitting). Shuttle daily 10-6:30, mid-June to mid-Sept. Park admission free. Farmyard and railway each $5; ages 13-18, $3.75; over 64, $3.50; ages 2-12, $2.50; family rate is available. Rates may vary; phone ahead. Phone (604) 257-8531 for railway.

Stanley Park Horse-drawn Tours depart from beside the information booth on Park Dr. off the

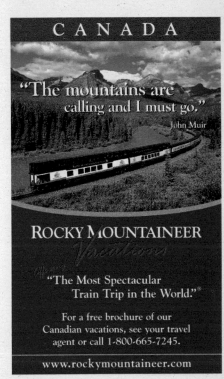

Georgia St. entrance. The narrated, 1-hour tour highlights the park's points of interest. Tours depart daily every 20-30 minutes 9:30-5:30, July 1-Labour Day; 9:40-5, Apr.-June and day after Labour Day-Sept. 30; 9:40-4, Mar. 15-31 and in Oct.; 10:30-3, Mar. 1-14. Fare $22.42; over 65 and students with ID $19.99; ages 3-12, $13.50. DC, MC, VI. Phone (604) 681-5115.

Vancouver Aquarium Marine Science Centre is at 845 Avison Way. More than 60,000 marine animals are exhibited, with emphasis on such diverse habitats as the Canadian Arctic, the Amazon Rain Forest and the Pacific Northwest. Sharks, moray eels and colorful fish populate the Tropic Zone, while the Strait of Georgia exhibit features divers interacting with marine life. Programs allowing animal encounters with sea lions, seals, otters and beluga whales are available for an additional fee.

Walk the BC Hydro Salmon Stream in Stanley Park to learn about a salmon's incredible life journey. Other highlights include daily whale and dolphin shows, shark dives and sea otter feedings as well as exhibits that feature sea lions and harbor seals.

Food is available. Allow 2 hours minimum. Daily 9:30-7, late June-Labour Day; 10-5:30, rest of year. Admission $16.12; over 64, students with ID and ages 13-18, $12.15; ages 4-12, $9.36. AX, MC, VI. Phone (604) 659-3474. *See color ad.*

Welcome to our world.

Meet sea otters, sharks, beluga whales and more, just minutes from downtown in famous Stanley Park. Open every day. 604-659-FISH or www.vanaqua.org

vancouver
AQUARIUM

UNIVERSITY OF BRITISH COLUMBIA is on Point Grey. Encompassing 2,470 hectares (6,103 acres) overlooking the Strait of Georgia, the university is the largest in the province.

The Pacific Museum of the Earth is just off the West Mall of the university on the main floor of the Earth and Ocean Science Building at 6339 Stores Rd. A highlight of the 30,000-piece mineral and fossil collection is an 80 million-year-old Lambeosaurus dinosaur. Also featured are a 7-foot-long amethyst tube and a large sedimentary structure. Allow 30 minutes minimum. Mon.-Fri. 9-5; closed statutory holidays. Donations. Phone (604) 822-6992.

UBC Botanical Garden is at 6804 S.W. Marine Dr. More than 10,000 plants from around the world are cultivated on 28 hectares (69 acres). Themed gardens include Asian, alpine, winter, perennial, food, medicinal and native plantings. Nitobe Memorial Garden, one of the most accurately represented Japanese gardens in North America, features a tea garden and stroll garden with seasonal displays of irises, Japanese maples and flowering cherries.

Allow 1 hour minimum. Main garden open daily 10-6. Nitobe Memorial Garden open daily 10-6, mid-Mar. to mid-Oct.; Mon.-Fri. 10-2:30, rest of year. Main garden $5, non-UBC students $2. Nitobe Memorial Garden $3; over 64, $2; non-UBC students $1.50. Phone (604) 822-9666.

UBC Museum of Anthropology is at 6393 N.W. Marine Dr. on the Point Grey Cliffs. Traditional post and beam construction is reflected in this striking concrete and glass building, which houses a major collection of Northwest Coast First Nations artwork. Displays include totem poles, feast dishes and canoes as well as artifacts from around the world. European ceramics also are displayed.

Allow 1 hour minimum. Daily 10-5 (also Tues. 5-9), Victoria Day-Labour Day; Tues.-Sun. 11-5 (also Tues. 5-9), rest of year. Closed Dec. 25-26. Admission $9; over 64, students with ID and ages 7-18, $7. MC, VI. Phone (604) 822-3825.

VANCOUVER AQUARIUM MARINE SCIENCE CENTRE—see Stanley Park p. 154.

VANCOUVER ART GALLERY is at 750 Hornby St. One of the largest art galleries in Western Canada features a full range of national and international art by contemporary artists and major historical figures. Allow 1 hour minimum. Daily 10-5:30 (also Thurs. 5:30-9), Apr.-Oct.; Tues.-Sun. 10-5:30 (also Thurs. 5:30-9), rest of year. Closed Jan. 1 and Dec. 25. Admission $15; over 64, $11; students with ID $10; under 12 free; by donation Thurs. 5-9. AX, MC, VI. Phone (604) 662-4719.

VANCOUVER LOOKOUT AT HARBOUR CENTRE is at 555 W. Hastings St. Two glass elevators ascend the outside of this tower, which is crowned with an observation deck that offers a spectacular panoramic view of the city and outlying districts. Hourly guided tours point out the city's landmarks; video kiosks, Internet terminals and information stations provide additional highlights. The complex includes a revolving restaurant and a shopping mall.

Allow 30 minutes minimum. Skylift elevator runs daily 8:30 a.m.-10:30 p.m., May-Oct.; 9-9, rest of year. Admission $9.35; over 60, $8.41; ages 11-17, $6.54; ages 5-10, $3.74. Rates may vary; phone ahead. Phone (604) 689-0421.

VANCOUVER MARITIME MUSEUM is at 1905 Ogden Ave. at n. foot of Chestnut and Cypress sts. Model ships, naval uniforms and other artifacts relate to man's interaction with the sea. Historic vessels are displayed outside in the harbor. The Alcan Children's Maritime Discovery Centre features hands-on activities to introduce youngsters to ships and pirates of the sea.

Allow 1 hour minimum. Daily 10-5, Victoria Day-Labour Day; Tues.-Sun. 10-5, rest of year. Museum admission (including the *St. Roch* National Historic Site) $8; over 64 and ages 6-19, $5.50; family rate $18. MC, VI. Phone (604) 257-8300.

***St. Roch* National Historic Site** is next to the Vancouver Maritime Museum. During World War II the *St. Roch* became the first vessel to travel from the Pacific to the Atlantic via the treacherous Northwest Passage in the Arctic; it completed the round trip in 1944. After the war, the schooner reached its destination via the Panama Canal, becoming the first ship to circumnavigate the North American continent. Preserved in dry dock, the vessel is displayed as it appeared in 1944.

Allow 1 hour minimum. Daily 10-4. Admission is included in the Vancouver Maritime Museum charge. Phone (604) 257-8300.

VANCOUVER MUSEUM is at the s.w. end of Burrard St. in Vanier Park at 1100 Chestnut St. Devoted to the art, natural history, anthropology and history of the lower mainland, the museum displays regional artifacts including pieces from First Nations peoples as well as ancient and contemporary objects from around the world. Daily 10-5, July 1-Sept. 5; Tues.-Sun. 10-5 (also Thurs. 5-9), rest of year. Closed Dec. 25. Admission $10; over 64, $8; ages 5-19, $6. MC, VI. Phone (604) 736-4431.

VANDUSEN BOTANICAL GARDEN is at 5251 Oak St. at W. 37th Ave. The 22-hectare (55-acre) area has an outstanding plant collection arranged to show geographical origin and botanical relationships. Gardens are set amid lawns, lakes and rock displays with vistas of the mountains and city. A hedge maze provides entertainment for children.

Food is available. Allow 1 hour minimum. Daily 10-9, June 1 through mid-Aug.; 10-8, mid-Aug. through Labour Day and in May; 10-6, day after Labour Day-Sept. 30 and in Apr.; 10-4, rest of year. Closed Dec. 25. Admission Apr.-Sept. $7; over 64

and ages 13-18, $5; ages 6-12, $3.50. Admission rest of year $5; over 64 and ages 13-18, $3.50; ages 6-12, $2. MC, VI. Phone (604) 878-9274.

What To Do

Sightseeing

Opportunities to watch bustling harbor activities are available at several vantage points in Vancouver. Seaplanes, barges, tugboats, cargo ships, ferries and the SeaBus can be observed from Granville Square at the foot of Granville Street; from Canada Place at the foot of Howe St.; from Lonsdale Quay at the foot of Lonsdale Ave.; and from Stanley Park. Fine views of the city, sea and mountains are available at CypressBowl, Simon Fraser University atop Burnaby Mountain, Grouse Mountain and Queen Elizabeth Park.

Boat Tours

HARBOUR CRUISES departs from the n. foot of Denman St., next to Stanley Park. Scenic 75-minute harbor tours are offered aboard an authentic paddlewheeler. Lunch and dinner cruises and an excursion to Bowen Island, off the coast of British Columbia, also are available.

Harbor tours board daily at 11:30, 1 and 2:30, mid-May to mid-Sept.; at 2:30, April 1 through mid-May and mid-Sept. through Oct. 31. Harbour tours $19; over 59 and ages 12-17, $16; ages 5-11, $7. Schedule and fares may vary; phone ahead. Phone (604) 688-7246 or (800) 663-1500. *See color ad.*

Bus Tours

SAVE Gray Line of Vancouver *(see color ad)* offers daily tours of Victoria, Whistler, the North Shore and other destinations departing from the Plaza of Nations at 700 Pacific Blvd. Its double-decker buses make a continuous loop past more than 21 attractions, allowing sightseers to reboard for 2 days. Phone Gray Line at (604) 879-3363 or (800) 667-0882.

West Coast City and Nature Sightseeing Ltd. features sightseeing trips of the city and its surrounding natural areas in 12- to 30-passenger minibuses. Full-day trips to Victoria and the Whistler resort area also are available; phone (604) 451-1600 or (604) 451-1777.

Industrial Tours

Tours are available of the Vancouver Post Office, (604) 662-5715, 349 W. Georgia St. Reservations are required.

Plane Tours

Another way to see Vancouver and its surroundings is by air. Harbour Air offers flights lasting from 35 minutes to 1.25 hours; departure is from downtown on Coal Harbour Rd., one block west of Canada Place. Fares vary, and reservations are required; phone (604) 274-1277.

Train Tours

Rocky Mountaineer Vacations *(see color ad p. 153)* offers scenic, 2-day, all daylight, narrated rail tours between Vancouver, British Columbia, and

Banff, Calgary, or Jasper, Alberta. Westbound or eastbound departures are offered mid-April to mid-October, with winter rail trips available in December. Onboard meals and snacks as well as overnight hotel accommodations in Kamloops are included. Phone (604) 606-7245 or (877) 460-3200.

Trolley Tours

Trolley tours provide a look at the city at a relaxed pace. The Downtown Historic Railway, comprised of two electric interurban railcars, skirts False Creek between Science World and Granville Island and runs from mid-May to mid-October; phone (604) 665-3903.

THE VANCOUVER TROLLEY CO. departs from many downtown accommodations and attractions. Narrated tours highlight Vancouver's major attractions. Passengers may board, depart or reboard at any stop on the route. Allow 2 hours minimum. Daily 8:40-6, Apr. 1-late Oct.; 9-4:30, rest of year. A 4-hour sunset tour leaves for Grouse Mountain at 6:15, mid-June to mid-Sept. Day tour pass, valid for one full circuit, $30; ages 4-12, $15. Sunset tour $55; senior citizens $52; ages 13-18, $48; ages 4-12, $30. A combination ticket is available. Phone (604) 801-5515 or (888) 451-5581. *See color ad.*

Sports and Recreation

Vancouver offers such a diversity of recreational opportunities that anyone with a yen for variety can ski on Grouse Mountain in the morning, golf on the banks of the Fraser River in the afternoon, fish for salmon in Horseshoe Bay at dusk and top off the day with a dip in English Bay.

Vancouver's park system has tennis courts, swimming pools, putting greens, golf courses, lawn bowling greens, hiking paths and a comprehensive

bike route. For park information phone the Vancouver Park Board at (604) 257-8400.

Swimming is available along English Bay, which is bordered by beaches from West Point Grey to Stanley Park. Beaches are easily accessible from Northwest Marine Drive in West Point Grey, Point Grey Road in Vancouver West and from Beach Avenue downtown.

White-water rafting is available April through September on the nearby Chilliwack River and a little farther afield on the Lillooet, Fraser and Thompson rivers. Vancouver rafting companies offering day trips as well as multiday trips include REO Rafting Adventure Resort, (604) 461-7238 or (800) 736-7238, and Kumsheen Raft Adventures, (250) 455-2296 or (800) 663-6667. Lotus Land Tours offers **sea kayaking** trips on Indian Arm and **whale-watching** tours from Steveston; phone (604) 684-4922 or (800) 528-3531.

Winter visitors with a penchant for **skiing** can tackle the challenging slopes of Grouse Mountain or Mount Seymour Park in North Vancouver. East of Vancouver are Hemlock Valley and Manning Park ski resorts, offering both downhill and cross-country treks. Cypress Provincial Park in West Vancouver also has cross-country and downhill skiing *(see Recreation Chart)*. Skiers can head north of Vancouver to Whistler and Blackcomb Mountains; site of the 2010 Olympic and Paralympic Winter Games.

When the waters sparkle from the summer sun, Vancouver becomes a **boating** paradise. For visitors without a boat, several companies have craft for hourly or daily rental. For charter yachts phone Harbour Cruises, (604) 688-7246, or Westin Bayshore Yacht Charters, (604) 691-6936. For **fishing** charters and boat rentals phone Sewell's Ltd., (604) 921-3474, at Horseshoe Bay.

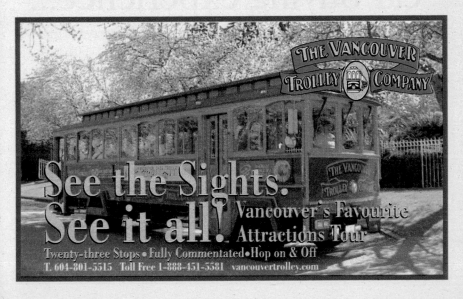

Vancouver residents love spectator sports, especially **football, hockey** and **soccer.** The B.C. Lions of the Canadian Football League play before capacity crowds in B.C. Place Stadium. The Canucks of the National Hockey League compete in General Motors Place. For football and hockey ticket information phone TicketMaster, (604) 280-4444. **Baseball** is played by the Vancouver Canadians at Nat Bailey Stadium; phone (604) 872-5232 for schedule and ticket information. Indoor **lacrosse** can be enjoyed at Bill Copeland Sports Centre in Burnaby, (604) 291-1261; and at Kerrisdale Arena, (604) 257-8121, and Queens Park Arena, (604) 777-5111, in New Westminster.

Thoroughbred racing with pari-mutuel betting is held at Hastings Park Race Course on the grounds of the Pacific National Exhibition; phone (604) 254-1631 *(see attraction listing p. 152).*

Note: Policies concerning admittance of children to pari-mutuel betting facilities vary. Phone for information.

Shopping

Befitting an international port, Vancouver has a wealth of marketplaces. These emporiums give definition to a metropolis that can be broken easily into a series of villages. From the cosmopolitan heart of the West End to historic Gastown to exotic Chinatown, Vancouver is a shopper's paradise.

Streets of fashionable boutiques are the signature of the West End. Representative of this area is Robson Street and its high-fashion boutiques. Enhancing the shops are the gardens, pools and waterfalls of Robson Square, a three-block area that stretches from the Vancouver Art Gallery to the glass-tiered pyramid of the Law Courts.

When the pleasure of the outdoors fades with the weather, there are nearby underground malls. The largest of these is Granville Street Mall, which includes Pacific Centre, anchored by the above-ground department stores Holt Renfrew and Sears, and the adjoining Vancouver Centre. Beneath the Hyatt Regency Hotel is Royal Centre with its fashion boutiques.

In Burnaby, MetroTown contains MetroTown Centre, Eaton Centre, Metropolis and Station Square. The area features more than 550 shops, restaurants and 22 motion-picture theaters as well as a virtual reality entertainment center. The Crystal Mall, 4500 Kingsway, is a 200-store mall and office complex.

Expo '86 created a world village and left a legacy of buildings and the light rail system known as SkyTrain. SkyTrain and its water counterpart, SeaBus, link two of the city's several marketplaces. Lonsdale Quay and Westminster Quay (in North Vancouver and New Westminster respectively) both offer shops, eateries and promenades along the waterfront.

Near the SeaBus terminal is the former Canadian Pavilion, now Canada Place. The distinctive white sails of this complex embrace the trade and convention center, cruise terminal, a hotel and the Promenade Shops, featuring the Made in BC shop and an IMAX theater.

East of the SeaBus terminal are the restored 19th-century buildings and cobblestone streets of Gastown. Carrall, Powell, Walter and Alexander streets meet at Maple Tree Square, defining this historic area and embracing specialty and antique shops, art galleries and restaurants. Most shops are open Sundays. Street vendors add to the area's charm, as does the 1.8-metric-ton (2-ton) Gastown Steam Clock at the corner of Cambie and Water streets.

The warehouses of the reclaimed industrial area of Granville Island have become a refuge for artists and casual shoppers. The centerpiece of this community is Granville Island Market, off W. Fourth Street by False Creek, an open market that offers fresh fruits, vegetables, seafood, meats, gourmet foods, baked goods, many fine restaurants (reservations are recommended), handicrafts and live theater.

Another cluster of abandoned warehouses has been rejuvenated into one of the trendiest areas of Vancouver—Yaletown. Bordered by Nelson and Homer streets and Pacific Boulevard, the community is filled with stores featuring everything from imported designer clothing to home furnishings and giftware by Canadian craftsmen. Old warehouse loading bays have been converted into cafes and restaurants, which use the wide sidewalks for patio dining.

South Vancouver features Oakridge Shopping Centre, 41st and Cambie streets; its vaulted glass ceilings shelter a collection of shops as well as giant fig trees. Across Burrard Inlet in West Vancouver are the twin malls of Park Royal. This complex has more than 190 shops offering everything from furnishings to groceries; the largest store being The Bay.

CHINATOWN centers on E. Pender St. between Carrall and Gore sts. The second largest area of its kind in North America, Chinatown is lined with elaborately carved and gilded shops displaying jade, bamboo, rattan, brassware, silk and brocade. Sidewalk markets feature Oriental produce. Even the phone booths are topped with pagoda roofs. The Chinese Cultural Centre Museum & Archives, 555 Columbia St., has some displays and photographs on its second floor relating to the history of the Chinese in British Columbia; phone (604) 658-8880. During Chinese New Year the streets resound with the din of drums and fireworks.

Theater and Concerts

The Centre in Vancouver for Performing Arts, 777 Homer St., is a premier facility for theater, dance and music; phone (604) 602-0616 for event information. The Queen Elizabeth Theatre at the intersection of Hamilton and Georgia streets, (604) 665-3050, is home to Ballet British Columbia,

(604) 732-5003, and the Vancouver Opera Association, (604) 683-0222. The adjacent Vancouver Playhouse presents professional theater, recitals and chamber music; phone (604) 873-3311. The Vancouver Symphony Orchestra performs at the Orpheum Theatre, Smithe and Granville streets; phone (604) 876-3434 for ticket information.

Other prominent metropolitan theaters presenting dramatic productions include the Arts Club Theatre, on Johnston Street on Granville Island, (604) 687-1644; the Metro Theatre, 1370 S.W. Marine Dr., (604) 266-7191; Studio 58, 100 W. 49th Ave., (604) 323-5227; and the Vancouver East Cultural Centre, 1895 Venables St., (604) 251-1363.

A theatrical presentation illustrating western Canada's history is featured at Storyeum; phone (604) 687-8142 *(see attraction listing p. 153)*.

During the summer concerts and musicals are presented in Stanley Park's Malkin Bowl. Kitsilano Showboat at Kitsilano Beach presents an outdoor variety show Monday, Wednesday and Friday at 7:30 p.m. during July and August (weather permitting). For more information phone (604) 734-7332.

Concerts in such genres as classical, country, pop and rock are presented year-round at the Pacific Coliseum, 100 N. Renfrew St., (604) 253-2311, and General Motors Place, 800 Griffiths Way, (604) 899-7444.

The daily papers carry listings of cultural events, as do weekly and monthly magazines. Ticket outlets include Ticketmaster Head Office, 1304 Hornby St.; and Ticketmaster, Pacific Centre Mall, 700 W. Georgia St.

Special Events

Life in a city where your office is only 25 minutes from a ski slope is worth celebrating, and the residents of Vancouver celebrate their setting throughout the year. New Year's Day sees the Polar Bear Swim at English Bay; the event draws many swimmers and hundreds of spectators.

The Vancouver Children's Festival in May ushers in summer, while cultural entertainment sails in with the Canadian International Dragon Boat Festival in mid-June. The Vancouver Folk Music Festival draws fans from as far away as Los Angeles for concerts during mid-July. HSBC Celebration of Light features 4 nights of fireworks displays and is held at English Bay the last week of July and the first week in August.

Virtually all facets of life and work in British Columbia are celebrated in the Pacific National Exhibition, held at the Exhibition Grounds from late August through Labour Day. In late September and early October the Oktoberfest is held at the Exhibition Grounds, where the revelry continues into the wee hours.

The Christmas season begins with the Christmas Carol Ships, which lead a flotilla of private watercraft decorated with Christmas lights around the harbor in mid-December. More information about events is available from your CAA or AAA club.

The Vancouver Vicinity

ALDERGROVE (H-11)
pop. 11,910, elev. 61 m/200′

A small town on the Lower Fraser Valley's southern side, Aldergrove is near the Fraser River and the Canada-United States border. Dairy, chicken, strawberry and raspberry farms dot the surrounding area. Just northeast of Aldergrove, Bradner grows about 400 varieties of daffodils.

Langley Chamber of Commerce—Aldergrove: 5761 Glover Rd., Suite 1, Langley, BC, Canada V3A 8M8; phone (604) 530-6656.

GREATER VANCOUVER ZOO is at 5048 264th St. The 48-hectare (120-acre) zoo is devoted to the preservation and breeding of endangered species. More than 800 animals represent 180 species from around the world, including elephants, leopards, monkeys, giraffes and tigers. A narrated train ride takes passengers around the zoo's perimeter; a bus tour travels through the North American Wilds exhibit.

Picnicking is permitted. Food is available. Allow 2 hours minimum. Daily 9-7, Apr.-Sept.; 9-4, rest of year. Closed Dec. 25. Admission $13; over 64 and ages 3-15, $10; family rate (two adults and two children) $40. Train ride $3. Parking $3. MC, VI. Phone (604) 856-6825.

BURNABY (G-11)
pop. 193,954, elev. 40 m/130′

Burnaby is more than just a suburban, bedroom community of hills, ridges, valleys, plain, and stunning views; it is an urban center which is home to Simon Fraser University and the British Columbia Institute of Technology.

DEER LAKE PARK is 14.5 km (9 mi.) s.e. at 6450 Deer Lake Ave. at Canada Way. The park contains the Century Gardens, with its distinctive rhododendron display and rose gardens. The Shadbolt Centre for the Arts offers community arts programs as well as theater and dance performances in its James Cowan Theatre. Several walking trails provide scenic views throughout the park. Daily 24 hours. Free. Phone (604) 294-7450 or (604) 291-6864.

(SAVE) Burnaby Village Museum is off Hwy. 1 Kensington Ave. S. exit to 6501 Deer Lake Ave. The 4-hectare (10-acre) village re-creates the sights and sounds of an 1890-1925 settlement in lower mainland British Columbia. Costumed townspeople welcome visitors to more than 30 shops and homes, including a printshop and schoolhouse. A restored 1912 Parker carousel is on the site.

Food is available. Allow 1 hour minimum. Daily noon-8, Dec. 15-Dec.30; 11-4:30, May 1-Labour Day; noon-5:30, mid-Nov. through Dec. 14 and Dec. 31-Jan. 2. Closed Dec. 24-25. Admission $8.14; over 64 and ages 13-18, $5.85; ages 6-12,

$4.95. Carousel ride $1. Prices and schedule may vary; phone ahead. MC, VI. Phone (604) 293-6500.

PLAYDIUM is in the MetroTown Shopping Centre at 4700 Kingsway. The high-tech virtual and physical entertainment complex offers more than 200 multisensory, interactive and virtual reality activities. Games include skateboarding, racing and combat simulators. Also featured are a roller coaster simulator, bowling and an adventure ride film. Food is available. Allow 30 minutes minimum. Sun.-Thurs. 10 a.m.-midnight, Fri.-Sat. 10 a.m.-2 a.m.; closed Dec. 25. Admission free. Pay-as-you-play individual attraction rates are 50c-$4 per use. Phone (604) 433-7529.

COQUITLAM (G-11)
pop. 112,890, elev. 137 m/449′

Named for a type of landlocked salmon, Coquitlam borders Pitt Lake and encompasses Burke Mountain. Recreational opportunities, including swimming, canoeing, hiking and fishing, are available throughout the area.

Nearby parks and lakes include Mundy Park, 4 kilometres (2.5 mi.) south off Mariner Way; Belcarra Park, 15 kilometres (9 mi.) northwest off Ioco and Bedwell Bay roads; Buntzen Lake, 12 kilometres (7 mi.) northwest off East and Sunnyside roads; Minnekhada Regional Park, 13 kilometres (8 mi.) northeast off Victoria Drive and Quarry Road; Town Centre Park and Lafarge Lake, on Pinetree Way just north of Lougheed Hwy.; and Burke Mountain, 11 kilometres (7 mi.) northeast off Coast Meridian and Harper roads.

Visitor InfoCentre/Tri-cities Chamber of Commerce: 1209 Pinetree Way, Coquitlam, BC, Canada V3B 7Y3; phone (604) 464-2716.

DELTA (H-11) pop. 96,950, elev. 10 m/33′

Delta, composed of the three distinct communities of Ladner, Tsawwassen and North Delta, is an amalgam of commerce, fisheries, industry, farmland, beaches and suburban residences. The warmwater beaches on Boundary Bay and Tsawwassen are popular spots for swimming and sunbathing. Other recreational opportunities in the area include fishing for salmon and boating on the Fraser River and the Strait of Georgia.

Delta Chamber of Commerce: 6201 60th Ave., Delta, BC, Canada V4K 4E2; phone (604) 946-4232.

DELTA MUSEUM AND ARCHIVES is at 4858 Delta St. The museum houses marine, fishing and farming exhibits, pioneer and First Nations displays, reconstructed rooms of a late Victorian household and an early 1900s Delta street scene. Allow 1 hour minimum. Museum open Tues.-Sat.

10-3:30. Archives open Tues.-Sat. 10-3; closed Nov. 11 and Dec. 24-Jan. 3. Donations. Phone (604) 946-9322.

GEORGE C. REIFEL MIGRATORY BIRD SANCTUARY

is at 5191 Robertson Rd. on Westham Island. More than 268 species of birds have been observed at the refuge, which comprises 344 hectares (850 acres) with 4 kilometres (2.5 mi.) of trails. Allow 1 hour minimum. Daily 9-4. Admission $4; over 59 and ages 2-14, $2. Bird seed 50c per bag. Phone (604) 946-6980.

LANGLEY (H-11) pop. 23,643, elev. 10 m/33′

Langley, the site of a Hudson's Bay Co. fort built in 1840 *(see Fort Langley National Historic Site of Canada p. 119)*, is in an important farming region. Orchards, strawberry and raspberry farms, horse ranches and dairy, chicken and mink farms make a patchwork of the countryside.

Langley Chamber of Commerce—Langley: Unit One, 5761 Glover Rd., Langley, BC, Canada V3A 8M8; phone (604) 530-6656.

(SAVE) **CANADIAN MUSEUM OF FLIGHT** is at Hangar 3, 5333 216th St., at the Langley Airport. The museum features a collection of more than 25 aircraft; some restored. Aircraft include a Handley-Page Hampden Bomber, helicopters and jets. The aircraft and artifacts displayed represent Canada's aviation history 1909 to the present day. A collection of other aviation memorabilia as well as a children's activity center is available.

Allow 30 minutes minimum. Daily 10-4; closed Jan. 1 and Dec. 25-26. Admission $5, over 59 and students with ID $4, under 6 free, family rate (includes two adults and up to four children) $12. MC, VI. Phone (604) 532-0035.

MAPLE RIDGE (H-11)
pop. 63,169, elev. 30 m/98′

Maple Ridge lies on the north shore of the Fraser River, with the Coast Mountains to the north and the Stave and Pitt Rivers forming its east and west boundaries. Snow-capped peaks overlook this Fraser Valley community.

The Fraser River Heritage Walk, which starts at Port Haney Wharf, passes many of the town's notable spots. The Haney House at 11612 224th St. was built in 1876 and contains many furnishings and artifacts owned by three generations of the Haney family. Displays at Maple Ridge Museum, 22520 116th Ave., reflect the history and geography of the area.

Kanaka Creek Regional Park *(see Recreation Chart)* offers hiking and horseback riding trails as well as canoeing, kayaking, fishing and picnic facilities. A fish hatchery is on the grounds. Phone (604) 530-4983. Maple Ridge also has a large per capita horse population and an extensive riding trail system.

Tourism Maple Ridge and Pitt Meadows: 12492 Harris Rd., Pitt Meadows, BC, Canada V3Y 2S4; phone (604) 460-8300 or (877) 465-8300.

UBC MALCOLM KNAPP RESEARCH FOREST is n. at 14500 Silver Valley Rd. Trails of various lengths lead visitors on tours through the forest, a research facility of the University of British Columbia. Bicycles and pets are not permitted. Daily dawn-dusk. Free. Phone (604) 463-8148.

MISSION (H-12) pop. 31,272, elev. 55 m/180′

Mission developed from a Roman Catholic mission built in 1861 to serve Indian tribes. The site became a popular stopping place for trappers, settlers and other river travelers.

The Fraser River provides opportunities for swimming, fishing, boating and water sports; its sandbars are good for rockhounds in search of agates, jades and garnets. Motocross and boat races are held at Mission Raceway from March through October.

Mission Regional Chamber of Commerce: 34033 Lougheed Hwy., Mission, BC, Canada V2V 5X8; phone (604) 826-6914.

WESTMINSTER ABBEY is 1.5 km (.9 mi.) e., .7 km (.5 mi.) n. of Hwy. 7 to 34224 Dewdney Trunk Rd. The Seminary of Christ the King is managed by Benedictine monks. Of interest are the view and architecture. Modest dress is required. Allow 30 minutes minimum. Mon.-Sat. 1:30-4:30, Sun. 2-4. Free. Phone (604) 826-8975.

XÁ:YTEM LONGHOUSE INTERPRETIVE CENTRE is at 35087 Lougheed Hwy. (Hwy. 7). Xá:ytem (pronounced HAY-tum) is said to be British Columbia's oldest known dwelling site. It is evidence of one of many large villages that were once inhabited by the ancestors of today's Stó:lō people. Of note is a replica of a *skumel*, or underground pithouse, and the "Rock"—a physical manifestation of Stó:lō spirituality. Among the items housed at the cedar longhouse are artifacts found at the site.

Guided tours are available. Picnicking is permitted. Allow 1 hour minimum. Mon.-Sun. 9-4:30, July-Aug.; Mon.-Fri. 9-4:30, rest of year. Hours may vary, phone ahead. Closed Dec. 25-Jan. 1. Admission $10; over 55 and students with ID $8; under 13, $7. VI. Phone (604) 820-9725.

NEW WESTMINSTER (G-11)
pop. 49,400, elev. 75 m/246′

The oldest incorporated city in Western Canada, New Westminster—also known as the Royal City— was named by Queen Victoria. Transformed into a boomtown by the lure of gold in 1857, it plunged into a depression when the gold rush subsided in the late 1860s. The city was the provincial capital until 1868.

New Westminster also is known for its architecture. Parts of the city were built by the Royal Engineers, sent in 1855 to keep order in the new crown colony. Former members of this organization later formed the New Westminster Regiment, whose history is recounted in the Museum of the Royal Westminster Regiment at Sixth St. and Queens Ave.; phone (604) 526-5116.

Other places of interest include old houses, many of which survived a devastating fire in 1898. The houses can be toured in May. Tickets must be purchased in advance; for information phone the New Westminster Hyack Festival Association at (604) 522-6894.

Westminster Quay Public Market, on the waterfront, maintains a tradition started in 1892 when farmers, hunters and settlers came to barter for goods. Fresh meat, baked goods, produce and local crafts can be purchased daily.

Antique Alley, on historic Front Street, is known for its heritage buildings housing stores featuring an array of antiques and collectibles.

Also of interest is *Sampson V* Maritime Museum aboard the stern-wheeler berthed on the Fraser River at the foot of Tenth Street. The stern-wheeler, the last steam-powered paddlewheeler to operate on the Fraser, can be toured; phone (604) 522-6894. The Canadian Lacrosse Hall of Fame, which celebrates Canada's national summer sport, is at 65 E. Sixth Ave., junction Sixth Avenue and McBride Boulevard; phone (604) 527-4640.

New Westminster Chamber of Commerce: 601 Queens Ave., New Westminster, BC, Canada V3M 1L1; phone (604) 521-7781 or (604) 526-1905.

IRVING HOUSE AND NEW WESTMINSTER MUSEUM AND ARCHIVES is at 302 Royal Ave. This 1864 mansion was built in the San Francisco Gothic Revival style for Capt. William Irving, a pioneer of the riverboat trade on the Fraser River. Furnished in period, the 14-room residence is bedecked in Victorian Christmas decor during December. The museum features artifacts, local history displays and an 1876 coach built to carry the governor general of Canada to the Cariboo goldfields. Allow 1 hour minimum. Wed.-Sun. 11:30-4:30, May 1-Labour Day; Sat.-Sun. 12:30-4:30, day after Labour Day-Apr. 30. Closed holidays. Donations. Phone (604) 527-4640.

JAPANESE FRIENDSHIP GARDEN is next to City Hall at 511 Royal Ave. Waterfalls, pathways and flowering trees and shrubs adorn the garden, which features 100 Yoshino cherry trees, a gift from the city of Moriguchi, Japan. Allow 1 hour, 30 minutes minimum. Daily dawn-dusk. Free. Phone (604) 527-4567.

SAVE **PADDLEWHEELER RIVERBOAT TOURS** departs from the boardwalk of the New Westminster Quay Public Market at 139-810 Quayside Dr. Narrated sightseeing tours of various lengths are offered aboard an authentic paddlewheeler. The MV *Native* is a replica of a late 19th-century riverboat that carried passengers on the historic Gold Rush Trail via the Fraser River. Evening entertainment cruises also are available.

Cruises depart daily year-round; phone for schedule. Fare $19.95-$39.95; some fares may include meals. Reservations are required. AX, MC, VI. Phone (604) 525-4465 or (877) 825-1302.

QUEENS PARK is at 6th St. and McBride Blvd. in the center of town. The park includes a Salish totem pole, a picnic area, tennis courts, botanical gardens, nature trails, a stadium, an arena and a band shell in which concerts are presented in July and August. Splash pools, playgrounds and a petting zoo are open in summer. In Centennial Lodge, the Art Gallery in the Park features works by emerging and established artists.

Allow 1 hour, 30 minutes minimum. Park open daily dawn-dusk. Art gallery daily 1-5, July-Aug.; Tues.-Sun. 1-5, rest of year. Splash pools and petting zoo daily 10-5:30, June-Aug. Donations. Phone (604) 527-4567 for the park or (604) 525-3244 for the gallery.

STARLINE TOURS depart from the Westminster Quay Public Market boardwalk. The narrated cruises along the Fraser River highlight the area's wildlife, natural history and development. A 6-hour Pitt Lake excursion includes lunch, while a 6-hour trip to the fishing village of Steveston allows time for exploring ashore. Sunset cruises and a combination boat and bus tour to Harrison Hot Springs also are offered.

Cruises depart at 10, Apr.-Oct.; phone for exact schedule. Sea lion cruises available Apr.-May. Fare for 6-hour cruises $65.75; over 60 and students 13-18 with ID $59.75; ages 6-12, $40. Reservations are required. MC, VI. Phone (604) 522-3506 or (604) 272-9187.

NORTH VANCOUVER (G-11)
pop. 44,303, elev. 99 m/325'

CAPILANO SALMON HATCHERY is at 4500 Capilano Park Rd. Self-guiding tours allow visitors to view this architecturally acclaimed facility. Displays trace the development of coho, chinook and steelhead salmon. Live adult salmon may be seen in the fish ladder July through November. Scenic picnic areas are available. Allow 30 minutes minimum. Daily 8-8, June-Aug.; 8-7 in May and Sept.; 8-6, in Oct.; 8-4, rest of year. Free. Phone (604) 666-1790.

GEM SAVE **CAPILANO SUSPENSION BRIDGE** is off Hwy. 1 exit 14, then 2 km (1.2 mi.) n. to 3735 Capilano Rd. The swinging 137-metre-long (450-ft.) footbridge spans a 70-metre-deep (230-ft.) densely wooded gorge above the Capilano River. George Grant Mackay, a Scottish civil engineer, built the original bridge in 1889 from hemp rope and cedar planks; the fourth structure on the site is reinforced with steel cables and concrete.

The site features gardens, a totem park and a story center that displays artifacts of the bridge. The Living Forest includes interactive displays and naturalist exhibits which guide visitors through a West Coast rain forest. Artisans sculpt totem poles, masks and life-size carvings of First Nations people in the Big House. First Nations dancers perform and costumed guides offer tours of the park and nature trails daily May through October.

Food is available. Allow 1 hour minimum. Daily 8:30-dusk, May-Oct.; 9-5, rest of year. Closed Dec. 25. Admission $23.95; over 65 and students with ID $17.95; ages 13-16, $11.45; ages 6-12, $5.95. Reservations are recommended for guided nature tours. AX, MC, VI. Phone (604) 985-7474. *See color ad p. 151.*

GROUSE MOUNTAIN is at 6400 Nancy Greene Way. From a height of 1,100 metres (3,609 ft.), the summit offers a panorama of the city. Skiing, snowshoeing, snowboarding, ice skating and sleigh rides are possible in the winter while helicopter and mountain biking tours are popular in the summer. Sports events and shows take place year-round. An aerial tramway operates all year to the chalet.

Each hour, Theatre in the Sky shows the film "Born to Fly," which provides an eagle's view of southwestern British Columbia. The Grouse Mountain Refuge for Endangered Wildlife is home to two orphaned grizzly bear cubs and four adult gray wolves. Also offered are a guided Eco Walk, a lumberjack show and a Birds in Motion demonstration. At the Híwus Feasthouse, First Nations traditions are presented through dance, song and storytelling during a potlatch-style meal.

Picnicking is permitted. Food is available. Allow 1 hour minimum. Grouse Mountain open daily 9 a.m.-10 p.m. Híwus Feasthouse performances Thurs.-Sat. at 7 p.m., June-Oct.; by appointment rest of year. Tram $26.95; over 64, $24.95; ages 13-18, $14.95; ages 5-12, $8.95. Fares may vary; phone ahead. Híwus Feasthouse performances $65; ages 13-18, $39; under 13, $29. AX, DC, MC, VI. Phone (604) 984-0661.

LYNN CANYON PARK AND ECOLOGY CENTRE is off Lynn Valley Rd. to the end of Peters Rd., following signs to 3663 Park Rd. The municipal park features paths, natural streams and rivers and a 50-metre-high (166-ft.) suspension bridge spanning a waterfall and the canyon. The ecology center offers films, interactive displays and nature programs. Food is available. Park open daily dawn-dusk; closed Jan. 1 and Dec. 25-26. Ecology center open daily 10-5, June-Sept.; Mon.-Fri. 10-5, Sat.-Sun. and holidays noon-4, rest of year. Guided nature walks offered Sat.-Sun. and holidays 10-5, Apr.-Sept.; noon-4, rest of year. Donations. Phone (604) 981-3103.

MAPLEWOOD FARM is at 405 Seymour River Pl. This park-farm specializes in the display of domestic farm animals and birds. Visitors may pet the inhabitants of Goathill and Rabbitat and view a cow-milking demonstration. Allow 1 hour minimum. Tues.-Sun. and Mon. holidays 10-4; closed Dec. 25. Cow-milking demonstrations daily at 1:15. Admission $3.12, over 54 and ages 19 months-16 years $1.54. Phone (604) 929-5610.

MOUNT SEYMOUR PROVINCIAL PARK is 24 km (15 mi.) n.e. The scenic area of 3,508 hectares (8,668 acres) is on the slopes of 1,433-metre (4,701-ft.) Mount Seymour. A good highway goes to the 1,006-metre (3,330-ft.) level. Hiking trails and downhill skiing are available in season. Picnicking is permitted. Daily 7 a.m.-11 p.m. Free. Phone (604) 582-5200. *See Recreation Chart.*

NORTH VANCOUVER MUSEUM AND ARCHIVES is in Presentation House at 209 W. Fourth St. The museum's artifacts document the community's growth from pioneer days. Documentary and photographic collections are housed in the archives. Allow 1 hour minimum. Museum open Tues.-Sun. noon-5. Archives open Tues.-Sat. noon-5. Complex closed Jan. 1 and Dec. 25. Donations. Phone (604) 987-5618.

ROCKWOOD ADVENTURES RAINFOREST WALKS departs from downtown hotels. Half- and full-day guided nature walks are offered to area ecological destinations including Lynn Canyon, a rain forest in Capilano River Canyon, a coastal forest at Burrard Inlet and Mount Gardner on Bowen Island. All trips include a snack or lunch. Trips daily Apr.-Oct. Fee $45-$130. Reservations are required. MC, VI. Phone (604) 980-7749 or (888) 236-6606.

PORT COQUITLAM (G-11)
pop. 51,257, elev. 10 m/33'

The 29-kilometre (18-mi.) Poco Trail passes through wooded areas and runs alongside the Pitt River, providing plenty of opportunities to observe waterfowl and other wildlife; the Pitt Dikes can be seen from the trail. Activities such as hiking, jogging, bicycling and horseback riding also can be enjoyed.

PORT MOODY (G-11)
pop. 23,816, elev. 10 m/33'

Port Moody once was the terminus of the Canadian Pacific Railway—the first train from Montréal to the Pacific arrived July 4, 1886. A year later the line was extended 20 kilometres (12 mi.) west to Vancouver. Rocky Point Park on Burrard Inlet offers picnicking, swimming, boating and nature trails.

PORT MOODY STATION MUSEUM is at 2734 Murray St. The museum displays local and railway artifacts and historical information about Port Moody in a former train depot with working and living areas restored to their early 1900s appearance. A heritage garden, typical of Canadian Pacific Railway stations 1882-1912, is on the grounds. A restored 1921 railroad car sits on tracks outside the museum. Daily 10-5, Labour Day-Victoria Day; noon-4, rest of year. Closed Jan. 1 and Dec.25-26. Donations. Phone (604) 939-1648.

RICHMOND (G-10) pop. 164,345, elev. 5 m/16'

On an island at the mouth of the Fraser River, Richmond first was settled in 1879. The town grew and prospered with its farming, fishing and waterborne trade industries. Today, Richmond's major industries include aviation, berry farming, high technology and manufacturing.

Steveston, an early fishing village now part of the southwest corner of Richmond, has been restored and is an area of shops, restaurants and businesses. Hundreds of boats line the docks as fishermen dry their nets and unload their catches for sale.

The Richmond Nature Park, 44 hectares (109 acres) at 11851 Westminster Hwy., has a bird pond, beehive displays, mounted birds, a quaking bog and plants identified by markers. A naturalist conducts hour-long tours of the park on Sunday.

Tourism Richmond: 11980 Deas Thruway, Richmond, BC, Canada V6W 1L1; phone (877) 247-0777.

GULF OF GEORGIA CANNERY NATIONAL HISTORIC SITE is at 12138 Fourth Ave. in Steveston Village. The 1894 salmon cannery has been restored to serve as an interpretive center for Canada's West Coast fishing industry. Interactive video presentations, guided tours of the plant and replicated 1900-50 canning line, and equipment demonstrations are offered. The Boiler House Theatre presents a film about the West Coast fishing industry every 30 minutes.

Daily 10-5, June 1-Labour Day; Thurs.-Mon. 10-5, early Apr.-May 31 and day after Labour Day-late Oct. Admission $6.50; over 64 and students with ID $5; ages 6-16, $3.25; family rate $16.25. VI. Phone (604) 664-9009.

RICHMOND CULTURAL CENTRE is off Granville St. at 7700 Minoru Gate. Home to the Richmond Arts Centre, Archives Museum and Art Gallery, the center presents programs and events in art, music, drama and dance. The gallery features works from local artists and traveling exhibits. The museum depicts Richmond's history through early household items, personal effects and articles relating to the area's agriculture, dairying, fishing and transportation.

Allow 1 hour minimum. Museum open Mon.-Fri. 9 a.m.-9:30 p.m.; Sat.-Sun. 10-5. Archives open Mon.-Thurs. 9-4:30. Complex closed holidays. Donations. Phone (604) 231-6457.

STARLINE TOURS—*see New Westminster p. 162.*

SURREY (H-11) pop. 347,825, elev. 80 m/262′

Surrey's sights are popular with nature buffs. Bear Creek Park features a garden area that includes rhododendrons, azaleas, ornamental grasses and bulb displays. A shoreline walk extends from Crescent Beach to Peace Arch Park. Walkers can observe tide pools, dig for clams or watch the myriad native birds.

Surrey Regional Chamber of Commerce: 14439 104th Ave., Suite 101, Surrey, BC, Canada V3R 1M1; phone (604) 581-7130.

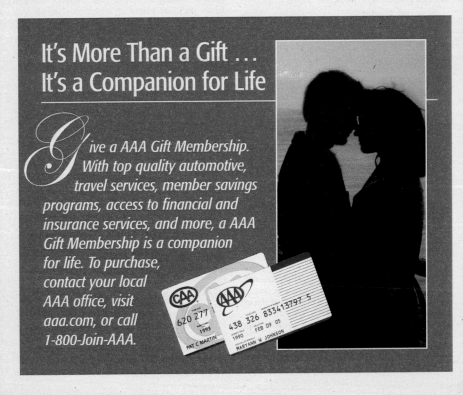

HISTORIC STEWART FARM is at 13723 Crescent Rd. An 1890s farmhouse has been restored to represent Victorian rural life. The site includes a restored pole barn, heritage gardens, a weaving center and an orchard. Picnicking is permitted. Allow 30 minutes minimum. Tues.-Fri. 10-4, Sat.-Sun. noon-4, mid-Feb. to mid-Dec. Donations. Phone (604) 502-6456.

NEWTON WAVE POOL is at 13730 72nd Ave. at the corner of King George Hwy. The indoor aquatic center houses, in addition to the wave pool, two water slides, a wading pool and a lagoon. The complex also includes an exercise, a steam and 5,000-square-foot weight room as well as a whirlpool. Tues. and Thurs.-Fri. 12:30-9, Sat.-Sun. 12:30-8, Mon. and Wed. 1:15-9, early July-early Sept.; Fri. 12:30-9, Sat.-Sun. 12:30-8, Mon. and Wed. 1:15-3:30 and 6-8 p.m., Tues. and Thurs. noon-3:30 and 6-8 p.m., rest of year. Pool admission $4.53; over 59 and students over 18 with ID $3.46; ages 2-18, $2.29. MC, VI. Phone (604) 501-5540.

RAINFOREST REPTILE REFUGE is 2 km (1.2 mi.) n. of the Pacific Border Crossing to 1395 176th St. The refuge is a haven for unwanted and abused reptiles and amphibians that once were pets and cannot be returned to their wilderness environments. Visitors can view crocodilians, snapping turtles and a 21-foot-long python. Cameras are not permitted. Allow 1 hour minimum. Tues.-Sun. 12:30-4:30. Admission $6.54; over 59 and students with ID $5.61; ages 3-12, $4.67. Hours and rates may vary; phone ahead. AX, MC, VI. Phone (604) 538-1711.

WEST VANCOUVER (G-11) pop. 41,421

CYPRESS PROVINCIAL PARK is off Trans-Canada Hwy. exit 8, then w. following signs. The park encompasses nearly 3,000 hectares (7,403 acres) of mountains, lakes and forests. Winter offers skiing and other snow-related activates, while summer features bird-watching and a wide range of hiking and nature trails. Picnicking is permitted. Daily 24 hours. Free. Phone (604) 924-2200. *See Recreation Chart.*

[SAVE] **SEWELLS SEA SAFARI TOURS** is off Trans-Canada Hwy. at Horseshoe Bay Ferry Terminal, following signs to village. Points of interest on the 2-hour high-speed tour of coastal British Columbia may include Bowyer Island, Pam Rocks—birthing ground to seal pups in July—Ragged Island and The Strait of Georgia. Tours depart daily at 10, 1 and 4, late Apr.-Oct. 31. Fare $55; over 64, $50; under 12, $25. AX, MC, VI. Phone (604) 921-3474.

This ends listings for the Vancouver Vicinity.
The following page resumes the alphabetical listings
of cities in British Columbia.

VANDERHOOF (E-4)
pop. 4,390, elev. 915 m/2,050'

When the last spike of the railroad was driven in 1914, the Grand Trunk Pacific Development Company offered land for sale. The decision of where to put the new settlement in the wilderness was decided by Herbert Vanderhoof, a railroad employee, and a town was built in just a few weeks. The site, unfortunately, was a poor choice, as the land flooded every spring. In 1919 the townspeople moved to higher ground on the opposite side of the tracks.

Mr. Vanderhoof's legacy to the town is its name, Dutch for "of the farm." The name is fitting, as farming has always been an economic mainstay in the area.

Vanderhoof & District Chamber of Commerce: 2353 Burrard Ave., P.O. Box 126, Vanderhoof, BC, Canada V0J 3A0; phone (250) 567-2124.

VANDERHOOF HERITAGE MUSEUM is w. on Hwy. 16 to 478 W. First St. The collection of reconstructed buildings depicts rural agriculture in the 1920s. Among the buildings restored and open are the 1914 Board of Trade Building, a café, a police office, a 1914 jail cell and a home typical of those built in the area by early Mennonite settlers. In the town square are examples of farm machines and equipment. Food is available. Allow 30 minutes minimum. Daily 10-7, Victoria Day weekend-Labour Day. Donations. Phone (250) 567-2991.

VERNON (C-9) pop. 33,494, elev. 383 m/1,256'

At the confluence of five valleys and bounded by three lakes, Vernon is an important shipping and trading center for the Okanagan region. The town's history is portrayed in 26 large murals painted on downtown buildings. On Hwy. 97 at 25th Avenue, Polson Park encompasses a Japanese garden, a Chinese tea house, a floral clock made of 3,500 plants and a children's water park.

Boating, fishing, hiking, mountain biking and golf are popular in summer; winter activities include skiing, dogsledding and snowshoeing. Several recreational opportunities are available at nearby Ellison Provincial Park *(see Recreation Chart and the AAA/CAA Western Canada & Alaska CampBook)* and Kalamalka Lake Provincial Park.

Silver Star Provincial Park offers mountain biking tours from late June to mid-September. A chairlift to the top of Silver Star Mountain operates daily, July 1 to mid-September.

For relaxation, the Kalamalka Lake viewpoint, 5 kilometres (3 mi.) south of 25th Avenue on Hwy. 97, provides an excellent view of the lake.

Vernon Travel InfoCentre: 701 Hwy. 97S, Vernon, BC, Canada V1B 3W4; phone (250) 542-1415 or (800) 665-0795. *See color ad.*

[SAVE] **ATLANTIS WATERSLIDES AND RECREATIONS LTD.** is 8 km (5 mi.) n. on Hwy. 97A at Pleasant Valley Rd. The water park has a slide with 10 flumes of varying lengths and slopes, a giant hot tub, miniature golf and a picnic area. Food is available. Allow 2 hours, 30 minutes minimum. Daily 10-8, early July to mid-Aug.; 10-6, mid-Aug. through Sept. 5; 9:30-5:30, mid-June to early July; 11-5, early June to mid-June. Admission $16.82; ages 4-11, $11.21; over 65, $7.48; family rate (two adults and two children) $48.60. MC, VI. Phone (250) 549-4121.

explore GREATER VERNON

1-800-665-0795
www.vernontourism.com

GREATER VERNON MUSEUM AND ARCHIVES is at 3009 32nd Ave. Exhibits include local and natural history items, Indian artifacts and period costumes and furniture. The Allan Brooks Gallery features works by the artist and naturalist. Archives and a research facility also are on the premises. Allow 1 hour minimum. Tues.-Sat. 10-5; closed holidays. Donations. Phone (250) 542-3142.

HISTORIC O'KEEFE RANCH is 12 km (7 mi.) n. on Hwy. 97. One of the earliest cattle empires in the Okanagan Valley, the 1867 O'Keefe homestead includes a dozen restored structures. Guided tours are offered of the family's Victorian mansion. Other buildings include a log house, a church, a general store, a blacksmith shop, a cowboy bunk house, barns and tool sheds. A museum depicts the family's history and the ranching way of life.

Picnicking is permitted. Food is available. Allow 1 hour, 30 minutes minimum. Daily 9-8, July-Aug.; 9-5, May-June and Sept. 1 through mid-Oct. Admission $8; over 64, $7; ages 6-18, $6; family rate $22. MC, VI. Phone (250) 542-7868.

OKANAGAN SCIENCE CENTRE is at 2704 Hwy. 6 in Polson Park. Housed in one of the oldest brick schoolhouses in British Columbia, the center features hands-on exhibits focusing on such topics as rocks, fossils, illusions, recycling and the environment. Allow 1 hour minimum. Mon.-Sat. 9-5, Sun. 1-5; closed Jan. 1 and Dec. 24-25. Admission $7; over 65 and ages 6-18, $4. Phone (250) 545-3644.

VERNON PUBLIC ART GALLERY is at 3228 31st Ave. on the ground level of the Parkade Bldg. Two exhibition rooms feature works of local, regional and nationally known artists. Some of the works by artist and naturalist Allan Brooks also are displayed. Allow 30 minutes minimum. Mon.-Fri. 10-5, Sat. 11-4; closed statutory holidays. Donations. Parking 60c per hour. Phone (250) 545-3173.

CASINOS

- **Lake City Casino** is at 4801 27th St. Daily 10 a.m.-2 a.m. Phone (250) 545-3505.

RECREATIONAL ACTIVITIES

Skiing

- **Silver Star Mountain Resort** is 22 km (15 mi.) n.e. on Silver Star Rd. Write Box 3002, Silver Star Mountain, BC, Canada V1B 3M1. Daily 8:30-3:30, mid-Nov. to mid-Apr. (also Thurs.-Sat. 3:30-8, Dec. 17 through mid-Apr.). Other activities are available. Phone (250) 542-0224 for information or (800) 663-4431 for reservations.

Victoria

"To realize Victoria," Rudyard Kipling wrote, "you must take all that the eye admires in Bournemouth, Torquay, the Isle of Wight, the Happy Valley at Hong Kong, the Doon, Sorrento, Camp's Bay, add reminiscences of the Thousand Islands and arrange the whole around the Bay of Naples with some Himalayas for the background."

Yet the capital of British Columbia remains quintessentially British. Along with its tearooms, double-decker buses, horse-drawn tallyho carriages and shops that sell china and woolens, Victoria proudly claims another, much older culture. Totem poles can be seen throughout local parks, reflecting the city's dual heritage.

Regarded as Canada's gentlest city, Victoria has uncluttered streets, gardens that bloom year-round and hotels that have been serving high tea for decades. Sharing a passion for gardening, Victoria residents tend their prim English gardens. The city's innumerable flower beds and hanging baskets, nurtured by the mild climate brought by the California Current, bloom in bright displays while the rest of Canada shivers.

The heart of the city curves around the stone-walled Inner Harbour, alive with bobbing pleasure craft, fishing boats and coastal shipping vessels. Facing the harbor are the Parliament Buildings and the block-long, ivy-covered Empress Hotel.

Emily Carr, a native of Victoria, devoted her artistic career to capturing on canvas the brilliant totem poles carved by the vanishing Indian civilizations of the Pacific coast. Like those she found in deserted Indian villages, the fanciful totems in Thunderbird Park evoke the highly developed ancient culture that dominated the area long before Victoria was settled in the mid-19th century.

Fort Victoria was built by Hudson's Bay Co. in 1843. Six years later Vancouver Island became a crown colony, and as British Columbia's only port, it became a passage to the Cariboo goldfields on the mainland in 1858. Violence around Bastion Square was so commonplace during this rowdy boomtown period that the *Victoria Gazette* reported no deaths "from natural causes in the city during the last 30 days." Local politicians supposedly settled their debates with fist fights on Government Street.

After the gold fever broke, Victoria began to assume its characteristic cool reserve. Lured by modest land prices, English settlers developed their queen's namesake city into a thriving government and commercial center. In 1868 Victoria became the capital of the newly joined crown colonies of Vancouver Island and British Columbia.

Since commercial supremacy passed to Vancouver after the completion of the Canadian Pacific Railway, Victoria has adopted a slower pace with few heavy

Thunderbird Park / © Gibson Stock Photography

City Centre / © SuperStock

industries. Victoria's harbor is a center for commercial trade. Lumber and fishing also contribute to the bustle of this port. The dry dock at the Canadian Forces Base-Pacific Command is one of the world's largest.

The city's strong tourism industry is buoyed by the continuous stream of travelers who come by ferry from Washington and throughout British Columbia.

Whether or not Victoria is more British than Britain remains an ongoing debate among Victoria's residents. Few would contest, however, that nature's blessings have endowed the city with ample charm in its own right. No one understood this better than its native Indians, whose awesome totems continue to speak the land's wonder.

Approaches

By Car

Victoria is the western terminus of the 7,760-kilometre (4,850-mi.) Trans-Canada Hwy. The highway traverses the mainland to Horseshoe Bay in West Vancouver and resumes at the Nanaimo ferry terminal. It then proceeds south along the island's eastern shore to Victoria. Hwy. 17, the other major artery into the city, connects Victoria with the ferry terminals at Swartz Bay and Sidney on the Saanich Peninsula.

By Boat

Several ferry systems connect Vancouver Island and Victoria with mainland Canada and the United States. The most direct route is the Tsawwassen-Swartz Bay automobile/passenger ferry service used by the intercity buses between Vancouver and Victoria. British Columbia Ferries also connects Nanaimo, 111 kilometres (69 mi.) north of Victoria, to Horseshoe Bay in West Vancouver. Phone (250) 386-3431 outside British Columbia or (888) 223-3779 within British Columbia for ferry information or reservations.

Ferries linking the southern end of the island and Victoria with the United States include Black Ball Transport Inc., (250) 386-2202, from Port Angeles, Wash.; and Washington State Ferries, (206) 464-6400, from Anacortes, Wash., to Sidney. Reservations are available for the Anacortes, Wash., to Sidney route; phone 1 day in advance to determine estimated waiting time.

Connecting Seattle and Victoria is the high-speed passenger ferry, the *Victoria Clipper (see color ad p. 176);* phone (250) 382-8100 or (800) 888-2535.

Departing from the north end of the island at Port Hardy, British Columbia Ferries' vessels voyage through the Inside Passage to Prince Rupert, where they connect with the Alaska State Ferry system. Information can be obtained from British Columbia Ferries, 1112 Fort St., Victoria, BC, Canada V8V

(continued on p. 172)

The Informed Traveler

City Population: 74,125

Elevation: 17m/56 ft.

Sales Tax: British Columbia's provincial sales tax is 7.5 percent. A room tax of 10 percent on lodgings also is levied in the Victoria area.

WHOM TO CALL

Emergency: 911

Police (non-emergency): (250) 995-7654

Hospitals: Royal Jubilee Hospital, (250) 370-8000; Victoria General Hospital, (250) 727-4212.

WHERE TO LOOK

Newspapers

Victoria's daily paper is the *Times-Colonist,* which is distributed in the morning.

Radio

Victoria radio stations CBC (90.5 FM), CIOC (98.5 FM), CFUV (102 FM), CJVI (900 AM) and C-FAX (1070 AM) have news and weather reports.

Visitor Information

Tourism Victoria Visitor Information Centre: 812 Wharf St., Victoria, BC, Canada V8W 1T3; phone (250) 953-2033.

The center provides maps and brochures outlining various self-guiding walking and driving tours. The center is open daily 8:30-6:30, mid-May to mid-Sept.; 9-5, rest of year.

TRANSPORTATION

Air Travel

Victoria International Airport is 22 kilometres (12 mi.) north on Hwy. 17 (Patricia Bay Hwy.). Air Canada makes frequent flights to Victoria from Vancouver and Seattle. International air connections are made in Vancouver.

Airport Bus Service runs between the airport and downtown hotels; phone (250) 386-2525. Fare $14, under 6 free.

Rental Cars

Auto rental agencies include Hertz, 1640 Electra Blvd. and 655 Douglas St., which offers discounts to AAA and CAA members; phone (250) 656-2312 or (250) 360-2822, or (800) 263-0600 in Canada, or (800) 654-3080 out of Canada. Additional agencies are listed in the telephone directory.

Rail Service

From its depot at 450 Pandora Ave., Via Rail has weekday passenger service between Victoria and Courtenay; phone (888) 842-7245 in Canada or in the United States.

Buses

Pacific Coach Lines, 700 Douglas St., provides daily bus service between Vancouver and Victoria via British Columbia Ferry. The vessels transport buses and personal vehicles; phone (604) 662-7575 or (800) 661-1725.

Island Coach Lines provides bus transportation between Victoria and Campbell River; Nanaimo; Port Alberni; Port Hardy, with connections to the *Queen of the North* ferry; and Port McNeill. For information phone (250) 385-4411 or (800) 663-8390.

Taxis

Taxis charge $2.50 minimum plus $1.45 per kilometre (.6 mi.). Companies include Blue Bird Cabs, (250) 382-4235; Empress Taxi, (250) 381-2222; and Victoria Taxi, (250) 383-7111.

Public Transport

BC Transit provides bus service for Greater Victoria. Buses serve the downtown area 6:30 a.m.-midnight. Fare $2; senior citizens, students and children $1.25. Buses run frequently between downtown and the ferry terminal. For route information phone (250) 382-6161.

Boats

Several ferry systems make connections with mainland Canada and the United States. *See Approaches By Boat for details.*

Destination Victoria

*T*he British legacy is indelibly stamped on the city. Here you will find massive stone castles, palatial government buildings, quaint cottages and gardens that bloom almost all year.

*B*ut look closer—another culture has left its mark: Native Indian icons are displayed with equal prominence throughout Victoria.

© Richard Cummins / Photophile

Butchart Gardens, Brentwood Bay. One of the Victoria vicinity's "must see" gardens dates to 1904. (See listing page 179)

© Gibson Stock Photography

Sightseeing in Victoria. A carriage ride is a romantic way to see the city. (See mention page 176)

© Gibson Stock Photography

Thunderbird Park, Victoria. This outdoor collection of First Nations totem poles includes many carvings of the mythical thunderbird. (See listing page 175)

BRITISH COLUMBIA
WASHINGTON.

Sidney

Saanichton

Brentwood Bay

Sooke

View Royal

Victoria

CANADA
UNITED STATES

See Downtown map page 172

Tourism Victoria

Whale watching, Victoria. Several excursion boats take passengers to see this exciting natural attraction. (See mention page 176)

*P*laces included in this AAA Destination City:

4V2; phone (250) 386-3431 outside British Columbia or (888) 223-3779 within British Columbia.

Getting Around

Street System

Most traffic activity is on Wharf, Government and Belleville streets, which embrace the Inner Harbour. Ferries arrive from Port Angeles, Wash., all year and from Seattle in summer. The main east-west streets are Yates, Fort and Johnson. Pandora Avenue, renamed Oak Bay Avenue in midtown, crosses the city from the Inner Harbour to Oak Bay.

Major north-south thoroughfares are Blanshard Street (Hwy. 17) and Douglas Street (Hwy. 1), which begins at Victoria's southern coast along the Juan de Fuca Strait. Dallas Road borders the shore and continues as Beach Drive along Victoria's eastern coast. Many Victoria streets are one-way.

Parking

On-street parking is controlled by meters and posted restrictions Mon.-Sat. 9-6. Vehicles parked on specially posted blocks are subject to towing during rush hours. Downtown off-street parking is available in civic parkades and shopping center lots.

What To See

ART GALLERY OF GREATER VICTORIA is at 1040 Moss St. The gallery presents contemporary, historical and Asian exhibitions, including a permanent Emily Carr exhibition. Daily 10-5 (also Thurs. 5-9); closed Nov. 11 and Dec. 25. Admission $6, over 64 and students with ID $4, under 12 free. Admission may increase for special exhibits. MC, VI. Phone (250) 384-4101.

BASTION SQUARE overlooks the harbor. James Douglas established Fort Victoria on this site in 1843. Restored and preserved buildings from the 19th-century boom days surround a courtyard plaza.

BEACON HILL PARK is at Douglas and Dallas sts. The 74-hectare (183-acre) park features attractive flowerbeds, small lakes, playing fields and lawns that slope to the sea, and a totem pole carved by Chief Mungo Martin. Daily dawn-dusk. Free.

BUTCHART GARDENS— *see Brentwood Bay p. 179.*

CANADIAN FORCES BASE ESQUIMALT NAVAL & MILITARY MUSEUM is 6 km (4 mi.) w. on Esquimalt Rd., then n. on Admirals Rd. to the main

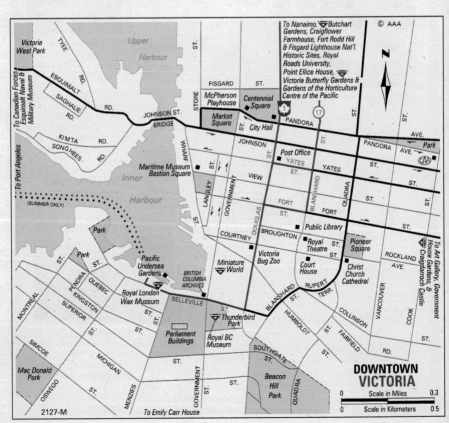

gate of Naden. Historic artifacts, documents and photographs relate to the naval and military heritage of the area. Allow 1 hour minimum. Mon.-Fri. 10-3:30, Jan. 2-Nov. 30; closed holidays. Admission $2; over 64, students with ID and under 17, $1; family rate $5. Phone (250) 363-4312 or (250) 363-5655.

Esquimalt Navy Base Summer Bus Tour departs from the Canadian Forces Base Esquimalt Naval & Military Museum. A 1-hour tour of the base also passes the harbor, where navy warships can be seen. Departures daily at 10, mid-June to mid-Aug. Free. Phone (250) 363-7060.

CENTRE OF THE UNIVERSE is at 5071 W. Saanich Rd. Housed within the Dominion Astrophysical Observatory, this interpretive center affords visitors a glimpse into the world of astronomy. The facility offers interactive exhibits, theater presentations and a look at the constellations in the Starlab Planetarium. Visitors may tour the 1.8-metre (5-ft.) Plaskett Telescope.

Guided tours are available. Allow 1 hour, 30 minutes minimum. Daily 1-11, May 23-Sept. 5; Sat. 1-11, Sun.-Fri. 10-6, Apr. 1-May 22 and Sept. 6-Oct. 31; Tues.-Sat. 10-5:30, rest of year. Closed Dec. 25-Jan. 1. Admission $9; over 64, $7; ages 6-17, $5; under 5 free when accompanied by a parent; family rate $23 (two adults and three children). Admission after 7 p.m. $12.50; over 64, $10.50;

ages 6-17, $7; family rate (two adults and three children) $31. AX, MC, VI. Phone (250) 363-8262.

CHRIST CHURCH CATHEDRAL is at Quadra and Rockland sts. The Anglican-Episcopal cathedral is reminiscent of the great Gothic churches of the Middle Ages. Originally founded in 1856, the present cathedral is the third church built on this site. Started in the late 1920s and completed in 1986, it is one of Canada's largest cathedrals. The bells are replicas of those at Westminster Abbey in London. A labyrinth is on the grounds. Daily 8-6. Free. Phone (250) 383-2714.

CRAIGDARROCH CASTLE is at 1050 Joan Crescent St. The sandstone mansion was built in the late 1880s for Robert Dunsmuir, a Scottish immigrant who attained wealth and fame through politics and coal mining. Dunsmuir died before the 39-room castle was completed. The building later served as a military hospital, a college and a music conservatory.

Visitors can appreciate the castle's stained-glass windows, intricate woodwork, ceiling murals and Victorian furnishings. There are numerous staircases, but no elevators. A self-guiding tour includes four floors of the castle and an 87-step climb to the tower, which offers stunning views of Victoria, the Strait and the Olympic Mountains.

Picnicking is permitted. Allow 1 hour minimum. Daily 9-7, June 15-Labour Day; 10-4:30, rest of

year. Closed Jan. 1 and Dec. 25-26. Admission $10; ages 13-17, $6.50; ages 6-12, $3.50 when accompanied by an adult. MC, VI. Phone (250) 592-5323.

EMILY CARR HOUSE is at 207 Government St. Built in 1864 a few blocks from the harbor, the house was the birthplace of artist and writer Emily Carr. The Victorian residence has been restored to the ambiance the Carr family experienced in the 1870s. Family possessions, including some of Carr's early pottery, are displayed. Daily 11-4, mid-May to mid-Oct. Last admission is at 4. Admission $5; under 18, $3.50; family rate $12. Guided tour $10; under 18, $5; family rate $25. MC, VI. Phone (250) 383-5843.

SAVE **GARDENS OF THE HORTICULTURE CENTRE OF THE PACIFIC** is off Hwy. 17 West Saanich/Quadra exit, then w. to Beaver Lake Rd., following signs to 505 Quayle Rd. Two hectares (5 acres) of educational gardens feature more than 10,000 plant varieties. Highlights of the developing site include the Winter Garden and the Takata Japanese Garden. The surrounding 36 hectares (90 acres) include forests, wetlands and a haven for migratory birds.

Picnicking is permitted. Allow 1 hour minimum. Daily 8-8, Apr.-Sept.; 9-4, rest of year. Closed Dec. 25. Admission $7.50, over 59 and students with ID $5.25, under 16 free. MC, VI. Phone (250) 479-6162.

GOVERNMENT HOUSE GARDENS is at 1401 Rockland Ave. The grounds in front of the lieutenant governor's residence consist of 5.7 hectares (14 acres) of formal gardens, featuring perennials, herbs, roses, irises, azaleas, rhododendrons and other floral varieties. The property behind the house—which is closed to the public—covers a 9-hectare (22-acre) rare Garry oak woodland that is native to southeast Vancouver Island.

Picnicking is permitted. Formal gardens daily dawn-dusk. Guided 90-minute tours of the woodland or gardens are available; phone ahead for times. Formal gardens by donations. Guided tours $10.

MARITIME MUSEUM OF BRITISH COLUMBIA is at 28 Bastion Sq. The Pacific Northwest's maritime heritage is presented through ship models, figureheads, ships' tools and naval uniforms. Also featured is the 1860 *Tilikum*, an 11-metre (36-ft.) dugout canoe converted to a schooner, which sailed from Victoria to England 1901-04. The museum's 1889 building features one of the oldest operating birdcage elevators in North America.

Allow 1 hour minimum. Daily 9:30-5, mid-June to mid-Sept.; 9:30-4:30, rest of year. Closed Dec. 25. Admission $7.48; over 65 and students with ID $4.67; ages 6-11, $2.80; family rate $20. MC, VI. Phone (250) 385-4222.

GEM **MINIATURE WORLD** is in the Fairmont Empress Hotel at 649 Humboldt St. Animation, lighting and sound effects enhance SAVE more than 80 highly detailed miniature scenes. Displays include a circus, two of the world's largest dollhouses, a Swiss Family Robinson tree house and a futuristic space diorama. Scenes illustrate historic battles, fairy tales, nursery rhymes, "Gulliver's Travels" and novels by Charles Dickens. The Great Canadian Railway exhibit recreates rail transportation in late 19th-century Canada.

Allow 1 hour minimum. Daily 8:30 a.m.-9 p.m., June 17-Labour Day; 9-7, May 20-June 16; 9-5, rest of year. Closed Dec. 25. Admission $9; ages 12-17, $8; ages 5-11, $7. AX, MC, VI. Phone (250) 385-9731.

SAVE **PACIFIC UNDERSEA GARDENS** is at 490 Belleville St. An observation room on the sea bottom allows visitors to view native marine life through large underwater windows. Daily 9-8:30, July-Aug.; 9-6, May-June; 9:30-5, rest of year. Admission $8.50; over 64, $7.50; ages 12-17, $6; ages 5-11, $4.50. MC, VI. Phone (250) 382-5717.

PARLIAMENT BUILDINGS overlook the Inner Harbour and yacht basin. The seat of British Columbia's Legislative Assembly, the buildings are elaborately carved facades and are surrounded by 5 hectares (12 acres) of lawns, gardens, fountains and statues of dignitaries. The rooms have mosaic tile

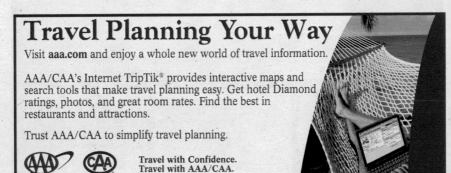

floors, rotundas, stained-glass windows, woodcarvings and murals. Guided tours, conducted in several languages, are given Mon.-Fri. 9-5, Sat.-Sun. 9-4:30, Victoria Day-Labour Day; Mon.-Fri. 9-5, rest of year. Contact the Tour Coordinator office to confirm times. Closed winter holidays. Free. Phone (250) 387-3046.

POINT ELLICE HOUSE is at 2616 Pleasant St. Built in 1861, the rambling Italianate residence contains many of its original furnishings. Lawns and a restored 19th-century garden surround the house. Self-guiding audiotapes are available. Food is available. Allow 30 minutes minimum. Daily 10-4, mid-May to mid-Sept.; Fri.-Sun. 10-4, mid-Sept. to late Oct. and in Dec. Admission $5 (includes tour). MC, VI. Phone (250) 380-6506.

ROYAL BC MUSEUM is next to the parliament buildings at 675 Belleville St. Two floors of displays reflect the human and natural history of British Columbia. A turn-of-the-20th-century frontier town has a theater with silent movies, a steam train pulling into its station and the aroma of apple pie wafting from a kitchen. A coastal rain forest exhibit is highlighted by live plants and ocean animals. Other features include the First Peoples Gallery, which includes an exhibit focusing on the historic Nisga'a agreement and the present-day Nisga'a community, and Haida argillite carvings.

The on-site National Geographic IMAX Theater *(see color ad)* offers films to complement the natural and human history theme of the museum. Local and international special exhibits are featured several times throughout the year.

Museum open daily 9-5. Theater open daily 10-8. Closed Jan. 1 and Dec. 25. Museum $12.50; over 64 and ages 6-18, $8.70; family rate $33.70. Combination ticket $21; over 64 and ages 6-18,

$16.95; under 5, $5. AX, MC, VI. Phone (250) 356-7226 or (888) 447-7977.

British Columbia Archives is in Heritage Court at 655 Belleville St. Extensive public and private records are available to those conducting historical, genealogical or other research. The archives are open to the public Mon.-Tues. and Thurs.-Fri. 9:30-4:30; closed 1 week in early May and holidays. A photo identification card is required. Free. Phone (250) 387-5885.

Helmcken House is next to the Royal BC Museum, behind Thunderbird Park. One of the oldest houses in British Columbia, the 1852 log structure was the home of John Sebastian Helmcken, a surgeon for Hudson's Bay Co. at Fort Victoria and a Father of Confederation. The restored house displays many original furnishings and a fine collection of period medical instruments.

Allow 30 minutes minimum. Daily 10-5, July-Sept. Hours vary; phone ahead. Admission $7; over 64 and students with ID $6; ages 5-12, $5; family rate $12. Phone (250) 356-7226.

The Netherlands Centennial Carillon is at the corner of Government and Belleville sts. The largest carillon in Canada houses 62 bells donated by British Columbians of Dutch origin as a tribute to the 1967 Canadian Confederation Centennial. Recitals are held Sun. at 3, Mar.-Dec. (also Fri. at 7, July-Aug.). Free. Phone (250) 356-7226.

Thunderbird Park is at the corner of Douglas and Belleville sts. on the grounds of the Royal BC Museum. The park's noted collection of Northwest Coast totem poles includes several carved by Kwakwaka'wakw artist Mungo Martin. Many poles are adorned with the mythical thunderbird, thought by some to be a representation of the California condor. Carvers can be seen at work in summer. Park open daily dawn-dusk. Carvers studio open daily 10-1. Free.

ROYAL LONDON WAX MUSEUM is at 470 Belleville in the Inner Harbour opposite the Parliament Buildings. Housed in the former customs office, the museum features some 300 wax figures in more than 50 scenes. Included are Albert Einstein, Mother Teresa, Martin Luther King and Princess Diana. Storytelling guides provide historical background about each figure. Themed collections include Royalty Row, Storybook Land, Martyrs of Hope, The Galaxy of Stars and The 20th Century.

A special exhibit celebrating Queen Elizabeth's Golden Jubilee includes Canadian prime ministers and American presidents during her reign. Frozen in Time, a multimedia theater presentation, focuses on the search for the Northwest Passage. Allow 1 hour minimum. Daily 9-7:30, May-Aug.; 9:30-5, rest of year. Closed Dec. 25. Admission $8.88; over 64, $7.95; ages 13-19, $6.54; ages 6-12, $4.67. AX, DC, MC, VI. Phone (250) 388-4461.

ROYAL ROADS UNIVERSITY is at 2005 Sooke Rd. The institution was one of Canada's three military colleges devoted to the training of officer cadets. Hatley Castle, built in 1908 for British Columbia's former lieutenant governor James Dunsmuir, is now used for university programs. A museum chronicles the history of the Dunsmuir family and Royal Roads. The 216.5-hectare (535-acre) facility contains natural forests, a formal lawn and Japanese, Italian and English rose gardens.

Guided tours are available. Grounds open daily dawn-dusk. Museum daily 11-4, early June-Labour Day; Mon.-Fri. 1-4, rest of year. Grounds, gardens and museum free. Hatley Castle tours $3, students with ID $1. Phone (250) 391-2600, ext. 4456.

UNIVERSITY OF VICTORIA is on McKenzie Ave. at Gordon Head Rd. The 160-hectare (395-acre) campus includes the Mystic Vale Ecological Protection Area, several totems carved by local artists and Finnerty Gardens, known for its collection of more than 200 rhododendron species. A self-guiding walking tour brochure is available from the MacPherson Library loans desk. Grounds open daily 24 hours. Guided tours are given Mon., Wed.

and Fri. at 12:30. Free. Parking $5. Reservations are required for tours. Phone (250) 721-8949.

VICTORIA BUG ZOO is at 631 Courtney St. More than 40 species of insects and spiders from around the world are on display. Highlights include a leaf-cutter ant farm and the giant African millipede. For the more adventurous, the zoo also provides the opportunity for and an environment conducive to a safe bug handling experience. Guided tours are available. Allow 30 minutes minimum. Mon.-Sat. 9:30-5:30, Sun. 11-5:30 (also 5:30-7 p.m., mid-June through Aug. 31); closed Jan. 1 and Dec. 25. Admission $7; senior citizens $5; over 16, $6; ages 3-16, $4.50. MC, VI. Phone (250) 384-2847.

What To Do

Sightseeing

Boat Tours

Sightseers using Victoria as a base for their travels can explore the Gulf Islands and Vancouver by ferry from Swartz Bay, north of Victoria via Hwy. 17; for schedule and toll phone the British Columbia Ferry Service at (250) 386-3431.

Opportunities for whale watching are offered by several boating companies, the oldest of which is Seacoast Expeditions, 146 Kingston St.; phone (250) 383-2254.

Bus and Carriage Tours

Guided tours of the city in red double-decker buses from London enhance Victoria's British atmosphere. Many of these tour operators are found along Belleville and Menzies streets by the harbor. Gray Line, 700 Douglas, (250) 388-5248, conducts bus tours.

The Tallyho offers horse-drawn narrated tours of the city from late March through September (weather permitting); phone (250) 383-5067. Black Beauty Victorian Carriage Tours offers horse-drawn carriage rides through downtown and Beacon Hill Park; phone (250) 361-1220. Both tours leave from the corner of Belleville and Menzies streets.

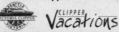

Driving Tours

The Greater Victoria Visitors Information Centre has information about such scenic drives as Marine Drive along the shoreline, a trip to Sooke Harbour on the west coast and the Malahat Drive, which runs along the east coast and reaches an elevation of 381 metres (1,250 ft.). The trip to Butchart Gardens is one of the most popular drives, following Hwy. 17 and Hwy. 17A through the rural communities and pastoral valleys of the Saanich Peninsula.

Walking Tours

Victoria is the perfect size for visitors keen on walking. A favorite thoroughfare of strollers and shoppers is Government Street, graced by banners and five-globe Victorian lampposts supporting baskets of geraniums and petunias.

Sports and Recreation

The English spirit still is manifest in such games as **lawn bowling** at the corner of Belleville Street and Douglas Street and **cricket** at Beacon Hill Park. Any notion, however, that Victoria's sports are too staid is dispelled quickly by a **box lacrosse** game. This offspring of the Indian game of *baggataway* is a rough-and-tumble version of field lacrosse confined to a smaller, enclosed area. Canada's Parliament designated boxla, as it also is called, the national sport in 1867. The game is played from April to August at Memorial Arena, 1925 Blanshard.

All-star **wrestling** and **ice hockey,** two other spectator sports that hardly could be considered sedate, also are held at the arena.

Water sports have obvious appeal in this island city. The wide variety of game fish around southern Vancouver Island includes rockfish, lingcod, sole and flounder; fishing licenses are required. Surf **fishing** often yields rewarding catches of salmon and black sea bass. Clamming and oyster harvesting are popular activities on any of the Gulf Islands, which are accessible by ferry from Swartz Bay.

Oak Bay Marina, 1327 Beach Dr., offers fishing charters at an hourly rate. Fishing equipment, a tackle shop and marine store are available; phone (250) 598-3369. Other nearby marinas include Anglers Anchorage Marina, 933 Marchant, Brentwood Bay; North Saanich Marina, 1949 Marina Way, Sidney; and the West Bay Marina, 453 Head St.

Boating is enjoyed in the Strait of Georgia and the Saanich Inlet. Uplands Park on Oak Bay is equipped with boat ramps. Fine beaches border Dallas Road and Beach Drive.

With its scenic coastal location and balmy climate, Victoria offers excellent playing conditions for **golf.** On a peninsula jutting into the Juan de Fuca Strait, Victoria Golf Club is open to members of other clubs.

Other golf clubs include Ardmore (nine holes), 930 Ardmore Dr., North Saanich; Cedar Hill (18 holes), 1400 Derby Rd.; Cordova Bay (18 holes), 5333 Cordova Bay Rd.; Glen Meadows (18 holes), 1050 McTavish Rd.; Green Acres (nine holes), 3970 Metchosin Rd.; Henderson Park (nine holes), 2291 Cedar Hill Crossroad; Mount Douglas (nine holes), 4225 Blenkinsop Rd.; Olympic View Golf Course (18 holes), 643 Latoria Rd.; Prospect Lake (nine holes), 4633 Prospect Lake Rd.; and Royal Oak Golf Club (nine holes), 540 Marsett Pl.

Many parks are scattered throughout Victoria and its surrounding municipalities of Oak Bay, Saanich and Esquimalt. Some offer **swimming,** such as Thetis Lake Park, Mount Work Park, Elk/Beaver Lake Park, Willows Beach Park and Island View Beach Park. Swimmers also might wish to try the Crystal Pool in Central Park.

Hiking, nature and horse trails are found at several parks. For more information contact Victoria Downtown Park; phone (250) 361-0600. Bamberton Provincial Park *(see Recreation Chart and the AAA/ CAA Western Canada & Alaska CampBook)* offers developed recreational facilities, including **camping.**

Hiking trails and floating walkways weave through the Swan Lake-Christmas Hill Nature Sanctuary, 6.5 kilometres (4 mi.) north via the Patricia Bay Hwy. Excellent views of Victoria and the sea are at Mount Douglas, Mount Tolmie and Beacon Hill Park.

Shopping

Lined with shops carrying English tweeds and fine china, Government Street maintains Victoria's heritage as a trading post of the British Empire. Such shops as E.A. Morris Tobacconist have distinguished Government Street since the 19th century. Established in 1833, Rogers' Chocolate Shop is a Victoria institution that counts British royalty in its clientele. The Rogers' factory, behind the store at 913 Government St., still produces its renowned bittersweet chocolate according to a guarded recipe.

Shoppers determined to bring home something other than a few extra pounds might want to explore the craft and specialty shops in the renovated squares and malls off Government Street. More than 30 quaint stores and restaurants in revitalized old buildings highlight Market Square, bounded by Johnson, Pandora and Store streets.

Trounce Alley, in the downtown core, is a hideaway of eclectic shops. Shops of mid-19th-century architecture display modern items in Bastion Square, once a hangout for prospectors and drifters. An attractive shopping arcade is in Centennial Square off Douglas Street. Nootka Court between Courtney and Humboldt streets contains small arts and crafts shops.

Popular items available in Victoria include handwoven woolens from Ireland and England, handknit Cowichan Indian sweaters, Eskimo jade sculpture and Northwest Indian masks and prints. The Bay department stores, 1150 and 3125 Douglas St., sell authentic Cowichan sweaters. Also in Victoria are Hillside Shopping Centre, 1644 Hillside Rd.; Mayfair Shopping Centre, 3147 Douglas St.; and Sears, 3190 Shelbourne St.

In keeping with its Victorian image, Victoria has more than 50 antique shops. Many are found along Government and Fort streets and Oak Bay Avenue.

Theater and Concerts

McPherson Playhouse in Centennial Square is the center of Vancouver Island's regional and professional theater. The restored old theater regularly presents noontime concerts and musical comedy productions in the evening; phone (250) 386-6121. The Pacific Opera Victoria, (250) 385-0222, performs at the Royal Theatre.

The Royal Theatre on Broughton Street is the home of the Victoria Symphony Orchestra, (250) 385-6515, which offers a pop and masterworks series September through May. The Victoria Conservatory of Music sometimes offers performances; phone (250) 386-5311.

Comedy revues and music hall shows also are staged frequently at the Belfry, (250) 385-6815, 1291 Gladstone, and the Royal Theatre, (250) 386-6121, 805 Broughton. The University of Victoria Auditorium on Finnerty Road also presents various cultural events; phone (250) 721-8480. Butchart Gardens mounts musical stage shows during the summer. Kaleidoscope Theatre, an open-air theater at the Inner Harbour, also offers summer productions.

Top-name entertainers, rock groups and other performers draw large audiences to Memorial Arena, 1925 Blanshard. A carillon at the Parliament Buildings can be heard daily at 3 during the summer.

Special Events

As a city of traditions, Victoria celebrates many events and festivals year after year. Victoria Day, a Canadian national holiday, launches a week of festivities highlighted by a parade. The weekend following Victoria Day features the classic Swiftsure Race, which has drawn an armada of more than 450 sailboats from all over the world since 1930. The Highlander Games take place in mid-May. The performing arts provide a theme for the Victoria Harbour Festival the last week in May.

Victoria Folkfest, held the last week in June, shows the costumes, dances and music of Victoria's cultural mélange. The Inner Harbour is the site of the Classic Boat Festival from late August to early September.

Autumn shows off its best colors along the rural Saanich Peninsula, where the Saanich Fair has been held in early September for more than a century. Fall's lower temperatures provide an energy boost for several major sports events, including the Victoria Open PGA Tournament Players Series and the Royal Victoria Marathon.

The Victoria Vicinity

BRENTWOOD BAY (H-10)

BUTCHART GARDENS is 2 km (1.2 mi.) s. on Saanich Rd., then w. to 800 Benvenuto Ave. The 20-hectare (50-acre) site contains the Rose Garden, Japanese Garden, Italian Garden, as well as the Star Pond and Ross Fountains. The Sunken Garden was created by the Butcharts on the site of their depleted limestone quarry.

The spring season brings azaleas, tulips, daffodils and other delicate blossoms. Breathtaking roses, annuals and perennials bloom in summer, while bursts of colorful foliage appear in autumn; subtle colored lighting illuminates the gardens June 15 through Sept. 15. July through August, nightly entertainment is offered with fireworks displays Saturday nights. Winter's starkness contrasts with the sparkle of holiday lights from Dec. 1 to Jan. 6.

Food is available. Allow 2 hours minimum. Gardens open daily at 9; (at 1 on Dec. 25); closing times vary depending on the season. Admission mid-June through Sept. 30, $22; ages 13-17, $11; ages 5-12, $2.50. Admission varies, rest of year. AX, MC, VI. Phone (250) 652-5256 or (866) 652-4422. *See color ad p. 173.*

VICTORIA BUTTERFLY GARDENS is 2 km (1.2 mi.) s. at jct. Saanich and Keating Cross rds. to 1461 Benvenuto Ave. This 1,110-square-metre (12,000-sq.-ft.) indoor tropical garden was designed specifically for the housing and breeding of more than 35 exotic butterfly and moth species. Guided tours and a videotape explain the transformations the butterflies undergo during their life cycle. More than 300 pupae are imported each week and displayed in the Emerging Room.

Up to 2,000 butterflies—from the 1.3-centimetre-long (.5-in.) Glasswing to the 30.5-centimetre-long (1-ft.) Atlas Moth—fly free among tropical plants and flowers, including an orchid exhibit and a carnivorous bog. Water falls into a stream that is home to fish, tropical ducks and such rare birds as the South African turacos.

Food is available. Allow 1 hour minimum. Daily 9-5:30, mid-May through Sept. 5; 9:30-4:30, Mar. 1 through mid-May and Sept. 6-Oct. 31. Opening and closing dates may vary; phone ahead. All-day admission $9.50; over 64, students with ID and ages 13-18, $8.50; ages 5-12, $5.50. MC, VI. Phone (250) 652-3822 or (877) 722-0272.

FORT RODD HILL AND FISGARD LIGHTHOUSE NATIONAL HISTORIC SITES (H-9)

Fifteen kilometres (9 mi.) west of Victoria via Hwy. 1A, Fort Rodd Hill was a coastal artillery fort 1895-1956. Of interest are the loophole walls, underground magazines, artillery stores, command posts, barracks and gun and searchlight emplacements. Audiotape and videotape presentations, along with period rooms, depict life at the fort. The 1860 Fisgard Lighthouse, restored to its 1873 appearance, was the first built on this part of the coast. Still operational, the lighthouse has two floors of historical exhibits. A nature trail follows the paths formerly used by soldiers. Historical exhibits also are featured. Picnic facilities are available.

Allow 1 hour, 30 minutes minimum. Park open daily 10-5:30, Mar.-Oct.; 9-4:30, rest of year. Lighthouse and fort exhibits daily 10-5, Mar.-Oct.; 9-4, rest of year. Closed Jan. 1 and Dec. 25-26. Limited services Nov.-Feb. Admission (includes fort and lighthouse) $4; over 64, $3.50; ages 6-16, $2; family rate $10. MC, VI. Phone (250) 478-5849.

SAANICHTON (H-10) elev. 58 m/194′

HERITAGE ACRES (SAANICH HISTORICAL ARTIFACTS SOCIETY) is off Hwy. 17, e. on Island View Dr., then n. to 7321 Lochside Dr. The society is dedicated to maintaining artifacts from the area's rural past on 12 hectares (29 acres) of parkland. A museum exhibits historic household items, furnishings and farm equipment. Also part of the complex are a blacksmith's shop, a sawmill, nature trails and a one-room log cabin. Rides are offered aboard model trains.

Picnicking is permitted. Allow 30 minutes minimum. Daily 9:30-4, June 1-Labour Day; 9:30-noon, rest of year. Closed Dec. 25. Donations. Admission is charged during events held Father's Day weekend and the third weekend in Sept. Phone (250) 652-5522.

SIDNEY (H-10) pop. 10,929, elev. 9 m/30′

Salish Indians were the earliest known inhabitants of the area now called Sidney. Incorporated into a town in 1967, Sidney is known for its fishing and waterfront activity. Picnicking, beachcombing and camping are popular at Sidney Spit Marine Provincial Park *(see the AAA/CAA Western Canada & Alaska CampBook).*

Saanich Peninsula Chamber of Commerce: 2480 Beacon Ave., P.O. Box 2014, Sidney, BC, Canada V8L 3S3. Phone (250) 656-3616.

BRITISH COLUMBIA AVIATION MUSEUM is at Victoria Airport at 1910 Norseman Rd. Displays of memorabilia and aircraft include World War II planes and bush planes, a model plane exhibit, photographs and aircraft engines. Guided tours are available. Allow 1 hour minimum. Daily 10-4 during DST; 11-3, rest of year. Closed Jan. 1 and Dec. 25. Admission $7; over 65, $5; students with ID $2; under 13 free. VI. Phone (250) 655-3300.

SIDNEY HISTORICAL MUSEUM is at 2423 Beacon Ave. The early lives of Sidney and North Saanich pioneers are portrayed through photographs and artifacts. Allow 1 hour minimum. Daily 10-4, May-Oct.; Sat.-Sun. 11-3, rest of year. Donations. Phone (250) 655-6355.

SOOKE (H-10) pop. 8,735, elev. 38 m/125′

A natural harbor off the Juan de Fuca Strait, Sooke was discovered and claimed by the Spanish in 1790. The area, soon traded to the British by treaty, was named after a local Indian tribe, T'Soke. It is a popular fishing site and the center of a large forest industry. A scenic portion of Hwy. 14 runs 43 kilometres (27 mi.) east from Sooke to Victoria.

Sooke Travel InfoCentre: 2070 Phillips Rd., Box 774, Sooke, BC, Canada V0S 1N0; phone (250) 642-6351.

SOOKE REGION MUSEUM is 1 km (.6 mi.) e. on Hwy. 14 at 2070 Phillips Rd. Exhibits about First Nations people, early settlers and industrialization illustrate the history and economy of the west coast region. The 1870 Moss Cottage depicts late 19th-century family life. Documentary films are shown. In the summer salmon barbecues are scheduled; reservations are required. Guided tours are available. Allow 30 minutes minimum. Daily 9-5. Museum by donations. Moss Cottage $2; students with ID and children over 12, $1. Phone (250) 642-6351.

VIEW ROYAL (H-10)
pop. 7,271, elev. 22 m/72′

CRAIGFLOWER FARMHOUSE is at jct. Craigflower and Admirals rds. Built in 1856 on an original homestead, the farmhouse is a fine example of early Georgian architecture. The heavy oak door reinforced with iron studs is a reminder of the British class system. Farm animals, on view in the summer, and a kitchen garden complement the atmosphere. The schoolhouse was built by the Craigflower farmhouse workers for their children.

Allow 30 minutes minimum. Wed.-Sun. 1-5, May-Sept. Admission $5; senior citizens and ages 6-18, $3. MC. Phone (250) 383-4627.

This ends listings for the Victoria Vicinity.
The following page resumes the alphabetical listings
of cities in British Columbia.

VIEW ROYAL—*see Victoria p. 180.*

WARDNER (D-12) pop. 100

KOOTENAY TROUT HATCHERY is 8 km (5 mi.) n. on the e. side of the Kootenay River. The facility raises 3 million trout annually. An aquarium contains fish species raised at the hatchery, including the rare white sturgeon. Displays explain fish raising. An outside moat holds large rainbow trout. Allow 30 minutes minimum. Daily 8-4. Free. Phone (250) 429-3214.

WESTBANK (C-9)
pop. 15,700, elev. 411 m/1,348′

Westbank was a link on the fur-trading route from the north-central part of the province, called New Caledonia, to the Columbia River. In the early 1860s fortune seekers en route to the Cariboo gold mines followed the old trail through the Okanagan Valley.

Ideal climatic conditions in the Okanagan Valley nurture Westbank's many orchards and vineyards. Vacationers also are drawn by the favorable weather in the valley. Downhill and cross-country skiing in the surrounding countryside are popular in winter.

Westbank Chamber of Commerce: 2375 Pamela St., Suite 4, Westbank, BC, Canada V4T 2H9; phone (250) 768-3378.

WINERIES

• **Mission Hill Family Estate** is 4.5 km (3 mi.) e. off Hwy. 97 via Boucherie Rd. to 1730 Mission Hill Rd. Daily 10-6, Nov.-May; closed Jan. 1 and Dec. 25-26. Tours are given at 11, 1 and 3. Times vary rest of year; phone ahead. Phone (250) 768-6448.

WEST VANCOUVER—*see Vancouver p. 165.*

WHISTLER (F-12)
pop. 8,896, elev. 640 m/2,009′

Whistler, a popular year-round resort village and skiing destination, is cradled by Whistler and Blackcomb mountains.

Walking trails start at Whistler Village for such destinations as Alta and Lost lakes, nearby alpine meadows and glacier regions. Mountain biking enthusiasts can test their mettle atop Whistler Mountain. Climbing to 6,000 feet, a gondola or chairlift ride up Whistler and Blackcomb mountains, respectively, affords a breathtaking view of the surround. The Valley Trail is available for roller skating, cycling and walking. Day excursions to the southern Cariboo region are available aboard the British Columbia Railway. This railway also makes daily runs to Whistler from North Vancouver; phone (604) 984-5246.

Several golf courses as well as tennis facilities and riding stables provide additional opportunities to enjoy the area in summer. The Whistler River is known for white-water rafting.

For information about the many private sightseeing companies, including float plane services, contact Whistler Resort Association, 4010 Whistler Way, Whistler, BC, Canada V0N 1B0; phone (604) 664-5625 or (800) 944-7853.

Whistler Chamber of Commerce: 4230 Gateway Dr., Whistler, BC V0N 1B4; phone (604) 932-5528, ext. 17 or (604) 932-5922, ext. 17.

Shopping areas: Whistler Village features more than 150 specialty shops in a pedestrian enclave.

BLACKCOMB HORSEDRAWN SLEIGH RIDES depart from Base II on Blackcomb Mountain, at the end of Glacier Dr. Tours of the wooded countryside stop at a warming cabin, where musical entertainment is provided. Lunch and dinner sleigh rides also are available by reservation. Trips daily on the hour 5-8, Nov. 25-Mar. 31. Fare $52; ages 13-18, $42; ages 3-12, $32. Phone (604) 932-7631.

WHISTLER AIR SERVICES is 3 km (1.9 mi.) n. on Hwy. 99, following signs. The company offers 30- to 70-minute floatplane tours over glaciers, ice caps or alpine lakes. Trips depart daily Apr.-Sept. (weather permitting). Fare $99-$189, under 12 half-price with two adults. Reservations are required. MC, VI. Phone (604) 932-6615 or (888) 806-2299.

RECREATIONAL ACTIVITIES

Dogsledding

- **Cougar Mountain Wilderness Adventures** is at 18-4314 Main St., Whistler, BC, Canada V0N 1B4. Other activities are offered. Daily 9-9, Dec.-Mar.; 8-7, June-Sept.; 9-5, rest of year. Phone (604) 932-4086 or (888) 297-2222.

Skiing

- **Whistler/Blackcomb Mountain** is on Hwy. 99. Write 4545 Blackcomb Way, Whistler, BC, Canada V0N 1B4. Other activities are offered. Whistler daily mid-Nov. to early June. Blackcomb mid-Nov. to early Apr. Phone (604) 932-3434 or (800) 766-0449.

White-water Rafting

- [SAVE] **Whistler River Adventures** departs from 4165 Springs Ln. at the base of the Whistler Mountain gondola in Whistler Village. Write P.O. Box 202, Whistler, BC, Canada V0N 1B0. Other activities are offered. Trips depart daily 8-8, mid-May through Sept. 12. Phone (604) 932-3532 or (888) 932-3532 within British Columbia.

WILLIAMS LAKE (F-5) pop. 11,153

The rush for gold brought prospectors to the heart of the Cariboo in the 1860s, but it was the 1920s Canadian Railway push that put Williams Lake on the map. Cattle ranching and timber production now are the economic mainstays. Twenty kilometres (12 mi.) north of Williams Lake, Bull Mountain Trails offers 30 kilometres (19 mi.) of trails for cross-country skiing, hiking and mountain biking.

Williams Lake and District Chamber of Commerce: 1148 S. Broadway, Williams Lake, BC, Canada V2G 1A2; phone (250) 392-5025.

MUSEUM OF THE CARIBOO CHILCOTIN is at 113 N. Fourth Ave. Highlights include the BC Cowboys Hall of Fame and displays portraying the ranching and rodeo history of the Cariboo Chilcotin. Artifacts and photographs depict the lifestyles of cowboys and ranchers as well as First Nations people. Allow 30 minutes minimum. Mon.-Sat. 10-4, June-Aug.; Tues.-Sat. 11-4, rest of year. Closed Jan. 1, Good Friday and Dec. 25. Admission $2, under 13 free. Phone (250) 392-7404.

SCOUT ISLAND NATURE CENTER is off Hwy. 97 just e. of jct. Hwy. 20, s. on McKenzie Ave., then e. on Borland Rd. Nature trails lead to views of the lake. The island and marsh are prime nesting grounds for migratory birds. A nature house offers interactive displays, a marsh aquarium and a beehive. Grounds daily 8-dusk. Nature house Wed.-Fri. 9-7, Sat.-Sun. noon-3, Mon.-Tues. 9-4, May-Aug. Free.

YALE (C-7) pop. 171

Settled at the southern entrance to Fraser Canyon, Yale was a major steamship port during the gold rush. The town was established in 1848 as a Hudson's Bay Co. fort, taking its name from the commander of Fort Langley. After gold was discovered on Hill's Bar in 1858, Yale's population swelled to 30,000. In later years the number dwindled to 200. Several buildings from the mid-1800s still stand, and a pioneer cemetery contains Victorian monuments to early settlers.

The Alexandra Suspension Bridge, 22 kilometres (14 mi.) north of town, was constructed in 1863 to ferry miners across the Fraser River. From the bridge, which was rebuilt in 1926 with the original foundations, the original wagon road to the Cariboo goldfields is visible. A hiking trail leading to the nearby Spirit Caves offers views of the canyon.

HISTORIC YALE MUSEUM AND CHURCH OF ST. JOHN THE DIVINE are at 31187 Douglas St. The museum displays artifacts about mining, paddlewheelers, the Canadian Pacific Railway and early settlers. The Church of St. John the Divine has served the area since it was built in 1863. Guided walking tours of the old townsite and pioneer cemetery are offered in the summer. Gold panning instructions and trips also are available.

Picnicking is permitted. Daily 10-5, Apr. 15-Oct. 15. Museum admission $5.50; senior citizens $5; ages 6-18, $3.50; family rate (two adults and two children under 18) $15. Walking tour (includes museum) $10; senior citizens $9.50; ages 6-18, $8. Gold panning (includes museum) $12; senior citizens $11; ages 6-18, $10. MC, VI. Phone (604) 863-2324.

RECREATIONAL ACTIVITIES

White-water Rafting

- **Fraser River Raft Expeditions** is 1 km (.6 mi.) w. on Hwy. 1. Write P.O. Box 10, Yale, BC, Canada V0K 2S0. Daily mid-Apr. to late Sept.; departure times vary with trip. Phone (604) 863-2336 or (800) 363-7238.

▼ YOHO NATIONAL PARK (A-11)

Elevations in the park range from 1,098 metres (3,600 ft.) at the West Gate of the park to 3,562 metres (11,686 ft.) on Mount Goodsir at the South Tower. Refer to CAA/AAA maps for additional elevation information.

Reached by hwys. 1 and 93, Yoho National Park covers 1,310 square kilometres (507 sq. mi.) just west of the Great Divide and Banff National Park. The word *yoho* is an exclamation of wonder or astonishment in the language of the Cree Indians.

In 1884 the Canadian Pacific Railway laid tracks through Kicking Horse Pass, discovered by Sir James Hector during his search for the best transportation route through the Rockies. The Trans-Canada Hwy. later was built along this same route.

Open mid-June through September 30 as weather permits, the 13-kilometre-long (7.8-mi.) Yoho Valley Road winds up a narrow valley between high, wooded mountain slopes. Takakkaw Falls ("magnificent" in the Cree language) drops 380 metres (1,265 ft.) in all, its highest sheer fall being 254 metres (833 ft.), making it one of the highest falls in Canada.

Other sights in the park include Natural Bridge, Emerald Lake, Wapta Falls and the Spiral Tunnels of the Canadian Pacific Railway. The lower Spiral Tunnel can be viewed from the Trans-Canada Hwy., 7 kilometres (4 mi.) east of Field. The upper Spiral Tunnel can be viewed from the Yoho Valley Road.

The park also contains the Burgess Shale fossil beds, which have preserved fossils of more than 120 species, including rare soft-bodied creatures dating back 515 million years to the Cambrian period. Specimens from the beds are displayed at the park's visitor information center.

General Information and Activities

Although the park is open all year, most facilities and interpretive programs operate only during July and August. A park information center on Hwy. 1 at Field is open in summer. The Trans-Canada Hwy. traverses the park and provides access to most of its roads and trails.

Access to the Burgess Shale fossil beds is limited to guided tours during July and August; fees range from $25-$55. Full-day round trips cover 19 kilometres (12 mi.) and are considered strenuous. Reservations are required; phone (800) 343-3006 Mon.-Fri. 10-3:30 in season.

There are several campgrounds in the park. Prices range from $14-$30 for sites and $6 for firewood. A wilderness pass is required to stay overnight in the backcountry. Passes are $8 per person each night and are available from the visitor information center.

Hiking trails range from nature walks to extended back-country trips; travelers on overnight outings should register at the visitor information center or with a park warden. Fishing, particularly rewarding to those in search of char and many other varieties of trout, requires a $20 annual permit, or a $7 1-day permit.

Horses, canoes and rowboats are available for rent at Emerald Lake. Winter activities include cross-country skiing, snowshoeing, ice climbing, back-country ski touring and winter camping. *See the Recreation Chart and the AAA/CAA Western Canada & Alaska CampBook.*

ADMISSION to the park is $7; over 64, $6; ages 6-16, $3; all occupants of a private vehicle (up to seven people) $14. AX, MC, VI.

ADDRESS inquiries to the Superintendent, Yoho National Park, P.O. Box 99, Field, BC, Canada V0A 1G0; phone (250) 343-6783.

Manitoba

Location is Everything

Winnipeg's position at the junction of two rivers led to its prominence as a trading post

Nature Made

Lakes, forests, rolling prairies and subarctic tundra are part of Manitoba's landscape

Polar Bears and Beluga Whales

Churchill is the place for viewing these magnificent creatures of the wild

The Water's Fine

Myriad lakes and rivers are popular with anglers, canoeists and boaters

Interpretive Sites

Manitoba's history is remembered at restored forts and trading posts

Whiteshell Provincial Park, Falcon Lake
© Terrance Klassen
Alamy Images

voice
of the
spirit

W aves pound a rock-strewn shore at the narrows of Lake Manitoba, producing a noise oddly like a beating drum. To the Cree Indians, this sound was the great spirit Manitou, whose name was given to the lake and, in 1870, the entire province.

From clear water lapping in giant lakes—Winnipeg, Winnipegosis and Manitoba—to the rustling sigh of wind across golden seas of wheat, the great spirit of this province speaks with many voices and conveys many moods.

It echoes in the plaintive cry of migrating geese winging south and the hoarse chuffing of a protective mother polar bear herding her cubs along Hudson Bay's icy shore.

The spirit sings within a chorus of steel wheels as trains carry freight across the prairies from west to east and back again. It proclaims itself in the bustling streets of Winnipeg, where sundry languages—French, English, Russian, Chinese and others—blend into a rich, evocative murmur, and laughs amid the joyous din of the city's various celebrations.

Even the silence deep within Manitoba's immense evergreen forests seems heavy with something left unsaid.

A province this vast has a lot to say; make the journey and let it speak to you.

Look north into the night sky. There. See it? A faint glow high above the horizon. . ..

Watch as an arc of yellow light gradually forms. As it drifts upward, shimmering yellow-green streamers rise from it, rippling like a breeze-blown curtain. New arcs appear lined with bright amber streaks that curl like wisps of smoke. Eventually the swirls of color fade and darkness returns, ending your encounter with the aurora borealis.

In Manitoba you won't have to wait long for a repeat performance. This far north you can count on basking in the aurora's eerie luminescence nearly 90 nights a year. Even citizens of Winnipeg, the capital, are often treated to this celestial light show, despite living in the province's extreme south.

Gem of the Prairies

Sky-obscuring pollution may be the bane of many cities, but Winnipeg's clean air isn't likely to spoil your auroral view. And while multihued lights dance overhead, visitors to the "Gem of the Prairies" can enjoy an equally colorful cultural spectrum spread out before them. Home to more than half of all Manitobans, Winnipeg is a city of surprising diversity; the Ellice-Sargent neighborhood

alone boasts 43 resident nationalities. Here it's not unusual to find a German butcher shop sandwiched between an Italian clothing store and a Vietnamese restaurant, all within a few steps of a Portuguese cafe.

Finding the cuisine you crave is a snap in this polyglot town. For Italian, follow your nose to the source of the garlic-tinged scents wafting from Corydon Avenue, Winnipeg's Little Italy. Here you'll find delicious pastas galore—from agnolotti to tufoli—and a table at a sidewalk bistro is perfect for people-watching while you nibble on a biscotti.

Those desiring a bit of Gallic flavor should saunter over to St. Boniface, home to Canada's largest French community west of the province of Québec. Restaurants serving French dishes are easy to find here, especially along Provencher Boulevard. And in winter St. Boniface comes alive during Le Festival du Voyageur, when Winnipegers turn out to celebrate the *joie de vivre* of the French fur traders who explored the area.

Red northern lights were once regarded as omens of war. If so, the skies must have shone red fairly often during the 18th century

© W. Perry Conway
Corbis

Manitoba Historical Timeline

Capt. Thomas Button winters at Port Nelson on Hudson Bay and claims the land for England.
1612

Henry Kelsey of the Hudson's Bay Co. spends 2 years exploring the province to find new sources of fur.
1690-92

The Red River Colony, Manitoba's first permanent settlement, is established with a land grant from the Hudson's Bay Co.
1812

1738
French fur-trader Pierre Gaultier de la Vérendrye arrives at the site now known as Winnipeg.

1869-70
The Métis, native people of mixed European and Indian ancestry, are led by Louis Riel in the Red River Rebellion to protect their language and property rights.

as conflicts escalated between French *voyageurs* and their English rivals. During this strife-ridden period, Fort Rouge—site of modern Winnipeg—was established where the Red and Assiniboine rivers meet.

Now known as The Forks, this riverfront area is a park where you can take a tree-shaded stroll past splashing fountains and vibrantly hued flower beds. During warm weather, people flock to the numerous festivals held here, including Winnipeg's International Children's Festival in early June.

Nearby, The Manitoba Museum invites visitors to take a whirlwind tour of the entire province by way of seven main galleries. And to learn more about auroras, stop by the museum's planetarium.

The Great White North

Follow your compass farther north and the chances of seeing Mother Nature's silent fireworks multiply. The northern lights not only occur more frequently in Manitoba's subarctic areas, but are brighter, too. In towns like Churchill, the lights are a major attraction.

But the real stars in this small community are its big, furry neighbors: polar bears.

Sightings of the great white animals are common in October, when they migrate onto rapidly freezing Hudson Bay to fish, and late June, when thawing ice forces a return to shore.

The best way to meet these deceptively cuddly looking carnivores is safely ensconced in a specially designed, balloon-tired tundra vehicle. Climb aboard one for an unforgettable in-the-wild encounter. And when you're ready to thaw out, visit Churchill's Eskimo Museum, which is filled with ancient Inuit tools and other artifacts, as well as the recent, burnished wildlife sculptures carved in serpentine that are prized by international collectors.

Well-acquainted with the aurora's haunting glow, the Inuits crafted stories as elaborate as their carvings to explain what they saw. According to one tale, the lights are torches lit by spirits to guide those who will follow across the narrow bridge to heaven.

But you don't have to study Inuit mythology to appreciate the northern lights' otherworldly beauty, nor must you understand the scientific principles behind the phenomenon. All you really need to know is that the skies in Manitoba are perfect for admiring them.

Manitoba becomes the fifth Canadian province.
1870

Manitoba's boundary is extended north to Hudson Bay.
1912

Manitoba's French speakers win an important victory when the Supreme Court rules that all provincial laws passed since 1870 are invalid because they were written only in English.
1986

1900-13
Manitoba's grain production increases dramatically, and Winnipeg becomes the trade center for the prairie region.

© PhotoDisc

1997
More than 25,000 residents between the U.S. border and Winnipeg are forced to evacuate as Red River flood waters surge north.

1999
The Pan Am Games are held in Winnipeg.

Recreation

The overwhelming bulk of Manitoba's populace resides in a thin strip just above the U.S. border, which leaves a vast region of unspoiled territory farther north that's prime for exploration.

Much of the province's outdoor fun involves its 100,000 lakes and the many rivers that link them.

Colorful sails glide across the surface of Lake Winnipeg as **windsurfing** enthusiasts take advantage of breezy days. Put in at Grand Beach Provincial Park, at the far southeast end of the lake. **Canoeing** down the Grass River, near the junction of hwys. 10 and 39, gives you the opportunity to see the beauty of the northern frontier.

Manitoba's lakes are home to dozens of species of fish, including walleye, northern pike, smallmouth bass, trout, arctic grayling, sturgeon and channel catfish. Fly-in fishing—at such isolated spots as Aikens and Dogskin lakes, northeast of Bissett in Atikaki Provincial Park; Gods Lake, Gods River, Knee Lake, and Island Lake, all in northeast Manitoba; and Big Sand, Egenolf, and Nueltin lakes in the northwest region—attracts anglers of all skill levels. Contact Manitoba Natural Conservation for information about licensing and regulations; phone (204) 945-6784.

Chilling Out

When the lakes freeze over, **ice fishing** and **ice skating** warm up as favored pursuits. Smooth blankets of snow—at such places as Assiniboine Park in Winnipeg—are irresistible for **snowshoeing** and **cross-country skiing.**

Many adventurers, too, have a hard time resisting the many **snowmobiling** trails that criss-cross the province. Kick up some powder in Duck Mountain and Turtle Mountain provincial parks.

Although **downhill skiing** is hard to come by in a province that's known mostly for its lowlands, skiers can take on 21 runs at Asessippi and Winter Park ski areas.

For **tobogganing** fun, head for the slides at Kildonan Park in Winnipeg.

Riding Mountain National Park rises from the flat prairie to provide a wealth of opportunity for activity. Self-guiding **hiking** trails range from the easy Beach Ridges Trail to the difficult Bald Hill Trail, named for the barren hill towering over scores of lush, green trees. Most memorable is the grueling but beautiful Ochre River Trail, which entices both trekkers and cross-country skiers.

The park's Clear Lake Trail is a challenging **cycling** route that traverses part of an unmaintained Indian reserve. Before tackling the entire 25-kilometre (16-mile) trail, obtain permission from the reserve; phone (204) 625-2004. **Mountain bikers** favor the exhilarating J.E.T. Trail, which rewards risk-takers with great views from the ridge. The multi-use Central Trail, the longest at 73 kilometres (45 miles), is especially popular for **horseback riding.**

Taking A Dive

Even **scuba divers** can indulge their passion in the crystal waters of Clear Lake. Register with the park before heading to facilities at Glen Beag day-use area. Divers also frequent West Hawk Lake, Manitoba's deepest. Formed by a meteorite, the lake is near the eastern entrance to Whiteshell Provincial Park.

Cree for "white bear," Wapusk National Park fittingly lives up to its name as a hot spot for polar bear viewing.

Black bears, whitetail deer, caribou and moose are among the big game species that contribute to the province's excellent rifle and bow **hunting** reputation.

An abundance of specimens draws **rockhounders** to Flin Flon, Souris, Thompson and Bissett, a former gold-mining town northwest of Nopiming Provincial Park. Contact the Deputy Office of Government Services for maps and information about rocks and minerals; phone (204) 945-1119.

Recreational Activities

Throughout the TourBook, you may notice a Recreational Activities heading with bulleted listings of recreation-oriented establishments listed underneath. Similar operations also may be mentioned in Destination City recreation sections. Since normal AAA inspection criteria cannot be applied, these establishments are presented only for information. Age, height and weight restrictions may apply. Reservations often are recommended and sometimes are required. Addresses and/or phone numbers are provided so visitors can contact the attraction for additional information.

Fast Facts

POPULATION: 1,119,583.

AREA: 647,797 sq km (250,114 sq mi); ranks 8th.

CAPITAL: Winnipeg.

HIGHEST POINT: 831 m (2,727 ft.), Baldy Mountain.

LOWEST POINT: Sea level, Churchill.

TIME ZONE(S): Central. DST.

MINIMUM AGE FOR UNRESTRICTED DRIVER'S LICENSE: 17 years, 6 months.

MINIMUM AGE FOR GAMBLING: 18.

SEAT BELT/CHILD RESTRAINT LAWS: Seat belts required for driver and all passengers; seat belt or child restraint required for ages 5-17; child safety seat required for under age 5 and under 22.6 kg (50 lbs.).

HELMETS FOR MOTORCYCLISTS: Required.

RADAR DETECTORS: Not permitted. The detectors will be confiscated. Visitors traveling in or passing through Manitoba should detach their units and store them inside their luggage.

FIREARMS LAWS: By federal law, all nonresidents entering Canada with a firearm must declare their weapon in writing and pay a fee of $50 (Canadian). Contact the Canadian Firearms Centre at (800) 731-4000 to receive a declaration form or for additional information.

HOLIDAYS: Jan. 1; Good Friday; Easter; Easter Monday; Victoria Day, May 24 (if a Mon.) or the closest prior Mon.; Canada Day, July 1; Civic Holiday, Aug. (1st Mon.); Labour Day, Sept. (1st Mon.); Thanksgiving, Oct. (2nd Mon.); Remembrance Day, Nov. 11; Dec. 25-26.

TAXES: In addition to Manitoba's provincial sales tax of 7 percent, there is a national 7 percent Goods and Services Tax (GST).

INFORMATION CENTERS: Free travel literature and information are available at the following locations: Canada/United States border, Hwy. 75 at Emerson (daily 8 a.m.-9 p.m., mid-May to early Sept.; Thurs.-Mon. 9-5, rest of year); Canada/United States border, Hwy. 10 at the International Peace Garden (daily 8 a.m.-9 p.m., mid-May to early Sept.); Manitoba/Ontario boundary, Hwy. 1E just east of West Hawk Lake (daily 8 a.m.-9 p.m., mid-May through Labour Day; Tues.-Sat. 9-4, day after Labour Day-second Mon. in Oct.); Manitoba/Saskatchewan boundaries on Hwy. 1W west of Kirkella, and Hwy. 16W near Russell (daily 8 a.m.-9 p.m., mid-May to early Sept.); and the Explore Manitoba Centre at The Forks in Winnipeg (daily 10-6).

FURTHER INFORMATION FOR VISITORS:

Travel Manitoba
155 Carlton St., 7th Floor
Winnipeg, MB, Canada R3C 3H8
(204) 945-3777, ext. RM5
(800) 665-0040, ext. RM5

Explore Manitoba Centre
The Forks
21 Forks Market Rd.
Winnipeg, MB, Canada R3C 4T7
(204) 945-3777
(800) 665-0040

RECREATION INFORMATION:

Manitoba Conservation
Parks and Natural Areas
200 Saulteaux Crescent
Winnipeg, MB, Canada R3J 3W3
(204) 945-6784
(800) 214-6497

ALCOHOL CONSUMPTION: Legal age 18.

SPECIAL REGULATIONS: Dogs and cats transported from the United States must have proof of rabies vaccination.

Manitoba Temperature Averages
Maximum / Minimum (Celsius)
From the records of the National Weather Service

	JAN	FEB	MAR	APR	MAY	JUNE	JULY	AUG	SEPT	OCT	NOV	DEC
The Pas	-16	-12	-4	7	16	21	25	23	16	8	-4	-13
	-27	-25	-17	-6	2	8	12	10	4	-2	-13	-22
Winnipeg	-13	-10	-2	9	18	23	27	26	19	11	-1	-10
	-22	-21	-13	-2	5	11	14	12	7	1	-9	-17

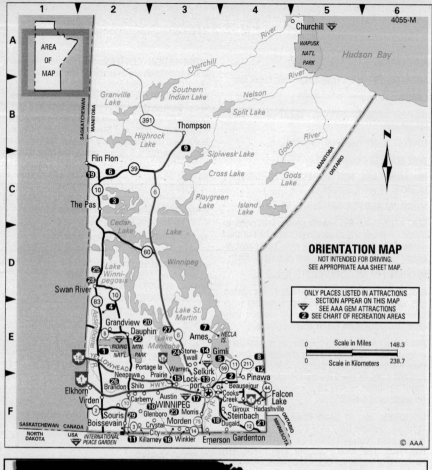

ORIENTATION MAP

NOT INTENDED FOR DRIVING.
SEE APPROPRIATE AAA SHEET MAP.

ONLY PLACES LISTED IN ATTRACTIONS
SECTION APPEAR ON THIS MAP.
SEE AAA GEM ATTRACTIONS
SEE CHART OF RECREATION AREAS

Scale in Miles   148.3
Scale in Kilometers 238.7

4055-M

© AAA

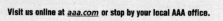
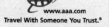

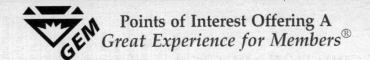

Points of Interest Offering A
Great Experience for Members®

Churchill (A-5)

ESKIMO MUSEUM—The museum's collections of Inuit artifacts are among the finest in the world. See p. 198.

International Peace Garden (F-2)

INTERNATIONAL PEACE GARDEN—The friendship shared by Canada and the United States along the world's longest unfortified border is celebrated at this park that straddles the Manitoba/North Dakota border. See p. 202.

Riding Mountain National Park (E-2)

RIDING MOUNTAIN NATIONAL PARK—The park's grasslands, forests and lakes are home to a diverse population that includes elk, bears and moose as well as pike and several varieties of trout. See p. 204.

Selkirk (E-3)

LOWER FORT GARRY NATIONAL HISTORIC SITE—Costumed interpreters re-create daily life during the 1850s at this restored stone fur-trading outpost. See p. 205.

Winnipeg (F-3)

DALNAVERT MUSEUM—The 1895 home of a prominent lawyer and politician is furnished with Victorian antiques. See p. 214.

THE FORKS—People meet today at The Forks just as they have for over 6,000 years; a national historic site, a marketplace and a children's museum currently occupy the area at the confluence of the Red and Assiniboine rivers. See p. 215.

MANITOBA CHILDREN'S MUSEUM—Fun and learning go hand-in-hand in this museum's six galleries. See p. 215.

THE MANITOBA MUSEUM—The museum's exhibits, audiovisual presentations and dioramas all center on a common theme—the historical relationship of Manitoba's citizens and the environment of the province. See p. 216.

ROYAL CANADIAN MINT—A production facility for Canadian and foreign coins, the facility is considered one of the world's most modern; a viewing gallery provides an observation point. See p. 217.

RECREATION AREAS	MAP LOCATION	CAMPING	PICNICKING	HIKING TRAILS	BOATING	BOAT RAMP	BOAT RENTAL	FISHING	SWIMMING	PETS ON LEASH	BICYCLE TRAILS	WINTER SPORTS	VISITOR CENTER	LODGE/CABINS	FOOD SERVICE
NATIONAL PARKS *(See place listings)*															
Riding Mountain (E-2) 2,978 square kilometres. Backpacking, cross-country skiing, golf, hiking, horseback riding, scuba diving, tennis, water skiing, wind surfing; boat cruises, paddleboats.		•	•	•	•	•	•	•	•	•	•	•	•	•	•
Wapusk (A-5) 11,475 square kilometres. Polar bear viewing.										•					
PROVINCIAL															
Asessippi (E-2) 2,330 hectares 13 km from Shellmouth Dam on Hwy. 83. Fishing, snowmobiling; nature trail.	**1**	•	•	•	•	•	•	•	•	•		•			•
Bakers Narrows (C-2) 145 hectares 27 km s. of Flin Flon on Hwy. 10. Board sailing, canoeing; playground, wildlife watching.	**19**	•	•		•	•		•		•			•		
Beaudry (F-3) 939 hectares 10 km w. of Winnipeg on Roblin Blvd./Hwy. 241.	**17**		•	•	•			•		•		•			

RECREATION AREAS

RECREATION AREAS	MAP LOCATION	CAMPING	PICNICKING	HIKING TRAILS	BOATING	BOAT RAMP	BOAT RENTAL	FISHING	SWIMMING	PETS ON LEASH	BICYCLE TRAILS	WINTER SPORTS	VISITOR CENTER	LODGE/CABINS	FOOD SERVICE
Birds Hill (F-4) 3,550 hectares 24 km n.e. of Winnipeg on Hwy. 59. Cross-country skiing, horseback riding, snowmobiling; interpretive programs, playground, wildlife watching.	2	●	●	●					●			●	●		
Clearwater Lake (C-2) 59,265 hectares 19 km n. of The Pas on Hwy. 10, then 2.5 km e. on Hwy. 287. Cross-country skiing, snowmobiling; interpretive trail.	3	●	●	●	●	●	●	●	●	●		●		●	●
Duck Mountain (E-2) 142,430 hectares 56 km n. of Roblin off Hwy. 83. Canoeing, cross-country skiing, snowmobiling.	4	●	●	●	●	●	●	●	●	●		●		●	●
Grand Beach (E-4) 2,490 hectares 80 km n.e. of Winnipeg on Hwy. 59, then 6 km w. on Hwy 12. Cross-country skiing, sailing, snowmobiling, tennis, windsurfing; interpretive programs, sand beaches.	5	●	●	●	●	●	●	●	●	●		●		●	●
Grass River (C-2) 228,018 hectares at Cranberry Portage off Hwy. 10. Canoeing; interpretive trail.	6	●	●	●	●	●	●	●	●					●	●
Hecla/Grindstone (E-3) 108,440 hectares 165 km n. of Winnipeg via Hwy. 8. Cross-country skiing, golf, sailing, snowmobiling, tennis, windsurfing; interpretive programs. *(See Hecla Island p. 201)*	7	●	●	●	●	●	●	●	●	●	●	●	●	●	●
Lundar Beach (E-3) 23 hectares 18 km w. of Lundar on Hwy. 419.	24	●	●	●	●	●			●	●			●		
Manipogo (E-2) 61 hectares 47 km n. of Dauphin on Hwy. 20. Board sailing; playground, wildlife watching.	20	●	●	●	●	●			●	●					
Moose Lake (F-4) 956 hectares 30 km n.e. of Sprague on Hwy. 308. Board sailing, canoeing, snowmobiling; playground, wildlife watching.	21	●	●	●	●	●			●	●			●		●
Nopiming (E-4) 142,910 hectares 70 km n.e. of Lac du Bonnet. Canoeing; interpretive trail.	8	●	●		●	●	●	●	●	●				●	
North Steeprock Lake (D-2) 13 hectares 3 km n. of Birch River on Hwy. 10, then 40 km w. on Hwy. 365.	25	●	●			●		●							
Paint Lake (B-3) 8,848 hectares 32 km s. of Thompson on Hwy. 6. Canoeing, cross-country skiing, ice skating, snowmobiling, tobogganing, windsurfing.	9	●	●	●	●	●	●	●	●	●		●		●	●
Rainbow Beach (E-2) 52 hectares 17 km e. of Dauphin on Hwy. 20. Board sailing, golfing; playground, wildlife watching.	22	●	●	●	●	●			●	●		●			
Rivers (F-2) 37 hectares 14 km n. of Brandon on Hwy. 10, then 26 km w. on Hwy. 25. Playground.	26	●	●		●				●	●					
St. Ambroise Beach (E-3) 46 hectares 47 km w. of Winnipeg on Hwy. 1, then 35 km n. on Hwy. 430. Windsurfing; interpretive trail.	15	●	●	●					●	●					
St. Malo (F-3) 148 hectares 64 km s. of Winnipeg on Hwy. 59. Motorized boats not allowed.	18	●	●	●	●				●	●				●	●
Spruce Woods (F-3) 26,950 hectares 20 km s.e. of Carberry on Hwy. 5. Canoeing, cross-country skiing, ice skating, snowmobiling, tobogganing; horseback riding trails, interpretive programs. *(See Carberry p. 197)*	10	●	●	●	●				●	●	●	●	●	●	
Stephenfield (F-3) 94 hectares 10 km w. of Carman on Hwy. 245. Board sailing, golfing; playground.	23	●	●	●					●	●					
Turtle Mountain (F-2) 18,570 hectares 23 km s. of Boissevain off Hwy. 10. Cross-country skiing, ice skating, snowmobiling, tobogganing; interpretive trail, horse trails. *(See Boissevain p. 196)*	11	●	●	●	●	●			●	●			●		
Watchorn (E-3) 10 hectares 11 km w. of Moosehorn on Hwy. 237. Playground.	27	●	●		●	●			●	●	●				

RECREATION AREAS

	MAP LOCATION	CAMPING	PICNICKING	HIKING TRAILS	BOATING	BOAT RAMP	BOAT RENTAL	FISHING	SWIMMING	PETS ON LEASH	BICYCLE TRAILS	WINTER SPORTS	VISITOR CENTER	LODGE/CABINS	FOOD SERVICE
Whitefish Lake (D-2) 24 hectares 13 km n. of Swan River, then 28 km w. on Hwy. 279. Playground.	28	•	•		•	•		•	•	•					
Whiteshell (E-4) 272,090 hectares 126 km e. of Winnipeg via Hwy. 1 near the Ontario border. Cross-country skiing, downhill skiing, golf, horseback riding, sailing, snowmobiling, tennis, tobogganing, windsurfing; interpretive programs, museum. *(See Falcon Lake p. 200)*	12	•	•	•	•	•	•	•	•	•	•	•	•	•	•
William Lake (F-2) 199 hectares 7 km e. of Horton, then 8 km s. Amphitheater, playground.	29	•	•	•				•	•	•					
OTHER															
Kildonan (F-3) 40 hectares at 2021 Main St. in Winnipeg. Cross-country skiing, ice skating, tobogganing; pool. *(See Winnipeg p. 216)*			•	•						•	•	•	•		
La Barriere (F-3) 21 hectares 6 km s. of jct. Waverley St. and Perimeter Hwy. in Winnipeg. Canoeing, cross-country skiing, naturalist-guided hikes, snowshoeing.			•	•				•		•	•	•			
Lake Minnewasta (F-3) 125 hectares 2 km w. of Morden on Hwy. 3, then 1 km s. on Hwy. 434.	16	•	•	•	•	•		•	•	•	•		•		
Selkirk Park (F-3) 81 hectares on the banks of the Red River at Eveline St. in Selkirk. Cross-country skiing, ice fishing; bird sanctuary.	13	•	•		•	•		•	•	•		•			
Stonewall Quarry (E-3) 30 hectares 4 blks. n. on Main St. in Stonewall. Nature programs. Cross-country skiing, ice skating, tobogganing. *(See Stonewall p. 206)*	14	•	•	•					•			•	•		•

Points of Interest

ARNES (E-3) elev. 225 m/739'

An old fishing village, Arnes today offers sandy beaches, a marina and a nine-hole golf course. A monument to writer and explorer Vilhjalmur Stefansson is inscribed "I know what I have experienced, and I know what it has meant to me," a statement from his autobiography. Born in 1879, Stefansson traveled by boat and dog sled across the Arctic, mapping large areas of the archipelago and collecting ethnological data from the central Arctic coast. He proved through his explorations that it was possible to live off the land in this forbidding area.

Lake Winnipeg Visitor Centre—Arnes: P.O. Box 1246, Gimli, MB, Canada R0C 1B0; phone (204) 642-4001.

AUSTIN (F-3) pop. 400, elev. 262 m/860'

SAVE **MANITOBA AGRICULTURAL MUSEUM,** 2.5 km (1.6 mi.) s. of Hwy. 1 on Hwy. 34, displays a large collection of steam engines, gasoline tractors, farm equipment and artifacts of pioneer farmers. The location also is home of the Manitoba Amateur Radio Museum. Daily 9-5, mid-May through Sept. 30. Admission $5, senior citizens and students with ID $4, under 12 free, family rate $15. MC, VI. Phone (204) 637-2354.

Homesteaders' Village, at the museum, depicts pioneer life in the late 19th century through furnished buildings of the period. Included are log cabins, an 1883 schoolhouse, two churches, a printing office, blacksmith's shop, grain elevator, pioneer-style store and gristmill. Daily 9-5, mid-May through Sept. 30. Admission included with Manitoba Agricultural Museum.

BEAUSEJOUR (F-4)
pop. 2,772, elev. 247 m/810'

Just 46 kilometres (29 mi.) northeast of Winnipeg, Beausejour is on one of the main roads to Whiteshell Provincial Park (see attraction listing p. 200). Nature enthusiasts take advantage of the walking, hiking and cross-country ski trails available at Wally Chryplywy Nature Park on First Street.

Beausejour and District Chamber of Commerce: P.O. Box 224, Beausejour, MB, Canada R0E 0C0; phone (204) 268-7550.

BROKEN BEAU HISTORICAL SOCIETY PIONEER VILLAGE MUSEUM, 1 blk. n. of Park Ave. and Seventh St. N., features a reassembled pioneer village with a restored railroad station, a blacksmith shop, a school, an old church, a community hall, a general store, a tailor's shop, a harness shop and a house, as well as pioneer artifacts and farm implements. Allow 1 hour minimum. Mon.-Fri. 1-5, July-Aug.; by appointment rest of year. Admission $3, under 15 free. Phone (204) 268-1357.

BOISSEVAIN (F-2) pop. 1,495

Nearby Turtle Mountain Provincial Park (see Recreation Chart) is named for the Western painted turtle, which lives in the park's many shallow lakes. The park is the year-round home of a large number of waterfowl and of migratory birds in spring and fall. A wildlife center also is available.

An outdoor art gallery throughout the town depicts the area's history by way of wall-size murals. Scenic Hwy. 10 leads south to the North Dakota border and the International Peace Garden (see place listing p. 202).

Boissevain & District Tourism Office: P.O. Box 368, Boissevain, MB, Canada R0K 0E0; phone (204) 534-6303 or (800) 497-2393.

BECKONING HILLS MUSEUM is at 425 Mill Rd. S. The museum exhibits pioneer artifacts, mementos such as uniforms from World Wars I and II, farming equipment, early photographs and items relating to culture, education and literature. Allow 1 hour minimum. Daily 1-5, June-Sept.; other times by appointment. Donations. Phone (204) 534-6544.

MONCUR GALLERY & MUSEUM, in the Civic Centre/Library Complex at 420 S. Railway St., contains 10,000 years of archeological history of early southwestern Manitoba. Included in the collection are projectile points, scrapers, ceremonial items and food preparation utensils. Allow 30 minutes minimum. Tues.-Sat. 9-5. Admission $2; ages 12-17, $1. Phone (204) 534-6478.

BRANDON (F-2)
pop. 39,716, elev. 409 m/1,300'

An agricultural and industrial center, Brandon is the second largest city in the province after Winnipeg and is known for its small-town warmth and big-city amenities.

The Keystone Centre, with more than 3.5 hectares (9 acres) under one roof, plays host to some of Manitoba's larger events, concerts and sports competitions; phone (204) 726-3500. The Canada Games Sportsplex offers both winter and summer recreational activities. Built for the 1979 Canada Winter Games, the structure houses racquetball courts, an ice arena, Olympic-size swimming pool, indoor water slide and an outdoor running track; phone (204) 729-2475.

The Brandon Hills Wildlife Management Area, just a short drive south of the city on Hwy. 10 and east along Beresford Road, provides a setting for a variety of recreational pursuits such as hiking, mountain bicycling and cross-country skiing.

Regional Tourism Centre/Riverbank Discovery Centre: #1-545 Conservation Dr., Brandon, MB, Canada R7A 7L8; phone (204) 729-2141.

Self-guiding tours: A historical walking tour of the residential area between 10th and 18th streets offers interesting architecture and turn-of-the-20th-century homes; a booklet describing the tour is available for $3 from the tourism center.

ART GALLERY OF SOUTHWESTERN MANITOBA, 710 Rosser Ave., features changing exhibits with an emphasis on contemporary Manitoba artists; displays change every 6-7 weeks. Workshops and art classes are offered for a fee. Allow 1 hour minimum. Mon.-Sat. 10-6 (also Thurs. 6-9 p.m.); closed major holidays. Donations. Phone (204) 727-1036.

COMMONWEALTH AIR TRAINING PLAN MUSEUM, in Hangar 1 at Brandon Airport, is dedicated to preserving the history of the British Commonwealth Air Training Plan of 1939-45. It has many of the aircraft used for training, photographs, artifacts and memorabilia. Three of the 11 aircraft displayed are in flying condition. A chapel has a book with names of more than 18,000 Canadian Air Force personnel who died during World War II.

Guided tours are available by appointment. Daily 10-4, May-Sept.; 1-4, rest of year. Closed Dec. 25. Admission $5, students with ID $3, under 6 free. MC, VI. Phone (204) 727-2444.

DALY HOUSE MUSEUM, 122 18th St., was built in 1882 as the home of Brandon's first mayor, Thomas Mayne Daly. It is furnished with late 19th-century upper middle-class pieces and houses photographs and artifacts that relate the city's history. Also featured are a general store and Brandon's old city hall council chambers. A research center on the third floor is available by appointment.

Guided tours are available. Allow 1 hour minimum. Mon.-Sat. 10-noon and 1-5, Sun. 1-4, July-Aug.; Tues.-Sat. 10-noon and 1-5, rest of year. Closed major holidays. Admission $3; over 65 and under 18, $2; family rate $7. Phone (204) 727-1722.

CARBERRY (F-3)
pop. 1,513, elev. 369 m/1,210′

The forests and sand dunes of nearby Spruce Woods Provincial Park *(see attraction listing)* inspired many of the works of artist, naturalist and writer Ernest Thompson Seton, including his stories "The Trail of the Sandhill Stag" and "Wild Animals I Have Known." He was appointed naturalist to the Manitoba government in 1892. A small highway park 15 kilometres (9 mi.) east of Carberry on Hwy. 1 has been dedicated to Seton.

Carberry Municipal Offices: P.O. Box 130, Carberry, MB, Canada R0K 0H0; phone (204) 834-2195.

CARBERRY PLAINS MUSEUM, at 520 4th Ave., contains pioneer artifacts relating to the area, including period clothing, pictures and furniture as well as displays of original 19th-century art, a schoolroom, a church, a store, a bedroom and a kitchen. Military memorabilia from World Wars I and II also are displayed. Allow 30 minutes minimum. Daily 1-6, June-Sept. Admission $2, students with ID $1, family rate $5. Phone (204) 834-2797, or (204) 834-2284 in the off-season.

THE SETON CENTRE, 116 Main St., features artwork and photographs depicting the life and philosophies of writer, artist, naturalist and early conservationist Ernest Thompson Seton. Allow 30 minutes minimum. Tues.-Sat. 9-5, June-July (other times by appointment); by appointment rest of year. Admission $1. Phone (204) 834-2509.

SPRUCE WOODS PROVINCIAL PARK is 20 km (12 mi.) s.e. on Hwy. 5. The 26,950-hectare (66,593-acre) park, a mosaic of geographic features, includes deciduous forests, creeping sand dunes, white spruce-covered sand hills, pots of quicksand and mixed grass prairie. The Assiniboine River winds through the park. Spirit Sands, rainwater trapped beneath the sandy surface that has emerged to create springs and quicksand, and Devil's Punch Bowl, a bowl-shaped depression, are highlights.

Comfortable walking shoes, a hat and drinking water are recommended. Allow 2 hours minimum. Park open daily 24 hours. Entrance fee $5 per vehicle for a 3-day pass, or $20 for an annual provincial park pass. Phone the visitor center at (204) 827-8850 May-Sept. or (204) 834-8800 rest of year. *See Recreation Chart and Glenboro in the AAA/CAA Western Canada & Alaska CampBook.*

Spirit Sands Wagon Outfitters, 27 km (17 mi.) s.e. on Hwy. 5 in Spruce Woods Provincial Park, offers 90-minute covered wagon rides through the Spirit Sands and Devil's Punch Bowl, providing views of sand dunes, cactuses, rare snakes and lizards, rolling grasslands and marshes. Trips depart daily mid-May through Labour Day. Fare $9; ages 3-16, $6. Phone (204) 827-2800 for wagon office or (204) 379-2007 off-season.

CHURCHILL (A-5) pop. 1,100, elev. 29 m/100′

Churchill, on the shore of Hudson Bay, is Canada's northernmost subarctic sea port. It also is the site of the Hudson's Bay Co.'s Prince of Wales Fort National Historic Site *(see attraction listing),* a partially restored ruin across from Churchill and Cape Merry Battery at the mouth of the Churchill River. Built over a period of 40 years during the 1700s to hold as many as 400 soldiers, the impressive stone fortress housed only 39 untrained men when three French warships mounted a surprise attack in 1782. The fort's governor wisely surrendered without engaging in battle.

After spending 3 unsuccessful days trying to demolish the 12-metre-thick (40-ft.) outer walls, the French abandoned the fort; it was never occupied again. The site is accessible by boat July through August (weather and tides permitting).

The area around Churchill holds an attraction for two giant mammals: the polar bear and the beluga whale. In fact the Churchill region is said to have the greatest concentration of accessible polar bears in the world. Having spent the winter hunting on the frozen bay, the bears come to shore south of Churchill as the ice melts, scatter along the coast and up to 50 kilometres (31 mi.) inland, and then return to the ice in autumn when the bay refreezes. Beluga whales are often sighted off the coast of Cape Merry during July and August.

Churchill Wilderness Encounter and Frontiers North Inc. are among the companies that offer boat tours to view the whales and seals after the ice melts. Tours last approximately 2.5 hours and usually include a stop at Prince of Wales Fort National Historic Site. Specially designed tundra vehicles provide half- and full-day tours to view the polar bears October through November. Regular bus tours of the area also are available. Reservations are advisable for all tours; phone (204) 675-2248.

Other natural features include flowers, arctic plant life, various wildlife and some 200 species of birds, which nest or pass through Churchill on their annual migrations. An excellent spot for bird-watching is Bird Cove, on the coast 16 kilometres (9 mi.) east of Churchill. The aurora borealis (northern lights) seen from Churchill during the fall and winter months are among the most brilliant in the world.

Churchill can be reached only by train or airplane. Via Rail Canada trains run from Winnipeg and Thompson to Churchill; phone (888) 842-7245. Calm Air offers flights from Winnipeg to Churchill; phone (800) 839-2256.

The Parks Canada Visitor Reception Centre offers information, interpretive displays and programs, historical exhibits and videotaped presentations June though November; by appointment rest of year. Phone (204) 675-8863.

Churchill Chamber of Commerce: P.O. Box 176, Churchill, MB, Canada R0B 0E0; phone (204) 675-2022 or (888) 389-2327.

CAPE MERRY NATIONAL HISTORIC SITE, accessible via the Cape Merry Centennial Pkwy., 3 km (1.9 mi.) w. to the e. shore of the Churchill River, is marked by a stone cannon battery built in 1746 to complement the defenses of the Prince of Wales Fort. An original cannon and powder magazine remain. A cairn commemorating Capt. Jens Munk, the first European to enter the Churchill River in 1619, is displayed. The cape offers views of harbor activity as well as whales, waterfowl and the Prince of Wales Fort.

Allow 30 minutes minimum. Daily 24 hours. Parks Canada offers guided tours June-Aug. Donations. Phone (204) 675-8863, or Parks Canada at (204) 675-8863 for tour times.

ESKIMO MUSEUM, 242 La Verendrye Ave., contains exhibits that depict the history and culture of the northern region of Canada. Founded in 1944 by Roman Catholic missionaries, it pays tribute to the creativity of the Canadian Inuit people. Highlights of the museum are Inuit carvings in bone, ivory, stone and antler as well as wildlife specimens, artifacts, and tools dating from 1700 B.C. Mon. 1-5, Tues.-Sat. 9-noon and 1-5, June-Nov.; Mon.-Sat. 1-4:30, rest of year. Closed holidays. Donations. Phone (204) 675-2030.

NORTH STAR TOURS, 204 La Verendrye St., conducts historical and land-based cultural tours of the Churchill area by bus. Wildlife tours, including beluga whale-watching tours, also are available. Allow 4 hours minimum. Daily 8-1, mid-June to mid-Nov. Fare $65; ages 13-20, $40; ages 3-12 free. AX, MC, VI. Phone (204) 675-2356 or (800) 665-0690.

PRINCE OF WALES FORT NATIONAL HISTORIC SITE, at the mouth of the Churchill River, is accessible by boat only. A huge stone fortress built 1731-71 by the Hudson's Bay Co., the fort fell to the French without incident in 1782. Independent whale-watching boat tours usually include the fort on their itineraries.

Allow 2 hours minimum. Access is possible on the changing tides 6 hours daily, July-Aug. (weather permitting); by appointment in Sept. Boat fare $65 (site admission included). For historic site information phone Parks Canada at (204) 675-8863.

SEA NORTH TOURS LTD., 39 Franklin St., offers boat tours to Prince of Wales Fort National Historic Site *(see attraction listing)* in craft ranging in size up to the 30-passenger *Sea North II*. This vessel is equipped with stereo hydrophones so that passengers can listen to the sounds made by the beluga whales that swim within feet of the boat. Tours also offer chances of sighting polar bears, ice formations and indigenous birds. Kayak tours also are available.

Allow 3 hours minimum. Daily dawn-dusk (times may vary depending on tides), mid-June to late Aug. Fare $75; under 12, $37.50. MC, VI. Phone (204) 675-2195 or (888) 348-7591.

TUNDRA BUGGY ADVENTURE is at 124 Kelsey Blvd. Specially designed vehicles carry passengers across the tundra to view the polar bears in the Cape Churchill Wildlife Management Area. Half-day bird-watching, whale-watching and ecological tours are offered.

Half-day tours Tues., Thurs. and Sat. 1-5, July-Sept. Full-day tundra tours Oct.-Nov.; phone for schedule. Half-day tour fare $89; under 12, $57. Reservations at least 2 weeks in advance are recommended. MC, VI. Phone (204) 675-2121 or (800) 663-9832. *See color ad p. 198.*

YORK FACTORY NATIONAL HISTORIC SITE is 250 km (150 mi.) s.e. near the mouth of the Hayes River; access to the site is limited to charter plane or boat. The site was established by the Hudson's Bay Co. as part of a series of fur trading posts. The 1832 depot is the oldest wooden structure still standing on permafrost. Interpretive tours of the site feature reconstructed buildings containing area artifacts.

Visitors should contact Parks Canada for transportation and safety information. Facilities at the site are limited; camping is not permitted. Allow 4 hours minimum. Daily 8-5, June 1-Sept. 15. Site free. Guided tour $8, under 5 free. Phone (204) 675-8863.

COOKS CREEK (F-4) elev. 238 m/780′

COOKS CREEK HERITAGE MUSEUM, jct. Hwy. 212 and Sapton Rd., houses artifacts pertaining to the life of the early settlers from Poland, Ukraine and other eastern European countries. Highlights include religious artifacts, folk art, clothing, a blacksmith shop, pioneer houses furnished in period and farm machines. Allow 1 hour minimum. Thurs.-Tues. 10-6, May 15-Aug. 31. Admission $3; over 65 and under 19, $2. Phone (204) 444-4448.

IMMACULATE CONCEPTION CHURCH AND THE GROTTO OF OUR LADY OF LOURDES is 3 km (1.9 mi.) n. on Hwy. 212 from jct. Hwy. 213

(Garvin Rd.). The Ukrainian Catholic church, built by Father Philip Ruh 1930-52, features onion domes and the Icon of Our Lady of Perpetual Help, a replica of the Miraculous Icon in Rome. The grotto adjacent to the church is a replica of the original Grotto of Lourdes in France.

Guided tours are available. Allow 1 hour minimum. Daily noon-8, July 1-Labour Day; Sat.-Sun. noon-8 in June and day after Labour Day-Sept. 30. Admission $1. Phone (204) 444-2478.

CRYSTAL CITY (F-3)
pop. 414, elev. 459 m/1,507′

CRYSTAL CITY COMMUNITY PRINTING MUSEUM INC., at 218 Broadway St. S., is said to be the oldest operating printing shop in western Canada. The museum features a collection of antique printing equipment still in operation. Guided tours are available. Allow 30 minutes minimum. Mon.-Fri. 9-5:30. Admission $2, students $1.50, under 5 free. Phone (204) 873-2293.

DAUPHIN (E-2) pop. 8,085, elev. 293 m/960′

Dauphin (DAW-fin) lies in a fertile farming valley between Duck Mountain Provincial Park *(see Recreation Chart)* and Riding Mountain National Park *(see place listing p. 204)*. Lake Dauphin, 15 kilometres (9 mi.) east of Dauphin, offers fishing.

Dauphin Economic Development: 100 Main St. S., Dauphin, MB, Canada R7N 1K3; phone (204) 622-3229 or (877) 566-5669.

FORT DAUPHIN MUSEUM, 140 Jackson St., is surrounded by a wooden palisade suggestive of an 18th-century fur trading fort of the North West Co. A trapper's cabin, schoolhouse, church, blacksmith shop, trading post and pioneer house inside the fort are furnished in the style of the early settlers. Archeological, fur trade and pioneer artifacts also are featured.

Allow 1 hour minimum. Daily 9-5, mid-June through Aug. 31; Mon.-Fri. 9-5, May 1 to mid-June and Sept. 1 to mid-Oct. Admission $3, students with ID $2, under 12 free if accompanied by an adult, family rate $5. Phone (204) 638-6630.

DUGALD (F-4) pop. 400, elev. 242 m/795′

Dugald is a hamlet east of Winnipeg's perimeter highway. Although many residents now commute to jobs in the city, farming is still important to the area.

[SAVE] COSTUME MUSEUM OF CANADA, n.w. of jct. Hwys. 15 and 206, features a 35,000-piece collection of textiles, clothing and accessories dating from 1565. The museum's exhibitions are presented in a *tableau vivant,* or living-picture style; each year a new exhibition is displayed. A visual storage room offers a close-up view of accessories.

Allow 1 hour minimum. Mon.-Sat. 10-4:30, Sun. noon-4:30, May-Sept.; by appointment in Apr. and

Oct.-Nov. Admission $5, senior citizens $4.50, students with ID $3.50, family rate $14. MC, VI. Phone (204) 853-2166 or (866) 853-2166.

Pioneer Home, n.w. of jct. Hwys. 15 and 206, was built in 1886 about 8 kilometres (5 mi.) from its present site on the Dugald property. The restored house has been decorated to resemble its appearance in the early 1900s. Guided tours explain the purpose of each room and its furnishings. Mon.-Sat. 10-4:30, Sun. noon-4:30, May-Sept.; by appointment in Apr. and Oct.-Nov. Admission $1 (included with Costume Museum of Canada admission).

ELKHORN (F-2) pop. 470, elev. 526 m/1,700'

THE MANITOBA ANTIQUE AUTOMOBILE MUSEUM is on Hwy. 1W. The museum displays some 90 vintage automobiles dating from 1908 to the mid-1960s; several are in operating condition. Also exhibited are steam engines, gas tractors and other farm machinery as well as aboriginal, household and pioneer artifacts. Allow 1 hour minimum. Daily 9-6, May-Sept. Admission $5; ages 5-16, $2. Phone (204) 845-2604, or (204) 845-2161 Oct.-Apr.

EMERSON (F-3) pop. 655

Emerson was named after American poet Ralph Waldo Emerson. When Manitoba became a province in 1870, this town on the border of the United States and Canada was the site of the province's first customs house. The original log buildings still stand just north of the Customs Port of Entry.

In 1874 the North West Mounted Police, later renamed the Royal Canadian Mounted Police, organized at Fort Dufferin, thus beginning their career of maintaining law and order in the untamed western areas of Canada. A 5-metre (15-ft.) bronze statue of a North West Mounted Police Officer and his horse is located next to the Tourist Information Centre on Hwy. 75. The statue is a tribute to the members of the force who made the historic "Trek West" from Emerson to Fort McLeod, Alberta.

The Boundary Commission Trail provides 3 kilometres (1.9 mi.) of hiking along the Red River north to the Historic Fort Dufferin Site. At the fort are the remains of old buildings, grave sites and a memorial to the North West Mounted Police.

Town of Emerson: P.O. Box 340, Emerson, MB, Canada R0A 0L0; phone (204) 373-2002.

FALCON LAKE (F-4) elev. 305 m/1,001'

As it winds its way across the country, the Trans Canada Trail enters Manitoba from Ontario at West Hawk Lake in Whiteshell Provincial Park *(see attraction listing)*, crossing the park diagonally as it heads westward to Pinawa. Incorporating many existing trails and utilizing abandoned railway lines, the trail offers hikers a diverse sampling of the province's topography.

WHITESHELL PROVINCIAL PARK is accessible via an especially scenic stretch of Hwy. 1E. The park's four districts encompass both wilderness and developed resort areas, more than 200 lakes and 12 rivers.

Alfred Hole Goose Sanctuary, east of Rennie on Hwy. 44, is a nesting ground for giant Canada geese, which can be seen from the interpretive center's observation deck. Rocks found throughout the park are part of the Precambrian Shield, the oldest geological formation in the world.

Park open daily 24 hours. An interpretive center at Whiteshell Fish Hatchery is open daily 9:30-4:30, June 1-Labour Day. One-hour tours of the center are given daily at 11 and 2. Entrance fee $5 per private vehicle for a 3-day pass or $20 for an annual provincial park pass. Phone the Falcon Lake District at (204) 349-2201, West Hawk District at (204) 349-2245, Rennie District at (204) 369-5246, Seven Sisters District at (204) 348-2203, or the interpretive center at the fish hatchery at (204) 349-8204. *See Recreation Chart and the AAA/CAA Western Canada & Alaska CampBook.*

RECREATIONAL ACTIVITIES
Horseback Riding

* **Falcon Beach Riding Stables and Guest Ranch** is off Hwy. 1 Falcon Lake exit. Write Falcon Beach Ranch, P.O. Box 179, Falcon Lake, MB, Canada R0E 0N0. Daily 9-9, July-Aug.; by appointment rest of year. Phone (204) 349-2410, or (877) 949-2410 in Canada.

FLIN FLON (C-2)
pop. 6,267, elev. 304 m/1,000'

Flin Flon was founded in 1915 when Tom Creighton, one of six prospectors, discovered an ore body which led to the development of Flin Flon as a mining town. The community owes its name to Josiah Flintabbatey Flonatin, the major character of "The Sunless City," a dime novel found in the area by the discoverers of the mineral deposits. Off Hwy. 10 is a humorous 7.5-metre (25-ft.) statue of Flintabbatey Flonatin designed by the American cartoonist Al Capp, of "L'il Abner" fame.

The Flin Flon Station Museum, north on Hwy. 10A, displays artifacts collected from mining, transportation and cultural sources; phone (204) 687-2946. Bordering Saskatchewan, Flin Flon is the northern terminus of the Manitoba stretch of scenic Hwy. 10.

Flin Flon and District Chamber of Commerce: P.O. Box 806, Flin Flon, MB, Canada R8A 1N6; phone (204) 687-4518.

GARDENTON (F-4) elev. 298 m/979'

Some of the earliest Ukrainian settlers in Manitoba came to Gardenton in 1896. St. Michael's Ukrainian Orthodox Historical Church, 4 kilometres (2.5 mi.) west, is purportedly North America's first Ukrainian Orthodox church; the church was built 1897-99. Lithographed icons from St. Petersburg, Moscow and Kiev ornament the sanctuary. A pilgrimage is held the third Sunday in August. Phone

(204) 425-3595 for an appointment to tour the church.

The Ukrainian Museum contains articles of clothing and hand tools depicting life in the late 1800s and early 1900s, a one-room schoolhouse and a thatched roof house. Also in the area is a tallgrass prairie. For further information about the museum phone (204) 425-3072 in summer, or (204) 425-3501 rest of year.

GIMLI (E-3) pop. 1,657, elev. 220 m/723′

Established in 1875, Gimli was the site of Canada's first permanent Icelandic settlement, the largest outside Iceland. The town's name, derived from Norse mythology, means "home of the gods." A Viking statue designed by Gissur Eliasson and the oldest Icelandic cemetery in Canada testify to Gimli's Nordic heritage. Gimli is located on the western shore of Lake Winnipeg, one of the largest freshwater lakes in the world.

Lake Winnipeg Visitor Centre—Gimli: P.O. Box 1246, Gimli, MB, Canada R0C 1B0; phone (204) 642-7974.

[SAVE] **NEW ICELAND HERITAGE MUSEUM** is at 94 First Ave. Displayed in the two buildings are exhibits that focus on the area's Icelandic roots, the fishing industry and Lake Winnipeg's natural history. Allow 30 minutes minimum. Daily 10-6, late May-early Sept. Museum only Mon.-Fri. 9-5, Sat.-Sun. noon-4, rest of year. Admission $5; over 60 and under 19, $4; family rate $15. AX, MC, VI. Phone (204) 642-4001.

GIROUX (F-4) pop. 100, elev. 271 m/888′

PHILIP'S MAGICAL PARADISE: MUSEUM OF MAGIC AND ILLUSION, 39 Municipal Rd. at jct. Hwy. 311, houses a variety of items donated by magicians from around the world. Allow 30 minutes minimum. Mon.-Fri. 7 p.m.-9 p.m., Sat.-Sun. 1-8, mid-May to late Sept. Donations. Phone (204) 326-5575 or (204) 326-1219.

GLENBORO (F-3) pop. 656, elev. 375 m/1,230′

Glenboro is known as the gateway to Spruce Woods Provincial Park (see Carberry p. 197) and the Manitoba Desert. At the junction of Hwys. 2 and 5 in Camel Park stands Sara the Camel, a 7-metre-high (24-ft.) symbol of the Spirit Sands. A portion of the SS Alpha, a steamship that ran aground on the Assiniboine River in 1885, also is displayed in the park.

Slightly northwest of Glenboro on Hwy. 2 is what is purported to be the last cable river ferry in southern Manitoba; phone (204) 827-2250.

GRANDVIEW (E-2)
pop. 839, elev. 434 m/1,425′

WATSON CROSSLEY COMMUNITY MUSEUM is on the w. side of town at the sports grounds on Railway Ave. The museum displays regional pioneer items including automobiles, horsedrawn

equipment, tractors, farm machinery and other artifacts. A restored 1896 homesteader's cabin, a pioneer church with a free-standing bell tower, a rural schoolhouse and a three-story 1918 pioneer house are furnished in their respective periods.

Allow 2 hours minimum. Daily 10-6, late June-early Sept.; by appointment rest of year. Admission $2, under 12 free. Phone (204) 546-2040 late June-early Sept., (204) 546-2661 or (204) 546-2764 rest of year.

HADASHVILLE (F-4)
pop. 100, elev. 297 m/975′

SANDILANDS FOREST CENTRE, about 2 km (1.2 mi.) s. of jct. Hwys. 1 and 11, tells visitors about forest conservation, reforestation and fire prevention. A train car used 1919-74 to promote the nationwide planting of trees is shown, an electronic display tests tree species knowledge and a museum has area plants and animals. The Old Beaver Dam Trail, reached by a suspension bridge over the Whitemouth River, penetrates aspen parkland and a boreal forest.

Guided tours of the center are available. Allow 1 hour minimum. Daily 10-5, July-Aug.; by appointment May-June and in Sept. Hours may vary; phone ahead. Donations. Guided tours $3. Reservations are required for guided tours. Phone (204) 453-3182.

HECLA ISLAND (E-4) elev. 210 m/690′

HECLA/GRINDSTONE PROVINCIAL PARK, 165 km (103 mi.) n. of Winnipeg, or 54 km (34 mi.) n. of Riverton, on Hwy. 8, is comprised of several islands in Lake Winnipeg, the largest of which is Hecla Island. The original settlers were Icelanders displaced from their homeland in 1876, fleeing poverty and Danish rule. Guided walks through the restored buildings of Hecla Village—a church, school, community hall, period house, dockside fish station, a tool display and a partially completed boarding house—are offered.

Park open daily 24 hours. Entrance fee $5 per private vehicle for a 3-day pass, or $20 for an annual provincial park pass. Phone (204) 279-2056 May-Sept., or (204) 378-2261 rest of year. See Recreation Chart.

Grassy Narrows Marsh and Wildlife Viewing Tower, at Hecla/Grindstone Provincial Park, offers wildlife viewing from trails and boardwalks along the marsh as well as from towers along the trails. Some trails are designated bicycling trails. The marsh, a nesting area for Canada geese and other waterfowl, is named after the Narrows, a channel between Hecla Island and the mainland. The tower was built for viewing moose as they feed in the marsh. **Note:** Visitors should bring drinking water and wear comfortable walking shoes. Daily 24 hours. Admission included with park.

Hecla Fish Station, at Hecla/Grindstone Provincial Park, is in an old ice house, or "fish station." The site provides a look at the commercial fishing industry of Lake Winnipeg through artifacts, wall plaques and a small museum. During fishing season visitors may view fishermen bringing in the day's catch. Wed.-Sun. 10-4, June 30-Aug. 30. Hours vary; phone ahead. Free.

Hecla Island Heritage Home Museum, at Hecla/Grindstone Provincial Park, depicts the lifestyle of an Icelandic family from the 1920s to the 1940s. The restored 1928 house is furnished in period with items donated by descendants of the original owners and by other islanders. Walking tours are available. Wed.-Sun. 10-4, June 15-Aug. 30. Schedule may vary; phone ahead. Donations.

▼ INTERNATIONAL PEACE GARDEN (F-2)

On US 281 and scenic Hwy. 10, the International Peace Garden consists of 586 hectares (1,451 acres) in Canada and an adjoining 360 hectares (888 acres) in North Dakota. Set among the lakes and streams of the wooded Turtle Mountains, the botanical garden and park commemorates the friendship between these two countries on the longest unfortified border in the world.

Centers of attraction include the Peace Tower, which represents people from the four corners of the world coming together for the common purpose of peace; an interpretive center depicting the history and development of the park; the Peace Chapel, which includes quotations etched in limestone walls; more than 150,000 annual flowers in the formal gardens that line the boundary; a floral clock; the Carillon Bell Tower, which chimes every 15 minutes; and a memorial cairn, constructed of steel salvaged from the destruction of the World Trade Center, commemorating the tragic events of September 11, 2001.

Other facilities include campgrounds, hiking and bicycling trails and picnic areas. Walking tours of the garden, nature hikes and arts and crafts classes are offered daily. Self-guiding walking and driving tours also are available. Flowers are in full bloom mid-July to early September (weather permitting).

The International Music Camp Summer School of Fine Arts is held at the garden June through July. The Canadian Legion Sports Camp, held during July through August, attracts coaches and athletes from many countries.

Allow 1 hour minimum. The garden and port of entry offices are open daily 24 hours. Daily vehicle permits $10; season permits $25; pedestrian permits $5. Permits are required mid-May to mid-Sept. Visitors are required to go through customs when leaving the garden. Phone (204) 534-2510 in Canada, (701) 263-4390 in the United States, or (888) 432-6733.

KILLARNEY (F-2)
pop. 2,221, elev. 495 m/1,625'

The area's resemblance to Ireland's Killarney Lakes prompted John Sidney O'Brien to change the name of the town of Oak Lake to Killarney. Green fire engines and a replica of the Blarney Stone are further evidence of the town's Irish heritage. A fountain statue of a leprechaun riding a turtle is in Erin Park.

Killarney and District Chamber of Commerce: P.O. Box 809, Killarney, MB, Canada R0K 1G0; phone (204) 523-4202.

J.A.V. DAVID MUSEUM, 414 Williams Ave., displays Indian and pioneer artifacts, local memorabilia, quilts and collections of birds, butterflies and animals. Also featured are an early 1900s schoolroom, a Ninette Sanitorium display, a post office display and a country store. Allow 1 hour minimum. Tues.-Sat. 10-noon and 1-5, July-Aug.; by appointment rest of year. Closed holidays. Admission $2, students $1, under 10 free, family rate $5. Phone (204) 523-7325.

LOCKPORT (F-3) elev. 313 m/1,000'

At Lockport Provincial Heritage Park, on Hwy. 44 just east of the Lockport bridge, is St. Andrews Lock and Dam. This rare structure on Canada's flat prairies was completed in 1910 to allow access and permit navigation on the Red River from Lake Winnipeg to the city of Winnipeg; it is purportedly the only lock and dam of its kind still standing in North America. Picnic sites and footpaths overlook the dam. A museum displays archeological exhibits. Phone (204) 757-2902.

Red River North Tourism—Lockport: 355 Main St., Selkirk, MB, Canada R1A 1T5; phone (204) 482-2022, or (800) 894-2621 in Canada.

ST. ANDREW'S CHURCH is 2 km (1.2 mi.) s. on Hwy. 9, then e. on St. Andrews Rd. (Hwy. 410) to jct. River Rd. (Hwy. 238) at 374 River Rd. Designed by its first rector 1844-49, this stone Gothic-Revival Anglican church is the oldest house of worship in continuous use in western Canada. It retains many of its original fixtures, such as buffalo-hide-covered kneeling benches. The church's cemetery is adjacent. Allow 30 minutes minimum. Tours daily 10-6, mid-May through Labour Day. Free. Phone (204) 334-6405.

St. Andrew's Rectory is across from the church. The two-story stone building, constructed in 1854 for the church's rectors, has exhibits on the ground floor about the building's architecture, the work of the early missionaries and life in the Red River Settlement. The building is home to the current church rector. Daily 10-6, mid-May through Labour Day. Free. Phone (204) 334-6405.

SKINNER'S WET N WILD WATERSLIDE PARK, on Hwy. 44 just w. of the Lockport bridge, includes four adult and two children's water slides, bumper boats, miniature golf, a hot tub, a wading pool, a video arcade, volleyball courts and horseshoe pits. Picnic areas and food are available. Daily 10-7 (weather permitting), July-Aug.; 10-6, in June. Admission $12; ages 4-12, $9.75; spectator pass $4.50;

family rate $50. Bumper boats and miniature golf $3 each. VI. Phone (204) 757-2623.

MORDEN (F-3) pop. 6,142, elev. 302 m/990′

Named after the area's first settler, Alvey Morden, the town grew almost overnight when the Canadian Pacific Railroad arrived in 1882. Located near the Boundary Commission-NWMP Trail in the Boundary Trail Heritage Region, Morden has a progressive industrial and business sector. Abundant recreational activities at Lake Minnewasta *(see Recreation Chart)* and Colert Beach include camping, swimming, fishing, water skiing, canoeing, sailing, bicycling and hiking in the summer. Winter activities include cross-country skiing, snowmobiling and ice fishing.

The Agriculture and Agri-Food Canada Research Station on Hwy. 100 develops field crops, fruits and ornamentals on 254 hectares (627 acres). Tours of the Morden area and the research station are offered May through September. For further information phone (204) 822-4471.

A mural on the corner of Stephen and Nelson streets is a re-creation of one of the earliest known photographs taken in the area. The scene depicts the supply train for Her Majesty's British North American Boundary Commission at Dead Horse Creek in June 1873.

Another mural, at the corner of Stephen and 7th streets, remembers the visit of Canada's first prime minister, Sir John A. MacDonald, to the town on July 15, 1886. The depiction features Sir John speaking from the rear of his railcar and Philip Locke presenting him with a bouquet of prairie flowers; a version of an Indian war dance also is depicted.

A third mural, at 306 N. Railway St., depicts the original uniform of the North West Mounted Police and provides a history of the force, now known as the Royal Canadian Mounted Police.

Morden and District Chamber of Commerce: 311 N. Railway St., Morden, MB, Canada R6M 1S9; phone (204) 822-5630.

Self-guiding tours: The Morden Mansion Book describes a self-guiding architectural/historical walking tour of Morden's turn-of-the-20th-century homes and buildings; it is available for $2 from the chamber of commerce.

MORDEN AND DISTRICT MUSEUM is in the lower level of the recreation center at 111-B Gilmour St. Fossil displays chronicle regional archeology and paleontology. Marine reptile fossils, such as mosasaurs and plesiosaurs, date from 80 million years ago when the Colorado Sea covered much of North America. The process of finding, excavating and displaying the fossils is depicted. Other exhibits deal with First Nations and pioneer life. Paleo Tours offers a chance to excavate fossils at a site nearby.

Allow 1 hour minimum. Daily 1-5, June-Aug.; Wed.-Sun. 1-5, rest of year. Closed Dec. 25. Admission $4; ages 6-17, $2; family rate $10. A fee is charged for Paleo Tours. Phone (204) 822-3406.

MORRIS (F-3) pop. 1,673, elev. 236 m/775′

Two rival fur-trading companies—the North West Co. and the Hudson's Bay Co.—set up shop on the Morris River in 1801. Not until 1874 did a permanent settlement take hold; incorporation took place in 1883. Both the town and the river on which it grew were named for Alexander Morris, the second lieutenant governor of Manitoba during the 1870s.

Morris & District Chamber of Commerce: P.O. Box 98, Morris, MB, Canada R0G 1K0; phone (204) 746-6275.

MORRIS & DISTRICT CENTENNIAL MUSEUM, on Main St. at jct. Hwys. 75 and 23, consists of two buildings. The main building is the original Carleton School, which contains pioneer era displays of farm tools and a laundry and dairy section. The second building contains five rooms featuring furniture and artifacts from the turn of the 20th century. A mural depicts the history of the Red River Valley. Daily noon-5, June-Aug. Donations. Phone (204) 746-2169.

NEEPAWA (E-3) pop. 3,325, elev. 400 m/1,300′

Neepawa, whose name derives from a native word for plenty, is a service center for the surrounding grain and livestock farms on the fertile plains northwest of Winnipeg. The city calls itself the World Lily Capital. This community of tree-lined streets is known around the world as the birthplace of author Margaret Laurence. Riverbend Park offers many pleasant diversions for residents and travelers alike, including a fitness trail and camping area.

Neepawa and District Chamber of Commerce: P.O. Box 726, Neepawa, MB, Canada R0J 1H0; phone (204) 476-5292 or (877) 633-7292.

BEAUTIFUL PLAINS MUSEUM, 91 Hamilton St. W., is housed in a former CNR station. The museum features several rooms of historical items. A children's room contains antique toys and books, and a military room has uniforms and pictures of local residents involved in World Wars I and II. Other rooms include items dedicated to nature, stores, Masonic lodges, sports and vintage clothing. An extensive doll collection also is displayed.

Allow 30 minutes minimum. Mon.-Fri. 9-5, Sat.-Sun. 1-5, July 1-early Sept.; Mon.-Fri. 9-5, late May-June 30. Donations. Phone (204) 476-3896.

MARGARET LAURENCE HOME, 312 First Ave., contains photographs, memorabilia, autographed books and research materials of the award-winning Canadian author, born here in 1926. Guided tours are available. Daily 10-6, July-Aug.; Mon.-Fri. 10-6, Sat.-Sun. noon-6, May-June; daily noon-5, Sept. 1-second Mon. in Oct.; by appointment rest of year. Admission $3, students $2, under 6 free, family rate $6. Phone (204) 476-3612.

PINAWA (F-4) pop. 1,500, elev. 282 m/925'

Named "Pinnawak," meaning calm waters, by the aboriginal people, Pinawa was first settled by families who operated one of the earliest hydroelectric power dams built between Sault Ste. Marie, Ontario, and the Rockies. The townsite was abandoned in 1951, and the historic site is now Pinawa Dam Provincial Heritage Park. The new Pinawa was built in 1963 when the Federal Crown Corp., Atomic Energy of Canada Limited (AECL) built its research center near the old townsite.

PORTAGE LA PRAIRIE (E-3)
pop. 12,976, elev. 332 m/1,100'

The city's name is derived from the prairie portage between the Red and Assiniboine rivers and Lake Manitoba. In the heart of the city at Crescent Road and Royal Road S. is Island Park. Surrounded by horseshoe-shaped Crescent Lake, this scenic park has a deer sanctuary, a large captive flock of Canada geese and offers opportunities for other bird-watching. Park features include exhibition grounds, seasonal harness racing, a golf course, an arboretum, tennis courts, picnic areas and bicycling and hiking trails.

Portage la Prairie City Hall, built in 1898, was designed by one of Canada's foremost architects, Thomas Fuller.

Portage and District Chamber of Commerce: 11 Second St. N.E., Portage la Prairie, MB, Canada, R1N 1R8; phone (204) 857-7778.

Self-guiding tours: A brochure detailing a self-guiding historic tour of Portage la Prairie is available at the chamber of commerce.

FORT LA REINE MUSEUM, PIONEER VILLAGE AND TOURIST BUREAU is at jct. Hwys. 26 and 1A E. The central museum includes pioneer household articles and implements, a log fort, school, doctor's office, trading post, furnished homestead and church as well as railway, farming and military displays. Canadian railway official Sir William Van Horne's business car also is displayed. A tourist bureau is available.

Picnicking is permitted. Allow 1 hour minimum. Daily 9-6, mid-May to mid-Sept. (also Wed. 6-9 p.m., July-Aug.). Admission $5; senior citizens $4; ages 6-12, $2. Phone (204) 857-3259.

◤◢ RIDING MOUNTAIN NATIONAL PARK (E-2)

Elevations in the park range from 230 metres (755 ft.) at Henderson Creek in the northeastern area to 756 metres (2,480 ft.) at Bald Hill in the eastern side of the park. Refer to CAA/AAA maps for additional elevation information.

Accessible from the north and south via scenic Hwy. 10, or from the east via Hwy. 19, Riding Mountain National Park lies on the plateau of the Manitoba escarpment, 197 kilometres (123 mi.) north of the U.S. border and 259 kilometres (162 mi.) northwest of Winnipeg. This 2,978-square-kilometre (1,150-sq.-mi.) area is blanketed with forests, lakes and meadows. The park is home to elk, moose, deer, bears and a wide variety of birds and vegetation. Waterfowl and beavers populate the waterways, and a herd of bison grazes in a large enclosure near Lake Audy.

General Information and Activities

Although the park is open year-round, complete facilities are available only from mid-May to mid-October. The park also encompasses the historic resort town of Wasagaming on Clear Lake, which offers the amenities of a resort destination.

Recreational activities available within the park include tennis, golfing, lawn bowling, swimming, hiking, fishing, canoeing, sailing, cross-country skiing, horseback riding, bicycling, camping and snowshoeing. More than 400 kilometres (250 mi.) of hiking, bicycling and horseback trails lead to lakes, meadows and evergreen forests. Bicycle and boat rentals are available.

Several forms of recreation can be pursued nearby. Guides and outfitters offer horseback riding and wagon excursions along with other wilderness activities. Located at Lake Katherine, the Native Cultural Anishinabe Village, or "Shawenequanape Kipichewin," offers cultural tours, interpretation programs and powwows. There are boat launching facilities at Clear Lake. Snowshoeing and dog sledding are other popular activities. *See Recreation Chart and the AAA/CAA Western Canada & Alaska CampBook.*

ADMISSION is $5; over 64, $4.25; ages 6-16, $2.50; family rate (up to seven people) $12.50; senior group (up to seven people) $10.50. Annual pass $25; over 64, $20; family rate $63. AX, MC, VI.

PETS are allowed in the park. Dogs must be leashed at all times.

ADDRESS inquiries to Visitor Information, Riding Mountain National Park, Wasagaming, MB, Canada R0J 2H0; phone (204) 848-7275 or (204) 848-7272.

VISITOR INFORMATION CENTRE OF WASAGAMING is on the s. shore of Clear Lake. The center maintains exhibits and displays about the natural and human history of the area. Interpretive programs include nature walks, campfires, theater programs and guided hikes. A campground is available. Daily 9-8, Victoria Day weekend-early Sept. Phone (204) 848-7275 or (204) 848-7272.

SELKIRK (E-3) pop. 9,752, elev. 231 m/800'

Selkirk's name honors Lord Selkirk, the Scottish philanthropist whose 1803 settlement in the Red River Valley to the south laid the foundation for Winnipeg. During the late 19th and early 20th centuries, Selkirk's position on the Red River made it a base for trade and communication with the more isolated settlements around Lake Winnipeg.

Chuck the Channel Catfish, a 9-metre (30-ft.) fiberglass statue, greets visitors on Main Street. The oversized catfish is an apt representation of the live version: Catfish weighing more than 9 kilograms (20 lbs.) abound in the Red River between Selkirk and Lockport.

St. Peter's Dynevor Church, 6.5 kilometres (4 mi.) northeast off Hwy. 59, was built in 1853. The original church, erected in 1836, was the center for Anglican missionary work among the Saulteaux Indians.

Red River North Tourism—Selkirk: 18 Main St., Selkirk, MB, Canada R1A 1P5; phone (204) 482-2022, or (800) 894-2621 in Canada.

LOWER FORT GARRY NATIONAL HISTORIC SITE, 5 km (3 mi.) s. on Hwy. 9, is purportedly the oldest intact stone fur-trading post in North America. The 19th-century buildings are restored and furnished as they might have been in their early days. Costumed staff members perform tasks and re-enact events that re-create the early 1850s atmosphere of the fort in its heyday. The Visitor Reception Centre offers exhibits and a slide presentation about the fort's history.

Picnic facilities and food are available. Allow 2 hours minimum. Daily 9-5, mid-May through Labour Day. Admission $5.75; over 65, $5; ages 6-16, $3; family rate $16.50. MC, VI. Phone (204) 785-6055 or (877) 534-3678.

MARINE MUSEUM OF MANITOBA, at the entrance to Selkirk Park at Eveline St. and Queen Ave., reflects Selkirk's nautical past through displays of outboard motors, tools used for early 1900s shipbuilding, two lighthouses and six restored ships. The 1897 passenger steamship SS *Keenora* houses nautical artifacts and photographs.

Other displays include early 1900s underwater diving and a graphite exhibit representing the species of fish caught in Lake Winnipeg and the Red River. Allow 1 hour minimum. Mon.-Fri. 9-5, Sat.-Sun. and holidays 10-6, mid-May through Labour Day. Admission $3.50; over 65, $3; ages 6-17, $2. Phone (204) 482-7761.

SHILO (F-2)

THE ROYAL REGIMENT OF CANADIAN ARTILLERY MUSEUM is on the Canadian Forces Base via Hwy. 340. This indoor-outdoor museum exhibits more than 10,000 articles of dress, technical instruments, ammunition, small arms, guns and World War II vehicles. Among the more than 150 pieces of major military equipment dating to 1796 are German, Russian and French guns.

Guided tours are available by appointment. Allow 1 hour minimum. Mon.-Fri. 9-5, Sat.-Sun. 1-5, Victoria Day-second Mon. in Oct.; Mon.-Fri. 9-5, rest of year. Donations. Phone (204) 765-3000, ext. 3531.

Bison

The Europeans who explored Canada in the 18th century were awed by the throngs of huge furry cattle that swarmed across the plains. Then, as many as 60 million North American bison, or plains buffalo, roamed the Canadian flatlands. They were the main food source for the Plains Indians, who had mastered the art of harvesting bison for food and clothing: Scaring the animals into a stampede, the Indians then ran them into corrals, where the bison could be killed as they were needed.

Later, the Métis, people of French and Indian heritage, became expert

Digital Archives

bison hunters as well. Hides were transformed into heavy robes that became the fashion in Europe; tongues were cooked and prized as delicacies; and bison meat, dried and pounded and mixed with fat and sometimes berries, was used to make pemmican, a Canadian aboriginal food which was packed in bags and stored.

As the Europeans fought the Indians and each other, the bison fell victim to reckless slaughter, the repeating rifle and politics. Carcasses of animals killed solely for their tongues or hides littered the plains. When the white settlers realized they could starve the natives by killing the bison, they set fire to the plains, killing thousands of the animals and driving others into what is now the United States. By 1885 the bison faced extinction in Canada.

Around 1900 a handful of conservation-minded cattlemen convinced the Canadian government to protect the bison, and the killing stopped. Manitoba acknowledges its debt to the bison by placing its image on the province's crest.

SOURIS (F-2) pop. 1,683, elev. 396 m/1,300′

The free-swinging 177-metre (581-ft.) footbridge built in 1904 over the Souris (SIR-iss) River is considered the longest free-suspension foot bridge in Canada. The bridge was reconstructed after being destroyed by a flood in 1976. Victoria Park has more than 6 kilometres (4 mi.) of walking trails, a viewing tower and a bird sanctuary containing geese, peacocks and swans *(see the AAA/CAA Western Canada & Alaska CampBook)*.

Rockhounding in nearby agate pits yields agate, dendrite, jasper, petrified wood and epidote; the area offers one of the largest varieties of semiprecious stones found in North America. Permits are required and cost $10 per private vehicle. Contact the Rock Shop, 8 First St. S., Souris, MB, Canada R0K 2C0; phone (204) 483-2561.

HILLCREST MUSEUM, Crescent Ave. and Sowden St. next to the swinging bridge, is a restored late 19th-century residence furnished with settler artifacts and antiques. Highlights include an agricultural display with a covered wagon, tractor and farm tools as well as a printing press, a collection of more than 500 butterflies and a caboose. Allow 30 minutes minimum. Daily 10-6, July 1-Labour Day. Admission $2; ages 6-15, $1. Phone (204) 483-2008.

STEINBACH (F-4)
pop. 9,227, elev. 261 m/900′

MENNONITE HERITAGE VILLAGE, 3 km (1.9 mi.) n. on Hwy. 12, centers on a replica of a Mennonite village with more than 20 completely furnished buildings that were moved to the site. On the 16-hectare (40-acre) grounds are a fruit garden, stock pens, a steam engine, gas tractors and other machinery. The village windmill is said to be the only one of its kind in Canada. A museum displays antiques and manuscripts.

Allow 1 hour minimum. Mon.-Sat. 10-9, Sun. noon-6, July-Aug.; Mon.-Sat. 10-5, Sun. noon-5, May-June and in Sept.; Mon.-Fri. 10-4, rest of year. Admission $8; over 65, $6; ages 13-18, $4; ages 6-12, $2; family rate $20. Admission may be increased during special events. MC, VI. Phone (204) 326-9661.

STONEWALL (E-3) pop. 4,012

Nobody knows for sure if Stonewall was named after founding father S.J. "Stonewall" Jackson or the limestone ridge on which the town is built. The name fits well, though, since limestone quarrying sustained the area's economy from the early 1880s until 1967. Stonewall's past is captured through the old stone buildings dotting its streets.

Stonewall and District Chamber of Commerce: P.O. Box 762, Stonewall, MB, Canada R0C 2Z0; phone (204) 467-8377.

[SAVE] **OAK HAMMOCK MARSH INTERPRETIVE CENTRE** is 13 km (8 mi.) e. on Hwy. 67, then 4 km (2.5 mi.) n. on Hwy. 220. This 3,600-hectare (9,000-acre) restored prairie wetland is home to more than 295 species of birds, 25 species of mammals and thousands of other plant and animal species. Scores of migrating birds and waterfowl can be seen in the spring and fall.

Hikers can explore 30 kilometres (19 mi.) of trails over a system of boardwalks and dikes. The interpretive center has displays, films and interpretive programs.

Picnicking is permitted. Food is available. Allow 2 hours minimum. Area open daily 24 hours. Interpretive center open daily 10-dusk, Sept.-May; 10-8, rest of year. Closed Dec. 25. Admission to interpretive center (includes guided tours of the center and the wetlands) $4; over 55 and ages 3-17, $3; family rate $14. AX, MC, VI. Phone (204) 467-3300 or (800) 665-3825.

STONEWALL QUARRY PARK, on the n. end of Main St., commemorates the important role limestone played in the town's development. The interpretive center has a museum, videotape presentations and exhibits; an observation tower affords a panorama of the area. Self-guiding tours around the 30-hectare (75 acre) grounds offer a closer look at kilns, fossil deposits in rock and wildlife. Kinsmen Lake has a sandy beach and swimming; tobogganing is a winter option.

Guided tours are available. Picnicking is permitted. Food and camping facilities are available. Allow 1 hour minimum. Interpretive center daily 11-5, May 1-Labour Day. Hours vary rest of year; phone ahead. Interpretive trail daily 8 a.m.-10 p.m. Park, museum and observation tower free. Admission to the lake area for swimming $4; over 65 and ages 2-17, $3. Prices may vary; phone ahead. Reservations are required for guided tours. Phone (204) 467-5354. *See Recreation Chart.*

SWAN RIVER (D-2)
pop. 4,032, elev. 340 m/1,116′

During the last 13 years of the 18th century, control of the Swan River Valley was sought by both the North West Co. and the Hudson's Bay Co. Each company built fur-trading posts in the area, but by 1800 the concentrated trapping generated by the rivalry had depleted the number of fur-bearing animals. The Hudson's Bay Co. abandoned the area until the two companies joined in 1821.

The Swan River Valley, nestled between the Duck and Porcupine mountains, offers fishing, hunting, boating, camping, swimming and picnicking. Scenic Hwy. 10 passes just east of town.

Swan River Chamber of Commerce: P.O. Box 1540, Swan River, MB, Canada R0L 1Z0; phone (204) 734-3102.

SWAN VALLEY HISTORICAL MUSEUM, 1.5 km (1 mi.) n. on Hwy. 10, reflects life in Manitoba's pioneer era through artifacts and restored buildings.

Highlights include two machine sheds, two log cabins, a CN railroad station, a telephone station, a blacksmith shop, a pioneer store, two churches and a 1900s one-room schoolhouse.

Allow 1 hour minimum. Mon.-Fri. 9-5, Sat.-Sun. and holidays 1-5, May-Sept.; by appointment rest of year. Admission $2, under 12 free. Phone (204) 734-3585, or (204) 734-2713 to schedule an appointment.

THE PAS (C-2) pop. 5,795, elev. 274 m/900′

A cairn in Devon Park at The Pas (pronounced "the paw") honors Henry Kelsey, the first known European to see the northern prairies in 1690. It is rumored that the first wheat on the prairies was planted in the area in 1734. Natural history exhibits, local historical materials and Indian and fur-trading artifacts are displayed in the Sam Waller Museum at 306 Fischer Ave. The museum also offers historic walking tours of the downtown and riverfront areas; phone (204) 623-3802.

Christ Church (Anglican), on Edwards Avenue, was founded in 1840 by Henry Budd, the first native Indian ordained to the Anglican ministry. The church contains hand-hewn furnishings made by ships' carpenters in 1847. Tours are offered by appointment; phone (204) 623-2119 or (204) 624-5433.

The Town of The Pas Tourism Commission: P.O. Box 870, The Pas, MB, Canada R9A 1K8; phone (204) 627-1134.

THOMPSON (B-3)
pop. 13,256, elev. 206 m/675′

Thompson sprang up after the discovery of one of the world's largest nickel deposits and is a major mining, communications, transportation, medical and retailing center. Inco Limited (Thompson Division) offers 90-minute walking tours of its nickel mining and processing complex; phone (204) 677-2216 for information.

Lakes and rivers abound in this rugged, picturesque area. Paint Lake Provincial Recreation Park *(see Recreation Chart and the AAA/CAA Western Canada & Alaska CampBook)* is 32 kilometres (20 mi.) south on Hwy. 6.

Also south of Thompson on Hwy. 6 is the starting point for a 10 kilometre (6-mi.) hiking trail that will take you over a bridge to Kwasitchewan Falls, the highest waterfall in the province. Between Wabowden and Thompson is Pisew Falls, the second-highest waterfall in Manitoba accessible by road. A 1.3-kilometre (.8-mi.) trail leads from the highway through the dense foliage to a platform overlooking the 12.8-metre (42-ft.) falls. Twelve site plaques describe the flora and fauna of this boreal forest. Picnic facilities are available.

Thompson Chamber of Commerce: 4 Nelson Rd., Thompson, MB, Canada R8N 1M2; phone (204) 677-4155 or (888) 307-0103.

HERITAGE NORTH MUSEUM, in a log cabin at jct. Princeton Dr. and Mystery Lake Rd., also serves as the tourist information center. Displayed are an assortment of stuffed and mounted animals native to the area, fossils, a mining exhibit, a woolly mammoth tusk found near Thompson, a boreal forest exhibit which includes a caribou-hide tepee, and changing exhibits. A second log building houses a mining exhibit. Archives are available.

Daily 9-5, in summer; Tues.-Sat. 1-5, rest of year. Admission $3.25; over 59 and ages 13-18, $2; ages 6-12, $1. Phone (204) 677-2216.

VIRDEN (F-2) pop. 3,109, elev. 439 m/1,440'

About 1,200 oil wells dot the landscape in and around Virden—the richest source of petroleum in Manitoba. The first oil-producing well was sunk in the 1950s in the Rosalee field northwest of Virden.

Many original fieldstone buildings, such as the 1892 St. Mary's Anglican Church at the corner of Queen Street and 9th Avenue, are still in use today. The site of Fort Montagne à la Bosse, built by the North West Co. in 1790, is northeast of Virden on the old Trans-Canada Highway. To help cool things off in the summer, the fairgrounds has a public pool and waterslides.

Virden and District Chamber of Commerce: P.O. Box 899, Virden, MB, Canada R0M 2C0; phone (204) 748-3955.

VIRDEN PIONEER HOME MUSEUM INC. is at 390 King St. W. The museum, in a large brick house, is a living memorial to the pioneers who came to the region. Built in 1888, it is furnished with family pieces donated by descendants of the pioneers. Allow 30 minutes minimum. Mon.-Sat. 9-6, Sun. 1-6, June-Aug.; by appointment rest of year. Donations. Phone (204) 748-1659, (204) 748-1897 or (204) 748-2740.

WAPUSK NATIONAL PARK (A-5)

Elevations in the park range from sea level along the Hudson Bay coastal areas to 94 metres (308 ft.) at Silcox Creek. Refer to CAA/AAA maps for additional elevation information.

South and east of Churchill on the shore of Hudson Bay, Wapusk (pronounced to rhyme with tusk) was established in 1996. The park consists of 11,475 square kilometres (7,119 sq. mi.). Translated from the Cree language, Wapusk means "white bear," a fitting name for a park that has an area where polar bears den and produce offspring.

Much of the national park, part of the Hudson Bay lowlands, is a flat plain covered by an extensive layer of peat; a layer of permafrost lies underneath. The treeless tundra consists mainly of wetlands—lakes, streams, bogs and rivers.

Polar bears congregate in the northern part of the park near Churchill around October, as they wait for freezing weather and the time when they can return to the ice in search of seals, their main food. The females dig their dens, and their young are born in late November and in December. The area around Churchill (*see place listing p. 197*) is one of the world's best places for viewing polar bears in their native habitat. Specialized tundra vehicles take visitors for close-up encounters.

The park, along a migratory flyway, also is a popular spring and fall feeding spot for waterfowl and shorebirds, including such rare species as the king eider, Ross' gull and gyrfalcon. Many build their nests here on the coast of Hudson Bay during the summer.

Churchill, in a somewhat remote location in northern Manitoba, can be reached by air and rail from Winnipeg. Since Wapusk is a wilderness park, it has no roads or trails. Several commercial operators provide tours into the park by plane, helicopter or tundra vehicle. The park office can provide a list. Park admission is free. For additional information contact Wapusk National Park, P.O. Box 127, Churchill, MB, Canada R0B 0E0; phone (204) 675-8863.

WARREN (E-3) pop. 600, elev. 248 m/815'

SAVE V. GROSS' DOLL MUSEUM, on Hwy. 3W, 3 km (1.9 mi.) n. of jct. Hwys. 6 and 67, displays some 3,500 dolls, ranging from those of late 1890s to the present. Allow 30 minutes minimum. Sun.-Fri. 10-5 (also Sat. and evenings by appointment), May-Oct.; by appointment rest of year. Admission $4, under 6 free. Phone (204) 322-5346.

WINKLER (F-3) pop. 7,943, elev. 271 m/890'

SAVE PEMBINA THRESHERMAN'S MUSEUM, 5 km (3 mi.) w. on Hwy. 3, features guided tours through displays of agricultural machinery, tools and household items as well as a steam threshing unit and a working sawmill. Allow 1 hour minimum. Mon.-Fri. 9-5, Sat.-Sun. and holidays 1-5, May-Sept. Admission $3, under 12 free. Phone (204) 325-7497.

Drive

See

Stay

Play

DO IT ALL WITH AAA/CAA!

Vacation planning, travel and destination information, AAA/CAA's famous maps and TripTiks®, TourBook® guides, air, cruise, tour, rail, and hotel reservations, attraction tickets and more! It's all part of the service for AAA/CAA members! Choose whatever method fits you best — online, in person, or by phone — to enjoy helpful services like these:

- Online TourBook® guide featuring hotel information and AAA/CAA Diamond ratings.
- Internet TripTik® itinerary planner rated No. 1 by the *Wall Street Journal.*
- Travel accessories such as luggage, travel guides, car games for the kids, and more.

- Ready-to-go, 2- to 5-day AAA/CAA Drive Trips vacations* for major U.S. and Canadian travel destinations.
- Flights, cruises and tours and expert advice from AAA/CAA Travel professionals.
- AAA/CAA Travel money options including no fee Travelers Cheques.

With AAA/CAA's expert travel information and pricing power behind you, you'll enjoy better quality and value than you'll find anywhere else. And, with AAA/CAA's extensive range of products and services, you'll enjoy complete, hassle-free vacation planning from a single source you know and trust.

Before your next vacation, visit aaa.com or your nearest AAA/CAA office. Discover the many ways AAA/CAA can help you drive more, see more, stay more and play more!

TRAVEL WITH SOMEONE YOU TRUST®

aaa.com

*PRODUCTS AND SERVICES AVAILABLE THROUGH PARTICIPATING AAA AND CAA CLUBS.

Winnipeg

The real estate agent's cry of "Location!" could have been invented in Winnipeg; the position of Manitoba's capital has determined both the city's past and present. Archeological evidence shows that Winnipeg has been an important place of settlement for more than 6,000 years.

The confluence of the Red River, which flows from south to north, and the Assiniboine River, whose eastward flowing waters were a main route of Western exploration, led to the founding of fur-trading posts in the early 18th century near the present site of Winnipeg. The fertile lands created by the rivers later drew farmers and other settlers.

Still later, the area's position south of the peaks of the Canadian Shield meant that roads and railroads were forced to converge at Winnipeg, making it the point through which the eastbound raw materials of the West and the westbound manufactured goods of the East passed. Profiting by the hydroelectric power generated from its rivers, the city emerged in the 20th century as a manufacturing center in its own right.

French Canadian explorer and trader Pierre Gaultier de la Vérendrye founded Fort Rouge at the confluence of the rivers in 1738. This fur-trading post was succeeded by Fort Gibraltar, built by the North West Co. in 1804, and Fort Garry, founded by the Hudson's Bay Co. in 1821. In the same year, Lord Selkirk brought a party of Scottish settlers to these fertile lands, a move that greatly disturbed the trappers and voyageurs who feared their livelihoods would be destroyed.

The small settlement managed to survive, and the shift from trapping and hunting to agriculture began. Because of aggressive Canadian advertising campaigns in Europe and a homestead policy similar to that being used to settle the plains of the United States, large numbers of immigrants began to flow into the area in the 1860s.

In 1873 the village that had grown about a half mile north of Fort Garry was incorporated and named for the Cree Indian words *win* ("muddy") and *nipee* ("water"). The railroad aided Winnipeg's growth still further: In 1876 the city began to ship wheat east, and when the Canadian Pacific Railway connected the coasts in 1885, freight and passengers began to flow through the city in both directions.

The diversity of today's Winnipeg mirrors the many nationalities who settled it, some drawn by agriculture, some by the railroad, some by industry. From countries throughout Great Britain and Europe they came, creating a cultural mix that is reflected in the city's skyline, which includes the neoclassical splendor of the Manitoba Legislative Building *(see attraction listing p. 216)*, the century-old buildings of Old Market Square and the rounded spires of the Ukrainian Greek Orthodox Cathedral.

© The Manitoba Museum

© Terrance Klassen / Alamy Images

The Golden Boy, sculpted by Charles Gardet of Paris, is a 5.25-metre-tall (17.2-ft.), 1,650-kilogram (3,638-lb.) statue sheathed in 24 karat gold leaf atop the dome of the Legislative Building. In many ways it symbolizes both the past and the future of the residents of Winnipeg. The statue was diverted on its journey from a French foundry during World War I, while the vessel that was carrying it served as a troop transport for 2 years.

After crossing the Atlantic many times, the golden immigrant was finally placed where he stands today, one hand holding aloft the torch of progress, the other cradling a symbolic sheaf of wheat. High above the city, he strides toward the increasingly important natural resources of the north, his color echoing the golden hue of the rolling fields of grain that brought the city below both population and prosperity.

Evidence has been uncovered through archeological digs that the current site of The Forks *(see attraction listing p. 215)* was a seasonal meeting place for aboriginal peoples more than 6,000 years ago. Tools, bones, footprints and pottery have been unearthed at the site located at the confluence of the Red and Assiniboine rivers.

Approaches

By Car

Forming a circle around Winnipeg is a perimeter highway. To the north of the Trans-Canada Highway, the major approach from the east and west, this perimeter road is designated Hwy. 101. To the south of the Trans-Canada Highway it is numbered Hwy. 100.

There are three major approaches to the perimeter highway: the Trans-Canada Highway, which approaches from both the east and west, and Hwy. 75, which approaches from the south. To the west of the city the Trans-Canada Highway is posted Hwy. 1W; from the east, Hwy. 1E.

Within the perimeter highway all three major approaches change designation: Hwy. 1W becomes Metro Rte. 85, Hwy. 1E becomes Metro Rte. 135, and Hwy. 75 becomes Metro Rte. 42.

Getting Around

Generally, rush hour in Winnipeg is from 7 to 9 a.m. and 3:30 to 5:30 p.m. As in most cities, stress can be alleviated if driving during rush hour is avoided. If driving during these times, be careful and be patient; the city's speed limit is 50 kilometres per hour (30 mph) unless otherwise posted.

Note the pedestrian crosswalks marked by pavement stripes and illuminated overhead signs. All vehicles must stop if the crosswalk is occupied by a pedestrian or if a pedestrian on the curb indicates an

(continued on p. 213)

The Informed Traveler

City Population: 619,544

Elevation: 229 m/763 ft.

Sales Tax: Manitoba's provincial sales tax is 7 percent. A 7 percent Goods and Services Tax (GST) also is levied in Canada on most sales and services. There is no additional local sales tax or tax on hotel/motel rooms or car rentals.

WHOM TO CALL

Emergency: 911

Police (non-emergency): (204) 986-6222

Time and Temperature: (204) 784-9000

Weather: (204) 983-2050

Hospitals: Concordia Hospital, (204) 667-1560; Health Sciences Centre, (204) 774-6511; Misericordia Health Centre, (204) 788-8364; St. Boniface General Hospital, (204) 233-8563; Seven Oaks General Hospital, (204) 632-7133; Victoria General Hospital, (204) 269-3570.

WHERE TO LOOK

Newspapers

Winnipeg has two daily newspapers, the *Free Press* and *The Sun,* both distributed in the morning.

Radio

The Canadian Broadcasting Corporation (CBC) has both AM (990) and FM (98.3) stations in Winnipeg as well as an AM (1050) station broadcasting in French.

Visitor Information

Destination Winnipeg: 259 Portage Ave., Winnipeg, MB, Canada R3B 2B4; phone (204) 943-1970 or (800) 665-0204.

Destination Winnipeg is open Mon.-Fri. 8:30-4:30. A second branch, at Winnipeg International Airport, is open daily 8 a.m.-9:45 p.m.; phone (204) 982-7543.

Travel Manitoba's Explore Manitoba Centre at The Forks: 21 Forks Market Rd., Winnipeg, MB, Canada R3C 4T7; phone (204) 945-3777 or (800) 665-0040.

Explore Manitoba Centre is staffed with on-site travel counselors daily 10-6. The telephones are manned daily 8:30-4:30, Victoria Day weekend-Labour Day; Mon.-Fri. 8:30-4:30, rest of year. The 24-hour Forks Hot Line, (204) 957-7618, also provides information. The center features dioramas depicting the various regions of the province.

TRANSPORTATION

Air Travel

Winnipeg International Airport is about 8 kilometres (5 mi.) northwest of downtown off Metro Route 90. Daily bus service between the airport and downtown is provided by Winnipeg Transit between 5:58 a.m. and 12:17 a.m. The one-way fare is $1.80; passengers must have exact change. Major hotels offer limousine service to and from the airport.

Rental Cars

Hertz, (204) 925-6600, (800) 263-0600 in Canada, or (800) 654-3080 out of Canada, offers discounts to AAA and CAA members. Winnipeg locations are at Winnipeg International Airport, Winnipeg Square and 1577 Erin St.

Rail Service

The VIA Rail Canada depot is downtown at 123 Main St.; phone (888) 842-7245.

Taxis

Cab companies include Blueline, (204) 925-8888; Duffy's, (204) 775-0101; and Unicity, (204) 925-3131. Base fare is $3, plus a charge of 10c for each additional 87 metres (285 ft.) or 14 seconds of metered waiting time.

Public Transport

Winnipeg Transit, the public bus system, serves downtown Winnipeg and its suburbs. Route maps and route information are available by phoning (204) 986-5700. The average bus fare is $1.80; riders must have exact change.

intention to cross. No vehicle may pass another that is stopped or slowing to yield to a pedestrian. Right turns on red are permitted after a stop, unless otherwise posted.

Street System

Winnipeg's streets are laid out in a number of grids, but each is oriented to a different compass direction. Visitors will find it easiest to orient themselves to the major thoroughfares, which have signs

carrying the word "Route" and a number. Routes ending in even numbers designate north-south thoroughfares, and those ending in odd numbers designate major east-west arteries.

The primary north-south routes that cross the downtown area are 42, 52 and 62. The major east-west highways include 105, 115, 57 and 85. A good street map will enable drivers to see how the various grids of named streets connect with the main numbered routes.

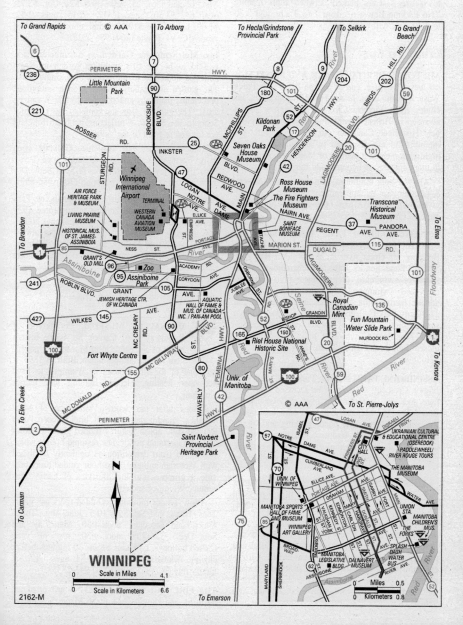

WINNIPEG

Parking

Visitors will do best to park in a commercial lot, where rates average about $1.10 to $1.35 for the first hour and $1.10 to $1.60 for subsequent hours. Daily rates are about $4 to $7. Parking meters downtown cost $1 an hour, but most carry a 1- or 2-hour limit. Some parking in downtown is free in designated metered areas.

Parking is strictly controlled along major downtown streets. Cars parked between signs reading "No Parking Between" from 7 to 9 a.m. and 3:30 to 5:30 p.m. will be towed.

What To See

AIR FORCE HERITAGE PARK AND MUSEUM is off Ness Ave. at n. end of Sharpe Blvd. (Air Force Way). The museum, in Air Force Headquarters, includes three Victoria Crosses, the highest medal awarded to British Commonwealth service personnel. Historical Canadian Air Force aircraft and memorabilia are displayed in an outdoor setting; highlights include a Garden of Memories as well as military fighters, helicopters and transport aircraft.

Allow 1 hour minimum. Museum open Mon.-Fri. 8-4, otherwise by appointment. Guided tours are given by request. Air park open daily 24 hours. Donations. Phone (204) 833-2500, ext. 6532.

AQUATIC HALL OF FAME AND MUSEUM OF CANADA INC./PAN-AM POOL is in the Pan-Am Building off Grant Ave. at 25 Poseidon Bay. The hall of fame honors Canadian champions in the sports of swimming, diving, water polo and synchronized swimming. Museum displays include aquatic memorabilia, a sports-stamp collection and The Cutty Sark Collection of models of well-known sailing ships. A library of aquatic literature is available. Mon.-Fri. 6 a.m.-9:30 p.m., Sat.-Sun. 9-5; closed Jan. 1 and Dec. 25-26. Free. Phone (204) 986-5890.

ASSINIBOINE PARK is at jct. Park Blvd. and Wellington Crescent; it also may be accessed from Portage Ave. via a footbridge over the Assiniboine River. The 153-hectare (378-acre) park has a zoo, miniature railway, duck pond, walking and biking paths, a conservatory, sculpture garden, a pavilion, Citizens Hall of Fame and gardens. Tobogganing, cross-country skiing and ice skating are available in the winter.

Assiniboine Forest, south of the park off Grant Avenue, is one of the largest urban nature parks in Canada. Daily dawn-dusk. Free. Phone (204) 986-7233.

Assiniboine Park Conservatory, in Assiniboine Park, features indoor gardens, changing floral and plant displays and art work by local artists. A tropical palm house contains orchids, ferns and banana plants. Food is available. Daily 9-8, mid-Apr. to mid-Sept.; 9-4:30, rest of year. Free. Phone (204) 986-5537.

Assiniboine Park Zoo, in Assiniboine Park, has more than 1,600 different animals in naturalistic settings. The zoo specializes in animals found in cooler climates from around the world as well as native North American species. Siberian tigers, snow leopards, polar bears, lynxes, elk, bison, and many other hardy species can be seen outside throughout the year. Large indoor facilities provide warm-weather viewing of many tropical animals.

Food is available. Daily 9-8; closed mornings of Nov. 11 and Dec. 25. Admission Mar.-Oct. $3.75; over 65, $3.50; ages 13-17, $2.15; ages 2-12, $1.60; family rate $10.95. Admission lower rest of year. MC, VI. Phone (204) 986-2327.

Leo Mol Sculpture Garden, in Assiniboine Park, is said to be the first sculpture garden in North America dedicated to the works of a single artist. The garden and gallery feature bronze sculptures, porcelains, paintings and sketches by the Winnipeg artist. The gardens also are home to the Leo Mol Schoolhouse Studio. A reflecting pool and fountain are located in front of the gallery.

Audiotape tours are available. Grounds open daily 7 a.m.-dusk. Gallery and studio open Tues.-Sun. 10-6, May-Aug.; Sat.-Sun. 11-5, in Sept. Donations. Audiotape tour $5. Phone (204) 986-6531.

Pavilion Gallery Museum is in Assiniboine Park at 55 Pavilion Crescent. Housed in a restored 1929 pavilion, the museum contains a permanent collection featuring the work of three prominent artists: Ivan Eyre, Walter Phillips and Clarence Tillenius. Allow 1 hour minimum. Tues.-Sun. 10-5, Victoria Day-Labour Day; Tues.-Sun. 11-5, rest of year. Free. Phone (204) 888-5466.

COSTUME MUSEUM OF CANADA— *see Dugald p. 199.*

DALNAVERT MUSEUM, .5 blk. s. of Broadway at 61 Carlton St., is the former home of Sir Hugh John Macdonald, prominent lawyer and politician. Built in 1895, it was one of the first houses in Winnipeg to have hot-water heating, electric lighting and indoor plumbing.

Named after the Scottish birthplace of Macdonald's grandmother, the red brick Queen Anne Revival-style house features stained glass windows and a wraparound porch. The restored house, which was saved from demolition, is opulently furnished with Victorian antiques. One-hour guided tours provide a glimpse into the lifestyles of early 20th-century Winnipeg society.

Allow 1 hour minimum. Guided tours are given Tues.-Thurs. and Sat.-Sun. 10-5, June-Aug.; Tues.-Thurs. and Sat.-Sun. noon-4:30, Mar.-May and Sept.-Dec.; Sat.-Sun. noon-4:30, rest of year. Closed holidays. Last tour begins 30 minutes before closing. Admission $4; over 64, $3; ages 5-17, $2; family rate $8. VI. Phone (204) 943-2835.

THE FIRE FIGHTERS MUSEUM is just e. of jct. Main St. and Higgins Ave. at 56 Maple St. Housed in a 1904 building used as a fire station until 1990, the museum features vintage firefighting equipment, such as an 1882 horse-drawn fire engine and a 1928 fire truck. Visitors can climb aboard a 1934 fire truck. Also featured are more than 10,000 photographs and information about firefighting in Winnipeg dating to 1882. Allow 1 hour minimum. Tues.-Sun. 11-3; closed major holidays. Admission $3; students with ID $2; ages 6-12, $1.50. Phone (204) 942-4817.

THE FORKS, at the confluence of the Red and Assiniboine rivers, has been a meeting place for more than 6,000 years, beginning with the aboriginal peoples. By virtue of location the 23-hectare (56-acre) site evolved into the center of the European fur trade in the 1730s. Métis, natives and eventually European settlers created a community along the rivers. More than a century later, the area became a transportation center as the railways laid tracks of steel across the prairie.

The Riverwalk follows the water's edge from the Manitoba Legislature to The Forks through downtown Winnipeg, and the Wall Through Time chronicles area history from glacial Lake Agassiz to the present.

A water bus service offers historical tours of the Red and Assiniboine rivers as well as transportation. Concerts and special events take place at The Forks throughout the year (see Special Events p. 220). Phone (204) 945-3777, (204) 783-6633 for water bus information or (800) 665-0040.

The Forks Market is at the confluence of the Red and Assiniboine rivers. Housed in refurbished stable buildings, the market contains shops that offer jewelry and crafts; fresh, specialty and ethnic foods; produce; and baked goods. A six-story glass tower affords a view of the rivers and the downtown area. Mon.-Sat. 9:30-9, Sun. 9:30-6:30, July-Aug.; daily 9:30-6:30 (also Fri. 6:30-9 p.m.), rest of year. Free. Phone (204) 942-6309.

The Forks National Historic Site, at the confluence of the Red and Assiniboine rivers, is a 3.5-hectare (9-acre) park that offers an outdoor playground and a riverside amphitheater with a view of historic St. Boniface. Interpretive programs and festivals are held Victoria Day through Labour Day. A variety of guided tours and theatrical presentations are available July through August. Daily 24 hours. Free. Phone (204) 983-6757.

Johnston Terminal, in the heart of The Forks, is a renovated railway cold storage warehouse. The four-story structure now features shops, boutiques and restaurants. Allow 1 hour minimum. Mon.-Sat. 10-9, Sun. 10-6. Free. Phone (204) 956-5593.

Manitoba Children's Museum, in the Kinsmen Building at 45 Forks Market Rd., is in western Canada's oldest train repair facility. The museum houses six galleries offering a wide variety of hands-on activities. At All Aboard children can pretend to be an engineer or conductor on the diesel train or Pullman car that are inside the museum.

They can climb into and slide down a 5-metre-tall (17-ft.) oak tree and see what life is like in a beaver lodge at The Tree & Me, or play with the latest technology in the Livewire gallery. They can be the star anchor in their own newscast at Our TV, then move on to Wonderworks and use child-size heavy equipment to design and build their own cities.

Picnicking is permitted. Allow 1 hour minimum. Daily 9:30-4:30 (also Fri.-Sat. 4:30-8); closed Easter, 4 days following Labour Day and Dec. 24-26. Ages 2-17, $6; adults $5.50; senior citizens $5. MC, VI. Phone (204) 924-4000.

FORT WHYTE CENTRE, 1961 McCreary Rd., is home to bison, deer, prairie dogs, red foxes, rabbits, muskrats, squirrels, waterfowl and songbirds. The center has trails, floating boardwalks, birdfeeding stations, a bison-viewing mound with a high-powered viewing scope, a family treehouse, fishing, summer boat and canoe rentals, snowshoeing, skating, tobogganing and an interpretive center. Vehicles for touring some areas are available for rent.

Picnic facilities are available. Allow 1 hour minimum. Mon.-Fri. 9-5, Sat.-Sun. and holidays 10-5; closed Dec. 25. Schedule varies summer and fall; phone for hours. Admission $5; over 65, $4; ages 3-17, $3. MC, VI. Phone (204) 989-8364.

FUN MOUNTAIN WATER SLIDE PARK, off Hwy. 1E on Murdock Rd., offers 10 waterslides, a swimming area, a hot tub, bumper boats, miniature golf, picnic areas and locker and changing facilities. Food is available. Daily 10-7, June-Aug. (weather permitting). Admission $13; ages 4-12, $10; over 55 and observers $6. Twilight rate $8. AX, MC, VI. Phone (204) 255-3910.

GRANT'S OLD MILL is at Portage Ave. and Booth Dr. This operational, reconstructed log flour mill—the original was built in 1829—marks the first use of water power in the Western provinces. Guided tours are available. Allow 30 minutes minimum. Daily 10-6, mid-May through Labour Day. Donations. Phone (204) 986-5613.

HISTORICAL MUSEUM OF ST. JAMES-ASSINIBOIA, 3180 Portage Ave., houses a collection of artifacts relating to the history of the St. James-Assiniboia area and a display building of pioneer activities. Guided interpretive tours through the mid-19th-century William Brown Log House offer a glimpse of the pioneer lifestyle. Allow 1 hour minimum. Daily 10-4, mid-May to early Sept.; by appointment rest of year. Donations. Phone (204) 888-8706.

JEWISH HERITAGE CENTRE OF WESTERN CANADA, 123 Doncaster St., site of the Fort Osborne Barracks, shares the history, experiences, achievements and culture of Jewish people in Western Canada. The museum's permanent exhibit depicts the settlement of Jews in Western Canada through artifacts, photographs and archival material.

The education center features items from the Holocaust. Changing exhibits and a library also are available.

Allow 30 minutes minimum. Sun.-Fri. noon-4 (also Wed.-Thurs. 4-8). Donations. Phone (204) 477-7466, or (204) 477-7460 for tours or appointments.

KILDONAN PARK is at 2021 Main St. In its 40 hectares (99 acres) along the Red River the park has some of the province's oldest and largest trees, flower and rock gardens, and a model of the witch's hut from "Hansel and Gretel."

Summer options include swimming; boating; bicycling; walking; in-line skating; and Rainbow Stage, Winnipeg's outdoor theater. Tobogganing, ice skating and cross-country skiing are winter sports. Food is available. Daily 8-dusk. Free. Phone (204) 986-7623. *See Recreation Chart.*

LIVING PRAIRIE MUSEUM is at 2795 Ness Ave. This 12-hectare (30-acre) unplowed tract supports more than 160 native plant species and is a remnant of the prairie that once covered much of North America. An interpretive center features displays of plants and animals of the tall grass prairie. Nature talks and hikes are offered, and a self-guiding trail brochure is available.

Allow 1 hour minimum. Interpretive center open daily 10-5, July-Aug.; Sun. 10-5, May-June; by appointment rest of year. Donations. Phone (204) 832-0167.

MANITOBA LEGISLATIVE BUILDING, bordered by Broadway Ave., Kennedy and Osborne sts. and the Assiniboine River, reflects neoclassical design in native limestone. The Italian marble grand staircase is guarded at its base by two life-size bronze bison, the emblems of Manitoba.

Atop the dome is Golden Boy by Parisian sculptor Charles Gardet. The torch, in the right hand, points to economic development and progress in the north; the sheaf of wheat in the left arm represents agriculture.

Guided tours are conducted daily on the hour 9-3, July 1-Labour Day. Self-guiding tours are available daily 8-8, year-round. Free. Phone (204) 945-5813.

THE MANITOBA MUSEUM, Main St. and Rupert Ave., illustrates the relationship of people and their environment in Manitoba's history. The Earth History Gallery shows geologic and organic evolution, the Arctic/Sub-Arctic Gallery explores Inuit culture and the zone's flora and fauna and the Boreal Forest Gallery features a diorama of a granite cliff, waterfall, marsh, Cree family and a wandering moose.

A replica of the ketch *Nonsuch* is shown docked in 17th-century England; the ship's 1668 voyage to Hudson Bay led to the opening of western Canada to commerce. The Hudson's Bay Company Gallery highlights fur trading and early exploration. The Grasslands Gallery covers southern Manitoba's early inhabitants, modern agriculture and urban settlement, and the Urban Gallery shows a 1920s boom-town Winnipeg.

Allow 1 hour minimum. Daily 10-5, Victoria Day-second Mon. in Oct.; Tues.-Sun. 10-5, rest of year. Admission $8; over 59, students with ID and ages 3-17, $6.50; family rate (up to six people with no more than two adults) $26.50. Combination ticket including museum, Planetarium and Science Gallery $18; ages 3-17, $12.50. Family pass (includes museum, Planetarium and Science Gallery) $60 (up to six people with no more than two adults). AX, MC, VI. Phone (204) 956-2830 or (204) 943-3139.

Planetarium, on the lower level of The Manitoba Museum, presents interactive and multimedia shows about our universe.

Allow 1 hour minimum. Shows are presented on the hour Tues.-Sun. beginning at 11, Victoria Day-second Mon. in Oct. Show schedule varies; phone ahead. Admission $6.50; over 60, students with ID and ages 3-17, $5. Combination ticket including The Manitoba Museum, Planetarium and Science Gallery $18; ages 3-17, $12.50. Family pass (includes museum, Planetarium and Science Gallery) $60 (up to six people with no more than two adults). AX, MC, VI. Phone (204) 956-2830, or (204) 943-3139 for show times.

Science Gallery, at The Manitoba Museum, depicts the ways in which the human senses perceive the universe through more than 100 hands-on exhibits. Allow 1 hour minimum. Daily 10-5, Victoria Day-second Mon. in Oct.; Tues.-Sun. 10-5, rest of year. Admission $6.50; over 60, students with ID and ages 3-17, $5. Combination ticket including The Manitoba Museum, Planetarium and Science Gallery $18; ages 3-17, $12.50. Family pass (includes museum, Planetarium and Science Gallery) $60 (up to six people with no more than two adults). AX, MC, VI. Phone (204) 956-2830 or (204) 943-3139.

MANITOBA SPORTS HALL OF FAME AND MUSEUM, on the fifth floor of The Bay, 450 Portage Ave., focuses on sports history and legendary athletes and teams. Interactive exhibits change every few months. Allow 1 hour minimum. Tues.-Sat. 10-5; closed major holidays. Donations. Phone (204) 774-0002.

RIEL HOUSE NATIONAL HISTORIC SITE, 330 River Rd., was the home of the mother of Louis Riel. Although this leader of the Métis and founder of the provisional government of Manitoba never lived in the house, his body lay in state for several days after his execution in 1885. The small log building with board siding is furnished in period.

The walkway to the house has signs explaining the history of the Métis and of the Riel family. Allow 30 minutes minimum. Guided tours daily 10-6, mid-May through Labour Day. Donations. Phone (204) 257-1783.

ROSS HOUSE MUSEUM, 140 Meade St. N. in Joe Zuken Heritage Park, was the first post office in western Canada in 1854. Displays reflect the life of the Ross family when their home served as the post office. Allow 30 minutes minimum. Wed.-Sun. 10-4:30, June-Aug. Free. Phone (204) 943-3958.

ROYAL CANADIAN MINT, 520 Lagimodière Blvd. at jct. Trans-Canada Hwy. and Hwy. 59, is considered one of the world's most modern mints. The Winnipeg Plant produces all of the circulation coinage for Canada and coinage for many foreign countries. The building includes a landscaped interior courtyard, a glass tower and a horseshoe-shaped tour route overlooking the manufacturing plant. A coin display provides historical information.

Guided tours are available. Mon.-Fri. 9-4, Sat. 10-1, Victoria Day-Labour Day; Mon.-Fri. 9-4, rest of year. Closed holidays. Last tour begins 1 hour before closing. Schedule may vary; phone ahead. Admission $3, under 6 free, family rate $10. Phone (204) 983-6429.

SAINT BONIFACE MUSEUM, s.e. on Main St. (Hwy. 1), then n. to 494 Taché Ave., was built 1846-51 as the first convent and hospital in western Canada. Displays depict the Red River Settlement and early French and Métis Manitoba; an exhibit is dedicated to Louis Riel, leader of the Red River Resistance. Visitors also can view the nearby ruins of the cathedral as well as the cemetery where Riel is buried.

Allow 30 minutes minimum. Mon.-Fri. 9-5, Sat. 10-5, Sun. 10-8, May-Sept.; Mon.-Fri. 9-5, Sun. noon-4, rest of year. Closed Dec. 24-25 and 31. Admission $3; over 60, physically impaired and students with ID $2; under 6 free; family rate $8. Phone (204) 237-4500.

SAINT NORBERT PROVINCIAL HERITAGE PARK is at 40 Turnbull Dr. at the fork of the Red and La Salle rivers. Near the former village of St. Norbert, this 7-hectare (17-acre) park is rich in history and linked to Manitoba's entry into the Confederation. A restored 19th-century farmhouse and village house are decorated in period.

A walking trail with information about native inhabitants and Manitoba history and a house belonging to a member of Riel's provisional government are available. Guided tours are available. Picnicking and fishing are permitted. Allow 1 hour minimum. Daily 10:30-5, May-Aug. Donations. Phone (204) 945-4236, or (204) 945-4375, Sept.-Apr.

SEVEN OAKS HOUSE MUSEUM, 1.5 blks. e. of Main St. off Rupertsland Blvd. and Jones St. in W. Kildonan, is said to be the oldest habitable house in Manitoba. This sturdy building, with its stone foundation, hand-hewn oak timbers, hand-split shingles and buffalo hair-bound plaster, was built 1851-53. The house displays belongings of the original occupants and other period furnishings. Guided tours are available. Allow 30 minutes minimum. Daily 10-5,

last weekend in May-Labour Day. Donations. Phone (204) 339-7429.

TRANSCONA HISTORICAL MUSEUM, 141 Regent Ave. W., is in a 1925 bank building. It contains items about the history of Transcona, a railroad town amalgamated into Winnipeg; railroad and military memorabilia; a butterfly collection; firearms; pioneer articles; and Manitoba First Nations artifacts. Highlights include the ship's wheel from the World War II HMCS *Transcona*, a 1923 hand-carved grandfather clock and hands-on exhibits.

Allow 30 minutes minimum. Mon.-Sat. 10-5, June-Aug.; Tues.-Fri. noon-5, Sat. 10-5, Feb.-May and Sept.-Dec. Donations. Phone (204) 222-0423.

UKRAINIAN CULTURAL AND EDUCATIONAL CENTRE (OSEREDOK), 184 Alexander Ave. E., at Main St. and Disraeli Frwy., is dedicated to the preservation of Canadian-Ukrainian culture. Highlights include a museum, an art gallery, a library and archives. Interpretive exhibits relate to the Ukrainian heritage around the world and include a wide range of artifacts, from fine art to farm implements to rare 16th-century maps. Guided tours are available by appointment. Allow 30 minutes minimum. Mon.-Sat. 10-4; Sun. 1-5, during summer months. Donations. Phone (204) 942-0218.

WESTERN CANADA AVIATION MUSEUM, in an aircraft hangar off Ellice Ave. at 958 Ferry Rd., displays 23 vintage aircraft. All aspects of aviation are exhibited, from bush planes to commercial airliners to combat planes and homemade aircraft. Children can explore the interactive Skyways exhibit and Spaceways, a simulated trip through the solar system. Videotaped presentations about historical aircraft are offered. A research library and archives can be seen by appointment.

Guided tours are available by appointment. Allow 1 hour minimum. Mon.-Sat. 10-4, Sun. and holidays 1-4; closed Jan. 1, Good Friday and Dec. 25-26. Admission $5; ages 3-17, $3; family rate $12. AX, MC, VI. Phone (204) 786-5503.

WINNIPEG ART GALLERY is at 300 Memorial Blvd. Eight galleries contain contemporary and historical works by Manitoba, Canadian and international artists. The Inuit art collection is reputed to be the largest public collection of contemporary Inuit art in the world. Guided tours are offered. Food is available. Allow 1 hour minimum. Tues.-Sun. 11-5. Admission $6; senior citizens and students with ID $4; ages 6-12, $3; family rate $15; free to all Sat. AX, MC, VI. Phone (204) 786-6641.

CASINOS

- **Club Regent** is at 1425 Regent Ave. Mon.-Sat. 10 a.m.-3 a.m., Sun. noon-3 a.m.; closed Jan. 1, Easter, Easter Monday, Nov. 11 and Dec. 24-25. Phone (204) 957-2700.

- **McPhillips Street Station** is at 484 McPhillips St. Mon.-Sat. 10 a.m.-3 a.m., Sun. noon-3 a.m.; closed Jan. 1, Easter, Easter Monday, Nov. 11 and Dec. 24-25. Phone (204) 957-3900.

What To Do

Sightseeing

The intersection of Portage Avenue and Main Street, a few blocks from the juncture of Winnipeg's two rivers, has been the major crossroads since the city's earliest days and is a good place to start a sightseeing foray.

Although now part of Winnipeg, the early settlement of St. Boniface has retained its French Canadian identity. A monument honoring the explorer Pierre Gaultier de la Vérendrye is on Taché Avenue opposite St. Boniface Hospital. Also in St. Boniface is the grave of Louis Riel, leader of the Métis and of the provisional government 1869-70. The grave is at Taché and Cathedral avenues in the churchyard of the St. Boniface Basilica.

Boat and Bus Tours

SAVE **PADDLEWHEEL/RIVER ROUGE TOURS** offers boat tour departures from the Alexander Docks at jct. Alexander Ave. and Waterfront Dr. and pickup service from downtown lodgings for bus tours. The company offers both boat and bus tours of Winnipeg. The MS *Paddlewheel Queen*, MS *Paddlewheel Princess* and the MS *River Rouge* offer daytime sightseeing cruises as well as evening dinner and dance cruises on the Assiniboine and Red rivers. Paddlewheel double-decker buses provide sightseeing excursions on land.

Food is available. Two-hour Winnipeg sightseeing cruise departs daily at 1, May-Oct. Historic cruise to Lower Fort Garry National Historic Site departs Thurs.-Fri. at 9 and returns at 4:30, July-Aug. Bus tour daily 9-noon, July-Aug. Combination cruise and bus tour departs at 9 and returns at 3, July-Aug. Fares range $12.75-$29.75; over 65, $11.20-$26.70; under 12, $7-$17.50. Reservations are recommended. MC, VI. Phone (204) 942-4500 or (204) 944-8000.

SPLASH DASH WATER BUS departs from the bottom of the river walk at The Forks. The boats provide 30-minute guided historical tours of a section of the Red and Assiniboine rivers. Points of interest are noted along the way. Allow 30 minutes minimum. Departures every 15 minutes daily 10-dusk (weather permitting), mid-May through second Mon. in Oct. Fare $8.50; over 55 and ages 4-18, $7.50. Phone (204) 783-6633.

Plane Tours

The Winnipeg Flying Club, (204) 338-7927, 16 kilometres (10 mi.) north of the perimeter on Hwy. 9 at St. Andrews Airport, offers scenic flights over Winnipeg, the Red River and the Lake Winnipeg area. Phone for information and reservations.

Train Tours

Antique rail cars pulled by a vintage locomotive take passengers on 2.5-hour trips departing from a 1910 station at Inkster Junction, 3 kilometres (1.9 mi.) west of Hwy. 90 and Inkster Boulevard. The Prairie Dog Central Railway makes stops at country markets in Grosse Isle and Warren. The scenic ride operates weekends May through September; phone (204) 832-5259, or (888) 780-7328 in Canada for reservations.

Walking Tours

Guided walking tours of the 20-block Historic Winnipeg area near Portage Avenue and Main Street in the Exchange District are available June through September. Departing from the Exchange District Information Booth in Old Market Square, these tours visit many of Manitoba's finest historical buildings; for schedule information phone (204) 942-6716.

One of the city's original ethnic neighborhoods, Selkirk Avenue is a mini-city that grew with the development of the railway in the 1880s. One-hour walking tours of the area depart from the Amphitheater on Selkirk Avenue, 4 blocks west of Main Street, from May to August; for information phone (204) 586-3445.

Walking tours of the old Saint Boniface area are available; phone (204) 233-8343 for information and reservations. A self-guiding walking tour of Osborne Village, a densely populated area with many shops and restaurants, includes more than 33 buildings; for information phone (204) 474-1008. Crescentwood, an area of stately homes, can be seen on a self-guiding tour; pamphlets are available at the McNally Robinson bookstore at Grant Park Shopping Centre, 1120 Grant Ave.

Sports and Recreation

Devotees of organized sports will find many opportunities to indulge themselves in Winnipeg. Canadians love **hockey,** and those who fancy flying sticks and flashing skates will find the American Hockey League's Manitoba Moose locking horns with their opponents at the Winnipeg Arena in the city's sports complex at 1430 Maroons Rd. Fans of **wrestling** will also find their sport at the arena.

Football fans can watch the Canadian Football League's Winnipeg Blue Bombers playing at the Canad Inns Stadium from June to November. The Northern **Baseball** League's Winnipeg Goldeyes play at CanWest Global Park from May to August.

To obtain additional information and tickets for sports and recreation events listed above, phone (204) 780-3333 for recorded information, (204) 780-7328, or (888) 780-7328 in Canada.

Sports car racing enthusiasts converge at the Victory Lanes Speedway, (204) 582-0527, on Hwy. 75, 4 kilometres (2.5 mi.) south of St. Norbert, from April through October (weather permitting).

Assiniboia Downs, 3975 Portage Ave. at the Perimeter Highway, offers **Thoroughbred racing** early May to mid-October. Simulcast races are offered year-round; phone (204) 885-3330.

Note: Policies concerning admittance of children to pari-mutuel betting facilities vary. Phone for information.

Other spectator sports include minor league hockey, **curling** and **ringette** games, held at municipal skating rinks, and **cricket** played in Assiniboine Park. Ringette, similar to hockey, is a popular women's sport developed in Canada.

There are 33 **golf** courses in Winnipeg. Nine-hole public courses include Crescent Drive, 781 Crescent Dr., (204) 986-5911, and Harbour View, 1867 Springfield Rd., (204) 222-2751. Among the 18-hole public courses are Kildonan Park, 2021 Main St., (204) 986-5679; Tuxedo, 400 Shaftesbury Blvd., (204) 888-2867; and Windsor Park, 10 Rue des Meurons, (204) 986-3006. John Blumberg, 4540 Portage Ave., (204) 986-3490, offers both nine- and 18-hole layouts.

Winnipeg has more than 280 **tennis** courts, some lighted for night matches. Many courts are at community centers. Championship matches are held during the summer at various locations throughout the city. **Squash, handball** and **racquetball** players can avail themselves of courts at a number of athletic clubs and local universities. For information contact Sport Manitoba; phone (204) 925-5600.

Fans of **bicycling** and **in-line skating** take to the marked paths in Winnipeg's city parks. Bicycle trails along less-traveled side streets in and around Winnipeg also have been established. **Cross-country skiing, tobogganing** and **ice skating** facilities are available at Assiniboine, Kildonan and St. Vital parks; facilities for ice skating also are found at numerous schools and community clubs.

Downhill skiing is available at Spring Hill Winter Park Ski Area, (204) 224-3051, near Birds Hill Provincial Park at the junction of Hwy. 59N at the Floodway; and Stony Mountain Winter Park, (204) 344-5977, 10 kilometres (6 mi.) north of the perimeter of Hwy. 7. Birds Hill Provincial Park, (204) 222-9151, also is a site for **snowmobiling** and cross-country skiing.

Swimming can be pursued all year in Winnipeg, where numerous indoor pools include those at four YM-YWCAs; phone (204) 947-3044. The Pan-Am Pool, 25 Poseidon Bay, is one of the largest indoor bodies of water in Canada and is open all year; phone (204) 986-5890 *(see attraction listing p. 214)*.

Many recreational activities are available at the Harbour View Recreation Complex in the northeastern section of Winnipeg in Kil-Cona Park, 1867 Springfield Rd. At this 162-hectare (400-acre) park are facilities for **miniature golf, lawn bowling, shuffleboard** and **horseshoes** as well as tennis courts, a golf course, a driving range and pedal boats during the summer. Golf and tennis lessons are available April to October. Ice skating, tobogganing and cross-country skiing are available during the winter. Phone (204) 222-2766.

Shopping

The intersection of Portage Avenue and Main Street is a good starting point for a shopping excursion. Winnipeg Square and the underground Lombard Concourse offer shops ranging from boutiques to bookstores. Portage Avenue also is the site of the city's largest department stores. Portage Place connects The Bay (The Hudson's Bay Co.) to other department stores with an extensive system of skywalks.

Winnipeg has a historic area where shoppers can browse through merchandise of today amid structures of the past. The Forks Market *(see attraction listing p. 215)* is behind Union Station, off Main Street (near Portage and Main). The shops and restaurants are located in an indoor market with more than 80 vendors selling everything from fresh fish and baked goods to arts and crafts items. The Johnston Terminal *(see attraction listing p. 215)*, across from the market, offers specialty boutiques and eateries.

Shopping for Western wear and accessories is possible at such factory outlet stores as Canada West Boots, 2188 McPhillips St., or MWG Factory Outlet, 1147 Notre Dame Ave.

More than 125 shops and restaurants can be found at Osborne Village, between River and Wardlaw avenues 2 blocks south of the Manitoba Legislative Building. Travelers in search of a truly representative souvenir may want to examine the native arts and crafts and western wear available at Winnipeg Outfitters Inc. at 250 McPhillips St.

Finally, visitors who like their shopping climate-controlled and under one roof can visit the malls at Cityplace, 333 St. Mary Ave. at Hargrave Street; Garden City, 2305 McPhillips St., with Sears and Winners as its anchor stores; Grant Park, 1120 Grant Ave., with Zellers; Kildonan Place, 1555 Regent Ave. W., with anchors Sears and Zellers; Polo Park, 1485 Portage Ave., which has The Bay and Sears for anchors; Portage Place, 393 Portage Ave.; or St. Vital Centre, 1225 St. Mary's Rd., with The Bay and Sears as its anchor stores.

Theater and Concerts

Canada's Royal Winnipeg Ballet, Winnipeg Symphony Orchestra and Manitoba Opera perform in Centennial Concert Hall, 555 Main St., opposite City Hall. The oldest company in Canada and the second oldest in North America, Canada's Royal Winnipeg Ballet is known for its versatile style and performs an eclectic mix of classical and contemporary ballets. At home performances are from October through May. For ticket information phone (204) 956-2792 or (800) 667-4792.

The Winnipeg Symphony Orchestra performs September to May and offers classical, contemporary and popular orchestral music; for concert information phone (204) 949-3999. The Manitoba Opera performs October through May; phone (204) 942-7479, or (204) 780-3333 for tickets.

Modern dance is presented by Winnipeg's Contemporary Dancers from December through April at the Centennial Concert Hall; for information phone (204) 452-0229.

Theater lovers can enjoy performances of the classics, comedies and modern dramas at the Manitoba Theatre Centre Mainstage, 174 Market St., from October to May; for general information or tickets phone (204) 942-6537. The MTC Warehouse Theatre, 140 Rupert Ave., (204) 942-6537, features alternative theater performances from November to April. The Lyric Theatre, just east of the Pavilion in Assiniboine Park, (204) 885-9742, is an outdoor theater showcasing drama festivals as well as performances by the Royal Winnipeg Ballet, the Winnipeg Symphony Orchestra and other musical groups.

For both adults and young people, the Prairie Theatre Exchange, at Portage Place, 393 Portage Ave., (204) 942-7291, or (204) 942-5483 for ticket information, presents a season of modern Canadian plays from October to April. Rainbow Stage in Kildonan Park offers musicals in a covered outdoor theater from July through August; phone (888) 780-3333. Celebrations Dinner Theatre, 1824 Pembina Hwy. in the Canad Inn Fort Garry, combines an original, three-act musical comedy with a four-course dinner for a one-stop evening out; phone (204) 982-8282.

The IMAX Theatre, Portage Place, 393 Portage Ave. in downtown Winnipeg, features a five-and-one-half-story-high by 22-metre-wide (72-ft.) screen; phone (204) 956-4629 for information or (204) 780-7328 to reserve tickets.

A variety of theatrical productions for children of all ages is presented at The Forks by the Manitoba Theatre for Young People; for information phone (204) 942-8898.

The French Canadian heritage of St. Boniface, in the heart of the French district, is remembered through the support of the Centre Culturel Franco-Manitobain at 340 Provencher Blvd.; phone (204) 233-8972. The center is the home of such cultural groups as Le Cercle Molière theater company (Canada's oldest active theater group), the dance group L'Ensemble Folklorique de la Rivière Rouge, and the choral groups L'Alliance Chorale Manitoba and La Chorale des Intrépides; phone (204) 233-8053 for more information.

Special Events

Winnipeg's calendar of events, with more than 130 days of festivals, reflects more than 43 nationalities that have made the city home. The *joie de vivre* spirit of the French voyageurs is revived each February during Le Festival du Voyageur, a 10-day-long celebration including winter sports, ice-sculpting contests, music and food. With the 18th-century fur trade as its theme, the event takes place in St. Boniface, Winnipeg's French Quarter.

The city plays host to the 4-day Winnipeg International Children's Festival at The Forks in early June. Music, theater, dance and comedy performances are offered as well as hands-on workshops and evening shows.

The weeklong Jazz Winnipeg Festival in late June features jazz performers on an outdoor stage. The Red River Exhibition, known locally as the "The Ex" is held during late June. The Ex's many rides, midway activities and games of chance as well as nightly concerts take place at Red River Exhibition Park off Perimeter Highway behind Assiniboia Downs.

In mid-July is the 10-day Winnipeg Fringe Festival, with various theater performances in the Exchange District. Mid-July also brings the 4-day Winnipeg Folk Festival to nearby Birds Hill Provincial Park, where more than 200 concerts, children's activities, music workshops and food are highlighted. In late July A Taste of Manitoba features some 30 restaurants offering samples of their food along with entertainment.

Early August brings the 2-week Folklorama multicultural celebration, Winnipeg's largest event and reputedly the largest multicultural festival of its kind. The following month those of German extraction host Oktoberfest, a celebration in mid-September with lively music and plenty of beer, wurst and Bavarian delicacies.

This ends listings for the Winnipeg Vicinity.

Northwest
Territori
and Nu

head
north

Near Yellowknife / © Dennis Fast / Alamy Images

T ake a journey into northern Canada and you may be surprised at your options for enjoyment.

Residents joke that the four seasons in the Northwest Territories and Nunavut—June, July, August and winter—are a bit unlike seasons in the rest of the world. The absence of a "real" spring or fall leaves busy summers and extra-long winters.

Arrive in June, July or August and you can dip your toes in the Arctic Ocean and marvel at the wildflower-dotted tundra under a midnight sun.

Or visit during the 8 months of winter and you can choose from myriad activities that involve snow and ice: snowmobiling, building an igloo, ice fishing, riding on a paw-powered sled or simply driving on an "ice highway," made of hard-packed snow piled on frozen lakes.

Celebrate the end of a long, dark winter by living it up at Inuvik's Sunrise Festival—held in honor of the sun's appearance after months of hiding.

Other diversions do not depend on snow or sun: Try a moose burger or dine on arctic char. Shop for such treasures as whalebone or soapstone carvings. Stay at a remote wilderness lodge and discover the specialized flora and fauna of the Arctic Circle. Learn about the traditions of the Inuit and Dene cultures. Set your sights on beluga whales or polar bears. See a shaggy musk-ox up close or listen to the roar of hooves from a migrating herd of caribous.

Whatever the season, the Northwest Territories and Nunavut invite you to refresh your senses in the north.

On April Fools' Day, 1999, in the eastern Northwest Territories, very few Inuit people were worried about such practical jokes as sugar in the salt shaker.

Instead, the focus was on celebrating the birth of Nunavut, Canada's newest territory. On this night, Inuit eyes were toward the heavens, watching as a grand display of colorful explosions lit up the black sky. Matching the glow of the fireworks were the sparks in the hearts of the Inuit, whose hopes are high for a bright future.

Twenty-four years after a separation was proposed, Nunavut (meaning *our land* in the Inuktitut language) officially seceded from the expansive Northwest Territories to form its own territory. A new line on the Canadian map allows its approximately 25,000 residents—85 percent of whom are Inuit—the chance to reclaim and govern what they have always believed to be their own.

Where the Streets Have No Name

Nunavut, a giant chunk of arctic earth stretching so far northeast it almost tickles the shores of Greenland, contains only one road within its 2 million square kilometres.

Above the tree line, it's a place where animals outnumber humans; where brightly colored rhododendron, lupines, yellow buttercups and mountain avens sprinkle treeless tundra; and where it may be easier to hook a 30-pound trout for dinner than pick up a cheeseburger at a drive-thru.

The tiny capital city of Iqaluit rests at the southern tip of mountainous Baffin Island, from which steep cliffs drop about 610 metres to the sea. Here it's no surprise to see caribou wander along unnamed streets, passing St. Jude's Anglican church—which, by the way, is shaped like an igloo. But don't worry; there are plenty of folks who can show you around, and during summer the midnight sun shines bright to light your way.

Even farther north is Quttinirpaaq National Park, which extends above the 80th parallel, just a snowball's throw from Santa's workshop. In this globe-top world of snowcapped peaks and glaciers, ice simply does not melt.

Despite the recent division of Nunavut and Northwest Territories, the two still share identical features. Take light, for example. During summer above the Arctic Circle, days have no end. A shining sun never dips below the

Sir Martin Frobisher, searching for the Northwest Passage to the Orient, arrives.
1576

The Treaty of Paris grants Canada to the British.
1763

Alexander Mackenzie establishes a trading post for the North West Co.
1789

© Chris Hellier/Corbis

1771
Hudson's Bay Co. explorer-trader Samuel Hearne arrives at Great Slave Lake.

NW Territories Historical Timeline

1845
Capt. Robert Le Mesurier McClure discovers the Northwest Passage.

horizon, and the sky is illuminated 24 hours a day. In winter, the opposite occurs as days and nights melt together under a cold, dark sky.

Sound dismal and depressing? Well, picture the sight of a black sky pin-pricked with stars surrounding a full, glowing moon, its light sprawling across wide, snow-covered tundra and frozen lakes. On such a clear winter night the flat, stark-white landscape glistens and appears endless.

Bright Lights, Small Cities

The Northern Lights, or "aurora borealis," painting the winter sky are no less impressive. A faint glow slightly above the horizon serves as the show's opening act. When the lights rise, they resemble curtains in shades of red, lavender and green. Feather-shaped and stretching across the night sky, the lights ripple and curl, forming watercolored waves.

In the Northwest Territories, you'll have a good chance to catch this dazzling display from October through February. A spot void of city lights is best; try giant Great Slave Lake, the fifth largest freshwater lake in North America (near Yellowknife). Frozen in winter, it provides a fine view of the vivid night sky.

Then visit Yellowknife, on the lake's north arm. Once glittering with gold, this former 1930s mining camp now flaunts its colorful past in Old Town, where shops and quaint neighborhoods nestle against the shore.

West of the city is Nahanni National Park, where 90-metre-high Virginia Falls plummets into South Nahanni River. The falls, arguably more spectacular than Niagara, form a pool of eddies and perilous rapids surrounded by cliffs taller than Toronto's CN Tower.

Roads are in short supply here, but sparkling falls and rivers await you on scenic drives. Mackenzie Highway, the territories' only paved highway, crosses the Mackenzie River near Fort Providence. Continue east along the "Waterfall Route" to Sambaa Deh Falls Park, where trails lead to two cascades.

Many motorists also choose to navigate the Dempster Highway, which dead-ends at Inuvik, the continent's farthest point north accessible by road.

In fact, visiting the lands north of the 60th parallel may be the brightest idea you've ever had.

Hudson's Bay Co. cedes the region to Canada.
1870

Northwest Territories divides into two territories; the eastern, Inuit-governed territory becomes Nunavut.
1999

A Soviet nuclear-powered satellite crashes into the Great Slave Lake area; debris is spread over 124,000 square kilometres.
1978

1911
Oil is discovered at Norman Wells.

© Galen Rowell/Corbis

1934
Gold is discovered at Yellowknife on Great Slave Lake.

1992
The Nunavut Land Claim Agreement, under which the Inuit give up any future aboriginal rights to their traditional land in return for the power to govern their own territory, is passed.

Recreation

Welcome to the top of the world. The vast Northwest Territories and Nunavut boast an area filled with wild rivers, icy seas, lofty mountains and Arctic tundra. Recreational diversions for both the adventure seeker and casual traveler are numerous.

Summer days, typically June through August, are long and surprisingly mild. With an average temperature of 21 C (70 F), visitors can enjoy the outdoors without the gear that winter demands. **Hikers** can check out a wide variety of topography, from steep mountain trails to Arctic tundra. The Canol Heritage Trail, en route to the Yukon, offers some challenging terrain.

Snowmobiling, snowshoeing, dog sledding and **cross-country skiing** are a way of life that has been known to extend into June—the warmer air and long days make this the perfect time for such outdoor pursuits. Recreational activities also can be combined with viewing the spectacular Northern Lights. Many outfitters offer snowmobile tours or flights to remote areas to observe this brilliant display. Hint: The best time for viewing these dancing lights is September through January.

Getting There is Half the Fun

Travel anywhere in the territories can include aircraft, boat, automobile, snowmobile, Inuit qomatiq (sled) and even dogsled. Of the Northwest Territories' four national parks, only Wood Buffalo can be reached by road. Nahanni is accessible solely by air; its rugged beauty is best explored by the experienced canoer. Only the hardy recreationalist should fly to the extremely remote Aulavik, where craggy badlands include thousands of archeological sites. The newest park, Tuktut Nogait, is a hiker's paradise where float planes begin landing on the Homaday River in mid-June.

High in Canada's eastern Arctic is Nunavut's Baffin Island. Auyuittuq National Park, reached by dog sled in winter and boat in summer, draws **climbers** to its lofty peaks. The sheer cliffs and arctic fiords of Quttinirpaaq National Park (formerly Ellesmere Island National Park Reserve), the northernmost national park in North America, can be explored by guided tour; outfitters are available in Grise Fiord, Iqaluit and Resolute.

Land of Adventure

Water challenges come in varying degrees of difficulty. **Canoeing** and **kayaking** conditions depend on the weather. Arctic rivers, while dangerous, can offer the ultimate thrill if explored cautiously. Sea kayakers can flow beside towering icebergs, while the many rivers stemming off the meandering Mackenzie are a canoeist's dream. Paddlers will be dazzled by the breathtaking scenery on the Nahanni. Hoist your sails on Great Slave Lake, where the wind is just right for **sailing,** or if you are brave enough, **scuba dive** in the frigid waters. Slave River rapids await **whitewater rafting** enthusiasts.

Cold northern waters yield excellent **fishing.** Plenty of lakes, streams and rivers are full of prize catches, from the feisty arctic char to the fierce northern pike. Some of the territories' waters are ranked the best in the world for angling, including Great Slave, Great Bear and Murky lakes and the Stark and Snowdrift rivers. **Ice fishing** is another way to reel in the big one. Don't forget your fishing license.

The land's beauty, combined with unspoiled wilderness and vast game selections, makes **hunting** quite a rewarding experience. For the ultimate hunt, sports enthusiasts can track down one of the world's largest predators—the polar bear—by dog sled. Musk ox hunting is another option. Other prized trophies include caribou, moose, wolverines, and grizzly and black bears. Hunts are strictly controlled; licensed guides and permits are required.

For those who like to shoot with a camera, **wildlife viewing** is rewarding. An outfitter will increase your chances of spotting the Arctic's resident polar bear. **Bird-watchers** flock to the Mackenzie River delta, one of the world's biggest nesting grounds.

Whether you are seeking adventure for a few hours or several days, an outfitter will help. NWT Arctic Tourism, (867) 873-7200 or (800) 661-0788, or Nunavut Tourism, (867) 979-6551 or (866) 686-2888, can offer information about tour companies and outfitters.

Recreational Activities

Throughout the TourBook, you may notice a Recreational Activities heading with bulleted listings of recreation-oriented establishments listed underneath. Similar operations also may be mentioned in Destination City recreation sections. Since normal AAA inspection criteria cannot be applied, these establishments are presented only for information. Age, height and weight restrictions may apply. Reservations often are recommended and sometimes are required. Addresses and/or phone numbers are provided so visitors can contact the attraction for additional information.

Fast Facts

POPULATION: 64,105.

AREA: Northwest Territories 1,346,106 sq km (519,731 sq mi); ranks 3rd. Nunavut 2,093,190 sq km (808,180 sq mi); ranks 1st.

CAPITAL: Yellowknife, Northwest Territories; Iqaluit, Nunavut.

HIGHEST POINT: 2,762 m/9,062 ft., Cirque of the Unclimbables Mountain northwest of Nahanni National Park Reserve.

LOWEST POINT: Sea level, Beaufort Sea.

TIME ZONE(S): Mountain/Central/Eastern/Atlantic. DST.

MINIMUM AGE FOR UNRESTRICTED DRIVER'S LICENSE: 16.

SEAT BELT/CHILD RESTRAINT LAWS: Seat belts required for driver and all passengers; child restraints required for children weighing less than 18 kilograms (40 lbs.).

HELMETS FOR MOTORCYCLISTS: Required for driver and passenger.

RADAR DETECTORS: Not permitted; visitors traveling in or passing through the Northwest Territories and Nunavut should detach their units and store them inside their luggage.

FIREARMS LAWS: By federal law, all nonresidents entering Canada with a firearm must declare their weapon in writing and pay a fee of $50 (Canadian).

HOLIDAYS: Jan. 1; Good Friday; Easter Monday; Victoria Day, May 24 (if a Mon.) or the closest prior Mon.; Aboriginal Day, June 21; Canada Day, July 1; Nunavut Day, July 9; Civic Holiday, Aug. (1st Mon.); Labour Day, Sept. (1st Mon.); Thanksgiving, Oct. (2nd Mon.); Remembrance Day, Nov. 11; Dec. 25-26.

TAXES: The Northwest Territories and Nunavut have no territorial sales tax. However, a 7 percent Goods and Services Tax (GST) is levied.

INFORMATION CENTERS: Territorial welcome centers in the Northwest Territories include an office on Hwy. 1 at the Alberta border (on the 60th parallel) near Enterprise; it is open 8 a.m.-10 p.m., late May to mid-September. A center at Km-post 77 on Hwy. 8 near Fort McPherson is open 10-10, early June to mid-September. The Northern Frontier Visitor's Centre in Yellowknife is open Mon.-Fri. 8:30-6:30, Sat.-Sun. 9-6, June-Sept.; Mon.-Fri. 8:30-5, Sat.-Sun. noon-4, rest of year. Phone (867) 873-4262 or (877) 881-4262. In Nunavut the Unikkaarvik Visitor Centre in Iqaluit is open Mon.-Fri. 8:30-5, Sat.-Sun. 10-6, June-Aug.; Mon.-Fri. 8:30-5, rest of year. Phone (867) 979-4636.

FURTHER INFORMATION FOR VISITORS:

NWT Arctic Tourism
Box 610
Yellowknife, NT, Canada X1A 2N5
(867) 873-7200
(800) 661-0788

Nunavut Tourism
Box 1450
Iqaluit, NU, Canada X0A 0H0
(867) 979-6551
(866) 686-2888

FISHING AND HUNTING REGULATIONS:

Northwest Territories Resources, Wildlife & Economic Development
Box 2668
Yellowknife, NT, Canada X1A 2P9
(867) 873-7184
(800) 661-0788

FERRY AND ROAD INFORMATION:
(800) 661-0750 (valid only in Canada)

ALCOHOL CONSUMPTION: Legal age 19.

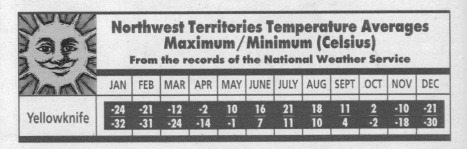

Northwest Territories Temperature Averages Maximum/Minimum (Celsius)
From the records of the National Weather Service

	JAN	FEB	MAR	APR	MAY	JUNE	JULY	AUG	SEPT	OCT	NOV	DEC
Yellowknife	-24	-21	-12	-2	10	16	21	18	11	2	-10	-21
	-32	-31	-24	-14	-1	7	11	10	4	-2	-18	-30

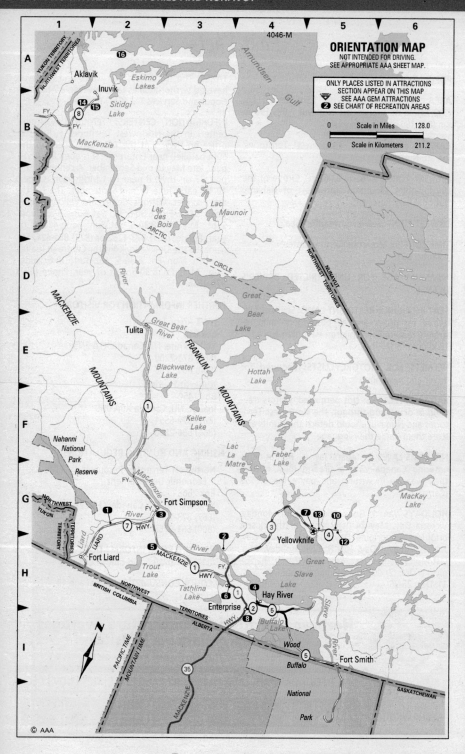

4046-M

ORIENTATION MAP
NOT INTENDED FOR DRIVING.
SEE APPROPRIATE AAA SHEET MAP.

ONLY PLACES LISTED IN ATTRACTIONS
SECTION APPEAR ON THIS MAP
▽ SEE AAA GEM ATTRACTIONS
② SEE CHART OF RECREATION AREAS

Scale in Miles   128.0

Scale in Kilometers   211.2

© AAA

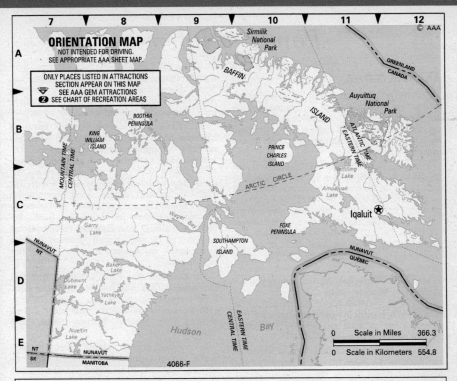

ORIENTATION MAP
NOT INTENDED FOR DRIVING.
SEE APPROPRIATE AAA SHEET MAP.

ONLY PLACES LISTED IN ATTRACTIONS
SECTION APPEAR ON THIS MAP
▽ SEE AAA GEM ATTRACTIONS
❷ SEE CHART OF RECREATION AREAS

RECREATION AREAS	MAP LOCATION	CAMPING	PICNICKING	HIKING TRAILS	BOATING	BOAT RAMP	BOAT RENTAL	FISHING	SWIMMING	PETS ON LEASH	BICYCLE TRAILS	WINTER SPORTS	VISITOR CENTER	LODGE/CABINS	FOOD SERVICE
NATIONAL PARKS *(See place listings)*															
Nahanni (G-1) 4,784 square kilometres 145 km w. of Fort Simpson. The park is not accessible by road; no motor boats allowed.		●	●	●	●	●		●	●	●			●		
Wood Buffalo (I-4) 44,980 square kilometres on Hwy. 5.		●	●	●	●			●	●	●			●	●	
TERRITORIAL															
Blackstone (G-2) 161 km s. of Fort Simpson. on Hwy. 7.	❶	●	●	●	●	●		●		●			●		
Chuk (B-2) s. of Inuvik on Hwy. 8.	⑮	●	●	●				●		●			●		
Fort Providence (H-3) at Fort Providence on Hwy. 3.	❷	●	●	●				●		●			●		
Fort Simpson (G-3) in Fort Simpson on Hwy. 1.	❸	●	●	●				●		●			●		
Fred Henne (G-5) on Hwy. 3 across from Yellowknife airport. *(See Yellowknife p. 234)*	❼	●	●	●	●			●	●	●			●		●
Gwich'in Reserve (B-1) s. of Inuvik on Hwy. 8.	⑭	●	●	●				●		●			●		
Hay River (H-4) in Hay River.	❹	●	●	●				●	●	●			●		
Lady Evelyn Falls (H-3) 6.5 km off Hwy. 1 near Kakisa.	❻	●	●	●	●			●		●			●		
Paniksak (A-2) w. of Tuktoyaktuk.	⑯	●	●							●			●		●
Prelude Lake (G-5) 29 km w. of Yellowknife on Hwy. 4.	⑩	●	●	●	●	●		●	●	●			●		
Reid Lake (G-5) 61 km n.w. of Yellowknife on Hwy. 4.	⑫	●	●	●	●	●	●	●	●	●			●		
Sambaa Deh Falls (H-2) s. of Fort Simpson on Hwy. 1.	❺	●	●	●				●		●			●		
Twin Falls Gorge (I-4) at Km-post 75 on Hwy. 1.	❽	●	●	●				●		●			●		
Yellowknife River (G-5) 8 km n.w. of Yellowknife on Hwy. 4.	⑬		●		●	●	●	●		●					

Points of Interest

AKLAVIK (A-1) pop. 700

Aklavik, which means "the place of the Barrenland grizzly," was founded in 1912 as the Mackenzie River delta outpost of Hudson's Bay Co. A thriving company base in addition to a trading and trapping center, the town became the administrative center of the Western Arctic region.

However, since the community rested in the middle of the largest delta in Canada, it faced constant change as the powerful Mackenzie River built up new land and flooded the old. These conditions prevented the construction of major roads and airstrips. As a result, the newer town of Inuvik *(see place listing p. 232)* absorbed Aklavik's administrative role. There are no roads into Aklavik; it is accessible by air from Inuvik or by ice roads during winter.

Many Aklavik residents refuse to move. The descendants of the early traders and trappers work on oil rigs in the Beaufort Sea or trap muskrat in the delta, which is rich in wildlife. A museum, the original company store and restored log cabins serve as reminders of the past.

Just off Main Street is a tree stump in which Albert Johnson, the suspected "Mad Trapper of Rat River," carved his initials. The town also contains his grave. Johnson, who allegedly killed prospectors and trappers for the gold in their teeth, was shot in 1932 after one of the most intensive manhunts in Canadian history. Whether he actually was the "mad trapper" has been a subject explored in both books and film.

BAFFIN ISLAND pop. 7,500

High in Nunavut's Eastern Arctic lies Baffin Island, the homeland of the Inuit. It is a land of majestic fiords, icebergs, bountiful wildlife and the midnight sun, which shines until 3 a.m. from March to June. Although Baffin Island is not accessible by car, Iqaluit *(see place listing p. 232)*, Nunavut's capital city, is served by two airlines.

Qaummaarviit Historic Park, 12 kilometres (7 mi.) west of Iqaluit, can be reached by boat in summer or by dog sled and snowmobile in spring. An easy-to-follow trail links the island's ruins with signs depicting aspects of prehistoric life and culture.

Auyuittuq National Park, 32 kilometres (20 mi.) from Pangnirtung, is accessible by dog sled, snowmobile or boat. The park is notable for its fiords and glaciated valleys and mountains and for being the first national park established above the Arctic Circle. Polar bears, arctic foxes, caribou, seals, walruses, whales and narwhals inhabit the region.

Included in the approximately 40 bird species spotted in the park are the rare gyrfalcon and whistling swan. Remains of the 1,000-year-old Thule Eskimo culture have been found in Cumberland Sound. Hikers and mountain campers traversing Auyuittuq's Pangnirtung Pass will find challenging trails, abundant wildlife and spectacular scenery.

Quttinirpaaq National Park (formerly known as Ellesmere Island National Park Reserve) is the most northerly land mass in Canada and contains 2,604-metre (8,544-ft.) Mount Barbeau, the highest mountain in eastern North America, and Lake Hazen, one of the largest lakes north of the Arctic Circle. The reserve is primarily a polar desert encompassing 39,500 square kilometres (15,250 sq. mi.) of mountain ranges, glaciers, ice shelves and fiords. Remains of buildings from European expeditions can be found on the rocky terrain. Outfitters in Grise Fiord, Iqaluit and Resolute Bay can arrange trips into the park.

The Katannilik Park Reserve, between Kimmirut and Iqaluit, is rich with wildlife and unique flora. River tours, hiking and northern survival challenge even the hardiest adventurers. Information can be obtained from Nunavut Tourism; phone (866) 686-2888.

In spring and summer licensed guides from Angmarlik Visitors Centre lead expeditions into Kekerten Historic Park, 50 kilometres (32 mi.) south of Pangnirtung; phone (867) 473-8737. Visitors can see remains of whale lookouts, blubber vats, whalers' houses and Inuit homes. A self-guiding trail connects dozens of ruins.

In the northeasternmost part of Baffin Island is Sirmilik National Park, approximately 22,000 square kilometres (8,494 sq. mi.) of rugged mountains, glaciers, ice fields, ocean fiords and coastal lowlands. In fact, Sirmilik translates to "the place of glaciers." Pond Inlet, the closest community to the park, is 25 kilometres (16 mi.) south. Travel to the park—by boat, dog sled or snowmobile (depending on the season)—can be arranged through outfitters in Pond Inlet or Arctic Bay.

The park is accessible year-round, except in October and November when the ice freezes up and in July during ice break up. Popular with mountain climbers, Sirmilik is also a haven for bird-watchers. Colonies of seabirds, including thick-billed murres, black-legged kittiwakes and greater snow geese, inhabit Bylot Island. For additional information phone the park office in Pond Inlet, (867) 899-8504.

ENTERPRISE (H-4) pop. 100

Enterprise is the first Northwest Territories community encountered by travelers heading north on Mackenzie Highway. A major service center for commercial traffic, the town is best known for its spectacular view of Hay River Gorge near the local Esso station.

Scenic 33-metre (108-ft.) Alexandra Falls and 15-metre (50-ft.) Louise Falls in Twin Falls Gorge Territorial Park *(see Recreation Chart and the AAA/ CAA Western Canada & Alaska CampBook)* are about 9 kilometres (6 mi.) south on Mackenzie Highway. Camping and picnicking are permitted.

FORT LIARD (H-1) pop. 500

Fort Liard is in the Territories' southwest corner. Nearby archeological digs have revealed strata showing 9,000 years of human occupancy. Prior to 1807 Northwest Co. founded a post that was taken over by Hudson's Bay Co. in 1821 when the companies merged. An earnest fur trade continues.

The opening of Liard Highway in the early 1980s put the quiet village on the map. The community is characterized by lush growth and a relatively mild climate, despite its northern location. Bird-watchers will find many songbirds during spring and summer. A small lakefront campground is nearby.

Boat launching is possible on the Petitot and Liard rivers, where visitors can see interesting rock formations and fish for pickerel at the rivers' mouth. Fort Liard is a good jumping-off point for exploring the surrounding mountains or Nahanni National Park Reserve *(see place listing p. 232).* Chartered flights and a forestry office are available in town.

FORT SIMPSON (G-2) pop. 1,300

Established in 1804 at the fork of the Mackenzie and Liard rivers, Fort Simpson is the oldest continuously occupied trading post in the Mackenzie River Valley. Once a district headquarters for Hudson's Bay Co., the town developed into a center of river trade. Originally Fort of the Forks, the town was renamed to honor Thomas Simpson, first governor of the merged Northwest and Hudson's Bay companies.

Fort Simpson has always been a gathering place for people. It serves as a center for territorial government administration and oil and mining exploration. It also serves as a departure point for air, raft and canoe trips into Nahanni National Park Reserve *(see place listing p. 232).*

A visitor center offers interpretive films, historical walking tours and a native crafts display; phone (867) 695-3182.

The Village of Fort Simpson Tourist Information Centre: P.O. Box 438, Fort Simpson, NT, Canada X0E 0N0; phone (867) 695-3182.

FORT SMITH (I-5) pop. 2,400

Initially a link in a strategic chain of 19th-century trading posts along the Mackenzie portage route to the Arctic, Fort Smith became an autonomous town in 1966. It is regional headquarters for the government of the Northwest Territories and contains several governmental offices. The town also is the site of the Thebacha Campus of Aurora College.

Permafrost

Permafrost, or permanently frozen ground, is a fact of life in most of the Northwest Territories. In his "Observations on Hudson's Bay 1743," James Isham wrote "the shortness of the summers is not sufficient to thaw the ice...therefore it gathers more and more every year." The permafrost layer is estimated to be as deep as 500 metres (1,640 ft.) in some areas.

Settlers found that attempts to build on the ice-filled ground were

© PhotoDisc

thwarted when heat from their structures melted the permafrost's top layer, causing foundations to crack and buildings to sink. Nearby Yukon Territory gold miners had to thaw and remove permafrost before they could extract the gold that lay beneath it.

In the 20th century Canadians began to work with permafrost. They found they could maintain its frozen state by insulating or preserving the top layer, making a surface strong enough to support any construction. Gravel pads 3 to 4 feet thick were used beneath smaller structures; pilings driven into the permafrost elevated larger buildings, preventing heat from penetrating the ground beneath them. In some instances, permafrost was excavated and replaced with various forms of fill.

In 1954 the Canadian government spent $34 million to build the new town of Inuvik on stilts. Pilings support buildings and connecting "utilidors," insulated corridors that house heating, water and sewage pipes.

Although the number of successful settlements built on top of permafrost is growing, mining is still a problem. To prevent shaft collapses resulting from a permafrost thaw, miners must shore open their holes with timbers or concrete.

Nearby Wood Buffalo National Park *(see place listing p. 233)* is home to one of the largest buffalo herds in the world.

Fort Smith Visitor Information Centre: 108 King St., P.O. Box 147, Fort Smith, NT, Canada X0E 0P0; phone (867) 872-3065 or (867) 872-8400.

NORTHERN LIFE MUSEUM is at 110 King St. The museum examines area history through collections of native artifacts, tools, crafts, manuscripts and paintings. Exhibits cover the history of the fur trade, aboriginal culture and the unique aspects of transportation in the north. Traveling exhibits from other Canadian museums sometimes are featured. Mon.-Fri. 10-7, Sat.-Sun. 10-5, early June-late Aug.; Mon.-Fri. 10-5, rest of year. Donations. Phone (867) 872-2859.

HAY RIVER (H-4) pop. 3,600

Recent archeological finds show that the Slavey Dene have used the area around Hay River for thousands of years, but the first buildings did not appear until 1868 when Hudson's Bay Co. established a trading post. The town's strategic location prompts its occasional reference as the "Hub of the North."

Hay River is the southernmost port of the Mackenzie River system. During the 5-month shipping season barges, fishing boats and Coast Guard craft clog the protected river channels. The town serves as headquarters of the Great Slave Lake commercial fishing industry, which supplies the demand for Great Slave Lake whitefish. Dene Cultural Institute, on the Hay River Dene Reserve, is open for tours mid-May to mid-September. A visitor center on Mackenzie Highway is open mid-May to mid-September; phone (867) 874-3180.

Hay River Chamber of Commerce: 10 K. Gagnier St., Hay River, NT, Canada X0E 1G1; phone (867) 874-2565.

INUVIK (B-2) pop. 3,300

Inuvik, meaning "place of man," was erected in 1958 to replace nearby Aklavik *(see place listing p. 230)*, which appeared to be sinking into the Mackenzie River delta. The town boomed in the 1970s as the center of the Beaufort Sea oil exploration, which since has shifted to other areas. As well as being the communications, commerce and government center for the Western Arctic, the town was the site of a Canadian Forces station until 1986.

Accessible via Dempster Highway, Inuvik is one of the northernmost points on the North American continent that can be reached by public road. During June and most of July there are 24 hours of daylight. The town also serves as a departure point for plane trips to the Arctic Ocean and the Mackenzie River delta system.

IQALUIT, NUNAVUT (C-12) pop. 4,200

In 1576 British explorer Martin Frobisher arrived at Iqaluit's bay in present-day Nunavut and assumed that he had discovered the Northwest Passage. A discovery he had believed to be gold proved to be iron pyrite, or "fools gold." The Baffin Island town honored his memory in its name—Frobisher Bay—until 1987, when its name officially was changed back to the traditional Inuit name, Iqaluit (ih-KA-loo-it), which means "many fish."

Iqaluit, now the capital of Nunavut, began as a small trading post. During the 19th century European and American whalers frequented the bay waters hoping to supply their home ports with whalebone for women's corsets and blubber for lamp oil. Hiking opportunities are plentiful on the outskirts of town or through the nearby mountains. Unaccessible by car, Iqaluit can be reached by air from Calgary and Edmonton via Yellowknife, Winnipeg via Rankin Inlet, Montréal and Ottawa.

With the construction of the Distant Early Warning (DEW) Line in 1954, the town became an important defense site and a major refueling station for both commercial and military aircraft. Iqaluit is the largest community in Nunavut and the educational, administrative, transportation and economic center for the Baffin region. A focal point for Inuit art, the town boasts numerous galleries.

In 1971 the Astro Hill Complex, which includes retail stores, a hotel, movie theater, high-rise apartments, offices and a swimming pool, was completed using modular precast concrete units. Of architectural interest at the time, the complex was designed to withstand northern climatic extremes.

Nunavut Tourism: Box 1450, Iqaluit, NU, Canada X0A 0H0; phone (866) 686-2888.

NUNATTA SUNAKKUTAANGIT is on Frobisher Bay in Bldg. 212. The museum's name translates to "things of the land." Exhibits of various art forms and artifacts, housed in a renovated Hudson's Bay Co. warehouse, focus on the Inuit culture of the Baffin region through displays. Tues.-Sun. 1-5; closed Good Friday, July 1, Nov. 11 and Dec. 25. Donations. Phone (867) 979-5537.

NAHANNI NATIONAL PARK RESERVE (G-1)

Elevations in the park range from 1,853 metres (6,079 ft.) at the South Nahanni River to 2,652 metres (8,700 ft.) on the north end of the park near Hole-in-the-Wall Lake. Refer to CAA/AAA maps for additional elevation information.

About 145 kilometres (90 mi.) west of Fort Simpson and accessible only by air, the park uses Fort Liard and Fort Simpson in the Territories, Muncho Lake in British Columbia, and Watson Lake and Whitehorse in the Yukon Territory as its major supply and jumping-off points. Steeped in myth, mystery and adventure, Nahanni National Park Reserve covers 4,766 square kilometres (1,840 sq. mi.) of wilderness in the South Nahanni country.

Liard Highway, linking Fort Nelson and Fort Simpson *(see place listing p. 231)*, passes Blackstone Territorial Park, east of Nahanni National Park Reserve, providing access to Liard River and Nahanni Butte, 30 kilometres (19 mi.) upriver.

A land of rivers, ragged peaks, more than 30 species of mammals and a waterfall twice the height of Niagara Falls, Nahanni National Park Reserve was created in 1972. It was placed on the UNESCO (United Nations Educational, Scientific and Cultural Organization) World Heritage list 6 years later and cited as an "exceptional natural site forming part of the heritage of mankind."

In the early 1900s the area received a reputation for myth and adventure. Gold prospectors, drawn by rumors of placer deposits, began to arrive. When the decapitated bodies of the two MacLeod brothers were found, stories of huge mountain men proliferated.

Although no real mountain men ever were seen, the park remains a place of rugged beauty with little development, including accommodations for visitors. Those who come to raft and canoe on the rivers and hike the forests, alpine tundra and canyons of Nahanni will find it a bracing experience. Travel by water is an excellent way to enjoy the park; however, it can be dangerous and should be attempted only by those experienced in canoeing and rafting. Reservations are required for river trips. Due to the trips' popularity, reservations should be made well in advance; phone the park office for information.

Less experienced river travelers should hire a licensed outfitter for guided river trips down the South Nahanni River. Tours pass Virginia Falls, where the South Nahanni River plunges more than 90 metres (295 ft.); the Gate, a 90-degree river bend below 213-metre (700-ft.) vertical cliffs; and hot springs such as those at First Canyon and Rabbitkettle. Visitors to Rabbitkettle **must** register at the warden's cabin and have park staff accompany them to the springs. Daytime air trips to Virginia Falls should be prearranged through an air charter company in Fort Simpson, Fort Liard, Watson Lake, Whitehorse or Muncho Lake.

Fishing for arctic grayling, lake and bull trout and northern pike is permitted with a national park fishing license (annual pass $20), which can be obtained at the Fort Simpson Administration Office or at the warden's cabin at Rabbitkettle Lake. All national park regulations apply. Firearms are not permitted.

Wildlife species include moose, beavers, woodland caribou, Dall sheep, grizzly and black bears, white-tailed deer and mountain goats. Visitors should take particular care when traveling in areas where they are likely to encounter bears.

The park is open year-round. The park administration office at Fort Simpson is open daily 8:30-5, mid-June to mid-Sept.; Mon.-Fri., rest of year. Overnight visitors and those planning river rafting or canoe trips must register before entering the park and upon leaving.

One-day admission to the park is $10 per person. For route information, park regulations, weather conditions and park activities write to the Superintendent, Nahanni National Park Reserve, P.O. Box 348, Fort Simpson, NT, Canada X0E 0N0; phone (867) 695-3151. *See Recreation Chart.*

TULITA (E-2) pop. 400

Because of the lack of roads on the frontier, most towns were founded along rivers. Originally called Fort Norman, Tulita was established in 1810 when Northwest Co. built a trading post at the confluence of the Great Bear and Mackenzie rivers. The town's name means "where two rivers meet."

Later years brought additional industries. In 1920 pitchblende—the chief ore-mineral source of uranium—was discovered, and the early 1980s brought the construction of the Wells-Zama oil pipeline.

Tulita is accessible via air service from Norman Wells. No all-weather roads lead into the community, but a winter road—open from late January to mid-March—connects Tulita to surrounding communities. Nearby is one of the Northwest Territories' oldest Anglican churches, built of squared logs in the 1860s. The restored church can be visited.

About 20 kilometres (12 mi.) away is a bed of low-grade coal that has been burning for centuries. Although the fire likely was ignited by lightning, Dene legend attributes it to a giant's campfire. During the summer the surface of the bed sometimes rises and the coals are exposed. Firefighters' attempts to extinguish the smoldering coals have failed.

Hamlet Office: Box 91, Tulita, NT, Canada X0E 0K0; phone (867) 588-4471.

WOOD BUFFALO NATIONAL PARK (I-4)

Elevations in the park range from 183 metres (600 ft.) at the Little Buffalo River to 945 metres (3,100 ft.) in the Caribou Mountains. Refer to CAA/AAA maps for additional elevation information.

Accessible by Hwy. 5, which connects with Mackenzie Highway at Hay River, Wood Buffalo National Park is the second largest park in the world. Covering about the same area as the states of Maryland and New Jersey combined, the national park straddles the border between the Northwest Territories and Alberta.

This vast subarctic wilderness contains such remarkable geological features as the Salt Plains, Alberta Plateau, the deltas and lowlands of the Peace and Athabasca rivers, and extensive gypsum karst formations. The park was established in 1922 to protect one of the world's largest free-roaming herds of wood bison; approximately 4,300 of these animals now live there. Moose, caribou, muskrats, beavers and black bears are among other park residents.

The Peace Athabasca Delta is an important stop-over for North America's four major waterfowl fly-ways. A large variety of waterfowl as well as hawks, eagles and pelicans, are present for part of the year. The northeastern corner of the park is one of the last nesting grounds in the world for the en-dangered whooping crane. Some of the park's lakes and rivers contain pike, pickerel, trout, whitefish and goldeye. Wildflowers and berries abound in the rolling meadows.

Boating, picnicking and camping are permitted at Pine Lake. The park has hiking trails, which can be used for snowshoeing and cross-country skiing in winter. Contact the park for information about guided nature hikes and other interpretive events.

The 400-kilometre (250-mi.) Fort Chipewyan Winter Road is open December 15 to March 15 (weather permitting). The road runs from Fort Mc-Murray, Alberta, to Fort Smith; part of the road is formed by ice. Phone the park office to check road conditions between Fort Chipewyan and Fort Smith.

Visitors can see such magnificent snow-covered scenery as boreal forest, lakes and wide-open mead-ows. Before departure travelers should contact the park office for a list of driving regulations and rec-ommended travel supplies.

The park's campgrounds and facilities are open Victoria Day weekend through October. The Fort Smith Visitor Reception Center at 149 McDougal Rd. is open Mon.-Fri. 9-5, Sat.-Sun. 1-5, mid-June through Labour Day; Mon.-Fri. 9-5, rest of year.

Admission to the park is free. For route informa-tion, road conditions or details about park activities contact the Superintendent, Wood Buffalo National Park, Box 750, Fort Smith, NT, Canada X0E 0P0; phone (867) 872-7960. *See Recreation Chart and the AAA/CAA Western Canada & Alaska CampBook.*

YELLOWKNIFE (G-5) pop. 16,541

Although the Dene hunted the Yellowknife re-gion for thousands of years and Europeans explored it in 1771, a permanent settlement was not estab-lished until the discovery of gold in 1934. Taking the name of the copper knives carried by the Chipewyan Indians, the town is now the capital of the Northwest Territories and the site of a function-ing gold mine and a booming diamond industry.

In 1967 Yellowknife replaced Ottawa as the seat of government for the Northwest Territories. Tours of the Legislative Assembly are available Mon.-Fri. at 10:30, 1:30 and 3:30, Sun. at 1:30, June-Aug.; Mon.-Fri. at 10:30, rest of year; phone (867) 669-2200. On the northern shore of Great Slave Lake, this "metropolis" of the north lies less than 500 kilometres (311 mi.) from the Arctic Circle and is an excellent place to shop for Northern arts.

The city's historic Old Town retains the gold rush excitement of the 1930s with quaint restau-rants, art galleries, shops, and boat, kayak, canoe and yacht rentals. Planes are available for flightsee-ing and fishing trips. The visitor center on 49th

Street can provide information about rentals and ex-cursions. The visitor center also is the starting point for guided tours of the Capital Park area, conducted in July and August.

Best viewed from November to March, the *au-rora borealis,* or northern lights, is produced when atomic particles from outside the atmosphere strike and excite atoms within the upper atmosphere. The lights sweep mysteriously across the clear night sky as luminescent curtains of red, green, pink and purple light in patterns called rayed bands. Guided viewing trips are available.

The scenic 71-kilometre (44-mi.) Ingraham Trail (Hwy. 4) to Tibbett Lake allows year-round access to several chains of lakes and streams. Seven boat launches and two campgrounds lie along the road. Prelude Nature Trail runs from Prelude Lake Camp-ground *(see Recreation Chart and the AAA/CAA Western Canada & Alaska CampBook)* through the wilderness to several lookout points, while another trail leads to Cameron Falls.

Prospector's Trail is in Fred Henne Park *(see Recreation Chart and the AAA/CAA Western Canada & Alaska CampBook),* west near Long Lake. The 4-kilometre (2.5-mi.) loop points out the region's varied geological features and is of interest to rock hounds; sturdy footwear and insect repellent are necessary. Other hiking trails lead from Ingra-ham Trail; information and brochures are available at the visitor center.

Easily accessible area lakes include Prosperous, Pontoon, Prelude, Reid and Tibbett. Walsh Lake has good trout fishing, but is accessible only by going through Reid Lake.

The scenic portion of Hwy. 3 runs north from Mackenzie Bison Sanctuary to Edzo, then parallels the northern shore of Great Slave Lake. Driving anywhere in the area, or throughout the Northwest Territories, demands that a vehicle be in top me-chanical condition.

Northern Frontier Regional Visitor Center: 4807 49th St., Yellowknife, NT, Canada X1A 3T5; phone (867) 873-4262 or (877) 881-4262.

Self-guiding tours: The visitor center provides brochures for a walking tour of Old Town and New Town.

THE PRINCE OF WALES NORTHERN HERITAGE CENTRE is .4 km (.25 mi.) w. on Hwy. 4. The cen-ter preserves area history through exhibits depicting aspects of Dene and Inuit cultures. Displays pertain to geology, archeology, exploration, fur trading, transportation, aviation and bush pilots, natural his-tory, artwork and handicrafts. Daily 10:30-5:30, June-Aug.; Mon.-Fri. 10:30-5, Sat.-Sun. noon-5, rest of year. Closed Jan. 1 and Dec. 25. Donations. Phone (867) 873-7551.

Saskatchewan

The Last Frontier
Rolling grasslands and evergreen forests create an unspoiled paradise

Big Muddy Badlands
Trace Butch Cassidy's Outlaw Trail through this colorfully rugged terrain

Call of the Wild
Whistling swans and white-tailed deer are among the many wilderness residents

Qu'Appelle Valley
The sun seems a little brighter as it shines upon this region's golden farmland

The Mounties
Explore the history of those who brought law and order to the Canadian West

a pastoral portrait

Near Kindersley
© Darrell Lecorre / Alamy Images

A visit to Saskatchewan is a perfect escape from the hustle and bustle.

Named after the Plains Indian term *kisiskatchewan,* meaning "the river that flows swiftly," Saskatchewan boasts more than just a great river with an unusual name.

Along country roads, you'll encounter prairies, mountains, grasslands and even sand dunes. While approximately half the province is covered in pine, white spruce and other trees, a good portion is blanketed with fields of wheat.

Look for signs marked with a barn symbol; they designate bed and breakfast inns and vacation farms, where you can take part in milking cows and—if you're lucky—enjoy homemade berry preserves or baked goods.

Take a dip into one of more than 100,000 freshwater lakes, some of which can be found in the Qu'Appelle Valley. Nestled among the water holes in this region are resorts and golf courses with rolling fairways.

For history, head to towns that preserve the origin of the Mounted Police, the heritage of Métis culture or the rough-and-tumble cowboy lifestyle.

Or visit the Beaver Lodge Cabin on Ajawaan Lake in Prince Albert National Park, residence of naturalist author Grey Owl, who coined the now-popular belief that "you belong to nature, not it to you."

The hues of Saskatchewan's palette were determined both with and without man's help. Painted by nature and the history of the plains, vibrant gold, green and red are the prominent colors in the province's scheme.

Sheaves of Golden Wheat

Shimmering fields of grain, glinting gold in the sunlight, are probably the image most associated with Saskatchewan. Captured on innumerable postcards and snapshots, the plains seem to stretch to the horizon in a never-ending series of undulating waves, interrupted only by an occasional silo. And the fields are certainly productive—more than 50 percent of Canada's wheat crop comes from this land.

Proof of the grain's economic importance to the province is the three golden wheat sheaves on its coat of arms. Saskatchewan's flag provides further evidence; its lower half, a solid band of gold, represents the grain fields dominating the province's southern portion.

You can experience early 20th-century pioneer prairie life at Motherwell Homestead National Historic Site, near Abernethy. Costumed interpreters busily carry out typical daily tasks of the period at the 1912 farmstead of William Richard Motherwell, farmer, politician and agricultural innovator. Motherwell developed techniques enabling early settlers to overcome the region's dry soil and short growing season.

If a more modern approach to rural life appeals to you, spend a few days at one of Saskatchewan's vacation farms. Helping with chores can offset the pounds you might gain from the hearty meals provided by your hosts. More than 70 Saskatchewan families offer visitors a chance to experience what living on a farm is all about.

Landscapes of Green

Color Regina green—the city is known for having more than 350,000 trees. A particularly verdant section of town is Wascana Centre, a 930-hectare urban park that is truly the heart of Saskatchewan's capital.

The center, lining the rambling shoreline of Wascana Lake, is home to cultural and educational institutions as well as the architecturally impressive Legislative Building, the seat of provincial government. Works by Canadian artists grace the building's walls. Galleries at the nearby Royal Saskatchewan Museum are devoted to earth and life sciences and the First Nations People. Young

Henry Kelsey, an English fur trader, explores Saskatchewan.
1690

The first permanent settlement is built by the Hudson's Bay Company.
1774

The massacre of a band of Assiniboine Indians by U.S. wolf hunters prompts the creation of the Mounted Police.

© Lee Foster

1873

1870
Canada acquires present-day Saskatchewan as part of the Northwest Territories.

Saskatchewan Historical Timeline

1885
Louis Riel leads the Métis tribe's battle for land rights in the Northwest Rebellion.

guests will have fun visiting a robotic dinosaur and digging into the hands-on exhibits in the Paleo Pit.

Initially known as Pile-O-Bones (the translation of the Cree word *Oscana*), Regina's early name is a reference to the buffalo remains left behind when the site served as a hunters' camp. Its present name was adopted in honor of Queen Victoria—Regina being Latin for queen. And the good monarch's husband was not forgotten when provincial town names were assigned—the city of Prince Albert was named for Victoria's consort in 1886.

The nearly 1 million acres of nearby Prince Albert National Park encompass other shades of green, primarily those of aspens and evergreens. Its woodlands, boreal landscapes and grasslands form just a small portion of the forests covering half the province.

Within the park is the simple lakeside cabin of Grey Owl, the Indian name assumed by Englishman Archibald Belaney. This early environmentalist, writer and lecturer, accepted into the Ojibwa tribe in the 1930s, was dedicated to the preservation of the Canadian wilderness and its wildlife. His gravesite is close by on a wooded hill.

Red Coats of the Canadian West

The Royal Canadian Mounted Police are immediately recognizable by their scarlet tunics. In fact, the route they took across the prairie in 1874 to establish law and order in western Canada is retraced along Hwy. 13, the Red Coat Trail. Many of their early posts are now national historic sites, including Fort Battleford, off Hwy. 4 near Battleford, and Fort Walsh, southwest of Maple Creek.

Regina is home to the RCMP's only training academy. Visitors are welcome to tour the facility, known as the Royal Canadian Mounted Police Depot, as well as a museum recounting the force's history. If your timing is right, you can watch the cadets drill at the Sergeant Major's Parade, usually held Monday through Friday at 12:45 p.m.

If you're in town in July or early August and truly want to be inspired by the colors of the province, try to catch the Sunset Retreat Ceremony. Culminating in the lowering of the Canadian flag at dusk, the golden glow cast by the fading sun seems a fitting background as the cadets, in traditional red jackets, proudly march against the backdrop of lush greenery bordering the parade grounds.

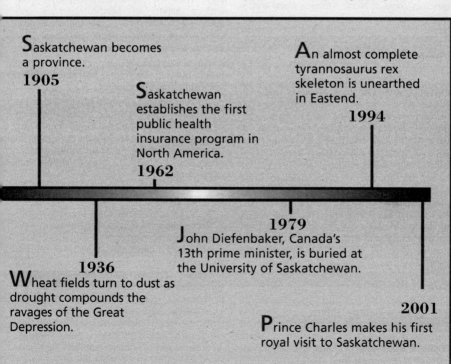

Saskatchewan becomes a province.
1905

Saskatchewan establishes the first public health insurance program in North America.
1962

An almost complete tyrannosaurus rex skeleton is unearthed in Eastend.
1994

1979
John Diefenbaker, Canada's 13th prime minister, is buried at the University of Saskatchewan.

1936
Wheat fields turn to dust as drought compounds the ravages of the Great Depression.

2001
Prince Charles makes his first royal visit to Saskatchewan.

Recreation

Contrary to popular belief, Saskatchewan is not all prairie. Even in the southern half, where farming is predominant, lakes and parks abound with recreational options.

Angling Heaven

With more than 100,000 lakes, rivers and streams to choose from, you're never really far from a good freshwater **fishing** spot. While northern pike, rainbow trout and walleye will take your bait at fishin' holes throughout the province, you'll have to head for northern waters to land trophy-size lake trout, Arctic grayling and other sport fish.

Lake Diefenbaker, south of Outlook, is a favorite fishing destination with both locals and visitors; this is the place to go if you're after walleye or northern pike. The Precambrian Shield, in the northern third of the province, is just about as good as it gets for anglers, with almost 40 percent of its area consisting of H20. Try Lac la Ronge if you're a trout fishing devotee. Outfitters will be happy to fly you to some of the more remote northern fishing lakes.

Tumbling east to west across the province north of the 55th parallel, the Churchill River provides some of North America's best whitewater **canoeing.** Should you choose to experience white water by **rafting,** check out the Clearwater River. Both of these bodies of water flow in northern Saskatchewan.

If the rush of white-water action is too intense, consider paddling your boat along calmer waters. The Bagwa Canoe Route, in Prince Albert National Park, will take you through several pristine lakes. Late May through September, when the lakes are at their warmest, is the best time to dip your oars. A bonus is the chance to sight bald eagles, ospreys and loons.

For the ultimate in calm, head to Little Manitou Lake, near the resort community of Manitou Beach. Indians knew about the lake's curative powers long before the arrival of European settlers. And there's no danger of sinking in these waters—the high concentration of minerals makes this impossible, so float to your heart's content.

Fun in the Snow

When the weather turns cold, bundle up and try **cross-country skiing.** Groomed and marked trails are easily accessible throughout the province—even in cities. Prince Albert National Park, almost in the middle of Saskatchewan, has more than 100 kilometres (60 mi.) of trails. Moose Mountain Provincial

Park, north of Carlyle, adds another 50 kilometres (30 mi.) to explore, while the forests, lakes and valleys of Duck Mountain Provincial Park, east of Kamsack, provide a picturesque backdrop for cross-country excursions.

If you prefer to stay within city limits, the Meewasin Valley Trail follows the Saskatchewan River through the middle of Saskatoon, the province's largest city.

Snowmobiling enthusiasts love the thousands of kilometres of interconnected, groomed trails linking towns and parks along Canada's version of Route 66, in this case a cross-country snowmobile route. Popular put-in points include Hudson Bay, Nipawin, North Battleford and Yorkton. Trail permits are mandatory; phone Tourism Saskatchewan, (877) 237-2273, for a provincial snowmobile trail map.

Warm Weather Choices

When the weather turns warm, everyone flocks to Prince Albert National Park. You don't even need **hiking** boots on a few of the park's short trails. Boundary Bog, Mud Creek and Treebeard, all loop trails, traverse fairly level terrain and take no longer than an hour each. They will, however, put you in touch with a variety of Mother Nature's creations—a black spruce and tamarack bog; sightings of beavers, otters and great blue herons; and forests of aspens and balsam firs.

An abundance of lakes and trails also makes **boating, bicycling, horseback riding** and fishing popular choices.

Another popular summer playground is the Qu'Appelle Valley, a broad swath of land in southern Saskatchewan bordered by rolling hills. A chain of lakes and three provincial parks are the setting for resort villages where guests enjoy boating, **water skiing** and **swimming.**

Recreational Activities

Throughout the TourBook, you may notice a Recreational Activities heading with bulleted listings of recreation-oriented establishments listed underneath. Similar operations also may be mentioned in Destination City recreation sections. Since normal AAA inspection criteria cannot be applied, these establishments are presented only for information. Age, height and weight restrictions may apply. Reservations often are recommended and sometimes are required. Addresses and/or phone numbers are provided so visitors can contact the attraction for additional information.

Fast Facts

POPULATION: 978,933.

AREA: 651,036 sq km (251,365 sq mi.); ranks 7th.

CAPITAL: Regina.

HIGHEST POINT: 1,392 m/4,566 ft., Cypress Hills.

LOWEST POINT: 65 m/213 ft., Lake Athabasca.

TIME ZONE(S): Central and Mountain.

MINIMUM AGE FOR UNRESTRICTED DRIVER'S LICENSE: 16 years, 6 months.

MINIMUM AGE FOR GAMBLING: 19.

SEAT BELT/CHILD RESTRAINT LAWS: Seat belts required for driver and all passengers; age-appropriate child restraints or safety seats are required for children under 16 years of age and weighing less than 22 kilograms (49 pounds).

HELMETS FOR MOTORCYCLISTS: Required.

RADAR DETECTORS: Permitted.

FIREARMS LAWS: By federal law, all nonresidents entering Canada with a firearm must declare their weapon in writing and pay a fee of $50 (Canadian). Contact the Canadian Firearms Centre at (800) 731-4000 for additional information or to receive a declaration form.

HOLIDAYS: Jan. 1; Good Friday; Victoria Day, May 24 (if a Mon.) or the closest prior Mon.; Canada Day, July 1; Saskatchewan Day, Aug. (1st Mon.); Labour Day, Sept. (1st Mon.); Thanksgiving, Oct. (2nd Mon.); Remembrance Day, Nov. 11; Dec. 25; Boxing Day, Dec. 26.

TAXES: Saskatchewan's provincial sales tax is 7 percent.

INFORMATION CENTERS: Provincial welcome centers are along Hwy. 1 east of Fleming; at 1922 Park St. in Regina; near Maple Creek on Hwy. 1; Hwy. 16 at Langenburg and Lloydminster; and Hwy. 39 at North Portal. All information centers are open daily mid-May to early September except the center in Regina, which is open Mon.-Fri. 8-5.

FURTHER INFORMATION FOR VISITORS:

Tourism Saskatchewan
1922 Park St.
Regina, SK, Canada S4P 3V7
(306) 787-2300 or (877) 237-2273
See color ad opposite Title page

FISHING AND HUNTING REGULATIONS:

Saskatchewan Environment
3211 Albert St.
Regina, SK, Canada S4S 5W6
(306) 787-2080

ALCOHOL CONSUMPTION: Legal age 19.

Saskatchewan Temperature Averages Maximum / Minimum (Celsius)
From the records of the National Weather Service

	JAN	FEB	MAR	APR	MAY	JUNE	JULY	AUG	SEPT	OCT	NOV	DEC
Prince Albert	-13 / -24	-10 / -22	-2 / -15	9 / -3	18 / 3	22 / 8	25 / 12	24 / 10	17 / 4	10 / -1	-2 / -11	-10 / -21
Regina	-11 / -22	-9 / -21	-2 / -13	10 / -3	19 / 3	23 / 8	27 / 11	26 / 10	20 / 4	12 / -2	-1 / -11	-8 / -18

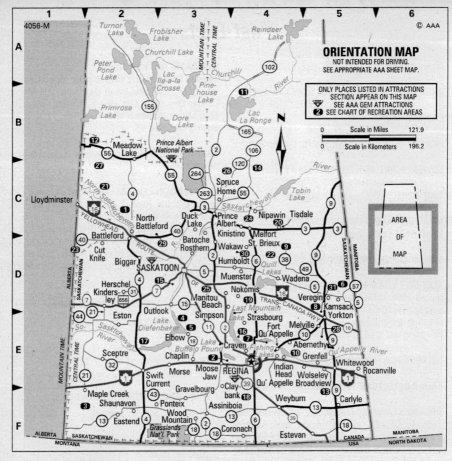

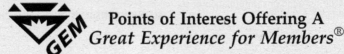

Points of Interest Offering A *Great Experience for Members*®

Prince Albert National Park (B-3)

PRINCE ALBERT NATIONAL PARK—This wilderness area is a beautiful example of Saskatchewan's transition from poplar bluffs and prairie lands to the evergreen forests and spruce bogs of the north. See p. 255.

Regina (E-4)

GOVERNMENT HOUSE MUSEUM AND HERITAGE PROPERTY—The elegance of the Victorian era and the power and prestige of former lieutenant governors, occupants from 1891-1945, are reflected in this Italianate-style mansion. See p. 256.

ROYAL CANADIAN MOUNTED POLICE DEPOT AND CENTENNIAL MUSEUM—More than a century of history is depicted through the photographs and related artifacts on display. See p. 257.

ROYAL SASKATCHEWAN MUSEUM—The museum comprises galleries that focus on the evolution of the province, such as geology and paleontology, culture and heritage, and natural history and environment. See p. 258.

Saskatoon (D-3)

WANUSKEWIN HERITAGE PARK—The Cree word for "seeking peace of mind," Wanuskewin is a fitting name for this park, once a center of spiritual renewal used by the Northern Plains Indians. See p. 260.

RECREATION AREAS

	MAP LOCATION	CAMPING	PICNICKING	HIKING TRAILS	BOATING	BOAT RAMP	BOAT RENTAL	FISHING	SWIMMING	PETS ON LEASH	BICYCLE TRAILS	WINTER SPORTS	VISITOR CENTER	LODGE/CABINS	FOOD SERVICE
NATIONAL PARKS *(See place listings)*															
Grasslands 906 square kilometres.		●	●	●						●			●		
Prince Albert 3,875 square kilometres. Horse rental.		●	●	●	●	●	●	●	●	●	●	●	●	●	●
PROVINCIAL															
The Battlefords (C-2) 600 hectares 4.75 km n. of Cochin off Hwy. 4. Cross-country skiing; golf.	❶	●	●	●	●	●	●	●	●	●	●	●		●	●
Blackstrap (D-3) 530 hectares 8 km e. of Dundurn via Hwy. 211. Cross-country and downhill skiing; sailboard rental.	25	●	●					●	●	●		●			●
Buffalo Pound (E-3) 1,930 hectares 19 km n. of Moose Jaw on Hwy. 2, then 13 km e. on Hwy. 202. Cross-country and downhill skiing; tennis; pool.	❷	●	●	●	●	●		●	●	●		●			●
Candle Lake (C-3) 1,270 hectares 60 km n.e. of Prince Albert on hwys. 55 and 120. Cross-country skiing.	26	●	●	●	●	●	●	●	●	●		●		●	●
Clearwater River 224,040 hectares 50 km n.e. of La Loche on Hwy. 955 (north of area shown on map). Canoeing.		●	●	●				●							
Crooked Lake (E-5) 190 hectares 30 km n. of Broadview on Hwy. 605. Golf.	28	●	●	●	●	●	●	●	●	●		●		●	●
Cypress Hills (F-1) 18,410 hectares 30 km s. of Maple Creek on Hwy. 21. Cross-country skiing, golf, tennis; horse rental, pool. Five horsepower limit for boats.	❸	●	●	●	●		●	●	●	●	●	●	●	●	●
Danielson (E-3) 2,910 hectares on n. end of Lake Diefenbaker via hwys. 44, 45 or 219.	❹	●	●		●	●	●	●	●	●			●	●	
Douglas (E-3) 4,430 hectares 11 km s.e. of Elbow on Hwy. 19. Houseboat rental.	❺	●	●	●	●	●	●	●	●	●			●		●
Duck Mountain (D-5) 26,160 hectares 25 km e. of Kamsack on Hwy. 57. Cross-country and downhill skiing; golf, tennis; horse rental.	❻	●	●	●	●	●	●	●	●	●		●		●	●
Echo Valley (E-4) 640 hectares 8 km w. of Fort Qu'Appelle off Hwy. 10. Cross-country skiing; horse rental.	❼	●	●	●	●	●		●	●	●		●	●		●
Good Spirit Lake (D-5) 1,900 hectares 24 km n.e. of Springside via Hwy. 47. Cross-country skiing, tennis.	❽	●	●	●	●	●		●	●	●		●		●	●
Greenwater Lake (D-4) 20,720 hectares 38 km n. of Kelvington on Hwy. 38. Cross-country skiing, golf, tennis.	❾	●	●	●	●	●	●	●	●	●		●		●	●
Katepwa Point (E-4) 8 hectares 10 km s.e. of Lebret on Hwy. 56.	10		●		●	●		●	●	●					●
Lac la Ronge (B-4) 344,470 hectares 48.25 km n. of La Ronge on Hwy. 102. Cross-country skiing; houseboat rental.	11	●	●	●	●	●	●	●	●	●		●		●	●
Makwa Lake (C-2) 2,560 hectares n.w. of Loon Lake off Hwy. 26. Cross-country skiing; horse rental.	27	●	●	●	●	●	●	●	●	●		●		●	●
Meadow Lake (B-2) 156,970 hectares 5 km n. of Goodsoil via Hwy. 26. Cross-country skiing, tennis; horse rental, sailboat rental.	12	●	●	●	●	●	●	●	●	●		●		●	●
Moose Mountain (F-5) 40,060 hectares 22.5 km n. of Carlyle on Hwy. 9. Cross-country skiing, golf (18 holes), tennis; horse rental.	13	●	●	●	●			●	●	●	●	●	●	●	●
Narrow Hills (C-4) 53,610 hectares 64.25 km n. of Smeaton on Hwy. 106. Canoeing, cross-country skiing, snowmobiling; playground.	14	●	●	●	●	●	●	●	●	●		●		●	●
Pike Lake (D-3) 500 hectares 30.5 km s. of Saskatoon on Hwy. 60. Golf, tennis; pool. Ten horsepower limit for boats.	15	●	●		●	●		●	●	●		●	●		●
Rowan's Ravine (E-4) 270 hectares 22.5 km w. of Bulyea on Hwy. 220.	16	●	●	●	●	●	●	●	●	●			●		●

RECREATION AREAS

RECREATION AREAS	MAP LOCATION	CAMPING	PICNICKING	HIKING TRAILS	BOATING	BOAT RAMP	BOAT RENTAL	FISHING	SWIMMING	PETS ON LEASH	BICYCLE TRAILS	WINTER SPORTS	VISITOR CENTER	LODGE/CABINS	FOOD SERVICE
Saskatchewan Landing (E-2) 5.600 hectares 45 km n. of Swift Current via Hwy. 4. Horse rental, windsurfing rental.	⑰	•	•	•	•	•	•	•	•	•			•	•	•
OTHER															
Bright Sand Lake (C-2) 648 hectares 27 km e. of St. Walburg off Hwy. 26 on a gravel road. Bird-watching, canoeing, cross-country skiing, golf, miniature golf, mountain biking, snowmobiling; beach, canoe rental, nature trails with interpretive signs, playground.	㉑	•	•	•	•	•	•	•	•	•	•	•	•	•	•
Dunnet (F-4) 50 hectares 7 km s. of Avonlea on Hwy. 334. Cross-country skiing, ice fishing, snowmobiling.	⑱	•	•	•	•	•		•	•	•	•	•	•		•
Kipabiskau (D-4) 16 hectares 35 km s.w. of Tisdale off Hwy. 3 or Hwy. 35. Cross-country skiing, ice fishing, snowmobiling; beach, canoe and kayak rental, nature trails, playground.	㉒	•	•	•	•	•	•	•	•	•					•
Last Mountain Lake (D-4) 65 hectares 20 km n.w. of Govan off Hwy. 20 on a gravel road. Bird-watching, ice fishing; pool. *(See Simpson p. 261).*	⑲	•	•	•	•	•		•	•	•			•		•
Macklin Lake (D-1) 154 hectares .4 km s. of Macklin on Hwy. 31. Golf; beach, playground, wildlife preserve.	㉓	•	•	•	•			•	•	•					•
Nipawin and District (C-4) 121 hectares 3 km n.w. of Nipawin on Hwy. 55. Cross-country skiing, golf, snowmobiling; petting zoo, playground, spray pool.	㉔	•	•	•	•	•		•	•	•		•	•		•
Pasquia (C-4) 65 hectares 12 km n. of Arborfield on Hwy. 23. Cross-country and downhill skiing, golf; Andy Jamault nature trail to the Pasquia paleontological site, pool.	⑳	•	•	•				•	•	•		•			•
Redberry Lake (D-3) 5,600 hectares 12.8 km e. of Hafford on Hwy. 40. Cross-country skiing, golf.	㉙	•	•	•	•	•		•	•	•	•	•	•		•
St. Brieux (D-4) 65 hectares 1 km w. of St. Brieux on Hwy. 368. Historic. Cross-country skiing, golf, miniature golf; beach, playground.	㉚	•	•	•	•	•		•	•	•			•		•
Whitesand (D-5) 49 hectares 9 km n.e. of Theodore off Hwy. 16. Golf, miniature golf; playground.	㉛	•	•	•	•			•		•	•				•

When you're on the road and get into a jam...

Emergency Services

24 hours a day, 7 days a week, AAA Emergency Road Service is there. AAA has rescued stranded members for more than 100 years. So if you get a flat tire, run out of gas, or just can't get your car started, call **1-800-AAA-HELP** and AAA is at your service.

Hearing Impaired: 1-800-955-4TDD.

Points of Interest

ABERNETHY (E-4) pop. 213

In 1882, about 2 decades before he began his distinguished career in Canadian politics, William Richard Motherwell arrived in southeastern Saskatchewan from his Ontario birthplace and acquired a 64-hectare (160-acre) homestead grant near Abernethy. He farmed the land using several techniques of scientific agriculture then considered revolutionary.

Motherwell was later instrumental in launching the Territorial Grain Growers Association. His knowledge of the land groomed him for later roles as Saskatchewan's minister of agriculture 1905-18 and federal minister of agriculture during the 1920s.

MOTHERWELL HOMESTEAD NATIONAL HISTORIC SITE is 8 km (5 mi.) s. on Hwy. 22. The site commemorates William Richard Motherwell and his contributions to Canadian agriculture. Motherwell's farmstead, including 8 acres of landscaped grounds, Ontarian-style barn and six-bedroom fieldstone house, have been restored to the pre-World War I era. Guided tours are available. Allow 1 hour minimum. Daily 9-5, Victoria Day-Labour Day. Admission $5.75; over 64, $5; ages 6-16, $3; family rate $14.50. Phone (306) 333-2116.

ASSINIBOIA (F-3) pop. 2,483

Assiniboia is an Ojibwa Indian word meaning "one who cooks with stones." Southeast of town off Hwy. 2 is St. Victor Petroglyphs Provincial Historic Park, the site of a sandstone cliff etched with prehistoric Indian carvings. The carvings at the top of the cliff depict human faces, footprints and animal tracks. Since they have faded with time, the designs are best seen late in the afternoon or on a cloudy day. There is a picnic site near the base of the cliff that is open June 1-Labour Day. Phone (306) 694-3659 for more information.

ASSINIBOIA AND DISTRICT MUSEUM is at 506 3rd Ave. W. The museum depicts the growth of Assiniboia from 1913 to the present. A guided tour includes exhibits such as a collection of antique cars dating from 1916-50 as well as vintage heavy farm equipment. Picnicking is permitted. Allow 30 minutes minimum. Daily 9-noon and 1-5, July-Aug.; Mon.-Fri. 9:30-11:30 and 1-4, rest of year. Closed major holidays. Admission $2.50; over 65, $2; ages 13-18, 50c. Phone (306) 642-5353.

BATOCHE (D-3)

Having had their lands in Manitoba's Red River Valley divided and bought out from under them by the swelling numbers of homesteaders, the Métis, a people of mixed Indian and French heritage, migrated to Batoche, in the valley of the South Saskatchewan River, around 1870. After farming and hunting buffalo for almost 15 years, they petitioned the Canadian government for rights to the land, but their requests were ignored.

Finally, in March 1885, their leader Louis Riel declared a provisional Métis government with Batoche as capital. With the fall of Batoche after a 4-day siege in early May, the group's dream of independence ended.

BATOCHE NATIONAL HISTORIC SITE is w. on Hwy. 225. The decisive battle of the Northwest Rebellion/Métis Resistance of 1885 was fought at this site, which covers 914 hectares (2,258 acres). Features include the ruins of a Batoche village, the St. Antoine de Padoue church, a rectory and a Visitor Reception Centre, with an audiovisual presentation. There are interpretive signs and costumed interpreters at key locations throughout the park.

Daily 9-5, May 8-Sept. 30. Admission $5.75; over 64, $5; ages 6-16, $3; family rate $14.50. Phone (306) 423-6227 or (306) 423-6228.

BATTLEFORD (D-2) pop. 3,820

Once capital of the Northwest Territories, Battleford is one of Saskatchewan's oldest communities. As soon as the Canadian Pacific Railway began construction, citizens made plans for their town to become a western metropolis. But the railroad took a more southerly route, and in 1883 the capital was moved to Regina.

Battleford's hopes revived in 1905 when the Canadian Northern Railway proposed a westward route, but the line was built north of town on the other side of the Saskatchewan River, spawning the new town of North Battleford *(see place listing p. 254).* Battleford and its sister city have continued to grow as the province's vast northwest region has become more developed.

FORT BATTLEFORD NATIONAL HISTORIC SITE is 2 km (1.2 mi.) off Hwy. 4. The North West Mounted Police district headquarters was established here in 1876 to enforce law and order. The fort became the site of armed confrontations between the First Nations and federal troops in 1885. Five buildings have been preserved; various illustrative exhibits are featured. Costumed staff members provide interpretive information. Historic weapons demonstrations are given, and historic trails also are on site.

Guided tours are available. Picnicking is permitted. Allow 1 hour, 30 minutes minimum. Daily 9-8, July 1-Labour Day; 9-6, May-June. Tours are offered every 30 minutes. Admission $5.75; over 64, $5; ages 6-16, $3; family rate $14.50. Phone (306) 937-2621.

BIGGAR (D-2) pop. 2,243

Named after W.H. Biggar, General Counsel for the Grand Trunk Pacific Railroad, Biggar was incorporated as a village in 1909 and as a town in 1911. In 1910 the GTPR established a divisional point. A construction boom resulted, and so did an increase in population. The town became one of the home terminals where train crews changed: The station was one of the largest in the West. During the years that followed the population remained stable, and it wasn't until the 1950s that Biggar experienced renewed growth.

The name Sandra Schmirler is synonymous with Biggar. A three-time world curling champion (1993, 1994 and 1997) and 1998 Olympic gold medalist for the sport of curling, Schmirler was born and schooled in Biggar. Sandra Schmirler Olympic Gold Park was opened in her honor on Aug. 6, 2000.

BIGGAR MUSEUM AND GALLERY is at 105 3rd Ave. W. Highlighting the story of settlement in Biggar, the museum features two outdoor murals, a plesiosaur diorama, First Peoples display and replicas of a CN railway station, the Hanson Buck, and a silent film theater. Also included is an art gallery. Changing exhibits are presented regularly in the museum and art gallery. Allow 30 minutes minimum. Mon.-Sat. 9-5, June-Sept.; 1-5, rest of year. Closed holidays. Donations. Phone (306) 948-3451.

HOMESTEAD MUSEUM is 1.6 km (1 mi.) w. on Hwy. 51. The museum houses an early 20th-century wooden home, a replica of a sod house, a store with a barbershop, a school, a restored 1923 homestead with a collection of character dolls, a bunkhouse, a church, a barn and a general display building. Allow 2 hours minimum. Mon.-Sat. 9-9, Sun. noon-9, Victoria Day weekend-second Mon. in Oct. Free. Phone (306) 948-3427.

BROADVIEW (E-5) pop. 669

Broadview began as a division point on the Canadian Pacific Railway. A marker in a park on the west side of town marks the location of the original tracks laid in 1882. Also in town is a sanctuary for Canada geese.

Broadview Chamber of Commerce: P.O. Box 367, Broadview, SK, Canada S0G 0K0; phone (306) 696-2533.

BROADVIEW MUSEUM is 1 blk. s. of Hwy. 1 on N. Front St. An Indian log house, an 1897 rural school and a Canadian Pacific Railroad station and caboose are displayed at the museum. Exhibits include Indian and pioneer artifacts, old photographs, and maps of early homesteads and trails. Daily 9:30-5:30, June-Aug. Donations. Phone (306) 696-3244.

CARLYLE (F-5) pop. 1,260

North of Carlyle is Moose Mountain Provincial Park (see Recreation Chart and the AAA/CAA Western Canada & Alaska CampBook), which began as

a resort beach on Lake Kenosee in 1906. The park is home to herds of moose and elk and is a nesting place for geese and other birds. There also are more than 450 beaver lodges.

Recreational facilities include an 18-hole golf course, hiking and equestrian trails, riding stables, a clubhouse and a swimming beach. Across from the entrance is Kenosee Superslide, a water park.

CANNINGTON MANOR PROVINCIAL HISTORIC PARK is e. on Hwy. 13 to Grid Rd. 603, then 2 km (1.2 mi.) n. on gravel roads. The village of Cannington Manor, founded in 1882, was an attempt to duplicate the upper-middle-class English way of life, including cricket matches and fox hunts. The museum and seven buildings contain antiques, artifacts and farming implements used by the settlers.

Guides in period costumes demonstrate activities typical of the settlement in the last 2 decades of the 19th century. Picnicking is permitted. Wed.-Mon. 10-5, Victoria Day-Labour Day. Admission $2, students with ID $1, under 6 free, family rate $5. Phone (306) 577-2600 or (306) 739-5251.

CARLYLE RUSTY RELIC MUSEUM AND TOURIST INFORMATION CENTRE is at Railway Ave. and 3rd St. W. Housed in the former Canadian National Railway Station, the museum features historical items from the area. Thirteen rooms contain such exhibits as a dentistry collection, farm equipment, World War II military uniforms, medical equipment, a restored kitchen and photographs. A restored one-room schoolhouse and a tourist information center also are on the grounds.

Allow 1 hour minimum. Mon.-Sat. 9-5, Sun. 1-5, mid-June through Labour Day. Admission $2; ages 6-18, $1. Phone (306) 453-2266.

CHAPLIN (E-3) pop. 292, elev. 674 m/2,214′

CHAPLIN NATURE CENTRE is at the western approach to town via Hwy. 1. The center is in the midst of the Chaplin Lake area, which encompasses some 6,000 hectares (15,000 acres) of inland saline water. More than 30 species of shorebirds, some endangered, either rest and refuel here during migratory journeys or nest and raise their young in the summer, feasting on brine shrimp that teem in the salty, shallow water.

Guided bus tours are available; binoculars are provided. Allow 1 hour, 30 minutes minimum. Daily 9-5, May 1-Labour Day. Center displays free. Guided tour $10, students with ID $5, family rate $30. Reservations are recommended. MC, VI. Phone (306) 395-2770 or (877) 746-7273.

CLAYBANK (E-3) pop. 20

CLAYBANK BRICK PLANT NATIONAL HISTORIC SITE is 1 km (.6 mi.) e. on Hwy. 339. This plant is said to be North America's most intact early 20th-century brick factory and was active 1914-89. Visitors may tour the large site, which comprises more than 20 structures. The plant also is open on special event days to afford visitors an opportunity to see the brick-making process.

Picnicking is permitted. Food is available. Allow 1 hour minimum. Daily 10-5, Victoria Day weekend-Labour Day; Sat.-Sun. 11-5, mid-May to day before Victoria Day weekend; by appointment rest of year. Admission $5, family rate $15. Phone (306) 868-4474.

CORONACH (F-4) pop. 822

POPLAR RIVER POWER STATION AND STRIP MINE is 10 km (6 mi.) s.e. Two-hour bus tours depart from the information center at jct. Centre St. and Railway Ave. (Hwy. 18). Guides provide interpretive explanations during a walking tour of the power plant and the bus tour of the strip-mining site. Durable clothing and flat-heeled shoes are recommended. Tours are given daily at 9:30 and 1, Mar.-Dec. (weather permitting). Free. Phone (306) 267-2078, or (306) 267-2157 Sat.-Sun.

CRAVEN (E-4) pop. 264

Last Mountain Provincial Historic Park, 8 kilometres (5 mi.) north of town on Hwy. 20, preserves the site of a fur-trade outpost that operated 1869-71. Park interpreters offer guided tours of the site's three reconstructed buildings Thurs.-Sun. 10-5, July 1-Labour Day; phone (306) 787-0731.

CUT KNIFE (D-2) pop. 556

In 1885 Cut Knife was the site of several Indian uprisings that were inspired by the Métis rebellion (*see Batoche p. 245*). The Battle of Cut Knife Hill, between the Cree tribe led by Chief Poundmaker and the North West Mounted Police under Col. W.D. Otter, ended in the retreat of the Mounties to Battleford.

Poundmaker, who stopped his warriors from pursuing and ambushing Otter's troops, later surrendered to the authorities to help restore peace between the Indians and settlers. A national historic plaque and a framework of tepee poles mark the chief's grave at the Poundmaker Reserve.

Dominating Cut Knife's horizon is the massive tomahawk in Tomahawk Park. The handle, carved from a British Columbian fir tree, is 16.4 metres (54 ft.) long and weighs 5.5 metric tons (6 tons); the fiberglass blade weighs 1,250 kilograms (2,750 lbs.).

Cut Knife Chamber of Commerce: P.O. Box 91, Cut Knife, SK, Canada S0M 0N0; phone (306) 398-2391.

CLAYTON McLAIN MEMORIAL MUSEUM is 3 blks. w. on Hill Ave. in Tomahawk Park. Indian artifacts, local historical records and articles used by early settlers are exhibited in the museum, which also includes several buildings depicting an early pioneer settlement. A trout pond is on the grounds. Allow 1 hour minimum. Mon.-Sat. 9-7, Sun. 1-5, July 1-Labour Day. Admission $1; under 12, 50c; family rate $3. Phone (306) 398-2345.

DUCK LAKE (C-3) pop. 624

The town of Duck Lake lies between the North Saskatchewan and South Saskatchewan rivers. The actual lake is a few kilometres west of town. A nearby cairn marks the site of the Battle of Duck Lake, in which the Métis Indians defeated the North West Mounted Police on Mar. 26, 1885.

SAVE DUCK LAKE REGIONAL INTERPRETIVE CENTRE is at the jct. of hwys. 11 and 212. The center focuses on the historical contributions made by Indian, Métis and pioneer populations in the area's development. A museum features collections ranging from traditional clothing to tools used in buffalo hunts. The history and cultures of the area are presented in a 15-minute video, and a tower provides panoramic views.

Allow 30 minutes minimum. Daily 10-5:30, Victoria Day weekend-Labour Day weekend. Admission $4, senior citizens $3, students with ID $2, under 6 free, family rate $10. MC, VI. Phone (306) 467-2057 or (866) 467-2057.

FORT CARLTON PROVINCIAL HISTORIC PARK is 26 km (16 mi.) w. on Hwy. 212. The fort that played a part in the settlement of north-central Saskatchewan has been reconstructed at the site, which features three tepees depicting the Plains Cree culture as it existed 1860-70. A replica of the Hudson's Bay Store is a museum of fur-trading history. The visitor center is a reconstruction of the 1879 home of the trading post overseer.

Camping is available. Allow 30 minutes minimum. Daily 10-6, Victoria Day-Labour Day. Admission $2.50; ages 6-17, $1; family rate $6. MC, VI. Phone (306) 467-5205.

EASTEND (F-2) pop. 576

EASTEND MUSEUM-CULTURAL CENTRE is downtown at 306 Redcoat Dr. Items of local interest are displayed, including early settler, business and Indian artifacts and a collection of dinosaur bones found in the area. Adjoining the museum is a rancher's restored log house dating from around 1911. Allow 30 minutes minimum. Daily 9-7, Victoria Day-Labour Day; by appointment rest of year. Admission $3, under 12 free. Phone (306) 295-3375.

T.REX DISCOVERY CENTRE is at 1 T-rex Dr. In partnership with the Royal Saskatchewan Museum, the center houses fossils and replicas of dinosaurs, a 98-seat theater and interpretive displays. Educational activities also are offered. A nearly complete T-rex skeleton was discovered in the area in 1991. Visitors may take a tour to an active fossil quarry or accompany a paleontologist for a hands-on digging experience.

Guided tours are available. Allow 1 hour minimum. Daily 9-5, Victoria Day-Labour Day; Mon.-Fri. 9-5, Sat.-Sun. 10-4, rest of year. Dig tours daily (weather permitting) at 9 and 1, July-Aug. Admission $7.50; ages 5-17, $5. A fee is charged for dig tours. Reservations are suggested. MC, VI. Phone (306) 295-4009.

ELBOW (E-3) pop. 298

ELBOW MUSEUM is at 239 Saskatchewan St. The area's history is depicted from 1905 to the present. Items displayed include arrowheads, photographs and maps. A replica of a sod house, furnished in pioneer style, also is on-site. The house reflects the ingenuity of early settlers in surviving the harsh environment with a scarcity of building materials. Allow 30 minutes minimum. Daily 1-5, July-Aug.; by appointment rest of year. Donations. Phone (306) 854-2277.

ESTEVAN (F-5)
pop. 10,242, elev. 570 m/1,870′

Estevan, founded in 1892 just north of the Souris River, is one of Saskatchewan's major centers for coal and oil. The sun shines an average of 2,540 hours annually, making the town among the sunniest spots in Canada.

Southeast of town off Hwy. 39 is Roche Percée, a group of strangely eroded rock formations that were once venerated by local Indians. Although most of the animals and initials carved on the rocks can no longer be seen, the site is still supposedly visited by spirits whose murmurs can be heard when the wind blows.

On Hwy. 39 at 118 4th St. is the Estevan Art Gallery & Museum. The facility provides information about local events and also presents changing exhibitions and occasional interpretive programs or tours; phone (306) 634-7644.

The Wood End Building, next to the center, was the 1893 barracks for the North West Mounted Police and contains artifacts that relate to the organization's early days. Also nearby is Eli Mandel Heritage Park, which contains an oil field display.

Tours to Shand Power Station and Luscar Boundary Mine can be arranged June through August through the Estevan Tourism Booth; phone (306) 634-6044.

Estevan Chamber of Commerce: 303-1133 4th St., Estevan, SK, Canada S4A 0W6; phone (306) 634-2828.

BOUNDARY DAM POWER STATION is 5 km (3 mi.) w. on Hwy. 18. This power station, which contains one of the largest lignite-burning plants in Canada, utilizes southeast Saskatchewan's vast coal reserves to produce more kilowatts than any other dam in the province. Swimming and boating are permitted. Allow 2 hours minimum. Guided tours are given Tues.-Sat. at 9 and 1, June-Aug. Tour schedule may vary; phone ahead. Free. Phone (306) 634-6044.

RECREATIONAL ACTIVITIES
Recreational Complex
• **Souris Valley Aquatic and Leisure Center**, 701 Souris Ave., Estevan, SK, Canada S4A 2T1.

Mon.-Fri. 6 a.m.-9:30 p.m., Sat. 8 a.m.-9:30 p.m., Sun. noon-9:30. Phone (306) 634-1888.

ESTON (E-2) pop. 1,048, elev. 682 m/2,240′

Founded in 1916, Eston has developed into a major grain center. More than one million bushels of grain are produced annually.

PRAIRIE WEST HISTORICAL CENTRE is at 946 2nd St. S.E. The restored 1910 Evans house contains more than 3,000 artifacts that include period furnishings and photographs, agricultural displays and the Heritage Art Gallery. A pioneer schoolroom is depicted at the Lovedale school. Allow 30 minutes minimum. Mon.-Sat. 9-noon and 1-5, Sun. 1-5, July-Aug.; daily 1:30-4:30, in June and Sept. Free. Phone (306) 962-3772.

FORT QU'APPELLE (E-4) pop. 1,940

With the 1874 signing of Treaty Number IV, representatives of the Cree and Saulteaux Indians gave away their legal right to vast tracts of southern Saskatchewan; near the center of Fort Qu'Appelle (kwah-PELL) a cairn marks the site of the signing. The fort for which the town is named was built in 1864 mainly for use as a trading post.

Fort Qu'Appelle is on the Qu'Appelle River in a broad valley of lush farmland. The area is known for the wide variety of berries growing on the moist, north-facing slopes. The dry, south-facing slopes are carpeted with wildflowers. Several kinds of hawks soar above this peaceful valley, and pelicans, herons, ducks and geese nest in the marshes. Near Fort Qu'Appelle the river widens into a chain of lakes.

The river's unusual name is the French translation of the Cree word *catabuysepu*, or "the river that calls." According to Indian legend, the river was haunted by a spirit that could be heard crying as it moved up and down the water.

Also taking its name from this Cree expression is nearby Katepwa Point Provincial Park, a lakeside recreation area offering day-use facilities. Another provincial park, Echo Valley, is west of town. *See Recreation Chart and the AAA/CAA Western Canada & Alaska CampBook.*

Fort Qu'Appelle Chamber of Commerce: P.O. Box 1273, Fort Qu'Appelle, SK, Canada S0G 1S0; phone (306) 332-5500.

FISH CULTURE STATION is 6 km (4 mi.) w. on Hwy. 210. The station raises such fish as northern pike, arctic grayling, whitefish, walleye and rainbow, brown, lake and brook trout through their life cycle from the egg stage to adult and distributes them to various lakes and rivers to bolster fish population. Guided tours are available. Allow 30 minutes minimum. Daily 9-noon and 1-4, May 1-Labour Day. Free. Phone (306) 332-3200.

FORT QU'APPELLE MUSEUM is at Bay Ave. and 3rd St. A small log building remaining from the original 1864 Hudson's Bay Co. trading post adjoins a modern structure displaying relics of the past, Indian crafts and a model of Fort Qu'Appelle. Daily 10-noon and 1-5, June 1-Labour Day; other times by appointment. Admission $2.50, children $1, family rate $5. Phone (306) 332-6443 or (306) 332-4319.

GRASSLANDS NATIONAL PARK (F-2)

Elevations in the park range from 747 metres (2,450 ft.) at the Frenchman River to 998 metres (3,275 ft.) at Horse Creek. Refer to CAA/AAA maps for additional elevation information.

Grasslands National Park of Canada encompasses the grasslands in two separate blocks between Val Marie and Killdeer in the southern part of the province. When completed, the park will preserve 900 square kilometres (350 sq. mi.) of Saskatchewan's original mixed-grass prairie, including such topographic features as buttes and coulees. Among the wildlife species found in the park are prairie dogs, golden eagles, rattlesnakes, pronghorn antelopes and mule deer.

The Grasslands also claim a rich history. The first recorded discovery of dinosaur remains in Canada was made in the Killdeer Badlands in 1875. Proof of early First Nations habitation includes remnants of tepee rings left by the Plains Indians.

Ranching operations exist in the area, and some of the proposed parkland is still under private ownership. Before entering the park, visitors are asked to contact or stop at the reception desk of the visitor center located in Val Marie, which offers park information, maps and permits as well as interpretive programs, guided hikes and special events. Write Grasslands National Park, P.O. Box 150, Val Marie, SK, Canada S0N 2T0; phone (306) 298-2257. *See Recreation Chart.*

GRAVELBOURG (F-3) pop. 1,187

CATHÉDRALE NOTRE-DAME DE L'ASSOMPTION is at 1st Ave. and Main St. The 1918 Cathedral of Our Lady of the Assumption is noted for the beauty of its interior murals, painted over a 10-year period by founding pastor Monsignor Charles Maillard, as well as its stained-glass windows. Guided tours are available. Open daily 9-5, July-Aug.; by appointment rest of year. Admission $2. Phone (306) 648-3322, or (306) 648-3105 to schedule a guided tour.

GRENFELL (E-5) pop. 1,067

Grenfell is located about 124 kilometres (77 mi.) east of Regina at the junction of Hwys. 1 and 47. Hwy. 47 north from town leads to scenic Hwy. 247, which runs east along the northern shores of Crooked and Round lakes to the junction with Hwy. 9; from there, Hwy. 9 offers another scenic stretch of roadway south to Whitewood.

GRENFELL MUSEUM is at Wolseley Ave. and Stella St. Adare, the former home of the editor/publisher of Grenfell's first newspaper, is furnished in

period. The 1904 house contains a brass bed, a wood-burning kitchen range, an icebox, a hand-operated vacuum cleaner and a dining table set with china. A separate building houses antiques, pioneer artifacts and military displays. Allow 2 hours minimum. Fri.-Sun. 2-8, early July-Aug. 31; other times by appointment. Donations. Phone (306) 697-2930.

HERSCHEL (D-2) pop. 35

ANCIENT ECHOES INTERPRETIVE CENTRE is on 1st Ave. The first part of this attraction—the interpretive center—depicts the area's natural history. Items include fossils, aboriginal artifacts and examples of taxidermy. The second part leads visitors on a guided tour, using their own vehicle, to 1,800-year-old petroglyphs located 3.2 kilometres (2 mi.) away. At the destination, a hiking trail reveals glacial ravines, freshwater springs and a variety of flora and fauna. A video of the hike is available for viewing.

Food is available. Picnicking is permitted. Allow 1 hour, 30 minutes minimum. Daily 9-5, May 15-Sept. 1; by appointment rest of year. Interpretive center $3; over 64 and ages 5-12, $2. Guided tour to the petroglyphs $5; ages 5-12, $3. Reservations are required for archeological site tours. Phone (306) 377-2045.

HUMBOLDT (D-4) pop. 5,161

Named after German author, explorer and scientist Baron Friedrich Heinrich Alexander von Humboldt, the city's heritage is evident in its architecture, folk art, festivals and murals. The murals are located on downtown buildings within a six-block area and depict the city's early history. A map detailing the location and background information of each mural may be obtained at the Willkommen Centre.

The 65-hectare (160-acre) Kloppenburg Wildlife Refuge, west of Humboldt off Hwy. 5, offers nature enthusiasts an opportunity to wander its informal trails and view flora and fauna existing in a natural, undeveloped state; phone (306) 682-3444.

Willkommen Centre: 601 Main St., P.O. Box 1598, Humboldt, SK, Canada S0K 2A0; phone (306) 682-3444 or (306) 682-3144.

HUMBOLDT AND DISTRICT MUSEUM AND GALLERY is at Main St. and Sixth Ave. Housed in a restored, early 20th-century post office, the museum contains exhibits about local wildlife, art and history. Allow 30 minutes minimum. Tues.-Sat. 10-5, Sun. 1-5, July-Aug.; Tues.-Sat. 1-5, rest of year. Donations. Phone (306) 682-5226.

INDIAN HEAD (E-4) pop. 1,758

SAVE **INDIAN HEAD MUSEUM** is at 610 Otterloo St. Housed in an old fire hall, this museum displays an extensive collection of artifacts dating back to the district's pioneer beginnings. Also on the grounds is an 1883 cottage that farm laborers lived in, as well as a 1926 school. A 1952 Pontiac in mint condition resides in a replicated 1930s village garage. A large assortment of farm machinery also is on display.

Guided tours are available by appointment. Allow 1 hour minimum. Daily 1-4, July-Aug.; by appointment rest of year. Admission $2; ages 12-19, 50c. Phone (306) 695-3908.

PFRA SHELTERBELT CENTRE is 1.6 km (1 mi.) s. of jct. hwys. 1 and 56. A short, self-guiding nature trail and picnic areas are part of the Prairie Farm Rehabilitation Administration (PFRA). Outdoor areas open daily dawn-dusk. Free. Phone (306) 695-2284.

KAMSACK (D-5) pop. 2,009

KAMSACK AND DISTRICT MUSEUM is 1.5 km (1 mi.) w. of Hwy. 5 to the Riverside Golf Course, following signs. Housed in a 1914 power plant, the museum features a 1914 generator, old farm equipment, household artifacts, a printing press, vintage clothing and replicas of an early 1900s doctor's office, hospital room and barbershop. Daily 10-5, June 1-Labour Day; by appointment rest of year. Admission $3, under 18 free. Phone (306) 542-4415.

KINDERSLEY (D-2) pop. 4,548

Kindersley is a popular stop for bird-watchers. The surrounding region annually attracts thousands of migrating geese, more than 10 species of ducks, and a few whistling swans and whooping cranes.

The town also is home to the Cape Kindersley Spaceport, part of an Ontario-based project to develop privately built spacecraft capable of launching three people 100 kilometres (62 mi.) into space and returning them safely. The site was chosen in part because of favorable winds and the surrounding flat terrain, which offers unhindered visibility. Kindersley celebrates the annual Goose Festival in September.

Kindersley Chamber of Commerce: 305 Main St., Box 1537, Kindersley, SK, Canada S0L 1S0; phone (306) 463-2320.

KINDERSLEY PLAINS MUSEUM is 1 km (.6 mi.) e. on Hwy. 7 to 903 11th Ave. Geological displays, Indian artifacts and farming and military items are featured. Guided tours are available. Allow 30 minutes minimum. Daily 9-5, May 13-Aug. 31. Admission $2; ages 12-18, $1. Phone (306) 463-6620 or (306) 463-2971.

KINISTINO (D-4) pop. 702

One of the oldest purely agricultural settlements in the province, Kinistino takes its name from *kinistineaux*, meaning "they who were the first to arrive." The allusion refers to the Cree Indians, who lived in the area before the arrival of homesteaders.

KINISTINO DISTRICT PIONEER MUSEUM is on Main St. The museum displays pioneer and aboriginal artifacts. Allow 30 minutes minimum. Daily

1-6, late June-Aug. 31. Donations. Phone (306) 864-2461.

LLOYDMINSTER (C-1) pop. 18,900

Lloydminster has the unusual distinction of sitting astride the Alberta-Saskatchewan border. A downtown monument consisting of four survey markers, erected in 1994, denotes the city's bi-provincial status. For outdoor enthusiasts, Lloydminster's several regional parks and campgrounds and many nearby lakes offer opportunities for fishing, bird-watching and water recreation.

Lloydminster Tourism: 4420 50th Ave., Lloydminster, AB, Canada T9V 0W2; phone (780) 875-6184, ext. 280, or (800) 825-6180.

BARR COLONY HERITAGE CULTURAL CENTRE is on Hwy. 16E at 45th Ave. This complex of museums, galleries and changing exhibits chronicles the history of one of North America's largest organized colonizations, led by Rev. Isaac Barr. It is next to Weaver Park, where the English colonists built their first settlement in 1903. The facilities and exhibits include The Richard Larsen Museum, The Fuchs Wildlife Exhibit, The Imhoff Art Collection and The Oil Technical Society Heavy Oil Science Centre.

Cultural center open daily 9-8, Victoria Day weekend-Labour Day; Wed.-Fri. 9-5, Sat.-Sun. 1-5, rest of year. Admission $4.50; senior citizens and students with ID $4; ages 5-12, $3.50; ages 2-4, $1. MC, VI. Phone (306) 825-5655.

BUD MILLER ALL SEASONS PARK is at 2902 59th Ave. The park consists of 81 hectares (200 acres) of walking and bicycling trails, gardens, picnic areas, playgrounds, sports facilities and a water park. Fishing, paddleboating and miniature golf are among the activities offered. An aquatic complex offers a wave pool, waterslide, whirlpool, steam room and sauna. Self-guiding interpretive trails are available.

Picnicking is permitted. Park open daily 7 a.m.-11 p.m. Aquatic complex hours vary with seasons and events; phone ahead. Park admission free. Aquatic complex $5.50; over 60 and ages 13-17, $4.50; ages 5-12, $3.50; ages 2-4, $2; family rate $17.50. Phone (780) 875-4497, (780) 875-4499 or (800) 825-6180.

MANITOU BEACH (D-3) pop. 212

The resort community of Manitou Beach is on the shore of Little Manitou Lake. The mineral waters of this lake were believed by the Indians to possess curative powers, and the sick of the tribe were brought for treatment long before Europeans knew of the land. Akin to the Dead Sea, the 19-kilometre-long (12-mi.) lake is three times saltier than the ocean. The town has a nine-hole golf course, hotel, convention center, mini-mall, tennis courts, cross-country ski trails and an indoor heated mineral pool.

Along the lake lies Camp Easter Seal, which provides summer recreation for the physically impaired; visitors are welcome.

MAPLE CREEK (F-2) pop. 2,270

The town of Maple Creek was named by the Canadian Pacific Railway workers who spent the winter of 1882 on the banks of Maple Creek. Livestock, grain, tourism, natural gas and oil development provide the area with a stable economy. Maple Creek also has a golf course and campgrounds.

South of town on Hwy. 21 is Cypress Hills Interprovincial Park *(see attraction listing in Alberta p. 77, Recreation Chart and the AAA/CAA Western Canada & Alaska CampBook)*. The lofty hills are characterized by forest-covered buttes, plateaus and ridges interspersed with large areas of ranchland.

Cypress Hills Regional Economic Development Authority: 124 Jasper St., P.O. Box 428, Maple Creek, SK, Canada S0N 1N0; phone (306) 662-4299.

FORT WALSH NATIONAL HISTORIC SITE is 55 km (34 mi.) s.w. on Hwy. 271. The site preserves an early North West Mounted Police fort. Reconstructed period buildings house exhibits of original post artifacts. Tours include trips to a reconstructed whiskey trading post and the fort. A bus trip around the park includes an interpretive commentary.

Allow 2 hours minimum. Daily 9:30-5:30, Victoria Day weekend-Labour Day. Admission (includes bus tour) $7.75; over 65, $6.50; ages 6-16, $4; family rate $17. MC, VI. Phone (306) 662-3590.

THE JASPER CULTURAL AND HISTORICAL CENTRE is at 311 Jasper St. Several rooms of historical displays and art are housed in a 1913 two-story brick school building. Exhibits include ranching, railroad, rodeo and school memorabilia. Allow 30 minutes minimum. Daily 10-4, May-Sept.; Mon. and Fri. 10-4, Tues.-Thurs. 1-4, rest of year. Admission $4; students with ID $2; ages 6-12, $1. Phone (306) 662-2434.

OLDTIMER'S MUSEUM is at 218 Jasper St. The museum contains collections of photographs, artifacts and archival material relating to the First Nations people, the North West Mounted Police, ranching and early settlement. Daily 9-5:30, Victoria Day weekend-Labour Day. Admission $3, students with ID $1. Phone (306) 662-2474.

MEADOW LAKE (B-2) pop. 4,582

Meadow Lake functions as a retail, service and distribution center for northwestern Saskatchewan's major industries as well as a shopping destination for communities in the region. Pastimes include fishing for lake trout, pike, pickerel and arctic grayling and hunting for big game, ducks, geese and sharp-tailed grouse.

With 25 sparkling lakes, Meadow Lake Provincial Park *(see Recreation Chart and the AAA/CAA*

Western Canada & Alaska CampBook) is a haven for fishing, swimming, boating and camping. The park offers hiking trails, beaches, interpretive and recreational programs, cabins, a miniature golf course and a 179-kilometre (111-mi.) canoe route stretching along the Waterhen and Beaver rivers. The town's recreational facilities include an 18-hole golf course and an indoor swimming pool.

Of historical interest is Steele Narrows Provincial Historic Park, 72 kilometres (45 mi.) southwest via hwys. 304 and 26. The last armed conflict on Canadian soil occurred between Big Bear and his band of Cree Indians and Maj. Sam Steele of the North West Mounted Police. The defeat of Big Bear on June 3, 1885, was the end of the Métis and Indian rebellion that began in March 1885 *(see Batoche p. 245)*. Tours of Meadow Lake's historical and industrial sites are available through the chamber of commerce; reservations are required.

Meadow Lake & District Chamber of Commerce: P.O. Box 1168, Meadow Lake, SK, Canada S9X 1Y8; phone (306) 236-4447.

MEADOW LAKE MUSEUM is at Hwy. 4 and 9th St. Local pioneer artifacts and antiques are displayed. Daily 9-9, Victoria Day weekend-Labour Day. Donations. Phone (306) 236-4447.

MELFORT (C-4) pop. 5,559, elev. 457 m/1,500'

Known as the City of Northern Lights due to the visibility of the aurora borealis in the night sky for much of the year, Melfort is in the Carrot River Valley, an area known for its fertile black loam. Agriculture has been the major industry in the area since the days of early settlement in the late 19th century. Melfort was incorporated as a village in 1903, as a town in 1907 and as the province's twelfth city on Sept. 2, 1980.

Melfort & District Chamber of Commerce: Box 2002, Melfort, SK, Canada S0E 1A0; phone (306) 752-4636.

MELFORT & DISTRICT MUSEUM is at 401 Melfort St. W. Historic buildings include a 1912 power house, reconstructed log farmhouse, general store and post office, barbershop, schoolhouse, blacksmith shop and real estate office. The museum also features farm machinery, equipment and tools used in the development of the local agricultural industry.

Guided tours are available. Allow 1 hour minimum. Mon.-Sat. 9-4:30, mid-May to early Sept.; closed holidays. Admission $3; ages 6-10, $2; family rate $10. Phone (306) 752-5870.

MELVILLE (E-5) pop. 4,453, elev. 555 m/1,820'

Situated on the east-west main line of the Canadian National Railway and also on an important north-south line of that company, Melville is known as "The Rail Centre." It came to provincial prominence when it was selected as a major railway service center early in the 20th century. The railway is still the city's largest employer, and its facilities are essential in marketing agricultural products as well as potash from nearby Esterhazy.

Melville & District Chamber of Commerce: P.O. Box 429, Melville, SK, Canada S0A 2P0; phone (306) 728-4177.

MELVILLE HERITAGE MUSEUM is at 100 Heritage Dr. Formerly the Luther Academy, the restored 1913 building now houses this regional museum. Exhibits include artifacts from various churches and denominations; sports, recreation and railway exhibits; military memorabilia; and more than 100 original photographs depicting Melville's early 20th-century progress. The oldest artifact, a German pulpit Bible, dates to 1721. A chapel and library also are on-site.

Guided tours are available. Allow 1 hour minimum. Tues.-Sun. 10-noon and 1-4, mid-May to mid-Oct.; by appointment rest of year. Donations. Phone (306) 728-2070.

MOOSE JAW (E-3)
pop. 32,131, elev. 542 m/1,778'

Moose Jaw's unusual name is probably derived from the big bend in Moose Jaw Creek. The Indians called this creek *moosichappishannissippi*, or "the creek that bends like a moose's jaw." Another popular theory is that an early traveler through the area fixed his cart wheel with a moose's jawbone found in the vicinity. Today's visitors are greeted by "Mac", a 30-foot-tall statue said to be the world's largest moose.

During Prohibition in the United States Moose Jaw was the home of an industrious band of bootleggers and American gangsters, earning the town the nickname "Little Chicago of the Prairies." Moose Jaw is an important western Canadian industrial city, and hard spring wheat also is grown in the area. The Canadian Forces base just south of the city is home to one of Canada's busiest airports and headquarters of the Snowbirds, the Canadian armed forces aerobatic team.

The Murals of Moose Jaw, painted on several downtown buildings, are a collection of more than 30 scenes depicting the town's history. Tours of the murals and heritage buildings can be arranged at the Tourist Information Centre on Diefenbaker Drive; phone (306) 693-8097.

A historic landmark south of town is Hwy. 2, once part of the Powder River Trail used by freighters and ranchers to reach Denver before the advent of the railroad. About 42 kilometres (26 mi.) north on Hwy. 2 is Buffalo Pound Provincial Park *(see Recreation Chart and the AAA/CAA Western Canada & Alaska CampBook)*, where 350 hectares (865 acres) are set aside as grazing land for a herd of buffaloes.

Wakamow Valley, in Moose Jaw, is a recreational development that includes Plaxton's Lake, North River Park, Kiwanis River Park, Kinsmen Wellesley Park, Connor Park and the Devonian

Trail, a pedestrian and bicycle trail system. Visitors can enjoy picnicking, camping, bird-watching, hiking, jogging and bicycling.

Moose Jaw Chamber of Commerce: 88 Saskatchewan St. E., Box 1359, Moose Jaw, SK, Canada S6H 4R3; phone (306) 692-6414.

Self-guiding tours: Brochures outlining a self-guiding tour of some of downtown Moose Jaw's most significant historic sites are available at the Moose Jaw Art Museum and National Exhibits in Crescent Park *(see attraction listing).*

CRESCENT PARK is at Fairford and Athabasca sts. An outdoor swimming pool, war memorial gardens and recreational facilities are contained on 11 hectares (27 acres). Free entertainment is presented Wednesday evenings July through August. The Moose Jaw Art Museum and National Exhibits, next to the public library, displays historical items of local, regional and national interest.

Museum open Tues.-Sun. noon-5 (also Tues. and Thurs. 7-9 p.m.); closed Good Friday, Easter and Dec. 25. Outdoor pool open daily 1-4 and 7-8:30, June 1-Labour Day. Museum free. Admission to pool $3.25; ages 13-17, $2.25; ages 3-12, $2; family rate $7. Phone (306) 692-4471, or (306) 694-4500 for the pool.

MOOSE JAW TROLLEY COMPANY tours depart from the spa at 24 Fairford St. E. Visitors are led on a guided tour of the city's quaint streets and can experience its rich history while riding on board a replicated electric streetcar that operated 1911-32. Allow 1 hour minimum. Tours depart daily at 11, 1:15, 3:15, 4:30 and 7, June-Aug.; Thurs.-Sun. at 1:15, 3:15 and 4:30, in May and Sept.-Oct. Fare $10; over 64, $9; ages 13-17, $7; ages 6-12, $5. Tickets can be purchased in Trudy's Gift Shop, in the lobby of Temple Gardens Mineral Spa. MC, VI. Phone (306) 693-8097.

SUKANEN SHIP, PIONEER VILLAGE AND MUSEUM is 13 km (8 mi.) s. on Hwy. 2. The large, unfinished ship was built by Tom Sukanen, a Finnish settler who had planned to sail the boat home to his native country by way of the South Saskatchewan River, Hudson Bay, Greenland and Iceland. A village preserves an old post office, blacksmith shop, school, church, railroad station and general store as well as a collection of antique tractors, trucks and cars.

Mon.-Sat. 9-5, Sun. noon-8, mid-May to mid-Sept. Admission $5; over 65 and students with ID $4; ages 8-12, $2. Phone (306) 693-7315.

TUNNELS OF MOOSE JAW is at 18 N. Main St. Two themed 45-minute tours take visitors through the underground passages connecting many downtown businesses. Costumed guides re-create characters from Moose Jaw's history, including the bootleggers who hid underground during Saskatchewan's Prohibition era 1916-24. Gangster

Al Capone is said to have used the tunnels to escape American authorities.

Guided tours are offered Sun.-Thurs. 10-7, Fri.-Sat. 10-9, July-Aug.; Mon.-Fri. 10-5:30, Sat. noon-7:30, Sun. noon-5:30, Mar.-June and Sept.-Dec.; Sun.-Fri. noon-5:30, Sat. noon-7:30, rest of year. Closed Jan. 1 and Dec. 25. Schedule may vary; phone ahead. Fare $13; over 60, $10; ages 13-17, $9.50; ages 6-12, $6.50. Combination ticket $21; over 60, $17; ages 13-17, $16; ages 6-12, $10. AX, MC, VI. Phone (306) 693-5261.

WESTERN DEVELOPMENT MUSEUM'S HISTORY OF TRANSPORTATION is at 50 Diefenbaker Dr. Displays illustrate air, water, rail and land transportation. The museum also houses an observatory. The Snowbird Gallery contains aircraft and memorabilia from the Canadian armed forces aerobatic team. Trips aboard the Short Line, a miniature steam locomotive, are available on weekends.

Picnicking is permitted. Allow 2 hours minimum. Museum open daily 9-5 (closed Mon., Jan.-Mar.); closed Jan. 1 and Dec. 25-26. Train rides Sat.-Sun., Victoria Day-Labour Day (weather permitting); phone to confirm schedule. Museum $7.25; over 64, $6.25; students with ID $5.25; ages 6-12, $2; family rate $16. Train rides $1. AX, MC, VI. Phone (306) 693-5989.

CASINOS

• **Casino Moose Jaw**, 21 Fairford St. E. Sun.-Thurs. 9 a.m.-2 a.m., Fri.-Sat. 9 a.m.-3 a.m.; closed Dec. 25. Phone (306) 694-3888. *See color ad p. 257.*

RECREATIONAL ACTIVITIES

Recreational Complex

• **Kinsmen Sportsplex**, 855 McDonald St. W., Moose Jaw, SK, Canada S6H 2W3. Daily 1-4 and 7-9, mid-Mar. to mid-Oct.; Sat. 2-3, Sun. 7-8, rest of year. Closed Jan. 1, Good Friday and Dec. 25. Phone (306) 694-4483.

MORSE (E-3) pop. 248

MORSE MUSEUM & CULTURAL CENTRE is at 410 McKenzie St. Housed in a brick school built in 1912, the exhibits focus on the town's development from the time of the early settlers to the 1970s. Included among the displays are artifacts detailing the history of the pioneer era in the West and a replica of a '30s kitchen. There also is a small art gallery showcasing the work of local, regional and provincial artists.

Guided tours are available. Food is available. Allow 1 hour minimum. Mon.-Sat. 9-5, Sun. 2-5, May-Dec.; Mon.-Fri. 9-5, rest of year. Closed Jan. 1, Good Friday and Dec. 25-26. Donations. Phone (306) 629-3230 or (306) 629-3626.

MUENSTER (D-4) pop. 379

ST. PETER'S ABBEY is 1 km (.6 mi.) e. off Muenster access rd. on Hwy. 5. A self-guiding walking tour of the abbey complex enables visitors to learn about monastic life. Brochures are available at Severin Hall. Sts. Peter and Paul Church, recreational facilities, a farm, gardens, an orchard, trails, print shop, workshops, a cemetery and a greenhouse are points of interest. Allow 1 hour minimum. Daily 8-dusk. Free. Phone (306) 682-1777.

ST. PETER'S CATHEDRAL is 1 km (.6 mi.) n. of Hwy. 5 on the Muenster access rd. The cathedral's walls and ceiling are lined with paintings by Berthold von Imhoff, who created the 80 life-size figures as a gift to the abbot of St. Peter's Abbey. Allow 30 minutes minimum. Daily 9-9, Mar.-Dec. Free. Phone (306) 682-1777 or (306) 682-1789.

NIPAWIN (C-4) pop. 4,275

The Nipawin Hydroelectric Station, northwest of town, uses water impounded in Codette Lake by the Francois-Finlay Dam to generate 1.1 billion kilowatt hours of electricity annually. Guided tours of the facility are conducted by the chamber of commerce on Fridays, June through August; phone ahead to confirm tour availability. SaskPower also conducts tours, but requires 2 weeks' advance notice; phone (306) 862-3148.

Nipawin & District Chamber of Commerce: Box 177, Nipawin, SK, Canada S0E 1E0; phone (306) 862-5252.

LIVING FORESTRY MUSEUM is just w. on Hwy. 35N. The museum contains rotating exhibits that describe the history of the area. Several historic buildings have been relocated to the vicinity, including a sawmill, schoolhouse, shingle mill, church and the 1924 Hornseth House. Demonstrations of the saw and shingle mills and a steam engine are provided during the summer months. Allow 1 hour minimum. Daily 9:30-5, June 15-Aug. 31; Mon.-Fri. 9:30-5, mid-May to June 14. Admission $2, under 12 free. Phone (306) 862-9299.

NOKOMIS (D-4) pop. 436

First named Blakemore and then Blaikie by railroad officials, Nokomis began as the junction of the Old Grand Trunk Railway and the Canadian Provincial Railway. Arriving from England, Mrs. Thomas Halstead, the town's postmistress, was intrigued by the West and the romantic domain of the Indians and chose the name Nokomis, from Henry Wadsworth Longfellow's poem "Hiawatha," for the young town.

NOKOMIS AND DISTRICT MUSEUM is at 3rd Ave. and Queen St. Housed in the former railway station, the museum features re-creations of a post office, schoolhouse, dentist's office, hospital room and equipment, hardware store, a garage with a 1930 Chevrolet and a church. Photographs, vintage clothing and antiques are displayed. Junction City 1907, behind the museum, is a replica of a small town. Allow 1 hour minimum. Daily 10-5, June

1-Labour Day. Admission $2, family rate $5. Phone (306) 528-2979.

NORTH BATTLEFORD (C-2) pop. 13,692

On the bank of the North Saskatchewan River, North Battleford is a gateway to the province's northwest parkland area. Agriculture is the backbone of the area's economy, with farms producing cereal grains, oil seeds and hay crops as well as cattle, hogs, poultry and bison. Forestry, manufacturing and heavy crude oil development also are important industries.

The Battlefords Provincial Park (see Recreation Chart and Cochin in the AAA/CAA Western Canada & Alaska CampBook) is approximately 42 kilometres (26 mi.) north off Hwy. 4 and offers fishing, water skiing, boating and hiking trails. Cross-country skiing and ice fishing are popular winter activities at the park.

Battlefords Chamber of Commerce: Junction hwys. 16 and 40E, P.O. Box 1000, North Battleford, SK, Canada S9A 3E6; phone (306) 445-6226.

ALLEN SAPP GALLERY is at 1 Railway Ave. This award-winning gallery features powerful and sensitive images of the Northern Plains Cree by renowned Cree artist Allen Sapp. Sapp's works depict Cree culture and his 1930s childhood on the Red Pheasant Reserve. Other exhibits include large-screen videos and historical artifacts.

Daily 10:30-5:30, June-Sept.; Wed.-Sun. 1-5, rest of year. Donations. Phone (306) 445-1760.

THE CHAPEL GALLERY is at 891 99th St., just e. of S. Railway Ave. Formerly a chapel, the building was converted to a gallery in 1986. The collection includes local, regional and provincial works; exhibits change regularly. There also is a seasonal labyrinth garden. Guided tours are available. Allow 30 minutes minimum. Daily 1-5, June-Aug.; Wed.-Sun. 1-5, rest of year. Closed Jan. 1 and Dec. 25. Donations. Phone (306) 445-1757.

WESTERN DEVELOPMENT MUSEUM'S HERITAGE FARM AND VILLAGE is at jct. hwys. 16 and 40. The story of agriculture and pioneer life is the focus of the museum, which preserves a 1920s pioneer village. A working farm offers demonstrations of early agricultural equipment and techniques.

Picnicking is permitted. Allow 2 hours minimum. Daily 9-5, May-Sept.; Wed.-Sun. 12:30-4:30, rest of year. Closed provincial holidays. Admission (good for 2 consecutive days) $7.25; over 64, $6.25; students with ID $5.25; ages 6-12, $2; family rate $16. AX, MC, VI. Phone (306) 445-8033.

CASINOS

• **Gold Eagle Casino**, 11902 Railway Ave. E. Mon.-Wed. 9 a.m.-3 a.m., Thurs.-Sat. 9 a.m.-4 a.m., Sun. noon-3 a.m.; closed Dec. 24 and 25. Phone (306) 446-3833.

OUTLOOK (D-3) pop. 2,129

Agriculture has traditionally sustained Outlook, where such crops as corn, potatoes, vegetables and sunflowers are grown. The town came upon its name in an unusual way. As two Canadian Pacific Railway officials stood quietly on the edge of an expansive valley, intensely watching the raging South Saskatchewan River gushing below them, the silence was broken when one uttered the words, "What a wonderful outlook!"

Outlook and District Regional Park, located along the South Saskatchewan River on the west edge of town, covers of 40 hectares (100 acres) and features a golf course, swimming pool, campgrounds and hiking trails. Nature enthusiasts will especially appreciate the many species of birds as well as the venerable elm trees. Phone (306) 867-8846.

A large salt and pepper shaker collection is the highlight of the Outlook & District Heritage Museum, in the center of town at 100 Railway Ave. E.

Town of Outlook: 400 Saskatchewan St., Box 518, Outlook, SK, Canada S0L 2N0; phone (306) 867-8663.

SOUTH SASKATCHEWAN RIVER PROJECT, on the South Saskatchewan and Qu'Appelle rivers, consists of two dams. Gardiner Dam, midway between Elbow and Outlook, is 5 kilometres (3 mi.) long, 64 metres (210 ft.) high and 1,615 metres (5,300 ft.) wide at its base. The impounded water forms Lake Diefenbaker, about 225 kilometres (140 mi.) long, up to 5 kilometres (3 mi.) wide and 56 metres (184 ft.) deep. The second, smaller structure is Qu'Appelle Dam. There is a visitor center at Gardiner Dam.

Food is available. Allow 30 minutes minimum. Tours of the power station at Coteau Creek are offered Mon.-Fri. 10-3. Visitor center open daily 9-5, Victoria Day weekend-Labour Day. Free. Phone (306) 857-2122 for the dam, (306) 857-5900 for the power station or (306) 857-5500 for the visitor center.

PONTEIX (F-2) pop. 550

NOTUKEU HERITAGE MUSEUM is at 110 Railway St. An extensive collection of First Nations artifacts, including arrowheads, is displayed. Guided tours are available in French or English. Picnicking is permitted. Allow 30 minutes minimum. Daily 10-6; closed major holidays. Admission $3, children $2. Phone (306) 625-3340.

PRINCE ALBERT (C-3) pop. 34,291

The gateway to Saskatchewan's north country, Prince Albert is one of the province's oldest communities. Trapper Peter Pond built a trading post on the north side of the North Saskatchewan River in 1776. Credited with founding the town, the Rev. James Nisbet settled on the south shore in 1866.

The log Presbyterian church that Nisbet built that year is now in Kinsmen Park. A blockhouse next to the church dates from the Northwest Rebellion/Métis Resistance of 1885. The Prince Albert Historical Museum *(see attraction listing)* occupies the site of the church built by Nisbet.

Prince Albert Tourism & Convention Bureau: 3700 2nd Ave. W., Prince Albert, SK, Canada S6W 1A2; phone (306) 953-4386.

DIEFENBAKER HOUSE MUSEUM is at 246 19th St. W. The 1947-75 home of the Right Honourable John G. Diefenbaker contains furniture and other possessions of the prime minister of Canada 1957-63. Allow 30 minutes minimum. Daily 10-6, May 12-Aug. 31. Donations. Phone (306) 953-4863.

EVOLUTION OF EDUCATION MUSEUM is at the corner of Marquis Rd. and Hwy. 2 at 3700 2nd Ave. W. The one-room, 1920 schoolhouse was designed to provide maximum warmth and light, with all large windows on the building's east side and desks facing south. Exhibits relate to area education and include pencil boxes, Dick and Jane readers and chalk clamps once used to draw lines on a blackboard. An interpreter is available to answer questions; a visitor information center also is in the building.

Allow 30 minutes minimum. Daily 10-6, Victoria Day weekend-Labour Day; by appointment rest of year. Free. Phone (306) 763-3506 Victoria Day weekend-Labour Day, or (306) 764-2999 rest of year.

LITTLE RED RIVER PARK is at the confluence of the North Saskatchewan and Little Red rivers on Hwy. 55. A scenic drive follows the north bank of the North Saskatchewan River. Picnic facilities and winter sports are available. Swimming in the river is not recommended. Free.

PRINCE ALBERT HISTORICAL MUSEUM is at 10 River St. E. at Central Ave. The museum is housed in an old fire hall that overlooks the North Saskatchewan River. Featured is the first fire engine pumper used in the territory. Other displays include Indian, fur trade and pioneer artifacts as well as a table and benches carved by the Rev. James Nisbet. A tearoom provides a view of the river. Allow 1 hour minimum. Daily 10-6, May 15-Aug. 31. Admission $1, under 6 free. Phone (306) 764-2992.

ROTARY MUSEUM OF POLICE AND CORRECTIONS is at the corner of Marquis Rd. and Hwy. 2 at 3700 2nd Ave. W. Displays pertain to the Royal Canadian Mounted Police, local police, provincial police and corrections services. Exhibits include corporal punishment items, police uniforms and weapons. The museum is in a landscaped park with a visitor center; an interpreter is available to answer questions. Allow 30 minutes minimum. Daily 10-6, Victoria Day weekend-Labour Day; by appointment rest of year. Free. Phone (306) 922-3313.

CASINOS

• **Northern Lights Casino**, 44 Marquis Rd. Mon.-Wed. 10 a.m.-3 a.m., Thurs.-Sat. 10 a.m.-4 a.m.,

Sun. noon-3 a.m.; closed Dec. 25. Phone (306) 764-4777.

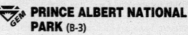 **PRINCE ALBERT NATIONAL PARK (B-3)**

Elevations in the park range from 488 metres (1,600 ft.) on the western side of the park to 724 metres (2,375 ft.) on the southern side of the park. Refer to CAA/AAA maps for additional elevation information.

The main entrance to Prince Albert National Park is 81 kilometres (50 mi.) north of the city of Prince Albert via hwys. 2 and 264.

The park covers 3,875 square kilometres (1,496 sq. mi.) of wilderness in central Saskatchewan. Its lakes, ponds, streams, bogs and rolling hills are a legacy of the glacial epoch. Notable are Sandy, Waskesiu, Kingsmere, Namekus, Crean and the Hanging Heart lakes. There also are several hundred smaller lakes and ponds and many sand beaches.

Heavy growths of conifers and several species of hardwoods surround the lakes, along with numerous shrubs and wildflowers. Fall foliage is especially colorful. Such wild animals as elk, deer, moose and bears are plentiful. A herd of bison roams the southwest corner of the park.

Early morning and evening provide the best chances of seeing wildlife along park roads, especially the Narrows and Kingsmere roads along Waskesiu Lake. Although some animals may seem tame, they are wild and should be observed only from a safe distance.

The park also preserves the legacy of Grey Owl. Born as Archibald Stansfeld Belaney, this controversial Englishman arrived in Canada in 1905. Adopted by the Ojibwa Indians and later married into the tribe, Grey Owl turned his love of nature to the re-establishment of the region's beaver population, which had been decimated by hunters and trappers. For 7 years he lived at Beaver Lodge on Ajawaan Lake, where he continued his restoration and conservation efforts.

General Information and Activities

Although the park is open throughout the year, complete facilities are provided Victoria Day-Labour Day only. Information is available from the information bureau in the Waskesiu Lake Visitor Services Centre, 8 kilometres (5 mi.) from the park's main gate on Hwy. 264.

Roads traverse the park and lead to Waskesiu, Namekus, Sandy and the Hanging Heart lakes and to the Kingsmere River. Although no roads lead directly to Kingsmere and Crean lakes, access is possible by boat. A light railway with handcars assists in portaging around the unnavigable stretch of the Kingsmere River.

There are more than 100 kilometres (60 mi.) of hiking trails traversing the park. Some are suitable for day walks, while others require an overnight stop. Pamphlets outlining self-guiding tours are available for the Mud Creek and Boundary Bog nature trails. From the boat dock on the north shore of Kingsmere Lake a 3-kilometre (1.9-mi.) trail leads to the home and grave of Grey Owl.

Park facilities include boat launching and berthing areas at the Hanging Heart Lakes, the Narrows and the main marina on Waskesiu Lake. Boats, canoes and outboard motors can be rented at all three marinas; paddle-wheeler tours are offered daily in summer. There are bicycle rentals, tennis and volleyball courts and bowling greens at the Waskesiu Lake Visitor Services Centre.

Waskesiu Lake's 18-hole golf course ranks among the finest in Canada. A 150-kilometre (93-mi.) network of groomed cross-country ski trails is open in winter. Snowshoeing and ice fishing also are permitted. Fishing licenses are required and can be obtained at the park information center, park entrances and campground offices.

Park naturalists offer a free summer interpretive program that includes car caravans on park roadways and special daily events. Interpretive programs are regularly presented at the outdoor theaters at the Narrows and Beaver Glen campgrounds.

At the Waskesiu Lake Visitor Services Centre is the Park Nature Centre, which has natural history exhibits, a bookstore and a theater; the nature center is open in July and August. *See Recreation Chart and the AAA/CAA Western Canada & Alaska CampBook.*

ADMISSION to the park is $5 per day; over 65, $4.25; ages 6-16, $2.50. Admission any 3 consecutive days $28 per family. A 7-day pass is $40 per family.

PETS (dogs and cats) are permitted in the park as long as they are on leashes.

ADDRESS inquiries to the Superintendent, Prince Albert National Park, P.O. Box 100, Waskesiu Lake, SK, Canada S0J 2Y0; phone (306) 663-4522.

QU'APPELLE (E-4) pop. 648

CREEKSIDE GARDENS is .4 km (.25 mi.) e. of town on Hwy. 1, following signs (about 35 minutes east of Regina). The gardens encompass approximately 2 hectares (5 acres) and feature lawns, shrubs, trees, perennials and more than 50,000 annuals. Picnicking is permitted. Allow 30 minutes minimum. Daily 9-9, mid-June to mid-Sept. Admission $2, under 12 free. Phone (306) 699-2233.

REGINA (E-4) pop. 178,225, elev. 578 m/1,896′

Indians once used the banks of Wascana Creek for drying buffalo meat and cleaning and stretching the hides. Thus the area became known as *Oscana*, a Cree word meaning "pile of bones." In 1882 the Canadian Pacific Railway completed its track across the plains, and the settlement of Pile-O-Bones sprang up at the rail terminal on Wascana Creek.

The seat of government of the Northwest Territories and the headquarters of the North West Mounted Police were established the same year. A few years later Princess Louise, the wife of Canada's governor-general, renamed the city Regina (Latin for queen) to honor her mother, Queen Victoria. In 1905 Saskatchewan became a province, with Regina as its capital.

In the heart of downtown is City Centre, the site of such buildings as the municipal government offices and the public library. The Prairie History Room, which documents local history, and the Dunlop Art Gallery, which displays works by regional artists, are both housed in the library. The Gallery on the Roof, in the Saskatchewan Power Building, contains changing art exhibits. A glockenspiel chimes at the corner of 12th Avenue and Scarth Street in tribute to the city's ethnic vitality.

The Globe Theatre in the old City Hall is the home of Regina's professional acting company. The city's No. 1 spectator sport is summer football played by the Canadian Football League's Saskatchewan Roughriders at Taylor Field.

Following Wascana Creek for 11 kilometres (7 mi.) is the Devonian Pathway, a paved bicycle trail that passes through six city parks and is used for jogging and walking as well as other activities; in winter it is groomed and lighted for cross-country skiing. The Condie Nature Refuge, just north of the city on Hwy. 11, offers nature trails that afford views of the refuge's grassland and marsh animals.

Further information is available from Tourism Saskatchewan, 1922 Park St., Regina, SK, Canada S4P 3V7; phone (306) 787-2300 or (877) 237-2273.

Regina Convention and Visitors Bureau: Hwy. 1 E., P.O. Box 3355, Regina, SK, Canada S4P 3H1; phone (306) 789-5099 or (800) 661-5099.

Shopping areas: Regina's major shopping malls include Cornwall Centre, 2101 11th Ave. It has 87 stores, including The Bay and Sears. Northgate Mall, 489 Albert St. N., has more than 70 stores. Victoria Square, 2223 Victoria E., is another suburban mall and has more than 50 stores. The specialty shops of Scarth Street Mall, downtown between 11th and 12th avenues, line a pedestrian-only street.

GOVERNMENT HOUSE MUSEUM AND HERITAGE PROPERTY is at 4607 Dewdney Ave. This Italianate-style mansion was the home of the lieutenant governors of the Northwest Territories 1891-1905 and the lieutenant governors of Saskatchewan 1905-45. Flanked by 2.5 hectares (6 acres) of gardens and orchards, the official residence has been restored to its Victorian elegance. Picnicking is permitted. Allow 1 hour minimum. Tues.-Sun. 10-4; closed Good Friday and Dec. 25. Guided tours depart every 30 minutes. Free. Phone (306) 787-5773.

HOLY ROSARY CATHEDRAL is at 3125 13th Ave., just w. of jct. with Albert St. This Cruciform/Romanesque structure, built in 1912, features 43 stained-glass windows installed in 1951 by French artisan Andre Rault, who designed windows for more than 50 other Canadian churches. Their artistry is best appreciated on a sunny day. A Casavant pipe organ, known for its exceptional sound quality, plays during Sunday services.

Guided tours are available. Allow 30 minutes minimum. Thurs.-Fri. 9-noon and 1-4, Wed. 1-5, July-Aug.; Mon.-Fri. 8:30-noon and 1-4:30, rest of year. The cathedral is kept locked for security purposes; phone ahead. Donations. Phone (306) 565-0909.

LEGISLATIVE BUILDING (Capitol) is off Albert St. in Wascana Centre. Surrounded by 67 hectares (165 acres) of landscaped grounds, the imposing landmark is the seat of provincial government. Completed in 1912, the building reflects the architecture of the English Renaissance and Louis XIV of France. The building houses several art galleries, including the Cumberland Gallery, a showcase for works of the Native Heritage Foundation of Canada.

Tours in French are available. Allow 30 minutes minimum. Daily 8 a.m.-9 p.m., Victoria Day-Labour Day; Mon.-Fri. 8-5, rest of year. Closed Jan. 1, Good Friday and Dec. 25. Guided tours of the building are offered. Tours depart every 30 minutes. Free. Phone (306) 787-5358.

REGINA PLAINS MUSEUM is on the second floor at 1835 Scarth St. It features Saskatchewan artist Jacqueline Berting's sculpture "The Glass Wheatfield," consisting of 14,000 waist-high stalks of hand-crafted glass. Also on display is a mural by aboriginal artist Sherry Farrell Racette. Mon.-Fri.

10-4 (also Sat. 10-4, June-Aug.). Free. Phone (306) 780-9435.

ROYAL CANADIAN MOUNTED POLICE DEPOT AND CENTENNIAL MUSEUM is on Dewdney Ave. W. The regimental museum of the Royal Canadian Mounted Police recounts its history of more than a century of service. Photographs, weapons, personal items, uniforms and related artifacts on display reflect the tragedies, successes, history and human side of this well-known Canadian institution.

At the training academy for cadets, a colorful Sergeant Major's parade is usually held Monday through Friday at 12:45 p.m., except for Fridays that precede a holiday weekend. Sunset ceremonies are held Tuesday at 6:30 p.m., July 1 to the first week in August. Depot and chapel tours are available and begin at the museum.

Guided tours are available. Allow 1 hour minimum. Museum open daily 8-6:45, Victoria Day weekend-Labour Day (also Tues. 6:30-8:30 p.m., July 1 to first week in Aug.); 10-4:45, rest of year. Closed Jan. 1 and Dec. 25. Depot and chapel tours depart Mon.-Fri. at 9, 10, 11, 1:30, 2:30 and 3:30, Victoria Day weekend-Labour Day; at 1:30, rest of year. Donations. Phone (306) 780-5838.

ST. PAUL'S CATHEDRAL is at 1861 McIntyre St. This Gothic Revival-style church is said to be the oldest in Regina; its cornerstone was laid in 1894. A museum, which is located under the church and is open by appointment, houses books and artifacts dating to the 1600s. Guided tours are available. Allow 30 minutes minimum. Mon.-Fri. 9-4, Sun. 9-noon. Donations. Phone (306) 522-6439.

[SAVE] **SASKATCHEWAN SCIENCE CENTRE** is on Winnipeg St. at Wascana Dr. in Wascana Centre. The Powerhouse of Discovery houses more than 100 permanent hands-on science exhibits and

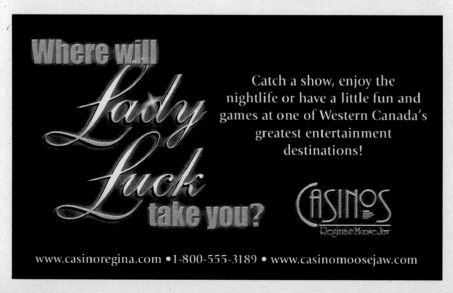

features live stage shows and demonstrations. Visitors who want to test their physical skills can tackle one of the tallest climbing walls in Canada. The 165-seat Kramer IMAX Theatre uses a five-story screen and four-way sound system to present science and nature films in a giant format.

Allow 2 hours minimum. Mon.-Fri. 9-6 (also Fri. 6-8:30 p.m.), Sat.-Sun. 11-6, Victoria Day-Labour Day; Tues.-Fri. and Monday holidays 9-5, Sat.-Sun. noon-6, rest of year. Admission $7; over 60 and ages 4-13, $5. IMAX shows $7; over 60 and ages 4-13, $5. Combination tickets are available. MC, VI. Phone (306) 522-4629, or (800) 667-6300 in Canada.

SASKATCHEWAN SPORTS HALL OF FAME is at 2205 Victoria Ave. Photographs, trophies, records and other memorabilia represent noted athletes and teams from Saskatchewan. Mon.-Fri. 9-5, Sat.-Sun. and holidays 1-5, Victoria Day-Labour Day; Mon.-Fri. 9-5, rest of year. Free. Phone (306) 780-9232.

WASCANA CENTRE surrounds Wascana Lake. The 930-hectare (2,300-acre) park is the center of recreational and cultural activity in Regina and includes the Saskatchewan Centre of the Arts. Wascana Place is both a departure point for sightseeing tours and a reservation office for special events. Ferry boat rides to the Willow Island picnic area are available. Wascana Waterfowl Park and Speakers' Corner also are in the area.

Ferry boat rides Mon.-Fri. noon-4, Sat.-Sun. noon-9. Ferry tours of Wascana Lake also are available by appointment; phone for more information. Ferry boat fare $3. Advance reservations are required. Phone (306) 347-1810 for reservations.

MacKenzie Art Gallery is in the T.C. Douglas Building at the s.w. corner of Wascana Centre at Albert St. and 23rd Ave. A major exhibition center for Saskatchewan, it contains permanent and changing exhibits of Canadian and international art. Allow 30 minutes minimum. Daily 10-5:30 (also Thurs.-Fri. 5:30-10). Guided tours are available Sat.-Sun. 2-4. Donations. Phone (306) 584-4250.

Royal Saskatchewan Museum is at College Ave. and Albert St. in Wascana Centre. The Earth Sciences Gallery focuses on the geological and paleontological evolution of Saskatchewan and includes Canada's only resident robotic dinosaur. The Paleo Pit features hands-on exhibits. The First Nations Gallery portrays the culture and heritage of the province's aboriginal population through artwork and artifacts.

The Life Sciences Gallery explores Saskatchewan's natural history and current environmental issues. Exhibits depict life in a beaver pond, a Costa Rican rain forest and hurricane actions that are disturbing the global ecosystem.

Allow 1 hour minimum. Daily 9-5, May 1-Labour Day; 9-4:30, rest of year. Closed Dec. 25. Donations. Phone (306) 787-2815.

CASINOS

- **Casino Regina**, 1880 Saskatchewan Dr. Daily 9 a.m.-4 a.m.; closed Dec. 24-25. Phone (306) 565-3000 or (800) 555-3189. *See color ad p. 257.*

ROCANVILLE (E-5) pop. 887

ROCANVILLE AND DISTRICT MUSEUM is at Qu'Appelle Ave. and Saint Albert St. A variety of local artifacts include steam tractors, a train station, blacksmith shop and schoolhouse. Allow 2 hours minimum. Daily 10-noon and 1-5, July-Aug.; by appointment rest of year. Admission $3, students with ID $2, under 12 free. Phone (306) 645-2113 or (306) 645-2164.

ROSTHERN (D-3) pop. 1,504

[SAVE] **SEAGER WHEELER FARM** is 7 km. (4 mi.) e. on Hwy. 312, following signs. One of the most noted farmers in Canada, Wheeler won five international wheat championships 1911-18 and was a prominent educator in progressive agricultural techniques. The farm features restored buildings and equipment. Also on the grounds are English flower gardens, orchards, a 24-hectare (60-acre) bird sanctuary and a visitor center with interpretive displays.

Guided tours are available. Picnicking is permitted. Allow 1 hour minimum. Tues.-Sun. 9-8, in July; 9-5, May 9-June 30 and Aug. 1-Sept. 7. Admission $5, under 13 free. Guided tour $1. MC, VI. Phone (306) 232-5959.

ST. BRIEUX (D-4)
pop. 505, elev. 547 m/1,797'

ST. BRIEUX MUSEUM is at 300 Barbier Dr., the main access road to the village. Originally a Roman Catholic rectory, it displays pioneer tools, furniture, period clothing and other artifacts and memorabilia related to the early 20th-century settlement of the St. Brieux district. Guided tours are available. Mon.-Fri. 10-5, Victoria Day-Labour Day; by appointment rest of year. Donations. Guided tour fee $2, under 19 free. Phone (306) 275-2229, or (306) 752-3707 off season.

SASKATOON (D-3)
pop. 196,811, elev. 487 m/1,598'

Saskatoon was founded in 1882 as a temperance colony under leader John Lake. According to legend a Cree Indian brought Lake a handful of the purple berries that grew in abundance alongside the river. Lake was so taken with the fruit he named his settlement Saskatoon, after *misaskquatoomina*, the Indian name for the wild berries. Today a slice of Saskatoon pie is a traditional treat recalling the city's past.

Straddling the South Saskatchewan River, Saskatoon is known as "The City of Bridges" because of the seven spans connecting its banks. It also is home to the University of Saskatchewan, which is building a reputation for research and development in science, medicine and agriculture. The Diefenbaker Canada Centre on campus showcases memorabilia of Canada's 13th prime minister.

The Local History Room on the second floor of the Frances Morrison Library, 311-23rd St. E., serves as a research facility for information that focuses on prairie history relating to Saskatoon in particular and western Canada in general. Collections include more than 60,000 historic photographs, thousands of books, pamphlets, maps, artifacts and periodicals. An art gallery is next to the room. Phone (306) 975-7578.

The Saskatchewan Railway Museum, 6 kilometres (4 mi.) west on Hwy. 7, then 2 kilometres (1.2 mi.) south on Hwy. 60, is operated by the Saskatchewan Railroad Historical Association and displays old railroad buildings and artifacts, including locomotives, cabooses and streetcars; phone (306) 382-9855 June-Sept.

The Centennial Auditorium, 35 22nd St. E., is a convention center as well as a cultural and civic center. The auditorium is home to the Saskatoon Symphony and the site of traveling shows throughout the year. The Meewasin Valley Centre, 402 3rd Ave. S., features interpretive displays pertaining to the area's history. Saskatchewan Place features rock concerts; trade shows; hockey, basketball and baseball games; and other sporting events. The facility is on the north side of the city next to hwys. 2 and 16.

The Meewasin Valley Trail, following the South Saskatchewan River through the heart of the city, has bicycle and jogging trails, picnic areas and playgrounds and provides opportunities for cross-country skiing and ice skating. Recreational activities are available at nearby Pike Lake and Blackstrap provincial parks (see Recreation Chart and the AAA/CAA Western Canada & Alaska CampBook).

Racing fans can enjoy horse racing at Marquis Downs from late May to early September. Races are held Fri.-Sat. 7-10 p.m.; phone (306) 242-6100 or (306) 683-8839. Drag racing heats up the Saskatchewan International Raceway from early May to mid-September; phone (306) 955-3724. Stock car racing takes place at the Bridge City Speedway from May through September; phone (306) 651-3278.

Note: Policies concerning admittance of children to pari-mutuel betting facilities vary. Phone for information.

Tourism Saskatoon: 6-305 Idylwyld Dr. N., Saskatoon, SK, Canada S7L 0Z1; phone (306) 242-1206 or (800) 567-2444.

BEAVER CREEK CONSERVATION AREA is 13 km (8 mi.) s. on Hwy. 219 (Lorne Ave.). Self-guiding

nature trails and interpretive displays are offered. Allow 2 hours minimum. Daily 9-9, July-Aug.; daily 9-5, May-June; Mon.-Fri. 9-5, Sat.-Sun. and holidays noon-5, Sept.-Oct.; Mon.-Fri. 9-5, Sat.-Sun. noon-5, rest of year. Free. Phone (306) 374-2474 or (306) 665-6887.

DIEFENBAKER CANADA CENTRE is at 101 Diefenbaker Pl. on the University of Saskatchewan campus. The archives and personal belongings of prime minister John Diefenbaker are housed at the center; his grave site is on the grounds. The museum also offers changing exhibits about Canadian history, art, politics, science, culture and current affairs.

Mon.-Fri. 9:30-4:30, Sat.-Sun. and holidays noon-4:30; closed Jan. 1, Good Friday, Nov. 11 and Dec. 25-26. Admission $2; ages 4-15, $1; family rate $5 (parents and dependent children). Phone (306) 966-8384.

GLADYS' DOLL HOUSE is 4 km (2.5 mi.) n. on Hwy. 12 from 71st St., then 1.6 km (1 mi.) e. and 1 km (.6 mi.) n. More than 1,000 new and antique dolls are featured. Each group of dolls is displayed depicting a scene best describing its history and background. Allow 1 hour minimum. Daily 1-7, June-Aug.; by appointment rest of year. Admission $3; students with ID $2.50; ages 6-12, $1. Phone (306) 933-2638.

MENDEL ART GALLERY AND CIVIC CONSERVATORY is at 950 Spadina Crescent E. in a park between Queen and 25th sts. This attractive complex overlooks the South Saskatchewan River. In the art gallery are exhibitions of international, national and regional works, including historical and contemporary art. Visitors may view the display of tropical and native plants in the conservatory. Programs and activities are presented in combination with each series of exhibitions. Allow 30 minutes minimum. Daily 9-9; closed Dec. 25. Free. Phone (306) 975-7610.

MUSÉE UKRAINA MUSEUM is next to St. George's Ukrainian Greek Catholic Cathedral at 202 Ave. M. South. Ethnographic collections represent the spiritual, material and folkloric cultural heritage of Ukraine. Interpretive tours portray Ukrainian civilization from prehistory to the commencement of emigration. The adjacent cathedral, with its Ukrainian Eastern Byzantine Rite architecture, art and iconography, may be viewed upon request. Allow 1 hour, 30 minutes minimum. Mon.-Sat. 11-5, Sun. 1-5. Admission $2, family rate (two adults and two children) $5. Phone (306) 244-4212.

SASKATCHEWAN INDIAN CULTURAL CENTRE is at 120 33rd St. E. The center is dedicated to preserving First Nations cultures in Saskatchewan such as the Woodland, Swampy and Plains Cree; Dene; Saulteaux; Dakota; Lakota; and Nakota. Exhibits include historic artifacts as well as contemporary arts and crafts. Allow 30 minutes minimum. Mon.-Fri. 8:30-4:30. Tours are given Tues.-Wed. by appointment. Free. Phone (306) 373-9901, or (306) 244-1146, ext. 22 to schedule a guided tour.

SASKATOON ZOO AND FORESTRY FARM PARK is n.e. off Attridge Dr., following signs. Displayed in settings resembling their natural habitats are 350 species of birds and animals native to Saskatchewan and western Canada. The park offers a children's petting zoo, a reptile and tropical fish display, stocked fishing pond and nature walkways. The Kinsmen Express train provides a tour around the park and zoo.

Allow 1 hour minimum. Zoo and park open daily 9-9, May 1-Labour Day; 10-4, rest of year. Admission $5.25; ages 6-18, $3.25; family rate $10.50. An additional $2 fee per vehicle is charged May 1-Labour Day. Fishing pond $2; ages 6-16, $1. Phone (306) 975-3382.

SHEARWATER BOAT CRUISES is off Spadina Crescent opposite Kinsmen Park, at the Mendel Art Gallery dock. Scenic 1-hour cruises aboard the *Saskatoon Princess* take in the downtown waterfront and include commentary about the city's history. Cruises depart daily at 2:30, 4 and 5:30, May 12-Sept. 30. Schedule may vary; phone ahead. Fare $12; over 60 and ages 7-19, $10; under 7, $8. AX, MC, VI. Phone (888) 747-7572.

UKRAINIAN MUSEUM OF CANADA is at 910 Spadina Crescent E. Exhibits include folk and fiber art, domestic and agricultural tools, and documents and photographs of Ukrainian immigrants. Guided tours are available. Allow 30 minutes minimum. Tues.-Sat. 10-5, Sun. 1-5; closed Jan. 1 and 7, Good Friday, Ukrainian Good Friday, Victoria Day, Labour Day and Dec. 25. Admission $3; over 64, $2; ages 6-16, $1. Phone (306) 244-3800.

◥◢ **WANUSKEWIN HERITAGE PARK** is 5 km (3.1 mi.) n. on Hwy. 11, 3 km (1.9 mi.) s. on Warman Rd., then 2 km (1.2 mi.) e. on Penner Rd., following signs. Cree for "seeking peace of mind," Wanuskewin is a 116-hectare (290-acre) First Nation heritage park that traces more than 6,000 years of area history. The park showcases 19 archeological sites where such artifacts as a medicine wheel and tipi rings have been unearthed. An interpretive center overlooks a valley where stampeding bison plunged over a cliff to their death. Hands-on exhibits, computer-activated displays and two audiovisual presentations portray the Northern Plains Indian culture.

An outdoor activity area allows visitors to help build a tipi or tan a hide. Native performers present Indian dances, songs and storytelling in a 500-seat amphitheater. Self-guiding trails meander through the park and feature interpretive signs explaining past uses of the land.

Food is available. Allow 2 hours minimum. Daily 9-9, Victoria Day weekend-Labour Day weekend; 9-5, rest of year. Closed Good Friday and Dec. 25. Admission $6.50; over 65, $5.50; ages 6-18, $4.50; family rate $25. MC, VI. Phone (306) 931-6767.

WESTERN DEVELOPMENT MUSEUM'S 1910 BOOMTOWN is at 2610 Lorne Ave. This indoor representation of a typical prairie town features more than 30 buildings. Displays include transportation artifacts and vintage agricultural equipment. Food is available. Allow 2 hours minimum. Daily 9-5, Apr.-Dec.; Tues.-Sun. 9-5, rest of year. Closed Jan. 1 and Dec. 25. Admission $7.25; over 64, $6.25; students with ID $5.25; ages 6-12, $2; family rate $16. Phone (306) 931-1910.

CASINOS

- **Saskatoon Prairieland Park Corp. Emerald Casino**, at Ruth St. W. and Lorne Ave. S. Mon.-Thurs. 10:30 a.m.-2 a.m., Fri.-Sat. 10:30 a.m.-4 a.m., Sun. noon-2 a.m.; closed Easter and Dec. 24-25. Phone (306) 683-8840.

SCEPTRE (E-2) pop. 136, elev. 671 m/2,200′

GREAT SANDHILLS MUSEUM is off Hwy. 32. Rooms represent historic buildings in the community, including a boarding house, library, hospital, blacksmith shop, dentist office, schoolhouse, barn and church. An interpretive center provides information about the great sandhills. Allow 30 minutes minimum. Mon.-Sat. 9-noon and 1-4, Sun. 1-5, May-Sept.; by appointment rest of year. Admission $3; ages 6-18, $2. Phone (306) 623-4345.

SHAUNAVON (F-2) pop. 1,775

GRAND COTEAU HERITAGE AND CULTURAL CENTRE is 2 blks. n. of Third Ave. at 440 Centre St. Natural history exhibits include fossils, birds,

mammals, fish and rocks. Human history is depicted through pioneer artifacts. An art gallery hosts local, regional and provincial exhibitions. Also located at the museum is the Shaunavon Tourist Information Centre. Picnicking is permitted. Allow 30 minutes minimum. Mon.-Sat. 9-5, May-Sept.; Tues.-Sat. 1:30-5, rest of year. Free. Phone (306) 297-3882.

SIMPSON (E-3) pop. 194

LAST MOUNTAIN LAKE SANCTUARY is 14 km (9 mi.) e. on Hwy. 748, then 3 km (1.9 mi.) s. via a gravel road. Said to be the oldest bird sanctuary in North America, the wildlife refuge was established in 1887 and covers 1,012 hectares (2,500 acres). The area's favorable habitats and location make it a haven for more than 280 species of birds. Each year during May and between mid-August and mid-September more than 20,000 sandhill cranes stop at the sanctuary during their seasonal migration.

Picnicking is permitted. Allow 1 hour minimum. Daily dawn-dusk. Free. Phone (306) 836-2022. *See Recreation Chart.*

SPRUCE HOME (C-3)

THE BUCKLAND HERITAGE MUSEUM AND THE NATURAL RESOURCES MUSEUM is on Hwy. 2. Featuring items donated by area residents and the local Conservation Officers of Saskatchewan, museum exhibits include the wreckage of a Vickers

Vedette airplane, a Bombardier snow bus and a Ford Model T car. Agricultural equipment and early 20th-century household items also are on display. A large mural depicts rural life in the region.

Allow 30 minutes minimum. Thurs.-Mon. 10-6:30, late June-Labour Day. Admission $1, under 12 free. Phone (306) 764-8470 or (306) 764-8394.

STRASBOURG (E-4) pop. 760

STRASBOURG AND DISTRICT MUSEUM is at Mountain St. and Railway Ave. Nature displays, handicrafts and pioneer artifacts are exhibited. Tues.-Sat. 10-4, Sun. 1-5, July-Sept. Donations. Phone (306) 725-3443.

SWIFT CURRENT (E-2) pop. 14,821

Once the site of transient Indian and fur trader camps, Swift Current began as a North West Mounted Police encampment on Swift Current Creek in 1874. Soon after, the Canadian Pacific Railway built a depot, and the settlement became the freight terminus for western Canada. From this point goods were hauled by wagon on overland trails; deep ruts can still be seen on the old North Battleford Trail north of Swift Current.

With the turn of the 20th century came the farmers and ranchers whose trades formed the backbone of the city's economy. Since the discovery of oil in the area in 1952, Swift Current has developed rapidly as a base for oil exploration; agriculture, however, remains the most important industry.

Swift Current Creek runs through town, and two nearby lakes offer recreational facilities. At Saskatchewan Landing Provincial Park (see Recreation Chart), a plaque marks the spot where pioneers once forded the South Saskatchewan River on their way into the wilds of the northern province. In the park's hills are several Indian grave sites and tepee rings.

Swift Current Chamber of Commerce & Tourist Information Centre: 1703 22nd Ave. N.E., Swift Current, SK, Canada S9H 5B7; phone (306) 773-7268.

ART GALLERY OF SWIFT CURRENT is at 411 Herbert St. E. This public art gallery offers exhibitions of local, provincial and national artwork. Guided tours are given upon request. Mon.-Thurs. 2-5 and 7-9 p.m., Fri.-Sat. 1-5, Sun. 1-4:30, Sept.-June; Mon.-Thurs. 2-5 and 7-9 p.m., Fri.-Sat. 1-5, rest of year. Closed major holidays and during exhibition changes. Free. Phone (306) 778-2736.

SWIFT CURRENT MUSEUM is at 105 Chaplin St. E. Exhibits depict the natural and human history of southwest Saskatchewan. Mon.-Fri. 10-5, Sat.-Sun. 1-5, June-Aug.; Mon.-Fri. 1:30-4:30, rest of year. Closed major holidays. Free. Phone (306) 778-2775.

TISDALE (C-4) pop. 3,063

This rural community in northeastern Saskatchewan provides easy access to several provincial parks offering recreational activities from fishing and boating in summer to skiing in winter. A roadside attraction, claimed to be the world's largest honeybee, stands on the south side of Hwy. 3 in town.

Greville Jones Wildlife Sanctuary is reached by a gravel access road about 6.4 kilometres (4 mi.) southwest of Tisdale off Hwy. 3, following signs. The site of an old farmstead, it is a pleasant place for a summer picnic or hike along one of several nature trails. Another scenic route is the Doghide River Trail, a system of walking, cycling and skiing trails that run along several sections of the riverbank. The trail can be accessed from the junction of Hwys. 3 and 35; proceed east .8 kilometre (.5 mi.), then north .5 kilometre (.3 mi.) and turn right into Kinsmen McKay Park.

TISDALE & DISTRICT MUSEUM, HERITAGE CENTRE AND DOGHIDE VILLAGE, at jct. Hwy. 3 and Heritage Rd. at the western approach to town, comprises three main areas. The Station houses a bee farming display, while Doghide Village features the furnished 1920 Pearse House, a log barn and milk house and a fire hall complete with antique water wagon. The Heritage Centre contains the Dagg Collection of vintage automobiles, which range from standard Fords and Chevrolets to such unusual makes as Star, Whippet and Essex.

Guided tours are available. Picnicking is permitted. Allow 30 minutes minimum. Daily 9-5, May 21-Sept. 11. Admission $2, family rate $5. (306) 873-4999.

VEREGIN (D-5) pop. 83

Emigrating from Russia in 1899 due to persecution, the Doukhobours named their village after their theocratic leader, Peter Vasilovich Veregin. The Doukhobour way of life centers on communal living and renounces violence and war. Its followers do not eat meat or use alcohol or tobacco. The community flourished for 2 decades before a majority of the sect relocated to British Columbia. A prayer house built by Veregin and a machine shed are all that remain of the original Doukhobour colony.

NATIONAL DOUKHOBOUR HERITAGE VILLAGE is across the tracks s. of Hwy. 5. The village is composed of the original Doukhobour prayer home and several reconstructed buildings typical of Veregin's Doukhobour dwellings at the turn of the 20th century. A museum displays Doukhobour handicrafts, clothing, hand tools, a collection of Leo Tolstoy's works and other artifacts.

Allow 30 minutes minimum. Daily 10-6, mid-May to mid-Sept.; by appointment rest of year. Admission $5; students with ID $2; ages 5-15, $1. Phone (306) 542-4441.

WADENA (D-4) pop. 1,412, elev. 488 m/1,600′

WADENA & DISTRICT MUSEUM is at 302 Main St. S. Housed in a 1904 train station, the museum preserves items relating to the history of the pioneers who settled the area in the early 20th century. Exhibits include antique farm equipment, a 1914 farm house, country schoolhouse and blacksmith shop. A caboose is adjacent to the station. Allow 30 minutes minimum. Tues.-Fri. 9-5, Sat.-Sun. 1-5, June 1-Labour Day; closed holidays. Donations. Phone (306) 338-3454.

WAKAW (D-3) pop. 884

WAKAW HERITAGE MUSEUM is in the center of town at 300 1st St. S. Exhibits include Ukrainian artworks and implements, mementos from both world wars, homestead displays and a wide assortment of items dating from the early to late 1900s. Allow 1 hour minimum. Thurs.-Mon. 10-5. Admission $3; ages 10-18, $2; senior citizens free. Phone (306) 233-4223.

John Diefenbaker's Law Office is off 1st St. S. at 3rd Ave. S. The site is a replica of the original office where the 13th prime minister of Canada practiced law 1919-25. Guides are available at the Wakaw Heritage Museum. Daily 10-5, July-Aug. Phone (306) 233-4223.

WEYBURN (F-4) pop. 9,534

Weyburn's name was coined in 1893 by Scottish railroad workers, who called this marshy area at the headwaters of the Souris River "wee burn." From these humble beginnings the town has grown into a major marketing center for the surrounding agricultural area. Weyburn is the southeastern terminus of scenic Hwy. 39, which continues to Moose Jaw.

The town was immortalized as "Crocus, Saskatchewan" in the works of W.O. Mitchell, who was born and reared in Weyburn and penned the book "Who Has Seen the Wind." A summary of Weyburn's history since its earliest days is depicted on the "Wheel of Progress" at the Weyburn Library. Between the spokes of the brass-rimmed mahogany wheel, which weighs 909 kilograms (2,000 lbs.) and has a diameter of 3.9 metres (13 ft.), are 10 mosaic panels showing highlights of the city's past.

Weyburn Chamber of Commerce: 405 Coteau Ave., Weyburn, SK, Canada S4H 3G5; phone (306) 842-4738.

Shopping areas: A major outlet mall in the Weyburn area is Weyburn Square Mall, off Hwy. 39 at 110 Souris Ave.; it contains 28 stores.

SAVE **SOO LINE HISTORICAL MUSEUM** is e. on Hwy. 39 at 411 Industrial Ln. Local pioneer artifacts trace the area's early history. The museum houses more than 5,000 pieces of silver, glass and antique furniture dating 1750-1970. Donated by Charles Wilson, the exhibit is reputed to be one of the country's largest private collections. Allow 30 minutes minimum. Mon.-Sat. 9-7:30, Sun. 11:30-7:30, June-Aug.; Mon.-Fri. 1-5, rest of year. Admission $5; students with ID $4; under 12, $2. Phone (306) 842-2922.

WEYBURN HERITAGE VILLAGE is 1 km (.6 mi.) s. from jct. Hwys. 35 and 39, then 1 km (.6 mi.) e. on 10th Ave. S. This historical village has been replicated to depict community life from the turn of the 20th century to the 1940s. All the buildings have been restored. Farm machinery is on display and visitors also may view a one-room school, rural municipality office, country church and blacksmith shop.

Guided tours are available. Picnicking is permitted. Allow 1 hour minimum. Daily 1-8, May-Aug.; closed Victoria Day, July 1 and first weekend in Aug. Admission $3; ages 13-19, $2; ages 5-12, $1; family rate $10. Phone (306) 842-6377.

WHITEWOOD (E-5) pop. 947

OLD GEORGE'S AUTHENTIC COLLECTIBLES is on Hwy. 1 just w. of town. On this 12-acre property, a 30-room brick dwelling houses such collectibles as oil lamps, clocks, crocks and jugs, Indian artifacts, antique bottles and spinning wheels. Hidden Village consists of 30 buildings representative of pioneer life, including a school, saloon, trapper's cabin and the first wooden hotel built in Saskatchewan.

Allow 1 hour minimum. Daily 10-6, mid-May to mid-Oct.; by appointment rest of year. Schedule may vary; phone ahead. Admission $5; under 12, $1. Phone (306) 735-2255.

WOLSELEY (E-4) pop. 766

WOLSELEY & DISTRICT MUSEUM is on Blanchard St. A collection of locally obtained artifacts reflecting life in the area circa 1880-1945 is displayed in a two-story boarding house built in 1901. Exhibits include medical, real estate and lumber offices as well as clothing from the various eras. Guided tours are available. Allow 30 minutes minimum. Daily 2-4, July-Aug.; by appointment rest of year. Donations. Phone (306) 698-2360.

WOOD MOUNTAIN (F-3) pop. 100

RODEO RANCH MUSEUM is 6 km (4 mi.) s. on Hwy. 18 at Wood Mountain Post Historic Site. The museum features exhibits about local ranching, Indians and saddle making. An adjacent adobe and log building houses blacksmithing tools. A rodeo is held on the grounds during the second weekend in July. Camping and picnic facilities are available. Allow 1 hour minimum. Daily 10-noon and 1-5, mid-May through Labour Day. Admission $2, students with ID $1, under 10 free with adult. Phone (306) 266-4953.

WOOD MOUNTAIN POST PROVINCIAL HISTORIC PARK is 8 km (5 mi.) s. on Hwy. 18. Two buildings are on the site of the North West Mounted Police post that stood 1874-1918; small stumps outline the rest of the post. Inside the buildings are displays on the Mounted Police, Sioux Indians and local history. An interpretive staff is on duty to answer questions. Allow 1 hour minimum. Thurs.-Mon. 9-5, June 1 to mid-Aug. Donations. Phone (306) 787-2700.

YORKTON (E-5) pop. 15,107

In 1882 some 200 settlers from Ontario bought land in the Northwest Territories in what is now southeastern Saskatchewan. They called the community around their trading post York City. In 1890 the railroad arrived in the area 5 kilometres (3 mi.) to the south. The York City colonists relocated to be near the railroad and named the new settlement Yorkton. A plaque marks the site of York City; nearby are millstones from the original colony's gristmill.

Recreation is available at nearby Good Spirit Lake Provincial Park *(see Recreation Chart and the AAA/CAA Western Canada & Alaska CampBook)*. The park, originally a Hudson's Bay Co. post in the 1880s, is noted for its miles of sandy beaches and fine dunes.

Tourism Yorkton Visitor Information Centre: Hwy. 9, Box 460, Yorkton, SK, Canada S3N 2W4; phone (306) 783-8707.

Self-guiding tours: The Yorkton Heritage Walking Tour affords visitors the opportunity to view gardens and historic buildings. The City Cemetery Walking Tour features the grave sites of many of the city's early pioneers. Materials outlining each tour are available at the information center.

GODFREY DEAN ART GALLERY is in the Godfrey Dean Centre at 49 Smith St. E. Assorted art forms are displayed, along with works by contemporary Canadian artists. Exhibits change monthly. Mon.-Fri. 11-5 (also Tues.-Thurs, 6-9 p.m.), in summer; Tues.-Fri. 11-5 (also Thurs. 6-9 p.m.), Sun. 1-4, in winter. Closed holidays. Free. Phone (306) 783-2992.

WESTERN DEVELOPMENT MUSEUM'S STORY OF PEOPLE is .4 km (.25 mi.) w. on Hwy. 16A. The museum focuses on the cultural roots of the settlers of western Canada. Picnic facilities are on the grounds. Allow 1 hour minimum. Daily 9-6, May 1 to mid-Sept. Admission $3.50; over 64, $3; students with ID $2.50; ages 6-12, $1; family rate $8. Phone (306) 783-8361.

CASINOS

• **Painted Hand Casino**, 30 3rd Ave. N. Mon.-Thurs. 9 a.m.-2 a.m., Fri.-Sat. 9 a.m.-3 a.m., Sun. noon-2 a.m.; closed Dec. 25. Phone (306) 786-6777.

Yukon Territory

A Panful of Nuggets

Miners still find gold a century after the great Klondike Gold Rush

Spirit of Adventure

Wild waterways, rugged mountains and unexplored wilderness await

All That Glitters

Black diamond jade, amber, topaz, malachite, obsidian and gold bejewel the territory

Lofty Mount Logan

Canada's highest peak rises from the icy St. Elias Mountains

The Northern Lights

Aurora borealis offers nature's nightly light show

Bennett Lake, near Carcross
© Natural Moments Photography
PictureQuest

unspoiled majesty

Near Whitehorse / © Terrence Klassen / Alamy Images

To find gleaming gifts of topaz in outcroppings of rock. To wander trails once trodden by miners and trappers. To cry "Mush!" behind a stalwart team of sturdy Alaskan huskies.

To do any of these is to begin to understand the majestic allure of the endless Yukon.

The roughly triangular territory is aland of adventure, a lonely wilderness, a rugged and pristine land of splendor and beauty.

Turbulent rivers of splashing white water weave through soaring mountain ranges. Soft blankets of white pull up snugly over a serene countryside.

The very essence of the sprawling territory is aptly captured in one moving

stanza from poet Robert Service's homage, "The Spell of the Yukon":

There's gold, and
it's haunting and haunting;

It's luring me on as of old;

Yet it isn't the gold that I'm wanting
so much as just finding the gold.

It's the great, big, broad land
'way up yonder,

It's the forests
where silence has lease;

It's the beauty
that thrills me with wonder,

It's the stillness
that fills me with peace.

"Thick between the flaky slabs, like cheese sandwiches"—this was how prospector George Washington Carmack described the gold he saw glimmering between rocks in Bonanza Creek near Dawson City in August 1896.

On July 14, 1897, the steamship *Excelsior* arrived in San Francisco carrying a treasure worth more than $500,000; a few days later the *Portland* docked in Seattle with one ton of gold piled on its deck. News of these recently discovered riches spread like wildfire, and thousands of get-rich-quick hopefuls began to head for the wealth that lay in Yukon Territory.

Klondike or Bust

That following winter, some 100,000 prospectors began a long, arduous journey to the Yukon to seek their fortunes. While the rush only lasted about 5 years, history was left in its trampled tracks. Following the Yukon River from British Columbia's border to Dawson City, you can explore the past on a course pursued by gold diggers more than 100 years ago.

If stampeders survived the trek through Chilkoot Pass—a climb over frozen mountains

with heavy packs full of supplies strapped to their backs—they crossed the border into the Yukon Territory at Bennett Lake.

The lake, surrounded by mighty peaks and woodlands, links to the Yukon River. Most fortune seekers waited out the harsh winter at the southern shore, which quickly transformed into a crowded tent city. Transients built boats, temporary shelter and a little log church out of timber hewn from the forest. In late May of 1898, the lake's ice broke and 7,000 handmade vessels headed across its waters, leaving memories of a bitter season behind.

Today, original miners' cabins still line Bennett Lake's northern shore at Carcross, a town chock full of gold rush history. The Caribou Hotel, built in 1898 to welcome gold rushers, is downtown, and graves of such early pioneers as Kate Carmack, Skookum Jim Mason and Dawson Charlie dot the city's cemetery.

From Carcross the gold route followed the Yukon River to Miles Canyon, just south of Whitehorse. Currents here were so dangerous that hundreds of boats capsized, and licensed

---

Yukon Territory Historical Timeline

The Hudson's Bay Co. sets up trading posts in the Yukon.
1800

Yukon Territory becomes a provisional district of the Northwest Territories.
1895

1898-1904
More than $100 million in gold is mined in the region.

Gold rush veteran Martha Black is elected to the House of Commons.
1935

© Gunter Marx Photography
Corbis

1942
The Alaska Highway is constructed, creating a new overland transportation route.

guides were a must for piloting would-be miners with smaller vessels through the rocks and whirlpools.

Cheechakos, or newcomers, relied upon their own floating devices until sternwheelers became a popular means of travel; by the early 1950s, more than 250 steamboats plied the Yukon. Boats were specifically designed for the river, employing flat bottoms that allowed for docking on sandbars. Nevertheless, many ran aground or were smashed by rapids or rocks on the Yukon's perilous waters.

A few stout vessels remain from this turbulent time. The restored steamer SS *Klondike II* resides in Whitehorse, while Dawson City is home to the dry-docked SS *Keno*.

The River to Riches

After stopping to relax and dry out in Whitehorse, miners pressed on, traversing Lake Laberge to enter a stretch of the Yukon called Thirty Mile. Due to swift currents and rocks, it was perhaps the most dangerous portion of the entire route. Historical sites along Thirty Mile—which is designated a Historic River—include abandoned Northwest Mounted Police posts, simple grave markers, woodcutters' cabins, telegraph stations, old log buildings and remains of beached paddlewheelers. They all bring yesteryear into focus.

More dangerous eddies had to be negotiated at Five Finger Rapids, just outside Carmacks, before exhausted voyagers passed Fort Selkirk and reached Dawson City—the golden ticket.

Downtown Dawson City remains much as it was when prospectors arrived, thanks to codes requiring new buildings to sport fronts reminiscent of the gold rush era. And old buildings have been restored: Cancan dancing takes place at Diamond Tooth Gertie's Gambling Hall and the log cabins once inhabited by author Jack London and poet Robert Service remain as examples of gold rush housing. A 1912 dredge can be seen along a tributary of the Klondike, and placer mining still occurs at nearby creeks such as the Eldorado.

And don't forget to stop by where it all began—a brass plaque on Bonanza Creek Road marks the spot that caused a great many to risk life and limb for a golden nugget that promised a change of fate.

Yukon's capital is moved from Dawson City to Whitehorse.
1953

© Paul A. Souders/Corbis

Kluane National Park is declared a Natural World Heritage Site.
1979

The Council for Yukon Indians and the Canadian and Yukon Territory governments sign an agreement stating the terms for final land claim settlements in the territory.
1993

1959
At a cost of $1 million, a large fish ladder is built at the Whitehorse Rapids for migrating chinook salmon.

1997
Yukon spends $37 million on mining exploration.

1999
Yukon signs an accord with the Vuntut Gwitchin people, thereby recognizing a First Nation tribe as a legitimate government for the first time in the territory's history.

Recreation

Through its pristine waterways, rugged mountains and unexplored wilderness, the Yukon evokes a spirit of adventure in visitors.

Highways to Adventure

There is no better place than the Chilkoot Trail to understand the challenges faced by early pilgrims—the gold-rush stampeders—coming into Yukon Territory. The Yukon's original inroad, with its trail head in Dyea, Alaska, affords today's experienced **hiking** enthusiasts a 53-kilometre (33-mi.), one-way walk through history that can take 3 to 5 days to complete.

Preparation—proper gear, provisions, permits—is key to enjoying this demanding trip through boreal forests and over alpine tundra and snow-patched mountains. You must reserve a campsite for each night you plan to spend on the trail. The Trail Centre in Skagway, Alaska, is the official registration point and offers maps, safety tips and a few words about bears during the Chilkoot hiking season, May through early September. For information phone Parks Canada year-round at (800) 661-0486.

At trail's end in Bennett, British Columbia, reward yourself with a railroad ride back to Skagway aboard the White Pass & Yukon Route, which shuttles returning Chilkoot hikers regularly. Reservations are a must; phone (907) 983-2217 or (800) 343-7373. Another return option is to hop a bus at Log Cabin, British Columbia.

Camping in summer, June through mid-September, truly is a wilderness experience. While you won't have to chop firewood (it's there and it's free), you will have to pump your own water. Government campgrounds are spread throughout the Yukon roughly 81-121 kilometres (50-75 mi.) apart. Many are beside lakes, rivers or streams, where you might hook a few Arctic graylings for dinner. Of the 10 campgrounds along the Alaska Hwy. (Hwy. 1), Watson Lake is one of the first you'll find as you enter the Yukon from British Columbia; it has 55 campsites. Farther west bordering the Kluane region is Congdon Creek; with 78 campsites, it's one of the largest in the territory. Both areas offer **fishing, swimming** and hiking.

Take scenic Dempster Hwy. (Hwy. 5) from Dawson City to Rock River Campground, the northernmost public facility at Km-post 447. Congratulate yourself upon arriving: You've crossed the Continental Divide—twice—*and* the Arctic Circle! There is no well water for the 14 sites at Rock River, so be sure to stock up on supplies in Dawson City or when you get to Eagle Plains—your last chance—at Km-post 371.

The Klondike Hwy. (Hwy. 2), open all year, is dotted with roadside respites for camping and **picnicking.** You also can camp just off the Robert Campbell and Silver Trail hwys. (hwys. 4 and 11, respectively). Travelers can access daily road condition reports by dialing the Department of Community and Transportation Services' hotline; phone (877) 456-7623 within the Yukon or (867) 456-7623 outside the Yukon. Wherever the road leads, watch for wildlife, especially around viewing areas identified with a sign picturing binoculars.

The Other Extremes

With almost 8 months of winter (October through May), **snow skiing** is a way of life in the Yukon. Near Whitehorse, a chalet and night lighting attract cross-country skiers to Mount McIntyre's world-class trails, while Mount Sima, one of the largest ski areas in the Yukon, appeals to downhill skiers with its nine runs and one chairlift. **Snowboarding,** too, is a favorite at Mount Sima's snowpark. Power up a snowmobile and glide on groomed trails around Whitehorse, or venture over more rugged terrain out of Dawson City, said to be the **snowmobiling** capital of the Yukon.

The territory's rich "veins"—its wild rivers—yield excitement other than gold finds. Outfitters are available in Whitehorse to take you **kayaking** or **white-water rafting** on the Tatshenshini's class three and four rapids, or through Kluane National Park and Reserve on the Alsek, a designated heritage river. Many sections of the Yukon River, which once ushered fortune seekers north to the Klondike goldfields, are easily navigated by canoe. And there are tons more nuggets of adventure to be discovered in the Yukon Territory.

Recreational Activities

Throughout the TourBook, you may notice a Recreational Activities heading with bulleted listings of recreation-oriented establishments listed underneath. Similar operations also may be mentioned in Destination City recreation sections. Since normal AAA inspection criteria cannot be applied, these establishments are presented only for information. Age, height and weight restrictions may apply. Reservations often are recommended and sometimes are required. Addresses and/or phone numbers are provided so visitors can contact the attraction for additional information.

Fast Facts

POPULATION: 28,674.

AREA: 482,443 sq km (186,271 sq mi); ranks 9th.

CAPITAL: Whitehorse.

HIGHEST POINT: 5,959 m/19,545 ft., Mount Logan.

LOWEST POINT: Sea level, Beaufort Sea.

TIME ZONE(S): Pacific.

MINIMUM AGE FOR UNRESTRICTED DRIVER'S LICENSE: 17 years, 6 months.

MINIMUM AGE FOR GAMBLING: 19.

SEAT BELT/CHILD RESTRAINT LAWS: Seat belts required for driver and all passengers; ages 7-15 must wear a seat belt. Child restraints and safety seats required for under age 7 and up to 22 kg (48 pounds).

HELMETS FOR MOTORCYCLISTS: Required for rider and passenger.

RADAR DETECTORS: Prohibited.

FIREARMS LAWS: By federal law, all nonresidents entering Canada with a firearm must declare their weapon in writing and pay a fee of $50 (Canadian). Contact the Canadian Firearms Centre at (800) 731-4000 to receive a declaration form or for additional information.

HOLIDAYS: Jan. 1; Heritage Day, Feb. 25; Good Friday; Easter Monday; Victoria Day, May 24 or the closest prior Mon.; Canada Day, July 1; Discovery Day, Aug. (3rd Mon.); Labour Day, Sept. (1st Mon.); Thanksgiving, Oct. (2nd Mon.); Remembrance Day, Nov. 11; Dec. 25 and 26.

TAXES: The Yukon Territory has no territorial sales tax.

FERRY SCHEDULES AND INFORMATION: The Department of Highways runs ferries along Dempster Hwy. and at Dawson City. Phone (867) 667-3710.

ROAD CONDITIONS: Through its Yukon Network the Canadian Broadcasting Corporation reports road conditions on the Alaska Hwy. and all other Yukon highways. Major participating stations, with their frequencies in kilohertz (kHz), are listed from south to north: Watson Lake, 990; Swift River, 970; Teslin, 940; Whitehorse, 570; Haines Junction, 860; Destruction Bay, 940; Beaver Creek, 690; Carmacks, 990; Mayo, 1230; Elsa, 560; Dawson City, 560; Faro, 105.1 FM; and Ross River, 990.

For changes on Yukon road conditions, phone (867) 456-7623 or (877) 456-7623 within the Yukon Territory.

INFORMATION CENTERS: Territorial information centers in Beaver Creek, Carcross, Dawson City, Haines Junction, Watson Lake and Whitehorse are open 12 hours a day, mid-May to mid-September. The Whitehorse Visitor Reception Center also is open 9-noon and 1-4:30, in winter.

FURTHER INFORMATION FOR VISITORS:

Department of Tourism & Culture
P.O. Box 2703
Whitehorse, YT, Canada Y1A 2C6
(867) 667-5340

FISHING AND HUNTING REGULATIONS:

Yukon Government Fish and Wildlife Branch
P.O. Box 2703
Whitehorse, YT, Canada Y1A 2C6
(867) 667-5221

ALCOHOL CONSUMPTION: Legal age 19.

Yukon Territories Temperature Averages Maximum/Minimum (Celsius)
From the records of the National Weather Service

	JAN	FEB	MAR	APR	MAY	JUNE	JULY	AUG	SEPT	OCT	NOV	DEC
Watson Lake	-11	-12	-2	6	15	7	21	20	13	5	-9	-18
	-30	-25	-18	-7	1	3	8	6	2	-3	-17	-27
Whitehorse	-14	-9	-2	5	14	20	20	18	13	5	-5	-11
	-22	-19	-13	-6	1	6	7	6	3	-2	-12	-19

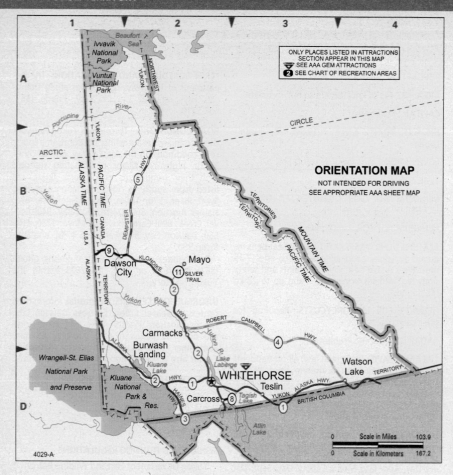

ORIENTATION MAP
NOT INTENDED FOR DRIVING
SEE APPROPRIATE AAA SHEET MAP

ONLY PLACES LISTED IN ATTRACTIONS
SECTION APPEAR IN THIS MAP
SEE AAA GEM ATTRACTIONS
2 SEE CHART OF RECREATION AREAS

4029-A

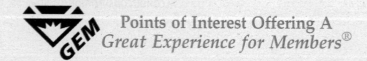

Points of Interest Offering A
Great Experience for Members®

Whitehorse (F-10)

YUKON BERINGIA INTERPRETIVE CENTRE—Life-size fossils
of woolly mammoths, giant beavers and scimitar cats as
well as First Nations exhibits are showcased in this centre
that depicts the Yukon Beringia from the ice age to the
present. See p. 278.

YUKON RIVER CRUISE—Narrated trips on the Yukon River
travel through Miles Canyon and pass the remains of a
wooden tramway, the site of Canyon City and the ruins of
the Camp McCrae laundry. See p. 278.

Points of Interest

Map coordinates relate to the map on page 272.

BURWASH LANDING (C-2)

In 1904, a year after gold was discovered in Fourth of July Creek, Morley Bones staked a discovery claim on Burwash Creek. Soon after the small community of Burwash sprang up around a trading post. Burwash Landing, with an airstrip and a resort, lies between the Kluane Lake and Kluane Game Sanctuary.

KLUANE MUSEUM OF NATURAL HISTORY is at Historic Mile 1093 on the Alaska Hwy. The museum contains a nature and taxidermy display, handmade First Nations crafts and costumes, a mineral and fossil collection and a large topographical map of the surrounding area. Allow 1 hour minimum. Daily 9-8, June-Aug.; 10-6, May 15-31 and Sept. 1-15. Admission $4.25; over 60, $3.50; ages 6-16, $2.25; family rate $9.75. Phone (867) 841-5561.

CARCROSS (D-2) pop. 152

Carcross, 74 kilometres (46 mi.) from Whitehorse on the S. Klondike Hwy., originally was called Caribou Crossing. The town's current name is a combination of the first syllable of each word. From this settlement George Carmack's party set out on the prospecting trip that began the gold rush of 1898. On July 29, 1900, the railroad's final spike was driven, marking the completion of the White Pass and Yukon Route, which linked Alaska and the Yukon Territory by rail.

Recalling the feverish gold rush days is the Caribou Hotel, regarded as the Yukon's oldest operating hotel, which opened in 1898 to accommodate gold seekers heading north.

Near the town's train depot is the "Duchess," a tiny locomotive that ran the 6.4-kilometre (4-mi.) line from Taku Arm on Tagish Lake to Atlin Lake in the early 1900s. It supposedly was the shortest and most expensive rail trip in the world—one-way fare was $2—and passengers had to sit on their baggage in the cramped compartment.

The Carcross Visitor Reception Centre on the Klondike Hwy. at Km-post 106 is in the historic White Pass and Yukon Route train depot. The center provides extensive information about Carcross— one of the Yukon's most picturesque areas; phone (867) 821-4431.

Just north of town along the Klondike Hwy. lies the Carcross Desert, considered the smallest desert in the world. The 260-hectare (650-acre) area was created by retreating glaciers that left a sandy lake bottom; today winds from Lake Bennett constantly shift the sand, limiting vegetation to such plants as kinnikinnick and lodgepole pine.

SAVE **CARIBOU CROSSING TRADING POST** is 3.2 km (2 mi.) n. on S. Klondike Hwy. to Km-post 109. At this 12-hectare (30-acre) park, visitors can view mounted animals in dioramas representing their natural habitats, explore an outdoor heritage area depicting the region's frontier days and climb to a lookout that provides a view of Lake Bennett, Carcross and surrounding mountains. The park includes a nature trail, petting farm and miniature golf.

Food is available. Allow 1 hour, 30 minutes minimum. Daily 9-5, mid-May to mid-Sept. Admission $7; ages 3-12, $4.50. Miniature golf tickets $4; ages 3-12, $2.50. Phone (867) 821-4055.

CARMACKS (C-2) pop. 500

Carmacks, named for George Washington Carmack, one of the discoverers of gold in the Klondike, was an important stopover point on the Overland Trail that linked Whitehorse and Dawson City before the Klondike Hwy. was built. Items from early travelers still can be found along the trail near town.

About 22 kilometres (14 mi.) north of Carmacks are the Five Fingers Rapids, which claimed the lives of many prospectors trying to reach Dawson City by way of the Yukon River.

DAWSON CITY (C-1) pop. 1,251

Dawson City was the center of the excitement caused by one of the world's most fabulous gold strikes. On Aug. 16, 1896, George Washington Carmack and his companions Skookum Jim and Dawson Charlie made the first strike on Bonanza Creek, a tributary of the Klondike River.

In the summer of 1897 miners from Dawson City arrived in Seattle and San Francisco with nearly $2 million as they carried word of the discovery to the United States, then in the midst of a depression. By the next spring more than 60,000 men and women had passed through Seattle and Alaska's Chilkoot and White passes on their way to the Klondike.

The Dawson settlement, which sprang up at the confluence of the Yukon and Klondike rivers, became a thriving city with some 30,000 inhabitants by the summer of 1898, making it the largest city west of Winnipeg and north of San Francisco.

All the creeks in the area had been staked by the spring of 1899. Hillside and bench claims were made, some yielding rich gold finds in the White Channel gravels. Between 1896 and 1904 Klondike creeks brought in more than $100 million in gold.

This period of Dawson City's history has been preserved by Rex Beach, Jack London, Robert W. Service and others who wrote colorful tales of personal experiences.

It was in Dawson City that London became acquainted with a large dog that he named Buck, a cross between a St. Bernard and a German shepherd that became the prototype for the dog in "Call of the Wild." Daily readings from the works of Jack London are given 10-6, mid-May to mid-Sept. at his cabin on Eighth Avenue.

Many historic buildings, some still in use, survive from the days when Dawson City was the gold capital of the world. The Midnight Sun and Eldorado hotels conjure memories of a lively past.

Harrington's Store, Princess Street and Third Avenue, has a free photographic exhibit titled "Dawson as They Saw It." The 1901 Post Office, King Street and Third Avenue, offers a visitor information exhibit; phone (867) 993-7200. Both are open June through September.

The SS *Keno*, in dry-dock on First Avenue between King and Queen streets, is typical of the stern-wheelers of the gold rush era. Built in 1922, it was one of the last riverboats to run between Dawson City and Whitehorse.

The summit of Midnight Dome, 7 kilometres (4 mi.) southeast via Front Street, offers a panorama of Dawson City, the Yukon and Klondike rivers and the gold fields. Many Dawson City pioneers are buried in cemeteries on the hillsides flanking the dome.

South on Bonanza Creek Road is the Discovery Claim, which started the great rush. Panning for gold is possible at several locations along the Klondike Hwy.: Claim 33, Guggieville RV Park, Dawson City RV Park, Gold Bottom Mines and Eureka Mines.

Yukon Queen River Cruises has one-way and round-trip cruises to Eagle, Alaska; for schedule and information phone (867) 993-5599.

The Dawson City Visitor Reception Centre features exhibits about Klondike history as well as offers walking tours around the city. The center is open daily 8-8, mid-May to late Sept.

Dawson City Visitor Reception Centre: Front and King streets, Dawson City, YT, Canada Y0B 1G0; phone (867) 993-5566.

Self-guiding tours: A brochure describing walking tours of historic sites is available at the visitor reception center.

BONANZA CREEK DISCOVERY CLAIM is 14.8 km (9.3 mi.) s. on Bonanza Creek Rd. Signs portray the story of gold mining along this famous creek. Discovery Claim #1 is the spot where gold first was discovered. A historical marker at Km-post 17.71 identifies the town of Grand Forks, which had a population of 5,000 during its prime. Dredge #4 at Km-post 12.3 was used to recover gold from creekbeds.

A trailer with exhibits about the dredge is open daily 9-5, mid-June to mid-Sept. Free. Phone (867) 993-7200.

DAWSON CITY MUSEUM is on Fifth Ave. Gold rush items are displayed at the museum, which contains a smithy, a general store, an old miner's cabin, a saloon and Chilkoot Hall. First Nations artifacts and an outdoor transportation exhibit with locomotives from the Klondike Mines railway also are featured. Daily 10-6, June 1-Labour Day; limited hours in May and day after Labour Day-Sept. 30. Admission $7, senior citizens and students with ID $5, family rate $16. Phone (867) 993-5291.

GOLD CITY TOURS departs from Front St., across from the SS *Keno*. Tours of Dawson and local gold fields include panning for gold. The 3.5-hour bus tours depart daily at 1, mid-May to mid-Sept. The 1.5-hour Midnight Dome Tour departs daily at 10 p.m. Fare for 3.5-hour tour $40. Midnight Dome Tour $15. Reservations are required. AX, CB, DC, MC, VI. Phone (867) 993-5175.

ROBERT SERVICE CABIN is 1 blk. s. of Church St. on Eighth Ave. The restored 1898 log cabin of the Bard of the Yukon is furnished as it was 1909-12 when Service was a resident and many of his ballads and poems. Guided tours are available. Allow 30 minutes minimum. Daily 10-noon and 1-4:30, end of May to mid-Sept. Admission $5, children free. Rates may vary; phone ahead to confirm. Phone (867) 993-7200.

CASINOS

- **Diamond Tooth Gertie's Gambling Hall,** Queen St. and Fourth Ave. Daily 7 p.m.-2 a.m., May 12-Sept. 17 (opens at 2 p.m. Sat.-Sun., mid-June through Labour Day). Phone (867) 993-5575.

IVVAVIK NATIONAL PARK (A-1)

Ivvavik National Park is in the extreme northwestern corner of the Yukon. Virtually untouched by humans, the Arctic wilderness is of great geologic interest; it is one of the few regions in Canada that contains areas never covered by glaciers.

Every spring it becomes the calving grounds of porcupine caribous that arrive after a long, difficult migration from the south and east. The park provides an important nesting area for North American waterfowl and a home to grizzly, black and polar bears. The only access to the park is by air.

KLUANE NATIONAL PARK AND RESERVE (D-1)

Elevations in the park range from 400 metres (1,300 ft.) in the Alsek River to 5,959 metres (19,545 ft.) at Mount Logan. Refer to CAA/AAA maps for additional elevation information.

Kluane (kloo-AH-nee) National Park and Reserve is bounded by the Haines (Hwy. 3) and Alaska (Hwy. 1) hwys. along its northeastern border. The park covers 22,015 square kilometres (8,500 sq. mi.) of wilderness.

Near its southeastern boundary was the Dalton Trail, a route used during the Klondike Rush of 1898. In 1904 a North West Mounted Police post was established on the south shore of Kluane Lake, and in 1942 the lake became a meeting place for crews building the Alaska Hwy.

During the building of the highway the wilderness area was preserved as the Kluane Game Sanctuary. In 1979 Kluane was declared a World Heritage Site for its impressive topographical features and its massive nonpolar ice fields.

The park is dominated by the Saint Elias Mountains, which run through the park in a southeasterly direction. Mount Logan, Canada's highest peak at 5,959 metres (19,545 ft.), and Mount St. Elias at 5,489 metres (18,008 ft.) dominate the range. The Saint Elias Mountains hold extensive ice fields that date from the last ice age and constitute the largest nonpolar glacier systems in the world.

An extensive network of glaciers, together with the ice fields, covers more than half of the park's area throughout the year. Notable are the Steele Glacier, which moves sporadically at a relatively rapid rate, and the Kaskawulsh and Lowell glaciers, which are flanked by moraines—accumulations of earth and stones carried and deposited by the glaciers. The movement and debris of the glaciers contribute to such park features as sand dunes and dust storms.

The park has a variety of flora. Such coniferous species as white spruce characterize the boreal forest of the river valleys. Lichens, dwarf birch trees and low shrubs distinguish the tundra uplands in the northern section, and colorful Arctic flowers cling to the crevices and ledges of the mountains. In the southeastern section where the Pacific Ocean's moderating influence is felt in the climate, the vegetation is more luxuriant.

Arctic grayling, lake trout, northern pike and kokanee salmon are found in lakes and streams. Other park species include golden eagles, ptarmigans, Dall sheep, mountain goats, caribou, moose and wolves. Kluane has one of the largest populations of grizzly bears and subspecies of moose in the world.

General Information and Activities

The park is open all year, but access may be limited in the winter, depending on weather conditions. The Kluane National Park and Reserve headquarters, at Km-post 1635 in Haines Junction, is open year-round. The Sheep Mountain Visitor Centre at Km-post 1707 is open mid-May to early September.

The park primarily is a wilderness area, so there are no roads except on the eastern and northern perimeters, traversed by Hwy. 3 and Hwy. 1, respectively. Hiking is the most popular activity in the park, with approximately 250 kilometres (155 mi.) of hiking trails. Hiking is possible along a few old mining roads, creekside paths and marked trails. Some trails are self-guiding. All overnight hikers must register at one of the information centers or with a park warden before and after hikes.

Sourdoughs and Cheechakos

To distinguish between the fortune seekers who entered the Yukon Territory during the 1897-98 Klondike Gold Rush, veterans of the '49 California Rush labeled the seasoned arrivals "Sourdoughs" and the greenhorns "Cheechakos" (CHE-cha-kos). Named after the staple bread of the frontier, Sourdoughs were prospectors who had survived a Yukon winter. The term Cheechako came from the Chinook Indian word for "new to come."

Once off the steamer at Skagway, Alaska, these newcomers had to transport thousands of pounds of survival gear—the Northwest

© PhotoDisc

Mounted Police wisely required each prospector to bring a year's supply of food—over the precipitous Chilkoot Pass. After that they had to float their unwieldy cargo over the treacherous rapids of the Yukon River.

More obstacles awaited the greenhorns at the gold sites. By the time the Cheechakos arrived, much of the gold field already was depleted or staked. To make things worse, Cheechakos were often directed to the hills by unscrupulous Sourdoughs who knew the gold nuggets tended to settle in creek beds. Nonetheless, some did tap into a channel of an ancient gold-bearing stream on Cheechako Hill.

Those who had survived to see the ice melt were dubbed Sourdoughs; the graveyards of those who had not succeeded dotted the route all the way back to Skagway. As one cynical Sourdough put it: "We were SOUR on the Yukon and didn't have enough DOUGH to get out."

Mountain climbing should be done only by well-trained climbers, who must obtain a climbing permit and register with the Warden Service before and after climbs.

Other recreational pursuits include fishing, backpacking, boating, cross-country skiing and ice fishing. All anglers within the park must obtain a national park fishing license, available at the park visitor centers and from area stores and lodges. Camping, fishing and picnic facilities are available at Kathleen Lake, 27 kilometres (17 mi.) south of Haines Junction.

During the summer the Kluane National Park and Reserve headquarters sponsors interpretive activities including campfire talks and guided walks. A relief map and an interactive computer touch screen are available. Information about recreational opportunities, sightseeing by small aircraft and other guided tours is available.

ADMISSION to the park is free.

PETS are permitted in the park if kept on a leash, but visitors are advised not to bring them.

ADDRESS inquiries about the park to Kluane National Park and Reserve, P.O. Box 5495, Haines Junction, YT, Canada Y0B 1L0; phone (867) 634-7250.

MAYO (C-2) pop. 400

Mayo lies 53 kilometres (33 mi.) northeast of the Klondike Hwy. at the confluence of the Stewart and Mayo rivers. Both the town and the river were named for the pioneer prospector and trader Alfred Mayo. In the early 1900s Mayo Landing became a shipping point for the gold and silver that was mined farther north in Elsa.

Mayo Lake to the northeast provides excellent fishing. The summit of nearby 1,890-metre (6,200-ft.) Keno Mountain provides a scenic view of the mining village of Keno. This once bustling community has a mining museum.

Further details about the silver mining towns of Mayo, Elsa and Keno, known collectively as the Silver Trail, are available at the information booth at Stewart Crossing.

BINET HOUSE INTERPRETIVE CENTRE is at jct. 2nd Ave. and Centre St. The two-story building features exhibits that include a collection of historic photographs, artifacts and a 3-D relief map of the region identifying the location of mineral deposits. Guided tours are available. Picnicking is permitted. Allow 30 minutes minimum. Daily 10-6, June-Aug. Admission $2, under 12 free. Phone (867) 996-2926.

TESLIN (D-3) pop. 189

The Nisutlin Bay Bridge, the longest water span on the Alaska Hwy., crosses an arm of Teslin Lake at Teslin. The highway parallels the 116-kilometre (72-mi.) lake for about 55 kilometres (34 mi.), providing a scenic drive bordered on both sides by mountains. The area is noted for abundant game, and the fjord-like lake provides excellent fishing. The economy of the community depends heavily on hunting, fishing and trapping.

Teslin has one of the largest First Nations populations in the Yukon, with many of its residents descended from the coastal Tlingit tribe. The original First Nations settlement is reached by a loop road. In the old village are Catholic and Anglican missions as well as a Royal Canadian Mounted Police station.

SAVE **GEORGE JOHNSTON MUSEUM** is 1 km (.6 mi.) w. of the Alaska Hwy. at Km-post 296. George Johnston, a Tlingit Indian, recorded his culture through his camera. A selection of Johnston's work, displays of the Tlingit tribe's rich and colorful history, Tlingit dancing costumes and pioneer items are exhibited. Daily 9-5, mid-May through Aug. 31. Admission $5; over 60 and college students with ID $4; ages 6-17, $3; family rate $15. Phone (867) 390-2550.

TESLIN TLINGIT HERITAGE CENTRE is 4 km (2.5 mi.) w. on Hwy. 1. Totem poles, hand-carved masks, crafts, artifacts and photographs relay the life and culture of the Teslin Tlingit people. Picnicking is permitted. Allow 30 minutes minimum. Mon.-Sat. 9-5, Sun. 11-5, June-Aug. Admission $5; over 54 and students with ID $4; ages 6-17, $3; family rate $15. MC, VI. Phone (867) 390-2532.

WATSON LAKE (D-4) pop. 1,000

At Km-post 1016.8 on the Alaska Hwy., Watson Lake is an important transportation, distribution and communication center for the southern Yukon. The town was named for Frank Watson, a trapper from England who settled there in 1898.

Watson Lake is known for the signpost collection that was begun by a homesick soldier during construction of the Alaska Hwy. in 1942. Over the years, tourists have continued adding signs showing the names of their hometowns, and now the collection includes more than 50,000 signs.

From Watson Lake the historic Robert Campbell Hwy. loops north and west through the wilderness of southeastern Yukon.

NORTHERN LIGHTS CENTRE is at 807 Frank Tr. Images of the aurora borealis are displayed in a planetarium-like dome theater. Narration details the myths and science behind the luminous phenomena. Allow 1 hour minimum. Daily 12:30-9:30, mid-May to mid-Sept. Admission $10; over 65 and students with ID $9; ages 6-12, $6; family rate (two adults and three children) $24. AX, MC, VI. Phone (867) 536-7827.

WATSON LAKE VISITOR RECEPTION CENTRE is at jct. Alaska and Robert Campbell hwys. A DVD presentation explains the history and hardship surrounding the construction of the Alaska Hwy. Allow 30 minutes minimum. Daily 8-8, mid-May to late Sept. Free. Phone (867) 536-7469.

WHITEHORSE (D-2)
pop. 19,058, elev. 689 m/2,260'

Whitehorse began during the Klondike gold rush when thousands of prospectors journeyed by ship to Skagway, Alaska, then climbed the rugged mountain passes to the headwaters of the Yukon River. They constructed nearly anything floatable for the more than 900-kilometre (559-mi.) trip to Dawson City via Whitehorse. Above Whitehorse many prospectors died in the dangerous Whitehorse Rapids.

When stern-wheeler service to Dawson became available, the trip from Whitehorse took 2.5 days; the return trip against the current took 5 days. The first rails of the White Pass and Yukon Route railway were laid at Skagway in May 1898, and the line to Whitehorse opened in July 1900.

During World War II Canadian and United States Army personnel building the Alaska Hwy. moved to Whitehorse, which became the capital of the Yukon Territory in 1953.

Evolving into the transportation, communication and distribution center of the Yukon, Whitehorse also became the territorial headquarters of the Royal Canadian Mounted Police as well as the heart of the territorial government and federal departments.

Attractions on a much larger scale include Lake Laberge, the setting for Robert W. Service's "The Cremation of Sam McGee," and the Robert Lowe Suspension Bridge across Miles Canyon.

The Whitehorse Power Dam features one of the world's longest wooden fish ladders; the salmon, running in late July or early August, can be seen from viewing windows. Lake Schwatka, impounded by the power dam, was named after Frederick Schwatka, the first U.S. army lieutenant to navigate the entire length of the Yukon River.

Visible from the Alaska Hwy., 24 kilometres (15 mi.) south of Whitehorse, is Marsh Lake Lock, the northernmost lock in the Western Hemisphere. It is used by small craft navigating the upper Yukon River.

Several guided tours of the town and surrounding area are available. [SAVE] Gray Line/Yukon offers guided bus tours of Whitehorse and Miles Canyon as well as cruises from Lake Schwatka through Miles Canyon. Several companies provide Yukon River cruises, guided hikes, and canoe, boat and raft trips on area rivers. The Yukon Conservation Society gives guided nature walks in the summer.

Whitehorse Visitor Reception Centre, on 2nd Avenue and Hanson Street, features exhibits and audiovisual presentations about the Yukon. The center is open daily 8-8, mid-May to late Sept.; Mon.-Fri. 9-noon and 1-4:30, rest of year. Phone (867) 667-3084.

Tourism & Culture, Government of Yukon: P.O. Box 2703, Whitehorse, YT, Canada Y1A 2C6; phone (867) 667-5036.

Self-guiding tours: Books detailing walking tours are available for $8.95 plus postage from the Yukon Historical and Museums Association, 3126 Third Ave., P.O. Box 4357, Whitehorse, YT, Canada Y1A 3T5; phone (867) 667-4704.

"FRANTIC FOLLIES" is presented in the Village Square room of the Westmark Whitehorse Hotel at 201 Wood St. The Gay '90s vaudeville revue has a cast of professional actors, dancers and musicians and recaptures the spirit and enthusiasm of the Klondike gold rush. The 1.7-hour family-style show includes music, comedy, magic, dancing and the poetry of Robert W. Service, Bard of the Yukon.

Performances are given nightly at 7 and 9:15, June 14-July 25; at 8:30, May 26-June 13 and June 26-Sept. 5. Phone to verify schedule. Admission $19; under 12, $9.50. Phone (867) 668-2042.

[SAVE] **THE GRAY LINE WHITEHORSE CITY TOUR** leaves from the Westmark Whitehorse Hotel, 201 Wood St. The narrated tour acquaints visitors with the city by calling upon such landmarks as the stern-wheeler SS *Klondike II*, the Whitehorse Power Dam and the Miles Canyon lookout. Other places of interest include museums, the longest wooden fish ladder in North America and a log skyscraper. Bus tours depart daily at 9, May 10-Sept. 15. Fare $23; ages 1-12, $11.50. Phone (867) 668-3225.

[SAVE] **MACBRIDE MUSEUM** is at 1124 First Ave. The museum offers an in-depth look at the Yukon heritage with exhibits ranging from prehistoric mammals to the 1898 gold rush. Displays include Sam McGee's 1899 cabin, First Nations relics and sample minerals of the territory. On the grounds are an old steam locomotive, a sleigh wagon and a giant nugget of copper weighing about 1,170 kilograms (2,580 lbs.).

Daily 10-6, June 1-Labour Day; daily noon-4, Apr.-May; Mon.-Sat. 10-4, day after Labour Day-Sept. 30; Thurs.-Sat. noon-4, rest of year. Admission $5; over 49, $4.50; ages 6-12, $3.50. Phone (867) 667-2709.

OLD LOG CHURCH MUSEUM is at Third Ave. and Elliott St. Built in 1900, the church houses many missionary, First Nations and Inuit items as well as an audiovisual presentation about the history of the Anglican church in the Yukon. Guided tours are available. Allow 30 minutes minimum. Mon.-Sat. 9-5, late May-Aug. 31. Admission $2.50; over 55 and students with ID $2; ages 6-12, $1; family rate $6. Phone (867) 668-2555.

THE SS *KLONDIKE II* NATIONAL HISTORIC SITE is next to the river at Second Ave. and Robert Campbell Bridge. One of the largest stern-wheelers on the Yukon River, the *Klondike II* ran its route 1937-55. The original *Klondike* struck a reef in 1936; a replacement was built the same year.

Tours are available. A videotape, "In the Days of the Riverboat," is presented prior to each tour. Allow 30 minutes minimum. Daily 9-6, mid-June to mid-Sept. Last tour begins 30 minutes before closing. Admission $5; over 60, $4.50; under 18, $3;

family rate (two adults and six children under 18) $15. Phone (867) 667-4511.

TAKHINI HOT SPRINGS is 10 km (6 mi.) w. off Klondike Hwy. at Km-post 10. Natural mineral hot spring pools are maintained at 36 degrees C (96.8 degrees F) for year-round swimming. Other activities include horseback riding, hiking, camping and cross-country skiing. Pool open daily 8 a.m.-10 p.m., July 1 through mid-Sept. Admission $7; ages 13-18, $6.50; ages 6-12, $5.25; over 65, $5.50. Phone (867) 633-2706.

WHITEHORSE FISHWAY is at the end of Nisutlin Dr. via Lewes Blvd. Said to be the longest wooden fish ladder in the world, the fishway enables chinook salmon and other fish to bypass the Whitehorse Rapids Dam during their 3,000-kilometre (1,860-mi.) migration between the Bering Sea and their freshwater spawning grounds in southern Yukon. Underwater windows provide a close-up view of the migrating fish. Allow 30 minutes minimum. Daily 9-9, late July-early Sept. Donations. Phone (867) 633-5965.

YUKON ARTS CENTRE is at 80 Range Rd. An art gallery features contemporary revolving exhibits and a theater presents concerts, dramas and musicals throughout the year. Phone for schedules and show information. Allow 1 hour minimum. Mon.-Fri. 11-5, Sat.-Sun. noon-5; closed major holidays. Donations. Phone (867) 667-8578.

YUKON BERINGIA INTERPRETIVE CENTRE is 2 km (1.2 mi.) e. on the Alaska Hwy. to Km-post 1473 (mi. 914) by Whitehorse Airport. An area of the Yukon, Alaska and Siberia never covered by glaciers during the ice age, Beringia is believed to be the route traveled by the first people who entered the Americas from Asia.

Fossils, life-size animal and First Nation exhibits, interactive computer kiosks, and murals and dioramas of Beringia's landscape illustrate the area's history, geographical events and culture, from the ice age to the present. Highlights include fossils of woolly mammoths, scimitar cats, giant beavers, short-faced bears and steppe bison. A diorama depicts the Bluefish Caves, an important North American archeological site.

Daily 8:30-7, May-Sept.; Mon.-Sat. by appointment and Sun. 1-5, rest of year. Admission $6; over 55, $5; family rate $25. Combination ticket with Yukon Transportation Museum $9. MC, VI. Phone (867) 667-8855 or (800) 661-0408.

YUKON HISTORICAL AND MUSEUMS ASSOCIATION GUIDED TOURS depart from the Donnenworth House, 3126 Third Ave. Guides in period costume describe the architecture, history and local color of Whitehorse on 1-hour walking tours. Historic sights include the 1901 telegraph office, the log church and rectory, the city fire station, the Klondike Airways building, the Royal Canadian Mounted Police compound, the Mast house and Sam McGee's cabin.

Self-guiding walking tour brochures also are available. Allow 1 hour minimum. Tours depart Mon.-Sat. at 9, 11, 1 and 3, June-Aug. Fee $2, under 12 free. Self-guiding walking tour brochure $8.95. Phone (867) 667-4704.

YUKON RIVER CRUISE docks 3.2 km (2 mi.) s. of downtown at 68 Miles Canyon Rd. Two-hour narrated excursions of the Yukon River through Miles Canyon are offered aboard the MV *Schwatka*. The boat passes the remains of a wooden tramway built to carry freight around the rapids, the site of Canyon City and the ruins of the Camp McCrae laundry, which served 30,000 troops stationed nearby during the construction of the Alaska Hwy.

Gray Line/Yukon provides shuttle service to the departure site from downtown hotels. Cruises depart daily at 2 and 7, in July; at 2 in June and Aug. Hours may vary; phone ahead. Shuttle departs hotels about 30 minutes before cruise time. Cruise fare $25. A fee is charged for shuttle. Fare may vary; phone ahead. Phone (867) 668-4716 for reservations or (867) 668-3225 for the shuttle service.

YUKON TRANSPORTATION MUSEUM is off Alaska Hwy. at Km-post 1475.7 by Whitehorse Airport. Exhibits highlight various modes of transportation, including snowshoes, dog sleds, stage coaches, boats, aircraft and military vehicles used during the construction of the Alaska Hwy. The *Queen of the Yukon*, the sister plane of Charles A. Lindbergh's *Spirit of St. Louis*, also is displayed.

Allow 30 minutes minimum. Daily 10-6, mid-May to mid-Sept. Hours may vary; phone ahead. Admission $6; over 55, $5; students ages 13-17 with ID $4; ages 6-12, $3. Phone (867) 668-4792.

RECREATIONAL ACTIVITIES

White-water Rafting

- **Tatshenshini Expeditions**, 1602 Alder St., Whitehorse, YT, Canada Y1A 3W8. Daily mid-June to early Sept. Phone (867) 633-2742.

Alaska

Batter-up at Midnight

Fairbanks hosts late-night baseball as the Arctic Circle is blanketed with continuous sunshine

Dancing Northern Lights

Brilliant bands of yellow, green and red quietly jump across night skies

"The Mountain"

Mount McKinley, North America's tallest mountain, towers over Denali National Park

Seward's Folly

Bought at just 2 cents per acre, Alaska surprised the world with its wealth of natural resources

Pacific Ring of Fire

Erupting volcanoes are commonplace in the Valley of Ten Thousand Smokes

Lake Clark National Park and Preserve
© Kennan Ward imagestate

sounds of The Great Land

Sitka / © Ernest Manewal / SuperStock

W hile the sights of The Last Frontier can be described as splendid, its sounds are no less spectacular.

A breathy blow accompanied by a geyserlike spray of seawater alerts you to the presence of a humpback whale. It's hard to ignore the loud, slapping sound associated with tail lobbing or breaching—when a whale will throw itself completely out of the water and smack the sea upon return—and it's usually followed by hoots and hollers from observers.

Sea lions make music all their own. Their squawky barking can be heard as you approach a rock packed with the huge creatures.

Drop anchor in ice-filled waters to experience the most spectacular sounds:

A popping noise similar to a firecracker signals a calving, when ice separates from a glacier. As chunks detach and fall, a thunderous roar echoes against the mountains, followed by a crash as they hit the sea. The show ends with the soft hiss of settling water.

Alaskan sounds identify the state's history and culture: Drumbeats, clapping, rattle-shaking, foot-tapping and rhythmic chanting resonate from native performances.

A sharp cry of "Mush!" or "All right!" from a musher gets a team of sled dogs moving; a command of "Come gee!" alerts the huskies to a right turn.

And just when a hush falls over The Great Land, the low hum of a floatplane is heard from the clouds, ready to take you to another adventure.

Totem poles—slender cedar logs with intricately carved and brightly painted bears, eagles, fish, whales, ravens or frogs—are true artistic works representing the history and customs of native Alaskans. Features of these poles give insight to the blessings of the 49th state.

When visiting Alaska, a stop at a totem pole park should be high on your list of things to do. To get the full effect, choose a tall, colorful totem and stand about 2 feet from it. After admiring the details, look up. Your first impression? Massive. At 85 feet tall and too big to hug, you may have to step back just to be able to catch a glimpse of the figure at the top of the pole. A glance at an Alaska state map also may elicit amazement—it's *huge*, and there's much to see and do.

Natives didn't call this state *Alyeska*—the Great Land—for nothing. It looms larger than life. There are approximately 3 million lakes, 3,000 rivers, 1,800 islands and 100,000 glaciers in Alaska's 586,000 square miles of untamed wilderness. And if that isn't enough, nine national parks and preserves and two expansive national forests total about 66 million acres of undisturbed land. Don't be upset when you find that little of this grandiose scenery fits nicely into your camera lens.

Tales from The Last Frontier

When examined in sequence, the array of symbolic figures on totem poles describe native tales. Likewise, Alaska's diversity is illustrated through its distinct natural features, which leave most anyone speechless. The state is home to towering Mount McKinley—so high that it's cloaked in clouds most of the time. Long, bright days are typical during the summer solstice, when the sun accompanies your every move and never completely disappears.

Options for excitement in The Land of the Midnight Sun seem endless. You can walk on an ice field and feel the crunch of ice under your boots; explore muted, willow-covered desert tundra; peer over chunky glaciers and sweeping mountain ranges from the seat of a helicopter; gaze at a sky painted with watercolored northern lights; enjoy a ride on a boat navigating through blue-green waters packed with bobbing icebergs; marvel at 25-foot-tall sand dunes; or board a bush plane to catch a glimpse of steam from an active volcano.

© Corbis

U.S. Secretary of State William H. Seward purchases Alaska from Russia for less than 2 cents per acre; the unpopular deal becomes known as "Seward's Folly."

1867

Russian explorer Vitus Bering, sent by Peter the Great to explore the North Pacific, is the first European to set foot on Alaskan soil.

1725

A submarine cable links Seattle to Sitka and Sitka to Valdez, increasing communication between Alaska and the rest of the world.

1903

1880

"Seward's Folly" becomes a gold mine as vast deposits of precious metals are discovered in Juneau, followed by discoveries in Skagway in 1897, Nome in 1898 and Fairbanks in 1903.

Alaska Historical Timeline

© Natali Fobes/Corbis

1942

Japan attacks Dutch Harbour and consequently occupies the Aleutian Islands for nearly a year during World War II.

Tribe members, ingenious at adapting to their variable and sometimes hostile surroundings, made the most of the state's natural offerings, which included the creatures portrayed in their art.

Salmon and orcas are just a couple of animals that appear on totems. Used for sustenance, they were often depicted in oral tales; today animals remain the focus of many pictures and the subjects of travelogues. Visitors relish the opportunity to snap a photograph of a moose cow nibbling grass alongside her twins or grizzly cubs wrestling under the protective watch of mama bear.

Affluent Alaska

For many residents Alaska's riches are liquid: The creation of the Trans-Alaska Pipeline made it possible to transport crude oil almost 800 miles from Prudhoe Bay south to Valdez. The pipeline, an amazing engineering feat crossing three mountain ranges and three fault lines, is able to withstand an earthquake measuring up to 8.5 on the Richter scale as well as temperatures as low as minus 80 F.

Oil isn't Alaska's only rich resource. Discoveries of gold in Fairbanks, Fort Yukon, Juneau, Nome, Skagway and Wrangell lured prospectors from the "Lower 48" to seek their fortune. Visit abandoned gold dredges, camps and mines scattered throughout the state and imagine the fervor that once pervaded these sites, many of which now serve as attractions.

And there was more money to be made. Russian trappers came in search of valuable sea otter pelts, placing the term "fur trade" in Alaskan history books. The first capital of Russian America, Kodiak is graced by the onion-shaped domes of a historic Russian Orthodox church.

But Alaska's native tribes have left the most enduring impact. Traditions of the Aleut, Alutiiq, Athabascan, Cup'ik, Haida, Inupiaq, Tlingit, Tsimpshian and Yup'ik tribes can be appreciated through the acts of proud dancers and storytellers who keep family legacies alive. And artisans create soapstone and whalebone carvings, clothing adorned with intricate beading and baskets made from white birch bark—all coveted by visitors.

And totem poles, Alaska's silent, symbolic sentries, are just one reminder of what makes this land truly great.

A Good Friday earthquake destroys Anchorage, the Northwest Panhandle and Cook Inlet and sends a tsunami that wipes out the town of Valdez.
1964

International efforts to rescue two whales trapped in ice off the Barrow coast captures worldwide attention.
1988

© Galen Rowell/Corbis

One of the most devastating fires in state history destroys homes and property in the south central area near Big Lake.
1996

1968
"Black Gold" is discovered on Prudhoe Bay, spurring the construction of an 800-mile pipeline to transport the oil to an ice-free port at Valdez.

1989
The worst oil spill in U.S. history occurs when the *Exxon Valdez* spills some 11 million gallons of crude oil into Prince William Sound.

© Kennan Ward/Corbis

1977
Construction of the Trans-Alaska Pipeline is complete.

Recreation

In the Land of the Midnight Sun, it's a far better idea to set your itinerary by "sight" rather than time. While there are lots of activities to keep your blood pumping, most people visit Alaska for what there is to *see:* Chances for **wildlife viewing** are as plentiful as snowflakes during winter.

Oh, *Another* Bald Eagle?

This phrase, overheard on a small boat weaving through the watery inlets of the Tongass National Forest, testifies to the fact that Alaska has one of the largest bald eagle populations in the world. If you know what to look for—white dots on dark spruce tree branches—you may lose count of all these stately birds. They aren't difficult to spot at the Chilkat Bald Eagle Preserve near Haines; more than 3,500 visit the area to feed.

Many **wildlife cruises** headed for the Inside Passage depart from Juneau. Arm yourself with some good binoculars, a camera and a journal to record your sightings. Entries might include descriptions of huge, barking Stellar sea lions lounging on top of each other; Dall's porpoises frolicking in a boat's wake; Sitka black- or white-tailed deer sipping from a stream; soaring peregrine falcons; or furry otters doing the backstroke.

Black bears fish for salmon in Anan Creek near Wrangell Island, and the west coast of Prince of Wales Island (near Ketchikan) is a great spot for watching tufted puffins. It's no "fluke" to see a whale tail—humpbacks often make appearances in Prince William Sound, and wherever there's an iceberg, you can be sure to find harbor seals resting upon floating ice chunks.

Day cruises depart from Seward and Whittier to explore Prince William Sound and Kenai Fjords National Park, home to sea mammals galore. Along the Kenai Peninsula, both humpback and beluga whales perform aquatic acrobatics near the Turnagain Arm. Nearby, Dall sheep can be seen grazing atop steep cliffs that grace Cook Inlet.

Looking for bears? The Kodiak National Wildlife Refuge is home to some 3,000 Kodiak bears, and Brooks Camp in Katmai National Park and Preserve safeguards one of the world's largest brown bear populations.

Grizzlies as well as caribou and moose roam the desertlike tundra of Denali National Park; take a narrated bus tour into the interior to catch a glimpse. Near the park entrance, forest rangers give a demonstration of sled dogs at work, which is a howling good show.

Even better, hang on tight for a **sled ride** pulled by Iditarod huskies in Seward.

And a View, Too

Seward Highway, connecting Seward and Anchorage, is Alaska's most traveled scenic byway, and it's easy to see why. Snaking along the coast of Turnagain Arm, scenes from the road include the lush Kenai Mountains, saltwater bays, jagged ridges and green alpine meadows. **Rock climbers** dangle from cliffs between Potters Marsh and Bird Creek.

As a matter of fact, any activity in Alaska includes a magnificent view: Try **rafting** in Denali on the Nenana River Gorge or **canoeing** near Admiralty Island National Monument. **Kayakers** also enjoy the Sarkar Lake Canoe Route in Tongass National Forest. Winter options include **cross-country skiing, dog sledding** or **snowmobiling** on the Twin Ridge or Upper Twin ski trails in Tongass National Forest, or **downhill skiing** at Mount Alyeska in Girdwood.

Want to stand on a glacier? **Hikers** in Kenai Fjords National Park follow rangers on **nature walks** to a nearby ice field. For a bit of history, try **bicycling** or **walking** the first mile of the original Iditarod Trail, now a paved beach path in Seward. Horseshoe Lake Trail provides a leisurely walk through the woods of Denali National Park.

Floatplane or **helicopter sightseeing** is an excellent way to see glaciers, ice fields, mountain ranges, waterfalls, lakes or stark tundra. Nearly every city has **flightseeing** tour operators.

A **fishing** charter from one of various harbors is a good way to hook steelhead, grayling or rainbow trout. **Sport fishing** yields red snapper or cod—and Resurrection Bay (near Seward), Sitka and Wrangell are home to world-class halibut and salmon.

Recreational Activities

Throughout the TourBook, you may notice a Recreational Activities heading with bulleted listings of recreation-oriented establishments listed underneath. Similar operations also may be mentioned in Destination City recreation sections. Since normal AAA inspection criteria cannot be applied, these establishments are presented only for information. Age, height and weight restrictions may apply. Reservations often are recommended and sometimes are required. Addresses and/or phone numbers are provided so visitors can contact the attraction for additional information.

Fast Facts

POPULATION: 626,932.

AREA: 586,412 square miles, ranks 1st.

CAPITAL: Juneau.

HIGHEST POINT: 20,320 ft., Mount McKinley.

LOWEST POINT: Sea level, Pacific Ocean.

TIME ZONE(S): Alaska for most of the state; Hawaii-Aleutian for the extreme western portion of the Aleutian Islands. DST.

MINIMUM AGE FOR UNRESTRICTED DRIVER'S LICENSE: 16 years, 6 months.

SEAT BELT/CHILD RESTRAINT LAWS: Seat belts required for driver and passengers; child restraints required for under 4.

HELMETS FOR MOTORCYCLISTS: Required for driver under 18 and all passengers.

RADAR DETECTORS: Permitted.

FIREARMS LAWS: Vary by state and/or county. Contact the Division of State Troopers, Headquarters, 5700 E. Tudor Rd., Dept. P, Anchorage, AK 99507; phone (907) 269-5511.

HOLIDAYS: Jan. 1; Martin Luther King Jr. Day, Jan. (3rd Mon.); Presidents Day, Feb. (3rd Mon.); Seward's Day, Mar. (last Mon.); Memorial Day, May (last Mon.); July 4; Labor Day, Sept. (1st Mon.); Columbus Day, Oct. (2nd Mon.); Alaska Day, Oct. 18; Veterans Day, Nov. 11; Thanksgiving and Dec. 25.

TAXES: Alaska does not have a statewide sales tax, but cities and boroughs may levy a sales tax of up to 6 percent, plus special taxes on goods and services.

INFORMATION CENTERS: Tok Information Center, jct. SR 2 (Alaska Hwy.) and SR 1, provides general tourist literature as well as reports on highway and weather conditions. The center is open daily 8-7, early May to mid-Sept.

FURTHER INFORMATION FOR VISITORS:

> Alaska Travel Industry
> Association
> 2600 Cordova St., Suite 201
> Anchorage, AK 99501
> (907) 929-2200

FISHING AND HUNTING REGULATIONS:

> Alaska Department of Fish
> and Game
> P.O. Box 25526
> Juneau, AK 99802-5526
> (907) 465-4180 (Division of
> Sport Fishing)
> (907) 465-4190 (Division of
> Wildlife Conservation)

ALASKA FERRY INFORMATION:

> Alaska Marine Highway
> 6858 Glacier Hwy.
> Juneau, AK 99801
> (800) 642-0066

NATIONAL FOREST INFORMATION:

> U.S. Forest Service
> 8465 Old Dairy Rd.
> Juneau, AK 99801
> (907) 586-8800
> (877) 444-6777 (reservations)

NATIONAL PARK INFORMATION:

> Alaska Public Lands
> 250 Cushman St.
> Fairbanks, AK 99701
> (907) 456-0527

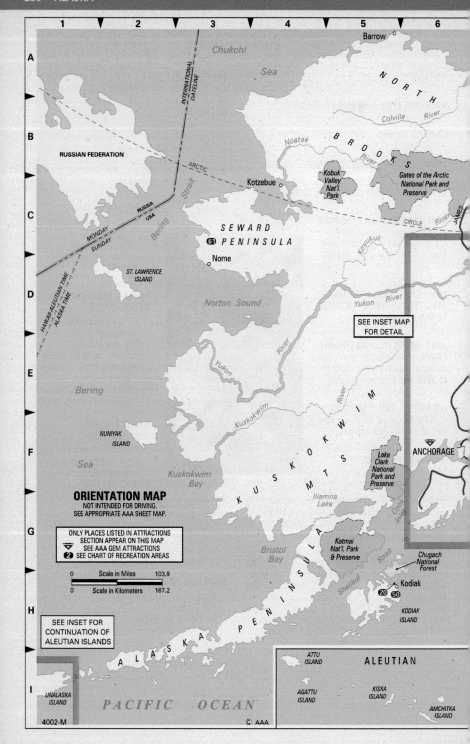

ORIENTATION MAP
NOT INTENDED FOR DRIVING.
SEE APPROPRIATE AAA SHEET MAP.

ONLY PLACES LISTED IN ATTRACTIONS
SECTION APPEAR ON THIS MAP.
SEE AAA GEM ATTRACTIONS
2 SEE CHART OF RECREATION AREAS

0   Scale in Miles   103.9
0   Scale in Kilometers   167.2

SEE INSET FOR
CONTINUATION OF
ALEUTIAN ISLANDS

4002-M

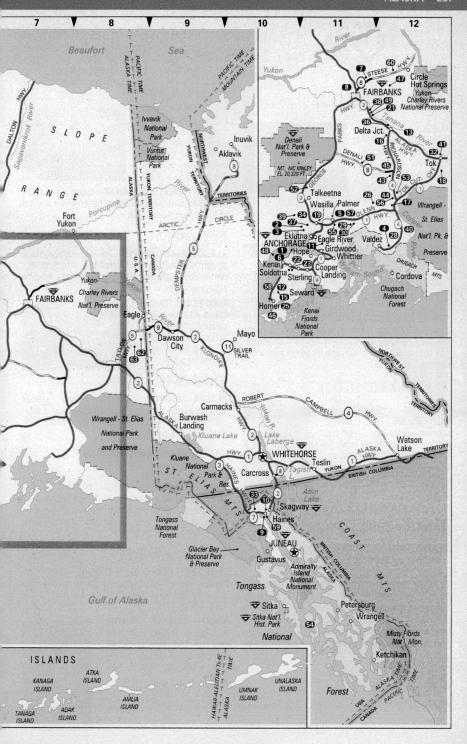

Points of Interest Offering A
Great Experience for Members®

Anchorage (C-10, F-6)

ALASKA NATIVE HERITAGE CENTER—Why did Tlingit tribe members carve totem poles? Learn about this and other traditions of native Alaskans. See p. 297.

ANCHORAGE MUSEUM OF HISTORY AND ART—The art, history and culture of the 49th state are presented in various exhibits. See p. 299.

Denali National Park & Preserve (B-10)

DENALI NATIONAL PARK & PRESERVE—Home of Mount McKinley, North America's highest peak, the park covers 9,375 square miles of native wildlife, active glaciers, snowcapped peaks and arctic tundra. See p. 303.

Fairbanks (B-11, D-7)

RIVERBOAT DISCOVERY—A trip aboard the sternwheeler *Discovery III* offers views of the Alaskan wilderness and an old Athabascan Indian village. See p. 308.

Juneau (G-10)

ALASKA STATE MUSEUM—Displays chronicle the state's history. See p. 315.

GLACIER GARDENS RAINFOREST ADVENTURE—Shuttles meander through a lush rain forest to the top of Thunder Mountain. See p. 317.

MACAULAY SALMON HATCHERY—More than 160 million salmon eggs hatch here annually. See p. 317.

MENDENHALL GLACIER—Trails on both sides of the 12-mile-long glacier offer spectacular views of the river of blue ice. See p. 317.

MOUNT ROBERTS TRAMWAY—Trams ascend the side of Mount Roberts to an observation station at 1,800 feet. See p. 318.

Seward (D-11)

ALASKA SEALIFE CENTER—Touch a starfish, stare at puffins and watch playful sea otters at this center dedicated to enriching the Alaska wildlife experience. See p. 327.

KENAI FJORDS TOURS—Cruises into the waters surrounding Kenai Fjords National Park offer views of marine life and active glaciers. See p. 328.

Sitka (H-10)

ALASKA RAPTOR CENTER—Success stories abound at this bald eagle rehabilitation and education center—just watch the raptors-in-residence. See p. 330.

Sitka National Historical Park (H-10)

SITKA NATIONAL HISTORICAL PARK—This 107-acre park commemorating the Tlingit Indian heritage contains a fort that was the site of the 1804 Battle of Sitka as well as the 1853 Russian Bishop's House. See p. 330.

Skagway (G-10)

KLONDIKE GOLD RUSH NATIONAL HISTORICAL PARK—Find out what happened after a gold nugget was found in Rabbit Creek on August 14, 1896. See p. 331.

WHITE PASS & YUKON ROUTE—A 3-hour narrated ride on this narrow-gauge railroad chugs across mountain rivers and chasms. See p. 331.

RECREATION AREAS

	MAP LOCATION	CAMPING	PICNICKING	HIKING TRAILS	BOATING	BOAT RAMP	BOAT RENTAL	FISHING	SWIMMING	PETS ON LEASH	BICYCLE TRAILS	WINTER SPORTS	VISITOR CENTER	LODGE/CABINS	FOOD SERVICE
NATIONAL PARKS AND PRESERVES *(See place listings)*															
Denali (B-10) 6,000,000 acres.		•	•	•				•		•		•	•	•	•
Gates of the Arctic (C-6) 8,500,000 acres.		•		•				•					•	•	
Glacier Bay (G-9) 3,283,168 acres.		•		•	•	•	•	•		•			•	•	•
Katmai (G-5) 4,159,097 acres.		•	•	•	•	•	•	•					•	•	•
Kenai Fjords (D-11) 600,000 acres.		•	•	•	•			•		•			•	•	
Kobuk Valley (C-5) 1,710,000 acres.		•		•	•			•							
Lake Clark (F-5) 4,000,000 acres.		•		•				•		•			•	•	
Wrangell-St. Elias (C-12, F-8) 3,000,000 acres.		•	•	•				•		•			•	•	
Yukon-Charley Rivers (B-12, D-8) 500,000 acres.		•		•				•					•		
NATIONAL FORESTS *(See place listings)*															
Chugach (D-12) 5,400,000 acres in south central Alaska.		•	•	•	•			•		•		•	•	•	
Tongass (G-9) 17,000,000 acres in southeastern Alaska.		•	•	•	•			•		•		•		•	
STATE															
Anchor River (D-10) 264 acres near Anchor Point on Sterling Hwy., Milepost 157.	**46**	•	•	•				•		•					
Bernice Lake (D-10) 152 acres 10 mi. n. of Kenai on N. Kenai Rd.	**1**	•	•		•	•		•	•	•					
Big Lake (North) (C-10) 19 acres 10 mi. w. of Wasilla on Parks Hwy., then 6 mi. s.w. on Big Lake Rd.	**2**	•	•		•	•		•	•	•		•			
Big Lake (South) (C-10) 16 acres 10 mi. w. of Wasilla on Parks Hwy., then 4 mi. s.w. on Big Lake Rd. and 2 mi. s.	**3**	•	•		•	•		•	•			•			
Bings Landing (D-10) 126 acres e. of Soldotna on Sterling Hwy., Milepost 79.	**48**	•	•	•	•			•		•					
Birch Lake (B-12) 191 acres n.e. of Delta Junction on Richardson Hwy., Milepost 305.5.	**49**	•			•	•		•	•						
Blueberry Lake (C-12) 192 acres e. of Valdez on Richardson Hwy., Milepost 23.	**4**	•	•	•				•		•					
Bonnie Lake (C-11) 129 acres e. of Palmer on Glenn Hwy., Milepost 83. Canoeing.	**5**	•			•	•		•	•	•					
Buskin River (H-5) 168 acres 4 mi. s.e. on Base-Town Rd. in Kodiak.	**50**	•	•	•				•		•					
Captain Cook (D-10) 3,466 acres 24 mi. n. of Kenai on N. Kenai Rd.	**6**	•	•	•	•			•	•	•			•		
Chena River (A-12) 254,000 acres 27 mi. e. of Fairbanks on Chena Hot Springs Rd.	**47**	•	•	•	•			•		•		•		•	
Chilkat (G-10) 9,837 acres 7 mi. s. of Haines on Haines Hwy.	**9**	•	•	•	•			•		•				•	
Chilkoot Lake (G-10) 80 acres 11 mi. n. of Haines on Lutak Rd., Milepost 10.	**10**	•	•		•	•		•	•	•					
Chugach (C-11) 495,204 acres just e. of Anchorage on Glenn Hwy. Numerous access points. Horse rental. *(See Anchorage p. 299)*	**11**	•	•	•	•			•		•	•	•	•		
Clam Gulch (D-10) 129 acres s. of Soldotna on Sterling Hwy., Milepost 117.	**12**	•						•							
Clearwater (B-12) 27 acres 11 mi. s.e. of Delta Junction on Alaska Hwy., Milepost 1415, then 8 mi. n.e. on side road.	**13**	•			•	•		•							
Deep Creek (D-10) 155 acres near Ninilchik on Sterling Hwy., Milepost 138.	**15**	•	•		•	•		•		•					
Denali (C-10) 324,240 acres n. of Talkeetna on Parks Hwy., Milepost 135-164.	**52**	•	•	•	•	•		•							

RECREATION AREAS

Recreation Area	Map Location	Camping	Picnicking	Hiking Trails	Boating	Boat Ramp	Boat Rental	Fishing	Swimming	Pets on Leash	Bicycle Trails	Winter Sports	Visitor Center	Lodge/Cabins	Food Service
Donnelly Creek (B-12) 42 acres s. of Delta Junction on Richardson Hwy., Milepost 238.	16	•	•					•		•					
Dry Creek (C-12) 372 acres n. of Glennallen on Richardson Hwy., Milepost 117.5.	17	•	•	•				•		•					
Eagle Trail (C-12) 280 acres 16 mi. s. of Tok on Tok Cut-off, Milepost 109.5.	18	•	•	•						•					
Fielding Lake (C-12) 300 acres s. of Delta Junction on Richardson Hwy., Milepost 201.	53	•			•	•		•		•					
Finger Lake (C-11) 47 acres 4 mi. w. of Palmer on Palmer-Wasilla Rd., then 1 mi. n. and .5 mi. w.	19	•	•	•				•	•	•			•		
Fort Abercrombie (H-5) 183 acres 4.5 mi. s.e. of Kodiak on Miller Point. Historic. *(See Kodiak p. 323)*	20	•	•	•	•			•	•	•			•		
Halibut Point (H-11) 40 acres 4 mi. n.e. of Sitka on Halibut Rd.	54		•	•				•		•					
Harding Lake (B-12) 169 acres .5 mi. n.e. from Milepost 321 on the Richardson Hwy.	21	•	•		•	•		•	•	•					
Izaak Walton (D-10) 8 acres e. of Soldotna off Glenn Hwy.	22	•	•		•	•				•					
Johnson Lake (D-11) 332 acres 16 mi. s. of Soldotna on Glenn Hwy.	23	•	•		•	•		•	•	•					
Kachemak Bay (D-10) 368,290 acres near Seldovia, at the end of Sterling Hwy., then by boat or plane across Kachemak Bay.	25	•	•	•	•			•		•					
Kepler-Bradley Lakes (C-11) 344 acres e. of Palmer on Glenn Hwy., Milepost 36.4.	55		•	•				•		•					
Lake Louise (C-11) 90 acres n.w. of Glennallen on Glenn Hwy., Milepost 160.	26	•	•		•	•		•		•					
Little Nelchina (C-12) 22 acres s.e. of Glennallen on Glenn Hwy., Milepost 137.4.	56	•		•	•			•		•					
Little Tonsina (C-12) 103 acres near Copper Center on Richardson Hwy., Milepost 65.	28	•	•					•		•					
Long Lake (C-11) 480 acres 7 mi. e. of Sutton on Glenn Hwy.	29	•	•		•	•		•	•	•					
Lower Chatanika River (A-11) 120 acres n.w. of Fairbanks off SR 2, Milepost 9.	8	•	•		•			•		•					
Matanuska Glacier (C-11) 229 acres e. of Palmer on Glenn Hwy., Milepost 101.	30	•	•	•						•					
Moon Lake (B-12) 22 acres 18 mi. w. of Tok on Alaska Hwy.	32	•	•		•	•		•	•	•					
Moose Creek (C-11) 40 acres near Palmer on Glenn Hwy., Milepost 54.4.	57	•	•	•						•					
Mosquito Lake (G-10) 10 acres 27.5 mi. w. of Haines on Haines Hwy., then 2.5 mi. on Mosquito Lake Rd.	33	•	•					•		•		•			
Nancy Lake, South (C-11) 22,685 acres 3.5 mi. s. of Willow on Parks Hwy., then 7 mi. w. on side road.	34	•	•		•			•		•		•		•	
Ninilchik (D-10) 97 acres n. of Homer on Sterling Hwy., Milepost 135.	58	•	•					•		•					
Portage Cove (G-10) 7 acres s. of Haines at 1 Beach Rd.	59	•	•					•		•					
Quartz Lake (B-11) 600 acres 2 mi. n.w. of Delta Junction on Alaska Hwy.	36	•	•		•	•	•	•	•	•		•			•
Rocky Lake (C-10) 48 acres 28 mi. w. of Palmer via Wasilla off Parks Hwy. at Milepost 3.5 of Big Lake Rd.	37	•	•		•	•		•	•	•					
Salcha River (B-12) 61 acres s.e. of North Pole on Alaska Hwy., Milepost 323. Canoeing.	38		•		•	•		•		•					
South Rolly Lake (C-10) 200 acres just w. of Wasilla off Parks Hwy. at Milepost 6.5 of Nancy Lake Pkwy.	39	•	•		•	•		•	•	•		•			

RECREATION AREAS

	MAP LOCATION	CAMPING	PICNICKING	HIKING TRAILS	BOATING	BOAT RAMP	BOAT RENTAL	FISHING	SWIMMING	PETS ON LEASH	BICYCLE TRAILS	WINTER SPORTS	VISITOR CENTER	LODGE/CABINS	FOOD SERVICE
Squirrel Creek (C-12) 350 acres near Copper Center on Richardson Hwy., Milepost 79.5.	40	•	•					•		•					
Tok River (B-12) 9 acres 5 mi. e. of Tok Junction on Alaska Hwy., Milepost 1309.	41	•			•	•		•	•	•			•		
Upper Chatanika River (A-11) 73 acres n.e. of Fairbanks off Steese Hwy.	7	•	•		•			•		•					
OTHER															
Brushkana (B-11) 15 acres 30 mi. e. of Cantwell on Denali Hwy., Milepost 104.	51	•	•					•		•					
Cripple Creek (A-12) 5 acres 50 mi. n.e. of Fairbanks on Steese Hwy., Milepost 60.	60	•	•					•		•					
Paxson Lake (C-12) 80 acres 10 mi. s. of Paxson on Richardson Hwy., Milepost 175.	43	•	•		•	•		•		•					
Salmon Lake (C-3) 20 acres 40 mi. n. of Nome.	61	•	•		•	•		•		•					
Sourdough (C-12) 140 acres 35 mi. n. of Glennallen on the Richardson Hwy., Milepost 148.	44	•	•		•	•		•		•					
Tangle Lakes (B-12) 100 acres 22 mi. w. of Paxson on Denali Hwy., Milepost 22.	45	•	•		•	•		•		•					
Walker Fork (E-8) 10 acres 80 mi. n.e. of Tok on Taylor Hwy., Milepost 82.	62	•	•	•				•		•					
West Fork (E-8) 10 acres 65 mi. n.e. of Tok on Taylor Hwy., Milepost 49.	63	•	•					•		•					

Alaska Temperature Averages
Maximum / Minimum (Fahrenheit)
From the records of the National Weather Service

	JAN	FEB	MAR	APR	MAY	JUNE	JULY	AUG	SEPT	OCT	NOV	DEC
Anchorage	21 / 3	27 / 10	33 / 14	45 / 28	54 / 37	63 / 43	64 / 50	63 / 48	55 / 39	63 / 28	28 / 16	21 / 7
Barrow	-9 / -24	-13 / -24	-8 / -22	7 / -8	25 / 12	36 / 28	45 / 33	43 / 33	33 / 27	21 / 12	5 / -8	-6 / -17
Fairbanks	-8 / -22	10 / -15	59 / 36	43 / 18	59 / 36	72 / 46	72 / 48	64 / 43	54 / 33	36 / 18	12 / -6	1 / -17
Juneau	30 / 19	32 / 21	37 / 25	45 / 30	54 / 37	63 / 45	63 / 48	63 / 46	55 / 43	46 / 37	39 / 28	33 / 25
Kotzebue	1 / -13	3 / -11	7 / -11	23 / 3	37 / 25	50 / 37	59 / 46	55 / 45	46 / 36	30 / 19	12 / 1	3 / -11
Nome	12 / -2	12 / -2	16 / 0	28 / 14	41 / 28	52 / 39	55 / 45	54 / 45	48 / 36	36 / 25	23 / 10	12 / -2

Points of Interest

ADMIRALTY ISLAND NATIONAL MONUMENT (H-11)

Accessible by floatplane from Juneau and Sitka or via ferries of the Alaska Marine Highway to Angoon, Admiralty Island is part of Tongass National Forest *(see place listing p. 333)*. Between the rocky beaches and high mountain peaks lie a million acres of coastal rain forests, freshwater lakes and streams, alpine meadows and dense thickets of wild currants and other berries.

Alaskan brown bears outnumber human beings, and the greatest concentration of bald eagles in North America nests along the coast. Beavers, martens, minks, river otters, Sitka black-tailed deer and weasels share the island with Vancouver Canada geese and trumpeter and whistling swans. Offshore are harbor seals, sea lions and whales.

Motorboating and sea kayaking are popular in protected saltwater bays, and a canoe portage trail connects nine interior lakes to bays on the east and west shores. Rustic cabins can be reserved, and campsites and open shelters are available on a first-come-first-served basis. Most of the island is a wilderness area; be prepared for rain and follow no-trace camping practices.

For more information write the U.S. Forest Service *(see Fast Facts)*.

ANCHORAGE (C-10, F-6)
pop. 260,283, elev. 118′

See map page 293.

Anchorage, on a high bluff enfolded by the two branches of Cook Inlet, lies as far west as the Hawaiian Islands and as far north as Helsinki, Finland. The tides in the inlet rise from 30 to 33 feet; the surrounding mountains loom several thousand feet overhead. The protective mountain barrier and the proximity of the ocean afford Anchorage a surprisingly moderate climate, relative to most of Alaska.

Anchorage is Alaska's largest city and is home to almost half of the state's residents. While not a dazzling metropolis, each summer the city is beautifully decorated with almost 100,000 hanging flower baskets brimming with brightly-colored blooms.

Established in 1915 as the construction headquarters for the Alaska Railroad *(see attraction listing)*, it is the transportation and business center of south-central Alaska and a major winter recreation area. Anchorage's heritage as a road town is recalled by a number of historic buildings, notably the Pioneer Schoolhouse in Ben Crawford Memorial Park and two nearby one-room log cabins. As well, landmarks denote both Russian and American Indian heritage.

Anchorage suffered from the effects of the 1964 Good Friday earthquake, one of the strongest in history, which destroyed much of downtown. Earthquake Park, at the west end of Northern Lights Boulevard, has a walking trail and interpretive signs that provide information about the massive temblor. The park also provides a stunning vista of Cook Inlet.

The dramatic beauty of the nearby mountains, inlets and glaciers offers an easily accessible sampling of Alaska's natural splendors. Two roads affording beautiful views link to Anchorage; scenic SR 1/9 extends south to Seward, and SR 1 extends north to Glennallen.

From Anchorage visitors also can take various sightseeing tours of the area, including the Kenai Peninsula and places of interest inaccessible by road. Trolley, flightseeing and other types of tours given by Anchorage City Trolley Tours depart daily May through September from 612 W. 4th Avenue between F and G streets; phone (907) 276-5603. Among the more novel sightseeing trips are dog sled tours, which leave from the Alyeska Resort and Ski Area *(see Girdwood p. 312)* December through March.

The Alaska Backpacker Shuttle offers daily shuttle service from Anchorage to Denali National Park and Fairbanks mid-May to mid-September; phone (907) 344-8775.

One-hour float trips on the Matanuska River depart by van from Anchorage to the launch point. Panning for gold is available an hour from downtown. For a different perspective, try flightseeing—operators can be found at the airport and Lake Hood.

Alaska Sightseeing Tours, SAVE Gray Line of Alaska (*see color ad p. 294*) and Princess Tours offer a float adventure on Eagle River; tours to Barrow, Kodiak Island, Kotzebue, Matanuska Valley, Nome, Portage Glacier and Prudhoe Bay; fishing on the Kenai River; cruises on Prince William Sound to Columbia Glacier; and a tour of Anchorage.

These agencies also offer 2-, 3- and 4-day round trips between Anchorage and Denali National Park. The trips include travel in railway cars equipped with glass ceiling panels. These same three companies also offer longer excursions to the interior and cruises up the Inside Passage.

The Alaska Center for the Performing Arts Discovery Theatre, at 621 W. 6th Ave., presents a large-screen slide show called "Sky Song" that displays a series of stunning images of the aurora borealis synchronized to classical music. Also shown is a narrated film titled "Alaska: Spirit of the Wild," which introduces visitors to the state through dramatic aerial footage. Phone (907) 242-4291.

Anchorage serves as the starting line for the 1,049-mile Iditarod Trail Race, which begins the first Saturday in March. The actual mileage of the race is 1,161 miles; however, 1,049 is often used as a symbolic figure because the distance is always more than 1,000 miles, and 49 was added to signify Alaska's rank as the 49th state. Dogs and mushers travel over the Alaska Range and across frozen Norton Bay, arriving in Nome nearly 2 weeks later.

Anchorage Convention and Visitors Bureau: 524 W. Fourth Ave., Anchorage, AK 99501-2212; phone (907) 276-4118, or (800) 478-1255 to request a visitors guide. *See color ad p. 294.*

Self-guiding tours: A guide outlining a walking tour and driving tours north and south of the city is available at Log Cabin Visitor Information Center, Fourth Avenue and F Street; phone (907) 274-3531.

26 GLACIER CRUISE BY PHILLIPS' CRUISES—*see Whittier p. 336.*

SAVE **ALASKA AVIATION HERITAGE MUSEUM** is at 4721 Aircraft Dr. On display are 29 vintage aircraft, including a 1931 American Pilgrim. Visitors also can observe restorations in progress. Memorabilia and photographs chronicle the history

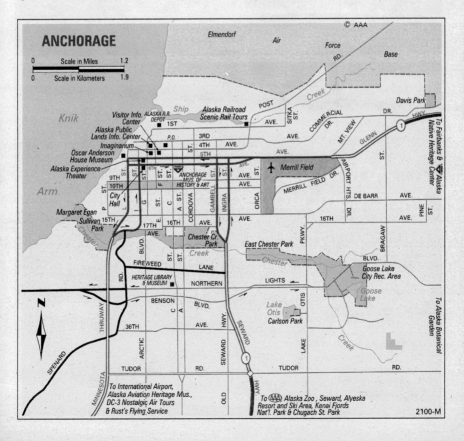

Anchorage:
base camp for adventure

Experience Wild Adventure!
For non-stop Anchorage itineraries, visit the experts at
the Downtown Visitor Information Center at Fourth
Avenue and F Street. Develop a personal itinerary
online! Explore www.Anchorage.net.

ALASKA
ANCHORAGE
Anchorage Convention & Visitors Bureau

of civilian and military aviation in Alaska; films are shown continuously. Allow 30 minutes minimum. Wed.-Mon. 10-6, late May to mid-Sept.; Fri.-Sat. 10-4, Sun. noon-4, rest of year. Closed major holidays in winter. Admission $5; over 62 and ages 12-18, $4; ages 5-11, $3. Phone (907) 248-5325.

ALASKA BOTANICAL GARDEN is 3 mi. e. of New Seward Hwy. on Tudor Rd, then just s. on Campbell Airstrip Rd. Arctic horticulture is showcased in a 110-acre birch and spruce woodland replete with more than 900 varieties of plants in demonstration, herb, perennial and alpine rock gardens. The park includes a wildflower walk, an interpretive nature trail and a creek where salmon spawn in the summer. Peak blooming season is late May to mid-September. Allow 1 hour, 30 minutes minimum. Daily 9-9. Admission $5; over 59 and ages 2-17, $3. Phone (907) 770-3692.

ALASKA EXPERIENCE THEATER, 705 W. Sixth Ave., presents "Alaska the Greatland," a 40-minute documentary projected onto a domed screen. Filmed from planes, river rafts and trains, the narrated documentary dramatizes the splendors of Alaska's great outdoors. An earthquake exhibit presents information about the 1964 Alaska earthquake, which measured 9.2 on the Richter scale.

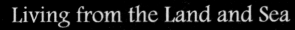

Shows daily on the hour 9-9, early June-Sept. 15; noon-6, rest of year. Admission to theater $8; ages 5-12, $4. Earthquake exhibit $6; ages 5-12, $4. Combined admission $12; ages 5-12, $7. AX, DS, MC, VI. Phone (907) 276-3730.

ALASKA NATIVE HERITAGE CENTER is approx. 3 mi. e. on Glenn Hwy. to N. Muldoon Rd. exit, then .5 mi. n. to 8800 Heritage Center Dr. Situated on 26 wooded acres, the center presents information about the five regional, native groups that inhabit Alaska: the Aleut and Alutiiq; Athabascan; Eyak, Tlingit, Haida and Tsimshian; Inupiaq and St. Lawrence Island Yupik; and Yup'ik and Cup'ik tribes.

The main building offers the Gathering Place for storytelling, dance and musical performances as well as a theater for films. The Hall of Cultures exhibit is divided into five areas in which multimedia displays about weaving, fishing, philosophy, moose hunting and dance are presented. Artisans create and display their crafts in adjacent studios.

Outside, life-size replicas of different types of housing (built by natives) surround a pond; tribal members at each locale give insight to traditions and customs. Allow 2 hours minimum. Daily 9-6, mid-May to mid-Sept. Admission $20.95; ages 7-16, $15.95. MC, VI. Phone (907) 330-8000 or (800) 315-6608. *See color ad p. 295.*

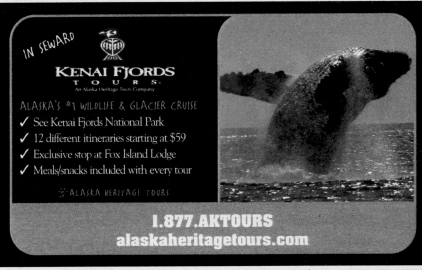

ALASKA PUBLIC LANDS INFORMATION CENTER, 605 W. Fourth Ave., offers information about Alaska's state and federal public lands. Exhibits include displays about Alaska's native culture and wildlife; films and interpretive programs are offered during the summer season. Visitors can plan their own trips with assistance from the staff. State and national park permits also are available. Daily 9-5, June-Aug.; Mon.-Fri. 10-5:30, rest of year. Closed winter holidays. Free. Phone (907) 271-2737.

ALASKA RAILROAD SCENIC RAIL TOURS departs from 411 W. First Ave. Narrated sightseeing tours are offered northward between Anchorage and Fairbanks with stops at Wasilla, Talkeetna and Denali National Park and Preserve. Southbound rail trips from Anchorage to Whittier follow the Turnagain Arm of Cook Inlet. Additional sightseeing excursions and connections to a variety of extended air, rail and boat tours also are available. Trips depart daily, early May to mid-Sept.; phone for schedule. One-way fares range $45-$175. Reservations are recommended. AX, MC, VI. Phone (907) 265-2494 or (800) 544-0552. *See color ad p. 296.*

ALASKA ZOO, 7.5 mi. s. on SR 1 (Seward Hwy.), then 2 mi. e. on O'Malley Rd., embraces a 20-acre wooded area with many arctic and Alaskan native animals, including Amur tigers, snow leopards, Tibetan yaks and several bear species. Allow 1 hour, 30 minutes minimum. Daily 9-6, May 1 to mid-Sept.; 10-5, rest of year. Closed Thanksgiving and Dec. 25. Admission $9; senior citizens $8; ages 12-17, $5; ages 3-11, $4. Phone (907) 346-3242.

ALYESKA RESORT AND SKI AREA—
see Girdwood p. 312.

ANCHORAGE MUSEUM OF HISTORY AND ART, 121 W. Seventh Ave., has exhibits focusing on the art, history and cultures of Alaska. The Alaska Gallery includes objects dating from prehistoric times through European exploration, Russian settlement, the gold rush era, World War II and statehood. Full-scale dioramas of an Athabascan tent; Yupik Eskimo, Tlingit and Aleut houses; a gold miner's cabin; an early Anchorage house; Quonset huts (in use during World War II); and moose boats provide insight to early Alaskan life.

In addition, a display about the Alaska Pipeline features a sample of the 4-foot-tall pipe. "Art of the Far North" contains drawings and paintings by Alaska's first explorers to current artists. Other highlights include summer films, a children's gallery and traveling exhibitions.

Food is available. Allow 1 hour minimum. Daily 9-6 (also Thurs. 6-9 p.m.), May 15-Sept. 15; Wed.-Sat. 10-6, Sun. noon-5, rest of year. Closed Jan. 1, Thanksgiving and Dec. 25. Admission $6.50; over 65, $6; under 18 free. Phone (907) 343-4326.

CHUGACH STATE PARK is e. on Glenn Hwy. Wildlife populations flourish within the park's 700 square miles of mountains, rivers, lakes and glaciers, providing many opportunities for viewing

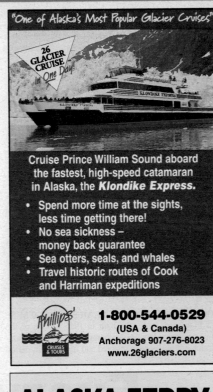

moose and beavers, as well as the occasional bear or wolf. Major areas are Eklutna Lake, Eagle River, Anchorage Hillside and Turnagain Arm. The park's headquarters is in the historic Potter Point Section House, at mile 115 of the Seward Highway.

Headquarters open Mon.-Fri. 10-4:30. Free. Parking $5 at many trailheads. Phone (907) 345-5014. *See Recreation Chart and the AAA Western Canada & Alaska CampBook.*

HERITAGE LIBRARY AND MUSEUM, at Northern Lights Blvd. and C St. in the Wells Fargo Bank Building, displays Eskimo and other native artifacts, an extensive collection of walrus ivory carvings and paintings by Alaskan artists. Allow 30 minutes minimum. Mon.-Fri. noon-4. Free. Phone (907) 265-2834.

SAVE **THE IMAGINARIUM,** Fifth Ave. and G St., is a hands-on science discovery center offering exhibits that explore nature, science and technology. Highlights include a marine wildlife area, reptile exhibits, a bubble lab and a planetarium. Allow 1 hour minimum. Mon.-Sat. 10-6, Sun. noon-5; closed major holidays. Admission $5.50; over 65 and ages 2-12, $5. Phone (907) 276-3179.

MAJOR MARINE TOURS—*see Whittier p. 336.*

OSCAR ANDERSON HOUSE MUSEUM, 420 M St. in Elderberry Park, was built in 1915 on one of the first townsite lots in Anchorage. The small woodframe house has been restored and furnished in period

and offers a fine view of Cook Inlet. Allow 30 minutes minimum. Mon.-Fri. noon-5, June 1 to mid-Sept. Admission $3; ages 5-12, $1. Phone (907) 274-2336.

PORTAGE GLACIER RECREATION AREA— *see Chugach National Forest p. 302.*

TRANS ARCTIC CIRCLE TREKS AND GLACIER BLUE TOURS—*see Fairbanks p. 310.*

RUST'S FLYING SERVICE departs from the south shore of Lake Hood off International Airport Rd. at Anchorage International Airport. Narrated sightseeing tours by seaplane offer views of Knik and Columbia glaciers, Mount McKinley and Denali National Park. Wildlife and marine life viewing opportunities, such as bear sightings, vary with tours. Ten-hour fishing trips, glacier landings and river float trips also are available. Flights require a minimum of two passengers.

Inquire about weather policies. Allow 1 hour, 30 minutes minimum. Daily by appointment; closed Jan. 1, Thanksgiving and Dec. 25. Fare $89-$349. AX, MC, VI. Phone (907) 243-1595, or (800) 544-2299 out of Alaska.

RECREATIONAL ACTIVITIES

Fishing

• **Jake's Alaska Wilderness Outfitters,** 2910 W. 31st Ave. Write P.O. Box 104179, Anchorage, AK 99510. Daily June-Sept. Phone (907) 522-1133.

Know *Before* You Go

Travel plans become crystal clear in the pages of AAA TourBooks® or online at **aaa.com**.

Each of the advertisers makes your travel choices easier by featuring photographs, detailed descriptions, toll-free numbers and Web addresses for their hotels, restaurants or attractions.

Travel with Confidence.
Travel with AAA

BARROW (A-5) pop. 4,581, elev. 2'

The northernmost settlement in Alaska, Barrow is 340 miles north of the Arctic Circle on the edge of the omnipresent Arctic icepack. The sun does not go below the horizon for 82 days from early May to early August or rise above the horizon for 51 days between November and January. The town is reached by daily scheduled flights from Anchorage and Fairbanks. Husky sled dogs still are used, but snowmobiles have become more popular.

Barrow is one of the world's largest Eskimo settlements. Although to some extent the people continue to follow their old traditions, the trend is toward a more modern way of life: The North Slope oil discovery created great wealth in the area.

The Post-Rogers Memorial, at the airport, commemorates the deaths of Will Rogers and his pilot, Wiley Post, who were killed in a 1935 plane crash 12 miles down the coast.

CHUGACH NATIONAL FOREST (D-12, G-6)

Elevations in the forest range from sea level at the Pacific Ocean at Prince William Sound to 13,176 ft. at Mount Marcus Baker. Refer to AAA maps for additional elevation information.

Extending along the Gulf of Alaska from Cape Suckling to Seward, Chugach (CHEW-gatch) National Forest covers 5,400,000 acres, roughly as large as New Hampshire. It is second in size only to the Tongass National Forest (see place listing p. 333) and includes many of the islands and much of the land bordering Prince William Sound and the northeastern portion of the Kenai Peninsula.

Within the 700,000-acre Copper River Delta Wildlife Management Area just east of Cordova is one of the largest concentrations of trumpeter swans in North America. Also in abundance are dusky Canada geese, short-billed dowitchers, red-throated loons and green-winged teal. Prince William Sound has spectacular scenic opportunities with its 3,500 miles of coastline as well as dramatic tidewater glaciers and marine life that includes many species of whales.

Both saltwater and freshwater fishing are available in abundance in the forest. Halibut, red snapper, salmon and crabs are plentiful along the more than 3,500 miles of saltwater shoreline. Popular spots are Resurrection Bay at Seward and in Prince William Sound around Valdez and Cordova. Freshwater lakes and streams provide red salmon, Dolly Varden char and rainbow trout. A sportfishing license is required for all types of fishing within the forest.

For photographers and sport hunters, the forest offers a variety of big game, including black and brown bears, moose and Dall sheep. Hunting is subject to Alaska's fish and game management laws, seasons and bag limits.

Seward Highway offers 127 miles of scenic driving along saltwater bays, ice-blue glaciers and valleys dotted with native wildlife. The highway connects the cities of Anchorage and Seward. Bordering the forest on the northwest is SR 4; its scenic portion extends from Valdez to the junction of SR 10 west of Chitina. Portions of one of the most famous trails, The Historic Iditarod Trail, can be hiked, skied, dog sledded or explored on snowmobile.

In addition to 14 road-accessible campgrounds and 200 miles of hiking trails, the Forest Service operates 42 cabins in remote areas near lakes, bays and streams. Accessible by trail, boat or floatplane, the cabins are equipped with bunks, tables, chairs, wood or oil stoves and outdoor sanitary facilities, but not electricity.

The fee is $25-$45 per night per party. Reservations are required and can be made up to six months in advance. Further information also can be obtained from the Chugach National Forest, 3301 C St., Suite 300, Anchorage, AK 99503, phone (907) 743-9500, (877) 444-6777 for reservations or the U.S. Forest Service in Juneau (see Fast Facts). Also see Recreation Chart and the AAA Western Canada & Alaska CampBook.

ALASKA WILDLIFE CONSERVATION CENTER, Seward Hwy. Milepost 79, is a 100-acre, drive-through wild animal park. Among the animals to be seen are musk oxen, red foxes, lynx, buffaloes, Sitka blacktail deer, caribous, eagles, moose, reindeer, elk and bears. Allow 30 minutes minimum. Daily 10-dusk (weather permitting). Last admission is 30 minutes before closing. Admission $7; over 54 and ages 4-12, $5. The maximum fee is $25 per carload. Pets are not permitted. MC, VI. Phone (907) 783-2025.

[SAVE] **PORTAGE GLACIER CRUISES** depart 1.5 mi. s. of the Begich-Boggs Visitor Center in the Portage Glacier Recreation Area (see attraction listing). A 1-hour narrated cruise takes passengers to the face of Portage Glacier. Sections of the glacier "calving" or breaking away into the lake below often can be seen. The 200-passenger ship has a climate-controlled cabin with oversized windows and an open-air observation deck. Shuttle and tour packages from Anchorage also are available.

Inquire about weather policies. Cruises depart daily at 10:30, noon, 1:30, 3 and 4:30, mid-May to late Sept. Fare $26; ages 3-11, $13. MC, VI. Phone (907) 277-5581.

PORTAGE GLACIER RECREATION AREA is 5.5 mi. e. from Milepost 79 of the Seward-Anchorage Hwy. Large icebergs calve off the face of the glacier into 650-foot-deep Portage Lake. An observation platform and a wayside exhibit are at the entrance to Williwaw Campground. Wayside exhibits also are available at Explorer Glacier. Iceworm safaris are offered. Guided tours and food are available. Picnicking is permitted. The road to and within the area is open all year. Phone (907) 783-3242.

Begich-Boggs Visitor Center contains an observatory, orientation area and exhibit hall. A 20-minute film titled "Voices from the Ice" is shown 20 minutes past every hour. Daily 9-6, Memorial Day-Labor Day; Sat.-Sun. 10-4, rest of year. Film $1. Phone (907) 783-2326.

CIRCLE HOT SPRINGS (A-12)

Circle Hot Springs is 8 miles off SR 6 (Steese Hwy.) via the gravel Circle Hot Springs Road. The town was discovered when George Crowe, a prospector on Deadwood Creek, wounded and trailed a moose across an unusually warm creek. Crowe traced the heat to the hot springs, which run 140 degrees Fahrenheit at the source. This discovery opened the way in 1897 for Circle Hot Springs Resort, which still attracts local miners in winter and out-of-town visitors all year.

COOPER LANDING (D-11) pop. 369

RECREATIONAL ACTIVITIES

Boating

- **Alaska Wildland Adventures** departs from the launch site on Sterling Hwy. (SR 1) Milepost 50.1. Write 16520 Sterling Hwy., Cooper Landing, AK 99572. Daily May-Sept. Other activities are offered. Phone (907) 783-2928 or (800) 478-4100.

CORDOVA (D-12) pop. 2,454, elev. 100'

Cordova is located on the eastern shores of Prince William Sound and is surrounded by the Chugach Mountain Range and the Chugach National Forest. The town can be reached by air from Juneau and Anchorage or via the Alaska Marine Highway from Valdez and Whittier. In the early 1900s, Cordova was the terminus of the Copper River Northwest Railroad that carried copper ore from the Kennecott Mines in McCarthy. Today the town's industry focuses on commercial fishing.

Cordova Chamber of Commerce: P.O. Box 99, Cordova, AK 99574; phone (907) 424-7260.

DELTA JUNCTION (B-11) pop. 840

The official northern terminus of the Alaska Highway, Delta Junction is one of the state's strongest agricultural producers. The town offers panoramic views of the Alaska Range as well as the Trans-Alaska Pipeline, the Delta Bison Range and glaciers.

BIG DELTA STATE HISTORICAL PARK AND RIKA'S ROADHOUSE AND LANDING, at Milepost 275 on Richardson Hwy., is a restored 10-acre homestead with a museum, historic cabins, a roadhouse, a garden and livestock and poultry pens. Guided tours are available. Food is available. Daily 9-5, May 15-Sept. 15; by appointment rest of year. Free. Phone (907) 895-4201 May 15-Sept. 15, or (907) 895-4938 rest of year.

DENALI NATIONAL PARK AND PRESERVE (B-10)

Elevations in the park and preserve range from 626 ft. at the northwest corner of the park at Chilcukabena Lake to the 20,320 ft. Mount McKinley. Refer to AAA maps for additional elevation information.

In the interior of Alaska, primitive and wild Denali National Park and Preserve covers 9,375 square miles and offers spectacular views of quiet lakes, snowcapped peaks and varicolored tundra. In addition to 20,320-foot Mount McKinley, the highest peak in North America, the park encompasses 17,400-foot Mount Foraker, 13,220-foot Silverthrone and 11,670-foot Mount Russell.

Mount McKinley, known to the early Athabascan Indians as Denali, "the high one," has two peaks: South Peak, the true summit, and 2 miles away, 19,470-foot North Peak. Most of the mountain is covered by ice and snow all year. Excellent views of Mount McKinley are possible along the park road (weather permitting); clouds hide the summit about 75 percent of the time in summer and 60 percent the rest of the year.

The park's many glaciers originate on the slopes of the Alaska Range. Muldrow Glacier, the largest northward-flowing glacier in Alaska, stretches from between Mount McKinley's twin peaks to within a few miles of the park road; it can be seen from several vantage points.

More than 167 species of birds and 39 kinds of mammals inhabit the park; grizzly bears, moose, Dall sheep, wolves and caribou are some of the larger mammals. Equally varied is the vegetation. The chief conifers are black and white spruce, while dwarf birch grow in thickets on the lower slopes and along the intermountain valleys. Low, boggy meadows are the habitat of stunted, twisted black spruce.

Above the river valleys, forests give way to vast stretches of wet tundra supporting shrubby plants and often underlain by permafrost. Dry alpine tundra blankets the slopes and ridges at the higher elevations.

General Information and Activities

From Anchorage and Fairbanks, the George Parks Highway (SR 3) provides access to the park all year, and SR 8 from Paxson is usually open from early June to mid-October. The park also is accessible from Anchorage or Fairbanks via the Alaska Railroad; there is daily service from late May to mid-September. Trains run northbound to Fairbanks on Saturday and southbound to Anchorage on Sunday the rest of the year. Charter flights are available from principal airports.

Denali Park Road, beginning at SR 3 at the park's eastern boundary, runs about 90 miles westward through the park, terminating at a partly abandoned mining town, Kantishna. Only the first 14.8

miles to Savage River are paved, and most of the road is narrow with many sharp curves. It is usually open from early June to mid-September.

Private vehicles may be used only on the first 14.8 miles of road unless you have a registered campsite at Teklanika Campground. Transportation beyond Savage River or to Sanctuary, Igloo and Wonder Lake campgrounds is provided by shuttle buses that operate to Eielson Visitor Center, Wonder Lake and other points in the park.

Fare for the shuttle varies with destination. The fare to Wonder Lake is $31.75; a ride to Eielson Visitor Center is $23. The fare to Toklat and Polychrome is $18. Kids under 15 ride for free; ages 15-17 ride for half price. Three- and 6-day trip passes are available; prices vary by destination. These fares do not include the $4 registration fee or the park admission fees.

More than half of the shuttle seats are available for telephone reservation. Phone (907) 272-7275 or (800) 622-7275 in advance. The rest of the spaces can be reserved only in person within 2 days of departure. Buses depart approximately every half-hour beginning at 5 a.m. from the Visitor Center near the entrance and stop to view wildlife when conditions are safe. Shuttle buses also drop off and pick up passengers along the park road on a space-available basis.

If you want to camp outside the established campgrounds, stop at the Visitor Center for a backcountry permit. Reservations for all campgrounds may be made here.

The George Parks Highway (SR 3) runs along the eastern border of the park and offers sweeping views of the park's alpine scenery from Willow to Nenana.

Sled dog demonstrations are given by rangers at the park kennels, mile 3 on Denali Park Road. The 40-minute presentations are offered daily at 10, 2 and 4, June through August. Ranger-naturalists also present various lectures, hikes and other activities daily at various campgrounds. Information about activities is available at the park visitor center, ranger stations and Eielson Visitor Center, or pick up a copy of the park's informational newspaper, *Denali Alpenglow.*

Guided and self-guiding hikes are available along several nature trails with trailheads along the paved portion of the park road. Throughout the rest of the park, hiking is generally cross-country.

Do not feed or disturb wildlife. Grizzly bears in particular can be dangerous; inquire at the Visitor Center about how to avoid close encounters with grizzlies. Firearms must be declared and made inoperative when you enter the park; hunting and shooting are forbidden.

Most fishing is poor in the park; only streams that are free of glacial silt are good fishing spots.

No license is required within the national park; the daily creel limit is 10 fish, only two of which may be lake trout. An Alaska fishing license is required in the national preserve areas. Check at a ranger station for further information.

Temperatures during the park season can vary from 40 to 80 degrees Fahrenheit, with an average of 50 to 54 degrees June through August. Daylight generally lasts for more than 18 hours during the summer months.

A store near the park entrance contains supplies, but no gas is available; the store is open approximately 7 a.m.-9 p.m. during peak season, shorter hours at other times. A gas station north of the park entrance on George Parks Highway is open in the summer. Food and supplies also are available at Riley Creek campground just inside the park boundaries. *See Recreation Chart and the AAA Western Canada & Alaska CampBook.*

ADMISSION is $5 per person or $10 per family.

PETS are permitted in the park only if they are leashed or otherwise physically restrained; they are not allowed on trails, shuttle buses or in the back country.

ADDRESS inquiries to the Superintendent, Denali National Park and Preserve, P.O. Box 9, Denali Park, AK 99755; phone (907) 683-2294.

ALASKA CABIN NIGHT DINNER THEATRE is 1.7 mi. n. of the park entrance on George Parks Hwy. at Milepost 239. The theater presents a 1915-style dinner show that highlights Alaska's gold-mining history. Costumed characters serve the all-you-can-eat meal. Allow 2 hours minimum. Shows daily at 5:30 and 8:30 p.m., mid-May to mid-Sept. Admission $49; under 12, $24.50. Reservations are recommended. AX, DS, MC, VI. Phone (907) 683-8200 or (800) 276-7234 (within 48 hours) for reservations.

CLIMB DENALI SHOW is presented at Grand Denali Lodge, Milepost 238.2 on George Parks Hwy. Through a 90-minute multimedia presentation in the Peak Experience Theater, mountaineers demonstrate climbing techniques while giving personal accounts of mountain climbing adventures. A pre-show meal is available in the lodge restaurant. Dinner daily at 6. Show starts at 7:30, mid-May to mid-Sept. Admission (dinner and show) $39.95; under 6, $19.95. Show only $15; under 6, $5. AX, DC, DS, MC, VI. Phone (907) 683-8500 or (907) 683-5100.

DENALI AIR is 10 mi. s. on George Parks Hwy. (SR 3) at Milepost 229.5. Commentary about history, scenery and topography complements an hourlong flight along the Alaska Range and around Mount McKinley. Allow 1 hour minimum. Flights depart every even hour daily 8-8 (weather permitting). Fare $240; ages 2-12, $120. AX, DS, MC, VI. Phone (907) 683-2261.

DENALI WILDERNESS SAFARIS, at Milepost 215 on George Parks Hwy., offers 3-hour heated jet boat rides to a camp in the Alaskan "bush" country, where locals share their methods of hunting, prospecting and trapping. Gold panning opportunities also are offered. Free transportation is provided from all area hotels. Trips depart daily at 8, 9, 12:30, 2:30 and 6. Fare, including a snack, $89; under 12, $45. Reservations are recommended. MC, VI. Phone (907) 768-2550.

[SAVE] **ERA HELICOPTERS FLIGHTSEEING TOURS,** is at 1 Glacier Way. The company offers a narrated, 50-minute aerial tour of North America's highest mountain, Mount McKinley, as well as 75-minute glacier landing tours. Four-hour heli-hiking excursions also are available. Caribous, moose and Dall sheep can be seen in the valleys. Free transportation is provided from area hotels. Daily 8-6, May-Sept. Aerial tour $259. Heli-hiking or glacier tour $359. Flights require a minimum of four passengers. AX, DS, MC, VI. Phone (907) 683-2574 or (800) 843-1947. *See color ad.*

NATURAL HISTORY TOUR, departing from area hotels, takes visitors on a bus tour across sections of the park where they can enjoy views of the Alaska Range from Mount McKinley to Mount Deborah. Driver-guides explain the region's natural history, unusual geological formations and local flora and fauna. The 4-hour trip departs daily 7-8:30, 11-2:30 and 4-5:30, mid-May to mid-Sept. Hours may vary; phone ahead. Fare, including a snack, $51.70; under 14, $33.45. AX, DS, MC, VI. Phone (907) 276-7234 or (800) 276-7234.

TUNDRA WILDERNESS TOURS picks up visitors at local hotels. Buses travel to Toklat River, making frequent stops en route for photography. Driver-guides explain in detail the region's geology, flora and fauna on the 6- to 8-hour tours. Binoculars are recommended for spotting moose, caribous, bears and other wildlife. Inquire about weather policies. Trips depart daily 5:30-7 a.m. and 1:30-3:30 p.m., mid-May to mid-Sept. Fare, including a box lunch, $87.25; under 15, $51. Reservations are recommended. AX, MC, VI. Phone (907) 276-7234, (907) 683-8200 or (800) 276-7234.

RECREATIONAL ACTIVITIES
White-water Rafting

- **Alaska Raft Adventures** departs from the McKinley Chalet at Milepost 238 on George Parks Hwy. (SR 3). Write P.O. Box 87, Denali National Park, AK 99755. Trips depart daily at 8, noon, 1:30 and 6. Phone (907) 276-7234, (907) 683-2215 or (800) 276-7234

- SAVE **Denali Raft Adventures, Inc.** is .5 mi. n. of the park entrance. Write Drawer 190, Denali National Park, AK 99755. Trips depart daily mid-May to mid-Sept., check-in at 7:30, 9, 10, 12:30, 3 and 6:30. Phone (907) 683-2234.

EAGLE (D-8) pop. 129

Eagle was settled in 1897 by 28 miners who named the town after the bald eagles that nested on the nearby bluff. In 1899, the Army established Fort Egbert and within several years, some 37 military buildings were constructed. Founded along the Yukon River near the Canadian border, Eagle is the only planned town of the gold rush.

Eagle Historical Society: P.O. Box 23, Eagle, AK 99738; phone (907) 547-2325.

EAGLE MUSEUMS are all within 1 sq. mi. of town. Tours depart from the courthouse at First and Berry sts. Visitors can join a walking tour that includes six restored buildings, including James Wickersham's original courthouse, the Army Mule Barn, Redman Lodge, Customs House, NCO Quarters and the Waterwagon Shed. Each building contains memorabilia portraying the small town's history. Allow 3 hours minimum. Daily 9-noon, Memorial Day-Labor Day. Admission $5, under 13 free. Phone (907) 547-2325.

EAGLE RIVER (C-11)

EAGLE RIVER NATURE CENTER is 12 mi. s.e. on Eagle River Rd. to its end at 32750 Eagle River Rd. The center sponsors interpretive programs including guided hikes along the four trails it maintains. A hands-on area allows visitors to touch antlers, bones, pelts and other collected items. Allow 30 minutes minimum. Mon.-Sat. 10-5 (also Fri.-Sat. 5-7), early May-early Sept.; Tues.-Sun. 10-5, early Sept.-Sept. 30; Fri.-Sun. 10-4, rest of year. Free. Parking $5. Phone (907) 694-2108.

EKLUTNA (C-11)

More than 150 years ago Russian missionaries came to Eklutna to convert the Athabascan Indians. Devotees constructed the St. Nicholas Russian Orthodox Church; the log structure still stands in Eklutna Historical Park along Glenn Highway, Milepost 26. In the nearby cemetery gaily colored "spirit houses," built to hold the souls of the deceased, adorn the burial sites. Guided tours of the historical park are available mid-May to mid-September.

FAIRBANKS (B-11, D-7)
pop. 30,224, elev. 432'
See map page 308.

Fairbanks, near the geographical center of Alaska, is a major visitor center and the northern terminus of the Alaska Railroad. The military, transportation and market nucleus of the Alaskan interior, Fairbanks is a supply point for arctic oil operations and a departure point for airlines statewide.

In 1901 Capt. E.T. Barnette founded a trading post where Fairbanks now stands—a riverboat captain refused to ferry him any farther up the Chena River due to the low water level. Gold was discovered nearby a year later, and the first wave of prospectors flooded up the river. The settlement was named for Charles Warren Fairbanks of Indiana, a U.S. senator who later became vice president to Theodore Roosevelt.

The construction of the Alaska Highway and the influx of the military into Fairbanks heralded a second boom. And in 1968 the discovery of oil in Prudhoe Bay, 390 miles north, triggered a third wave of development. Of interest is Pioneer Park, a frontier theme park at Airport and Peger roads.

Fairbanks offers a variety of winter sports and other activities, including aurora viewing, cross-country and downhill skiing, curling, ice hockey and dog mushing. The city's geographical location allows the semiprofessional Alaska Goldpanners baseball team to play its Midnight Sun Game at 10:30 p.m. on June 18 without using artificial lighting.

Local sightseeing tours to Alaska's arctic zone and other remote places throughout the state are available through Northern Alaska Tour Company; phone (907) 474-8600 *(see color ad p. 310).* Using railway cars with skylights, Alaska Sightseeing Tours, SAVE Gray Line of Alaska and Princess Tours also offer trips between Anchorage and Fairbanks via Denali National Park. Canoes for trips on the Chena River can be rented from several outfitters.

Interesting drives include visits to Chena Hot Springs and the town of Ester. Abandoned gold dredges can be seen outside of Fairbanks along the roads to Chatanika and Ester. The Alaska Public Lands Information Center, on the lower level of Courthouse Square at Third Avenue and Cushman Street, shows free movies and has information about public lands and parks; phone (907) 456-0531.

Fairbanks Log Cabin Visitor Information Center: 550 First Ave., Fairbanks, AK 99701; phone (907) 456-5774 or (800) 327-5774. *See color ad p. 309.*

Self-guiding tours: Information about a historical walking and driving tour is available from the Fairbanks Log Cabin Visitor Information Center.

EL DORADO GOLD MINE is 9 mi. n. off Steese Hwy. at Milepost 1.3. A 2-hour narrated trip aboard a replica of a Tanana Valley Railroad train passes through a permafrost tunnel into a working gold mine where mining techniques are demonstrated. Passengers have the opportunity to pan for gold. Allow 2 hours minimum. Tours depart Mon.-Fri. and Sun. at 9:45 and 3, Sat. at 3, mid-May to mid-Sept. Fare $29.95; ages 3-12, $19.95. Reservations are required. AX, DS, MC, VI. Phone (907) 479-6673 or (866) 479-6673. *See color ad p. 309.*

ESTER GOLD CAMP, 5 mi. w. via SR 3 (George Parks Hwy.), contains buildings that date back to the Ester townsite of 1904 and Fairbanks Exploration Co., which operated a gold camp there until 1958. Transportation is available from many local hotels. Food is available. Allow 1 hour minimum. Daily 24 hours, mid-May to mid-Sept. Free. Phone (907) 479-2500 or (800) 676-6925.

"Photosymphony" at Firehouse Theater presents "The Crown of Light," an audiovisual re-creation of the aurora borealis, or northern lights. "The Crown of Light" is shown nightly at 6:45 and 7:45, mid-May to mid-Sept. Admission $8; ages 3-12, $4. Reservations are recommended. The show is not recommended for infants and young children.

"Service with a Smile" in the Malemute Saloon, is a 1.5-hour performance that recounts the gold rush days in story and song. The poetry of Robert Service, author of "The Shooting of Dan McGrew," is featured. The saloon, with swinging doors and sawdust-covered floors, is filled with historical relics. Shows nightly at 9, mid-May to mid-Sept. Admission $15; ages 3-12, $7.50. Reservations are recommended.

GOLD DREDGE NUMBER 8, n. on SR 2 (Old Steese Hwy.) to Goldstream Rd. following signs, is a five-deck ship more than 250 feet long that was built in 1928 to ply Goldstream and Engineer creeks for the precious metal. Following the 90-minute tour, visitors can pan for gold and search for bison and mammoth bones. Food is available. Daily 9:30-3:30, mid-May to mid-Sept. Admission $24; ages 6-12, $12. Phone (907) 457-6058.

RIVERBOAT DISCOVERY, departing from a pier on Discovery Rd. off Airport Way, provides 3.5-hour trips on the Chena and Tanana rivers aboard the stern-wheeler *Discovery III.* Guides discuss area wildlife, history, anthropology, geology and customs. Views vary from wilderness to elegant houses, and the trip includes a guided walking tour of the Chena Indian village. Inquire about weather policies. Trips depart daily at

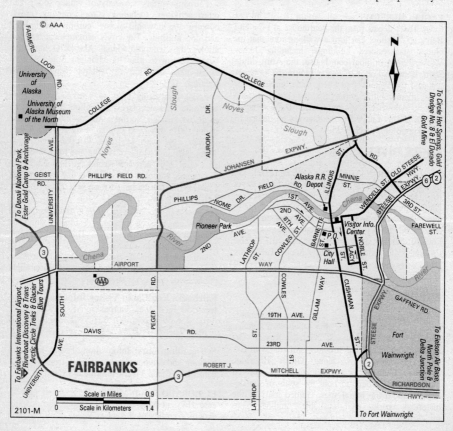

© AAA

FAIRBANKS

Scale in Miles 0.9
Scale in Kilometers 1.4
2101-M

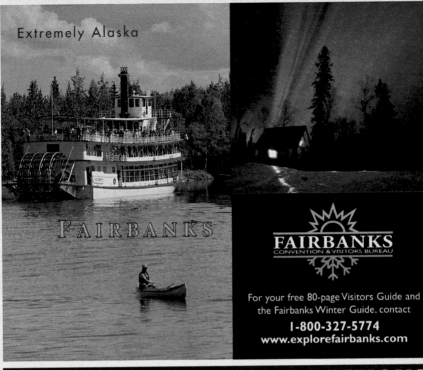

Extremely Alaska

FAIRBANKS

FAIRBANKS
CONVENTION & VISITORS BUREAU

For your free 80-page Visitors Guide and
the Fairbanks Winter Guide, contact
1-800-327-5774
www.explorefairbanks.com

FAIRBANKS' PREMIER ATTRACTIONS
Call Toll Free 1-866-479-6673

•Riverboat Discovery•

AAA GEM
Attraction

Daily Sailing 8:45am & 2pm
www.riverboatdiscovery.com

*Join the Binkley
family aboard the
authentic sternwheeler
Riverboat Discovery*

reservations@riverboatdiscovery.com

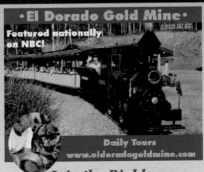

•El Dorado Gold Mine•

Featured nationally
on NBC!

Daily Tours
www.eldoradogoldmine.com

*Join the Binkley
family for an adventure
into Fairbanks'
gold mining history*

El Dorado
Gold Mine

reservations@eldoradogoldmine.com

Call for reservations **Local Calls 479-6673**

8:45 and 2, late May to mid-Sept. Fare $44.95; ages 3-12, $29.95. Reservations are required. Phone (907) 479-6673 or (866) 479-6673. *See color ad p. 309.*

TRANS ARCTIC CIRCLE TREKS AND GLACIER BLUE TOURS is at 4825 Glasgow Dr., with pick-up service available from area hotels and RV parks. This tour company offers a variety of guided excursions including day trips to the Arctic Circle and multi-day trips to the Arctic Ocean, Prudhoe Bay and Point Barrow. Visitors on the 1-day tour can enjoy mountain scenery, a walk through alpine tundra and a hands-on Trans-Alaska Pipeline demonstration. Add-on land and air excursions are available.

One-day tour departs daily May 15-Sept. 15. Other tours depart throughout the year. Fare for 1-day tour $119. Rates vary according to tour; phone ahead. Reservations are required. AX, DS, MC, VI. Phone (907) 479-5451 or (800) 336-8735. *See color ad & p. 298.*

[SAVE] **UNIVERSITY OF ALASKA MUSEUM OF THE NORTH,** on the West Ridge of the University of Alaska campus, contains natural and cultural history exhibits. Also displayed are an extensive gold collection and a steppe bison killed by a lion 36,000 years ago and preserved in the permafrost. Twenty-minute talks are given about such topics as native Alaska games and culture,

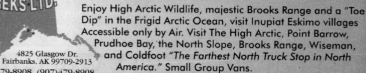

bears and wolves. "Dynamic Aurora" is a multimedia presentation that explains the northern lights.

Allow 30 minutes minimum. Daily 9-7, June-Aug.; 9-5 in May and Sept.; Mon.-Fri. 9-5, Sat.-Sun. noon-5, rest of year. Talks daily at 11:30 and 2, June-Aug. "Dynamic Aurora" daily at 10 and 3, June-Aug. Admission $5; over 59, $4.50; ages 7-17, $3. Talks free. "Dynamic Aurora" show $5. Phone (907) 474-7505.

Student-guided Walking Tours of the University of Alaska Fairbanks depart from the University of Alaska Museum of the North. Tours of the campus last 1.5 to 2 hours. Comfortable shoes are recommended. Other activities include the Arctic Region Supercomputing tour (Wed. at 2); the International Arctic Research Center tour (Wed. at 3); the Poker Flat Research Range tour (Thurs. at 1:30, select dates only); and the Georgeson Botanical Garden tour (Fri. at 2; self-guiding tour available daily 8-8). Campus walking tour Mon.-Fri. at 10, June-Aug.; closed July 3-4. Phone (907) 474-7581.

FORT YUKON (C-7) pop. 595

Just north of the Arctic Circle at a point where the Yukon River is almost 3 miles wide, the Athabascan Indian village of Fort Yukon was established as a trading post by the Hudson's Bay Co. in 1847. The village was an important port during the gold rush days, and the post office has remained popular for those who wish to mail from above the Arctic Circle.

Fort Yukon is reached by daily air service from Fairbanks. Visitors can see fish wheels in operation and purchase craftwork and fine furs. Temperatures have ranged as high as 100 degrees Fahrenheit in the summer and as low as minus 78 Fahrenheit in winter.

GATES OF THE ARCTIC NATIONAL PARK AND PRESERVE (C-6)

Elevations in the park and preserve range from 300 ft. along the Kobuk River to 8,510 ft. at Mount Igikpak. Refer to AAA maps for additional elevation information.

Lying north of the Arctic Circle, Gates of the Arctic National Park and Preserve's 8.5 million acres features a raw, austere landscape of sparse vegetation and jagged spires. The rocky spine of the Brooks Range forms the park's backbone, and a boreal forest, or taiga, of spruce, birch and poplar meets the almost treeless tundra that rolls uninterrupted to the Arctic Ocean.

Despite being four times the size of Yellowstone National Park, Gates of the Arctic is a meager larder for the caribous, moose, wolves and bears that roam the park in search of food. Fortunately much

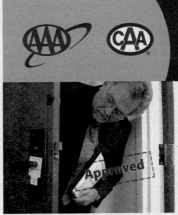

of their arctic range is protected, as Gates of the Arctic is joined on either side by Noatak National Preserve and nearby Arctic National Wildlife Refuge.

It was a forester on leave, Bob Marshall, who, in exploring this uncharted region in the late 1930s, christened this land Gates of the Arctic. The term both describes and evokes the grandeur of this wilderness—the soaring immensity of sky and mountains, the burst of wildflowers in summer and the cyclical abundance of wildlife.

But as Marshall remarked, the greatest pleasure is its undeveloped and wild character, which gives the visitor the sense of being the first to visit the tundra foothills or one of the park's nameless peaks. Today a good way to enjoy the park is to follow Marshall's example and hike the park's rugged terrain, which offers challenging backpacking. A popular alternative is to canoe or raft the network of rivers and lakes.

Most visitors use various air charter services from Fairbanks and Bettles Field to reach the park's interior. The Dalton Highway skirts the park's eastern edge and is the only road that approaches the park. Because of Gates of the Arctic's fragile ecology, there are no park facilities, trails or campgrounds within the park. For trip planning assistance and a list of outfitters, guides and air taxi operators, write Gates of the Arctic National Park and Preserve, P.O. Box 26030, Bettles, AK 99726; phone (907) 692-5494. *See Recreation Chart.*

GIRDWOOD (C-11) elev. 23′

Initially called Glacier City, Girdwood was established at the turn of the 20th century as a gold mining town. The community prospered until mine closures in the 1930s reduced it to a virtual ghost town. Misfortune struck again when the 1964 Good Friday earthquake caused massive destruction along the coast, forcing residents to move the town 2.5 miles inland to its present location. Today Girdwood thrives as a year-round recreation destination and one of the state's largest ski resorts.

Girdwood is on Turnagain Arm, a fjord carved by glaciers and known for its dramatic bore tides, which can be 6 feet high and travel at speeds of up to 15 miles an hour. The town also is located at the base of 3,939-foot Mount Alyeska; a 60-passenger tramway ascends to the 2,300-foot level and offers a panorama of the valley and Turnagain Arm.

RECREATIONAL ACTIVITIES

Skiing

- **Alyeska Resort and Ski Area** is on SR 1 (Seward Hwy.). Write P.O. Box 249, Girdwood, AK 99587. Other activities are offered. Open mid-Nov. to mid-Apr. Phone (907) 754-1111.

GLACIER BAY NATIONAL PARK AND PRESERVE (G-9)

Elevations in the park and preserve range from sea level at Glacier Bay to 15,320 ft. at Mount Fairweather. Refer to AAA maps for additional elevation information.

Stretching northward from Cross Sound to the Canadian border, Glacier Bay National Park is one of the most scenic spots in Alaska. In this 3,283,168-acre park, blue-white glaciers flow from the snow-clad peaks of the Fairweather Range to fiordlike inlets.

The park features 15,320-foot Mount Fairweather and Glacier Bay. The bay, about 65 miles long and 2.5 to 10 miles wide, was filled with ice 5,000 feet thick as recently as 200 years ago. The park contains some of the world's most impressive tidewater glaciers. Icebergs that crack off, or calve, from the nearly vertical ice cliffs dot the waters of the upper bay. Boaters are likely to encounter numerous harbor seals and an occasional whale.

This spectacular region is accessible only by plane or boat. Alaska Airlines offers flights from Juneau daily June through early September. A 10-mile road connects the park headquarters with the small community of Gustavus, where charter vessels and air and boat service to Juneau are available.

A boat tour of the bay departs from Glacier Bay Lodge each morning, late May to mid-September; phone (800) 451-5952.

Due to concern for the endangered humpback whale, permits are required from June through August for private vessels to enter Glacier Bay. An Alaska fishing license is required for fishing. Boaters should contact the National Park Service for current regulations; phone (907) 697-2627. For further information about the park contact the Superintendent, Glacier Bay National Park and Preserve, P.O. Box 140, Gustavus, AK 99826; phone (907) 697-2230. *See Recreation Chart.*

GUSTAVUS (G-10) pop: 429

FOUR SEASONS TOURS departs from Gustavus dock. During a 3-hour whale watch tour, passengers view a variety of local wildlife, including bald eagles, humpback whales, seals, sea otters, orca whales and Stellar sea lions. An on-board naturalist provides background about these animals and their environment. Allow 4 hours minimum. Daily departures at 2, late May to early Sept. Fare $79; ages 3-12, $49. MC, VI. Phone (877) 774-8687.

HAINES (G-10) pop. 1,811, elev. 66′

Haines lies in a spectacular setting on the Chilkat Peninsula near the northern end of Lynn Canal between the waters of the Inside Passage and the Chilkat River. The Alaska Marine Highway links Haines with Prince Rupert, British Columbia, and

Bellingham, Wash., and enables visitors to connect with the Alaska Highway at Haines Junction, Milepost 1016, via SRs 7 and 4. For information about the Alaska Marine Highway phone (907) 766-2111 or (800) 642-0066, ext. 9604 *(see color ad p. 292)*.

From late October through February the 48,000-acre Chilkat Bald Eagle Preserve, between Mileposts 9 and 31 on scenic Haines Highway, harbors one of the largest congregations of bald eagles in the world. More than 3,500 of the birds gather to feed on the salmon in the Chilkat River; sometimes as many as 30 eagles roost in a tree during this time. Use roadside pulloffs for viewing; stopping on the road is prohibited. Tour information is available at Haines Visitor Center.

Other interesting drives near Haines include Lutak Road, leading to Chilkoot Lake, and Mud Bay Road, which passes Pyramid Harbor and an old cannery with its salmon boats before approaching Chilkat State Park *(see Recreation Chart and the AAA Western Canada & Alaska CampBook)*. Davidson and Rainbow glaciers also are visible from this route.

The fishing industry that once was so vital to Alaska's economy sustained several area salmon canneries in the early part of the 20th century. Tsirku Canning Co. at Fifth and Main streets offers demonstrations of the only known working three-piece canning machinery. A museum contains photographs, a videotape and exhibits about the packing process; phone (907) 766-3474.

Fjord Express, (800) 320-0146, and Chilkat Cruises Fast Ferry, (888) 766-2103, provide efficient transportation between Haines, Skagway and Juneau.

Haines Visitor Center: 122 Second Ave., P.O. Box 530, Haines, AK 99827; phone (907) 766-2234 or (800) 458-3579. *See color ad.*

Self-guiding tours: Brochures featuring walking tours of Haines and Fort William H. Seward are available from Haines Visitor Center.

SAVE **CHILKAT BALD EAGLE PRESERVE FLOAT TRIPS,** on Sawmill Rd., pass through the Bald Eagle Preserve on the Chilkat River and offer views of the Chilkat Mountains and bald eagles in their natural habitat. Transportation to and from the river is provided. Bring warm clothes, binoculars, camera, sunglasses and rain gear. Inquire about weather policies. The 4-hour float trip departs daily, May-Sept. Departure times vary; phone ahead. Fare $79; ages 7-14, $62.50. Reservations are recommended. Phone (907) 766-2491.

CHILKOOT LAKE TOURS, 1183 Haines Hwy., offers sightseeing and fishing cruises of Chilkoot Lake. Brown bears, bald eagles and spawning salmon can be seen. Inquire about weather policies. Allow 3 hours minimum. Daily at 9 and 2, May 1-Sept. 15; other times by appointment. Fare for sightseeing cruise $85; fishing cruise $99. AX, CB, MC, VI. Phone (907) 766-3779.

FORT WILLIAM H. SEWARD is at the s. end of Haines Hwy. The site of the first permanent Army post in Alaska contains a replica of a tribal house, a trapper's cabin and several caches. The old hospital houses carvers who use traditional Tlingit Indian methods. Chilkat Indian storytelling dances are performed most weekdays in the tribal house. Walking tour maps are available at the Haines Visitor Center and at Hotel Halsingland. Fort open daily. Performance schedule varies; phone ahead. Fort free. Performances $10; under 12, $5. Phone (907) 766-2234 for fort information or (907) 766-2540 for performance times.

SHELDON MUSEUM AND CULTURAL CENTER, on Main St. above the boat harbor, allows visitors to experience the art and culture of the Tlingit

native people and to learn about the early pioneer history of Haines Mission, the Porcupine Goldrush and Fort Seward, a frontier army post. Videotape presentations about the Haines Highway, Chilkat weaving and local community lifestyles also are featured. Allow 1 hour, 30 minutes minimum. Daily 11-6, late May to mid-Sept.; Mon.-Fri. 1-4, rest of year. Admission $3, under 13 free. Phone (907) 766-2366.

RECREATIONAL ACTIVITIES
Fishing

- **Weeping Trout Sports Resort** is downtown at 144 Second Ave. S. Write P.O. Box 129, Haines, AK 99827. Trips depart June-Sept. Other activities are offered. Phone (907) 766-2827.

HOMER (D-10) pop. 3,946, elev. 67′

Homer Pennock landed a party of gold and coal prospectors in the schooner *Excelsior* in 1896 and established Homer. Gold was not found, but an abundance of coal was and the settlement remained.

Healthy fishing and tourism industries support Homer's economy. Kachemak Bay, a 30-mile arm of lower Cook Inlet, provides a usually ice-free deepwater harbor for Homer. A small boat harbor has launching facilities and charter boats. Charter planes are available in town for hunting, fishing, wildlife viewing and sightseeing expeditions. Cross-country skiing is popular in winter. The city is linked by daily air service with Anchorage, and by the Alaska Marine Highway with Seward, Kodiak and Seldovia.

Skyline Drive, accessible from West and East Hill roads, follows the rim of the plateau behind the town and offers access to ski slopes and views of the bay, Homer Spit and the Kenai Mountains. Chartered bush flights afford panoramas of the bay, open coal seams and Harding Icefield to the southeast.

Homer Chamber of Commerce: P.O. Box 541, Homer, AK 99603; phone (907) 235-7740 or (907) 235-5300.

ALASKA ISLANDS & OCEAN VISITOR CENTER is at 95 Sterling Hwy. The center presents an overview of the area through interpretive exhibits about Kachemak Bay; local estuaries; research ships; and the seabird and marine inhabitants of the Alaska Marine National Wildlife Refuge. Outdoor nature trails link the 60-acre site with Bishop's Beach Park on Kachemak Bay. Naturalist-led tours are offered, and a short movie about the Aleutian Islands is shown. Allow 2 hours minimum. Daily 9-6, Memorial Day-Labor Day; varies, rest of year. Closed holidays. Donations. Phone (907) 226-4619.

SAVE **PRATT MUSEUM** is .5 blks. n. of Pioneer Ave. at 3779 Bartlett St. Highlights include a botanical garden; a marine gallery; fishing boat models; sea birds and marine mammals; a forest trail; an exhibit detailing the impact of the *Exxon Valdez* oil spill; and cultural displays, which feature

Russian, Eskimo and American Indian artifacts. Alaskan art from the Kenai Peninsula also is exhibited.

Allow 1 hour minimum. Sun.-Wed. 10-6, Thurs.-Sat. 10-8, June-Sept.; Tues.-Sun. noon-5, Feb.-Apr. and Oct.-Dec. Closed Thanksgiving and Dec. 25. Admission $6; over 65 and students with ID $5.50; ages 6-18, $3. Phone (907) 235-8635.

RECREATIONAL ACTIVITIES
Fishing

- **Homer Ocean Charters** is at Cannery Row boardwalk on Homer Spit Rd. Write P.O. Box 2543, Homer, AK 99603. Trips depart daily by appointment. Phone (907) 235-6212.

HOPE (F-6) pop. 137, elev. 32′

RECREATIONAL ACTIVITIES
White-water Rafting

- **Chugach Outdoor Center** departs from Milepost 7.5, Hope Hwy. Write P.O. Box 28, Hope, AK 99605. Other activities are offered. Trips daily 8-7, May-Sept. Phone (907) 277-7238 or (866) 277-7238.

JUNEAU (G-10) pop. 30,711, elev. 12′

Juneau, Alaska's capital city, lies along the beautiful Gastineau Channel at the foot of snowcapped mounts Roberts and Juneau. The borough of Juneau covers 3,108 square miles of towering mountains, islands, saltwater bays, forested valleys and residential flatlands. Its road system extends from Thane, 6 miles southeast of downtown, northwest to Echo Cove at Milepost 40.2 on the Glacier Highway. The city is accessible by air or by sea.

When Joe Juneau and Richard Harris discovered gold in 1880, they started the first rush in American Alaska. At one time the Alaska-Juneau and Treadwell mines were producing about 20,000 tons of ore daily. Not until 1944, when the low price of gold and the high cost of extraction rendered it impractical, did mining operations cease.

The Alaska State Capitol, Fourth and Main streets, offers free 30-minute tours in summer. One block west of the capitol is the State Office Building, which contains a century-old totem pole and a Kimball Theatre pipe organ equipped with such accessories as a glockenspiel, sleigh bells and bird whistles. Free concerts are held Friday at noon in the eighth-floor atrium. Also on the eighth floor, a terrace affords panoramas of the harbor and the surrounding mountains.

Tours of one of the oldest churches in southeastern Alaska are available mid-May to mid-September. Built in 1894, St. Nicholas Russian Orthodox Church is at Fifth and Gold streets. The Shrine of St. Terese, near Milepost 23 on the Glacier Highway, is a stone chapel on an island connected to shore by a gravel causeway.

There are many ways to tour Juneau. Nearby hiking trails, which vary in length and difficulty, lead to fishing spots, scenic mountain areas, old mine ruins and points near Mendenhall Glacier. Bus tours circle points of interest in Juneau and visit Mendenhall Glacier and the log Chapel-by-the-Lake at Auke Lake. Tours depart from the cruise ship docks during the summer. Visitors also can charter boats for sightseeing or fishing.

Charter flights provide views of the ice field; among the companies that provide such service are Alaska Seaplane Service, L.A.B. Flying, Skagway Air Service, Ward Air and Wings of Alaska. In addition to flightseeing tours Alaska Fly 'n' Fish Charters offers floatplane fishing trips. Helicopter tours, float trips, gold-panning excursions and several tours of nearby and more distant points of interest are available through SAVE Gray Line of Alaska and other local tour companies.

Salmon bakes are held in Salmon Creek and at Thane Ore House daily in summer.

Juneau Convention and Visitors Bureau: 101 Egan Dr., Juneau, AK 99801; phone (907) 586-2201 or (888) 581-2201.

Self-guiding tours: Free walking tour maps of the historical and governmental districts are available at Juneau Visitor Information Center in Centennial Hall, 101 Egan Dr.

 ALASKA STATE MUSEUM, w. of Egan Dr. at 395 Whittier St., chronicles the state's history and preserves and exhibits Tlingit and Athabascan Indian, Eskimo and Aleut culture. Wildlife and mining displays, Russian-American historical exhibits and art of Alaska are featured. Highlights include a bald eagle nesting tree.

Guided tours are available in summer. Allow 1 hour minimum. Daily 8:30-5:30, mid-May to late Sept.; Tues.-Sat. 10-4, rest of year. Closed holidays. Admission mid-May to late Sept. $5, under 19 free. Admission rest of year $3, under 19 free. Phone (907) 465-2901.

DOLPHIN WHALE WATCH TOURS depart from Merchant's Wharf at 2 Marine Way. Three-hour tours on a jet boat offer the opportunity to view humpback and killer whales, porpoises, sea lions, seals and eagles. Daily 7-7, May 15-Sept. 15; Mon.-Thurs. 10-3, Apr. 15-May 14 and Sept. 16-30. Fare $105; ages 2-12, $84. AX, DS, MC, VI. Phone (907) 463-3422.

ERA HELICOPTERS FLIGHTSEEING TOURS depart from the North Douglas Airport. Narrated,

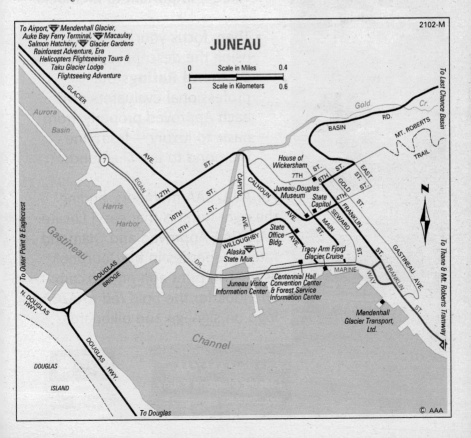

2102-M

JUNEAU

To Airport, Mendenhall Glacier, Auke Bay Ferry Terminal, Macaulay Salmon Hatchery, Glacier Gardens Rainforest Adventure, Era Helicopters Flightseeing Tours & Taku Glacier Lodge Flightseeing Adventure

Scale in Miles 0 0.4
Scale in Kilometers 0 0.6

To Last Chance Basin

Gold Cr.

RD.

BASIN

MT. ROBERTS TRAIL

Aurora Basin

GLACIER

AVE.

EGAN

7

Harris Harbor

12TH ST.

10TH ST.

9TH ST.

CAPITOL ST.

CALHOUN AVE.

House of Wickersham

7TH ST.

6TH ST.

5TH ST.

GOLD ST.

4TH ST.

EAST ST.

Juneau-Douglas Museum

State Capitol

FRANKLIN

SEWARD ST.

MAIN ST.

State Office Bldg.

WILLOUGHBY AVE.

Alaska State Mus.

DR.

AVE.

Tracy Arm Fjord Glacier Cruise

MARINE

WAY

GASTINEAU AVE.

FRANKLIN ST.

To Thane & Mt. Roberts Tramway

Juneau Visitor Information Center

Centennial Hall Convention Center & Forest Service Information Center

Mendenhall Glacier Transport, Ltd.

Gastineau

To Outer Point & Eaglecrest

DOUGLAS BRIDGE

N. DOUGLAS HWY.

DOUGLAS HWY.

DOUGLAS ISLAND

Channel

To Douglas

© AAA

Find Hotels As Easy As 1-2-3-4-5!

For reliable hotel stays matched to your needs every time, use AAA/CAA's valuable two-part rating system:

- First, rest assured that *every* hotel designated **AAA/CAA Approved** upholds qualities like cleanliness, service, and value – important to members.

- Then, focus your selection using the descriptive **AAA/CAA Diamond Ratings** our professional evaluators give each Approved property, from basic to luxury — from one Diamond to five Diamonds.

For AAA/CAA members, finding the right hotel is that easy! Locate AAA/CAA Approved and Diamond rated properties in the TourBook® listings, in print and on aaa.com, and look for the bold red AAA/CAA logo on signage and billboards.

Read about **AAA/CAA Lodging Diamond Rating** requirements on page **16**.

Show Your Card
Approved Lodging

1-hour tours offer views of the capital city, abandoned mines and four glaciers in the Juneau Icefield. Highlights include a glacier landing to explore the blue ice. Flights combined with glacier trekking and dog sledding trips also are available. Free transportation is provided from downtown hotels. Allow 2 hours minimum. Daily 8-6. Fare $225-$389. Flights require a minimum of four passengers. AX, DS, MC, VI. Phone (907) 586-2030 or (800) 843-1947. *See color ad p. 306.*

FOREST SERVICE INFORMATION CENTER is at 8465 Old Dairy Rd. Trail guides, maps, current conditions and recreation and cabin reservation information about Tongass National Forest and Glacier Bay National Park are available. Mon.-Fri. 8-5. Free. Phone (907) 586-8751.

GLACIER GARDENS RAINFOREST ADVENTURE is at 7600 Glacier Hwy. A motorized shuttle takes passengers up Thunder Mountain through botanical gardens nestled in a lush Alaskan rain forest. Guests travel past streams, ponds, waterfalls and such flora as rhododendrons, Japanese maples and ferns. A scenic overlook at the 580-foot marker offers a spectacular view of the Mendenhall Valley and Chilkat Mountains. Allow 1 hour minimum. Daily 9-6, May-Sept. Admission $17.95; ages 6-12, $12.95. AX, MC, VI. Phone (907) 790-3377.

HOUSE OF WICKERSHAM, 213 Seventh St., was the residence of Judge James Wickersham, noted Alaskan statesman, historian and pioneer judge. Built 1898-99 on "Chicken Ridge," this large Victorian house offers panoramic views of Gastineau Channel. Wherever the judge traveled in Alaska he collected ivory pieces, basketry and carvings, which are on display. Thurs.-Tues. 10-noon and 1-5, mid-May to late Sept.; by appointment rest of year. Donations. Phone (907) 586-9001.

JUNEAU-DOUGLAS MUSEUM, Fourth and Main sts., features exhibits about the area's early gold mining days, Tlingit culture and life in the Juneau-Douglas areas. Special exhibits about the greater Juneau area change annually. A relief map of the city's topography and a video presentation titled "Juneau: City Built on Gold" are other features. Free maps outlining a historic walking tour are available. Mon.-Fri. 9-5, Sat.-Sun 10-5, May-Sept.; Tues.-Sat. noon-4 and by appointment, rest of year. Closed winter holidays. Admission $3, under 18 free. Phone (907) 586-3572.

MACAULAY SALMON HATCHERY, 2697 Channel Dr., hatches more than 122 million salmon eggs annually, including chum, pink, coho and king. The hatchery features many exhibits and saltwater aquariums that contain live adult salmon and more than 100 species of southeast Alaska sea life. Guided tours are available. Allow 30 minutes minimum. Mon.-Fri. 10-6, Sat.-Sun. 10-5, mid-May to mid-Sept.; by appointment rest of year. Admission $3.25; ages 3-12, $1.75. AX, MC, VI. Phone (907) 463-4810.

MENDENHALL GLACIER, 13 mi. n.w. via SR 7 and Mendenhall Loop Rd., is an impressive river of blue ice, 13 miles long and 1.5 miles wide at its widest point. The glacier is fed by the 1,500-square-mile Juneau Icefield, part of the Tongass National Forest *(see place listing p. 333).*

Trails on either side of the glacial valley afford scenic views. To the east are Mendenhall Lake and Nugget Creek Falls; the west trail ascends above the glacier. Camping and picnic facilities are available at Mendenhall Lake. An easily traversable .5-mile nature trail begins near the visitor center; brochures are available.

The Steep Creek viewing platform near the visitor center parking lot is a good vantage point from which to see spawning sockeye salmon mid-July through mid-September. The salmon run attracts bald eagles and black bears mid-September through November.

Mendenhall Glacier Visitor Center contains a model depicting glacier dynamics, dioramas and display cases that interpret five evolving ecosystems at the glacier and a naturalistic salmon-filled stream that tumbles over rocks and flows under a glass floor. A film is shown three times every hour during the summer, otherwise by request. Interpretive talks and nature hikes also are offered. Daily 8-6:30, May-Sept.; 10-4, rest of year. Admission $3, under 13 free. Phone (907) 789-0097 or (907) 789-6640.

MENDENHALL GLACIER TRANSPORT LTD., departing from the cruise ship dock downtown, provides sightseeing excursions of Juneau by bus. The tour stops at the Chapel by the Lake and Mendenhall Glacier. Other tours are available. Allow 2 hours, 30 minutes minimum. Daily 9-3:30, May-Sept. Fare $20. Phone (907) 789-5460. *See color ad p. 317.*

MOUNT ROBERTS TRAMWAY, 490 S. Franklin St. on the cruise ship dock, offers a 6-minute ride to the 1,800-foot-level of Mount Roberts. At the top, visitors can stop at the nature center, see a live bald eagle displayed by the Juneau Raptor Center, take wildlife or nature walks and view the spectacular scenery. "Seeing Daylight," a movie about Alaska's native Tlingit, is presented in the Chilkat Theater. Food is available. Allow 1 hour, 30 minutes minimum. Daily 9-9, May 5-Sept. 25. Fare $21.95; ages 7-12, $12.60. AX, CB, MC, VI. Phone (907) 463-3412 or (888) 461-8726.

TAKU GLACIER LODGE FLIGHTSEEING ADVENTURE departs from the wharf near the cruise ship docks. A floatplane takes passengers to a 1923 fishing and hunting lodge in the Taku River Valley for a salmon feast. Aerial views include mountains, Taku Inlet, waterfalls and five glaciers. Walking trails explore the area surrounding the historic lodge, which is across the river from the Hole-in-the-Wall Glacier. Allow 3 hours minimum. Trips depart daily at 9, 11, 1 and 3, May-Sept. Fare $199; under 12, $156. AX, MC, VI. Phone (907) 586-6275.

TRACY ARM FJORD GLACIER CRUISE departs the Goldbelt Tour Center Dock at 76 Egan Dr. The boat traverses iceberg-laden fjords that larger ships cannot. Visitors come in close proximity to glaciers, cliffs and cascading waterfalls. Food is available. Allow 8 hours minimum. Daily 9-5, May 17-Sept. 7. Fare $119; ages 2-12, $70. AX, MC, VI. Phone (907) 586-8687 or (800) 820-2628.

RECREATIONAL ACTIVITIES
Fishing

- **Juneau Sportfishing** offers round-trip transportation from local hotels and ships. Write P.O. Box 20438, Juneau, AK 99802. Trips depart daily. Reservations are required. Phone (907) 586-1887.

- **Salmon Guaranteed Charters**, 4510 Prospect Way, Juneau, AK 99801. Daily May-Oct. Reservations are required. Phone (907) 364-3474.

Skiing

- **Eaglecrest Ski Area** is 12 mi. n.w. off the N. Douglas Hwy. Write 155 S. Seward St., Juneau, AK 99801. Thurs.-Mon. 9-4, Dec.-Mar. (also Thurs. 4-9, early Jan. to mid-Mar.). Phone (907) 790-2000.

KATMAI NATIONAL PARK AND PRESERVE (G-5)

Elevations in the park and preserve range from sea level at the Shelikof Strait to 7,606 ft. at Mount Dennison. Refer to AAA maps for additional elevation information.

On the northern portion of the Alaska Peninsula, 4.1-million-acre Katmai National Park and Preserve displays an outstanding example of volcanism. In 1912 one of the greatest volcanic explosions in recorded history turned a nameless green valley into what became known as the Valley of Ten Thousand

Before you hit the open road, tear along the dotted line!

For reservations call **1-800-HOLIDAY**

For reservations call
1 800 HOLIDAY

Valid at participating Holiday Inn® and Holiday Inn Express® hotels One coupon per room per stay Valid on each night of stay; no copies or facsimiles accepted Not valid for groups or in conjunction with any other discount, promotion or special event as established by each independent operator Not valid with employee or travel industry discounts Blackout dates apply Rooms limited and subject to availability Void where taxed, restricted or otherwise prohibited by law Coupon has no cash value Offer valid March 1, 2005 to May 31, 2005 ®Trademarks of members of InterContinental Hotels Group ©2004 InterContinental Hotels Group All rights reserved Most hotels are independently owned and/or operated 2005CAA Western

Offer valid March 1 - May 31, 2005

$10 OFF CAA/AAA room rate

See back for participating hotels.

For reservations call
1 800 HOLIDAY

Valid at participating Holiday Inn® and Holiday Inn Express® hotels One coupon per room per stay Valid on each night of stay; no copies or facsimiles accepted Not valid for groups or in conjunction with any other discount, promotion or special event as established by each independent operator Not valid with employee or travel industry discounts Blackout dates apply Rooms limited and subject to availability Void where taxed, restricted or otherwise prohibited by law Coupon has no cash value Offer valid June 1, 2005 to August 31, 2005 ®Trademarks of members of InterContinental Hotels Group ©2004 InterContinental Hotels Group All rights reserved Most hotels are independently owned and/or operated 2005CAA Western

Offer valid June 1 - August 31, 2005

$5 OFF CAA/AAA room rate

See back for participating hotels.

For reservations call
1 800 HOLIDAY

Valid at participating Holiday Inn® and Holiday Inn Express® hotels One coupon per room per stay Valid on each night of stay; no copies or facsimiles accepted Not valid for groups or in conjunction with any other discount, promotion or special event as established by each independent operator Not valid with employee or travel industry discounts Blackout dates apply Rooms limited and subject to availability Void where taxed, restricted or otherwise prohibited by law Coupon has no cash value Offer valid September 1, 2005 to November 30, 2005 ®Trademarks of members of InterContinental Hotels Group ©2004 InterContinental Hotels Group All rights reserved Most hotels are independently owned and/or operated 2005CAA Western

Offer valid September 1 - November 30, 2005

$10 OFF CAA/AAA room rate

See back for participating hotels.

For reservations call
1 800 HOLIDAY

Valid at participating Holiday Inn® and Holiday Inn Express® hotels One coupon per room per stay Valid on each night of stay; no copies or facsimiles accepted Not valid for groups or in conjunction with any other discount, promotion or special event as established by each independent operator Not valid with employee or travel industry discounts Blackout dates apply Rooms limited and subject to availability Void where taxed, restricted or otherwise prohibited by law Coupon has no cash value Offer valid December 1, 2005 to February 28, 2006 ®Trademarks of members of InterContinental Hotels Group ©2004 InterContinental Hotels Group All rights reserved Most hotels are independently owned and/or operated 2005CAA Western

Offer valid December 1, 2005 February 28, 2006

$15 OFF CAA/AAA room rate

See back for participating hotels

For reservations call **1-800-HOLIDAY**
or your travel professional

ALBERTA
★ Calgary Dwtn Conference Centre
● Calgary University
▲ Edmonton
▼ Fort McMurray
★ Hinton
▲ Lethbridge
● Red Deer
● Rocky Mountain House
BRITISH COLUMBIA
★ International Vancouver Airport
● Kamloops
● Kelowna
▼ North Vancouver
◆ Osoyoos
▲ Salmon Arm
● Vancouver
● Vancouver Airport
★ Vancouver Centre (Broadway)
▼ Vancouver Downtown

★ Victoria
★ Westbank
◆ Whistler Village Centre
MANITOBA
▼ Winnipeg Downtown
▼ Winnipeg Airport/West
★ Winnipeg South
NEW BRUNSWICK
▲ Moncton
● Saint John *Opening Soon*
NEWFOUNDLAND & LABRADOR
★ Stephenville
NOVA SCOTIA
● Halifax/Bedford
■ Halifax Centre
★ Halifax Harbourview
ONTARIO
▲ Barrie
★ Barrie Hotel & Conference Centre
★ Brantford
★ Burlington Hotel & Conference Center

★ Cambridge
● Cornwall
● Dryden
★ Fort Erie/ Niagara Convention Centre
★ Guelph
▲ Guelph
● Hamilton Stoney Creek
★ Kingston Waterfront
★ Kitchener Waterloo
■ Mississauga
★ Oakville Centre
● Oshawa
▼ Ottawa Downtown
▼ Ottawa Kanata
● Peterborough Waterfront
★ Sarnia
★ Sault Ste Marie Waterfront
★ St Catharines/Niagara
■ Toronto Airport
● Toronto Airport Area (Dixie Rd)
★ Toronto Airport East

■ Toronto Brampton
● Toronto East
▼ Toronto Markham
★ Toronto Mississauga
● Toronto North York
★ Toronto West
★ Toronto Yorkdale
★ Trenton
■ Windsor (Ambassador Bridge)
PRINCE EDWARD ISLAND
▲ Charlottetown
QUEBEC
★ Gatineau Ottawa Plz Chaudière
★ Montreal Airport
■ Montreal Centre Ville (Dwtn Conv Ctr)
★ Montreal Longueuil
★ Montreal Midtown
★ Pte Claire Airport
● Quebec City Downtown
★ Saguenay Convention Centre

★denotes Holiday Inn® hotels ■denotes Holiday Inn Select® hotels ▼denotes Holiday Inn® Hotel & Suites ◆denotes Holiday Inn SunSpree® Resort
● denotes Holiday Inn Express® hotels ▲denotes Holiday Inn Express® Hotel & Suites

ALBERTA
★ Calgary Dwtn Conference Centre
● Calgary University
▲ Edmonton
▼ Fort McMurray
★ Hinton
▲ Lethbridge
● Red Deer
● Rocky Mountain House
BRITISH COLUMBIA
★ International Vancouver Airport
● Kamloops
● Kelowna
▼ North Vancouver
◆ Osoyoos
▲ Salmon Arm
● Vancouver
● Vancouver Airport
★ Vancouver Centre (Broadway)
▼ Vancouver Downtown

★ Victoria
★ Westbank
◆ Whistler Village Centre
MANITOBA
▼ Winnipeg Downtown
▼ Winnipeg Airport/West
★ Winnipeg South
NEW BRUNSWICK
▲ Moncton
● Saint John *Opening Soon*
NEWFOUNDLAND & LABRADOR
★ Stephenville
NOVA SCOTIA
● Halifax/Bedford
■ Halifax Centre
★ Halifax Harbourview
ONTARIO
▲ Barrie
★ Barrie Hotel & Conference Centre
★ Brantford
★ Burlington Hotel & Conference Center

★ Cambridge
● Cornwall
● Dryden
★ Fort Erie/ Niagara Convention Centre
★ Guelph
▲ Guelph
● Hamilton Stoney Creek
★ Kingston Waterfront
★ Kitchener Waterloo
■ Mississauga
★ Oakville Centre
● Oshawa
▼ Ottawa Downtown
▼ Ottawa Kanata
● Peterborough Waterfront
★ Sarnia
★ Sault Ste Marie Waterfront
★ St Catharines/Niagara
■ Toronto Airport
● Toronto Airport Area (Dixie Rd)
★ Toronto Airport East

■ Toronto Brampton
● Toronto East
▼ Toronto Markham
★ Toronto Mississauga
● Toronto North York
★ Toronto West
★ Toronto Yorkdale
★ Trenton
■ Windsor (Ambassador Bridge)
PRINCE EDWARD ISLAND
▲ Charlottetown
QUEBEC
★ Gatineau Ottawa Plz Chaudière
★ Montreal Airport
■ Montreal Centre Ville (Dwtn Conv Ctr)
★ Montreal Longueuil
★ Montreal Midtown
★ Pte Claire Airport
● Quebec City Downtown
★ Saguenay Convention Centre

★denotes Holiday Inn® hotels ■denotes Holiday Inn Select® hotels ▼denotes Holiday Inn® Hotel & Suites ◆denotes Holiday Inn SunSpree® Resort
● denotes Holiday Inn Express® hotels ▲denotes Holiday Inn Express® Hotel & Suites

ALBERTA
★ Calgary Dwtn Conference Centre
● Calgary University
▲ Edmonton
▼ Fort McMurray
★ Hinton
▲ Lethbridge
● Red Deer
● Rocky Mountain House
BRITISH COLUMBIA
★ International Vancouver Airport
● Kamloops
● Kelowna
▼ North Vancouver
◆ Osoyoos
▲ Salmon Arm
● Vancouver
● Vancouver Airport
★ Vancouver Centre (Broadway)
▼ Vancouver Downtown

★ Victoria
★ Westbank
◆ Whistler Village Centre
MANITOBA
▼ Winnipeg Downtown
▼ Winnipeg Airport/West
★ Winnipeg South
NEW BRUNSWICK
▲ Moncton
● Saint John *Opening Soon*
NEWFOUNDLAND & LABRADOR
★ Stephenville
NOVA SCOTIA
● Halifax/Bedford
■ Halifax Centre
★ Halifax Harbourview
ONTARIO
▲ Barrie
★ Barrie Hotel & Conference Centre
★ Brantford
★ Burlington Hotel & Conference Center

★ Cambridge
● Cornwall
● Dryden
★ Fort Erie/ Niagara Convention Centre
★ Guelph
▲ Guelph
● Hamilton Stoney Creek
★ Kingston Waterfront
★ Kitchener Waterloo
■ Mississauga
★ Oakville Centre
● Oshawa
▼ Ottawa Downtown
▼ Ottawa Kanata
● Peterborough Waterfront
★ Sarnia
★ Sault Ste Marie Waterfront
★ St Catharines/Niagara
■ Toronto Airport
● Toronto Airport Area (Dixie Rd)
★ Toronto Airport East

■ Toronto Brampton
● Toronto East
▼ Toronto Markham
★ Toronto Mississauga
● Toronto North York
★ Toronto West
★ Toronto Yorkdale
★ Trenton
■ Windsor (Ambassador Bridge)
PRINCE EDWARD ISLAND
▲ Charlottetown
QUEBEC
★ Gatineau Ottawa Plz Chaudière
★ Montreal Airport
■ Montreal Centre Ville (Dwtn Conv Ctr)
★ Montreal Longueuil
★ Montreal Midtown
★ Pte Claire Airport
● Quebec City Downtown
★ Saguenay Convention Centre

★denotes Holiday Inn® hotels ■denotes Holiday Inn Select® hotels ▼denotes Holiday Inn® Hotel & Suites ◆denotes Holiday Inn SunSpree® Resort
● denotes Holiday Inn Express® hotels ▲denotes Holiday Inn Express® Hotel & Suites

ALBERTA
★ Calgary Dwtn Conference Centre
● Calgary University
▲ Edmonton
▼ Fort McMurray
★ Hinton
▲ Lethbridge
● Red Deer
● Rocky Mountain House
BRITISH COLUMBIA
★ International Vancouver Airport
● Kamloops
● Kelowna
▼ North Vancouver
◆ Osoyoos
▲ Salmon Arm
● Vancouver
● Vancouver Airport
★ Vancouver Centre (Broadway)
▼ Vancouver Downtown

★ Victoria
★ Westbank
◆ Whistler Village Centre
MANITOBA
▼ Winnipeg Downtown
▼ Winnipeg Airport/West
★ Winnipeg South
NEW BRUNSWICK
▲ Moncton
● Saint John *Opening Soon*
NEWFOUNDLAND & LABRADOR
★ Stephenville
NOVA SCOTIA
● Halifax/Bedford
■ Halifax Centre
★ Halifax Harbourview
ONTARIO
▲ Barrie
★ Barrie Hotel & Conference Centre
★ Brantford
★ Burlington Hotel & Conference Center

★ Cambridge
● Cornwall
● Dryden
★ Fort Erie/ Niagara Convention Centre
★ Guelph
▲ Guelph
● Hamilton Stoney Creek
★ Kingston Waterfront
★ Kitchener Waterloo
■ Mississauga
★ Oakville Centre
● Oshawa
▼ Ottawa Downtown
▼ Ottawa Kanata
● Peterborough Waterfront
★ Sarnia
★ Sault Ste Marie Waterfront
★ St Catharines/Niagara
■ Toronto Airport
● Toronto Airport Area (Dixie Rd)
★ Toronto Airport East

■ Toronto Brampton
● Toronto East
▼ Toronto Markham
★ Toronto Mississauga
● Toronto North York
★ Toronto West
★ Toronto Yorkdale
★ Trenton
■ Windsor (Ambassador Bridge)
PRINCE EDWARD ISLAND
▲ Charlottetown
QUEBEC
★ Gatineau Ottawa Plz Chaudière
★ Montreal Airport
■ Montreal Centre Ville (Dwtn Conv Ctr)
★ Montreal Longueuil
★ Montreal Midtown
★ Pte Claire Airport
● Quebec City Downtown
★ Saguenay Convention Centre

★denotes Holiday Inn® hotels ■denotes Holiday Inn Select® hotels ▼denotes Holiday Inn® Hotel & Suites ◆denotes Holiday Inn SunSpree® Resort
● denotes Holiday Inn Express® hotels ▲denotes Holiday Inn Express® Hotel & Suites

Smokes. For more than 45 years the eruption was attributed to Mount Katmai, but recent studies indicate that the source was a new volcanic vent called Novarupta, some 6 miles distant.

During or shortly after the eruption, the peak of Mount Katmai collapsed, forming a caldera that subsequently filled with water. Molten material released from Novarupta and surrounding vents flowed down the valley, and thousands of holes from which smoke and gases arose formed as gases and vaporized surface water percolated through the volcanic deposits. These fumaroles, which gave the valley its name, lasted only about 20 years.

Although nearly all of the "smokes" have died out, steam columns from nearby volcanoes sometimes can be seen. By air it is possible to see the jade-green lake in the crater of Mount Katmai and to circle over still-active mounts Trident, Mageik and Martin.

In addition to its superlative scenery—large lakes, rivers, glaciers and active volcanoes—the park is noted for its abundant wildlife. The most prominent mammal is the Alaskan brown bear, the world's largest carnivore, averaging 500 pounds with some reaching 1,200 pounds. It is recommended that visitors maintain at least 50 yards from individual bears and 100 yards from sows with young. Visitors also should make noises while walking or hiking.

Katmai National Park can be reached only by boat or plane. A boat ramp is at Lake Camp, 10 miles by dirt road from King Salmon. Commercial airlines serve King Salmon, 35 miles from Brooks Camp. Amphibious aircraft make daily scheduled flights between King Salmon and Brooks Camp. Bush planes can be chartered.

Daily tours to the Valley of 10,000 Smokes begin at Brooks Camp and include lunch; the fare is $96. For more information phone Katmai Land, (800) 544-0551. *See Recreation Chart.*

KENAI (D-10) pop. 6,942, elev. 86′

Established as Fort St. Nicholas by Russian fur traders in 1791, Kenai (KEEN-eye) is one of the oldest permanent settlements in Alaska. Until 1953 the town grew under a squatters' rights policy. Kenai is the closest settlement to the south-central region's most promising oil-development fields and is the site of major petrochemical plants.

Kenai's Russian Orthodox Church, established in 1894, contains religious and art objects brought from Russia in 1841.

A popular and colorful pastime during the summer months in Kenai is berry picking. Such berries as Alaska blueberries (a smaller version of its common cousin), nagoonberries (reddish purple in color), cloudberries and salmonberries (both peach in color), crowberries (black in color), northern red currants, wild raspberries and cranberries grow on the peninsula.

Mountains of Ice

Glaciers—blue-white in color, with long frozen tongues reaching into the water—cover more than 75,000 square miles in the United States, and most are found in Alaska.

If you've explored the waters of the Inside Passage or Prince William Sound, you've certainly seen them.

But how is a glacier formed? Here are the basics: Glaciers are created when more snow falls each winter than melts the following summer. As areas receive snowfall year after year, new snow layers create pressure on existing layers of snow and ice. This creates firn, small granules of compacted snow. Firn from previous years is buried and turns to ice

Laura Breen

through crystallization. The process continues, increasing the pressure on the ice field until air diminishes, and solid crystalline ice is formed.

As the layers of snow, firn and ice thicken, the lower ice can no longer support the weight of the mass, and it moves downward, smoothing surrounding mountain walls and floors and leaving grooves in a U-shaped valley.

You may be wondering why glacial ice is blue. It's actually not. Glacial ice is so concentrated that it absorbs all colors in the light spectrum except blue, which is reflected back at the viewer—making the ice *appear* blue. The lack of oxygen in the ice causes it to melt much more slowly than ice created in your freezer.

Some of the more popular glaciers to visit are Columbia, Exit, Hubbard, Le Conte, Mendenhall and Portage. But while you're gazing at these giant frozen wonders, keep in mind that almost 90 percent of an iceberg is below water!

Kenai Visitors and Convention Bureau: 11471 Kenai Spur Hwy., Kenai, AK 99611; phone (907) 283-1991.

KENAI VISITORS & CULTURAL CENTER, 11471 Kenai Spur Hwy., offers visitor information as well as displays about Kenai's history and culture. Exhibit rooms showcase Dena'ina Athabascan art and artifacts, Russian relics and educational displays describing Alaskan wildlife. The center also hosts traveling and temporary exhibitions of photography, art, crafts, native culture and Alaska history throughout the year. Allow 30 minutes minimum. Mon.-Fri. 9-7, Sat.-Sun. 10-6, mid-May to mid-Sept.; Mon.-Fri. 9-5, rest of year. Admission $3. Phone (907) 283-1991.

KENAI NATIONAL WILDLIFE REFUGE— *see Soldotna p. 332.*

KENAI FJORDS NATIONAL PARK (D-11)

Elevations in the park range from sea level at Nuka Bay to 6,400 ft. at a peak on the Harding Icefield. Refer to AAA maps for additional elevation information.

On the southeastern side of the Kenai Peninsula, Kenai Fjords National Park covers more than 600,000 acres. Access to the park is by private vehicle, plane or boat from Seward. Air charters also are available from other communities on the Kenai Peninsula. Scheduled bus service is available between Seward and Anchorage. Several tour companies offer trips to Exit Glacier and boat trips to the fjords.

The park encompasses a coastal mountain range that includes most of Harding Icefield, one of the four largest ice fields in the United States. A remnant of the ice age, it blankets all but the top of the Kenai Mountains. Along the coast is the rugged shoreline of the glacier-carved Kenai Fjords. Seals, porpoises, whales and sea otters are some of the 23 marine mammal species that inhabit the coastal waters.

Exit Glacier is the most accessible of the glaciers that flow from Harding Icefield. Three miles north of Seward via the Seward Highway and Exit Glacier Road, the glacier is reached by a .7-mile trail that begins at the Exit Glacier parking area. A strenuous 7-mile round-trip journey from the base of Exit Glacier to Harding Icefield departs from the visitor center at 9, July through August. Bald eagles, bears, moose, mountain goats and Stellar sea lions inhabit the area.

Picnicking and back-country camping are permitted; a 12-site walk-in tent campground is available. Hikes to the glacier and nature walks are conducted daily at Exit Glacier by park rangers on duty, Memorial Day through Labor Day. Winter activities at Exit Glacier include skiing, snowmobiling, snowshoeing and dog sledding. Boat and air charters provide access to the coast during the summer.

Both park headquarters and a visitor center are in Seward. Park headquarters is at 500 Adams St., Suite 103, and the visitor center is at 1212 4th Ave. next to the harbor master's office. Slide shows, exhibits and information about ranger-conducted activities are available. Headquarters and visitor center open daily 9-6, Memorial Day-Labor Day; Mon.-Fri. 8-5, rest of year. Admission to Exit Glacier is $5 per vehicle. For information write the Superintendent, Kenai Fjords National Park, P.O. Box 1727, Seward, AK 99664; phone (907) 224-7500 or (907) 224-2132 for mailing information. *See Recreation Chart.*

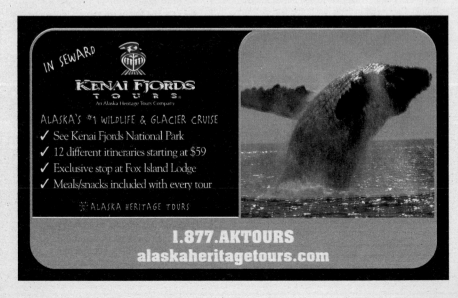

KETCHIKAN (I-12) pop. 7,922

Alaska's southernmost city sits on stilts at the base of the Tongass National Forest *(see place listing p. 333)*. On Revillagigedo Island, separated from the mainland by Behm Canal, Ketchikan claims to be the salmon capital of the world. An average annual rainfall of 156 to 162 inches makes it the wettest community in North America. The city's economic base relies on fishing, canning, mineral exploration, tourism and logging and cold-storage operations.

The town is populated with native culture and contains the largest concentration of Tlingit (KLINK-it), Haida (HY-dah), and Tsimshian (SIMP-shee-ane) people in Alaska. This heritage can be seen in the many totem poles that populate the area. Totem poles—tall cedar logs carved with eagles, ravens, wolves, bears, whales and other figures—depict stories or designate clans or lineage, and Ketchikan is reputed to contain the most in the world.

Creek Street is a relic of Ketchikan's rough-and-tumble past. Built on stilts over Ketchikan Creek, the street was once the site of a thriving red-light district. Highlights include art galleries, shops and a museum. The creek is a spawning ground for salmon.

Alaska Sightseeing Tours, (SAVE) Gray Line of Alaska and Princess Tours are among the companies that offer tours of the city. Ketchikan Visitors Center can provide a more complete list. Charter aircraft, boats, rental cars, buses and taxis are available at the Ketchikan Visitors Bureau, the airport and the ferry terminal.

Southeast Alaska Discovery Center: 50 Main St., Ketchikan, AK 99901; phone (907) 228-6220 or TTY (907) 228-6237.

Self-guiding tours: Maps of a 2-hour walking tour of downtown are available at Ketchikan Visitors Bureau, 131 Front St., Ketchikan, AK 99901; phone (907) 225-6166 or (800) 770-3300.

Shopping areas: The Creek Street boardwalk area in downtown contains a number of specialty shops and boutiques.

CLASSIC TOURS picks up passengers at the downtown cruise ship dock or local accommodation. Passengers ride in a restored 1955 Chevy, which is driven by a retired schoolteacher clad in a poodle skirt and saddle shoes. Narrated tours can accommodate up to five passengers and include visits to Saxman Native Village, Totem Heritage Center, the Creek Street boardwalk and a remote bald eagle's nest. Wildlife viewing is possible. Custom tours also can be arranged. Allow 1 hour minimum. Daily 8-6, early May-Sept. 30. Fare $70-$90. Reservations are recommended. Phone (907) 225-3091.

DEER MOUNTAIN TRIBAL HATCHERY AND EAGLE CENTER, .5 mi. n.e. at 1158 Salmon Rd. across the bridge from the Totem Heritage Center, raises king (chinook) and coho (silver) salmon, and steelhead and rainbow trout. A videotape presentation is offered, and visitors can taste samples of smoked salmon. Bald eagles also are featured in a landscaped enclosure. Allow 30 minutes minimum. Daily 8-4:30. Guided tour $7.95. Phone (907) 225-6760.

SAXMAN NATIVE VILLAGE, 2.5 mi. s. on S. Tongass Hwy., is a Tlingit (KLINK-it) Indian village of about 350 residents. The totem park contains 30 totem poles, and master carvers can be seen at work in the carving center. Other highlights include the Beaver Tribal House and the Old School House.

The Cape Fox Dancers perform based on audience attendance.

Guided tours are available. Allow 30 minutes minimum. Daily 8-5, holidays 9-3, mid-May through Sept. 30; varies rest of year. Free. Tour fee $35; under 12, $17.50. MC, VI. Phone (907) 225-4846, ext. 100.

TONGASS HISTORICAL MUSEUM, 629 Dock St. in Ketchikan's Centennial Building, displays pioneer items, artwork, and artifacts of the southeast Alaskan Indian tribes. Allow 30 minutes minimum. Daily 8-5, early May-Sept.; Wed.-Fri. 1-5, Sat.-Sun. 1-4, rest of year. Also open when cruise ships are in port. Closed winter holidays. Admission $2. Phone (907) 225-5600.

TOTEM BIGHT STATE HISTORIC PARK, 10 mi. n. on N. Tongass Hwy., displays more than a dozen poles and a model of a Tlingit clan house. The site is reached by a short trail through a forest from the parking area. A brochure describes typical totem characters and gives insight to the art of totem carving. More totem poles are in Saxman Native Village, 2.5 miles south on S. Tongass Highway. Allow 30 minutes minimum. Daily 6 a.m.-10 p.m. Donations. Phone (907) 247-8574.

TOTEM HERITAGE CENTER, 601 Deermount St., displays original 19th-century totem poles retrieved from native villages and emphasizes traditional Tlingit, Haida and Tsimshian art. Guided tours are available. Allow 30 minutes minimum. Daily 8-5, mid-May through Sept. 30; Mon.-Fri. 1-5 and during classes, rest of year. Closed winter holidays. Admission $5, mid-May through Sept. 30; free to all rest of year. Phone (907) 225-5900.

KLONDIKE GOLD RUSH NATIONAL HISTORICAL PARK—*see Skagway p. 331.*

KOBUK VALLEY NATIONAL PARK (C-5)

Elevations in the park range from 100 ft. at the point where the Kobuk River flows out of the southwest corner of the park to 4,700 ft. in the Brooks Range, which forms the park's northern border. Refer to AAA maps for additional elevation information.

Some 25 miles north of the Arctic Circle, Kobuk Valley National Park covers 1,710,000 acres in the heart of the arctic wildlands, where the boreal forest gives way to the frozen tundra. The broad Kobuk Valley is enclosed almost completely by the Baird Mountains to the north and the Waring Mountains to the south. Traversing the valley from east to west, the wide and placid Kobuk River offers good fishing and idyllic float trips. The swifter Salmon River, a designated Wild and Scenic River, flows south from the Baird Mountains.

Preserved within the park are the 25-square-mile Great Kobuk Sand Dunes, the largest active dunes in the Arctic. Created by the grinding action of ancient glaciers, the sand was carried by wind and water to a wide area south of the Kobuk River. The 100-foot dunes are accessible by a difficult hike from the river along Kavet Creek.

Home to seminomadic tribes for more than 12,500 years, the region still supports the native Inupiats; they are granted by law the right to continue subsistence hunting, trapping and other practices. Important to their survival is North America's largest caribou herd, numbering some 500,000. Many can be seen crossing the Kobuk River in September during their migration southward.

Other wildlife common to the region include moose, grizzly and black bears, wolves, red foxes, lynxes, wolverines and martens. Golden eagles can be seen in the northern latitudes; other birds include sandhill cranes, arctic loons, American golden plovers and arctic terns.

The park attracts experienced backpackers, campers and river travelers. Though the park is open year-round, the elements limit most visits to June through September. Fishing is good when the rivers are clear of silt; catches include salmon, pike, arctic char, whitefish and grayling. An Alaska fishing license is required. Hunting is not permitted, but it is legal to carry a firearm for protection from bears.

Access to the region is by daily commercial flights from Anchorage and Fairbanks to Kotzebue (*see place listing p. 324*), where connections to the villages of Kiana and Ambler can be made. Air taxi service into the park is available from Kotzebue, Kiana and Ambler. There are no facilities, services, trails or campgrounds in the park; a ranger station near Onion Portage is open June through September. The park headquarters in Kotzebue is open late May through September.

Due to its location, the area is subject to harsh weather and high winds. It is advisable to carry protection against hypothermia, mosquitoes and biting flies.

For trip planning assistance and a list of authorized outfitters, guides and air taxi operators, write the Superintendent, Western Arctic National Parklands, P.O. Box 1029, Kotzebue, AK 99752; phone (907) 442-3760 or (907) 442-3890. *See Recreation Chart.*

KODIAK (H-6) pop. 6,334

A Russian explorer-trader's quest for sea otter pelts led to the European settlement of Kodiak Island in 1784. The community of Kodiak was established about 1792 when Alexander Baranov moved his headquarters from the original 1784 settlement at Three Saints Bay, making Kodiak the first capital of Russian America. The blue, onion-shaped domes of the Holy Resurrection Russian Orthodox Church recall the days when the Russian Empire in the North Pacific was administered from Kodiak.

One of the oldest communities in Alaska, Kodiak also is a leading commercial fishing port. The town is on the northeastern tip of Kodiak Island, which is home to the Kodiak brown bear.

Kodiak was nearly destroyed twice; in June 1912, an eruption from Mount Novarupta covered the town with ash. On Good Friday in 1964 an earthquake in south central Alaska created tsunamis that enveloped the islands. Citizens found refuge on nearby Pillar Mountain and returned with the task of rebuilding the city.

Kodiak can be reached by air service from Anchorage or by the Alaska Marine Highway, a passenger/vehicle ferry, from Homer and Seward. Reservations are required well in advance for the ferry; write Alaska Marine Highway, P.O. Box 703, Kodiak, AK 99615, or phone (907) 486-3800 or (800) 526-6731 *(see color ad p. 292).*

Kodiak Island Convention and Visitors Bureau: 100-AAA Marine Way, Suite 200, Kodiak, AK 99615; phone (907) 486-4782.

BARANOV MUSEUM, in the Erskine House on the harbor front, has collections of early Russian and Alaskan artifacts as well as American household furnishings from the early 20th century. The building, which dates from 1808, was used by Alexander Baranov as a warehouse for storing furs. Original log construction methods can be examined inside. Allow 1 hour minimum. Mon.-Sat. 10-4, Memorial Day-Labor Day; Tues-Sat. 10-3, day after Labor Day-Jan. 31 and Mar. 1-day before Memorial Day. Closed major holidays. Admission $3, under 12 free. Phone (907) 486-5920.

FORT ABERCROMBIE STATE HISTORICAL PARK, 4.5 mi. n.e. on Miller Point, is a World War II fortification. The 183-acre park offers a view of the rocky coastline and nearby islands. Interpretive programs are given, and hiking trails are available. World War II artifacts remain; the visitor center offers natural-history displays and information about Alaska's participation in World War II. Tidal pools are within walking distance of the visitor center. Picnicking is permitted. Daily 24 hours. Free. Phone (907) 486-6339. *See Recreation Chart and the AAA Western Canada & Alaska CampBook.*

KODIAK ALUTIIQ DANCERS perform at 312 W. Marine Way. Traditional Alutiiq dances are presented in an authentic "barabara," or underground earthen hut. The elaborately costumed dancers express cultural and spiritual values that have survived for thousands of years. Narration is provided. Allow 30 minutes minimum. Performances daily at 3:30, June-Sept.; by appointment rest of year. Closed legal holidays. Admission $15. Reservations are recommended. Phone (907) 486-4449.

KODIAK NATIONAL WILDLIFE REFUGE occupies the southwestern two-thirds of Kodiak Island and 50,000 acres on Ban Island and the northwestern tip of Afognak Island. The 1,865,000 acres were set aside to preserve the habitat of the Kodiak bear, some of which weigh up to 1,500 pounds. Among other inhabitants are Sitka black-tailed deer,

Stories in Cedar

The art of totem pole carving in Alaska originated with the Tlingit, Haida and Tsimshian native tribes. Abundant food supplies along the Inside Passage allowed the natives the leisure time necessary to develop their elaborate craft.

Cedar totem poles served many purposes. Each figure on the pole represented an element in a story, and together the figures recorded the legends and histories of the tribes, who

Laura Breen

have no written language.

Genealogy poles, erected in front of an owner's house, identified a clan, told a family story or conveyed the family's status. Crests (usually in the shapes of eagles or ravens) denoted the clans of the husband and wife. Mortuary poles included a compartment for the ashes of a deceased clan member or chief and were carved in honor of that individual. Shame poles were created to chastise someone who wronged the clan or village—the pole remained standing until the debt was repaid tenfold. Other totem poles conveyed mythological or legendary stories, or commemorated a notable event, such as a birth or a good deed.

Colors were limited to natural pigments made from salmon eggs or hematite. Black was the primary color; red was used for secondary elements; and blue-green was used for highlighting.

An intimate knowledge of native traditions is necessary to fully interpret the totem poles, but there are common figures that are relatively easy to identify: the raven, a symbol of the creator, who changes form at will; the eagle, representing peace and friendship; the killer whale, a symbol of strength; and the beaver, bear and wolf.

sea lions, sea otters and bald eagles. The refuge is accessible only by plane and boat. Cabins are available. Phone (907) 487-2600.

Visitor Center, .2 mi. n. of the state airport, offers displays, videotapes, audiovisual presentations and information about the refuge. Allow 1 hour minimum. Mon.-Fri. 8-4:30, Sat.-Sun. noon-4; closed holidays.

KODIAK TOURS offers transportation from local hotels. Narrated tours of the island are tailored to the interests of the visitor. The U.S. Coast Guard Base, Kodiak Island National Wildlife Refuge Center, Fort Abercrombie and Buskin River state parks, Pillar Mountain and Lake Iliamma are among the sites. The tour stops to view the island's wildlife and scenery.

Inquire about weather policies. Six-hour tours depart daily at 10. Evening tours also are available. Full-day fare (includes all attraction admission fees) $50. Evening fare $15, senior citizens $12. Reservations are recommended. Phone (907) 486-2628.

KOTZEBUE (C-4) pop. 3,082, elev. 20′

Kotzebue, on the Baldwin Peninsula, sits on glacial moraine on the eastern edge of Kotzebue Sound. It was named after Otto Von Kotzebue, a German sailor exploring for Russia around 1818. Inhabited by the Kikiktagruk Inupiat Eskimos since the early 19th century, the area later became a seasonal trading center for the various Eskimo tribes due to its position at the confluence of the Noatak and Kobuk rivers. Its establishment as a permanent city began in 1899 with a Quaker mission.

Kotzebue is situated 33 miles above the Arctic Circle in the treeless tundra; the sun rises each year in early June and remains above the horizon for only 38 days. A spectacular ice breakup takes place for 2 weeks between mid-May and mid-June.

The second-largest Eskimo village in Alaska, Kotzebue is reached only by daily air service from Anchorage, Nome and Fairbanks. Arrangements for bush plane flights over the surrounding tundra and to the Kobuk River for hunting and fishing expeditions can be made at the airport. Short air and boat excursions to most of the surrounding villages also are available through independent operators. Nana Museum of the Arctic, near the airport, offers a slide show and a tour.

Big Dipper Community Circle Information: P.O. Box 1030, Kotzebue, AK 99752; phone (907) 442-4172.

LAKE CLARK NATIONAL PARK AND PRESERVE (F-5)

Elevations in the park and preserve range from sea level along Cook Inlet to 10,197 ft. at Mount Redoubt. Refer to AAA maps for additional elevation information.

West of Cook Inlet, Lake Clark National Park and Preserve is an almost 4-million-acre mountainous crossroads where ice and fire meet. The Pacific crust grinds beneath the North American plate, creating the Chigmit Mountains, a jagged array of spires and two steaming volcanoes, Mount Redoubt and Mount Iliamna. Mount Redoubt, the more active, last erupted in December 1989; it continues to emit steam and, less frequently, ash.

Covered by massive ice fields, the seemingly impenetrable Chigmit Mountains are formed by the linkage of two great ranges, the Alaska and the Aleutian. Together the ranges divide the park into distinct areas: the eastern flank's coastal plain bordering Cook Inlet and the lake and tundra region on the western flank. Lake Clark, 50 miles long, juts in from the southwest.

Moisture abounds along the park's coastal area, which is characterized by rocky cliffs along its southern portion, giving way to tidal marshes and grasslands in the north. In contrast to the luxuriant alder thickets and Sitka spruce along Cook Inlet, lakes, boreal forests and rolling tundra highlands distinguish the park's western landscape.

Numerous glacier-fed rivers and creeks are channeled through Lake Clark, creating one of the richest sockeye salmon spawning grounds in the world. The park was created primarily to protect this fruitful breeding area.

Although the park is open all year, most people visit during the peak of the summer season, late June through August. Even in summer months, weather conditions vary in the interior; it is advisable to bring protection against insects as well as clothing for sunny, wet or freezing weather. Visitors should outfit themselves in Kenai, Homer or Anchorage, as the communities closer to the park have limited supplies.

For anglers the rivers and lakes on the park's western side provide a variety of trophy-size fish, including salmon, arctic grayling and trout. A 2- to 3-mile trail to Tanalian Falls and Kontrashibuna Lake is accessible from Port Alsworth, near Lake Clark. The open foothills are ideal for backpacking. River-running also is popular on the Mulchatna, Tlikakila and Chilikadrotna rivers, all federally designated wild and scenic rivers.

As there are no roads in the park, access is almost exclusively by air. Most travelers charter aircraft; the closest airport is south of the park in Iliamna. A 1- to 2-hour flight from Anchorage, Homer or Kenai will provide access to most points within the park and preserve.

The National Park Service facility is at Port Alsworth and contains a visitor center with displays regarding natural history topics. While there are minimal National Park facilities—staffed patrol cabins at Telaquana Lake, Twin Lakes, Crescent Lake and Chinitna Bay—there are a number of private lodges and cabins in the park.

For information about accommodations as well as a list of outfitters and maps, write the Superintendent, Lake Clark National Park and Preserve, 4230 University Dr., Suite 311, Anchorage, AK 99508; phone (907) 271-3751. *See Recreation Chart.*

MISTY FIORDS NATIONAL MONUMENT (H-12)

East of Ketchikan and within the Tongass National Forest *(see place listing p. 333)*, Misty Fiords National Monument covers about 3,580 square miles of wilderness. The area is accessible by float plane from Ketchikan and other communities near the national forest. An information center and cruises to the monument are available in Ketchikan *(see place listing p. 321)*.

Behm Canal, a deep inlet of the Pacific Ocean, leads to the interior of the monument, where rock walls that rise 3,000 feet surround Walker Cove and Rudyerd Bay. Geological features include mineral springs, 237-foot-tall New Eddystone Rock, 3,150-foot-tall Punchbowl Face, lava flows, five major rivers and hundreds of small streams. The region receives more than 120 inches of precipitation each year. Bald eagles, brown and black bears, wolves and mountain goats inhabit the area; whales, porpoises, seals and sea lions can be sighted in Behm Canal or in the ocean nearby.

Recreational activities include backpacking, picnicking, birdwatching, hunting, fishing and crabbing. Rustic cabins are available for $25-$45 per day; reservations may be made by calling Reserve America, (877) 444-6777. For further information contact the Southeast Alaska Discovery Center, 50 Main St., Ketchikan, AK 99901; phone (907) 228-6220.

NOME (D-3) pop. 3,505, elev. 13′

Placer gold washed from the hillsides to the beaches at Nome lured thousands to the remote shores of the Bering Sea in 1898. At the height of the gold rush, 20,000 people lived in Nome, once the largest settlement in Alaska.

On the Seward Peninsula, Nome is the judicial and commercial center of northwestern Alaska and the main supply point for nearby mining districts and Eskimo villages. The city is accessible daily by plane from Anchorage. Regularly scheduled and charter flights are available to various Eskimo villages.

Cruise ships serve Nome during the summer, and rental cars provide visitors with opportunities for self-guiding trips to nearby villages.

When a diphtheria epidemic threatened the town in 1925, the necessary serum was delivered by dog team. The annual Iditarod Trail Race commemorates this emergency mission. The race, which begins in Anchorage *(see place listing p. 292)* in early March, encompasses treacherous climbs, river passages and bone-chilling blizzards. Mushers cross the finish line in Nome after traveling roughly 1,100 miles, exhausted but invigorated by cheers from supporters lining the chute on Front Street.

One of the activities during the final week of the race is the Bering Sea Ice Classic, a six-hole golf tournament played on frozen Norton Sound.

The Last Great Race

To commemorate the 1925 event in which 20 mushers relayed serum to Nome to save children who contracted diphtheria, the first Iditarod Race took place on Mar. 3, 1973.

Beginning in Anchorage and culminating in Nome, the race trail covers some 1,000 miles of rugged terrain, takes between 9-17 days to complete and can reach temperatures of minus 60 F.

In preparation for the great race, the trail is broken and marked with  reflector tape, and checkpoints are chosen where teams stop to eat and rest. Since it's not feasible for mushers to carry all of their provisions in

© PhotoDisc

their sleds, the bulk of food and supplies is shipped to the checkpoints prior to the race.

To aid in endurance, dogs ingest 5,000 calories or more each day, gobbling such delicacies as moose, caribou or even seal meat. Concern for the dogs' health is strong: Booties are worn for paw protection, and about 25 veterinarians man the checkpoints to examine each dog.

While teams may begin the race with as many as 16 dogs, some drop from the race. "Dropped dogs"—dogs that do not finish the race due to dehydration, flu or fatigue—are carried to the nearest checkpoint and flown back to Anchorage. A musher must finish the race with at least five dogs.

Teams travel at night as well as during the day, and dogs rest about 10-12 hours per 24-hour period. But mushers don't enjoy that luxury: Responsible for feeding and caring for the dogs (including changing their booties every 100 miles), they rarely sleep more than 2 hours per night.

The goal? Nome's Burled Arch on Front Street. At this finish line, teams are greeted by cheering crowds and the sounding of the city's fire siren.

The Midnight Sun Festival celebrates the summer solstice, the longest day of the year with almost 24 hours of sunlight. The mid-June festival lasts several days and includes a parade and The Nome River Raft Race.

Nome Convention and Visitors Bureau: P.O. Box 240-AAA, Nome, AK 99762; phone (907) 443-6624.

CARRIE M. McLAIN MEMORIAL MUSEUM is at 223 E. Front St. The museum showcases the history of the Nome gold rush, the lifestyles of Bering Strait Eskimos and the early days of sled dog racing. Daily 9-5:30, June-Sept.; Tues.-Sat. noon-6, rest of year. Closed holidays. Donations. Phone (907) 443-6630.

PALMER (C-11) pop. 4,533, elev. 240'

The peaks of the Chugach and Talkeetna mountains rise above Palmer, a city surrounded by the lush pastures and dairy and vegetable farms of the fertile Matanuska Valley, where cabbages can grow to weigh more than 70 pounds. A drive to Wasilla *(see place listing p. 335)* provides a good view of the valley and its farms. The Matanuska Agricultural Experimental Farm, 7 miles southwest, welcomes visitors.

Palmer lies near the intersection of the Glenn and George Parks highways (SRs 1 and 3), both of which are scenic highways. An interesting drive is along a narrow, rough, winding road that follows Willow Creek through formerly rich gold areas. The road crosses Hatcher Pass en route to Willow.

Palmer Visitor and Information Center: Valley Way between Fireweed and Elmwood, Box 115, Palmer, AK 99645; phone (907) 745-2880.

Self-guiding tours: Brochures describing a walking tour of downtown Palmer are available at the Visitor and Information Center.

INDEPENDENCE MINE STATE HISTORICAL PARK, 19 mi. n. on Hatcher Pass Rd., is a 761-acre park in the 221,000-acre Hatcher Pass region. The park preserves 15 buildings and numerous artifacts from its heyday as a gold boom town in the 1930s and 1940s. The history of the mine is chronicled in a museum and at the visitor center. Walking trails lead visitors past many of the mine camp's buildings, including bunkhouses, warehouses, the commissary and mess halls.

Guided tours are available. Park open daily. Visitor center open daily 10-7, June 15-Labor Day; Sat.-Sun. 11-7, day after Labor Day-Sept. 15. Tours are given Mon.-Fri. at 1 and 3, Sat.-Sun. at 1, 3 and 4:30, second week of June-Labor Day. Admission $5 per private vehicle. Tour fee $5; senior citizens and under 8, $3. Phone (907) 745-2827 or (907) 745-3975.

MUSK OX FARM, 2 mi. n. at Milepost 50 on Glenn Hwy., is said to be the only musk ox domestication

project in the world. The shaggy creatures are valued for their fine underwool called "qiviut." Eskimos knit the hair, eight times warmer by weight than wool, into hats and scarves. Hands-on exhibits are available. Guided tours offer insight into the animal's history and behavior and allow observation from fenced walkways. Picnicking is permitted. Daily 10-6, mid-May to late Sept. Admission $8.50; over 65 and ages 13-18, $7; ages 6-12, $5.50. Phone (907) 745-4151.

PETERSBURG (H-11) pop. 3,224, elev. 28'

Petersburg, at the north end of Mitkof Island, is an Alaska Marine Highway port. In 1897 Norwegian Peter Buschmann decided to build a cannery on Mitkof Island at the head of picturesque Wrangell Narrows, but first he had to build a sawmill to supply lumber for the cannery.

The cannery at the north end of Nordic Drive was completed in 1900; the facility packed 32,750 cases of salmon during its first production year. Now Petersburg Fisheries, the firm is a pioneer in Alaska's expanding bottom-fishing and shrimping industries.

Nicknamed "Little Norway," Petersburg boasts brightly painted wooden houses decorated with hand-painted floral designs, a traditional craft called rosemaling.

Among the nearby points of interest is Le Conte Glacier, an active tidewater glacier south of Petersburg; it can be reached via chartered plane, helicopter or boat. In nearby Frederick Sound whale-watching is popular; the area is home to orca and humpback whales as well as other sea mammals.

Petersburg Visitor Information Center: First and Fram sts., P.O. Box 649, Petersburg, AK 99833; phone (907) 772-4636 or (866) 484-4700.

CLAUSEN MEMORIAL MUSEUM, 203 Fram St., features exhibits about commercial fishing and canning, a dugout Tlingit Indian canoe, tools and artifacts. A "Fisk" fountain and a 126.5-pound king salmon, said to be a world record catch, also are on display. Guided tours are available. Open Mon.-Fri. 10-5, May 1-Sept. 6; Sat. 10-4:30, rest of year. Closed holidays. Winter hours may vary; phone ahead. Admission $3, under 12 free. Phone (907) 772-3598.

SEWARD (D-11) pop. 2,830, elev. 70'

Named for William H. Seward, who negotiated the purchase of Alaska, Seward is an ice-free port in a setting of great beauty. At the northeast end of a bay named Resurrection by Russians who arrived in its waters on Easter, the city is surrounded by lush, tall mountains and ice fields.

Charter boats and planes can be hired for fishing, hunting and sightseeing trips. Seward is the southern terminus of the Seward Highway, a scenic highway that extends north to Anchorage through an alpine terrain of glaciers and lakes. Seward also is the main access point to Kenai Fjords National Park *(see place listing p. 320),* which includes Exit Glacier, one of the few accessible glaciers.

Seward Community Library at 5th Avenue and Adams Street shows movies and slides of the havoc wreaked by the 1964 Good Friday earthquake.

Seward Chamber of Commerce: P.O. Box 749, Seward, AK 99664; phone (907) 224-8051. *See color ad.*

Self-guiding tours: Guides containing information about a walking tour are available at the chamber of commerce office on Seward Highway or at the Information Center, 3rd Avenue and Jefferson Street.

ALASKA SEALIFE CENTER, Seward Hwy. (SR 9) at Milepost 0, is dedicated to understanding and maintaining the integrity of Alaska's marine ecosystem through research, rehabilitation and public education. Highlights include habitats featuring Stellar sea lions, harbor seals and colorful diving seabirds. Exhibits include the Chiswell Island kiosk, featuring an interactive display with live video from a Stellar sea lion rookery; and the hands-on Discovery Pool. Guided Behind-the-Scenes tours are available.

Allow 1 hour, 30 minutes minimum. Daily 8-8, May 1-Labor Day; 9-6 in Apr. and Sept.; 10-5, rest of year. Closed Thanksgiving and Dec. 25. Admission $14; ages 7-12, $11. Tour fee $6. Reservations are required for tours. AX, DS, MC, VI. Phone (907) 224-6300 or (800) 224-2525.

GODWIN GLACIER DOG SLED TOURS offers excursions departing from the Seward Airport off Seward Hwy. Beginning with a helicopter flight to Godwin Glacier, the guided tour includes a 2.5-mile dog sled ride traversing the glacier's ancient snowfield. During the round-trip flight, passengers may spot mountain goats, bears, moose and eagles. Allow 2 hours minimum. Mon.-Sat. 8-6, May 20-Sept. 10 (weather permitting). Fare $360; ages 2-12, $325; family rate (four people) $1,290. AX, CB, DC, DS, MC, VI. Phone (907) 224-8239 or (888) 989-8239.

IDIDARIDE SLED DOG TOURS is off Seward Hwy. (SR 9) Milepost 3.6, 1 mi. w. on Exit Glacier Rd, .4 mi. n. on Old Exit Glacier Rd. (gravel road) following signs. An experienced

Iditarod racer offers a summer version of a sled dog ride aboard a wheeled sled during a 2-mile trip through Box Canyon. Visitors can tour the dog kennel to socialize with the husky puppies and witness a sled dog training demonstration. Allow 1 hour, 30 minutes minimum. Daily 8-8, May-Sept. Fare $44; ages 2-11, $22. MC, VI. Phone (907) 224-8607 or (800) 478-3139.

KENAI FJORDS TOURS depart from the Seward small boat harbor. The company offers glacier and wildlife cruises into the waters that surround Kenai Fjords National Park. Cruises also explore Resurrection Bay and the northwestern fjords, where active tidewater glaciers are a highlight. A variety of marine mammals can be seen; gray whales often are spotted on whale-watching tours. Meals are included.

Inquire about weather policies. Tours depart daily, late Mar.-Oct. 31. Six-hour Kenai Fjords National Park tours depart at 8, 11:30 and 3. Northwestern Fjords tours last 9.5 hours and depart at 9. Three-hour Resurrection Bay wildlife tours depart at 2:30. Fox Island Salmon Bake cruises last 5 or 7.5 hours and depart at noon and 5:30. Park tour $115; under 12, $57.50. Fjord tour $139; under 12, $69. Bay tour $59; under 12, $29.50. Salmon Bake cruises $79; under 12, $39.50. Reservations are recommended. AX, DS, MC, VI. Phone (907) 224-8068 or (800) 478-8068. *See color ads p. 297, p. 320 & p. 327.*

MAJOR MARINE TOURS depart from the Seward small boat harbor, 1 blk. e. of Seward Hwy. Narrated glacier and wildlife sightseeing cruises visit Kenai Fjords National Park. Passengers spot bald eagles, otters, porpoises, sea lions and whales. Food is available. Inquire about weather policies. Cruises depart daily, mid-May to mid-Sept. Half-day cruise departs at 12:45 (also at 6, mid-June to mid-Aug.), full-day cruise departs at 11:45. Half-day fare $54-$69; ages 2-11, $27-$34 (depending on time of departure). Full-day fare $117; ages 2-11, $58. AX, DS, MC, VI. Phone (907) 274-7300 or (800) 764-7300. *See color ad.*

RENOWN CHARTERS & TOURS offers cruises departing from bldg. #4 of the Seward small boat harbor on the boardwalk. Two tours are available: a 4-hour whale-watching cruise in Resurrection Bay; and a 7-hour cruise into Kenai Fjords National Park. Lunch is available on all tours.

Whale-watching cruise departs at noon and 4:30, Apr.-Sept. National park cruise departs at 10:30, mid-May through Sept. 30. Check-in is 30 minutes prior to departure. Whale-watching cruise $59; ages 3-12, $30. National park cruise fare $109; ages 3-12, $50. Reservations are recommended. AX, DS, MC, VI. Phone (907) 224-3806, (907) 272-1961, or (800) 655-3806 out of Alaska.

SCENIC MOUNTAIN AIR (FLIGHTSEEING) operates wheeled planes from Seward Airport

and float planes from Trail Lake in Moose Pass. Sights on the varied tours include Kenai Fjords, Harding Icefield and wildlife. Flying/fishing and flying/hiking tours also are available. Flights depart daily 8 a.m.-7 p.m., May 1-Sept. 15 (weather permitting). Fares $89-$189, depending on length of tour. DS, MC, VI. Phone (907) 288-3646.

SEWARD HISTORICAL SOCIETY MUSEUM, 336 Third Ave., has exhibits about the main events in Seward's history. A collection of native baskets and ivory carvings is displayed. Daily 9-5, May-Sept.; otherwise varies. Admission $3; ages 5-18, 50c. Phone (907) 224-3902.

RECREATIONAL ACTIVITIES
Kayaking

• **Sunny Cove Sea Kayaking** departs from Lowell's Point on Resurrection Bay, 2 mi. from downtown. Write P.O. Box 3332, Seward, AK 99664. Other activities are offered. Tours depart daily at 10, 1 and 7. Phone (907) 224-8810.

SITKA (H-10) pop. 8,835

Surrounded by high peaks and small wooded islands, historic Sitka is accessible by air or the Alaska Marine Highway.

In 1804 Russians led by Alexander Baranov established a settlement on the site of an ancient Tlingit (KLINK-it) village; that settlement became the capital of Russian America. Originally named New Archangel, it was a thriving port of nearly 3,000 when San Francisco was just a mission village. Castle Hill marks the site of Baranov's headquarters and commemorates the 1867 ceremony that transferred ownership of Alaska from Russia to the United States. St. Michael's Cathedral, a restored Russian church with an onion-shaped dome, contains a collection of religious icons and artwork.

The colorfully costumed New Archangel Dancers perform Russian dances in the Harrigan Centennial Hall auditorium when large ships are in port in summer. Performances by the Sheet'ka Kwaan Naa Kahadi Native Dancers are given at the Tribal Community House on Katlian Street.

For cruise ship and ferry passengers, Sitka Tours offers a short bus tour of Sitka, which includes guide service and round-trip transportation from the port. Boat tours to view wildlife and the surrounding area also are available.

Sitka Convention and Visitors Bureau: Dept. A, Box 1226, Sitka, AK 99835; phone (907) 747-5940.

ALASKA RAPTOR CENTER, .8 mi. e. of Lake St. at 1101 Sawmill Creek Rd., is home to 25 "raptors in residence," including bald and golden eagles, ravens, falcons and owls. The 17-acre rehabilitation center, surrounded by muskeg, mountains and the Indian River, provides medical treatment to more than 200 eagles and other birds of prey each year. A videotape, live demonstrations and a .25-mile nature trail are available.

Raptors unable to be released into the wild help educate visitors and travel to schools nationwide to raise awareness of wild birds and their habitats. Feathers, bones, photographs and a national map indicating where birds have been released are displayed, and visitors can view raptors perched outside the center and in the clinic's treatment room and recuperation areas.

Guide tours are available. Allow 1 hour, 30 minutes minimum. Daily 8-4, May-Sept. Admission $12; under 13, $6. Phone (907) 747-8662 or (800) 643-9425.

ISABEL MILLER MUSEUM is in Harrigan Centennial Building. The museum features exhibits depicting the history of Sitka, including the area's earliest inhabitants and the legacy of World War II. Displays illustrate the lifestyles of the Tlingit along with the town's Russian and American settlers. An 8-foot-square diorama shows Sitka as it appeared in 1867, the time Alaska was transferred to the United States from Russia. Allow 30 minutes minimum. Daily 8-5, early May to late Sept.; Tues.-Sat. 10-noon and 1-4, rest of year. Donations. Phone (907) 747-6455.

SHELDON JACKSON MUSEUM is at 104 College Dr. on the Sheldon Jackson College campus. Housed in one of the first concrete structures built in Alaska, it is reputed to be the oldest continuing museum in Alaska. Displays of Eskimo, Aleut and Northwest Coast and Athabaskan Indian artifacts include pelts, sleds, kayaks, ceremonial masks, and tools and utensils of wood, bone and ivory. Allow 30 minutes minimum. Daily 9-5, mid-May to mid-Sept.; Tues.-Sat. 10-4, rest of year. Closed holidays. Admission $4, under 18 free, mid-May to mid-Sept. Admission $3, rest of year. Phone (907) 747-8981.

SITKA NATIONAL HISTORICAL PARK (H-10)

Near downtown Sitka on Lincoln Street, this urban park commemorates the Battle of Sitka, fought in 1804 between the Kiksadi Tlingit Indians and the fur hunters and Aleut natives of the Russian-American Co. The battle marked the last major resistance by Alaskan natives to European domination. The 113-acre park preserves the Tlingit fort site, the battlefield and the 1842 Russian Bishop's House.

A fine collection of Tlingit (KLINK-it) and Haida (HY-dah) totem poles, some more than a century old, is displayed along a 2-mile trail through the park's temperate rain forest and coastal intertidal area. During August and September visitors may view salmon spawning in the Indian River.

The visitor center contains exhibits and audio-visual presentations about the area's Tlingit Indian heritage as well as its Russian legacy. Within the visitor center skilled native artisans demonstrate traditional crafts at the Southeast Alaska Indian Cultural Center, which is open daily.

Visitor center open daily 8-5, mid-May through Sept. 30; Mon.-Fri. 8-5, rest of year. Park free. Visitor center $3. Address inquiries to the Superintendent, Sitka National Historical Park, 103 Monastery St., Sitka, AK 99835; phone (907) 747-0110.

THE RUSSIAN BISHOP'S HOUSE, 501 Lincoln St. across from Crescent Harbor, is a two-story log structure completed in 1843. It is one of the last surviving colonial Russian buildings in North America. Restored to its 1853 appearance, the building reflects the influence of the Russian Orthodox Church and the traders of the Russian-American Co., who made Sitka the capital of colonial Russian America.

Allow 30 minutes minimum. Daily and holidays 9-5, May 15-Sept. 30; by appointment rest of year. Admission $3, under 12 free, family rate $6. Phone (907) 747-0110.

SKAGWAY (G-10) pop. 862, elev. 2'

During the icy winter of 1897-98 hordes of enthusiastic would-be prospectors who had heard of the Klondike gold strike swarmed ashore at Skagway. They assembled their gear and began the trek over treacherous mountains and down raging rivers to the Klondike. Within 3 months of the first gold strike, the settlement at Skagway grew from one cabin into a thriving city of more than 20,000 people. But the gold rush ended suddenly, and those who had come to Skagway moved on.

The notorious outlaw Jefferson R. "Soapy" Smith and Frank Reid, who represented the outraged citizenry, shot it out in a battle that cost both men their lives. Gold Rush Cemetery, 1.5 miles from town, contains the graves of both "Soapy" Smith and Frank Reid.

A stop on many summer cruises along the Inside Passage, Skagway is the northern terminus of the Alaska Marine Highway. Sightseeing opportunities include visits to Reid's Falls and flower gardens; tours of the city and the harbor; flightseeing tours to Glacier Bay, gold rush trails and the Juneau Ice Cap; bus excursions to Dyea and Carcross, Yukon Territory; and hiking trips to AB Mountain and the Dewey Lakes.

[SAVE] Gray Line of Alaska offers historical points-of-interest tours daily; phone (800) 544-2206.

Skagway Convention & Visitors Bureau: P.O. Box 10295, Skagway, AK 99840; phone (907) 983-2854 or (888) 762-1898.

THE DAYS OF '98 SHOW WITH SOAPY SMITH, presented at Eagles' Hall, 6th Ave. and Broadway, includes a stage show with original songs, a cancan line, a historic shoot-out and mock gambling. Mock gambling nightly at 7. Stage shows daily at 10:30, 2:30 and 8, mid-May to late Sept. Evening shows $16; ages 3-15, $8. Matinees $14; ages 3-12, $7. Phone (907) 983-2545.

KLONDIKE GOLD RUSH NATIONAL HISTORICAL PARK includes the Skagway Historic District and Chilkoot and White Pass trails, over which each prospector was required to haul nearly a ton of supplies during the gold rush of 1897-98. It was during this stampede that Skagway's population boomed from 5 to 5,000.

The park visitor center is in the White Pass and Yukon Route Railroad Depot, one of Alaska's oldest. At Broadway and Second Avenue, it contains exhibits and interpretive programs about the era. Two films are shown: an orientation film about the gold rush, and a film about hiking the Chilkoot Trail. Walking tours led by a park ranger explore the Skagway Historic District, where nearly 100 restored buildings represent a colorful history. The Trail Center provides information about day hikes and backpacking on the Chilkoot Trail.

Visitor center daily 8-6, early May-late Sept. Orientation film is shown on the hour at 8, 9, 11-2, 4 and 5. Walking tours depart the visitor center daily on the hour 9-11 and at 2 and 3, early May-late Sept. Trail Center daily 8-4:30, June-Aug. Visitor and trail centers free. Fees apply and reservations are recommended for Chilkoot Trail backpacking. Phone (907) 983-2921 for the visitor center, or (907) 983-9234 for trail information June-Aug., or (800) 661-0486 for trail information rest of year.

SKAGWAY MUSEUM is at Seventh and Spring sts. in the McCabe College Building. Displays pertain to Alaskan history and native cultures, including a Tlingit war canoe, photographs, documents, gold rush relics and native artifacts. Mon.-Fri. 9-5, Sat.-Sun. 1-4, May-Sept.; hours vary, rest of year. Admission $2, students with ID $1, under 13 free. Phone (907) 983-2420.

WHITE PASS & YUKON ROUTE is at Second Ave. and Spring St. A vintage train chugs across mountain rivers and chasms during full-day and half-day narrated narrow-gauge rides on a rail line built in 1898 to carry people and supplies to the Klondike gold rush. Passengers travel round-trip in a period parlor car to the summit of White Pass past granite gulches, cascading waterfalls, Lake Bennett, B.C., and spectacular scenery. A narrator tells the story of the stampede north into the gold fields through some of the most rugged terrain in the United States and Canada.

Ticket office open daily 8-5. Trips depart daily at 8:15 and 12:45 (weather permitting), mid-May to late Sept. Inquire about additional departures. Fare for half-day trip $89; ages 3-12, $44.50. AX, DS, MC, VI. Phone (907) 983-2217 or (800) 343-7373. *See color ad.*

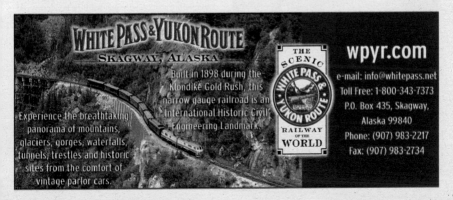

SOLDOTNA (D-11) pop. 3,759

Soldotna's location on the Kenai Peninsula at the junction of Sterling and Kenai Spur highways has ensured its steady growth since homesteading began in 1947. World War II veterans were among the first homesteaders; they were given a 90-day preference right in choosing and filing for land.

The area is rich with opportunities for year-round recreation—hiking, fishing, camping, canoeing and ice fishing are favored activities. Nearby Kenai River yields record catches of salmon and rainbow trout.

Soldotna Chamber of Commerce and Visitor Information Center: 44790 Sterling Hwy., Soldotna, AK 99669; phone (907) 262-9814.

KENAI NATIONAL WILDLIFE REFUGE, with its headquarters in Soldotna, covers about 1,920,000 acres. The refuge was established in 1941 by President Franklin D. Roosevelt to preserve the area's large moose population. Other wildlife include Dall sheep, coyotes, black bears and bald eagles. Fishing and hunting are subject to state and federal regulations. Boat ramps, trails and camping are available. Picnicking is permitted. The refuge is open all year, except when roads are impassable. Phone (907) 262-7021. *See the AAA Western Canada & Alaska CampBook.*

Visitor Center, 1 mi. s.e. of the Kenai River Bridge on Ski Hill Rd., exhibits wildlife dioramas and presents films. Mon.-Fri. 8-4:30, Sat.-Sun. 9-6, June 1-Labor Day.

STERLING (D-10) pop. 4,705, elev. 198'

RECREATIONAL ACTIVITIES

Fishing

- **Great Alaska Fish Camp**, 33881 Sterling Hwy., Sterling, AK 99672. Trips are offered mid-May through Sept. 30. Other activities are offered. Phone (800) 544-2261.

TALKEETNA (C-11) pop. 772, elev. 355'

Situated at the confluence of the Talkeetna, Susitna and Chulitna rivers, Talkeetna takes its name from the Tanaina Indian word for "river of plenty." The village was an important supply station for gold prospectors from the late 1800s to 1940, but is now a popular staging area for outdoors enthusiasts.

Mat-Su Convention & Visitors Bureau: Milepost 35.5, Parks Hwy., HC 01 Box 6166 J21, Palmer, AK 99645; phone (907) 746-5000. *See color ad p. 296.*

Self-guiding tours: A map of a downtown walking tour is available at Talkeetna Historical Society Museum *(see attraction listing)* and the visitor center next to Village Park on Main Street.

[SAVE] **K-2 AVIATION** is at Talkeetna State Airport off Talkeetna Spur Rd. Flightseeing tours of varying types and lengths include a 1-hour flight to the summit of Mount McKinely; extended tours that encircle the mountain; and mountain tours with a glacier landing. Daily 7 a.m.-9 p.m. Fare for 1-hour tour $140. Rates vary according to tour. Reservations are recommended. AX, MC, VI. Phone (907) 733-2291 or (800) 764-2291.

MUSEUM OF NORTHERN ADVENTURE, on Main St. across from the post office, recounts the eras, lore and natural history of northern Alaska through dioramas, life-size wax figures, sound effects, photographs and newspaper articles. A trophy room contains big game and other wildlife taxidermy. Allow 30 minutes minimum. Daily 10-6, May 1 to mid-Sept. Admission $2; over 65 and under 13, $1; family rate $5. AX, MC, VI. Phone (907) 733-3999.

TALKEETNA AERO SERVICES/FLY DENALI is at Talkeetna State Airport off Talkeetna Spur Rd. Passengers are treated to views of Mt. McKinley, Denali Park or the Kahiltna Glacier from 20,000 feet as well as glacier landings on Mt. McKinley. Flights from Anchorage and Talkeetna to Denali National Park are available. Allow 2 hours minimum. Daily 7 a.m.-8 p.m., mid-May to mid-Sept.; 9-5, rest of year. Fare $140-$250 (depending on tour). DS, AX, MC, VI. Phone (907) 683-2899, or (800) 660-2688.

SAVE **TALKEETNA AIR TAXI** is at Talkeetna State Airport off Talkeetna Spur Rd. Flightseeing tours of the area are offered. Scenic views from the air include Denali National Park, Mount McKinley and nearby glaciers. Other activities such as mountain climbing, glacier landings and support and wilderness tours also are offered. Daily 8-8, May-Sept.; 9-4, rest of year. Fare $140-$260. DS, MC, VI. Phone (907) 733-2218 or (800) 533-2219. *See color ad.*

TALKEETNA HISTORICAL SOCIETY MUSEUM, in four buildings at the corner of First Alley and Village Airstrip Rd., displays a wealth of local history memorabilia within re-creations of a log cabin, a one-room schoolhouse, a railroad depot and section house. Of interest is a large-scale model of Mount McKinley and the surrounding area. Allow 30 minutes minimum. Daily 10-6, May-Sept.; Fri.-Sun. 11-4 in Apr. and Oct.; Sat.-Sun. 11-5, rest of year. Hours may vary; phone ahead. Admission $3, under 12 free. Phone (907) 733-2487.

TOK (B-12) pop. 1,393

On the Alaska Highway 93 miles from the Canadian border, Tok is a trade center for nearby Athabascan villages. Some claim that Tok's name derives from the native word meaning "peace crossing"; others say Tok was the name of a survey crew's dog.

A center for dog breeding, training and mushing, Tok claims the title "Dog Capital of Alaska."

Tok Chamber of Commerce: P.O. Box 389, Tok, AK 99780; phone (907) 883-5775.

ALASKA PUBLIC LANDS INFORMATION CENTER, Milepost 1314 on Alaska Hwy., includes displays, state and federal information, a trip planning room and interpretive programs. Daily 8-7, Memorial Day-Labor Day; 8-4:30, rest of year. Free. Phone (907) 883-5666 or (907) 883-5667.

TETLIN NATIONAL WILDLIFE REFUGE is in e. central Alaska, directly s. of the Alaska Hwy. and n. of Wrangell-St. Elias National Park and Preserve; the visitor center is at Milepost 1229, Alaska Hwy. The gateway to Alaska, the refuge occupies 730,000 acres. More than 143 nesting bird species and 47 migrant species—including bald eagles, trumpeter swans and ospreys—flock here. Black and grizzly bears, moose, wolves and caribou are permanent residents.

Hunting and fishing are permitted. The refuge operates two public campgrounds. Refuge open daily 24 hours. Free. Phone (907) 883-5312.

TONGASS NATIONAL FOREST (G-9)

Elevations in the forest range from sea level at the Pacific Ocean to 10,290 ft. at Mount Ratz. Refer to AAA maps for additional elevation information.

In southeastern Alaska, Tongass National Forest covers about 17 million acres, making it the largest national forest. In 1907 Teddy Roosevelt created the forest, taking the name from the "Tongass" clan of Tlingit Indians that lived along the southern edge of the forest's present-day boundaries. It boasts more than 5 million acres of preserved wilderness, including Misty Fiords National Monument *(see place listing p. 325)* and Admiralty Island National Monument *(see place listing p. 292).*

Consisting mostly of islands, the forest also includes a mountainous mainland strip deeply cleft by rock-walled fiords, bays, inlets and channels with glaciers, ice fields and waterfalls. The abundant wildlife includes trumpeter swans, bald eagles and Alaskan brown (grizzly) bears. Licenses are required for hunting and fishing.

The largest island within the National Forest and one of the largest islands in the United States is Prince of Wales Island. Long inlets and deep bays mark its 900-mile coastline, while u-shaped valleys and low mountains rising up to 3,800 feet distinguish its interior. Thanks to a moist climate, a dense forest of spruce and hemlock blankets the landscape.

One of the most interesting features of the island is its caves, including El Capitan, a large limestone cave system with 11,000 feet of mapped passages. Grizzly bear bones more than 12,000 years old

have been found inside. The Forest Service provides free 2-hour tours of El Capitan from mid-May to early September; reservations are required. Access to the cave entrance is via a steep 1,300-foot-long trail and visitors need to bring their own equipment for the tour, including flashlights, hard hats and sturdy footgear. Phone (907) 828-3304 for information and reservations.

The Forest Service provides cabins at several locations within Tongass National Forest. Many rental cabins are near lakes and streams or high in alpine meadows. Although a few can be reached by boat or trail, most are accessible only by charter plane from Craig, Hoonah, Juneau, Ketchikan, Petersburg, Sitka, Wrangell and Yakutat. Charter planes seating two to five people cost about $325-$550 an hour.

A $25-$45 per-party, per-night fee is charged for cabins. There is a 7-night limit May through September; a 10-night limit the rest of the year. Cabin permits are necessary and can be requested up to 180 days prior to use; full payment is required at the time the reservation is made. Forest information centers with exhibits, films and cabin reservation information are in Juneau *(see place listing p. 314)*, Ketchikan *(see place listing p. 321)* and Petersburg *(see place listing p. 326)*.

For further information write Southeast Alaska Discovery Center, 50 Main St., Ketchikan, AK 99901; phone (907) 228-6220. *See Recreation Chart and the AAA Western Canada & Alaska CampBook.*

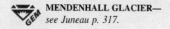 **MENDENHALL GLACIER—** *see Juneau p. 317.*

VALDEZ (C-11) pop. 4,036, elev. 15′

Called the "Switzerland of Alaska," Valdez (val-DEEZ) is ringed by snowcapped mountains. As the northernmost ice-free port, the town was established in 1898 as an outfitting point for miners taking the hazardous pack trail over Valdez Glacier to the northern gold fields.

In addition to the gold rush, Valdez's rich history includes a 5-minute, 9.2-magnitude earthquake in 1964; construction of the Trans-Alaska Pipeline and Marine Terminal in the 1970s; and the 1989 *Exxon Valdez* oil spill and cleanup.

Access into Valdez is by scheduled air service, ferry or via the scenic Richardson Highway. Near Milepost 16 are Bridal Veil and Horsetail falls and the Historic 1899 Trans-Alaska Military Trail & Wagon Road. Thompson Pass, Milepost 26, offers a spectacular view of the Chugach Mountains, valley rivers and historic Keystone Canyon. At Milepost 29 is Worthington Glacier State Park, which has walking trails.

Nearby glaciers in Prince William Sound include Mears, Shoup and Columbia, the second largest tidewater glacier in North America. Cruises are available to Mears and Columbia.

Valdez Convention and Visitors Bureau: P.O. Box 1603-3A, Valdez, AK 99686; phone (907) 835-2984. *See color ad.*

SAVE **STAN STEPHENS GLACIER & WILDLIFE CRUISES** departs from 112 N. Harbor Dr., 3 blks. e. of jct. Richardson Hwy. and Meals St. The outfit offers 6- to 9-hour narrated sightseeing cruises on Prince William Sound to Columbia and

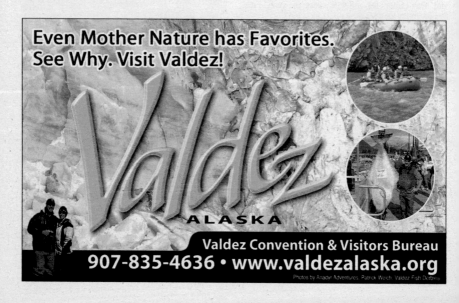

Meares glaciers. Along the way, guests might glimpse bald eagles, Dall's porpoises, black bears, sea otters, Stellar sea lions, puffins, mountain goats and humpback, minke and orca whales. A narrator details area history and information about the Trans-Alaska Pipeline. A light meal is included.

Trips depart daily, mid-May to mid-Sept. Fare $85-$125; ages 3-12, $42-$62. Reservations are recommended. MC, VI. Phone (907) 835-4731 or (866) 867-1297. *See color ad.*

VALDEZ MUSEUM & HISTORICAL ARCHIVE, at 217 Egan Dr., has exhibits about pioneers, gold seekers, local history, glaciers and the pipeline as well as photographs of Valdez before and after the 1964 earthquake. A 1907 Ahrens fire truck and a Fresnel lighthouse lens also are featured. In addition to an exhibit that describes oil industry history, there is one that illustrates the effects and the cleanup efforts of the *Exxon Valdez* oil spill of March 1989.

Allow 30 minutes minimum. Museum daily 9-6, May 15-Sept. 15; Mon.-Sat. 1-5, rest of year. Annex daily 9-4, May 15-Sept. 15; by appointment rest of year. Admission $5; over 64, $4.50; ages 14-17, $4. Museum annex $1.50, under 18 free. Phone (907) 835-2764.

WORTHINGTON GLACIER, about 30 mi. e. on the Richardson Hwy., is Alaska's most accessible glacier. Milepost 28.7 provides an excellent viewpoint; a road leads to the glacier. Camping at the foot of the glacier is permitted.

WASILLA (C-11) pop. 5,469

Founded in 1917, Wasilla is a growing community in the Matanuska-Susitna Valley named after a respected Athabascan Indian chief. Home to the Iditarod Trail Committee headquarters, the town has two warm-water lakes. Dorothy G. Page Museum on Main Street contains historical artifacts; the Old Wasilla Town Site behind the museum preserves Wasilla's first school, two log cabins, a smithy and the town's first public bath. Wasilla lies near the intersection of SRs 1 and 3, both of which are scenic highways.

Greater Wasilla Chamber of Commerce: 415 E. Railroad Ave., Wasilla, AK 99654; phone (907) 376-1299.

MUSEUM OF ALASKA TRANSPORTATION AND INDUSTRY, Milepost 47 on Parks Hwy., displays various items relating to Alaska's transportation and industrial history. Fifteen acres of outdoor exhibits include aircraft, boats, tractors, dog sleds, snowmobiles, farm implements, railroad cars, fire trucks, antique automobiles and memorabilia from early railroading days. Also featured are aviation photographs, vintage farm equipment and engines. Steam train rides are given every third Saturday and holidays during summer.

Picnicking is permitted. Daily 10-5, May-Sept.; Tues.-Sat. 10-5 and by appointment, rest of year. Admission $8; over 65 and ages 3-18, $5; family rate $18. Phone (907) 376-1211.

WHITTIER (D-11) pop. 1,658

Nearly surrounded by mountains and perched at the edge of beautiful Prince William Sound, Whittier remained relatively isolated until June 2000 when a 2.5-mile railroad tunnel was converted to accommodate automobile traffic. The unusual Anton Anderson Memorial Tunnel is a single-lane combination highway and railway that enables cars and trains to take turns passing through the tunnel. Because the tunnel has only one lane, the direction of traffic alternates, ceasing altogether while trains travel through. For the tunnel's traffic schedule phone (907) 611-2586. Tunnel information also is broadcasted by radio on 530 AM in Whittier and 1610 AM in Portage and Bear Valley. A toll of $12 per car is charged at the tunnel's western entrance; toll increases with size of vehicle.

[SAVE] **26 GLACIER CRUISE BY PHILLIPS' CRUISES** departs from the port of Whittier. Cruises explore the calm, protected waters of Prince William Sound. Passengers aboard the company's high-speed catamaran can see tidewater glaciers plus an array of wildlife.

Allow a full day. Cruises depart daily early May-late Sept. Fare $129; under 12, $69. Bus or rail service is offered from Anchorage at an additional cost. Reservations are recommended. AX, DS, MC, VI. Phone (907) 276-8023 or (800) 544-0529. *See color ad p. 299.*

[SAVE] **MAJOR MARINE TOURS** depart from the tour boat dock. A 5-hour narrated sightseeing cruise takes passengers to see spectacular tidewater glaciers and picturesque waterfalls in Prince William Sound. Eagles, otters and harbor seals can be spotted. Food is available. Inquire about weather policies. Allow 6 hours minimum. Departures daily at 1, mid-May to mid-Sept. Reservations are recommended. Fare $99; under 12, $49. AX, DS, MC, VI. Phone (907) 274-7300 or (800) 764-7300. *See color ad p. 328.*

RECREATIONAL ACTIVITIES

Kayaking

- **Alaska Sea Kayakers** depart from the Whittier Boat Harbor. Daily 8-7, May-Sept. Phone (877) 472-2534.

WRANGELL (H-11) pop. 2,308, elev. 37'

Petroglyphs pecked into shale rock and elaborately carved totem poles, cedar monuments of the Stikine (STIK-een) and Tlingit (KLINK-it) Indians, are interesting aspects of Wrangell. Although European and American explorers visited the area in the late 1700s, Russians began trading here by 1811 and established a redoubt in Wrangell in 1834. The only Alaskan town to have existed under Russian, British and American rule, it also survived three gold rushes—In 1861, 1872 and 1898 the lure of riches brought a rush of miners and settlers.

Petroglyphs can be seen on a beach at the north end of Wrangell Island. Of undetermined age, some carvings face the water, others the shore or sky. They are best viewed at low tide. Nearby Anan Creek allows the opportunity to observe sea lions and seals and watch black bear fish for salmon.

Other attractions include the nine totem poles (some are replicas carved by the Civilian Conservation Corps in the late 1930s) on Shakes Island in Wrangell Harbor, as well as the four totem poles in Kiksadi Totem Park at Front and Episcopal streets. Artifacts are displayed in Chief Shakes Tribal House, also on the island. A large concentration of bald eagles gather in Wrangell from January to mid-April waiting for smelt to run up the Stikine River. A visitor center is in the Stikine Inn, at Front Street and Stikine Avenue.

Wrangell Chamber of Commerce: P.O. Box 49, Wrangell, AK 99929; phone (907) 874-3901 or (800) 367-9745.

WRANGELL MUSEUM, 296 Outer Dr., contains local natural history and mineral displays, original totems, petroglyphs, photographs, a collection of spruceroot and cedarbark baskets, beadwork, stone tools and other artifacts crafted by Alaskan natives. Also featured are representations of other cultures that influenced the settlement of the area. Of interest are four original house posts from the Bear Tribal House that were carved in the late 1700s.

Allow 30 minutes minimum. Mon.-Sat. 10-5 and when cruise ships are in port, June 12-Sept. 30; Tues.-Sat. 1-5, Oct.-Apr. Closed holidays. Admission $5; senior citizens $3; ages 6-12, $2; family rate $12. Phone (907) 874-3770.

The Alaska Highway

On March 9, 1942, the U.S. Army Corps of Engineers began bulldozing its way through mountains and forests to create a direct land route linking the United States to the Alaska Territory. The Alaska Highway originated as an emergency passage for American troops during World War II following the Japanese occupation of the Aleutian Islands, which extend southwestward from the Alaska Peninsula.

More than 11,000 troops worked on the road, and American Indians, trappers and prospectors were hired to help. Canada supplied the right of way and materials in exchange for use of the road following the war. The workers built 133 log and pontoon bridges and dug more than 8,000 culverts. Despite untold hardships and the worst winter in recorded history, the highway was completed in just 8 months. In 1943 the highway became public, and for the next 7 years more than 70 companies and 16,000 civilian workers labored to turn it into a year-round, all-weather road.

© Gunter Marx Photography Corbis

The 1,523-mile Alaska Highway takes its travelers on a wilderness tour starting at Dawson Creek, British Columbia, through the Yukon Territory and on through Delta Junction to Fairbanks. The scenery is picture perfect, with an abundance of spruce forests, magnificent mountain passes, lakes, rivers and glacial ice formations. Bears, moose and other wildlife can appear at any time.

The road is maintained daily, but be aware that conditions often change depending on the weather. Take your time, drive with your headlights on and drive defensively. Always be alert for bumps and holes in the road. Gas, food and lodging are conveniently found every 20 to 50 miles.

WRANGELL-ST. ELIAS NATIONAL PARK AND PRESERVE (C-12, F-8)

Elevations in the park and preserve range from sea level at the Gulf of Alaska to 18,008 ft. at Mount St. Elias. Refer to AAA maps for additional elevation information.

In south central Alaska bordering Canada's Yukon Territory, Wrangell-St. Elias National Park and Preserve is the country's largest national park. It is a place of overpowering dimensions, embracing an area larger than Massachusetts, Rhode Island and Connecticut combined; glaciers five times the size of Manhattan; and nine of the 16 highest peaks in North America.

In this 13-million-acre park, the collision of two continental plates has produced some of the world's highest coastal ranges. Forming a barrier along the Gulf of Alaska are the Chugach Mountains, and paralleling them to the north are the Wrangell Mountains.

Between these two ranges are the St. Elias Mountains, extending like the stem of the letter "Y" into Canada's Kluane National Park. Atop these towering peaks are ice fields so immense that they act as a natural cooling system, affecting areas as far south as Chicago and the Central Plains.

As imposing as its ice fields are, it was, another commodity traded by the Ahtna Dene or "people of the Copper River" that caught the world's attention. These and other tribes forged tools of locally mined copper. The first person of European descent to verify the source of the copper trading was Lt. Henry Allen, who in 1885 explored much of Alaska's interior.

Fifteen years later two miners discovered the malachite cliffs above the Kennicott Glacier, which became one of the world's richest sources of copper. The subsequent founding of the Kennecott Mine became one of the most significant events in Alaska's history: The great wealth and development it spawned affected not only Alaska but the entire nation. Currently the ruined mine is all that remains of this immense enterprise.

Legacies of the Kennecott Mine and the Yukon gold fields are some of the area's roads, which provide limited access to the park. One of Alaska's oldest roadways is the Richardson Highway, which was completed in 1919 and was the first all-Alaska route to the Yukon gold fields. Both the Richardson and Glenn highways follow the curve of the park's western boundary and offer several spectacular views of 12,010-foot Mount Drum, 14,163-foot Mount Wrangell and 16,237-foot Mount Sanford.

Two other roads penetrate the park's interior—the Chitina-McCarthy and the Nabesna. Both of these gravel roads offer good views of the mountains and are convenient jumping-off places for hiking and river-running. The 60-mile McCarthy Road follows an abandoned railroad bed. Visitors should allow a minimum of 3 hours to drive between Chitina and McCarthy. Before using either of these routes, check with the ranger stations in Slana and Chitina.

The park's visitor center, 3 miles north of Copper Center on Richardson Highway, provides trip-planning assistance and information about park activities. Fishing, hiking, rafting and wildlife- viewing, especially of the park's large population of Dall sheep, are just some of the activities pursued in the park.

On the southeastern edge of the park and accessible only by sea is Hubbard Glacier on Disenchantment Bay. In 1986 this vast, active tidewater glacier advanced so quickly that for several months it blocked the entrance to Russell Fjord behind a dam of ice, briefly turning it into a lake.

For more information write the Superintendent, Wrangell-St. Elias National Park and Preserve, P.O. Box 439, Copper Center, AK 99573; phone (907) 822-5234. *See Recreation Chart.*

YUKON-CHARLEY RIVERS NATIONAL PRESERVE (B-12, D-8)

Elevations in the preserve range from 600 ft. on the Yukon River where it leaves the preserve near Circle to 6,435 ft. in the Cirque Lakes area on the Charley River drainage. Refer to AAA maps for additional elevation information.

Near the Canadian border in east central Alaska, more than 140 miles of the Yukon River and the entire watershed of the Charley River are encompassed within the 2.5 million acres of the Yukon-Charley Rivers National Preserve. John McPhee remarked in his book "Coming into the Country" that New Jersey could easily fit into this vast emptiness between Eagle and Circle.

Although only 10 year-round residents now live within the preserve's boundaries, it was not always so sparsely populated. During the gold rush, the Yukon—a summer waterway and winter highway—was thronged with people who briefly transformed such communities as Circle into the "Paris of the North." This rough-and-tumble gold rush region was the grist of Robert Service's poetry and Jack London's stories.

Now quiet has returned, and where riverboats once departed from Eagle, river runners make the 5- to 7-day float down the river to Circle. One of the pleasures of this trip is the opportunity to see Peregrine falcons, a threatened species that makes its home in the bluffs along the river. Hikers can catch a glimpse of caribou and Dall sheep in the preserve's upland regions and moose in the lowlands.

The Taylor and Steese highways are the primary summer access routes to the national preserve, terminating respectively in Eagle and Circle just outside the preserve's boundaries. The scenic portion of the Taylor Highway from Chicken to Eagle runs through mountains, rolling tundra and river valleys. Most people, however, reach the park by boat or float on the Yukon River and its tributaries.

The preserve has no roads and no established trails or maintained public airstrips. Seven public-use cabins are available on a first-come, first-served basis. Food service, basic supplies, lodgings and charter boat and air service are available during the summer months in nearby Eagle and Circle. A list of authorized guides can be obtained from the preserve headquarters and visitor center in Eagle.

In addition, the Bureau of Land Management administers Fort Egbert and a campground in Eagle (see the AAA Western Canada & Alaska CampBook). A visitor center, open Mon.-Fri. 8-5, Memorial Day-Labor Day, can be contacted at P.O. Box 167, Eagle, AK 99738; phone (907) 547-2233. For more information write the Superintendent, Yukon-Charley Rivers National Preserve, P.O. Box 74718, Fairbanks, AK 99707-4718. See Recreation Chart.

Smithsonian
National Museum of American History
Behring Center

America on the Move is made possible by generous support from
General Motors Corporation, AAA, State Farm Companies Foundation, The History Channel,
United States Congress, U.S. Department of Transportation, ExxonMobil, American Public
Transportation Association, American Road & Transportation Builders Association,
Association of American Railroads, National Asphalt Pavement Association, The UPS Foundation.

See how we got here.

Immerse yourself in a new museum experience and explore how transportation has changed America. **National Museum of American History, Washington, D.C.** americanhistory.si.edu/onthemove.

AMERICA
ON THE MOVE

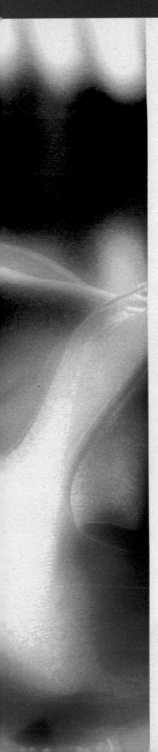

Because she believes that dreams really do come true.

With enchanting Disney vacation rates at AAA/CAA Travel—they can.

We have a magical vacation for every Disney dream. And when you book your *AAA Vacations*® or *Disney Cruise Line*® package through your AAA/CAA Travel office, you'll enjoy special benefits and great values, too. Visit AAA/CAA Travel today and let the fairytale begin.

Travel
www.aaa.com

Disneyland® Resort
Walt Disney World® Resort
Disney Cruise Line®

Howard Johnson®

We've gone from 28 flavors of ice cream to over 475 flavors of hotel.

We started as a modest chain of restaurant/ice cream stands sprinkled along the roadside. That was then. Today we have hotels everywhere from Charlottetown to Victoria. For every type of traveler. So whether you're on the road for pleasure or business we've got you covered. Also, be sure to check out our "Best Rate or it's Free" Guarantee*, as well as our loyalty program, TripRewards.®

howardjohnson.com
1-800-446-4656
Ask for SRP - SA3

triprewards
It's fun to get more.®

Howard Johnson
Go anywhere. Stay Here.℠

Go anywhere. Stay Here.℠

Alberta

Maligne Lake,
Jasper National Park
© SuperStock

AIRDRIE —See Calgary p. 391.

ATHABASCA pop. 2,415

──── WHERE TO STAY ────

BEST WESTERN ATHABASCA INN *Book at aaa.com* Phone: (780)675-2294

(CAA) (SAVE)

| 3/1-5/1 & 10/1-2/28 [CP] | 1P: $119-$139 | 2P: $119-$139 |
| 5/2-9/30 [CP] | 1P: $109-$129 | 2P: $109-$129 |

Small-scale Hotel **Location:** 1 km s on Hwy 2. 5211 41st Ave T9S 1A5. Fax: 780/675-3890. **Facility:** 65 one-bedroom standard units. 4 stories (no elevator), interior corridors. **Parking:** on-site, winter plug-ins. **Terms:** small pets only ($10 fee, in designated units). **Amenities:** voice mail, irons, hair dryers. *Some:* high-speed Internet, fax. **Dining:** 5:30 am-10 pm, Sat & Sun 6 am-9 pm, cocktails, nightclub. **Leisure Activities:** whirlpool, exercise room. **Guest Services:** valet laundry. **Business Services:** meeting rooms, business center. **Cards:** AX, DC, DS, MC, VI. **Special Amenities:** free continental breakfast and free local telephone calls.

SOME UNITS

[S⊘ D] [🐕] [❨]] [Y] [🍽] [DATA PORT] [🔌] [💻] / [☒] [🖨] /
FEE

BANFF pop. 7,135

──── WHERE TO STAY ────

BANFF ASPEN LODGE *Book at aaa.com* Phone: (403)762-4401

6/1-9/30	1P: $195-$205	2P: $195-$205	XP: $15	F16
12/25-2/28	1P: $135-$155	2P: $135-$155	XP: $15	F16
3/1-5/31 & 10/1-12/24	1P: $100-$120	2P: $120-$140	XP: $15	F16

Small-scale Hotel **Location:** At Moose St. 401 Banff Ave T1L 1A9 (PO Box 1017). Fax: 403/762-5905. **Facility:** Smoke free premises. 89 units. 69 one- and 20 two-bedroom standard units. 3 stories, interior/exterior corridors. **Parking:** on-site, winter plug-ins. **Terms:** package plans. **Amenities:** hair dryers. *Some:* irons. **Leisure Activities:** sauna, whirlpool. **Guest Services:** gift shop, valet and coin laundry, area transportation (fee). **Business Services:** meeting rooms, PC (fee). **Cards:** AX, MC, VI.

SOME UNITS

[A$K] [S⊘ D] [❨]] [☒] [☒] [⚙] [📷] [💻] / [🔌] [🖨] /

BANFF CARIBOU LODGE *Book at aaa.com* Phone: (403)762-5887

6/1-9/24	1P: $179-$235	2P: $179-$235	XP: $15	F16
9/25-2/28	1P: $109-$175	2P: $109-$175	XP: $15	F16
3/1-5/31	1P: $109-$159	2P: $109-$159	XP: $15	F16

Small-scale Hotel **Location:** Banff Ave and Marmot St. Located opposite Rotary Park. 521 Banff Ave T1L 1A4 (PO Box 279). Fax: 403/762-5918. **Facility:** 200 one-bedroom standard units, some with whirlpools. 4 stories, interior corridors. **Parking:** on-site. **Terms:** check-in 4 pm, 3 day cancellation notice-fee imposed, [AP], [BP], [CP] & [MAP] meal plans available, package plans. **Amenities:** video games, high-speed Internet (fee), hair dryers. *Some:* irons. **Leisure Activities:** sauna, whirlpool, steamroom, exercise room. **Guest Services:** gift shop, valet laundry, area transportation (fee). **Business Services:** meeting rooms, PC (fee). **Cards:** AX, DC, DS, JC, MC, VI. *(See color ad p 347)*

SOME UNITS

[A$K] [S⊘ D] [❨]] [Y] [☒] [⚙] [📷] [DATA PORT] [💻] / [☒] /

BANFF INTERNATIONAL HOTEL *Book at aaa.com* Phone: (403)762-5666

6/1-10/8	1P: $229-$279	2P: $229-$279	XP: $20	F16
5/1-5/31	1P: $149-$199	2P: $149-$199	XP: $20	F16
3/1-4/30 & 10/9-2/28	1P: $129-$179	2P: $129-$179	XP: $20	F16

Small-scale Hotel **Location:** Corner of Elk St; centre. 333 Banff Ave T1L 1B1 (PO Box 1040). Fax: 403/760-3281. **Facility:** 165 one-bedroom standard units. 3 stories, interior corridors. **Parking:** on-site, winter plug-ins. **Terms:** check-in 4 pm, 3 day cancellation notice-fee imposed, [BP] meal plan available, package plans. **Amenities:** video games, voice mail, irons, hair dryers. **Leisure Activities:** sauna, whirlpool, steamroom, exercise room. **Guest Services:** gift shop, valet and coin laundry. **Business Services:** PC (fee). **Cards:** AX, DC, MC, VI.

SOME UNITS

[A$K] [S⊘ D] [❨]] [Y] [☒] [⚙] [📷] [💻] / [☒] [DATA PORT] /

BANFF PARK LODGE RESORT HOTEL & CONFERENCE CENTRE   *Book at aaa.com*

Phone: (403)762-4433

CAA SAVE	6/1-9/30	1P: $251-$371	2P: $251-$371	XP: $15 F16
	12/26-2/28	1P: $179-$299	2P: $179-$299	XP: $15 F16
	10/1-12/25	1P: $161-$281	2P: $161-$281	XP: $15 F16
	3/1-5/31	1P: $152-$272	2P: $152-$272	XP: $15 F16

Large-scale Hotel **Location:** Between Caribou and Wolf sts; downtown. 222 Lynx St T1L 1K5 (PO Box 2200). Fax: 403/762-3553. **Facility:** Designated smoking area. 211 units. 208 one-bedroom standard units, some with whirlpools. 3 one-bedroom suites with whirlpools. 3 stories, interior corridors. **Parking:** on-site (fee) and valet. **Terms:** 3 day cancellation notice-fee imposed. **Amenities:** voice mail, safes, irons, hair dryers. *Some:* high-speed Internet. **Dining:** 2 restaurants, 6:30 am-midnight, cocktails. **Pool(s):** heated indoor, saltwater. **Leisure Activities:** whirlpool, steamroom, hiking trails. *Fee:* bicycles. **Guest Services:** gift shop, complimentary evening beverages, valet laundry, area transportation (fee)-major ski areas. **Business Services:** conference facilities, PC (fee). **Cards:** AX, DC, JC, MC, VI. *(See color ad p 346)*

SOME UNITS

BANFF PTARMIGAN INN
Book at aaa.com

6/1-10/15	1P: $189-$235	2P: $189-$235	XP: $15	F16
3/1-5/31 & 10/16-2/28	1P: $109-$159	2P: $109-$159	XP: $15	F16

Phone: (403)762-2207

Small-scale Hotel
Location: Sw of Moose St. 337 Banff Ave T1L 1A9 (PO Box 1984, T1L 1B7). **Fax:** 403/762-3577. **Facility:** Smoke free premises. 134 one-bedroom standard units, some with whirlpools. 2-3 stories, interior corridors. **Parking:** on-site, winter plug-ins. **Terms:** check-in 4 pm, 3 day cancellation notice, [AP], [BP], [CP], [ECP] & [MAP] meal plans available, package plans. **Amenities:** high-speed Internet, hair dryers. **Leisure Activities:** sauna, whirlpools, steamroom, limited exercise equipment. **Fee:** massage. **Guest Services:** valet laundry, area transportation (fee). **Business Services:** meeting rooms, PC (fee). **Cards:** AX, DC, DS, JC, MC, VI. *(See color ad p 347)*

SOME UNITS

BANFF ROCKY MOUNTAIN RESORT
Book at aaa.com

All Year	1P: $155-$435	2P: $155-$435	XP: $15	F16

Phone: (403)762-5531

Resort Condominium
Location: Banff Ave and Tunnel Mountain Rd; just s of Trans-Canada Hwy 1. 1029 Banff Ave T1L 1A2 (PO Box 100). **Fax:** 403/762-5166. **Facility:** Just outside of town, this condo-style resort features a mix of guest rooms, all with gas fireplaces. 171 units. 54 one-bedroom standard units. 60 one- and 57 two-bedroom suites ($165-$435), some with efficiencies, kitchens and/or whirlpools. 2 stories (no elevator), exterior corridors. **Parking:** on-site, winter plug-ins. **Terms:** check-in 5 pm, 2 night minimum stay - seasonal, 3 day cancellation notice-fee imposed, pets ($15 extra charge). **Amenities:** video games, voice mail, irons, hair dryers. **Pool(s):** heated outdoor, heated indoor. **Leisure Activities:** sauna, whirlpools, 2 tennis courts, recreation programs, playground, exercise room, basketball, volleyball. **Fee:** bicycles, massage. **Guest Services:** valet and coin laundry, area transportation. **Business Services:** meeting rooms, PC (fee). **Cards:** AX, DC, DS, MC, VI.

SOME UNITS

FEE

THE BANFF VOYAGER INN
Book at aaa.com

6/1-9/30	1P: $165-$195	2P: $165-$195	XP: $15	F17
3/1-5/31	1P: $75-$110	2P: $75-$110	XP: $15	F17
10/1-2/28	1P: $75-$100	2P: $75-$100	XP: $15	F17

Phone: (403)762-3301

CAA SAVE

Small-scale Hotel
Location: 1.2 km ne; corner of Marmot St. 555 Banff Ave T1L 1B5 (PO Box 1540). **Fax:** 403/760-7775. **Facility:** 88 one-bedroom standard units, some with whirlpools. 2 stories (no elevator), interior corridors. **Parking:** on-site, winter plug-ins. **Terms:** check-in 4 pm, cancellation fee imposed. **Amenities:** voice mail. *Some:* hair dryers. **Dining:** 7 am-11 & 5:30-9:30 pm, cocktails. **Pool(s):** heated outdoor. **Leisure Activities:** sauna, whirlpool. **Guest Services:** valet laundry. **Business Services:** meeting rooms, PC (fee). **Cards:** AX, JC, MC, VI. **Special Amenities:** free local telephone calls and free newspaper.

SOME UNITS

BEST WESTERN SIDING 29 LODGE
Book at aaa.com

7/1-8/31 [CP]	1P: $199-$305	2P: $199-$305	XP: $10	F
9/1-9/30 [CP]	1P: $185-$260	2P: $185-$260	XP: $10	F
3/1-6/30 & 10/1-2/28 [CP]	1P: $95-$205	2P: $95-$205	XP: $10	F

Phone: (403)762-5575

CAA SAVE

Small-scale Hotel
Location: 1.3 km ne off Banff Ave. Located in a residential area. 453 Marten St T1L 1B3 (PO Box 1387). **Fax:** 403/762-8866. **Facility:** 57 units. 55 one-bedroom standard units, some with kitchens and/or whirlpools. 2 one-bedroom suites with whirlpools. 3 stories, interior corridors. **Parking:** on-site. **Terms:** 2 night minimum stay - seasonal, package plans. **Amenities:** irons, hair dryers. **Pool(s):** heated indoor. **Leisure Activities:** whirlpool. **Business Services:** PC (fee). **Cards:** AX, DC, JC, MC, VI. **Special Amenities:** free continental breakfast and free local telephone calls.

SOME UNITS

BOW VIEW MOTOR LODGE

6/1-9/30	1P: $160-$175	2P: $160-$175	XP: $10	F8
5/1-5/31	1P: $115-$125	2P: $115-$125	XP: $10	F8
3/1-4/30 & 10/1-2/28	1P: $100-$120	2P: $100-$120	XP: $10	F8

Phone: 403/762-2261

Motel
Location: Between Lynx St and Bow Ave; on Wolf St. 228 Bow Ave T1L 1A5 (PO Box 339). **Fax:** 403/762-8093. **Facility:** Smoke free premises. 57 units. 54 one- and 3 two-bedroom standard units. 3 stories, interior corridors. **Parking:** on-site, winter plug-ins. **Terms:** check-in 4 pm, 7 day cancellation notice. **Amenities:** voice mail. **Pool(s):** small heated outdoor. **Leisure Activities:** whirlpool. **Cards:** AX, DC, DS, JC, MC, VI.

BREWSTER'S MOUNTAIN LODGE
Book at aaa.com

6/24-10/1	1P: $189-$249	2P: $189-$249	XP: $15	F12
10/2-1/2	1P: $99-$219	2P: $99-$219	XP: $15	F12
1/3-2/28	1P: $109-$189	2P: $109-$189	XP: $15	F12
3/1-6/23	1P: $139-$179	2P: $139-$179	XP: $15	F12

Phone: (403)762-2900

CAA SAVE

Small-scale Hotel
Location: Just w off Banff Ave; centre. 208 Caribou St T1L 1C1 (PO Box 2286). **Fax:** 403/762-2970. **Facility:** Smoke free premises. 77 one-bedroom standard units, some with whirlpools. 3 stories, interior corridors. **Parking:** on-site (fee). **Terms:** check-in 4 pm, 3 night minimum stay - seasonal, 3 day cancellation notice, [BP] & [CP] meal plans available, package plans. **Amenities:** hair dryers. **Dining:** Cafe Soleil, see separate listing. **Leisure Activities:** sauna, whirlpool, exercise room. **Guest Services:** gift shop, valet laundry, area transportation (fee). **Business Services:** meeting rooms, PC (fee). **Cards:** AX, JC, MC, VI. *(See color ad p 349)*

SOME UNITS

FEE

BUFFALO MOUNTAIN LODGE

6/1-9/30	1P: $199-$299		XP: $25	F12
3/1-5/31 & 10/1-2/28	1P: $139-$199		XP: $25	F12

Phone: (403)762-2400

Small-scale Hotel
Location: 1.6 km ne. 700 Tunnel Mountain Rd T1L 1B3 (PO Box 1326). **Fax:** 403/760-4492. **Facility:** 108 units. 92 one-bedroom standard units, some with efficiencies. 16 one-bedroom suites with efficiencies. 2 stories (no elevator), exterior corridors. **Parking:** on-site, winter plug-ins. **Terms:** check-in 4 pm, 3 day cancellation notice-fee imposed, package plans. **Amenities:** video library, voice mail, irons, hair dryers. **Dining:** dining room, see separate listing. **Leisure Activities:** whirlpool, steamroom, recreation programs, exercise room. **Guest Services:** valet laundry, area transportation (fee). **Business Services:** conference facilities, business center. **Cards:** AX, MC, VI.

SOME UNITS

BUMPER'S INN

	6/1-9/30	1P: $125-$135	2P: $125-$135	XP: $10 F12
	10/1-2/28	1P: $55-$85	2P: $55-$85	XP: $10 F12
Motel	3/1-5/31	1P: $55-$85	2P: $85	XP: $10 F12

Phone: (403)762-3386

Location: 1.2 km ne on Banff Ave at jct Marmot St. 603 Banff Ave T1L 1B3 (PO Box 1328). Fax: 403/762-8842. **Facility:** 39 one-bedroom standard units. 2 stories (no elevator), exterior corridors. **Parking:** on-site, winter plug-ins. **Terms:** office hours 7 am-11 pm, cancellation fee imposed. **Amenities:** voice mail, hair dryers. **Dining:** Bumper's The Beef House, see separate listing. **Guest Services:** area transportation (fee). **Cards:** AX, MC, VI.

SOME UNITS

(ASK) (TI) (AC) (R) (B) / (X) /

CASTLE MOUNTAIN CHALETS *Book at aaa.com* Phone: 403/762-3868

(CAA) (SAVE)	All Year	1P: $145-$335	2P: $145-$335

Location: 32 km w on Trans-Canada Hwy 1, jct Castle, 1 km ne on Hwy 1A (Bow Valley Pkwy). (PO Box 1655). Fax: 403/762-8629. **Facility:** Smoke free premises. 23 units. 2 one-bedroom suites with kitchens. 21 cabins. 1 story, exterior corridors. *Bath:* combo or shower only. **Parking:** on-site, winter plug-ins. **Terms:** office hours 7 am-10 pm, 2 night minimum stay - seasonal and/or weekends, 14 day cancellation notice-fee imposed, package plans, pets ($25 extra charge). **Amenities:** video library, hair dryers. **Leisure Activities:** steamroom, cross country skiing, recreation programs, telephone & library in central recreation building, exercise room. *Fee:* fishing rods, bicycles. **Guest Services:** gift shop, coin laundry. **Cards:** AX, MC, VI. *(See color ad below)*

SOME UNITS

(FEE) (図) (区) (AC) (VCR) (R) (Z) (目) (匣) / (匣) /

CHARLTON'S CEDAR COURT ◆◆ ◆◆ Motel

Book at aaa.com

6/3-9/30	1P: $199-$229	2P: $199-$229	XP: $25	F16
10/1-2/28	1P: $126-$229	2P: $126-$229	XP: $25	F16
3/1-6/2	1P: $132-$162	2P: $132-$162	XP: $25	F16

Phone: (403)762-4485

Location: 1 km ne. 513 Banff Ave T1L 1B4 (PO Box 1478). Fax: 403/762-2744. **Facility:** Smoke free premises. 57 units. 41 one- and 16 two-bedroom standard units, some with efficiencies. 2-3 stories, exterior corridors. **Parking:** on-site, winter plug-ins. **Terms:** office hours 7 am-11 pm, check-in 4 pm, 5 day cancellation notice-fee imposed, package plans. **Amenities:** video games, voice mail, hair dryers. **Pool(s):** heated indoor, saltwater. **Leisure Activities:** whirlpool, steamroom. **Guest Services:** valet laundry, area transportation (fee). **Business Services:** meeting rooms, PC (fee). **Cards:** AX, DC, JC, MC, VI. *(See color ad below)*

SOME UNITS

(ASK) (S🛇) (🛏↑) (⊐) (✕) (📷) (DATA PORT) (🔌) (⬛) / (🖨) /

Royal Canadian Lodge
459 Banff Avenue

One of Banff's Finest Hotels
Outstanding Accommodations • Hotel Spa
Award Winning Restaurant

The Evergreen
Casual Fine Dining

Charlton's Cedar Court
513 Banff Avenue

Indoor Pool • Kitchenette Suites
Loft Suites with Fireplace

Toll Free in North America: 1-800-661-1225
www.charltonresorts.com

Member Discounts

DOUGLAS FIR RESORT & CHALETS *Book at aaa.com* **Phone:** (403)762-5591

CAA SAVE

Condominium

6/11-10/10	1P: $198-$420	2P: $198-$420	XP: $15	F14
10/11-2/28	1P: $155-$355	2P: $155-$355	XP: $15	F14
3/1-4/17	1P: $143-$338	2P: $143-$338	XP: $15	F14
4/18-6/10	1P: $115-$335	2P: $115-$335	XP: $15	F14

Location: 1.6 km ne. 525 Tunnel Mountain Rd T1L 1B2 (PO Box 1228). Fax: 403/762-8774. **Facility:** On a wooded hillside with scenic mountain views, the resort offers a mix of chalets and condos featuring upscale decor. Smoke free premises. 133 units. 34 one-bedroom standard units with kitchens. 56 one-, 33 two- and 1 three-bedroom suites with kitchens, some with whirlpools. 9 cottages. 2-3 stories, interior/exterior corridors. **Parking:** on-site, winter plug-ins. **Terms:** check-in 4 pm, cancellation fee imposed, package plans. **Amenities:** video library (fee), dual phone lines, voice mail, safes, irons, hair dryers. **Pool(s):** heated indoor, wading. **Leisure Activities:** saunas, whirlpools, waterslide, tennis court, racquetball court, ice skating, playground, exercise room. *Fee:* game room. **Guest Services:** sundries, coin laundry. **Business Services:** PC (fee). **Cards:** AX, DC, MC, VI. *(See color ad p 350)*

SOME UNITS / VCR FEE

THE FAIRMONT BANFF SPRINGS *Book at aaa.com* **Phone:** (403)762-2211

CAA SAVE

Resort
Large-scale Hotel

6/1-9/30	1P: $439-$649	2P: $439-$649	XP: $25	F18
5/1-5/31	1P: $299-$439	2P: $299-$439	XP: $25	F18
3/1-4/30 & 10/1-2/28	1P: $209-$379	2P: $209-$379	XP: $25	F18

Location: Just s on Banff Ave over the bridge, 0.5 km e. 405 Spray Ave T1L 1J4 (PO Box 960). Fax: 403/762-5755. **Facility:** With a distinctive design that brings to mind a castle, this engaging hotel offers impressive public areas that serve to offset its small guest rooms. 770 units. 720 one-bedroom standard units, some with whirlpools. 39 one- and 11 two-bedroom suites, some with whirlpools. 3-9 stories, interior corridors. **Parking:** on-site (fee) and valet, winter plug-ins ($40 fee). **Amenities:** video games (fee), voice mail, honor bars, irons, hair dryers. *Some:* CD players, high-speed Internet (fee), safes. **Dining:** 7 restaurants, 24 hours, cocktails, also, The Banffshire Club, see separate listing. **Pool(s):** heated outdoor, heated indoor, wading, lap. **Leisure Activities:** saunas, whirlpools, steamrooms, 5 tennis courts, ice skating, recreation programs, audio visual theatre, hiking trails, jogging, spa. *Fee:* golf-27 holes, tobogganing, bowling, bicycles, horseback riding. **Guest Services:** gift shop, valet laundry, beauty salon. **Business Services:** conference facilities, business center. **Cards:** AX, CB, DC, DS, JC, MC, VI.

SOME UNITS

HIDDEN RIDGE RESORT *Book at aaa.com* **Phone:** (403)762-3544

Condominium

6/1-10/15	1P: $189-$499	2P: $189-$499	XP: $15	F16
3/1-5/31	1P: $139-$399	2P: $139-$399	XP: $15	F16
10/16-2/28	1P: $109-$299	2P: $109-$299	XP: $15	F16

Location: 2.4 km ne. 901 Coyote Dr at Tunnel Mountain Rd T1L 1B7 (PO Box 1984). Fax: 403/762-2804. **Facility:** Smoke free premises. 94 units. 40 one- and 44 two-bedroom suites with kitchens, some with whirlpools. 10 cottages. 2 stories (no elevator), exterior corridors. **Parking:** on-site, winter plug-ins. **Terms:** check-in 4 pm, 3 day cancellation notice, package plans. **Amenities:** hair dryers. **Leisure Activities:** whirlpool, recreation programs. **Guest Services:** area transportation. **Business Services:** meeting rooms, PC (fee). **Cards:** AX, DC, DS, JC, MC, VI. *(See color ad p 347)*

HIGH COUNTRY INN

	6/1-9/30 [BP]	1P: $171-$181		XP: $15	F12
	3/1-4/3 [BP]	1P: $109-$119		XP: $15	F12
Small-scale Hotel	4/4-5/31 & 10/1-2/28 [BP]	1P: $98-$108		XP: $15	F12

Phone: (403)762-2236

Location: N of Rabbit St. 419 Banff Ave T1L 1A7 (PO Box 700). Fax: 403/762-5084. **Facility:** Smoke free premises. 70 units. 68 one-bedroom standard units, some with whirlpools. 2 one-bedroom suites ($118-$275). 3 stories, interior corridors. *Bath:* combo or shower only. **Parking:** on-site, winter plug-ins. **Terms:** check-in 4 pm, package plans. **Amenities:** hair dryers. *Some:* video games. **Dining:** Ticino Swiss-Italian Restaurant, see separate listing. **Pool(s):** small heated indoor. **Leisure Activities:** sauna, whirlpools. **Guest Services:** valet and coin laundry, area transportation (fee). **Business Services:** meeting rooms. **Cards:** AX, MC, VI. *(See color ad p 351)*

SOME UNITS

(ASK) 〔🍽️〕 〔🏊〕 〔✕〕 〔DATA PORT〕 〔📶〕 〔💻〕 / 〔🖨️〕 /

HOMESTEAD INN

	6/1-9/30	1P: $139-$149	2P: $149	XP: $15	F12
	10/1-2/28	1P: $69-$95	2P: $79-$95	XP: $15	F12
Motel	5/1-5/31	1P: $75-$85	2P: $85	XP: $15	F12
	3/1-4/30	1P: $69-$79	2P: $79	XP: $15	F12

Phone: 403/762-4471

Location: Between Caribou and Wolf sts; downtown. 217 Lynx St T1L 1A7 (PO Box 669). Fax: 403/762-8877. **Facility:** 27 one-bedroom standard units. 3 stories (no elevator), exterior corridors. **Parking:** on-site, winter plug-ins. **Terms:** office hours 7 am-11 pm. **Amenities:** hair dryers. **Guest Services:** area transportation (fee). **Cards:** AX, MC, VI.

SOME UNITS

〔🍽️+〕 〔📶〕 〔💻〕 / 〔✕〕 /

INNS OF BANFF   *Book at aaa.com*

	5/16-12/31	1P: $110-$285	2P: $110-$285	XP: $20	F16
	1/1-2/28	1P: $110-$240	2P: $110-$240	XP: $20	F16
Small-scale Hotel	3/1-4/18	1P: $135-$190	2P: $135-$190	XP: $20	F16
	4/19-5/15	1P: $110-$165	2P: $110-$165	XP: $20	F16

Phone: (403)762-4581

Location: Trans-Canada Hwy 1, exit Tunnel Mountain Rd, 2.8 km s. 600 Banff Ave T1L 1H8 (PO Box 1077). Fax: 403/762-2434. **Facility:** Designated smoking area. 180 units. 161 one-bedroom standard units, some with whirlpools. 19 one-bedroom suites. 4 stories, interior corridors. **Parking:** on-site, winter plug-ins. **Terms:** check-in 4 pm, cancellation fee imposed, package plans. **Amenities:** voice mail, hair dryers. **Pool(s):** heated indoor. **Leisure Activities:** saunas, whirlpools. *Fee:* downhill & cross country skiing, snowmobiling, bicycles, massage. **Guest Services:** gift shop, valet and coin laundry, beauty salon. **Business Services:** meeting rooms, PC (fee). **Cards:** AX, DC, JC, MC, VI.

SOME UNITS

(ASK) 〔🛟〕 〔🍽️〕 〔🍷〕 〔🏊〕 〔✕〕 〔📷〕 〔DATA PORT〕 〔📶〕 〔💻〕 / 〔🍴〕 〔🖨️〕 /

IRWIN'S MOUNTAIN INN

〔CAA〕 〔SAVE〕

	5/27-9/24	1P: $130-$160	2P: $130-$160	XP: $15	F16
	3/1-5/26	1P: $75-$100	2P: $75-$100	XP: $10	F16
	9/25-2/28	1P: $65-$80	2P: $65-$80	XP: $5	F16

Phone: (403)762-4566

Location: 1 km ne. 429 Banff Ave T1L 1B2 (PO Box 1198). Fax: 403/762-8220. **Facility:** 65 units. 59 one- and 6 **Small-scale Hotel** two-bedroom standard units, some with whirlpools. 3 stories, interior corridors. **Parking:** on-site, winter plug-ins. **Terms:** check-in 4 pm, cancellation fee imposed, [MAP] meal plan available. **Amenities:** high-speed Internet, voice mail, hair dryers. **Dining:** 7 am-11 & 5-11 pm; hours vary seasonally, cocktails. **Leisure Activities:** sauna, whirlpool, steamroom, ski lockers, exercise room. *Fee:* game room. **Guest Services:** sundries, coin laundry, area transportation (fee)-ski areas. **Business Services:** meeting rooms. **Cards:** AX, MC, VI. **Special Amenities:** free local telephone calls.

SOME UNITS

〔🛟〕 〔🍽️〕 〔✕〕 〔📷〕 〔DATA PORT〕 〔💻〕 / 〔✕〕 〔📶〕 〔🖨️〕 /

JOHNSTON CANYON RESORT

| | 6/17-9/17 | 1P: $129-$279 | 2P: $129-$279 | XP: $10 | F12 |
| Cabin | 5/20-6/16 & 9/18-10/2 | 1P: $116-$249 | 2P: $116-$249 | XP: $10 | F12 |

Phone: 403/762-2971

Location: 24 km nw on Hwy 1A (Bow Valley Pkwy). Located at Johnston Canyon. Hwy 1A T1L 1A9 (PO Box 875). Fax: 403/762-0868. **Facility:** Designated smoking area. 41 cabins. 1 story, exterior corridors. *Bath:* combo or shower only. **Parking:** on-site. **Terms:** open 5/20-10/2, office hours 8 am-10 pm, check-in 4 pm, cancellation fee imposed. **Amenities:** video library (fee). **Leisure Activities:** tennis court, bicycles, hiking trails. **Guest Services:** gift shop. **Cards:** MC, VI. *(See color ad below)*

〔🛏️〕 〔🍽️〕 〔✕〕 〔✕〕 〔🍴〕 〔📺〕 〔VCR〕 〔🎿〕 〔📶〕 〔💻〕

RED CARPET INN — *Book at aaa.com*

CAA SAVE

Motel

6/24-9/26 [CP]	1P: $119-$149	2P: $139-$159	XP: $10	F16
5/20-6/23 [CP]	1P: $90-$119	2P: $95-$135	XP: $10	F16
3/1-5/19 [CP]	1P: $75-$99	2P: $79-$110	XP: $10	F16
9/27-2/28 [CP]	1P: $69-$99	2P: $79-$110	XP: $10	F16

Phone: (403)762-4184

Location: 1 km ne. 425 Banff Ave T1L 1B6 (PO Box 1800). Fax: 403/762-4894. **Facility:** 52 one-bedroom standard units, some with whirlpools. 3 stories, interior/exterior corridors. **Parking:** on-site, winter plug-ins. **Terms:** check-in 4 pm, small pets only ($10 fee). **Amenities:** hair dryers. **Leisure Activities:** whirlpools. **Guest Services:** valet laundry, area transportation (fee)-ski shuttle. **Business Services:** PC (fee). **Cards:** AX, JC, MC, VI. **Special Amenities:** free continental breakfast and free local telephone calls.

SOME UNITS

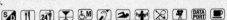

THE RIMROCK RESORT HOTEL

CAA SAVE

Large-scale Hotel

6/1-10/7	1P: $400-$550	2P: $400-$550	XP: $25	F18
12/23-2/28	1P: $345-$470	2P: $345-$470	XP: $25	F18
3/1-5/31 & 10/8-12/22	1P: $255-$345	2P: $255-$345	XP: $25	F18

Phone: (403)762-3356

Location: 4 km s via Sulphur Mountain Rd; adjacent to Upper Hot Springs Pool. Located in a quiet, secluded area. 100 Mountain Dr T1L 1J2 (PO Box 1110). Fax: 403/762-4132. **Facility:** Tucked away in the mountains just on the outside of town, this luxurious resort hotel features elegant rooms and upscale dining. 346 one-bedroom standard units. 9 stories, interior corridors. **Parking:** on-site and valet, winter plug-ins. **Terms:** 3 day cancellation notice-fee imposed, package plans. **Amenities:** video games, dual phone lines, voice mail, honor bars, irons, hair dryers. **Dining:** 6 am-10 pm, cocktails, also, Eden, see separate listing, entertainment. **Pool(s):** heated indoor. **Leisure Activities:** sauna, whirlpool, steamrooms, ice skating, hiking trails, spa, aerobics, sports court. *Fee:* ski shuttle. **Guest Services:** gift shop, valet laundry, area transportation-downtown. **Business Services:** conference facilities, business center. **Cards:** AX, CB, DC, DS, JC, MC, VI. **Special Amenities:** free local telephone calls.

SOME UNITS

ROYAL CANADIAN LODGE BANFF — *Book at aaa.com*

Small-scale Hotel

6/3-9/30	1P: $325-$450	2P: $325-$450	XP: $25	F16
10/1-2/28	1P: $200-$450	2P: $200-$450	XP: $25	F16
3/1-6/2	1P: $200-$350	2P: $200-$350	XP: $25	F16

Phone: (403)762-3307

Location: 1 km ne. 459 Banff Ave T1L 1B4 (PO Box 1478). Fax: 403/762-4094. **Facility:** Designated smoking area. 99 one-bedroom standard units, some with whirlpools. 3 stories, interior corridors. **Parking:** on-site (fee) and valet. **Terms:** check-in 4 pm, 5 day cancellation notice-fee imposed, package plans. **Amenities:** video games, high-speed Internet, voice mail, safes, hair dryers. **Dining:** The Evergreen, see separate listing. **Pool(s):** small heated indoor. **Leisure Activities:** whirlpool, steamroom, exercise room. *Fee:* massage. **Guest Services:** valet laundry, area transportation (fee). **Business Services:** meeting rooms. **Cards:** AX, DC, JC, MC, VI. *(See color ad p 350)*

RUNDLESTONE LODGE *Book at aaa.com* Phone: (403)762-2201

Small-scale Hotel

7/1-8/31	1P: $165-$185	2P: $165-$185
6/1-6/30	1P: $130-$165	2P: $140-$165
9/1-2/28	1P: $95-$155	2P: $110-$165
3/1-5/31	1P: $95-$120	2P: $110-$130

Location: 0.9 km ne. 537 Banff Ave T1L 1A6 (PO Box 489). Fax: 403/762-4501. **Facility:** 96 units. 94 one-bedroom standard units, some with whirlpools. 2 one-bedroom suites with kitchens and whirlpools. 3 stories, interior corridors. **Parking:** on-site. **Amenities:** high-speed Internet, hair dryers. **Pool(s):** heated indoor, lap. **Leisure Activities:** whirlpool, exercise room. **Guest Services:** valet and coin laundry, area transportation (fee). **Business Services:** meeting rooms, PC (fee). **Cards:** AX, DC, DS, MC, VI. *(See color ad p 353)*

SOME UNITS

TUNNEL MOUNTAIN RESORT Phone: (403)762-4515

Condominium

6/1-9/30	1P: $205-$275	2P: $205-$275	XP: $15	F15
10/1-2/28	1P: $110-$275	2P: $110-$275	XP: $15	F15
3/1-5/31	1P: $160-$219	2P: $160-$219	XP: $15	F15

Location: 1.6 km ne. Tunnel Mountain Rd T1L 1B1 (PO Box 1137). Fax: 403/762-5183. **Facility:** 94 units. 24 one-bedroom standard units with whirlpools. 15 one- and 55 two-bedroom suites, some with whirlpools. 2 stories, exterior corridors. **Parking:** on-site, winter plug-ins. **Terms:** check-in 4 pm, 2 night minimum stay, 3 day cancellation notice-fee imposed. **Amenities:** voice mail, hair dryers. *Some:* DVD players, high-speed Internet (fee), dual phone lines. **Pool(s):** small heated indoor. **Leisure Activities:** sauna, whirlpools, steamroom, playground, exercise room. *Fee:* massage. **Guest Services:** valet and coin laundry. **Business Services:** meeting rooms, PC (fee). **Cards:** AX, MC, VI.

SOME UNITS

─── WHERE TO DINE ───

THE BANFFSHIRE CLUB   **Dinner:** $100-$120   **Phone:** 403/762-6860

Location: Just s on Banff Ave over the bridge, 0.5 km e; in The Fairmont Banff Springs. 405 Spray Ave T1L 1J4. **Hours:** 6 pm-10 pm, Tues-Thurs to 9 pm. Closed: Sun & Mon. **Reservations:** required. **Features:** A meal at the sophisticated, exquisite restaurant likely will be remembered for a lifetime. Harp music permeates the air and sets the tone for an evening of fine dining, where meals are as pleasant as a finely tuned orchestra. Scottish furnishings are plentiful, and the servers don kilts. Each dish is a work of art and almost too
Continental   beautiful to eat. Guests should be prepared for fine food, fine wine and fine service. Dressy casual; cocktails. **Parking:** on-site and valet. **Cards:** AX, DC, DS, JC, MC, VI.

BUFFALO MOUNTAIN LODGE DINING ROOM   **Lunch:** $9-$15   **Dinner:** $22-$35   **Phone:** 403/760-4484

Location: 1.6 km ne; in Buffalo Mountain Lodge. 700 Tunnel Mountain Rd T1L 1B3. **Hours:** 7 am-10 pm. **Reservations:** suggested. **Features:** You'll appreciate the casual elegance in this restaurant's mountain setting. Its Rocky Mountain cuisine features wild-game meat, robust flavors and an excellent wine list. After-
Regional   dinner drinks and a cigar menu are offered fireside in the lounge. Casual dress; cocktails. **Parking:** on-site.
Canadian   **Cards:** AX, DC, MC, VI.

BUMPER'S THE BEEF HOUSE   **Dinner:** $10-$35   **Phone:** 403/762-2622

Location: 1.2 km ne on Banff Ave at jct Marmot St; in Bumper's Inn. 603 Banff Ave T1L 1A9. **Hours:** 4:30 pm-10 pm; to 9:30 pm in fall. Closed: 12/24, 12/25. **Reservations:** suggested. **Features:** Established in 1975, the
Steak House   restaurant occupies an A-frame building. The decor is a blend of the Old West and a mountain chalet, with the loft-lounge overlooking the dining room. Patrons can enjoy the all-you-can-eat salad bar with each entree. Although the succulent hamburgers are a favorite, the menu also features prime rib and steaks, all served by the friendly staff. Cocktails. **Parking:** on-site. **Cards:** AX, DC, MC, VI.

CAFE SOLEIL   **Lunch:** $8-$14   **Dinner:** $8-$20   **Phone:** 403/762-2090

Location: Just w off Banff Ave; centre; in Brewster's Mountain Lodge. 208 Caribou St T1L 1A9. **Hours:** 7 am-2 & 6-10:30 pm. Closed major holidays. **Features:** The Mediterranean-style bistro is owned by the same folks who
Mediterranean   run Typhoon, and is fast becoming a popular spot in Banff. Guests can sit for hours sampling and sharing the distinctive tapas, including lamb lollipops, eggplant and homemade soup. Casual dress; cocktails.
Parking: street. **Cards:** AX, DC, MC, VI.

CILANTRO MOUNTAIN CAFE   **Lunch:** $10-$12   **Dinner:** $14-$26   **Phone:** 403/762-2400

Location: 2.3 km n; in Buffalo Mountain Lodge. Tunnel Mountain Rd T0L 0C0. **Hours:** Open 5/15-10/30; 11 am-10 pm. **Reservations:** suggested. **Features:** The seasonal restaurant treats patrons to fine, friendly service in
Southwest   a casual atmosphere. However, the food—an eclectic mix of designer wood-fired pizzas, pasta dishes and
California   fantastic desserts, all relying heavily on regional ingredients—is anything but casual. On summer days, locals often congregate on the patio. Casual dress; cocktails. **Parking:** on-site. **Cards:** AX, DC, JC,
MC, VI.

COYOTES DELI & GRILL   **Lunch:** $8-$11   **Dinner:** $14-$22   **Phone:** 403/762-3963

Location: Just w of Banff Ave; centre. 206 Caribou St T1L 1A2. **Hours:** 7:30-11 am, 11:30-4 & 5-11 pm. Closed: 12/25. **Reservations:** suggested, for dinner. **Features:** Set in a relaxed yet lively deli-bistro, Coyotes
Regional American   focuses on contemporary Southwest cuisine with an accent on creativity and color. A large open kitchen allows you to watch your food being prepared. Casual dress; cocktails. **Parking:** street. **Cards:** AX, DC,
MC, VI.

EDEN   **Dinner:** $95-$125   **Phone:** 403/762-1833

Location: 4 km s via Sulphur Mountain Rd; adjacent to Upper Hot Springs Pool; in The Rimrock Resort Hotel. 100 Mountain Ave T1L 1J2. **Hours:** 6 pm-10 pm. **Reservations:** suggested. **Features:** Tastes, textures, creativity and imagination mingle to produce an exquisite meal from beginning to end. A touch of something magical is evident at the intimate restaurant, where hours pass unnoticed as diners unwind in plush wingback chairs, gazing out at the spectacular mountains. The finest crystal touches guests' lips, and the finest food teases
French   their taste buds. A team of professional servers will provide attentive and knowledgeable service, creating a memorable experience. Dressy casual; cocktails. **Parking:** on-site and valet. **Cards:** AX, DC, DS, JC, MC, VI.

THE EVERGREEN   **Lunch:** $10-$14   **Dinner:** $23-$43   **Phone:** 403/762-3307

Location: 1 km ne; in Royal Canadian Lodge Banff. 459 Banff Ave T1L 1B4. **Hours:** 6:30 am-10 pm; hours may vary seasonally. **Reservations:** suggested. **Features:** An open-concept kitchen, innovative Continental
International   menu and comfortable yet elegant ambience make the restaurant a popular choice. Dishes highlight fresh local and regional ingredients. This place is within easy walking distance of the town center. Casual dress;
cocktails. **Parking:** valet and street. **Cards:** AX, DC, DS, JC, MC, VI. *(See color ad p 350)*

GIORGIO'S TRATTORIA   **Dinner:** $12-$24   **Phone:** 403/762-5114

Location: Centre. 219 Banff Ave T0L 0C0. **Hours:** 5 pm-10:30 pm; to 10 pm off season. Closed: Sun-Wed 11/1-11/30. **Features:** This restaurant's Southern and Mediterranean decor offers a warm, relaxed ambience. The dishes include fresh pasta made in-house, meat and seafood specialties, and pizza cooked in a traditional wood-burning oven. Casual dress; cocktails. **Parking:** street. **Cards:** AX, MC, VI.
Italian

GRIZZLY HOUSE   **Lunch:** $10-$18   **Dinner:** $14-$35   **Phone:** 403/762-4055

Location: Between Caribou and Wolf sts. 207 Banff Ave T0L 0C0. **Hours:** 11:30 am-midnight. **Reservations:** suggested. **Features:** The eclectic and rustic downtown restaurant treats patrons to a
Fondue   distinctive fondue experience. Beef, buffalo, chicken, ostrich, rattlesnake, lobster and shark are among meats available for dipping. Finish the meal with a decadent chocolate fondue. Hot rock fondues are a particularly memorable experience. The bustling atmosphere is fun and lively. Casual dress; cocktails. **Parking:** street.
Cards: AX, MC, VI.

LE BEAUJOLAIS

Dinner: $30-$55   **Phone:** 403/762-2712

French

MC, VI.

Location: Northwest corner of Banff Ave and Buffalo St; upstairs; near bridge. 212 Buffalo St T1L 1B5. **Hours:** Open 3/1-10/31 & 12/1-2/28; 6 pm-11 pm. **Reservations:** suggested. **Features:** Guests ascend the stairs to the elegant dining room, which overlooks one of the main streets. The restaurant offers an experience, not just a meal. Professional servers ensure a memorable event from beginning to end. The cuisine, a harmony of traditional elements prepared with a contemporary flair, is available as a prix fixe menu or a la carte. The wine list is among the most impressive in town. Dressy casual; cocktails. **Parking:** street. **Cards:** AX, MC, VI.

THE MAPLE LEAF GRILLE & SPIRITS

Lunch: $8-$14   **Dinner:** $17-$39   **Phone:** 403/760-7680

Canadian

Location: Corner of Banff Ave and Caribou St. 137 Banff Ave T1L 1C8. **Hours:** 11 am-11 pm. Closed: for lunch 12/25. **Reservations:** required. **Features:** The restaurant is a favorite for a truly Canadian experience, both in food and decor. The cozy, rock-and-wood interior displays Canadian art, as well as a canoe on the ceiling and snowshoes on the walls. The chef creates artistic regional dishes, using organic, free-range, locally grown ingredients when possible. Among selections are preparations of elk, venison, salmon and char, all made to complement the season. Cocktails. **Parking:** street. **Cards:** AX, DC, MC, VI.

ST-JAMES'S GATE OLDE IRISH PUB

Lunch: $9-$25   **Dinner:** $9-$25   **Phone:** 403/762-9355

Irish

Location: Just w of Banff Ave; centre. 207 Wolf St T1L 1C2. **Hours:** 11 am-1 am, Fri & Sat-2 am. **Features:** For a casual place to kick back in the typical Irish way, look no further. The modern-day version of a rustic pub serves traditional food, such as shepherd's pie, steak and Guinness pie. Lamb stew is a fantastic, hearty choice, served with a chunk of soda bread. Guests can savor a pint of locally brewed beer or try some of the ales from overseas. Also on hand is an impressive selection of single-malt scotches, local and imported draft beers and cigars. Cocktails; entertainment. **Parking:** street. **Cards:** AX, DC, MC, VI.

SALTLIK A RARE STEAKHOUSE

Lunch: $9-$21   **Dinner:** $14-$30   **Phone:** 403/762-2467

Steak House

Location: Jct Caribou and Bear sts. 221 Bear St T1L 1B3. **Hours:** 11 am-11 pm. Closed: 12/25. **Reservations:** accepted. **Features:** True to its name, the restaurant truly is a "rare steak house" and a superb place. From the moment guests ascend the stairs to the upscale, contemporary dining room, they're impressed by the atmosphere. Also praiseworthy is the incredibly friendly, attentive service. Servers take the time to explain the different cuts of meat and accompanying sauces. All entrees are a la carte, and the side orders are large enough to split. Casual dress; cocktails. **Parking:** street. **Cards:** AX, MC, VI.

SILVER DRAGON RESTAURANT

Lunch: $6-$12   **Dinner:** $8-$15   **Phone:** 403/762-3939

Chinese

Location: Centre. 211 Banff Ave T1L 1E4. **Hours:** 11:30 am-10:30 pm; to 10 pm in winter. **Features:** Two flights up from street level, the restaurant is a definite stop for those who crave Chinese food. Portions of seafood, pork, noodles and beef are certain to satisfy any appetite. Patrons discover a contemporary decor, complete with a fish tank that the kids will enjoy. Casual dress; cocktails. **Parking:** street. **Cards:** AX, DC, JC, MC, VI.

SUKIYAKI HOUSE

Lunch: $8-$15   **Dinner:** $9-$27   **Phone:** 403/762-2002

Japanese

Location: Downtown; 2nd floor, Park Avenue Mall. 211 Banff Ave T1L 1B8. **Hours:** 4:30 pm-10 pm; also noon-2:30 pm 6/1-9/30. Closed: 12/24, 12/25. **Reservations:** suggested. **Features:** Diners who crave sushi might try the traditional sushi house decor includes an open-concept sushi bar, where guests can choose from love boat platters, varied sushi and sashimi and traditional miso soup. Casual dress; cocktails. **Parking:** street. **Cards:** AX, MC, VI.

SUNFOOD CAFE

Lunch: $5-$8   **Dinner:** $10-$15   **Phone:** 403/760-3933

Vegetarian

Location: Downtown; 2nd level of Sundance Mall. 215 Banff Ave T1L 1B4. **Hours:** 11 am-9 pm; 10 am-10 pm 6/1-9/15. **Reservations:** not accepted. **Features:** Upon arrival at the small, intimate bistro, tucked upstairs off the beaten path, guests most likely will be greeted by Christian, the energetic owner of the city's only vegetarian restaurant. He has cultivated a reputation for hearty and healthy options, ranging from curry to soups to daily specials. Casual dress; cocktails. **Parking:** on-site. **Cards:** MC, VI.

TICINO SWISS-ITALIAN RESTAURANT

Dinner: $13-$33   **Phone:** 403/762-3848

Swiss

Location: N of Rabbit St; in High Country Inn. 415 Banff Ave T1L 1B5. **Hours:** Open 3/1-11/9 & 12/8-2/28; 7 am-10:30 & 5:30-10 pm. **Reservations:** suggested. **Features:** Amid Swiss-inspired decor, diners can sample finely presented specialties from the Ticino area, including the famous fondue. To start off the day right, stop in for the morning Alpine breakfast buffet, which includes a wide range of fruits, pastries and other fine treats. Casual dress; cocktails. **Parking:** on-site. **Cards:** AX, DC, JC, MC, VI.

TOMMY'S NEIGHBOURHOOD PUB

Lunch: $6-$12   **Dinner:** $6-$12   **Phone:** 403/762-8888

American

Location: Downtown. 120 Banff Ave T1L 1A4. **Hours:** 11 am-2 am. Closed: 12/25. **Features:** After a day on the ski hills or hiking in the mountains, the restaurant is a good stop for a great burger and a pint of ale. Locals frequent the place not only for its food but also for its casual, pub-style atmosphere. Menu offerings also include soups, salads and sandwiches. Guests can settle into a booth or belly up to the bar for great conversation and good times. Casual dress; cocktails. **Parking:** street. **Cards:** MC, VI.

TYPHOON

Lunch: $6-$10   **Dinner:** $16-$22   **Phone:** 403/762-2000

International

Location: Downtown. 211 Caribou St T1L 1B5. **Hours:** 11:30 am-3 & 6-10:30 pm. **Reservations:** suggested. **Features:** Funky, eclectic, chic and upbeat all are words that describe the atmosphere at the laid-back, intimate bistro, where the food is anything but casual. The owners label the fare as "eclectic Asian," and the menu proves it, with Thai, Vietnamese, Japanese and other Asian influences. Fast becoming a popular spot with the locals, this place prepares innovative food in an eclectic environment. Bright and bold, the decor features artwork by one of the owners. Casual dress; cocktails. **Parking:** street. **Cards:** AX, CB, DS, JC, MC, VI.

BEAVER MINES pop. 65

——— WHERE TO STAY ———

ASPEN GROVE B & B
Phone: 403/627-2928

All Year [BP]   1P: $60-$65   2P: $75-$80   XP: $15

Bed & Breakfast

Location: Hwy 6, 19 km w on SR 507, 7 km s on SR 744, then 2 km w; Hwy 3, 20 km s on SR 744, then 2 km w at Buckhorn Rd. Buckhord Rd T0K 1W0 (PO Box 250, PINCHER CREEK). Fax: 403/627-2928. **Facility:** This upscale B&B nestled in the mountains offers sweeping views and proximity to skiing. Smoke free premises. 4 one-bedroom standard units. 2 stories (no elevator), interior corridors. *Bath:* combo or shower only. **Parking:** on-site, winter plug-ins. **Terms:** 2 night minimum stay - seasonal and/or weekends, 7 day cancellation notice. **Amenities:** *Some:* hair dryers. **Leisure Activities:** whirlpool, fishing, hiking trails. *Fee:* horseback riding. **Guest Services:** complimentary laundry. **Business Services:** meeting rooms. **Cards:** VI.

BROOKS pop. 11,604

——— WHERE TO STAY ———

BEST WESTERN BROOKS INN   *Book at aaa.com*
Phone: (403)363-0080

5/15-9/30   1P: $99-$139   2P: $109-$149   XP: $10   F12
3/1-5/14 & 10/1-2/28   1P: $89-$109   2P: $99-$139   XP: $10   F12

Small-scale Hotel

Location: Just s off Trans-Canada Hwy 1. 115 Fifteenth Ave W T1R 1C4. Fax: 403/363-0088. **Facility:** 59 units. 54 one-bedroom standard units, some with efficiencies and/or whirlpools. 5 one-bedroom suites. 3 stories, interior/exterior corridors. **Parking:** on-site, winter plug-ins. **Terms:** 30 day cancellation notice, pets ($10 extra charge). **Amenities:** high-speed Internet, voice mail, irons, hair dryers. *Some:* video games. **Pool(s):** small heated indoor. **Leisure Activities:** whirlpool, waterslide, exercise room. **Guest Services:** coin laundry. **Business Services:** meeting rooms. **Cards:** AX, DC, DS, MC, VI. **Special Amenities:** free continental breakfast and free local telephone calls.

SOME UNITS

THE DOUGLAS COUNTRY INN
Phone: 403/362-2873

All Year   1P: $65   2P: $75

Bed & Breakfast

Location: Hwy 873, 6.5 km n of jct Trans-Canada Hwy 1. (PO Box 1833, T1R 1C6). **Facility:** Smoke free premises. 7 one-bedroom standard units. 1 story, interior corridors. *Bath:* combo or shower only. **Parking:** on-site, winter plug-ins. **Terms:** pets ($10 fee). **Leisure Activities:** whirlpool. **Guest Services:** coin laundry.

Cards: MC, VI.

HERITAGE INN
Phone: (403)362-6666

All Year   1P: $87   2P: $97   XP: $5   F16

Small-scale Hotel

Location: Hwy 873, 0.8 km s of jct Trans-Canada Hwy 1. 1217 2nd St W T1R 1B8 (PO Box 907). Fax: 403/362-7319. **Facility:** 106 units. 103 one-bedroom standard units. 3 one-bedroom suites ($117-$130), some with efficiencies. 2 stories (no elevator), interior corridors. **Parking:** on-site, winter plug-ins. **Terms:** package plans, pets ($5 extra charge). **Amenities:** voice mail. *Some:* high-speed Internet, dual phone lines. **Leisure Activities:** sauna, whirlpool, exercise room. **Guest Services:** valet laundry. **Business Services:** meeting rooms. **Cards:** AX, DC, DS, MC, VI.

SOME UNITS

HOLIDAY INN EXPRESS HOTEL & SUITES BROOKS   *Book at aaa.com*
Phone: (403)362-7440

All Year [ECP]   1P: $119-$135   2P: $125-$141   XP: $6   F12

Small-scale Hotel

Location: Trans-Canada Hwy 1, exit 2nd St W. 1307 2nd St W T1R 1B3 (PO Box 289). Fax: 403/362-7477. **Facility:** 78 units. 63 one-bedroom standard units, some with whirlpools. 15 one-bedroom suites ($199-$205). 3 stories, interior corridors. **Parking:** on-site, winter plug-ins. **Terms:** cancellation fee imposed, pets ($25 extra charge, in designated units). **Amenities:** high-speed Internet, dual phone lines, irons, hair dryers. **Pool(s):** heated indoor. **Leisure Activities:** whirlpool, exercise room. **Guest Services:** valet and coin laundry. **Business Services:** meeting rooms. **Cards:** AX, DC, DS, MC, VI.

SOME UNITS

TRAVELODGE BROOKS   *Book at aaa.com*
Phone: (403)362-8000

5/1-9/30   1P: $81   2P: $96   XP: $10   F12
3/1-4/30 & 10/1-2/28   1P: $77   2P: $91   XP: $10   F12

Small-scale Hotel

Location: Trans-Canada Hwy 1, 0.3 km sw on SR 542, exit E Brooks. 1240 Cassils Rd E T1R 1C3 (PO Box 1417). Fax: 403/362-8008. **Facility:** 61 one-bedroom standard units. 2 stories (no elevator), interior/exterior corridors. **Parking:** on-site, winter plug-ins. **Terms:** check-in 4 pm, pets ($5 extra charge, in smoking units). **Amenities:** video games. **Guest Services:** coin laundry. **Business Services:** meeting rooms. **Cards:** AX, DC, DS, MC, VI.

SOME UNITS

——— WHERE TO DINE ———

LUIGI'S PIZZA AND STEAKHOUSE
Lunch: $5-$8   Dinner: $10-$20   Phone: 403/501-5995

Steak House

Location: Trans-Canada Hwy 1, 2 km s. 1020 2nd St W T1R 0C3. **Hours:** 11 am-midnight, Fri & Sat-1 am, Sun 11:30 am-midnight. Closed: 12/25. **Features:** The simple family restaurant serves a variety of options sure to satisfy even the pickiest of eaters. Whether ordering pizza, a Greek specialty or a steak, patrons can anticipate fast service and a hearty meal. Casual dress; cocktails. **Parking:** on-site. **Cards:** AX, MC, VI.

Destination Calgary
pop. 878,866

A versatile city with an abundance of theaters and shopping malls, Calgary seems to have something for everyone.

Y ou can attend a horse show, join in a rousing celebration of the Wild West or browse through unique marketplaces. Want to ride down a rushing river? Calgary won't leave you high and dry.

Travel Alberta

Calgary skyline.
A welcoming skyline and the Calgary Tower make this city stand out.

© Gibson Stock Photography

Shopping for Western wear, Calgary.
If you're going to the Calgary Stampede, you've just got to dress the part. (See mention page 60)

© Gibson Stock Photography

Chinatown, Calgary.
Chinese heritage is on display in Calgary's Chinatown section.

Airdrie

Cochrane

② See Vicinity map page 361

See Downtown map page 359

Strathmore

Calgary

Okotoks

© Paul A. Souders
Corbis

Boogie boarding.
Nearby lakes provide ample opportunities for boogie boarding, power boating and other water-based recreation.

P *laces included in this AAA Destination City:*

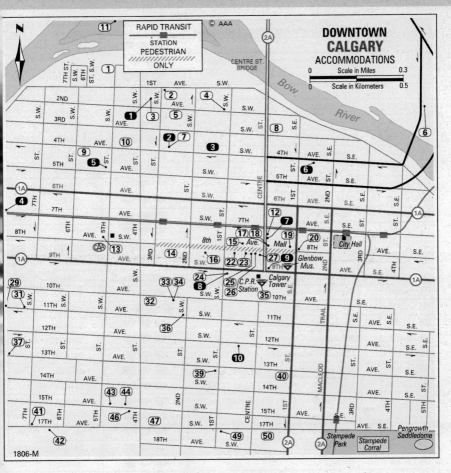

Downtown Calgary

This index helps you "spot" where approved accommodations and restaurants are located on the corresponding detailed maps. Lodging rate ranges are for comparison only and show the property's high season; rates are per night, unless only weekly (W) rates are available. Restaurant rate range is for dinner, unless only lunch (L) is served. Turn to the listing page for more detailed rate information and consult display ads for special promotions.

Spotter/Map Page Number	OA	DOWNTOWN CALGARY - Lodgings	Diamond Rating	Rate Range High Season	Listing Page
1 / above	CAA	**Sheraton Suites Calgary Eau Claire - see color ad p 5**	◇◇◇◇	$145-$235 SAVE	368
2 / above	CAA	**The Westin Calgary - see color ad p 5, p 366**	◇◇◇◇	$99-$399 SAVE	368
3 / above	CAA	**International Hotel of Calgary**	◇◇	$229-$259 SAVE	366
4 / above		Sandman Hotel Downtown Calgary	◇◇◇	$119-$190	368
5 / above		Hawthorn Hotel & Suites	◇◇	$169-$199	365
6 / above		Delta Bow Valley	◇◇◇	$289	365
7 / above	CAA	**Hyatt Regency Calgary - see ad p 366**	◇◇◇◇	$109-$249 SAVE	366
8 / above		The Fairmont Palliser	◇◇◇◇	$129-$440	365
9 / above	CAA	**Calgary Marriott Hotel - see color ad p 365**	◇◇◇	$113-$208 SAVE	365
10 / above		Holiday Inn Conference Centre Calgary Downtown - see color ad card insert	◇◇◇	$129	365

Spotter/Map Page Number	OA	DOWNTOWN CALGARY - Restaurants	Diamond Rating	Rate Range High Season	Listing Page
1 / p. 359		La Caille Restaurant	◆◆◆	$22-$30	370
2 / p. 359		Brewster's Brewing Company and Restaurant	◆◆	$7-$18	368
3 / p. 359		Barclay's	◆◆◆	$10-$20	368
4 / p. 359		Sakana Grill	◆◆	$8-$17	372
5 / p. 359		Don Quijote	◆◆	$12-$22	370
6 / p. 359	AAA	Il Sogno	◆◆◆	$16-$22	370
7 / p. 359		O. N. Bar & Grill	◆◆◆◆	$25-$42	371
8 / p. 359	AAA	Silver Dragon Restaurant	◆◆	$6-$17	372
9 / p. 359		The Glory Of India	◆◆	$10-$16	370
10 / p. 359	AAA	Caesar's Steakhouse	◆◆◆	$18-$35	369
11 / p. 359		River Cafe	◆◆◆	$14-$32	372
12 / p. 359		Thomson's Restaurant	◆◆◆	$19-$34	372
13 / p. 359		Chicago Chophouse	◆◆◆	$16-$30	369
14 / p. 359		The Orchid Room Fusion Cuisine	◆◆	$15-$30	371
15 / p. 359		Prairie Ink Restaurant & Bakery	◆◆	$6-$13	372
16 / p. 359		Rose Garden Thai Restaurant	◆◆	$10-$15	372
17 / p. 359		Catch Restaurant & Oyster Bar	◆◆◆	$10-$40	369
18 / p. 359		Catch Restaurant	◆◆◆◆	$20-$40	369
19 / p. 359		Centini Restaurant and Lounge	◆◆◆	$12-$35	369
20 / p. 359		Teatro	◆◆◆	$22-$42	372
22 / p. 359		Murrieta's Westcoast Grill	◆◆◆	$12-$22	371
23 / p. 359		The Conga Room	◆◆◆	$15-$25	369
24 / p. 359		The Rimrock Dining Room	◆◆◆	$16-$34	372
25 / p. 359		The Belvedere	◆◆◆	$29-$39	368
26 / p. 359		Divino Wine & Cheese Bistro	◆◆◆	$18-$35	370
27 / p. 359		Saltlik, A Rare Steakhouse	◆◆◆	$18-$30	372
29 / p. 359		Bonterra Trattoria	◆◆◆	$16-$25	368
31 / p. 359		The King & I	◆◆◆	$8-$25	370
32 / p. 359		Thai Sa-On Restaurant	◆◆	$6-$13	372
33 / p. 359		Cannery Row	◆◆	$11-$20	369
34 / p. 359		McQueens Upstairs	◆◆◆	$17-$35	371
35 / p. 359		The Panorama Dining Room	◆◆◆	$27-$38	371
36 / p. 359		Vintage Chophouse	◆◆◆	$16-$28	373
37 / p. 359		Gnocchi's Ristorante	◆◆◆	$12-$23	370
39 / p. 359		Mescalero	◆◆◆	$17-$24	371
40 / p. 359		Manuel Latruwe Belgian Patisserie & Bread Shop	◆◆	$4-$7(L)	371
41 / p. 359		Nellie's Kitchen	◆	$4-$9(L)	371
42 / p. 359		Brava Bistro	◆◆◆	$9-$29	368
43 / p. 359		The Living Room	◆◆◆	$16-$30	371
44 / p. 359		El Sombrero Restaurant	◆◆	$11-$20	370
46 / p. 359		The Kashmir	◆◆	$6-$15	370
47 / p. 359		Cilantro	◆◆◆	$15-$30	369
49 / p. 359		La Chaumiere Restaurant	◆◆◆◆	$19-$29	370
50 / p. 359		Da Paolo Ristorante	◆◆◆	$14-$29	369

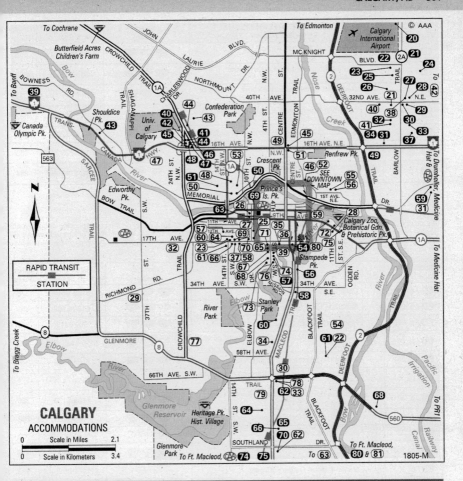

© AAA

CALGARY
ACCOMMODATIONS

| 0 | Scale in Miles | 2.1 |
| 0 | Scale in Kilometers | 3.4 |

1805-M

✈ Airport Accommodations

Spotter/Map Page Number	OA	CALGARY INTERNATIONAL AIRPORT	Diamond Rating	Rate Range High Season	Listing Page
34 / above	CAA	**Best Western Airport Inn, 10 km s of airport**	▽▽	$129-$149 SAVE	373
23 / above	CAA	**Best Western Port O'Call Hotel, 6 km s of airport**	▽▽▽	$115-$145 SAVE	373
59 / above		Coast Plaza Hotel & Conference Centre, 12 km s of airport	▽▽▽	$129-$189	376
29 / above	CAA	**Comfort Inn And Suites-Airport, 8 km s of airport**	▽▽▽	$99-$219 SAVE	376
25 / above	CAA	**Country Inn & Suites By Carlson, 5.7 km s of airport**	▽▽▽	$119-$175 SAVE	377
37 / above		Days Inn Calgary Airport, 8 km s of airport	▽▽▽	$108-$125	378
20 / above		Delta Calgary Airport, at airport	▽▽▽	$139-$249	378
32 / above		Executive Royal Inn North Calgary, 8.2 km s of airport	▽▽▽	$110-$150	379
28 / above	CAA	**Greenwood Inn Hotels, 7.5 km s of airport**	▽▽▽	$99-$139 SAVE	380
26 / above		Hampton Inn & Suites-Calgary Airport, 5.8 km s of airport	▽▽▽	$129-$179	380
22 / above		Hilton Garden Inn-Calgary Airport, 10 km s of airport	▽▽▽	$99-$115	382

Spotter/Map Page Number	OA	CALGARY INTERNATIONAL AIRPORT (continued)	Diamond Rating	Rate Range High Season	Listing Page
49 / p. 361	CAA	**Holiday Inn Calgary-Airport, 10 km s of airport**	◈◈◈	$114-$199 [SAVE]	382
24 / p. 361		Marriott Residence Inn-Calgary Airport, 6 km s of airport	◈◈◈	$189-$219	382
31 / p. 361	CAA	**Radisson Hotel Calgary Airport, 10 km s of airport**	◈◈◈	$99-$135 [SAVE]	383
21 / p. 361		Sandman Hotel Suites & Spa Calgary Airport, 3 km s of airport	◈◈◈	$139-$169	383
27 / p. 361		Sheraton Cavalier Hotel, 7.5 km s of airport	◈◈◈	$189-$269	383
30 / p. 361	CAA	**Super 8 Motel Calgary Airport, 8 km s of airport**	◈◈	$112-$125 [SAVE]	383
33 / p. 361	CAA	**Travelodge Hotel Calgary Airport, 8 km s of airport**	◈◈	$119-$149 [SAVE]	384

Calgary

This index helps you "spot" where approved accommodations and restaurants are located on the corresponding detailed maps. Lodging rate ranges are for comparison only and show the property's high season; rates are per night, unless only weekly (W) rates are available. Restaurant rate range is for dinner, unless only lunch (L) is served. Turn to the listing page for more detailed rate information and consult display ads for special promotions.

Spotter/Map Page Number	OA	CALGARY - Lodgings	Diamond Rating	Rate Range High Season	Listing Page
20 / p. 361		Delta Calgary Airport	◈◈◈	$139-$249	378
21 / p. 361		Sandman Hotel Suites & Spa Calgary Airport	◈◈◈	$139-$169	383
22 / p. 361		Hilton Garden Inn-Calgary Airport	◈◈◈	$99-$115	382
23 / p. 361	CAA	**Best Western Port O'Call Hotel - see color ad p 374**	◈◈◈	$115-$145 [SAVE]	373
24 / p. 361		Marriott Residence Inn-Calgary Airport	◈◈◈	$189-$219	382
25 / p. 361	CAA	**Country Inn & Suites By Carlson - see color ad p 377**	◈◈◈	$119-$175 [SAVE]	377
26 / p. 361		Hampton Inn & Suites-Calgary Airport - see color ad p 381	◈◈◈	$129-$179	380
27 / p. 361		Sheraton Cavalier Hotel - see color ad p 5	◈◈◈	$189-$269	383
28 / p. 361	CAA	**Greenwood Inn Hotels**	◈◈◈	$99-$139 [SAVE]	380
29 / p. 361	CAA	**Comfort Inn And Suites-Airport - see color ad p 376**	◈◈◈	$99-$219 [SAVE]	376
30 / p. 361	CAA	**Super 8 Motel Calgary Airport**	◈◈	$112-$125 [SAVE]	383
31 / p. 361	CAA	**Radisson Hotel Calgary Airport - see color ad p 377**	◈◈◈	$99-$135 [SAVE]	383
32 / p. 361		Executive Royal Inn North Calgary	◈◈◈	$110-$150	379
33 / p. 361	CAA	**Travelodge Hotel Calgary Airport - see color ad p 367**	◈◈	$119-$149 [SAVE]	384
34 / p. 361	CAA	**Best Western Airport Inn**	◈◈	$129-$149 [SAVE]	373
37 / p. 361		Days Inn Calgary Airport	◈◈◈	$108-$125	378
39 / p. 361	CAA	**Four Points by Sheraton Hotel and Suites, Calgary West - see color ad p 5**	◈◈◈	$144-$219 [SAVE]	379
40 / p. 361	CAA	**Super 8 Motel-Motel Village**	◈◈	$79-$169 [SAVE]	383
41 / p. 361	CAA	**Quality Inn University**	◈◈	$99-$169 [SAVE]	383
42 / p. 361	CAA	**Best Western Village Park Inn**	◈◈	$109-$189 [SAVE]	374
43 / p. 361	CAA	**Budgetlodge - see color ad p 375**	◈◈	$69-$89 [SAVE]	375
44 / p. 361	CAA	**Econo Lodge Inn & Suites University - see color ad p 379**	◈◈	$89-$199 [SAVE]	378
45 / p. 361	CAA	**Econo Lodge Motel Village - see color ad p 379**	◈◈	$80-$159 [SAVE]	378
46 / p. 361	CAA	**Holiday Inn Express Calgary-University - see color ad card insert**	◈◈	$108-$158 [SAVE]	382
47 / p. 361	CAA	**Hampton Inn & Suites Calgary-University - see color ad p 381**	◈◈◈	$149-$249 [SAVE]	381

Spotter/Map Page Number	OA	**CALGARY** - Lodgings (continued)	Diamond Rating	Rate Range High Season	Listing Page
48 / p. 361	CAA	Comfort Inn & Suites-Motel Village - see color ad p 376	◇◇◇	$99-$219 [SAVE]	377
49 / p. 361	CAA	Holiday Inn Calgary-Airport	◇◇◇	$114-$199 [SAVE]	382
50 / p. 361	CAA	Kensington Riverside Inn	◇◇◇◇	$259-$349 [SAVE]	382
51 / p. 361		A Good Knight Bed & Breakfast	◇◇	$115-$150	373
54 / p. 361	CAA	Elbow River Inn & Casino - see color ad p 380	◇	$109-$159 [SAVE]	379
56 / p. 361	CAA	Best Western Calgary Centre Inn	◇◇◇	$139-$149 [SAVE]	373
57 / p. 361	CAA	Calgary Westways Guest House	◇◇◇	$85-$139 [SAVE]	375
58 / p. 361	CAA	Days Inn Calgary South - see color ad p 378	◇◇	$149-$179 [SAVE]	378
59 / p. 361		Coast Plaza Hotel & Conference Centre	◇◇◇	$129-$189	376
60 / p. 361	CAA	Comfort Inn & Suites-South - see color ad p 376	◇◇◇	$99-$199 [SAVE]	377
61 / p. 361		Blackfoot Inn	◇◇◇	$99-$189	375
62 / p. 361	CAA	Calgary South Travelodge	◇◇	$105-$150 [SAVE]	375
63 / p. 361	CAA	Holiday Inn Express Hotel & Suites Calgary Downtown	◇◇◇	$99-$179 [SAVE]	382
64 / p. 361	CAA	Econo Lodge South	◇◇	$129-$189 [SAVE]	379
65 / p. 361	CAA	Carriage House Inn	◇◇	$109-$129 [SAVE]	375
66 / p. 361	CAA	Travelodge Hotel Calgary Macleod Trail - see color ad p 367	◇◇	$119-$159 [SAVE]	384
68 / p. 361		Glenmore Inn and Convention Centre	◇◇	Failed to provide	380
69 / p. 361	CAA	Best Western Suites Downtown - see color ad p 374	◇◇◇	$110-$175 [SAVE]	374
70 / p. 361	CAA	Best Western Hospitality Inn	◇◇◇	$169-$179 [SAVE]	373
74 / p. 361		Holiday Inn Express Hotel & Suites Calgary-South	◇◇◇	$149-$249	382
75 / p. 361		Wingate Inn	◇◇◇	$169-$255	384
80 / p. 361		Cindy's Bed & Breakfast	◇◇◇	$80-$185	376
		CALGARY - Restaurants			
21 / p. 361		Thai Boat	◇◇	$9-$12	390
22 / p. 361		Wildwood Brewing Pub	◇◇	$9-$15	390
23 / p. 361		Wrapture	◇	$5-$8	390
25 / p. 361		Steeps The Urban Teahouse	◇	$3-$6	390
26 / p. 361		Gruman's Deli	◇◇	$15-$26	386
27 / p. 361		Red Saffron	◇◇	$8-$15	389
28 / p. 361		Kane's Harley Diner	◇	$4-$10	387
29 / p. 361		Janine's Bistro	◇◇	$6-$14	386
30 / p. 361		Bagolac Saigon Restaurant	◇◇	$6-$10	385
31 / p. 361		Forbidden City Seafood & Dim Sum Restaurant	◇	$8-$12	386
32 / p. 361		Crete Souvlaki	◇	$3-$7	385
33 / p. 361		Smuggler's Inn	◇◇	$20-$25	389
34 / p. 361		Boyd's Seafood Restaurant	◇◇	$12-$35	385
35 / p. 361		Peking Dragon	◇◇	$7-$12	388
36 / p. 361		Latin Corner Restaurant	◇◇◇	$10-$30	387
37 / p. 361		Athens By Night	◇◇	$14-$22	385
38 / p. 361		Carver's Steakhouse	◇◇◇	$28-$35	385
39 / p. 361		Sushi Kawa	◇◇	$7-$14	390

Spotter/Map Page Number	OA	CALGARY - Restaurants (continued)	Diamond Rating	Rate Range High Season	Listing Page
40 / p. 361		Misai Japanese Restaurant	◆◆	$9-$15	387
41 / p. 361		Oriental Phoenix	◆◆◆	$6-$15	388
42 / p. 361		Alberta King of Subs	◆	$2-$10	384
43 / p. 361		Madisons Cafe & Bar	◆◆	$8-$21	387
44 / p. 361		Nick's Steakhouse & Pizza	◆◆	$8-$25	388
45 / p. 361		Atlas Specialty Supermarket & Restaurant	◆	$5-$13	385
46 / p. 361		Boogie's Burgers	◆	$5-$10	385
47 / p. 361		Gus's Cafe & Pizzeria	◆◆	$7-$15	386
48 / p. 361		Charly Chan's Rice House	◆◆	$9-$14	385
49 / p. 361		Lina's Italian Market & Cappuccino Bar	◆	$4-$9	387
50 / p. 361		Maurya	◆◆	$8-$15	387
51 / p. 361		Santorini Greek Taverna	◆◆	$14-$28	389
52 / p. 361		Diner Deluxe	◆◆	$10-$15	386
53 / p. 361		Muse Restaurant & Lounge	◆◆◆	$23-$35	388
54 / p. 361		Rocky's Burger Bus	◆	$3-$6(L)	389
55 / p. 361	CAA	**La Dolce Vita Ristorante Italiano**	◆◆◆	$11-$25	387
56 / p. 361		La Brezza	◆◆	$12-$25	387
57 / p. 361		Pegasus	◆◆	$8-$16	388
58 / p. 361		Sultan's Tent	◆◆	$15-$22	390
59 / p. 361		Deane House Historic Site Restaurant at Fort Calgary	◆◆	$8-$10(L)	386
60 / p. 361		Restaurant Indonesia	◆◆	$7-$11	389
61 / p. 361		Moti Mahal	◆◆	$10-$16	388
62 / p. 361		Cornerstone Grill	◆◆◆	$7-$30	385
63 / p. 361	CAA	**The Newport Grill at the Inn on Lake Bonavista**	◆◆◆	$15-$25	388
64 / p. 361		Palace of Eats	◆	$5-$8	388
65 / p. 361		Ouzo Greek Taverna	◆◆	$8-$16	388
66 / p. 361		Codo Vietnamese Restaurant	◆	$5-$11	385
67 / p. 361		Fleur de Sel	◆◆◆	$15-$19	386
68 / p. 361		The Joyce on 4th Irish Pub	◆◆	$8-$15	386
69 / p. 361		The Arden	◆◆	$8-$17	384
70 / p. 361		Kyoto 17	◆◆	$8-$16	387
71 / p. 361		Hana Sushi	◆◆	$8-$20	386
72 / p. 361		Rouge	◆◆◆	$22-$34	389
73 / p. 361		Wildwood	◆◆◆	$11-$24	390
74 / p. 361		Aida's	◆◆	$5-$12	384
75 / p. 361		Spolumbo's Deli	◆	$4-$8(L)	389
76 / p. 361		The Planet Coffee Roasters	◆	$3-$6	389
77 / p. 361	CAA	**Pfanntastic Pannenkoek Haus**	◆◆	$7-$13	389
78 / p. 361		Open Sesame	◆◆	$7-$11	388
79 / p. 361		Leo Fu's	◆◆	$8-$15	387
80 / p. 361		Sugo	◆◆◆	$15-$32	390
81 / p. 361		The Ranche Restaurant	◆◆◆	$22-$30	389

DOWNTOWN CALGARY (See map and index starting on p. 359)

—— WHERE TO STAY ——

CALGARY MARRIOTT HOTEL   *Book at aaa.com*   **9**
Phone: (403)266-7331

(CAA) (SAVE)

▼▼▼▼

Large-scale Hotel

All Year — 1P: $113-$208 — 2P: $113-$208 — XP: $20 — F18

Location: Jct 9th Ave and Centre St; attached to Telus Convention Centre. Located across from Calgary Tower. 110 9th Ave SE T2G 5A6. Fax: 403/269-1961. **Facility:** 384 units. 374 one-bedroom standard units. 10 one-bedroom suites. 22 stories, interior corridors. **Parking:** on-site (fee) and valet, winter plug-ins. **Terms:** cancellation fee imposed, pets (with prior approval). **Amenities:** video games, high-speed Internet (fee), voice mail, irons, hair dryers. **Dining:** 6:30 am-2 & 5-midnight, Sun from 7 am, cocktails. **Pool(s):** heated indoor. **Leisure Activities:** sauna, whirlpool, exercise room. *Fee:* massage. **Guest Services:** gift shop, valet laundry. **Business Services:** meeting rooms, business center. **Cards:** AX, CB, DC, DS, JC, MC, VI. *(See color ad below)*

SOME UNITS

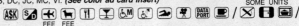

DELTA BOW VALLEY   *Book at aaa.com*   **6**
Phone: 403/266-1980

▼▼▼

Large-scale Hotel

7/7-7/16 — 1P: $289 — 2P: $289 — XP: $15 — F18
3/1-7/6 & 7/17-2/28 — 1P: $199 — 2P: $199 — XP: $15 — F18

Location: 1st St SE and 4th Ave SE. 209 4th Ave SE T2G 0C6. Fax: 403/205-5460. **Facility:** 398 one-bedroom standard units, some with whirlpools. 25 stories, interior corridors. **Parking:** on-site (fee) and valet. **Terms:** package plans. **Amenities:** video games, high-speed Internet (fee), dual phone lines, voice mail, irons, hair dryers. *Some:* honor bars. **Pool(s):** small heated indoor. **Leisure Activities:** saunas, whirlpool, exercise room. **Business Services:** conference facilities, business center. **Cards:** AX, DC, DS, MC, VI.

SOME UNITS

THE FAIRMONT PALLISER   *Book at aaa.com*   **8**
Phone: (403)262-1234

▼▼▼▼ ▼▼▼▼

Large-scale Hotel

All Year — 1P: $129-$440 — 2P: $129-$440 — XP: $25 — F18

Location: 9th Ave SW and 1st St SW. 133 9th Ave SW T2P 2M3. Fax: 403/260-1260. **Facility:** A sense of history and nostalgia reigns at this grand hotel, which features an imperial theme throughout its luxurious and upscale guest rooms. 405 units. 388 one-bedroom standard units. 17 one-bedroom suites ($299-$2000). 12 stories, interior corridors. **Parking:** on-site (fee) and valet, winter plug-ins. **Terms:** check-in 4 pm, cancellation fee imposed, [CP] meal plan available, package plans, small pets only ($25 extra charge). **Amenities:** video games, high-speed Internet, dual phone lines, voice mail, honor bars, irons, hair dryers. *Some:* DVD players, CD players, safes. **Dining:** The Rimrock Dining Room, see separate listing. **Pool(s):** heated indoor. **Leisure Activities:** whirlpool, steamroom. *Fee:* massage, esthetics. **Guest Services:** gift shop, valet laundry, beauty salon. **Business Services:** conference facilities, business center. **Cards:** AX, DC, DS, MC, VI.

SOME UNITS

FEE

HAWTHORN HOTEL & SUITES   *Book at aaa.com*   **5**
Phone: (403)263-0520

▼▼▼ ▼▼

Large-scale Hotel

6/1-9/30 [BP] — 1P: $169-$199 — 2P: $169-$199
10/1-2/28 [BP] — 1P: $151-$181 — 2P: $151-$181
3/1-5/31 [BP] — 1P: $149-$179 — 2P: $149-$179

Location: Corner of 5th Ave SW and 5th St SW. 618 5th Ave SW T2P 0M7. Fax: 403/298-4888. **Facility:** 304 units. 44 one-bedroom standard units with kitchens. 194 one- and 66 two-bedroom suites with kitchens. 28 stories, interior corridors. **Parking:** on-site (fee), winter plug-ins. **Terms:** cancellation fee imposed, weekly rates available, package plans, pets ($10 extra charge). **Amenities:** voice mail, irons, hair dryers. *Fee:* video games, high-speed Internet. **Pool(s):** heated outdoor. **Leisure Activities:** sauna, steamroom, exercise room. **Guest Services:** gift shop, valet and coin laundry. **Business Services:** meeting rooms, PC. **Cards:** AX, DC, DS, MC, VI.

SOME UNITS

FEE

HOLIDAY INN CONFERENCE CENTRE CALGARY DOWNTOWN   *Book at aaa.com*   **10**
Phone: (403)266-4611

▼▼▼

Small-scale Hotel

All Year — 1P: $129 — 2P: $129 — XP: $10 — F19

Location: At 1st St SW; centre. 119 12th Ave SW T2R 0G8. Fax: 403/237-0978. **Facility:** 188 one-bedroom standard units, some with whirlpools. 11 stories, interior corridors. *Bath:* combo or shower only. **Parking:** on-site (fee), winter plug-ins. **Terms:** package plans, pets ($25 extra charge, in smoking units). **Amenities:** video games, high-speed Internet (fee), voice mail, irons, hair dryers. *Some:* dual phone lines. **Pool(s):** small heated outdoor. **Leisure Activities:** limited exercise equipment. **Guest Services:** valet laundry. **Business Services:** meeting rooms, business center. **Cards:** AX, CB, DC, JC, MC, VI. *(See color ad card insert)*

SOME UNITS

FEE   FEE

(See map and index starting on p. 359)

HYATT REGENCY CALGARY *Book at aaa.com* Phone: (403)717-1234 **7**

(CAA) (SAVE)

▽▽▽▽ ▽▽▽▽

3/1-7/17 & 9/6-11/30   1P: $109-$249   2P: $109-$249
7/18-9/5 & 12/1-2/28   1P: $99-$229   2P: $99-$229

Location: Corner of Centre St and 7th Ave SW. Located adjacent to Telus Convention Centre. 700 Centre St SE T2G 5P6. Fax: 403/537-4444. **Facility:** Featuring a Canadian theme throughout, this downtown hotel with a

Large-scale Hotel luxurious ambience offers attentive service, upscale rooms and a new spa. 355 units. 342 one-bedroom standard units. 13 one-bedroom suites, some with whirlpools. 22 stories, interior corridors. *Bath:* combo or shower only. **Parking:** on-site (fee) and valet. **Terms:** 14 day cancellation notice-fee imposed. **Amenities:** high-speed Internet (fee), dual phone lines, voice mail, safes, honor bars, irons, hair dryers. *Some:* DVD players, CD players. **Dining:** Thomson's Restaurant, see separate listing. **Pool(s):** heated indoor. **Leisure Activities:** sauna, whirlpool, exercise room, spa. **Guest Services:** gift shop, valet laundry. **Business Services:** conference facilities, business center. **Cards:** AX, CB, DC, DS, JC, MC, VI. *(See ad below)*

SOME UNITS

🍴 🍸 ⬚ 📷 🐦 ✕ 🎞 DATAPORT 💻 / ✕ VCR FEE 🖥 /

INTERNATIONAL HOTEL OF CALGARY *Book at aaa.com* Phone: (403)265-9600 **3**

(CAA) (SAVE)

▽▽▽ ▽▽

All Year   1P: $229-$259   2P: $229-$259   XP: $15   F18

Location: Corner of 4th Ave and 2nd St SW. 220 4th Ave SW T2P 0H5. Fax: 403/290-7879. **Facility:** 248 one-bedroom suites, some with kitchens. 35 stories, interior corridors. **Parking:** on-site (fee) and valet.

Large-scale Hotel **Terms:** cancellation fee imposed, weekly rates available, package plans, pets ($5 fee). **Amenities:** video games, high-speed Internet (fee), voice mail, honor bars, irons, hair dryers. **Dining:** 6:30 am-2 & 5-11 pm, Sat from 6:30 pm, cocktails. **Pool(s):** small heated indoor. **Leisure Activities:** saunas, whirlpool, exercise room. **Guest Services:** area transportation (fee). **Business Services:** meeting rooms. **Cards:** AX, CB, DC, JC, MC, VI. **Special Amenities:** free newspaper and early check-in/late check-out.

SOME UNITS

Ⓢ🄳 FEE 🄺 FEE 🛏 🍴 🍸 🐦 ✕ 🎞 DATAPORT 💻 / ✕ 🖥 /

DISCOUNTS & REWARDS GALORE!

Enjoy another **5%** off the already discounted CAA/AAA rates, earn Guest Rewards and Hbc Rewards bonus points at participating Travelodge properties.

Ask for the Discounts Galore Rate!
Travelodge Reservations:
1-800-578-7878

Participating properties:

Travelodge Hotel Calgary Airport
403-291-1260   whg7102@whg.com
Travelodge Hotel Calgary Macleod Trail
403-253-7070   whg7103@whg.com

Travelodge Edmonton South
780-436-9770   whg7104@whg.com
Travelodge Edmonton West
780-483-6031   whg7105@whg.com
Travelodge Regina East
306-565-0455   whg7115@whg.com

(See map and index starting on p. 359)

SANDMAN HOTEL DOWNTOWN CALGARY   *Book at aaa.com*   Phone: (403)237-8626 4

5/1-9/30	1P: $119-$190	2P: $119-$190	XP: $10	F14
3/1-4/30 & 10/1-2/28	1P: $109-$160	2P: $109-$160	XP: $10	F14

Large-scale Hotel **Location:** Corner of 7th Ave SW and 8th St. 888 7th Ave SW T2P 3J3. Fax: 403/290-1238. **Facility:** 301 one-bedroom standard units. 23 stories, interior corridors. **Parking:** on-site (fee). **Terms:** [BP] meal plan available, pets ($10 fee). **Amenities:** video games, dual phone lines, voice mail, irons, hair dryers. *Some:* high-speed Internet. **Pool(s):** small heated indoor. **Leisure Activities:** whirlpool, exercise room. **Guest Services:** valet laundry. **Business Services:** meeting rooms, administrative services, PC. **Cards:** AX, DC, DS, JC, MC, VI.

SOME UNITS

SHERATON SUITES CALGARY EAU CLAIRE   *Book at aaa.com*   Phone: (403)266-7200 1

All Year	1P: $145-$235	2P: $145-$235	XP: $10	F18

Location: At 3rd St SW and 2nd Ave SW. Located adjacent to Eau Claire Market. 255 Barclay Parade SW T2P 5C2. Fax: 403/266-1300. **Facility:** Set along the river's edge, and with a prime location next to the Eau Claire market, this all-suite hotel offers upscale rooms and attentive service. 323 units. 313 one- and two-Large-scale Hotel bedroom suites ($180-$454), some with whirlpools. 15 stories, interior corridors. **Parking:** on-site (fee) and valet. **Terms:** cancellation fee imposed, package plans. **Amenities:** video games, high-speed Internet, dual phone lines, voice mail, honor bars, irons, hair dryers. *Some:* DVD players, CD players, fax, safes. **Dining:** 2 restaurants, 6 am-midnight, cocktails, also, Barclay's, see separate listing. **Pool(s):** heated indoor. **Leisure Activities:** sauna, whirlpool, waterslide, jogging, exercise room. **Fee:** bicycles, massage. **Guest Services:** gift shop, valet and coin laundry. **Business Services:** conference facilities, business center. **Cards:** AX, DC, MC, VI. *(See color ad p 5)*

SOME UNITS

THE WESTIN CALGARY   *Book at aaa.com*   Phone: (403)266-1611 2

All Year	1P: $99-$399	2P: $99-$399	XP: $20	F16

Location: Corner of 4th Ave SW and 3rd St. 320 4th Ave SW T2P 2S6. Fax: 403/233-7471. **Facility:** Refinement can be found in both towers of this upscale hotel; one side features contemporary decor, the other a more plush, royal atmosphere. 525 units. 467 one-bedroom standard units. 58 one-bedroom suites. 20 stories, Large-scale Hotel interior corridors. **Parking:** on-site (fee) and valet. **Terms:** [BP] meal plan available, package plans, small pets only. **Amenities:** video games, high-speed Internet (fee), dual phone lines, voice mail, safes, honor bars, irons, hair dryers. **Dining:** 6:30 am-midnight, cocktails, also, O. N. Bar & Grill, see separate listing. **Pool(s):** heated indoor. **Leisure Activities:** saunas, whirlpool, exercise room, spa. **Guest Services:** gift shop, valet laundry. **Business Services:** conference facilities, business center. **Cards:** AX, CB, DC, DS, JC, MC, VI. *(See color ad p 5 & p 366)*

SOME UNITS

———— **WHERE TO DINE** ————

BARCLAY'S

Lunch: $8-$14	Dinner: $10-$20	Phone: 403/517-6666 3

International **Location:** At 3rd St SW and 2nd Ave SW; in Sheraton Suites Calgary Eau Claire. 255 Barclay Parade SW T2P 5C2. **Hours:** 6 am-10 pm, Fri & Sat-11 pm. **Reservations:** suggested. **Features:** Patrons can choose from the regular a la carte menu or share selections from the new fondue menu. The casually upscale eatery offers fine service and good value for the dollar. Casual dress; cocktails. **Parking:** on-site (fee) and valet. **Cards:** AX, DC, MC, VI.

THE BELVEDERE

Lunch: $23-$26	Dinner: $29-$39	Phone: 403/265-9595 25

Continental **Location:** Just e of 1st St SW. 107 8th St SW T2P 1B4. **Hours:** 11:30 am-2 & 5:30-10 pm, Sat from 5 pm. Closed major holidays; also Sun. **Reservations:** suggested. **Features:** New York meets Calgary at the upscale, intimate restaurant, tucked amid the shops and restaurants of Stephen Avenue. The decor is all New York, a long, narrow space with exposed brick walls, mirrors, walnut trim and exposed lighting. The menu changes every few months but might list such innovative creations as gingered ahi tuna, venison or duck. The romantic setting is fitting for special occasions. Dressy casual; cocktails. **Parking:** street. **Cards:** AX, DC, MC, VI.

BONTERRA TRATTORIA

Lunch: $10-$18	Dinner: $16-$25	Phone: 403/262-8480 29

Nouvelle Italian **Location:** 10th Ave and 8th St SW. 1016 8th St SW T2R 1K2. **Hours:** 11:30 am-2:30 & 5-10 pm, Fri-11 pm, Sat 5 pm-11 pm, Sun 5 pm-10 pm. Closed major holidays. **Reservations:** suggested. **Features:** For an upscale, Italian dining experience, look no further than Bonterra. Sumptuous smells waft from the open concept kitchen, where contemporary Italian dishes are created. The romantic dining room is a great place for a special occasion, and in the summer a garden oasis patio awaits in the back. With an extensive wine list, and superb professional service, this is one fine place for a great meal. Casual dress; cocktails. **Parking:** on-site. **Cards:** AX, DC, MC, VI.

BRAVA BISTRO

Lunch: $8-$16	Dinner: $9-$29	Phone: 403/228-1854 42

Canadian **Location:** Just e of 7th St. 723 17th Ave SW T2S 0B6. **Hours:** 11:30 am-10 pm, Fri & Sat-midnight, Sun 5 pm-10 pm. Closed: 1/1, 12/25, 12/26. **Reservations:** suggested. **Features:** Old World inspiration combines with New World ingredients at the upscale, trendy addition to the dining options on 17th Avenue. The restaurant is an ideal place for a first date or special occasion. Artistic and creative dishes—ranging from risotto with squash and duck confit to linguine with saffron and seafood—emphasize freshness, simplicity and seasonality. Diners can complete their meal with a selection from the award-winning wine list. Dressy casual; cocktails. **Parking:** on-site. **Cards:** AX, MC, VI.

BREWSTER'S BREWING COMPANY AND RESTAURANT

Lunch: $7-$18	Dinner: $7-$18	Phone: 403/233-2739 2

Canadian **Location:** Across from Eau Claire Market. 101 Barclay Parade SW T2P 4R5. **Hours:** 11 am-midnight, Thurs-Sat to 2 am. Closed: 12/25, 12/26. **Features:** The popular brew pub prepares its own ales and lagers, which match well with selections from the extensive menu. The lounge is upbeat. Featured promotions can include a burger and movie night. Service is quick and efficient, and the portions are hearty. Cocktails. **Parking:** street. **Cards:** AX, MC, VI.

(See map and index starting on p. 359)

CAESAR'S STEAKHOUSE — Lunch: $18-$30 — Dinner: $18-$35 — Phone: 403/264-1222 — ⑩
CAA
▼▼▼▼
Steak House
Location: Just e of 5th St. 512 4th Ave SW T2P 0J6. **Hours:** 11 am-midnight, Sat from 4:30 pm. Closed major holidays; also Sun. **Reservations:** suggested, for lunch. **Features:** One of the city's original steakhouses, the dark, dimly lit restaurant speaks to years gone by, with professionally dressed servers, intimate corners and a booming lunch business. A trip to the West is not complete without a stop at the popular restaurant. An extensive selection of Alberta AAA beef is prepared to the diner's liking from the glassed-in barbecue area. This place buzzes at lunch, as many corporate types nosh on a Caesar alongside their steak. Semi-formal attire; cocktails. **Parking:** street. **Cards:** AX, CB, DC, DS, JC, MC, VI. 🍸 ✖

CANNERY ROW — Lunch: $10-$16 — Dinner: $11-$20 — Phone: 403/269-8889 — ㉝
▼▼ ▼▼
Seafood
Location: At 2nd St SW. 317 10th Ave SW T2R 0A5. **Hours:** 11:30 am-midnight. Closed: 1/1, 12/25. **Reservations:** required, for lunch Mon-Fri. **Features:** The restaurant has a fun, exciting atmosphere, an open kitchen and an oyster bar. On the menu are superb seafood and pasta entrees, as well as noteworthy appetizers. The attractive wine list includes several by-the-glass selections. This spot is popular with the downtown business crowd. Casual dress; cocktails. **Parking:** on-site. **Cards:** AX, DC, DS, MC, VI. 🍸 ✖

CATCH RESTAURANT — Lunch: $16-$22 — Dinner: $20-$40 — Phone: 403/206-0000 — ⑱
▼▼▼ ▼▼▼
Seafood
Location: At Centre St and 8th Ave SE (Stephen Ave). 100 Stephen Ave SE T2G 0K6. **Hours:** 11:30 am-2 & 5-11 pm. Closed major holidays; also Sun. **Reservations:** suggested. **Features:** There are three levels to this restaurant. On the first floor, you'll find a fun, casual oyster bar. On the third level, an atrium and nestled in the middle, a stunning, upscale dining room, with lofty ceilings, warm wood tones, and exquisite table presentations. If you have a craving for seafood, this is the place to go. With an impressive selection of seafood from around the world, including Alaskan sablefish, Atlantic halibut cheeks, and Pacific salmon, seafood lovers will be in heaven. Dressy casual; cocktails. **Parking:** on-site (fee). **Cards:** AX, DC, MC, VI. ✖

CATCH RESTAURANT & OYSTER BAR — Lunch: $10-$40 — Dinner: $10-$40 — Phone: 403/206-0000 — ⑰
▼▼▼▼
Seafood
Location: Corner of 8th Ave (Stephen Ave) and 1st St SE; main level. 100 8th Ave SE T2P 1B3. **Hours:** 11:30 am-2 & 5-11 pm. Closed major holidays; also for dinner Sun. **Reservations:** suggested. **Features:** Down the stairs from Catch, which offers a more upscale experience, the oyster bar is more casual yet still boasts the same fine food. The bustling, nautical place prepares an extensive selection of fresh seafood, flown in each day. Guests can enjoy not only oysters but also other distinctive choices, including salmon, traditional fish and chips and the catch of the day. Casual dress; cocktails. **Parking:** street. **Cards:** AX, DC, MC, VI. ✖

CENTINI RESTAURANT AND LOUNGE — Lunch: $7-$17 — Dinner: $12-$35 — Phone: 403/269-1600 — ⑲
▼▼▼▼
Italian
Location: Corner of 8th Ave SE (Stephen Ave) and 1st St SE; in Telus Convention Centre. 160 8th Ave SE T2G 0K6. **Hours:** 11:30 am-2:30 & 5-midnight. Closed major holidays; also Sun. **Reservations:** suggested. **Features:** Relaxed elegance and finely prepared food are part of the experience at one of the city's trendiest new restaurants. Simple decor is stark and light in color. Imaginative dishes are created in the open kitchen. With its interesting menu and fine service, this place caters to those looking for a place to lunch or enjoy pre- or post-theater cocktails. Casual dress; cocktails. **Parking:** street. **Cards:** AX, DC, MC, VI. ✖

CHICAGO CHOPHOUSE — Lunch: $9-$26 — Dinner: $16-$30 — Phone: 403/265-3000 — ⑬
▼▼▼▼
Steak House
Location: Corner of 8th Ave SW and 5th St. 604 8th Ave SW T2P 1G5. **Hours:** 11 am-11 pm, Fri-midnight, Sat 5 pm-midnight, Sun 5 pm-10 pm. Closed major holidays. **Reservations:** required, for lunch. **Features:** Guests can see and be seen at the ultra-modern, contemporary steakhouse, in the heart of the city. Efficient, professional servers help make this place popular with the business crowd at lunchtime. The menu blends a wide selection of top-quality cuts of beef with sandwiches and meal-size salads. The chic, lofty interior has an open-concept kitchen, and the selection of by-the-glass wines is one of the best in the city. Casual dress; cocktails. **Parking:** street. **Cards:** AX, DC, MC, VI. ♿M 🍸 ✖

CILANTRO — Lunch: $10-$14 — Dinner: $15-$30 — Phone: 403/229-1177 — ㊼
▼▼▼▼
Southwest California
Location: Just e of 4th St SW. 338 17th Ave SW T2S 0A8. **Hours:** 11 am-midnight, Sat 5 pm-11 pm, Sun 5 pm-10 pm. Closed major holidays. **Reservations:** suggested. **Features:** The dark wood interior and lovely stained-glass windows combine to create an intimate atmosphere in the small dining room, where guests can enjoy an interesting selection of California-inspired cuisine. Good choices include melts-in-the-mouth sea bass, various pastas and salads and any of the delectable desserts. Service is professional and friendly. Casual dress; cocktails. **Parking:** on-site. **Cards:** AX, DC, DS, JC, MC, VI. 🍴 ✖

THE CONGA ROOM — Lunch: $9-$20 — Dinner: $15-$25 — Phone: 403/262-7248 — ㉓
▼▼▼▼
Nouvelle Latino
Location: Jct 1st St and 8th Ave SW; centre. 109 8th Ave SW T2T 1B4. **Hours:** 11 am-10 pm, Fri & Sat-2 am. Closed major holidays; also Sun. **Reservations:** suggested. **Features:** Meals are presented with a flourish at the festive, feisty cantina, along Stephen Avenue downtown. The long dining room extends past the bar and kitchen, with a stone wall providing an interesting focal point. The spot is great for an exciting, action-packed dining experience in a fascinating atmosphere. Casual dress; cocktails; entertainment. **Parking:** street. **Cards:** AX, DC, MC, VI. 🍸 ✖

DA PAOLO RISTORANTE — Lunch: $8-$15 — Dinner: $14-$29 — Phone: 403/228-5556 — ㊿
▼▼▼▼
Italian
Location: Just w on 17th Ave SE from MacLeod Tr S (becomes Hwy 2A S). 121 17th Ave SE T2G 1H3. **Hours:** 11:30 am-2 & 5-11 pm, Sat from 5 pm. Closed major holidays; also Sun & 7/15-7/28. **Reservations:** suggested. **Features:** The popular restaurant serves traditional fare with a warm, welcoming attitude. Dozens of fresh pasta and seafood dishes are complemented by chicken and veal entrees. The wine list includes well-chosen Italian selections. Formal service is the standard. Semi-formal attire; cocktails. **Parking:** on-site. **Cards:** AX, DC, MC, VI. ✖

(See map and index starting on p. 359)

DIVINO WINE & CHEESE BISTRO   **Lunch:** $12-$29   **Dinner:** $18-$35   **Phone:** 403/410-5555   26
▽▽▽▽   **Location:** On Stephen Ave (8th Ave); downtown. 113 8th Ave SW T2P 1B4. **Hours:** 11:30 am-10 pm, Fri & Sat-
International   midnight. Closed major holidays. **Reservations:** suggested. **Features:** There is more than just wine and
cheese at the upscale bistro, and the variety makes it a good reason to come. Cheese from around the
world, including Alberta varieties, is paired with fresh artisan bread. Those in the mood for something more
can expect decadent, beautiful food, ranging from mushroom risotto appetizers to roasted halibut to lobster cannelloni. Upscale
decor and professional service complete the experience. Casual dress; cocktails. **Parking:** street. **Cards:** AX, MC, VI.

DON QUIJOTE   **Lunch:** $9-$19   **Dinner:** $12-$22   **Phone:** 403/205-4244   5
▽▽ ▽▽   **Location:** Across from Eau Claire Market. 309 2nd Ave SW T2P 0C5. **Hours:** 11:30 am-2 & 5-10 pm, Sat & Sun
Spanish   from 5 pm. Closed major holidays; also for dinner Mon. **Reservations:** suggested. **Features:** This
restaurant is a great place to have tapas and dance the salsa. Focusing on the seafood of the Spanish
ports, it relies heavily on the tradition of butter, garlic and lemon. For a decadent finish, try the rich custard-
filled cake soaked in cinzano. Dressy casual; cocktails; entertainment. **Parking:** street. **Cards:** AX, DC, MC, VI.

EL SOMBRERO RESTAURANT   **Lunch:** $11-$15   **Dinner:** $11-$20   **Phone:** 403/228-0332   44
▽▽ ▽▽   **Location:** Between 5th and 4th sts SW, upper level. 520 17th Ave SW T2S 0B1. **Hours:** 11:30 am-2 pm, Thurs &
Mexican   Fri also 5 pm-10 pm, Sat 5 pm-11 pm, Sun 5 pm-9 pm. Closed: 12/25, 12/26; also Mon. **Features:** A taste
of Mexico awaits at the cozy bistro-style restaurant, where one staircase up from street level in the trendy 17th
Avenue district. A guitarist adds ambience to the evening, strumming and singing in the background as
guests enjoy hearty Mexican fare. Casual dress; cocktails. **Parking:** street. **Cards:** AX, DC, MC, VI.

THE GLORY OF INDIA   **Lunch:** $13   **Dinner:** $10-$16   **Phone:** 403/263-8804   9
▽▽ ▽▽   **Location:** Jct 5th St and 4th Ave SW; on ground floor of apartment building. 515 4th Ave SW T2P 0J8. **Hours:** 11:30
Indian   am-2 & 5-10 pm, Sat from 5 pm. Closed major holidays; also Sun. **Features:** The casual Indian restaurant
serves tasty portions of traditional Indian cuisine. The lunch buffet is popular, and reservations are
recommended. A la carte dinner items are best enjoyed with several people to allow for sampling of the
varied dishes, including ali goobi, lamb and beef curries and chicken tikka. Casual dress; cocktails. **Parking:** street. **Cards:** AX,
DC, JC, MC, VI.

GNOCCHI'S RISTORANTE   **Lunch:** $8-$16   **Dinner:** $12-$23   **Phone:** 403/262-2887   37
▽▽▽▽▽   **Location:** Corner of 8th St SW and 13th Ave. 1238 8th St SW T2R 1A9. **Hours:** 11:30 am-10 pm, Sat & Sun from
Italian   5 pm. Closed major holidays. **Reservations:** suggested. **Features:** An elegant, upscale dining room awaits
guests of the bistro, which prepares a wide array of traditional Italian cuisine. Hearty portions of minestrone
soup, pasta, veal and the namesake gnocchi are sure to please. Casual dress; cocktails. **Parking:** on-site.
Cards: AX, MC, VI.

IL SOGNO   **Lunch:** $10-$18   **Dinner:** $16-$22   **Phone:** 403/232-8901   6
(CAA)   **Location:** Just n of Memorial Dr, at Edmonton Tr and 4th St NE. 24 4th St NE T2E 3R7. **Hours:** 11:20 am-2 & 5-10
▽▽▽▽   pm. Closed major holidays. **Reservations:** suggested. **Features:** Italian for "the dream," Il Sogno is a
Italian   simply elegant restaurant with an upscale decor and sumptuous Italian food. Classically prepared dishes on
the seasonally inspired menu include some new twists on old favorites. Ravioli with walnut-cream sauce,
veal and a trilogy of surprise desserts are among choices that might be found. The building originally was
used as a rooming house, and the owners have maintained the history and integrity in the decor. Casual
dress; cocktails. **Parking:** on-site. **Cards:** AX, MC, VI. **Historic**

THE KASHMIR   **Lunch:** $6-$15   **Dinner:** $6-$15   **Phone:** 403/244-2294   46
▽▽ ▽▽   **Location:** At 4th St SW. 507 17th Ave SW T2S 0A9. **Hours:** 11:30 am-1:30 & 5-10 pm, Sat & Sun 5 pm-9 pm.
East Indian   Closed: 12/25, 12/26. **Features:** For a taste of East Indian food, patrons need look no further than the
family-run restaurant on trendy 17th Avenue. Among traditional dishes are pakoras and samosas. Casual
dress; cocktails. **Parking:** street. **Cards:** AX, MC, VI.

THE KING & I   **Lunch:** $8-$25   **Dinner:** $8-$25   **Phone:** 403/264-7241   31
▽▽▽▽   **Location:** Corner of 11th Ave SW and 8th St. 822 11th Ave SW T2R 0E5. **Hours:** 11:30 am-10:30 pm, Fri-11:30
Thai   pm, Sat 4:30 pm-11:30 pm, Sun 4:30 pm-9:30 pm. **Reservations:** suggested. **Features:** An upscale,
contemporary atmosphere awaits you at the King & I, where modern furnishings and decor set the scene for
authentic, tasty Thai dishes. The menu features a wide variety of appetizers, including calamari and fresh
spring rolls. Arrive with an appetite, as the main dishes are heaping, and you can choose from traditional Pad Thai to various
curry dishes. If you are looking for a taste of Thailand in modern surroundings, look no further. Casual dress; cocktails. **Parking:**
street. **Cards:** AX, DC, MC, VI.

LA CAILLE RESTAURANT   **Lunch:** $15-$20   **Dinner:** $22-$30   **Phone:** 403/262-5554   1
▽▽▽▽   **Location:** Corner of 1st Ave and 7th St SW. 100 La Caille Pl SW T2P 5E2. **Hours:** 11 am-2:30 & 5-1 am, Sat &
Nouvelle   Sun from 5 pm. **Reservations:** required. **Features:** Along the Eau Claire Pathway and affording views of
Continental   the Bow River, the longstanding restaurant is an upscale and elegant place for a special occasion. The
romantic setting complements the rich decor inside. From the greeting at the door to the presentation of the
check, diners enjoy fine and attentive service. Buffalo tenderloin, beef, salmon and scallops are among
menu options. Dressy casual; cocktails. **Parking:** valet and street. **Cards:** AX, DS, MC, VI.

LA CHAUMIERE RESTAURANT   **Lunch:** $9-$16   **Dinner:** $19-$29   **Phone:** 403/228-5690   49
▽▽▽ ▽▽▽   **Location:** Corner of 1st St SW and 17th Ave SW. 139 17th Ave SW T2S 0A1. **Hours:** 11:45 am-2:30 & 5:30-10 pm,
Continental   Sat 5:30 pm-midnight. Closed major holidays; also Sun. **Reservations:** required. **Features:** The upscale
restaurant's impressive, almost castle-like building has a peaked roof and elegant exterior, making it an
ideal spot for fine French dining. Patrons cross the threshold over polished granite floors into an exquisitely
appointed dining room, where servers dressed in formal attire await. Superb entrees range from various seafood dishes to
mouthwatering preparations of beef. Semi-formal attire; cocktails. **Parking:** on-site. **Cards:** AX, DC, MC, VI.

(See map and index starting on p. 359)

THE LIVING ROOM   Lunch: $10-$16   Dinner: $16-$30   Phone: 403/228-9830   43
▼▼▼   **Location:** Just e of 5th St SW. 514 17th Ave SW T5W 4X6. **Hours:** 11:30 am-2 & 5-11 pm. Closed major
Canadian   holidays. **Features:** The contemporary restaurant serves imaginative Canadian fare, including a five-course
menu surprise. As the name suggests, the decor—including oversize couchlike chairs—contributes to a
cozy and comfortable dining environment. Casual dress; cocktails. **Parking:** on-site. **Cards:** AX, MC, VI.
⊠

MANUEL LATRUWE BELGIAN PATISSERIE &
BREAD SHOP   Lunch: $4-$7   Phone: 403/261-1092   40
▼▼▼   **Location:** 1st St SE at 13th Ave. 1333 1st St SE T2G 5L1. **Hours:** Open 3/1-12/31 & 1/21-2/28; 7:30 am-6 pm,
Bakery/Desserts   Sat-5 pm. Closed major holidays; also Sun & Mon. **Features:** Elegance and refinement characterize the
upscale bakery, which features the divine dessert creations of Manuel Latruwe. The display case is filled
with gorgeous mousses, cheesecakes, tarts and pastries, as well as artisan breads. Although there are
three small cafe tables, most people, including business folks en route to work and skiers headed to the mountains, get their
selections to go. Ice creams and sorbets also are concocted here. **Parking:** on-site. **Cards:** MC, VI.
&M ⊠

MCQUEENS UPSTAIRS   Dinner: $17-$35   Phone: 403/269-4722   34
▼▼▼   **Location:** At 2nd St SW. 317 10th Ave SW T2R 0A5. **Hours:** 5:30 pm-10 pm, Fri & Sat 5 pm-11 pm. Closed: 1/1,
Seafood   12/24, 12/25; also Sun. **Reservations:** suggested. **Features:** Music from a pianist or jazz duo enlivens the
inviting, elegant atmosphere. The restaurant's selection of flavorful seafood, steak and chicken is prepared
with creativity, style and color. An extensive wine list enhances the menu. On-site parking is limited, but
meters and lots are nearby. Casual dress; cocktails; entertainment. **Parking:** on-site. **Cards:** AX, DC, DS, MC, VI.
⊠

MESCALERO   Lunch: $7-$12   Dinner: $17-$24   Phone: 403/266-3339   39
▼▼▼   **Location:** Corner of 1st St SW and 13th Ave SW. 1315 1st St SW T2R 0V5. **Hours:** 11:30 am-2 & 5-10 pm, Thurs-
Southwest   11 pm, Fri & Sat-midnight. Closed: 12/24-12/26. **Reservations:** suggested. **Features:** A charming, rustic
Mexican   Mexican decor and warm, lively atmosphere greet diners. The restaurant has an appealing menu of lamb,
beef, veal, chicken and seafood dishes, many of which are grilled over an applewood fire and creatively
presented. Casual dress; cocktails. **Parking:** street. **Cards:** AX, MC, VI.
⊠

MURRIETA'S WESTCOAST GRILL   Lunch: $9-$18   Dinner: $12-$22   Phone: 403/269-7707   22
▼▼▼   **Location:** Corner of 8th Ave SW and 1st St SW; upstairs from street level. 200-800 1st St SW T2P 7N2. **Hours:** 11
am-midnight, Thurs-1 am, Fri & Sat-2 am, Sun 4 pm-10 pm. Closed: 12/25. **Reservations:** suggested.
West Pacific Rim   **Features:** The lively, airy dining room buzzes with sounds from the open-concept kitchen and animated
conversations. The bustling restaurant has an energy and liveliness that makes it a popular spot for a
gathering of friends. For a more intimate experience, smaller areas are tucked away from the main dining room. Among
offerings are mussels, ahi tuna, salmon and various pasta dishes. Casual dress; cocktails. **Parking:** street. **Cards:** AX, DC, DS,
MC, VI.
&M Ⅰ ⊠

NELLIE'S KITCHEN   Lunch: $4-$9   Phone: 403/244-4616   41
▼   **Location:** Corner of 7th St and 17th Ave SW. 738B 17th Ave SW T2S 0B7. **Hours:** 7:30 am-3:30 pm, Sat & Sun
Canadian   from 8:30 am. Closed: 12/25. **Features:** Particularly popular on weekends, the bustling, cozy diner is a
favorite for fabulous home-cooked breakfast. In addition to all-day breakfasts, ranging from omelets to
French toast to pancakes, the menu also lists some lunch options. Homemade banana bread is well worth a
splurge. Casual dress. **Parking:** street.
Ⓚ ⊠

O. N. BAR & GRILL   Lunch: $10-$18   Dinner: $25-$42   Phone: 403/266-1611   7
▼▼▼ ▼▼▼   **Location:** Corner of 4th Ave SW and 3rd St; in The Westin Calgary. 320 4th Ave SW T2P 2S6. **Hours:** 11:30 am-2 &
Continental   5:30-10 pm, Sat from 5:30 pm. Closed major holidays; also Sun. **Reservations:** suggested.
Features: Superior meal selection, taste and appearance exceed diners' expectations at this formal
restaurant tucked in an intimate corner of the Westin Calgary. The dark, elegant decor creates a wonderful
environment in which to enjoy tasty, creative dishes. Known for Alberta beef, the menu also features many seafood selections.
The wine list is extensive. Dressy casual; cocktails; entertainment. **Parking:** on-site (fee) and valet. **Cards:** AX, DC, DS, JC,
MC, VI.
Ⅰ ⊠

THE ORCHID ROOM FUSION CUISINE   Lunch: $14-$21   Dinner: $15-$30   Phone: 403/263-4457   14
▼▼ ▼▼   **Location:** Corner of 2nd St SW; Bankers Hall, 2nd Floor. 315 8th Ave SW T2P 4K1. **Hours:** 10 am-6 pm, Thurs-Sat
Vietnamese   to 8 pm; to 7 pm, Thurs-Sat to 9 pm in winter. Closed major holidays; also Sun. **Reservations:** suggested,
for lunch. **Features:** A combination of Vietnamese and French cuisine makes for an eclectic menu with an
accent on healthy choices. Colorful plate presentations include banana leaves, yellow daisies and orchids.
Among choices are many unusual vegan dishes. The cozy setting has an open annex. Cocktails. **Parking:** street. **Cards:** AX,
MC, VI.
⊠

THE PANORAMA DINING ROOM   Lunch: $11-$19   Dinner: $27-$38   Phone: 403/266-7171   35
▼▼▼   **Location:** At top of Calgary Tower; in Palliser Square. 101 9th Ave SW T2P 1J9. **Hours:** 7:30 am-2:30 & 5-9 pm;
Continental   from 8 am in winter. **Reservations:** suggested. **Features:** Mouthwatering selections of regional Canadian
cuisine range from pan-seared Atlantic salmon to grilled strip loin of New Zealand venison to grilled
tenderloin of Alberta beef. The revolving room atop the city's tallest building offers a spectacular view of the
city and Rocky Mountains. An elevation fee is charged. Casual dress; cocktails. **Parking:** no self-parking. **Cards:** AX, DC,
MC, VI.
Ⅰ ⊠

(See map and index starting on p. 359)

PRAIRIE INK RESTAURANT & BAKERY   Lunch: $6-$13   Dinner: $6-$13   Phone: 403/538-1798   15
Canadian
Location: Between Centre and 1st sts SW; in top floor of McNally Robinson bookstore. 120 8th Ave SW T2P 1B3. **Hours:** 9 am-9 pm, Fri & Sat-10 pm, Sun 11 am-6 pm. Closed major holidays. **Features:** The tranquil setting is a superb spot for a great meal. Guests can sit by the window overlooking the street below and enjoy heaping portions of food, ranging from crab cakes to pear and goat cheese salad to pizza and pasta cooked in a wood-burning oven. The bakery generates mouthwatering dessert creations. Bookshelves offer literary inspiration. Cocktails. **Parking:** street. **Cards:** AX, MC, VI.

THE RIMROCK DINING ROOM   Lunch: $11-$20   Dinner: $16-$34   Phone: 403/260-1219   24
Continental
Location: 9th Ave SW and 1st St SW; in The Fairmont Palliser. 133 9th Ave SW T2P 2M3. **Hours:** 6:30 am-2 & 5:30-10 pm, Sun from 7 am. **Reservations:** suggested. **Features:** Tucked in a corner of the Palliser Hotel, the fine dining room has a reputation for steaks and fine service. Patrons celebrating anniversaries or other special occasions are treated by attentive servers. In addition to quality beef, the menu also lists seafood dishes and exquisite desserts. Dressy casual; cocktails. **Parking:** on-site (fee) and valet. **Cards:** AX, CB, DC, DS, JC, MC, VI.

RIVER CAFE   Lunch: $7-$14   Dinner: $14-$32   Phone: 403/261-7670   11
Regional
Canadian
Location: On Prince's Island, on the Bow River. **Hours:** Open 3/1-1/1 & 2/5-2/28; 11 am-11 pm, Sat & Sun from 10 am. Closed: 12/25. **Reservations:** suggested. **Features:** In the heart of Prince's Island Park, the enchanting, tree house-like restaurant features a decor that includes natural wood accents and a large fireplace. The focus of the menu is on Canadian Rocky Mountain cuisine. During summer, seating is available on the patio, and in winter, the atmosphere is cozy inside. Parking is not available on the island, but city lots are just a short walk away. Casual dress; cocktails. **Parking:** no self-parking. **Cards:** AX, DC, MC, VI.

ROSE GARDEN THAI RESTAURANT   Lunch: $8-$10   Dinner: $10-$15   Phone: 403/263-1900   16
Thai
Location: At 8th Ave and 2nd St. 207 8th Ave SW T2P 1B7. **Hours:** 11:30 am-9 pm, Fri & Sat-10 pm. Closed: 12/25. **Features:** The family-owned restaurant in the heart of downtown serves Thai favorites. The menu includes pad Thai, savory curries and salad rolls. Servers are friendly. Casual dress; cocktails. **Parking:** street. **Cards:** AX, MC, VI.

SAKANA GRILL   Lunch: $7-$9   Dinner: $8-$17   Phone: 403/290-1118   4
Japanese
Location: Corner of 1st St and 2nd Ave SW. 116 2nd Ave SW T2P 0B9. **Hours:** 11 am-2 & 5-11 pm. Closed: 1/1, 12/25. **Reservations:** suggested. **Features:** On the fringe of Chinatown near the Eau Claire market, the bustling Japanese restaurant has many distinctive features, including a sushi bar, teppanyaki grill and private dining rooms. Business folks frequent the place at lunch time, grabbing seats at the sushi bar and making selections from the boat that floats by. Fantastic sushi and sashimi options offer exceptional value for the dollar. Casual dress; cocktails. **Parking:** on-site (fee) and street. **Cards:** AX, DC, MC, VI.

SALTLIK, A RARE STEAKHOUSE   Lunch: $12-$18   Dinner: $18-$30   Phone: 403/537-1160   27
Steak House
Location: Jct Stephen Ave (8th Ave) and 1st St SW. 101 8th Ave SW T6E 1H1. **Hours:** 11 am-10 pm, Fri & Sat-midnight. **Reservations:** suggested. **Features:** True to its name, the restaurant is a "rare steakhouse" and a superb one at that. In the heart of downtown along the trendy Stephen Avenue pedestrian shopping district, the upscale, contemporary dining room and atmosphere is impressive. Also praiseworthy is the incredibly friendly, attentive service. Servers take time to explain the different cuts of meat and accompanying sauces. All entrees are a la carte, and side orders are large enough to split. Casual dress; cocktails. **Parking:** street. **Cards:** AX, DC, DS, MC, VI.

SILVER DRAGON RESTAURANT   *Menu on aaa.com*   Lunch: $6-$17   Dinner: $6-$17   Phone: 403/264-5326   8
CAA
Chinese
Location: In Chinatown. 106 3rd Ave SE T2G 0B6. **Hours:** 10 am-midnight, Fri & Sat-2 am, Sun 9:30 am-10 pm. **Reservations:** suggested. **Features:** The restaurant specializes in Cantonese and Szechuan cuisine, including excellent ginger beef. A delicious dim sum selection is served each day. The contemporary decor comprises nouveau Oriental artwork. Servers are cordial. Cocktails. **Parking:** on-site (fee) and street. **Cards:** AX, DC, JC, MC, VI.

TEATRO   Lunch: $14-$22   Dinner: $22-$42   Phone: 403/290-1012   20
Nouvelle Italian
Location: Corner of 8th Ave SE and 1st St SE. 200 8th Ave SE T2G 0K7. **Hours:** 11:30 am-11 pm, Sat from 5 pm, Sun 5 pm-10 pm. Closed major holidays. **Reservations:** suggested. **Features:** Located in the theatre district, this upsale Italian trattoria is a great place to dine before the show. Featured several times on the Food Network, the chef will surprise and delight you with many inventive creations. Whether you're in the mood for seafood, pasta or meat dishes, you'll find something exquisite to satisfy your appetite. A perfect place for a special occasion or a first date. Dressy casual; cocktails. **Parking:** street. **Cards:** AX, DC, MC, VI.

THAI SA-ON RESTAURANT   Lunch: $6-$13   Dinner: $6-$13   Phone: 403/264-3526   32
Thai
Location: At 4th St SW. 351 10th Ave SW T2R 0A5. **Hours:** 11:30 am-2 & 5-10 pm, Fri & Sat-10:30 pm. Closed major holidays; also Sun. **Reservations:** suggested. **Features:** Decorative presentation and good use of spices and condiments characterize offerings of well-prepared cuisine, including many vegetarian items. The quiet, casual ambience is enhanced by music and artwork from Thailand. Casual dress; cocktails. **Parking:** street. **Cards:** AX, MC, VI.

THOMSON'S RESTAURANT   Lunch: $10-$17   Dinner: $19-$34   Phone: 403/537-4449   12
Canadian
Location: Corner of Centre St and 7th Ave SW; in Hyatt Regency Calgary. 700 Centre St SE T2G 5P6. **Hours:** 6:30 am-2 & 5-11 pm, Fri & Sat-midnight. **Reservations:** suggested. **Features:** The restaurant presents a varied menu of seafood, steaks and other regional meats. Thursday prime rib nights pack the place with locals. Guests can expect casual yet attentive service in the upscale dining room. Casual dress; cocktails. **Parking:** on-site. **Cards:** AX, CB, DC, DS, MC, VI.

(See map and index starting on p. 359)

VINTAGE CHOPHOUSE   **Lunch:** $10-$15   **Dinner:** $16-$28   **Phone:** 403-262-7262   **36**

▼▼▼▼

Steak House

Location: Corner of 3rd St and 11th Ave SW. 322 11th Ave SW T2E 0Z1. **Hours:** 11:30 am-11 pm, Fri-2 am, Sat 5 pm-2 am, Sun 5 pm-10 pm. **Closed:** 12/25. **Reservations:** suggested. **Features:** An upscale and elegant experience awaits at the fine steakhouse, which is in a historic building. Inside, the atmosphere is anything but historic. A large lounge caters to the after-work crowd, and the dining room allows for a more leisurely and romantic meal. Steaks feature prominently on the menu, but diners also will find salmon, pasta dishes and ribs. Finely executed service, including tableside preparation of Caesar salad, adds to the overall experience. Casual dress; cocktails. **Parking:** street. **Cards:** AX, DC, MC, VI.

🍸 ✕

CALGARY pop. 878,866   (See map and index starting on p. 361)

———— WHERE TO STAY ————

A GOOD KNIGHT BED & BREAKFAST   **Phone:** 403-270-7628   **51**

▼▼▼ ▼▼▼

7/1-7/17 [BP]	1P: $115-$150	2P: $115-$150	XP: $25
7/18-10/10 [BP]	1P: $89-$125	2P: $89-$125	XP: $15
3/1-6/30 [BP]	1P: $79-$125	2P: $79-$125	XP: $15
10/11-2/28 [BP]	1P: $79-$99	2P: $79-$99	XP: $15

Bed & Breakfast

Location: Trans-Canada Hwy 1 (16th Ave NW), 3 km s to 6th Ave NW, just w to 16th St NW, just n to 7th Ave NW, then just w. 1728 7th Ave NW T2N 0Z4. **Fax:** 403/284-0010. **Facility:** Smoke free premises. 4 one-bedroom standard units, some with kitchens and/or whirlpools. 2 stories (no elevator), interior corridors. **Parking:** street. **Terms:** 2 night minimum stay - seasonal, 7 day cancellation notice. **Amenities:** irons, hair dryers. **Cards:** MC, VI.

SOME UNITS

✕ 🖐 DATA PORT 💻 / VCR 📟 📠 /

BEST WESTERN AIRPORT INN   *Book at aaa.com*   **Phone:** (403)250-5015   **34**

CAA SAVE

7/1-7/20	1P: $129-$149	2P: $129-$149	XP: $10 F12
3/1-6/30 & 7/21-8/31	1P: $109-$139	2P: $109-$149	XP: $10 F12
9/1-2/28	1P: $99-$119	2P: $99-$129	XP: $10 F12

▼▼▼ ▼▼▼

Small-scale Hotel

Location: 1 km e of jct Hwy 2 (Deerfoot Tr) and 16th Ave NE (Trans-Canada Hwy 1). 1947 18th Ave NE T2E 7T8. **Fax:** 403/250-5019. **Facility:** 76 one-bedroom standard units, some with whirlpools. 3 stories, interior corridors. **Parking:** on-site, winter plug-ins. **Amenities:** high-speed Internet, voice mail, irons, hair dryers. **Dining:** 5 pm-10 pm, cocktails. **Pool(s):** small heated indoor. **Leisure Activities:** whirlpool, exercise room. **Guest Services:** valet and coin laundry. **Business Services:** PC (fee). **Cards:** AX, DC, DS, MC, VI. **Special Amenities:** free expanded continental breakfast and free local telephone calls.

SOME UNITS

🅂🄳 🍽 🏊 🎥 DATA PORT 💻 / ✕ VCR 📟 📠 /

BEST WESTERN CALGARY CENTRE INN   *Book at aaa.com*   **Phone:** (403)287-3900   **56**

CAA SAVE

5/20-9/6 [ECP]	1P: $139-$149	2P: $139-$149
9/7-2/28 [ECP]	1P: $129-$139	2P: $129-$139
3/1-5/19 [ECP]	1P: $119-$129	2P: $119-$129

▼▼▼ ▼▼▼

Small-scale Hotel

Location: East side of Hwy 2A (MacLeod Tr) at 36th Ave SE. 3630 MacLeod Tr S T2G 2P9. **Fax:** 403/287-3906. **Facility:** 71 units. 69 one-bedroom standard units, some with whirlpools. 2 one-bedroom suites ($129-$179) with whirlpools. 4 stories, interior corridors. **Parking:** on-site, winter plug-ins. **Terms:** 7 day cancellation notice, package plans. **Amenities:** video games, high-speed Internet, dual phone lines, voice mail, irons, hair dryers. **Pool(s):** heated indoor, wading. **Leisure Activities:** whirlpool, exercise room. **Guest Services:** valet and coin laundry. **Cards:** AX, CB, DC, DS, JC, MC, VI. **Special Amenities:** free expanded continental breakfast and free local telephone calls.

SOME UNITS

🅂🄳 🍽 🏋 🏊 🎥 DATA PORT 💻 / ✕ 📟 📠 /

BEST WESTERN HOSPITALITY INN   *Book at aaa.com*   **Phone:** (403)278-5050   **70**

CAA SAVE

All Year	1P: $169-$179	XP: $10 F12

▼▼▼ ▼▼▼

Small-scale Hotel

Location: On Hwy 2A (MacLeod Tr); corner of Southland Dr. 135 Southland Dr SE T2J 5X5. **Fax:** 403/225-5834. **Facility:** 260 units. 251 one-bedroom standard units. 9 one-bedroom suites, some with whirlpools. 3-8 stories, interior corridors. **Bath:** combo or shower only. **Parking:** on-site, winter plug-ins. **Terms:** cancellation fee imposed, [AP] meal plan available, small pets only (in smoking units). **Amenities:** video games, voice mail, irons, hair dryers. Some: high-speed Internet. **Dining:** 6:30 am-11 pm, Sun 7 am-10 pm, cocktails, also, Cornerstone Grill, see separate listing. **Pool(s):** 2 heated indoor. **Leisure Activities:** whirlpool, waterslide, limited exercise equipment. **Guest Services:** gift shop, valet laundry. **Business Services:** conference facilities, business center. **Cards:** AX, DS, MC, VI. **Special Amenities:** free newspaper and early check-in/late check-out.

SOME UNITS

🅂🄳 🐾 🍽 🍸 🏊 ✕ 🎥 DATA PORT 💻 / ✕ 📟 /

BEST WESTERN PORT O'CALL HOTEL   *Book at aaa.com*   **Phone:** (403)291-4600   **23**

CAA SAVE

3/1-9/30	1P: $115-$145	2P: $115-$145	XP: $5 F18
10/1-2/28	1P: $109-$139	2P: $109-$139	XP: $5 F18

▼▼▼ ▼▼▼

Small-scale Hotel

Location: 2.5 km ne of jct Hwy 2 (Deerfoot Tr); at 19th St NE. 1935 McKnight Blvd NE T2E 6V4. **Fax:** 403/250-6827. **Facility:** 201 units. 199 one-bedroom standard units, some with whirlpools. 2 one-bedroom suites ($199-$299) with whirlpools. 6-7 stories, interior corridors. **Parking:** on-site. **Terms:** check-in 4 pm. **Amenities:** high-speed Internet, voice mail, irons, hair dryers. Some: dual phone lines, safes. **Dining:** 2 restaurants, 6 am-midnight, cocktails. **Pool(s):** heated indoor. **Leisure Activities:** whirlpool, steamrooms, racquetball court, exercise room. **Fee:** massage. **Guest Services:** gift shop, valet laundry. **Business Services:** conference facilities, PC. **Cards:** AX, DC, DS, MC, VI. **Special Amenities:** free local telephone calls and free newspaper. *(See color ad p 374)*

SOME UNITS

🅂🄳 ✈ 🍽 🍸 ♿ 🏊 ✕ 🎥 DATA PORT 💻 / ✕ 📟 /
FEE

(See map and index starting on p. 361)

BEST WESTERN SUITES DOWNTOWN *Book at aaa.com* Phone: (403)228-6900 **69**

CAA SAVE

5/1-7/17 [ECP]	1P: $110-$175	2P: $110-$175	XP: $10	F17
3/1-4/30 & 7/18-2/28 [ECP]	1P: $89-$155	2P: $89-$155	XP: $10	F17

Location: Corner of 8th St and 13th Ave SW. 1330 8th St SW T2R 1B6. Fax: 403/228-5535. **Facility:** 123 units. 82 one-bedroom standard units, some with efficiencies and/or whirlpools. 17 one- and 24 two-bedroom suites Small-scale Hotel ($135-$175), some with kitchens and/or whirlpools. 16 stories, interior corridors. **Parking:** on-site, winter plug-ins. **Terms:** cancellation fee imposed, weekly rates available. **Amenities:** high-speed Internet, voice mail, irons, hair dryers. *Some:* dual phone lines. **Leisure Activities:** sauna, exercise room. **Guest Services:** sundries, valet and coin laundry. **Business Services:** meeting rooms, PC. **Cards:** AX, DC, MC, VI. **Special Amenities: free expanded continental breakfast and free local telephone calls.** *(See color ad below)*

SOME UNITS

 FEE

BEST WESTERN VILLAGE PARK INN *Book at aaa.com* Phone: (403)289-0241 **42**

CAA SAVE

6/1-8/31	1P: $109-$179	2P: $119-$189	XP: $10	F17
3/1-5/31 & 9/1-2/28	1P: $89-$149	2P: $99-$159	XP: $10	F17

Location: Just ne of jct Trans-Canada Hwy 1 and Crowchild Tr. Located in Motel Village. 1804 Crowchild Tr NW T2M 3Y7. Fax: 403/289-4645. **Facility:** 159 units. 156 one-bedroom standard units. 3 one-bedroom suites ($175-Small-scale Hotel $275) with whirlpools. 5 stories, interior corridors. **Parking:** on-site. **Terms:** small pets only (in designated units). **Amenities:** video games, high-speed Internet, voice mail, irons, hair dryers. *Some:* DVD players, CD players, safes. **Dining:** 6:30 am-11 pm, cocktails. **Pool(s):** small heated indoor. **Leisure Activities:** whirlpool. **Guest Services:** gift shop, valet and coin laundry. **Business Services:** meeting rooms, business center. **Cards:** AX, DC, DS, MC, VI. **Special Amenities: free local telephone calls and free newspaper.**

SOME UNITS

(See map and index starting on p. 361)

BLACKFOOT INN — *Book at aaa.com* — Phone: (403)252-2253 — **61**

7/18-2/28	1P: $99-$189	2P: $99-$189	XP: $20 F18
3/1-7/17	1P: $99-$165	2P: $99-$165	XP: $20 F18

Small-scale Hotel **Location:** At 58th Ave SE; access to property from 58th Ave only. 5940 Blackfoot Tr SE T2H 2B5. Fax: 403/252-3574. **Facility:** 200 units. 199 one-bedroom standard units. 1 one-bedroom suite ($165-$180). 7 stories, interior corridors. **Parking:** on-site, winter plug-ins. **Terms:** 3 day cancellation notice. **Amenities:** video games, voice mail, irons, hair dryers. *Some:* CD players, high-speed Internet (fee), fax, safes. **Pool(s):** heated outdoor. **Leisure Activities:** whirlpool, steamroom, exercise room. **Guest Services:** gift shop, valet laundry. **Business Services:** conference facilities, business center. **Cards:** AX, DC, MC, VI.

SOME UNITS
ASK SD 🐾 🍽 🍸 🕎 🛥 ✕ 🐾 DATA PORT 💻 / ✕ VCR /

BUDGETLODGE — Phone: (403)288-7115 — **43**

3/1-7/18	1P: $69-$79	2P: $74-$89	XP: $5 D12
7/19-9/30	1P: $59-$89	2P: $64-$79	XP: $5 D12
10/1-2/28	1P: $55-$65	2P: $60-$75	XP: $5 D12

Motel **Location:** On 16th Ave NW (Trans-Canada Hwy 1) at 43rd St NW. 4420 16th Ave NW T3B 0M4. Fax: 403/286-4899. **Facility:** 72 one-bedroom standard units, some with efficiencies. 2 stories, interior corridors. **Parking:** on-site, winter plug-ins. **Terms:** cancellation fee imposed, weekly rates available. **Amenities:** voice mail. **Guest Services:** coin laundry. **Cards:** AX, MC, VI. **Special Amenities:** free local telephone calls. *(See color ad below)*

SOME UNITS
SD 🕎 DATA PORT / ✕ 🔋 /

CALGARY SOUTH TRAVELODGE — *Book at aaa.com* — Phone: (403)253-1111 — **62**

5/31-9/10 [ECP]	1P: $105	2P: $150	XP: $10 F17
3/1-5/30 & 9/11-2/28 [ECP]	1P: $82-$92	2P: $82-$92	XP: $10 F17

Location: On Hwy 2A (MacLeod Tr S); at 70th Ave S. 7012 MacLeod Tr S T2H 0L3. Fax: 403/253-2879. **Facility:** 62 one-bedroom standard units. 2 stories (no elevator), interior/exterior corridors. **Parking:** on-site, winter plug-ins. **Terms:** cancellation fee imposed. **Amenities:** video library (fee), voice mail, irons, hair dryers. *Some:* DVD players. **Pool(s):** small heated outdoor, saltwater. **Guest Services:** valet laundry. **Cards:** AX, DC, MC, VI. **Special Amenities:** free expanded continental breakfast and free local telephone calls.

SOME UNITS
SD 🕎 🛥 🐾 DATA PORT 🔋 💻 / ✕ VCR 🔋 /

CALGARY WESTWAYS GUEST HOUSE — *Book at aaa.com* — Phone: (403)229-1758 — **57**

6/1-9/30 [BP]	1P: $85-$119	2P: $95-$139	XP: $25 D14
10/1-11/30 [BP]	1P: $79-$99	2P: $89-$119	XP: $20 D14
3/1-5/31 & 12/1-2/28 [BP]	1P: $69-$99	2P: $79-$119	XP: $20 D14

Historic Bed & Breakfast **Location:** 1.7 km s on Hwy 2A (MacLeod Tr S), 0.5 km w. Located in a residential area. 216 25th Ave SW T2S 0L1. Fax: 403/228-6265. **Facility:** This unassuming 1912 house offers a variety of upscale lodgings ranging from smaller original units to deluxe, spacious rooms. Smoke free premises. 5 one-bedroom standard units, some with whirlpools. 3 stories (no elevator), interior corridors. *Bath:* combo or shower only. **Parking:** on-site, winter plug-ins. **Terms:** 2 night minimum stay - seasonal, age restrictions may apply, 7 day cancellation notice-fee imposed, package plans, pets ($8 fee, owner's dogs on premises). **Amenities:** video library, DVD players, CD players, high-speed Internet, voice mail, irons, hair dryers. **Leisure Activities:** bicycles, hiking trails. **Guest Services:** complimentary laundry, area transportation (fee). **Business Services:** PC. **Cards:** AX, MC, VI. **Special Amenities:** free full breakfast and free local telephone calls.

SD 🚭 🐾 ✕ VCR 📷 DATA PORT
FEE FEE

CARRIAGE HOUSE INN — *Book at aaa.com* — Phone: (403)253-1101 — **65**

6/1-9/1	1P: $109-$129	2P: $109-$129	XP: $10 F16
3/1-5/31	1P: $89-$119	2P: $89-$119	XP: $10 F16
9/2-2/28	1P: $89-$109	2P: $89-$109	XP: $10 F16

Small-scale Hotel **Location:** On Hwy 2A (MacLeod Tr); corner of 90th Ave SW. 9030 MacLeod Tr S T2H 0M4. Fax: 403/259-2414. **Facility:** 157 one-bedroom standard units, some with whirlpools. 4-10 stories, interior corridors. **Parking:** on-site, winter plug-ins. **Terms:** 3 day cancellation notice, weekly rates available, [BP] meal plan available, package plans, pets ($5 extra charge). **Amenities:** high-speed Internet, voice mail, irons, hair dryers. *Some:* dual phone lines. **Dining:** 2 restaurants, 6:30 am-11 pm, Sun 7 am-10 pm, cocktails. **Pool(s):** heated outdoor. **Leisure Activities:** saunas, whirlpool, limited casino, exercise room. **Guest Services:** gift shop, valet laundry. **Business Services:** conference facilities. **Cards:** AX, CB, DC, DS, JC, MC, VI. **Special Amenities:** free local telephone calls and free newspaper.

SOME UNITS
🚭 🐾 🍽 🍸 🛥 ✕ 🐾 DATA PORT 💻 / ✕ 🔋 🔋 /
FEE FEE

(See map and index starting on p. 361)

CINDY'S BED & BREAKFAST
Bed & Breakfast
All Year [BP] 1P: $80-$170 2P: $95-$185 XP: $20
Phone: (403)254-6698 80 F8
Location: From Deerfoot Tr (Hwy 2), exit Dunbow Rd E, 3.2 km e to 44th St, then just n; outside Calgary city limits. 44th St & Dunbow Rd T0L 0X0 (PO Box 2, Site 8 RR 1, DE WINTON). Fax: 403/201-6770. **Facility:** Just south of the Calgary city limits, this elegant B&B is removed from the hustle of the city on five-plus acres of manicured lawns and gardens. Smoke free premises. 4 one-bedroom standard units, some with whirlpools. 2 stories (no elevator), interior corridors. *Bath:* combo or shower only. **Parking:** on-site. **Terms:** 2 night minimum stay - seasonal and/or weekends, 14 day cancellation notice-fee imposed, weekly rates available. **Amenities:** video library, DVD players, hair dryers. *Some:* high-speed Internet. **Leisure Activities:** whirlpool, limited exercise equipment, game room. **Guest Services:** complimentary laundry. **Business Services:** PC. **Cards:** AX, JC, MC, VI.

SOME UNITS
(ASK) [X] [X] [CTV] [DATA PORT] [ ] / [VCR] /

COAST PLAZA HOTEL & CONFERENCE CENTRE *Book at aaa.com*
Large-scale Hotel
All Year 1P: $129-$189 2P: $129-$189 XP: $15
Phone: (403)248-8888 59 F18
Location: Just s of jct 16th Ave (Trans-Canada Hwy 1) and 36th St NE, just w on 12th Ave NE. Located adjacent to Pacific Place Mall. 1316 33rd St NE T2A 6B6. Fax: 403/248-0749. **Facility:** 248 units. 245 one-bedroom standard units. 3 one-bedroom suites ($275-$299) with whirlpools. 6-12 stories, interior corridors. **Parking:** on-site, winter plug-ins. **Terms:** cancellation fee imposed, package plans, pets ($20 deposit). **Amenities:** video games, high-speed Internet, voice mail, irons, hair dryers. *Some:* CD players. **Pool(s):** small heated indoor. **Leisure Activities:** sauna, whirlpool, exercise room. **Guest Services:** gift shop, valet laundry. **Business Services:** conference facilities, business center. **Cards:** AX, CB, DC, DS, JC, MC, VI.

SOME UNITS
(ASK) [+] [🐾] [🍴] [24] [Y] [&M] [🛏] [�"] [X] [🐾] [DATA PORT] [ ] / [X] [■] [📷] /
FEE

COMFORT INN AND SUITES-AIRPORT *Book at aaa.com*
Small-scale Hotel
(CAA) (SAVE)
5/1-9/30 1P: $99-$199 2P: $109-$219 XP: $10 29 F18
3/1-4/30 & 10/1-2/28 1P: $89-$119 2P: $99-$149 XP: $10 F18
Phone: 403/735-1966
Location: Just se of jct 32nd Ave NE and Barlow Tr NE. 3111 26th St NE T1Y 7E4. Fax: 403/735-1955. **Facility:** 74 units. 56 one-bedroom standard units, some with whirlpools. 18 one-bedroom suites. 4 stories, interior corridors. **Parking:** on-site, winter plug-ins. **Amenities:** high-speed Internet, voice mail, safes (fee), irons, hair dryers. **Pool(s):** heated indoor. **Leisure Activities:** whirlpool, steamroom, waterslide, limited exercise equipment. **Guest Services:** valet and coin laundry. **Business Services:** meeting rooms, PC (fee). **Cards:** AX, DC, DS, MC, VI. **Special Amenities:** free continental breakfast and free local telephone calls. *(See color ad below)*

SOME UNITS
[S🅳] [+] [🍴+] [�"] [X] [DATA PORT] [ ] / [X] [VCR] [■] [📷] /
FEE

(See map and index starting on p. 361)

COMFORT INN & SUITES-MOTEL VILLAGE
CAA SAVE
Phone: (403)289-2581 **48**

	1P: $99-$199	2P: $109-$219	XP: $10	F18
5/1-9/30				
3/1-4/30 & 10/1-2/28	1P: $79-$109	2P: $89-$149	XP: $10	F18

Small-scale Hotel **Location:** Just n of jct Trans-Canada Hwy 1 and Crowchild Tr. Located in Motel Village. 2369 Banff Tr NW T2M 4L2. Fax: 403/284-3897. **Facility:** 82 units. 58 one-bedroom standard units, some with whirlpools. 24 one-bedroom suites. 4 stories, interior corridors. **Parking:** on-site, winter plug-ins. **Terms:** [CP] meal plan available. **Amenities:** high-speed Internet, voice mail, safes (fee), irons, hair dryers. **Pool(s):** small heated indoor. **Leisure Activities:** whirlpool, waterslide, limited exercise equipment. **Guest Services:** valet and coin laundry. **Business Services:** meeting rooms. **Cards:** AX, CB, DC, DS, MC, VI. **Special Amenities:** free continental breakfast and free local telephone calls. (See color ad p 376)

SOME UNITS

COMFORT INN & SUITES-SOUTH   Book at aaa.com
CAA SAVE
Phone: (403)287-7070 **60**

7/1-9/30 [CP]	1P: $99-$179	2P: $99-$199	XP: $10	F18
10/1-2/28 [CP]	1P: $89-$139	2P: $99-$199	XP: $10	F18
3/1-6/30 [CP]	1P: $89-$139	2P: $99-$149	XP: $10	F18

Small-scale Hotel **Location:** Hwy 2A (MacLeod Tr), w on 45th Ave. 4611 MacLeod Tr SW T2G 0A6. Fax: 403/287-8855. **Facility:** 93 units. 68 one-bedroom standard units, some with whirlpools. 25 one-bedroom suites ($109-$229). 4 stories, interior corridors. **Parking:** on-site, winter plug-ins. **Terms:** cancellation fee imposed. **Amenities:** video games, high-speed Internet, voice mail, irons, hair dryers. **Leisure Activities:** whirlpool, waterslide, limited exercise equipment. **Fee:** massage. **Guest Services:** valet and coin laundry. **Business Services:** meeting rooms, business center. **Cards:** AX, CB, DC, DS, MC, VI. **Special Amenities:** free continental breakfast and free local telephone calls. (See color ad p 376)

SOME UNITS

COUNTRY INN & SUITES BY CARLSON   Book at aaa.com
CAA SAVE
Phone: (403)250-1800 **25**

| 6/1-9/30 [ECP] | 1P: $119-$175 | 2P: $129-$175 | XP: $10 | F18 |
| 3/1-5/31 & 10/1-2/28 [ECP] | 1P: $109-$150 | 2P: $119-$150 | XP: $10 | F18 |

Small-scale Hotel **Location:** Barlow Tr and 39th Ave NE. 2481 39th Ave NE T2E 8V8. Fax: 403/250-2121. **Facility:** 106 units. 54 one-bedroom standard units, some with whirlpools. 52 one-bedroom suites. 3 stories, interior corridors. **Bath:** combo or shower only. **Parking:** on-site, winter plug-ins. **Terms:** 3 day cancellation notice. **Amenities:** high-speed Internet, dual phone lines, voice mail, irons, hair dryers. **Pool(s):** small heated indoor. **Leisure Activities:** whirlpool, exercise room. **Guest Services:** valet and coin laundry. **Business Services:** meeting rooms. **Cards:** AX, DC, DS, JC, MC, VI. **Special Amenities:** free expanded continental breakfast and free local telephone calls. (See color ad below)

SOME UNITS

(See map and index starting on p. 361)

DAYS INN CALGARY AIRPORT   *Book at aaa.com*   Phone: (403)250-3297   **37**

6/1-8/31 [ECP]	1P: $108-$125	2P: $108-$125	XP: $10 F12
3/1-5/31 & 9/1-2/28 [ECP]	1P: $100-$120	2P: $100-$120	XP: $5 F12

Small-scale Hotel   **Location:** Barlow Tr, just e of Sunridge Way NE. 2799 Sunridge Way NE T1Y 7K7. Fax: 403/291-2533. **Facility:** 76 units. 60 one-bedroom standard units, some with whirlpools. 16 one-bedroom suites, some with whirlpools. 4 stories, interior corridors. **Parking:** on-site, winter plug-ins. **Terms:** cancellation fee imposed, pets ($10 fee). **Amenities:** voice mail, irons, hair dryers. *Some:* high-speed Internet, dual phone lines. **Pool(s):** heated indoor. **Leisure Activities:** whirlpool, waterslide, exercise room. **Guest Services:** sundries, valet and coin laundry. **Business Services:** PC (fee). **Cards:** AX, DC, MC, VI.

SOME UNITS

(ASK) (SO) (➔) (🐾) (†↑+) (♨M) (➷) (✕) (📽) (DATA PORT) (🖥) (📠) (🖨) / (✕) /
FEE

DAYS INN CALGARY SOUTH   *Book at aaa.com*   Phone: (403)243-5531   **58**

(CAA) (SAVE)

7/1-7/16 [CP]	1P: $149-$179	2P: $149-$179	XP: $10 F16
7/17-8/31 [CP]	1P: $99-$119	2P: $99-$119	XP: $10 F16
3/1-6/30 & 9/1-2/28 [CP]	1P: $89-$109	2P: $89-$109	XP: $10 F16

Small-scale Hotel   **Location:** Corner of MacLeod Tr and 38th Ave SE. Located in a busy commercial area. 3828 MacLeod Tr S T2G 2R2. Fax: 403/243-6962. **Facility:** 134 one-bedroom standard units. 4 stories, interior corridors. **Parking:** on-site, winter plug-ins. **Terms:** package plans, small pets only ($10 extra charge, in smoking units). **Amenities:** video games, high-speed Internet, voice mail, irons, hair dryers. **Dining:** 11 am-midnight, cocktails. **Pool(s):** heated indoor. **Leisure Activities:** whirlpool, exercise room. *Fee:* game room. **Guest Services:** gift shop, valet and coin laundry, beauty salon. **Business Services:** conference facilities, PC (fee). **Cards:** AX, CB, DC, DS, JC, MC, VI. *(See color ad below)*

SOME UNITS

(SO) (🐾) (†↑+) (Y) (➷) (✕) (📽) (DATA PORT) (🖨) / (✕) (🖥) (📠) /
FEE

DELTA CALGARY AIRPORT   *Book at aaa.com*   Phone: (403)291-2600   **20**

All Year	1P: $139-$249	2P: $139-$249	XP: $25 F18

Large-scale Hotel   **Location:** At Calgary International Airport. 2001 Airport Rd NE T2E 6Z8. Fax: 403/291-8722. **Facility:** 296 units. 284 one-bedroom standard units. 12 one-bedroom suites ($229-$389), some with whirlpools. 3-8 stories, interior corridors. **Parking:** on-site (fee) and valet. **Terms:** check-in 4 pm, cancellation fee imposed, pets (in smoking units). **Amenities:** video games, voice mail, irons, hair dryers. *Some:* high-speed Internet (fee). **Pool(s):** small heated indoor. **Leisure Activities:** whirlpool, jogging, exercise room. **Guest Services:** gift shop, valet laundry. **Business Services:** conference facilities, business center. **Cards:** AX, CB, DC, MC, VI.

SOME UNITS

(ASK) (SO) (🐾) (†↑) (Y) (➷) (✕) (📽) (DATA PORT) (🖨) (🖥) / (✕) /

ECONO LODGE INN & SUITES UNIVERSITY   *Book at aaa.com*   Phone: (403)289-1921   **44**

(CAA) (SAVE)

5/1-9/30 [CP]	1P: $89-$169	2P: $99-$199	XP: $10 F18
10/1-12/31 [CP]	1P: $70-$99	2P: $70-$109	XP: $10 F18
3/1-4/30 & 1/1-2/28 [CP]	1P: $70-$99	2P: $70-$99	XP: $10 F18

Motel   **Location:** Just n of jct 16th Ave NW (Trans-Canada Hwy 1) and Banff Tr NW. Located in Motel Village. 2231 Banff Tr NW T2M 4L2. Fax: 403/282-2149. **Facility:** 82 units. 78 one- and 4 two-bedroom standard units, some with efficiencies or kitchens. 2 stories, exterior corridors. **Parking:** on-site, winter plug-ins. **Terms:** 3 day cancellation notice. **Amenities:** voice mail, irons, hair dryers. *Some:* high-speed Internet. **Pool(s):** heated indoor. **Leisure Activities:** whirlpool, exercise room. **Guest Services:** coin laundry. **Cards:** AX, CB, DC, MC, VI. **Special Amenities:** free continental breakfast and free local telephone calls. *(See color ad p 379)*

SOME UNITS

(SO) (†↑+) (➷) (📽) (DATA PORT) (🖨) (🖥) (📠) / (✕) /

ECONO LODGE MOTEL VILLAGE   *Book at aaa.com*   Phone: (403)289-2561   **45**

(CAA) (SAVE)

5/1-9/30 [CP]	1P: $80-$129	2P: $89-$159	XP: $10 F18
1/1-2/28 [CP]	1P: $69-$79	2P: $79-$99	XP: $10 F18
3/1-4/30 & 10/1-12/31 [CP]	1P: $60-$79	2P: $69-$99	XP: $10 F18

Motel   **Location:** Jct 16th Ave NW (Trans-Canada Hwy 1) and Banff Tr NW. Located in Motel Village. 2440 16th Ave NW T2M 0M5. Fax: 403/282-9713. **Facility:** 56 units. 54 one-bedroom standard units, some with efficiencies. 2 one-bedroom suites with efficiencies. 2 stories (no elevator), interior/exterior corridors. **Parking:** on-site, winter plug-ins. **Terms:** 3 day cancellation notice, weekly rates available. **Amenities:** irons, hair dryers. **Leisure Activities:** sauna, exercise room. **Guest Services:** valet and coin laundry. **Cards:** AX, DC, MC, VI. **Special Amenities:** free continental breakfast and free local telephone calls. *(See color ad p 379)*

SOME UNITS

(SO) (†↑+) (📽) (DATA PORT) (🖥) / (✕) (🖨) (📠) /

(See map and index starting on p. 361)

ECONO LODGE SOUTH   *Book at aaa.com*   Phone: (403)252-4401   64

ⓒ SAVE   7/1-7/18   1P: $129-$179   2P: $139-$189   XP: $10   F18

◆◆◆   6/1-6/30 & 7/19-2/28   1P: $89-$119   2P: $99-$129   XP: $10   F18

Motel   3/1-5/31   1P: $79-$99   2P: $89-$109   XP: $10   F18

Location: Corner of MacLeod Tr and 75th Ave. 7505 MacLeod Tr S T2H 0L8. Fax: 403/252-2780. **Facility:** 73 units. 71 one-bedroom standard units, some with efficiencies. 2 one-bedroom suites ($159-$249) with efficiencies. 2 stories (no elevator), interior/exterior corridors. **Parking:** on-site, winter plug-ins. **Terms:** pets ($10 extra charge). **Amenities:** voice mail, hair dryers. *Some:* irons. **Pool(s):** heated indoor, wading. **Leisure Activities:** sauna, whirlpool. **Guest Services:** valet and coin laundry. **Cards:** AX, DC, MC, VI. **Special Amenities:** free continental breakfast and free local telephone calls.

SOME UNITS
[⬛ symbols] FEE

ELBOW RIVER INN & CASINO   Phone: (403)269-6771   54

ⓒ SAVE   4/1-9/30   1P: $109-$159   2P: $109-$159   XP: $10   F16

◆◆   3/1-3/31 & 10/1-2/28   1P: $99   2P: $99   XP: $10   F16

Small-scale Hotel   **Location:** Jct MacLeod Tr and 1st St SE. Located opposite Stampede Park. 1919 MacLeod Tr SE T2G 4S1. Fax: 403/237-5181. **Facility:** This motel is set along the banks of the Elbow River. 60 one-bedroom standard units. 3 stories, interior corridors. **Parking:** on-site, winter plug-ins. **Terms:** 3 night minimum stay - seasonal, package plans, pets ($10 fee). **Dining:** 7 am-2 & 5-10 pm, cocktails. **Leisure Activities:** jogging. **Guest Services:** valet laundry. **Cards:** AX, DC, MC, VI. *(See color ad p 380)*

SOME UNITS
[⬛ symbols] FEE

EXECUTIVE ROYAL INN NORTH CALGARY   *Book at aaa.com*   Phone: 403/291-2003   32

◆◆◆   All Year   1P: $110-$150   2P: $110-$150   XP: $10   F18

Small-scale Hotel   **Location:** 27th Ave NE and Barlow Tr. 2828 23rd St NE T2E 8T4. Fax: 403/291-2019. **Facility:** 201 units. 191 one-bedroom standard units. 10 one-bedroom suites with whirlpools. 6 stories, interior corridors. **Parking:** on-site, winter plug-ins. **Terms:** check-in 4 pm, cancellation fee imposed, pets ($20 fee, in smoking units). **Amenities:** video games, high-speed Internet, dual phone lines, voice mail, irons, hair dryers. **Leisure Activities:** whirlpools, steamrooms, exercise room. **Guest Services:** gift shop, valet laundry. **Business Services:** conference facilities, administrative services (fee). **Cards:** AX, DC, DS, MC, VI.

SOME UNITS
[ASK] [⬛ symbols] FEE

FOUR POINTS BY SHERATON HOTEL AND SUITES,
CALGARY WEST   *Book at aaa.com*   Phone: (403)288-4441   39

ⓒ SAVE   6/1-10/15   1P: $144-$219   2P: $144-$219   XP: $10   F10

◆◆◆   3/1-5/31   1P: $124-$169   2P: $124-$169   XP: $10   F10

            10/16-2/28   1P: $114-$159   2P: $114-$159   XP: $10   F10

Large-scale Hotel   **Location:** Opposite Canada Olympic Park. 8220 Bowridge Cres NW T3B 2V1. Fax: 403/288-4442. **Facility:** 150 units. 100 one-bedroom standard units, some with whirlpools. 50 one-bedroom suites ($144-$239). 4 stories, interior corridors. **Parking:** on-site, winter plug-ins. **Terms:** cancellation fee imposed, package plans. **Amenities:** high-speed Internet, dual phone lines, voice mail, irons, hair dryers. **Dining:** 6 am-10 pm, cocktails. **Pool(s):** heated indoor. **Leisure Activities:** whirlpool, steamroom, waterslide, exercise room, spa. **Guest Services:** gift shop, valet and coin laundry. **Business Services:** conference facilities, business center. **Cards:** AX, DC, MC, VI. **Special Amenities:** free newspaper and free room upgrade (subject to availability with advance reservations). *(See color ad p 5)*

SOME UNITS
[⬛ symbols]

(See map and index starting on p. 361)

GLENMORE INN AND CONVENTION CENTRE Phone: 403/279-8611 [68]

Property failed to provide current rates

▼▼ ▼▼
Small-scale Hotel
Location: 3 km e of Hwy 2 (Deerfoot Tr), exit Glenmore Tr E; at Ogden Rd. 2720 Glenmore Tr SE T2C 2E6. **Fax:** 403/236-8035. **Facility:** 169 units. 161 one-bedroom standard units, some with whirlpools. 8 one-bedroom suites, some with whirlpools. 2-8 stories, interior corridors. **Parking:** on-site, winter plug-ins. **Terms:** check-in 4 pm, small pets only (on garden level, in smoking units). **Amenities:** high-speed Internet, dual phone lines, voice mail, irons, hair dryers. **Leisure Activities:** saunas, whirlpool, exercise room. **Guest Services:** valet laundry. **Business Services:** conference facilities, business center.

SOME UNITS
🛏 🍴 ⛉ ☒ 🎥 DATA PORT ▣ / ☒ VCR ▤ ▣ /

GREENWOOD INN HOTELS *Book at aaa.com* Phone: (403)250-8855 [28]

(AAA) [SAVE] All Year 1P: $99-$139 2P: $99-$139 XP: $10 F18

▼▼▼ **Location:** From Barlow Tr N, just e on 32nd Ave NE, then just n. 3515 26th St NE T1Y 7E3. **Fax:** 403/250-8050. **Facility:** 213 units. 208 one-bedroom standard units. 5 one-bedroom suites ($279-$299), some with whirlpools. 6 stories, interior corridors. *Bath:* combo or shower only. **Parking:** on-site, winter plug-ins. Small-scale Hotel **Terms:** cancellation fee imposed, pets ($10 fee, in designated units). **Amenities:** high-speed Internet, voice mail, irons, hair dryers. **Dining:** 6 am-11 pm, Sat & Sun from 6:30 am, cocktails. **Pool(s):** heated indoor, saltwater. **Leisure Activities:** whirlpool, steamroom, exercise room. **Guest Services:** gift shop, valet laundry. **Business Services:** conference facilities, PC (fee). **Cards:** AX, DC, MC, VI. **Special Amenities:** free local telephone calls and free newspaper.

SOME UNITS
✈ 🛏 🍴 ⛉ 🛋 ⊼ ☒ 🎥 DATA PORT ▤ ▣ / ☒ ▣ /
FEE

HAMPTON INN & SUITES-CALGARY AIRPORT *Book at aaa.com* Phone: (403)250-4667 [26]

▼▼ ▼▼ 5/16-9/15 [BP] 1P: $129-$169 2P: $134-$179
3/1-5/15 & 9/16-11/15 [BP] 1P: $119-$169 2P: $124-$169
Small-scale Hotel 11/16-2/28 [BP] 1P: $109-$149 2P: $114-$159
Location: Barlow Tr at 37th Ave NE. 2420 37th Ave NE T2E 8S6. **Fax:** 403/250-5788. **Facility:** 103 units. 72 one-bedroom standard units. 31 one-bedroom suites, some with efficiencies. 4 stories, interior corridors. *Bath:* combo or shower only. **Parking:** on-site, winter plug-ins. **Amenities:** video games, high-speed Internet, dual phone lines, voice mail, irons, hair dryers. **Pool(s):** heated indoor. **Leisure Activities:** exercise room. **Guest Services:** valet and coin laundry, area transportation. **Business Services:** meeting rooms, PC. **Cards:** AX, DC, DS, MC, VI. *(See color ad p 381)*

SOME UNITS
A$K S🄳 ✈ 🍴 🛋 🎥 ⊼ 🎥 DATA PORT ▣ / ☒ ▤ ▣ /

(See map and index starting on p. 361)

HAMPTON INN & SUITES CALGARY-UNIVERSITY

Book at aaa.com   Phone: (403)289-9800 [47]

7/1-8/31 [ECP]	1P: $149-$229	2P: $169-$249	XP: $15 F18
9/1-2/28 [ECP]	1P: $109-$179	2P: $119-$189	XP: $10 F18
5/1-6/30 [ECP]	1P: $109-$149	2P: $124-$164	XP: $15 F18
3/1-4/30 [ECP]	1P: $99-$139	2P: $114-$154	XP: $15 F18

Small-scale Hotel **Location:** Just n of jct 16th Ave NW (Trans-Canada Hwy 1). 2231 Banff Tr NW T2M 4L2. Fax: 403/289-9200. **Facility:** 96 units. 72 one-bedroom standard units. 24 one-bedroom suites ($139-$249) with efficiencies, some with whirlpools. 4 stories, interior corridors. **Parking:** on-site, winter plug-ins. **Terms:** cancellation fee imposed, weekly rates available. **Amenities:** high-speed Internet, voice mail, irons, hair dryers. *Some:* DVD players. **Pool(s):** heated indoor. **Leisure Activities:** whirlpool, waterslide, exercise room. **Guest Services:** sundries, valet and coin laundry. **Business Services:** meeting rooms, business center. **Cards:** AX, CB, DC, DS, MC, VI. **Special Amenities:** free expanded continental breakfast and free local telephone calls. *(See color ad below)*

SOME UNITS

(See map and index starting on p. 361)

HILTON GARDEN INN-CALGARY AIRPORT
Book at aaa.com   **Phone:** (403)717-1999   **22**

All Year	1P: $99-$115	2P: $99-$115	XP: $20	F18

Location: Barlow Tr, w on McKnight Blvd, n on 19th St NE, then e. 2335 Pegasus Rd NE T2E 8C3.
Small-scale Hotel   Fax: 403/717-1901. **Facility:** 135 units. 131 one-bedroom standard units. 4 one-bedroom suites with whirlpools. 5 stories, interior corridors. **Parking:** on-site, winter plug-ins. **Terms:** 7 day cancellation notice-fee imposed, [BP] & [CP] meal plans available. **Amenities:** video games, high-speed Internet, dual phone lines, voice mail, irons, hair dryers. **Pool(s):** heated indoor. **Leisure Activities:** whirlpool, exercise room. **Guest Services:** sundries, valet and coin laundry, area transportation. **Business Services:** meeting rooms, business center. **Cards:** AX, CB, DC, DS, JC, MC, VI.

SOME UNITS

HOLIDAY INN CALGARY-AIRPORT
Book at aaa.com   **Phone:** (403)230-1999   **49**

6/1-9/30	1P: $114-$199	2P: $114-$199	XP: $15	F18
3/1-5/31 & 10/1-2/28	1P: $99-$139	2P: $99-$139	XP: $15	F18

Location: 1 km of jct Hwy 2 (Deerfoot Tr) and 16th Ave NE (Trans-Canada Hwy 1). 1250 McKinnon Dr NE T2E 7T7.
Small-scale Hotel   Fax: 403/277-2623. **Facility:** 170 one-bedroom standard units. 5 stories, interior corridors. **Parking:** on-site, winter plug-ins. **Terms:** 2 night minimum stay - seasonal, cancellation fee imposed, package plans. **Amenities:** video games, high-speed Internet, voice mail, irons, hair dryers. **Dining:** 6 am-11 pm, Sun-10 pm, cocktails. **Pool(s):** heated indoor. **Leisure Activities:** saunas, exercise room. **Guest Services:** valet and coin laundry, area transportation. **Business Services:** meeting rooms, business center. **Cards:** AX, CB, DC, DS, JC, MC, VI. **Special Amenities:** free local telephone calls and free newspaper.

SOME UNITS

HOLIDAY INN EXPRESS CALGARY-UNIVERSITY
Book at aaa.com   **Phone:** (403)289-6600   **46**

4/15-8/28 [ECP]	1P: $108-$158	2P: $108-$158	XP: $10	F19
8/29-2/28 [ECP]	1P: $90-$115	2P: $90-$115	XP: $10	F19
3/1-4/14 [ECP]	1P: $90-$105	2P: $90-$105	XP: $10	F19

Location: 16th Ave (Trans-Canada Hwy 1) and Banff Tr NW. Located in Motel Village, across from McMahon Stadium.
Small-scale Hotel   2227 Banff Tr NW T2M 4L2. Fax: 403/289-6767. **Facility:** 64 one-bedroom standard units. 3 stories, interior corridors. **Bath:** combo or shower only. **Parking:** on-site, winter plug-ins. **Terms:** check-in 4 pm, cancellation fee imposed, small pets only (1st floor units). **Amenities:** dual phone lines, voice mail, irons, hair dryers. **Leisure Activities:** pool privileges, exercise room. **Guest Services:** valet laundry. **Business Services:** meeting rooms. **Cards:** AX, DC, MC, VI. *(See color ad card insert)*

SOME UNITS

HOLIDAY INN EXPRESS HOTEL & SUITES
CALGARY DOWNTOWN
Phone: (403)269-8262   **63**

All Year [ECP]	1P: $99-$179	2P: $99-$179	XP: $10	F18

Location: 8th Ave at 10th St SW. 1020 8th Ave SW T2P 1J2. Fax: 403/269-4868. **Facility:** 56 units. 49 one-bedroom standard units. 7 one-bedroom suites with whirlpools. 9 stories, interior corridors. **Parking:** on-site, winter plug-ins. **Terms:** package plans, pets ($50 extra charge, in smoking units). **Amenities:** high-speed **Small-scale Hotel**   Internet, dual phone lines, voice mail, irons, hair dryers. **Leisure Activities:** exercise room. **Guest Services:** valet and coin laundry. **Business Services:** meeting rooms, PC. **Cards:** AX, DC, DS, JC, MC, VI. **Special Amenities:** free expanded continental breakfast and free newspaper.

SOME UNITS
FEE

HOLIDAY INN EXPRESS HOTEL & SUITES
CALGARY-SOUTH
Phone: (403)225-3000   **74**

All Year [ECP]	1P: $149-$249		XP: $10	F19

Location: Hwy 2 (Deerfoot Tr), exit Anderson Rd w, then just s on MacLeod Tr. 12025 Lake Fraser Dr SE (MacLeod Tr S) T2J 7G5. Fax: 403/252-0994. **Facility:** 106 units. 63 one-bedroom standard units. 43 one-bedroom suites **Small-scale Hotel**   ($183-$266), some with whirlpools. 4 stories, interior corridors. **Parking:** on-site, winter plug-ins. **Terms:** pets ($20 extra charge, in smoking units). **Amenities:** video games, high-speed Internet, dual phone lines, voice mail, irons, hair dryers. **Pool(s):** heated indoor. **Leisure Activities:** whirlpool, waterslide, exercise room. **Guest Services:** valet and coin laundry. **Business Services:** meeting rooms, business center. **Cards:** AX, DC, DS, JC, MC, VI.

SOME UNITS
FEE

KENSINGTON RIVERSIDE INN
Book at aaa.com   **Phone:** (403)228-4442   **50**

All Year [BP]	1P: $259-$334	2P: $274-$349	XP: $25	F8

Location: Just w of 10th St NW; downtown. Located in Kensington area. 1126 Memorial Dr NW T2N 3E3.
Fax: 403/228-9608. **Facility:** Upscale and exquisite, this high-end B&B features original artwork, gourmet breakfasts and rooms well equipped for business travelers. Smoke free premises. 19 one-bedroom standard **Bed & Breakfast**   units, some with whirlpools. 2 stories, interior corridors. **Parking:** on-site. **Terms:** 3 day cancellation notice, 3% service charge. **Amenities:** video library, CD players, high-speed Internet, dual phone lines, voice mail, irons, hair dryers. **Leisure Activities:** jogging. **Guest Services:** sundries, valet laundry. **Business Services:** meeting rooms. **Cards:** AX, CB, DC, DS, JC, MC, VI. **Special Amenities:** free full breakfast and free newspaper.

FEE

MARRIOTT RESIDENCE INN-CALGARY AIRPORT
Book at aaa.com   **Phone:** 403/735-3336   **24**

7/8-8/31 [BP]	1P: $189-$219	2P: $189-$219		
3/1-7/7 & 9/1-2/28 [BP]	1P: $149-$199	2P: $149-$199		

Location: Corner of Barlow Tr and 39th Ave NE. 2622 39th Ave NE T1Y 7J9. Fax: 403/735-1121. **Facility:** 120 units. 48 one-bedroom standard units, some with efficiencies or kitchens. 48 one- and 24 two-bedroom **Small-scale Hotel**   suites, some with efficiencies or kitchens. 4 stories, interior corridors. **Bath:** combo or shower only. **Parking:** on-site, winter plug-ins. **Terms:** 10 day cancellation notice, pets ($100 fee). **Amenities:** video games, CD players, high-speed Internet, voice mail, irons, hair dryers. *Some:* dual phone lines. **Pool(s):** heated indoor. **Leisure Activities:** whirlpool, limited exercise equipment, sports court. **Guest Services:** sundries, complimentary evening beverages: Mon-Thurs, valet and coin laundry, area transportation. **Business Services:** meeting rooms, PC. **Cards:** AX, CB, DC, JC, MC, VI.

SOME UNITS
FEE

(See map and index starting on p. 361)

QUALITY INN UNIVERSITY   *Book at aaa.com*   Phone: (403)289-1973   41

(CAA) (SAVE)

6/1-9/30	1P: $99-$169	2P: $99-$169	XP: $10 F12
5/1-5/31	1P: $89-$149	2P: $89-$149	XP: $10 F12
3/1-4/30 & 10/1-2/28	1P: $79-$139	2P: $79-$139	XP: $10 F12

Location: Just n of jct Trans-Canada Hwy 1 and Crowchild Tr. Located in Motel Village. 2359 Banff Tr NW T2M 4L2.
Small-scale Hotel Fax: 403/282-1241. **Facility:** 105 units. 104 one-bedroom standard units, some with whirlpools. 1 one-bedroom suite with whirlpool. 2 stories (no elevator), interior/exterior corridors. *Bath:* combo or shower only.
Parking: on-site, winter plug-ins. **Terms:** check-in 4 pm, 3 day cancellation notice-fee imposed, small pets (with approval). **Amenities:** high-speed Internet, voice mail, irons, hair dryers. **Dining:** 10 am-2 & 5-10 pm, Fri & Sat 10 am-10 pm, cocktails. **Pool(s):** heated indoor. **Leisure Activities:** steamroom, exercise room. *Fee:* game room. **Guest Services:** valet and coin laundry. **Business Services:** meeting rooms, PC (fee). **Cards:** AX, CB, DC, MC, VI. **Special Amenities:** free expanded continental breakfast.

SOME UNITS

RADISSON HOTEL CALGARY AIRPORT   *Book at aaa.com*   Phone: (403)291-4666   31

(CAA) (SAVE)

5/1-7/17	1P: $99-$135	2P: $99-$135	XP: $10 F17
3/1-4/30 & 7/18-2/28	1P: $94-$130	2P: $94-$130	XP: $10 F17

Location: 0.5 km e of jct 16th Ave NE (Trans-Canada Hwy 1) and Hwy 2 (Deerfoot Tr). 2120 16th Ave NE T2E 1L4.
Fax: 403/291-6498. **Facility:** 185 units. 177 one-bedroom standard units, some with whirlpools. 8 one-bedroom suites ($159-$190). 10 stories, interior corridors. *Bath:* combo or shower only. **Parking:** on-site,
Small-scale Hotel winter plug-ins. **Terms:** [AP], [BP], [CP] & [ECP] meal plans available, pets ($10 extra charge, in smoking unit). **Amenities:** video games, dual phone lines, voice mail, irons, hair dryers. *Some:* high-speed Internet. **Dining:** 6:30 am-11 pm, cocktails, nightclub. **Pool(s):** heated indoor. **Leisure Activities:** whirlpool, exercise room. **Guest Services:** gift shop, valet laundry. **Business Services:** conference facilities, PC (fee). **Cards:** AX, DC, MC, VI. **Special Amenities:** free newspaper and free room upgrade (subject to availability with advance reservations). *(See color ad p 377)*

SOME UNITS

FEE

SANDMAN HOTEL SUITES & SPA CALGARY
AIRPORT   *Book at aaa.com*   Phone: (403)219-2475   21

5/1-10/15	1P: $139-$169	2P: $139-$169	
3/1-4/30 & 10/16-2/28	1P: $109-$139	2P: $109-$139	

Location: Just n of jct Barlow Tr and McKnight Blvd. 25 Hopewell Way NE T3J 4V7. Fax: 403/219-2476.
Small-scale Hotel **Facility:** 177 units. 113 one-bedroom standard units. 64 one-bedroom suites ($139-$189), some with whirlpools. 4 stories (no elevator), interior corridors. **Parking:** on-site, winter plug-ins. **Terms:** package plans, pets ($10 fee).
Amenities: video games, high-speed Internet, dual phone lines, voice mail, irons, hair dryers. **Pool(s):** heated indoor. **Leisure Activities:** saunas, whirlpool, exercise room. *Fee:* massage. **Guest Services:** valet laundry. **Business Services:** meeting rooms, PC. **Cards:** AX, DC, DS, MC, VI.

SOME UNITS

FEE

SHERATON CAVALIER HOTEL   *Book at aaa.com*   Phone: (403)291-0107   27

All Year	1P: $189-$269	XP: $15 F18

Location: Barlow Tr at 32nd Ave NE. 2620 32nd Ave NE T1Y 6B8. Fax: 403/291-2834. **Facility:** 306 units. 286
one-bedroom standard units. 20 one-bedroom suites with whirlpools. 7 stories, interior corridors. **Parking:**
Large-scale Hotel on-site and valet, winter plug-ins. **Amenities:** video games, high-speed Internet (fee), dual phone lines,
voice mail, honor bars, irons, hair dryers. *Some:* fax. **Dining:** Carver's Steakhouse, see separate listing. **Pool(s):** heated indoor.
Leisure Activities: sauna, whirlpools, waterslide, exercise room. **Guest Services:** gift shop, valet laundry. **Business Services:** conference facilities, business center. **Cards:** AX, DC, DS, MC, VI. *(See color ad p 5)*

SOME UNITS

FEE

SUPER 8 MOTEL CALGARY AIRPORT   *Book at aaa.com*   Phone: 403/291-9888   30

(CAA) (SAVE)

6/1-9/30	1P: $112-$125	2P: $112-$125	XP: $10 F12
4/1-5/31	1P: $73-$99	2P: $75-$111	XP: $10 F12
3/1-3/31 & 10/1-2/28	1P: $63-$89	2P: $65-$92	XP: $10 F12

Location: Corner of 32nd Ave and Barlow Tr NE. 3030 Barlow Tr NE T1Y 1A2. Fax: 403/291-3000. **Facility:** 61
Small-scale Hotel one-bedroom standard units. 4 stories, interior corridors. **Parking:** on-site, winter plug-ins. **Terms:** small pets only ($10 fee). **Amenities:** safes (fee), irons, hair dryers. **Guest Services:** coin laundry. **Business Services:** meeting rooms. **Cards:** AX, DC, DS, MC, VI. **Special Amenities:** free continental breakfast and free local telephone calls.

SOME UNITS

FEE

SUPER 8 MOTEL-MOTEL VILLAGE   *Book at aaa.com*   Phone: (403)289-9211   40

(CAA) (SAVE)

5/31-9/30 [CP]	1P: $79-$159	2P: $89-$169	XP: $10 F12
3/1-5/30 & 10/1-2/28 [CP]	1P: $59-$99	2P: $59-$99	XP: $10 F12

Location: Just n of jct Trans-Canada Hwy 1 and Crowchild Tr. Located in Motel Village, across from McMahon Stadium.
1904 Crowchild Tr NW T2M 3Y7. Fax: 403/282-7824. **Facility:** 59 units. 49 one- and 10 two-bedroom standard
Motel units. 2 stories (no elevator), exterior corridors. **Parking:** on-site, winter plug-ins. **Terms:** cancellation fee imposed, small pets only ($10 fee). **Amenities:** safes (fee). *Some:* hair dryers. **Pool(s):** small heated outdoor. **Guest Services:** sundries, valet and coin laundry. **Business Services:** PC (fee). **Cards:** AX, CB, DC, DS, MC, VI.
Special Amenities: free continental breakfast and free local telephone calls.

SOME UNITS

FEE

(See map and index starting on p. 361)

TRAVELODGE HOTEL CALGARY AIRPORT *Book at aaa.com* Phone: (403)291-1260 ③③

(CAA) (SAVE)

♦♦♦♦

Small-scale Hotel

| 7/1-7/31 | 1P: $119-$139 | 2P: $129-$149 | XP: $10 | F18 |
| 3/1-6/30 & 8/1-2/28 | 1P: $95-$115 | 2P: $95-$115 | XP: $10 | F18 |

Location: Barlow Tr, then e. 2750 Sunridge Blvd NE T1Y 3C2. Fax: 403/291-9170. **Facility:** 203 one-bedroom standard units. 6 stories, interior corridors. **Parking:** on-site, winter plug-ins. **Terms:** [BP] & [CP] meal plans available, package plans. **Amenities:** video games, voice mail, irons, hair dryers. *Some:* high-speed Internet. **Dining:** 7 am-11 pm, cocktails. **Pool(s):** heated indoor. **Leisure Activities:** whirlpool, exercise room. **Guest Services:** valet and coin laundry. **Business Services:** meeting rooms, PC. **Cards:** AX, DC, MC, VI. *(See color ad p 367)*

SOME UNITS

[icons] ⬛ ✈ 🐴 ❗ 🍸 📶 🐕 🎥 DATA PORT 💻 / ✕ VCR 🔌 /

TRAVELODGE HOTEL CALGARY MACLEOD TRAIL *Book at aaa.com* Phone: (403)253-7070 ⑥⑥

(CAA) (SAVE)

♦♦♦♦

Small-scale Hotel

7/1-7/31	1P: $119-$159	2P: $119-$159	XP: $10	F18
8/1-2/28	1P: $89-$109	2P: $99-$109	XP: $10	F18
3/1-6/30	1P: $89-$109	2P: $89-$109	XP: $10	F18

Location: On Hwy 2 (Deerfoot Tr) at 90th Ave SW. 9206 MacLeod Tr S T2J 0P5. Fax: 403/255-6740. **Facility:** 254 units. 253 one-bedroom standard units. 1 one-bedroom suite. 6 stories, interior corridors. **Parking:** on-site, winter plug-ins. **Terms:** [BP] & [CP] meal plans available, package plans, small pets only ($15 fee, in designated units). **Amenities:** video games, high-speed Internet, voice mail, irons, hair dryers. **Dining:** 6:30 am-10 pm, cocktails. **Pool(s):** small heated indoor. **Leisure Activities:** whirlpool. **Guest Services:** valet and coin laundry. **Business Services:** meeting rooms, fax (fee). **Cards:** AX, DC, MC, VI. *(See color ad p 367)*

SOME UNITS

[icons] 🛏 ❗ 🍸 🐕 🐾 🎥 DATA PORT 💻 / ✕ 🔌 🖨 /
FEE

WINGATE INN *Book at aaa.com* Phone: (403)514-0099 ⑦⑤

♦♦♦

Small-scale Hotel

| 6/1-9/15 [ECP] | 1P: $169-$255 | 2P: $169-$255 | |
| 3/1-5/31 & 9/16-2/28 [ECP] | 1P: $135-$199 | 2P: $135-$199 | |

Location: Hwy 2A (MacLeod Tr), 0.5 km e on Sun Valley, 0.3 km n on Midpark Way, then just s. 400 Midpark Way T2X 3S4. Fax: 403/514-0090. **Facility:** 103 units. 87 one-bedroom standard units, some with whirlpools. 16 one-bedroom suites, some with whirlpools. 4 stories, interior corridors. **Bath:** combo or shower only. **Parking:** on-site, winter plug-ins. **Terms:** package plans, pets ($25 fee, on smoking floor). **Amenities:** video games, high-speed Internet, dual phone lines, voice mail, safes, irons, hair dryers. **Pool(s):** small heated indoor. **Leisure Activities:** whirlpool, waterslide, exercise room. **Guest Services:** valet and coin laundry, area transportation. **Business Services:** meeting rooms, business center. **Cards:** AX, DC, DS, MC, VI.

SOME UNITS

[icons] (ASK) 🛏 ❗ 🛁 ♿ 🏊 ✕ 🎥 DATA PORT 🔌 🖨 💻 / ✕ /
FEE

WHERE TO DINE

AIDA'S Lunch: $5-$12 Dinner: $5-$12 Phone: 403/541-1189 ⑦④

♦♦♦

Lebanese

Location: At 4th St and 23rd Ave. 2208 4th St SW T2S 1W9. **Hours:** 11 am-10 pm, Mon-9 pm, Fri & Sat-11 pm, Sun 4 pm-9 pm. Closed major holidays. **Reservations:** suggested, weekends. **Features:** Hearty portions of tasty, traditional Lebanese food await patrons of the cozy, bistro-style restaurant. A taste of Lebanon infuses such dishes as falafel and flavorful tabbouleh salad. Save room for dessert, particularly the delicious layali loubnan, a Lebanese version of tiramisu. Casual dress; cocktails. **Parking:** street. **Cards:** AX, MC, VI.

[icons] 🍷 ✕

ALBERTA KING OF SUBS Lunch: $2-$10 Dinner: $2-$10 Phone: 403/293-5809 ④②

♦

Canadian

Location: McKnight Blvd and 52nd St NE, just s on 52nd St NE. 7196 Temple Dr NE #22 T1Y 4E8. **Hours:** 10 am-9 pm, Thurs-Sat to 10 pm. Closed: 3/28, 12/25. **Reservations:** not accepted. **Features:** Montreal-style smoked-meat sandwiches and hot grilled subs are specialties at the strip-mall eatery, which has only nine tables and a counter. French fries, coleslaw and sugar also are on the menu. Service is friendly and polite. Casual dress; beer only. **Parking:** on-site. **Cards:** VI.

[icons] ✕

THE ARDEN Lunch: $8-$17 Dinner: $8-$17 Phone: 403/228-2821 ⑥⑨

♦♦♦

Continental

Location: Corner of 10 St SW. 1112 17th Ave SW T2T 0B4. **Hours:** 11 am-10 pm, Thurs & Fri-midnight, Sat 9 am-midnight, Sun 9 am-4 pm. Closed: 1/1, 12/25, 12/26. **Features:** Co-owned by singer/songwriter Jann Arden, the restaurant features an upscale, eclectic menu with options ranging from pot sticker appetizers to sea bass for the main course. The atmosphere is funky and upbeat, and the owner is often known to greet her guests. Cocktails. **Parking:** on-site. **Cards:** AX, DC, MC, VI.

[icons] 🅰 ✕

(See map and index starting on p. 361)

ATHENS BY NIGHT   **Lunch:** $9-$15   **Dinner:** $14-$22   **Phone:** 403/244-1771   ③⑦
Greek
Location: Corner of 17th Ave SW and 11th St SW. 1137 17th Ave SW T2T 0L2. **Hours:** 11:30 am-10 pm, Thurs & Fri-11 pm, Sat & Sun 4 pm-10 pm. Closed major holidays; also Sun. **Reservations:** suggested. **Features:** Tasty Greek food is served in hearty portions at this Mediterranean-style oasis on a busy stretch of 17th Avenue. Don't be surprised if the owner comes to say hello. Patrons who return often find that he remembers their name. Casual dress; cocktails. **Parking:** on-site. **Cards:** MC, VI.

ATLAS SPECIALTY SUPERMARKET &
RESTAURANT   **Lunch:** $5-$13   **Dinner:** $5-$13   **Phone:** 403/230-0990   ④⑤
Persian
Location: 9th Ave (Trans-Canada Hwy 1) and 9th St SW, just e of Centre St. 116 16th Ave NE T2P 2Y6. **Hours:** 10 am-9 pm, Sun 11 am-7 pm. Closed: 1/1, 12/25; also Mon in winter. **Features:** Tucked away from the hectic 16th Avenue roadway, the simple eatery and supermarket is a Persian oasis. Among traditional dishes are kebabs, eggplant soup and delicious teas. On the shelves are hard-to-find spices and ingredients. Guests order at the counter and then have a seat. **Parking:** on-site. **Cards:** MC, VI.

BAGOLAC SAIGON RESTAURANT   **Lunch:** $6-$10   **Dinner:** $6-$10   **Phone:** 403/252-5588   ③⓪
Vietnamese
Location: Just e off MacLeod Tr near Chinook Centre. #8, 6130-1A St SW T2R 0B2. **Hours:** 11 am-9:30 pm. Closed major holidays; also Sun. **Features:** Upscale decor awaits at this fancy Vietnamese restaurant, where a mixture of Thai and Vietnamese dishes are available. The selection on the menu is so outstanding that you may have a hard time selecting. It is best to order a variety of dishes to truly experience the tastes and flavors of this cuisine, starting with salad rolls, a traditional bun or noodle soup. Casual dress; cocktails. **Parking:** on-site. **Cards:** AX, MC, VI.

BOOGIE'S BURGERS   **Lunch:** $5-$10   **Dinner:** $5-$10   **Phone:** 403/230-7070   ④⑥
American
Location: Corner of 8th Ave NE. 908 Edmonton Tr NE T2E 3K1. **Hours:** 10:30 am-10 pm, Sat 10 am-9 pm. Closed: Sun. **Features:** A favorite neighborhood haunt, the burger joint whips up creamy milkshakes, huge burgers and crispy fries. Guests can grab a seat at the counter and chat with the friendly owners, or in the summer, enjoy a shake at a picnic table. Beer & wine only. **Parking:** on-site.

BOYD'S SEAFOOD RESTAURANT   **Lunch:** $8-$12   **Dinner:** $12-$35   **Phone:** 403/253-7575   ③④
Seafood
Location: Corner of 52nd and MacLeod Tr. 5211 MacLeod Tr T2H 0J3. **Hours:** 11 am-9 pm, Wed-Sat to 10 pm, Sun noon-9 pm. Closed: 12/25. **Reservations:** suggested. **Features:** A long and varied menu of seafood is presented at the casual family restaurant, which transports guests to the east coast of Nova Scotia for a taste of the maritime. Fish and chips, mussels, Alaskan halibut, clams and more are dished in heaping portions. Most selections are flown in fresh daily, and there is something for everyone. This place offers a great value for the dollar. Service is friendly. Casual dress; cocktails. **Parking:** on-site. **Cards:** MC, VI.

CARVER'S STEAKHOUSE   **Dinner:** $28-$35   **Phone:** 403/250-6327   ③⑧
Steak House
Location: Barlow Tr at 32nd Ave NE; in Sheraton Cavalier Hotel. 2620 32nd Ave NE T1Y 6B8. **Hours:** 5:30 pm-10:30 pm, Sun 5 pm-9 pm. Closed major holidays. **Reservations:** required. **Features:** One of Calgary's finest steak houses, the formal restaurant is the place to go for beef. The contemporary, upscale dining room features superb steaks and decadent desserts. Made-to-order steaks are mouthwatering. Casual dress; cocktails. **Parking:** on-site and valet. **Cards:** AX, DC, DS, MC, VI.

CHARLY CHAN'S RICE HOUSE   **Lunch:** $9-$14   **Dinner:** $9-$14   **Phone:** 403/283-6165   ④⑧
Sichuan
Location: From 10th St NW, just w at Kensington Rd. 1140 Kensington Rd NW T4V 0S2. **Hours:** 11 am-11 pm, Fri & Sat-midnight. **Features:** In the heart of Kensington and just below street level, the simple restaurant serves Szechuan food. Dishes are hearty and tasty, and the service pleasant and friendly. Those seeking good value for the dollar will like this place. Casual dress; cocktails. **Parking:** street. **Cards:** AX, DC, MC, VI.

CODO VIETNAMESE RESTAURANT   **Lunch:** $5-$8   **Dinner:** $5-$11   **Phone:** 403/228-7798   ⑥⑥
Vietnamese
Location: Just e of jct 14th St and 17th Ave SW. 1411 17th Ave SW T2T 0L4. **Hours:** 11 am-10 pm, Sun noon-9 pm. **Features:** A favorite among locals, the simple restaurant is one of the city's best-kept secrets. Huge portions of fresh Vietnamese food mean great value for the dollar. Representative of traditional fare are spring rolls, vermicelli rice dishes and a variety of curries. Although it can often be busy, especially on weekends, the restaurant's service is quick and attentive. Casual dress; cocktails. **Parking:** street. **Cards:** MC, VI.

CORNERSTONE GRILL   **Lunch:** $7-$30   **Dinner:** $7-$30   **Phone:** 403/225-5805   ⑥②
International
Location: On Hwy 2A (MacLeod Tr); corner of Southland Dr; in Best Western Hospitality Inn. 135 Southland Dr SE T2J 5X5. **Hours:** 11 am-10 pm. Closed: 12/25. **Features:** The casual restaurant marks its menu with an International flair. Asian, Thai and even some Vietnamese influences are apparent. However, even pasta and steak standards, including AAA Sterling beef, make appearances. Service is pleasant and friendly, and the decor is upbeat and casual. Casual dress; cocktails. **Parking:** on-site. **Cards:** AX, MC, VI.

CRETE SOUVLAKI   **Lunch:** $3-$7   **Dinner:** $3-$7   **Phone:** 403/246-4777   ③②
Greek
Location: 26th St SW. 2623 17th Ave SW T3E 0A5. **Hours:** 9 am-10 pm, Sat & Sun 11:30 am-9:30 pm. Closed: 1/1, 12/25. **Features:** Fast, fresh and cheap are all words to describe the distinctive eatery. Heaping portions of Greek food are dished at the quick-serve eatery, which is attached to the OK gas station on 17th Avenue. Most people get their food to go, but there are a few tables available. **Parking:** on-site. **Cards:** AX, MC, VI.

(See map and index starting on p. 361)

DEANE HOUSE HISTORIC SITE RESTAURANT AT FORT CALGARY

Lunch: $8-$10   **Phone:** 403/269-7747   59

Canadian

Location: Corner of 8th St. 806 9th Ave SE T2P 2M5. **Hours:** 11 am-3 pm, Sat & Sun from 10 am. Closed major holidays. **Reservations:** suggested. **Features:** The glassed-in, veranda dining room offers a lovely view of the Elbow River. Menu offerings include fresh scones, homemade soup, eggs Benedict, French toast, quiche, bacon and eggs and gingerbread cake. On Friday from 6:30 pm to 10:30 pm, the Mystery from History dinner theater takes the stage. Casual dress; cocktails. **Parking:** on-site. **Cards:** AX, MC, VI. **Historic**

DINER DELUXE

Lunch: $4-$9   **Dinner:** $10-$15   **Phone:** 403/276-5499   52

Canadian

Location: Corner of Edmonton Tr NE and 7th Ave NE. 804 Edmonton Tr NE T2E 3J6. **Hours:** 7:30 am-9 pm, Sat 8 am-3 & 5-9 pm, Sun 8 am-3 pm. Closed: 12/25. **Features:** Everything old is new again, and such is the case at this funky retro diner, where you can find all day breakfasts made with gourmet and specialty ingredients. If you're looking for a nostalgic atmosphere, this is the place. You can enjoy a taste of the fifties, including formica countertops, boldly coloured vinyl chairs, tall milkshakes and hearty burgers. Friendly servers are quick and knowledgeable, and can offer great detail about the various dishes. Casual dress; cocktails. **Parking:** street. **Cards:** AX, MC, VI.

FLEUR DE SEL

Lunch: $9-$15   **Dinner:** $15-$19   **Phone:** 403/228-9764   67

Nouvelle French

Location: 4th St and 21st Ave SW; in the Tivoli Theatre Building. 2015 4th St SW, #2 T2S 1W6. **Hours:** 11 am-2 & 5-midnight, Sat & Sun from 5 pm. Closed: 1/1, 12/25. **Reservations:** required. **Features:** Elegantly funky describes the atmosphere at this small brasserie, where diners appreciate nouveau French cuisine and a fine wine selection. The memorable experience here is about more than just the creative, sophisticated food, encompassing the inviting atmosphere and charming decor. Cocktails. **Parking:** street. **Cards:** AX, DC, DS, MC, VI.

FORBIDDEN CITY SEAFOOD & DIM SUM RESTAURANT

Lunch: $3-$10   **Dinner:** $8-$12   **Phone:** 403/250-1848   31

Chinese

Location: 16th Ave NE (Trans-Canada Hwy 1), exit 36th St S; in Pacific Place Shopping Plaza. 220 Pacific Pl, 999 36th St NE T2E 2K9. **Hours:** 11 am-10:30 pm, Fri & Sat-midnight. Closed major holidays. **Features:** In the Northeast, the large, contemporary restaurant serves wonton soup, ginger beef, Peking-style sesame prawns and the specialty, dim sum. Best enjoyed with a group of people, dim sum items include steamed shrimp dumplings and onion cakes. Service is quick and efficient, and the atmosphere is bustling. Casual dress; cocktails. **Parking:** on-site. **Cards:** AX, DC, MC, VI.

GRUMAN'S DELI

Lunch: $8-$11   **Dinner:** $15-$26   **Phone:** 403/261-9003   26

Deli/Subs
Sandwiches

Location: 7th Ave SW and 9th St SW. Plaza 1000 7th Ave SW T2P 5L5. **Hours:** 7:30 am-7:30 pm, Sat from 10:30 am. Closed major holidays; also Sun. **Features:** Named after the owner's mother, the upscale Jewish delicatessen serves traditional favorites, such as chicken liver pate, potato latke and Montreal smoked meat. Patrons can order at the counter to take away or enjoy table service. Although the delicious food is hearty, don't eat so much that you won't have room for dessert. Casual dress; beer & wine only. **Parking:** street. **Cards:** AX, MC, VI.

GUS'S CAFE & PIZZERIA

Lunch: $5-$10   **Dinner:** $7-$15   **Phone:** 403/282-4005   47

Pizza

Location: 16th Ave (Trans-Canada Hwy 1), just s at 29th St NW. 1620 29th St NW T2W 4L7. **Hours:** 9 am-10 pm, Thurs & Fri-11 pm, Sat 4 pm-10 pm. Closed major holidays; also Sun. **Features:** Ideally located just off Trans-Canada Highway 1 and near the hospital, this family-run restaurant serves simply good food. Though they specialize in pizza, you'll also find a variety of other items on the menu including soups, salads and sandwiches. Service is quick and prompt, and if you become a regular, don't be surprised to see the owner sit and chat with you! Casual dress; cocktails. **Parking:** on-site. **Cards:** MC, VI.

HANA SUSHI

Lunch: $5-$10   **Dinner:** $8-$20   **Phone:** 403/229-1499   71

Japanese

Location: Corner of 18th Ave SW. 1803 4th St SW T2S 1W2. **Hours:** 11:30 am-2 & 5-10 pm, Sun-9 pm. Closed major holidays. **Reservations:** suggested. **Features:** The small, traditional restaurant is a great spot for good sushi at a great value. In addition to a wide variety of sushi and sashimi, the menu lists full dinners that include miso soup, salad and a selection of sushi. Casual dress; cocktails. **Parking:** street. **Cards:** AX, DC, MC, VI.

JANINE'S BISTRO

Lunch: $5-$7   **Dinner:** $6-$14   **Phone:** 403/233-0995   29

Polish

Location: From Sarcee Tr, just e at Richmond Rd; in Glamorgan Shopping Centre. #6, 3919 Richmond Rd SW T3E 4P2. **Hours:** 8 am-8 pm, Thurs-Sat to 9 pm. Closed major holidays; also Sun & holiday weekends. **Features:** Eastern European is the way Janine describes her fare, and her menu boasts such specialties as pierogies, pork schnitzel, cabbage rolls and, on Fridays, borscht for those who arrive early enough. Burgers are another good choice. Only 12 tables are available at the cozy, family-run restaurant, which serves huge portions of tasty food. In a small plaza, this little place is easy to miss, but it's well worth the drive. Casual dress; cocktails. **Parking:** on-site. **Cards:** VI.

THE JOYCE ON 4TH IRISH PUB

Lunch: $6-$12   **Dinner:** $8-$15   **Phone:** 403/541-9168   68

Irish

Location: Jct 24th Ave SW and 4th St SW. 506 24th Ave SW T2S 0K4. **Hours:** 11 am-1 am, Thurs-Sat to 2 am, Sun-midnight. Closed: 12/25. **Reservations:** suggested. **Features:** A wide selection of ales and whiskeys complements traditional fare, including boxty, an Irish dish made with a potato pancake and various fillings, and Guinness and beef pie. Saturday visitors can expect live music and Celtic dancers. The rich decor incorporates oversized couches and a long bar. The mood is lively and upbeat. Casual dress; cocktails. **Parking:** on-site. **Cards:** AX, MC, VI.

(See map and index starting on p. 361)

KANE'S HARLEY DINER Lunch: $4-$10 Dinner: $4-$10 Phone: 403/269-7311 (28)
Canadian
Location: 9th Ave SE at 12th St; in Inglewood. 1209 9th Ave SE T2G 3E8. **Hours:** 7 am-10 pm. **Closed:** 12/25. **Reservations:** not accepted. **Features:** Orange and brown retro decor sets the scene at the popular diner in the town's heart. Guests seat themselves in booths and admire Harley motorcycles as they peruse the menu, which is laden with comfort foods. Among choices are grilled cheese and ham sandwiches, poutine, hearty hamburgers and even liver and onions. Breakfast is served all day, and service always comes with a smile. Casual dress; cocktails. **Parking:** street. **Cards:** MC, VI.

KYOTO 17 Lunch: $6-$10 Dinner: $8-$16 Phone: 403/245-3188 (70)
Japanese
Location: Corner of 17th Ave SW and 8th St SW; basement level of the Devenish Building. 908 17th Ave SW T2T 0A3. **Hours:** 11:30 am-10 pm, Sat 5 pm-11 pm, Sun 5 pm-9 pm. **Closed** major holidays. **Reservations:** accepted. **Features:** The restaurant features a sushi bar, rice, curry, Japanese noodles and full dinners with teriyaki chicken and steak. The decor is contemporary in the smoke-free main dining room, while the traditional private rooms offer a more authentic experience. Metered parking is available during the day. Cocktails. **Parking:** street. **Cards:** AX, DC, JC, MC, VI.

LA BREZZA Lunch: $9-$15 Dinner: $12-$25 Phone: 403/262-6230 (56)
Italian
Location: 9th St NE; in Bridgeland. 990 1st Ave NE T2E 4J9. **Hours:** 11:30 am-2:30 & 5-midnight, Sat & Sun from 5 pm. **Reservations:** suggested. **Features:** In a small house, the physical setting enhances the warm, relaxed atmosphere. Funky lighting crisscrosses the ceiling. Whether for a first date or a reunion of old friends, the restaurant's eclectic atmosphere, refined service and creative Italian cuisine will create a lingering memory. Casual dress; cocktails. **Parking:** on-site. **Cards:** AX, MC, VI.

LA DOLCE VITA RISTORANTE ITALIANO Lunch: $9-$16 Dinner: $11-$25 Phone: 403/263-3445 (55)
(AAA)
Italian
Location: At 9th St NE; in Bridgeland. 916 1st Ave NE T2E 0C5. **Hours:** 11:30 am-2 & 5:30-10:30 pm, Sat 5:30 pm-11 pm. Closed major holidays; also Sun. **Reservations:** suggested. **Features:** In the city's "Little Italy" area, the restaurant features casual dining upstairs and more formal dining downstairs. Fresh pasta, seafood and veal are prepared with a balance of traditions and imaginative presentations. Vine-covered, lemon walls, warm terra cotta tiles and Mediterranean decor will make patrons think they are in a small villa in Italy. Semi-formal attire; cocktails.. **Parking:** street. **Cards:** AX, DC, MC, VI.

LATIN CORNER RESTAURANT Lunch: $8-$10 Dinner: $10-$30 Phone: 403/228-5377 (36)
Nouvelle Latino
Location: Between 20th and 21st aves; 4 blks s of 17th Ave SW. 2116 4th St SW T2S 1W7. **Hours:** 11:30 am-2 & 5-10 pm, Fri & Sat-midnight. Closed major holidays. **Features:** On 4th Street, the funky bistro-style eatery is a fitting stop for a taste of Latin cuisine. This place is in the heart of the restaurant district. Casual dress; cocktails. **Parking:** street. **Cards:** AX, MC, VI.

LEO FU'S Lunch: $7-$8 Dinner: $8-$15 Phone: 403/255-2528 (79)
Chinese
Location: Just w of Hwy 2A (MacLeod Tr); across from "Ikon" Building. 511 70th Ave SW T2V 0P5. **Hours:** 11:30 am-2 & 4:30-10 pm, Fri-11:30 pm, Sat 4:30 pm-11:30 pm, Sun 4:30 pm-10 pm. **Closed:** 12/25. **Features:** The out-of-the-way restaurant serves consistently adventurous Szechuan and Mandarin cuisine. Dishes include crispy chunks of beef served in a savory orange sauce, a delicious salt-and-pepper squid and mouthwatering shrimp kung pao, which will challenges diners' thresholds for spice. Casual dress; cocktails. **Parking:** on-site. **Cards:** AX, DC, MC, VI.

LINA'S ITALIAN MARKET & CAPPUCCINO BAR Lunch: $4-$9 Dinner: $4-$9 Phone: 403/277-9166 (49)
Italian
Location: Corner of 21st Ave NW. 2202 Centre St NE T2E 2T4. **Hours:** 9 am-7 pm, Sat & Sun-5 pm. **Closed:** 3/28, 12/25. **Features:** The family-owned, coffee-bar-style restaurant has eight tables and over-the-counter ordering. Big food comes at small prices. On the menu are homemade pizzas, pasta dishes, soups, salads and Italian pastries. Check out the family-size tiramisu in the cooler. Service is casual and friendly. Cocktails. **Parking:** on-site. **Cards:** MC, VI.

MADISONS CAFE & BAR Lunch: $6-$10 Dinner: $8-$21 Phone: 403/220-9888 (43)
West Canadian
Location: Just nw of Crowchild Tr and 32nd Ave NW; in Brentwood Shopping Complex. 17-3802 Brentwood Rd NW T2L 1K8. **Hours:** 10 am-midnight, Sun-10 pm. **Closed:** 1/1, 12/25. **Reservations:** suggested. **Features:** The restaurant's atmosphere is cheerful, upbeat and funky, providing something for everyone. West Coast and Asian influences are reflected in imaginative versions of popular dishes, including brie and mango quesadillas, vermicelli salad rolls and traditional crust pizza. Cocktails. **Parking:** on-site. **Cards:** AX, MC, VI.

MAURYA Lunch: $10 Dinner: $8-$15 Phone: 403/270-3133 (50)
East Indian
Location: At 12th St NW. #100 1204 Kensington Rd NW T2N 3P5. **Hours:** 11:30 am-2 & 5-10 pm, Fri & Sat-11 pm. **Closed:** 12/25. **Reservations:** suggested. **Features:** You'll find excellent and tasty East Indian cuisine at Maurya's, with a menu that specializes in tandoori and includes many vegetarian dishes. The extensive lunch buffet has more than a dozen items, and you can spend hours dining in this relaxing, simple ambience. Casual dress; cocktails. **Parking:** street. **Cards:** AX, DC, MC, VI.

MISAI JAPANESE RESTAURANT Lunch: $9-$15 Dinner: $9-$15 Phone: 403/250-1688 (40)
Japanese
Location: From Barlow Tr, 1 km w at 32nd Ave. #7 1915-32 Ave NE T2E 7C8. **Hours:** 11 am-10 pm, Fri & Sat-11 pm. **Closed:** for dinner on holidays. **Reservations:** suggested. **Features:** Traditional decor awaits at the Northeast establishment, which is near many hotels and not far from the airport. The restaurant offers shuttle service to and from local hotels. Japanese art decorates individual booths, as well as rooms, in the dark-wood interior. The selection of sushi, sashimi, tempura and stir-fries offers good value for the dollar. Casual dress; cocktails. **Parking:** on-site. **Cards:** AX, DC, MC, VI.

(See map and index starting on p. 361)

MOTI MAHAL Lunch: $8-$12 Dinner: $10-$16 Phone: 403/228-9990 **61**

Northern Indian
Location: Just s of jct 17th Ave SW and 14th St SW; in a small strip mall. 1805 14th St SW T2T 3P1. **Hours:** 11:30 am-1:30 & 5:30-10 pm, Sat-11 pm, Sun 11:30 am-2 & 5:30-10 pm. Closed: for lunch holidays. **Reservations:** suggested. **Features:** Based on the cuisine of Northern India, the varied menu lists such dishes as buttery masalas, curries and the specialty chicken tikka with spicy yogurt and tomato sauce. Tapestries hang around the dining room, creating a royal environment. Casual dress; cocktails. **Parking:** on-site. **Cards:** AX, DC, MC, VI.

MUSE RESTAURANT & LOUNGE Dinner: $23-$35 Phone: 403/670-6873 **53**

International
Location: From Memorial Dr, just n on 10th St, just w on Kensington Rd, then just s at 10A St NW. 107-10A St NW T2N 4M7. **Hours:** 4 pm-midnight. Closed: 12/25. **Reservations:** suggested. **Features:** As one of the city's best new restaurants, the establishment presents a dazzling, innovative menu. The decor sets the scene for an upscale evening. The chef emphasizes regional items in the imaginative dishes. Desserts are delicious. Dressy casual; cocktails. **Parking:** street. **Cards:** AX, MC, VI.

THE NEWPORT GRILL AT THE INN ON
LAKE BONAVISTA Lunch: $14-$17 Dinner: $15-$25 Phone: 403/271-6711 **63**

Nouvelle
Continental
Location: 11.2 km se via MacLeod Tr, 0.8 km e on Anderson Rd to Bonaventure Dr, just s to Lake Bonavista Dr, then 1.2 km e to Lake Bonavista Shopping Centre. 205-747 Lake Bonavista Dr SE T2J 0N2. **Hours:** 11:30 am-2 & 5-11 pm. Closed: 5/23, 9/5. **Reservations:** suggested. **Features:** Lovely views of Lake Bonavista can be had from almost every table at the upscale restaurant. Among interesting and eclectic entrees are preparations of salmon, linguine and buffalo. Formerly called the Inn on Lake Bonavista, the restaurant has undergone a complete renovation and now boasts good food in fine surroundings. Casual dress; cocktails. **Parking:** on-site. **Cards:** AX, DC, MC, VI.

NICK'S STEAKHOUSE & PIZZA Lunch: $6-$12 Dinner: $8-$25 Phone: 403/282-9278 **44**

Steak House
Location: Just nw of Motel Village. 2430 Crowchild Tr NW T2M 4N5. **Hours:** 11:30 am-midnight. Closed: 12/24, 12/25. **Features:** A favorite with families, the restaurant has been a local fixture for more than 20 years. Steaks are grilled to perfection, and pizza is prepared with a variety of unusual toppings. The cozy decor and simple menu suit the tastes of all kinds of patrons. Casual dress; cocktails. **Parking:** on-site. **Cards:** AX, MC, VI.

OPEN SESAME Lunch: $7-$11 Dinner: $7-$11 Phone: 403/259-0123 **78**

Asian
Location: Just s of Hwy 8 (Glenmore Tr). 6920 MacLeod Tr S T2H 0L3. **Hours:** 11:30 am-10 pm, Fri & Sat-11 pm, Sun 4:30 pm-10 pm. Closed: 12/24, 12/25. **Reservations:** suggested. **Features:** Guests must descend the stairs to discover the restaurant's treasures. The Pan Asian noodle house features a do-it-yourself stir-fry station, as well as a full menu. Made-to-order dishes include sumptuous pot sticker appetizers and varied stir-fried noodle preparations. The rich decor of mahogany woods and dark, intimate corners sets the stage for a memorable meal. Casual dress; cocktails. **Parking:** on-site. **Cards:** AX, DC, DS, MC, VI.

ORIENTAL PHOENIX Lunch: $6-$10 Dinner: $6-$15 Phone: 403/250-8813 **41**

Vietnamese
Location: Corner of 27th Ave NE and Barlow Tr. 2493 27th Ave NE T2E 8M1. **Hours:** 11 am-8:30 pm, Fri-9:30 pm, Sat noon-9:30 pm. Closed major holidays; also Sun; ten days during Christmas. **Features:** Traditional Vietnamese food is served simply, but the service and decor is anything but. Upscale and sleek, the modern dining room is a busy place at lunch and around the dinner hour. Guests can sample tasty food in fine surroundings characterized by bold, contemporary colors and art. Among choices are salad rolls, rice vermicelli dishes and noodle soups. Semi-formal attire; cocktails. **Parking:** on-site. **Cards:** AX, DC, MC, VI.

OUZO GREEK TAVERNA Lunch: $6-$10 Dinner: $8-$16 Phone: 403/229-1400 **65**

Greek
Location: Corner of 20th Ave and 4th St SW. 2005 B 4th St SW T2S 1W6. **Hours:** 11:30 am-9 pm, Fri & Sat-10 pm. Closed major holidays. **Reservations:** suggested. **Features:** One of the newest additions to the Fourth Street restaurant scene, the family-owned Greek restaurant serves hearty, delicious fare prepared in the traditional sense. This spot is popular with the locals for its large seasonal patio, healthy portions and friendly service. Casual dress; cocktails. **Parking:** street. **Cards:** AX, MC, VI.

PALACE OF EATS Lunch: $5-$8 Dinner: $5-$8 Phone: 403/244-6602 **64**

Deli/Subs
Sandwiches
Location: Just n of 17th Ave SW. 1411 11th St SW T2R 1G7. **Hours:** 11 am-8 pm. Closed major holidays. **Features:** The funky, table-free eatery takes its name from a restaurant that stood in downtown Calgary from 1920 to the mid-60s. A true gem, this place specializes in Montreal-style bagels, creamy milkshakes and hand-sliced, stacked Montreal smoked meat sandwiches on Winnipeg rye. Check out the original mahogany paneling and benches, which give the restaurant an antique feel. Casual dress. **Parking:** street.

PEGASUS Lunch: $8-$16 Dinner: $8-$16 Phone: 403/229-1231 **57**

Greek
Location: At 11th Ave SW. 1101 14th St SW T3C 1C2. **Hours:** 11:30 am-2 & 5-10 pm, Fri-11 pm, Sat 5 pm-11 pm, Sun 5 pm-10 pm. Closed: 1/1, 12/25, 12/26. **Reservations:** suggested. **Features:** A favorite among the locals, the homey, traditional restaurant features a wide selection of Greek dishes, such as souvlaki and moussaka. Patrons who visit on the weekend may enjoy traditional Greek dancing and entertainment. Casual dress; cocktails. **Parking:** on-site. **Cards:** AX, DC, MC, VI.

PEKING DRAGON Lunch: $7-$12 Dinner: $7-$12 Phone: 403/228-1205 **35**

Chinese
Location: At 19th Ave SW. 1904 4th St SW T2S 1W3. **Hours:** 11 am-11 pm, Fri-midnight, Sat 4:30 pm-midnight, Sun 4:30 pm-10 pm. Closed major holidays. **Features:** A popular spot with the locals, the casual Chinese restaurant prepares traditional selections and offers fine, friendly service. Among choices are egg rolls, Peking duck and egg foo yong. Casual dress; cocktails. **Parking:** on-site. **Cards:** MC, VI.

(See map and index starting on p. 361)

PFANNTASTIC PANNENKOEK HAUS   Lunch: $7-$13   Dinner: $7-$13   Phone: 403/243-7757   77
Location: Just ne of jct Hwy 8 (Glenmore Tr) and Crowchild Tr; in a small strip mall. 2439 54th Ave SW T3E 1M4.
Hours: 11 am-8 pm, Sat & Sun from 8 am. Closed: Mon. **Reservations:** accepted, except Sun.
Features: The restaurant prepares 75 varieties of meal-size Dutch crepes served with various toppings. A
savory selection for dinner and a sweet choice for dessert make for a tasty meal. Diners should come with
an appetite since servings are huge. Soups and salads are also offered. Casual dress; cocktails. **Parking:**
on-site. **Cards:** AX, MC, VI.

Dutch

THE PLANET COFFEE ROASTERS   Lunch: $3-$6   Dinner: $3-$6   Phone: 403/244-3737   76
Location: At 4th St and 23rd Ave SW. 2212 4th St SW T2S 1W9. **Hours:** 7 am-11 pm, Sun from 8 am. Closed:
12/25. **Features:** The smell of coffee permeates the air at the simple coffeehouse in the heart of the trendy
Fourth Street district. A coffee roaster is inside, and patrons can buy their own freshly roasted beans or
Coffee/Espresso   settle in to sip a tasty "cuppa." Representative of the small selection of food are Jamaican patties, various
salads and sweet treats. **Parking:** street. **Cards:** MC, VI.

THE RANCHE RESTAURANT   Lunch: $12-$18   Dinner: $22-$30   Phone: 403/225-3939   81
Location: Off Bow Bottom Tr; in Fish Creek Provincial Park. 9005 15979 Bow Bottom Tr SE T2P 0Y8. **Hours:** 11:30
am-3 & 5-9 pm, Fri & Sat-10 pm, Sun 10:30 am-2:30 & 5-9 pm. Closed major holidays. **Reservations:** required. **Features:** Originally built more than 100 years ago as a wealthy gent's mansion
Regional   that lapsed into disuse, the house has been restored to its former grandeur. Creative, well-executed
Canadian   preparations draw on a variety of prairie ingredients and flavours. In a park in the southern part of Calgary,
the restaurant offers a superb setting and experience. Casual dress; cocktails. **Parking:** on-site. **Cards:** AX, DC, MC, VI.
Historic

RED SAFFRON   Lunch: $8-$15   Dinner: $8-$15   Phone: 403/541-1041   27
Location: 17th Ave SW at 8th St. 924 B 17th Ave SW T2T 0A2. **Hours:** 11:30 am-9 pm, Thurs-Sat to 10 pm.
Closed major holidays; also Mon. **Features:** In the trendy 17th Avenue area, the small, Persian kebab
house boasts a simple, chic decor, but the food is anything but simple. Representative of traditional food are
Persian   varied kebabs, salads and soups. The owners take the time to explain the history and tastes of the cuisine.
Casual dress. **Parking:** street. **Cards:** MC, VI.

RESTAURANT INDONESIA   Lunch: $7-$8   Dinner: $7-$11   Phone: 403/244-0645   60
Location: Corner of 16th Ave SW and 14th St SW. 1604 14th St SW T3C 1E2. **Hours:** 11:30 am-2:30 & 5-11 pm,
Sat 5 pm-11:30 pm, Sun 5 pm-9 pm. Closed major holidays; also Mon. **Reservations:** suggested.
Features: Choices such as satay, chili-basil chicken and gado-gado are among palate-pleasing offerings
Indonesian   that tease with rich, intense flavors. Fresh, colorful food jumps with memories of the Spice Islands. Try the
favourite aduk-aduk tempeh. Dressy casual; cocktails. **Parking:** street. **Cards:** AX, MC, VI.

ROCKY'S BURGER BUS   Lunch: $3-$6   Phone: 403/243-0405   54
Location: From MacLeod Tr, 2 km e at 46th Ave to 12th St. 4645 12th St SE T3E 4R7. **Hours:** 9 am-4 pm, Sat from
10 am. Closed major holidays; also Sun. **Features:** Inside an old transit bus in an industrial section of the
city are some of the best hamburgers in the province. Hand-made beef burgers, hand-cut fries and creamy
Canadian   milkshakes make this spot popular and distinctive. Plus, the food is cheap. Casual dress. **Parking:** on-site.

ROUGE   Lunch: $12-$24   Dinner: $22-$34   Phone: 403/531-2767   72
Location: Corner of 12th St and 8th Ave SE. 1240 8th Ave SE T2G 0M7. **Hours:** 11 am-2 & 5:30-10 pm, Sat from
5:30 pm. Closed major holidays; also Sun. **Reservations:** suggested. **Features:** In a residential area near
the zoo, the historic house has been converted into a quaint restaurant featuring contemporary French
French   cuisine. Seasonally inspired dishes range from ricotta ravioli to salmon and specialty soups. Each dish is a
work of art, and servers are highly attentive. The home maintains its historic roots with Victorian decor in each of its small dining
rooms. Casual dress; cocktails. **Parking:** on-site. **Cards:** AX, DC, MC, VI. **Historic**

SANTORINI GREEK TAVERNA   Lunch: $9-$15   Dinner: $14-$28   Phone: 403/276-8363   51
Location: Just s of 16th Ave and Centre St N. 1502 Centre St N T2E 2R9. **Hours:** 11 am-11 pm, Fri-midnight, Sat
noon-midnight, Sun 4 pm-10 pm. Closed: 1/1, 12/25, 12/26; also Mon. **Reservations:** suggested,
weekends. **Features:** Hearty Greek food, friendly service and a bustling, festive atmosphere define the cozy
Greek   taverna, which makes guests feel as though they've stepped into small town Greece. The menu features
traditional dishes, including mouthwatering moussaka, sumptuous souvlaki and spanakopita. Save some room for bougasta, a
distinctive custard dessert. Casual dress; cocktails. **Parking:** on-site. **Cards:** AX, DC, MC, VI.

SMUGGLER'S INN   Lunch: $9-$11   Dinner: $20-$25   Phone: 403/253-5355   33
Location: Just s of Glenmore Tr; attached to Open Sesame. 6920 MacLeod Tr T2H OL3. **Hours:** 11:30 am-11 pm.
Closed: 12/25. **Features:** One of the city's oldest steak and prime rib houses, this place lets guests sample
the all-you-can-eat soup and salad bar with any entree. The menu centers on steak, prime rib and chicken.
Steak House   The dark, cozy interior is a favorite with the business-lunch crowd. Casual dress; cocktails. **Parking:** on-site.
Cards: AX, DC, MC, VI.

SPOLUMBO'S DELI   Lunch: $4-$8   Phone: 403/264-6452   75
Location: Corner of 9th Ave SE and 13th St SE; in Inglewood. 1308 9th Ave SE T2G 0T3. **Hours:** 8 am-5:30 pm.
Closed major holidays; also Sun. **Features:** Owned by a group of former Canadian Football League
Stampeders players, the bustling, energetic deli serves varied meats, including outstanding, high-quality
Deli/Subs   sausage. This is a popular place at lunch, when patrons order at the counter and have their basket of food
Sandwiches   delivered to them. Casual dress. **Parking:** street. **Cards:** AX, MC, VI.

(See map and index starting on p. 361)

STEEPS THE URBAN TEAHOUSE **Lunch:** $3-$6 **Dinner:** $3-$6 **Phone:** 403/209-0076 ㉕

Canadian

Location: At 8th St SW; in Mount Royal Shops. 880 16th Ave SW T2T OA3. **Hours:** 10 am-11 pm, Fri & Sat-midnight. Closed major holidays. **Reservations:** not accepted. **Features:** The teahouse lures those who yearn for a pot of tea. It's a little-known fact that the Americanization of tea involved the creation of the tea bag, but loose teas—150 types, ranging from the rare and exotic to more common varieties—are the preference at the urban spot. Guests can take their time choosing from one of the many tins, which can be paired with soup and a sandwich, a samosa or wrap or one of the homemade desserts. Casual dress. **Parking:** street. **Cards:** MC, VI.

SUGO **Dinner:** $15-$32 **Phone:** 403/263-1115 (80)

Italian

Location: Corner of 9th Ave SE and 12th St; in Inglewood. 1214 9th Ave SE T2G 0S9. **Hours:** 5 pm-11 pm. Closed: 12/25, 12/26. **Reservations:** suggested. **Features:** In the funky Inglewood area, the upscale Italian eatery has a cozy decor to complement its innovative menu. Although the ingredients are not classically Italian, guests still can find daily selections of pasta and traditionally prepared food. The service is fine, and the atmosphere is casually elegant. Casual dress; cocktails. **Parking:** street. **Cards:** AX, DC, MC, VI.

SULTAN'S TENT **Dinner:** $15-$22 **Phone:** 403/244-2333 (58)

Traditional Moroccan

Location: Just w of 8th St SW. 909 17th Ave SW T2T 0A4. **Hours:** 5:30 pm-10:30 pm, Fri & Sat 5 pm-11 pm. Closed major holidays; also Sun. **Reservations:** suggested. **Features:** Eating is a communal event at the cozy Moroccan restaurant. Representative of the food are such delicacies as couscous, merguez, lamb, a five-course sultan's feast and other traditional dishes. And the traditional method of eating such creations is with the hands. The decor, which is inspired by the Berber culture of North Africa, offers intimate seating. Casual dress; cocktails. **Parking:** on-site. **Cards:** AX, DC, MC, VI.

SUSHI KAWA **Lunch:** $6-$10 **Dinner:** $7-$14 **Phone:** 403/802-0058 ㊴

Japanese

Location: Jct 4th St SW and 22nd Ave. 2204 4th St SW T2S 1W9. **Hours:** 11:30 am-2 & 5-9:30 pm, Thurs & Fri-10:30 pm, Sat 5 pm-10:30 pm, Sun 5 pm-9 pm. Closed major holidays. **Reservations:** suggested. **Features:** Fourth Street is a popular area for sushi restaurants, but what sets this one apart is the incredible and imaginative variety of appetizers and sushi platters. Patrons might try a vegetable sushi bowl—fresh vegetables atop sushi rice. Sushi pizzas, vegetable gyozas and an incredible variety of other appetizers are pictured on the colorful menu, making decisions difficult. Sumo wrestling often is shown on the large-screen TV, and the decor is simple and contemporary. Casual dress; cocktails. **Parking:** street. **Cards:** AX, MC, VI.

THAI BOAT **Lunch:** $5-$9 **Dinner:** $9-$12 **Phone:** 403/291-9887 ㉑

Thai

Location: Just w of Barlow Tr at 32nd Ave. 2323 32 Ave NE #108 T2E 6Z3. **Hours:** 11 am-2 & 5-10 pm, Fri-11 pm, Sat 5 pm-11 pm, Sun 5 pm-10 pm. Closed major holidays. **Features:** The restaurant is a must-stop for folks staying out by the airport. A sister property to Thai SaOn downtown, this place displays casual Thai decor inside, but the food—an array of traditional items—is anything but casual. Thai salad rolls wow the taste buds. This place is affordable and enjoyable at lunch, and the service is friendly and efficient. Casual dress; cocktails. **Parking:** on-site. **Cards:** AX, MC, VI.

WILDWOOD **Lunch:** $9-$13 **Dinner:** $11-$24 **Phone:** 403/228-0100 (73)

Regional Canadian

Location: Corner of 4th St SW and 25th Ave. 2417 4th St SW T2S 1X5. **Hours:** 11:30 am-3 & 5-10 pm, Fri & Sat-11 pm, Sun 5 pm-9 pm. Closed: 12/25. **Reservations:** suggested, weekends. **Features:** Rocky Mountain cuisine is the specialty at the upscale brew pub and dining room. Upstairs, diners enter into a beautiful loft-like dining room done in rich, warm tones and where sounds and smells float from the open-concept kitchen. The food, including Arctic char, flatbreads and chicken, is beautiful and imaginative. Guests can expect to enjoy some regional dishes in a warm, cozy atmosphere. Casual dress; cocktails. **Parking:** on-site. **Cards:** AX, MC, VI.

WILDWOOD BREWING PUB **Lunch:** $9-$15 **Dinner:** $9-$15 **Phone:** 403/228-0100 ㉒

Canadian

Location: Corner of 4th St SW and 25th Ave; downstairs from Wildwood Restaurant. 2417 4th St SW T2S 1X5. **Hours:** 11:30 am-midnight, Fri & Sat-1 am. Closed: 12/25. **Features:** In the basement of the Wildwood restaurant, the casual brewpub serves the same quality food in a more laid-back setting. Large vats of beer sit behind a glassed-in room, and the restaurant bustles particularly in the evenings and on weekends. A fantastic selection of locally brewed ales and lagers pairs with regional Canadian cuisine. Casual dress; cocktails. **Parking:** on-site. **Cards:** AX, DC, MC, VI.

WRAPTURE **Lunch:** $5-$8 **Dinner:** $5-$8 **Phone:** 403/228-5777 ㉓

Deli/Subs Sandwiches

Location: 17th Ave at 11th St. 1208 17th Ave SW T2T 0L2. **Hours:** 11 am-10 pm, Fri & Sat-11 pm. Closed major holidays. **Features:** If you're looking for something a little different, try Wrapture, where everything is made fresh to order. Located in the trendy 17th Ave district, this small fast food restaurant specializes in healthy choices, with a variety of wraps, salads and smoothies on the menu. For a quick, healthy inexpensive meal, this is an ideal choice. **Parking:** on-site. **Cards:** MC, VI.

The Calgary Vicinity

AIRDRIE pop. 20,382

———— **WHERE TO STAY** ————

SUPER 8 MOTEL-AIRDRIE   *Book at aaa.com*   Phone: 403/948-4188
(AA) (SAVE)   All Year [CP]   1P: $68-$80   2P: $70-$94   XP: $5   F12
▼▼▼ ▼▼▼   **Location:** Hwy 2, exit E Airdrie, 0.8 km e on Hwy 587 E, then 1.8 km s. 815 E Lake Blvd T4A 2G4.
    Fax: 403/948-4299. **Facility:** 49 units. 47 one- and 2 two-bedroom standard units. 3 stories, interior
Small-scale Hotel corridors. **Parking:** on-site, winter plug-ins. **Terms:** 3 day cancellation notice, weekly rates available, small
    pets only ($10 fee). **Amenities:** hair dryers. **Guest Services:** coin laundry. **Cards:** AX, DC, MC, VI.
    Special Amenities: free continental breakfast and free local telephone calls.

SOME UNITS

[icons] SD ▦ ⑪ ⊕ ⌨ DATA PORT ▤ / ✕ ▣ ▭ /
                    FEE

———— *The following lodging was either not evaluated or did not* ————
meet AAA rating requirements but is listed for your information only.

RAMADA INN & SUITES   Phone: 403/945-1288
[fyi]   Not evaluated. **Location:** 191 Eastlake Cres T4B 2B8. Facilities, services, and decor characterize a mid-range
    property.

COCHRANE pop. 11,798

———— **WHERE TO STAY** ————

BEST WESTERN HARVEST COUNTRY INN   *Book at aaa.com*   Phone: (403)932-1410
▼▼▼ ▼▼▼   5/16-2/28   1P: $109-$129   2P: $109-$129   XP: $7   F16
    3/1-5/15   1P: $89-$119   2P: $89-$119   XP: $7   F16
Small-scale Hotel   **Location:** Hwy 1A, 1 km sw on Hwy 22. 11 West Side Dr T4C 1M1. Fax: 403/932-8997. **Facility:** 49 one-bedroom
    standard units, some with whirlpools. 3 stories (no elevator), interior/exterior corridors. **Parking:** on-site,
winter plug-ins. **Terms:** small pets only ($7 extra charge, in designated units). **Amenities:** voice mail, irons, hair dryers. **Leisure
Activities:** sauna, exercise room. **Guest Services:** valet and coin laundry. **Cards:** AX, CB, DC, DS, JC, MC, VI.

SOME UNITS

[icons] ASK SD ▦ ⑪ ⌨ DATA PORT ▤ ▣ ▭ / ✕ VCR /
                    FEE

BOW RIVER INN

▼▼ ▼▼	6/1-10/31	1P: $99-$109	2P: $99-$109	XP: $10	F12
	5/1-5/31	1P: $79-$89	2P: $79-$89	XP: $10	F12
Motel	3/1-4/30 & 11/1-2/28	1P: $69-$79	2P: $69-$79	XP: $10	F12

Phone: 403/932-7900

Location: Hwy 1A, 1 km sw on Hwy 22. 3 West Side Dr T4C 1M1. Fax: 403/932-1880. **Facility:** 44 units. 41 one-bedroom standard units, some with efficiencies. 3 one-bedroom suites ($149-$169) with kitchens. 1 story, exterior corridors. **Parking:** on-site, winter plug-ins. **Terms:** office hours 7 am-midnight, small pets only ($7 fee). **Amenities:** hair dryers. **Guest Services:** valet laundry. **Cards:** AX, MC, VI.

SOME UNITS

(ASK) (S/D) [FEE] 🐾 (TI→) 📷 (DATA PORT) 🖥 🖨 🖵 / ⊠ /

SUPER 8 MOTEL-COCHRANE   *Book at aaa.com*

▼▼ ▼▼ ▼	5/16-8/31 [ECP]	1P: $130-$170	2P: $130-$170	XP: $10	F18
	3/1-5/15 & 9/1-2/28 [ECP]	1P: $100-$160	2P: $100-$160	XP: $10	F18

Phone: (403)932-6355

Small-scale Hotel   **Location:** Hwy 1A, 1 km sw on Hwy 22. 10 West Side Dr T4C 1M1. Fax: 403/851-0808. **Facility:** 72 one-bedroom standard units. 4 stories, interior corridors. *Bath:* combo or shower only. **Parking:** on-site, winter plug-ins. **Terms:** pets ($10 extra charge). **Amenities:** voice mail, irons, hair dryers. *Some:* video games, high-speed Internet. **Pool(s):** heated indoor. **Leisure Activities:** whirlpool, waterslide, exercise room. **Guest Services:** valet and coin laundry. **Business Services:** meeting rooms, PC (fee). **Cards:** AX, DC, DS, MC, VI.

SOME UNITS

(ASK) (S/D) [FEE] 🐾 (TI→) 🛏 ⊠ 📷 (DATA PORT) 🖥 🖨 🖵 / ⊠ / (VCR)

——— WHERE TO DINE ———

BLUE DOG CAFE

Lunch: $6-$10   **Dinner:** $8-$16   Phone: 403/932-4282

▼▼ ▼▼

Cajun

Location: Hwy 1A, 2 blks w. 110 Third Ave W T0L 0W0. **Hours:** 11 am-10 pm, Fri & Sat-midnight. Closed: 1/1, 12/25, 12/26, 12/26. **Reservations:** suggested. **Features:** With a touch of jazz and a taste of funk, the eclectic cafe offers an intimate, memorable dining experience in this small town. The dining room has a mere 15 tables. On the menu are Cajun specialty dishes, including jambalaya and catfish. Casual dress; cocktails. **Parking:** on-site. **Cards:** AX, MC, VI.

⊠

COFFEE CO & PIE EMPORIUM

Lunch: $6-$12   **Dinner:** $8-$17   Phone: 403/932-2111

▼▼ ▼▼

Continental

Location: Downtown. 216 1st St W T4C 1B3. **Hours:** 10 am-9 pm, Sat & Sun from 9 am. Closed: 1/1, 12/25. **Reservations:** suggested. **Features:** A cozy, country atmosphere awaits at the restaurant, known throughout the province for its "splurgeworthy" homemade pies, of which there are usually more than 54 varieties. Homemade comfort foods range from quiches to soups to sandwiches. Also available are afternoon tea and an extensive breakfast menu. Casual dress; cocktails. **Parking:** on-site. **Cards:** DC, MC, VI.

🍸 ⊠

OKOTOKS pop. 11,664

——— WHERE TO STAY ———

BEST WESTERN OKOTOKS LODGE   *Book at aaa.com*

(CAA) (SAVE)	6/1-10/15 [ECP]	1P: $119-$129	2P: $129-$139	XP: $7	F12
	10/16-2/28 [ECP]	1P: $109-$119	2P: $119-$139	XP: $7	F12
▼▼ ▼▼ ▼	3/1-5/31 [ECP]	1P: $109-$119	2P: $119-$129	XP: $7	F12

Phone: (403)938-7400

Location: Hwy 2, exit 2A, 4 km s to Southridge Dr. 22 Southridge Dr T1S 1N1. Fax: 403/938-1474. **Facility:** 64 Small-scale Hotel   units. 41 one-bedroom standard units. 23 one-bedroom suites, some with whirlpools. 2 stories, interior corridors. **Parking:** on-site. **Terms:** check-in 4 pm, cancellation fee imposed, [AP], [BP] & [MAP] meal plans available, pets ($5 extra charge). **Amenities:** dual phone lines, irons, hair dryers. *Some:* high-speed Internet. **Leisure Activities:** whirlpool, limited exercise equipment. **Guest Services:** complimentary laundry. **Business Services:** meeting rooms. **Cards:** AX, DC, DS, MC, VI. **Special Amenities:** free expanded continental breakfast and free room upgrade (subject to availability with advance reservations).

SOME UNITS

(S/D) 🐾 [FEE] (DATA PORT) 🖥 🖨 🖵 / ⊠ /

——— WHERE TO DINE ———

LA P'TITE TABLE

Lunch: $6-$9   **Dinner:** $14-$24   Phone: 403/938-2224

▼▼ ▼▼

French

Location: From Northridge Dr, 1 km e via Elizabeth Ave; across from information center. 52 N Railway St T1S 1J3. **Hours:** 11 am-1:30 & 5:30-8:30 pm, Sat from 5:30 pm. Closed: 3/28, 7/1, 12/25; also Sun & Mon. **Reservations:** suggested. **Features:** You'll enjoy this lovely gem tucked away in the suburbs. Its historic-looking exterior is complemented by artwork inside, and its menu specializes in eye-appealing contemporary-traditional French cooking. The friendly service is cordial and welcoming. Dressy casual; cocktails. **Parking:** street. **Cards:** MC, VI.

⊠

ON THE FRINGE

Lunch: $5-$8   **Dinner:** $5-$8   Phone: 403/938-1101

▼▼

Coffee/Espresso

Location: 1 km e; across from railway station. 66 N Railway St T1S 1J3. **Hours:** 7 am-8 pm, Sat 10 am-6 pm, Sun 10 am-5 pm. **Features:** For a quick and healthy bite to eat, look no further than On the Fringe. This funky coffee house serves up a good variety of healthy sandwiches, all served on multigrain organic breads, daily soups and superb salads. You might also be tempted by the dessert case, which features temptations such as rhubarb squares and lemon desserts. In the summer, you can pass away an afternoon on their patio, sipping lattes and enjoying this quiet neighborhood favourite. Beer & wine only. **Parking:** street. **Cards:** MC, VI.

⊠

STRATHMORE pop. 7,621

——— WHERE TO STAY ———

BEST WESTERN STRATHMORE INN   *Book at aaa.com*   Phone: (403)934-5777

CAA SAVE
	6/1-9/30	1P: $84-$179	2P: $90-$179	XP: $6	F12
	10/1-2/28	1P: $79-$179	2P: $84-$179	XP: $6	F12
	3/1-5/31	1P: $79-$149	2P: $84-$149	XP: $6	F12

Location: Trans-Canada Hwy 1, jct SR 817; centre. 550 Hwy 1 T1P 1M6. Fax: 403/934-5730. **Facility:** 81 units. 54 Small-scale Hotel one- and 14 two-bedroom standard units. 11 one- and 2 two-bedroom suites, some with whirlpools. 3 stories (no elevator), interior corridors. **Parking:** on-site, winter plug-ins. **Terms:** check-in 4 pm, [ECP] meal plan available, pets ($10 extra charge). **Amenities:** high-speed Internet (fee), voice mail, irons, hair dryers. **Pool(s):** small heated indoor. **Leisure Activities:** whirlpool, exercise room. **Guest Services:** valet and coin laundry. **Business Services:** meeting rooms, PC. **Cards:** AX, CB, DC, DS, JC, MC, VI. **Special Amenities:** free continental breakfast.

SOME UNITS

(S⊘ ⌂ ¶↕ ➥ ⬚ DATA PORT ⊟ ⊞ ⊡ / ✕ VCR /)
FEE

SUPER 8 MOTEL   *Book at aaa.com*   Phone: (403)934-1808

| | 7/8-8/1 [CP] | 1P: $107-$151 | 2P: $112-$151 | XP: $5 | F12 |
| | 3/1-7/7 & 8/2-2/28 [CP] | 1P: $77-$122 | 2P: $82-$122 | XP: $5 | F12 |

Motel   **Location:** Just n on SR 817. 450 Westlake Rd T1P 1H8. Fax: 403/934-1952. **Facility:** 49 one-bedroom standard units, some with whirlpools. 2 stories (no elevator), interior/exterior corridors. **Parking:** on-site, winter plug-ins. **Terms:** pets ($10 fee, in smoking units). **Amenities:** voice mail, hair dryers. *Some:* irons. **Guest Services:** coin laundry. **Cards:** AX, DC, MC, VI.

SOME UNITS

(ASK) (S⊘ ⌂ ¶↕ ⬚ DATA PORT ⊟ ⊞ ⊡ / ✕ VCR /)
FEE   FEE

TRAVELODGE STRATHMORE   *Book at aaa.com*   Phone: (403)901-0000

| | 6/1-9/15 | 1P: $89-$99 | 2P: $99-$109 | XP: $10 | F17 |
| | 3/1-5/31 & 9/16-2/28 | 1P: $79-$89 | 2P: $89-$99 | XP: $10 | F17 |

Small-scale Hotel   **Location:** Just n of Trans-Canada Hwy 1; at Ridge Rd. 350 Ridge Rd T1P 1B5. Fax: 403/901-0016. **Facility:** 121 units. 116 one-bedroom standard units, some with whirlpools. 2 one- and 3 two-bedroom suites ($139-$199), some with whirlpools. 3 stories, interior corridors. **Parking:** on-site, winter plug-ins. **Terms:** check-in 4 pm, package plans, pets ($10 fee). **Amenities:** high-speed Internet, dual phone lines, voice mail, irons, hair dryers. **Pool(s):** heated indoor. **Leisure Activities:** whirlpool, waterslide, exercise room. **Guest Services:** valet and coin laundry. **Business Services:** conference facilities, business center. **Cards:** AX, MC, VI.

SOME UNITS

(ASK) (S⊘ ⌂ ¶↕ ➥ ✕ DATA PORT ⊟ ⊞ ⊡ / ✕ /)
FEE

——— WHERE TO DINE ———

**STRATHMORE STATION
RESTAURANT & PUB**   Lunch: $6-$13   Dinner: $9-$16   Phone: 403/934-0000

CAA
Location: Trans-Canada Hwy 1, just w of jct SR 817. 380 Ridge Rd T1P 1B5. **Hours:** 8 am-1 am, Sun & Mon-midnight. Closed: 12/25. **Features:** Families and groups alike will enjoy the nostalgia of the Strathmore Station, which has a medley of comfort foods, including pizza, steak, pasta and oversize salad. Railway enthusiasts will enjoy the railway decor, complete with black and white photos from the railway days, large colourful murals and a special caboose dining car. Casual dress; cocktails. **Parking:** on-site. **Cards:** AX,
International   MC, VI.

✕

This ends listings for the Calgary Vicinity.
The following page resumes the alphabetical listings of
cities in Alberta.

CAMROSE pop. 14,854

——— WHERE TO STAY ———

NORSEMEN INN
▼▼ ▼▼

Small-scale Hotel

Phone: (780)672-9171

All Year   1P: $85-$179   2P: $85-$179
Location: Hwy 13 (48th Ave) at 65th St; west end of town. 6505 48th Ave T4V 3K3. Fax: 780/672-0130. **Facility:** 76 one-bedroom standard units. 4 stories, interior corridors. *Bath:* combo or shower only. **Parking:** on-site, winter plug-ins. **Terms:** weekly rates available. **Amenities:** irons, hair dryers. *Some:* high-speed Internet. **Leisure Activities:** Fee: game room. **Guest Services:** valet laundry. **Business Services:** conference facilities. **Cards:** AX, DC, MC, VI.

SOME UNITS

(ASK) [🛏] [🍴] [🍷] [📷] [DATA PORT] [💻] / [✕] [🔒] /

R & R INN AND SUITES CAMROSE
▼▼ ▼▼

Small-scale Hotel

Phone: (780)672-2292
F12

All Year [CP]   1P: $60-$149   2P: $70-$149   XP: $10
Location: Hwy 13 (48th Ave) at 66th St. 6508 48th Ave (Hwy 13) T4V 3A3. Fax: 780/672-2289. **Facility:** 44 one-bedroom standard units, some with whirlpools. 2 stories (no elevator), interior/exterior corridors. **Parking:** on-site, winter plug-ins. **Amenities:** voice mail, hair dryers. **Leisure Activities:** sauna, whirlpool. **Guest Services:** coin laundry. **Business Services:** meeting rooms. **Cards:** AX, MC, VI.

SOME UNITS

(ASK) [🍴] [📷] [DATA PORT] [🔒] [💼] [💻] / [✕] /

THE TRAVELLERS INN
▼▼ ▼▼

Motel

Phone: 780/672-3377

All Year [CP]   1P: $50-$89   2P: $64-$99
Location: Hwy 13 E (48th Ave) at 62nd St. 6216 48th Ave T4V 0K6. Fax: 780/679-6200. **Facility:** 40 one-bedroom standard units. 2 stories (no elevator), exterior corridors. **Parking:** on-site, winter plug-ins. **Terms:** office hours 7 am-11 pm, weekly rates available, pets ($10 extra charge). **Amenities:** high-speed Internet, voice mail. *Some:* hair dryers. **Guest Services:** valet laundry. **Cards:** DC, MC, VI.

SOME UNITS

(ASK) [S/D] [🛏] [🍴] [🔒] [💼] [💻] / [✕] /
FEE

——— WHERE TO DINE ———

MONTE CARLO RESTAURANT
▼▼ ▼▼

Continental

Lunch: $7-$10   **Dinner: $10-$17**   **Phone: 780/672-1040**
Location: Corner of 49th St and 48th Ave (Hwy 13). 4907 48th Ave T4V 0J4. **Hours:** 11 am-9 pm, Fri-10 pm, Sat 11:30 am-10 pm, Sun 11:30 am-9 pm. Closed major holidays. **Features:** One of the most popular places in town, the restaurant draws flocks of locals for lunch. Among menu choices are steaks, pizzas, pasta dishes and entree-size salads. Service is fast and friendly, and the atmosphere is casual. Cocktails. **Parking:** on-site. **Cards:** MC, VI.

[♿M] [✕]

CANMORE pop. 10,792

——— WHERE TO STAY ———

BANFF BOUNDARY LODGE
(CAA) (SAVE)
▼▼ ▼▼

Condominium

Book at aaa.com

Phone: (403)678-9555

3/1-10/9	2P: $99-$259	XP: $15	F17
12/23-2/28	2P: $99-$129	XP: $15	F17
10/10-12/22	2P: $99-$139	XP: $15	F17

Location: Just e of Banff National Park east gate, parallel to Trans-Canada Hwy 1, exit Harvie Heights Rd. 1000 Harvie Heights Rd T1W 2W2. Fax: 403/678-2851. **Facility:** 42 units. 4 one- and 38 two-bedroom units with kitchens. 1-2 stories (no elevator), exterior corridors. **Parking:** on-site, winter plug-ins. **Terms:** check-in 4 pm, 3 day cancellation notice, weekly rates available, package plans, pets ($15 extra charge). **Amenities:** video library (fee), hair dryers. **Leisure Activities:** whirlpool, childern's play area, picnic area with gas barbecue. **Guest Services:** coin laundry. **Business Services:** meeting rooms. **Cards:** AX, MC, VI.

SOME UNITS

[S/D] [🛏] [🐾] [VCR] [DATA PORT] [🔒] [💼] [💻] / [✕] /
FEE

BEST WESTERN GREEN GABLES INN
(CAA) (SAVE)
▼▼ ▼▼

Small-scale Hotel

Book at aaa.com

Phone: (403)678-5488

6/3-10/15 [CP]	1P: $119-$169	2P: $119-$169	XP: $10	F17
10/16-2/28 [CP]	1P: $99-$129	2P: $99-$129	XP: $10	F17
3/1-6/2 [CP]	1P: $99-$119	2P: $99-$119	XP: $10	F17

Location: 5.2 km e of Banff National Park east gate on Hwy 1A (Bow Valley Tr). 1602 2nd Ave T1W 1M8. Fax: 403/678-2670. **Facility:** 61 one-bedroom standard units, some with efficiencies. 2 stories (no elevator), interior corridors. **Parking:** on-site, winter plug-ins. **Terms:** check-in 4 pm, cancellation fee imposed, package plans. **Amenities:** irons, hair dryers. **Dining:** Chez Francois, see separate listing. **Leisure Activities:** whirlpool, steamroom, limited exercise equipment. **Guest Services:** valet laundry, area transportation (fee)-ski hills. **Business Services:** meeting rooms, PC (fee). **Cards:** AX, DC, DS, MC, VI. **Special Amenities:** early check-in/late check-out and free room upgrade (subject to availability with advance reservations).

SOME UNITS

[S/D] [🍴] [✕] [📷] [DATA PORT] [🔒] [💻] / [✕] [📠] /

BEST WESTERN POCATERRA INN
(CAA) (SAVE)
▼▼ ▼▼

Small-scale Hotel

Book at aaa.com

Phone: (403)678-4334

6/25-10/13 [ECP]	1P: $179-$199	2P: $179-$199	XP: $10	F17
5/21-6/24 [ECP]	1P: $129-$179	2P: $129-$179	XP: $10	F17
10/14-2/28 [ECP]	1P: $99-$159	2P: $99-$159	XP: $10	F17
3/1-5/20 [ECP]	1P: $99-$139	2P: $99-$139	XP: $10	F17

Location: 5.8 km e of Banff National Park east gate on Hwy 1A (Bow Valley Tr). 1725 Mountain Ave T1W 2W1. Fax: 403/678-3999. **Facility:** 83 units. 81 one-bedroom standard units, some with whirlpools. 2 one-bedroom suites ($199-$279) with whirlpools. 4 stories, interior corridors. **Parking:** on-site, winter plug-ins. **Terms:** check-in 4 pm, package plans, small pets only ($15 fee, in smoking units). **Amenities:** dual phone lines, voice mail, irons, hair dryers. **Pool(s):** heated indoor. **Leisure Activities:** sauna, whirlpool, steamroom, waterslide, exercise room. *Fee:* game room. **Guest Services:** valet and coin laundry, area transportation (fee)-ski areas. **Business Services:** meeting rooms, PC (fee). **Cards:** AX, CB, DC, DS, MC, VI. **Special Amenities:** free expanded continental breakfast and free local telephone calls.

SOME UNITS

[S/D] [🛏] [♿M] [🏊] [✕] [📷] [DATA PORT] [🔒] [💼] [💻] / [✕] /
FEE

BOW VALLEY MOTEL

Phone: (403)678-5085

CAA SAVE

6/18-9/22	1P: $100-$110	2P: $105-$120	XP: $10	F12
5/20-6/17	1P: $75-$85	2P: $80-$90	XP: $5	F12
9/23-2/28	1P: $55-$85	2P: $55-$85	XP: $5	F12
3/1-5/19	1P: $55-$65	2P: $55-$65	XP: $5	F12

Motel **Location:** Centre of downtown. 610 8th St T1W 2B5. Fax: 403/678-6560. **Facility:** 25 one-bedroom standard units, some with efficiencies. 1-3 stories (no elevator), exterior corridors. **Parking:** on-site, winter plug-ins. **Terms:** office hours 8 am-11 pm, weekly rates available, package plans. **Amenities:** voice mail, hair dryers. **Leisure Activities:** whirlpool. **Guest Services:** coin laundry. **Cards:** DS, MC, VI. **Special Amenities:** free local telephone calls.

SOME UNITS

CANADIAN ROCKIES CHALETS   *Book at aaa.com*

Phone: (403)678-3799

CAA SAVE

12/23-1/1	1P: $179-$269	2P: $179-$269	XP: $15	F17
3/1-10/9	1P: $99-$269	2P: $99-$269	XP: $15	F17
1/2-2/28	1P: $129-$219	2P: $129-$219	XP: $15	F17
10/10-12/22	1P: $99-$179	2P: $99-$179	XP: $15	F17

Condominium **Location:** 5.8 km e of Banff National Park east gate on Hwy 1A (Bow Valley Tr); Trans-Canada Hwy 1, exit Canmore. 1206 Bow Valley Tr T1W 1N6. Fax: 403/678-3413. **Facility:** Smoke free premises. 39 units. 19 two- and 20 three-bedroom suites with kitchens. 3 stories (no elevator), exterior corridors. **Parking:** on-site. **Terms:** office hours 8 am-10 pm, check-in 4 pm, 3 day cancellation notice, weekly rates available, package plans, pets ($15 fee, with prior approval). **Amenities:** high-speed Internet, voice mail, hair dryers. **Leisure Activities:** whirlpool, barbecue area. **Guest Services:** coin laundry. **Business Services:** meeting rooms, PC (fee). **Cards:** AX, DC, MC, VI. **Special Amenities:** free local telephone calls.

SOME UNITS
FEE / FEE

DAYS INN & SUITES   *Book at aaa.com*

Phone: 403/609-0075

6/1-9/15 [ECP]	1P: $149-$259	2P: $159-$259	XP: $10	F12
12/21-2/28 [ECP]	1P: $99-$200	2P: $119-$200	XP: $10	F12
3/1-5/31 [ECP]	1P: $89-$185	2P: $99-$185	XP: $10	F12
9/16-12/20 [ECP]	1P: $79-$185	2P: $89-$185	XP: $10	F12

Small-scale Hotel **Location:** 5.8 km e of Banff National Park east gate on Hwy 1A (Bow Valley Tr); Trans-Canada Hwy 1, exit Canmore, 1 km s, then just w. 815 Bow Valley Tr T1W 3B1. Fax: 403/678-2288. **Facility:** 29 units. 28 one-bedroom standard units, some with whirlpools. 1 one-bedroom suite ($185-$259) with whirlpool. 3 stories, interior corridors. *Bath:* some combo or shower only. **Parking:** on-site, winter plug-ins. **Terms:** check-in 4 pm, cancellation fee imposed. **Amenities:** irons, hair dryers. **Guest Services:** coin laundry. **Cards:** AX, DC, DS, JC, MC, VI.

SOME UNITS

FOUR POINTS BY SHERATON CANMORE   *Book at aaa.com*

Phone: (403)609-4422

CAA SAVE

6/1-10/15	1P: $149-$284	2P: $149-$284	XP: $15	F17
3/1-5/31 & 10/16-2/28	1P: $79-$204	2P: $79-$204	XP: $15	F17

Small-scale Hotel **Location:** Trans-Canada Hwy 1, exit 2nd St westbound; exit 3rd St eastbound, located on north side of Trans-Canada Hwy 1. #1 Silver Tip Tr T1W 2Z7. Fax: 403/609-0008. **Facility:** 99 units. 94 one-bedroom standard units, some with whirlpools. 5 one-bedroom suites. 3 stories, interior corridors. *Bath:* combo or shower only. **Parking:** on-site, winter plug-ins. **Terms:** cancellation fee imposed. **Amenities:** video games, high-speed Internet (fee), voice mail, irons, hair dryers. **Dining:** 6:30 am-2 & 5-10:30 pm, cocktails. **Leisure Activities:** whirlpool, hiking trails, exercise room. *Fee:* golf course privileges. **Guest Services:** valet laundry, area transportation-Canmore. **Business Services:** meeting rooms, PC (fee). **Cards:** AX, DC, JC, MC, VI. *(See color ad below & p 5)*

SOME UNITS

THE GEORGETOWN INN

Phone: (403)678-3439

6/20-9/19	1P: $139-$179	2P: $139-$179
3/1-6/19 & 9/20-2/28	1P: $109-$149	2P: $109-$149

Country Inn **Location:** 5.7 km e of Banff National Park east gate on Hwy 1A (Bow Valley Tr); Trans-Canada Hwy 1, exit Canmore. 1101 Bow Valley Tr T1W 1N4. Fax: 403/678-6909. **Facility:** Smoke free premises. 20 units. 19 one-bedroom standard units, some with whirlpools. 1 one-bedroom suite with whirlpool. 3 stories, interior corridors. **Parking:** on-site, winter plug-ins. **Terms:** office hours 7 am-11 pm, 3 day cancellation notice-fee imposed, [BP] meal plan available, package plans. **Amenities:** hair dryers. *Some:* DVD players. **Guest Services:** coin laundry. **Cards:** AX, DS, MC, VI.

SOME UNITS

GRAND CANADIAN RESORT VACATION CLUB   Book at aaa.com

Phone: (403)678-0018

CAA SAVE

6/1-9/30	1P: $309-$329	2P: $309-$329
3/1-5/31 & 10/1-2/28	1P: $259-$279	2P: $259-$279

Condominium

Location: Trans-Canada Hwy 1, exit Three Sisters Pkwy, 4 km n. Located at Residence Inn by Marriott. 91 Three Sisters Dr T1W 2X4. Fax: 403/609-0191. **Facility:** These luxurious, fully equipped condos, attached to the Residence Inn by Marriott, are in a scenic mountain setting just outside of town. Smoke free premises. 32 two-bedroom suites with kitchens and whirlpools. 3 stories, interior corridors. **Parking:** on-site, winter plug-ins. **Terms:** office hours 8 am-9 pm, check-in 4 pm, cancellation fee imposed. **Amenities:** video games, dual phone lines, voice mail, irons, hair dryers. **Pool(s):** heated outdoor. **Leisure Activities:** whirlpools, cross country skiing, exercise room. **Fee:** game room. **Guest Services:** complimentary laundry. **Business Services:** PC. **Cards:** AX, DC, DS, JC, MC, VI. **Special Amenities:** free local telephone calls.

HOWARD JOHNSON CANMORE/BANFF   Book at aaa.com

Phone: (403)609-4656

CAA SAVE

7/1-9/30 [CP]	1P: $124-$240	2P: $124-$240	XP: $15	F17
5/1-6/30 [CP]	1P: $79-$199	2P: $79-$199	XP: $15	F17
3/1-4/30 & 10/1-2/28 [CP]	1P: $59-$140	2P: $59-$140	XP: $15	F17

Small-scale Hotel

Location: 5.6 km e of Banff National Park east gate on Hwy 1A (Bow Valley Tr); Trans-Canada Hwy 1, exit Canmore. Located next to railway tracks. 1402 Bow Valley Tr T1W 1N5. Fax: 403/609-2773. **Facility:** 202 units. 200 one-bedroom standard units, some with whirlpools. 1 one- and 1 two-bedroom suites with whirlpools. 3 stories, interior corridors. **Bath:** combo or shower only. **Parking:** on-site, winter plug-ins. **Terms:** check-in 4 pm, package plans, pets ($15 extra charge). **Amenities:** voice mail, irons, hair dryers. **Fee:** video games, safes. **Dining:** 7 am-11 & 4-11 pm; 7 am-10 & 4-9 pm in winter. **Pool(s):** small heated indoor. **Leisure Activities:** whirlpool, waterslide. **Guest Services:** gift shop, valet and coin laundry. **Business Services:** meeting rooms, fax (fee). **Cards:** AX, CB, DC, DS, JC, MC, VI. **Special Amenities:** free local telephone calls and free newspaper.

SOME UNITS

THE LADY MACDONALD COUNTRY INN

Phone: (403)678-3665

CAA SAVE

6/1-9/30 [BP]	1P: $150-$225	2P: $150-$225	XP: $10	F12
3/1-5/31, 10/1-10/31 & 12/1-2/28 [BP]	1P: $110-$180	2P: $110-$180	XP: $10	F12

Country Inn

Location: Trans-Canada Hwy 1, exit Canmore; 5.7 km e of Banff National Park east gate on Hwy 1A (Bow Valley Tr). 1201 Bow Valley Tr T1W 1P5. Fax: 403/678-9714. **Facility:** A retreatlike ambience enhances this upscale country inn, which features individually decorated rooms and a Victorian-style dining room. Designated smoking area. 12 units. 11 one- and 1 two-bedroom standard units, some with whirlpools. 2 stories (no elevator), interior corridors. **Bath:** combo or shower only. **Parking:** on-site, winter plug-ins. **Terms:** open 3/1-10/31 & 12/1-2/28, office hours 9 am-5 pm, package plans. **Amenities:** voice mail, hair dryers. **Fee:** massage. **Leisure Activities:** **Guest Services:** gift shop, coin laundry, area transportation (fee)-ski shuttle. **Cards:** AX, MC, VI. **Special Amenities:** free full breakfast and free local telephone calls.

SOME UNITS

MYSTIC SPRINGS CHALETS & HOT POOLS   Book at aaa.com

Phone: (403)609-0333

12/24-2/28	1P: $259-$299	2P: $259-$299	XP: $20	F15
5/20-10/9	1P: $199-$299	2P: $199-$299	XP: $20	F15
3/1-5/19	1P: $179-$199	2P: $179-$199	XP: $20	F15
10/10-12/23	1P: $159-$179	2P: $159-$179	XP: $20	F15

Condominium

Location: Trans-Canada Hwy 1, exit Three Sisters Pkwy; 3 km w to Kananaskis Way. 140 Kananaskis Way T1W 2X2. Fax: 403/609-0264. **Facility:** Featuring an outdoor saltwater pool, a barbecue area and upscale accommodations, this property offers amenities from martini glasses to DVD players. Smoke free premises. 44 two-bedroom suites with kitchens. 2 stories (no elevator), exterior corridors. **Parking:** on-site. **Terms:** office hours 7 am-2 am, check-in 4 pm, 5 day cancellation notice-fee imposed, weekly rates available, package plans, pets ($15 fee). **Amenities:** DVD players, CD players, high-speed Internet, voice mail, irons, hair dryers. **Pool(s):** heated outdoor. **Leisure Activities:** whirlpool, limited exercise equipment. **Fee:** massage. **Guest Services:** valet and coin laundry. **Business Services:** meeting rooms. **Cards:** AX, DC, MC, VI. *(See color ad p 353)*

FEE

QUALITY RESORT-CHATEAU CANMORE   Book at aaa.com

Phone: (403)678-6699

CAA SAVE

7/1-9/30	1P: $184-$204	2P: $184-$204	XP: $15	F17
12/22-2/28	1P: $114-$169	2P: $114-$169	XP: $15	F17
3/1-6/30	1P: $114-$149	2P: $114-$149	XP: $15	F17
10/1-12/21	1P: $114-$134	2P: $114-$134	XP: $15	F17

Small-scale Hotel

Location: Trans-Canada Hwy 1, exit Canmore; 4.8 km e of Banff National Park east gate on Hwy 1A (Bow Valley Tr). 1720 Bow Valley Tr T1W 2X3. Fax: 403/678-6954. **Facility:** 93 units. 26 one-bedroom standard units. 67 one-bedroom suites, some with whirlpools. 4 stories, interior/exterior corridors. **Parking:** on-site, winter plug-ins. **Terms:** check-in 4 pm, cancellation fee imposed. **Amenities:** video library (fee), voice mail, hair dryers. *Some:* DVD players. **Dining:** 7 am-10 pm, cocktails. **Pool(s):** heated indoor. **Leisure Activities:** sauna, hot tub, lighted tennis court, ice skating, sports court. **Fee:** bicycles, massage. **Guest Services:** gift shop, valet and coin laundry, tanning facility. **Business Services:** meeting rooms, fax (fee). **Cards:** AX, DC, JC, MC, VI. **Special Amenities:** free newspaper.

SOME UNITS

RADISSON HOTEL & CONFERENCE CENTRE   Book at aaa.com

Phone: (403)678-3625

CAA SAVE

6/1-10/9	1P: $189-$269	2P: $189-$269	XP: $15	F17
5/1-5/31	1P: $124-$204	2P: $124-$204	XP: $15	F17
3/1-4/30 & 10/10-2/28	1P: $114-$194	2P: $114-$194	XP: $15	F17

Small-scale Hotel

Location: Trans-Canada Hwy 1, exit Canmore; 6 km e of Banff National Park east gate on Hwy 1A (Bow Valley Tr). 511 Bow Valley Tr T1W 1N7. Fax: 403/678-3765. **Facility:** 224 units. 214 one-bedroom standard units, some with efficiencies. 2 one- and 8 two-bedroom suites ($194-$269), some with kitchens and/or whirlpools. 2-3 stories, interior/exterior corridors. **Parking:** on-site, winter plug-ins. **Terms:** check-in 4 pm, [BP] & [CP] meal plans available, package plans, pets ($10 extra charge). **Amenities:** voice mail, irons, hair dryers. **Dining:** 6:30 am-10 pm, cocktails. **Pool(s):** heated indoor. **Leisure Activities:** whirlpool, steamroom, picnic area, playground, exercise room. **Fee:** massage. **Guest Services:** gift shop, valet and coin laundry, area transportation (fee)-ski hills. **Business Services:** conference facilities, administrative services (fee). **Cards:** AX, DC, MC, VI. **Special Amenities:** early check-in/late check-out and free room upgrade (subject to availability with advance reservations). *(See color ad p 377)*

SOME UNITS

FEE

RESIDENCE INN BY MARRIOTT

Book at aaa.com

Phone: 403-678-3400

CAA SAVE

6/1-9/30 [BP]	1P: $219-$279	2P: $219-$279	XP: $10	F17
5/1-5/31 [BP]	1P: $165-$225	2P: $165-$225	XP: $10	F17
3/1-4/30 & 10/1-2/28 [BP]	1P: $149-$209	2P: $149-$209	XP: $10	F17

Location: Trans-Canada Hwy 1, exit Three Sisters Pkwy, then 4 km n. 91 Three Sisters Dr T1W 2X4. **Small-scale Hotel** Fax: 403/609-0190. **Facility:** 119 units. 21 one-bedroom standard units with efficiencies. 85 one- and 13 two-bedroom suites with efficiencies. 5 stories, interior corridors. **Parking:** on-site, winter plug-ins. **Terms:** cancellation fee imposed, pets ($85 fee, $10 extra charge). **Amenities:** video games (fee), high-speed Internet, dual phone lines, voice mail, irons, hair dryers. **Pool(s):** small heated outdoor. **Leisure Activities:** whirlpools, cross country skiing, hiking trails, exercise room. **Guest Services:** complimentary evening beverages: Mon-Thurs, valet and coin laundry, area transportation-within 5 km. **Business Services:** meeting rooms, PC (fee). **Cards:** AX, DC, DS, MC, VI. **Special Amenities:** free expanded continental breakfast and free local telephone calls.

SOME UNITS

ROCKY MOUNTAIN SKI LODGE

Phone: (403)678-5445

CAA SAVE

6/27-9/18	1P: $110-$230	2P: $110-$230
6/1-6/26	1P: $85-$165	2P: $85-$165
3/1-5/31 & 9/19-2/28	1P: $65-$145	2P: $65-$145

Motel

Location: Trans-Canada Hwy 1, exit Canmore; 4.8 km e of Banff National Park east gate on Hwy 1A (Bow Valley Tr). Located in a commercial area. 1711 Bow Valley Tr T1W 2T8 (Box 8070). Fax: 403/678-6484. **Facility:** 82 units. 59 one- and 23 two-bedroom standard units, some with efficiencies or kitchens. 1-2 stories (no elevator), exterior corridors. **Parking:** on-site, winter plug-ins. **Terms:** office hours 7 am-11 pm, cancellation fee imposed, pets ($5 fee, in designated units). **Amenities:** voice mail, hair dryers. *Some:* high-speed Internet. **Leisure Activities:** sauna, whirlpool, ski & bike storage, playground. **Guest Services:** coin laundry. **Business Services:** meeting rooms, PC (fee). **Cards:** AX, MC, VI. *(See color ad below)*

SOME UNITS

RUNDLE MOUNTAIN LODGE

Phone: (403)678-5322

6/24-9/4	1P: $125-$135	2P: $125-$135	XP: $10	F17
12/26-2/28	1P: $64-$98	2P: $64-$108	XP: $10	F17
9/5-12/25	1P: $64-$79	2P: $64-$89	XP: $10	F17
3/1-6/23	1P: $69-$79	2P: $69-$79	XP: $10	F17

CAA SAVE

Motel

Location: Trans-Canada Hwy 1, exit Canmore; 4.8 km e of Banff National Park east gate on Hwy 1A (Bow Valley Tr). 1723 Bow Valley Tr T1W 1L7. Fax: 403/678-5813. **Facility:** 61 units. 47 one- and 6 two-bedroom standard units, some with efficiencies, kitchens and/or whirlpools. 8 one-bedroom suites ($179-$250) with kitchens. 1-2 stories (no elevator), exterior corridors. **Parking:** on-site, winter plug-ins. **Terms:** office hours 7 am-11 pm, check-in 4 pm, 7 day cancellation notice, pets ($7 fee, in designated units). **Amenities:** Some: DVD players, hair dryers. **Pool(s):** small heated indoor. **Leisure Activities:** whirlpool, playground. **Guest Services:** sundries, coin laundry. **Business Services:** meeting rooms. **Cards:** AX, CB, DC, JC, MC, VI.

RUNDLE RIDGE CHALETS

Phone: (403)678-5387

6/15-9/15	1P: $109-$215	2P: $109-$215	XP: $10	F17
3/1-6/14 & 9/16-2/28	1P: $84-$159	2P: $84-$159	XP: $10	F17

CAA SAVE

Cabin

Location: Trans-Canada Hwy 1, exit Harvie Heights Rd; 1 km e of Banff National Park east gate. Located in a quiet, rustic area. 1100 Harvie Heights Rd T1W 2W2. Fax: 403/678-2690. **Facility:** 37 units. 5 one-, 5 two- and 2 three-bedroom suites. 25 cabins. 1 story, exterior corridors. *Bath:* combo or shower only. **Parking:** on-site, winter plug-ins. **Terms:** office hours 9 am-10 pm, check-in 4 pm, 3 night minimum stay - seasonal, weekly rates available, pets ($10 extra charge, in designated units). **Leisure Activities:** cross country skiing, hiking trails, playground. **Guest Services:** sundries. **Cards:** AX, DC, MC, VI. *(See color ad p 354)*

THE STOCKADE LOG CABINS

Phone: 403/678-5212

6/16-9/15 [ECP]	1P: $109-$225	2P: $109-$225	XP: $15	F16
3/1-6/15 & 9/16-2/28 [ECP]	1P: $78-$145	2P: $78-$145	XP: $15	F16

CAA SAVE

Cabin

Location: Trans-Canada Hwy 1, exit Harvie Heights Rd; 1 km e of Banff National Park east gate. Located in a quiet, rustic area. 1050 Harvie Heights Rd T1W 2W2. Fax: 403/678-6463. **Facility:** Smoke free premises. 13 units. 5 one-bedroom standard units. 8 cabins. 1 story, exterior corridors. *Bath:* combo or shower only. **Parking:** on-site, winter plug-ins. **Terms:** office hours 8 am-11 pm, check-in 4 pm, pets ($10 extra charge). **Cards:** AX, MC, VI.

WINDTOWER LODGE & SUITES

Book at aaa.com

Phone: (403)609-6600

6/1-10/15	1P: $119-$399	2P: $119-$399	XP: $20	F
3/1-5/31	1P: $89-$399	2P: $89-$399	XP: $20	F
10/16-2/28	1P: $89-$299	2P: $89-$299	XP: $20	F

CAA SAVE

Condominium

Location: Trans-Canada Hwy 1, exit 1A (Bow Valley Tr), 1 km w, then n at Montane Dr. 160 Kananaskis Way T1W 3E2. Fax: 403/609-9328. **Facility:** Designated smoking area. 105 units. 49 one-bedroom standard units, some with whirlpools. 56 one-bedroom suites with kitchens. 2 stories, interior corridors. *Bath:* combo or shower only. **Parking:** on-site (fee) and street. **Terms:** check-in 4 pm, 3 day cancellation notice-fee imposed, weekly rates available, [BP] meal plan available, package plans, pets ($15 extra charge). **Amenities:** voice mail, hair dryers. **Dining:** 7 am-6:30 pm; to 3 pm in winter, cocktails. **Leisure Activities:** whirlpool, exercise room. **Business Services:** meeting rooms, PC (fee). **Cards:** AX, DC, MC, VI. *(See color ad p 397)*

─────── **WHERE TO DINE** ───────

BEAMER'S COFFEE BAR

Lunch: $3-$7   **Dinner:** $3-$7   **Phone:** 403/678-3988

Coffee/Espresso

Location: Trans-Canada Hwy 1, exit Canmore, 1 km w. 1702A Bow Valley Tr T1W 1N5. **Hours:** 6 am-9 pm. Closed: 12/25. **Features:** In a convenient spot, the contemporary coffeehouse draws both locals and those en route to the ski hills. Among healthy offerings are magnificent muffins, soups, breakfast bagels and, of course, Beamer's coffee. Big boy sandwiches are built on the premises with fresh, multigrain bread and a choice of toppings. For those with a sweet tooth, the display case features some tempting choices. Cocktails. **Parking:** on-site. **Cards:** AX, MC, VI.

BOLO RANCHHOUSE RESTAURANT & PUB

Lunch: $6-$10   **Dinner:** $8-$24   **Phone:** 403/678-5211

CAA

Steak House

Location: Corner of 8th St and 8th Ave. 838 8th St T1W 2B7. **Hours:** 8 am-midnight. Closed: 12/25. **Reservations:** suggested. **Features:** The restaurant is known for its Rocky Mountain-inspired preparations of seafood, chicken and AAA Alberta beef. Prime rib is served Thursday through Saturday. The log cabin and rustic stone fireplace contribute to a relaxed atmosphere. The patio is open in pleasant weather. On the menu are steaks, baby back ribs, fresh fish, seared chicken, beef tenderloin medallions, peppered shrimp, burgers and salads. Casual dress; cocktails. **Parking:** on-site. **Cards:** AX, DC, MC, VI.

CHEZ FRANCOIS

Lunch: $8-$10   **Dinner:** $15-$26   **Phone:** 403/678-6111

French

Location: 5.2 km e of Banff National Park east gate on Hwy 1A (Bow Valley Tr); in Best Western Green Gables Inn. 1602 2nd Ave T1W 1P7. **Hours:** 7 am-2:30 & 5-10 pm, Sat & Sun 7 am-3 & 5-10 pm. **Reservations:** suggested. **Features:** This fine-dining establishment features classic French cuisine, seafood and pasta. This is a popular place with locals. Casual dress; cocktails. **Parking:** on-site. **Cards:** AX, DC, MC, VI.

CRAZY WEED KITCHEN **Lunch:** $10-$15 **Dinner:** $15-$25 **Phone:** 403/609-2530
Location: Centre. 626 8th St T1W 2B5. **Hours:** 11:30 am-3:30 & 5:30-10:30 pm. **Reservations:** suggested.
Features: First-timers who aren't careful might pass by this gem. There are but 10 tables in the bright, airy,
Canadian lemon-yellow interior, which has a casual bistro feel to it. The food, however, is anything but casual. The
artistic chef mixes distinctive and flavorful ingredients to create delicious dishes. Choose the mixed green
salad with lemon grass vinaigrette or any of the specials of the day, which might include tea-smoked salmon or pomegranate
chicken. Service is friendly and casual. Casual dress; beer & wine only. **Parking:** street. **Cards:** MC, VI.

THE GRIZZLY PAW BREWING COMPANY **Lunch:** $8-$10 **Dinner:** $10-$12 **Phone:** 403/678-9983
Location: Downtown. 622 Main St T1W 2B5. **Hours:** 11 am-midnight, Fri & Sat-1 am. Closed: 12/25.
Features: A taste of local ales awaits at the popular brew pub, where beer is made on site. The menu
Canadian features a variety of hearty pub food, ranging from hamburgers to fish and chips, jalapeno poppers, soups
and salads. For a casual meal, this is a popular spot. Casual dress; cocktails. **Parking:** on-site. **Cards:** AX,
MC, VI.

LUNA BLUE **Lunch:** $8-$12 **Dinner:** $18-$22 **Phone:** 403/609-3221
Location: At 7th Ave; downtown. 107-721 Main St T1W 1J6. **Hours:** noon-3 & 5-10 pm. Closed: 12/25; also Wed
in winter. **Features:** Melange means "medley," a theme reflected in the entrees of the chic restaurant and
French tapas bar. French fusion influences are reflected in the dish preparations and ingredients. Guests might
choose a few of the extensive tapas selections and split them or instead decide on several entrees. The
cozy decor is conducive to lingering dinners and lunches. Service is fantastic. Semi-formal attire; cocktails. **Parking:** street.
Cards: MC, VI.

LUNA BLUE FRESH PASTA RESTAURANT **Lunch:** $9-$15 **Dinner:** $9-$15 **Phone:** 403/609-3221
Location: Downtown. 107-721 8th (Main) St T2S 0J6. **Hours:** 11:30 am-3 & 5-10 pm; hours vary in winter.
Closed major holidays; also Wed 10/1-6/14. **Reservations:** suggested. **Features:** Almost every pasta dish
Italian on the extensive menu contains fresh pasta made locally every day. On the main drag, the casual eatery
serves hearty and healthy options in a cozy environment. Casual dress; cocktails. **Parking:** street.
Cards: MC, VI.

MURRIETA'S WESTCOAST GRILL **Lunch:** $12-$24 **Dinner:** $12-$24 **Phone:** 403/609-9500
Location: Corner of 7th St and Main, on second level; downtown. 200, 737 Main St T1W 2B2. **Hours:** 11 am-10 pm,
Thurs-Sat to 1 am. **Reservations:** suggested. **Features:** Upstairs from street level, the classy, upbeat
West Pacific Rim restaurant boasts West Coast cuisine, including a variety of sandwiches and salads at lunch and heartier
dishes at dinner. Reservations are recommended at the popular spot in this mountain town, especially for
the dinner hour. Lending to the restaurant's atmosphere are cozy mountain decor, wooden accents, a lounge and a fireplace.
Casual dress; cocktails. **Parking:** street. **Cards:** AX, DC, MC, VI.

PATRINOS STEAKHOUSE & PUB **Lunch:** $7-$11 **Dinner:** $8-$20 **Phone:** 403/678-4060
Location: At 15th St. 1602 Bow Valley Tr T1W 1N5. **Hours:** 11 am-11 pm, Sun from 10 am. Closed: 12/25.
Features: The simple, family-run, roadside restaurant features a good selection of comfort foods, ranging
Continental from pizza and pasta to steaks. Guests can eat in the casual dining room or grab something in the lounge
next door. Expect friendly, attentive service. Casual dress; cocktails. **Parking:** on-site. **Cards:** AX, MC, VI.

QUARRY BISTRO **Lunch:** $8-$17 **Dinner:** $14-$28 **Phone:** 403/678-6088
Location: Downtown. 718 Main St T2E V36. **Hours:** 11:30 am-2:30 & 5-10 pm, Mon & Tues from 5 pm, Sat &
Sun 9 am-2:30 & 5-10 pm. Closed major holidays; also Tues in winter. **Reservations:** suggested.
Provincial French **Features:** Along the city's main street, the restaurant shows a contemporary, simple and chic decor. Guests
find comfortable surroundings and outdoor seating in the warmer months. The menu, a collection of locally
and seasonally inspired dishes, is rooted in the classic French and Italian Provincial style. On the menu might be macaroni and
cheese with three cheeses, veal saltimbocca and cranberry-ricotta ravioli. Servers are efficient and extremely friendly. Casual
dress; cocktails. **Parking:** street. **Cards:** AX, MC, VI.

SINCLAIRS **Lunch:** $8-$12 **Dinner:** $15-$25 **Phone:** 403/678-5370
Location: Corner of 6th Ave and 8th St. 637 8th St, Unit 1 T1W 2B1. **Hours:** 11:30 am-10 pm; 11:30 am-2:30 &
5:30-9 pm 10/15-4/30. Closed: 1/1, 12/25. **Reservations:** suggested. **Features:** In the heart of a small,
Rocky Mountain town, the quaint, two-story house is hard to recognize as a cozy restaurant. The varied
Canadian menu lists pasta dishes, sumptuous salads and regional specialties such as buffalo burgers. The
atmosphere is inviting, and the service is friendly. Casual dress; cocktails. **Parking:** street. **Cards:** AX, DC, MC, VI.

TAPAS RESTAURANT **Lunch:** $9-$20 **Dinner:** $9-$35 **Phone:** 403/609-0583
Location: Downtown; next to Paintbox Lodge. 633 10th St T1W 2A2. **Hours:** 8 am-11 pm. Closed major holidays.
Reservations: suggested. **Features:** Diners should come in groups to sample and savor the widest variety
Mediterranean of memorable tapas preparations. Drawing on influences from both Spain and Portugal, selections are
mouthwatering. Delicious favorites include fiery sweet potato tapas, eggplant and paella for two. A relatively
new addition to the city scene, the casual spot is popular with locals and visitors alike for its comfortable surroundings and
superb food. Casual dress; cocktails. **Parking:** street. **Cards:** MC, VI.

ZONA'S LATE NIGHT BISTRO **Dinner:** $10-$20 **Phone:** 403/609-2000
Location: Corner of 7th Ave and 9th St. 701 9th St T1W 2V7. **Hours:** 5 pm-10 pm. Closed: 1/1, 12/25.
Reservations: suggested. **Features:** The small bistro's cozy wooden interior sets the stage for a
Canadian memorable meal. Among hearty, healthy menu options are vegetarian lasagna and curry. Each dish is
served on a one-of-a-kind piece of pottery, created by the owner. A favorite with the locals, this place often
bustles on weekends. Casual dress; cocktails. **Parking:** street. **Cards:** AX, MC, VI.

——— *The following restaurants have not been evaluated by AAA* ———
but are listed for your information only.

CHEF'S STUDIO JAPAN   Phone: 403/609-8383
[fyi]   Not evaluated. **Location:** Just off Main St. 108-709 Main St. **Features:** If you are craving sushi, this restaurant, located between two art galleries, is a treat. This influence is also seen in the dishes, which are Japanese works of art!

SAGE BISTRO   Phone: 403/678-4878
[fyi]   Not evaluated. **Location:** Hwy 1A. 1712 Bow Valley Tr. **Features:** Along Highway 1A, the restaurant presents a menu of regionally inspired dishes. The setting is comfortable.

CARDSTON pop. 3,475

——— **WHERE TO STAY** ———

SOUTH COUNTRY INN   Phone: 403/653-8000
(CAA) (SAVE)   5/15-10/14   1P: $81   2P: $94   XP: $7   F12
🔷🔷🔷   3/1-5/14 & 10/15-2/28   1P: $58-$64   2P: $67-$74   XP: $7   F12
Location: On Hwy 2; centre. 404 Main St T0K 0K0 (PO Box 1710). Fax: 403/653-8004. **Facility:** 45 one-bedroom standard units, some with whirlpools. 2 stories (no elevator), interior corridors. **Parking:** on-site, winter plug-
Small-scale Hotel ins. **Terms:** package plans. **Dining:** 6 am-11 pm. **Pool(s):** small indoor. **Leisure Activities:** whirlpool. **Guest Services:** coin laundry. *Fee:* tanning facility. **Business Services:** meeting rooms. **Cards:** AX, MC, VI. **Special Amenities:** free local telephone calls.

SOME UNITS
[S/D] [🍴] [🏊] [🐾] [DATA PORT] / [✕] /

THOMSON'S RANGEVIEW RANCH [AP]   Phone: (403)653-2292
🔷   5/15-9/15 [AP]   1P: $165
Ranch   **Location:** 4 km s on Hwy 2, 10.7 km e on Hwy 501, from Jefferson sign, 16 km n on dirt road. (PO Box 28, Site 10). Fax: 403/653-1650. **Facility:** 4 one-bedroom standard units. 1 story, exterior corridors. **Parking:** on-site. **Terms:** open 5/15-9/15, 30 day cancellation notice-fee imposed. **Amenities:** video library. **Leisure Activities:** fishing, horseback riding. **Guest Services:** TV in common area, complimentary laundry, area transportation. **Cards:** MC, VI.

SOME UNITS
[✈] [W] [🕿] / [✕] [🛢] /

——— **WHERE TO DINE** ———

PIZZAS & CREAM   **Lunch:** $3-$7   **Dinner:** $3-$7   Phone: 403/653-4143
🔷   **Location:** Downtown. 325 Main St T0K 0K0. **Hours:** 11 am-10 pm, Fri-midnight, Sat-11 pm. Closed: Sun.
Pizza   **Features:** A play on words, the retro diner's name aptly describes its food: pizza and ice cream. Guests seat themselves in a red and silver booth and phone orders to the front. Whimsical, nostalgic memorabilia ranges from Trivial Pursuit to Lite Brite. Piping-hot pizza delivered atop an old-fashioned pizza stand tastes great with a frothy milkshake. Casual dress. **Parking:** street. **Cards:** AX, MC, VI.

[✕]

CLARESHOLM pop. 3,622

——— **WHERE TO STAY** ———

BLUEBIRD MOTEL   Phone: 403/625-3395
🔷🔷🔷   All Year   1P: $69-$74   2P: $69-$80   XP: $7   F
Motel   **Location:** 0.5 km n on Hwy 2. 5505 1st St W T0L 0T0 (PO Box 1888). Fax: 403/625-3395. **Facility:** 23 units. 15 one-bedroom standard units, some with efficiencies or kitchens. 7 one- and 1 two-bedroom suites ($74-$90), some with efficiencies or kitchens. 1 story, exterior corridors. *Bath:* combo or shower only. **Parking:** on-site, winter plug-ins. **Terms:** office hours 8 am-11 pm, cancellation fee imposed, pets (in smoking units). **Amenities:** hair dryers. **Guest Services:** coin laundry. **Cards:** AX, MC, VI.

SOME UNITS
(ASK) [S/D] [🐾] [🐾] [DATA PORT] [🛢] [▭] / [✕] (VCR) [📷] /

COCHRANE —See Calgary p. 391.

DEAD MAN'S FLATS

——— **WHERE TO STAY** ———

PIGEON MOUNTAIN MOTEL   Phone: 403/678-5756
(CAA) (SAVE)   6/1-9/30   1P: $95-$120   2P: $95-$120   XP: $5
🔷   3/1-5/31 & 10/1-2/28   1P: $65-$75   2P: $75-$80   XP: $5
Motel   **Location:** On Trans-Canada Hwy 1. Located at Dead Man's Flats Service Centre. 250 1st Ave T1W 2T8 (PO Box 8038, CANMORE). Fax: 403/678-5761. **Facility:** 16 units. 8 one- and 8 two-bedroom standard units. 2 stories (no elevator), exterior corridors. **Parking:** on-site, winter plug-ins. **Terms:** 4 day cancellation notice-fee imposed, small pets only. **Cards:** AX, MC, VI. **Special Amenities:** free local telephone calls and preferred room (subject to availability with advance reservations).

SOME UNITS
[S/D] [🐾] [🍴] [🍳] [🐾] [▭] / [✕] [🛢] [📷] /

DRUMHELLER pop. 7,785

——— WHERE TO STAY ———

BEST WESTERN JURASSIC INN   *Book at aaa.com*
CAA SAVE
Phone: 403/823-7700

3/1-10/15	1P: $130	XP: $10 F18
10/16-2/28	1P: $100	XP: $10 F18

Location: Hwy 9, se access to town. 1103 Hwy 9 S T0J 0Y0 (Box 3009). Fax: 403/823-5002. **Facility:** 48 units. 45 one-bedroom standard units, some with efficiencies. 3 one-bedroom suites with efficiencies, some with
Small-scale Hotel whirlpools. 2 stories (no elevator), interior/exterior corridors. **Parking:** on-site, winter plug-ins. **Terms:** check-in 4 pm, pets ($10 extra charge). **Amenities:** voice mail, irons, hair dryers. **Dining:** 6 am-10 pm, cocktails. **Pool(s):** small heated indoor. **Leisure Activities:** whirlpool, exercise room. **Guest Services:** valet and coin laundry. **Business Services:** meeting rooms. **Cards:** AX, MC, VI. **Special Amenities:** free local telephone calls and free room upgrade (subject to availability with advance reservations).

SOME UNITS

HEARTWOOD HAVEN COUNTRY INN
Phone: 403/823-4956

5/16-10/15	1P: $99-$260	2P: $110-$260	XP: $10 F13
3/1-5/15 & 10/16-2/28	1P: $99-$260	2P: $110-$260	XP: $10 F13

Bed & Breakfast   **Location:** Just w of Hwy 9; downtown. 356 4th St W T0J 0Y3. Fax: 403/823-4935. **Facility:** Smoke free premises. 5 units. 4 one-bedroom standard units, some with whirlpools. 1 one-bedroom suite ($260) with kitchen and whirlpool. 2 stories (no elevator), interior/exterior corridors. *Bath:* combo or shower only. **Parking:** on-site, winter plug-ins. **Terms:** office hours 9 am-9 pm, 2 night minimum stay - weekends, cancellation fee imposed, weekly rates available, package plans. **Amenities:** video library, hair dryers. **Leisure Activities:** spa. *Fee:* exercise room. **Cards:** AX, MC, VI.

SOME UNITS

INN AT HEARTWOOD MANOR
CAA SAVE
Phone: 403/823-6495

5/16-10/15	1P: $99-$260	2P: $110-$260	XP: $10 F13
3/1-5/15 & 10/16-2/28	1P: $79-$225	2P: $89-$225	XP: $10 F13

Country Inn   **Location:** Just e of Hwy 9; downtown. 320 N Railway Ave E T0J 0Y4. Fax: 403/823-4935. **Facility:** Classic old-fashioned touches like high beds with step stools distinguish this commercial-district inn, skillfully renovated to modern standards. Smoke free premises. 10 units. 9 one- and 2 two-bedroom standard units, some with whirlpools. 2 stories (no elevator), interior corridors. *Bath:* combo or tub only. **Parking:** on-site, winter plug-ins. **Terms:** office hours 9 am-9 pm, 2 night minimum stay - seasonal and/or weekends, cancellation fee imposed, weekly rates available, package plans, small pets only ($10 fee). **Amenities:** video library, hair dryers. **Leisure Activities:** spa. **Guest Services:** gift shop. **Cards:** MC, VI.

SOME UNITS

NEWCASTLE COUNTRY INN
Phone: 403/823-8356

5/15-10/15 [CP]	1P: $80-$100	2P: $95-$125	XP: $15
4/1-5/14 & 10/16-2/28 [CP]	1P: $65-$85	2P: $80-$100	XP: $15
3/1-3/31 [CP]	1P: $50-$80	2P: $65-$95	XP: $15

Country Inn   **Location:** 1.7 km sw on 3rd Ave W (turns into Newcastle Tr). Located in a residential area. 1130 Newcastle Tr T0J 0Y2. Fax: 403/823-2373. **Facility:** Smoke free premises. 11 one-bedroom standard units. 2 stories (no elevator), interior corridors. **Parking:** on-site, winter plug-ins. **Amenities:** hair dryers. **Cards:** MC, VI.

SUPER 8 MOTEL
Phone: (403)823-8887

5/15-9/30	1P: $129	2P: $149	XP: $10 F12
3/1-5/14 & 10/1-2/28	1P: $99	2P: $109	XP: $10 F12

Motel   **Location:** Off Hwy 9. 600-680 2nd St SE T0J 0Y0 (Box 447). Fax: 403/823-8884. **Facility:** 73 units. 69 one-bedroom standard units, some with whirlpools. 4 one-bedroom suites ($149-$219), some with whirlpools. 2 stories, interior/exterior corridors. **Parking:** on-site, winter plug-ins. **Terms:** cancellation fee imposed, [ECP] meal plan available, pets ($10 extra charge). **Amenities:** voice mail, irons, hair dryers. **Pool(s):** small heated indoor. **Leisure Activities:** whirlpool, waterslide, exercise room. **Guest Services:** valet and coin laundry. **Cards:** AX, DC, DS, MC, VI.

SOME UNITS

TASTE THE PAST BED & BREAKFAST
Phone: 403/823-5889

All Year	1P: $85	2P: $95-$100

Historic Bed & Breakfast   **Location:** Hwy 9, exit 2nd St W; centre. 281 2nd St W T0J 0Y0 (PO Box 865). **Facility:** This large home was built by a coal baron in 1910. Smoke free premises. 3 one-bedroom standard units. 3 stories (no elevator), interior corridors. *Bath:* combo or shower only. **Parking:** on-site, winter plug-ins. **Terms:** check-in 4 pm, 14 day cancellation notice-fee imposed. **Guest Services:** TV in common area. **Cards:** MC, VI.

——— WHERE TO DINE ———

SIZZLING HOUSE
CAA
Chinese
Lunch: $8   **Dinner:** $8-$16   **Phone:** 403/823-8098

Location: Downtown. 160 Centre St T0J 0Y0. **Hours:** 11 am-10 pm, Fri & Sat-11 pm; to 9 pm off season. Closed: 12/25, 12/26. **Features:** This is the place for Chinese food with Thai and Szechuan twists. The decor is simple, the service is friendly, and the food is delicious. The lunch buffet is a great value, but diners also can opt to order a la carte from the menu. Casual dress; cocktails. **Parking:** street. **Cards:** AX, MC, VI.

THAT'S CRAFTY CRAFT BARN & TEA ROOM
Canadian
Lunch: $5-$8   **Phone:** 403/677-2207

Location: 26 km w on Hwy 9. Box 1477 T0J 0Y0. **Hours:** Open 3/15-12/26; 10 am-5 pm. Closed major holidays; also Sun. **Features:** Located just outside of town, this craft shop and tea shop is a lovely place for fresh tea biscuits and a good bowl of soup. Casual dress. **Parking:** on-site. **Cards:** AX, MC, VI.

Destination Edmonton

pop. 666,104

E dmonton, nicknamed "Gateway to the North," was once a place for gold miners to stop and gather provisions for their rough journey into the icy Klondike.

D isappointed prospectors who eventually returned to help build Edmonton indeed struck gold: Today the shining city is a mecca of culture and recreation with its lovely theaters, parks and gardens.

Town of Stony Plain CVB

Heritage Walk Murals, Stony Plain. The history of Stony Plain is depicted on 22 murals painted by local artists on buildings throughout the city. (See mention page 76)

Golfing. Edmonton boasts more than 70 golf courses in its metropolitan area, including what is claimed to be Canada's oldest municipal course.

Town of Stony Plain CVB

© Paul A. Souders Corbis

A young equestrian. Horseback riding, popular with all ages, is available at many parks in Edmonton's North Saskatchewan River valley.

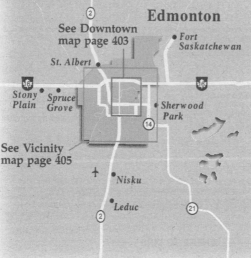

Edmonton

See Downtown map page 403

St. Albert

Stony Plain

Spruce Grove

Fort Saskatchewan

Sherwood Park

See Vicinity map page 405

Nisku

Leduc

Travel Alberta

Edmonton skyline. The city's contemporary skyline blends well with the greenery of its urban parklands and open spaces.

P laces included in this AAA Destination City:

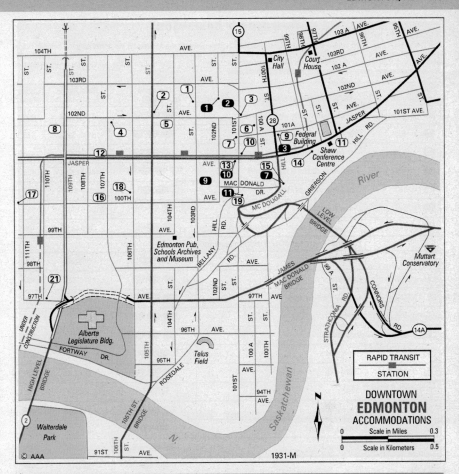

DOWNTOWN
EDMONTON
ACCOMMODATIONS

RAPID TRANSIT
■ STATION

Scale in Miles   0   0.3
Scale in Kilometers   0   0.5

1931-M

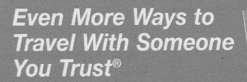

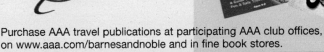

Downtown Edmonton

This index helps you "spot" where approved accommodations and restaurants are located on the corresponding detailed maps. Lodging rate ranges are for comparison only and show the property's high season; rates are per night, unless only weekly (W) rates are available. Restaurant rate range is for dinner, unless only lunch (L) is served. Turn to the listing page for more detailed rate information and consult display ads for special promotions.

Spotter/Map Page Number	OA	DOWNTOWN EDMONTON - Lodgings	Diamond Rating	Rate Range High Season	Listing Page
❶ / p. 403		Delta Edmonton Centre Suite Hotel	◆◆◆	$160-$279	408
❷ / p. 403		The Sutton Place Hotel, Edmonton	◆◆◆	$152-$202	408
❸ / p. 403		The Westin Edmonton - see color ad p 5	◆◆◆	$299	408
❼ / p. 403	CAA	**The Fairmont Hotel Macdonald**	◆◆◆◆	$169-$199 (SAVE)	408
❾ / p. 403		Alberta Place Suite Hotel	◆◆	$99-$149	408
❿ / p. 403	CAA	**Union Bank Inn**	◆◆◆	$162-$184 (SAVE)	408
⓫ / p. 403		Crowne Plaza Edmonton-Chateau Lacombe	◆◆◆	$99-$159	408
		DOWNTOWN EDMONTON - Restaurants			
① / p. 403		The Creperie	◆◆	$10-$23	409
② / p. 403		Characters	◆◆◆	$16-$39	409
③ / p. 403		Capitals Restaurant	◆◆◆	$16-$20	409
④ / p. 403		Khazana	◆◆◆	$10-$20	410
⑤ / p. 403		Ric's Grill	◆◆◆	$15-$27	410
⑥ / p. 403		Bistro Praha	◆◆	$6-$16	409
⑦ / p. 403		Chance	◆◆◆	$20-$35	409
⑧ / p. 403		Mikado	◆◆	$8-$16	410
⑨ / p. 403		Pradera Cafe	◆◆◆	$12-$30	410
⑩ / p. 403		Zenari's On First	◆◆	$8-$12	411
⑪ / p. 403		Hardware Grill	◆◆◆	$24-$37	409
⑫ / p. 403		Doan's	◆◆	$5-$15	409
⑬ / p. 403		Madison's Grill	◆◆◆	$22-$34	410
⑭ / p. 403		Riverside Bistro	◆◆	$13-$25	410
⑮ / p. 403		The Harvest Room	◆◆◆	$26-$42	410
⑯ / p. 403	CAA	**Il Portico**	◆◆◆	$18-$30	410
⑰ / p. 403		Il Pasticcion Trattoria	◆◆	$16-$25	410
⑱ / p. 403		Cafe Select	◆◆	$10-$20	409
⑲ / p. 403		La Ronde Revolving Restaurant	◆◆◆	$18-$35	410
㉑ / p. 403		The Copper Pot Restaurant	◆◆◆	$16-$29	409

EDMONTON
ACCOMMODATIONS

Scale in Miles 0 — 2.0
Scale in Kilometers 0 — 3.2

1930-M

© AAA

✈ Airport Accommodations

Spotter/Map Page Number	OA	EDMONTON INTERNATIONAL AIRPORT	Diamond Rating	Rate Range High Season	Listing Page
N/A	CAA	**Best Western Denham Inn and Suites, 8 km se of airport**	▽▽▽	$99-$129 SAVE	422
N/A		Edmonton International Airport-Super 8 Motel, 6 km se of airport	▽▽	$85-$101	422
N/A		Executive Royal Inn Hotel & Conference Centre, 3.5 km e of airport	▽▽▽	$150	422
N/A	CAA	**Ramada Inn Edmonton International Airport, 3.5 km e of airport**	▽▽	$89-$99 SAVE	422
67 / above		Nisku Inn & Conference Centre-Edmonton Airport, 3.5 km e of airport	▽▽	$139	423
68 / above		Quality Inn-Airport, 3.7 km e of airport	▽▽▽	$95-$115	424
69 / above	CAA	**Holiday Inn Express Edmonton Int'l Airport, 3.7 km e of airport**	▽▽▽	$99 SAVE	423

Edmonton and Vicinity

This index helps you "spot" where approved accommodations and restaurants are located on the corresponding detailed maps. Lodging rate ranges are for comparison only and show the property's high season; rates are per night, unless only weekly (W) rates are available. Restaurant rate range is for dinner, unless only lunch (L) is served. Turn to the listing page for more detailed rate information and consult display ads for special promotions.

Spotter/Map Page Number	OA	EDMONTON - Lodgings	Diamond Rating	Rate Range High Season	Listing Page
27 / p. 405		Hilton Garden Inn-West Edmonton	◆◆◆	$94-$194	414
28 / p. 405	CAA	Travelodge Edmonton West - see color ad p 367	◆◆	$99-$119 SAVE	416
29 / p. 405	CAA	Rosslyn Inn & Suites	◆◆	$92-$139 SAVE	416
30 / p. 405	CAA	Chateau Louis Hotel & Conference Centre - see color ad p 412	◆◆	$109-$199 SAVE	412
31 / p. 405	CAA	Mayfield Inn & Suites at West Edmonton	◆◆◆	$129-$189 SAVE	415
32 / p. 405	CAA	Best Western Westwood Inn - see color ad p 411	◆◆◆	$109-$160 SAVE	411
33 / p. 405	CAA	Days Inn & Suites West Edmonton - see color ad p 415	◆◆	$126-$289 SAVE	413
34 / p. 405	CAA	West Harvest Inn - see color ad p 417	◆◆	$89-$149 SAVE	417
35 / p. 405	CAA	Continental Inn	◆◆	$90-$105 SAVE	413
36 / p. 405		Glenora Bed & Breakfast Inn	◆◆◆	$70-$145	414
37 / p. 405	CAA	Chateau Edmonton Hotel & Suites	◆◆◆	$99-$349 SAVE	412
38 / p. 405	CAA	Wingate Inn Edmonton West	◆◆◆	$126-$171 SAVE	418
39 / p. 405	CAA	Holiday Inn Express Hotel & Suites Edmonton - see color ad card insert, p 415	◆◆◆	$139-$189 SAVE	415
40 / p. 405	CAA	Executive Royal Inn West Edmonton	◆◆	$125-$232 SAVE	413
41 / p. 405	CAA	Comfort Inn West	◆◆	$80-$110 SAVE	412
42 / p. 405		The Met Hotel	◆◆◆	$290-$350	416
43 / p. 405	CAA	Fantasyland Hotel	◆◆◆	$189-$329 SAVE	414
44 / p. 405	CAA	West Edmonton Mall Inn	◆◆	$129 SAVE	417
45 / p. 405		Campus Tower Suite Hotel	◆◆	$109	412
46 / p. 405	CAA	Holiday Inn Convention Centre (S.E. Edmonton)	◆◆◆	$109 SAVE	414
47 / p. 405	CAA	Argyll Plaza Hotel	◆	$84-$129 SAVE	411
48 / p. 405		The Varscona Hotel	◆◆◆	$225-$310	416
49 / p. 405	CAA	Best Western Cedar Park Inn	◆◆	$109-$169 SAVE	411
51 / p. 405		Hotel Selkirk	◆◆◆	$184	415
52 / p. 405	CAA	Delta Edmonton South Hotel and Conference Centre - see color ad p 413	◆◆◆	$111-$169 SAVE	413
55 / p. 405	CAA	Greenwood Inn Hotels	◆◆◆	$99-$139 SAVE	414
56 / p. 405	CAA	Holiday Inn Edmonton-The Palace - see color ad p 415	◆◆	$96-$182 SAVE	414
58 / p. 405	CAA	Travelodge Edmonton South - see color ad p 367	◆◆	$89-$115 SAVE	416
59 / p. 405	CAA	Travelodge Beverly Crest	◆◆	$87-$97 SAVE	416
60 / p. 405	CAA	Super 8 Hotel	◆◆	$89-$219 SAVE	416
		EDMONTON - Restaurants			
21 / p. 405		The Dish Bistro	◆◆	$8-$14	419
22 / p. 405		Fife N' Dekel	◆	$2-$6(L)	419
23 / p. 405		Mayfield Dinner Theatre	◆◆	$39-$89	420

Spotter/Map Page Number	OA	EDMONTON - Restaurants (continued)	Diamond Rating	Rate Range High Season	Listing Page
24 / p. 405		Tapestry Bistro	♦♦	$6-$15	421
25 / p. 405		Yiannis Taverna	♦♦	$14-$21	421
26 / p. 405		Royal Fork Buffet Restaurant	♦	$13	420
27 / p. 405		La Spiga	♦♦♦	$15-$35	419
28 / p. 405		Cafe Mosaics	♦	$5-$10	418
29 / p. 405		Highlevel Diner	♦♦	$10-$15	419
30 / p. 405		Packrat Louie's Kitchen & Bar	♦♦♦	$19-$30	420
31 / p. 405		Da-De-O New Orleans Diner & Bar	♦♦	$6-$13	418
32 / p. 405		O'Byrne's Irish Pub	♦	$6-$15	420
33 / p. 405		The King & I	♦♦	$7-$17	419
34 / p. 405		Von's Steak & Fish House	♦♦	$14-$32	421
35 / p. 405		Nagano	♦♦	$6-$10	420
36 / p. 405		The Blue Pear	♦♦♦	$59	418
37 / p. 405		Turtle Creek Cafe	♦♦	$6-$15	421
38 / p. 405		Unheardof Restaurant	♦♦♦	$23-$36	421
39 / p. 405		Three Muskateers French Creperie	♦♦	$12-$18	421
40 / p. 405		Death By Chocolate	♦	$6-$10	419
41 / p. 405		Bee-Bell Bakery	♦	$2-$9(L)	418
42 / p. 405		Billingsgate Seafood Market Lighthouse Cafe	♦♦	$11-$30	418
47 / p. 405		Chianti	♦♦	$7-$16	418
48 / p. 405		New Asian Village	♦♦	$10-$25	420
49 / p. 405		Manor Cafe	♦♦	$12-$25	420
50 / p. 405		Lemongrass Cafe	♦♦	$6-$17	420
51 / p. 405		Parkallen Restaurant	♦♦♦	$9-$17	420
52 / p. 405		Barb & Ernie's	♦	$10-$15	418
53 / p. 405		Jack's Grill	♦♦♦	$19-$24	419
54 / p. 405		Century Grill	♦♦♦	$22-$30	418
55 / p. 405		Sweetwater Cafe	♦♦	$10-$15	421
56 / p. 405		Seasons Grill	♦♦	$8-$20	420
57 / p. 405		The Funky Pickle Pizza Co	♦	$4-$10	419
58 / p. 405		Dante's Bistro	♦♦♦	$14-$22	419
		NISKU - Lodgings			
67 / p. 405		Nisku Inn & Conference Centre-Edmonton Airport	♦♦	$139	423
68 / p. 405		Quality Inn-Airport	♦♦♦	$95-$115	424
69 / p. 405	CAA	Holiday Inn Express Edmonton Int'l Airport	♦♦♦	$99 SAVE	423
		ST. ALBERT - Restaurant			
61 / p. 405		Ric's Grill	♦♦♦	$17-$30	424

DOWNTOWN EDMONTON (See map and index starting on p. 403)

——— **WHERE TO STAY** ———

ALBERTA PLACE SUITE HOTEL　*Book at aaa.com*　Phone: (780)423-1565　**9**
All Year　1P: $99-$149　XP: $10　F16
Location: Just s of Jasper Ave. 10049 103rd St T5J 2W7. Fax: 780/426-6260. **Facility:** 85 units. 24 one-bedroom
Condominium　standard units with kitchens. 61 one-bedroom suites with kitchens. 19 stories, interior corridors. **Parking:**
on-site, winter plug-ins. **Terms:** check-in 4 pm, cancellation fee imposed, pets ($10-$50 fee).
Amenities: high-speed Internet, voice mail, irons, hair dryers. **Pool(s):** heated indoor. **Leisure Activities:** whirlpool, exercise
room. **Guest Services:** valet and coin laundry. **Business Services:** meeting rooms, PC (fee). **Cards:** AX, JC, MC, VI.

SOME UNITS

CROWNE PLAZA EDMONTON-CHATEAU LACOMBE　*Book at aaa.com*　Phone: (780)428-6611　**11**
All Year　1P: $99-$159　2P: $99-$159　XP: $10
Location: Jct 101st St, MacDonald Dr and Bellamy Hill. 10111 Bellamy Hill T5J 1N7. Fax: 780/425-6564.
Large-scale Hotel　**Facility:** 307 units. 290 one-bedroom standard units. 17 one-bedroom suites. 24 stories, interior corridors.
Parking: on-site (fee) and valet, winter plug-ins. **Terms:** cancellation fee imposed, small pets only. **Dining:** La
Ronde Revolving Restaurant, see separate listing. **Leisure Activities:** exercise room. **Guest Services:** gift shop, valet laundry.
Business Services: conference facilities, business center. **Cards:** AX, DC, DS, JC, MC, VI.

SOME UNITS

DELTA EDMONTON CENTRE SUITE HOTEL　Phone: (780)429-3900　**1**
3/1-6/30 & 9/1-2/28　1P: $160-$279　XP: $10　F18
7/1-8/31　1P: $105-$279　XP: $10　F18
Large-scale Hotel　**Location:** At 102nd St at 103rd Ave. Located next to a shopping centre. 10222 102nd St T5J 4C5.
Fax: 780/426-0562. **Facility:** 169 units. 63 one-bedroom standard units with whirlpools. 106 one-bedroom
suites ($299-$399), some with whirlpools. 7 stories, interior corridors. **Parking:** on-site (fee) and valet, winter plug-ins.
Terms: cancellation fee imposed, small pets only (in smoking units). **Amenities:** video games (fee), high-speed Internet, dual
phone lines, voice mail, honor bars, irons, hair dryers. **Leisure Activities:** whirlpool, steamroom, exercise room. **Guest
Services:** valet laundry. **Business Services:** conference facilities, business center. **Cards:** AX, CB, DC, MC, VI.

SOME UNITS

THE FAIRMONT HOTEL MACDONALD　*Book at aaa.com*　Phone: (780)424-5181　**7**
(CAA) (SAVE)　All Year　1P: $169-$199　2P: $169-$199　XP: $10
Location: Just s of Jasper Ave. 10065 100th St T5J 0N6. Fax: 780/429-6481. **Facility:** Perched atop the river
valley, this historic hotel with a majestic ambience offers attentive service and upscale rooms, some with a
view. 198 units. 189 one-bedroom standard units. 9 one-bedroom suites ($379-$409) with whirlpools. 9
Large-scale Hotel　stories, interior corridors. **Parking:** on-site (fee) and valet, winter plug-ins. **Terms:** cancellation fee imposed,
pets ($20 fee). **Amenities:** video games, high-speed Internet, voice mail, honor bars, irons, hair dryers. *Some:* CD players. **Dining:** The Harvest Room, see separate listing. **Pool(s):** heated indoor, wading. **Leisure
Activities:** sauna, whirlpool, steamroom, 2 squash courts. *Fee:* massage. **Guest Services:** gift shop, valet laundry. **Business
Services:** conference facilities, business center. **Cards:** AX, DC, DS, JC, MC, VI.

SOME UNITS

THE SUTTON PLACE HOTEL, EDMONTON　*Book at aaa.com*　Phone: (780)428-7111　**2**
11/1-2/28　1P: $152-$192　2P: $162-$202　XP: $20　F15
3/1-10/31　1P: $142-$182　2P: $152-$192　XP: $20　F15
Large-scale Hotel　**Location:** 102nd Ave at 101st St. 10235 101st St T5J 3E9. Fax: 780/441-3098. **Facility:** 313 one-bedroom
standard units. 26 stories, interior corridors. **Parking:** on-site (fee) and valet. **Terms:** package plans, small
pets only ($10 extra charge, in kennels). **Amenities:** video games, voice mail, irons, hair dryers. *Some:* CD players, high-speed
Internet, dual phone lines, safes. **Dining:** Capitals Restaurant, see separate listing. **Pool(s):** heated indoor. **Leisure
Activities:** saunas, whirlpool. **Guest Services:** gift shop, valet laundry. **Business Services:** conference facilities, business
center. **Cards:** AX, CB, DC, DS, JC, MC, VI.

SOME UNITS

UNION BANK INN　*Book at aaa.com*　Phone: (780)423-3600　**10**
(CAA) (SAVE)　All Year [BP]　1P: $162-$173　2P: $173-$184　XP: $10　D
Location: Corner of 101st St. 10053 Jasper Ave T5J 1S5. Fax: 780/423-4623. **Facility:** Smoke free premises. 34
units. 33 one-bedroom standard units, some with whirlpools. 1 one-bedroom suite with whirlpool. 3-5 stories,
Small-scale Hotel　interior corridors. **Parking:** on-site. **Terms:** 3 day cancellation notice-fee imposed, package plans.
Amenities: voice mail, irons, hair dryers. *Some:* high-speed Internet. **Dining:** Madison's Grill, see separate
listing. **Leisure Activities:** limited exercise equipment. **Guest Services:** complimentary evening beverages,
valet laundry. **Business Services:** meeting rooms, PC. **Cards:** AX, DC, DS, MC, VI. **Special Amenities:** free full breakfast
and free newspaper.

SOME UNITS

THE WESTIN EDMONTON　*Book at aaa.com*　Phone: (780)426-3636　**3**
1/1-2/28　1P: $299　XP: $25　F17
3/1-12/31　1P: $289　XP: $25　F17
Large-scale Hotel　**Location:** 101st Ave at 100th St. 10135 100th St T5J 0N7. Fax: 780/428-1454. **Facility:** 413 units. 402 one-
bedroom standard units. 8 one- and 3 two-bedroom suites. 20 stories, interior corridors. **Parking:** on-site
(fee) and valet. **Terms:** package plans, small pets only. **Amenities:** video games, high-speed Internet (fee), dual phone lines,
voice mail, honor bars, irons, hair dryers. *Some:* fax. **Dining:** Pradera Cafe, see separate listing. **Pool(s):** small heated indoor.
Leisure Activities: saunas, whirlpool, exercise room. **Guest Services:** gift shop, valet laundry. **Business Services:**
conference facilities, business center. **Cards:** AX, CB, DC, DS, JC, MC, VI. *(See color ad p 5)*

SOME UNITS

(See map and index starting on p. 403)

──────── *The following lodging was either not evaluated or did not* ────────
meet AAA rating requirements but is listed for your information only.

EDMONTON HOUSE SUITE HOTEL   Phone: 780/420-4000

[fyi]   Not evaluated. **Location:** Just se of jct 102nd St and 100th Ave. 10205 100th Ave T5J 4B5. Facilities, services, and decor characterize a mid-range property.

──────── **WHERE TO DINE** ────────

BISTRO PRAHA   Lunch: $6-$16   Dinner: $6-$16   Phone: 780/424-4218   ⑥
▼▼▼   **Location:** Just n of Jasper Ave. 10168 100A St T5J 0R6. **Hours:** 11 am-1 am, Sat noon-2 am, Sun 4 pm-
Czechoslovak   midnight. Closed major holidays. **Reservations:** suggested. **Features:** Guests can enjoy meals at a
leisurely pace, while relaxing in antique furniture and appreciating the sounds of classical music. The warm,
inviting decor creates a pleasant atmosphere. On the menu are hearty portions of steak tartare, various
schnitzels and a selection of crepes for dessert. Casual dress; cocktails. **Parking:** street. **Cards:** AX, DC, MC, VI.   ✕

CAFE SELECT   Lunch: $8-$13   Dinner: $10-$20   Phone: 780/428-1629   ⑱
▼▼▼   **Location:** Just s of Jasper Ave. 10018-106 St T5J 1G1. **Hours:** 11:30 am-midnight, Thurs & Fri-2
Continental   am, Sun 5 pm-midnight. Closed: 1/1, 12/25. **Reservations:** suggested. **Features:** Patrons unwind in a
comfortable, intimate atmosphere while contemplating a menu of traditional favorites, such as rack of lamb
and beef tenderloin, as well as lighter fare ranging from salads to fondue. Patio dining is available in
season. Cocktails. **Parking:** street. **Cards:** AX, CB, DC, MC, VI.   ✕

CAPITALS RESTAURANT   Lunch: $12-$20   Dinner: $16-$20   Phone: 780/428-7111   ③
▼▼▼   **Location:** 102nd Ave at 101st St; in The Sutton Place Hotel, Edmonton. 10235 101st St T5J 3E9. **Hours:** 6-10:30
Canadian   am, 11:30-2:30 & 5:30-11 pm. **Reservations:** suggested. **Features:** In Sutton Place Hotel, the upscale
restaurant prepares selections of regional cuisine. Service is fine and friendly. Casual dress; cocktails.
Parking: on-site (fee) and valet. **Cards:** AX, CB, DC, DS, JC, MC, VI.   ⵏ ✕

CHANCE   Lunch: $9-$20   Dinner: $20-$35   Phone: 780/424-0400   ⑦
▼▼▼   **Location:** Just n of Jasper Ave at 101st St. 10155 101st St, Commerce Place T5J 4G8. **Hours:** 11 am-10 pm, Sat
Regional   from 5 pm. Closed major holidays; also Sun. **Reservations:** suggested. **Features:** In the heart of
Continental   downtown, the upscale, contemporary restaurant prepares a good selection of entrees with a regional flair.
The intimate atmosphere incorporates booths, as well as a New York-style long bar. The dedicated staff
provides attentive service and delivers tasty entrees ranging from salmon to risotto to maybe even venison.
Cocktails. **Parking:** on-site (fee). **Cards:** AX, DC, MC, VI.   ⵏ ✕

CHARACTERS   Lunch: $14-$18   Dinner: $16-$39   Phone: 780/421-4100   ②
▼▼▼   **Location:** Just n of jct 102nd Ave and 105th St. 10257 105th St T5J 1E3. **Hours:** 11:30 am-2 & 5:30-10 pm.
Canadian   Closed major holidays; also Sun. **Reservations:** suggested. **Features:** Polished hardwood floors, brick
walls and a glimmering open concept kitchen set the tone for this fresh contemporary restaurant. The
seasonally inspired menu changes, but can include a variety of offerings including duck, lamb, Alberta pork
and beef. An impressive wine list will ensure a memorable experience. Dressy casual; cocktails. **Parking:** on-site. **Cards:** AX,
DC, MC, VI.   ⵏ ✕

THE COPPER POT RESTAURANT   Lunch: $9-$15   Dinner: $16-$29   Phone: 780/452-7800   ㉑
▼▼▼   **Location:** From 109th St, just w of 97th Ave (one way street), then just n. #101, 9707-110th St T5K 2L9. **Hours:** 11:30
International   am-10:30 pm, Fri-midnight, Sat 5 pm-midnight. Closed: 12/25; also Sun. **Reservations:** suggested.
Features: Near the legislative buildings and overlooking the river valley, the intimate restaurant is tucked
away on the ground floor of an office tower. The innovative and eclectic menu lists several pasta dishes,
Alberta bison and seafood selections, all plated in hearty portions. Service is relaxed yet professional. Casual dress; cocktails.
Parking: on-site. **Cards:** AX, DC, MC, VI.   ⵏ ✕

THE CREPERIE   Lunch: $7-$12   Dinner: $10-$23   Phone: 780/420-6656   ①
▼▼▼   **Location:** Just n of 102nd Ave. 10220 103rd St T5J 0Y8. **Hours:** 11:30 am-10 pm, Fri-11 pm, Sat 5 pm-11 pm,
French   Sun 5 pm-9 pm. Closed: 12/25. **Reservations:** suggested. **Features:** Patrons can prepare themselves for
delectable French cuisine—including outstanding stuffed crepes—in the cozy restaurant, just below street
level. Menu options, such as seafood and vegetarian dishes, are varied enough to tempt any palate. Dressy
casual; cocktails. **Parking:** on-site (fee). **Cards:** AX, DC, MC, VI.   ✕

DOAN'S   Lunch: $5-$15   Dinner: $5-$15   Phone: 780/424-3034   ⑫
▼▼▼   **Location:** Just n of Jasper Ave at 107st St. 10130 107th St T5J 1J4. **Hours:** 11 am-10 pm, Fri & Sat-11 pm.
Vietnamese   Closed: 12/25. **Reservations:** suggested. **Features:** Visitors to the simple, neatly furnished and spacious
dining room can enjoy classic Vietnamese dishes, such as hearty rice and noodle soup. Several meat
dishes are expertly spiced by the restaurant's signature sauces. Cocktails. **Parking:** on-site. **Cards:** AX,
DC, MC, VI.   ✕

HARDWARE GRILL   Lunch: $11-$15   Dinner: $24-$37   Phone: 780/423-0969   ⑪
▼▼▼   **Location:** Corner of 97th St. 9698 Jasper Ave T5H 3V5. **Hours:** 11:30 am-2 & 5-9:30 pm, Fri & Sat 5 pm-10:30
Regional   pm. Closed major holidays; also Sun. **Reservations:** suggested. **Features:** Superb service, fine
Canadian   surroundings and a wonderful menu combine to create a truly memorable dining experience in the former
hardware store. The warehouse-like dining room is open and airy, and there are hints of history throughout.
Representative of seasonally inspired Canadian cuisine are such choices as bison, duck sausage and
cedar-planked salmon. But the grand finale—exceptional desserts, including warm gingerbread cake—will make guests want to
come back again. Dressy casual; cocktails. **Parking:** street. **Cards:** AX, DC, MC, VI.   ✕

(See map and index starting on p. 403)

THE HARVEST ROOM **Lunch:** $16-$23 **Dinner:** $26-$42 **Phone:** 780/424-5181 15
▼▼▼▼▼ **Location:** Just s of Jasper Ave; in The Fairmont Hotel Macdonald. 10065 100th St T5J 0N6. **Hours:** 6:30 am-10 pm,
Canadian Sat & Sun from 7 am. **Reservations:** suggested. **Features:** The atmosphere is warm and vibrant in the elegant surroundings of this restaurant. Views of the North Saskatchewan River are beautiful. Creative Canadian Prairie cuisine is prepared in the open-concept kitchen. Among tempting entrees are preparations of Alberta beef and venison. Professional, upscale service complements the delicious, upscale food presentations. Dressy casual; cocktails. **Parking:** valet. **Cards:** AX, DC, DS, JC, MC, VI. ⓶Ⓜ Ⓨ Ⓧ

IL PASTICCION TRATTORIA **Dinner:** $16-$25 **Phone:** 780-488-9543 17
▼▼ ▼▼ **Location:** Corner of 115th St and 100th Ave. 11520 100th Ave T5K 0J7. **Hours:** 5 pm-10 pm. Closed: Sun.
Italian **Reservations:** not accepted. **Features:** Just a block south of Jasper Avenue, the funky little trattoria has a light and lively dining room, complete with an open concept kitchen. Boldly painted walls and checkered tablecloths set the scene. Guests can choose from homemade pastas and traditional Italian meat dishes. Servers are prompt and friendly. Casual dress; cocktails. **Parking:** on-site (fee). **Cards:** AX, MC, VI. Ⓧ

IL PORTICO *Menu on aaa.com* **Lunch:** $10-$15 **Dinner:** $18-$30 **Phone:** 780/424-0707 16
ⒸⒶⒶ **Location:** Corner of 100th Ave and 107th St. 10012 107th St T5J 1J2. **Hours:** 11:30 am-2:30 & 5:30-10:30 pm, Sat
▼▼▼▼ from 5:30 pm. Closed: Sun. **Reservations:** suggested. **Features:** A popular spot with the business crowd,
Italian the innovative downtown restaurant has been recognized for its notable wine selection. Among offerings on the seasonally inspired menus are beef tenderloin and various creative pasta dishes. Downstairs is a large wine cellar, suitable for small dinner gatherings. Casual dress; cocktails. **Parking:** on-site. **Cards:** AX, DC, MC, VI. Ⓨ Ⓧ

KHAZANA **Lunch:** $11 **Dinner:** $10-$20 **Phone:** 780/702-0330 4
▼▼▼▼▼ **Location:** Corner of 102nd Ave. 10177 107 St T5J 1J5. **Hours:** 11:30 am-2 & 5-9:30 pm, Fri-10:30 pm, Sat 5 pm-
Indian 10:30 pm, Sun 5 pm-9:30 pm. Closed major holidays. **Reservations:** suggested. **Features:** Khazana's features an authentic, tasty tandoori cuisine of papadams, fresh Nan bread, peshawari kebab (lamb), boti kebab (prime beef) and murgh tandoori (chicken). The inviting, upscale decor includes original artwork from New Delhi and costumed servers. Casual dress; cocktails. **Parking:** street. **Cards:** AX, DC, MC, VI. Ⓧ

LA RONDE REVOLVING RESTAURANT **Dinner:** $18-$35 **Phone:** 780/428-6611 19
▼▼▼▼ **Location:** Jct 101st St, MacDonald Dr and Bellamy Hill; in Crowne Plaza Edmonton-Chateau Lacombe. 10111 Bellamy
Canadian Hill T5J 1N7. **Hours:** 5:30 pm-10:30 pm, Sun also 10:30 am-2 pm. Closed: week after New Years. **Reservations:** suggested. **Features:** The revolving rooftop restaurant offers a panoramic view of the city. The atmosphere is elegant, yet casual, and classic European cuisine reflects Asian influences. Prix fixe selections cater to couples and include aperitifs and champagnes. Dressy casual; cocktails. **Parking:** on-site (fee) and valet. **Cards:** AX, DC, DS, JC, MC, VI. Ⓨ Ⓧ

MADISON'S GRILL **Lunch:** $10-$15 **Dinner:** $22-$34 **Phone:** 780/421-7171 13
▼▼▼▼ **Location:** Corner of 101st St; in Union Bank Inn. 10053 Jasper Ave T5J 1S5. **Hours:** 7 am-10 pm, Fri-11 pm, Sat 8
Continental am-11 & 5-11 pm, Sun 8 am-11 & 5-9 pm. **Reservations:** suggested. **Features:** The popular, trendy restaurant features food flavored with contemporary touches. Patrons can tempt their taste buds with crab cakes prepared in tempura batter. Among the wide selection of main courses are preparations of halibut, snapper and lamb chops. After dinner, guests can relax in the small library lounge with a sumptuous dessert. Dressy casual; cocktails. **Parking:** on-site. **Cards:** AX, DC, DS, MC, VI. Ⓨ Ⓧ

MIKADO **Lunch:** $6-$11 **Dinner:** $8-$16 **Phone:** 780/425-8096 8
▼▼▼ ▼▼▼ **Location:** Jct 103rd Ave and 109th St; in shopping plaza. 10350 109th St T5J 4X9. **Hours:** 11 am-10 pm, Fri & Sat-
Japanese 11 pm, Sun 4 pm-9 pm. Closed: 12/25. **Reservations:** suggested. **Features:** The eatery is a hot spot for sushi in the capital city. As they enter, patrons are greeted with a warm towel and a friendly smile. The bright, contemporary dining room offers a variety of seating options—in private dining rooms, in the main restaurant or at the sushi bar. The chef is a master, creating a wide variety of sushi and sashimi. **Parking:** on-site. **Cards:** AX, MC, VI. ⓶Ⓜ

PRADERA CAFE **Lunch:** $9-$15 **Dinner:** $12-$30 **Phone:** 780/493-8994 9
▼▼▼▼ **Location:** 101st St at 100th St; in the Westin Edmonton. 10135 100th St T5J 0N7. **Hours:** 6:30 am-10 pm, Sat &
Canadian Sun 7 am-10 pm. **Reservations:** suggested. **Features:** The elegant dining room invites diners to peruse an excellent menu, which blends International influences with regional ingredients. Among dishes to satisfy any appetite are superbly presented English-cut prime rib, fresh lake trout and chateaubriand. Casual dress; cocktails. **Parking:** on-site (fee) and valet. **Cards:** AX, DC, MC, VI. Ⓨ Ⓧ

RIC'S GRILL **Lunch:** $9-$17 **Dinner:** $15-$27 **Phone:** 780/429-4333 5
▼▼▼▼ **Location:** Corner of 104th St and 102nd Ave; in historic Metals building. 10190 104th St T5J 1A7. **Hours:** 11:30 am-2
Steak & Seafood & 4:30-10 pm. Closed major holidays. **Reservations:** suggested. **Features:** Downtown in the historic Metals Building, the upscale steak-and-seafood house offers a wide variety of Sterling Silver cuts, as well as an extensive appetizer collection. Casual dress; cocktails. **Parking:** street. **Cards:** AX, MC, VI. **Historic** ⓶Ⓜ Ⓨ Ⓧ

RIVERSIDE BISTRO **Lunch:** $10-$15 **Dinner:** $13-$25 **Phone:** 780/945-4747 14
▼▼▼▼ **Location:** Just s of Jasper Ave at Thornton Ct and 99th St; in Courtyard by Marriott Edmonton. One Thornton Ct T5J
Canadian ZE7. **Hours:** 6:30 am-10 & 11-11 pm, Sat & Sun from 7 am. **Reservations:** suggested. **Features:** The restaurant affords spectacular views. Guests can sit on one of the city's best and largest patios to take in sights along the river valley while savoring a glass of wine with contemporary Canadian cuisine. Inside, an upscale lobby lounge adjoins the restaurant, and the decor and service are just as upscale. Casual dress; cocktails. **Parking:** on-site (fee) and valet. **Cards:** AX, DC, MC, VI. ⓶Ⓜ Ⓨ Ⓧ

(See map and index starting on p. 403)

ZENARI'S ON FIRST   Lunch: $8-$12   Dinner: $8-$12   Phone: 780/425-6151   ⑩
♦♦♦ ♦♦♦   **Location:** Just n of Jasper Ave. 10117 101st St T5M 1G3. **Hours:** 11 am-10 pm, Fri-midnight, Sat 4 pm-10 pm.
Italian   Closed major holidays; also Sun. **Reservations:** suggested. **Features:** The small downtown bistro-style
eatery presents a menu of Italian food. Smells and sounds from the open-concept exhibition kitchen will
activate and trigger the senses. Among choices are risotto, focaccia sandwiches and oversize salads. This
is a popular spot with the lunch crowd. Casual dress; cocktails. **Parking:** street. **Cards:** AX, DC, MC, VI.   🚹Ⓜ ✕

EDMONTON pop. 666,104   (See map and index starting on p. 405)

──── WHERE TO STAY ────

ARGYLL PLAZA HOTEL   Phone: (780)438-5876   ㊼
Ⓐ Ⓢ   All Year [CP]   1P: $84-$129   2P: $84-$129   XP: $10   F17
♦♦♦   **Location:** 63rd Ave at 99th St. Located in a strip mall. 9933 63rd Ave T6E 6C9. Fax: 780/436-5813. **Facility:** 48
one-bedroom standard units, some with efficiencies and/or whirlpools. 3 stories, interior corridors. **Parking:**
Small-scale Hotel   on-site, winter plug-ins. **Terms:** check-in 4 pm, cancellation fee imposed, package plans, pets ($5 extra
charge, in smoking units). **Amenities:** voice mail, hair dryers. **Dining:** 6:30 am-10:30 pm, Sat & Sun from 7
am. **Leisure Activities:** sauna, whirlpool. **Guest Services:** valet laundry, area transportation-West
Edmonton Mall. **Business Services:** meeting rooms. **Cards:** AX, DC, MC, VI.

SOME UNITS
🐾 🍴 📺 📠 💻 / ✕ 🔌 /
FEE

BEST WESTERN CEDAR PARK INN   *Book at aaa.com*   Phone: (780)434-7411   ㊾
Ⓐ Ⓢ   All Year [ECP]   1P: $109-$169   2P: $119-$169   XP: $10   F17
♦♦♦ ♦♦♦   **Location:** Hwy 2 (Gateway Blvd) at 51st Ave. 5116 Gateway Blvd T6H 2H4. Fax: 780/437-4836. **Facility:** 190 units.
187 one-bedroom standard units, some with whirlpools. 3 one-bedroom suites, some with whirlpools. 5
Small-scale Hotel   stories, interior corridors. **Parking:** on-site, winter plug-ins. **Terms:** 3 day cancellation notice, package plans,
pets ($10 fee, in limited units). **Amenities:** video games, high-speed Internet (fee), voice mail, irons, hair
dryers. *Some:* dual phone lines. **Dining:** Seasons Grill, see separate listing. **Pool(s):** small heated indoor.
Leisure Activities: saunas, limited exercise equipment. **Guest Services:** gift shop, valet laundry, area transportation-West
Edmonton Mall. **Business Services:** conference facilities. **Cards:** AX, CB, DC, DS, JC, MC, VI. **Special Amenities:** early
check-in/late check-out and preferred room **(subject to availability with advance reservations).**

SOME UNITS
🅢 ✈ 🐾 🍴 🍽 🏊 🐕 🔌 💻 / ✕ /
FEE

BEST WESTERN WESTWOOD INN   *Book at aaa.com*   Phone: (780)483-7770   ㉜
Ⓐ Ⓢ   6/16-9/5   1P: $109-$160   2P: $119-$160   XP: $10   F17
♦♦♦ ♦♦♦   3/1-6/15 & 9/6-2/28   1P: $99-$160   2P: $109-$160   XP: $10   F17
Small-scale Hotel   **Location:** Hwy 16A (Stony Plain Rd) at 180th St. 18035 Stony Plain Rd T5S 1B2. Fax: 780/486-1769. **Facility:** 169
one-bedroom standard units, some with whirlpools. 3-6 stories, interior corridors. **Parking:** on-site, winter
plug-ins. **Terms:** [AP], [BP], [CP] & [ECP] meal plans available. **Amenities:** video games (fee), high-speed
Internet, voice mail, safes, irons, hair dryers. **Dining:** 6 am-11 pm, Sun-10 pm, cocktails. **Pool(s):** small
heated indoor. **Leisure Activities:** whirlpool, steamroom, squash court, exercise room. *Fee:* game room. **Guest Services:** valet
and coin laundry, beauty salon. **Business Services:** conference facilities, PC. **Cards:** AX, DC, DS, MC, VI. **Special Amenities:**
early check-in/late check-out. *(See color ad below)*

SOME UNITS
🅢 🍴 🍽 🎧 🏊 ✕ 🐕 🔌 🔌 💻 / ✕ /

(See map and index starting on p. 405)

CAMPUS TOWER SUITE HOTEL — Book at aaa.com
Phone: (780)439-6060 **45**
All Year 1P: $109 2P: $109 XP: $20 F18
Condominium
Location: At 111th St and 87th Ave. 11145 87th Ave T6G 0Y1. Fax: 780/433-4410. **Facility:** 90 units. 74 one- and 16 two-bedroom suites ($109-$170), some with efficiencies or kitchens. 16 stories, interior corridors. **Parking:** on-site, winter plug-ins. **Amenities:** voice mail, irons, hair dryers. *Some:* high-speed Internet, dual phone lines. **Leisure Activities:** exercise room. **Guest Services:** valet and coin laundry, area transportation. **Business Services:** meeting rooms. *Fee:* administrative services, PC. **Cards:** AX, DC, MC, VI.

SOME UNITS

(ASK) (SD) (YI) (Y) (X) (B) (X) (P) / (X) /

CHATEAU EDMONTON HOTEL & SUITES — Book at aaa.com
Phone: (780)465-7931 **37**
All Year 1P: $99-$199 2P: $129-$349 XP: $10 F15
Large-scale Hotel
Location: Hwy 2 (Gateway Blvd), 3.7 km e at 63rd Ave (turns into Argyll Rd); at 75th St. 7230 Argyll Rd T6C 4A6. Fax: 780/469-3680. **Facility:** 139 units. 109 one-bedroom standard units, some with whirlpools. 30 one-bedroom suites. 7 stories, interior corridors. **Parking:** on-site, winter plug-ins. **Terms:** package plans, 5% service charge, pets ($10 extra charge). **Amenities:** high-speed Internet, voice mail, irons, hair dryers. **Dining:** 2 restaurants, 6 am-midnight, cocktails. **Pool(s):** small heated indoor. **Leisure Activities:** whirlpool, exercise room. **Guest Services:** gift shop, valet laundry. **Business Services:** conference facilities, business center. **Cards:** AX, MC, VI.

SOME UNITS

(SD) (🐾) (YI) (Y) (🛥) (📹) (DATA PORT) (P) / (X) (VCR) (B) (X)
FEE FEE

CHATEAU LOUIS HOTEL & CONFERENCE CENTRE
Phone: (780)452-7770 **30**
All Year [BP] 1P: $109-$199 2P: $109-$199 XP: $10 F11
Small-scale Hotel
Location: On Kingsway and 117th St. 11727 Kingsway T5G 3A1. Fax: 780/454-3436. **Facility:** 141 units. 139 one-bedroom standard units, some with whirlpools. 2 one-bedroom suites ($279-$999), some with whirlpools. 3 stories, interior corridors. *Bath:* combo or shower only. **Parking:** on-site, winter plug-ins. **Terms:** weekly rates available, package plans, small pets only ($5 extra charge, in designated units). **Amenities:** high-speed Internet, voice mail. *Some:* CD players, irons, hair dryers. **Dining:** 6:30 am-midnight, Sat from 7 am, Sun 8 am-midnight, cocktails, nightclub. **Leisure Activities:** pool tables, gazebo, exercise room. **Guest Services:** valet laundry, airport transportation-City Centre Airport, area transportation-train station. **Business Services:** conference facilities. **Cards:** AX, DC, MC, VI. **Special Amenities:** free full breakfast and free local telephone calls. *(See color ad below)*

SOME UNITS

(SD) (✈) (🐾) (YI) (24†) (Y) (ᏑM) (⌨) (📷) (📹) (DATA PORT) (P) / (X) (B) (X)
FEE

COMFORT INN WEST — Book at aaa.com
Phone: (780)484-4415 **41**
All Year 1P: $80-$100 2P: $90-$110 XP: $10 F18
Small-scale Hotel
Location: At 176th St. 17610 100th Ave T5S 1S9. Fax: 780/481-4034. **Facility:** 100 one-bedroom standard units. 2 stories (no elevator), interior corridors. **Parking:** on-site, winter plug-ins. **Terms:** package plans, pets ($10 fee). **Amenities:** irons, hair dryers. **Dining:** 6:30 am-7 pm, cocktails. **Guest Services:** valet laundry. **Business Services:** meeting rooms. **Cards:** AX, DC, DS, MC, VI.

SOME UNITS

(SD) (✈) (🐾) (YI) (📹) (DATA PORT) (P) / (X) (B)
FEE FEE FEE

(See map and index starting on p. 405)

CONTINENTAL INN
(CAA) (SAVE)

Small-scale Hotel

Phone: (780)484-7751 **35**

All Year | 1P: $90-$105 | 2P: $90-$105 | XP: $5 | F12

Location: On Hwy 16A (Stony Plain Rd) at 166th St. 16625 Stony Plain Rd T5P 4A8. Fax: 780/484-9827. **Facility:** 100 one-bedroom standard units, some with whirlpools. 6 stories, interior corridors. **Parking:** on-site, winter plug-ins. **Terms:** 3 day cancellation notice. **Amenities:** high-speed Internet (fee), voice mail, hair dryers. *Some:* irons. **Dining:** 2 restaurants, 6 am-11 pm, Sun 7 am-10 pm, cocktails. **Guest Services:** valet and coin laundry. **Business Services:** meeting rooms. **Cards:** AX, MC. **Special Amenities:** free local telephone calls and free newspaper.

SOME UNITS

DAYS INN & SUITES WEST EDMONTON
(CAA) (SAVE)

Small-scale Hotel

Book at aaa.com

Phone: (780)444-4440 **33**

6/1-9/30 | 1P: $126-$289 | 2P: $126-$289 | XP: $10 | F17
3/1-5/31 & 10/1-2/28 | 1P: $117-$289 | 2P: $117-$289 | XP: $10 | F17

Location: Hwy 16, exit 170th St S. 10010 179A St T5S 2T1. Fax: 780/930-8777. **Facility:** Smoke free premises. 108 units. 84 one-bedroom standard units. 24 one-bedroom suites ($169-$289) with efficiencies, some with whirlpools. 4 stories, interior corridors. **Parking:** on-site, winter plug-ins. **Terms:** check-in 4 pm, cancellation fee imposed, weekly rates available. **Amenities:** high-speed Internet, dual phone lines, voice mail, irons, hair dryers. *Some:* CD players. **Dining:** 6:30 am-2 am, cocktails. **Pool(s):** saltwater. **Leisure Activities:** whirlpool, exercise room. **Guest Services:** valet laundry, area transportation-West Edmonton Mall. **Business Services:** meeting rooms, business center. **Cards:** AX, CB, DC, DS, JC, MC, VI. **Special Amenities:** free local telephone calls and free newspaper. *(See color ad p 415)*

SOME UNITS

FEE

DELTA EDMONTON SOUTH HOTEL AND
CONFERENCE CENTRE
(CAA) (SAVE)

Large-scale Hotel

Book at aaa.com

Phone: (780)434-6415 **52**

All Year | 1P: $111-$169 | 2P: $111-$169 | XP: $10 | F17

Location: Jct Calgary Tr (Hwy 2) and Whitemud Dr. 4404 Gateway Blvd T6H 5C2. Fax: 780/436-9247. **Facility:** 237 units. 229 one-bedroom standard units. 8 one-bedroom suites ($279-$499), some with whirlpools. 11 stories, interior corridors. **Parking:** on-site and valet, winter plug-ins. **Terms:** cancellation fee imposed, 12% service charge, small pets only ($10 fee). **Amenities:** video games, high-speed Internet, voice mail, irons, hair dryers. **Dining:** 6 am-11 pm, cocktails. **Pool(s):** heated indoor. **Leisure Activities:** whirlpool, exercise room. **Guest Services:** gift shop, valet laundry. **Business Services:** conference facilities, business center. **Cards:** AX, CB, DC, MC, VI. *(See color ad below)*

SOME UNITS

FEE

EXECUTIVE ROYAL INN WEST EDMONTON
(CAA) (SAVE)

Small-scale Hotel

Phone: (780)484-6000 **40**

All Year | 1P: $125-$232 | 2P: $125-$232 | XP: $12 | F12

Location: Corner of 178th St and 100th Ave. 10010 178th St T5S 1T3. Fax: 780/489-2900. **Facility:** 238 units. 233 one-bedroom standard units, some with whirlpools. 5 one-bedroom suites with whirlpools. 4 stories, interior corridors. *Bath:* combo or shower only. **Parking:** on-site, winter plug-ins. **Terms:** check-in 4 pm, package plans, pets ($15 extra charge). **Amenities:** video games, voice mail, irons, hair dryers. *Some:* high-speed Internet. **Dining:** 6:30 am-10 pm, cocktails. **Leisure Activities:** whirlpools, exercise room. *Fee:* game room. **Guest Services:** gift shop, valet laundry. **Business Services:** conference facilities, PC. **Cards:** AX, DC, MC, VI. **Special Amenities:** free local telephone calls and free newspaper.

SOME UNITS

FEE

(See map and index starting on p. 405)

FANTASYLAND HOTEL   *Book at aaa.com*   **Phone:** (780)444-3000 **43**
(CAA) (SAVE)   All Year   1P: $189-$329   2P: $189-$329   XP: $10   F16
Location: At 178th St. Located in West Edmonton Mall at southwest end. 17700 87th Ave T5T 4V4.
Fax: 780/444-3294. **Facility:** 355 units. 354 one-bedroom standard units, some with whirlpools. 1 one-
bedroom suite. 12 stories, interior corridors. *Bath:* combo or shower only. **Parking:** on-site and valet, winter
Large-scale Hotel plug-ins. **Terms:** check-in 4 pm, [BP] & [CP] meal plans available, package plans. **Amenities:** video games,
voice mail, safes, hair dryers. **Dining:** 2 restaurants, 7 am-10 pm, cocktails. **Pool(s):** wading. **Leisure
Activities:** exercise room. *Fee:* waterslide, miniature golf, ice skating, adjacent to amusement park, sea life caverns, dinner
theatre, movie theatres, world water park, massage. **Guest Services:** gift shop, valet laundry. **Business Services:** conference
facilities. **Cards:** AX, DC, MC, VI.
SOME UNITS

GLENORA BED & BREAKFAST INN   **Phone:** (780)488-6766 **36**
All Year [BP]   1P: $70-$130   2P: $85-$145   XP: $25
Location: At 124th St. Located in the Glenora District (art gallery district). 12327 102nd Ave T5N 0L8.
Bed & Breakfast Fax: 780/488-5168. **Facility:** Built in 1912, this restored B&B is partly furnished with antiques and offers a
variety of guest rooms ranging from apartment-style to traditional. Smoke free premises. 25 units. 17 one-
bedroom standard units. 8 one-bedroom suites, some with kitchens. 3 stories (no elevator), interior corridors. *Bath:*
shared or private, combo or shower only. **Parking:** on-site, winter plug-ins. **Terms:** office hours 7 am-9 pm, weekly rates
available, package plans. **Amenities:** video library, hair dryers. *Some:* high-speed Internet. **Guest Services:** coin laundry.
Cards: AX, MC, VI.
SOME UNITS

GREENWOOD INN HOTELS   *Book at aaa.com*   **Phone:** (780)431-1100 **55**
(CAA) (SAVE)   All Year   1P: $99-$139   2P: $99-$139   XP: $10   F18
Location: Hwy 2 (Gateway Blvd), just n of Whitemud Dr. 4485 Gateway Blvd T6H 5C3. Fax: 780/437-3455.
Facility: 224 units. 221 one-bedroom standard units. 3 one-bedroom suites ($249-$279), some with
whirlpools. 6 stories, interior corridors. *Bath:* combo or shower only. **Parking:** on-site, winter plug-ins.
Small-scale Hotel **Terms:** cancellation fee imposed, pets ($10 extra charge). **Amenities:** video games, high-speed Internet
(fee), voice mail, irons, hair dryers. **Dining:** 2 restaurants, 6 am-11 pm, Sun from 6:30 am, cocktails.
Pool(s): saltwater. **Leisure Activities:** whirlpool, steamroom, exercise room. **Guest Services:** gift shop, valet laundry.
Business Services: conference facilities, PC (fee). **Cards:** AX, CB, DC, MC, VI. **Special Amenities: free local telephone
calls and free newspaper.**
SOME UNITS
FEE

HILTON GARDEN INN-WEST EDMONTON   *Book at aaa.com*   **Phone:** 780/443-2233 **27**
All Year   1P: $94-$194   2P: $94-$194   XP: $20   F17
Location: From 176th St, just w. 17610 Stony Plain Rd T5S 1A2. Fax: 780/443-4171. **Facility:** 160 units. 155 one-
bedroom standard units. 5 one-bedroom suites with whirlpools. 6 stories, interior corridors. **Parking:** on-site,
Small-scale Hotel winter plug-ins. **Terms:** cancellation fee imposed. **Amenities:** video games, high-speed Internet, dual phone
lines, voice mail, irons, hair dryers. **Pool(s):** heated indoor. **Leisure Activities:** whirlpool, exercise room. **Guest Services:**
sundries, valet and coin laundry. **Business Services:** meeting rooms, business center. **Cards:** AX, DC, MC, VI.
SOME UNITS

HOLIDAY INN CONVENTION CENTRE (S.E.
EDMONTON)   *Book at aaa.com*   **Phone:** (780)468-5400 **46**
(CAA) (SAVE)   All Year   1P: $109   2P: $109
Location: Hwy 14, just s via 50th St exit, then just e. 4520 76th Ave T6B 0A5. Fax: 780/466-0451. **Facility:** 93 one-
bedroom standard units, some with whirlpools. 6 stories, interior corridors. **Parking:** on-site, winter plug-ins.
Terms: cancellation fee imposed, package plans, small pets only ($20 extra charge). **Amenities:** high-
Small-scale Hotel speed Internet (fee), dual phone lines, voice mail, irons, hair dryers. **Dining:** 6 am-2 & 5-10 pm, cocktails.
Pool(s): heated indoor. **Leisure Activities:** whirlpool, steamroom, exercise room. **Guest Services:** valet
laundry, area transportation-West Edmonton Mall. **Business Services:** conference facilities, PC. **Cards:** AX, CB, DC, DS, JC,
MC, VI.
SOME UNITS
FEE

HOLIDAY INN EDMONTON-THE PALACE   *Book at aaa.com*   **Phone:** (780)438-1222 **56**
(CAA) (SAVE)   All Year   1P: $96-$182   2P: $96-$182   XP: $10   F19
Location: Just s of Whitemud Dr. 4235 Gateway Blvd T6J 5H2. Fax: 780/438-0906. **Facility:** 137 units. 104 one-
and 20 two-bedroom standard units, some with whirlpools. 13 one-bedroom suites ($140-$500). 5 stories,
interior corridors. *Bath:* combo or shower only. **Parking:** on-site, winter plug-ins. **Terms:** [BP] & [CP] meal
Small-scale Hotel plans available, small pets only ($10 extra charge, 1st floor units). **Amenities:** video games, high-speed
Internet, dual phone lines, voice mail, irons, hair dryers. **Dining:** 6:30 am-10 pm, cocktails. **Leisure
Activities:** whirlpools, exercise room. **Guest Services:** gift shop, valet laundry, airport transportation-Edmonton International
Airport, area transportation-West Edmonton Mall, beauty salon. **Business Services:** conference facilities. **Cards:** AX, DC, DS,
JC, MC, VI. **Special Amenities: free local telephone calls and free newspaper.** *(See color ad p 415)*
SOME UNITS
FEE

(See map and index starting on p. 405)

HOLIDAY INN EXPRESS HOTEL & SUITES
EDMONTON *Book at aaa.com* **Phone:** (780)483-4000 **39**

CAA SAVE

6/2-9/30   1P: $139-$189   2P: $139-$189   XP: $10   F18
3/1-6/1 & 10/1-2/28   1P: $129-$179   2P: $129-$179   XP: $10   F18

Location: On 100th Ave, just w of 178th St. 10017 179A St T5S 2L4. **Fax:** 780/481-6227. **Facility:** 102 units. 68 one-bedroom standard units, some with whirlpools. 34 one-bedroom suites ($179-$269), some with whirlpools. 4 stories, interior corridors. **Parking:** on-site, winter plug-ins. **Terms:** check-in 4 pm, package plans. **Amenities:** video games, high-speed Internet, dual phone lines, voice mail, irons, hair dryers. *Some:* CD players. **Pool(s):** heated indoor. **Leisure Activities:** whirlpool, steamroom, exercise room. *Fee:* game room. **Guest Services:** valet and coin laundry, area transportation-West Edmonton Mall. **Business Services:** meeting rooms. **Cards:** AX, DC, DS, MC, VI. **Special Amenities:** free continental breakfast and free local telephone calls.
(See color ad card insert & below)

Small-scale Hotel

SOME UNITS
🛎️ 🚗 🍴 &M 📷 🏊 ✂️ 📹 📠 / ✕ VCR 🔌 🖨️ /
FEE

HOTEL SELKIRK *Book at aaa.com* **Phone:** (780)496-7227 **51**

5/12-9/21   1P: $184   2P: $184

Location: From Whitemud Dr, exit Fox Dr; follow signs for hotel. Located in Fort Edmonton Park. 7000 143rd St T5J 2R7 (PO Box 2359). **Fax:** 780/431-0946. **Facility:** Smoke free premises. 30 units. 28 one-bedroom standard units. 2 one-bedroom suites. 2 stories, interior corridors. **Parking:** on-site and valet. **Terms:** open 5/12-9/21, office hours 7 am-11 pm, check-in 4 pm, 3 day cancellation notice, [MAP] meal plan available, package plans. **Amenities:** voice mail, hair dryers. **Leisure Activities:** hiking trails. **Cards:** AX, DC, MC, VI.

Small-scale Hotel

ASK 🛎️ 🍴 🍸 ✕ 📹 📠

MAYFIELD INN & SUITES AT WEST EDMONTON *Book at aaa.com* **Phone:** (780)484-0821 **31**

CAA SAVE

All Year   1P: $129   2P: $189   XP: $10   F

Location: 1.6 km n of jct Hwy 2 (Gateway Blvd) and 16A on Mayfield Rd. 16615 109th Ave T5P 4K8. **Fax:** 780/486-1634. **Facility:** 327 units. 219 one-bedroom standard units, some with kitchens and/or whirlpools. 108 one-bedroom suites ($165-$189), some with whirlpools. 10 stories, interior corridors. **Parking:** on-site, winter plug-ins. **Terms:** package plans, pets ($15 extra charge). **Amenities:** video games, high-speed Internet, voice mail, irons, hair dryers. *Some:* dual phone lines, safes. **Dining:** 3 restaurants, 6:30 am-10 pm, cocktails, also, Mayfield Dinner Theatre, see separate listing, nightclub. **Pool(s):** heated indoor. **Leisure Activities:** saunas, whirlpool, steamroom, racquetball courts, 5 squash courts, spa. *Fee:* esthetics, game room. **Guest Services:** gift shop, valet and coin laundry. **Business Services:** conference facilities, business center. **Cards:** AX, CB, DC, DS, JC, MC, VI. **Special Amenities:** free full breakfast and free newspaper.

Large-scale Hotel

SOME UNITS
🛎️ 🐕 🍴 24🍴 🍸 🏊 ✝️ ✂️ 📹 📠 📠 / ✕ VCR 🔌 🖨️ /
FEE

(See map and index starting on p. 405)

THE MET HOTEL   **Phone: (780)465-8150** 42

Small-scale Hotel

All Year [CP] 1P: $290-$350
Location: Just e of 105th St. 10454 82nd Ave (Whyte Ave) T6E 4Z7. Fax: 780/465-8174. **Facility:** 98 units. 92 one-bedroom standard units. 6 one-bedroom suites ($550) with whirlpools. 8 stories, interior corridors. *Bath:* combo or shower only. **Parking:** valet and street. **Terms:** pets ($25 fee, in designated units). **Amenities:** CD players, high-speed Internet, voice mail, honor bars, irons, hair dryers. *Some:* safes. **Leisure Activities:** exercise room. **Guest Services:** complimentary evening beverages, valet laundry. **Business Services:** meeting rooms, PC. **Cards:** AX, DC, MC, VI.

SOME UNITS
ASK SD 🛏 🍴 🍽 Y DATA PORT 💻 / ✕ 🖼 /
FEE

ROSSLYN INN & SUITES *Book at aaa.com*   **Phone: (780)476-6241** 29

CAA SAVE

Small-scale Hotel

All Year 1P: $92-$139 2P: $92-$139 XP: $10 F18
Location: Hwy 16 (Yellowhead Hwy), 2 km n at 97th St. 13620 97 St T5E 4E2. Fax: 780/473-3021. **Facility:** 93 units. 77 one-bedroom standard units, some with whirlpools. 16 one-bedroom suites ($119-$159). 2-5 stories, interior corridors. *Bath:* combo or shower only. **Parking:** on-site, winter plug-ins. **Terms:** pets ($10 fee). **Amenities:** video games, voice mail. *Some:* high-speed Internet, dual phone lines, irons, hair dryers. **Dining:** 6 am-10 pm, Sun 7 am-9 pm, cocktails. **Leisure Activities:** exercise room. **Guest Services:** valet and coin laundry. **Business Services:** meeting rooms. **Cards:** AX, DC, DS, JC, MC, VI.

SOME UNITS
SD 🛏 🍴 Y 🍽 DATA PORT 💻 / ✕ VCR 🔒 🖼 /
FEE

SUPER 8 HOTEL *Book at aaa.com*   **Phone: (780)433-8688** 60

CAA SAVE

Small-scale Hotel

6/16-8/31 1P: $89-$219 2P: $89-$219 XP: $5 F16
3/1-6/15 & 9/1-2/28 1P: $89-$179 2P: $89-$179 XP: $5 F16
Location: Jct 36th Ave. 3610 Gateway Blvd T6J 7H8. Fax: 780/433-8823. **Facility:** 104 units. 69 one-bedroom standard units, some with whirlpools. 35 one-bedroom suites ($99-$189). 4 stories, interior corridors. *Bath:* combo or shower only. **Parking:** on-site, winter plug-ins. **Terms:** package plans, pets ($10 fee, main floor units). **Amenities:** dual phone lines, voice mail, irons, hair dryers. **Pool(s):** small heated indoor. **Leisure Activities:** whirlpool, waterslide. **Guest Services:** valet and coin laundry. **Cards:** AX, DC, JC, MC, VI. **Special Amenities:** free continental breakfast and free local telephone calls.

SOME UNITS
SD ✈ 🛏 🍴 🔥M 🚤 🍽 DATA PORT 🔒 💻 / ✕ 🖼 /
FEE FEE

TRAVELODGE BEVERLY CREST *Book at aaa.com*   **Phone: (780)474-0456** 59

CAA SAVE

Small-scale Hotel

5/2-9/1 1P: $87-$97 2P: $87-$97 XP: $8 F17
3/1-5/1 & 9/2-2/28 1P: $77-$87 2P: $77-$87 XP: $8 F17
Location: 8 km e of Capilano Dr, 1 km s from W Hwy 16 (Yellowhead Tr) on Victoria Tr exit. 3414 118th Ave T5W 0Z4. Fax: 780/479-3542. **Facility:** 86 one-bedroom standard units. 2 stories (no elevator), interior corridors. **Parking:** on-site, winter plug-ins. **Terms:** 12% service charge, small pets only (must be attended). **Amenities:** voice mail, hair dryers. **Dining:** 2 restaurants, 6 am-9:30 pm, cocktails, nightclub. **Guest Services:** valet laundry, barber shop. **Business Services:** meeting rooms, administrative services (fee). **Cards:** AX, DC, MC, VI. **Special Amenities:** free local telephone calls and free newspaper.

SOME UNITS
🛏 🍴 Y DATA PORT 💻 / ✕ VCR
FEE

TRAVELODGE EDMONTON SOUTH *Book at aaa.com*   **Phone: (780)436-9770** 58

CAA SAVE

Small-scale Hotel

7/1-8/31 1P: $89-$109 2P: $95-$115 XP: $10 F18
3/1-6/30 & 9/1-2/28 1P: $79-$99 2P: $79-$105 XP: $10 F18
Location: Jct Calgary Tr (Hwy 2) and 45th Ave, just n of Whitemud Dr. 10320 45th Ave S T6H 5K3. Fax: 780/436-3529. **Facility:** 219 units. 214 one-bedroom standard units. 5 one-bedroom suites. 3 stories, interior corridors. **Parking:** on-site, winter plug-ins. **Terms:** [BP], [CP] & [ECP] meal plans available, package plans, small pets ($10 extra charge, in smoking units). **Amenities:** video games, voice mail, irons, hair dryers. **Pool(s):** small heated indoor. **Leisure Activities:** whirlpool, limited exercise equipment. **Guest Services:** valet laundry. **Business Services:** meeting rooms. **Cards:** AX, DC, MC, VI. *(See color ad p 367)*

SOME UNITS
SD 🛏 🍴 🚤 🍽 DATA PORT 💻 / ✕ VCR 🔒 🖼 /
FEE

TRAVELODGE EDMONTON WEST *Book at aaa.com*   **Phone: (780)483-6031** 28

CAA SAVE

Small-scale Hotel

7/1-9/30 1P: $99-$109 2P: $99-$119 XP: $10 F17
3/1-6/30 & 10/1-2/28 1P: $84-$104 2P: $94-$114 XP: $10 F17
Location: From Hwy 16, exit 184 St. 18320 Stony Plain Rd T5S 1A7. Fax: 780/484-2358. **Facility:** 220 one-bedroom standard units. 5 stories, interior corridors. **Parking:** on-site. **Terms:** weekly rates available, package plans. **Amenities:** video games, voice mail, irons, hair dryers. *Some:* high-speed Internet. **Dining:** 6:30 am-11 pm, Sun from 7 am, cocktails. **Pool(s):** small heated indoor. **Leisure Activities:** whirlpool, waterslide. **Fee:** game room. **Guest Services:** gift shop, valet and coin laundry. **Business Services:** meeting rooms. **Cards:** AX, DC, DS, MC, VI. *(See color ad p 367)*

SOME UNITS
SD 🛏 🍴 🚤 ✕ 🍽 DATA PORT 💻 / ✕ 🔒 /
FEE

THE VARSCONA HOTEL *Book at aaa.com*   **Phone: (780)434-6111** 48

Small-scale Hotel

All Year [CP] 1P: $225-$310 XP: $20 F12
Location: Corner of 82nd Ave (Whyte Ave) and 106th St. 8208 106th St T6E 6R9. Fax: 780/439-1195. **Facility:** 89 units. 85 one-bedroom standard units. 4 one-bedroom suites ($420). 6 stories, interior corridors. *Bath:* combo or shower only. **Parking:** on-site and valet, winter plug-ins. **Terms:** package plans, small pets only ($25 fee). **Amenities:** CD players, high-speed Internet, voice mail, honor bars, irons, hair dryers. *Some:* dual phone lines. **Leisure Activities:** exercise room. **Guest Services:** complimentary evening beverages, valet laundry. **Business Services:** meeting rooms, PC. **Cards:** AX, CB, DC, MC, VI.

SOME UNITS
ASK SD 🛏 🍴 Y 🍽 DATA PORT 💻 / ✕ VCR 🔒 /
FEE

(See map and index starting on p. 405)

WEST EDMONTON MALL INN   *Book at aaa.com*   Phone: (780)444-9378   **44**
CAA SAVE   All Year   1P: $129   2P: $129   XP: $10   F16
Location: Whitemud Dr, exit 170th St N, just w on 90th Ave. Located next to the mall. 17504 90th Ave T5T 6L6.
Fax: 780/489-7899. **Facility:** 88 one-bedroom standard units. 3 stories, interior corridors. **Parking:** on-site,
winter plug-ins. **Terms:** check-in 4 pm, cancellation fee imposed, package plans, 12% service charge.
Small-scale Hotel **Amenities:** video games, voice mail, hair dryers. **Guest Services:** valet laundry. **Business Services:**
meeting rooms. **Cards:** AX, DC, MC, VI.
SOME UNITS

WEST HARVEST INN   *Book at aaa.com*   Phone: (780)484-8000   **34**
CAA SAVE   All Year   1P: $89-$149   2P: $89-$149   XP: $10   F17
Location: Hwy 16A (Stony Plain Rd) at 178th St. 17803 Stony Plain Rd NW T5S 1B4. Fax: 780/486-6060.
Facility: 160 one-bedroom standard units, some with whirlpools. 3 stories, interior corridors. **Bath:** combo or
shower only. **Parking:** on-site, winter plug-ins. **Terms:** check-in 4 pm, package plans. **Amenities:** voice
Small-scale Hotel mail, irons, hair dryers. *Some:* high-speed Internet. **Dining:** 6:30 am-11 pm, Sun-10 pm, cocktails. **Guest
Services:** valet laundry. **Business Services:** meeting rooms, PC (fee). **Cards:** AX, MC, VI.
Special Amenities: free local telephone calls and free newspaper. *(See color ad below)*
SOME UNITS

(See map and index starting on p. 405)

WINGATE INN EDMONTON WEST   Phone: (780)443-1000   🔳38

(CAA) (SAVE)

5/16-10/15	1P: $126-$171	2P: $126-$171	XP: $10	F17
10/16-2/28	1P: $117-$162	2P: $117-$162	XP: $10	F17
3/1-5/15	1P: $108-$153	2P: $108-$153	XP: $10	F17

Location: 100th Ave at 182nd St. 18220 100th Ave T5S 2V2. **Fax:** 780/443-0500. **Facility:** 106 units. 82 one-**Small-scale Hotel** bedroom standard units. 24 one-bedroom suites, some with whirlpools. 4 stories, interior corridors. **Parking:** on-site, winter plug-ins. **Terms:** pets ($10 extra charge). **Amenities:** video games, high-speed Internet, dual phone lines, voice mail, safes, irons, hair dryers. **Pool(s):** small heated indoor. **Leisure Activities:** whirlpool, waterslide, exercise room. **Guest Services:** valet and coin laundry, area transportation. **Business Services:** meeting rooms, business center. **Cards:** AX, DC, DS, MC, VI. **Special Amenities:** free expanded continental breakfast and free newspaper.

SOME UNITS

WHERE TO DINE

BARB & ERNIE'S   **Lunch:** $8-$10   **Dinner:** $10-$15   Phone: 780/433-3242   🔳52

German

Location: 99th St S, w at 72nd Ave. 9906 72nd Ave T6E 0Z3. **Hours:** 7 am-8 pm, Fri-9 pm, Sat 8 am-9 pm, Sun 9 am-8 pm. Closed major holidays; also Mon. **Reservations:** accepted. **Features:** Ask any local for a favorite breakfast place, and this is often mentioned. Lunch and dinner are popular as well. Ernie himself often greets guests as they enter. Among the homey restaurant's pleasing array of Bavarian dishes are sauerkraut and sausages. Casual dress; cocktails. **Parking:** on-site. **Cards:** AX, DC, DS, MC, VI.

BEE-BELL BAKERY   **Lunch:** $2-$9   Phone: 780/439-3247   🔳41

Bakery/Desserts

Location: E at 80th Ave to 104th St. 10416 80th Ave T6E 5T7. **Hours:** 9 am-5:30 pm, Sat from 8 am. Closed major holidays; also Sun. **Reservations:** not accepted. **Features:** Although there are no places to sit and eat, the bakery is a favorite for those planning a picnic in the park or a festival outing. Patrons step up to the counter to order a variety of breads, quiches and delectable desserts. **Parking:** street.

BILLINGSGATE SEAFOOD MARKET LIGHTHOUSE
CAFE   **Lunch:** $9-$12   **Dinner:** $11-$30   Phone: 780/433-0091   🔳42

Seafood

Location: Corner of 73rd Ave and 104th St. 7331 104th St T6E 4B9. **Hours:** 11:30 am-9 pm, Fri & Sat-10 pm, Sun 11 am-8 pm. Closed: 12/25. **Reservations:** suggested. **Features:** Patrons walk past displays of fresh seafood to the lively, bright restaurant, where seafood lovers indulge in jewels from the ocean. Fresh halibut, salmon, trout and a catch of the day are sure to delight, as does traditional fish and chips. Desserts made on the premises are well worth saving room for. The cafe-style restaurant bustles at lunchtime, and a distinctive East Coast flair characterizes the decor. Casual dress; cocktails. **Parking:** on-site. **Cards:** MC, VI.

THE BLUE PEAR   **Dinner:** $59   Phone: 780/482-7178   🔳36

French

Location: Southeast corner of 123rd St and 7th Ave. 10643 123rd St T5N 1P3. **Hours:** 6 pm-8:30 pm. Closed major holidays; also Sun-Tues. **Reservations:** required. **Features:** The distinctive name of the upscale restaurant is derived from its previous name, D'Anjou. After ringing the doorbell, guests enter the small dining room, where there are but 12 tables. The five-course prix fixe menu changes monthly, and the chef marries French cooking techniques with regional ingredients. Representative of typical menu fare are such creations as Arctic char with peppercorns, lamb or salmon. Service is exceptional. Casual dress; cocktails. **Parking:** on-site. **Cards:** AX, MC, VI.

CAFE MOSAICS   **Lunch:** $5-$10   **Dinner:** $5-$10   Phone: 780/433-9702   🔳28

Vegetarian

Location: 82nd Ave (Whyte Ave), just e of 109th St. 10844 82nd Ave T6E 2B3. **Hours:** 9 am-9 pm, Sun 11 am-2:30 pm. Closed major holidays. **Features:** An eclectic and funky respite for vegetarians, the small cafe is along trendy Whyte Avenue. Home-cooked meals, including a large selection of vegetarian entrees, are served in a cozy setting. Whether a hearty bowl of soup, a distinctive pizza or an entree-size spinach salad, the servings are large and a good value for the dollar. This place is nice for spending hours catching up with a friend over a cup of tea. Casual dress; beer & wine only. **Parking:** street. **Cards:** MC, VI.

CENTURY GRILL   **Lunch:** $9-$14   **Dinner:** $22-$30   Phone: 780/431-0303   🔳54

Northern Pacific Rim

Location: Calgary Tr S at 39th Ave. 3975 Calgary Tr T6J 6S6. **Hours:** 11 am-10 pm, Fri & Sat-11 pm, Sun 5 pm-10 pm. Closed major holidays. **Reservations:** suggested. **Features:** Chic and contemporary, the upscale restaurant features a lovely open-concept dining room with black and gray decor. Patrons can dine in the restaurant or the more casual lounge. Creative cuisine boldly pairs varied tastes and sensations. The menu focuses heavily on regional ingredients and also exhibits a Californian flair. Casual dress; cocktails. **Parking:** on-site. **Cards:** AX, MC, VI.

CHIANTI   **Lunch:** $7-$16   **Dinner:** $7-$16   Phone: 780/439-9829   🔳47

Italian

Location: Corner of 105th St. 10501 82nd Ave NW T6E 2A3. **Hours:** 11 am-11 pm, Fri & Sat-midnight. Closed: 1/1, 12/25. **Features:** In a former post office building on trendy Whyte Avenue, the lively, long-established restaurant serves entrees of pasta, veal, seafood and chicken, and most menu items can be served in half portions. This place is ideal for large gatherings or an evening out in a festive atmosphere. Tasty Italian food is a good value. Casual dress; cocktails. **Parking:** street. **Cards:** AX, DC, DS, MC, VI.

DA-DE-O NEW ORLEANS DINER & BAR   **Lunch:** $6-$13   **Dinner:** $6-$13   Phone: 780/433-0930   🔳31

Cajun

Location: On 82nd Ave (Whyte Ave) at 106th St. 105-48A 82nd Ave T6E 2A4. **Hours:** 11:30 am-11 pm, Fri & Sat-midnight, Sun 10 am-10 pm. **Reservations:** suggested. **Features:** Diners hankering for value for the dollar need look no further than this eclectic, retro Cajun diner in the trendy Whyte Avenue district. Famous for its po' boys, hearty jambalaya and Cajun sweet potato fries, the eatery projects the feel of Louisiana. With booths, individual jukeboxes and retro decor, the setting is fitting for a great meal with great service. Casual dress; cocktails. **Parking:** street. **Cards:** MC, VI.

(See map and index starting on p. 405)

DANTE'S BISTRO   Lunch: $7-$13   Dinner: $14-$22   Phone: 780/486-4448   ⑤⑧
▼▽▽▽◆   **Location:** At 173rd St. 17328 Stony Plain Rd T5S 1K6. **Hours:** 11:30 am-10 pm, Thurs-midnight, Fri & Sat-1 am,
International   Sun-9 pm. **Closed:** 12/25. **Reservations:** suggested. **Features:** Although it's difficult to classify the restaurant's cuisine, a possible description might be "food without borders." The eclectic, International menu features a huge range of options, with Asian, Mexican, French and fusion influences to name a few. Offerings include sushi, oven-fired pizza, entree salads and creative pasta dishes. The bustling atmosphere in the lofty, airy dining room creates a festive environment. Casual dress; cocktails. **Parking:** on-site. **Cards:** AX, DC, MC, VI.

DEATH BY CHOCOLATE   Lunch: $6-$10   Dinner: $6-$10   Phone: 780/486-2201   ④⓪
▼▽   **Location:** Corner of Bourbon St; in West Edmonton Mall. 87th Ave & 170th St T5T 4M2. **Hours:** 8 am-midnight, Fri-1
Bakery/Desserts   am, Sat 9 am-1 am, Sun 10 am-11 pm. **Closed:** 12/25. **Features:** A plethora of more than 30 desserts tempts from inside West Edmonton Mall. Such splurges as Callebaut dark and white chocolate mousse, tiramisu and the whimsical "ice burger"—which comprises chocolate ice cream "patties" on a sponge cake "bun" with raspberry coulis "ketchup," pineapple spear "fries" and whipped cream "mayo"—beckon to the sweet tooth. There is a contemporary coffeehouse feel to the cafe, where guests order at the counter and have desserts served to them. Casual dress. **Parking:** on-site. **Cards:** AX, MC, VI.

THE DISH BISTRO   Lunch: $5-$10   Dinner: $8-$14   Phone: 780/488-6181   ②①
▽▽▽▽ ▽▽▽▽   **Location:** Just w of jct Hwy 16A (Stony Plain Rd) and 124th St. 12417 Stony Plain Rd T5N 3N3. **Hours:** 11 am-9 pm.
International   Closed major holidays; also Sun. **Reservations:** suggested. **Features:** In the art district, the little bistro is a cozy place for a healthy quick bite or quaint, leisurely meal. Among interesting creations are curried egg sandwiches, crab cakes and sumptuous pastas. The dining room has original artwork, hardwood floors and large, street-view windows. Casual dress; cocktails. **Parking:** street. **Cards:** AX, MC, VI.

FIFE N' DEKEL   Lunch: $2-$6   Phone: 780/489-6436   ②②
▼   **Location:** 170th St at 106th Ave; in industrial shopping plaza on west side of road. 10646 170th St T5S 1P3. **Hours:** 7
Deli/Subs   am-4:30 pm, Sat 10 am-3 pm. **Closed** major holidays; also Sun. **Reservations:** not accepted.
Sandwiches   **Features:** Quick, healthy lunch options are plentiful at the cafeteria-style eatery. Guests order at the counter and watch their sandwich being made. In addition to such sandwiches as roasted turkey, beef, ham and vegetarian, the menu lists soups, salads and tempting selections from a dessert case full of sumptuous options. Because this place draws a good crowd at lunch, patrons should arrive early to avoid lines. Cocktails. **Parking:** on-site. **Cards:** AX, MC, VI.

THE FUNKY PICKLE PIZZA CO   Lunch: $4-$10   Dinner: $4-$10   Phone: 780/423-3865   ⑤⑦
▼   **Location:** Just n of West Edmonton Mall at 171st St. 17104 90th Ave T5T 4C8. **Hours:** 11 am-midnight, Thurs-Sat
Pizza   to 3:30 am. **Reservations:** not accepted. **Features:** The small pizza bar might do the trick for hungry folks looking for a quick bite to eat. Guests can order eclectic and designer pizza toppings on whole-wheat crust, and the large slices are sure to satisfy any appetite. Seating here is limited so many opt to get their food to go. Casual dress. **Parking:** on-site. **Cards:** AX, MC, VI.

HIGHLEVEL DINER   Lunch: $6-$9   Dinner: $10-$15   Phone: 780/433-0933   ②⑨
▽▽▽▽ ▽▽▽▽   **Location:** Jct 109th St and Saskatchewan Dr. 10912 88th Ave T6G 0Z1. **Hours:** 8 am-11 pm, Thurs-Sat 9 am-
Canadian   midnight, Sun 9 am-11 pm. Closed major holidays. **Reservations:** not accepted. **Features:** A longstanding favorite among Edmontonians for the past 30 years, the casual diner-style restaurant overlooks the South end of the High Level bridge. Known for its enormous cinnamon buns, blueberry crisp and breakfasts, the diner also serves comfort food, ranging from garlic mashed potatoes to prime rib to hearty soups. Casual dress; cocktails. **Parking:** street. **Cards:** AX, MC, VI.

JACK'S GRILL   Dinner: $19-$24   Phone: 780/434-1113   ⑤③
▼▼▼▼   **Location:** Whitemud Dr, exit 111th St, 0.8 km n, then just w on 57th Ave; in a strip mall. 5842 111th St T6H 3G1.
Regional   **Hours:** 5 pm-10 pm. **Closed:** 12/25, 12/26; also 1st week of January. **Reservations:** suggested.
Canadian   **Features:** The chef is an architect who builds unusual, inventive cuisine with fresh ingredients, bold flavors and French and West Coast influences. The relaxed, casual atmosphere sustains a feel of upscale elegance. Regardless of whether diners choose seating in the dining room or on the seasonal patio, they can expect superb service. Dressy casual; cocktails. **Parking:** on-site. **Cards:** AX, DC, MC, VI.

THE KING & I   Lunch: $7-$10   Dinner: $7-$17   Phone: 780/433-2222   ③③
▼▼ ▼▼   **Location:** Corner of 107th St, just n of 82nd Ave (Whyte Ave). 8208 107th St T6E 6P4. **Hours:** 11:30 am-10:30 pm,
Thai   Fri-11:30 pm, Sat 4:30 pm-11:30 pm. Closed: Sun. **Reservations:** suggested. **Features:** Zesty vegetarian, meat, seafood and poultry dishes provide sensational, savory variety at the pleasant southside curry house, just off Whyte Avenue. Steaming regional Thai curries are an aromatic and tasty choice to enjoy with friends. Casual dress; cocktails. **Parking:** street. **Cards:** AX, DC, MC, VI.

LA SPIGA   Dinner: $15-$35   Phone: 780/482-3100   ②⑦
▼▼▼▼   **Location:** Just s of 102nd Ave. 10133 125th St T5N 1S7. **Hours:** 5 pm-10 pm, Fri & Sat-11 pm. Closed major
Italian   holidays; also Sun. **Reservations:** suggested. **Features:** Dining is intimate, elegant and formal dining in the charming, two-story 1913 mansion. The menu centers on Northern Italian cuisine, with dishes ranging from creamy pasta to succulent veal. The exquisite tiramisu could rival even some created in Italy. The semi-casual atmosphere accents the superb food. Service is professional. Dressy casual; cocktails. **Parking:** on-site. **Cards:** AX, DC, MC, VI. **Historic**

(See map and index starting on p. 405)

LEMONGRASS CAFE   Lunch: $6-$17   Dinner: $6-$17   Phone: 780/413-0088   ⑤⓪
▼▼ ▼▼▼▼ **Location:** Just w of 104th St on Allard Way; in a small strip mall. 10417 51st Ave T6H 0K4. **Hours:** 11 am-9 pm, Fri
& Sat-10 pm, Sun noon-9 pm. Closed: 1/1, 12/25; also Mon. **Reservations:** suggested, weekends.
Vietnamese **Features:** This restaurant has a deceptively unassuming exterior. Just behind the doors is a bright, cheerful,
airy cafe, offering exciting, fresh, healthy entrees. Traditional Vietnamese fare includes salad rolls, curries
and the house specialty: spiced salmon wrapped in banana leaf with vermicelli. Guests can finish off the meal with a single malt
scotch or innovative dessert. Casual dress; cocktails. **Parking:** on-site. **Cards:** MC, VI.
✕

MANOR CAFE   Lunch: $9-$15   Dinner: $12-$25   Phone: 780/482-7577   ④⑨
▼▼ ▼▼ **Location:** Just s of 102nd Ave. 10109 125th St T5N 1S7. **Hours:** 11 am-11 pm, Fri & Sat-midnight, Sun 10 am-2
& 5-10 pm. Closed major holidays; also Sun in winter. **Reservations:** suggested. **Features:** The cafe
International occupies the beautifully restored home of one of Alberta's former Attorney Generals. Decor is charming,
warm and intimate, with a casual feel. The bistro-style menu includes progressive and innovative
international dishes. Casual dress; cocktails. **Parking:** on-site. **Cards:** AX, MC, VI.
✕

MAYFIELD DINNER THEATRE   Dinner: $39-$89   Phone: 780/483-4051   ㉓
▼▼ ▼▼ **Location:** 1.6 km n of jct Hwy 2 (Gateway Blvd) and 16A on Mayfield Rd; in Mayfield Inn & Suites at West Edmonton.
16615 109th Ave T5P 4K8. **Hours:** 6 pm-8 pm, Sun 10:30 am-noon & 5:30-7:15 pm. Closed: 12/24, 12/25;
American also Mon. **Reservations:** required. **Features:** Guests can combine live theater with an attractive, well-
stocked buffet at the distinctive establishment. Well-known TV stars perform on stage. Senior citizens
receive reduced rates during Wednesday matinees. Student specials are available Tuesday through Thursday and Sunday
evenings. Show times are Monday through Thursday at 8 p.m., Friday and Saturday at 8:15 p.m. and Sunday at noon and 7:30
p.m. Semi-formal attire; cocktails; entertainment. **Parking:** on-site. **Cards:** AX, DC, MC, VI.
✕

NAGANO   Lunch: $6-$10   Dinner: $6-$10   Phone: 780/487-8900   ㉟
▼▼ ▼▼ **Location:** Hwy 16A (Stony Plain Rd) at 178th St; next to West Harvest Inn. 10080 178th St T5H 1B4. **Hours:** 11 am-2
& 4:30-10 pm, Fri-11 pm, Sat 11 am-11 pm, Sun 4 pm-9:30 pm. Closed major holidays. **Features:** The
Japanese simple restaurant serves traditional food in a contemporary environment. Servers typically are dressed in
kimonos, and service comes with a smile. Bento boxes are a great value, and there is a full sushi bar as
well. Beer & wine only. **Parking:** on-site. **Cards:** AX, MC, VI.
✕

NEW ASIAN VILLAGE   Lunch: $8   Dinner: $10-$25   Phone: 780/433-3804   ④⑧
▼▼ ▼▼ **Location:** From 109th St, 1 km e. 10143 Saskatchewan Dr TZE 1V6. **Hours:** 11 am-2 & 5-10 pm, Fri & Sat-
midnight, Sun 5 pm-10 pm. Closed: 12/24, 12/25. **Features:** East Indian cuisine is served in a cozy
East Indian maharajah room or in the main dining room, which affords views of the city. Sounds of Indian music and
scents of curry pique the senses, arousing an appetite for dishes such as tasty tandoori chicken, goat, lamb
and vegetarian specialties. Casual dress; cocktails. **Parking:** on-site. **Cards:** AX, JC, MC, VI.
🍽 ✕

O'BYRNE'S IRISH PUB   Lunch: $6-$15   Dinner: $6-$15   Phone: 780/414-6766   ㉜
▼▼▼ **Location:** Corner of 106th St. 10616 82nd Ave (Whyte Ave) T6E 2A7. **Hours:** 11 am-2 am. Closed: 12/25.
Irish **Features:** In a trendy area, the Irish pub welcomes travelers from around the globe. The restaurant offers a
lively atmosphere, friendly service and live entertainment, as well as all-day Irish breakfast and an excellent
DC, MC, VI. selection of Irish beers on tap. Casual dress; cocktails; entertainment. **Parking:** on-site (fee). **Cards:** AX,

PACKRAT LOUIE'S KITCHEN & BAR   Lunch: $9-$16   Dinner: $19-$30   Phone: 780/433-0123   ㉚
▼▼▼▼ **Location:** Jct 103rd St and 83rd Ave, just 1 blk n of Jasper Ave. 10335 83rd Ave T6E 2C6. **Hours:** 11:30 am-10 pm,
Fri & Sat-11 pm. Closed major holidays; also Sun & Mon. **Reservations:** suggested. **Features:** In the heart
Continental of Old Strathcona, the bistro-style restaurant prepares fresh market cuisine. Guests can choose from pizza
made in a wood-burning oven, organic chicken breasts or fresh fish and weekly specials. Dessert is a must.
The Swiss owner is known for his fine desserts and Swiss chocolate truffles. Casual dress; cocktails. **Parking:** on-site.
Cards: AX, DC, MC, VI.
🍽 ✕

PARKALLEN RESTAURANT   Lunch: $8-$12   Dinner: $9-$17   Phone: 780/436-8080   ⑤①
▼▼▼▼ **Location:** Corner of 70th Ave and 109th St. 7018 109th St T6H 3C1. **Hours:** 11 am-11 pm. Closed: Sun.
Reservations: suggested. **Features:** A popular spot with the locals, the family-run restaurant is considered
Lebanese to be one of the city's best ethnic restaurants. The menu centers on selections of traditional Lebanese fare,
including fatouche salad, baba ghanoush and marinated kebabs. Those not in the mood for Lebanese
cuisine also can try award-winning pizza. The wine list is extensive. The casually elegant dining room displays traditional art.
Servers are friendly and knowledgeable. Casual dress; cocktails. **Parking:** on-site. **Cards:** AX, MC, VI.
✕

ROYAL FORK BUFFET RESTAURANT   Lunch: $9   Dinner: $13   Phone: 780/484-7025   ㉖
▼▼ **Location:** Hwy 16A (Stony Plain Rd) at 150th St. 15061 Stony Plain Rd T5P 4W1. **Hours:** 11 am-8:30 pm, Fri &
Sat-9 pm, Sun 10 am-8 pm; Sunday brunch. Closed: 12/25. **Features:** Diners with appetites frequent the
American casual, family-oriented buffet restaurant. After paying at the door, patrons grab a tray and wander up and
down the buffet tables as often as they like. The buffet lines up a nice selection of salads, seafood, beef and
pork dishes. Dinner prices go into effect at 4 pm, all day Sunday and on major holidays. **Parking:** on-site. **Cards:** MC, VI. ✕

SEASONS GRILL   Lunch: $8-$17   Dinner: $8-$20   Phone: 780/437-7011   ㊶
▼▼ ▼▼ **Location:** Hwy 2 (Gateway Blvd) at 51st Ave; in Best Western Cedar Park Inn. 5116 Gateway Blvd N T6H 2H4.
Hours: 6:30 am-11 pm, Sun 7 am-10 pm. **Reservations:** suggested. **Features:** The recently renovated
Canadian restaurant lets patrons peruse a seasonally inspired menu amid cozy, contemporary surroundings. Ranging
from prime rib to pumpkin seed-encrusted sole, the menu variety is surprising and delightful. Casual dress;
cocktails. **Parking:** on-site. **Cards:** AX, CB, DC, DS, JC, MC, VI.
🍽 ✕

(See map and index starting on p. 405)

SWEETWATER CAFE Lunch: $6-$12 Dinner: $10-$15 Phone: 780/488-1959 55
International **Location:** Just w of jct 124th St and 102nd Ave. 12427 102nd Ave T5N 0M2. **Hours:** 11 am-10 pm, Fri & Sat-11 pm, Sun 9 am-3 pm. Closed: 1/1, 12/25. **Features:** For a quick, casual lunch or a lingering dinner, the comfortable cafe fits the bill. The diverse menu lists many types of gourmet pizzas, pastas and burgers, as well as hearty salads and delectable desserts. Diners can admire local art while enjoying their meal. Service is casual, yet friendly. Semi-formal attire; cocktails. **Parking:** on-site. **Cards:** AX, MC, VI.

TAPESTRY BISTRO Lunch: $6-$12 Dinner: $6-$15 Phone: 780/481-0307 24
International **Location:** From 100th Ave, s at 175th St; in small shopping plaza. 17505 100th Ave T5S 2B8. **Hours:** 11 am-8 pm. Closed major holidays; also Sat & Sun. **Features:** With its lemon-yellow walls and cobalt-blue tablecloths, the bistro has a funky feel. Healthy items are made with the freshest of ingredients. In addition to its catering business, the small, cozy restaurant offers fast, friendly service. Among choices are sandwiches, wraps, soups and salads. Casual dress; beer & wine only. **Parking:** on-site. **Cards:** MC, VI.

THREE MUSKATEERS FRENCH CREPERIE Lunch: $8-$14 Dinner: $12-$18 Phone: 780/437-4239 39
French **Location:** Just w of 104th St. 10416 82nd Ave (Whyte Ave) T6E 2A2. **Hours:** 11:30 am-2 & 5-9 pm. Closed major holidays. **Features:** Romantic with dim lighting and original murals on the walls, the French creperie creates traditional and more distinctive crepes. On trendy Whyte Avenue, the restaurant is a welcome respite after a day of shopping. The friendly staff serves hearty portions. Casual dress; cocktails. **Parking:** street. **Cards:** AX, MC, VI.

TURTLE CREEK CAFE Lunch: $6-$10 Dinner: $6-$15 Phone: 780/433-4202 37
California **Location:** Just s of 109th St bridge; in shopping plaza. 8404 109th St T6G 1E2. **Hours:** 11:30 am-10 pm, Sat & Sun from 11 am. Closed major holidays. **Features:** The pleasant, casual eatery lists a variety of things on its menu. Whether diners are craving a sandwich, nachos, a hamburger or a large salad, there is something for everyone. The service is friendly, and Sunday brunches are well attended. Casual dress; cocktails. **Parking:** on-site. **Cards:** AX, MC, VI.

UNHEARDOF RESTAURANT Dinner: $23-$36 Phone: 780/432-0480 38
Canadian **Location:** Corner of 82nd Ave (Whyte Ave) and 96th St. 9602 82nd Ave T6C 1A1. Closed major holidays; also Mon. **Reservations:** suggested. **Features:** Where? Never heard of it! The owners and servers have heard the joke time and time again, yet regardless, the restaurant remains a must. In an old house along the east end of Whyte Avenue, the cozy eatery draws patrons for its fine food and splendid service. Food made from regional ingredients is offered from a prix fixe menu or a la carte. The wine list is fantastic. This place is a favorite for special occasions. Casual dress; cocktails. **Parking:** street. **Cards:** AX, DC, MC, VI.

VON'S STEAK & FISH HOUSE Lunch: $8-$12 Dinner: $14-$32 Phone: 780/439-0041 34
Steak & Seafood **Location:** Just s of 82nd Ave (Whyte Ave) at 103rd St. 10309 81st Ave T6E 1X3. **Hours:** 11 am-10 pm, Sun from 4 pm. Closed: 12/25. **Reservations:** suggested. **Features:** In Strathcona, an old part of town south of the river, the restaurant offers casual dining in a warm, quiet atmosphere. The dining room sports wood beams and a large riverstone fireplace. Beef and seafood are mainstays on a menu of choices that display Louisiana and Mediterranean influences. Casual dress; cocktails. **Parking:** street. **Cards:** AX, DC, MC, VI.

YIANNIS TAVERNA Lunch: $6-$14 Dinner: $14-$21 Phone: 780/433-6768 25
Greek **Location:** Corner of 104th St. 10444 82nd Ave NW (Whyte Ave) T6E 2A2. **Hours:** 11:30 am-11 pm, Fri & Sat-1 am, Sun & Mon from 5 pm. Closed: 1/1, 3/28, 12/25. **Reservations:** suggested, weekends. **Features:** The lively, traditional restaurant is reminiscent of a cozy tavern in Greece, complete with a quaint sidewalk patio. Music, art and atmosphere combine to provide an enjoyable experience. Weekend entertainment features the hasapiko dance, belly dancing at 8:30 pm and later in the evening, the Zorba dance, in which patrons are encouraged to participate. Casual dress; cocktails. **Parking:** street. **Cards:** AX, DC, MC, VI.

The Edmonton Vicinity

FORT SASKATCHEWAN pop. 13,121

——— WHERE TO STAY ———

BEST WESTERN FORT INN AND SUITE *Book at aaa.com* — Phone: (780)998-7888

(CAA) (SAVE)

All Year — 1P: $118-$142 — XP: $10 — F10
Location: Just e of Hwy 15/21 and 101st St. 10115 88th Ave T8L 2T3. Fax: 780/998-2540. **Facility:** 70 units. 63 one-bedroom standard units, some with whirlpools. 7 one-bedroom suites ($139-$229), some with whirlpools. 4 stories, interior corridors. **Parking:** on-site, winter plug-ins. **Terms:** check-in 4 pm.
Small-scale Hotel **Amenities:** video library (fee), dual phone lines, irons, hair dryers. **Dining:** 6 am-10 pm, cocktails. **Leisure Activities:** exercise room. **Guest Services:** coin laundry. **Business Services:** meeting rooms, PC (fee).
Cards: AX, CB, DC, DS, MC, VI. **Special Amenities:** free local telephone calls and free newspaper.

SOME UNITS
[icons]

LEDUC pop. 15,032

——— WHERE TO STAY ———

BEST WESTERN DENHAM INN AND SUITES *Book at aaa.com* — Phone: (780)986-2241

(CAA) (SAVE)

All Year [ECP] — 1P: $99-$129 — 2P: $99-$129 — XP: $10 — F12
Location: Hwy 2, exit Leduc/City Centre, just e. 5207 50th Ave T9E 6V3. Fax: 780/986-1511. **Facility:** 95 one-bedroom standard units, some with whirlpools. 2-5 stories, interior corridors. **Parking:** on-site, winter plug-ins. **Terms:** check-in 4 pm. **Amenities:** video games, voice mail, irons, hair dryers. *Some:* high-speed
Small-scale Hotel Internet. **Dining:** 6 am-9 pm, Fri & Sat-10 pm, Sun 7 am-9 pm, cocktails. **Leisure Activities:** whirlpool, exercise room. **Guest Services:** sundries, valet and coin laundry. **Business Services:** meeting rooms.
Cards: AX, CB, DC, DS, JC, MC, VI. **Special Amenities:** free expanded continental breakfast and free newspaper.

SOME UNITS
[icons]

EDMONTON INTERNATIONAL AIRPORT-SUPER 8 MOTEL *Book at aaa.com* — Phone: (780)986-8000

[diamond icons]

6/1-8/31 [ECP] — 1P: $85-$95 — 2P: $91-$101 — XP: $6 — F12
3/1-5/31 & 9/1-2/28 [ECP] — 1P: $75-$85 — 2P: $81-$91 — XP: $6 — F12
Location: Hwy 2, exit N Business Section, 32 km s. 8004 Sparrow Crescent T9E 7G1. Fax: 780/986-8222.
Small-scale Hotel **Facility:** 64 units. 53 one-bedroom standard units. 11 one-bedroom suites ($105-$145). 4 stories, interior corridors. **Parking:** on-site, winter plug-ins. **Terms:** pets ($10 fee). **Amenities:** high-speed Internet, hair dryers. **Guest Services:** valet and coin laundry. **Business Services:** PC (fee). **Cards:** AX, DC, MC, VI.

SOME UNITS
[icons]

EXECUTIVE ROYAL INN HOTEL & CONFERENCE CENTRE *Book at aaa.com* — Phone: (780)986-1840

[diamond icons]

All Year — 1P: $150 — 2P: $150 — XP: $10 — F18
Location: Hwy 2, 1 km e. 8450 Sparrow Dr T9E 7G4. Fax: 780/986-1864. **Facility:** 186 units. 178 one-bedroom standard units, some with whirlpools. 8 one-bedroom suites ($190-$250), some with whirlpools. 5 stories,
Small-scale Hotel interior corridors. **Parking:** on-site, winter plug-ins. **Terms:** pets ($20 fee, in smoking units).
Amenities: video games, high-speed Internet, voice mail, irons, hair dryers. **Leisure Activities:** whirlpools, exercise room.
Guest Services: gift shop, valet and coin laundry. **Business Services:** conference facilities. **Cards:** AX, DC, MC, VI.

SOME UNITS
[icons]

RAMADA INN EDMONTON INTERNATIONAL AIRPORT *Book at aaa.com* — Phone: (780)980-0986

(CAA) (SAVE)

All Year — 1P: $89-$99 — 2P: $89-$99 — XP: $7 — F12
Location: Hwy 2, exit Edmonton International Airport/Nisku Business Park (10th Ave), 0.5 km s. 8340 Sparrow Crescent T9E 8B7. Fax: 780/980-4003. **Facility:** 50 units. 48 one-bedroom standard units, some with whirlpools. 2 one-bedroom suites ($139). 2 stories, interior corridors. **Parking:** on-site. **Terms:** cancellation fee imposed.
Small-scale Hotel **Amenities:** high-speed Internet, voice mail, irons, hair dryers. **Leisure Activities:** sauna, whirlpool, limited exercise equipment. **Guest Services:** coin laundry. **Business Services:** meeting rooms. **Cards:** AX, DC, MC, VI. **Special Amenities:** free continental breakfast and free newspaper.

SOME UNITS
[icons]

——— WHERE TO DINE ———

RUTH'S DELI — Lunch: $3-$8 — Dinner: $3-$8 — Phone: 780/986-0433

Deli/Subs
Sandwiches

Location: Just n at 50th St; in City Centre Mall. #26, 5201 50th St T9E 6T4. **Hours:** 8 am-5 pm. Closed major holidays; also Sat & Sun. **Features:** The delicatessen appeals to hurried diners looking for a quick, healthy bite to eat. Guests can get a sandwich and soup to go or eat in at one of the small dinner tables. Check out the sandwich board for daily specials and order at the counter for a meal that's ready in minutes. Casual dress. **Parking:** on-site. **Cards:** MC, VI.

[icon]

ZAMBELLIS RESTAURANT   Lunch: $8-$12   Dinner: $10-$20   Phone: 780/980-9669

♦♦♦ ♦♦♦
International

Location: Hwy 2, exit Leduc Business Centre (50th St). 6210 50th St T9E 7G9. **Hours:** 11 am-10 pm. Closed major holidays. **Features:** Although it's described as a steak and pizza place, the restaurant presents a much more diverse menu. Greek food is a highlight, as are child- and senior-size portions. The large, bustling dining room features an open-concept kitchen and small sports lounge. Expect generous portions and friendly service. Casual dress; cocktails. **Parking:** on-site. **Cards:** AX, DC, MC, VI.   Ⓨ Ⓧ

NISKU   (See map and index starting on p. 405)

—— WHERE TO STAY ——

HOLIDAY INN EXPRESS EDMONTON INT'L
AIRPORT   *Book at aaa.com*   Phone: (780)955-1000   ⑥⑨

Ⓐ Ⓢⓐⓥⓔ
♦♦♦ ♦♦♦ ♦♦♦
Small-scale Hotel

All Year   1P: $99   2P: $99   XP: $10   F18
Location: Hwy 2, exit Edmonton International Airport/Nisku Business Park (10th Ave), 0.8 km e. 1102 4th St T9E 8E2. Fax: 780/955-3009. **Facility:** 83 units. 81 one-bedroom standard units. 2 one-bedroom suites ($108-$153) with whirlpools. 4 stories, interior corridors. *Bath:* combo or shower only. **Parking:** on-site, winter plug-ins. **Terms:** package plans, pets ($10 deposit). **Amenities:** video games, high-speed Internet, dual phone lines, voice mail, irons, hair dryers. **Leisure Activities:** whirlpool, exercise room. **Guest Services:** valet and coin laundry. **Business Services:** meeting rooms. **Cards:** AX, DC, DS, MC, VI.

SOME UNITS

Ⓢⓓ ⊀ 🐾 ▥ &M ❒ 🎦 🎥 ᴅᴀᴛᴀ🅟🅞🅡🅣 ❒ / Ⓧ 🗋 🖵 /
FEE

NISKU INN & CONFERENCE CENTRE-EDMONTON
AIRPORT   *Book at aaa.com*   Phone: (780)955-7744   ⑥⑦

♦♦♦ ♦♦♦
Small-scale Hotel

All Year   1P: $139   2P: $139   XP: $10   F18
Location: Hwy 2, exit Edmonton International Airport/Nisku Business Park (10th Ave), 0.5 km e. 1101 4th St T9E 7N1. Fax: 780/955-7743. **Facility:** 156 one-bedroom standard units, some with whirlpools. 2 stories (no elevator), interior corridors. **Parking:** on-site. **Terms:** package plans, pets ($20 fee). **Amenities:** video games, high-speed Internet, voice mail, hair dryers. *Some:* irons. **Pool(s):** heated indoor. **Leisure Activities:** whirlpool, exercise room. **Guest Services:** gift shop, valet laundry, beauty salon. **Business Services:** conference facilities, PC (fee). **Cards:** AX, DC, MC, VI.

SOME UNITS

Ⓐⓢⓚ ⊀ 🐾 ▥ Ⓨ &M 🛥 🎥 ᴅᴀᴛᴀ🅟🅞🅡🅣 ❒ / Ⓧ 🗋 /
FEE

(See map and index starting on p. 405)

QUALITY INN-AIRPORT   *Book at aaa.com*

▼▼▼▼   All Year   1P: $95   2P: $115   XP: $10   Phone: (780)955-3001   **68**
F
Small-scale Hotel   **Location:** Hwy 2, exit Edmonton International Airport/Nisku Business Park (10th Ave), 0.8 km e. 501 11th Ave T9E 7N5.
Fax: 780/955-3006. **Facility:** 30 units. 29 one-bedroom standard units, some with whirlpools. 1 one-bedroom suite. 2 stories (no elevator), interior corridors. **Parking:** on-site, winter plug-ins. **Amenities:** irons,
hair dryers. **Guest Services:** valet laundry. **Business Services:** meeting rooms, PC. **Cards:** AX, DC, DS, JC, MC, VI.

SOME UNITS

(ASK) (SD) (✈) (†¶) (⅄) (✦) (⚙) (DATA PORT) (🖥) (🖥) / (✕) (🖥) /
FEE

ST. ALBERT pop. 53,081   (See map and index starting on p. 405)

———— WHERE TO DINE ————

RIC'S GRILL   **Lunch:** $9-$17   **Dinner:** $17-$30   **Phone:** 780/460-6602   **61**

▼▼▼   **Location:** Hwy 2 N, just e at St. Anne; corner of St. Anne and Perron St. 24 Perron St T8N 1E7. **Hours:** 11:30 am-10
pm, Fri & Sat-11 pm, Sun 4:30 pm-10 pm. Closed: 12/25. **Features:** On the site of the old Bruin Inn, this
Steak & Seafood   once was the only place where women could enjoy a drink without a male escort. Now anyone can come in
and enjoy a great steak or tasty entree, such as salmon, chicken and pasta dishes. The upscale and
contemporary dining room is a popular spot for locals. Black and white pictures from the olden days are featured upstairs, en
route to the bathrooms. Cocktails. **Parking:** on-site. **Cards:** AX, MC, VI.

(⅄) (✕)

SHERWOOD PARK pop. 47,645

———— WHERE TO STAY ————

BEST WESTERN SHERWOOD HOTEL &
CONFERENCE CENTRE   *Book at aaa.com*   **Phone:** (780)464-4900

▼▼▼   All Year   1P: $136-$149   XP: $10   F10
Small-scale Hotel   **Location:** 1 km sw of Hwy 16, exit Broadmoor Blvd. 2100 Premier Way T8H 2G4. Fax: 780/464-4796. **Facility:** 125
units. 119 one- and 6 two-bedroom standard units, some with whirlpools. 3 stories, interior corridors. **Bath:**
combo or shower only. **Parking:** on-site, winter plug-ins. **Terms:** check-in 4 pm, cancellation fee imposed.
Amenities: video games, high-speed Internet, dual phone lines, voice mail, irons, hair dryers. **Leisure Activities:** bicycles. *Fee:*
game room. **Guest Services:** gift shop, valet and coin laundry. **Business Services:** conference facilities. **Cards:** AX, DC,
MC, VI.

SOME UNITS

(ASK) (SD) (†¶) (⅄) (✦) (⚙) (DATA PORT) (🖥) / (✕) (🖥) (🖥) /
FEE

FRANKLIN'S INN   **Phone:** (780)467-1234

(CAA) (SAVE)   All Year   1P: $75-$135   2P: $75-$135   XP: $10   F15
▼▼ ▼▼   **Location:** At Granada Blvd. Located next to a shopping complex. 2016 Sherwood Dr T8A 3X3. Fax: 780/467-3907.
Facility: 40 one-bedroom standard units, some with whirlpools. 3 stories, interior corridors. **Parking:** on-site, winter plug-ins. **Terms:** 7 day cancellation notice, pets ($5 fee, in smoking rooms). **Amenities:** voice
Small-scale Hotel   mail. *Some:* irons, hair dryers. **Dining:** 6 am-3 pm, cocktails. **Leisure Activities:** *Fee:* esthetics. **Guest
Services:** gift shop, valet laundry, beauty salon. **Business Services:** conference facilities. **Cards:** AX, DC,
MC, VI. **Special Amenities:** free local telephone calls.

SOME UNITS

(🛏) (†¶) (⅄) (⚙) (🖥) / (✕) (DATA PORT) (🖥) (🖥) /
FEE   FEE FEE

FRANKLIN'S INN / RAMADA LIMITED-EDMONTON EAST/SHERWOOD
PARK   *Book at aaa.com*   **Phone:** (780)467-6727

(CAA) (SAVE)   7/16-8/1 [ECP]   1P: $120   2P: $125   XP: $5   F17
▼▼ ▼▼   3/1-7/15 & 8/2-2/28 [ECP]   1P: $111   2P: $116   XP: $5   F17
Location: Hwy 14, 1.5 km e on Baseline Rd, 0.4 km n on Broadmoor Blvd; Hwy 16, exit Broadmoor Blvd, 2.5 km s. 30
Broadway Blvd T8H 2A2. Fax: 780/467-5685. **Facility:** 63 one-bedroom standard units. 4 stories, interior
Small-scale Hotel   corridors. **Parking:** on-site, winter plug-ins. **Terms:** small pets only ($10 fee, in smoking units).
Amenities: high-speed Internet (fee), voice mail, irons, hair dryers. **Leisure Activities:** whirlpool, exercise
room. **Guest Services:** valet and coin laundry. **Business Services:** meeting rooms. **Cards:** AX, DC, MC, VI.
Special Amenities: free expanded continental breakfast and free local telephone calls.

SOME UNITS

(SD) (🛏) (†¶) (♿) (GM) (DATA PORT) (🖥) (🖥) / (✕) /
FEE

ROADKING INNS   **Phone:** (780)464-1000

(CAA) (SAVE)   All Year   1P: $89-$99   2P: $89-$99   XP: $10   F18
▼▼ ▼▼   **Location:** Just sw of Hwy 16, exit Broadmoor Blvd. Located next to a truck stop facility. 26 Strathmoor Dr T8H 2B6.
Fax: 780/464-1043. **Facility:** 88 one-bedroom standard units. 2 stories, interior corridors. **Parking:** on-site.
Terms: package plans, pets ($100 deposit, in smoking units). **Amenities:** voice mail, irons, hair dryers.
Small-scale Hotel   **Dining:** 2 restaurants, 24 hours, cocktails. **Leisure Activities:** exercise room. *Fee:* game room. **Guest
Services:** gift shop, valet and coin laundry. **Business Services:** meeting rooms, fax (fee). **Cards:** AX, DC,
MC, VI. **Special Amenities:** free local telephone calls and free room upgrade (subject to availability with advance
reservations).

SOME UNITS

(SD) (🛏) (†¶) (⅄) (DATA PORT) (🖥) / (✕) (🖥) /
FEE

———— WHERE TO DINE ————

SORRENTINO'S BISTRO BAR   **Lunch:** $8-$13   **Dinner:** $10-$18   **Phone:** 780/449-1384

▼▼ ▼▼   **Location:** Hwy 16, exit Broadmoor Blvd S, 5 km to Wye Rd; northeast corner of Sherwood Dr and Wye Rd. 1020
Sherwood Dr T8A 2G4. **Hours:** 11 am-2:30 & 5-10 pm, Thurs-Sat 11 am-2:30 & 4-midnight, Sun 4 pm-10 pm.
Italian   Closed: 1/1, 12/25. **Reservations:** suggested. **Features:** Italian ambience and cuisine await at the cozy
restaurant, which prepares pizza, calzones and, of course, pasta dishes. There are daily specials, and the
service is friendly and attentive. Cocktails. **Parking:** on-site. **Cards:** AX, MC, VI.

(⅄) (✕)

SUMO SUMO SUSHI BAR & GRILL   **Lunch:** $5-$13   **Dinner:** $5-$13   **Phone:** 780/416-7866
Sushi
Location: Corner of Baseline Rd and Broadmoor; in Baseline Village Shopping Plaza. #390, 222 Baseline Rd T8H 1S8. **Hours:** 11:30 am-9 pm, Fri & Sat-9:30 pm, Sun noon-9 pm. Closed: 12/25. **Features:** In a small shopping plaza, this gem of a restaurant appeals to those with sumo appetites but who don't want to pay sumo prices. A wonderful selection of traditional and nouveau sushi is available, as is a teppanyaki bar. Locals frequent this place. Casual dress; cocktails. **Parking:** on-site. **Cards:** MC, VI.

VICKY'S RESTAURANT   **Lunch:** $7-$12   **Dinner:** $12-$20   **Phone:** 780/417-1750
International
Location: Corner of Broadmoor Blvd and Wye Rd; accessible from Broadmoor Blvd. #86, 993 Fir St T8A 4N5. **Hours:** 11 am-10 pm, Sat from 5 pm, Sun from 4 pm. Closed: 12/25, 12/26. **Features:** A well-known spot in the Sherwood Park community, the family-run restaurant has been serving excellent homemade food for many years. Patrons can choose from such Greek specialties as spanakopita and souvlaki or try one of the other International dishes. A visit is not complete without a trip to the restroom, where an eclectic mix of interesting trinkets is on display. Casual dress; cocktails. **Parking:** on-site. **Cards:** AX, MC, VI.

SPRUCE GROVE pop. 15,983

———— **WHERE TO STAY** ————

ROYAL INN EXPRESS HOTEL   **Phone:** (780)962-6050
Small-scale Hotel

| | 1P: $88-$94 | 2P: $88-$94 | XP: $10 | F16 |

All Year [CP]
Location: I-16A, just n. 20 Westgrove Dr T7X 3X3. Fax: 780/962-6588. **Facility:** 48 units. 47 one-bedroom standard units, some with whirlpools. 1 one-bedroom suite ($99-$150). 4 stories, interior corridors. **Bath:** combo or shower only. **Parking:** on-site, winter plug-ins. **Terms:** office hours 6 am-midnight, cancellation fee imposed, small pets only ($10 fee). **Amenities:** dual phone lines, voice mail, irons, hair dryers. **Guest Services:** valet and coin laundry. **Cards:** AX, DC, JC, MC, VI.

SOME UNITS

STONY PLAIN pop. 9,589

———— **WHERE TO STAY** ————

RAMADA INN & SUITES   *Book at aaa.com*   **Phone:** (780)963-0222
Small-scale Hotel

	1P: $88-$129	2P: $95-$129	XP: $7	F17
7/1-8/31				
3/1-6/30 & 9/1-2/28	1P: $68-$106	2P: $75-$106	XP: $7	F17

Location: Hwy 16A, exit Dunmore Rd, just s. 3301 43rd Ave T7Z 1L1. Fax: 780/963-6030. **Facility:** 88 units. 72 one-bedroom standard units, some with efficiencies and/or whirlpools. 16 one-bedroom suites ($98-$106), some with efficiencies, kitchens and/or whirlpools. 2 stories (no elevator), interior/exterior corridors. **Parking:** on-site, winter plug-ins. **Terms:** check-in 4 pm, pets ($4 extra charge). **Amenities:** irons, hair dryers. **Pool(s):** heated indoor. **Leisure Activities:** sauna, whirlpool. **Guest Services:** valet and coin laundry, area transportation (fee). **Business Services:** meeting rooms. **Cards:** AX, DC, DS, MC, VI.

SOME UNITS

STONY CONVENTION INN   **Phone:** (780)963-3444
Small-scale Hotel

1/1-2/28	1P: $64-$74	2P: $71-$81	XP: $7	F12
9/1-12/31	1P: $59-$69	2P: $66-$76	XP: $7	F12
7/1-8/31	1P: $69	2P: $76	XP: $7	F12
3/1-6/30	1P: $64-$74	2P: $64-$74	XP: $7	F12

Location: Hwy 16A, exit Stony Plain Rd, 0.8 km s on SR 779. 4620 48th St T7Z 1L4. Fax: 780/963-9492. **Facility:** 48 units. 46 one-bedroom standard units, some with efficiencies. 2 one-bedroom suites with whirlpools, some with efficiencies. 2 stories (no elevator), interior corridors. **Parking:** on-site, winter plug-ins. **Terms:** check-in 4 pm, cancellation fee imposed, small pets only ($3 fee). **Guest Services:** gift shop, valet and coin laundry, area transportation. **Business Services:** meeting rooms. **Cards:** AX, MC, VI.

SOME UNITS

This ends listings for the Edmonton Vicinity.
The following page resumes the alphabetical listings of
cities in Alberta.

EDSON pop. 7,585

──────── WHERE TO STAY ────────

BEST WESTERN HIGH ROAD INN   *Book at aaa.com*   **Phone:** 780/712-2378
All Year   1P: $99-$199   2P: $109-$199   XP: $10   F12
Location: On 2nd Ave; centre. 300 52nd St T7E 1V8 (PO Box 7770). Fax: 780/723-1868. **Facility:** 114 units. 107 one-bedroom standard units. 7 one-bedroom suites, some with whirlpools. 4 stories, interior corridors.
Small-scale Hotel   **Parking:** on-site, winter plug-ins. **Terms:** check-in 4 pm, small pets only ($10 fee). **Amenities:** high-speed Internet, voice mail, irons, hair dryers. *Some:* dual phone lines, fax. **Pool(s):** heated indoor. **Leisure Activities:** whirlpool, waterslide, exercise room. **Guest Services:** valet laundry. **Business Services:** meeting rooms. **Cards:** AX, DC, DS, MC, VI.

SOME UNITS
🛏 🍴 ⅄ 🐾 ⊠ 🎥 [DATA PORT] 🛗 💻 /⊠ 📷 /
FEE

GUEST HOUSE INN & SUITES   **Phone:** 780/723-4486
(CAA) (SAVE)   All Year   1P: $76-$86   2P: $84-$90   XP: $10   F6
Location: 1 km e on Hwy 16. 4411 4th Ave T7E 1B8. Fax: 780/723-2006. **Facility:** 108 units. 89 one-bedroom standard units, some with kitchens and/or whirlpools. 18 one- and 1 two-bedroom suites ($100-$180) with kitchens. 1-3 stories (no elevator), interior/exterior corridors. **Parking:** on-site, winter plug-ins. **Terms:** pets
Motel   ($6 fee). **Amenities:** voice mail, hair dryers. **Dining:** 5:30 am-11 pm, cocktails. **Leisure Activities:** sauna, steamroom, exercise room. **Guest Services:** coin laundry. **Business Services:** meeting rooms, PC.
Cards: AX, MC, VI. **Special Amenities:** free full breakfast and free local telephone calls.

SOME UNITS
[S D] 🛏 🍴 ⊠ 🎥 [DATA PORT] 🛗 💻 /⊠ 📷 /
FEE

SUPER 8 MOTEL   *Book at aaa.com*   **Phone:** 780/723-2500
All Year [CP]   1P: $73-$86   2P: $81-$94   XP: $8   F12
Location: 1.1 km e on Hwy 16. 4300 2nd Ave T7E 1B8. Fax: 780/723-2544. **Facility:** 45 one-bedroom standard units. 2 stories (no elevator), interior corridors. **Parking:** on-site, winter plug-ins. **Terms:** small pets only
Small-scale Hotel   ($50 deposit, $10 extra charge, in designated units). **Amenities:** *Some:* high-speed Internet (fee). **Guest Services:** coin laundry. **Business Services:** PC. **Cards:** AX, DC, DS, MC, VI.

SOME UNITS
🛏 🍴 🎥 [DATA PORT] 🛗 💻 /⊠ /
FEE

──────── WHERE TO DINE ────────

MJ STEAK & SEAFOOD RESTAURANT   **Lunch:** $5-$10   **Dinner:** $9-$25   **Phone:** 780/712-4388
Location: Hwy 16 W, just after the highway splits. 4332 4th Ave T7E 1P7. **Hours:** 5:30 am-10 pm, Sat & Sun from 5 am. Closed: 12/24, 12/25, 12/26. **Features:** The simple restaurant features a wide variety of sandwiches
International   and soups on its lunch menu, as well as lays out an all-you-can-eat lunch buffet. Dinner entrees center on reasonably priced choices of steaks and seafood. Service is attentive. Casual dress; cocktails. **Parking:** on-site. **Cards:** AX, MC, VI.

⊠

FORT MACLEOD pop. 2,990

──────── WHERE TO STAY ────────

FORT MOTEL   **Phone:** (403)553-3606
All Year   1P: $40-$55
Location: Centre. 451 Main St T0L 0Z0 (PO Box 1032). Fax: 403/553-2718. **Facility:** 14 units. 13 one-bedroom standard units, some with efficiencies. 1 two-bedroom suite ($40-$55) with kitchen. 1 story, exterior
Motel   corridors. **Parking:** on-site, winter plug-ins. **Terms:** office hours 8 am-11 pm, weekly rates available, pets ($10 fee, in smoking units, with prior approval). **Cards:** MC, VI.

SOME UNITS
[ASK] [S D] 🛏 🍴 🎥 🛗 📷 💻 /⊠ /
FEE

SUNSET MOTEL   **Phone:** 403/553-4448
(CAA) (SAVE)   5/16-9/30 [CP]   1P: $50-$56   2P: $50-$62   XP: $6
3/1-5/15 & 10/1-2/28 [CP]   1P: $42-$46   2P: $42-$50   XP: $4
Location: 1 km w on Hwy 2 and 3. 104 Hwy 3W T0L 0Z0 (PO Box 398). Fax: 403/553-2784. **Facility:** 22 units. 13 one- and 8 two-bedroom standard units, some with kitchens. 1 two-bedroom suite ($64-$90) with kitchen. 1
Motel   story, exterior corridors. **Bath:** combo or shower only. **Parking:** on-site, winter plug-ins. **Terms:** office hours 7 am-11 pm. **Guest Services:** gift shop. **Business Services:** meeting rooms. **Cards:** AX, DC, MC, VI.
Special Amenities: free continental breakfast and free local telephone calls.

SOME UNITS
[S D] 🛏 🎥 [DATA PORT] 🛗 📷 💻 /⊠ /

──────── WHERE TO DINE ────────

AUNTY LYNDA'S CAFE & GRILL   **Lunch:** $6-$8   **Dinner:** $10-$17   **Phone:** 403/553-2655
(CAA)   **Location:** East end of town. 2323 7th Ave T0L 0Z0. **Hours:** 7 am-9 pm. Closed: 12/25. **Features:** The charming restaurant's menu lists a good selection of seafood, veal, beef and pasta dishes, as well as creative burgers and home-baked pies and cheesecake. The clean, bright, homey decor has a country flair. Casual dress;
Canadian   cocktails. **Parking:** on-site. **Cards:** AX, MC, VI.

⊠

JOHNNY'S RESTAURANT   **Lunch:** $6-$9   **Dinner:** $6-$16   **Phone:** 403/553-3939
Location: Next to Empress Theatre. 225 24th St (Main St) T0L 0Z0. **Hours:** 10 am-9 pm, Sun 11 am-8 pm. Closed: 1/1, 12/25. **Reservations:** suggested. **Features:** The highly trained chef/owner prepares an
Chinese   extensive selection of Western and Chinese dishes. Fresh ingredients, generous portions and unsurpassed friendliness make this a gem of a place. Entrees include selections of salmon, veal, prawns, ribs and steak, as well as fresh pasta and lighter sandwiches. Casual dress; cocktails. **Parking:** on-site. **Cards:** AX, MC, VI.

⊠

FORT MCMURRAY

──── WHERE TO STAY ────

HOLIDAY INN HOTEL & SUITES FORT MCMURRAY   *Book at aaa.com*   Phone: (780)714-9444
▼▼▼▼
Small-scale Hotel
All Year   1P: $142-$179   XP: $10   F
Location: Hwy 63, exit Hospital St, just e to Franklin Ave, then 1 km se. 8200 Franklin Ave T9H 2H9. Fax: 780/714-9440. **Facility:** 92 units. 62 one-bedroom standard units, some with whirlpools. 30 one-bedroom suites. 3 stories, interior corridors. **Parking:** on-site. **Terms:** cancellation fee imposed. **Amenities:** high-speed Internet, dual phone lines, voice mail, irons, hair dryers. **Pool(s):** heated indoor. **Leisure Activities:** whirlpool, exercise room. **Guest Services:** valet laundry. **Business Services:** meeting rooms, PC. **Cards:** AX, DC, DS, MC, VI. *(See color ad card insert)*

SOME UNITS

QUALITY HOTEL & CONFERENCE CENTRE FORT MCMURRAY   *Book at aaa.com*   Phone: (780)791-7200
(CAA) (SAVE)
▼▼ ▼▼
Small-scale Hotel
All Year   1P: $150-$270   2P: $150-$270   XP: $10   F17
Location: Hwy 63, 1 km e at Gregoire Dr. Located on southside of the city. 424 Gregoire Dr T9H 3R2. Fax: 780/790-1658. **Facility:** 154 units. 150 one-bedroom standard units, some with whirlpools. 4 one-bedroom suites, some with kitchens and/or whirlpools. 3 stories, interior corridors. **Parking:** on-site, winter plug-ins. **Terms:** package plans, pets (in designated units). **Amenities:** video games, high-speed Internet, voice mail, hair dryers. *Some:* dual phone lines, irons. **Dining:** 5:30 am-10 pm, cocktails. **Pool(s):** small heated indoor. **Leisure Activities:** whirlpool, exercise room. **Guest Services:** valet laundry. **Business Services:** conference facilities, PC. **Cards:** AX, DC, DS, MC, VI. **Special Amenities:** free local telephone calls and free newspaper.

SOME UNITS

RADISSON HOTEL & SUITES   *Book at aaa.com*   Phone: (780)743-2400
▼▼▼
Small-scale Hotel
All Year   1P: $149-$299   XP: $10   F12
Location: From Hwy 63, 1 km e. 435 Gregoire Dr T9H 4K7. Fax: 780/743-2448. **Facility:** 134 units. 123 one-bedroom standard units. 11 one-bedroom suites, some with whirlpools. 5 stories, interior corridors. **Parking:** on-site. **Terms:** check-in 4 pm, cancellation fee imposed, package plans. **Amenities:** video games, high-speed Internet, voice mail, safes, irons, hair dryers. *Some:* dual phone lines. **Pool(s):** heated indoor. **Leisure Activities:** whirlpool, waterslide, exercise room. **Guest Services:** valet and coin laundry. **Business Services:** meeting rooms. **Cards:** AX, CB, DC, DS, JC, MC, VI. *(See color ad p 377)*

SOME UNITS

THE SAWRIDGE INN & CONFERENCE CENTRE   *Book at aaa.com*   Phone: (780)791-7900
▼▼ ▼
Small-scale Hotel
All Year   1P: $139-$189   2P: $149-$199   XP: $10   F
Location: 6 km s, just e of Hwy 63, exit MacKenzie Blvd. 530 MacKenzie Blvd T9H 4C8. Fax: 780/743-4654. **Facility:** 188 units. 185 one-bedroom standard units, some with whirlpools. 3 one-bedroom suites ($169-$399) with whirlpools. 3 stories, interior corridors. **Parking:** on-site, winter plug-ins. **Terms:** check-in 4 pm, 5 day cancellation notice, [AP] & [BP] meal plans available, package plans. **Amenities:** video games, high-speed Internet, voice mail, hair dryers. *Some:* honor bars, irons. **Pool(s):** heated indoor. **Leisure Activities:** whirlpool, exercise room. **Guest Services:** gift shop, valet laundry. **Business Services:** conference facilities, business center. **Cards:** AX, DC, JC, MC, VI.

SOME UNITS

SUPER 8 MOTEL   *Book at aaa.com*   Phone: (780)799-8450
▼▼ ▼
Small-scale Hotel
All Year [CP]   1P: $89-$150   2P: $99-$150
Location: Just w of Hwy 63, 5 km s. 321 Sakitawaw Tr T9H 5E7. Fax: 780/799-8464. **Facility:** 100 one-bedroom standard units, some with whirlpools. 2 stories (no elevator), interior corridors. **Parking:** on-site, winter plug-ins. **Terms:** pets ($10 fee). **Amenities:** high-speed Internet, voice mail. *Some:* irons, hair dryers. **Leisure Activities:** whirlpool, exercise room. **Guest Services:** valet and coin laundry. **Business Services:** meeting rooms. **Cards:** AX, DC, DS, MC, VI.

SOME UNITS
FEE

──── WHERE TO DINE ────

THE FISH PLACE   Lunch: $10-$15   Dinner: $15-$24   Phone: 780/791-4040
▼▼ ▼
Seafood
Location: Hwy 63, exit Thickwood Blvd, 1.8 km w; in small shopping plaza. 412 Thickwood Blvd T9K 1P1. **Hours:** 11 am-11 pm, Sun-10 pm. Closed major holidays. **Reservations:** suggested. **Features:** A well-known fact about Fort McMurray is that the largest population of Newfoundlanders outside of Newfoundland is found here. As a result, the superb fish restaurant was established to accommodate that population. Seven days a week, the nautical, cozy restaurant is busy serving seafood and evening specials. Seafood lovers looking for a hearty meal with speedy service should look no further. Casual dress; cocktails. **Parking:** on-site. **Cards:** AX, MC, VI.

FORT SASKATCHEWAN —*See Edmonton p. 422.*

GRANDE PRAIRIE pop. 36,983

──── WHERE TO STAY ────

AMERIHOST INN & SUITES   *Book at aaa.com*   Phone: (780)831-2999
(CAA) (SAVE)
▼▼ ▼
Small-scale Hotel
All Year [ECP]   1P: $109-$275   2P: $109-$275
Location: 102nd St at 117th Ave. 11710 102nd St T8V 7S7. Fax: 780/513-1146. **Facility:** 66 units. 29 one-bedroom standard units. 37 one-bedroom suites, some with kitchens and/or whirlpools. 3 stories, interior corridors. **Parking:** on-site, winter plug-ins. **Terms:** pets ($20 extra charge). **Amenities:** video games, high-speed Internet, voice mail, irons, hair dryers. **Pool(s):** heated indoor. **Leisure Activities:** whirlpool, waterslide, exercise room. **Guest Services:** valet and coin laundry. **Business Services:** meeting rooms, business center. **Cards:** AX, DC, MC, VI. **Special Amenities:** free expanded continental breakfast and free local telephone calls.

SOME UNITS
FEE

BEST WESTERN GRANDE PRAIRIE HOTEL &
SUITES   *Book at aaa.com*
Phone: (780)402-2378

(CAA) (SAVE)

All Year   1P: $99-$119   2P: $99-$119
Location: Corner of Hwy 43 and 117th Ave. 10745 117th Ave T8V 7N6. Fax: 780/402-8026. Facility: 100 units. 63
one-bedroom standard units, some with whirlpools. 37 one-bedroom suites. 4 stories, interior corridors.
Small-scale Hotel   Parking: on-site, winter plug-ins. Terms: pets ($20 fee). Amenities: video games, high-speed Internet, dual
phone lines, voice mail, irons, hair dryers. Dining: Sorrentino's, see separate listing. Pool(s): heated indoor.
Leisure Activities: whirlpool, exercise room. Guest Services: area transportation-within city limits, tanning
facility. Business Services: meeting rooms, business center. Cards: AX, DC, MC, VI. Special Amenities: free expanded
continental breakfast and free local telephone calls.

SOME UNITS
[icons] / [icons] /
FEE

QUALITY HOTEL & CONFERENCE CENTRE
GRANDE PRAIRIE   *Book at aaa.com*
Phone: (780)539-6000

All Year [BP]   1P: $90-$134   2P: $90-$134   XP: $10   F17
Location: 2.9 km w on Hwy 2. 11201 100th Ave T8V 5M6. Fax: 780/532-1961. Facility: 102 units. 98 one-
bedroom standard units. 4 one-bedroom suites ($120-$184) with efficiencies. 10 stories, interior corridors.
Small-scale Hotel   Parking: on-site, winter plug-ins. Terms: package plans, pets ($10 extra charge). Amenities: video games,
high-speed Internet, voice mail, irons, hair dryers. Leisure Activities: exercise room, game room. Guest Services: valet
laundry. Business Services: conference facilities, PC. Cards: AX, DC, DS, JC, MC, VI.

SOME UNITS
(ASK) [icons] / [icons] /
FEE

SERVICE PLUS INNS AND SUITES   *Book at aaa.com*
Phone: (780)538-3900

All Year   1P: $99-$250   2P: $99-$250
Location: 2.2 km w on Hwy 2, just n. Located adjacent to a casino. 10810 107th A Ave T8V 7A9. Fax: 780/532-8558.
Small-scale Hotel   Facility: 123 units. 120 one- and 2 two-bedroom standard units. 1 one-bedroom suite ($99-$250) with
whirlpool. 4 stories, interior corridors. Bath: combo or shower only. Parking: on-site, winter plug-ins.
Terms: package plans, pets ($10 extra charge in smoking units). Amenities: video games, voice mail, irons, hair dryers.
Some: high-speed Internet, dual phone lines, fax. Pool(s): heated indoor. Leisure Activities: whirlpool, waterslide, limited
exercise equipment. Guest Services: valet laundry. Business Services: meeting rooms, PC. Cards: AX, DC, MC, VI.

SOME UNITS
[icons] / [icons] /
FEE

STANFORD INN
Phone: (780)539-5678

All Year   1P: $69-$79   2P: $72-$82   XP: $5   F16
Location: 2.8 km w on Hwy 2. 11401 100th Ave T8V 5M6. Fax: 780/538-3913. Facility: 204 units. 202 one-
bedroom standard units, some with efficiencies, kitchens and/or whirlpools. 2 two-bedroom suites ($170)
Small-scale Hotel   with kitchens and whirlpools. 2 stories (no elevator), interior/exterior corridors. Parking: on-site, winter plug-
ins. Terms: pets ($5 extra charge). Amenities: video library, voice mail, irons, hair dryers. Some: high-speed Internet. Leisure
Activities: whirlpool, steamroom, exercise room. Guest Services: coin laundry. Business Services: meeting rooms.
Cards: AX, DC, MC, VI.

SOME UNITS
(ASK) [icons] / [icons] /
FEE

TRUMPETER HOTEL & MEETING CENTRE
Phone: (780)539-5561

(CAA) (SAVE)

All Year   1P: $89   2P: $99   XP: $10   F16
Location: 100th St at 121st Ave. 12102 100th St T8V 5P1. Fax: 780/538-4636. Facility: 122 units. 120 one-
bedroom standard units, some with whirlpools. 2 one-bedroom suites ($169) with whirlpools. 3 stories,
interior corridors. Parking: on-site, winter plug-ins. Amenities: voice mail, hair dryers. Some: high-speed
Small-scale Hotel   Internet, irons. Dining: 2 restaurants, 6 am-11 pm, cocktails. Leisure Activities: exercise room. Guest
Services: valet laundry. Business Services: meeting rooms. Cards: AX, DC, MC, VI. Special Amenities:
free local telephone calls and free newspaper.

SOME UNITS
[icons] / [icons] /

——— **WHERE TO DINE** ———

ACROPOLIS
Lunch: $8-$13   Dinner: $10-$21   Phone: 780/538-4424
Location: Corner of 100th St and 101st Ave; downtown. 10011 101st Ave T8V 0X9. Hours: 11 am-2 & 5-10 pm, Sat
from 5 pm. Closed major holidays; also Sun & Mon. Reservations: suggested. Features: A taste of Greece
Greek   is found at the downtown eatery, where diners find fare ranging from spanakopita and souvlaki to moussaka
and baklava. Portions are not skimpy and are served by friendly, attentive staff members. Casual dress;
cocktails. Parking: street. Cards: AX, DC, MC, VI.

[icons]

BARCELONA STEAKHOUSE & GRILL
Lunch: $10-$22   Dinner: $16-$28   Phone: 780/532-4201
Location: Corner of Hwy 40 and 98th Ave; in Holiday Inn. 9816 107th St T8V 1L4. Hours: 11 am-2 & 4:30-10 pm.
Closed major holidays. Reservations: suggested. Features: In the Holiday Inn Grande Prairie, the upscale
Steak House   steakhouse offers both an a la carte menu and a fantastic buffet at lunch. With fine surroundings, friendly
service and great AAA Alberta beef, this is a great place to dine. Casual dress. Parking: on-site.
Cards: MC, VI.

[icons]

THE GOLDEN STAR
Lunch: $6-$10   Dinner: $10-$14   Phone: 780/532-7549
Location: Centre. 10112 101st Ave T8V 0Y2. Hours: 11 am-11 pm, Sun-9 pm. Closed: 12/25.
Reservations: accepted. Features: Patrons can expect a friendly atmosphere and a contemporary setting.
Chinese   A few Western dishes show up on a menu that's predominantly Chinese. Dim sum is served on weekends.
Service is prompt and cordial. Casual dress; cocktails. Parking: street. Cards: AX, CB, DC, MC, VI.

[icons]

SORRENTINO'S

Italian

Dinner: $15-$26   **Phone:** 780/814-7171

Location: Corner of Hwy 43 and 117th Ave; in Best Western Grande Prairie Hotel & Suites. 10745 117th Ave T8V 7N6. **Hours:** 4:30 pm-11 pm. Closed major holidays. **Features:** This Italian eatery is intimately lit and employs an efficient staff. Representative of traditional dishes are risotto, lasagna, fettuccine and lamb. The decadent desserts shouldn't be overlooked. Casual dress; cocktails. **Parking:** on-site. **Cards:** AX, DC, MC, VI. ✉

HIGH RIVER pop. 9,345

———— WHERE TO STAY ————

HERITAGE INN

Small-scale Hotel

	1P: $89	2P: $97	XP: $5	F16
1/1-2/28	1P: $89	2P: $97	XP: $5	F16
3/1-12/31	1P: $87	2P: $95	XP: $5	F16

Phone: (403)652-3834

Location: Trans-Canada Hwy 2, exit 23, 2 km w of Hwy 2. 1104 11th Ave SE T1V 1M4. Fax: 403/652-4432. **Facility:** 73 units. 72 one-bedroom standard units, some with whirlpools. 1 one-bedroom suite ($115-$150) with whirlpool. 2 stories (no elevator), interior corridors. **Parking:** on-site, winter plug-ins. **Terms:** package plans, pets ($5 fee, in smoking units). **Pool(s):** small heated indoor. **Leisure Activities:** whirlpool, limited exercise equipment. **Business Services:** meeting rooms. **Cards:** AX, DC, DS, MC, VI.

SOME UNITS

(ASK) SⅮ [icons] FEE / ✉ VCR /

SUPER 8 MOTEL   *Book at aaa.com*

Small-scale Hotel

	1P: $100-$160	2P: $100-$160	XP: $10	F12
5/16-9/30 [CP]	1P: $100-$160	2P: $100-$160	XP: $10	F12
3/1-5/15 & 10/1-2/28 [CP]	1P: $90-$160	2P: $100-$160	XP: $10	F12

Phone: (403)652-4448

Location: Trans-Canada Hwy 2, exit High River, just w. 1601 13th Ave SE T1V 1M6 (Box 5505). Fax: 403/652-4649. **Facility:** 60 one-bedroom standard units, some with efficiencies and/or whirlpools. 3 stories, interior corridors. *Bath:* combo or shower only. **Parking:** on-site, winter plug-ins. **Terms:** package plans, pets ($10 extra charge). **Amenities:** voice mail, irons, hair dryers. *Some:* video games. **Pool(s):** small heated indoor. **Leisure Activities:** whirlpool, waterslide, exercise room. **Guest Services:** valet and coin laundry. **Business Services:** meeting rooms. **Cards:** AX, DC, DS, MC, VI.

SOME UNITS

(ASK) SⅮ [icons] FEE / ✉ VCR /

———— WHERE TO DINE ————

WHISTLESTOP CAFE

Canadian

Lunch: $5-$8   **Phone:** 403/652-7026

Location: 1 km n at 3rd Ave; next to museum. 129 3rd Ave SW T1V 1S2. **Hours:** 8 am-5 pm; 10 am-4 pm in winter. Closed major holidays. **Features:** Simple, well-prepared food is one of the reasons to come to the distinctive eatery. Its location in a 1947 Canadian Pacific rail coach car, complete with CP memorabilia, is another. On the menu is a wide variety of comfort foods, including sandwiches, quiche, quesadillas and fried green tomatoes. The dessert selection is extensive. Guests can enjoy lunch or afternoon tea and imagine the car swaying gently along the tracks as it did long ago. Casual dress. **Parking:** on-site. **Cards:** MC, VI. ✉

HINTON pop. 9,405

———— WHERE TO STAY ————

BEST WESTERN WHITE WOLF INN   *Book at aaa.com*

Small-scale Hotel

	1P: $110-$170	2P: $116-$170	XP: $10	F17
6/16-10/15 [CP]	1P: $110-$170	2P: $116-$170	XP: $10	F17
5/1-6/15 [CP]	1P: $96-$160	2P: $106-$160	XP: $10	F17
3/1-4/30 & 10/16-2/28 [CP]	1P: $84-$126	2P: $96-$126	XP: $10	F17

Phone: (780)865-7777

Location: At west end of town; just off Hwy 16. 828 Carmichael Ln T7V 1T1. Fax: 780/865-3484. **Facility:** 42 units. 39 one- and 2 two-bedroom standard units, some with whirlpools. 1 one-bedroom suite. 2 stories (no elevator), exterior corridors. **Parking:** on-site, winter plug-ins. **Terms:** cancellation fee imposed, pets ($10 fee). **Amenities:** irons, hair dryers. **Leisure Activities:** whirlpool, limited exercise equipment. **Guest Services:** valet laundry. **Cards:** AX, DC, DS, MC, VI.

SOME UNITS

(ASK) SⅮ [icons] FEE / ✉ /

CRESTWOOD HOTEL

Small-scale Hotel

	1P: $119-$175	2P: $119-$175	XP: $5	F12
5/1-9/30	1P: $119-$175	2P: $119-$175	XP: $5	F12
3/1-4/30 & 10/1-2/28	1P: $89-$125	2P: $89-$125	XP: $5	F12

Phone: (780)865-4001

Location: 1 km w on Hwy 16. 678 Carmichael Ln T7V 1S9. Fax: 780/865-8886. **Facility:** 97 one-bedroom standard units, some with kitchens. 3 stories (no elevator), interior corridors. **Parking:** on-site, winter plug-ins. **Terms:** cancellation fee imposed. **Amenities:** hair dryers. **Pool(s):** heated indoor. **Leisure Activities:** sauna. **Guest Services:** sundries, valet and coin laundry. **Business Services:** conference facilities, PC. **Cards:** AX, DC, MC, VI.

SOME UNITS

(ASK) SⅮ [icons] / ✉ /

DAYS INN   *Book at aaa.com*

CAA SAVE

Small-scale Hotel

| All Year | 1P: $99 | 2P: $159 | XP: $10 | F12 |

Phone: (780)817-1960

Location: 2.3 km e on Hwy 16. 358 Smith St T7V 2A1. Fax: 780/865-4064. **Facility:** 40 units. 39 one- and 1 two-bedroom standard units, some with efficiencies. 2 stories (no elevator), interior corridors. **Parking:** on-site, winter plug-ins. **Amenities:** hair dryers. **Leisure Activities:** whirlpool, exercise room. **Guest Services:** valet and coin laundry. **Business Services:** meeting rooms. **Cards:** AX, MC, VI. **Special Amenities:** free continental breakfast and free newspaper.

SOME UNITS

[icons] / ✉ /

HOLIDAY INN HINTON   *Book at aaa.com*

Phone: (780)865-3321

6/1-9/30	1P: $129	2P: $129
3/1-5/31 & 10/1-2/28	1P: $99	2P: $99

Small-scale Hotel

Location: 0.5 km w on Hwy 16. 393 Gregg Ave T7V 1N1. **Fax:** 780/865-7856. **Facility:** 104 units. 102 one-bedroom standard units. 1 one- and 1 two-bedroom suites ($159-$199), some with whirlpools. 2 stories (no elevator), interior corridors. **Parking:** on-site, winter plug-ins. **Terms:** [AP] meal plan available. **Amenities:** video games, high-speed Internet, dual phone lines, voice mail, irons, hair dryers. **Dining:** 5:30 am-11 pm, cocktails. **Pool(s):** heated outdoor. **Leisure Activities:** exercise room. **Guest Services:** valet and coin laundry. **Business Services:** meeting rooms, PC (fee). **Cards:** AX, DC, DS, MC, VI. **Special Amenities:** free local telephone calls and free newspaper. *(See color ad card insert)*

SOME UNITS

OVERLANDER MOUNTAIN LODGE

Phone: 780/866-2330

6/13-9/30	1P: $132-$194	2P: $132-$194	XP: $15	F15
10/1-1/2 & 1/16-2/28 [ECP]	1P: $120	2P: $120	XP: $15	F15
3/1-6/12 [ECP]	1P: $115	2P: $115	XP: $15	F15

Country Inn

Location: Hwy 16, 24 km w. Hwy 16 T7V 1X5 (PO Box 118). **Fax:** 780/866-2332. **Facility:** 41 units. 24 one-bedroom standard units, some with kitchens and/or whirlpools. 12 one-bedroom suites. 5 cottages ($235-$350). 1-2 stories (no elevator), interior/exterior corridors. *Bath:* combo or shower only. **Parking:** on-site, winter plug-ins. **Terms:** open 3/1-1/2 & 1/16-2/28, office hours 7 am-11 pm, check-in 4 pm, 3 day cancellation notice-fee imposed, [ECP] meal plan available, package plans. **Amenities:** hair dryers. *Some:* irons. **Dining:** Stone Peak Restaurant & Lounge, see separate listing. **Leisure Activities:** hiking trails. *Fee:* horseback riding. **Guest Services:** valet laundry. **Business Services:** meeting rooms. **Cards:** AX, DC, MC, VI. **Special Amenities:** free expanded continental breakfast and free newspaper.

SOME UNITS

RAMADA LIMITED & SUITES   *Book at aaa.com*

Phone: (780)865-2575

6/15-9/30 [ECP]	1P: $129-$149	2P: $129-$149	XP: $10	F17
3/1-6/14 & 10/1-2/28 [ECP]	1P: $94-$110	2P: $94-$110	XP: $10	F17

Small-scale Hotel

Location: 6 km w on Hwy 16. 500 Smith St T7V 2A1. **Fax:** 780/865-2976. **Facility:** 55 units. 46 one-bedroom standard units. 9 one-bedroom suites ($149-$200), some with kitchens and/or whirlpools. 2 stories (no elevator), interior/exterior corridors. *Bath:* combo or shower only. **Parking:** on-site, winter plug-ins. **Terms:** small pets only ($10 fee). **Amenities:** irons, hair dryers. **Leisure Activities:** whirlpool, limited exercise equipment. **Guest Services:** coin laundry. **Business Services:** meeting rooms. **Cards:** AX, CB, DC, DS, JC, MC, VI.

SOME UNITS

SUPER 8 MOTEL   *Book at aaa.com*

Phone: 780/817-2228

6/1-9/30	1P: $100-$107	2P: $107-$114	XP: $7	F12
3/1-5/31 & 10/1-2/28	1P: $80-$87	2P: $87-$94	XP: $7	F12

Small-scale Hotel

Location: 1.6 km on Hwy 16. 284 Smith St T7V 2A1. **Fax:** 780/817-2880. **Facility:** 48 units. 46 one-bedroom standard units. 2 one-bedroom suites ($99-$120). 2 stories (no elevator), interior corridors. **Parking:** on-site, winter plug-ins. **Terms:** [CP] meal plan available, pets ($10 extra charge, with prior approval). **Pool(s):** small heated indoor. **Leisure Activities:** whirlpool. **Guest Services:** coin laundry. **Cards:** AX, DC, DS, MC, VI.

SOME UNITS

──────── **WHERE TO DINE** ────────

L & W FAMILY RESTAURANT

Lunch: $4-$8   **Dinner:** $9-$15   Phone: 780/865-4892

Canadian

Location: West end of city on Hwy 16; across from Holiday Inn. 414 Carmichael Ln T7V 1X7. **Hours:** 10:30 am-1 am. **Closed:** 1/1, 12/25, 12/26. **Features:** Ask any local in town for a good place to eat, and the diner-style restaurant is mentioned time and time again. Guests order at the counter and pick up their food when their number is called. Among offerings are Greek specialties, such as souvlaki and spanakopita, and hamburgers, pizzas and steaks, which are served in ample portions. Cocktails. **Parking:** on-site. **Cards:** MC, VI.

STONE PEAK RESTAURANT & LOUNGE   *Menu on aaa.com*

Lunch: $5-$15   **Dinner:** $27-$31   Phone: 780/866-2330

International

Location: Hwy 16, 24 km w; in Overlander Mountain Lodge. Hwy 16 T7V 1X5. **Hours:** 7 am-9:30 pm; 7 am-10:30 & 5-9 pm in winter. **Closed:** 12/25, 12/26, 12/26; also 1st week of Jan. **Reservations:** suggested. **Features:** Just outside of town, the restaurant is worth the drive. Diners can enjoy seasonally inspired cuisine in the log interior, which features a cozy decor. Chocolate pecan pie, created from a recipe so secret that the chef won't allow his staff to see him make it, is a great way to finish a fine meal. The cozy surroundings afford views of the mountains in the distance. Casual dress; cocktails. **Parking:** on-site. **Cards:** AX, DC, MC, VI.

JASPER pop. 4,180

──────── **WHERE TO STAY** ────────

ALPINE VILLAGE

Phone: 780/852-3285

6/10-9/17	1P: $150-$230	2P: $150-$230	XP: $10	F7
5/20-6/9	1P: $100-$170	2P: $100-$170	XP: $10	F7
4/25-5/19 & 9/18-10/30	1P: $80-$130	2P: $80-$130	XP: $10	F7

Cabin

Location: Jct Hwy 16 and 93, 1.4 km s on Hwy 93, then just n on Hwy 93A. (PO Box 610). **Fax:** 780/852-1955. **Facility:** These upscale cabins, which range in size and decor, are in a wooded, riverfront setting outside of town. Designated smoking area. 41 units. 12 one-bedroom standard units. 29 cabins ($180-$330). 1 story, exterior corridors. *Bath:* combo or shower only. **Parking:** on-site. **Terms:** open 4/25-10/30, office hours 8 am-10 pm, check-in 4 pm, 14 day cancellation notice-fee imposed, weekly rates available. **Amenities:** *Some:* hair dryers. **Leisure Activities:** hiking trails, playground. **Guest Services:** sundries, valet laundry. **Cards:** MC, VI. *(See color ad p 431)*

SOME UNITS

AMETHYST LODGE   *Book at aaa.com*   Phone: (780)852-3394

CAA SAVE

	5/1-9/30	1P: $212-$270	2P: $212-$270	XP: $10	F15
	10/1-10/31	1P: $142-$190	2P: $142-$190	XP: $10	F15
	3/1-4/30	1P: $89-$135	2P: $89-$135	XP: $10	F15
	11/1-2/28	1P: $65-$125	2P: $65-$125	XP: $10	F15

Small-scale Hotel Location: 0.5 km e. 200 Connaught Dr T0E 1E0 (PO Box 1200). Fax: 780/852-5198. **Facility:** 97 units. 91 one-bedroom standard units. 6 one-bedroom suites. 3 stories, interior/exterior corridors. **Parking:** on-site, winter plug-ins. **Terms:** check-in 4 pm, package plans, pets (in smoking units). **Amenities:** voice mail, hair dryers. *Some:* high-speed Internet. **Dining:** 7 am-11 & 5-10 pm; seasonal hours vary, cocktails. **Leisure Activities:** whirlpools. **Guest Services:** valet laundry, area transportation-train station. **Business Services:** meeting rooms. **Cards:** AX, MC, VI. **Special Amenities:** free local telephone calls and preferred room (subject to availability with advance reservations).

SOME UNITS

BECKER'S CHALETS   Phone: 780/852-3779

CAA SAVE

| | 6/1-9/18 | 1P: $140-$170 | 2P: $140-$170 | XP: $10 | F12 |
| | 4/29-5/31 & 9/19-10/10 | 1P: $110-$150 | 2P: $110-$150 | XP: $10 | F12 |

Cabin

Location: 6.8 km s on Hwy 93. Located in a quiet rustic area. (PO Box 579). Fax: 780/852-7202. **Facility:** 118 units. 5 one-bedroom standard units. 52 one-, 14 two- and 2 three-bedroom suites with kitchens. 45 cabins ($230-$380). 2 stories (no elevator), exterior corridors. **Bath:** combo or shower only. **Parking:** on-site. **Terms:** open 4/29-10/10, office hours 7 am-11 pm, 2 night minimum stay - seasonal, 7 day cancellation notice. **Amenities:** hair dryers. **Dining:** 8 am-11 & 5:30-10 pm, cocktails. **Leisure Activities:** fishing, hiking trails, playground. **Fee:** bicycles. **Guest Services:** gift shop, coin laundry. **Cards:** AX, MC, VI.

SOME UNITS

CHATEAU JASPER   *Book at aaa.com*   Phone: (780)852-5644

6/2-10/1	1P: $330-$425	2P: $330-$425	XP: $10 F17
10/2-2/28	1P: $150-$180	2P: $150-$180	XP: $10 F17
5/1-6/1	1P: $175	2P: $175	XP: $10 F17
3/1-4/30	1P: $135	2P: $135	XP: $10 F17

Small-scale Hotel **Location:** Corner of Juniper and Geikie sts. Located in a residential area. 96 Geikie St T0E 1E0 (PO Box 1418). Fax: 780/852-4860. **Facility:** Designated smoking area. 119 one-bedroom standard units, some with whirlpools. 3 stories, interior corridors. **Parking:** on-site, winter plug-ins. **Terms:** check-in 4 pm, cancellation fee imposed, package plans. **Amenities:** video games, high-speed Internet, voice mail, safes, irons, hair dryers. **Dining:** Sorrentino's, see separate listing. **Pool(s):** heated indoor. **Leisure Activities:** whirlpool, exercise room. **Guest Services:** valet laundry, area transportation-train & bus station. **Business Services:** conference facilities. **Cards:** AX, DC, MC, VI. **Special Amenities:** free newspaper. *(See color ad p 431)*

THE FAIRMONT JASPER PARK LODGE   *Book at aaa.com*   Phone: (780)852-3301

5/21-10/31	1P: $449-$599	2P: $449-$599	XP: $25 F17
5/1-5/20	1P: $239-$309	2P: $239-$309	XP: $25 F17
3/1-4/30 & 11/1-2/28	1P: $199-$269	2P: $199-$269	XP: $25 F17

Resort   Large-scale Hotel **Location:** 4.8 km ne via Hwy 16; 3.2 km se off highway via Maligne Rd, follow signs for lodge. Lodge Rd T0E 1E0 (PO Box 40). Fax: 780/852-5107. **Facility:** It's said that at one time, Marilyn Monroe frequented this resort set along two lakes just outside of town; activities and scenic grounds await. 446 units. 331 one-bedroom standard units. 115 one-bedroom suites ($369-$839), some with whirlpools. 1-2 stories (no elevator), exterior corridors. **Parking:** on-site and valet, winter plug-ins. **Terms:** check-in 4 pm, 3 day cancellation notice-fee imposed, [AP], [CP] & [MAP] meal plans available, package plans, pets ($30 fee). **Amenities:** video games, voice mail, irons, hair dryers. *Some:* CD players, high-speed Internet (fee), dual phone lines, safes. **Dining:** The Edith Cavell, Moose's Nook, see separate listings. **Pool(s):** heated outdoor. **Leisure Activities:** saunas, whirlpool, steamroom, rental boats, rental canoes, rental paddleboats, 4 tennis courts, cross country skiing, ice skating, tobogganing, recreation programs, hiking trails, playground, exercise room, horseshoes, shuffleboard. *Fee:* fishing, golf-18 holes, bicycles, horseback riding, massage, game room. **Guest Services:** gift shop, valet laundry, area transportation (fee). **Business Services:** conference facilities, business center. **Cards:** AX, DC, DS, JC, MC, VI. *(See color ad below)*

SOME UNITS   FEE   FEE

JASPER HOUSE BUNGALOWS   Phone: 780/852-4535

6/10-9/25	1P: $140-$215	2P: $140-$215	XP: $10 F6
4/25-6/9 & 9/26-10/15	1P: $75-$140	2P: $75-$140	XP: $10 F6

Cabin **Location:** 4 km s on Hwy 93. Located in a quiet, rustic area. (PO Box 817). Fax: 780/852-5335. **Facility:** Smoke free premises. 56 cabins. 1 story, exterior corridors. *Bath:* combo or shower only. **Parking:** on-site. **Terms:** open 4/25-10/15, office hours 8 am-10 pm, 7 day cancellation notice-fee imposed, [MAP] meal plan available. **Amenities:** hair dryers. **Leisure Activities:** hiking trails, horseshoes. **Guest Services:** gift shop, coin laundry. **Cards:** AX, MC, VI.

SOME UNITS

JASPER INN ALPINE RESORT *Book at aaa.com* Phone: (780)852-4461

CAA SAVE

	6/1-9/30	1P: $217-$425	2P: $217-$425	XP: $10	F17
	5/1-5/31	1P: $125-$310	2P: $125-$310	XP: $10	F17
	10/1-2/28	1P: $111-$310	2P: $111-$310	XP: $10	F17
	3/1-4/30	1P: $109-$310	2P: $109-$310	XP: $10	F17

Small-scale Hotel Location: 1.2 km ne at Geikie and Bonhomme sts. 98 Geikie St T0E 1E0 (PO Box 879). Fax: 780/852-5916. **Facility:** 143 units. 101 one- and 26 two-bedroom standard units, some with kitchens and/or whirlpools. 16 one-bedroom suites. 2-3 stories (no elevator), interior/exterior corridors. **Parking:** on-site, winter plug-ins. **Terms:** check-in 4 pm, 3 day cancellation notice-fee imposed, package plans, pets ($10 extra charge, in limited units). **Amenities:** irons, hair dryers. *Some:* high-speed Internet. **Dining:** 6:30 am-11 & 5-11 pm; 7 am-10 & 5-10 pm in winter, cocktails. **Pool(s):** heated indoor, wading. **Leisure Activities:** sauna, whirlpool, steamroom, ski lockers. **Guest Services:** coin laundry. **Business Services:** meeting rooms, PC. **Cards:** AX, DC, DS, MC, VI. *(See color ad below)*

LOBSTICK LODGE *Book at aaa.com* Phone: (780)852-4431

CAA SAVE

	5/1-9/30	1P: $215-$237	2P: $215-$237	XP: $10	F15
	10/1-10/31	1P: $145-$167	2P: $145-$167	XP: $10	F15
	3/1-4/30	1P: $107-$129	2P: $107-$129	XP: $10	F15
	11/1-2/28	1P: $75-$97	2P: $75-$97	XP: $10	F15

Small-scale Hotel Location: 1.2 km ne at Geikie and Juniper sts. 94 Geikie St T0E 1E0 (PO Box 1200). Fax: 780/852-4142. **Facility:** 139 units. 134 one-bedroom standard units, some with kitchens. 5 one-bedroom suites with kitchens. 3 stories, interior corridors. **Parking:** on-site, winter plug-ins. **Terms:** check-in 4 pm, package plans, pets (in smoking units). **Amenities:** voice mail, irons, hair dryers. **Dining:** 6:30 am-11 & 5-10 pm; hours vary seasonally, cocktails. **Pool(s):** wading. **Leisure Activities:** sauna, whirlpools, steamroom, sun deck. **Guest Services:** gift shop, valet and coin laundry, area transportation-train station. **Business Services:** meeting rooms. **Cards:** AX, CB, DC, JC, MC, VI. **Special Amenities:** free local telephone calls and preferred room (subject to availability with advance reservations).

MARMOT LODGE *Book at aaa.com* Phone: (780)852-4471

CAA SAVE Motel

	5/1-9/30	1P: $209-$231	2P: $209-$231	XP: $10	F15
	10/1-10/31	1P: $139-$161	2P: $139-$161	XP: $10	F15
	3/1-4/30	1P: $99-$123	2P: $99-$123	XP: $10	F15
	11/1-2/28	1P: $70-$94	2P: $70-$94	XP: $10	F15

Location: 1.6 km ne. 86 Connaught Dr T0E 1E0 (PO Box 1200). Fax: 780/852-3280. **Facility:** 107 units. 81 one-bedroom standard units, some with kitchens. 25 one- and 1 two-bedroom suites with kitchens, some with whirlpools. 2 stories (no elevator), exterior corridors. **Parking:** on-site, winter plug-ins. **Terms:** check-in 4 pm, package plans, small pets only (in smoking units). **Amenities:** voice mail, hair dryers. **Dining:** 7 am-11 & 5-10 pm; seasonal hours vary, cocktails. **Pool(s):** heated indoor. **Leisure Activities:** sauna, whirlpools. **Guest Services:** coin laundry, area transportation-train station. **Business Services:** meeting rooms. **Cards:** AX, CB, DC, JC, MC, VI. **Special Amenities:** free local telephone calls and preferred room (subject to availability with advance reservations).

MOUNT ROBSON INN *Book at aaa.com*

Phone: (780)852-3327

CAA SAVE
WWW WWW

	6/10-9/30	1P: $194-$339	2P: $194-$339	XP: $10	F12
	5/1-6/9	1P: $129-$249	2P: $129-$249	XP: $10	F12
	3/1-4/30	1P: $89-$225	2P: $89-$225	XP: $10	F12
	10/1-2/28	1P: $85-$210	2P: $85-$210	XP: $10	F12

Motel **Location:** 1 km sw. 902 Connaught Dr T0E 1E0 (PO Box 88). Fax: 780/852-5004. **Facility:** 80 units. 74 one-bedroom standard units, some with whirlpools. 6 one-bedroom suites ($149-$339). 2 stories (no elevator), exterior corridors. **Parking:** on-site, winter plug-ins. **Terms:** cancellation fee imposed, package plans. **Amenities:** video library (fee), hair dryers. *Some:* video games, irons. **Dining:** 7 am-11 pm; seasonal hours vary, cocktails. **Leisure Activities:** whirlpools. **Guest Services:** coin laundry, area transportation-train station. **Business Services:** PC (fee). **Cards:** AX, DC, JC, MC, VI. **Special Amenities:** free local telephone calls. *(See color ad below)*

SOME UNITS
🅂🄳 🍴 📺 📠 📶 💻 / ⊠ 📼 🖥 /
FEE

PARK PLACE INN

Phone: 780/852-9770

CAA SAVE
WWW WWW WWW

	6/1-9/7	1P: $199-$259	2P: $199-$259	XP: $15	F14
	9/8-10/17	1P: $149-$219	2P: $149-$219	XP: $15	F14
	3/1-5/31 & 10/18-2/28	1P: $109-$179	2P: $109-$179	XP: $15	F14

Small-scale Hotel **Location:** Downtown. 623 Patricia St T0E 1E0 (Box 2112). Fax: 780/852-1180. **Facility:** Smoke free premises. 12 one-bedroom standard units, some with whirlpools. 2 stories, interior corridors. **Parking:** on-site. **Terms:** 5 day cancellation notice. **Amenities:** hair dryers. *Some:* DVD players. **Cards:** AX, JC, MC, VI.

🍴 ⊠ 📺 📶 💻 🖥

PATRICIA LAKE BUNGALOWS

Phone: 780/852-3560

WWW WWW

| | 6/10-9/11 | 1P: $81-$250 | 2P: $81-$250 | XP: $10 | F11 |
| | 5/1-6/9 & 9/12-10/16 | 1P: $59-$250 | 2P: $59-$250 | XP: $10 | F11 |

Cabin **Location:** 4.8 km nw via Pyramid Lake Rd. Pyramid Lake Rd T0E 1E0 (PO Box 657). Fax: 780/852-4060. **Facility:** Designated smoking area. 37 units. 9 one-bedroom standard units. 1 one- and 8 two-bedroom suites with kitchens. 19 cabins. 1 story, exterior corridors. *Bath:* combo or shower only. **Parking:** on-site. **Terms:** open 5/1-10/16, office hours 8 am-10 pm, check-in 3:30 pm, 7 day cancellation notice, pets ($10 fee, with prior approval). **Amenities:** hair dryers. **Leisure Activities:** whirlpool, rental boats, rental canoes, rental paddleboats, boat dock, fishing, playground. *Fee:* bicycles, horseback riding. **Guest Services:** gift shop, coin laundry. **Cards:** MC, VI.

SOME UNITS
🔥 🏠 ⊠ ⊠ 🎿 🐾 ☎ 🖥 💻 / 📼 🖥 /
FEE   FEE

PYRAMID LAKE RESORT   _Book at aaa.com_   Phone: (780)852-4900

CAA SAVE   6/9-9/6   1P: $269-$399   2P: $269-$399   XP: $15   F18
◆◆◆   3/1-6/8 & 9/7-2/28   1P: $125-$235   2P: $125-$235   XP: $15   F18
Location: Jct Connaught Dr and Cedar St, 6 km nw via Pyramid Lake Rd. Located in a quiet area. Pyramid Lake Rd
Small-scale Hotel T0E 1E0 (PO Box 388). Fax: 780/852-7007. **Facility:** Smoke free premises. 62 units. 34 one-bedroom
standard units. 26 one- and 2 two-bedroom suites with efficiencies. 2 stories (no elevator), exterior corridors.
Parking: on-site, winter plug-ins. **Terms:** check-in 4 pm, 7 day cancellation notice-fee imposed, package
plans, small pets only ($25 fee). **Amenities:** voice mail, hair dryers. **Dining:** The Pines, see separate listing. **Leisure
Activities:** whirlpool, steamroom, rental boats, rental canoes, rental paddleboats, boat ramp, cross country skiing, hiking trails,
exercise room. _Fee:_ fishing, 2 person kayaks, ice skating, barbecue patio, bicycles. **Guest Services:** gift shop. **Business
Services:** meeting rooms. **Cards:** AX, DC, MC, VI. _(See color ad p 434)_   SOME UNITS

THE SAWRIDGE INN AND CONFERENCE CENTRE   _Book at aaa.com_   Phone: (780)852-5111

CAA SAVE   6/1-9/30   1P: $235-$295   2P: $235-$295   XP: $25   F15
◆◆◆   5/1-5/31   1P: $165-$195   2P: $165-$195   XP: $20   F15
          10/1-2/28   1P: $135-$195   2P: $135-$195   XP: $10   F15
          3/1-4/30   1P: $115-$145   2P: $115-$145   XP: $10   F15
Small-scale Hotel **Location:** 1.7 km e. 82 Connaught Dr T0E 1E0 (PO Box 2080). Fax: 780/852-5942. **Facility:** 153 units. 149 one-
bedroom standard units. 4 one-bedroom suites ($200-$450) with whirlpools. 3 stories, interior corridors.
Parking: on-site, winter plug-ins. **Terms:** check-in 4 pm, 2 night minimum stay - seasonal, 5 day cancellation notice-fee
imposed, [BP], [ECP] & [MAP] meal plans available, package plans, small pets only ($20 fee, in designated rooms).
Amenities: video games, high-speed Internet (fee), voice mail, irons, hair dryers. _Some:_ CD players. **Dining:** 2 restaurants, 5
am-11 pm; hours vary seasonally, cocktails, nightclub. **Pool(s):** heated indoor. **Leisure Activities:** sauna, whirlpools, exercise
room, spa. **Guest Services:** gift shop, valet and coin laundry, area transportation-within Jasper. **Business Services:**
conference facilities, PC (fee). **Cards:** AX, DC, DS, JC, MC, VI. **Special Amenities:** free local telephone calls and free
newspaper.   SOME UNITS

SUNWAPTA FALLS RESORT   _Book at aaa.com_   Phone: (780)852-4852

CAA SAVE   6/21-9/20   1P: $139-$199   2P: $139-$199   XP: $10   F12
◆◆   5/8-6/20 & 9/21-10/14   1P: $79-$129   2P: $79-$129   XP: $10   F12
Motel   **Location:** 55 km s on Icefields Pkwy (Hwy 93). Located in a quiet secluded setting. Hwy 93 T0E 1E0 (PO Box 97).
Fax: 780/852-5353. **Facility:** Smoke free premises. 52 one-bedroom standard units. 1-2 stories (no
elevator), exterior corridors. **Parking:** on-site. **Terms:** open 5/8-10/14, check-in 4 pm, package plans, pets
($25 fee). **Dining:** 7 am-11 pm; hours vary off season, cocktails. **Leisure Activities:** fishing, hiking trails.
Fee: fishing equipment, whitewater rafting, bicycles. **Guest Services:** gift shop. **Business Services:** meeting rooms, PC.
Cards: AX, MC, VI. **Special Amenities:** early check-in/late check-out and preferred room (subject to availability with
advance reservations).** _(See color ad below)_

—— WHERE TO DINE ——

ANDY'S BISTRO
▼▼▼▼
International

Dinner: $18-$32   **Phone:** 780/852-4559

Location: Centre. 606 Patricia St T0E 1E0. **Hours:** 5 pm-9 pm. Closed: 12/23-12/26. **Reservations:** suggested. **Features:** It is difficult to choose one word to define the fine cuisine, as the International menu reflects influences from around the world. Guests might find salmon, veal, spaetzle or chicken, all prepared a la minute. The bistro nurtures a casual atmosphere. Casual dress; cocktails. **Parking:** street. **Cards:** MC, VI.

BEAR'S PAW BAKERY
▼▼
Bakery/Desserts

Lunch: $2-$7   **Dinner:** $5-$10   **Phone:** 780/852-3233

Location: Just w off Connaught Dr at Cedar Dr. 4 Cedar Ave T0E 1E0. **Hours:** Open 3/1-10/31 & 12/1-2/28; 6 am-8 pm. Closed: 1/1, 12/25. **Features:** Guests can savor the aroma of freshly baked goods at the cozy hideaway bakery. Eyes feast on European-style pastries, artisan breads and Vienna pastries. Beware: Standing too long in front of the display case will cause mouths to water. Representative of the many temptations are trail cookies, Bear's Paw cinnamon buns, carrot cake and date squares. Only one table is available, so most patrons grab a sweet and a cup of coffee and head out into the mountain air. **Parking:** street. **Cards:** MC, VI.

BECKER'S GOURMET RESTAURANT
(CAA)
▼▼▼
Continental

Dinner: $16-$30   **Phone:** 780/852-3535

Location: On Hwy 93, 6.8 km s. Hwy 93 T0E 1E0. **Hours:** Open 4/30-10/15; 8 am-11 & 5:30-10 pm. **Reservations:** suggested. **Features:** Along the river just south of the city, the restaurant is a favorite among Jasper residents. The dining room's warm oak and fir decor is distinctly Canadian and, set against the backdrop of the river, provides an idyllic setting. Regionally inspired Continental cuisine ranges from salmon and scallops to beef tenderloin and lamb. Casual dress; cocktails. **Parking:** on-site. **Cards:** AX, DS, MC, VI.

CALEDONIA GRILL
▼▼ ▼▼
International

Lunch: $5-$10   **Dinner:** $11-$26   **Phone:** 780/852-4070

Location: On Connaught Dr; in Whistler's Inn. 105 Miette Ave T0E 1E0. **Hours:** Open 3/1-10/31 & 12/1-2/28; 7 am-2:30 & 5-10 pm. **Reservations:** suggested, in summer. **Features:** The casual, family-owned restaurant is a local favorite. On the varied menu are pasta dishes, steaks and seafood—something for everyone to enjoy. Casual dress; cocktails. **Parking:** street. **Cards:** AX, MC, VI.

THE EDITH CAVELL
(CAA)
▼▼▼▼▼
Canadian

Dinner: $25-$40   **Phone:** 780/852-6052

Location: 4.8 km ne via Hwy 16; 3.2 km se off highway via Maligne Rd, follow signs for lodge; in The Fairmont Jasper Park Lodge. Lodge Rd T0E 1E0. **Hours:** 6 pm-10 pm. **Reservations:** required. **Features:** The sounds of the harp, views of Lac Beauvert and Mount Edith Cavell, and the rich, mahogany woodwork of the elegant dining room set the scene for a truly enchanting experience. The restaurant's delightful, complex nouvelle cuisine draws inspiration from the Northwest. Among delicacies are preparations of Arctic char, salmon and venison. In season, guests can savor a weekly changing tasting menu. Dressy casual; cocktails; entertainment. **Parking:** on-site and valet. **Cards:** AX, DC, DS, JC, MC, VI.

FIDDLE RIVER RESTAURANT
▼▼ ▼▼
Seafood

Dinner: $15-$35   **Phone:** 780/852-3032

Location: At Hazel Ave; upstairs. 620 Connaught Dr T0E 1E0. **Hours:** 5 pm-10 pm. Closed: 12/25, 12/26. **Features:** An ever-changing seafood menu is the highlight of the casual yet cozy restaurant, upstairs from street level. Fresh is the operative word, and patrons might find salmon, trout, sole, king crab, cod or blackened shrimp on the menu. For a view of the mountains, request a window seat. Service is friendly and attentive. Semi-formal attire; cocktails. **Parking:** street. **Cards:** AX, MC, VI.

JABA JAZZ
▼▼
Coffee/Espresso

Lunch: $5-$10   **Dinner:** $5-$10   **Phone:** 780/852-4046

Location: Centre; upstairs from street level. 610 Patricia St T0E 1E0. **Hours:** 8 am-10 pm; to 6 pm in winter. Closed: 12/25. **Reservations:** not accepted. **Features:** Tucked away in a corner, upstairs from street level, is a popular coffeehouse. An escalator leads to this spot, where patrons nosh on homemade bread, sandwiches, soups and preparations from the fresh juice and smoothie bar. An overhead atrium—which adds to the bright, cheery feel—and a patio overlooking the street make the hidden spot a favorite among locals. Casual dress. **Parking:** street. **Cards:** VI.

JASPER PIZZA PLACE
▼▼▼
Pizza

Lunch: $4-$15   **Dinner:** $4-$15   **Phone:** 780/852-3225

Location: Centre. 402 Connaugt St T0E 1E0. **Hours:** 11 am-11 pm. Closed: 12/25. **Features:** Those looking for pizza need search no further. Whether guests choose to eat in the restaurant, order at the counter or get it to go, they can anticipate great pizza, served with thick or thin crust. Unusual toppings—such as spinach, asparagus and artichokes—are available. Service is friendly and attentive. Casual dress; cocktails. **Parking:** street. **Cards:** MC, VI.

KAROUZO'S STEAKHOUSE
▼▼ ▼▼
Steak House

Lunch: $7-$14   **Dinner:** $12-$60   **Phone:** 780/852-4640

Location: Between Spruce and Hazel aves. 628 Connaught Dr T0E 1E0. **Hours:** Open 4/1-10/15; 11 am-11 pm. **Features:** On the main street leading into town, the family-run steak and seafood restaurant features a wide variety of entrees, including some pasta dishes. Cocktails. **Parking:** street. **Cards:** MC, VI.

LA FIESTA
▼▼ ▼▼
Spanish

Lunch: $6-$12   **Dinner:** $15-$23   **Phone:** 780/852-0404

Location: Between Elm and Miette aves; across from the Info Centre. 504 Patricia St T0E 1E0. **Hours:** 11:30 am-11 pm; noon-2:30 & 4:30-10 pm 11/1-5/31. Closed: 12/25; also Sun in winter. **Features:** An oasis of Spanish cuisine awaits in the cozy restaurant, a new addition to the city scene. Inside, guests can experience the wonders of tapas (Spanish appetizers) that range from lamb and chorizo sausage meatballs to goat cheese and artichoke dip. Group of friends often linger over a pitcher of sangria, especially the owner's specialty, made with white wine. The simple decor of white walls and dark woods is nonetheless festive and evocative of Spain. Semi-formal attire; cocktails. **Parking:** street. **Cards:** MC, VI.

L & W FAMILY RESTAURANT **Lunch:** $8-$15 **Dinner:** $8-$15 **Phone:** 780/852-4114
International
Location: Corner of Hazel and Patricia. **Hours:** 11 am-11 pm. Closed major holidays. **Features:** Those looking for good value for the dollar will find the family-run restaurant at the corner of Patricia and Hazel a good choice. There is something for everyone on the menu, including Greek dishes, burgers, pizza and sandwiches. Casual dress; cocktails. **Parking:** street. **Cards:** AX, MC, VI.

MOOSE'S NOOK **Dinner:** $25-$40 **Phone:** 780/852-6052
Regional Canadian
Location: 4.8 km ne via Hwy 16; 3.2 km se off highway via Maligne Rd, follow signs for lodge; in The Fairmont Jasper Park Lodge. Lodge Rd T0E 1E0. **Hours:** Open 5/15-10/15; 6 pm-10 pm. **Reservations:** suggested. **Features:** In the magnificent Jasper Park Lodge, this "nook" of a restaurant is casual, but the food is anything but. Representative of creative, inventive regional cuisine are Alberta beef and pork entrees, seasonal greens and tempting desserts. The service and ambience are upscale without being pretentious and laid-back yet classy. This spot shouldn't be missed for those looking for a taste of Canada. Casual dress; cocktails; entertainment. **Parking:** on-site and valet. **Cards:** AX, CB, DC, DS, MC, VI.

PAPA GEORGE'S RESTAURANT **Lunch:** $6-$10 **Dinner:** $12-$35 **Phone:** 780/852-3351
Continental
Location: Centre; in Astoria Hotel. 404 Connaught Dr T0E 1E0. **Reservations:** suggested. **Features:** You'll enjoy the family dining in Papa George's bistro setting. They have a varied menu with International flavour and specialize in hearty sandwiches, freshly baked bread and pastry, duck a l'orange, lamb, fresh seafood, pork and Alberta steak. Casual dress; cocktails. **Parking:** on-site. **Cards:** AX, MC, VI.

THE PINES **Lunch:** $9-$12 **Dinner:** $19-$28 **Phone:** 780/852-3810
Canadian
Location: Jct Connaught Dr and Cedar St, 6 km nw via Pyramid Lake Rd; in Pyramid Lake Resort. **Hours:** 7 am-10 pm. **Reservations:** suggested, in summer. **Features:** The cozy yet upscale dining room makes guests feel as through they are dining in a lodge, with wooden beams overhead and lovely views of the lake. Each preparation of regional cuisine is an artistic creation. The atmosphere and service are sure to please. Casual dress; cocktails. **Parking:** on-site. **Cards:** AX, DC, JC, MC, VI. *(See color ad p 434)*

SOFT ROCK CAFE' **Lunch:** $4-$10 **Dinner:** $4-$10 **Phone:** 780/852-5850
Deli/Subs Sandwiches
Location: South end of town. 632 Connaught Dr T0E 1E0. **Hours:** 7:30 am-10 pm; 7 am-4 pm in winter. Closed 12/25. **Features:** The cafe is a popular spot for a quick bite while surfing the 'net. Breakfast is available until 4 pm, but patrons also may choose a hearty soup, sandwich, baked good or croque monsieur/madame. Cocktails. **Parking:** street. **Cards:** MC, VI.

SOMETHING ELSE RESTAURANT **Lunch:** $6-$9 **Dinner:** $11-$17 **Phone:** 780/852-3850
Greek
Location: Just w of Connaught Dr. 621 Patricia St T0E 1E0. **Hours:** 11 am-11 pm. Closed: 12/25. **Features:** The menu lists large portions of lamb and chicken dishes and pizza. Preparations show a tasty mix of International flavor. The staff provides friendly, cheerful and prompt service in a modest, casual atmosphere. Casual dress; cocktails. **Parking:** on-site. **Cards:** AX, DC, DS, MC, VI.

SORRENTINO'S **Lunch:** $9-$14 **Dinner:** $11-$29 **Phone:** 780/852-5644
Italian
Location: Corner of Juniper and Geikie sts; in Chateau Jasper. 96 Geikie St T0E 1E0. **Hours:** 6:30 am-11 & 5-10:30 pm; seasonal hours may vary. **Reservations:** suggested. **Features:** This upscale Italian restaurant prepares a wide selection of pastas and traditional dishes. Professionally dressed staff members provide attentive service, and the decor lends an upscale ambience. Casual dress; cocktails. **Parking:** on-site. **Cards:** AX, DC, JC, MC, VI. *(See color ad p 431)*

TREELINE RESTAURANT **Lunch:** $4-$8 **Dinner:** $4-$8 **Phone:** 780/852-3093
Canadian
Location: 3 km s on Hwy 93, 4 km w at Whistlers Campground, follow signs; tram ride to restaurant. **Hours:** Open 4/30-10/1; 9:30 am-5:30 pm; to 6:30 pm 6/1-6/30; 8:30 am-10 pm 7/1-8/20; 9:30 am-4:30 pm 8/21-10/1. **Reservations:** accepted. **Features:** A spectacular view awaits above the trees in the tundra just south of town. A $20 tram ride whisks guests up past the tree line and affords views of five mountain ranges, lakes and the town. Diners can work up an appetite climbing to the summit of Whistler's Mountain and then enter the cafeteria-style restaurant for burgers, sandwiches and salads or perhaps a beer or glass of wine. A full menu is available only in high season; the early season offers light meals. Casual dress; beer & wine only. **Parking:** on-site. **Cards:** MC, VI.

TRUFFLES & TROUT **Lunch:** $5-$10 **Dinner:** $5-$10 **Phone:** 780/852-9676
Deli/Subs Sandwiches
Location: Corner of Hazel and Patricia sts; in Jasper Marketplace. 627 Patricia St T0E 1E0. **Hours:** 8 am-9 pm; hours vary seasonally. **Features:** For a quick pick-me-up or shot of caffeine, the homey delicatessen and coffee bar does the trick. The menu features a wide array of sandwiches, pitas, salads and delicious baked goods. Patrons can grab a quick bite to go or sit at the stool bar tables. A favorite with locals, this is a great place to meet and share a treat with a friend. **Parking:** street. **Cards:** VI.

VILLA CARUSO **Lunch:** $8-$15 **Dinner:** $15-$30 **Phone:** 780/852-3920

Steak House
Location: Connaught Dr and Hazel Ave; 2nd level. Connaught Dr & Hazel Ave T0E 1E0. **Hours:** 11 am-midnight; 3 pm-11 pm 11/1-4/30. Closed major holidays. **Features:** Established in 1977, the longstanding steakhouse sits above street level but is accessible via elevator. The spacious lodge-like setting has wood beams and hardwood floors, and guests seated near the windows are treated to a great view of the mountains. Alberta beef is the house specialty, but other Canadian specialties, including salmon, also find their way onto the menu. Casual dress; cocktails. **Parking:** street. **Cards:** AX, DC, MC, VI.

KANANASKIS

―――― **WHERE TO STAY** ――――

DELTA LODGE AT KANANASKIS   *Book at aaa.com*   Phone: (403)591-7711

6/1-9/30	1P: $229-$279	2P: $229-$279	XP: $25	F18
10/1-12/18	1P: $129-$279	2P: $129-$279	XP: $25	F18
12/19-2/28	1P: $129-$209	2P: $129-$209	XP: $25	F18
3/1-5/31	1P: $129-$189	2P: $129-$189	XP: $25	F18

Resort
Large-scale Hotel **Location:** Trans-Canada Hwy 1, 23.5 km s on Hwy 40 (Kananaskis Tr), then 3 km on Kananaskis Village access road, follow signs. Located in a quiet area. Kanasaskis Village T0L 2H0 (PO Box 249). Fax: 403/591-7770. **Facility:** This attractive resort, nestled in a tranquil mountain village, is near recreation areas and offers a mix of room styles. 321 units. 281 one- and 14 two-bedroom standard units, some with whirlpools. 26 one-bedroom suites ($250-$450), some with whirlpools. 3 stories, interior corridors. **Parking:** on-site (fee) and valet, winter plug-ins. **Terms:** check-in 4 pm, 3 day cancellation notice-fee imposed, package plans, pets ($100 fee). **Amenities:** video games, high-speed Internet, voice mail, irons, hair dryers. *Some:* CD players. **Pool(s):** heated indoor. **Leisure Activities:** whirlpool, steamroom, 6 lighted tennis courts, cross country skiing, ice skating, tobogganing, recreation programs, hiking trails, playground, sports court. *Fee:* bicycles, horseback riding, massage, game room. **Guest Services:** gift shop, valet laundry, area transportation. **Business Services:** conference facilities, business center. **Cards:** AX, DC, DS, MC, VI. *(See color ad below)*

SOME UNITS

EXECUTIVE RESORT AT KANANASKIS   *Book at aaa.com*   Phone: (403)591-7500

7/1-10/1	1P: $209-$219	2P: $209-$219	XP: $20	F17
5/13-6/30	1P: $139-$159	2P: $139-$159	XP: $20	F17
10/2-2/28	1P: $139-$149	2P: $139-$149	XP: $20	F17
3/1-5/12	1P: $129-$139	2P: $129-$189	XP: $20	F17

Small-scale Hotel **Location:** Trans-Canada Hwy 1, 23.5 km s on Hwy 40 (Kananaskis Tr), then 3 km on Kananaskis Village access road, follow signs. 2 Terrace Dr T0L 2H0 (PO Box 10). Fax: 403/591-7633. **Facility:** Designated smoking area. 90 units. 87 one-bedroom standard units, some with whirlpools. 3 one-bedroom suites. 3 stories, interior corridors. **Parking:** on-site, winter plug-ins. **Terms:** check-in 4 pm, 7 day cancellation notice, [AP], [BP] & [MAP] meal plans available, package plans. **Amenities:** high-speed Internet, dual phone lines, voice mail, irons, hair dryers. **Dining:** 6:30 am-10 pm, cocktails. **Leisure Activities:** whirlpool, rental bicycles, hiking trails, exercise room. **Guest Services:** coin laundry, area transportation (fee)-golf course & Nakiska Ski Resort. **Business Services:** conference facilities. **Cards:** AX, DC, MC, VI. **Special Amenities:** free local telephone calls and free newspaper.

LAKE LOUISE

—— **WHERE TO STAY** ——

THE FAIRMONT CHATEAU LAKE LOUISE   *Book at aaa.com*   **Phone:** (403)522-3511

CAA (SAVE)

▼▼▼▼

6/1-9/30	1P: $499-$839	2P: $499-$839	XP: $25	F17
3/1-5/31 & 12/23-2/28	1P: $289-$449	2P: $289-$449	XP: $25	F17
10/1-12/22	1P: $199-$379	2P: $199-$379	XP: $25	F17

Resort
Large-scale Hotel

Location: 3 km up the hill from the village. Located in a quiet area. 111 Lake Louise Dr T0L 1E0. **Fax:** 403/522-3834. **Facility:** Surrounded by mountains and set alongside Lake Louise, the property features a grand lobby; some rooms offer views of the Victoria Glacier. 550 units. 533 one-bedroom standard units, some with whirlpools. 17 one-bedroom suites ($2099-$2489) with whirlpools. 8 stories, interior corridors. **Parking:** on-site (fee) and valet, winter plug-ins. **Terms:** check-in 4 pm, 3 day cancellation notice-fee imposed, [BP] & [MAP] meal plans available, package plans, small pets only ($25 extra charge, in smoking units). **Amenities:** video games (fee), voice mail, honor bars, irons, hair dryers. *Some:* CD players, high-speed Internet (fee), dual phone lines, safes. **Dining:** 5 restaurants, 24 hours, cocktails, also, Fairview Dining Room, see separate listing. **Pool(s):** heated indoor. **Leisure Activities:** whirlpool, steamroom, rental canoes, recreation programs, hiking trails, exercise room, spa. *Fee:* cross country skiing, ice skating, horseback riding. **Guest Services:** gift shop, valet laundry, area transportation. **Business Services:** conference facilities, business center. **Cards:** AX, CB, DC, DS, JC, MC, VI. **Special Amenities:** free newspaper and early check-in/late check-out.

SOME UNITS

🅂🄳 🍴 🛏 🍴 24📺 🍸 🛋 🏊 ✕ 🐾 📠 ▣ / ✕ 🐾 /
　　　FEE FEE

LAKE LOUISE INN   *Book at aaa.com*   **Phone:** 403/522-3791

▼▼ ▼▼

Property failed to provide current rates

Small-scale Hotel

Location: Just w of 4-way stop. 210 Village Rd T0L 1E0 (PO Box 209). **Fax:** 403/522-2018. **Facility:** 232 units. 214 one-bedroom standard units, some with efficiencies. 18 one-bedroom suites. 2-3 stories, interior/exterior corridors. **Parking:** on-site, winter plug-ins. **Terms:** check-in 4 pm, pets ($100 deposit, except in main building). **Amenities:** voice mail, hair dryers. *Some:* irons. **Pool(s):** heated indoor. **Leisure Activities:** whirlpools, steamroom, ice skating, recreation programs, exercise room. *Fee:* massage. **Guest Services:** gift shop, coin laundry, area transportation. **Business Services:** meeting rooms, PC (fee).

SOME UNITS

🍴 🛏 🍴 🍸 🛋 🏊 ✕ 📠 ▣ / ✕ 🐾 🖥 📠 /
FEE FEE

MOUNTAINEER LODGE   **Phone:** (403)522-3844

▼▼ ▼▼

6/15-9/24	1P: $170-$275	2P: $180-$275	XP: $10	F10
6/1-6/14	1P: $110-$160	2P: $120-$160	XP: $10	F10
5/1-5/31 & 9/25-10/15	1P: $85-$130	2P: $90-$130	XP: $10	F10

Small-scale Hotel

Location: Just e of 4-way stop. 101 Village Rd T0L 1E0 (PO Box 150). **Fax:** 403/522-3902. **Facility:** Smoke free premises. 78 units. 74 one- and 4 two-bedroom standard units. 2 stories (no elevator), interior/exterior corridors. *Bath:* combo or shower only. **Parking:** on-site. **Terms:** open 5/1-10/15, office hours 7 am-midnight, check-in 4 pm, 7 day cancellation notice. **Amenities:** hair dryers. **Leisure Activities:** whirlpool, steamroom. **Business Services:** PC (fee). **Cards:** AX, MC, VI.

SOME UNITS

A$K 🅂🄳 🍴 ✕ 🐾 📺 📷 ▣ / 🖥 /

For the Traveller with Higher Expectations

POST HOTEL & SPA
LAKE LOUISE

1-800-661-1586 • www.posthotel.com

POST HOTEL & SPA *Book at aaa.com* Phone: (403)522-3989

▼▼▼▼ ▼▼▼▼ 5/26-10/16 1P: $215-$450 2P: $215-$450
3/1-5/25 & 12/8-2/28 1P: $195-$365 2P: $195-$365

Small-scale Hotel **Location:** Just w of main intersection; in village. 200 Pipestone Rd T0L 1E0 (PO Box 69). Fax: 403/522-3966. **Facility:** Mountain decor, luxurious bathrooms, upscale rooms and fine service await at this cozy hotel, located in the heart of Lake Louise village. Designated smoking area. 96 units. 65 one-bedroom standard units. 27 one-bedroom suites with whirlpools. 4 cabins. 3 stories, interior corridors. **Parking:** on-site. **Terms:** open 3/1-10/16 & 12/8-2/28, check-in 3:30 pm, 14 day cancellation notice-fee imposed. **Amenities:** video library, voice mail, safes, hair dryers. *Some:* irons. **Dining:** Post Hotel Dining Room, see separate listing. **Pool(s):** heated indoor. **Leisure Activities:** whirlpool, steamroom. **Guest Services:** complimentary evening beverages, valet laundry. **Business Services:** meeting rooms, PC (fee). **Cards:** AX, MC, VI. *(See color ad p 439)*

SOME UNITS

🍴 🍸 📶 🏊 ✕ VCR DATA/PORT / 📻 🔒 💻 /

The following lodging was either not evaluated or did not meet AAA rating requirements but is listed for your information only.

NUM-TI-JAH LODGE Phone: 403/522-2167

[fyi] Not evaluated. **Location:** Hwy 93, 40 km n. Located on Bow Lake. Mile 22, Bow Lake, Icefields Pkwy T0L 1E0 (PO Box 39). Facilities, services, and decor characterize a mid-range property.

——— WHERE TO DINE ———

BAKER CREEK BISTRO **Lunch:** $8-$12 **Dinner:** $20-$35 Phone: 403/522-2182

▼▼▼ ▼▼▼ **Location:** 11 km e on Hwy 1A (Bow Valley Pkwy). Bow Valley Pkwy T0L 1E0. **Hours:** 7 am-10, noon-2 & 5-10 pm; hours vary seasonally. **Reservations:** suggested. **Features:** The bistro's cozy, log-cabin setting sustains a warm-spirited ambience. Among regional dishes are lamb chops, baked chicken and beef tenderloin, with an accent on fresh herbs and spices and hearty portions. Cocktails. **Parking:** on-site. **Cards:** MC, VI.

Canadian

🍸 📻 ✕

ELKHORN DINING ROOM **Lunch:** $15-$25 **Dinner:** $20-$32 Phone: 403/522-2167

▼▼▼ ▼▼▼ **Location:** Hwy 93, 40 km n; in Num-Ti-Jah Lodge. Mile 22, Bow Lake, Icefields Pkwy T0L 1E0. **Hours:** 7:30 am-9:30 pm. Closed: 10/14-12/1. **Reservations:** required, for dinner. **Features:** The cozy dining room features a creative and fine selection of regional cuisine, ranging from sea bass to venison to salmon. The wood interior has high ceilings and a large fireplace. Friendly, attentive service and a cozy, alpine atmosphere add to the experience. Casual dress; cocktails. **Parking:** on-site. **Cards:** MC, VI.

Regional Canadian

🍸 📻 ✕

FAIRVIEW DINING ROOM **Dinner:** $25-$37 Phone: 403/522-3511

(CAA) **Location:** 3 km up the hill from the village; in The Fairmont Chateau Lake Louise. 111 Lake Louise Dr T0L 1E0. **Hours:** 5:30 pm-9:30 pm; hours may vary off season. **Reservations:** required. **Features:** Ask for a seat by ▼▼▼ ▼▼▼ the oversized windows and be rewarded with commanding views of Lake Louise and the Victoria Glacier. From start to finish, diners can expect professional and knowledgeable service amid exquisite surroundings. Canadian The menu explores a diverse selection of Canadian cuisine, ranging from venison to organic chicken, and decadent desserts. A trip to Lake Louise would be remiss without a meal in this elegant restaurant. Dressy casual; cocktails. **Parking:** on-site (fee) and valet. **Cards:** AX, DC, DS, JC, MC, VI. **Historic**

🍸 📻 ✕

LAKE LOUISE STATION **Lunch:** $7-$10 **Dinner:** $13-$28 Phone: 403/522-2600

▼▼▼ ▼▼▼ **Location:** From 4-way stop, just s via underpass, then 1 km w. 200 Sentinel Rd T0L 1E0. **Hours:** 11:30 am-10 pm; to 6 pm 10/1-5/15. Closed: 12/25. **Reservations:** suggested. **Features:** This restaurant is located in a beautifully restored heritage railway station that includes a 1925 dining car. The progressive Continental Canadian cuisine offers lasagna, chicken, pork ribs, stuffed halibut, salmon, rack of lamb and even build-your-own pizza. Casual dress; cocktails. **Parking:** on-site. **Cards:** MC, VI.

🍸 📻 ✕

POST HOTEL DINING ROOM **Lunch:** $9-$28 **Dinner:** $28-$46 Phone: 403/522-3989

(CAA) **Location:** Just w of main intersection; in village; in Post Hotel & Spa. 200 Pipestone Rd T0L 1E0. **Hours:** Open 3/1-10/17 & 12/9-2/28; 7-11 am, 11:30-2 & 5-10 pm. Closed: 12/25. **Reservations:** suggested, for dinner. ▼▼▼ ▼▼▼ **Features:** Delicious food lends to the restaurant's exceptional reputation. European classics are wonderfully flavorful and colorfully presented. A less extensive menu is offered at lunch. A cigar room is available. Continental Dressy casual; cocktails. **Parking:** on-site. **Cards:** AX, MC, VI.

🍸 📻 ✕

LEDUC —*See Edmonton p. 422.*

LETHBRIDGE pop. 67,374

——— WHERE TO STAY ———

BEST WESTERN HEIDELBERG INN *Book at aaa.com* Phone: (403)329-0555

(CAA) [SAVE] All Year 1P: $99-$119 2P: $104-$124 XP: $5 F18
▼▼▼ ▼▼▼ **Location:** 4 km se on Hwy 4 and 5. 1303 Mayor Magrath Dr T1K 2R1. Fax: 403/328-8846. **Facility:** 66 one-bedroom standard units. 9 stories, interior corridors. **Parking:** on-site, winter plug-ins. **Amenities:** voice mail, irons, hair dryers. *Some:* dual phone lines. **Dining:** 6 am-11 pm, Sun 7 am-10 pm, cocktails. **Leisure** Small-scale Hotel **Activities:** sauna, limited exercise equipment. **Guest Services:** valet laundry. **Cards:** AX, DC, DS, JC, MC, VI. **Special Amenities:** free newspaper and early check-in/late check-out.

SOME UNITS

🅂🄳 🍴 🍸 DATA/PORT 💻 / ✕ VCR 🔒 /

FEE

COMFORT INN

Book at aaa.com

Phone: (403)320-8874

5/1-8/31	1P: $95-$110	2P: $95-$110	XP: $5	F
3/1-4/30 & 9/1-2/28	1P: $85-$110	2P: $85-$110	XP: $5	F

Small-scale Hotel **Location:** Southeast end of city; Mayor Magrath Dr, exit n at Scenic Dr. 3226 Fairway Plaza Rd S T1K 7T5. Fax: 403/320-8824. **Facility:** 58 units. 55 one-bedroom standard units. 3 one-bedroom suites. 4 stories, interior corridors. **Bath:** combo or shower only. **Parking:** on-site, winter plug-ins. **Terms:** cancellation fee imposed, pets ($10 extra charge). **Amenities:** high-speed Internet, voice mail, irons, hair dryers. **Pool(s):** heated indoor. **Leisure Activities:** whirlpool, exercise room. **Guest Services:** valet and coin laundry. **Business Services:** PC. **Cards:** AX, DC, DS, JC, MC, VI.

SOME UNITS

DAYS INN LETHBRIDGE

Book at aaa.com

Phone: (403)327-6000

5/1-9/30	1P: $80-$90	2P: $86-$91	XP: $6	F12
3/1-4/30 & 10/1-2/28	1P: $74-$84	2P: $79-$89	XP: $5	F12

Small-scale Hotel **Location:** Corner of 3rd Ave and Scenic Dr; centre. 100 3rd Ave S T1J 4L2. Fax: 403/320-2070. **Facility:** 91 units. 90 one-bedroom standard units, some with whirlpools. 1 one-bedroom suite ($121-$156) with kitchen. 2 stories (no elevator), interior/exterior corridors. **Parking:** on-site, winter plug-ins. **Amenities:** video library (fee), hair dryers. *Some:* irons. **Pool(s):** heated indoor. **Leisure Activities:** whirlpool, exercise room. **Guest Services:** coin laundry. **Business Services:** PC, fax. **Cards:** AX, DC, DS, JC, MC, VI. **Special Amenities:** free expanded continental breakfast and free local telephone calls.

SOME UNITS

ECONO LODGE & SUITES LETHBRIDGE

Book at aaa.com

Phone: (403)328-5591

All Year	1P: $58-$69	2P: $58-$69	XP: $5	F18

Motel **Location:** Hwy 3, 4 or 5, exit Mayor Magrath Dr S. 1124 Mayor Magrath Dr S T1K 2P8. Fax: 403/380-4873. **Facility:** 44 units. 38 one-bedroom standard units, some with efficiencies and/or whirlpools. 6 one-bedroom suites ($74-$90) with efficiencies. 2 stories (no elevator), exterior corridors. **Bath:** combo or shower only. **Parking:** on-site, winter plug-ins. **Terms:** 7 day cancellation notice, pets ($5 extra charge). **Amenities:** *Some:* hair dryers. **Leisure Activities:** limited exercise equipment. **Guest Services:** coin laundry. **Business Services:** PC (fee). **Cards:** AX, DC, DS, JC, MC, VI.

SOME UNITS

HOLIDAY INN EXPRESS HOTEL & SUITES LETHBRIDGE

Book at aaa.com

Phone: (403)394-9292

All Year	1P: $84-$225	2P: $84-$225	XP: $10	D18

Small-scale Hotel **Location:** Hwy 3, exit Stafford Dr, just s; downtown. 120 Stafford Dr S T1J 4W4. Fax: 403/394-9202. **Facility:** 102 units. 82 one-bedroom standard units, some with whirlpools. 20 one-bedroom suites. 4 stories, interior corridors. **Parking:** on-site, winter plug-ins. **Terms:** package plans, pets ($30 fee). **Amenities:** high-speed Internet, dual phone lines, voice mail, irons, hair dryers. **Pool(s):** small heated indoor. **Leisure Activities:** whirlpool, waterslide, limited exercise equipment. **Guest Services:** valet and coin laundry. **Business Services:** meeting rooms. **Cards:** AX, DC, DS, JC, MC, VI. *(See color ad card insert)*

SOME UNITS

LETHBRIDGE LODGE HOTEL AND CONFERENCE CENTRE

Book at aaa.com

Phone: (403)328-1123

All Year	1P: $100-$165	2P: $110-$175	XP: $10	F18

Large-scale Hotel **Location:** Scenic Dr at 4th Ave S; centre. 320 Scenic Dr T1J 4B4. Fax: 403/328-0002. **Facility:** 190 units. 154 one-bedroom standard units. 36 one-bedroom suites ($120-$195), some with whirlpools. 4 stories, interior corridors. **Parking:** on-site, winter plug-ins. **Terms:** check-in 4 pm, small pets only ($10 fee). **Amenities:** video games, high-speed Internet, voice mail, irons, hair dryers. **Dining:** 6:30 am-11 pm, cocktails, also, Anton's, see separate listing, nightclub. **Pool(s):** heated indoor. **Leisure Activities:** whirlpool, exercise room. **Guest Services:** sundries, valet laundry. **Business Services:** conference facilities. **Cards:** AX, DC, DS, JC, MC, VI. **Special Amenities:** free local telephone calls and free newspaper.

SOME UNITS

RAMADA HOTEL & SUITES

Book at aaa.com

Phone: (403)380-5050

7/1-8/31 [ECP]	1P: $145	2P: $155	XP: $10	F18
3/1-6/30 & 9/1-2/28 [ECP]	1P: $135	2P: $145	XP: $10	F18

Large-scale Hotel **Location:** 4.5 km se on Hwy 4 and 5, exit Mayor Magrath Dr S. 2375 Mayor Magrath Dr S T1K 7M1. Fax: 403/380-5051. **Facility:** 119 units. 97 one-bedroom standard units. 22 one-bedroom suites ($165-$205), some with whirlpools. 4 stories, interior corridors. **Parking:** on-site, winter plug-ins. **Terms:** check-in 4 pm, 14 day cancellation notice, pets ($10 extra charge). **Amenities:** video games, dual phone lines, voice mail, irons, hair dryers. *Some:* high-speed Internet. **Pool(s):** heated indoor, wading. **Leisure Activities:** whirlpool, waterslide, exercise room. *Fee:* game room. **Guest Services:** gift shop, valet and coin laundry. **Business Services:** meeting rooms, business center. **Cards:** AX, DC, JC, MC, VI.

SOME UNITS

SOUTH COUNTRY INN

Phone: (403)380-6677

6/1-9/15 [BP]	1P: $89-$119	2P: $95-$125	XP: $10	F18
3/1-5/31 & 9/16-2/28 [BP]	1P: $65-$99	2P: $70-$109	XP: $10	F18

Small-scale Hotel **Location:** 4.5 km se on Hwy 4 and 5, exit Mayor Magrath Dr, then just w. 2225 Mayor Magrath Dr T1K 7M1. Fax: 403/320-2945. **Facility:** 50 units. 43 one- and 7 two-bedroom standard units. 4 stories, interior corridors. **Bath:** combo or shower only. **Parking:** on-site, winter plug-ins. **Terms:** weekly rates available. **Amenities:** high-speed Internet. **Leisure Activities:** whirlpool, exercise room. **Guest Services:** valet and coin laundry. **Business Services:** meeting rooms, PC. **Cards:** AX, CB, DC, DS, MC, VI.

SOME UNITS

THRIFTLODGE Book at aaa.com Phone: (403)328-4436

6/1-11/15	1P: $48-$59	2P: $59-$70	XP: $5	F17
3/1-5/31	1P: $44-$54	2P: $54-$64	XP: $5	F17
11/16-2/28	1P: $40-$50	2P: $50-$60	XP: $5	F17

Motel

Location: 4 km se on Hwy 4 and 5, exit Mayor Magrath Dr S. 1142 Mayor Magrath Dr S T1K 2P8. **Fax:** 403/328-4436. **Facility:** 56 one-bedroom standard units, some with efficiencies. 2 stories (no elevator), exterior corridors. **Parking:** on-site, winter plug-ins. **Terms:** pets ($5 extra charge). **Amenities:** video library (fee), voice mail. **Pool(s):** small outdoor. **Leisure Activities:** whirlpool. **Guest Services:** coin laundry. **Cards:** AX, DC, MC, VI. **Special Amenities:** free continental breakfast and free local telephone calls.

SOME UNITS

———— WHERE TO DINE ————

ANTON'S Lunch: $11-$16 Dinner: $18-$27 Phone: 403/328-1123

Continental

Location: Scenic Dr at 4th Ave S; centre; in Lethbridge Lodge Hotel and Conference Centre. 320 Scenic Dr T1J 4B4. **Hours:** 11:30 am-2 & 5-10 pm, Fri-11 pm, Sat 5 pm-11 pm, Sun 9:30 am-2 & 5-9 pm. Closed major holidays; also Mon. **Reservations:** suggested. **Features:** The excellent menu offers Continental cuisine with French influences, including some tableside preparations. Baked salmon in phyllo and rack of lamb Provencal are excellent. There is a noon weekday buffet and a brunch and evening buffet on Sundays. Some tables offer views of the valley. Guests can expect professional, exceptional service while enjoying fine food in a romantic environment. Casual dress; cocktails. **Parking:** on-site. **Cards:** AX, DS, JC, MC, VI.

THE CHEESECAKE CAFE RESTAURANT Lunch: $8-$15 Dinner: $8-$15 Phone: 403/394-2253

American

Location: At Stafford Dr and 2nd Ave S; downtown. 904 2nd Ave S T1J 0C6. **Hours:** 11 am-11 pm, Fri & Sat-1 am, Sun 10 am-11 pm. Closed: 12/24, 12/25. **Reservations:** not accepted. **Features:** As might be expected, cheesecake is the signature item, and it's worth saving room for one of the lip-smacking varieties made on the premises. A huge dessert display case greets patrons upon arrival. Offerings on the extensive lunch and dinner menu range from sandwiches and entree salads to pasta, pizza and seafood selections. It takes a while to get through the menu. Casual dress; cocktails. **Parking:** on-site. **Cards:** AX, MC, VI.

COCO PAZZO Lunch: $8-$11 Dinner: $10-$27 Phone: 403/329-8979

Italian

Location: Corner of 12th St. 1264 3rd Ave S T1J 0J9. **Hours:** 11 am-11 pm, Fri & Sat-midnight, Sun 5 pm-9 pm. Closed: 1/1, 12/25, 12/26. **Features:** The cozy Italian cafe has a fun, casual atmosphere. Finely tuned, guest-oriented service enhances the meals, which range from wood-fired-oven pizzas and fresh pasta to seafood and other nicely prepared meat and poultry dishes. Casual dress; cocktails. **Parking:** on-site. **Cards:** AX, MC, VI.

DOURO'S PIZZA & STEAKHOUSE Lunch: $6-$9 Dinner: $9-$18 Phone: 403/327-3067

Steak House

Location: From Mayor Magrath Dr, exit N at Scenic Dr to Fairway Plaza; southeast end of town. 2433 Fairway Plaza Rd S T1K 6Z2. **Hours:** 11 am-midnight, Fri & Sat-1 am. Closed: 12/25. **Reservations:** suggested. **Features:** A great place for families, the casual restaurant serves a wide range of pizzas and steaks, as well as other dishes, including large sandwiches, oversize salads and nachos. Patrons get great value for the dollar, and there's something for everyone. Casual dress; cocktails. **Parking:** on-site. **Cards:** AX, MC, VI.

THE PITA PIT Lunch: $4-$6 Dinner: $4-$6 Phone: 403/317-7788

Deli/Subs
Sandwiches

Location: Corner of 3rd Ave and 6th St; downtown. 602 3rd Ave T1J 2C7. **Hours:** 11 am-3 am, Thurs-Sat to 4 am, Sun-midnight; Mon-Wed to midnight in summer. **Features:** The simple eatery offers a healthy fast food option. Guests step up to the counter to order from among a selection of chicken, beef, vegetarian, ham and turkey pitas. Topping choices include lettuce, tomato, olives and other fresh ingredients. Topped with a sauce and coupled with a cup of soup, a pita makes for a quick and healthy lunch or dinner. Inside are six tables. Takeout service is a popular option. Casual dress. **Parking:** street.

SHANGHAI RESTAURANT Lunch: $3-$8 Dinner: $7-$14 Phone: 403/327-3552

Chinese

Location: Downtown. 610 3rd Ave S T1J 0H5. **Hours:** 11 am-midnight, Fri-2 am, Sat noon-2 am, Sun 4 pm-11 pm. Closed: 12/25. **Features:** As one of the city's oldest establishments, the simple Chinese restaurant has an enviable reputation. Typical fare can be savored in the dining room, which is one level up from the street. Also on the menu is a small selection of Western food. Among popular choices are chop suey, egg foo yong, goba, Cantonese-style chow mein and ginger beef. Casual dress; cocktails. **Parking:** street. **Cards:** MC, VI.

STREATSIDE EATERY Lunch: $9-$19 Dinner: $9-$19 Phone: 403/328-8085

Canadian

Location: At 3rd Ave and 8th St; downtown. 317 8th St S T1J 2J5. **Hours:** 11 am-10 pm, Fri & Sat-11:30 pm, Sun-8 pm. Closed: 12/25, 12/26. **Features:** A favorite among the locals, the casual downtown eatery prepares homemade comfort food from fresh ingredients. Although this place is known for its quiche of the day, guests also can also try entree-size salads and sandwiches. The red brick interior and outdoor patio contribute to a pleasant atmosphere. Casual dress; cocktails. **Parking:** street. **Cards:** AX, MC, VI.

SVEN ERICKSEN'S FAMILY RESTAURANT Lunch: $9-$12 Dinner: $13-$25 Phone: 403/328-7756

American

Location: 4.4 km se on Hwy 4 and 5, exit Mayor Magrath Dr. 1715 Mayor Magrath Dr T1K 2R7. **Hours:** 11 am-11 pm, Sun 9:30 am-9 pm. Closed: 12/24-12/26. **Reservations:** suggested. **Features:** The restaurant has a longstanding reputation for fine food. The varied lunch and dinner menu includes Alberta beef steak, prime rib, seafood, chicken, veal and pasta dishes, as well as salads. Its unpretentious service enhances the casual dining atmosphere. Casual dress; cocktails. **Parking:** on-site. **Cards:** AX, DC, MC, VI.

TREATS EATERY — Lunch: $7-$16 — Dinner: $7-$16 — Phone: 403/380-4880
ŵŵ ŵŵ
American
Location: 3.2 km se on Hwy 4 and 5, exit Mayor Magrath Dr at 10th Ave S. 1104 Mayor Magrath Dr T1K 2P9.
Hours: 11 am-10 pm, Fri & Sat-11 pm, Sun noon-10 pm. Closed: 1/1, 12/25. **Reservations:** suggested.
Features: Although the fun, casual establishment has an unusual Western theme, it doesn't offer Western-style dishes. On the menu are deli-style burgers, sandwiches and quiche, as well as health-conscious dishes and more elaborate dinner items. Cocktails. **Parking:** on-site. **Cards:** AX, DC, MC, VI.

LLOYDMINSTER pop. 20,988—See also LLOYDMINSTER, SK.

──── **WHERE TO STAY** ────

BEST WESTERN WAYSIDE INN & SUITES — *Book at aaa.com* — Phone: (780)875-4404
ŵŵ ŵŵ
Small-scale Hotel
All Year — 1P: $107-$119 — 2P: $115-$127 — XP: $8 — F18
Location: 0.8 km w on Hwy 16 from jct Hwy 17. 5411 44th St T9V 0A9. **Fax:** 780/875-7210. **Facility:** 128 units. 97 one-bedroom standard units. 31 one-bedroom suites ($149-$249), some with whirlpools. 6 stories, interior corridors. **Parking:** on-site, winter plug-ins. **Terms:** pets ($5 extra charge, in smoking units).
Amenities: voice mail, irons, hair dryers. **Pool(s):** small heated indoor. **Leisure Activities:** exercise room. *Fee:* massage.
Guest Services: valet laundry. **Business Services:** conference facilities, administrative services (fee). **Cards:** AX, DC, DS, MC, VI.
SOME UNITS
FEE

TROPICAL INN — Phone: (780)875-7000
(CAA) (SAVE)
ŵŵ ŵŵ
Small-scale Hotel
All Year — 1P: $88-$254 — 2P: $92-$254 — XP: $5 — D17
Location: Jct Hwy 16 and 17, 1 km w. 5621 44th St T9V 0B2. **Fax:** 780/875-7828. **Facility:** 165 units. 159 one-bedroom standard units, some with whirlpools. 6 one-bedroom suites ($114-$254) with whirlpools. 8 stories, interior corridors. **Parking:** on-site, winter plug-ins. **Terms:** check-in 4 pm, weekly rates available, small pets only (in designated units). **Amenities:** video games, high-speed Internet (fee), voice mail, hair dryers. *Some:* irons. **Dining:** 6 am-10 pm, Fri-Sun from 7 am, cocktails. **Pool(s):** small heated indoor. **Leisure Activities:** sauna, whirlpool, waterslide, exercise room. **Guest Services:** valet laundry. **Business Services:** meeting rooms, administrative services (fee). **Cards:** AX, DC, DS, JC, MC, VI.
SOME UNITS

WEST HARVEST INN — *Book at aaa.com* — Phone: (780)875-6113
ŵŵ ŵŵ
Small-scale Hotel
All Year — 1P: $95-$105 — 2P: $103-$111 — XP: $8 — F16
Location: Jct Hwy 16 and 17, 1 km w. 5620 44th St T9V 0B6. **Fax:** 780/875-2265. **Facility:** 97 one-bedroom standard units, some with whirlpools. 2 stories (no elevator), interior/exterior corridors. **Parking:** on-site, winter plug-ins. **Amenities:** video games, voice mail, hair dryers. *Some:* irons. **Pool(s):** heated indoor. **Leisure Activities:** steamrooms, exercise room. **Guest Services:** valet laundry. **Business Services:** meeting rooms, administrative services, PC (fee). **Cards:** AX, DC, DS, MC, VI.
SOME UNITS

──── **WHERE TO DINE** ────

MR BILL'S FAMILY RESTAURANT — Lunch: $5-$10 — Dinner: $8-$19 — Phone: 780/875-3388
ŵŵ ŵŵ
Continental
Location: Corner of Hwy 16 and 54th Ave. 10 5405 44th St T9V 0A9. **Hours:** 10 am-10 pm. Closed major holidays; also Sun. **Reservations:** suggested. **Features:** In a border town that features predominantly chain eateries, the excellent family restaurant serves burgers, sandwiches, pasta and a few Greek dishes. Popular with the locals, this spot offers fast, friendly service amid comfortable, trendy decor. For a delicious, hearty lunch, try the superb Greek avgolemono soup. Casual dress; cocktails. **Parking:** on-site. **Cards:** AX, MC, VI.

MEDICINE HAT pop. 51,249

──── **WHERE TO STAY** ────

BEST WESTERN INN — *Book at aaa.com* — Phone: (403)527-3700
ŵŵ ŵŵ
Small-scale Hotel
All Year [ECP] — 1P: $99-$249 — 2P: $99-$249
Location: On Trans-Canada Hwy 1; 0.4 km w of jct Hwy 3, access 7th St SW. 722 Redcliff Dr T1A 5E3. **Fax:** 403/526-8689. **Facility:** 122 units. 115 one-bedroom standard units, some with efficiencies and/or whirlpools. 7 one-bedroom suites, some with whirlpools. 2 stories (no elevator), interior/exterior corridors. **Parking:** on-site, winter plug-ins. **Terms:** small pets only (with prior approval). **Amenities:** video games, voice mail, irons, hair dryers. *Some:* high-speed Internet, dual phone lines. **Pool(s):** 2 small heated indoor. **Leisure Activities:** sauna, whirlpools, steamroom, exercise room. **Guest Services:** valet and coin laundry. **Business Services:** meeting rooms, PC. **Cards:** AX, DC, DS, JC, MC, VI.
SOME UNITS

COMFORT INN & SUITES — *Book at aaa.com* — Phone: (403)504-1700
ŵŵ ŵŵ
Small-scale Hotel
6/1-10/31 [ECP] — 1P: $80-$115 — 2P: $85-$115 — XP: $5 — F17
3/1-5/31 & 11/1-2/28 [ECP] — 1P: $75-$100 — 2P: $80-$115 — XP: $5 — F17
Location: 5 km se; just n off Trans-Canada Hwy 1; corner of Dunmore Rd. Located opposite Medicine Hat Mall. 2317 Trans-Canada Way SE T1B 4E9. **Fax:** 403/527-1579. **Facility:** 101 units. 72 one-bedroom standard units, some with whirlpools. 29 one-bedroom suites ($105-$350), some with whirlpools. 3 stories, interior corridors. **Parking:** on-site, winter plug-ins. **Terms:** check-in 4 pm. **Amenities:** high-speed Internet, voice mail, irons, hair dryers. **Pool(s):** small heated indoor. **Leisure Activities:** whirlpool, exercise room. **Guest Services:** valet and coin laundry. **Business Services:** meeting rooms, PC (fee). **Cards:** AX, DC, DS, MC, VI.
SOME UNITS

DAYS INN-MEDICINE HAT   *Book at aaa.com*

▼▼▼   All Year [ECP]   1P: $99-$109   2P: $99-$109   XP: $10   F12
                                                                                                Phone: (403)580-3297

Location: Trans-Canada Hwy 1, exit Dunmore Rd, just sw. 24 Strachan Ct SE T1B 4R7. Fax: 403/580-3299.
Small-scale Hotel **Facility:** 76 units. 61 one-bedroom standard units, some with whirlpools. 15 one-bedroom suites ($129-
$149), some with whirlpools. 4 stories, interior corridors. **Parking:** on-site, winter plug-ins. **Terms:** check-in
4 pm. **Amenities:** voice mail, irons, hair dryers. *Some:* video games, high-speed Internet. **Pool(s):** heated indoor. **Leisure
Activities:** whirlpool, waterslide. **Guest Services:** sundries, valet and coin laundry. **Business Services:** PC (fee). **Cards:** AX,
DC, MC, VI.

SOME UNITS

(ASK) (S☐) (†↓↑) (⊃) (⊷⊷) (🎥) (DATA PORT) (☐) (⌨) (▭) / (✕) /

IMPERIAL INN   Phone: (403)527-8811

(CAA) (SAVE)   6/24-9/5   1P: $69-$74   2P: $73-$84   XP: $4
                3/1-6/23 & 9/6-2/28   1P: $64-$69   2P: $68-$79   XP: $4
▼▼▼
Location: 3.6 km se; just n off Trans-Canada Hwy 1. Located opposite Southview Shopping Mall. 3282 13th Ave SE
Motel   T1B 1H8. Fax: 403/526-7039. **Facility:** 102 units. 97 one- and 5 two-bedroom standard units. 2 stories (no
elevator), interior/exterior corridors. **Parking:** on-site, winter plug-ins. **Terms:** pets ($5 extra charge).
Amenities: hair dryers. **Dining:** 2 restaurants, 7 am-10 & 5:30-8:30 pm, Sat & Sun-11 am, cocktails, also,
Beefeater Steakhouse, see separate listing. **Pool(s):** small heated indoor. **Leisure Activities:** sauna, whirlpools, steamroom.
Guest Services: valet and coin laundry. **Business Services:** meeting rooms. **Cards:** AX, DC, DS, JC, MC, VI.
Special Amenities: free local telephone calls and early check-in/late check-out. *(See color ad below)*

SOME UNITS

(S☐) (🐾) (†↓) (⊃) (✕) (🎥) (DATA PORT) (☐) (⌨) (▭) / (✕) /
      FEE

MEDICINE HAT LODGE HOTEL CASINO
   CONVENTION CENTRE HEALTH
   SPA & INDOOR WATERSLIDE PARK   *Book at aaa.com*
                                                                                                Phone: 403/529-2222

▼▼▼   7/1-9/6   1P: $99-$109   2P: $109-$119   XP: $10   F17
        3/1-6/30 & 9/7-2/28   1P: $91-$101   2P: $101-$109   XP: $10   F17
Large-scale Hotel **Location:** East end approach to city on Trans-Canada Hwy 1, at jct Dunmore Rd. 1051 Ross Glen Dr SE T1B 3T8.
Fax: 403/529-1538. **Facility:** Some rooms with pool view balconies are offered at this casino hotel; indoor
waterslides are featured for children. 221 units. 185 one-bedroom standard units, some with whirlpools. 36 one-bedroom suites,
some with whirlpools. 4 stories, interior corridors. *Bath:* combo or shower only. **Parking:** on-site, winter plug-ins. **Terms:** check-
in 4 pm, pets ($10 fee, in designated units). **Amenities:** video games, high-speed Internet, voice mail, irons, hair dryers.
Dining: Mamma's Ristorante, see separate listing. **Pool(s):** small heated indoor, wading. **Leisure Activities:** whirlpool,
waterslide, rental bicycles, exercise room, spa. *Fee:* game room. **Guest Services:** gift shop, valet and coin laundry, hair salon.
Business Services: conference facilities, PC. **Cards:** AX, DC, DS, MC, VI.

SOME UNITS

(🏌) (ASK) (S☐) (✛) (🍽) (†↓) (Y) (⊃) (✕) (🎥) (DATA PORT) (☐) (▭) / (✕) (⌨) /
                    FEE

RANCHMEN MOTEL   Phone: 403/527-2263

▼▼   All Year   1P: $50-$60   2P: $57-$67   XP: $5   D12
Location: Trans-Canada Hwy 1 at 16th St SW. 535 16th St SW T1A 5E7. Fax: 403/529-9775. **Facility:** 44 units. 38
Motel   one- and 6 two-bedroom standard units, some with efficiencies. 1-2 stories (no elevator), exterior corridors.
Parking: on-site, winter plug-ins. **Terms:** office hours 7 am-midnight, weekly rates available, small pets only
($5 fee). **Leisure Activities:** miniature golf. **Guest Services:** coin laundry. **Cards:** AX, MC, VI.

SOME UNITS

(🐾) (†↓) (🎥) (☐) (⌨) (▭) / (✕) /
      FEE

SUPER 8 MOTEL   Phone: 403/528-8888

▼▼ ▼▼   6/1-8/31 [CP]   1P: $79-$89   2P: $84-$94   XP: $5   F12
          9/1-11/30 [CP]   1P: $77-$87   2P: $82-$92   XP: $5   F12
Small-scale Hotel 3/1-5/31 [CP]   1P: $74-$84   2P: $79-$89   XP: $5   F12
          12/1-2/28 [CP]   1P: $68-$78   2P: $73-$83   XP: $5   F12
Location: Trans-Canada Way at 13 Ave SE; just n off Trans-Canada Hwy 1. 1280 Trans-Canada Way SE T1B 1J5. Fax: 403/526-4445.
Facility: 70 units. 69 one-bedroom standard units, some with kitchens. 1 one-bedroom suite with kitchen. 2-3 stories (no
elevator), interior/exterior corridors. **Parking:** on-site, winter plug-ins. **Terms:** check-in 4 pm, small pets only ($5 fee, in
designated units). **Amenities:** voice mail, hair dryers. **Pool(s):** small heated indoor. **Leisure Activities:** whirlpool, limited
exercise equipment. **Guest Services:** valet laundry. **Business Services:** PC (fee). **Cards:** AX, DC, DS, MC, VI.

SOME UNITS

(ASK) (S☐) (🐾) (†↓) (⅙M) (⊃) (DATA PORT) (☐) (⌨) (▭) / (✕) (VCR) /
              FEE   FEE

TRAVELODGE HOTEL MEDICINE HAT   *Book at aaa.com*   **Phone:** (403)527-2275

CAA SAVE
WWW WWW

	5/1-9/30	1P: $93-$125	2P: $93-$125
	1/1-2/28	1P: $85-$119	2P: $85-$119
	3/1-4/30 & 10/1-12/31	1P: $83-$115	2P: $83-$115

Location: 2.8 km sw on Trans-Canada Hwy 1 at jct Hwy 3. 1100 Redcliff Dr SW T1A 5E5. Fax: 403/526-7842.
Small-scale Hotel **Facility:** 129 one-bedroom standard units, some with efficiencies or kitchens. 2 stories (no elevator), interior/exterior corridors. **Parking:** on-site, winter plug-ins. **Terms:** check-in 4 pm, pets ($7 extra charge, in designated units). **Amenities:** high-speed Internet (fee), voice mail, irons, hair dryers. *Some:* video games. **Dining:** 6 am-11 pm, Sun 7 am-9 pm, cocktails. **Pool(s):** small heated outdoor, small heated indoor. **Leisure Activities:** sauna, whirlpool, waterslide, exercise room. **Guest Services:** gift shop, valet and coin laundry. **Business Services:** meeting rooms. **Cards:** AX, DC, DS, MC, VI. **Special Amenities:** free local telephone calls and free newspaper.

SOME UNITS

🅂🅳 🐾 ⊺⊹ 🍸 🌊 ✕ 🐾 DATA·PORT 💻 / ✕ 🔋 🖥 /
FEE

——— WHERE TO DINE ———

BEEFEATER STEAKHOUSE   **Lunch:** $7-$14   **Dinner:** $9-$30   **Phone:** 403-526-6925

CAA
WWW WWW

Location: 3.6 km se; just n off Trans-Canada Hwy 1; in Imperial Inn. 3286 13th Ave SE T1B 1H8. **Hours:** 11 am-midnight, Sat from 4:30 pm, Sun 4:30 pm-10 pm. **Closed:** 12/25, 12/26. **Reservations:** suggested.
Steak & Seafood **Features:** Patrons appreciate the good value they receive at the restaurant, which offers relaxed dining in an attractive library-like setting. The menu specializes in prime rib and seafood, with a good selection of sandwiches at lunch. Service is good and efficient. Casual dress; cocktails. **Parking:** on-site. **Cards:** AX, DC, MC, VI.

🍸

HAT'S RESTAURANT   **Dinner:** $7-$15   **Phone:** 403/529-9739

WWW WWW

Location: In Crestwood Shopping Centre. 1701 Dunmore Rd SE T1A 1Z8. **Hours:** 4 pm-10 pm, Fri & Sat-11 pm. **Closed:** Mon. **Reservations:** suggested, weekends. **Features:** Locals claim the wonderful Chinese
Chinese restaurant as a favorite for its flavorful, reasonably priced food. Traditional foods line the all-you-can-eat buffet, as well as the a la carte menu. Also offered is a smattering of Western cuisine. Casual dress; cocktails. **Parking:** on-site. **Cards:** AX, MC, VI.

✕

MAMMA'S RISTORANTE   **Lunch:** $7-$16   **Dinner:** $13-$29   **Phone:** 403/529-2222

WWW WWW WWW

Location: East end approach to city on Trans-Canada Hwy 1, at jct Dunmore Rd; in Medicine Hat Lodge Hotel Casino Convention Centre Health Spa & Indoor Waterslide Park. 1051 Ross Glen Dr SE T1B 3T8. **Hours:** 5 pm-10 pm, Sun
Continental also 10 am-2 pm. **Reservations:** suggested. **Features:** The varied menu includes preparations of pasta, seafood, veal and Alberta beef. The restaurant's elegant garden setting lends to a casual, relaxed atmosphere. Service is efficient and friendly. Casual dress; cocktails. **Parking:** on-site. **Cards:** AX, DC, DS, MC, VI.

🍸 ✕

MARIO'S RESTAURANT   **Lunch:** $6-$10   **Dinner:** $10-$18   **Phone:** 403/529-2600

WWW WWW

Location: Corner of 5th Ave and 5th St SE. 439 5th Ave SE T1A 2P9. **Hours:** 11:30 am-2 & 5-11 pm, Sat from 5
Italian pm. **Closed:** 1/1, 12/25, 12/26; also Sun. **Reservations:** suggested, weekends. **Features:** Guests are treated to delicious offerings from a Northern Italian dinner menu that lists nicely prepared homemade pasta, breast of chicken, veal, steak and seafood dishes. The Mediterranean setting is comfortable and casual. Service is fine. Cocktails. **Parking:** on-site. **Cards:** AX, DC, MC, VI.

🍸 ✕

TUSCANY MEDITERRANEAN GRILLE   **Dinner:** $10-$22   **Phone:** 403/529-0777

WWW WWW

Location: 2.4 km sw; just s of Trans-Canada Hwy 1 at 7th St. 925 7th St SW T1A 7H1. **Hours:** 4 pm-11 pm, Sun-
Italian 9:30 pm. **Closed:** 12/25, 12/26. **Reservations:** suggested. **Features:** Located just on the outskirts of town, you'll be able to enjoy fine food, great service and a cozy atmosphere. Featuring an array of Mediterranean food, everything is prepared to order and very tasty. Cocktails. **Parking:** on-site. **Cards:** AX, DC, MC, VI.

✕

MOUNTAIN VIEW pop. 80

——— WHERE TO STAY ———

ROCKY RIDGE COUNTRY RESORT   **Phone:** 403/653-2350

WWW WWW

	5/15-9/14 [BP]	2P: $80-$150	XP: $10	F6
	3/1-5/14 & 9/15-2/28 [BP]	2P: $64-$120	XP: $10	F6

Location: Hwy 5, 1 km n follow signs by village church. (Box 117). Fax: 403/653-1640. **Facility:** Smoke free
Bed & Breakfast premises. 7 units. 6 one-bedroom standard units. 1 cabin ($200-$250). 2 stories (no elevator), interior corridors. *Bath:* some shared or private, combo or shower only. **Parking:** on-site, winter plug-ins. **Terms:** check-in 4 pm, package plans. **Amenities:** hair dryers. **Leisure Activities:** sauna, whirlpool, game room. **Guest Services:** TV in common area. **Cards:** AX, MC, VI.

ASK ✕ ✕ 🅿 ☎

NISKU —*See Edmonton p. 423.*

OKOTOKS —*See Calgary p. 392.*

PEACE RIVER pop. 6,240

——— WHERE TO STAY ———

TRAVELLERS MOTOR HOTEL   Phone: (780)624-3621
(CAA) (SAVE)   All Year   1P: $59-$89   2P: $64-$94   XP: $5   F16
▼▼ ▼▼   **Location:** Just s off Hwy 2 S, exit town centre. 9510 100th St T8S 1S9 (PO Box 7290). Fax: 780/624-4855.
Motel   **Facility:** 137 units. 135 one- and 2 two-bedroom standard units, some with kitchens. 2 stories (no elevator), interior/exterior corridors. **Parking:** on-site, winter plug-ins. **Terms:** cancellation fee imposed, weekly rates available, pets ($20 deposit). **Amenities:** voice mail, hair dryers. *Some:* high-speed Internet, irons. **Dining:** 2 restaurants, 5:30 am-midnight, cocktails. **Leisure Activities:** sauna, golf course privileges. **Guest Services:** valet and coin laundry, area transportation. **Business Services:** meeting rooms, PC (fee). **Cards:** AX, CB, DC, DS, MC, VI.

SOME UNITS
⟨S/D⟩ ⟨✈⟩ ⟨🛏⟩ ⟨🍴⟩ ⟨🍸⟩ ⟨💪⟩ ⟨🎥⟩ ⟨DATA PORT⟩ ⟨💻⟩ / ⟨✕⟩ ⟨📵⟩ ⟨🖼⟩ /
FEE

PINCHER CREEK pop. 3,666

——— WHERE TO STAY ———

HERITAGE INN   Phone: (403)627-5000
▼▼ ▼▼   6/1-9/30   1P: $89   2P: $99   XP: $5   F16
         10/1-2/28   1P: $83   2P: $92   XP: $5   F16
Small-scale Hotel 3/1-5/31   1P: $81   2P: $90   XP: $5   F16
Location: SR 3, 4.7 km s on SR 6. 919 Waterton Ave (Hwy 6) T0K 1W0 (PO Box 399). Fax: 403/627-3936.
Facility: 42 one-bedroom standard units. 2 stories (no elevator), interior corridors. **Parking:** on-site, winter plug-ins. **Terms:** package plans, small pets only ($10 fee, in smoking units). **Guest Services:** coin laundry. **Business Services:** meeting rooms. **Cards:** AX, DC, DS, MC, VI.

SOME UNITS
⟨ASK⟩ ⟨S/D⟩ ⟨🛏⟩ ⟨🍴⟩ ⟨🍸⟩ ⟨💪⟩ ⟨DATA PORT⟩ ⟨💻⟩ / ⟨✕⟩ ⟨📵⟩ ⟨🖼⟩ /
FEE

——— WHERE TO DINE ———

SWISS ALPINE RESTAURANT   Lunch: $8-$22   Dinner: $8-$22   Phone: 403/627-5079
▼▼ ▼   **Location:** Jct Hwy 6 and Main St. 988 Main St T0K 1W0. **Hours:** 11 am-10 pm. Closed: 1/1, 12/25; also Sun &
Ethnic   Mon. **Reservations:** suggested, in summer. **Features:** This popular restaurant features Swiss croute, crepes, lamb, Alberta beef, sandwiches, pasta and stir-fry dishes, which are prepared with fresh ingredients and a Swiss flair. Sunday night has a prime rib special. The rustic decor displays art for sale. Cocktails.
Parking: on-site. **Cards:** AX, DC, MC, VI.

⟨🍸⟩ ⟨✕⟩

RED DEER pop. 67,707

——— WHERE TO STAY ———

CAPRI HOTEL TRADE & CONVENTION CENTRE   *Book at aaa.com*   Phone: (403)346-2091
(CAA) (SAVE)   All Year   2P: $90-$175   XP: $20   F18
▼▼ ▼▼   **Location:** 2 km s on Hwy 2A (Gaetz Ave). 3310 50th Ave T4N 3X9. Fax: 403/346-4790. **Facility:** 220 units. 196 one-bedroom standard units. 16 one- & 8 two-bedroom suites ($215-$500), some with whirlpools. 2-14 stories, interior corridors. **Parking:** on-site, winter plug-ins. **Terms:** 48 day cancellation notice-fee imposed,
Large-scale Hotel package plans, small pets only. **Amenities:** video games, voice mail, irons, hair dryers. *Some:* high-speed Internet (fee). **Dining:** 3 restaurants, 6 am-2 am, cocktails. **Pool(s):** small heated outdoor. **Leisure Activities:** sauna, whirlpool, exercise room. *Fee:* massage. **Guest Services:** gift shop, valet laundry, area transportation (fee), beauty salon. **Business Services:** conference facilities, business center. **Cards:** AX, DC, MC, VI.

SOME UNITS
⟨S/D⟩ ⟨✈⟩ ⟨🛏⟩ ⟨🍴⟩ ⟨🍸⟩ ⟨🏊⟩ ⟨✕⟩ ⟨🎥⟩ ⟨DATA PORT⟩ ⟨💻⟩ / ⟨✕⟩ ⟨📵⟩ ⟨🖼⟩ /
FEE

DEER PARK INN   Phone: (403)343-8444
(CAA) (SAVE)   All Year [CP]   1P: $69-$77   2P: $69-$77   XP: $5   F18
▼▼ ▼▼   **Location:** Hwy 2, exit S Red Deer on service road. 37557 Hwy 2 T4E 1B1. Fax: 403/342-4310. **Facility:** 76 one-bedroom standard units. 2 stories (no elevator), exterior corridors. **Parking:** on-site, winter plug-ins.
Motel   **Terms:** weekly rates available, package plans. **Amenities:** voice mail, hair dryers. **Guest Services:** coin laundry. **Cards:** AX, MC, VI.

SOME UNITS
⟨S/D⟩ ⟨🍴⟩ ⟨🎥⟩ ⟨DATA PORT⟩ ⟨💻⟩ / ⟨✕⟩ ⟨📵⟩ ⟨🖼⟩ /

HOLIDAY INN 67 STREET   *Book at aaa.com*   Phone: (403)342-6567
(CAA) (SAVE)   3/1-12/18 [CP]   1P: $100-$120   2P: $100-$120
         12/19-2/28 [CP]   1P: $90-$110   2P: $90-$110
▼▼ ▼▼   **Location:** 3.2 km nw, 0.8 km e of Hwy 2, exit 67th St. 6500 67th St T4P 1A2. Fax: 403/343-3600. **Facility:** 97 one-bedroom standard units, some with whirlpools. 4 stories, interior corridors. **Parking:** on-site, winter plug-ins.
Small-scale Hotel **Terms:** pets ($15 fee, in smoking units). **Amenities:** video games, high-speed Internet, dual phone lines, voice mail, irons, hair dryers. **Dining:** 6 am-midnight, Sun from 7 am, cocktails. **Pool(s):** heated indoor.
Leisure Activities: sauna, whirlpool, game room. *Fee:* massage. **Guest Services:** valet laundry. *Fee:* tanning facility.
Business Services: conference facilities, business center. **Cards:** AX, CB, DC, DS, JC, MC, VI. **Special Amenities:** free continental breakfast and free local telephone calls.

SOME UNITS
⟨S/D⟩ ⟨🛏⟩ ⟨🍴⟩ ⟨🍸⟩ ⟨🏊⟩ ⟨💪⟩ ⟨✕⟩ ⟨🎥⟩ ⟨DATA PORT⟩ ⟨📵⟩ ⟨💻⟩ / ⟨✕⟩ ⟨🖼⟩ /
FEE

HOLIDAY INN EXPRESS RED DEER *Book at aaa.com*
Phone: (403)343-2112

CAA SAVE All Year 1P: $119-$149 XP: $10 F18
Location: 1.8 km e on Hwy 2A (Gaetz Ave). 2803 50th Ave T4R 1H1. Fax: 403/340-8540. **Facility:** 92 one-bedroom standard units, some with whirlpools. 2 stories (no elevator), interior corridors. **Parking:** on-site,
Small-scale Hotel speed Internet, dual phone lines, voice mail, irons, hair dryers. **Pool(s):** small heated indoor, saltwater.
winter plug-ins. **Terms:** small pets only ($15 extra charge, in smoking units). **Amenities:** video games, high-
Leisure Activities: whirlpool, steamroom, exercise room. **Guest Services:** valet and coin laundry.
Cards: AX, DC, DS, JC, MC, VI. *(See color ad card insert)* SOME UNITS

RED DEER LODGE HOTEL & CONFERENCE
CENTRE *Book at aaa.com*
Phone: (403)346-8841

CAA SAVE 3/1-5/31 & 9/16-2/28 1P: $109-$159 2P: $109-$159 XP: $15 F17
6/1-9/15 1P: $99-$159 2P: $99-$159 XP: $15 F17
Location: Corner of 43rd St and 49th Ave; centre. 4311 49th Ave T4N 5Y7. Fax: 403/341-3220. **Facility:** 233 units.
201 one-bedroom standard units. 32 one-bedroom suites ($199-$259). 5-7 stories, interior corridors.
Large-scale Hotel **Parking:** on-site, winter plug-ins. **Terms:** check-in 3:30 pm, cancellation fee imposed, package plans, pets
($15 fee, in courtyard smoking units). **Amenities:** video games, voice mail, irons, hair dryers. *Some:* high-
speed Internet. **Dining:** 6:30 am-11 pm, cocktails. **Pool(s):** heated indoor. **Leisure Activities:** whirlpool, bicycles, hiking trails,
jogging, exercise room. *Fee:* massage, esthetics salon. **Guest Services:** gift shop, valet laundry. **Business Services:**
conference facilities, PC. Cards: AX, DC, DS, MC, VI. **Special Amenities: free newspaper and free room upgrade (subject
to availability with advance reservations).** SOME UNITS

SANDMAN HOTEL RED DEER *Book at aaa.com*
Phone: (403)343-7400

All Year 1P: $99-$109 2P: $99-$109 XP: $10 F16
Location: 2 km n. 2818 Gaetz Ave T4R 1M4. Fax: 403/343-7411. **Facility:** 143 units. 94 one-bedroom standard
Small-scale Hotel units, some with whirlpools. 49 one-bedroom suites. 4 stories, interior corridors. **Parking:** on-site, winter
plug-ins. **Terms:** check-in 4 pm, pets ($10 extra charge). **Amenities:** video games, dual phone lines, voice
mail, irons, hair dryers. **Pool(s):** heated indoor. **Leisure Activities:** whirlpool, exercise room. **Guest Services:** valet laundry.
Business Services: meeting rooms, PC (fee). Cards: AX, DC, DS, MC, VI. SOME UNITS

SERVICE PLUS INNS AND SUITES *Book at aaa.com*
Phone: (403)342-4445

CAA SAVE 5/1-11/16 [ECP] 1P: $94-$169 2P: $99-$199 XP: $10 F16
3/1-4/30 & 11/17-2/28 [ECP] 1P: $89-$169 2P: $94-$199 XP: $10 F16
Location: 3.6 km nw, 0.5 km e of Hwy 2, exit 67th St. 6853 66th St T4P 3T5. Fax: 403/342-4433. **Facility:** 90 units.
75 one- and 3 two-bedroom standard units, some with whirlpools. 12 one-bedroom suites, some with
Small-scale Hotel whirlpools. 4 stories, interior corridors. **Parking:** on-site, winter plug-ins. **Terms:** package plans, small pets
only ($15 fee, must be in kennel). **Amenities:** high-speed Internet, voice mail, irons, hair dryers. **Dining:** 11
am-11 pm, Fri & Sat-1 am, cocktails. **Pool(s):** heated indoor. **Leisure Activities:** whirlpool, waterslide, limited exercise
equipment. **Guest Services:** complimentary evening beverages: Wed, valet laundry. **Business Services:** meeting rooms.
Cards: AX, DC, DS, MC, VI. **Special Amenities: free expanded continental breakfast and free newspaper.** SOME UNITS

STANFORD INN *Book at aaa.com*
Phone: (403)347-5551

All Year 1P: $80-$100 2P: $80-$100 XP: $5 F12
Location: Hwy 2, exit Gaetz Ave to 49th St, just e. Located next to casinos. 4707 Ross St T4N 1X3.
Small-scale Hotel Fax: 403/347-8820. **Facility:** 61 units. 54 one-bedroom standard units, some with whirlpools. 7 one-
bedroom suites ($120-$140). 3 stories, interior corridors. **Parking:** on-site, winter plug-ins. **Terms:** check-in
4 pm, pets ($10 extra charge). **Amenities:** voice mail, irons, hair dryers. *Some:* CD players. **Guest Services:** valet and coin
laundry. **Business Services:** meeting rooms. Cards: AX, DC, MC, VI. SOME UNITS

───── *The following lodging was either not evaluated or did not* ─────
meet AAA rating requirements but is listed for your information only.

BEST WESTERN RED DEER
Phone: 403/346-3555

fyi Not evaluated. **Location:** From Hwy 2, just e at 66th St. 6839 66th St T4P 3T5. Facilities, services, and decor
characterize a mid-range property.

───── **WHERE TO DINE** ─────

MOHAVE GRILL Lunch: $9-$16 Dinner: $10-$20 Phone: 403/340-3463
Location: Hwy 2, exit 67th St, 0.5 km e; next to Service Plus Inns & Suites. 6608 Orr Dr T4P 3T5. **Hours:** 11 am-11
pm, Fri & Sat-midnight, Sun-10 pm. Closed: 12/25. **Features:** Diners will find mainly Mexican food at the
Mexican funky, festive restaurant, just off the highway. However, the eclectic menu takes some chances by delving
into Cajun, Southwestern and Jamaican influences. Each dish is sure to please, and the servings are
plentiful. Semi-formal attire; cocktails. **Parking:** on-site. Cards: AX, MC, VI.

RUSTY PELICAN Lunch: $7-$9 Dinner: $9-$18 Phone: 403/347-1414
Location: 2 km n on Gaetz Ave. 2079 50th Ave T4R 1Z4. **Hours:** 11 am-midnight. Closed: 12/25.
Reservations: suggested. **Features:** Ask any local for a great place to eat, and this place is mentioned
Continental often. The large, loft-like dining room creates a casual atmosphere, and most tables feature a large
umbrella. Many entrees amid the menu's eclectic array exhibit Asian influences. Among selections are
lettuce wraps, sumptuous salmon, pasta and assorted sandwiches. Cocktails. **Parking:** on-site. Cards: AX, DC, MC, VI.

SHAUNEY'S

▽▽▽ ▽▽▽

American

Lunch: $6-$9   **Dinner:** $10-$20   **Phone:** 403/342-2404
Location: Just w of 51st Ave; centre; opposite Millenium Building. 4909 48th St T4N 1S8. **Hours:** 11 am-10 pm. Closed major holidays; also Sun. **Reservations:** accepted. **Features:** The locally popular Shauney's has a bright and cheerful decor with a casual atmosphere. Its menu emphasizes beef and seafood dishes prepared with a Continental flair. An extensive sandwich selection is offered at lunch time. Parking is free and opposite restaurant after 5 pm. Casual dress; cocktails. **Parking:** street. **Cards:** AX, MC, VI.   ⊡ ⊠

ROCKY MOUNTAIN HOUSE pop. 6,208

——— WHERE TO STAY ———

CHINOOK INN

(CAA) (SAVE)

▽▽▽

Motel

All Year [ECP]   1P: $75-$85   2P: $80-$90   XP: $8   **Phone:** 403/845-2833
Location: 1.3 km w on Hwy 11, then s. 5321 59th Ave T4T 1J4. Fax: 403/845-6845. **Facility:** 19 one-bedroom standard units, some with whirlpools. 1 story, interior corridors. **Parking:** on-site, winter plug-ins. **Terms:** pets ($10 extra charge). **Amenities:** high-speed Internet (fee), voice mail, hair dryers. **Leisure Activities:** barbecue area, bicycles. **Guest Services:** valet laundry. **Business Services:** PC (fee). **Cards:** MC, VI. **Special Amenities:** free expanded continental breakfast and free local telephone calls.

SOME UNITS

🅂🅳 🐾 📶 [DATA PORT] 🛗 / ⊠ 🔌 📟 /
FEE

HOLIDAY INN EXPRESS ROCKY MOUNTAIN HOUSE   *Book at aaa.com*

(CAA) (SAVE)

▽▽▽ ▽▽▽

Small-scale Hotel

(See color ad card insert)

All Year   1P: $99-$109   2P: $99-$109   XP: $10   F   **Phone:** (403)845-2871
Location: Just nw of jct 47th Ave and 45th St. 4715 45th St T4T 1B1 (Box 1447). Fax: 403/845-5533. **Facility:** 40 units. 39 one-bedroom standard units. 1 one-bedroom suite with kitchen. 2 stories (no elevator), interior corridors. **Parking:** on-site, winter plug-ins. **Terms:** pets ($10 fee). **Amenities:** high-speed Internet, dual phone lines, voice mail, irons, hair dryers. **Guest Services:** valet laundry. **Business Services:** PC (fee). **Cards:** AX, MC, VI. **Special Amenities:** free continental breakfast and free local telephone calls.

SOME UNITS

🐾 🍴 📶 [DATA PORT] 🛗 📺 📟 / ⊠ /
FEE

SUPER 8 MOTEL

▽▽▽ ▽▽▽

Small-scale Hotel

5/16-9/30   1P: $109-$159   2P: $109-$159   **Phone:** (403)846-0088
3/1-5/15 & 10/1-2/28   1P: $99-$159   2P: $99-$159
Location: Just off Hwy 11 at east end of town. 4406 41st Ave T4T 1J6. Fax: 403/846-0089. **Facility:** 59 units. 54 one-bedroom standard units, some with whirlpools. 5 one-bedroom suites. 3 stories, interior corridors. *Bath:* combo or shower only. **Parking:** on-site, winter plug-ins. **Terms:** pets ($10 fee). **Amenities:** voice mail, irons, hair dryers. *Some:* video games. **Pool(s):** small heated indoor. **Leisure Activities:** whirlpool, waterslide, exercise room. **Guest Services:** coin laundry. **Business Services:** meeting rooms. **Cards:** AX, DC, DS, MC, VI.

SOME UNITS

(ASK) 🅂🅳 🐾 🍴 ⇆ ⊠ 📶 [DATA PORT] 🛗 📺 📟 / ⊠ (VCR) /
FEE

——— WHERE TO DINE ———

MERLIN'S FAMILY RESTAURANT & LOUNGE

▽▽▽ ▽▽▽

Continental

Lunch: $7-$10   **Dinner:** $9-$35   **Phone:** 403/845-7711
Location: Hwy 11, just s at 52nd Ave; corner of 52nd Ave and 50th St (Main St). 5203 50th St T4T 1G7. **Hours:** 11 am-10 pm. Closed major holidays; also Sun. **Features:** The relaxed, upstairs restaurant's menu lists something for everyone in the family. Patrons can choose from hamburgers, steak, salmon or pasta dishes, each served in hearty portions. Cocktails. **Parking:** on-site. **Cards:** AX, DC, MC, VI.   ⊡ ⊠

ST. ALBERT —*See Edmonton p. 424.*

SASKATCHEWAN RIVER CROSSING

——— WHERE TO STAY ———

COLUMBIA ICEFIELD CHALET AT COLUMBIA ICEFIELD

▽▽▽ ▽▽▽

Small-scale Hotel

6/16-9/15   1P: $185-$205   XP: $10   F16   **Phone:** 780/852-6550
5/1-6/15 & 9/16-10/1   1P: $110-$130   XP: $10   F16
Location: 50 km n on Hwy 93 (Icefield Pkwy). Hwy 93 N T1L 1J3 (PO Box 1140, BANFF). Fax: 877/766-7433. **Facility:** Smoke free premises. 32 units. 10 one- and 22 two-bedroom standard units. 3 stories, interior corridors. **Parking:** on-site. **Terms:** open 5/1-10/1, check-in 4 pm, cancellation fee imposed. **Amenities:** hair dryers. **Leisure Activities:** hiking trails. **Guest Services:** gift shop. **Cards:** AX, MC, VI.

🍴 ⊠ 🅺 (CPV) 📟

SHERWOOD PARK —*See Edmonton p. 424.*

SPRUCE GROVE —*See Edmonton p. 425.*

STONY PLAIN —*See Edmonton p. 425.*

STRATHMORE —*See Calgary p. 393.*

SYLVAN LAKE pop. 7,493

———— **WHERE TO DINE** ————

SYLVAN LAKE GOLF & COUNTRY CLUB   **Lunch:** $7-$10   **Dinner:** $12-$24   **Phone:** 403/887-6695
Canadian
Location: On Hwy 11A (Lakeshore Dr). 5331 Lakeshore Dr T4S 1E8. **Hours:** 8 am-10 pm; hours may vary seasonally. **Closed:** 1/1, 12/25. **Reservations:** required. **Features:** Next to the golf course are three venues: a spot for pub fare, a casual area and a more formal dining room that's open in the evening. Simple, yet hearty, dishes range from meal-sized salads to pastas. Service is friendly. Casual dress; cocktails. **Parking:** on-site. **Cards:** AX, MC, VI.

TABER pop. 7,671

———— **WHERE TO STAY** ————

HERITAGE INN   **Phone:** (403)223-4424
Small-scale Hotel
All Year	1P: $68-$76	2P: $76-$84	XP: $5 F16

Location: 1 km e of jct Hwy 3 and 36 S, on Hwy 3. 4830 46th Ave T1G 2A4. Fax: 403/223-1733. **Facility:** 74 units. 72 one-bedroom standard units. 2 one-bedroom suites, some with whirlpools. 2 stories (no elevator), interior corridors. **Parking:** on-site, winter plug-ins. **Terms:** package plans, pets ($5 extra charge, 1st floor smoking units). **Amenities:** high-speed Internet. *Some:* CD players. **Leisure Activities:** sauna, whirlpool. *Fee:* game room. **Guest Services:** valet laundry. **Business Services:** conference facilities. **Cards:** AX, MC, VI.

SOME UNITS

SUPER 8 MOTEL, TABER   *Book at aaa.com*   **Phone:** 403/223-8181
Small-scale Hotel
All Year	1P: $67-$79	2P: $73-$85	XP: $6 F17

Location: Hwy 3, west end of town. 5700 46th Ave T1G 2B1. Fax: 403/223-1811. **Facility:** 48 one-bedroom standard units. 2 stories (no elevator), interior/exterior corridors. **Parking:** on-site, winter plug-ins. **Terms:** [CP] meal plan available. **Guest Services:** coin laundry. **Cards:** AX, DC, MC, VI.

SOME UNITS

TROCHU pop. 1,033

———— **WHERE TO STAY** ————

ST. ANN RANCH COUNTRY INN   **Phone:** 403/442-3924
Historic Bed & Breakfast
All Year	1P: $50-$70	2P: $75-$95	XP: $35 D8

Location: Hwy 2, 55 km e on Hwy 27, 3 km n on Hwy 21, 1 km e on PR 585, then 0.5 km s on King George Ave. Located in a quiet secluded area. (PO Box 670). Fax: 403/442-4264. **Facility:** This vintage farmhouse is operated by descendants of the original owners. Smoke free premises. 9 units. 8 one-bedroom standard units. 1 cabin. 4 stories (no elevator), interior corridors. *Bath:* shared or private, combo, shower or tub only. **Parking:** on-site, winter plug-ins. **Terms:** check-in 4 pm, age restrictions may apply, cancellation fee imposed. **Leisure Activities:** whirlpool, cross country skiing, hiking trails. **Guest Services:** complimentary laundry. **Business Services:** meeting rooms. **Cards:** MC, VI.

SOME UNITS

WAINWRIGHT pop. 5,117

———— **WHERE TO DINE** ————

THE HONEY POT EATERY & PUB   **Lunch:** $5-$9   **Dinner:** $6-$18   **Phone:** 780/842-4094
American
Location: 1 km s on Main St from jct Hwy 14, just w at clock tower. 823 2nd Ave T9W 1C5. **Hours:** 11 am-9:30 pm, Wed-Sat to 10 pm, Sun-2 pm. **Closed** major holidays. **Reservations:** suggested. **Features:** Diners receive a good meal and excellent value at the tucked-away restaurant. Its friendly, casual ambience enhances the country charm of its Western-style barnwood exterior. The extensive menu lists homemade bread, pies, soup and sandwiches. Casual dress; cocktails. **Parking:** street. **Cards:** AX, DC, MC, VI.

WATERTON PARK pop. 155

———— **WHERE TO STAY** ————

ASPEN VILLAGE INN   **Phone:** 403/859-2255
Motel
5/15-9/15	1P: $153-$195	2P: $153-$195	XP: $20 F16
5/1-5/14 & 9/16-10/10	1P: $103-$129	2P: $103-$129	XP: $20 F16

Location: Centre. 111 Windflower Ave T0K 2M0 (PO Box 100). Fax: 403/859-2033. **Facility:** 51 units. 38 one- and 1 two-bedroom standard units, some with kitchens. 11 one- and 1 two-bedroom suites ($218-$270), some with kitchens. 1-2 stories (no elevator), exterior corridors. **Parking:** on-site. **Terms:** open 5/1-10/10, office hours 7 am-11 pm, [BP], [CP] & [ECP] meal plans available, package plans. **Amenities:** hair dryers. **Leisure Activities:** whirlpool, recreation programs, barbecues, playground. **Guest Services:** gift shop. **Cards:** AX, DC, DS, MC, VI.

SOME UNITS

BAYSHORE INN   *Book at aaa.com*   Phone: 403/859-2211

(CAA) (SAVE)   6/17-9/16   1P: $139-$225   2P: $139-$225   XP: $10   F12

◆◆ ◆◆   4/15-6/16 & 9/17-10/15   1P: $95-$175   2P: $95-$175   XP: $10   F12

Motel   **Location:** Centre. 111 Waterton Ave T0K 2M0 (PO Box 38). Fax: 403/859-2291. **Facility:** 70 units. 64 one- and 4 two-bedroom standard units, some with whirlpools. 2 one-bedroom suites. 2 stories (no elevator), exterior corridors. *Bath:* combo or shower only. **Parking:** on-site. **Terms:** open 4/15-10/15, 3 day cancellation notice-fee imposed, package plans, pets ($20 fee, in designated units). **Amenities:** hair dryers. **Dining:** 2 restaurants, 7 am-11 pm, cocktails, nightclub. **Leisure Activities:** live theatre, hiking trails. *Fee:* massage. **Guest Services:** gift shop, coin laundry. **Business Services:** meeting rooms, PC (fee). **Cards:** AX, MC, VI. *(See color ad below)*

SOME UNITS

CRANDELL MOUNTAIN LODGE   Phone: 403/859-2288

(CAA) (SAVE)   6/1-9/15   1P: $139-$219   2P: $139-$219   XP: $10

◆◆ ◆◆   3/1-5/31 & 9/16-2/28   1P: $99-$169   2P: $99-$169   XP: $10

Small-scale Hotel   **Location:** Centre. 102 Mt. View Rd T0K 2M0 (PO Box 114). Fax: 403/859-2288. **Facility:** Designated smoking area. 17 units. 13 one-bedroom standard units, some with efficiencies. 4 one-bedroom suites ($169-$219) with kitchens, some with whirlpools. 2 stories (no elevator), interior corridors. *Bath:* combo or shower only. **Parking:** on-site. **Terms:** office hours 8 am-10 pm, 7 day cancellation notice. **Amenities:** hair dryers. **Leisure Activities:** hiking trails. **Cards:** DS, MC, VI.

SOME UNITS

KILMOREY LODGE   Phone: 403/859-2334

(CAA) (SAVE)   5/15-10/15   1P: $130-$209   2P: $130-$209   XP: $20   F16

◆◆◆ ◆◆   3/1-5/14 & 10/16-2/28   1P: $99-$153   2P: $99-$153   XP: $20   F16

Historic Country Inn   **Location:** Centre. 117 Evergreen Ave T0K 2M0 (PO Box 100). Fax: 403/859-2342. **Facility:** As one of the original buildings in town, this quaint, historic country inn has cozy rooms that contribute to its retreat-like ambience. 23 units. 20 one- and 2 two-bedroom standard units, some with whirlpools. 1 one-bedroom suite ($242-$252). 3 stories (no elevator), interior corridors. *Bath:* combo or shower only. **Parking:** on-site, winter plug-ins. **Terms:** office hours 7 am-11 pm, [BP], [CP], [ECP] & [MAP] meal plans available, package plans. **Amenities:** hair dryers. **Dining:** The Lamp Post Dining Room, see separate listing. **Leisure Activities:** Nordic ski trails, hiking trails. *Fee:* snowshoes, Canadian wilderness tours. **Guest Services:** TV in common area, gift shop. **Business Services:** PC (fee). **Cards:** AX, DC, DS, MC, VI.

SOME UNITS

SHINTANGLE SPRING BED & BREAKFAST INN

Phone: 403/627-5751

6/1-9/30 [BP]	1P: $90	2P: $120	XP: $25
3/1-5/31 & 10/1-2/28 [BP]	1P: $65	2P: $85	XP: $15

Bed & Breakfast

Location: 7.4 km n of park entrance, then just w at Nixon Rd. (PO Box 71). **Fax:** 403/627-5758. **Facility:** Smoke free premises. 4 one-bedroom standard units. 1 story, interior corridors. **Parking:** on-site, winter plug-ins. **Terms:** check-in 3:30 pm, 2 night minimum stay - seasonal. **Guest Services:** TV in common area. **Cards:** MC, VI.

WATERTON GLACIER SUITES

Book at aaa.com

Phone: 403/859-2004

6/17-9/16	1P: $169-$259	2P: $169-$259	XP: $10	F12
3/1-6/16 & 9/17-2/28	1P: $125-$175	2P: $125-$175	XP: $10	F12

(CAA) (SAVE)

Small-scale Hotel

(See color ad p 450)

Location: Centre. 107 Windflower Ave T0K 2M0. **Fax:** 403/859-2118. **Facility:** Designated smoking area. 26 one-bedroom suites with whirlpools. 2 stories (no elevator), exterior corridors. **Parking:** on-site. **Terms:** office hours 7 am-midnight, 3 day cancellation notice-fee imposed, package plans. **Amenities:** voice mail, irons, hair dryers. **Guest Services:** sundries. **Business Services:** PC (fee). **Cards:** AX, MC, VI.

SOME UNITS

WATERTON LAKES LODGE

Book at aaa.com

Phone: (403)859-2150

6/16-9/15	1P: $225	2P: $245	XP: $20	F15
4/27-6/15 & 9/16-10/11	1P: $105	2P: $125	XP: $20	F15
10/12-10/31	1P: $99	2P: $99	XP: $20	F15

(CAA) (SAVE)

Large-scale Hotel

Location: Centre. 101 Clematis Ave T0K 2M0 (PO Box 4). **Fax:** 403/859-2229. **Facility:** Smoke free premises. 80 units. 75 one-bedroom standard units, some with efficiencies and/or whirlpools. 5 one-bedroom suites ($175-$290) with efficiencies. 2 stories (no elevator), interior/exterior corridors. *Bath:* combo or shower only. **Parking:** on-site, winter plug-ins. **Terms:** open 4/27-10/31, check-in 4 pm, 3 day cancellation notice-fee imposed, package plans, small pets only ($20 fee, in designated units). **Amenities:** video library (fee), voice mail, hair dryers. *Some:* CD players. **Dining:** Bighorn Grill, see separate listing. **Pool(s):** heated indoor. **Leisure Activities:** sauna, whirlpool, steamroom, recreation programs, hiking trails. *Fee:* massage, aerobic facilities. **Guest Services:** gift shop, coin laundry. **Business Services:** meeting rooms, PC (fee). **Cards:** AX, MC, VI. *(See color ad below)*

SOME UNITS

─────── *The following lodging was either not evaluated or did not* ───────
meet AAA rating requirements but is listed for your information only.

PRINCE OF WALES HOTEL   Phone: 403/859-2231
fyi   Not evaluated. **Location:** Through park gates, about 8 km, then just se. (PO Box 33). Facilities, services, and decor
                 characterize a mid-range property.

─────── **WHERE TO DINE** ───────

BIGHORN GRILL   **Lunch:** $9-$13   **Dinner:** $13-$23   Phone: 403/859-2150
◆◆ ◆◆   **Location:** Centre; in Waterton Lakes Lodge. 101 Clematis Ave T0K 2M0. **Hours:** Open 4/27-10/31; 7 am-10 pm.
             Features: This casual eatery is a great place for families. There is something for everyone, ranging from
Canadian   pastas to pizzas, steaks and seafood. Or, for something a little more regional, you could also sample bison
             or venison. Casual dress; cocktails. **Parking:** on-site. **Cards:** AX, MC, VI.
                                                                                          🍸 ⊠

THE LAMP POST DINING ROOM   **Lunch:** $8-$13   **Dinner:** $14-$28   Phone: 403/859-2334
◆◆ ◆◆   **Location:** Centre; in Kilmorey Lodge. 117 Evergreen Ave T0K 2M0. **Hours:** 7:30 am-10 pm. Closed: 12/25.
             Reservations: required, for dinner. **Features:** This charming country-inn-style restaurant features an
Canadian   exciting, appealing lunch menu and more extensive dinner selections. Specialties include Alberta beef, wild
             game and fresh British Columbia salmon. Casual dress; cocktails. **Parking:** on-site. **Cards:** AX, DC, DS,
MC, VI. **Country Inn**
                                                                                          🍸 ⊠

WESTEROSE

─────── **WHERE TO STAY** ───────

─────── *The following lodging was either not evaluated or did not* ───────
meet AAA rating requirements but is listed for your information only.

VILLAGE CREEK COUNTRY INN   Phone: 780/586-0006
fyi   Not evaluated. **Location:** Hwy 13, just n on Norris Beach Rd, 28 km w of Hwy 2. 9 Village Dr T0C 2V0 (General
                 Delivery). Facilities, services, and decor characterize a mid-range property.

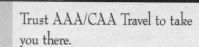

WETASKIWIN pop. 11,154

———— WHERE TO STAY ————

BEST WESTERN WAYSIDE INN   *Book at aaa.com*   **Phone:** (780)352-6681
◆◆◆ ◆◆◆   All Year   1P: $89-$99   2P: $89-$99
Small-scale Hotel   **Location:** Just n of Hwy 13 W, on Hwy 2A. 4103 56 St T9A 1V2. Fax: 780/352-2331. **Facility:** 28 one-bedroom standard units. 2 stories (no elevator), interior corridors. **Parking:** on-site, winter plug-ins. **Terms:** check-in 4 pm, cancellation fee imposed, pets ($100 deposit). **Amenities:** high-speed Internet, irons, hair dryers.
Leisure Activities: exercise room. **Business Services:** meeting rooms. **Cards:** AX, DC, DS, MC, VI.

SOME UNITS
[ASK] [S/D] [🛏] [🍴] [📺] [DATA PORT] [💻] / [✕] /
FEE

SUPER 8 MOTEL   *Book at aaa.com*   **Phone:** (780)361-3808
◆◆◆ ◆◆◆   All Year   1P: $89-$99   2P: $89-$99   XP: $5   F12
Small-scale Hotel   **Location:** On Hwy 2A, just s of jct Hwy 13 W. 3820 56th St T9A 2B2. Fax: 780/361-0388. **Facility:** 49 one-bedroom standard units. 2 stories (no elevator), interior/exterior corridors. **Parking:** on-site, winter plug-ins. **Terms:** check-in 4 pm, weekly rates available, pets ($50 deposit, with prior approval). **Guest Services:** coin laundry. **Business Services:** meeting rooms. **Cards:** AX, DC, MC, VI.

SOME UNITS
[ASK] [S/D] [🛏] [🍴] [🔊M] [DATA PORT] / [✕] [🛢] [🖥] /
FEE

———— WHERE TO DINE ————

HUCKLEBERRY'S CAFE   **Lunch:** $7-$16   **Dinner:** $7-$23   **Phone:** 780/352-3111
◆◆ ◆◆   **Location:** Just e of Hwy 2A, s of jct Hwy 13 W. 103-3840 St T9A 2B2. **Hours:** 9:30 am-10 pm, Sun-9 pm. Closed:
Continental   12/25, 12/26. **Reservations:** suggested. **Features:** For a taste of the Wild West, the bustling restaurant fits the bill. Friendly servers are dressed in typical Western wear, and the decor follows suit. On the menu is a wide variety of burgers, pasta dishes and sandwiches that emphasize local ingredients, such as Alberta turkey and beef, as well as the famous huckleberry, a berry from the mountains. Not surprisingly, the berry, which is plumper and juicier than the blueberry, found its way into the cafe's name and desserts. Cocktails. **Parking:** on-site. **Cards:** AX, MC, VI.   [✕]

THE MACEACHERN TEA HOUSE   **Lunch:** $7-$9   **Phone:** 780/352-8308
◆◆ ◆◆   **Location:** 50th Ave at 47th St. 4719 50th Ave T9A 0R9. **Hours:** 9:30 am-3:30 pm, Sat 10 am-3 pm. Closed major
Continental   holidays; also Sun, Sat 9/1-5/31. **Reservations:** suggested, for lunch. **Features:** In a charming turn-of-the-20th-century home, the delightful near-downtown restaurant presents a menu of homemade soups, salads, delicious orange rolls, cinnamon buns, muffins, bagels, sandwiches and desserts, as well as scones for afternoon tea. Servers are friendly. Casual dress; cocktails. **Parking:** on-site. **Cards:** MC, VI.   [✕]

WHITECOURT pop. 8,334

———— WHERE TO STAY ————

QUALITY INN   *Book at aaa.com*   **Phone:** (780)778-5477
[CAA] [SAVE]   All Year   1P: $59-$75   2P: $62-$78   XP: $6   F18
◆◆ ◆◆   **Location:** On Hwy 43, 0.5 km e of Hwy 32. 5420 49th Ave T7S 1P3 (PO Box 1438). Fax: 780/778-4219. **Facility:** 74 units. 70 one-bedroom standard units. 4 one-bedroom suites. 2 stories (no elevator), interior corridors.
Parking: on-site, winter plug-ins. **Terms:** weekly rates available, package plans, pets (in smoking units).
Small-scale Hotel   **Amenities:** *Some:* hair dryers. **Dining:** 6 am-11 pm, cocktails. **Leisure Activities:** sauna, whirlpool, exercise room. **Guest Services:** coin laundry. **Business Services:** meeting rooms. **Cards:** AX, DC, MC, VI.

SOME UNITS
[S/D] [✈] [🛏] [🍴] [Y] [✕] [DATA PORT] [💻] / [✕] [🛢] /

———— The following lodging was either not evaluated or did not ————
meet AAA rating requirements but is listed for your information only.

SUPER 8 MOTEL   **Phone:** 780/778-8908
[fyi]   Not evaluated. **Location:** 4121 Kepler St T7S 1P6. Facilities, services, and decor characterize a mid-range property.

British Columbia

Purcell Mountains,
north of Kimberley
© George Hunter
SuperStock

100 MILE HOUSE

─── WHERE TO STAY ───

100 MILE HOUSE SUPER 8 *Book at aaa.com*
◆◆◆ ◆◆◆

4/1-9/30	1P: $79	2P: $88	XP: $7 F12
3/1-3/31 & 10/1-2/28	1P: $72	2P: $79	XP: $7 F12

Motel **Location:** 1 km s on Hwy 97. 989 Alder Ave V0K 2E0 (Box 759). Fax: 250/395-8880. **Facility:** 28 one-bedroom standard units. 2 stories (no elevator), exterior corridors. **Parking:** on-site, winter plug-ins. **Terms:** office hours 7 am-11 pm, small pets only ($10 extra charge, in smoking units). **Amenities:** hair dryers. **Cards:** AX, MC, VI.

Phone: (250)395-8888

SOME UNITS
(ASK) (SD) 🛏 🎥 🖥 🖳 / ⊠ 🔌 🖼 /
FEE

RAMADA LIMITED *Book at aaa.com*
◆◆◆ ◆◆◆

5/16-9/30	1P: $92	2P: $98	XP: $5 F17
3/15/15 & 10/1-2/28	1P: $84	2P: $89	XP: $5 F17

Motel **Location:** 1 km s on Hwy 97. 917 Alder Rd V0K 2E0 (Box 2020). Fax: 250/395-2037. **Facility:** 36 one-bedroom standard units, some with efficiencies and/or whirlpools. 3 stories, interior corridors. *Bath:* combo or shower only. **Parking:** on-site. **Terms:** office hours 6 am-11 pm, cancellation fee imposed, [CP] meal plan available, small pets only ($5 extra charge). **Amenities:** voice mail, irons, hair dryers. *Some:* high-speed Internet. **Leisure Activities:** sauna, whirlpool. **Guest Services:** coin laundry. **Cards:** AX, DC, MC, VI.

Phone: 250/395-2777

SOME UNITS
(ASK) (SD) 🛏 🎥 🔌 🖳 / ⊠ 🔌 🖼 /
FEE

RED COACH INN
◆◆◆

5/1-10/31	1P: $65-$91	2P: $65-$97	XP: $6 F16
3/1-4/30 & 11/1-2/28	1P: $65-$79	2P: $65-$85	XP: $6 F16

Small-scale Hotel **Location:** On Hwy 97, on the north end of town. 170 Cariboo Hwy N V0K 2E0 (PO Box 760). Fax: 250/395-2446. **Facility:** 49 one-bedroom standard units. 2 stories (no elevator), interior/exterior corridors. *Bath:* combo or shower only. **Parking:** on-site, winter plug-ins. **Terms:** pets ($6 extra charge). **Pool(s):** heated indoor. **Leisure Activities:** whirlpool, limited exercise equipment. **Guest Services:** gift shop, valet laundry. **Business Services:** meeting rooms, business center. **Cards:** AX, DC, JC, MC, VI.

Phone: (250)395-2266

SOME UNITS
(ASK) (SD) 🛏 🍴 🍷 🏋 🚣 📷 🔌 🖳 / ⊠ 🔌 /
FEE

─── WHERE TO DINE ───

HAPPY LANDING RESTAURANT   **Lunch:** $6-$13   **Dinner:** $10-$34   **Phone:** 250/395-5359
◆◆◆ ◆◆◆

Swiss **Location:** Hwy 97, 1 km s (Service Rd). 725 Alder Ave V0K 2E0. **Hours:** 5 pm-9 pm, Tues, Wed & Fri also 11:30 am-2 pm. Closed major holidays; also Sun. **Reservations:** suggested. **Features:** Behind the village restaurant's charming blue shutters, diners are welcomed to savor the flavors of traditional Swiss cuisine. Among choices are steak tartare, veal sausages with onions, schnitzels, roestis and other Continental favorites. Casual dress; cocktails. **Parking:** on-site. **Cards:** MC, VI.

⊠

108 MILE HOUSE

─── WHERE TO STAY ───

108 RESORT & CONFERENCE CENTRE *Book at aaa.com*
(CAA) (SAVE)
◆◆◆ ◆◆◆ ◆◆◆

6/2-9/30		2P: $100-$120	XP: $10 F5
4/1-6/1 & 10/1-10/15		2P: $80-$100	XP: $10 F5

Resort **Location:** From Hwy 97, 1.6 km nw on access road, follow signs. Located on the 108 Recreational Ranch. 4816 Telqua
Small-scale Hotel Dr V0K 2Z0 (PO Box 2, 108 MILE RANCH). Fax: 250/791-6537. **Facility:** Many activities are offered at this 600-acre resort, which features spacious guest rooms overlooking a golf course and lake. 62 units. 61 one-bedroom standard units. 1 one-bedroom suite. 2 stories (no elevator), exterior corridors. **Parking:** on-site, winter plug-ins. **Terms:** open 4/1-10/15, cancellation fee imposed, package plans, small pets only ($10 extra charge, in designated units). **Amenities:** *Some:* irons, hair dryers. **Dining:** 7 am-10 pm; hours may vary seasonally, cocktails. **Leisure Activities:** saunas, whirlpool, rental canoes, fishing, 4 tennis courts (2 lighted), 5000 ft airstrip with hangar, hiking trails, jogging, playground. *Fee:* golf-18 holes, bicycles, horseback riding. **Guest Services:** coin laundry, airport transportation (fee)-108 Airport. **Business Services:** conference facilities. **Cards:** AX, DC, MC, VI. **Special Amenities:** free local telephone calls and free room upgrade (subject to availability with advance reservations).

Phone: (250)791-5211

SOME UNITS
(SD) ⊞ 🛏 🍴 🍷 🏋 ➕ ⊠ 📷 🖳 / ⊠ 🔌 /
FEE FEE

ABBOTSFORD pop. 115,463

─── WHERE TO STAY ───

BEST WESTERN BAKERVIEW INN *Book at aaa.com*
(CAA) (SAVE)
◆◆◆ ◆◆◆

All Year	1P: $69-$89	2P: $89-$99	XP: $6 F12

Motel **Location:** Trans-Canada Hwy 1, exit 92 (Town Centre), just n on Hwy 11. 1821 Sumas Way V2S 4L5. Fax: 604/854-1385. **Facility:** 61 one-bedroom standard units, some with efficiencies. 2 stories (no elevator), exterior corridors. **Parking:** on-site. **Terms:** 3 day cancellation notice. **Amenities:** irons, hair dryers. **Dining:** 6:30 am-10 pm, wine/beer only. **Pool(s):** heated indoor. **Leisure Activities:** whirlpool. **Guest Services:** valet laundry. **Cards:** AX, DC, MC, VI. **Special Amenities:** free local telephone calls and free room upgrade (subject to availability with advance reservations).

Phone: 604/859-1341

SOME UNITS
🍴 🏊 🔌 🖳 / ⊠ 🔌 /

BEST WESTERN REGENCY INN & CONFERENCE CENTRE _Book at aaa.com_ Phone: (604)853-3111

CAA SAVE

7/1-9/7 [ECP]	1P: $109-$139	2P: $109-$139	XP: $10	F12
3/1-6/30 [ECP]	1P: $89-$119	2P: $89-$119	XP: $10	F12
9/8-2/28 [ECP]	1P: $79-$119	2P: $79-$119	XP: $10	F12

Location: Trans-Canada Hwy 1, exit 87 (Clearbrook Rd). Located behind an elementary school. 32110 Marshall Rd V2T 1A1. Fax: 604/852-1750. **Facility:** 128 one-bedroom standard units, some with efficiencies, kitchens and/or whirlpools. 2-3 stories, interior corridors. **Parking:** on-site. **Terms:** package plans. **Amenities:** video games (fee), voice mail, irons, hair dryers. **Dining:** 6 am-11 pm, wine/beer only. **Pool(s):** small heated indoor. **Leisure Activities:** whirlpools, limited exercise equipment. **Guest Services:** valet and coin laundry. **Business Services:** conference facilities, business center. **Cards:** AX, DC, DS, MC, VI. **Special Amenities: free expanded continental breakfast and free room upgrade (subject to availability with advance reservations).**
Small-scale Hotel

SOME UNITS

COAST ABBOTSFORD HOTEL & SUITES _Book at aaa.com_ Phone: (604)853-1880

5/1-9/15	1P: $94-$104	2P: $104-$114	XP: $10	F
3/1-4/30 & 9/16-2/28	1P: $84-$94	2P: $94-$104	XP: $10	F

Location: Trans-Canada Hwy 1 (Town Centre), just n on Hwy 11. 2020 Sumas Way V2S 2C7. Fax: 604/853-1951. **Facility:** 60 one-bedroom standard units, some with whirlpools. 4 stories, interior corridors. **Parking:** on-site. **Terms:** 14 day cancellation notice, pets ($10 extra charge). **Amenities:** high-speed Internet, voice mail, irons, hair dryers. **Pool(s):** heated indoor. **Leisure Activities:** whirlpool, limited exercise equipment. **Guest Services:** valet laundry. **Business Services:** meeting rooms. **Cards:** AX, DC, DS, JC, MC, VI.
Small-scale Hotel

SOME UNITS

COMFORT INN ABBOTSFORD _Book at aaa.com_ Phone: 604/859-6211

CAA SAVE

6/1-9/1	1P: $99-$109	2P: $109-$129	XP: $10	F18
3/1-5/31 & 9/2-2/28	1P: $89-$99	2P: $99-$109	XP: $10	F18

Location: Trans-Canada Hwy 1, exit 87 (Clearbrook Rd). 2073 Clearbrook Rd V2T 2X1. Fax: 604/859-6200. **Facility:** 41 one-bedroom standard units, some with efficiencies and/or whirlpools. 2 stories (no elevator), interior/exterior corridors. **Parking:** on-site. **Terms:** small pets only ($10 extra charge). **Amenities:** voice mail, irons, hair dryers. **Dining:** 6 am-9 pm, wine/beer only. **Pool(s):** heated indoor. **Leisure Activities:** sauna, whirlpool, limited exercise equipment. **Guest Services:** valet and coin laundry. **Business Services:** meeting rooms. **Cards:** AX, DC, DS, JC, MC, VI. **Special Amenities: free continental breakfast and free local telephone calls.**
Small-scale Hotel

SOME UNITS

THE INN AT KING'S CROSSING Phone: (604)859-2220

5/1-8/31 [CP]	1P: $80-$190	2P: $85-$190	XP: $7	F12
3/1-4/30 & 9/1-2/28 [CP]	1P: $75-$185	2P: $80-$190	XP: $7	F12

Location: Trans-Canada Hwy 1, exit 90, just s, then e on King Rd. 1515 College Dr V2S 8J1. Fax: 604/859-2292. **Facility:** 18 one-bedroom standard units, some with whirlpools. 2 stories, interior corridors. **Parking:** on-site. **Business Services:** conference facilities. **Cards:** AX, MC, VI.
Small-scale Hotel

SOME UNITS

RAMADA INN & CONFERENCE CENTRE-ABBOTSFORD _Book at aaa.com_ Phone: (604)870-1050

5/1-9/30	1P: $99-$109	2P: $99-$109	XP: $10	F17
3/1-4/30 & 10/1-2/28	1P: $89-$99	2P: $89-$99	XP: $10	F17

Location: Trans-Canada Hwy 1, exit 95 (Whatcom Rd). 36035 N Parallel Rd V3G 2C6. Fax: 604/870-1060. **Facility:** 116 one-bedroom standard units, some with whirlpools. 4 stories, interior corridors. **Parking:** on-site. **Terms:** package plans, pets ($10 extra charge). **Amenities:** voice mail, irons, hair dryers. **Pool(s):** small heated indoor. **Leisure Activities:** whirlpool, limited exercise equipment, game room. **Guest Services:** valet and coin laundry. **Business Services:** meeting rooms. **Cards:** AX, MC, VI.
Small-scale Hotel

SOME UNITS

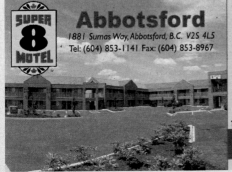

SUPER 8 MOTEL ABBOTSFORD *Book at aaa.com* Phone: (604)853-1141

CAA SAVE

Motel

5/1-9/30 [ECP]	1P: $75-$115	2P: $80-$120	XP: $10	F12
10/1-2/28 [ECP]	1P: $70-$110	2P: $75-$115	XP: $10	F12
3/1-4/30 [ECP]	1P: $65-$105	2P: $70-$110	XP: $10	F12

Location: Trans-Canada Hwy 1, exit 92 (Town Centre), just n on Hwy 11. 1881 Sumas Way V2S 4L5. **Fax:** 604/853-8967. **Facility:** 40 one-bedroom standard units, some with efficiencies. 2 stories, interior/exterior corridors. **Parking:** on-site. **Terms:** check-in 4 pm, small pets only ($10 extra charge). **Amenities:** hair dryers. **Guest Services:** valet and coin laundry. **Business Services:** meeting rooms. **Cards:** AX, DC, DS, MC, VI. **Special Amenities:** free expanded continental breakfast and free local telephone calls. *(See color ad p 457)*

SOME UNITS

AINSWORTH HOT SPRINGS

------- WHERE TO STAY -------

AINSWORTH HOT SPRINGS RESORT Phone: (250)229-4212

CAA SAVE

Small-scale Hotel

All Year   1P: $93-$176   2P: $93-$176   XP: $15   D13

Location: On Hwy 31. 3609 Hwy 31 V0G 1A0 (PO Box 1268). **Fax:** 250/229-5600. **Facility:** Smoke free premises. 43 one-bedroom standard units, some with efficiencies and/or whirlpools. 4 stories, interior/exterior corridors. **Parking:** on-site. **Terms:** package plans. **Amenities:** hair dryers. **Dining:** 7 am-9:30 pm, cocktails. **Leisure Activities:** hot springs pool, whirlpool & cave, cross country skiing, bicycles, hiking trails. *Fee:* helicopter tours, massage. **Guest Services:** gift shop, complimentary laundry. **Business Services:** meeting rooms. **Cards:** AX, MC, VI.

SOME UNITS

ALDERGROVE —See Vancouver p. 579.

BARRIERE

------- WHERE TO STAY -------

MOUNTAIN SPRINGS MOTEL & RV PARK Phone: (250)672-0090

CAA SAVE

Motel

5/1-9/30	1P: $48-$53	2P: $57-$62	XP: $5
3/1-4/30 & 10/1-2/28	1P: $45-$48	2P: $48-$53	XP: $5

Location: 1 km s on Hwy 5 (Yellowhead Hwy). 4253 Yellowhead Hwy V0E 1E0 (PO Box 1169). **Fax:** 250/672-2373. **Facility:** 12 one-bedroom standard units, some with efficiencies. 1 story, exterior corridors. **Parking:** on-site, winter plug-ins. **Terms:** office hours 7 am-midnight, cancellation fee imposed, pets ($5 extra charge, small dogs only). **Guest Services:** coin laundry. **Cards:** AX, DS, MC, VI.

SOME UNITS

BLUE RIVER

------- WHERE TO STAY -------

GLACIER MOUNTAIN LODGE Phone: (250)673-2393

Motel

All Year   1P: $79-$119   2P: $79-$129   XP: $10   F8

Location: On Hwy 5 (Yellowhead Hwy) at Shell Rd, follow signs. 869 Shell Rd V0E 1J0 (PO Box 27, V0E 1J0). **Fax:** 250/673-8225. **Facility:** Smoke free premises. 33 one-bedroom standard units. 2 stories (no elevator), interior corridors. **Parking:** on-site, winter plug-ins. **Terms:** pets ($10 extra charge). **Amenities:** hair dryers. **Leisure Activities:** whirlpool. **Cards:** AX, DC, MC, VI.

MIKE WIEGELE HELICOPTER SKIING Phone: (250)673-8381

Resort
Small-scale Hotel

3/1-10/31 & 12/1-2/28   1P: $85-$290   2P: $85-$290   XP: $30   F

Location: On Hwy 5 (Yellowhead Hwy) at Harwood Dr, follow signs. 1 Harwood Dr V0E 1J0 (Box 159). **Fax:** 250/673-8464. **Facility:** Heli-skiing, helicopter fishing and mountain biking are among the activities offered at this resort nestled in a valley near picturesque mountains. Smoke free premises. 80 units. 72 one-bedroom standard units, some with kitchens and/or whirlpools. 8 cabins ($195-$290) with whirlpools. 2 stories (no elevator), exterior corridors. **Parking:** on-site, winter plug-ins. **Terms:** open 3/1-10/31 & 12/1-2/28, office hours 8 am-4 pm, 3 day cancellation notice-fee imposed, package plans, pets ($25 extra charge). **Amenities:** voice mail, hair dryers. **Leisure Activities:** saunas, whirlpool, rental canoes, fishing, rental bicycles, hiking trails, jogging. **Guest Services:** gift shop, coin laundry. **Business Services:** meeting rooms, PC. **Cards:** AX, MC, VI.

SOME UNITS

BOSTON BAR pop. 233

------- WHERE TO DINE -------

SALMON HOUSE RESTAURANT Lunch: $8-$13   Phone: 604/867-9277

CAA

Canadian

Location: 11 km s on Trans-Canada Hwy 1; at Hell's Gate Airtram. **Hours:** Open 5/15-10/10; 10 am-4 pm; 9:30 am-5:30 pm 5/20-9/1. **Features:** You travel to this restaurant on a thrilling Hell's Gate Airtram ride over the mighty Fraser River. Regular Airtram admission applies with a $1.50 discount to CAA/AAA members. The menu features homemade salmon chowder, salmon lasagna, sandwiches and burgers. Well worth the stop. Casual dress; cocktails. **Parking:** on-site. **Cards:** MC, VI.

BOWEN ISLAND

──────── **WHERE TO STAY** ────────

WILDWOOD LANE COTTAGES
▼▼▼ ▼▼▼ 3/1-9/12   2P: $125-$175   XP: $25   F
             9/13-2/28   2P: $119-$149   XP: $25   F

Phone: (604)947-2253

Cottage   **Location:** From ferry terminal, 5.6 km w on Grafton Rd, then 1 km n. 1291 Adams Rd V0N 1G0 (PO Box 248). **Fax:** 604/947-2268. **Facility:** Smoke free premises. 5 cottages. 1 story, exterior corridors. *Bath:* shower only. **Parking:** on-site. **Terms:** office hours 8 am-10 pm, 2 night minimum stay - seasonal and/or weekends, 14 day cancellation notice-fee imposed, weekly rates available, package plans, pets ($20 extra charge). **Amenities:** video library, hair dryers. **Leisure Activities:** sauna, whirlpool. **Cards:** AX, MC, VI.

(ASK) (S/D) 🛏 ⊠ (K) (CTV) (VCR) 🖥 💻
        FEE

BRENTWOOD BAY — See Victoria p. 633.

BURNABY — See Vancouver p. 579.

CACHE CREEK pop. 1,056

──────── **WHERE TO STAY** ────────

BONAPARTE MOTEL
(CAA) (SAVE)   5/16-10/15   1P: $60-$70   2P: $75-$100   XP: $10   D10
▼▼▼ ▼▼▼   3/1-5/15 & 10/16-2/28   1P: $40-$50   2P: $50-$60   XP: $5   D10

Phone: (250)457-9693

Motel   **Location:** 1 km n of jct Trans-Canada Hwy 1. 1395 Hwy 97 N V0K 1H0 (PO Box 487). **Fax:** 250/457-9697. **Facility:** 24 one-bedroom standard units, some with efficiencies or kitchens. 1 story, exterior corridors. **Parking:** on-site, winter plug-ins. **Terms:** office hours 7 am-midnight, small pets only ($10 extra charge, in limited units). **Pool(s):** heated outdoor. **Leisure Activities:** sauna, whirlpool. **Cards:** AX, DS, MC, VI.

SOME UNITS
(S/D) 🛏 (↑↑) 🏊 (📷) 🖥 / ⊠ /
      FEE

SAGE HILLS MOTEL
(CAA) (SAVE)   5/15-10/15   1P: $60   2P: $60   XP: $10
▼▼▼   3/1-5/14 & 10/16-2/28   1P: $50   2P: $50   XP: $10

Phone: (250)457-6451

Motel   **Location:** Just n of jct Hwy 97 and Trans-Canada Hwy 1. 1390 Hwy 97 N V0K 1H0 (Box 126). **Fax:** 250/457-6451. **Facility:** 18 units. 13 one- and 5 two-bedroom standard units, some with efficiencies. 1 story, exterior corridors. *Bath:* combo or shower only. **Parking:** on-site. **Terms:** office hours 8 am-11 pm. **Pool(s):** heated outdoor. **Cards:** AX, DC, MC, VI.

SOME UNITS
(S/D) (↑↑) 🏊 (📷) / ⊠ /

──────── **WHERE TO DINE** ────────

WANDER INN RESTAURANT   *Menu on aaa.com*   **Lunch:** $5-$10   **Dinner:** $7-$16   Phone: 250/457-6511
(CAA)   **Location:** Just s of jct Hwy 97. Trans-Canada Hwy 1 V0K 1H0. **Hours:** 11 am-10 pm. **Closed:** 12/25, 12/26.
▼▼▼   **Features:** The cuisine features Cantonese dishes such as the emperor's plate with chicken, beef and stir-fry, as well as burgers, sandwiches, soup, steak and chops. Seniors and visitors like this place, which has a coffee shop and dining room section. Casual dress; cocktails. **Parking:** on-site. **Cards:** AX, MC, VI.

Chinese   🍽 ⊠

CAMPBELL RIVER pop. 28,456

──────── **WHERE TO STAY** ────────

ARBOUR'S GUEST HOUSE
▼▼▼   All Year   1P: $75-$85   2P: $85-$99   XP: $10

Phone: (250)287-9873

  Location: 2 km s on Island Hwy 19A, just e on 1st Ave, then 0.8 km s on Murphy St, on water side of street. Located in a residential area. 375 S Murphy St V9W 1Y8. **Fax:** 250/287-9825. **Facility:** Smoke free premises. 4 one-
Bed & Breakfast   bedroom standard units. 2 stories (no elevator), interior corridors. *Bath:* some shared or private. **Parking:** on-site. **Terms:** office hours 8 am-10 pm, age restrictions may apply, 14 day cancellation notice-fee imposed, weekly rates available, package plans. **Amenities:** *Some:* hair dryers. **Cards:** MC, VI.

SOME UNITS
(ASK) (S/D) ⊠ (K) (📷) / (W) /

BEST WESTERN AUSTRIAN CHALET   *Book at aaa.com*
(CAA) (SAVE)   5/1-9/30   1P: $119-$169   2P: $129-$179   XP: $10   F12
▼▼▼ ▼▼▼   3/1-4/30 & 10/1-2/28   1P: $89-$109   2P: $99-$119   XP: $10   F12

Phone: (250)923-4231

Motel   **Location:** 3.2 km s on Island Hwy 19A. 462 S Island Hwy V9W 1A5. **Fax:** 250/923-2840. **Facility:** 55 one-bedroom standard units, some with efficiencies and/or whirlpools. 2 stories (no elevator), interior/exterior corridors. **Parking:** on-site. **Terms:** cancellation fee imposed, small pets only ($5 extra charge). **Amenities:** irons, hair dryers. **Pool(s):** heated indoor. **Leisure Activities:** sauna, whirlpool, fishing, fish freezing facilities, putting green, table tennis, barbecue, limited exercise equipment. **Guest Services:** valet and coin laundry. **Business Services:** meeting rooms. **Cards:** AX, CB, DC, DS, MC, VI. **Special Amenities:** free local telephone calls and free newspaper. (See color ad p 460)

SOME UNITS
(S/D) 🛏 (↑↑) 🏊 ⊠ (K) (DATA PORT) 🖥 💻 / ⊠ (VCR) 📷 /
      FEE

CAMPBELL RIVER LODGE FISHING & ADVENTURE RESORT

CAA (SAVE)
◇◇ (diamond)
Motel

Phone: (250)287-7446

3/1-9/30 [CP]	1P: $59-$79	2P: $64-$89	XP: $10 F5
10/1-2/28 [CP]	1P: $59-$69	2P: $64-$74	XP: $10 F5

Location: On Island Hwy 19A, 2 km nw of downtown; just e from Hwy 19 and 28. 1760 Island Hwy V9W 2E7. Fax: 250/287-4063. **Facility:** 28 one-bedroom standard units, some with efficiencies. 2 stories (no elevator), interior/exterior corridors. *Bath:* combo or shower only. **Parking:** on-site. **Terms:** office hours 7:30 am-11:30 pm, 3 day cancellation notice-fee imposed, package plans, small pets only ($8 extra charge). **Dining:** noon-2 & 5-9 pm 6/1-8/31, cocktails. **Leisure Activities:** whirlpool, saltwater & freshwater charter fishing with guides. *Fee:* custom fish canning, freezing & shipping. **Guest Services:** gift shop, coin laundry. **Business Services:** meeting rooms. **Cards:** AX, MC, VI. **Special Amenities:** free continental breakfast and free local telephone calls.

SOME UNITS
🆘 🛏️ 🍽️ 🍸 🎾 / ⊗ 🔌

CAMPBELL RIVER SUPER 8   *Book at aaa.com*

◇◇◇
Motel

Phone: 250/286-6622

5/20-9/30	1P: $82	2P: $90	XP: $6 F12
4/16-5/19 & 10/1-2/28	1P: $66	2P: $74	XP: $6 F12
3/1-4/15	1P: $60	2P: $68	XP: $6 F12

Location: 3 km s on Island Hwy 19A. 340 S Island Hwy V9W 1A5. Fax: 250/286-6622. **Facility:** 39 one-bedroom standard units. 2 stories (no elevator), interior corridors. **Parking:** on-site. **Terms:** [CP] meal plan available, 15% service charge, pets ($6 extra charge). **Pool(s):** heated indoor. **Leisure Activities:** whirlpool. **Cards:** AX, DC, DS, MC, VI.

SOME UNITS
(ASK) 🆘 🛏️ 🍽️ 🔥 ♿ 🏊 DATA PORT 🔌 / ⊗ 📷

ELK FALLS FISHING RESORT MOTEL

◇◇◇ ◇◇◇
Cabin

Phone: (250)286-6796

All Year	1P: $79-$129	2P: $79-$139	XP: $10 F10

Location: Jct Hwy 19 and 28, just w on Hwy 28. 2320 Campbell River Rd V9W 4N7. Fax: 250/286-6119. **Facility:** Smoke free premises. 10 cabins. 1 story, exterior corridors. *Bath:* combo or shower only. **Parking:** on-site. **Terms:** office hours 7 am-10 pm, 30 day cancellation notice-fee imposed. **Leisure Activities:** fishing. *Fee:* charter fishing. **Cards:** AX, MC, VI.

SOME UNITS
(ASK) 🆘 ⊗ 🎾 🔌 📺 / 📷

RAMADA HOTEL & SUITES   *Book at aaa.com*

CAA (SAVE)
◇◇◇ ◇◇◇ ◇◇◇
Small-scale Hotel

Phone: (250)286-1131

5/16-9/15	1P: $139-$159	2P: $139-$159	XP: $10 F17
3/1-5/15 & 9/16-2/28	1P: $109-$139	2P: $109-$139	XP: $10 F17

Location: On Island Hwy 19A, 2 km s. 261 Island Hwy V9W 2B3. Fax: 250/287-4055. **Facility:** 65 one-bedroom standard units, some with whirlpools. 7 stories, interior corridors. **Parking:** on-site. **Terms:** small pets only ($8 extra charge, 1st floor units). **Dining:** 2 restaurants, 6:30 am-11 & 4-10 pm, cocktails. **Pool(s):** heated indoor. **Leisure Activities:** whirlpool, limited exercise equipment. **Guest Services:** valet and coin laundry. **Business Services:** conference facilities, PC (fee). **Cards:** AX, DC, DS, MC, VI. **Special Amenities:** free local telephone calls.

SOME UNITS
🆘 🛏️ 🍽️ 🍸 🎾 🔥 🎾 DATA PORT 📺 / ⊗ 🔌 📷

TOWN CENTRE INN

◇◇◇ ◇◇◇
Motel

Phone: (250)287-8866

3/1-9/30 [BP]	1P: $69-$74	2P: $84-$89	XP: $10 F10
10/1-2/28 [BP]	1P: $56-$59	2P: $64-$74	XP: $10 F10

Location: Follow Island Hwy 19A through town, watch for signs, just e on Dogwood St; corner of 16th Ave. 1500 Dogwood St V9W 3A6. Fax: 250/287-3944. **Facility:** 34 one-bedroom standard units, some with efficiencies. 2 stories (no elevator), exterior corridors. **Parking:** on-site. **Terms:** office hours 7:30 am-midnight. **Amenities:** hair dryers. **Leisure Activities:** sauna. **Guest Services:** coin laundry. **Cards:** AX, MC, VI.

SOME UNITS
(ASK) 🆘 🔥 🎾 DATA PORT 🔌 📺 / ⊗ /

PAINTER'S LODGE **Phone:** 250/286-1102
[fyi] Not evaluated. **Location:** 2 km n on Hwy 19 from jct Hwy 19 and 28, just e, follow signs. Located in a quiet area. 1625 MacDonald Rd V9W 5C1 (PO Box 460). Facilities, services, and decor characterize a mid-range property.

———— **WHERE TO DINE** ————

BAAN THAI RESTAURANT **Lunch:** $9-$10 **Dinner:** $8-$15 **Phone:** 250/286-4853
▼▼▼ **Location:** At 11th Ave; downtown. 1090B Shoppers Row V9W 2C6. **Hours:** 11 am-2:30 & 5-9 pm, Fri & Sat-9:30 pm, Sun 5 pm-9 pm. Closed major holidays. **Reservations:** suggested. **Features:** The traditional flavors and aromas of Thailand's distinctive cuisine are honored at the contemporary downtown restaurant. The second-floor spot also features a small rooftop patio. Casual dress; cocktails. **Parking:** street.
Thai
Cards: MC, VI. [K] [X]

BEE HIVE SEAFOOD GRILL & CAFE **Lunch:** $8-$15 **Dinner:** $19-$21 **Phone:** 250/286-6812
▼▼ **Location:** Just s on Island Hwy 19A from downtown. 921 Island Hwy V9W 2C2. **Hours:** 11 am-10 pm. Closed: 12/25. **Features:** Near the start of the downtown shopping district, the waterfront restaurant offers views of Seafood Quadra Island just across the water. In addition to local seafood, such as oysters, mussels, salmon and halibut, the menu includes low-carbohydrate dishes. All are priced reasonably. Casual dress; cocktails.
Parking: on-site. **Cards:** AX, MC, VI. [X]

BEST WOK **Lunch:** $4-$10 **Dinner:** $6-$15 **Phone:** 250/287-2831
▼▼ **Location:** From Shoppers Row, just e on 10th Ave, then just s. 968 Alder St V9W 2P9. **Hours:** 11 am-9:30 pm. Closed: 12/25. **Features:** Contemporary Chinese and Western food is on the menu at the downtown restaurant. Combination meals serve two, four, six or eight to 10 diners. Plenty of on-site parking is available. Casual dress; cocktails. **Parking:** on-site. **Cards:** MC, VI.
Chinese [X]

FUSILLI GRILL **Lunch:** $8-$22 **Dinner:** $8-$22 **Phone:** 250/830-0090
▼▼ **Location:** Island Hwy 19A, 2.4 km se. 4-220 Dogwood St V9W 2X9. **Hours:** 11 am-9:30 pm, Fri-10:30 pm, Sat & Sun 4:30 pm-10 pm. Closed: 1/1, 12/25. **Reservations:** suggested, Fri & Sat night. **Features:** Contemporary West Coast creations inspired by Italian cuisine highlight the menu of the youthful Nouvelle Italian and casual bistro-restaurant. This place is in a small strip mall, away from the busy town center and highways. Daily specials and British Columbia wines are featured. Casual dress; cocktails. **Parking:** on-site. **Cards:** MC, VI.
 [X]

HARBOUR GRILL **Lunch:** $8-$11 **Dinner:** $19-$27 **Phone:** 250/287-4143
▼▼ **Location:** On Island Hwy 19A; in Discovery Harbour Mall. 112 1334 Island Hwy V9W 2C2. **Hours:** 11:30 am-2 & 5:30-10 pm, Sat & Sun from 5:30 pm. Closed: 12/25. **Reservations:** accepted. **Features:** Floor-to-ceiling windows overlook the harbor, where the people-watching is great. Offerings include a soup of the day, Steak & Seafood sandwiches and burgers for lunch and more elaborate fare for dinner. Cocktails. **Parking:** on-site.
Cards: AX, MC, VI. [X]

CHASE pop. 2,460

———— **WHERE TO STAY** ————

CHASE COUNTRY INN MOTEL **Phone:** (250)679-3333
▼▼ 5/1-10/31 1P: $65-$79 2P: $79-$95 XP: $10 D12
3/1-4/30 & 11/1-2/28 1P: $55-$69 2P: $59-$79 XP: $7 D12
Motel **Location:** Trans-Canada Hwy 1 and Coburn St. 576 Coburn St V0E 1M0 (Box 1031). Fax: 250/679-8018. **Facility:** 21 one-bedroom standard units, some with efficiencies or kitchens. 2 stories (no elevator), exterior corridors. **Parking:** on-site, winter plug-ins. **Terms:** office hours 8 am-11 pm, 3 day cancellation notice-fee imposed, small pets only ($5 extra charge). **Amenities:** hair dryers. **Guest Services:** gift shop. **Cards:** AX, MC, VI. SOME UNITS
[ASK] [S▢] [♦] [▮] [✦] [DATA PORT] [▯] [▭] /[X]/
FEE

QUAAOUT RESORT & CONFERENCE CENTRE **Phone:** (250)679-3090
▼▼ 5/1-9/30 1P: $120-$180 2P: $120-$180 XP: $10 F12
3/1-4/30 & 10/1-2/28 1P: $79-$140 2P: $79-$140 XP: $10 F12
Resort **Location:** Trans-Canada Hwy 1, exit Squilax Bridge, 2.5 km w on Little Shuswap Rd. Located in a quiet, secluded area.
Small-scale Hotel (PO Box 1215). Fax: 250/679-3039. **Facility:** Native interpretative trails crisscross the grounds of this lakefront lodge offering brightly decorated guest rooms. 72 one-bedroom standard units, some with whirlpools. 3 stories, interior corridors. **Parking:** on-site. **Terms:** office hours 7 am-11 pm, check-in 4 pm, weekly rates available, package plans, pets ($10 extra charge, in designated units). **Amenities:** hair dryers. **Pool(s):** heated indoor. **Leisure Activities:** whirlpool, steamroom, rental canoes, boat dock, fishing, rental bicycles, hiking trails, jogging, exercise room. **Guest Services:** gift shop, coin laundry. **Business Services:** conference facilities. **Cards:** AX, MC, VI. SOME UNITS
[S▢] [♦] [▮] [&M] [▱] [X] [✦] [DATA PORT] [▭] /[X] [▯]/
FEE

CHEMAINUS pop. 2,706

———— **WHERE TO DINE** ————

THE WATERFORD RESTAURANT **Lunch:** $7-$13 **Dinner:** $15-$25 **Phone:** 250/246-1046
▼▼ **Location:** From Chemainus Rd, s on Oak St to Maple St. 9875 Maple St V0R 1K1. **Hours:** Open 4/1-10/31; 11:30 am-2 & 5:30-close. Closed: Sun & Mon. **Reservations:** suggested, in season. **Features:** The Waterford Restaurant features Canadian West Coast and French cuisine, prepared by chef Dwayne Maslen. Try the Canadian rack of lamb dijon, or the classic filet mignon, with mushrooms and Bernaise sauce, but be sure to leave room for one of their sumptuous Italian gelato desserts. Casual dress; cocktails. **Parking:** street. **Cards:** AX, MC, VI.
 [K] [X]

CHETWYND pop. 2,591

-------- WHERE TO DINE --------

THE SWISS INN
(CAA)
♦♦ ◊◊
Continental

Lunch: $6-$11   **Dinner: $8-$40**   **Phone: 250/788-2566**
Location: 1 km e on Hwy 97. 4812 N Access Rd V0C 1J0. **Hours:** 11 am-2 & 5-10 pm, Sat from 5 pm. Closed major holidays; also Sun. **Features:** The casual, lively Swiss Inn features European and International specialties. Among choices are homemade sausage, spaetzle and schnitzel, as well as popular pizzas, charbroiled steaks and Friday and Saturday night prime rib dinners. The atmosphere is cozy and warm. Cocktails. **Parking:** on-site. **Cards:** AX, MC, VI.
[X]

CHILLIWACK pop. 62,927

-------- WHERE TO STAY --------

BEST WESTERN RAINBOW COUNTRY INN   *Book at aaa.com*
(CAA) (SAVE)
♦♦ ♦♦
Small-scale Hotel

5/1-9/30	1P: $99-$120	2P: $109-$130	XP: $10 F15
3/1-4/30 & 10/1-2/28	1P: $84-$109	2P: $94-$119	XP: $10 F15

Phone: (604)795-3828

Location: Trans-Canada Hwy 1, exit 116 (Lickman Rd). 43971 Industrial Way V2R 3A4. Fax: 604/795-5039. **Facility:** 74 one-bedroom standard units, some with whirlpools. 2 stories (no elevator), interior corridors. **Parking:** on-site. **Terms:** package plans, small pets only ($5 extra charge). **Amenities:** irons, hair dryers. **Dining:** 2 restaurants, 6 am-11 pm, cocktails. **Pool(s):** heated indoor. **Leisure Activities:** sauna, whirlpool. **Guest Services:** valet and coin laundry. **Business Services:** meeting rooms. **Cards:** AX, DC, DS, MC, VI. **Special Amenities:** free local telephone calls and free room upgrade (subject to availability with advance reservations).

SOME UNITS
[S/D] [icons] FEE / [X] [icons]

CHILLIWACK TRAVELODGE   *Book at aaa.com*
(CAA) (SAVE)
♦♦ ♦♦
Small-scale Hotel

6/1-9/30	1P: $68-$80	2P: $73-$87	XP: $6 F17
3/1-5/31 & 10/1-2/28	1P: $52-$65	2P: $59-$71	XP: $6 F17

Phone: (604)792-4240

Location: Trans-Canada Hwy 1, exit 119, just n. 45466 Yale Rd W V2R 3Z8. Fax: 604/792-2325. **Facility:** 82 units. 81 one- and 1 two-bedroom standard units, some with efficiencies. 2 stories (no elevator), interior corridors. **Parking:** on-site. **Terms:** small pets only ($5 extra charge). **Amenities:** high-speed Internet, voice mail, hair dryers. **Dining:** 6 am-10 pm, wine/beer only. **Pool(s):** heated indoor. **Leisure Activities:** whirlpool. **Guest Services:** coin laundry. **Business Services:** meeting rooms. **Cards:** AX, DC, DS, MC, VI. **Special Amenities:** free local telephone calls and free newspaper.

SOME UNITS
[S/D] [icons] FEE / [X] [icons] /

COMFORT INN   *Book at aaa.com*
♦♦ ♦♦
Motel

7/1-9/15	1P: $91-$111	2P: $99-$119	XP: $10 F18
5/1-6/30	1P: $88-$108	2P: $96-$116	XP: $10 F18
9/16-2/28	1P: $87-$107.	2P: $95-$115	XP: $10 F18
3/1-4/30	1P: $82-$102	2P: $90-$110	XP: $10 F18

Phone: (604)858-0636

Location: Trans-Canada Hwy 1, exit 119, s on Vedder Rd, then 1 km w. 45405 Luckakuck Way V2R 3C7. Fax: 604/858-0116. **Facility:** 83 one-bedroom standard units. 2 stories (no elevator), interior corridors. **Parking:** on-site. **Terms:** pets ($5 extra charge). **Amenities:** irons, hair dryers. **Guest Services:** valet laundry. **Cards:** AX, CB, DC, DS, JC, MC, VI.

SOME UNITS
[ASK] [S/D] [icons] FEE / [X] /

DAYS INN CHILLIWACK   *Book at aaa.com*
♦♦ ♦♦
Motel

7/1-9/30	1P: $79-$89	2P: $79-$89	XP: $10 F13
3/1-6/30 & 10/1-2/28	1P: $69-$79	2P: $69-$79	XP: $10 F13

Phone: (604)792-1955

Location: Hwy 1, exit 119B eastbound, 1 km n on Yale Rd, then just e on Hocking Ave; exit 120 westbound, just n. 8583 Young Rd S V2P 4P3. Fax: 604/795-2664. **Facility:** 29 one-bedroom standard units. 2 stories (no elevator), interior corridors. **Parking:** on-site. **Terms:** 7 day cancellation notice-fee imposed, weekly rates available, [CP] meal plan available, package plans. **Amenities:** hair dryers. **Cards:** AX, DC, JC, MC, VI.

SOME UNITS
[ASK] [S/D] [icons] / [X] [icons]

RHOMBUS HOTELS & RESORTS-DOWNTOWN
CHILLIWACK   *Book at aaa.com*
(CAA) (SAVE)
♦♦ ♦♦
Small-scale Hotel

5/16-9/15	1P: $91-$130	2P: $91-$130	XP: $10 F18
9/16-2/28	1P: $80-$120	2P: $80-$120	XP: $10 F18
3/1-5/15	1P: $78-$117	2P: $78-$117	XP: $10 F18

Phone: (604)795-4788

Location: Trans-Canada Hwy 1, exit 119, 3 km n on Yale Rd, then just w; downtown. 45920 First Ave V2P 7K1. Fax: 604/795-4680. **Facility:** 110 one-bedroom standard units. 9 stories, interior corridors. **Parking:** on-site. **Terms:** check-in 4 pm, cancellation fee imposed, [AP], [BP], [CP], [ECP] & [MAP] meal plans available, package plans, small pets only ($10 extra charge). **Dining:** 7 am-10 pm, cocktails. **Pool(s):** heated indoor. **Leisure Activities:** sauna, whirlpool. **Guest Services:** valet laundry. **Business Services:** conference facilities. **Cards:** AX, DC, MC, VI.

SOME UNITS
[S/D] [icons] FEE / [X] /

-------- WHERE TO DINE --------

EARLS
♦♦ ♦♦
Canadian

Lunch: $7-$12   **Dinner: $7-$12**   **Phone: 604/858-3360**
Location: Trans-Canada Hwy 1, exit 119, just w on Vedder Rd; in Cottonwood Shopping Center. 45583 Luckakuck Way V2R 1A1. **Hours:** 11:30 am-11 pm. Closed: 12/25. **Features:** Offering tempting burgers, fresh salads, chicken wings and plenty of beer on tap, the eatery also features great food, friendly service and lots of free parking. Casual dress; cocktails. **Parking:** on-site. **Cards:** AX, MC, VI.
[Y] [X]

Nobody ever said you had to stay on the highlighted route.

Whether you're travelling the major highways or scenic country roads, Choice Hotels® gives you everything you need to experience the West. Plus, CAA members always save at any of our 49 locations across Western Canada.* Just call to book your next stay. Then get out and hit the road.

1.800.228.1222
choicehotels.ca

British Columbia
- Abbotsford
- Chilliwack
- Fernie
- Fort St. John
- Hope
- Kamloops (2)
- Kelowna
- Princeton
- Vancouver (4)
- Vancouver/Langley
- Vancouver/Richmond (2)

- Vancouver/Surrey
- Victoria (3)
- Victoria/Saanichton

Alberta
- Banff/Canmore
- Calgary (7)
- Edmonton
- Edmonton/Nisku
- Fort McMurray
- Grande Prairie
- Lethbridge (2)
- Medicine Hat

- Whitecourt

Saskatchewan
- Moose Jaw
- Prince Albert
- Regina (2)
- Saskatoon (2)
- Swift Current
- Yorkton

Manitoba
- Brandon
- Winnipeg (3)

We'll see you there.
CHOICE HOTELS CANADA℠

CAA & Choice Hotels.
No one knows Canada better.

When travelling within Canada, CAA members always save at participating Choice Hotels.

With 228 locations across Canada, Choice Hotels® fits your travel plans and your budget. To book now and save, call today and ask for CAA preferred rates,* and for hotel information visit us online.

1.800.228.1222
choicehotels.ca

We'll see you there.
CHOICE HOTELS CANADA™

LA MANSIONE RISTORANTE
▼▼▼
Italian

Dinner: $19-$29

Location: Trans-Canada Hwy 1, exit 119 to downtown, then 3.6 km n. 46290 Yale Rd E V2P 2P6. **Hours:** 5:30 pm-10 pm. Closed: 12/25; also Mon & Sun 9/15-4/30. **Reservations:** suggested. **Features:** La Mansione's beautiful downtown site was built in 1911 and has long been one of the area's most important historical buildings. The restaurant's menu features steak, seafood, lamb, veal and pasta specialties, and its setting is cozy and informal. Casual dress; cocktails. **Parking:** on-site. **Cards:** AX, MC, VI.

Phone: 604/792-8910

☒

CHRISTINA LAKE pop. 1,035

———— WHERE TO STAY ————

NEW HORIZON MOTEL
▼▼ ▼▼
Motel

	1P: $95-$145	2P: $95-$145	XP: $10	D12
5/16-9/25 [CP]				
3/1-5/15 & 9/26-2/28 [CP]	1P: $79-$105	2P: $85-$110	XP: $10	D12

Phone: (250)447-9312

Location: Just e. 2037 Hwy 3 V0H 1E2. Fax: 250/447-9488. **Facility:** 25 units. 19 one-bedroom standard units, some with kitchens and/or whirlpools. 6 one-bedroom suites ($165-$275) with kitchens. 1-2 stories (no elevator), exterior corridors. **Parking:** on-site. **Terms:** office hours 7 am-10 pm, 2 night minimum stay - seasonal and/or weekends, 30 day cancellation notice-fee imposed, small pets only ($10 extra charge, with prior approval in designated units). **Amenities:** hair dryers. *Some:* high-speed Internet. **Leisure Activities:** basketball, volleyball. **Guest Services:** sundries. **Cards:** AX, DC, MC, VI.

SOME UNITS
🐾 [DATA PORT] 💻 / ☒ [VCR] 📶 🖥 /
FEE

CLEARWATER

———— WHERE TO STAY ————

CLEARWATER LODGE
▼▼ ▼▼
Small-scale Hotel

| 5/15-2/28 | 1P: $109-$120 | 2P: $123-$145 | XP: $10 | F12 |
| 3/1-5/14 | 1P: $109 | 2P: $123 | XP: $10 | F12 |

Phone: (250)674-3080

Location: Jct Clearwater Valley Rd and Hwy 5 (Yellowhead Hwy). 331 Eden Rd V0E 1N0 (PO Box 1946). Fax: 250/674-3084. **Facility:** 64 one-bedroom standard units, some with efficiencies and/or whirlpools. 2 stories (no elevator), interior/exterior corridors. **Parking:** on-site, winter plug-ins. **Terms:** office hours 7 am-11 pm, pets ($10 extra charge). **Amenities:** *Some:* high-speed Internet. **Pool(s):** heated indoor. **Leisure Activities:** sauna, whirlpool, exercise room. **Guest Services:** coin laundry. **Business Services:** meeting rooms. **Cards:** AX, DC, JC, MC, VI.

SOME UNITS
[ASK] [S/D] 🐾 🍴 🍸 [&M] [&] 🏊 ☒ [DATA PORT] 📶 🖥 💻 / ☒ /
FEE

DUTCH LAKE MOTEL AND CAMPGROUND
▼▼ ▼▼
Motel

| 5/21-9/30 | 1P: $89 | 2P: $93-$98 | XP: $10 | F12 |
| 3/1-5/20 & 10/1-2/28 | 1P: $55 | 2P: $60-$65 | XP: $5 | F12 |

Phone: 250/674-3325

Location: Hwy 5 (Yellowhead Hwy) at Roy Rd. 333 Roy Rd V0E 1N0 (RR 2 Box 5116). Fax: 250/674-2916. **Facility:** 27 units. 21 one-bedroom standard units, some with efficiencies. 6 one-bedroom suites ($110-$160) with efficiencies (utensils extra charge). 2 stories (no elevator), exterior corridors. **Parking:** on-site. **Terms:** office hours 7 am-11 pm. **Amenities:** *Some:* hair dryers. **Leisure Activities:** rental boats, rental canoes, fishing. **Guest Services:** coin laundry. **Cards:** AX, MC, VI.

SOME UNITS
[ASK] [S/D] 🍴 [&M] ☒ 💻 / ☒ [AC] 📶 🖥 /

JASPER WAY INN MOTEL ON BEAUTIFUL DUTCH LAKE
[CAA] [SAVE]
▼▼
Motel

| 5/1-9/30 | 1P: $56-$90 | 2P: $62-$95 | XP: $6 | F5 |
| 3/1-4/30 & 10/1-2/28 | 1P: $50-$85 | 2P: $56-$85 | XP: $6 | F5 |

Phone: (250)674-3345

Location: 1 km w on Old N Thompson Hwy, just off Hwy 5 (Yellowhead Hwy). 57 E Old N Thompson Hwy V0E 1N0 (RR 2 Box 2127). Fax: 250/674-2687. **Facility:** 16 units. 12 one- and 4 two-bedroom standard units, some with kitchens. 2 stories (no elevator), exterior corridors. *Bath:* combo or shower only. **Parking:** on-site, winter plug-ins. **Terms:** office hours 9 am-10 pm, small pets only. **Leisure Activities:** rental boats, rental canoes, boat dock, fishing. **Cards:** AX, DC, MC, VI. **Special Amenities:** free local telephone calls.

SOME UNITS
[S/D] 🐾 🍴 ☒ 📶 / ☒ [AC] 💻 /

CLINTON pop. 621

———— WHERE TO STAY ————

———— *The following lodging was either not evaluated or did not* ————
meet AAA rating requirements but is listed for your information only.

CARIBOO LODGE RESORT
[fyi]

Not evaluated. **Location:** Hwy 97 and Dewoney Ave. 1414 Cariboo Hwy V0K 1K0 (PO Box 459). Facilities, services, and decor characterize a mid-range property.

Phone: 250/459-7992

COQUITLAM —See Vancouver p. 581.

COURTENAY pop. 18,304

—— WHERE TO STAY ——

THE COAST WESTERLY HOTEL *Book at aaa.com*
Phone: (250)338-7741

Small-scale Hotel

All Year   1P: $119-$229   2P: $129-$239   XP: $10   F18
Location: Corner of Cliffe Ave and Island Hwy 19A N. 1590 Cliffe Ave V9N 2K4. Fax: 250/338-5442. **Facility:** 108 units. 105 one-bedroom standard units, some with whirlpools. 3 one-bedroom suites. 4 stories, interior corridors. **Parking:** on-site. **Terms:** package plans, small pets only ($10 extra charge). **Amenities:** irons, hair dryers. **Pool(s):** small heated indoor. **Leisure Activities:** saunas, whirlpool, exercise room. **Guest Services:** valet laundry. **Business Services:** meeting rooms. **Cards:** AX, DC, DS, JC, MC, VI.

SOME UNITS

CROWN ISLE RESORT & GOLF COMMUNITY
Phone: (250)703-5050

Resort
Small-scale Hotel

6/1-9/30   1P: $119-$325   2P: $119-$325   XP: $15   F12
5/1-5/31 & 10/1-2/28   1P: $99-$279   2P: $99-$279   XP: $15   F12
3/1-4/30   1P: $99-$249   2P: $99-$249   XP: $15   F12
Location: Island Hwy 19A N, 1.5 km n on Comox Rd, then 2.5 km ne on Ryan Rd, follow signs. 399 Clubhouse Dr V9N 9G3. Fax: 250/703-5051. **Facility:** World-class golfing awaits at the Crown Isle Resort, where many of the guest rooms overlook the golf course; also featured is an on-site car museum. Smoke free premises. 82 units. 75 one- and 7 two-bedroom standard units, some with efficiencies, kitchens and/or whirlpools. 2-3 stories (no elevator), exterior corridors. **Parking:** on-site. **Terms:** 7 day cancellation notice-fee imposed, package plans. **Amenities:** video library, voice mail, irons, hair dryers. *Some:* DVD players, CD players. **Leisure Activities:** whirlpool, steamrooms, exercise room. *Fee:* golf-18 holes. **Guest Services:** gift shop. **Business Services:** conference facilities. **Cards:** AX, DC, DS, MC, VI.

SOME UNITS

GREYSTONE MANOR BED & BREAKFAST
Phone: 250/338-1422

Historic Bed
& Breakfast

All Year [BP]   1P: $75   2P: $95
Location: 4 km s on Island Hwy 19A S. Located in a quiet secluded area. 4014 Haas Rd V9N 9T4. **Facility:** An English-style garden is featured at this B&B set on acreage overlooking the water. Smoke free premises. 3 one-bedroom standard units. 2 stories (no elevator), interior corridors. **Bath:** combo or shower only. **Parking:** on-site. **Terms:** office hours 7:30 am-10 pm, check-in 4 pm, age restrictions may apply, cancellation fee imposed. **Amenities:** hair dryers. **Cards:** MC, VI.

KINGFISHER OCEANSIDE RESORT & SPA
Phone: (250)338-1323

Small-scale Hotel

6/1-9/30 & 12/16-2/28   1P: $155-$165   2P: $155-$165   XP: $10   F16
3/1-5/31 & 10/1-12/15   1P: $125-$165   2P: $125-$165   XP: $10   F16
Location: 5 km s on Hwy 19A S. 4330 S Island Hwy V9N 9R9. Fax: 250/338-0058. **Facility:** Smoke free premises. 64 units. 44 one-bedroom standard units, some with efficiencies and/or whirlpools. 20 one-bedroom suites ($180-$450) with efficiencies, some with whirlpools. 2 stories, exterior corridors. **Bath:** combo or shower only. **Parking:** on-site. **Terms:** office hours 7 am-11 pm, 2 night minimum stay - seasonal and/or weekends, 7 day cancellation notice, small pets only ($7 extra charge, in limited units). **Amenities:** video library (fee), irons, hair dryers. *Some:* high-speed Internet, dual phone lines. **Pool(s):** heated outdoor. **Leisure Activities:** sauna, whirlpool, steamroom, tennis court, exercise room, spa. **Guest Services:** valet laundry. **Business Services:** meeting rooms. **Cards:** AX, DC, DS, MC, VI.

SOME UNITS

TRAVELODGE COURTENAY *Book at aaa.com*
Phone: (250)334-4491

(CAA) (SAVE)

Motel

All Year [ECP]   1P: $75-$120   2P: $83-$128   XP: $8   F17
Location: 1.2 km s on Island Hwy 19A S. Located adjacent to Driftwood Mall. 2605 S Island Hwy (Cliffe Ave) V9N 2L8. Fax: 250/334-4694. **Facility:** 91 one-bedroom standard units, some with efficiencies. 2 stories (no elevator), exterior corridors. **Parking:** on-site. **Terms:** weekly rates available, package plans, pets ($50 deposit, $5 extra charge). **Amenities:** voice mail, hair dryers. **Pool(s):** heated outdoor. **Leisure Activities:** sauna. **Guest Services:** valet and coin laundry. **Business Services:** meeting rooms. **Cards:** AX, CB, DC, DS, JC, MC, VI. **Special Amenities:** free expanded continental breakfast and free local telephone calls.

SOME UNITS

—— WHERE TO DINE ——

MCSWIGGINS CAFE
Lunch: $5-$9   **Phone:** 250/338-2966

Canadian

Location: 1 km s on Island Hwy 19A. 2270 Cliffe Ave V9N 2L4. **Hours:** 6 am-4 pm. Closed major holidays; also Sun. **Features:** The popular breakfast and lunch cafe professes: "We're not fast food. All food is freshly prepared and may take longer; your patience is appreciated." Wonderful aromas greet those who walk in the door. Only cash is accepted. Casual dress. **Parking:** on-site.

MONTE CHRISTO ON THE RIVER
Lunch: $9-$12   **Dinner:** $12-$21   **Phone:** 250/338-1468

Continental

Location: Island Hwy 19A N. 975 Comox Rd V9N 3P7. **Hours:** 11:30 am-10 pm, Sat & Sun 4 pm-11 pm. Closed: 12/25. **Features:** Along the river, the well-established restaurant presents a casual lunch menu with daily specials and homemade soups. At the heart of the dinner menu are steak, seafood, pasta and barbecue dishes. Also offered are many seniors' and children's choices. Casual dress; cocktails. **Parking:** on-site. **Cards:** AX, MC, VI.

THE OLD HOUSE RESTAURANT
Lunch: $8-$12   **Dinner:** $12-$32   **Phone:** 250/338-5406

Canadian

Location: From Island Hwy 19A, jct 17th St; before the 17th St Bridge. 1760 Riverside Ln V9N 8C7. **Hours:** 11:30 am-9 pm. Closed: 12/25. **Features:** This locally popular dining spot is housed in a rustic 1938 home with cozy fireplaces and tantalizing wood aromas. Sitting on two acres of beautiful gardens, the site overlooks the grounds and a working mill across the river. Friendly, attentive service. Casual dress; cocktails. **Parking:** on-site. **Cards:** AX, DC, MC, VI.

CRANBROOK pop. 18,476

WHERE TO STAY

DELTA ST. EUGENE MISSION RESORT   *Book at aaa.com*   **Phone:** (250)420-2000

(CAA) (SAVE)

| | 5/1-9/30 | 1P: $139 | 2P: $139 | XP: $20 | F18 |
| | 3/1-4/30 & 10/1-2/28 | 1P: $129 | 2P: $129 | XP: $20 | F18 |

Location: Hwy 3, exit Kimberley/Airport (Hwy 95A) to Mission Rd, 4.5 km n. Spectacular mountain setting outside of town on golf course. 7731 Mission Rd V1C 7E5. Fax: 250/420-2001. **Facility:** This upscale hotel, in a picturesque setting, was built in an old mission school dating to the 1800s. Designated smoking area. 125 units. 122 one-bedroom standard units. 3 one-bedroom suites, some with whirlpools. 3 stories, interior corridors. **Parking:** on-site and valet. **Terms:** check-in 4 pm, cancellation fee imposed, package plans, pets ($10 fee). **Amenities:** video games, high-speed Internet, dual phone lines, voice mail, irons, hair dryers. **Dining:** 6:30 am-11 pm, also, Purcell Grill, see separate listing. **Leisure Activities:** fishing, cross country skiing, ice skating, billards,, hiking trails. *Fee:* golf-18 holes, helitours, rafting, horseback riding. **Guest Services:** sundries, valet laundry, airport transportation-Cranbrook Airport, area transportation. **Business Services:** conference facilities, administrative services. **Cards:** AX, CB, DC, DS, JC, MC, VI. *(See color ad below)*

Historic Resort
Large-scale Hotel

SOME UNITS

[icons] FEE /[icon]/

HERITAGE INN   *Book at aaa.com*   **Phone:** (250)489-4301

	6/1-9/30	1P: $100	2P: $105	XP: $5	F16
	10/1-2/28	1P: $95	2P: $100		
	3/1-5/31	1P: $95	2P: $100	XP: $5	F16

Small-scale Hotel

Location: Hwy 3 and 95; centre. 803 Cranbrook St N V1C 3S2. Fax: 250/489-5758. **Facility:** 100 units. 97 one-bedroom standard units. 2 one- and 1 two-bedroom suites ($140-$199). 3 stories (no elevator), interior corridors. **Parking:** on-site, winter plug-ins. **Terms:** package plans, small pets only ($5 fee). **Amenities:** voice mail. *Some:* high-speed Internet (fee), safes, irons. **Pool(s):** heated indoor. **Leisure Activities:** whirlpool, limited exercise equipment. **Guest Services:** valet laundry. **Business Services:** conference facilities. **Cards:** AX, DC, DS, MC, VI.

SOME UNITS

(ASK) [icons] FEE FEE /[X][VCR][icon]/

MODEL A INN   **Phone:** (250)489-4600

(CAA) (SAVE)

| | 5/1-9/30 | 1P: $90-$175 | 2P: $100-$175 | XP: $5 | F10 |
| | 3/1-4/30 & 10/1-2/28 | 1P: $70-$120 | 2P: $80-$120 | XP: $5 | F10 |

Motel

Location: 2.5 km n on Hwy 3 and 95. 1908 Cranbrook St N V1C 3T1. Fax: 250/489-0906. **Facility:** 46 units. 42 one-bedroom standard units, some with whirlpools. 4 one-bedroom suites with efficiencies. 2 stories (no elevator), exterior corridors. **Parking:** on-site, winter plug-ins. **Terms:** small pets only ($5 fee). **Guest Services:** valet laundry. **Cards:** AX, DC, MC, VI. **Special Amenities:** free local telephone calls and early check-in/late check-out.

SOME UNITS

[icons] FEE /[X][icon][icon]/

SUPER 8 MOTEL   *Book at aaa.com*   **Phone:** (250)489-8028

(CAA) (SAVE)

| | 7/1-9/30 | 1P: $97-$105 | 2P: $105-$115 | XP: $10 | F12 |
| | 3/1-6/30 & 10/1-2/28 | 1P: $80-$90 | 2P: $90-$100 | XP: $10 | F12 |

Small-scale Hotel

Location: Just w of jct Hwy 93 and 95; corner of 30th Ave. 2370 Cranbrook St N V1C 3T2. Fax: 250/489-1223. **Facility:** 48 one-bedroom standard units. 2 stories (no elevator), interior corridors. **Parking:** on-site, winter plug-ins. **Terms:** cancellation fee imposed, pets ($10 fee, in smoking units). **Leisure Activities:** whirlpool. **Guest Services:** coin laundry. **Business Services:** PC (fee). **Cards:** AX, MC, VI.

SOME UNITS

[icons] FEE /[X][VCR][icon]/

WHERE TO DINE

BAVARIAN CHALET   **Lunch:** $5-$10   **Dinner:** $8-$25   **Phone:** 250/489-3305

Continental

Location: 2 km n on Hwy 3 and 95. 1617 Cranbrook St V1C 3S7. **Hours:** 11 am-3 & 5-10 pm. Closed major holidays; also Sun. **Reservations:** required. **Features:** The restaurant is a favorite for good, hearty food, a relaxing atmosphere and European touches. Among menu choices are ribs, chicken cordon bleu, schnitzels and German spaetzle, as well as excellent prime rib specials Thursday-Saturday nights. Save room for the delicious apple strudel. Cocktails. **Parking:** on-site. **Cards:** AX, MC, VI.

[X]

HEIDI'S EUROPEAN &
INTERNATIONAL CUISINE   *Menu on aaa.com*   **Lunch:** $6-$12   **Dinner:** $9-$25   **Phone:** 250/426-7922

Location: On 9th Ave S; centre. 821 C Baker St V1C 1A3. **Hours:** 11 am-2:30 & 5-10 pm, Sat from 11:30 am, Sun 5 pm-9 pm. **Features:** The cozy, comfortable, European-style restaurant serves an extensive menu of International fare, including rotisserie chicken, schnitzel, bratwurst and steak. Prime rib is offered Fridays and Saturdays. Casual dress; cocktails. **Parking:** street. **Cards:** AX, DC, MC, VI.   ⊠

International

PURCELL GRILL   **Lunch:** $10-$14   **Dinner:** $16-$26   **Phone:** 250/420-2025
▼▼▼ **Location:** Hwy 3, exit Kimberley/Airport (Hwy 95A) to Mission Rd, 4.5 km n; in Delta St. Eugene Mission Resort. 7731
Regional Mission Rd V1C 7E5. **Hours:** 6:30 am-11 pm, Sun 7 am-10 pm; hours vary off season.
Canadian **Reservations:** suggested. **Features:** Creative, artistic dishes are created with many regional ingredients at the casually upscale restaurant. The setting, in the old quarters of the Delta St. Eugene Mission school, lends a sense of history. Exposed brick walls, heavy overhead beams and views of the golf course set the scene for a luxurious meal. Service is friendly and attentive. Casual dress; cocktails. **Parking:** on-site and valet. **Cards:** AX, DC, MC, VI.
♿Ⓜ 🍽 ⊠

CRESTON pop. 4,795

―――― **WHERE TO STAY** ――――

DOWNTOWNER MOTOR INN   **Phone:** (250)428-2238
▼▼ 3/1-10/31   1P: $47-$50   2P: $52-$64   XP: $5   F
11/1-2/28   1P: $37-$42   2P: $45-$54   XP: $5   F
Small-scale Hotel **Location:** Corner of 12th Ave N. 1218 Canyon St V0B 1G0 (PO Box 490, V0B 1G0). Fax: 250/428-9974. **Facility:** 23 one-bedroom standard units. 2 stories (no elevator), interior corridors. **Parking:** on-site, winter plug-ins. **Terms:** office hours 7 am-11 pm, cancellation fee imposed, pets ($4 extra charge). **Leisure Activities:** sauna, whirlpool. **Business Services:** meeting rooms. **Cards:** AX, DC, MC, VI.

SOME UNITS
🛏 🍴▸ / ⊠ 🖥 /
FEE

SKIMMERHORN INN   **Phone:** (250)428-4009
ⒸⒶⒶ ⓈⒶⓋⒺ All Year   1P: $60-$80   2P: $70-$90   XP: $5
▼▼ ▼▼ **Location:** On Hwy 3, 0.8 km e. 2711 Hwy 3 V0B 1G0 (Box 262). Fax: 250/428-4069. **Facility:** 25 units. 16 one-
Motel bedroom standard units, some with efficiencies. 9 one-bedroom suites, some with efficiencies. 2 stories (no elevator), exterior corridors. **Parking:** on-site, winter plug-ins. **Terms:** package plans, pets ($5 fee, dogs only). **Pool(s):** small heated outdoor. **Leisure Activities:** playground. **Business Services:** fax (fee). **Cards:** MC, VI. **Special Amenities:** free local telephone calls and free room upgrade (subject to availability with advance reservations).

SOME UNITS
🛏 🍴▸ 🏊 🖥📠 🖥 / ⊠ 📼 🖥 🖼 /
FEE   FEE

SUNSET MOTEL   **Phone:** (250)428-2229
ⒸⒶⒶ ⓈⒶⓋⒺ All Year   1P: $58-$69   2P: $64-$84   XP: $5
▼▼ ▼▼ **Location:** 1 km e on Hwy 3. 2705 Canyon St, Hwy 3 E V0B 1G0 (PO Box 186). Fax: 250/428-2251. **Facility:** 24
Motel one-bedroom standard units, some with efficiencies, kitchens and/or whirlpools. 2 stories (no elevator), exterior corridors. **Parking:** on-site, winter plug-ins. **Terms:** package plans, small pets only ($5 extra charge). **Pool(s):** small heated outdoor. **Cards:** AX, DC, MC, VI. **Special Amenities:** free local telephone calls and preferred room (subject to availability with advance reservations).

SOME UNITS
🅂🅳 🛏 🍴▸ 🏊 🎣 📠 🖥 🖥 / ⊠ 🖼 /
FEE

―――― **WHERE TO DINE** ――――

GRANNY'S PLACE   **Lunch:** $5-$9   **Dinner:** $5-$9   **Phone:** 250/428-3990
▼ **Location:** On Hwy 3, just n. 2808 Hwy 3 V0B 1G1. **Hours:** 6 am-10 pm; 7 am-8 pm 10/31-5/24. Closed: 12/25,
Canadian 12/26. **Features:** All day breakfasts can be found at this simple roadside restaurant, which is a favorite amongst the locals. Vinyl booths line one wall of the dining room, with an outdoor patio in season. You can choose from a variety of omelettes, salads and sandwiches, but a note of caution: the pies are known throughout the town to be the best, so save room! **Parking:** on-site. **Cards:** MC, VI.   ⊠

DAWSON CREEK pop. 10,754

―――― **WHERE TO STAY** ――――

DAWSON CREEK SUPER 8   *Book at aaa.com*   **Phone:** (250)782-8899
ⒸⒶⒶ ⓈⒶⓋⒺ 6/1-9/15 [ECP]   1P: $90-$150   2P: $90-$150   XP: $10   F18
3/1-5/31 & 9/16-2/28 [ECP]   1P: $85-$140   2P: $85-$140   XP: $10   F18
▼▼ ▼▼ **Location:** Just s of jct Hart Hwy 97 S and Alaska Hwy 97 N. 1440 Alaska Ave V1G 1Z5. Fax: 250/784-1988.
Small-scale Hotel **Facility:** 66 one-bedroom standard units. 2 stories (no elevator), interior corridors. **Parking:** on-site, winter plug-ins. **Terms:** pets ($10 fee, in designated units). **Amenities:** irons, hair dryers. *Some:* high-speed Internet. **Leisure Activities:** limited exercise equipment. **Guest Services:** coin laundry. **Business Services:** meeting rooms, PC. **Cards:** AX, DC, DS, MC, VI. **Special Amenities:** free expanded continental breakfast and free local telephone calls.

SOME UNITS
🅂🅳 🛏 🎣 📠 🖥 🖥 / ⊠ 📼 🖼 /
FEE

RAMADA LIMITED   Phone: 250/782-8595
[fyi]   Not evaluated. **Location:** Jct Alaska Hwy 97 N and Hart Hwy 97 S. 1748 Alaska Ave V1G 1P4. Facilities, services,
           and decor characterize a mid-range property.

———— **WHERE TO DINE** ————

ALASKA CAFE & DINING ROOM   **Lunch:** $6-$20   **Dinner:** $6-$20   **Phone:** 250/782-7040
▼▼ ▼▼   **Location:** Just s of Mile O' Post; centre. 10213 10th St V1G 4G7. **Hours:** 11:30 am-9:30 pm, Fri & Sat-10 pm;
           from 11 am 6/1-9/6. Closed major holidays. **Reservations:** accepted. **Features:** Patrons enjoy the unusual
American   Alaskan-style setting of the restaurant, in a landmark building with a hotel and public house. The extensive
           menu centers on International cuisine, with an emphasis on American and seafood creations. Casual dress;
cocktails. **Parking:** street. **Cards:** AX, MC, VI.
                                                                                                     ⊠

DELTA —See Vancouver p. 582.

DUNCAN pop. 4,699

———— **WHERE TO STAY** ————

BEST WESTERN COWICHAN VALLEY INN   *Book at aaa.com*   Phone: (250)748-2722
(CAA) [SAVE]   6/27-9/5   1P: $105-$129   2P: $111-$135   XP: $6   F16
               4/16-6/26 & 9/6-2/28   1P: $95-$119   2P: $101-$125   XP: $6   F16
▼▼ ▼▼   3/1-4/15   1P: $89-$115   2P: $95-$119   XP: $6   F16
               Location: 3 km n. 6474 Trans-Canada Hwy 1 V9L 6C6. Fax: 250/748-2207. **Facility:** 42 one-bedroom standard
Small-scale Hotel units. 2 stories (no elevator), interior corridors. **Parking:** on-site. **Terms:** small pets only. **Amenities:** voice
               mail, irons, hair dryers. **Dining:** 6:30 am-2 & 5-9 pm, cocktails. **Pool(s):** small heated outdoor. **Leisure**
Activities: limited exercise equipment. **Guest Services:** valet laundry. **Business Services:** meeting rooms. **Cards:** AX, CB,
DC, DS, JC, MC, VI. **Special Amenities:** free local telephone calls and free newspaper.
                                                                                            SOME UNITS
        [S/D] [🛏] [🍴] [Y] [🐟] [📷] [DATA PORT] [⊟] [▭] / [⊠] [VCR] /

FALCON NEST MOTEL   Phone: (250)748-8188
▼▼▼   6/1-9/30   1P: $54-$61   2P: $60-$67   XP: $10
◆   3/1-5/31 & 10/1-2/28   1P: $44-$51   2P: $50-$57   XP: $10
Motel   **Location:** 1.5 km n. 5867 Trans-Canada Hwy 1 V9L 3R9. Fax: 250/748-7829. **Facility:** 24 one-bedroom standard
           units, some with efficiencies or kitchens. 2 stories (no elevator), exterior corridors. **Parking:** on-site.
Terms: office hours 8 am-midnight, weekly rates available, small pets only ($7 extra charge). **Amenities:** hair dryers. **Pool(s):**
small heated outdoor. **Cards:** MC, VI.
                                                                                            SOME UNITS
        [ASK] [S/D] [🛏] [🍴+] [🐟] [DATA PORT] [▭] / [⊠] [AC] [⊟] /
                       FEE

THUNDERBIRD MOTOR INN   Phone: (250)748-8192
▼▼▼   6/16-9/30   1P: $69-$74   2P: $79-$84   XP: $10   F12
           3/1-6/15   1P: $62-$67   2P: $72-$77   XP: $10   F12
Motel   10/1-2/28   1P: $59-$64   2P: $69-$74   XP: $8   F12
           Location: Trans-Canada Hwy 1, just e on James St. 5849 York Rd V9L 3S3. Fax: 250/748-7360. **Facility:** 32 one-
bedroom standard units, some with efficiencies. 2 stories (no elevator), exterior corridors. **Parking:** on-site. **Terms:** office hours
8 am-11 pm. **Guest Services:** coin laundry. **Cards:** AX, MC, VI.
                                                                                            SOME UNITS
        [ASK] [S/D] [🍴] [📷] [▭] / [⊠] [⊟] /

TRAVELODGE SILVER BRIDGE INN DUNCAN   *Book at aaa.com*   Phone: (250)748-4311
▼▼▼▼   5/1-9/30   1P: $99-$109   2P: $109-$119   XP: $10   F12
           3/1-4/30 & 10/1-2/28   1P: $89-$99   2P: $99-$109   XP: $10   F12
Small-scale Hotel **Location:** Just n of the Silver Bridge. 140 Trans-Canada Hwy 1 V9L 3P7. Fax: 250/748-1774. **Facility:** 33 one-
           bedroom standard units, some with efficiencies, kitchens and/or whirlpools. 2 stories (no elevator), exterior
corridors. **Parking:** on-site. **Terms:** cancellation fee imposed, pets ($10 extra charge). **Amenities:** irons, hair dryers. **Guest
Services:** valet laundry. **Business Services:** conference facilities. **Cards:** AX, DC, MC, VI.
                                                                                            SOME UNITS
        [ASK] [S/D] [🍴] [Y] [📷] [DATA PORT] [⊟] [▱] [▭] / [⊠] /
                       FEE

———— **WHERE TO DINE** ————

DOGHOUSE A FAMILY RESTAURANT   **Lunch:** $6-$10   **Dinner:** $7-$13   **Phone:** 250/746-4614
▼▼ ▼▼   **Location:** Corner of Trunk Rd and Trans-Canada Hwy 1. 271 Trans-Canada Hwy 1 V9L 3R1. **Hours:** 6 am-10 pm.
           Closed: 12/25. **Features:** You'll enjoy the quality home-style cooking, generous family servings and
Canadian   reasonable prices at this restaurant, which has been in business since 1955. Known locally for their special
           fish 'n' chips, they also offer veal cutlets and homemade desserts. Casual dress; cocktails. **Parking:** on-site.
Cards: AX, MC, VI.
                                                                                                     ⊠

ENDERBY pop. 2,818

---- WHERE TO STAY ----

HOWARD JOHNSON INN FORTUNES LANDING *Book at aaa.com* Phone: (250)838-6825

(CAA) (SAVE) 5/16-9/16   1P: $79-$99   2P: $89-$109   XP: $10   F17
▼▼ ▼▼   3/1-5/15 & 9/17-2/28   1P: $69-$89   2P: $79-$99   XP: $10   F17
Location: 1 km n on Hwy 97A. 1510 George St V0E 1V0 (Box 168). Fax: 250/838-6887. **Facility:** 32 units. 31 one-bedroom standard units. 1 two-bedroom suite with kitchen. 2 stories (no elevator), exterior corridors.
Small-scale Hotel **Parking:** on-site. **Terms:** small pets only ($5 extra charge, in smoking units). **Dining:** 7 am-9 pm, cocktails. **Pool(s):** heated outdoor. **Leisure Activities:** whirlpool. **Business Services:** meeting rooms. **Cards:** AX, DC, MC, VI. **Special Amenities:** free local telephone calls and free newspaper.

SOME UNITS
[S/D] [🛏] [🍴] [Y] [🌊] [DATA PORT] [▭] / [✕] [🛢] [📷] /
FEE

FAIRMONT HOT SPRINGS pop. 429

---- WHERE TO STAY ----

FAIRMONT HOT SPRINGS RESORT   Phone: (250)345-6311

▼▼ ▲▲▲▼   5/20-10/9   1P: $169-$209   2P: $169-$209   XP: $6   F5
   3/18-5/19   1P: $129-$179   2P: $129-$179   XP: $6   F5
Resort   3/1-3/17 & 10/10-2/28   1P: $109-$169   2P: $109-$169   XP: $6   F5
Large-scale Hotel **Location:** 1.6 km e off Hwy 93 and 95. 5225 Fairmont Resort Rd V0B 1L0 (PO Box 10). Fax: 250/345-6616. **Facility:** The resort's outstanding feature is an area with natural hot-spring pools on its landscaped grounds. Smoke free premises. 140 units. 125 one- and 4 two-bedroom standard units, some with efficiencies. 6 one-bedroom suites ($241-$299). 5 cottages ($169-$219). 3 stories, interior/exterior corridors. **Parking:** on-site, winter plug-ins. **Terms:** check-in 4 pm, 3 day cancellation notice, package plans. **Amenities:** voice mail, irons, hair dryers. **Leisure Activities:** saunas, fishing, 2 tennis courts, cross country skiing, recreation programs in summer, jogging, playground, spa. *Fee:* golf-36 holes, miniature golf, downhill skiing, horseback riding. **Guest Services:** gift shop, coin laundry. **Business Services:** conference facilities. **Cards:** AX, DC, DS, MC, VI. *(See color ad below)*

[🔪] [🍴] [Y] [🏊] [✕] [DATA PORT] [🛢] [▭]

FANNY BAY pop. 744

---- WHERE TO STAY ----

SHIPS POINT INN   Phone: (250)335-1004

(CAA) (SAVE) 5/31-9/30   1P: $41-$53   2P: $41-$53
▼▼ ▼▼▼   3/1-5/30 & 10/1-2/28   1P: $38-$45   2P: $38-$45
Location: Hwy 19, exit 87 to Hwy 19A, 7 km n, then 3 km e, follow signs. 7584 Ships Point Rd V0R 1W0. Fax: 250/335-1014. **Facility:** This secluded property is at the water's edge of a bay that is frequented by Bed & Breakfast resident seals and otters. Smoke free premises. 6 one-bedroom standard units. 2 stories (no elevator), interior corridors. *Bath:* combo or shower only. **Parking:** on-site. **Terms:** office hours 8 am-10 pm, age restrictions may apply, 7 day cancellation notice, package plans. **Amenities:** hair dryers. **Leisure Activities:** whirlpool. **Cards:** AX, MC, VI. **Special Amenities:** free full breakfast and free newspaper.

[S/D] [✕] [🍴] [W] [Z]

FERNIE pop. 4,611

---- WHERE TO STAY ----

BEST WESTERN FERNIE MOUNTAIN LODGE *Book at aaa.com*   Phone: (250)423-5500

(CAA) (SAVE) 3/1-3/28   1P: $131-$279   2P: $131-$279   XP: $10   F16
▼▼ ▼▼▼   3/29-12/18   1P: $97-$279   2P: $97-$279   XP: $10   F16
   12/19-2/28   1P: $131   2P: $131   XP: $10   F16
Location: Hwy 3, exit 7th Ave, on Hwy 3; east end of Fernie. 1622 7th Ave V0B 1M0 (PO Box 2680).
Small-scale Hotel Fax: 250/423-5501. **Facility:** 95 units. 85 one-bedroom standard units, some with efficiencies and/or whirlpools. 10 one-bedroom suites, some with efficiencies and/or whirlpools. 3 stories, interior corridors. **Parking:** on-site, winter plug-ins. **Terms:** cancellation fee imposed, pets ($20 fee, in smoking units). **Amenities:** high-speed Internet, voice mail, irons, hair dryers. **Dining:** 6:30 am-11 pm, cocktails. **Pool(s):** small heated indoor. **Leisure Activities:** whirlpools, exercise room. **Guest Services:** gift shop, valet and coin laundry. **Business Services:** meeting rooms, PC (fee). **Cards:** AX, DC, MC, VI. **Special Amenities:** free newspaper and early check-in/late check-out.

SOME UNITS
[S/D] [🛏] [🍴] [Y] [🌊] [📺] [DATA PORT] [🛢] [📷] [▭] / [✕] /
FEE

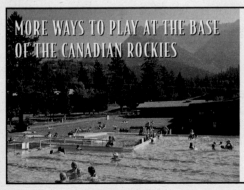

FERNIE LOG INN   Phone: (250)423-6222

◆◆◆
Motel

All Year   1P: $59-$85   2P: $65-$95   XP: $10   F6
Location: 1.8 km e on Hwy 3. Located adjacent to information centre. 141 Commerce Rd V0B 1M5.
Fax: 250/423-6221. **Facility:** Smoke free premises. 6 one-bedroom standard units. 2 stories (no elevator),
exterior corridors. **Parking:** on-site, winter plug-ins. **Terms:** office hours 2 pm-10:30 pm, check-in 4 pm,
weekly rates available, package plans, pets ($10 fee). **Leisure Activities:** whirlpool. **Cards:** MC, VI.

(ASK) (S/D) ▭ ✕ (AC) (📹) (DATA PORT) ▯ ▭ ▭
FEE

**LIZARD CREEK LODGE AND CONDOMINIUMS AT
FERNIE ALPINE RESORT**   Phone: 250/423-2057

(CAA) (SAVE)
▽▼▽▼▽

Condominium

3/1-4/17	1P: $195-$485	2P: $195-$485	XP: $25 F16
6/27-9/6	1P: $129-$345	2P: $129-$345	XP: $25 F16
4/18-6/26 & 9/7-2/28	1P: $95-$255	2P: $95-$255	XP: $25 F16

Location: 6.5 km w on Hwy 3, 1.4 km on Ski Area Rd, follow signs. 5346 Highline Dr V0B 1M6. Fax: 250/423-2058.
Facility: Featuring ski-in/ski-out access, this luxurious property offers a mix of lodge rooms in the main
building as well as upscale, fully equipped condos. Designated smoking area. 99 units. 7 one-bedroom
standard units with kitchens. 47 one-, 34 two- and 11 three-bedroom suites with kitchens. 3 stories, interior corridors. **Parking:**
on-site. **Terms:** check-in 4 pm, 2 night minimum stay - seasonal, 30 day cancellation notice, [AP] meal plan available, package
plans. **Amenities:** dual phone lines, voice mail, irons, hair dryers. **Dining:** Lizard Creek Lodge Dining Room, see separate
listing. **Pool(s):** small heated outdoor. **Leisure Activities:** whirlpools, steamroom, cross country skiing, recreation programs,
hiking trails, exercise room. **Fee:** downhill skiing, snowmobiling, bicycles, horseback riding, massage. **Guest Services:** gift
shop, valet and coin laundry, area transportation-Fernie townsite. **Business Services:** meeting rooms, PC (fee). **Cards:** AX,
MC, VI.

(❚❙) (🚲) (✕) (✕) (VCR) (📹) (DATA PORT) ▯ ▭ ▭

PARK PLACE LODGE   *Book at aaa.com*   Phone: (250)423-6871

(CAA) (SAVE)
▽▼▽▼▽

Small-scale Hotel

3/1-4/2 & 12/23-2/28	1P: $110-$204	2P: $129-$229	XP: $10 D17
4/3-12/22	1P: $80-$164	2P: $99-$189	XP: $10 D17

Location: At 7th St. 742 Hwy 3 V0B 1M0 (PO Box 2560). Fax: 250/423-3773. **Facility:** 64 one-bedroom standard
units, some with efficiencies or kitchens. 2 stories, interior corridors. **Parking:** on-site, winter plug-ins.
Terms: check-in 4 pm, cancellation fee imposed, package plans, small pets only. **Amenities:** DVD players,
video games, CD players, high-speed Internet, dual phone lines, voice mail, irons, hair dryers. **Dining:** 6
am-9 pm, cocktails. **Pool(s):** small heated indoor. **Leisure Activities:** saunas, whirlpool, bicycles, hiking trails, exercise room.
Guest Services: sundries, valet laundry, area transportation-within 2 km. **Business Services:** meeting rooms. **Cards:** AX, DC,
DS, MC, VI. **Special Amenities:** free local telephone calls and free room upgrade (subject to availability with advance
reservations).

SOME UNITS

(S/D) ▭ (❚❙) (🍸) (🚲) (✕) (📹) (DATA PORT) ▯ ▭ ▭ /✕/

RIVERSIDE MOUNTAIN LODGE   *Book at aaa.com*   Phone: (250)423-5000

CAA SAVE

Resort
Condominium

3/1-4/2 & 1/22-2/28	1P: $69-$159	2P: $69-$159	XP: $10 F10
4/3-1/21	1P: $59-$139	2P: $59-$139	XP: $10 F10

Location: Hwy 3, 2 km w. 100 Riverside Way V0B 1M1. Fax: 250/423-5067. **Facility:** Set just outside of town along the river, this luxurious condo property offers many services found at full-scale hotels. Smoke free premises. 231 units. 121 one-bedroom standard units. 11 one-, 66 two- and 33 three-bedroom suites ($139-$978), some with kitchens and/or whirlpools. 3 stories, interior/exterior corridors. **Parking:** on-site, winter plug-ins. **Terms:** check-in 4 pm, 30 day cancellation notice, in winter-fee imposed, pets ($25 fee, in designated units). **Amenities:** video library (fee), voice mail, irons. *Some:* video games, CD players, high-speed Internet, hair dryers. **Dining:** 7 am-11 pm, cocktails. **Pool(s):** heated indoor. **Leisure Activities:** sauna, whirlpools, waterslide, fishing, downhill & cross country skiing, ice skating, rental bicycles, hiking trails, playground, exercise room, spa, movie theatre. *Fee:* game room. **Guest Services:** gift shop, coin laundry, area transportation-ski hills. **Business Services:** meeting rooms, business center. **Cards:** AX, MC, VI. *(See color ad p 469)*

SOME UNITS

[icons] FEE

SUPER 8 MOTEL-FERNIE   Phone: 250/423-6788

Small-scale Hotel

3/1-3/31 & 12/21-2/28	1P: $92	2P: $99	XP: $8 F12
4/1-12/20	1P: $80	2P: $87	XP: $8 F12

Location: 1.5 km w. 2021 Hwy 3 V0B 1M1. Fax: 250/423-6799. **Facility:** 43 one-bedroom standard units. 3 stories, interior corridors. **Parking:** on-site, winter plug-ins. **Terms:** pets ($6 fee, $25 deposit, in smoking units). **Leisure Activities:** whirlpool. *Fee:* game room. **Guest Services:** coin laundry. **Business Services:** meeting rooms, PC (fee). **Cards:** AX, DS, MC, VI.

SOME UNITS

[icons] ASK ... FEE

——— *The following lodgings were either not evaluated or did not* ———
meet AAA rating requirements but are listed for your information only.

KERRIN LEE-GARTNER'S SNOW CREEK LODGE   Phone: 250/423-7669

[fyi] Not evaluated. **Location:** Hwy 3, follow signs for Fernie Alpine Resort. 5258 Highline Dr V0B 1M1. Facilities, services, and decor characterize a mid-range property.

KING FIR LODGE   Phone: 250/423-6878

[fyi] Not evaluated. **Location:** Hwy 3, follow signs for Fernie Alpine Resort. 4559 Timberline Crescent V0B 1M6. Facilities, services, and decor characterize a mid-range property.

TIMBERLINE LODGE CONDOMINIUMS   Phone: 250/423-6878

[fyi] Not evaluated. **Location:** Hwy 3, follow signs for Fernie Alpine Resort. 4559 Timberline Crescent V0B 1M1. Facilities, services, and decor characterize a mid-range property.

——— **WHERE TO DINE** ———

LIZARD CREEK LODGE DINING ROOM   Lunch: $8-$14   Dinner: $20-$25   Phone: 250/423-2057

Canadian

Location: 6.5 km w on Hwy 3, 1.4 km on Ski Area Rd, follow signs; in Lizard Creek Lodge and Condominiums at Fernie Alpine Resort. 5346 Highline Dr V0B 1M1. **Hours:** 7 am-11 pm; 8 am-9 pm 5/1-11/30. **Reservations:** suggested, winter. **Features:** Considered to be one of the best places in Fernie, this upscale dining room is a superb place for a fine meal. With a regional menu and creative dishes, you'll enjoy a great meal after a day on the ski hill. Casual dress; cocktails. **Parking:** on-site. **Cards:** AX, MC, VI.

MUGSHOTS BISTRO   Lunch: $4-$8   Dinner: $4-$8   Phone: 250/423-8018

Coffee/Espresso

Location: Corner of 5th St and 3rd Ave; downtown. 592 3rd Ave V0B 1M0. **Hours:** 7 am-9 pm; to 6 pm 5/1-11/1. Closed: 12/25; also Sun 5/1-11/1. **Features:** Quirky and eclectic best describes the funky coffeehouse, which prepares a wide selection of soups, sandwiches, ground coffees and sumptuous desserts. The downtown spot is popular with locals and visitors alike not only for its hearty, healthy food but also for the Internet cafe. **Parking:** street. **Cards:** VI.

THE OLD ELEVATOR   Dinner: $13-$30   Phone: 250/423-7115

Canadian

Location: 1st Ave and 2nd St. 291 1st Ave V0B 1M0. **Hours:** 5 pm-10:30 pm; to 10 pm 6/1-12/1. Closed: Sun & Mon 6/1-12/1. **Reservations:** suggested. **Features:** On the outskirts is the town's original grain elevator, which dates back to 1908. Today, it houses an intimate restaurant, which presents a menu with regional flair. Representative of taste bud-tempting choices are preparations of salmon, veal or even Alaskan cod. Selections change seasonally. Wood accents lend to an atmosphere of coziness, and guests can check out the original grain shaft. Casual dress; cocktails. **Parking:** street. **Cards:** AX, MC, VI. **Historic**

YAMAGOYA   Dinner: $8-$11   Phone: 250/259-4141

Japanese

Location: Just n of Hwy 3 at 7th St. 741 7th Ave V0B 1M0. **Hours:** 5 pm-10 pm. Closed major holidays. **Reservations:** not accepted. **Features:** Although classified as a sushi restaurant, this place also prepares other Japanese dishes, including teppanyaki, gyoza and spring rolls. The dining room is upscale in decor, yet casual in nature. At the heart of the menu are varied sushi selections, as well as traditional sashimi, nigiri and rolls. Casual dress; cocktails. **Parking:** street. **Cards:** MC, VI.

——— *The following restaurant has not been evaluated by AAA* ———
but is listed for your information only.

THE CURRY BOWL   Phone: 250/423-2695

[fyi] Not evaluated. **Location:** Hwy 3, across from arena at 9th St. 931 7th Ave. **Features:** A mix of Thai, Japanese and Asian cuisine awaits at the popular spot. Reservations are not accepted, and the small restaurant fills up quickly. After a day on the slopes, it is best to arrive early.

FIELD

KICKING HORSE LODGE
Phone: 250/343-6303

	6/1-2/28	1P: $145-$180	2P: $145-$180	XP: $15	D11
	5/1-5/31	1P: $95-$150	2P: $95-$150	XP: $10	D11
Small-scale Hotel	3/1-4/30	1P: $70-$115	2P: $70-$115	XP: $10	D11

Location: Centre. 100 Centre St V0A 1G0 (PO Box 174). Fax: 250/343-6355. **Facility:** Designated smoking area. 14 one-bedroom standard units, some with efficiencies, kitchens and/or whirlpools. 3 stories (no elevator), exterior corridors. **Parking:** on-site, winter plug-ins. **Terms:** office hours 7:30 am-11 pm, check-in 4 pm, 2 night minimum stay - seasonal, 7 day cancellation notice-fee imposed, package plans. **Leisure Activities:** cross country skiing, hiking trails, jogging. **Guest Services:** coin laundry. **Cards:** MC, VI.

SOME UNITS

──────── The following lodging was either not evaluated or did not ────────
meet AAA rating requirements but is listed for your information only.

EMERALD LAKE LODGE & CONFERENCE CENTRE
Phone: 250/343-6321

[fyi] Not evaluated. **Location:** Hwy 1, exit Emerald Lake Rd, 8 km n. Emerald Lake Rd V0A 1G0 (Box 10). Facilities, services, and decor characterize a mid-range property.

TRUFFLE PIGS CAFE
Lunch: $4-$8   **Dinner:** $9-$15   **Phone:** 250/343-6462

Canadian

Location: Centre; across from Kicking Horse Lodge. 318 Stephen Ave V0A 1G0. **Hours:** 8 am-10 pm; 8:30 am-7 pm in winter. Closed: 12/25. **Features:** The funky cafe has a wonderful selection of home-cooked food, ranging from delicious baked goods to sandwiches to all-day breakfast items. Guests can enjoy a casual meal in the contemporary dining room, which features a light, airy decor. Casual dress; beer & wine only. **Parking:** street. **Cards:** AX, MC, VI.

FORT ST. JOHN pop. 16,034

BEST WESTERN COACHMAN INN   *Book at aaa.com*
Phone: (250)787-0651

(AAA) (SAVE)

| All Year | 1P: $110 | 2P: $115 | XP: $5 | F17 |

Location: 2 km s on Hwy 97. 8540 Alaska Rd V1J 5L6. Fax: 250/787-5266. **Facility:** 70 one-bedroom standard units. 2 stories (no elevator), interior corridors. **Parking:** on-site, winter plug-ins. **Terms:** [BP] meal plan available, small pets only ($15 extra charge, in designated units). **Amenities:** high-speed Internet, irons, hair dryers. *Some:* DVD players. **Dining:** 6 am-11 pm, cocktails. **Leisure Activities:** sauna, whirlpool, limited exercise equipment. **Business Services:** meeting rooms, PC. **Cards:** AX, DC, DS, MC, VI. **Special Amenities:** early check-in/late check-out.

Small-scale Hotel

SOME UNITS
FEE

QUALITY INN NORTHERN GRAND   *Book at aaa.com*
Phone: (250)787-0521

(AAA) (SAVE)

| All Year | 1P: $99-$119 | 2P: $109-$129 | XP: $10 | F17 |

Location: Centre. 9830 100th Ave V1J 1Y5. Fax: 250/787-2648. **Facility:** 125 units. 124 one-bedroom standard units, some with whirlpools. 1 one-bedroom suite. 6 stories, interior corridors. **Parking:** on-site, winter plug-ins. **Terms:** cancellation fee imposed, package plans, pets ($15 fee). **Amenities:** voice mail, irons, hair dryers. *Some:* CD players, dual phone lines. **Dining:** 6 am-10 pm, Sat & Sun from 8 am, cocktails. **Pool(s):** small heated indoor. **Leisure Activities:** sauna, whirlpool, exercise room. **Guest Services:** valet laundry. **Business Services:** conference facilities. **Cards:** AX, DC, DS, MC, VI.

Large-scale Hotel

SOME UNITS
FEE

RAMADA LIMITED   *Book at aaa.com*
Phone: (250)787-0779

| | 1/1-2/28 [ECP] | 1P: $107-$113 | 2P: $107-$123 | XP: $10 | F18 |
| | 3/1-12/31 [ECP] | 1P: $105-$111 | 2P: $105-$121 | XP: $10 | F18 |

Small-scale Hotel

Location: Corner of 100th Ave; centre of downtown. 10103 98th Ave V1J 1P8. Fax: 250/787-0709. **Facility:** 73 one-bedroom standard units, some with efficiencies and/or whirlpools. 3 stories (no elevator), interior corridors. *Bath:* combo or shower only. **Parking:** on-site, winter plug-ins. **Terms:** check-in 4 pm, small pets only ($10 extra charge). **Amenities:** high-speed Internet, voice mail, irons, hair dryers. **Leisure Activities:** whirlpool, exercise room. **Guest Services:** valet and coin laundry. **Business Services:** meeting rooms. **Cards:** AX, DC, DS, MC, VI.

SOME UNITS
FEE

SUPER 8 MOTEL-FORT ST. JOHN
Phone: 250/785-7588

| All Year | 1P: $109-$275 | 2P: $109-$275 |

Location: Just s on Hwy 97 (Alaska Hwy). 9500 Alaska Hwy V1J 6S7. Fax: 250/785-1118. **Facility:** 94 units. 86 one-bedroom standard units. 8 one-bedroom suites, some with whirlpools. 4 stories, interior corridors. *Bath:* combo or shower only. **Parking:** on-site, winter plug-ins. **Terms:** 7 day cancellation notice, package plans, pets ($10 fee). **Amenities:** high-speed Internet, voice mail, irons, hair dryers. **Pool(s):** small heated indoor. **Leisure Activities:** whirlpool, waterslide, exercise room. **Guest Services:** valet and coin laundry, area transportation. **Business Services:** meeting rooms, business center. **Cards:** AX, DC, DS, MC, VI.

Small-scale Hotel

SOME UNITS
FEE

FORT STEELE

―――――― WHERE TO STAY ――――――

BULL RIVER GUEST RANCH
Phone: 250/429-3760

(CAA) (SAVE)

▼▼▼ ▼▼▼
Ranch

| 5/1-12/31 | 1P: $125 | 2P: $125-$145 | XP: $20 | F15 |

Location: Hwy 95, 21.9 km se of town on Ft Steele-Wardner Rd, 12 km ne on gravel road, follow signs; Hwy 3 W, 41 km e of Cranbrook, use Ft Steele Rd. Located in a quiet, rustic area. (PO Box 133, CRANBROOK). Fax: 250/429-4045. **Facility:** Smoke free premises. 7 cabins. 1 story, exterior corridors. *Bath:* shower only. **Parking:** on-site. **Terms:** open 5/1-12/31, 2 night minimum stay, 14 day cancellation notice-fee imposed, weekly rates available. **Leisure Activities:** sauna, whirlpool, boating, canoeing, fishing, water rafting, badminton, barbecue area, bicycles, hiking trails, jogging, horseshoes, volleyball. *Fee:* horseback riding. **Guest Services:** coin laundry. **Business Services:** meeting rooms. **Cards:** VI.

🛏 ✕ ✕ 🅐 🎞 ☎ 🗄 🖥 🖳

GALIANO ISLAND —*See Gulf Islands National Park Reserve p. 476.*

GIBSONS pop. 3,906

―――――― WHERE TO STAY ――――――

BONNIEBROOK LODGE BED & BREAKFAST
Phone: 604/886-2887

▼▼▼▼▼▼
Country Inn

| 3/1-1/1 & 2/10-2/28 [BP] | 2P: $150-$190 | XP: $30 | D11 |

Location: Hwy 101, 6 km s on Veterans Rd to Fichett St, just sw to King St, 1 km sw to Chaster, then 8 km sw to Gowers Pt Rd, follow signs. 1532 Oceanbeach Esplanade, RR #5 V0N 1V5. Fax: 604/886-8853. **Facility:** The renovated guest rooms in this 1922 lodge include amenities such as hot tubs and gas fireplaces; breakfast is delivered to each room. Smoke free premises. 7 one-bedroom standard units with whirlpools. 3 stories (no elevator), interior/exterior corridors. **Parking:** on-site. **Terms:** open 3/1-1/1 & 2/10-2/28, office hours 8 am-11 pm, 7 day cancellation notice. **Amenities:** video library, CD players, hair dryers. **Dining:** Chez Philippe, see separate listing. **Cards:** AX, DC, MC, VI.

🍴 ✕ 🅐 🆅🅲🆁 ☎ 🗄 🖳

CEDARS INN
Phone: (604)886-3008

(CAA) (SAVE)

▼▼▼ ▼▼
Motel

6/21-9/5		2P: $116-$136	XP: $10	F12
9/6-11/30		2P: $116-$126	XP: $10	F12
3/1-6/20		2P: $106-$126	XP: $10	F12
12/1-2/28		2P: $96-$116	XP: $10	F12

Location: Hwy 101 and Shaw Rd; 6 km n from ferry terminal. Located opposite Sunnycrest Mall. 895 Gibsons Way V0N 1V8 (PO Box 739, V0n 1V0). Fax: 604/886-3046. **Facility:** 45 one-bedroom standard units, some with efficiencies. 2 stories (no elevator), interior/exterior corridors. *Bath:* combo or shower only. **Parking:** on-site. **Terms:** office hours 7 am-11 pm, cancellation fee imposed, package plans, small pets ok ($15 extra charge). **Amenities:** irons, hair dryers. **Dining:** 11 am-10 pm, cocktails. **Pool(s):** heated outdoor. **Leisure Activities:** sauna, whirlpool, limited exercise equipment. **Guest Services:** valet laundry. **Business Services:** meeting rooms. **Cards:** AX, MC, VI. **Special Amenities:** free local telephone calls.

SOME UNITS

🆂🅓 🛏 🍴 ➤ ✕ 🅳🅐🆃🅰 🖳 / ✕ 🖥
FEE

―――――― WHERE TO DINE ――――――

CHEZ PHILIPPE
Dinner: $18-$27
Phone: 604/886-2188

▼▼▼ ▼▼
French

Location: Hwy 101, 6 km s on Veterans Rd to Fichett St, just sw to King St, 1 km sw to Chaster, then 8 km sw to Gowers Pt Rd, follow signs; in Bonniebrook Lodge Bed & Breakfast. 1532 Ocean Beach Esplanade RR5 V0N 1V5. **Hours:** 5:30 pm-8:30 pm. Closed: 3/28, 10/10, 12/25, 12/26; also Tues-Thurs 9/15-5/18 & 1/1-2/11. **Reservations:** required. **Features:** Located in a stately bed and breakfast and across the street from a public beach, it features a pleasant yet cozy dining experience where the large windows overlook a special view of the ocean, during the spring and summer watch as the cruise ships pass by on their way to Alaska. Choose from a la cart menu items like breast of chicken or steak or try the table d'hote selection that is offered nightly. Nice selection of reasonable priced wines. Casual dress; cocktails. **Parking:** on-site. **Cards:** AX, DC, MC, VI. **Country Inn**

🅐 ✕

HAUS UROPA RESTAURANT
Lunch: $10-$14
Dinner: $12-$20
Phone: 604/886-8326

▼▼▼ ▼▼
Swiss

Location: Hwy 101, just s on School Rd (towards ocean), then just w. 426 Gower Pointe Rd V0N 1V0. **Hours:** 11:30 am-2 & 5-10 pm, Sun from 5 pm. Closed major holidays; also Tues & Wed. **Reservations:** required. **Features:** The charming Bavarian chalet-style restaurant serves a mix of Swiss and German dishes, along the lines of Wiener Schnitzel, bratwurst and weisswurst. Daily lunch specials are popular. The owner/chef makes sure everything served is of high quality. Casual dress; cocktails. **Parking:** on-site. **Cards:** MC, VI.

🅐 ✕

MOLLY'S REACH RESTAURANT
Lunch: $6-$8
Dinner: $10-$14
Phone: 604/886-9710

▼▼▼
Canadian

Location: School Rd and Gibsons Way; on the waterfront. **Hours:** 7 am-9 pm; from 8 am 10/15-5/1. Closed: 12/25. **Reservations:** accepted. **Features:** The famous landmark originally was built as a set for "The Beachcombers," a popular CBC TV series of the late 70s and early 80s. Today, it's a family restaurant that serves a mix of seafood, steaks, sandwiches and soups. This place is well worth the stop for the memories alone. Cocktails. **Parking:** on-site. **Cards:** MC, VI.

🅐 ✕

GOLD BRIDGE

―――――― WHERE TO STAY ――――――

MORROW CHALETS
Phone: 250/238-2462

▼▼▼ ▼▼
Cottage

| All Year | 1P: $200 | 2P: $200 | XP: $25 | F16 |

Location: 8 km n from the Tyaughton Lake turnoff, follow signs. (General Delivery). Fax: 250/238-2462. **Facility:** Fully self-contained log cabins on Tyaughton Lake, these lodgings can accommodate six or more persons; summer and winter activities are available. 4 cottages, some with whirlpools. 2 stories (no elevator), exterior corridors. **Parking:** on-site. **Terms:** office hours 8 am-8 pm, check-in 4 pm, 30 day cancellation notice-fee imposed, weekly rates available. **Amenities:** hair dryers. **Guest Services:** complimentary laundry. **Cards:** MC, VI.

(ASK) 🆂🅓 🛏 ✕ 🅐 🕅 🗄 🖥

TYAX MOUNTAIN LAKE RESORT

▼▼▼ ▼▼▼

Resort
Small-scale Hotel

Phone: (250)238-2221

| | 1P: $118-$148 | 2P: $134-$168 | XP: $24 | F12 |

All Year
Location: 8 km n from the Tyaughton Lake turnoff, follow signs. Tyaughton Lake Rd V0K 1P0. Fax: 250/238-2528. **Facility:** A log lodge and log chalets are featured at this resort offering family-oriented wilderness activities. 34 units. 29 one-bedroom standard units. 5 three-bedroom suites with kitchens, some with whirlpools. 3 stories (no elevator), interior corridors. **Parking:** on-site. **Terms:** office hours 8 am-10 pm, check-in 4 pm, 2 night minimum stay - seasonal, 30 day cancellation notice, [AP] & [MAP] meal plans available, package plans. **Amenities:** voice mail, hair dryers. **Leisure Activities:** sauna, whirlpool, rental boats, canoeing, paddleboats, fishing, tennis court, cross country skiing, ice skating, tobogganing, hiking trails, playground. *Fee:* snowmobiling, bicycles, horseback riding. **Guest Services:** gift shop, coin laundry. **Business Services:** meeting rooms. **Cards:** AX, MC, VI.

SOME UNITS
(ASK) (SD) (🍴) (Y) (X) (AC) / (X) (🔌) (🖥) /

GOLDEN pop. 4,020

—————— **WHERE TO STAY** ——————

BEST WESTERN MOUNTAIN VIEW INN — *Book at aaa.com*

Phone: (250)344-2333

(CAA) (SAVE)
▼▼▼ ▼▼

Small-scale Hotel

	7/1-8/31	1P: $129-$189	2P: $129-$189	XP: $15	F16
	9/1-11/30	1P: $119-$189	2P: $119-$189	XP: $10	F16
	12/1-2/28	1P: $109-$189	2P: $119-$189	XP: $10	F16
	3/1-6/30	1P: $109-$159	2P: $109-$189	XP: $10	F16

Location: On Trans-Canada Hwy 1, south service road; 0.7 km w of jct Hwy 95 and Trans-Canada Hwy 1. 1024 11th St N V0A 1H0 (PO Box 2400). Fax: 250/344-2317. **Facility:** 72 one-bedroom standard units. 3 stories, interior corridors. **Parking:** on-site, winter plug-ins. **Terms:** cancellation fee imposed, pets ($20 fee). **Amenities:** video games, high-speed Internet, irons, hair dryers. **Pool(s):** heated indoor. **Leisure Activities:** ATV tours. *Fee:* whitewater rafting, snowmobile tours. **Guest Services:** valet and coin laundry. **Cards:** AX, CB, DC, DS, MC, VI.

SOME UNITS
(SD) (🛏) (🍴) (🏊) (🛗) (X) (🎥) (DATA PORT) (🔌) (🖥) / (X) (VCR) FEE

COLUMBIA VALLEY LODGE

▼▼▼

Small-scale Hotel

Phone: 250/348-2508

| | 4/15-10/31 [ECP] | 1P: $60-$90 | 2P: $70-$105 | XP: $15 | F6 |

Location: 23 km s. 2304 Hwy 95 S V0A 1H0 (PO Box 2669). Fax: 250/348-2505. **Facility:** 12 one-bedroom standard units. 2 stories (no elevator), interior/exterior corridors. *Bath:* combo or shower only. **Parking:** on-site, winter plug-ins. **Terms:** open 4/15-10/31, office hours 7 am-midnight, 3 day cancellation notice-fee imposed, weekly rates available, package plans. **Leisure Activities:** rental canoes. **Business Services:** PC (fee). **Cards:** MC, VI.

SOME UNITS
(ASK) (SD) (🍴) (AC) (CTV) (Z) / (X) /

GOLDEN GATE MOTEL

▼▼▼

Motel

Phone: (250)344-2252

	6/16-9/15	1P: $50-$60	2P: $65-$70	XP: $5	F6
	3/1-6/15	1P: $40-$45	2P: $50-$55	XP: $5	F6
	1/1-2/28	1P: $40-$45	2P: $45-$50	XP: $5	F6
	9/16-12/31	1P: $35-$40	2P: $45-$50	XP: $5	F6

Location: On Trans-Canada Hwy 1, 1.5 km e of jct Hwy 95. 1408 Golden View Rd V0A 1H0 (PO Box 566). Fax: 250/344-2230. **Facility:** 38 one-bedroom standard units. 2 stories (no elevator), exterior corridors. **Parking:** on-site, winter plug-ins. **Terms:** office hours 8 am-11 pm, cancellation fee imposed, package plans, pets ($5 fee, with prior approval). **Cards:** AX, MC, VI.

SOME UNITS
(ASK) (SD) (🛏) (🍴) / (X) (AC) (🔌) /
FEE

GOLDEN RIM MOTOR INN

▼▼▼ ▼▼▼

Motel

Phone: (250)344-2216

	6/1-9/15	1P: $89-$98	2P: $99-$110	XP: $8	F6
	3/1-5/31	1P: $60-$69	2P: $69-$79	XP: $5	F6
	9/16-2/28	1P: $60-$69	2P: $69-$79	XP: $6	F6

Location: 1.5 km e on Trans-Canada Hwy 1 from jct Hwy 95. 1416 Golden View Rd V0A 1H0 (PO Box 510). Fax: 250/344-6673. **Facility:** 81 units. 78 one-bedroom standard units, some with kitchens. 1 one- and 2 two-bedroom suites ($135-$165) with whirlpools. 2-3 stories (no elevator), exterior corridors. **Parking:** on-site, winter plug-ins. **Terms:** office hours 6 am-midnight, cancellation fee imposed, package plans, small pets only ($6 extra charge). **Amenities:** hair dryers. **Pool(s):** heated indoor. **Leisure Activities:** sauna, whirlpool, waterslide. **Guest Services:** coin laundry. **Business Services:** PC. **Cards:** AX, CB, DC, MC, VI.

SOME UNITS
(ASK) (SD) (🛏) (🍴) (🏊) (X) (🎥) (🖥) / (X) (🔌) (🖥) /
FEE

HILLSIDE LODGE & CHALETS

(CAA) (SAVE)
▼▼▼ ▼▼▼

Cabin

Phone: (250)344-7281

	3/1-9/15		2P: $128-$145	XP: $20	
	12/15-1/10		2P: $118-$145	XP: $20	
	1/11-2/28		2P: $118-$135	XP: $20	
	9/16-12/14		2P: $108-$135	XP: $20	

Location: 15 km w on Hwy 1, follow signs n off highway. Located in a quiet area. 1740 Seward Frontage Rd V0A 1H0 (PO Box 2603). Fax: 250/344-7281. **Facility:** Spectacular mountain scenery and the sound of moving water give this lodge's grounds a serene sense of place; offerings include cabins and B&B rooms. Smoke free premises. 12 units. 4 one-bedroom standard units. 8 cabins ($125-$195). 1-2 stories, exterior corridors. *Bath:* combo or shower only. **Parking:** on-site, winter plug-ins. **Terms:** 5 day cancellation notice, pets ($10 deposit, in cabins only). **Amenities:** *Some:* hair dryers. **Leisure Activities:** sauna, whirlpool, steamroom, cross country skiing, hiking trails, limited exercise equipment. *Fee:* massage. **Cards:** DC, MC, VI.

SOME UNITS
(🛏) (X) (X) (AC) (CTV) (Z) (🔌) (🖥) / (TV) (VCR) (🖥) /
FEE

KAPRISTO LODGE

CAA SAVE

Bed & Breakfast

Phone: (250)344-6048

3/1-4/15 & 5/15-11/1 [BP]   1P: $150-$190   2P: $180-$240   XP: $45   D12

Location: Jct Trans-Canada Hwy 1 and 95, 14 km s on Hwy 95, 1 km se on Austin Rd, then 0.7 km se, follow signs. Located in a quiet, secluded area. 1297 Campbell Rd V0A 1H7 (PO Box 90). Fax: 250/344-6755. **Facility:** This B&B is in a picturesque mountain setting and features cozy, comfortable gathering spaces enhanced by sweeping views. Smoke free premises. 6 units. 3 one- and 1 two-bedroom standard units, some with kitchens and/or whirlpools. 2 one-bedroom suites. 2 stories (no elevator), interior corridors. **Parking:** on-site, winter plug-ins. **Terms:** open 3/1-4/15 & 5/15-11/1, 21 day cancellation notice-fee imposed, [AP] meal plan available, package plans, no pets allowed (owner's pets on premises). **Amenities:** video library, hair dryers. *Some:* DVD players. **Dining:** lunch & dinner served to guests upon request. **Leisure Activities:** sauna, outdoor whirlpool, snowshoeing, heliport, hiking trails, basketball. *Fee:* river floating, kayaks, heli-hiking, horseback riding. **Guest Services:** TV in common area. *Fee:* airport transportation-Calgary Airport, area transportation. **Cards:** MC, VI. **Special Amenities: free full breakfast and free local telephone calls.**

SOME UNITS
[icons] FEE

QUANTUM LEAPS LODGE LTD

Small-scale Hotel

Phone: (250)344-2114

All Year   1P: $65-$85   2P: $80-$100   XP: $25

Location: 17 km n of town; from Hwy 1, exit Moberly Branch Rd, 2.1 km ne on Moberly Branch Rd to Golden Donald Upper, 2.7 km e on Golden Donald Upper, then 3.3 km ne. 2119 Blaeberry Rd V0A 1H1. Fax: 250/344-4809. **Facility:** Smoke free premises. 5 units. 3 one- and 1 two-bedroom standard units, some with kitchens. 1 cottage. 2 stories (no elevator), exterior corridors. *Bath:* some shared or private. **Parking:** on-site. **Terms:** check-in 3:30 pm, 2 night minimum stay - weekends, 30 day cancellation notice-fee imposed, weekly rates available, [MAP] meal plan available, package plans, pets ($10 fee). **Amenities:** video library. **Leisure Activities:** sauna, whirlpool, bicycles, hiking trails. *Fee:* massage. **Guest Services:** TV in common area, coin laundry. **Cards:** AX, MC, VI.

SOME UNITS
[icons] FEE / VCR

RAMADA LIMITED   *Book at aaa.com*

CAA SAVE

Small-scale Hotel

Phone: (250)439-1888

6/25-9/10 [CP]	1P: $129-$149	2P: $139-$159	XP: $10	F17
12/16-2/28 [CP]	1P: $109-$139	2P: $119-$149	XP: $10	F17
9/11-12/15 [CP]	1P: $89-$119	2P: $99-$129	XP: $10	F17
3/1-6/24 [CP]	1P: $89-$109	2P: $99-$119	XP: $10	F17

Location: Jct Trans-Canada Hwy 1 and 95, 1 km n. 1311 12th St N (Hwy 1) V0A 1H0 (Box 487). Fax: 250/439-1889. **Facility:** 60 units. 48 one-bedroom standard units, some with kitchens and/or whirlpools. 10 one- and 2 two-bedroom suites ($139-$199). 3 stories, interior corridors. **Parking:** on-site, winter plug-ins. **Terms:** cancellation fee imposed. **Amenities:** voice mail, irons, hair dryers. *Some:* high-speed Internet. **Pool(s):** small heated indoor. **Leisure Activities:** whirlpool. **Guest Services:** coin laundry. **Business Services:** PC. **Cards:** AX, DS, MC, VI. *(See color ad below)*

SOME UNITS
[icons] DATA PORT / X

RONDO MOTEL

CAA SAVE

Motel

Phone: 250/344-5295

6/25-9/5	1P: $70-$78	2P: $80-$88	XP: $8	F12
3/1-6/24	1P: $55-$70	2P: $65-$80	XP: $8	F12
9/6-12/15	1P: $50-$70	2P: $60-$80	XP: $8	F12
12/16-2/28	1P: $55-$65	2P: $65-$75	XP: $8	F12

Location: Jct Trans-Canada Hwy 1 and 95, 2 km s on 10th Ave, just w on Park Dr; downtown. Located just past metal bridge. 824 Park Dr V0A 1H0 (Box 258). Fax: 250/344-2645. **Facility:** 42 units. 34 one- and 8 two-bedroom standard units, some with kitchens. 1-2 stories (no elevator), exterior corridors. **Parking:** on-site, winter plug-ins. **Terms:** office hours 9 am-midnight, pets ($5 fee, in designated units). **Leisure Activities:** sauna, whirlpool. **Business Services:** meeting rooms, PC (fee). **Cards:** AX, MC, VI. **Special Amenities: free local telephone calls.**

SOME UNITS
[icons] FEE / X

——— WHERE TO DINE ———

CEDAR HOUSE CAFE & RESTAURANT **Dinner: $13-$34** **Phone: 250/344-4679**
(CAA)
▽▽▽
Canadian

Location: 7.4 km s of town, just e at Almberg Rd, follow signs. 735 Hefti Rd V0A 1H2. **Hours:** 4:30 pm-10 pm. Closed: 1/1. **Reservations:** suggested. **Features:** Casual mountain dining is what's to be expected at the small, bistro-style restaurant. The cozy, comfortable dining room has many rustic features, yet a surprising elegance. Menu selections ranging from salmon to lamb to other Canadian specialties often incorporate produce grown in the chef's own garden. Service is laid-back and friendly, and even the owner has been known to come out and greet guests. Casual dress; cocktails. **Parking:** on-site. **Cards:** MC, VI. 🎫 ✕

ELEVEN 22 GRILL & LIQUIDS **Dinner: $10-$28** **Phone: 250/344-2443**
▽▽ ▽▽
West Canadian
Cards: MC, VI.

Location: Just e at 12th St; centre. 1122 10th Ave S V0A 1H0. **Hours:** 5 pm-10 pm. Closed: 10/15-11/01. **Reservations:** suggested. **Features:** The charming eatery's International menu lists health-conscious curries, pastas, salads, hummus, tzatziki, spanakopita and burgers, plus fondue is offered weekly in winter. The restored centennial home nurtures a warm, casual ambience. Casual dress; cocktails. **Parking:** on-site. ♿Ⓜ 🎫 ✕

GOLDEN BAKERY & DELI **Lunch: $3-$6** **Dinner: $3-$6** **Phone: 250/344-2928**
▽▽
Deli/Subs
Sandwiches

Location: Just w off Hwy 95; downtown. 415 9th St N V0A 1H0. **Hours:** 6:30 am-6 pm. Closed major holidays; also Sun. **Features:** One of the town's best-kept secrets, the simple delicatessen and bakery serves homemade soups, salads and sandwiches, along with a huge selection of sweets. Just off the highway, the eatery invites guests to dine in or get their food to go. Don't bypass the display case of treats. **Parking:** street. **Cards:** VI. ✕

THE KICKING HORSE GRILL **Dinner: $7-$21** **Phone: 250/344-2330**
▽▽▽
International

Location: Hwy 95, just e; downtown. 1105 9th St S V0A 1H0. **Hours:** 4:30 pm-11 pm. Closed: 1/1. **Reservations:** suggested. **Features:** The restaurant's small lodge-like interior is perfect for a casual meal with friends. Dark wood beams crisscross the ceiling and line the walls, creating a true Rocky Mountain feel. The food draws upon many influences, ranging from Asian to Swedish and even some Canadian elements, resulting in an interesting and eclectic menu. Casual dress; cocktails. **Parking:** on-site. **Cards:** AX, MC, VI. 🎫 ✕

GRAND FORKS pop. 4,054

——— WHERE TO STAY ———

RAMADA LIMITED **_Book at aaa.com_** **Phone: (250)442-2127**
▽▽▽▽
Motel

5/1-9/30	1P: $99-$109	2P: $99-$109	XP: $15	F12
3/1-4/30 & 10/1-2/28	1P: $89-$99	2P: $89-$99	XP: $10	F12

Location: West end of town on Hwy 3. 2729 Central Ave V0H 1H2. Fax: 250/442-2844. **Facility:** 45 units. 38 one- and 6 two-bedroom standard units, some with kitchens (utensils extra charge) and/or whirlpools. 1 one-bedroom suite ($119-$149). 2 stories (no elevator), exterior corridors. **Parking:** on-site, winter plug-ins. **Terms:** cancellation fee imposed, small pets only ($15 fee). **Amenities:** voice mail, irons, hair dryers. **Pool(s):** heated outdoor. **Guest Services:** coin laundry. **Cards:** AX, MC, VI.

SOME UNITS
(A$K) (S🅳) 🐾 🍴 🏊 📺 (DATA PORT) 💻 / ✕ 🖥 🍽 /
FEE

WESTERN TRAVELLER MOTEL **Phone: (250)442-5566**
(CAA) (SAVE)
▽▽▽
Motel

6/1-9/30	1P: $60-$119	2P: $65-$129	XP: $7	D12
3/1-5/31	1P: $55-$109	2P: $59-$119	XP: $5	D12
10/1-2/28	1P: $55-$99	2P: $59-$109	XP: $5	D12

Location: West end of town on Hwy 3. 1591 Central Ave V0H 1H0 (PO Box 1780). Fax: 250/442-2019. **Facility:** 29 one-bedroom standard units, some with efficiencies. 2 stories (no elevator), exterior corridors. **Parking:** on-site, winter plug-ins. **Terms:** office hours 7 am-11 pm, package plans, small pets only ($7 fee). **Amenities:** *Some:* irons, hair dryers. **Business Services:** meeting rooms. **Cards:** AX, MC, VI. **Special Amenities:** free local telephone calls and preferred room (subject to availability with advance reservations).

SOME UNITS
(S🅳) 🍴 / ✕ 🖥 💻 /
FEE

Gulf Islands
National Park Reserve

GALIANO ISLAND pop. 1,071

——— WHERE TO STAY ———

THE BELLHOUSE INN   **Phone:** (250)539-5667

	6/1-9/15 [BP]	1P: $125-$195	2P: $125-$195	XP: $20
	9/16-10/31 [BP]	1P: $100-$150	2P: $110-$150	XP: $20
Historic Bed	11/1-2/28 [BP]	1P: $85-$150	2P: $95-$150	XP: $20
& Breakfast	3/1-5/31 [BP]	1P: $75-$150	2P: $85-$150	XP: $20

Location: From Sturdies Bay ferry terminal, 0.5 km nw on Main Rd, 0.5 km w on Burrill Rd, then 0.5 km s on Jack Rd. 29 Farmhouse Rd V0N 1P0 (Box 16, Site 4). Fax: 250/539-5316. **Facility:** A waterfront location enhances this 1890s farmhouse. Smoke free premises. 4 one-bedroom standard units, some with whirlpools. 2 stories (no elevator), interior corridors. *Bath:* combo or shower only. **Parking:** on-site. **Terms:** office hours 8 am-10 pm, 2 night minimum stay - seasonal and/or weekends, age restrictions may apply, 7 day cancellation notice. **Amenities:** hair dryers. **Cards:** MC, VI.

GALIANO INN AND SPA   **Phone:** (250)539-3388

All Year   2P: $250-$350   XP: $35

Country Inn

Location: From Sturdies Bay ferry terminal, just ne on Sturdies Bay Rd. 134 Madrona Dr V0N 1P0 (Box S24-C47). Fax: 250/539-3338. **Facility:** A luxury spa is featured and every room has an ocean view at this property said to be Galiano Island's only oceanfront inn and restaurant. Smoke free premises. 10 one-bedroom standard units, some with whirlpools. 2 stories (no elevator), interior corridors. **Parking:** on-site. **Terms:** office hours 8 am-8 pm, 7 day cancellation notice-fee imposed, package plans. **Amenities:** honor bars, hair dryers. **Dining:** Atrevida Restaurant, see separate listing. **Leisure Activities:** whirlpool, spa. **Business Services:** meeting rooms. **Cards:** MC, VI.

WOODSTONE COUNTRY INN   **Phone:** (250)539-2022

3/1-11/30 & 2/1-2/28 [BP]   1P: $135-$225   2P: $135-$225   XP: $40

Country Inn

Location: From Sturdies Bay ferry terminal, 3.5 km nw on Sturdies Bay Rd. 743 Georgeson Bay Rd V0N 1P0. Fax: 250/539-5198. **Facility:** A wood-burning fireplace in the common area sets the tone for this warm, modern inn with attractive rooms and country views. Smoke free premises. 12 one-bedroom standard units, some with whirlpools. 2 stories (no elevator), interior corridors. **Parking:** on-site. **Terms:** open 3/1-11/30 & 2/1-2/28, office hours 8 am-10 pm, 2 night minimum stay - seasonal, age restrictions may apply, 7 day cancellation notice-fee imposed, package plans. **Amenities:** hair dryers. **Leisure Activities:** Fee: massage. **Business Services:** meeting rooms. **Cards:** AX, MC, VI.

——— WHERE TO DINE ———

ATREVIDA RESTAURANT   **Lunch:** $9-$15   **Dinner:** $20-$24   **Phone:** 250/539-3388

Pacific Rim

Location: From Sturdies Bay ferry terminal, just ne on Sturdies Bay Rd; in Galiano Inn and Spa. 134 Madrona Dr V0N 1P0. **Hours:** 5 pm-9 pm; 7 am-10 pm 5/15-9/15; weekends 7 am-9 pm 3/1-5/14 & 9/16-2/28. **Reservations:** required, for dinner. **Features:** The waterfront restaurant serves delightful West Coast cuisine prepared with fresh local ingredients, including Salt Spring Island organic goat cheese and West Coast seafood. A fine selection of British Columbia wines complements the fare. Hours vary in the off-season, so call ahead. Casual dress; cocktails. **Parking:** on-site. **Cards:** MC, VI.

——— The following restaurant has not been evaluated by AAA ——— but is listed for your information only.

HUMMINGBIRD INN PUB   **Phone:** 250/539-5472

[fyi]

Not evaluated. **Location:** From Sturdies Bay Ferry Terminal, 3 km nw. 47 Sturdies Bay Rd V0N 1P0. **Features:** Dining choices on the island are limited, but those who visit the adult-oriented pub can expect pub-style food.

MAYNE ISLAND pop. 880

——— WHERE TO STAY ———

——— The following lodging was either not evaluated or did not ——— meet AAA rating requirements but is listed for your information only.

OCEANWOOD COUNTRY INN   **Phone:** 250/539-5074

[fyi]

Not evaluated. **Location:** From ferry terminal right on Dalton Dr to Mariners Way; right turn then immediate left onto Dinner Bay Rd, follow for 0.8 km. Located in a quiet area. 630 Dinner Bay Rd V0N 2J0. Facilities, services, and decor characterize a basic property.

PENDER ISLAND

POETS COVE RESORT & SPA   *Book at aaa.com*   Phone: (250)629-2100

▽▽▽ ▽▽▽

5/1-9/30 [CP]	1P: $345	2P: $345	XP: $50	D12
3/25-4/30 [CP]	1P: $245	2P: $245	XP: $50	D12
10/1-2/28 [CP]	1P: $215	2P: $215	XP: $50	D12
3/1-3/24 [CP]	1P: $195	2P: $195	XP: $50	D12

Small-scale Hotel

Location: From Otter Bay Ferry Terminal, follow signs to South Pender Island 16 km s; Otter Bay Rd to Bidwell Harbour Rd to Canal Rd. 9801 Spalding Rd, South Pender Island V0N 2M3. Fax: 250/629-2105. **Facility:** Smoke free premises. 46 units. 25 one-bedroom standard units. 21 cottages ($495-$895). 1-3 stories, interior/exterior corridors. **Parking:** on-site. **Terms:** check-in 4 pm, 2 night minimum stay - seasonal, 14 day cancellation notice-fee imposed, package plans, $10 service charge, small pets only ($25 extra charge, in cottages). **Amenities:** video library (fee), DVD players, high-speed Internet, voice mail, irons, hair dryers. **Dining:** Aurora Restaurant, see separate listing. **Pool(s):** 2 heated outdoor. **Leisure Activities:** whirlpools, steamroom, exercise room. *Fee:* marina. **Guest Services:** coin laundry. **Business Services:** meeting rooms. **Cards:** AX, MC, VI.

SOME UNITS

(ASK) (SD) 🛏️ 📶 🍽️ 🍸 ⓜ 🏊 ✖️ ✖️ 👤 (DATA PORT) 📧 📺 / 🅰️ /
FEE

──────── WHERE TO DINE ────────

AURORA RESTAURANT   **Dinner:** $20-$30   Phone: 250/629-2115

▽▽▽▽▽

Canadian

Location: From Otter Bay Ferry Terminal, follow signs to South Pender Island 16 km s; Otter Bay Rd to Bidwell Harbour Rd to Canal Rd; in Poets Cove Resort & Spa. 9801 Spalding Rd V0N 2M3. **Hours:** 7 am-10:30 & 6-9:30 pm. Closed: Tues. **Reservations:** required. **Features:** You will find this restaurant inside Pender Island's newest upscale lodging; all tables overlook the marina. Enjoy a cuisine that uses only the highest quality ingredients specially brought in just for this restaurant. Dinner is very popular so reservations are a must. Casual dress; cocktails. **Parking:** on-site and valet. **Cards:** AX, DC, MC, VI.

🍸 ✖️

QUADRA ISLAND pop. 2,548

──────── WHERE TO STAY ────────

TAKU RESORT   Phone: (250)285-3031

(CAA) (SAVE)

▽▽▽ ▽▽▽

7/1-9/5	1P: $90-$265	2P: $90-$265	XP: $20	D12
3/1-6/30	1P: $85-$195	2P: $85-$195	XP: $15	D12
9/6-10/31	1P: $85-$195	2P: $85-$195	XP: $20	D12
11/1-2/28	1P: $55-$130	2P: $55-$130	XP: $10	D12

Motel

Location: From Campbell River ferry terminal, 6.6 km n on West Rd, then just e on Heriot Bay Rd, follow signs to Heriot Bay. 616 Taku Rd V0P 1H0 (PO Box 1, HERIOT BAY). Fax: 250/285-3712. **Facility:** Smoke free premises. 9 units. 5 one- and 4 two-bedroom standard units, some with efficiencies, kitchens and/or whirlpools. 5 cabins. 1 story, exterior corridors. **Parking:** office hours 8 am-8 pm, check-in 4 pm, 2 night minimum stay - seasonal, 30 day cancellation notice-fee imposed, small pets only ($8 extra charge, in cabins). **Leisure Activities:** whirlpool, rental canoes, fishing, tennis court, bocci, basketball, horseshoes, volleyball. *Fee:* boat dock, kayaks, laser sailboats. **Guest Services:** coin laundry. **Business Services:** PC. **Cards:** AX, MC, VI.

SOME UNITS

🛏️ 📶 ✖️ ✖️ 🅰️ 📧 📺 / 🆅 (VCR) (DATA PORT) 🔒 📠 /
FEE

TSA-KWA-LUTEN LODGE   Phone: (250)285-2042

▽▽▽ ▽▽▽

7/1-9/15	1P: $120-$125	2P: $125-$130	XP: $20	F12
5/3-6/30 & 9/16-10/12	1P: $75-$80	2P: $80-$85	XP: $10	F12

Small-scale Hotel

Location: From Campbell River ferry terminal, 0.3 km se on Green Rd, 1 km e on Noble Rd, 2.9 km se on Cape Mudge Rd to Joyce Rd, then 1 km sw, 2.2 km s. 1 Lighthouse Rd V0P 1N0 (PO Box 460, QUATHIASKI COVE). Fax: 250/285-2532. **Facility:** Smoke free premises. 34 units. 30 one-bedroom standard units, some with whirlpools. 4 cottages ($180), some with whirlpools. 1-2 stories (no elevator), interior/exterior corridors. **Parking:** on-site. **Terms:** open 5/3-10/12, 3 day cancellation notice. **Amenities:** irons, hair dryers. **Dining:** Hama Elas Dining Room, see separate listing. **Leisure Activities:** sauna, whirlpool, horseshoes. *Fee:* charter fishing, bicycles. **Business Services:** meeting rooms. **Cards:** AX, DC, JC, MC, VI.

SOME UNITS

(ASK) (SD) 🍽️ 🍸 ✖️ ✖️ 🅰️ 🆅 (DATA PORT) 📺 / 🔒 📠 /

──────── The following lodging was either not evaluated or did not ────────
meet AAA rating requirements but is listed for your information only.

APRIL POINT RESORT & MARINA   Phone: 250/285-2222

(fyi)

Resort
Large-scale Hotel

Did not meet all AAA rating requirements for some property operations at time of last evaluation on 06/18/2003. **Location:** From Campbell River terminal, n on Ferry Rd, 1 km to Pidcock and April Point rds, then 3.2 km n. 900 April Point Rd V0P 1N0 (PO Box 248, CAMPBELL RIVER, V9W 4Z9). Facilities, services, and decor characterize a mid-range property.

──────── WHERE TO DINE ────────

APRIL POINT RESORT & MARINA   **Lunch:** $8-$13   **Dinner:** $16-$25   Phone: 250/285-2222

▽▽▽▽ ▽▽

Pacific Rim

Location: From Campbell River ferry terminal, n on Ferry Rd, 1 km to Pidcock and April Point rds, then 3.2 km n; in April Point Resort & Marina. 900 April Point Rd V0P 1N0. **Hours:** Open 5/1-10/15; 5:30 am-10 pm. **Reservations:** suggested. **Features:** Guests are treated to wonderful water views from every table, and during summer they can watch cruise ships heading up to Alaska. The menu lists such items as locally caught fish, standard sandwiches and burgers, as well as sushi bar preparations. Guests can catch the free water taxi from its sister property, Painter's Lodge. Casual dress; cocktails. **Parking:** on-site. **Cards:** AX, DC, JC, MC, VI.

🍸 🅰️ ✖️

HAMA ELAS DINING ROOM   **Lunch:** $8-$15   **Dinner:** $15-$23   **Phone:** 250/285-2042

Seafood

Location: From Campbell River ferry terminal, just e on Green Rd, 1 km se on Noble Rd, 3 km s on Cape Mudge Rd to Joyce Rd, then 1.8 km w; in Tsa-Kwa-Luten Lodge. 1 Lighthouse Rd V0P 1N0. **Hours:** Open 5/3-10/12; 7:30 am-9 pm. **Reservations:** suggested. **Features:** The menu centers on a native theme and lists North American dishes familiar to many guests, such as steak, chicken and pasta. Casual dress; cocktails. **Parking:** on-site.
Cards: AX, DC, DS, JC, MC, VI.

SALTSPRING ISLAND pop. 9,381

──────── **WHERE TO STAY** ────────

ANNE'S OCEANFRONT HIDEAWAY B & B   **Phone:** (250)537-0851

5/1-9/30 [BP]	1P: $205-$275	2P: $205-$275
10/1-2/28 [BP]	1P: $190-$230	2P: $190-$230
3/1-4/30 [BP]	1P: $185-$225	2P: $185-$225

Bed & Breakfast   **Location:** From Ganges township, just n, 3 km w on Vesuvius Bay Rd, 6 km n on Sunset Dr. Located in a quiet secluded area. 168 Simson Rd V8K 1E2. Fax: 250/537-0861. **Facility:** On a hillside, this modern B&B with an ocean view offers a wraparound veranda for boat-watching; guest rooms have spa tubs. 4 one-bedroom standard units with whirlpools. 2 stories, interior corridors. **Parking:** on-site. **Terms:** office hours 6 am-11 pm, 2 night minimum stay - seasonal and/or weekends, age restrictions may apply, 10 day cancellation notice-fee imposed. **Amenities:** CD players, hair dryers. **Leisure Activities:** whirlpool. **Cards:** AX, MC, VI.

HARBOUR HOUSE   **Phone:** (250)537-5571

5/20-9/30	1P: $84-$295	2P: $89-$295	XP: $10	F12
3/1-5/19 & 10/1-2/28	1P: $54-$195	2P: $59-$195	XP: $10	F12

Small-scale Hotel   **Location:** 1 km n on Lower Ganges Rd, then just e, towards Long Harbour ferry terminal. 121 Upper Ganges Rd V8K 2S2. Fax: 250/537-4618. **Facility:** 35 one-bedroom standard units, some with whirlpools. 2 stories (no elevator), interior/exterior corridors. **Parking:** on-site. **Terms:** office hours 8 am-9 pm, cancellation fee imposed, small pets only ($20 extra charge, with prior approval). **Amenities:** irons. *Some:* hair dryers. **Dining:** Porters Restaurant & Lounge, see separate listing. **Business Services:** meeting rooms. **Cards:** AX, MC, VI.

SOME UNITS

THE OLD FARMHOUSE BED & BREAKFAST   **Phone:** 250/537-4113

5/16-9/30	1P: $185	2P: $185	XP: $50	F10
3/1-5/15 & 10/1-2/28	1P: $155	2P: $155	XP: $50	F10

Historic Bed & Breakfast   **Location:** From Ganges township, 4 km n on Lower Ganges North End Rd. 1077 North End Rd V8K 1L9. Fax: 250/537-4969. **Facility:** Tall trees, orchards and a garden enhance the grounds of this 100-year-old farmhouse. Smoke free premises. 4 one-bedroom standard units. 2 stories (no elevator), interior corridors.
Parking: on-site. **Terms:** office hours 8 am-10 pm, 7 day cancellation notice, weekly rates available. **Cards:** MC, VI.

SALT SPRINGS SPA RESORT   **Phone:** (250)537-4111

6/25-8/31	1P: $199-$299	2P: $199-$299	XP: $20	D16
3/1-6/24 & 9/1-10/31	1P: $129-$219	2P: $129-$219	XP: $20	D16
11/1-2/28	1P: $109-$199	2P: $109-$199	XP: $20	D16

Cottage   **Location:** From Ganges township, 8 km n on North End Rd, 1.1 km ne on Fernwood Rd, then 1.8 km nw. 1460 N Beach Rd V8K 1J4. Fax: 250/537-2939. **Facility:** Fully self-contained cottages are offered at this resort featuring natural mineral baths drawn from underground springs; spa/wellness center on site. Smoke free premises. 13 cottages with whirlpools. 1 story, exterior corridors. *Bath:* shower only. **Parking:** on-site. **Terms:** office hours 8 am-8 pm, check-in 4 pm, 7 day cancellation notice. **Amenities:** hair dryers. **Leisure Activities:** bicycles, spa. **Guest Services:** coin laundry. **Cards:** AX, MC, VI.

SEABREEZE INNE
Phone: (250)537-4145

♦♦♦ ♦♦♦	6/17-9/24	1P: $115-$185	2P: $115-$185	XP: $25	F12
Motel	3/16-6/16	1P: $85-$175	2P: $85-$175	XP: $25	F12
	9/25-2/28	1P: $59-$175	2P: $59-$175	XP: $25	F12
	3/1-3/15	1P: $59-$145	2P: $59-$145	XP: $25	F12

Location: From Ganges township, 1 km s on Fulford-Ganges Rd. 101 Bittancourt Rd V8K 2K2. Fax: 250/537-4323. **Facility:** Smoke free premises. 28 one-bedroom standard units, some with efficiencies and/or whirlpools. 2 stories (no elevator), exterior corridors. **Parking:** on-site. **Terms:** office hours 8 am-11 pm, 2 night minimum stay - weekends, 30 day cancellation notice-fee imposed, package plans, pets ($20 extra charge, with prior approval, no cats). **Amenities:** high-speed Internet, voice mail. **Leisure Activities:** whirlpool, rental bicycles, playground, horseshoes. **Guest Services:** coin laundry. **Cards:** AX, MC, VI.

SOME UNITS

(ASK) (SD) (≡) (⊠) (⊠) (K) (▼) (▭) / (VCR) (▤) (▦) /
FEE

The following lodging was either not evaluated or did not meet AAA rating requirements but is listed for your information only.

HASTINGS HOUSE COUNTRY HOUSE HOTEL
Phone: 250/537-2362

[fyi] Not evaluated. **Location:** 1 km n on Lower Ganges Rd, then just e, towards Long Harbour ferry terminal. 160 Upper Ganges Rd V8K 2S2. Facilities, services, and decor characterize an upscale property.

——— WHERE TO DINE ———

BARB'S BUNS LICENSED BAKERY & CAFE
Lunch: $6-$10   Phone: 250/537-4491

♦♦♦ **Location:** In Ganges township; from Lower Ganges Rd, just w; centre. #1, 121 McPhillips Ave V8K 2T6. **Hours:** 7 am-5:30 pm, Sun 10 am-4 pm. **Features:** Delightfully Bohemian, the bright and bustling cafe/bakery tantalizes guests with the tempting aromas of fresh bread, pastries and coffee. Vegetarian breakfast and lunch items that emphasize healthfulness are prepared with organic ingredients. Casual dress. **Parking:** street.

Bakery/Desserts
Cards: MC, VI.

(K) (⊠)

CALVIN'S SALTSPRING ISLAND BISTRO
Lunch: $6-$9   Dinner: $11-$18   Phone: 250/538-5551

♦♦♦ ♦♦♦ **Location:** In Ganges township; corner of Hereford Ave. 133 Lower Ganges Rd V8K 2T2. **Hours:** Open 3/1-12/31 & 2/1-2/28; 11 am-2 & 5-9 pm, Sun 10 am-2:30 pm. Closed: Mon. **Features:** Located in the heart of the Ganges township right near the water, this simple bistro type restaurant offers hearty meals like burgers, sandwiches and soups, as well as a number of hearty desserts. There's a choice of booth seating or tables that are set up near the large windows with a great view of the water. Casual dress; cocktails. **Parking:** street. **Cards:** AX, MC, VI.

Canadian

(K) (⊠)

HASTINGS HOUSE DINING ROOM
Dinner: $75-$95   Phone: 250/537-2362

(CAA) **Location:** 1 km n on Lower Ganges Rd, then just e, towards Long Harbour ferry terminal; in Hastings Country House Hotel. 160 Upper Ganges Rd V8K 2S2. **Hours:** Open 3/15-11/15; 6 pm-8 pm. **Reservations:** suggested.
♦♦♦ ♦♦♦ **Features:** This restaurant holds a truly wonderful dining experience. There is only one sitting each night, so reservations are a must. Each dinner guest gets their own personalized menu which features your pre-set course meal along with the featured wines. Dressy casual; cocktails. **Parking:** on-site. **Cards:** AX, MC, VI.
Pacific Rim

(K) (⊠)

MOBY'S MARINE PUB
Lunch: $7-$11   Dinner: $8-$15   Phone: 250/537-5559

♦♦ **Location:** 1 km n on Lower Ganges Rd, then just e. 124 Upper Ganges Rd V8K 2S2. **Hours:** 10 am-midnight, Fri & Sat 11 am-1 am, Sun 11 am-midnight. Closed: 12/25, 12/26. **Features:** Across from the Harbour House Hotel, this unpretentious working man's pub located in the marina has great views of the water and surrounding islands. You won't find table cloths here, but you will find hearty pub food served late into the evening seven days a week. Patrons must be at least 19 years old to enter the pub. Casual dress; cocktails. **Parking:** on-site.
Canadian
Cards: MC, VI.

(⊠)

PORTERS RESTAURANT & LOUNGE
Lunch: $6-$10   Dinner: $6-$18   Phone: 250/537-4700

♦♦ **Location:** 1 km n on Lower Ganges Rd, then just e, towards Long Harbour ferry terminal; in Harbour House. 121 Upper Ganges Rd V8K 2S2. **Hours:** 8 am-9 pm; from 11 am 10/1-6/30. Closed major holidays. **Reservations:** suggested. **Features:** Featuring an extensive menu with daily specials, a casual and pleasant type of decor with tables set up against the window plus a large outdoor garden patio gives everyone a pleasant view of the Ganges Harbour. Down home Canadian fare is served with a smile from the attentive staff. Casual dress; cocktails. **Parking:** on-site. **Cards:** AX, MC, VI.
Canadian

(K) (⊠)

RESTAURANT HOUSE PICCOLO
Dinner: $18-$29   Phone: 250/537-1844

♦♦♦ ♦♦ **Location:** In Ganges township; cross street Lower Ganges Rd. 108 Hereford Ave V8K 2V9. **Hours:** 5 pm-10 pm. Closed: 12/25, 12/26. **Reservations:** required. **Features:** You'll enjoy this restaurant's cozy setting, tucked away from the busy shops of Ganges. The menu offers delightful Scandinavian and European classics and seafood dishes. An impressive selection of reasonably priced wines is offered. Casual dress; cocktails.
Continental
Parking: street. **Cards:** MC, VI.

(K) (⊠)

SATURNA ISLAND pop. 319

——— WHERE TO STAY ———

SATURNA LODGE & RESTAURANT
Phone: 250/539-2254

♦♦♦ ♦♦	3/15-12/31 [BP]		2P: $120-$195	XP: $35	D5

Country Inn **Location:** From BC ferry terminal, just s on Narvaez Bay Rd, then just e, follow signs. 130 Payne Rd V0N 2Y0 (PO Box 175, SATURNA). Fax: 250/539-3091. **Facility:** Smoke free premises. 7 one-bedroom standard units. 2 stories (no elevator), interior corridors. *Bath:* some shared or private. **Parking:** on-site. **Terms:** open 3/15-12/31, office hours 7 am-10 pm, 2 night minimum stay - seasonal and/or weekends, 14 day cancellation notice, package plans. **Amenities:** *Some:* hair dryers. **Dining:** restaurant, see separate listing. **Leisure Activities:** whirlpool. **Cards:** MC, VI.

(¶) (⊠) (K) (▦) (Z)

——— **WHERE TO DINE** ———

SATURNA LODGE & RESTAURANT   **Dinner: $35**   **Phone: 250/539-2254**

Pacific Rim

Location: From BC ferry terminal, just s on Narvaez Bay Rd, then just e, follow signs; in Saturna Lodge & Restaurant. 130 Payne Rd V0N 2Y0. **Hours:** Open 3/15-12/31; 6 pm-8 pm. **Reservations:** suggested. **Features:** Part of the lodge, the restaurant opens for dinner not only for guests but also for locals. Options include a set course of three items or a la carte offerings. Wonderful water views are available from just about every table. Casual dress; cocktails. **Parking:** on-site. **Cards:** MC, VI.

The previous listings were for the Gulf Islands National Park Reserve.
This page resumes the alphabetical listings of cities in British Columbia.

HARRISON HOT SPRINGS pop. 1,343

——— **WHERE TO STAY** ———

HARRISON HOT SPRINGS RESORT & SPA   *Book at aaa.com*   **Phone: (604)796-2244**

(AAA) (SAVE)

	7/1-9/30	1P: $164-$544	2P: $165-$544	XP: $20	F15
	3/1-6/30 & 10/1-12/31	1P: $154-$424	2P: $154-$424	XP: $20	F15
	1/1-2/28	1P: $134-$360	2P: $134-$360	XP: $20	F15

Large-scale Hotel

Location: Just w. Located on the lakefront. 100 Esplanade Ave V0M 1K0. Fax: 604/796-3682. **Facility:** Smoke free premises. 334 one-bedroom standard units. 8 stories, interior corridors. *Bath:* combo or shower only. **Parking:** on-site and valet. **Terms:** check-in 4 pm, 3 day cancellation notice-fee imposed, package plans, small pets only ($100 extra charge, with prior approval). **Amenities:** video games (fee), voice mail, irons, hair dryers. *Some:* high-speed Internet. **Dining:** 7 am-3 & 5-10 pm, cocktails, also, The Copper Room, see separate listing, entertainment. **Pool(s):** 3 heated outdoor, 2 heated indoor. **Leisure Activities:** steamrooms, rental boats, indoor/outdoor hot therapeutic mineral pools, 2 tennis courts, rental bicycles, hiking trails, jogging, playground, exercise room, spa. *Fee:* golf-9 holes. **Guest Services:** gift shop, valet laundry. **Business Services:** conference facilities. **Cards:** AX, DC, DS, MC, VI. **Special Amenities: free newspaper.**

SOME UNITS

HARRISON VILLAGE MOTEL   **Phone: 604/796-2616**

Motel

All Year	1P: $79-$89	2P: $79-$89	XP: $10

Location: On the lakefront. 280 Esplanade Ave V0M 1K0 (PO Box 115). Fax: 604/796-3032. **Facility:** 18 units. 15 one-bedroom standard units, some with kitchens. 3 two-bedroom suites ($129-$185) with kitchens. 2 stories, interior/exterior corridors. *Bath:* combo or shower only. **Parking:** on-site. **Terms:** 7 day cancellation notice-fee imposed. **Cards:** MC, VI.

SOME UNITS

——— **WHERE TO DINE** ———

BLACK FOREST RESTAURANT   **Lunch: $8-$15**   **Dinner: $14-$26**   **Phone: 604/796-9343**

German

Location: Just w; on the lakefront. 180 Esplanade Ave V0M 1K0. **Hours:** 5 pm-10 pm; from noon 6/1-9/30. Closed: 12/25. **Reservations:** suggested, in summer. **Features:** You'll enjoy the steak and West Coast salmon at the Black Forest, which also serves German specialties of beef rouladen and schnitzel. The Alpine decor features a central European flair in its paintings and murals. Visitors like the warm, cozy atmosphere. Casual dress; cocktails. **Parking:** street. **Cards:** AX, MC, VI.

THE COPPER ROOM   **Dinner: $25-$36**   **Phone: 604/796-2244**

Pacific Rim

Location: Just w; in Harrison Hot Springs Resort & Spa. 100 Esplanade Ave V0M 1K0. **Hours:** 6 pm-10 pm. **Reservations:** required. **Features:** You'll appreciate the Copper Room for its popular evening dining and dancing. This restaurant is also known for its delicious prime rib and Fraser Valley local produce. Nightly entertainment is featured and a dress code is imposed. Dressy casual; cocktails; entertainment. **Parking:** on-site. **Cards:** AX, DC, DS, MC, VI.

HARRISON MILLS pop. 141

——— **WHERE TO STAY** ———

HISTORIC FENN LODGE BED & BREAKFAST   **Phone: (604)796-9798**

Historic Bed & Breakfast

All Year [BP]	1P: $115-$160	2P: $115-$160	XP: $30	D10

Location: Hwy 7, 4 km n of the Sasquatch Inn, watch for signs. 15500 Morris Valley Rd V0M 1L0 (PO Box 67). Fax: 604/796-9274. **Facility:** This distinctive hotel built in 1903 retains many of its original furnishings. Smoke free premises. 7 one-bedroom standard units. 2 stories (no elevator), interior corridors. *Bath:* shower or tub only. **Parking:** on-site. **Terms:** 2 night minimum stay - seasonal and/or weekends, 7 day cancellation notice. **Pool(s):** outdoor. **Cards:** MC, VI.

HEDLEY pop. 272

——— **WHERE TO STAY** ———

——— *The following lodging was either not evaluated or did not* ———
meet AAA rating requirements but is listed for your information only.

COLONIAL INN   **Phone: 250/292-8131**

[fyi]

Not evaluated. **Location:** Just e on Hwy 3. 608 Colonial Rd V0X 1K0 (PO Box 198). Facilities, services, and decor characterize a basic property.

HOPE pop. 6,184

ALPINE MOTEL

CAA SAVE

Motel

Phone: (604)869-9931

6/16-9/30	1P: $68-$85	2P: $75-$85	XP: $10	D5
5/15-6/15	1P: $64-$75	2P: $72-$80	XP: $10	D5
3/1-5/14	1P: $58-$70	2P: $68-$72	XP: $10	D5
10/1-2/28	1P: $55-$65	2P: $65-$70	XP: $10	D5

Location: Trans-Canada Hwy 1, exit 173 westbound; exit 170 eastbound, just n from lights. 505 Old Hope-Princeton Way V0X 1L0 (PO Box 708). Fax: 604/869-7290. **Facility:** 14 one-bedroom standard units, some with efficiencies. 1 story, exterior corridors. **Parking:** on-site. **Terms:** office hours 7 am-midnight, small pets only ($5 extra charge). **Cards:** AX, DC, MC. **Special Amenities:** free local telephone calls.

SOME UNITS

BEST CONTINENTAL MOTEL

CAA SAVE

Motel

Phone: 604/869-9726

6/16-10/15	1P: $60-$70	2P: $69-$80	XP: $6	F6
5/1-6/15	1P: $54-$64	2P: $64-$74	XP: $6	F6
3/1-4/30 & 10/16-2/28	1P: $50-$60	2P: $55-$70	XP: $6	F6

Location: Trans-Canada Hwy 1, exit 170 to downtown; at Fort St. 860 Fraser Ave V0X 1L0 (PO Box 1396). Fax: 604/869-3164. **Facility:** 13 one-bedroom standard units. 2 stories, exterior corridors. **Parking:** on-site. **Terms:** office hours 8 am-midnight, small pets only ($5 extra charge). **Cards:** AX, MC, VI. **Special Amenities:** free local telephone calls and free room upgrade (subject to availability with advance reservations).

SOME UNITS

BEST WESTERN HERITAGE INN   *Book at aaa.com*

CAA SAVE

Motel

Phone: (604)869-7166

8/1-8/31 [CP]	1P: $109-$119	2P: $119-$129	XP: $10	F12
5/15-7/31 [CP]	1P: $99-$109	2P: $109-$119	XP: $10	F12
9/1-2/28 [CP]	1P: $79-$109	2P: $89-$119	XP: $10	F12
3/1-5/14 [CP]	1P: $79-$89	2P: $89-$99	XP: $10	F12

Location: Trans-Canada Hwy 1, exit 173 westbound; exit 170 eastbound, then just n from lights. 570 Old Hope-Princeton Way V0X 1L0 (PO Box 1787). Fax: 604/869-7106. **Facility:** 26 one-bedroom standard units, some with kitchens. 1-2 stories, exterior corridors. **Parking:** on-site. **Terms:** office hours 6:30 am-midnight, 3 day cancellation notice. **Amenities:** irons, hair dryers. **Leisure Activities:** whirlpool, limited exercise equipment. **Guest Services:** coin laundry. **Cards:** AX, DC, DS, MC, VI. **Special Amenities:** free continental breakfast and early check-in/late check-out.

SOME UNITS

COLONIAL '900' MOTEL

CAA SAVE

Motel

Phone: (604)869-5223

5/15-10/15	1P: $85-$95	2P: $95-$105	XP: $10	D12
3/1-5/14 & 10/16-2/28	1P: $65-$75	2P: $85-$95	XP: $10	D12

Location: Trans-Canada Hwy 1, exit 173 westbound; exit 170 eastbound, 1 km n from lights. 900 Old Hope-Princeton Way V0X 1L0 (PO Box 849). Fax: 604/869-5228. **Facility:** Smoke free premises. 16 one-bedroom standard units, some with efficiencies or kitchens. 1 story, exterior corridors. **Parking:** on-site, winter plug-ins. **Terms:** office hours 9 am-11 pm, cancellation fee imposed. **Amenities:** hair dryers. **Guest Services:** gift shop. **Cards:** AX, DC, MC, VI. **Special Amenities:** free local telephone calls and preferred room (subject to availability with advance reservations).

SOME UNITS

INN TOWNE MOTEL

CAA SAVE

Motel

Phone: 604/869-7276

5/15-10/14	1P: $60-$80	2P: $70-$110	XP: $10	
3/1-5/14 & 10/15-2/28	1P: $50-$80	2P: $65-$100	XP: $10	

Location: Trans-Canada Hwy 1, exit 170, 1 km n to downtown. Located near the south end of the Fraser River Bridge. 510 Trans-Canada Hwy V0X 1L0 (PO Box 1037). Fax: 604/869-7222. **Facility:** 26 one-bedroom standard units, some with efficiencies, kitchens and/or whirlpools. 1-2 stories, exterior corridors. **Parking:** on-site. **Terms:** office hours 7 am-11 pm, small pets only ($5 extra charge). **Pool(s):** heated indoor. **Leisure Activities:** sauna, whirlpool. **Guest Services:** coin laundry. *Fee:* tanning facility. **Cards:** AX, DC, DS, MC, VI.

SOME UNITS

QUALITY INN   *Book at aaa.com*

CAA SAVE

Motel

Phone: (604)869-9951

6/15-9/30 [CP]	1P: $87-$92	2P: $97-$102	XP: $10	F18
3/1-6/14 & 10/1-2/28 [CP]	1P: $64-$69	2P: $70-$75	XP: $6	F18

Location: Trans-Canada Hwy 1, exit 173 westbound; exit 170 eastbound, just n from lights. 350 Old Hope-Princeton Way V0X 1L0 (PO Box 353). Fax: 604/869-9421. **Facility:** 25 one-bedroom standard units, some with efficiencies. 2 stories, interior corridors. **Parking:** on-site. **Terms:** office hours 8 am-midnight, check-out 1 am, small pets only (must be attended). **Amenities:** hair dryers. **Pool(s):** heated indoor. **Leisure Activities:** sauna, whirlpool. **Cards:** AX, CB, DC, DS, JC, MC, VI. **Special Amenities:** free continental breakfast and free local telephone calls.

SOME UNITS

ROYAL LODGE MOTEL

Motel

Phone: (604)869-5358

7/1-8/30	1P: $70-$80	2P: $70-$80	XP: $5	F12
3/1-6/30	1P: $65-$80	2P: $65-$80	XP: $5	F12
8/31-12/31	1P: $75-$85	2P: $80	XP: $5	F12
1/1-2/28	1P: $60-$65	2P: $60-$65	XP: $5	F12

Location: Trans-Canada Hwy 1, exit 173 westbound; exit 170 eastbound, just n from lights. 580 Old Hope-Princeton Way V0X 1L4. Fax: 604/869-9484. **Facility:** 21 one-bedroom standard units, some with efficiencies. 2 stories, exterior corridors. **Parking:** on-site. **Terms:** office hours 7 am-11 pm, cancellation fee imposed. **Cards:** AX, DC, MC, VI.

SOME UNITS

SKAGIT MOTOR INN

Phone: 604/869-5220

CAA SAVE
Motel

5/15-10/15	1P: $85-$95	2P: $95-$105	XP: $10 F16
3/1-5/14 & 10/16-2/28	1P: $75-$85	2P: $85-$95	XP: $10 F16

Location: Trans-Canada Hwy 1, exit 170 to downtown; just e of Water Ave. Located in a residential area. 655 3rd Ave V0X 1L0 (PO Box 908). Fax: 604/869-5856. **Facility:** 31 one-bedroom standard units, some with efficiencies. 1 story, exterior corridors. **Parking:** on-site. **Terms:** office hours 7 am-11 pm, 3 day cancellation notice-fee imposed. **Amenities:** voice mail, hair dryers. **Leisure Activities:** whirlpool. **Guest Services:** coin laundry. **Business Services:** meeting rooms. **Cards:** AX, CB, DC, JC, MC, VI. **Special Amenities:** free local telephone calls and free room upgrade (subject to availability with advance reservations).

SOME UNITS

——— WHERE TO DINE ———

THE GOLDRUSH PUB

Lunch: $8-$12   **Dinner:** $8-$12   **Phone:** 604/860-4333

Canadian

Location: Trans-Canada Hwy 1, exit 170 eastbound; exit 173 westbound. 629 Old Hope Princeton Hwy V0X 1L2. **Hours:** 11 am-midnight, Fri & Sat-1 am. **Features:** Examples of the good pub food include burgers, sandwiches and many appetizers. Various beers on tap or in the bottle are available. Weekends mean live music, and karaoke nights also are planned. Provincial liquor laws do not allow entry to those under age 19. Casual dress; cocktails. **Parking:** on-site. **Cards:** MC, VI.

HOME RESTAURANT

Lunch: $4-$8   **Dinner:** $7-$12   **Phone:** 604/869-5558

Canadian

Location: Trans-Canada Hwy 1, exit 173 westbound; exit 170 eastbound, just n from lights. 665 Old Hope-Princeton Way V0X 1L4. **Hours:** 6 am-9 pm; to 11 pm 7/1-8/31. Closed: 12/25. **Features:** You'll enjoy this very popular family-style eatery, which features all your favorites—burgers, meat loaf, club-house sandwiches, mountain-men breakfasts and homemade soup, sauce and pie. Food is king here, and you'll want to come back again and again. Beer & wine only. **Parking:** on-site. **Cards:** MC, VI.

HOPE DRIVE-IN & RESTAURANT

Lunch: $6-$10   **Dinner:** $9-$15   **Phone:** 604/869-5380

Canadian

Location: Trans-Canada Hwy 1, exit 173 westbound; exit 170 eastbound, just n from lights. 590 Old Hope-Princeton Way V0X 1L0. **Hours:** 6 am-10 pm. Closed: 1/1, 12/25, 12/26. **Features:** The casual drive-in is a good stop for good food at reasonable prices. Guests can eat in or order from the take-out window. On the menu are freshly made sandwiches, burgers and homemade soups and desserts. Casual dress; cocktails. **Parking:** on-site. **Cards:** MC, VI.

ROLLY'S RESTAURANT

Lunch: $6-$10   **Dinner:** $8-$15   **Phone:** 604/869-7448

Canadian

Location: Trans-Canada Hwy 1, exit 170 to downtown; Hudson Bay St. 888 Fraser Ave V0X 1L0. **Hours:** 6 am-9 pm; to 10 pm 7/1-8/31. Closed: 12/25. **Features:** Rolly's is a great casual, family-dining experience with breakfast served all day. Their home-style cooking menu features chicken teriyaki, halibut, salmon, pasta, Angus beef, fish 'n' chips and more. The open and casual atmosphere is very comfortable. Casual dress; cocktails. **Parking:** on-site. **Cards:** AX, MC, VI.

INVERMERE pop. 2,858

——— WHERE TO STAY ———

BEST WESTERN INVERMERE INN   *Book at aaa.com*

Phone: (250)342-9246

CAA SAVE
Small-scale Hotel

7/15-9/30	1P: $135-$155	2P: $135-$155	XP: $15 F12
5/1-7/14	1P: $105-$125	2P: $105-$125	XP: $15 F12
3/1-4/30 & 10/1-2/28	1P: $89-$99	2P: $89-$99	XP: $15 F12

Location: 3 km w of Hwy 93 and 95 at Invermere exit; centre. 1310 7th Ave V0A 1K0 (PO Box 2340). Fax: 250/342-6079. **Facility:** 45 units. 43 one- and 1 two-bedroom standard units. 1 one-bedroom suite ($150-$250). 3 stories, interior corridors. **Parking:** on-site, winter plug-ins. **Terms:** check-in 4 pm, cancellation fee imposed, package plans, pets ($10 fee). **Amenities:** voice mail, irons, hair dryers. **Dining:** 9 am-2 & 6-10 pm; hours vary off season, cocktails, nightclub. **Leisure Activities:** whirlpool, limited exercise equipment. **Business Services:** meeting rooms. **Cards:** AX, DC, DS, MC, VI. **Special Amenities:** early check-in/late check-out.

SOME UNITS

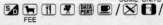

FEE

——— The following lodging was either not evaluated or did not meet AAA rating requirements but is listed for your information only. ———

INVERMERE SUPER 8

Phone: 250-342-8888

fyi

Not evaluated. **Location:** On Hwy 95. 8888 Arrow Rd V0A 1K0. Facilities, services, and decor characterize a mid-range property.

——— WHERE TO DINE ———

BLACK FOREST STEAK & SCHNITZEL HOUSE

Dinner: $13-$24   **Phone:** 250/342-9417

CAA
Continental

Location: On Hwy 93 and 95. 540 Hwy 93 & 95 V0A 1K0. **Hours:** 5 pm-11 pm; to 10 pm off season. **Reservations:** suggested. **Features:** On the menu is a good selection of schnitzels, bratwurst, steak and seafood finely prepared with a respect for tradition. Table d'hotes are offered daily, and the decor and relaxed ambience are inspired by Europe. The restaurant is a favorite with birders, who can enjoy watching the owner's pets while dining. Cocktails. **Parking:** on-site. **Cards:** AX, DC, MC, VI.

STRAND'S OLD HOUSE RESTAURANT   **Dinner:** $13-$30   **Phone:** 250/342-6344
Location: Centre. 818 12th St V0A 1K0. **Hours:** 5 pm-10 pm; Mon-Fri to 10:30 pm in summer. Closed: 12/25.
Continental   **Reservations:** suggested. **Features:** The restaurant offers intimate dining in a restored historic house. The varied menu includes sumptuous venison in blackberry sauce, a selection of pastas and dinner-size salads. The covered porch provides a bright, airy alternative to the more secluded corners of the main dining room. Servers are friendly and courteous. Casual dress; cocktails. **Parking:** on-site. **Cards:** AX, MC, VI. **Historic**

KAMLOOPS pop. 77,281

———— **WHERE TO STAY** ————

ACCENT INNS   *Book at aaa.com*   **Phone:** (250)374-8877

7/1-9/30	1P: $109-$139	2P: $119-$149	XP: $10 F16
5/1-6/30	1P: $99-$119	2P: $109-$129	XP: $10 F16
3/1-4/30 & 10/1-2/28	1P: $89-$109	2P: $99-$119	XP: $10 F16

Motel   **Location:** Trans-Canada Hwy 1, exit 369 (Columbia St) eastbound at Notre Dame Dr; exit 370 (Summit Dr) westbound at Notre Dame Dr. 1325 Columbia St W V2C 6P4. Fax: 250/372-0507. **Facility:** 83 one-bedroom standard units, some with efficiencies. 3 stories, exterior corridors. **Parking:** on-site, winter plug-ins. **Terms:** small pets only ($10 extra charge, in selected units). **Amenities:** video games (fee), voice mail, hair dryers. **Pool(s):** heated outdoor. **Leisure Activities:** sauna, whirlpool, limited exercise equipment. **Guest Services:** valet and coin laundry. **Business Services:** meeting rooms. **Cards:** AX, DC, JC, MC, VI. **Special Amenities:** free local telephone calls and free newspaper.
(See color ad p 488 & p 608)

BEST VALUE SUPER VIEW INN   *Book at aaa.com*   **Phone:** 250/374-8100

5/1-9/30	1P: $70-$80	2P: $89	XP: $6 D15
3/1-4/30 & 10/1-2/28	1P: $55-$60	2P: $65	XP: $5 D15

Motel   **Location:** Trans-Canada Hwy 1, exit 368 (Hillside Ave), just s. 1200 Rogers Way V1S 1N5. Fax: 250/374-3749. **Facility:** 38 one-bedroom standard units, some with efficiencies and/or whirlpools. 2 stories (no elevator), exterior corridors. **Parking:** on-site. **Terms:** office hours 7 am-11 pm, small pets only ($5 extra charge, in selected units). **Pool(s):** small heated outdoor. **Guest Services:** coin laundry. **Cards:** AX, CB, DC, DS, JC, MC, VI.

COMFORT INN & SUITES   *Book at aaa.com*   **Phone:** (250)372-0987

5/1-9/30 [CP]	1P: $135-$159	2P: $135-$159	XP: $10 F18
3/1-4/30 & 10/1-2/28 [CP]	1P: $99-$125	2P: $99-$125	XP: $10 F18

Small-scale Hotel   **Location:** Trans-Canada Hwy 1, exit 368 (Hillside Ave), just w. 1810 Rogers Pl V1S 1T7. Fax: 250/372-0967. **Facility:** 128 units. 118 one-bedroom standard units, some with efficiencies and/or whirlpools. 10 one-bedroom suites, some with efficiencies and/or whirlpools. 3 stories, interior corridors. **Parking:** on-site, winter plug-ins. **Amenities:** high-speed Internet, voice mail, irons, hair dryers. **Dining:** 6 am-11 pm, cocktails. **Pool(s):** heated outdoor, heated indoor. **Leisure Activities:** whirlpools, waterslide, limited exercise equipment. **Guest Services:** valet and coin laundry. **Business Services:** meeting rooms, PC. **Cards:** AX, CB, DC, DS, JC, MC, VI. **Special Amenities:** free continental breakfast and free local telephone calls. *(See color ad below)*

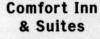

COURTESY MOTEL
Phone: 250/372-8533

▼▼ ▼▼

5/15-9/30	1P: $69-$75	2P: $85-$89	XP: $10	F12
3/1-5/14 & 10/1-2/28	1P: $59-$65	2P: $75-$79	XP: $10	F12

Motel **Location:** 2.4 km e on Trans-Canada Hwy 1, south side of service access road. 1773 Trans-Canada Hwy E V2C 3Z6. Fax: 250/374-2877. **Facility:** 45 one-bedroom standard units, some with kitchens. 2 stories (no elevator), exterior corridors. **Parking:** on-site, winter plug-ins. **Terms:** office hours 7 am-midnight, small pets only ($10 extra charge). **Pool(s):** heated indoor. **Leisure Activities:** whirlpool. **Guest Services:** coin laundry. **Cards:** AX, DC, MC, VI.

SOME UNITS
(ASK) (SD) ... FEE

DAYS INN *Book at aaa.com*
Phone: (250)374-5911

▼▼ ▼▼

6/16-9/30	1P: $109-$119	2P: $119-$129	XP: $10	F14
5/1-6/15	1P: $104-$114	2P: $114-$124	XP: $10	F14
3/1-4/30 & 10/1-2/28	1P: $99-$109	2P: $109-$119	XP: $10	F14

Small-scale Hotel **Location:** Trans-Canada Hwy 1, exit 368 (Hillside Ave), just s. 1285 Trans-Canada Hwy W V2E 2J7. Fax: 250/374-6922. **Facility:** 62 one-bedroom standard units. 3 stories, interior corridors. **Parking:** on-site. **Terms:** package plans, pets ($40 deposit, $10 extra charge). **Amenities:** high-speed Internet, hair dryers. **Pool(s):** heated indoor. **Leisure Activities:** whirlpool. **Guest Services:** valet laundry. **Business Services:** meeting rooms. **Cards:** AX, DC, MC, VI.

SOME UNITS
(ASK) ... FEE ... (DATA PORT)

FOUR POINTS BY SHERATON *Book at aaa.com*
Phone: (250)374-4144

(CAA) (SAVE)

5/16-9/15	1P: $129-$219	2P: $129-$219	XP: $20	F16
3/1-5/15 & 9/16-2/28	1P: $109-$169	2P: $109-$169	XP: $20	F16

▼▼▼▼ ▼▼ **Location:** Trans-Canada Hwy 1, exit 368 (Hillside Ave), just s. 1175 Rogers Way V1S 1R5. Fax: 250/374-0449. **Facility:** 78 units. 77 one- and 1 two-bedroom standard units, some with efficiencies, kitchens and/or Small-scale Hotel whirlpools. 4 stories, interior corridors. **Parking:** on-site, winter plug-ins. **Terms:** cancellation fee imposed, package plans. **Amenities:** high-speed Internet, dual phone lines, voice mail, irons, hair dryers. **Dining:** 6:30 am-10:30 pm, cocktails. **Pool(s):** heated indoor. **Leisure Activities:** sauna, whirlpool, waterslide, limited exercise equipment. **Guest Services:** valet and coin laundry. **Business Services:** meeting rooms, PC. **Cards:** AX, DS, MC, VI. **Special Amenities:** free local telephone calls and free newspaper. *(See color ad p 5)*

SOME UNITS
(SD) ... (DATA PORT)

GRANDVIEW MOTEL
Phone: (250)372-1312

(CAA) (SAVE)

6/15-9/15	1P: $69-$72	2P: $75-$89	XP: $10	F16
4/1-6/14	1P: $58-$60	2P: $63-$73	XP: $5	F16
3/1-3/31	1P: $52-$54	2P: $56-$63	XP: $5	F16
9/16-2/28	1P: $48-$50	2P: $55-$60	XP: $5	F16

▼▼ ▼▼

Motel **Location:** Trans-Canada Hwy 1, exit 369 (Columbia St) eastbound, 2 km n; exit 370 (Summit Dr) westbound to Columbia St via City Centre. 463 Grandview Terrace V2C 3Z3. Fax: 250/372-0847. **Facility:** 28 one-bedroom standard units, some with efficiencies. 2 stories (no elevator), exterior corridors. **Parking:** on-site, winter plug-ins. **Terms:** office hours 8 am-11 pm, 10% service charge, small pets only ($5 extra charge). **Pool(s):** heated outdoor. **Leisure Activities:** gas barbecue area. **Guest Services:** coin laundry. **Cards:** DC, JC, MC, VI. **Special Amenities:** free local telephone calls and free newspaper. *(See color ad below)*

SOME UNITS
(SD) ... FEE

HAMPTON INN *Book at aaa.com*   **Phone:** (250)571-7897

(CAA) (SAVE)

4/1-9/30 [ECP]	1P: $130-$250	2P: $130-$250	XP: $10 F18
3/1-3/31 & 10/1-2/28 [ECP]	1P: $99-$149	2P: $99-$149	XP: $10 F18

Location: Trans-Canada Hwy 1, exit 368 (Hillside Ave), just s via Hillside Way. 1245 Rogers Way V1S 1R9. Fax: 250/571-7896. **Facility:** 81 one-bedroom standard units, some with whirlpools. 3 stories, interior corridors. *Bath:* combo or shower only. **Parking:** on-site, winter plug-ins. **Terms:** package plans.
Small-scale Hotel
Amenities: video games (fee), high-speed Internet, voice mail, irons, hair dryers. **Pool(s):** heated indoor. **Leisure Activities:** whirlpool, waterslide, limited exercise equipment. **Guest Services:** valet and coin laundry. **Business Services:** meeting rooms, PC. **Cards:** AX, DC, DS, MC, VI. **Special Amenities:** free expanded continental breakfast and free newspaper. *(See color ad below)*

SOME UNITS

(icons) ⓈD 🍴 🏊 ⊗ 📶 DATA PORT 💻 / ⊠ 📱 🖥 /

HOLIDAY INN EXPRESS KAMLOOPS *Book at aaa.com*   **Phone:** (250)372-3474

(CAA) (SAVE)

5/1-9/15 [ECP]	1P: $125-$150	2P: $125-$150	
9/16-10/31 [ECP]	1P: $115-$125	2P: $115-$125	
3/1-4/30 & 11/1-2/28 [ECP]	1P: $109-$119	2P: $109-$119	

Location: Trans-Canada Hwy 1, exit 367 (Pacific Way), just w. 1550 Versatile Dr V1S 1X4. Fax: 250/372-1585.
Small-scale Hotel Facility: 80 units. 79 one-bedroom standard units. 1 one-bedroom suite ($160-$230) with whirlpool. 4 stories, interior corridors. **Pool(s):** heated indoor. **Leisure Activities:** whirlpool, limited exercise equipment. **Guest Services:** valet laundry. **Business Services:** meeting rooms. **Cards:** AX, DC, DS, JC, MC, VI. **Special Amenities:** free expanded continental breakfast and free local telephone calls. *(See color ad card insert)*

SOME UNITS

ⓈD 🍴 🚹M 🏊 📶 DATA PORT / ⊠ 📱 /

HOSPITALITY INN *Book at aaa.com*   **Phone:** (250)374-4164

6/16-9/30	1P: $67-$79	2P: $71-$83	XP: $5 F12
4/16-6/15	1P: $59-$71	2P: $63-$75	XP: $5 F12
3/1-4/15 & 10/1-2/28	1P: $50-$60	2P: $55-$60	XP: $5 F12

Motel
Location: Trans-Canada Hwy 1, exit 369 (Columbia St) eastbound, 2 km n; exit 370 (Summit Dr) westbound to Columbia St via City Centre. 500 W Columbia St V2C 1K6. Fax: 250/374-6971. **Facility:** 76 one-bedroom standard units, some with efficiencies. 2 stories (no elevator), exterior corridors. **Parking:** on-site, winter plug-ins. **Terms:** office hours 7 am-midnight, small pets only ($10 extra charge). **Pool(s):** heated outdoor. **Leisure Activities:** sauna, whirlpool. **Cards:** AX, DC, DS, JC, MC, VI.

SOME UNITS

(ASK) ⓈD 🐾 🍴 🏊 📶 📱 💻 / ⊠ /
FEE

KAMLOOPS SUPER 8 MOTEL *Book at aaa.com*   **Phone:** 250/374-8688

(CAA) (SAVE)

6/16-9/15	1P: $84-$150	2P: $92-$150	XP: $8 F12
3/1-6/15 & 9/16-2/28	1P: $56-$120	2P: $62-$120	XP: $6 F12

Motel
Location: Trans-Canada Hwy 1, exit 367 (Pacific Way). 1521 Hugh Allan Dr V1S 1P4. Fax: 250/374-8688.
Facility: 47 one-bedroom standard units. 2 stories (no elevator), interior corridors. **Parking:** on-site. **Terms:** pets ($6 extra charge, with prior approval). **Cards:** AX, DC, DS, MC, VI. **Special Amenities:** free continental breakfast and free local telephone calls.

SOME UNITS

ⓈD 🐾 🍴 🚹M DATA PORT / ⊠ /
FEE

KAMLOOPS TRAVELODGE MOUNTVIEW *Book at aaa.com*   **Phone:** (250)374-4788

5/1-9/30 [CP]	1P: $99	2P: $109	XP: $10 F17
3/1-4/30 & 10/1-2/28 [CP]	1P: $79	2P: $89	XP: $10 F17

Motel
Location: Trans-Canada Hwy 1, exit 368 (Hillside Ave), just s. 1225 Rogers Way V1S 1R9. Fax: 250/374-4017.
Facility: 53 units. 52 one-bedroom standard units, some with efficiencies and/or whirlpools. 1 two-bedroom suite ($120-$165). 3 stories, exterior corridors. **Parking:** on-site. **Terms:** office hours 7 am-midnight. **Amenities:** *Some:* high-speed Internet. **Pool(s):** heated outdoor. **Leisure Activities:** whirlpool. **Guest Services:** coin laundry. **Business Services:** meeting rooms. **Cards:** AX, DC, DS, MC, VI. *(See color ad p 486)*

SOME UNITS

(ASK) ⓈD 🍴 🚹M 🏊 📶 DATA PORT 💻 / ⊠ 📱 🖥 /

MAVERICK MOTOR INN

Motel

All Year [ECP]   1P: $75-$149   2P: $85-$149   XP: $10   F10

Phone: (250)374-9666

Location: Trans-Canada Hwy 1, exit 368 (Hillside Ave). 1250 W Trans-Canada Hwy 1 V2C 6R3. Fax: 250/374-5645. **Facility:** 42 one-bedroom standard units, some with efficiencies. 2 stories (no elevator), interior corridors. **Parking:** on-site. **Terms:** office hours 7 am-11 pm. **Amenities:** video library (fee), voice mail, irons, hair dryers. **Pool(s):** heated indoor. **Leisure Activities:** sauna, whirlpool, waterslide, limited exercise equipment. **Guest Services:** coin laundry. **Business Services:** meeting rooms. **Cards:** AX, CB, DC, MC, VI.

SOME UNITS

QUALITY INN   *Book at aaa.com*

(CAA) (SAVE)

Motel

5/1-10/15   1P: $90-$115   2P: $105-$125   XP: $15   F12
3/1-4/30 & 10/16-2/28   1P: $65-$80   2P: $75-$85   XP: $10   F12

Phone: (250)851-0111

Location: Trans-Canada Hwy 1, exit 368 (Hillside Ave). 1860 Rogers Pl V1S 1T7. Fax: 250/851-0380. **Facility:** 63 one-bedroom standard units, some with efficiencies and/or whirlpools. 2 stories (no elevator), interior corridors. **Parking:** on-site, winter plug-ins. **Terms:** package plans. **Amenities:** irons, hair dryers. **Pool(s):** small heated outdoor. **Leisure Activities:** sauna, whirlpool, limited exercise equipment. **Guest Services:** coin laundry. **Business Services:** meeting rooms. **Cards:** AX, DC, DS, JC, MC, VI. **Special Amenities:** free local telephone calls and early check-in/late check-out.

SOME UNITS

RAMADA INN-KAMLOOPS   *Book at aaa.com*

(CAA) (SAVE)

Small-scale Hotel

5/16-10/15   1P: $99-$109   2P: $99-$109   XP: $10   F17
3/1-5/15 & 10/16-2/28   1P: $69-$89   2P: $69-$89   XP: $10   F17

Phone: (250)374-0358

Location: Trans-Canada Hwy 1, exit 369 (Columbia St) eastbound, 2 km n; exit 370 (Summit Dr) westbound to Columbia St via City Centre. 555 W Columbia St V2C 1K7. Fax: 250/374-0691. **Facility:** 90 one-bedroom standard units, some with efficiencies. 2-3 stories, interior corridors. **Parking:** on-site, winter plug-ins. **Terms:** [BP] & [CP] meal plans available, pets ($10 extra charge). **Amenities:** video library, voice mail, irons, hair dryers. **Dining:** 6:30 am-10 & 5-10 pm, cocktails. **Pool(s):** heated outdoor. **Leisure Activities:** sauna, whirlpool, limited exercise equipment. **Guest Services:** valet laundry. **Business Services:** meeting rooms, PC. **Cards:** AX, DC, MC, VI. **Special Amenities:** free local telephone calls and free newspaper.

SOME UNITS

RANCHLAND MOTEL

Phone: (250)828-8787

	6/1-9/15	1P: $59-$63	2P: $67-$71	XP: $8
	3/1-5/31	1P: $40-$63	2P: $55-$67	XP: $8
	9/16-11/30	1P: $49-$55	2P: $55-$59	XP: $5
Motel	12/1-2/28	1P: $49	2P: $59	XP: $5

Location: 4.5 km e on Trans-Canada Hwy 1, exit River Rd, then just w along service access road. 2357 Trans-Canada Hwy E V2C 4A8. **Fax:** 250/828-8786. **Facility:** 36 one-bedroom standard units, some with efficiencies. 2 stories (no elevator), exterior corridors. **Parking:** on-site, winter plug-ins. **Terms:** office hours 7 am-11 pm, small pets only ($10 extra charge). **Leisure Activities:** sauna, whirlpool. **Guest Services:** coin laundry. **Cards:** AX, DC, DS, JC, MC, VI.

SOME UNITS

(ASK) (S/D) [⊞] [¶†] [⊟] [⊡] / [✕] /
FEE

SCOTT'S INN & RESTAURANT

Phone: (250)372-8221

	6/1-8/31 [CP]	1P: $59-$79	2P: $69-$99	XP: $10	D16
	9/1-11/30 [CP]	1P: $49-$65	2P: $69-$89	XP: $10	D16
	3/1-5/31 [CP]	1P: $49-$69	2P: $59-$89	XP: $10	D16
Motel	12/1-2/28 [CP]	1P: $49-$59	2P: $59-$79	XP: $10	D16

Location: Trans-Canada Hwy 1, exit 369 (Columbia St) eastbound, 5 km n; exit City Centre westbound, 1.6 km s on Columbia St. Located in a residential area across from a playground. 551 11th Ave V2C 9444. **Fax:** 250/372-9444. **Facility:** 51 units. 48 one- and 3 two-bedroom standard units, some with efficiencies or kitchens. 2 stories (no elevator), exterior corridors. *Bath:* combo or shower only. **Parking:** on-site, winter plug-ins. **Terms:** office hours 7 am-11 pm, package plans, small pets only ($6-$10 extra charge). **Amenities:** hair dryers. **Dining:** 7 am-9 pm, wine/beer only. **Pool(s):** heated indoor. **Leisure Activities:** whirlpool. **Guest Services:** coin laundry. **Cards:** AX, DC, DS, JC, MC, VI. **Special Amenities:** free continental breakfast and free local telephone calls. *(See color ad p 486)*

SOME UNITS

(S/D) [⊞] [¶] [⊃] [⊡] / [✕] [⊟] [⊡] /
FEE

***The following lodgings were either not evaluated or did not
meet AAA rating requirements but are listed for your information only.***

BEST WESTERN KAMLOOPS

Phone: 250/828-6660

[fyi] Not evaluated. **Location:** Trans-Canada Hwy 1, exit 368 (Hillside Ave), just s. 1250 Rogers Way V1S 1N5. Facilities, services, and decor characterize a mid-range property.

PLAZA HERITAGE HOTEL

Phone: 250/377-8075

[fyi] Not evaluated. **Location:** Trans-Canada Hwy 1, exit 369 (Columbia St) eastbound; exit 370 (Summit Dr) westbound, Columbia St to City Centre, then just n on 4th Ave. 405 Victoria St V2C 2A9. Facilities, services, and decor characterize a mid-range property.

--- **WHERE TO DINE** ---

CHAPTERS VIEWPOINT

Lunch: $4-$13   **Dinner:** $11-$39   **Phone:** 250/374-3224

Canadian

Location: Trans-Canada Hwy 1, exit 369 (Columbia St) eastbound, 2 km n; exit 370 (Summit Dr) westbound to Columbia St via City Centre Rt; in Panorama/Howard Johnson Inn. 610 W Columbia St V2C 1L1. **Hours:** 8 am-10 pm. Closed: 12/25, 12/26. **Reservations:** suggested. **Features:** This restaurant's great location offers a spectacular view of the city and surrounding hills. The well-prepared menu features New Mexican cuisine, beef and prime rib, chicken and seafood. The decor is Pacific Northwest and makes use of the Douglas fir for beams. Casual dress; cocktails. **Parking:** on-site. **Cards:** AX, DC, MC, VI. [✕]

LEGENDS WEST

Lunch: $7-$15   **Dinner:** $15-$40   **Phone:** 250/372-3418

International

Location: Trans-Canada Hwy 1, exit 367 (Pacific Way); adjacent to Holiday Inn Express. 1550 Versatile Dr V1S 1X4. **Hours:** 11 am-10 pm. Closed: 1/1, 12/25. **Reservations:** suggested. **Features:** While Chef Bentley may reserve his most playful creative ideas for the dinner specials, the eclectic menu keeps its focus on fresh seafood, meats, pasta and stir-frys. Dishes borrow inspiration from Asia, Europe and America. An intimate, lovingly landscaped garden patio awaits patrons while in season. Casual dress; cocktails. **Parking:** on-site. **Cards:** AX, MC, VI. [✕]

ON THE ROCKS PUB & GRILL

Lunch: $7-$13   **Dinner:** $7-$13   **Phone:** 250/374-9761

Canadian

Location: Trans-Canada Hwy 1, exit 368 (Hillside Ave), just s. 1265 Rogers Way V1S 1R9. **Hours:** 11 am-midnight. Closed: 12/25. **Features:** The sports bar and grill features tons of appetizers, burgers, sandwiches, pitas and wraps, plus daily specials and lots of beers on tap. No one younger than 19 is permitted. The enclosed smoking room has a cozy fireplace. Casual dress; cocktails. **Parking:** on-site. **Cards:** MC, VI. [✕]

ORIENTAL GARDENS RESTAURANT

Dinner: $10-$20   **Phone:** 250/372-2344

Chinese

Location: Victoria St at 5th Ave; downtown. 545 Victoria St V2C 2B1. **Hours:** 5 pm-11 pm, Fri & Sat-midnight. Closed: 12/25. **Reservations:** suggested. **Features:** Delicious Japanese and Chinese entrees are featured at this restaurant, where a full sushi bar and Japanese-style private dining booths are also offered. If you park in the lot to the side, ask the restaurant staff to validate your ticket stub. Casual dress; cocktails. **Parking:** on-site (fee) and street. **Cards:** AX, MC, VI. [✕]

RIC'S MEDITERRANEAN GRILL

Lunch: $9-$16   **Dinner:** $15-$29   **Phone:** 250/372-7771

Steak & Seafood

Location: At 2nd Ave; downtown. 227 Victoria St V2C 2A1. **Hours:** 11 am-10 pm, Sat & Sun from 4:30 pm; to 9:30 pm, Fri-10 pm, Sat 4 pm-10 pm, Sun 4 pm-9:30 pm in winter. Closed: 12/25. **Reservations:** suggested. **Features:** A youthful and bustling ambience characterizes the popular downtown restaurant. The food blends Mediterranean ingredients with seafood, fish and steaks to create dishes that show sensitivity to International influences. The long list of appetizers and by-the-glass wine choices let diners turn dinner into a sampling event. Casual dress; cocktails. **Parking:** street. **Cards:** AX, MC, VI. [✕]

THIS OLD STEAK & FISH HOUSE

Lunch: $6-$12   **Dinner:** $14-$32   **Phone:** 250/374-3227

Steak & Seafood

Location: Trans-Canada Hwy 1, exit 369 (Columbia St), just n to 2nd Ave, then just w at 2nd Ave and Battle St. 172 Battle St V2C 2L2. **Hours:** 11:30 am-2 & 5-10 pm, Sat & Sun from 5 pm. Closed major holidays. **Reservations:** suggested. **Features:** Steak and seafood are at the heart of the menu at the cozy bistro-style restaurant near downtown. The weekly changing fish menu might feature such creations as stuffed halibut, lobster and salmon. Also offered are some Mexican dishes, as well as entree salads. The upstairs meeting room overlooks the city. Cocktails. **Parking:** on-site. **Cards:** AX, MC, VI. [✕]

WARUNEE'S THAI RESTAURANT   Lunch: $8-$15   Dinner: $8-$15   Phone: 250/554-7080
Thai   **Location:** From Overlander Bridge, 1 km nw; at Aspen Ave. 413 Tranquille Rd V2B 3G9. **Hours:** 11 am-3 & 5-11 pm, Sat & Sun from 5 pm. Closed: Mon. **Reservations:** suggested. **Features:** Visitors experience the delightful fragrances of coconut, fresh mint and kaffir lime. The traditions of Thai cuisine are proudly sustained in the quaint North Shore restaurant, which is decorated with sculptures, maps and artifacts from the beloved country. Casual dress; cocktails. **Parking:** street. **Cards:** AX, DC, MC, VI.

The following restaurant has not been evaluated by AAA
but is listed for your information only.

UNIVERSITY COLLEGE OF THE CARIBOO DINING
ROOM   Phone: 250/828-5354
[fyi]   Not evaluated. **Location:** Trans-Canada Hwy 1, exit 369 (Columbia St) eastbound; exit 370 (Summit Dr) westbound, Columbia St to City Center, then just w on McGill Rd. 900 College Way V2C 5N3. **Features:** UCC student chefs invite the public to sample the culinary delights as they prepare two or four course meals evenings in the dining room or stop in for breakfast or lunch weekdays. Pay lot in effect during the day, complimentary parking in the evening. Look for the Food Training Centre.

KELOWNA pop. 96,288

--- WHERE TO STAY ---

"ABBOTT VILLA" TRAVELODGE KELOWNA   *Book at aaa.com*   Phone: (250)763-7771

	5/1-9/30	1P: $97-$126	2P: $97-$126	XP: $10	F16
	10/1-12/31	1P: $81-$102	2P: $81-$102	XP: $10	F16
Motel	1/1-2/28	1P: $78-$102	2P: $78-$102	XP: $10	F16
	3/1-4/30	1P: $76-$99	2P: $76-$99	XP: $10	F16

Location: Hwy 97 N (Harvey Ave), just w; between Leon and Lawrence aves. 1627 Abbott St V1Y 1A9. Fax: 250/762-2402. **Facility:** Smoke free premises. 52 units. 49 one-bedroom standard units, some with kitchens. 3 two-bedroom suites ($150-$225), some with whirlpools. 1-3 stories (no elevator), exterior corridors. **Parking:** on-site. **Terms:** cancellation fee imposed, package plans. **Amenities:** hair dryers. **Pool(s):** small heated outdoor. **Leisure Activities:** sauna, whirlpool. **Guest Services:** valet laundry. **Cards:** AX, DC, MC, VI.

SOME UNITS
[icons: ASK S⊃ ➤ ✕ 🎦 DATA PORT 🔲 📷 / 🖥]

ACCENT INNS   *Book at aaa.com*   Phone: (250)862-8888

	7/1-9/30	1P: $129-$149	2P: $139-$159	XP: $10	F16
	5/1-6/30	1P: $99-$119	2P: $109-$129	XP: $10	F16
	3/1-4/30 & 10/1-2/28	1P: $89-$109	2P: $99-$119	XP: $10	F16

Location: Corner of Hwy 97 N (Harvey Ave) and Gordon Dr. Located across from a shopping mall. 1140 Harvey Ave
Small-scale Hotel   V1Y 6E7. Fax: 250/862-8884. **Facility:** 102 units. 89 one-bedroom standard units, some with efficiencies. 13 one-bedroom suites, some with efficiencies or kitchens. 3 stories, exterior corridors. **Parking:** on-site, winter plug-ins. **Terms:** check-in 4 pm, pets ($10 fee, with prior approval). **Amenities:** video games, voice mail, hair dryers. *Some:* dual phone lines, irons. **Dining:** 7 am-10 pm, cocktails. **Pool(s):** heated outdoor. **Leisure Activities:** sauna, whirlpool, limited exercise equipment. **Guest Services:** sundries, valet and coin laundry. **Business Services:** meeting rooms, PC. **Cards:** AX, DC, JC, MC, VI. **Special Amenities:** free local telephone calls and free newspaper. *(See color ad below & p 608)*

SOME UNITS
[icons: S⊃ FEE 🛏 🍽 &M ➤ ✕ 🎦 🔲 📷 / ✕ DATA PORT 🖥]

A VISTA VILLA BED, BBQ & SPA   Phone: 250/762-7837

	5/16-10/15 [MAP]	2P: $239-$269
	10/16-2/28 [MAP]	2P: $229-$259
Bed & Breakfast	3/1-5/15 [MAP]	2P: $219-$249

Location: Hwy 97 (Harvey Ave), 2 km n on Spall to Summit, just e to Valley, follow Valley which changes to Ryder Dr. 962 Ryder Dr V1Y 7T5. Fax: 250/762-7167. **Facility:** Though classified as a B&B, this is a decadent Bed & BBQ; a continental breakfast is in your room, and a BBQ dinner is served nightly on the deck. Designated smoking area. 4 one-bedroom standard units with whirlpools. 2 stories (no elevator), interior/exterior corridors. **Parking:** on-site, winter plug-ins. **Terms:** check-in 4 pm, 2 night minimum stay - seasonal, age restrictions may apply, 21 day cancellation notice-fee imposed, package plans. **Amenities:** video library, CD players, hair dryers. **Pool(s):** small heated outdoor. **Leisure Activities:** limited exercise equipment, spa. **Guest Services:** gift shop, complimentary evening beverages, complimentary laundry. **Business Services:** PC, fax. **Cards:** AX, MC, VI.

SOME UNITS
[icons: ➤ ✕ 🎦 🅩 🔲 📷 / 📺 🖥 /]

BEST WESTERN INN-KELOWNA

Book at aaa.com   Phone: (250)860-1212

CAA SAVE

6/10-10/2 [ECP]	1P: $165-$269	2P: $165-$269	XP: $15	F17
4/28-6/9 [ECP]	1P: $145-$259	2P: $145-$259	XP: $15	F17
10/3-2/28 [ECP]	1P: $115-$259	2P: $115-$259	XP: $15	F17
3/1-4/27 [ECP]	1P: $125-$249	2P: $125-$249	XP: $15	F17

Small-scale Hotel **Location:** 1 km s of jct Hwy 33 and 97 N; corner of Leckie Rd. 2402 Hwy 97 N V1X 4J1. Fax: 250/860-0675. **Facility:** 145 units. 123 one-bedroom standard units, some with whirlpools. 22 one-bedroom suites with efficiencies. 8 stories, interior/exterior corridors. *Bath:* combo or shower only. **Parking:** on-site. **Terms:** check-in 4 pm, cancellation fee imposed, pets ($15 extra charge). **Amenities:** video games, voice mail, irons, hair dryers. *Some:* high-speed Internet, honor bars. **Dining:** 7 am-9 pm, Sat & Sun from 7:30 am, cocktails. **Pool(s):** heated indoor. **Leisure Activities:** whirlpools, steamroom, exercise room, spa. **Guest Services:** gift shop, valet and coin laundry. **Business Services:** conference facilities, PC (fee). **Cards:** AX, DC, DS, MC, VI. **Special Amenities:** free expanded continental breakfast and free local telephone calls. *(See color ad below)*

SOME UNITS

COMFORT INN

Book at aaa.com   Phone: (250)769-2355

CAA SAVE

5/1-9/30	1P: $109-$139	2P: $109-$139	XP: $10	F16
10/1-10/31	1P: $99-$129	2P: $99-$129	XP: $10	F16
3/1-4/30 & 11/1-2/28	1P: $89-$129	2P: $89-$129	XP: $10	F16

Small-scale Hotel **Location:** Jct Hwy 97 (Harvey Ave) and Bartley Rd, s to Ross Rd. 1655 Westgate Rd V1Z 3P1. Fax: 250/769-2370. **Facility:** 81 units. 80 one-bedroom standard units, some with kitchens and/or whirlpools. 1 one-bedroom suite ($159-$229) with kitchen. 2 stories (no elevator), interior corridors. **Terms:** cancellation fee imposed, package plans, small pets only ($10 fee, in designated units). **Pool(s):** heated indoor. **Leisure Activities:** whirlpool, exercise room. **Guest Services:** valet and coin laundry. **Business Services:** meeting rooms. **Cards:** AX, DC, DS, JC, MC, VI. **Special Amenities:** free continental breakfast and free newspaper.

SOME UNITS

DILWORTH MOTOR LODGE

Phone: (250)762-9666

7/1-9/30	1P: $99-$119	2P: $99-$119	XP: $10	F16
5/1-6/30	1P: $89-$109	2P: $89-$109	XP: $10	F16
3/1-4/30 & 10/1-2/28	1P: $69-$89	2P: $69-$89	XP: $10	F16

Small-scale Hotel **Location:** Hwy 97 N (Harvey Ave), just w. Located behind the White Spot Restaurant. 1755 Dilworth Dr V1Y 8R1. Fax: 250/862-8484. **Facility:** 50 units. 48 one-bedroom standard units, some with efficiencies or kitchens. 2 one-bedroom suites with kitchens. 3 stories (no elevator), interior corridors. **Parking:** on-site. **Terms:** weekly rates available, package plans. **Amenities:** voice mail, hair dryers. **Pool(s):** small heated indoor. **Leisure Activities:** sauna, whirlpool. **Guest Services:** coin laundry. **Cards:** AX, DC, MC, VI.

SOME UNITS

THE GRAND OKANAGAN LAKEFRONT RESORT & CONFERENCE CENTRE

Book at aaa.com   Phone: (250)763-4500

6/14-10/6	1P: $299-$539	2P: $299-$539	XP: $15	F17
3/1-6/13 & 10/7-11/30	1P: $189-$420	2P: $189-$420	XP: $15	F17
12/1-2/28	1P: $179-$300	2P: $179-$300	XP: $15	F17

Resort Large-scale Hotel **Location:** Hwy 97 (Harvey Ave), 1 km w. 1310 Water St V1Y 9P3. Fax: 250/763-4565. **Facility:** Featuring a spa, a casino and waterfront views, this luxurious, full-service, resort hotel has a retreat-like ambience. 320 units. 253 one-bedroom standard units, some with whirlpools. 17 one- and 50 two-bedroom suites, some with kitchens and/or whirlpools. 10 stories, interior corridors. *Bath:* combo or shower only. **Parking:** on-site (fee) and valet. **Terms:** check-in 4 pm, package plans, small pets only ($10 fee). **Amenities:** video games, high-speed Internet (fee), voice mail, irons, hair dryers. *Some:* CD players, dual phone lines, honor bars. **Dining:** Grand Bay Cafe, see separate listing. **Pool(s):** heated outdoor, heated indoor/outdoor. **Leisure Activities:** sauna, whirlpools, rental boats, rental canoes, rental paddleboats, boat dock, fishing, rental bicycles, jogging, spa. *Fee:* waterskiing, game room. **Guest Services:** gift shop, valet and coin laundry. **Business Services:** conference facilities, business center. **Cards:** AX, DC, DS, MC, VI.

SOME UNITS

THE GRAPEVINE BED & BREAKFAST

▼▼▼

Bed & Breakfast

5/1-10/15 [BP]		2P: $135-$150	XP: $20
3/1-4/30 & 10/16-2/28 [BP]		2P: $80-$90	XP: $20

Phone: (250)860-5580

Location: Hwy 97 N (Harvey Ave), 4 km w on Dilworth Dr, then just n. 2621 Longhill Rd V1V 2G5. **Fax:** 250/860-5586. **Facility:** A private garden and surrounding vineyards add country charm to this B&B located close to the city. Designated smoking area. 4 one-bedroom standard units. 2 stories (no elevator), interior corridors. *Bath:* combo or shower only. **Parking:** on-site. **Terms:** check-in 4 pm, 2 night minimum stay - weekends, age restrictions may apply, 14 day cancellation notice-fee imposed, weekly rates available. **Amenities:** video library, hair dryers. *Some:* CD players. **Pool(s):** small heated outdoor, saltwater. **Leisure Activities:** whirlpool. **Guest Services:** coin laundry. **Cards:** AX, MC, VI.

SOME UNITS

🛋 ✕ 🐾 / 📼 /

HOLIDAY INN EXPRESS KELOWNA   *Book at aaa.com*

▼▼▼

Small-scale Hotel

6/24-10/9 [ECP]	1P: $169-$189	2P: $169-$189	XP: $10	F19
4/1-6/23 [ECP]	1P: $149-$169	2P: $149-$169	XP: $10	F19
3/1-3/31 & 10/10-2/28 [ECP]	1P: $129-$149	2P: $129-$149	XP: $10	F19

Phone: (250)763-0500

Location: 1 km s of jct Hwy 97 N (Harvey Ave) and 33. 2429 Hwy 97 N V1X 4J2. Fax: 250/763-7555. **Facility:** 120 one-bedroom standard units, some with whirlpools. 4 stories, interior corridors. *Bath:* combo or shower only. **Parking:** on-site. **Terms:** check-in 4 pm, package plans. **Amenities:** video games, voice mail, irons, hair dryers. *Some:* dual phone lines. **Pool(s):** heated indoor. **Leisure Activities:** whirlpool, exercise room. **Guest Services:** valet laundry. **Business Services:** meeting rooms, PC. **Cards:** AX, CB, DC, DS, JC, MC, VI. *(See color ad card insert)*

SOME UNITS

(ASK) 🅂🄳 🍽 ♿🅼 🛋 📹 DATA PORT 🛏 🖥 / ✕ 📠 /

THE HOTEL ELDORADO

▼▼

Small-scale Hotel

6/11-8/25	1P: $169-$299	2P: $169-$299	XP: $15	F17
8/26-2/28	1P: $139-$219	2P: $139-$219	XP: $15	F17
5/1-6/10	1P: $119-$199	2P: $119-$199	XP: $15	F17
3/1-4/30	1P: $69-$159	2P: $69-$159	XP: $15	F17

Phone: (250)763-7500

Location: Hwy 97, 4 km s on Pandosy, turns into Lakeshore Dr, just w. 500 Cook Rd V1W 3G9. **Fax:** 250/861-4779. **Facility:** Designated smoking area. 19 one-bedroom standard units, some with whirlpools. 3 stories, interior corridors. *Bath:* combo or shower only. **Parking:** on-site. **Terms:** office hours 7 am-11 pm, 7 day cancellation notice-fee imposed, package plans. **Amenities:** voice mail, hair dryers. **Dining:** The Eldorado Restaurant, see separate listing. **Leisure Activities:** rental boats. *Fee:* marina, waterskiing. **Guest Services:** sundries, valet laundry. **Business Services:** meeting rooms, PC. **Cards:** AX, DC, MC, VI.

(ASK) 🍽 🍸 ✕ ✕ 📹 DATA PORT

THE KELOWNA LAKESHORE INN   *Book at aaa.com*

(CAA) (SAVE)

▼▼▼▼

Motel

All Year [CP]	1P: $69-$199	2P: $69-$199	XP: $10	F14

Phone: 250/763-4717

Location: Hwy 97 (Harvey Ave), 4 km s on Pandosy (which becomes Lakeshore Rd). 3756 Lakeshore Rd V1W 3L4. **Fax:** 250/712-3285. **Facility:** Designated smoking area. 46 units. 44 one-bedroom standard units. 2 one-bedroom suites with kitchens. 2 stories (no elevator), exterior corridors. **Parking:** on-site. **Terms:** 3 night minimum stay - seasonal, package plans. **Amenities:** voice mail, hair dryers. *Some:* DVD players. **Pool(s):** heated outdoor. **Leisure Activities:** whirlpool, boat dock, badminton, barbecues. **Guest Services:** valet and coin laundry. **Cards:** AX, MC, VI. **Special Amenities:** free continental breakfast and free newspaper.

SOME UNITS

🍽 🛋 ✕ ✕ DATA PORT 🛏 🖥 🖥 / 📼 /

KELOWNA MOTOR INN

(CAA) (SAVE)

▼▼▼▼

Motel

6/1-9/30	1P: $105-$139	2P: $109-$159	XP: $10	F12
3/1-5/31	1P: $85-$119	2P: $89-$119	XP: $10	F12
10/1-2/28	1P: $75-$99	2P: $79-$109	XP: $10	F12

Phone: (250)762-2533

Location: Corner of Hwy 97 N (Harvey Ave) and Gordon Dr. Located across from the mall. 1070 Harvey Ave V1Y 8S4. **Fax:** 250/868-3874. **Facility:** 112 units. 100 one-bedroom standard units, some with efficiencies (utensils extra charge) and/or whirlpools. 8 one- and 4 two-bedroom suites ($119-$169), some with efficiencies. 2 stories (no elevator), exterior corridors. **Parking:** on-site. **Terms:** cancellation fee imposed. **Amenities:** voice mail, hair dryers. **Dining:** Mekong Restaurant, see separate listing. **Pool(s):** heated indoor. **Leisure Activities:** whirlpool, steamroom. **Guest Services:** coin laundry. **Cards:** AX, MC, VI. **Special Amenities:** free local telephone calls and free newspaper.

SOME UNITS

🅂🄳 🍽 🛋 📹 🖥 / ✕ 📼 🛏 🖥 /

FEE

MANTEO RESORT-WATERFRONT HOTEL & VILLAS   *Book at aaa.com*

(CAA) (SAVE)

▼▼▼

Resort
Condominium

7/1-9/4		2P: $240-$620	XP: $15	F17
4/22-6/30		2P: $215-$470	XP: $15	F17
3/1-4/21 & 9/5-2/28		2P: $149-$350	XP: $15	F17

Phone: (250)860-1031

Location: Hwy 97 (Harvey Ave), 3.2 km s on Pandosy (which becomes Lakeshore Rd). 3762 Lakeshore Rd V1W 3L4. **Fax:** 250/860-1041. **Facility:** Set along the lake, this resort offers extensive recreational facilities as well as large, upscale rooms ranging from studio to condo style. Designated smoking area. 102 units. 48 one-bedroom standard units. 30 one-, 17 two- and 7 three-bedroom suites with kitchens. 4 stories, interior/exterior corridors. **Parking:** on-site. **Terms:** check-in 4 pm, 7 day cancellation notice, package plans. **Amenities:** voice mail, irons, hair dryers. *Some:* video games, CD players, high-speed Internet. **Dining:** Wild Apple Grill, see separate listing. **Pool(s):** 2 heated outdoor, heated indoor, wading. **Leisure Activities:** saunas, whirlpools, steamrooms, waterslide, rental boats, rental canoes, rental paddleboats, boat dock, fishing, putting green, lighted tennis court, recreation programs, movie theatre, library, water playground, playground, exercise room. *Fee:* massage, game room. **Guest Services:** valet and coin laundry. **Business Services:** conference facilities, PC. **Cards:** AX, DC, MC, VI. **Special Amenities:** free newspaper.

SOME UNITS

🅂🄳 🍽 ♿ 🛋 ✕ ✕ 📹 DATA PORT 🖥 / 📼 🛏 🖥 /

OTELLA'S WINE COUNTRY INN

Phone: 250/763-4922

▼▼▼▼ All Year — 2P: $125-$175

Bed & Breakfast
Location: Hwy 97 (Harvey Ave), 2 km n on Spall/Glenmore rds, just w on High Summit Rd, 0.8 km on Clifton Rd, just ne on Caramillo, then just n. Located in a secluded residential area. 42 Altura Rd V1V 1B6. Fax: 250/763-4982. **Facility:** The inn's owners are wine enthusiasts who have created picturesque gardens and serve up gourmet meals on a vine-covered patio. Smoke free premises. 4 one-bedroom standard units. 3 stories (no elevator), interior corridors. **Bath:** some shared or private, combo or shower only. **Parking:** on-site. **Terms:** check-in 3:30 pm, 2 night minimum stay, age restrictions may apply, 14 day cancellation notice-fee imposed, package plans. **Amenities:** hair dryers. **Leisure Activities:** cross country skiing, hiking trails. **Guest Services:** gift shop, complimentary evening beverages, coin laundry. **Cards:** VI.

SOME UNITS

⊠ / 📺 [VCR] 🔌 /

THE ROYAL ANNE HOTEL

Phone: (250)763-2277

▼▼ ▼▼				
6/30-9/5	1P: $129-$189	2P: $129-$189	XP: $10	F15
5/20-6/29	1P: $129-$159	2P: $129-$159	XP: $10	F15
3/1-5/19 & 9/6-2/28	1P: $89-$159	2P: $89-$159	XP: $10	F15

Small-scale Hotel
Location: Corner of Pandosy and Bernard St; downtown. 348 Bernard St V1Y 6N5. Fax: 250/763-2636. **Facility:** Smoke free premises. 52 one-bedroom standard units. 5 stories, interior corridors. **Parking:** on-site. **Terms:** cancellation fee imposed, package plans, $2 service charge, pets ($10 fee). **Amenities:** voice mail, irons, hair dryers. **Leisure Activities:** saunas, exercise room. **Guest Services:** valet laundry. **Business Services:** meeting rooms, PC. **Cards:** AX, DC, MC, VI.

[ASK] [S🔒] 🔁 🐾 📺 ⊠ 🎥 [DATA PORT] 💻
FEE FEE

SAFARI INN   *Book at aaa.com*

Phone: (250)860-8122

▼▼▼				
5/15-10/1	1P: $69-$149	2P: $69-$149	XP: $5	F16
10/2-2/28	1P: $54-$94	2P: $54-$94	XP: $5	F16
3/1-5/14	1P: $59-$89	2P: $59-$89	XP: $5	F16

Motel
Location: Just s of Hwy 97 N (Harvey Ave) and 33. 1651 Powick Rd V1X 4L1. Fax: 250/860-0828. **Facility:** 37 units. 26 one-bedroom standard units, some with kitchens. 11 two-bedroom suites ($89-$149) with kitchens. 2 stories (no elevator), exterior corridors. **Parking:** on-site. **Terms:** office hours 8 am-11 pm, cancellation fee imposed, [CP] meal plan available, package plans. **Amenities:** voice mail. **Pool(s):** heated outdoor. **Guest Services:** coin laundry. **Cards:** AX, MC, VI.

SOME UNITS

[ASK] [S🔒] 🏊 🎥 💻 / ⊠ 🔌 🖥 /

SIESTA MOTOR INN

Phone: (250)763-5013

▼▼▼ ▼▼				
6/20-9/20	1P: $108-$160	2P: $108-$160	XP: $10	F16
3/1-6/19 & 9/21-2/28	1P: $79-$134	2P: $79-$134	XP: $10	F16

Motel
Location: Hwy 97 (Harvey Ave), 2.8 km s on Pandosy which becomes Lakeshore Rd. 3152 Lakeshore Rd V1W 3T1. Fax: 250/763-1265. **Facility:** 96 units. 24 one-bedroom standard units, some with efficiencies. 68 one- and 4 two-bedroom suites ($209-$280) with kitchens. 2 stories (no elevator), exterior corridors. **Parking:** on-site. **Terms:** 4 night minimum stay - seasonal. **Amenities:** voice mail. *Some:* irons. **Pool(s):** heated outdoor, heated indoor. **Leisure Activities:** sauna, whirlpools, playground, exercise room. **Guest Services:** coin laundry. **Business Services:** fax (fee). **Cards:** AX, DC, MC, VI.

SOME UNITS

🍴 🏊 ⊠ 🎥 [DATA PORT] 🔌 💻 / ⊠ 🖥 /

SUPER 8 MOTEL   *Book at aaa.com*

Phone: (250)762-8222

▼▼▼ ▼▼▼				
7/1-10/20	1P: $89-$109	2P: $106-$120	XP: $10	F12
5/1-6/30	1P: $86-$96	2P: $91-$106	XP: $10	F12
10/21-2/28	1P: $76-$86	2P: $86-$98	XP: $10	F12
3/1-4/30	1P: $74-$84	2P: $81-$95	XP: $10	F12

Motel
Location: 0.5 km n on Hwy 97 N (Harvey Ave) from jct Hwy 33. 2592 Hwy 97 N V1X 4J4. Fax: 250/762-3398. **Facility:** 60 one-bedroom standard units. 2 stories (no elevator), exterior corridors. **Parking:** on-site. **Amenities:** hair dryers. **Pool(s):** small heated outdoor. **Leisure Activities:** whirlpool. **Business Services:** PC. **Cards:** DC, MC, VI.

SOME UNITS

[ASK] [S🔒] 🍴 🔁 🎥 [DATA PORT] 💻 / ⊠ /

TOWN & COUNTRY MOTEL   *Book at aaa.com*

Phone: (250)860-7121

▼▼▼				
6/17-9/30	1P: $109-$119	2P: $119-$129	XP: $10	F
10/1-2/28	1P: $73-$83	2P: $83-$93	XP: $5	F
3/1-6/16	1P: $73-$83	2P: $83-$93	XP: $10	F

Motel
Location: 0.5 km n on Hwy 97 N (Harvey Ave) from jct Hwy 33. 2629 Hwy 97 N V1X 4J6. Fax: 250/868-3376. **Facility:** 32 one-bedroom standard units, some with kitchens. 2 stories (no elevator), exterior corridors. **Bath:** combo or shower only. **Parking:** on-site. **Terms:** office hours 7:30 am-11 pm, weekly rates available, package plans, small pets only ($10 extra charge, in smoking units). **Amenities:** video library (fee), voice mail, hair dryers. **Pool(s):** heated indoor. **Cards:** AX, MC, VI.

SOME UNITS

[ASK] 🐾 🍴 ♿ 🔁 🎥 [DATA PORT] 🔌 🖥 💻 / ⊠ [VCR] /
FEE   FEE

TRAVELLER'S CHOICE MOTOR INN

Phone: 250/762-3221

(AA) [SAVE]

▼▼ ▼▼				
6/29-9/30	1P: $109	2P: $109-$119	XP: $8	F12
3/1-6/28 & 10/1-10/31	1P: $79	2P: $79-$89	XP: $8	F12
11/1-2/28	1P: $69	2P: $69-$79	XP: $8	F12

Motel
Location: Hwy 97 N (Harvey Ave), just e. Located across from the mall. 1780 Gordon Dr V1Y 3H2. Fax: 250/762-7261. **Facility:** 43 units. 34 one- and 2 two-bedroom standard units, some with kitchens. 7 one-bedroom suites with kitchens. 2 stories (no elevator), exterior corridors. **Parking:** on-site. **Terms:** office hours 7 am-midnight, cancellation fee imposed, package plans. **Amenities:** voice mail, hair dryers. **Pool(s):** heated indoor. **Leisure Activities:** whirlpool, barbecue. *Fee:* bicycles. **Guest Services:** valet and coin laundry. **Cards:** AX, CB, DC, DS, MC, VI. **Special Amenities:** free local telephone calls and free room upgrade (subject to availability with advance reservations).

SOME UNITS

[S🔒] 🍴 🔁 ⊠ 🎥 [DATA PORT] 🔌 💻 / ⊠ 🖥 /

VINEYARD INN

▼▼▼ ▼▼▼
Motel

6/16-9/15	1P: $89-$139	2P: $89-$159	XP: $5	F12
3/1-6/15 & 9/16-10/31	1P: $74-$89	2P: $74-$99	XP: $5	F12
11/1-2/28	1P: $59-$79	2P: $59-$89	XP: $5	F12

Phone: (250)860-5703

Location: Southwest corner of jct Hwy 97 (Harvey Ave) and 33. 2486 Hwy 97 N V1X 4J3. **Fax:** 250/861-8610.
Facility: Smoke free premises. 26 units. 10 one-bedroom standard units. 14 one- and 2 two-bedroom suites, some with efficiencies or kitchens. Exterior corridors. **Parking:** on-site. **Terms:** office hours 7:30 am-11:30 pm, package plans, small pets only ($5 fee). **Amenities:** voice mail, hair dryers. **Pool(s):** small heated outdoor. **Leisure Activities:** whirlpool, putting green, playground, basketball, volleyball. **Guest Services:** coin laundry. **Cards:** AX, DC, MC, VI.

SOME UNITS

ASK ⬛ 🛏 🍴 🏊 ✕ ✕ 🎥 🖥 ⬛ / 🖨 /
FEE

The following lodgings were either not evaluated or did not meet AAA rating requirements but are listed for your information only.

LAKE OKANAGAN RESORT

[fyi]

Phone: 250/769-3511

Not evaluated. **Location:** 2.5 km sw on Hwy 97 (Harvey Ave), then 17 km nw on Westside Rd (narrow winding road), follow signs. 2751 Westside Rd V1Z 3T1. Facilities, services, and decor characterize a mid-range property.

RAMADA LODGE HOTEL

[fyi]

Phone: 250/860-9711

Not evaluated. **Location:** Hwy 97 N (Harvey Ave) at Dilworth Dr. 2170 Harvey Ave V1Y 6G8. Facilities, services, and decor characterize a mid-range property.

WHERE TO DINE

CHRISTOPHER'S

▼▼▼ ▼▼▼
Steak & Seafood

Dinner: $15-$30   **Phone:** 250/861-3464

Location: Downtown. 242 Lawrence Ave V1Y 6L3. **Hours:** 4:30 pm-10 pm, Fri & Sat-11 pm. Closed: 1/1, 12/25, 12/26. **Reservations:** suggested. **Features:** Patrons appreciate the restaurant's quaint dining room, personalized attention and fresh seafood. Selections also include steak, salad bar offerings and desserts. Large groups are accommodated at this local favorite, and the atmosphere can be boisterous. Casual dress; cocktails. **Parking:** street. **Cards:** AX, DC, MC, VI.

✕

COYOTE'S RESTAURANT UPSTAIRS

▼▼▼ ▼▼▼
International

Lunch: $8-$15   **Dinner:** $11-$23   **Phone:** 250/860-1266

Location: Hwy 97 (Harvey Ave), 1 km w; in Grand Okanagan. 1352 Water St V1Y 9P3. **Hours:** 11:30 am-10 pm, Fri & Sat-11 pm. Closed: 12/25. **Features:** Patrons can access the restaurant from the waterfront entrance or walk through the Grand Okanagan Hotel. Inside are a modern, upbeat atmosphere and a menu with preparations from around the world. Mexican, Pacific Rim and Japanese influences all are evident, but traditional steak and seafood entrees are every bit as satisfying. Casual dress; cocktails. **Parking:** street. **Cards:** AX, MC, VI.

✕

DAWETT FINE INDIAN CUISINE

▼▼▼ ▼▼▼
Indian

Lunch: $4-$9   **Dinner:** $10-$17   **Phone:** 250/717-1668

Location: Downtown. 1435 Ellis St V1Y 2A3. **Hours:** 11 am-2:30 & 4:30-9:45 pm, Fri-10:45 pm, Sat & Sun 1 pm-9:45 pm. Closed: 12/25. **Features:** Considered one of the best Indian restaurants in the Okanagan, this place doesn't disappoint with its traditional ethnic cuisine. Guests can tantalize their taste buds with tandoori chicken, chicken masala, pakoras and samosas, all made with top-quality ingredients. Vegetarians will find many choices of fine food to enjoy in a simple, comfortable dining room. Semi-formal attire; cocktails. **Parking:** on-site. **Cards:** AX, MC, VI.

✕

THE ELDORADO RESTAURANT

▼▼▼ ▼▼▼
Regional Canadian

Lunch: $15-$20   **Dinner:** $18-$30   **Phone:** 250/763-7500

Location: Hwy 97, 4 km s on Pandosy (which becomes Lakeshore Dr), just w; in The Hotel Eldorado. 500 Cook Rd V1W 3G9. **Hours:** 7 am-10 pm; to midnight in summer. **Reservations:** suggested. **Features:** The casual yet elegant restaurant is right along the water and offers views of Lake Okanagan and the valley. Preparations of regionally diverse cuisine exceed expectations. In addition to seafood and pasta options, diners can select from several meat dishes. Known for its brunch, this place is a must stop for those visiting Kelowna. Casual dress; cocktails. **Parking:** on-site. **Cards:** AX, DC, MC, VI.

🍸 ✕

THE FINER CHOICE IN DINING

(AAA)
▼▼▼ ▼▼▼
Continental

Lunch: $5-$11   **Dinner:** $10-$30   **Phone:** 250/763-0422

Location: Between Abbott and Water sts. 237 Lawrence Ave V1Y 6L2. **Hours:** 5 pm-11 pm, Thurs & Fri 11:30 am-2 pm. Closed: 1/1-2/13 & Sun 9/15-5/1. **Reservations:** required, in summer. **Features:** The restaurant's extensive menu includes veal, chicken, seafood, beef and vegetarian dishes. Portions are generous, and the good-quality local wines are worth a try. For free parking, be sure to ask for a voucher as you enter. Service is friendly. Casual dress; cocktails. **Parking:** on-site. **Cards:** AX, CB, DC, MC, VI.

✕

FORSTER'S AT THE SUMMERHILL SUNSET BISTRO

▼▼▼ ▼▼▼
Regional Canadian

Lunch: $9-$15   **Dinner:** $14-$26   **Phone:** 250/764-8000

Location: 15 km e at Pandosy (which becomes Lakeshore Rd), just s at Chute Lake Rd, follow signs. 4870 Chute Lake Rd V1W 4M3. **Hours:** 11 am-10 pm. Closed: 12/25. **Reservations:** suggested. **Features:** Overlooking the Okanagan Valley, the winery restaurant affords nice views. Food presentations are artistic. Guests can make their way to the eatery after a tour and tasting or come directly for a special meal. Several menu items incorporate regional ingredients and the Bavarian smokehouse cooking technique. Starters are large enough to share, and meals are exquisite. Casual dress; cocktails. **Parking:** on-site. **Cards:** AX, DC, MC, VI.

♿M ✕

FRESCO RESTAURANT & MARTINI LOUNGE

Dinner: $22-$30   **Phone:** 250/868-8805

(CAA)

▼▼▼ ▼▼▼

Regional Canadian

Location: Hwy 97 (Harvey Ave), 3 blks n on Water St; at jct of Bernard and Water sts. 1560 Water St V1Y 1J7. **Hours:** Open 3/1-12/31 & 2/1-2/28; 5:30 pm-10 pm. Closed: 12/24, 12/25, 12/26; also Sun & Mon 2/1-4/30. **Reservations:** suggested. **Features:** In a historic brick building, the restaurant offers fine dining at its best in the heart of the Okanagan. The experience is memorable and lovely. Creative seasonal cuisine emphasizes the products of the area, as does the extensive list of regional wines. Artistic and delicious, each dish is prepared in an open kitchen and served by staff who are attentive and knowledgeable. Casual dress; cocktails. **Parking:** street. **Cards:** AX, MC, VI.

GRAND BAY CAFE

Lunch: $10-$15   **Dinner:** $13-$30   **Phone:** 250/763-4500

▼▼▼ ▼▼▼

Canadian

Location: Hwy 97 (Harvey Ave), 1 km w; in The Grand Okanagan Lakefront Resort & Conference Centre. 1310 Water St V1Y 9P3. **Hours:** 6:30 am-10 pm. **Reservations:** suggested. **Features:** This restaurant's menu lines up a wide variety of fare, ranging from seafood to pasta to prime rib. Most tables offer a view overlooking the lake and river paths, and the service is attentive. Casual dress; cocktails. **Parking:** on-site (fee) and valet. **Cards:** AX, CB, DC, DS, JC, MC, VI.

JAKX NEIGHBOURHOOD GRILL

Lunch: $6-$16   **Dinner:** $6-$16   **Phone:** 250/763-0773

▼▼ ▼▼

Continental

Location: 3 km e on Pandosy (which becomes Lakeshore Rd) at jct Pandosy and Klo Rd; in shopping plaza. 203-595 KLO Rd V1Y 8E7. **Hours:** 11 am-9 pm. Closed major holidays; also Sun. **Reservations:** suggested. **Features:** A favorite among locals, the family-owned restaurant is on the second floor of a shopping center, with wheelchair access via an elevator. A wine list focused on bottles from area wineries matches with pizzas and pasta and meat entrees. Families are welcomed. Casual dress; cocktails. **Cards:** MC, VI.

THE JAMMERY

Lunch: $6-$17   **Dinner:** $6-$17   **Phone:** 250/766-1139

▼▼▼ ▼▼▼

International

Location: Hwy 97 N (Harvey Ave), 12 km n. 8038 Hwy 97 N V1X 6A6. **Hours:** 7 am-5 pm; to 8 pm 5/24-9/30. Closed: 1/1, 12/25, 12/26. **Reservations:** suggested. **Features:** A play on the winery concept, the restaurant uses locally grown fruits in its creations. Guests can learn about the jam being made on site or just come for afternoon tea. The menu lays out an excellent selection of breakfast choices, many sandwiches and wraps, as well as afternoon tea items. **Parking:** on-site. **Cards:** MC, VI.

LAUGHING MOON RESTAURANT

Lunch: $9-$12   **Dinner:** $11-$13   **Phone:** 250/764-0674

▼▼▼ ▼▼▼

Continental

Location: 7 km w at Pandosy (which becomes Lakeshore Rd). 4600 Lakeshore Rd V1W 1X4. **Hours:** 7:30 am-9:30 pm, Sun-Tues to 4 pm. Closed: 1/1, 12/25. **Features:** The distinctive restaurant's simple dining room pipes with live local music on weekends. Although the menu is not extensive, its meals, which incorporate blends of Thai, Vietnamese and Canadian ingredients, are fantastic. The system of ordering is unusual, and servers are friendly. Casual dress; beer & wine only. **Parking:** on-site. **Cards:** MC, VI.

MAMMA ROSA

Dinner: $10-$15   **Phone:** 250/763-4114

▼▼▼ ▼▼▼

Italian

Location: Downtown. 561 Lawrence Ave V1Y 6L8. **Hours:** Open 3/1-1/1 & 2/1-2/28; 5 pm-10 pm, Sun 5:30 pm-9 pm. Closed: 5/23, 7/1, 8/1. **Reservations:** suggested. **Features:** As the name suggests, the restaurant is known for Italian food, just as Mama might have made it. The extensive menu lists homemade in various forms, ranging from cannelloni and lasagna to manicotti and penne. Also tempting is a fine selection of pizzas. Red- and white-checked tablecloths and Italian decor lend to a cozy atmosphere. The service is super. Casual dress; cocktails. **Parking:** street. **Cards:** AX, MC, VI.

MEKONG RESTAURANT

Lunch: $6-$9   **Dinner:** $8-$14   **Phone:** 250/763-8000

▼▼▼ ▼▼▼

Traditional Chinese

Location: Corner of Hwy 97 N (Harvey Ave) and Gordon Dr; in Kelowna Motor Inn. 1030 Harvey Ave V1Y 8S4. **Hours:** 11:30 am-10 pm. Closed: 12/25. **Reservations:** accepted. **Features:** The restaurant prepares fresh, mouthwatering Szechuan cuisine. Ask about the signature deluxe meals for two to 10 people: ginger chicken and steak strips with black pepper sauce. The decor is bright, fresh and contemporary. Peak meal times can be busy. Cocktails. **Parking:** on-site. **Cards:** AX, DC, MC, VI.

MINI O-ZEKI

Lunch: $8-$14   **Dinner:** $8-$14   **Phone:** 250/862-8022

▼▼▼

Sushi

Location: Hwy 97 (Harvey Ave), 3 km s on Pandosy (which becomes Lakeshore Rd); in South Gate Plaza. 2684 Pandosy V1W 3L4. **Hours:** 11:30 am-8:30 pm, Sat & Sun from noon. Closed: Mon. **Features:** The eat-in/take-out eatery has but seven small tables, and diners can watch sushi and sashimi being made at the counter. Many locals patronize the popular, busy spot for take-out sushi. Regardless of where the food is eaten, patrons are tempted by artistic, traditional displays of delicious Japanese fare. Casual dress. **Parking:** on-site. **Cards:** VI.

MINSTREL CAFE

Lunch: $6-$10   **Dinner:** $14-$20   **Phone:** 250/764-2301

▼▼▼▼▼

International

Location: Hwy 97 (Harvey Ave), 9 km s at Pandosy (which becomes Lakeshore Rd). 4638 Lakeshore Rd V1W 3T4. **Hours:** 11:30 am-2 & 5:30-10 pm, Fri & Sat-11 pm. Closed major holidays. **Features:** A little off the beaten path, the distinctive cafe is considered to be one of Kelowna's best-kept secrets, especially for lunch. Upon entry, guests notice a large tree in the middle of the dining room, set against soft olive walls which boast original local art. The menu lists a wide range of soups, salads, frittatas and all-day breakfast items, which can be enjoyed in the open, airy dining room or on the patio outside. Live entertainment is featured on weekends. Casual dress; cocktails. **Parking:** on-site. **Cards:** MC, VI.

PEARSON'S EUROPEAN DELI

Lunch: $5-$9   **Phone:** 250/762-0800

▼

Deli/Subs Sandwiches

Location: Hwy 95 S; in a strip mall at jct Cooper Ave. #30-2070 Harvey Ave V1Y 8P8. **Hours:** 7:30 am-5 pm, Sat 9 am-3 pm. Closed major holidays; also Sun. **Reservations:** not accepted. **Features:** As diners enter the small delicatessen, they are hit with the smell of fresh bread. Before them is a case of salads, ranging from pasta to curried chicken. Behind the counter is a chalkboard with several sandwich options, as well as such listings as cabbage rolls and pierogies. Made on thick slabs of fresh bread, sandwiches are incredible. This spot fits the bill for a healthy, quick meal. Casual dress. **Parking:** on-site. **Cards:** AX, MC, VI.

PHEASANT & QUAIL PUB
▼▼▼ ▼▼▼ American
Lunch: $8-$12   **Dinner:** $8-$16   **Phone:** 250/860-1066
Location: 3 km s on Pandosy (which becomes Lakeshore Rd). 3110 Lakeshore Rd V1W 3T1. **Hours:** 11 am-midnight. Closed: 12/25. **Reservations:** accepted. **Features:** Modeled after an English ale house, the cozy restaurant invites patrons to drop in for a pint and some good pub food. Comfortable armchairs for lounging, a bar area and an enclosed smoking area encourage relaxing. Fish and chips, sandwiches, pastas and salads make up the menu, and the friendly servers share information about the local brews. Casual dress; cocktails. **Parking:** on-site. **Cards:** AX, DC, MC, VI.

[Y] [X]

RIC'S GRILL
▼▼▼ ▼▼▼ Steak & Seafood
Lunch: $12-$18   **Dinner:** $15-$25   **Phone:** 250/869-1586
Location: Corner of Lawrence Ave and Abbott St; downtown. 210 Lawrence Ave V1Y 6L3. **Hours:** 11 am-midnight, Sat 4 pm-midnight, Sun 4 pm-11 pm. **Reservations:** suggested. **Features:** Funky and modern describe the decor and the food at the upscale steakhouse, a new addition to the Kelowna scene. This place bustles with activity; reservations are definitely recommended. The steaks are well worth it. A wide variety of distinctive appetizers rounds out the menu. Servers are friendly and attentive. Casual dress; cocktails. **Parking:** street. **Cards:** AX, DC, MC, VI.

[Y] [X]

THE TEAHOUSE RESTAURANT
▼▼▼ ▼▼▼ Canadian
Lunch: $8-$12   **Dinner:** $14-$28   **Phone:** 250/763-1080
Location: From Hwy 97, 3 km s on Gordon Rd, 4 km e on KLO Rd, then just n on E Kelowna Rd to Dunster Rd; follow signs. 3002 Dunster Rd V1W 4A6. **Hours:** Open 5/1-10/14; 11:30 am-2:30 & 5:30-9 pm. Closed: for dinner Mon. **Features:** It's worth the short drive out to the Kelowna Land Orchard, where visitors can spend the day wandering in the orchards and learning about the industry. Afterward, they can stop into the quaint, country-style tea house, which presents a menu that emphasizes local and regional ingredients. Casual dress; cocktails. **Parking:** on-site. **Cards:** AX, MC, VI.

[&M] [X]

WILD APPLE GRILL   *Menu on aaa.com*
(AAA)
▼▼▼ ▼▼▼ Regional Canadian
Lunch: $8-$16   **Dinner:** $10-$21   **Phone:** 250/860-4488
Location: Hwy 97 N (Harvey Ave), 3.2 km s on Pandosy (which becomes Lakeshore Rd); in Manteo Resort-Waterfront Hotel & Villas. 3762 Lakeshore Rd V1W 3L4. **Hours:** 6 am-10 pm. **Reservations:** suggested. **Features:** A fresh, bright, contemporary dining room awaits guests of the restaurant along the waterfront. Featuring an open-concept kitchen and light, bright colors, the dining room transforms in the evening to become a bit more intimate. Upbeat, creative meals include pasta and sandwiches at lunch and creative seafood and meat preparations at dinner. Casual dress; cocktails. **Parking:** on-site. **Cards:** AX, DC, MC, VI.

[X]

THE WILLIAMS INN RESTAURANT
▼▼▼ ▼▼▼ Continental
Lunch: $8-$16   **Dinner:** $12-$24   **Phone:** 250/763-5136
Location: Downtown. 526 Lawrence Ave V1Y 6L7. **Hours:** 11:30 am-2 & 5-10 pm, Sat & Sun from 5 pm. Closed major holidays. **Features:** In a small downtown house, the pub-style eatery is popular with the lunch crowd. Entrees range from salmon and steak to hearty salads. Save room for dessert. This is a lovely spot for a special-occasion outing. The patio opens in season. Casual dress; cocktails. **Parking:** street. **Cards:** AX, MC, VI.

[X]

YAMAS TAVERNA RESTAURANT
▼▼ ▼▼ Greek
Lunch: $8-$14   **Dinner:** $10-$16   **Phone:** 250/763-5823
Location: From Hwy 97, just w at Ellis St. 1630 Ellis St V1L 2Y7. **Hours:** 11 am-2 & 5-10 pm, Sat & Sun from 5 pm. **Features:** A typical and traditional Greek feel envelops the downtown restaurant, which is popular with the business crowd at lunch. Guests can choose from the all-you-can-eat lunch buffet or from delicious entrees on the menu. Casual dress; cocktails. **Parking:** street. **Cards:** AX, MC, VI.

[X]

KIMBERLEY pop. 6,484

———— WHERE TO STAY ————

MARK CREEK LODGE   *Book at aaa.com*
▼▼▼ ▼▼▼
Small-scale Hotel

7/1-9/15	1P: $99-$109	2P: $99-$109	XP: $15	F12
3/1-6/30 & 9/16-2/28	1P: $89-$99	2P: $89-$99	XP: $15	F12

Phone: (250)427-2266

Location: Centre. 300 Wallinger Ave V1A 1Z4. Fax: 250/427-7621. **Facility:** 43 one-bedroom standard units. 3 stories (no elevator), interior corridors. **Parking:** on-site. **Terms:** check-in 4 pm, weekly rates available, [AP] & [BP] meal plans available, package plans, pets ($10 fee, in smoking units). **Amenities:** hair dryers. **Business Services:** meeting rooms. **Cards:** AX, MC, VI.

SOME UNITS
[ASK] [S&] [🛏] [⊤⊤] [▣] / [X] [DATA PORT] [▤] /
FEE

TRICKLE CREEK RESIDENCE INN BY MARRIOTT   *Book at aaa.com*
(AAA) [SAVE]
▼▼▼ ▼▼▼
Small-scale Hotel

12/17-1/3	1P: $235-$345	2P: $235-$345	XP: $15	F16
7/1-12/16	1P: $160-$270	2P: $160-$270	XP: $15	F16
1/4-2/28	1P: $149-$269	2P: $149-$269	XP: $15	F16
3/1-6/30	1P: $137-$234	2P: $137-$234	XP: $15	F16

Phone: 250/427-5175

Location: Hwy 95A, 3.1 km w on Ross St, follow signs for Alpine Village, then just e. 500 Stemwinder Dr V1A 2Y6 (PO Box 220). Fax: 250/427-5176. **Facility:** Smoke free premises. 80 units. 19 one-bedroom standard units with kitchens. 41 one- and 20 two-bedroom suites ($137-$345) with kitchens. 3 stories, interior corridors. **Bath:** combo or shower only. **Parking:** on-site. **Terms:** check-in 4 pm, 2 night minimum stay - weekends, cancellation fee imposed, package plans, pets ($25 extra charge). **Amenities:** dual phone lines, voice mail, irons, hair dryers. **Dining:** 11 am-midnight, Sun-11 pm, cocktails. **Pool(s):** small heated outdoor. **Leisure Activities:** whirlpools, downhill skiing, hiking trails, exercise room. Fee: golf-18 holes. **Guest Services:** gift shop, valet and coin laundry. **Business Services:** meeting rooms, PC (fee). **Cards:** AX, DC, MC, VI. **Special Amenities:** free newspaper and early check-in/late check-out.

[🛏] [⊤⊤] [❄] [⊘] [⇲] [X] [X] [DATA PORT] [▤] [▱] [▣]
FEE

CHICAMON SPRINGS LODGE   Phone: 250/427-4770
[fyi]   Not evaluated. **Location:** From Gerry Sorensen Way, right on Dogwood Dr, follow signs. Located on ski hill. 890 Dogwood Dr V1A 2Y5 (PO Box 114). Facilities, services, and decor characterize a mid-range property.

INNWEST KIRKWOOD CONDOMINIUMS   Phone: 250/427-7616
[fyi]   Not evaluated. **Location:** From Gerry Sorensen Way, follow signs. 880 North Star Dr V1A 2Y6 (PO Box 247). Facilities, services, and decor characterize a basic property.

LADYSMITH pop. 6,587

——— **WHERE TO STAY** ———

KIWI COVE LODGE   Phone: 250/245-8051
[fyi]   Did not meet all AAA rating requirements for some guest rooms at time of last evaluation on 03/10/2003. **Location:** 4.5 km n on Trans-Canada Hwy 1, then 1.2 km e, follow signs. Located in a rural area. 5131 Bretton Page Rd
Bed & Breakfast   V9G 7L6. Facilities, services, and decor characterize a basic property.

LANGLEY —*See Vancouver p. 583.*

LOGAN LAKE pop. 2,185

——— **WHERE TO STAY** ———

LOGAN LAKE LODGE   Phone: (250)523-9466
◆◆◆   All Year   1P: $55-$60   2P: $60-$65   XP: $5   F12
     Location: Centre at Meadow Creek Rd and Chartrand Cresent. 111 Chartrand Ave V0K 1W0 (4221 Rockridge
Motel   Crescent, WEST VANCOUVER, V7W 1A9). Fax: 250/523-9467. **Facility:** 21 one-bedroom standard units. 2 stories (no elevator), interior corridors. **Parking:** on-site, winter plug-ins. **Terms:** office hours 8 am-11 pm, 7 day cancellation notice, pets ($15 extra charge). **Business Services:** meeting rooms. **Cards:** AX, MC, VI.

SOME UNITS
(ASK) (S/D) (🛏) (¶¶) (Y) (⚡) (🖥) / (✕) /
FEE

LUND pop. 265

——— **WHERE TO STAY** ———

THE LUND HOTEL   Phone: 604/414-0474
[fyi]   Did not meet all AAA rating requirements for some guest rooms at time of last evaluation on 10/22/2002. **Location:** At Hwy 101; on the Sunshine Coast. 1436 Hwy 101 V0N 2G0 (General Delivery). Facilities, services, and
Small-scale Hotel   decor characterize a basic property.

MADEIRA PARK

——— **WHERE TO STAY** ———

SUNSHINE COAST RESORT   Phone: (604)883-9177
◆◆◆◆◆   6/15-9/30   1P: $100-$145   2P: $100-$145   XP: $20   D12
     3/1-6/14   1P: $75-$110   2P: $75-$110   XP: $20   D12
     10/1-2/28   1P: $60-$85   2P: $60-$85   XP: $20   D12
Condominium   **Location:** Just n of Madeira Park Rd, follow signs. 12695 Sunshine Coast (Hwy 101) V0N 2H0 (Box 213). Fax: 604/883-9171. **Facility:** New condo units plus the original four self-contained cottage-style rooms all overlook the deep-water marina and surrounding mountains. Smoke free premises. 14 units. 4 one-bedroom standard units. 9 one-bedroom suites ($95-$195) with efficiencies, some with whirlpools. 1 cottage ($110-$205) with whirlpool. 3 stories, interior/exterior corridors. *Bath:* combo or shower only. **Parking:** on-site. **Terms:** office hours 8 am-midnight, 2 night minimum stay - seasonal and/or weekends, 21 day cancellation notice-fee imposed, weekly rates available, $25 service charge, pets ($10 extra charge, in limited units). **Amenities:** video library, voice mail, irons, hair dryers. **Leisure Activities:** whirlpool, rental boats, canoeing, fishing. *Fee:* charter fishing. **Guest Services:** coin laundry. **Cards:** AX, MC, VI.

SOME UNITS
(🛏) (&M) (📶) (✕) (✕) (AC) (VCR) (DATA PORT) (📟) (🖥) / (📠) /
FEE

RUBY LAKE RESORT   Phone: 604/883-2269
[fyi]   Not evaluated. **Location:** 16 km w on Sunshine Coast (Hwy 101). (RR 1 S20 C-25). Facilities, services, and decor characterize a mid-range property.

—— *The following restaurant has not been evaluated by AAA* ——
but is listed for your information only.

RUBY LAKE RESORT RESTAURANT   **Phone:** 604/883-2269
[fyi]   Not evaluated. **Location:** 16 km w on Sunshine Coast (Hwy 101); in Ruby Lake Resort. RR 1, S-20, C-25 V0N 2H0.
        Features: Good word of mouth brings guests from all over to dine at this restaurant on the lake, enjoy an array of different pasta dishes and some very reasonably priced wines.

MALAHAT —See Victoria p. 633.

MANNING PARK

—— WHERE TO STAY ——

MANNING PARK RESORT   *Book at aaa.com*   **Phone:** (250)840-8822

▼▼▼ ▼▼▼	9/11-2/28	1P: $89-$149	2P: $94-$154	XP: $5	F11
▼▼ ▼▼	7/1-9/10	1P: $129-$144	2P: $134-$149	XP: $5	F11
Small-scale Hotel	3/1-4/2	1P: $119-$144	2P: $124-$149	XP: $5	F11
	4/3-6/30	1P: $69-$99	2P: $74-$104	XP: $5	F11

Location: Crowsnest Hwy 3; midway between Hope and Princeton. Hwy 3 V0X 1R0 (46244 Airport Rd, Suite 21, CHILLIWACK, V2P 1A5). Fax: 250/840-8848. **Facility:** 73 units. 49 one-bedroom standard units. 24 cabins. 2 stories (no elevator), interior/exterior corridors. **Parking:** on-site. **Terms:** check-in 4 pm, 2 night minimum stay - weekends, 30 day cancellation notice-fee imposed, package plans, 15% service charge, pets ($25 extra charge, in cabins only). **Amenities:** video library (fee). *Some:* voice mail. **Leisure Activities:** sauna, whirlpool, steamroom, rental canoes, fishing, 2 lighted tennis courts, cross country skiing, ice skating, rental bicycles, playground, exercise room. *Fee:* game room. **Guest Services:** gift shop, coin laundry. **Business Services:** meeting rooms. **Cards:** AX, MC, VI.

ASK SD 🛏 🍽 🍸 ✕ 🚫 🎥 🎬 🖥 / ✕ VCR DATA/PORT ⓩ 📷 /

MAPLE RIDGE —See Vancouver p. 585.

MAYNE ISLAND —See Gulf Islands National Park Reserve p. 476.

MCBRIDE pop. 711

—— WHERE TO STAY ——

NORTH COUNTRY LODGE   **Phone:** (250)569-0001

CAA SAVE	All Year	1P: $65-$99	2P: $65-$99	XP: $5	F12

Location: Just w of village main exit, on Hwy 16 north service road. 868 Frontage Rd N V0J 2E0 (PO Box 567). Fax: 250/569-0002. **Facility:** 48 units. 44 one-bedroom standard units, some with efficiencies. 4 two-bedroom suites ($105-$125) with efficiencies. 2 stories (no elevator), exterior corridors. **Parking:** on-site, winter plug-ins. **Terms:** office hours 7:30 am-11 pm, pets ($5 fee, in designated units). **Amenities:** hair dryers. **Dining:** 6 am-10 pm, Sat & Sun-11 pm, cocktails. **Leisure Activities:** whirlpool, limited exercise equipment. **Cards:** AX, MC, VI. **Special Amenities:** free local telephone calls.

SD 🛏 🍽 🍸 🎬 DATA/PORT 🖥 / ✕ 🖥 /

MERRITT pop. 7,088

—— WHERE TO STAY ——

BEST WESTERN NICOLA INN   *Book at aaa.com*   **Phone:** (250)378-4253

CAA SAVE	6/22-8/31	1P: $95	2P: $105	XP: $10	F12
	3/1-6/21	1P: $79	2P: $85	XP: $10	F12
▼▼▼ ▼▼▼	9/1-2/28	1P: $72	2P: $79	XP: $10	F12

Location: Hwy 5, exit 290, 1 km w. 4025 Walters St V1K 1K1. Fax: 250/378-6869. **Facility:** 56 units. 52 one-bedroom standard units. 4 one-bedroom suites ($120-$150). 2 stories (no elevator), exterior corridors. **Parking:** on-site, winter plug-ins. **Terms:** cancellation fee imposed, small pets only ($10 extra charge). **Amenities:** irons, hair dryers. **Dining:** 6:30 am-9 pm, cocktails. **Pool(s):** heated indoor. **Leisure Activities:** whirlpool, limited exercise equipment. **Guest Services:** coin laundry. **Business Services:** meeting rooms. **Cards:** AX, DC, DS, MC, VI. **Special Amenities:** free local telephone calls and early check-in/late check-out.

SD 🛏 🍽 ➰ 🎬 DATA/PORT 🖥 📷 🖥 / ✕ VCR /

MERRITT MOTOR INN   **Phone:** (250)378-9422

CAA SAVE	5/1-10/1 [CP]	1P: $90-$100	2P: $95-$105	XP: $7	D10
	10/2-2/28 [CP]	1P: $75-$80	2P: $80-$85	XP: $7	D10
▼▼▼ ▼▼▼	3/1-4/30 [CP]	1P: $75-$80	2P: $75-$85	XP: $7	D10

Location: Hwy 5, exit 290, just w. 3561 Voght St V1K 1C5. Fax: 250/378-5465. **Facility:** 35 one-bedroom standard units, some with efficiencies or kitchens. 2 stories, exterior corridors. **Parking:** on-site. **Terms:** office hours 7 am-11 pm, package plans, small pets only ($5 extra charge, in designated units). **Dining:** 6:30 am-9:30 pm, wine/beer only. **Pool(s):** heated indoor. **Leisure Activities:** whirlpool. **Cards:** AX, DS, MC, VI. **Special Amenities:** free continental breakfast and free local telephone calls.

SD 🛏 🍽 ➰ 🖥 🖥 / ✕ 📷 /

RAMADA LIMITED   *Book at aaa.com*   **Phone:** (250)378-3567

5/1-9/30 [ECP]	1P: $85-$95	2P: $90-$100	XP: $5 F
3/1-4/30 & 10/1-2/28 [ECP]	1P: $70-$80	2P: $75-$85	XP: $5 F

Motel   **Location:** Hwy 5, exit 290, just w. 3571 Voght St V1K 1C5. Fax: 250/378-4016. **Facility:** 50 units. 46 one-bedroom standard units, some with efficiencies and/or whirlpools. 4 one-bedroom suites, some with kitchens and/or whirlpools. 3 stories (no elevator), exterior corridors. **Parking:** on-site, winter plug-ins. **Terms:** office hours 6:30 am-11:30 pm, package plans, small pets only ($5 extra charge, in designated units). **Amenities:** high-speed Internet. *Some:* irons, hair dryers. **Pool(s):** heated indoor. **Leisure Activities:** sauna, whirlpool, limited exercise equipment. **Guest Services:** coin laundry. **Business Services:** meeting rooms. **Cards:** AX, DS, MC, VI.

SOME UNITS

(ASK) (S/D) 🛏 📶 🍽 🏊 ⊗ 🐾 (DATA PORT) 🖥 / ⊗ 📠 🖥 /
          FEE

MISSION —*See Vancouver p. 585.*

NAKUSP pop. 1,698

———— **WHERE TO STAY** ————

THE SELKIRK INN   **Phone:** 250-265-3666

(CAA) (SAVE)	7/1-10/31	1P: $58-$70	2P: $58-$79	XP: $5
	5/1-6/30	1P: $54-$67	2P: $54-$72	XP: $5
▼▼▼ ▼▼▼	3/1-4/30 & 11/1-2/28	1P: $45-$52	2P: $45-$55	XP: $5

Small-scale Hotel   **Location:** Just n. 210 W 6th Ave V0G 1R0 (PO Box 370). Fax: 250/265-4799. **Facility:** 39 one-bedroom standard units, some with efficiencies (utensils extra charge). 2 stories (no elevator), interior corridors. *Bath:* combo or shower only. **Parking:** on-site. **Terms:** office hours 7 am-11 pm, package plans, small pets only ($8 fee, in designated units). **Leisure Activities:** sauna. **Business Services:** meeting rooms. **Cards:** AX, MC, VI.

SOME UNITS

🛏 📶 🐾 🖥 / ⊗ 🕅 🖥 🖥 /
          FEE

NANAIMO pop. 73,000

———— **WHERE TO STAY** ————

BEST WESTERN DORCHESTER HOTEL   *Book at aaa.com*   **Phone:** (250)754-6835

(CAA) (SAVE)	6/1-9/30	1P: $90-$140	2P: $90-$140	XP: $10 F12
	3/1-5/31 & 10/1-2/28	1P: $80-$120	2P: $80-$120	XP: $10 F12

▼▼ ▼▼ ▼▼   **Location:** Trans-Canada Hwy 1 to Comox Rd; downtown. 70 Church St V9R 5H4. Fax: 250/754-2638. **Facility:** 65 one-bedroom standard units. 4 stories, interior corridors. **Parking:** on-site. **Amenities:** irons, hair dryers. Small-scale Hotel **Dining:** 7 am-10 pm, cocktails. **Guest Services:** valet laundry. **Business Services:** meeting rooms. **Cards:** AX, DC, MC, VI. **Special Amenities:** early check-in/late check-out and free room upgrade (subject to availability with advance reservations).

SOME UNITS

(S/D) 🍽 🍸 🐾 (DATA PORT) 🖥 / ⊗ 🕅 🖥 /

BEST WESTERN NORTHGATE INN   *Book at aaa.com*   **Phone:** (250)390-2222

(CAA) (SAVE)	5/1-8/31	1P: $99-$129	2P: $99-$129	XP: $10 F12
	3/1-4/30 & 9/1-10/31	1P: $89-$109	2P: $89-$109	XP: $10 F12
▼▼ ▼▼	11/1-2/28	1P: $79-$99	2P: $79-$99	XP: $10 F12

Location: Hwy 19A (Island Hwy), just w on Aulds Rd, then just s. 6450 Metral Dr V9T 2L8. Fax: 250/390-2412. Small-scale Hotel **Facility:** 72 one-bedroom standard units, some with efficiencies and/or whirlpools. 3 stories, interior corridors. **Parking:** on-site. **Terms:** cancellation fee imposed, package plans, small pets only ($20 extra charge, 1st floor units). **Amenities:** voice mail, irons, hair dryers. **Dining:** 6 am-9 pm, Sat & Sun from 7 am, cocktails. **Leisure Activities:** sauna, whirlpool, limited exercise equipment. **Guest Services:** valet and coin laundry. **Business Services:** meeting rooms. **Cards:** AX, DC, MC, VI. **Special Amenities:** free newspaper. *(See color ad below)*

SOME UNITS

(S/D) 🛏 🍽 ⊗ 🐾 (DATA PORT) 🖥 🖥 🖥 / ⊗ /
          FEE

DAYS INN NANAIMO HARBOURVIEW   *Book at aaa.com*   **Phone:** (250)754-8171

5/1-9/30	1P: $129-$149	2P: $139-$159	XP: $10	F12
10/1-2/28	1P: $109-$119	2P: $119-$129	XP: $10	F12
3/1-4/30	1P: $99-$119	2P: $109-$129	XP: $10	F12

Small-scale Hotel   **Location:** On Island Hwy 1, 2 km s. 809 Island Hwy S V9R 5K1. Fax: 250/754-8557. **Facility:** 79 one-bedroom standard units, some with efficiencies. 2 stories (no elevator), interior corridors. **Parking:** on-site. **Terms:** cancellation fee imposed, package plans, small pets only ($5 extra charge, 1st floor units). **Amenities:** video library (fee), hair dryers. *Some:* high-speed Internet, irons. **Pool(s):** heated indoor. **Leisure Activities:** whirlpool. **Guest Services:** valet and coin laundry. **Business Services:** meeting rooms. **Cards:** AX, DC, DS, JC, MC, VI.

SOME UNITS
[ASK] [S/D] [🛏] [🍴FEE] [➰] [▣] / [✕] [VCR FEE] [DATA PORT] [🔌] /

THE GRAND HOTEL NANAIMO   *Book at aaa.com*   **Phone:** (250)758-3000

7/1-2/28	1P: $129-$289	2P: $129-$289	XP: $15	F11
3/1-4/30	1P: $119-$279	2P: $119-$279	XP: $15	F11
5/1-6/30	1P: $109-$269	2P: $109-$269	XP: $15	F11

Small-scale Hotel   **Location:** 6 km n on Hwy 19A (Island Hwy) from Departure Bay ferry terminal, then just e. 4898 Rutherford Rd V9T 4Z4. Fax: 250/729-2808. **Facility:** 72 one-bedroom standard units, some with whirlpools. 4 stories, interior corridors. **Parking:** on-site. **Terms:** cancellation fee imposed, [BP] meal plan available, package plans. **Amenities:** high-speed Internet, voice mail, irons, hair dryers. **Pool(s):** heated indoor. **Leisure Activities:** limited exercise equipment. **Guest Services:** valet laundry. **Business Services:** meeting rooms. **Cards:** AX, DC, MC, VI.

SOME UNITS
[🍴] [🍷] [&M] [🔥] [➰] [DATA PORT] [▣] / [✕] [🔌] [🖼] /

RAMADA LIMITED ON LONG LAKE   *Book at aaa.com*   **Phone:** (250)758-1144

6/1-9/30 [ECP]	1P: $119-$149	2P: $139-$169	XP: $20	F18
3/1-5/31 & 10/1-2/28 [ECP]	1P: $109-$129	2P: $109-$139	XP: $10	F18

Small-scale Hotel   **Location:** 5 km n on Hwy 19A (Island Hwy) from Departure Bay ferry terminal. 4700 Island Hwy N V9T 1W6. Fax: 250/758-5832. **Facility:** 62 one-bedroom standard units, some with efficiencies, kitchens and/or whirlpools. 3 stories, exterior corridors. **Parking:** on-site. **Terms:** package plans, small pets only ($20 extra charge). **Amenities:** video library (fee), high-speed Internet, voice mail, irons, hair dryers. **Leisure Activities:** sauna, whirlpool, rental canoes, rental paddleboats, boat dock, limited exercise equipment, horseshoes, volleyball. **Guest Services:** valet and coin laundry. **Business Services:** meeting rooms. **Cards:** AX, CB, DC, DS, JC, MC, VI. **Special Amenities:** free expanded continental breakfast and free local telephone calls.

SOME UNITS
[S/D] [🛏] [&M] [✕] [VCR] [DATA PORT] [🔌] [▣] / [✕] [🖼] /

TRAVELODGE NANAIMO   *Book at aaa.com*   **Phone:** (250)754-6355

6/1-9/30 [CP]	1P: $88-$94	2P: $94-$106	XP: $7	F17
10/1-2/28 [CP]	1P: $78-$84	2P: $84-$90	XP: $7	F17
3/1-5/31 [CP]	1P: $77-$83	2P: $83-$89	XP: $7	F17

Motel   **Location:** Jct Hwy 19A (Terminal Ave) and Island Hwy 1, access from either highway. 96 Terminal Ave N V9S 4J2. Fax: 250/754-1301. **Facility:** 78 one-bedroom standard units, some with efficiencies. 3 stories, interior corridors. **Parking:** on-site. **Terms:** cancellation fee imposed, $2 service charge, pets ($10 extra charge, 1st floor units). **Amenities:** *Some:* high-speed Internet, hair dryers. **Leisure Activities:** sauna. **Guest Services:** valet and coin laundry. **Business Services:** meeting rooms. **Cards:** AX, DC, MC, VI. **Special Amenities:** free continental breakfast and free local telephone calls. *(See color ad below)*

SOME UNITS
[S/D] [🛏] [🍴FEE] [🎬] [▣] / [✕] [AC] [🔌] [🖼] /

———— WHERE TO DINE ————

BLUE GINGER SUSHI BAR & SATAY GRILL   **Lunch:** $5-$10   **Dinner:** $10-$20   **Phone:** 250/751-8238

Japanese   **Location:** Hwy 19A (Island Hwy), at Turner Rd; in Longwood Station. 5769 Turner Rd V9T 6L8. **Hours:** 11 am-2:30 & 4:30-10 pm, Fri-11 pm, Sat noon-11 pm, Sun 4:30 pm-10 pm. Closed: 12/25. **Features:** The restaurant represents an interesting idea: combining three Asian tastes—Japanese, Chinese and Thailand—on a single menu. Dishes reflect a melange of flavors and are a fun twist on the typical Asian dining experience. Casual dress; cocktails. **Parking:** on-site. **Cards:** AX, MC, VI.

[✕]

EARLS

♦♦ ♦♦

Canadian

Lunch: $9-$25 **Dinner:** $9-$25 **Phone:** 250/756-4100
Location: 4 km n on Hwy 19A (Island Hwy) from departure Bay Ferry Terminal. 100-2980 N Island Hwy V9T 5V4.
Hours: 11 am-11 pm, Fri & Sat-midnight, Sun 10:30 am-10 pm. Closed: 12/25. **Features:** Juicy burgers,
fresh salads, chicken wings and beer: What could be better? The food is great and the service friendly.
There is plenty of free parking. Casual dress; cocktails. **Parking:** on-site. **Cards:** AX, DC, MC, VI. ⊠

LONGWOOD BREWPUB

♦♦ ♦♦

Canadian

Lunch: $8-$15 **Dinner:** $10-$20 **Phone:** 250/729-8225
Location: Hwy 19A (Island Hwy) at Turner Rd; in the Longwood Station. 5775 Turner Rd V9T 6L8. **Hours:** 11 am-11
pm, Sun 9 am-10 pm. Closed: 1/1, 12/25. **Features:** Families are welcomed in the restaurant section, but
the pub, which offers all the amenities of the restaurant, is strictly for adults. Patrons can sample hand-
crafted lagers and ales, as well as hearty pub food, such as sandwiches, burgers, pastas and varied dinner
entrees. Casual dress; cocktails. **Parking:** on-site. **Cards:** AX, DC, MC, VI. ⊠

ZOUGLA

♦♦ ♦♦

Mediterranean

Lunch: $8-$15 **Dinner:** $14-$26 **Phone:** 250/716-3233
Location: Hwy 19A (Island Hwy) and Brechin Rd, on the road to Departure Bay ferry terminal. 2021 Estevan Rd V9S
3Y9. **Hours:** 11 am-11 pm. Closed: 12/25, 12/26. **Features:** You'll enjoy this restaurant's offerings of steak,
seafood and Mediterranean specialties such as moussaka, spanakopita and souvlakia. Floor-to-ceiling
windows offer a great view of the ocean and mountains. Couples and travellers like the relaxing ambience.
Casual dress; cocktails. **Parking:** on-site. **Cards:** AX, MC, VI. ⊠

NANOOSE BAY pop. 4,723

——— WHERE TO STAY ———

FAIRWINDS SCHOONER COVE RESORT & MARINA

♦♦ ♦♦

Small-scale Hotel

Phone: (250)468-7691

	1P: $139-$159	2P: $139-$159	XP: $10	F16
5/1-9/30				
3/1-4/30 & 10/1-2/28	1P: $89-$109	2P: $89-$109	XP: $10	F16

Location: Island Hwy 1, 8.5 km se, follow signs via Powderpoint Rd (becoming Fairwinds Dr). 3521 Dolphin Dr V9P
9J7. Fax: 250/468-5744. **Facility:** 31 one-bedroom standard units. 2 stories, interior corridors. **Parking:** on-
site. **Terms:** weekly rates available, package plans, small pets only ($10 extra charge, in designated units). **Amenities:** irons,
hair dryers. **Pool(s):** heated outdoor. **Leisure Activities:** whirlpool, rental boats, fishing, 2 tennis courts, recreation programs,
rental bicycles, exercise room, volleyball. *Fee:* marina, charter fishing, golf-18 holes. **Guest Services:** gift shop, coin laundry.
Business Services: meeting rooms. **Cards:** AX, DC, MC, VI.

SOME UNITS

ASK ⓢⒹ 🐕 🍽 🍸 &M 🛶 ⊠ 🎿 ▣ ·/⊠/
FEE

NARAMATA pop. 1,791

——— WHERE TO STAY ———

THE VILLAGE MOTEL

♦♦ ♦♦

Motel

Phone: (250)496-5535

7/1-9/15	1P: $71-$127	2P: $71-$127	XP: $10
5/16-6/30 & 9/16-2/28	1P: $65-$114	2P: $65-$114	XP: $10
3/1-5/15	1P: $59-$95	2P: $59-$95	XP: $10

Location: 14 km n on Naramata Rd from Penticton. 244 Robinson Dr V0H 1N0 (PO Box 194). Fax: 250/496-5744.
Facility: Designated smoking area. 9 units. 5 one-bedroom standard units, some with efficiencies. 4 one-bedroom suites with
efficiencies. 1 story, exterior corridors. **Parking:** on-site. **Terms:** 14 day cancellation notice, small pets only ($15 extra charge).
Amenities: hair dryers. **Leisure Activities:** bicycles. **Business Services:** fax (fee). **Cards:** AX, JC, MC, VI.

SOME UNITS

ⓢⒹ 🐕 🍽 ⊠ 🎿 🐾 ✆ 🛏 ▣ /▣/
FEE

——— WHERE TO DINE ———

**COBBLESTONE WINE BAR &
RESTAURANT**

Ⓐ

♦♦ ♦♦ ♦♦

Canadian

Lunch: $8-$14 **Dinner:** $12-$24 **Phone:** 250/496-5064
Location: 19 km ne of Penticton; from Naramata Rd, w along Robinson to 1st St, just s; in Naramata Heritage Inn &
Spa. 3625 First St V0H 1N0. **Hours:** Open 3/1-12/31 & 2/7-2/28; 11 am-10 pm. Closed: 1st week of February.
Features: There is an intimate and cozy feel amongst the brick floors and walls of this restaurant, set in the
basement of the Naramata Heritage Inn & Spa. This is casual dining at its best, with a menu that features
many artistic dishes with regional ingredients. Your server will impress you with an extensive wine
knowledge, helping to create a lovely and enjoyable meal. Semi-formal attire; cocktails; entertainment.
Parking: on-site. **Cards:** AX, MC, VI. &M ⊠

NELSON pop. 9,298

——— WHERE TO STAY ———

**BEST WESTERN BAKER STREET INN &
CONVENTION CENTRE** *Book at aaa.com*

Ⓐ SAVE

♦♦ ♦♦ ♦♦

Small-scale Hotel

Phone: (250)352-3525

| 7/1-9/30 | 1P: $129 | 2P: $129 | XP: $10 | F |
| 3/1-6/30 & 10/1-2/28 | 1P: $109 | 2P: $109 | XP: $10 | F |

Location: Jct of Hwy 6 and 3A. 153 Baker St V1L 4H1. Fax: 250/352-2995. **Facility:** 70 units. 69 one-bedroom
standard units, some with whirlpools. 1 one-bedroom suite. 4 stories, interior corridors. **Parking:** on-site.
Terms: check-in 4 pm, cancellation fee imposed, package plans. **Amenities:** high-speed Internet, voice
mail, irons, hair dryers. **Dining:** 6:30 am-9 pm, cocktails. **Leisure Activities:** whirlpool, exercise room.
Guest Services: valet and coin laundry, area transportation (fee)-ski hill. **Business Services:** meeting rooms, PC. **Cards:** AX,
DC, DS, MC, VI. **Special Amenities:** free local telephone calls and free newspaper.

SOME UNITS

ⓢⒹ 🕃 🐕 🍽 🍸 &M 🐾 DATA PORT ▣ /⊠ 🛏 ▣/
FEE

NORTH SHORE INN

Phone: (250)352-6606

| | 5/1-9/30 | 1P: $62-$80 | 2P: $72-$92 | XP: $10 | F6 |
| | 3/1-4/30 & 10/1-2/28 | 1P: $55-$67 | 2P: $65-$77 | XP: $7 | F6 |

Motel

Location: 3 km n on Hwy 3A via Nelson Bridge. 687 Hwy 3A V1L 5P7 (PO Box 119). Fax: 250/354-1772. **Facility:** 30 units. 29 one-bedroom standard units, some with kitchens. 1 one-bedroom suite. 3 stories (no elevator), interior/exterior corridors. **Parking:** on-site. **Terms:** office hours 7:30 am-11 pm, cancellation fee imposed, weekly rates available, package plans. **Leisure Activities:** whirlpool. **Business Services:** meeting rooms. **Cards:** AX, MC, VI.

SOME UNITS

(ASK) (S D) (†↑→) (🎥) (🖼) / (╳) (🖥) (🖥) /

--------- WHERE TO DINE ---------

ALL SEASONS CAFE

Dinner: $14-$28

Phone: 250/352-0101

Canadian

Location: Just e of Baker St; between Josephine and Hall sts. 620 Herridge Ln V1L 6A7. **Hours:** 5 pm-10 pm. Closed: 12/25. **Reservations:** suggested. **Features:** True to its name, this funky restaurant features a regional and seasonal menu, incorporating the best of the area and time of year in terms of ingredients. Everything is made from scratch, and the dishes are quite beautiful. Located in a small house-like setting a block away from downtown, this is a true gem in the heart of Nelson. You can eat in the dimly lit romantic dining room or in the glass-enclosed veranda, with a view of the rock garden. Casual dress; cocktails. **Parking:** street. **Cards:** MC, VI.

(╳)

FIDDLERS GREEN RESTAURANT

Dinner: $11-$25

Phone: 250/825-4466

(CAA)

Continental

Location: 10 km n on Hwy 3A. 2710 Lower 6 Mile Rd V1L 5P4. **Hours:** 5:30 pm-9 pm. Closed: 12/25. **Reservations:** suggested. **Features:** Located in a heritage house with large gardens and country charm, this restaurant features a progressive menu with an accent on fresh herbs and spices, eye-appealing presentations and British Columbia wines. Charming service. Garden and fireside dining. Casual dress; cocktails. **Parking:** on-site. **Cards:** MC, VI.

(K) (╳)

MAZATLAN MEXICAN RESTAURANT

Lunch: $6-$8   Dinner: $10-$12

Phone: 250/352-1388

Mexican

Location: Downtown; next to Savoy Hotel. 198 Baker St V1L 4H2. **Hours:** 11 am-10 pm, Fri & Sat-11 pm. Closed: 12/25; also Mon. **Features:** Upbeat and funky describes the decor at the homey, family-run restaurant. Delicious dishes—including black bean soup, chimichangas, burritos and enchiladas—come from the Mazatlan area of Mexico. Portions are huge. The festive eatery is popular with longtime town residents. Cocktails. **Parking:** street. **Cards:** AX, MC, VI.

(╳)

--------- *The following restaurants have not been evaluated by AAA* ---------
but are listed for your information only.

CAFE DANUBE

Phone: 250/354-0566

[fyi]

Not evaluated. **Location:** Downtown. 415 Hall St V7L 7Y9. **Features:** The culinary pleasures of Europe and the Middle East are featured in such preparations as crepes, quiches, tapenades, pates maison, Middle Eastern meatballs, pierogies and cabbage rolls. Traditional knowledge inspires the attractive, eclectic menu.

THE RICE BOWL

Phone: 250/354-4129

[fyi]

Not evaluated. **Location:** Downtown. 301 Baker St V1L 4H6. **Features:** A favorite among locals, the popular downtown restaurant serves a variety of Asian dishes.

NEW DENVER pop. 538

--------- WHERE TO STAY ---------

SWEET DREAMS GUESTHOUSE & DINING

Phone: (250)358-2415

All Year   1P: $55-$60   2P: $80-$95   XP: $25   F12

Country Inn

Location: 0.4 km w of Hwy 6 on Slocan Ave. Located across the street from lake. 702 Eldorado St V0G 1S0 (PO Box 177). Fax: 250/358-2556. **Facility:** Smoke free premises. 5 one-bedroom standard units. 2 stories (no elevator), interior corridors. **Bath:** some shared or private, shower only. **Parking:** on-site. **Terms:** check-in 5 pm, 7 day cancellation notice, pets (with prior approval). **Leisure Activities:** rental canoes, hiking trails. **Cards:** MC, VI.

(ASK) (🛏) (†↑) (╳) (K) (🅿) (☎)

NEW WESTMINSTER —See Vancouver p. 585.

NORTH VANCOUVER —See Vancouver p. 586.

OLIVER pop. 4,224

--------- WHERE TO DINE ---------

JACQUES' WINE COUNTRY RESTAURANT

Dinner: $15-$25

Phone: 250/498-4418

(CAA)

Continental

Location: Just s on Hwy 97 from 350th Ave. 34646 Hwy 97 V0H 1T0. **Hours:** 5 pm-close. Closed: Mon. **Reservations:** suggested. **Features:** The French-born chef/owner Jacques combines French cuisine with regional ingredients to create flavorful dishes. In the heart of wine country, the small-town eatery nurtures a cozy, country-inn atmosphere, in part thanks to its distinctive wine-cellar theme. Casual dress; cocktails. **Parking:** on-site. **Cards:** AX, DC, MC, VI.

(╳)

—— WHERE TO STAY ——

BELLA VILLA RESORT MOTEL
Phone: (250)495-6751

CAA SAVE

6/25-9/5	1P: $80-$110	2P: $100-$130	XP: $10
3/1-6/24	1P: $45-$60	2P: $55-$80	XP: $5
9/6-11/1	1P: $50-$65	2P: $55-$70	XP: $5
11/2-2/28	1P: $45-$55	2P: $50-$60	XP: $5

Motel
Location: Just off Hwy 3 E (Main St), turn on Ponderosa Dr, then just e of bridge on Hwy 3 E (Main St). 6904 Ponderosa Dr V0H 1V3. Fax: 250/495-6753. **Facility:** Smoke free premises. 14 units. 8 one-bedroom standard units with kitchens. 6 one-bedroom suites with kitchens. 2 stories (no elevator), exterior corridors. **Parking:** on-site. **Terms:** office hours 6 am-midnight, 14 day cancellation notice-fee imposed. **Leisure Activities:** boating, boat dock, barbecue area. **Cards:** MC, VI.

BEST WESTERN SUNRISE INN *Book at aaa.com*
Phone: (250)495-4000

CAA SAVE

6/1-9/30 [CP]	1P: $179-$259	2P: $179-$259	XP: $10 F17
3/1-5/31 [CP]	1P: $99-$179	2P: $99-$179	XP: $10 F17
10/1-2/28 [CP]	1P: $89-$149	2P: $89-$149	XP: $10 F17

Small-scale Hotel
Location: Jct Hwy 97, 3 km on Hwy 3 (Main St). 5506 Main St V0H 1V0 (PO Box 305). Fax: 250/495-4001. 37 one-bedroom standard units, some with efficiencies and/or whirlpools. 29 one-bedroom suites with kitchens. 3 stories, interior corridors. *Bath:* combo or shower only. **Parking:** on-site, winter plug-ins. **Terms:** check-in 4 pm, 7 day cancellation notice-fee imposed, weekly rates available. **Amenities:** high-speed Internet, voice mail, irons, hair dryers. **Dining:** 11 am-2 & 4-9 pm, cocktails. **Pool(s):** heated indoor. **Leisure Activities:** whirlpool, exercise room. *Fee:* game room. **Guest Services:** coin laundry. **Business Services:** meeting rooms, PC. **Cards:** AX, DC, DS, MC, VI. **Special Amenities:** free continental breakfast and early check-in/late check-out.

SOME UNITS

HOLIDAY INN HOTEL & SUITES *Book at aaa.com*
Phone: (250)495-7223

6/30-9/5	1P: $170-$175	2P: $170-$175	XP: $20 F18
9/6-2/28	1P: $89-$99	2P: $89-$99	XP: $20 F18
4/1-6/29	1P: $99	2P: $99	XP: $20 F18
3/1-3/31	1P: $85	2P: $85	XP: $20 F18

Condominium
Location: Jct Hwy 97, 1.9 km e on Hwy 3 (Main St). 7906 Main St V0H 1V0 (PO Box 1019). Fax: 250/495-6899. **Facility:** Set on the shores of a lake, the hotel offers guest rooms, all of which have a balcony, and many rooms also have full kitchens. 122 units. 50 one-bedroom standard units, some with kitchens and/or whirlpools. 17 one- and 55 two-bedroom suites ($129-$295) with kitchens, some with whirlpools. 4 stories, interior corridors. *Bath:* combo or shower only. **Parking:** on-site. **Terms:** check-in 4 pm, 30 day cancellation notice-fee imposed. **Amenities:** video games, high-speed Internet, voice mail, irons, hair dryers. *Some:* dual phone lines. **Pool(s):** heated indoor. **Leisure Activities:** whirlpool, rental paddleboats, marina, exercise room, horseshoes, volleyball. *Fee:* boats, game room. **Guest Services:** sundries, valet and coin laundry. **Business Services:** meeting rooms. **Cards:** AX, DC, MC, VI. *(See color ad card insert)*

SOME UNITS

SUPER 8 MOTEL-OSOYOOS *Book at aaa.com*
Phone: 250/495-6525

6/20-9/10	1P: $129-$269	2P: $129-$269	XP: $10 F12
9/11-2/28	1P: $79-$189	2P: $79-$189	XP: $10 F12
3/1-6/19	1P: $79-$189		

Small-scale Hotel
Location: Jct Hwy 97, 2 km e. 7702 Main St (Hwy 3 E) V0H 1V0 (PO Box 458). Fax: 250/495-6226. **Facility:** 60 units. 47 one-bedroom standard units, some with kitchens. 9 one- and 4 two-bedroom suites with kitchens. 3 stories, interior/exterior corridors. **Parking:** on-site, winter plug-ins. **Terms:** office hours 7 am-11 pm, check-in 4 pm, cancellation fee imposed, package plans. **Amenities:** voice mail, hair dryers. **Pool(s):** heated indoor. **Leisure Activities:** whirlpool, waterslide. **Guest Services:** coin laundry. **Business Services:** meeting rooms, PC. **Cards:** AX, DC, MC, VI.

SOME UNITS

The following lodging was either not evaluated or did not meet AAA rating requirements but is listed for your information only.

WESTRIDGE MOTOR INN
Phone: 250/495-7322

[fyi]
Not evaluated. **Location:** Jct Hwy 3 (Main St) and 97. 9913 Hwy 3 V0H 1V0 (PO Box 431). Facilities, services, and decor characterize a mid-range property.

—— WHERE TO DINE ——

CAMPO MARINA
Dinner: $5-$15
Phone: 250/495-7650

Italian
Location: At east end of town on Hwy 3 (Main St). 5907 Main St V0H 1V0. **Hours:** 5 pm-9:30 pm. **Features:** The established, family-run restaurant is sure to please with its hearty Italian dishes. The cozy, comfortable dining room welcomes guests to linger over linguine, tantalize their taste buds with tiramisu and savor pan-seared scallops. Semi-formal attire; cocktails. **Parking:** on-site. **Cards:** MC, VI.

THE CHALET HELVETIA
Lunch: $9-$12   **Dinner:** $14-$21
Phone: 250/495-7552

Continental
Location: Just s off Hwy 3 (Main St) at 85th St. 8312 74th Ave V0H 1V0. **Hours:** 11 am-2 & 5-9 pm; hours vary in winter. Closed: Mon & Sun off season. **Reservations:** suggested, in summer. **Features:** Just off Main Street in the center of town, the cozy, casual restaurant is a short distance from the lake. The cuisine is predominantly Swiss, offering several types of schnitzels, spaetzle and chicken and beef dishes. The owner and his wife make diners feel special by their desire to please. Casual dress; cocktails. **Parking:** on-site. **Cards:** AX, DC, JC, MC, VI.

DIAMOND STEAK AND SEAFOOD HOUSE

Steak & Seafood

Dinner: $10-$55   **Phone:** 250/495-6223
Location: Hwy 3 (Main St) at 89th St; centre. 8903 Main St V0H 1V0. **Hours:** Open 3/1-1/31; 4 pm-10 pm. Closed: 1/1, 12/25. **Reservations:** required, in summer. **Features:** Tasty food and attentive service are hallmarks at the excellent family restaurant. The menu lists a nice selection of pasta, pizza and Greek specialties. Broiled chicken breast with peppercorn and brandy demi-glace sauce is simply delectable. Casual dress; cocktails. **Parking:** street. **Cards:** AX, MC, VI.

WILDFIRE GRILL

Canadian

Lunch: $8-$10   **Dinner:** $14-$18   **Phone:** 250/495-2215
Location: Just e of jct Hwy 97 and 3 (Main St), on Hwy 3 (Main St); downtown. 8526 Main St V0H 1V0. **Hours:** 11 am-11 pm; 11 am-2 & 5-9 pm, Sat & Sun 5 pm-9 pm in winter. Closed: 12/25. **Features:** As patrons enter the downtown restaurant's small dining room, they are greeted by warm orange walls and tables that sparkle. The dining patio opens seasonally. "Globally inspired" is the motto of the contemporary bistro, which serves salmon, chicken and pasta dishes, as well as hearty salads. Cocktails. **Parking:** street. **Cards:** AX, MC, VI.

PARKSVILLE pop. 10,323

—— WHERE TO STAY ——

BAYSIDE OCEANFRONT INN

CAA SAVE

Small-scale Hotel

7/1-9/30	1P: $129-$189	2P: $139-$189	XP: $15	F17
5/1-6/30	1P: $99-$159	2P: $109-$159	XP: $15	F17
3/1-4/30 & 10/1-2/28	1P: $89-$149	2P: $99-$149	XP: $15	F17

Phone: (250)248-8333

Location: Island Hwy 19, exit 51 (Parksville/Coombs), 2 km e, then 1 km n on Hwy 19A. 240 Dogwood St V9P 2H5 (PO Box 1720). Fax: 250/248-4689. **Facility:** Smoke free premises. 59 one-bedroom standard units. 3 stories, interior corridors. **Parking:** on-site. **Terms:** small pets only ($10 extra charge). **Amenities:** voice mail, irons, hair dryers. **Dining:** 7 am-10 pm, cocktails. **Pool(s):** heated indoor. **Leisure Activities:** sauna, whirlpool, steamroom, volleyball. **Fee:** squash, massage. **Guest Services:** valet laundry, area transportation-train & bus station. **Business Services:** meeting rooms. **Cards:** AX, DC, MC, VI. **Special Amenities:** free local telephone calls and free newspaper.

SOME UNITS

BEACH ACRES RESORT

CAA SAVE

Cottage

6/24-9/4 Wkly	2P: $1350-$2095	XP: $12	F9
3/1-6/23 & 9/5-12/31 Dly	2P: $125-$218	XP: $12	F9
1/1-2/28 Dly	2P: $138-$212	XP: $12	F9

Phone: (250)248-3424

Location: Island Hwy 19, exit 46 (Parksville), 2.5 km n on Hwy 19A. 1015 Resort Dr #25 V9P 2E4. Fax: 250/248-6145. **Facility:** This mix of condos is dispersed over several acres; some are set back and secluded, some sit on a cliff overlooking the ocean and some are beachfront. Smoke free premises. 55 units. 2 one- and 20 two-bedroom standard units, some with kitchens. 33 cottages. 1-2 stories (no elevator), exterior corridors. *Bath:* combo or shower only. **Parking:** on-site. **Terms:** check-in 4 pm, 7 night minimum stay - seasonal, cancellation fee imposed, weekly rates available, package plans. **Amenities:** video library (fee), voice mail, irons. **Dining:** 8 am-9:30 pm; hours vary off season, cocktails. **Pool(s):** heated indoor. **Leisure Activities:** sauna, whirlpool, 3 tennis courts, recreation programs, playground, basketball, horseshoes, shuffleboard, volleyball. **Guest Services:** gift shop, coin laundry. **Business Services:** meeting rooms. **Cards:** AX, DC, MC, VI. *(See color ad below)*

SOME UNITS

MARINA VIEW BED & BREAKFAST

Bed & Breakfast

5/16-9/15 [BP]	1P: $80-$90	2P: $85-$95	XP: $20
9/16-10/31 [BP]	1P: $70-$80	2P: $85-$95	XP: $20
4/1-5/15 [BP]	1P: $70-$80	2P: $75-$85	XP: $20

Phone: 250/248-9308

Location: Island Hwy 19, exit 51 (Parksville/Coombs), 2 km e, 3 km n on Hwy 19A, then just e on Wright Rd, follow signs. 895 Glenhale Crescent V9P 1Z7. Fax: 250/248-9408. **Facility:** Smoke free premises. 3 one-bedroom standard units. 2 stories (no elevator), interior corridors. *Bath:* combo or shower only. **Parking:** on-site. **Terms:** open 4/1-10/31, age restrictions may apply, 7 day cancellation notice. **Amenities:** hair dryers. **Cards:** MC, VI.

SANDCASTLE INN

Phone: (250)248-2334

7/1-9/4 [CP]	1P: $99-$209	2P: $99-$209	XP: $10	F12
9/5-9/30 [CP]	1P: $79-$169	2P: $79-$169	XP: $10	F12
3/1-6/30 [CP]	1P: $69-$169	2P: $69-$169	XP: $10	F12
10/1-2/28 [CP]	1P: $69-$159	2P: $69-$159	XP: $10	F12

CAA SAVE

Small-scale Hotel **Location:** Island Hwy 19, exit 51 (Parksville/Coombs), 2 km e, then just n on Hwy 19A. 374 W Island Hwy V9P 1K8. Fax: 250/248-7330. **Facility:** 36 one-bedroom standard units, some with efficiencies. 3 stories, interior corridors. *Bath:* combo or shower only. **Parking:** on-site. **Terms:** office hours 7 am-11 pm, cancellation fee imposed. **Leisure Activities:** barbecue area. **Guest Services:** coin laundry. **Business Services:** meeting rooms. **Cards:** AX, MC, VI. **Special Amenities:** free continental breakfast.

SOME UNITS

SKYLITE MOTEL

Phone: (250)248-4271

7/1-9/6 [CP]	1P: $109-$119	2P: $109-$129	XP: $10	F12
9/7-2/28 [CP]	1P: $69-$89	2P: $69-$89	XP: $10	F12
5/15-6/30 [CP]	1P: $69-$79	2P: $69-$89	XP: $10	F12
3/1-5/14 [CP]	1P: $62-$72	2P: $62-$82	XP: $10	F12

Motel

Location: Island Hwy 19, exit 46 (Parksville), 3.5 km n on Hwy 19A. 459 E Island Hwy V9P 2G5. Fax: 250/248-4128. **Facility:** 27 one-bedroom standard units, some with efficiencies or kitchens. 1-2 stories (no elevator), exterior corridors. **Parking:** on-site. **Terms:** office hours 7 am-11 pm, weekly rates available. **Cards:** AX, MC, VI.

SOME UNITS

TIGH-NA-MARA SEASIDE SPA RESORT   *Book at aaa.com*

Phone: (250)248-2072

5/1-9/30	1P: $129-$229	2P: $129-$229	XP: $15	F5
3/1-4/30 & 10/1-2/28	1P: $99-$209	2P: $99-$209	XP: $15	F5

CAA SAVE

Resort
Large-scale Hotel

Location: Island Hwy 19, exit 46 (Parksville), 2 km n on Hwy 19A. 1155 Resort Dr V9P 2E5. Fax: 250/248-4140. **Facility:** This all-season resort offers log cottages and deluxe condo units fronting on a sandy beach; conference and spa facilities are available. Smoke free premises. 192 units. 89 one-bedroom standard units, some with efficiencies and/or whirlpools. 66 one- and 4 two-bedroom suites ($149-$309), some with kitchens and/or whirlpools. 33 cottages ($169-$289). 1-3 stories (no elevator), exterior corridors. **Parking:** on-site. **Terms:** 5 day cancellation notice-fee imposed, package plans, pets ($2 extra charge, in cottages off season). **Amenities:** video library (fee), voice mail. *Some:* irons, hair dryers. **Dining:** Cedar Dining Room at Tigh-Na-Mara Resort, see separate listing. **Pool(s):** heated indoor. **Leisure Activities:** whirlpool, steamroom, rental paddleboats, tennis court, recreation programs, playground, limited exercise equipment, spa, horseshoes, volleyball. *Fee:* bicycles. **Guest Services:** gift shop, coin laundry, airport transportation-Qualicum Airport, area transportation-bus & train station. **Business Services:** conference facilities, business center. **Cards:** AX, DC, JC, MC, VI.

SOME UNITS

TRAVELODGE PARKSVILLE   *Book at aaa.com*

Phone: (250)248-2232

6/16-9/30 [ECP]	1P: $129-$169	2P: $145-$189	XP: $10	F12
3/1-6/15 & 10/1-2/28 [ECP]	1P: $89-$129	2P: $99-$139	XP: $10	F12

Small-scale Hotel

Location: Island Hwy 19, exit 51 (Parksville/Coombs), 2 km e, then just n on Hwy 19A. 424 W Island Hwy V9P 1K8. Fax: 250/248-3273. **Facility:** 84 one-bedroom standard units, some with whirlpools. 3 stories, interior corridors. **Parking:** on-site. **Terms:** small pets only ($10 extra charge). **Amenities:** hair dryers. **Pool(s):** heated indoor. **Leisure Activities:** whirlpool, limited exercise equipment. **Guest Services:** coin laundry. **Business Services:** meeting rooms. **Cards:** AX, DC, DS, JC, MC, VI.

SOME UNITS

V.I.P. MOTEL

Phone: (250)248-3244

5/16-9/30 [ECP]	1P: $109-$119	2P: $119-$129	XP: $10	F12
3/16-5/15 & 10/1-2/28 [ECP]	1P: $74-$79	2P: $84-$89	XP: $10	F12

CAA SAVE

Motel

JC, MC, VI.

Location: Island Hwy 19, exit 51 (Parksville/Coombs), 2 km e, then just n on Hwy 19A. 414 W Island Hwy V9P 1K8. Fax: 250/248-0018. **Facility:** 21 one-bedroom standard units, some with efficiencies. 1 story, exterior corridors. **Parking:** on-site. **Terms:** office hours 7 am-11 pm, 7 day cancellation notice-fee imposed. **Amenities:** hair dryers. **Leisure Activities:** barbecue patio. **Guest Services:** coin laundry. **Cards:** AX, DC,

SOME UNITS

—————— *The following lodging was either not evaluated or did not* ——————
meet AAA rating requirements but is listed for your information only.

OCEAN TRAILS RESORT

Phone: 250/248-3636

fyi

Condominium

Did not meet all AAA rating requirements for. **Location:** Island Hwy 19, exit Parksville, 1.5 km n on Hwy 19A. 1135 Resort Dr V9P 2T6. Facilities, services, and decor characterize a mid-range property.

—————— **WHERE TO DINE** ——————

CEDAR DINING ROOM AT
TIGH-NA-MARA RESORT

Lunch: $12-$15   **Dinner:** $19-$34   **Phone:** 250/248-2333

CAA

Pacific Rim

Location: Island Hwy 19, exit 46 (Parksville), 2 km n on Hwy 19A; in Tigh-Na-Mara Seaside Spa Resort. 1155 Resort Dr V9P 2E5. **Hours:** 7 am-9:30 pm. **Reservations:** required, for dinner. **Features:** Although the menu focuses on West Coast seafood, it also lists pasta and steak dishes and more casual breakfast and lunch offerings. Sunday brunch is popular. The authentic log restaurant is nestled in a forest by the sea. The country-elegant setting is informal, warm and friendly. Cocktails. **Parking:** on-site. **Cards:** AX, DC, MC, VI.

KALVAS RESTAURANT
♦♦♦ ♦♦♦
Steak & Seafood
Cozy setting. Casual dress; cocktails. **Parking:** on-site. **Cards:** MC, VI.

Dinner: $12-$22   **Phone:** 250/248-6933
Location: Island Hwy 19, exit 51 (Parksville/Coombs), 2 km e, then just n on Hwy 19A. 180 Moilliet St V0R 2S0. **Hours:** 5 pm-10 pm, Sat-11 pm. Closed: 12/25. **Reservations:** suggested. **Features:** You'll surely enjoy the Alpine, log-cabin decor and high-quality, home cooking with fresh ingredients at this restaurant. It features an extensive menu of fresh seafood such as lobster, crab and oysters, as well as duck, pheasant and steak.
☒

LEFTY'S
♦♦♦ ♦♦♦
Canadian
motto here: "Everyone is born right-handed; only the greatest overcome it.". Casual dress. **Parking:** on-site. **Cards:** MC, VI.

Lunch: $6-$9   **Dinner:** $6-$15   **Phone:** 250/954-3886
Location: Island Hwy 19, exit 46 (Parksville), 4 km n on Hwy 19A. 101-280 E Island Hwy V9P 2G3. **Hours:** 8 am-8 pm, Fri & Sat-9 pm. Closed: 12/25. **Features:** Three friends realized they all were left-handed, and a new restaurant was born. The kitchen is committed to fresh ingredients in such dishes as the signature "southpawtatoes," which are oven roasted in special seasoning, and the made-from-scratch desserts. The
☒

TRISKELL RESTAURANT
♦♦♦ ♦♦♦
Regional French
veau aux poires. The owners themselves deliver warm and attentive service. Semi-formal attire; cocktails. **Parking:** on-site.
Cards: MC, VI.

Lunch: $5-$15   **Dinner:** $16-$26   **Phone:** 250/248-2011
Location: Island Hwy 19, exit 51 (Parksville/Coombs), 2 km e, then just n on Hwy 19A. 3-220 W Island Hwy V9P 2P3. **Hours:** Open 3/1-12/31 & 2/1-2/28; 11 am-2 & 5-9 pm. Closed major holidays; also Sun. **Features:** Charming simplicity awaits guests at the restaurant, where traditional specialties of Brittany are featured. Savory, sweet crepes are offered alongside such dishes as coquille St. Jacques, lapin braise and
☒

PARSON

──────── WHERE TO STAY ────────

TIMBER INN & CHALETS
♦♦♦ ♦♦♦
Small-scale Hotel

7/1-10/15 & 12/15-1/5	1P: $65-$95	2P: $75-$95	XP: $15	D16
3/1-6/30 & 1/6-2/28	1P: $49	2P: $65-$75	XP: $15	D16

Phone: (250)348-2228

Location: Just off Hwy 95 in Parson; 34 km s of Golden. 3483 Hwy 95 V0A 1L0 (Box 139). **Fax:** 250/348-2228. **Facility:** Smoke free premises. 10 units. 5 one-bedroom standard units. 5 cabins ($135-$180). 2 stories (no elevator), interior/exterior corridors. *Bath:* combo or shower only. **Parking:** on-site. **Terms:** open 3/1-10/15 & 12/15-2/28, office hours 7 am-11 pm, check-in 4 pm, 30 day cancellation notice-fee imposed, [ECP] & [MAP] meal plans available, package plans, pets ($5 fee, in designated cabins). **Amenities:** hair dryers. **Leisure Activities:** sauna, whirlpool, hiking trails, limited exercise equipment, basketball, horseshoes, volleyball. *Fee:* massage. **Guest Services:** TV in common area, complimentary laundry. **Business Services:** PC. **Cards:** MC, VI.
SOME UNITS
🛏 🍴 ☒ ☒ 🎽 🄰 🕿 / 🔌 💻 /
FEE

PEMBERTON pop. 1,637

──────── WHERE TO STAY ────────

PEMBERTON VALLEY LODGE   *Book at aaa.com*
(CAA) (SAVE)
♦♦♦ ♦♦♦
Small-scale Hotel

All Year	1P: $169-$269	2P: $169-$269	XP: $15	F18

Phone: (604)894-2000

Location: Just e on Hwy 99 from Pioneer Junction. 1490 Portage Rd V0N 2L1. **Fax:** 604/894-2002. **Facility:** Smoke free premises. 84 units. 31 one-bedroom standard units with efficiencies. 43 one- and 10 two-bedroom suites with kitchens. 3 stories, interior corridors. **Parking:** on-site. **Terms:** cancellation fee imposed, pets ($20 extra charge). **Amenities:** video library, DVD players, high-speed Internet, voice mail, irons, hair dryers. **Pool(s):** heated outdoor. **Leisure Activities:** whirlpool. **Guest Services:** complimentary laundry, area transportation-Whistler Ski Hills. **Business Services:** meeting rooms. **Cards:** AX, CB, DC, DS, JC, MC, VI. **Special Amenities:** early check-in/late check-out and preferred room (subject to availability with advance reservations).
🆂🅳 🛏 🄼 🏊 ☒ 🔌 💾 🖥 💻
FEE

PENDER ISLAND —See Gulf Islands National Park Reserve p. 477.

PENTICTON pop. 30,985

──────── WHERE TO STAY ────────

BEST WESTERN INN AT PENTICTON   *Book at aaa.com*
♦♦♦ ♦♦♦
Small-scale Hotel

5/1-9/14	1P: $115-$119	2P: $119-$127	XP: $10	F16
9/15-10/31	1P: $89-$98	2P: $98-$109	XP: $10	F16
3/1-4/30 & 11/1-2/28	1P: $81-$89	2P: $89-$99	XP: $10	F16

Phone: (250)493-0311

Location: 4 km s. 3180 Skaha Lake Rd V2A 6G4. **Fax:** 250/493-5556. **Facility:** 67 units. 55 one-bedroom standard units, some with whirlpools. 9 one- and 3 two-bedroom suites, some with efficiencies or kitchens. 2 stories (no elevator), exterior corridors. **Parking:** on-site. **Terms:** cancellation fee imposed, [AP] meal plan available, package plans, small pets only ($10 fee, in smoking units). **Amenities:** voice mail, irons, hair dryers. *Some:* high-speed Internet. **Pool(s):** heated outdoor. **Leisure Activities:** whirlpool, playground. **Guest Services:** valet and coin laundry. **Business Services:** meeting rooms. **Cards:** AX, DC, DS, MC, VI.
SOME UNITS
(A$K) 🆂🅳 🛏 🍴 🏊 🎽 🔌 💻 / ☒ 💾 🖥 /
FEE

DAYS INN PENTICTON   *Book at aaa.com*
(CAA) (SAVE)
♦♦♦ ♦♦♦
Small-scale Hotel

All Year	1P: $79-$199	XP: $10	F14

Phone: (250)493-6616

Location: Hwy 97, just n. 152 Riverside Dr V2A 5Y4. **Fax:** 250/493-6615. **Facility:** Smoke free premises. 84 one-bedroom standard units, some with whirlpools. 2 stories (no elevator), interior/exterior corridors. **Parking:** on-site. **Terms:** 3 night minimum stay - seasonal and/or weekends, small pets only ($10 extra charge). **Amenities:** voice mail, irons, hair dryers. *Some:* video games, high-speed Internet. **Pool(s):** heated outdoor. **Leisure Activities:** children's splash park, exercise room. **Guest Services:** coin laundry. **Business Services:** meeting rooms. **Special Amenities:** free continental breakfast and free newspaper.
SOME UNITS
🆂🅳 🛏 🍴 🏊 ☒ 🎽 🔌 💾 💻 / 🖥 /
FEE

EMPIRE MOTEL

Motel

6/25-9/7	1P: $89-$130	2P: $95-$150	XP: $5
3/1-6/24 & 9/8-2/28	1P: $60-$75	2P: $65-$80	XP: $5

Phone: 250/493-2323

Location: 4.5 km s. 3495 Skaha Lake Rd V2A 6G6. Fax: 250/493-4270. **Facility:** Smoke free premises. 32 units. 17 one- and 5 two-bedroom standard units, some with efficiencies. 10 one-bedroom suites with kitchens. 2 stories (no elevator), exterior corridors. **Parking:** on-site. **Terms:** office hours 7 am-11 pm, 30 day cancellation notice-fee imposed. **Amenities:** hair dryers. **Pool(s):** heated outdoor. **Leisure Activities:** playground. **Cards:** AX, MC, VI.

SOME UNITS

GOLDEN SANDS RESORT MOTEL

CAA SAVE

Condominium

6/22-9/15	2P: $109-$295	XP: $10
5/16-6/21	2P: $85-$175	XP: $10
5/1-5/15 & 9/16-2/28	2P: $69-$160	XP: $10

Phone: 250/492-4210

Location: Riverside Dr and Lakeshore Dr W. 1028 Lakeshore Dr W V2A 1C1. Fax: 250/492-0339. **Facility:** Smoke free premises. 47 units. 11 one-bedroom standard units, some with kitchens. 24 one-, 11 two- and 1 three-bedroom suites with kitchens. 2 stories (no elevator), exterior corridors. **Parking:** on-site. **Terms:** office hours 8 am-11 pm, check-in 4 pm, 14 day cancellation notice-fee imposed, small pets only ($10 fee, in designated units). **Amenities:** voice mail. **Pool(s):** heated outdoor. **Leisure Activities:** whirlpool, barbecues. **Guest Services:** coin laundry. **Cards:** MC, VI.

SOME UNITS
FEE

PENTICTON LAKESIDE RESORT, CONVENTION CENTRE & CASINO *Book at aaa.com*

CAA SAVE

Large-scale Hotel

6/24-9/4	1P: $199-$259	2P: $199-$259	XP: $20	F16
5/20-6/23 & 9/5-2/28	1P: $161-$199	2P: $161-$199	XP: $20	F16
3/1-5/19	1P: $151-$189	2P: $151-$189	XP: $20	F16

Phone: (250)493-8221

Location: Main St at Lakeshore Dr W. 21 Lakeshore Dr W V2A 7M5. Fax: 250/493-0607. **Facility:** With an on-site casino, lakeside location and balconies in some rooms, this full-service, resort-style hotel is a destination property. 204 units. 197 one-bedroom standard units, some with whirlpools. 7 one-bedroom suites. 6 stories, interior corridors. **Parking:** on-site (fee) and valet. **Terms:** check-in 4 pm, [CP] meal plan available, package plans, small pets only ($10 extra charge). **Amenities:** video games, voice mail, irons, hair dryers. **Dining:** 2 restaurants, 7 am-11 pm; patio dining in summer, cocktails. **Pool(s):** heated indoor. **Leisure Activities:** whirlpool, rental boats, rental canoes, rental paddleboats, boat dock, fishing, recreation programs in summer. *Fee:* massage. **Guest Services:** gift shop, valet laundry. **Business Services:** conference facilities. **Cards:** AX, CB, DC, DS, MC, VI.

SOME UNITS
FEE

PENTICTON SLUMBER LODGE

CAA SAVE

Motel

5/16-7/23 & 9/1-2/28	1P: $88-$168	2P: $98-$208	XP: $10
7/24-8/31	1P: $98-$190	2P: $128-$200	XP: $10
3/1-5/15	1P: $68-$118	2P: $78-$150	XP: $10

Phone: (250)492-4008

Location: Corner of Lakeshore Dr and Winnipeg St; Hwy 97, n on Riverside. 1.5 km e. Located in a residential area. 274 Lakeshore Dr W V2A 1B8. Fax: 250/492-7528. **Facility:** 42 units. 22 one-bedroom standard units, some with kitchens. 17 one-, 2 two- and 1 three-bedroom suites with kitchens. 2 stories (no elevator), exterior corridors. **Parking:** on-site. **Terms:** office hours 8 am-10 pm, 7 night minimum stay - seasonal, 14 day cancellation notice-fee imposed, weekly rates available, package plans, small pets only ($10 fee, in smoking units, with prior approval). **Amenities:** voice mail, hair dryers. **Pool(s):** heated indoor. **Guest Services:** coin laundry. **Cards:** AX, DC, MC, VI.

SOME UNITS
FEE

PENTICTON TRAVELODGE *Book at aaa.com*

Small-scale Hotel

5/13-10/10	1P: $109-$199	2P: $109-$199	XP: $15	F17
3/25-5/12	1P: $79-$169	2P: $79-$169	XP: $15	F17
3/1-3/24 & 10/11-2/28	1P: $69-$139	2P: $69-$139	XP: $15	F17

Phone: (250)492-0225

Location: Hwy 97 (Eckhart Ave), just ne. 950 Westminster Ave W V2A 1L2. Fax: 250/493-8340. **Facility:** Smoke free premises. 34 units. 32 one-bedroom standard units. 2 one-bedroom suites with efficiencies. 3 stories, interior/exterior corridors. **Parking:** on-site, winter plug-ins. **Terms:** office hours 6:30 am-11 pm, 2 night minimum stay - seasonal, cancellation fee imposed, small pets only ($10 extra charge). **Amenities:** irons, hair dryers. **Pool(s):** heated outdoor, heated indoor. **Leisure Activities:** sauna, whirlpool, waterslide, playground, limited exercise equipment. **Guest Services:** coin laundry. **Cards:** AX, DC, DS, MC, VI.

ASK   SOME UNITS
FEE

RAMADA INN & SUITES *Book at aaa.com*

CAA SAVE

Small-scale Hotel

5/13-10/10	1P: $129-$299	2P: $129-$299	XP: $20	F17
3/25-5/12	1P: $99-$249	2P: $99-$249	XP: $20	F17
3/1-3/24 & 10/11-2/28	1P: $89-$219	2P: $89-$219	XP: $20	F17

Phone: (250)492-8926

Location: 1.2 km w on Hwy 97. 1050 Eckhardt Ave W V2A 2C3. Fax: 250/492-2778. **Facility:** 125 units. 110 one-bedroom standard units, some with whirlpools. 15 one-bedroom suites with kitchens. 2-3 stories, exterior corridors. **Parking:** on-site, winter plug-ins. **Terms:** 2 night minimum stay - seasonal, cancellation fee imposed, package plans, small pets only ($10 fee, in designated units). **Amenities:** voice mail, irons, hair dryers. *Some:* high-speed Internet. **Dining:** 11:30 am-midnight, cocktails. **Leisure Activities:** whirlpool, playground, limited exercise equipment, game room. **Guest Services:** valet and coin laundry. **Business Services:** meeting rooms, PC. **Cards:** AX, DC, DS, MC, VI. **Special Amenities:** free newspaper and preferred room (subject to availability with advance reservations).

SOME UNITS
FEE

RIORDAN HOUSE BED & BREAKFAST

Phone: 250/493-5997

All Year [ECP]   2P: $60-$95   XP: $20

Historic Bed & Breakfast

Location: Corner of Winnipeg St and Hwy 97 (Eckhardt Ave). 689 Winnipeg St V2A 5N1. Fax: 250/493-5997. **Facility:** The owners create a welcoming ambience at this 1920 home distinguished by a collection of gesso art dating from 1887. Smoke free premises. 3 one-bedroom standard units. 2 stories (no elevator), interior corridors. *Bath:* shared, combo, shower or tub only. **Parking:** on-site. **Terms:** age restrictions may apply, 3 day cancellation notice, weekly rates available, package plans, no pets allowed (owner's pet on premise). **Amenities:** video library. *Some:* hair dryers. **Leisure Activities:** Fee: bicycles. **Guest Services:** gift shop, area transportation. **Business Services:** fax (fee). **Cards:** AX, DC, MC, VI.

SPANISH VILLA RESORT

Phone: (250)492-2922

5/16-7/23 & 9/1-2/28	1P: $88-$168	2P: $98-$208	XP: $10
7/24-8/31	1P: $98-$190	2P: $128-$200	XP: $10
3/1-5/15	1P: $68-$118	2P: $78-$150	XP: $10

Motel

Location: Corner of Power St and Lakeshore Dr W. 890 Lakeshore Dr W V2A 1C1. Fax: 250/492-2922. **Facility:** Smoke free premises. 60 units. 16 one-bedroom standard units. 38 one-, 5 two- and 1 three-bedroom suites with kitchens. 2 stories (no elevator), exterior corridors. **Parking:** on-site. **Terms:** office hours 8 am-10 pm, 7 night minimum stay - seasonal, 14 day cancellation notice-fee imposed, weekly rates available, small pets only ($10 extra charge). **Amenities:** voice mail, hair dryers. **Pool(s):** heated indoor. **Guest Services:** coin laundry. **Cards:** AX, DC, MC, VI.

SOME UNITS

SUPER 8 MOTEL PENTICTON   *Book at aaa.com*

Phone: 250/492-3829

6/16-9/15 [CP]	1P: $90-$105	2P: $90-$116	XP: $11	F16
4/1-6/15 [CP]	1P: $80-$85	2P: $80-$95	XP: $11	F16
3/1-3/31 & 9/16-2/28 [CP]	1P: $64-$70	2P: $64-$80	XP: $11	F16

Motel

Location: Jct Main St and Industrial. 1706 Main St V2A 5G8. Fax: 250/492-5278. **Facility:** 51 units. 43 one-bedroom standard units, some with kitchens and/or whirlpools. 3 one- and 5 two-bedroom suites ($99-$162). 2 stories (no elevator), interior/exterior corridors. *Bath:* combo or shower only. **Parking:** on-site. **Terms:** office hours 7 am-11 pm, small pets only ($10 fee, in smoking units). **Pool(s):** heated indoor. **Leisure Activities:** whirlpool. **Guest Services:** coin laundry. **Cards:** AX, MC, VI.

SOME UNITS

SWISS SUNSET INN

Phone: 250/492-8209

6/28-9/2	1P: $75-$85	2P: $79-$89	XP: $8	F5
5/1-6/27	1P: $59-$69	2P: $69-$74	XP: $8	F5
3/1-4/30 & 9/3-2/28	1P: $49-$59	2P: $55-$65	XP: $8	F5

Motel

Location: 3.4 km s. 2604 Skaha Lake Rd V2A 6G1. Fax: 250/492-5170. **Facility:** 25 units. 14 one- and 1 bedroom standard units. 10 one-bedroom suites ($69-$129), some with efficiencies or kitchens. 2 stories (no elevator), exterior corridors. **Parking:** on-site. **Terms:** office hours 7 am-11 pm, 10 day cancellation notice-fee imposed. **Amenities:** hair dryers. **Pool(s):** small heated outdoor. **Guest Services:** coin laundry. **Cards:** DC, MC, VI.

SOME UNITS

WATERFRONT INN

Phone: (250)492-8228

6/16-9/5	1P: $75-$125	2P: $75-$125	XP: $15	D9
9/6-10/15	1P: $65-$95	2P: $65-$95	XP: $10	D9
5/1-6/15	1P: $65-$85	2P: $65-$85	XP: $10	D9

Motel

Location: Hwy 97 to Channel Pkwy and Skaha Lake Rd, just ne to Lee Ave, then just s. Located adjacent to Skaha Park. 3688 Parkview St V2A 6H1. Fax: 250/492-8228. **Facility:** Smoke free premises. 20 units. 4 one-bedroom standard units. 16 one-bedroom suites with kitchens. 2 stories (no elevator), exterior corridors. **Parking:** on-site. **Terms:** open 5/1-10/15, office hours 7 am-10 pm, 30 day cancellation notice, small pets only ($10 extra charge). **Leisure Activities:** sauna, whirlpool. **Guest Services:** coin laundry. **Cards:** AX, MC, VI.

SOME UNITS

—————— **WHERE TO DINE** ——————

CEILI'S INN ON THE LAKE

Lunch: $9-$16   **Dinner:** $9-$21   **Phone:** 250/492-4092

Irish

Location: Between Riverside Dr and Power St. 950 Lakeshore Dr V2A 1B8. **Hours:** Open 5/1-9/30; 11 am-10 pm. **Features:** The inn serves many Irish favorites, including steak and kidney pie, with a selection of good old-fashioned Irish beers. Views of Okanagan Lake are stunning from the renovated outdoor deck. Casual dress; cocktails. **Parking:** street. **Cards:** MC, VI.

GRANNY BOGNER'S

Dinner: $19-$25   **Phone:** 250/493-2711

Continental

Location: 2 blks w of Main St; corner of Argyle St. 302 Eckhardt Ave W V2A 2A9. **Hours:** Open 3/1-12/31 & 2/1-2/28; 5:30 pm-9:30 pm. Closed: Sun & Mon. **Reservations:** accepted. **Features:** For somewhere special to eat, the 100-year-old heritage mansion fits the bill. On a quiet residential street, the rustic restaurant has an elegant dining room and attentive servers. Guests can sit back and enjoy flavorful creations from the kitchen. Drawing largely on regional ingredients, the chef also chooses many local wines for the menu. Casual dress; cocktails. **Parking:** on-site. **Cards:** AX, MC, VI.

HOG'S BREATH COFFEE CO

Lunch: $4-$6   **Dinner:** $4-$6   **Phone:** 250/493-7800

Coffee/Espresso

Location: End of Main St at Front St; downtown. 202 Main St V2A 5B2. **Hours:** 7 am-11 pm; to 5:30 pm in winter. Closed: 12/25. **Features:** The festive downtown cafe bustles with the lunchtime crowd, who come for hearty healthy food that is prepared daily. Whether veggie lasagna, soup, salad or an all-day breakfast special, each dish is sure to sate the heartiest of appetites. This spot also is great for a good cup of coffee and a sweet treat. The delicious cinnamon buns are sizeable. Beer & wine only. **Parking:** street. **Cards:** MC, VI.

JADE GARDEN

Chinese

Dinner: $7-$14 **Phone:** 250/492-7259
Location: Between Comox and Alberni sts. 902 Westminster Ave W V2A 1L2. **Hours:** 4:30 pm-9 pm. Closed: 12/25. **Features:** You'll find a large buffet of traditional Chinese foods to choose from at the long-standing family-style restaurant. Casual dress; cocktails. **Parking:** on-site. **Cards:** AX, MC, VI.

LA CASA OUZERIA

Italian

Lunch: $6-$10 **Dinner:** $10-$23 **Phone:** 250/492-9144
Location: Corner of Main St and Nelson Ave. 1090 Main St V2A 5E5. **Hours:** 11:30 am-2 & 5-10 pm. Closed: 1/1, 12/25, 12/26; also Mon. **Reservations:** suggested, weekends. **Features:** A family-run operation, the homey restaurant satisfies those who can't decide what to have. The menu lists both Greek and Italian cuisine. The service and ambience merge to create a cozy, comfortable experience. Casual dress; cocktails. **Parking:** on-site. **Cards:** MC, VI.

MON THONG THAI RESTAURANT

Thai

Lunch: $5-$13 **Dinner:** $8-$13 **Phone:** 250/770-9791
Location: 4 km s. 2985 Skaha Lake Rd V2A 5J6. **Hours:** 11:30 am-2:30 & 5-9 pm, Fri-Sun 9:30 pm. Closed: 12/25. **Features:** In the south end of town toward Skaha Lake, the friendly restaurant serves authentic Thai cuisine from an extensive menu that includes dishes from mild to hot and spicy. Bangkok-trained chefs prepare fresh, delicious food, while eschewing the use of monosodium glutamate. Casual dress; cocktails. **Parking:** on-site. **Cards:** AX, DC, MC, VI.

SHADES FAMILY RESTAURANT

American

Lunch: $6-$8 **Dinner:** $10-$12 **Phone:** 250/493-0465
Location: Corner of Main St and Okanagan Rd. 1909 Main St V2A 5H5. **Hours:** 6 am-9 pm, Fri & Sat-10 pm. **Features:** For a quick, affordable meal that will please everyone in the family, the family-run restaurant hits the mark. On the menu is everything from grilled cheese sandwiches to burgers and fries. Guests shouldn't be surprised if the server addresses them as "honey" and knows almost all the regulars by name. Cocktails. **Parking:** on-site. **Cards:** AX, DC, MC, VI.

THEO'S RESTAURANT

Greek

Lunch: $6-$12 **Dinner:** $11-$30 **Phone:** 250/492-4019
Location: Main St at Eckhardt Ave. 687 Main St V2A 5C9. **Hours:** 11 am-midnight, Sun 4 pm-11 pm. Closed: 12/25. **Reservations:** suggested. **Features:** The established downtown restaurant specializes in traditional Greek salads, souvlaki, moussaka and roast lamb, as well as steak and seafood. The Mediterranean decor is warm and family-oriented. Parking is available on the street or behind the restaurant. Casual dress; cocktails. **Parking:** on-site. **Cards:** AX, DC, MC, VI.

PITT MEADOWS — See Vancouver p. 588.

PORT ALBERNI pop. 17,743

———— **WHERE TO STAY** ————

BEST WESTERN BARCLAY HOTEL *Book at aaa.com* **Phone:** (250)724-7171

Small-scale Hotel

5/1-9/30	1P: $119-$129	2P: $129-$149	XP: $10 F17
10/1-2/28	1P: $89-$99	2P: $99-$119	XP: $10 F17
3/1-4/30	1P: $79-$89	2P: $89-$109	XP: $10 F17

Location: Johnston Rd (Hwy 4), just s on Gertrude St. 4277 Stamp Ave V9Y 7X8. Fax: 250/724-9691. **Facility:** 86 one-bedroom standard units, some with whirlpools. 5 stories, interior corridors. **Parking:** on-site. **Terms:** cancellation fee imposed, package plans, small pets only ($20 extra charge). **Amenities:** high-speed Internet, voice mail, irons, hair dryers. **Dining:** 6 am-9 pm, cocktails. **Pool(s):** heated outdoor. **Leisure Activities:** sauna, whirlpool, exercise room. **Guest Services:** valet laundry. **Business Services:** meeting rooms. **Cards:** AX, MC, VI.

SOME UNITS

CEDAR WOOD LODGE **Phone:** (250)724-6800

Bed & Breakfast

6/25-9/30 [ECP]	1P: $125-$129	2P: $135-$140	XP: $15 D13
10/1-2/28 [ECP]	1P: $90-$105	2P: $105-$115	XP: $15 D13
3/1-6/24 [ECP]	1P: $90-$99	2P: $100-$110	XP: $15 D13

Location: 3 km w on River Rd (Hwy 4) from Johnston Rd. 5895 River Rd V9Y 6Z5. Fax: 250/724-6887. **Facility:** Smoke free premises. 8 one-bedroom standard units with whirlpools. 2 stories (no elevator), interior corridors. **Parking:** on-site. **Terms:** office hours 7 am-11 pm, weekly rates available, package plans. **Business Services:** meeting rooms. **Cards:** AX, JC, MC, VI.

COAST HOSPITALITY INN *Book at aaa.com* **Phone:** (250)723-8111

Small-scale Hotel

6/1-2/28	1P: $115	2P: $125	XP: $10 F18
3/1-5/31	1P: $110	2P: $120	XP: $10 F18

Location: 3.2 km sw of jct Hwy 4 via City Centre/Port Alberni South Rt. 3835 Redford St V9Y 3S2. Fax: 250/723-0088. **Facility:** 50 one-bedroom standard units. 2 stories (no elevator), interior corridors. **Parking:** on-site. **Terms:** cancellation fee imposed, package plans, small pets only ($10 extra charge). **Amenities:** high-speed Internet, voice mail, irons, hair dryers. **Leisure Activities:** limited exercise equipment. **Guest Services:** valet laundry. **Business Services:** meeting rooms. **Cards:** AX, CB, DC, DS, JC, MC, VI.

SOME UNITS

RIVERSIDE MOTEL

CAA SAVE	6/20-9/20	1P: $69-$73	2P: $75-$93	XP: $7	D
	3/1-6/19	1P: $63-$77	2P: $69-$83	XP: $5	D
	9/21-11/1	1P: $60-$65	2P: $65-$79	XP: $5	D
Motel	11/2-2/28	1P: $49-$55	2P: $55-$70	XP: $5	D

Phone: (250)724-9916

Location: Johnston Rd (Hwy 4), just s on Gertrude St, then just w. 5065 Roger St V9Y 3Y9. Fax: 250/724-9916. **Facility:** Smoke free premises. 10 one-bedroom standard units, some with efficiencies or kitchens. 1 story, exterior corridors. *Bath:* combo or shower only. **Parking:** on-site. **Terms:** office hours 7:30 am-11 pm, cancellation fee imposed, small pets only. **Amenities:** hair dryers. **Guest Services:** coin laundry. **Cards:** AX, MC, VI. **Special Amenities:** free local telephone calls and early check-in/late check-out.

------- WHERE TO DINE -------

LITTLE BAVARIA RESTAURANT *Menu on aaa.com* **Lunch:** $8-$10 **Dinner:** $8-$20 **Phone:** 250/724-4242

CAA

German

Location: Between Argyle and Angus. 3035 4th Ave V9Y 2B8. **Hours:** 11 am-2 & 5-10 pm. Closed: 12/24-12/29. **Reservations:** suggested. **Features:** This quaint restaurant features a pleasant Bavarian decor with an accent on good old-fashioned German food. Schnitzel, Hungarian goulash, cabbage rolls, steak, seafood, and fondue for two are on the menu. Couples and business people like this place. Casual dress; cocktails. **Parking:** street. **Cards:** AX, MC, VI.

PORT COQUITLAM —*See Vancouver p. 588.*

PORT HARDY pop. 4,574

------- WHERE TO STAY -------

AIRPORT INN

	7/1-9/30	1P: $85-$95	2P: $95-$105	XP: $10	F12
	5/16-6/30	1P: $75-$85	2P: $85-$95	XP: $10	F12
Small-scale Hotel	10/1-2/28	1P: $70-$80	2P: $75-$85	XP: $5	F12
	3/1-5/15	1P: $65-$75	2P: $70-$80	XP: $10	F12

Phone: (250)949-9434

Location: Hwy 19, 5 km ne, follow signs. 4030 Byng Rd V0N 2P0 (PO Box 2039). Fax: 250/949-6533. **Facility:** 45 one-bedroom standard units, some with efficiencies. 2 stories (no elevator), interior corridors. **Parking:** on-site. **Terms:** small pets only (ground floor units). **Amenities:** voice mail, hair dryers. *Some:* irons. **Dining:** Airport Inn Restaurant, see separate listing. **Guest Services:** coin laundry. **Business Services:** meeting rooms, PC. **Cards:** AX, MC, VI.

SOME UNITS

GLEN LYON INN

	5/15-10/5	1P: $99-$115	2P: $115-$130	XP: $10	F
	10/6-2/28	1P: $80-$90	2P: $90-$100	XP: $10	F
Small-scale Hotel	3/1-5/14	1P: $75-$85	2P: $85-$95	XP: $10	F

Phone: 250/949-7115

Location: Hwy 19, 1.5 km n, follow signs. 6435 Hardy Bay Rd V0N 2P0 (Box 103). Fax: 250/949-7415. **Facility:** 44 one-bedroom standard units, some with efficiencies and/or whirlpools. 3 stories, exterior corridors. **Parking:** on-site. **Terms:** 3 day cancellation notice-fee imposed, package plans, small pets only ($5 extra charge, ground floor units). **Amenities:** voice mail, hair dryers. *Some:* CD players. **Leisure Activities:** limited exercise equipment. **Guest Services:** coin laundry. **Business Services:** meeting rooms, PC. **Cards:** AX, MC, VI.

SOME UNITS

FEE

PIONEER INN

CAA SAVE	5/15-10/15	1P: $85-$112	2P: $95-$112	XP: $10	F12
	3/1-5/14 & 10/16-2/28	1P: $49-$69	2P: $57-$77	XP: $8	F12

Phone: (250)949-7271

Motel

Location: Hwy 19, 1 km w, follow signs. 8405 Byng Rd V0N 2P0 (Box 699). Fax: 250/949-7334. **Facility:** 36 units. 35 one- and 1 two-bedroom standard units, some with efficiencies or kitchens. 2 stories (no elevator), exterior corridors. *Bath:* combo or shower only. **Parking:** on-site. **Terms:** office hours 7 am-11 pm, small pets only ($5 extra charge). **Dining:** 7 am-9:30 pm, cocktails. **Guest Services:** coin laundry. **Business Services:** PC. **Cards:** AX, MC, VI. **Special Amenities:** free local telephone calls.

SOME UNITS

FEE

------- *The following lodging was either not evaluated or did not* -------
meet AAA rating requirements but is listed for your information only.

QUARTERDECK INN

Phone: 250/902-0455

fyi

Not evaluated. **Location:** Hwy 19, 1.5 km n. 6555 Hardy Bay Rd V0N 2P0 (Box 910). Facilities, services, and decor characterize a mid-range property.

------- WHERE TO DINE -------

AIRPORT INN RESTAURANT **Lunch:** $7-$15 **Dinner:** $7-$15 **Phone:** 250/949-9434

Chinese

Location: Hwy 19, 5 km ne, follow signs; in Airport Inn. 4030 Byng Rd V0N 2P0. **Hours:** 6:30 am-9:30 pm, Sat & Sun from 7 am. Closed: 1/1, 3/28, 12/25. **Features:** Locals and visitors alike enjoy the restaurant, near Port Hardy's airport. It prepares many Cantonese/Chinese selections, as well as some Western fare, including burgers, hot and cold sandwiches and appetizers. Families are welcomed. Cocktails. **Parking:** on-site. **Cards:** AX, MC, VI.

MALONE'S OCEANSIDE BISTRO   **Lunch:** $7-$11   **Dinner:** $7-$20   **Phone:** 250/949-3050

Canadian

Location: 1 km se on Hwy 19, then just sw; in The North Island Mall. 9300 Trustee Rd. **Hours:** 11 am-9 pm. Closed major holidays; also Sun. **Features:** In a former shopping mall now housing North Island College, the popular family restaurant presents a menu of local seafood, steak, pizza and traditional Greek specialties. Casual dress; cocktails. **Parking:** on-site. **Cards:** MC, VI.

SPORTSMAN'S CLUB   **Lunch:** $8-$10   **Dinner:** $15-$24   **Phone:** 250/949-7811

Steak & Seafood

Location: Corner of Market and Hastings sts; across from Visitor Info Centre. 6400 Market St V0N 2P0. **Hours:** 11 am-1:30 & 5-9 pm. **Closed:** 12/25. **Features:** The longstanding restaurant's decor is reflective of the 70s, which is apropos given that it opened in 1975. Locals say this is the place to come for steak, but Italian items and some seafood also are on the menu. A smoking area is offered. Casual dress; cocktails. **Parking:** on-site. **Cards:** AX, MC, VI.

STINK CREEK CAFE   **Lunch:** $3-$8   **Phone:** 250/949-8117

Canadian

Location: Hwy 19, 1 km nw (towards water) on Granville St, then just ne. 7030 Market St V0N 2P0. **Hours:** 5:30 am-5 pm. Closed major holidays. **Features:** Don't let the name fool you, the food is excellent! Homemade soup and sandwiches along with mouth-watering pastry, pie and muffins. Try the specialty "rhubarb muffins." Located downtown. **Parking:** street. **Cards:** AX, MC, VI.

PORT MCNEILL pop. 2,821

──────── WHERE TO STAY ────────

HAIDA-WAY MOTOR INN   **Phone:** (250)956-3373

6/1-9/30	1P: $85-$99	2P: $99-$109	XP: $10 F6
3/1-5/31 & 10/1-2/28	1P: $65-$70	2P: $69-$75	XP: $10 F6

Small-scale Hotel   **Location:** Hwy 19, 2 km e. 1817 Campbell Way V0N 2R0 (Box 399). Fax: 250/956-4710. **Facility:** 52 one-bedroom standard units, some with efficiencies or kitchens. 3 stories (no elevator), interior/exterior corridors. **Parking:** on-site. **Terms:** office hours 6 am-2 am, check-in 4 pm. **Dining:** Northern Lights Restaurant, see separate listing. **Guest Services:** coin laundry. **Business Services:** meeting rooms, PC. **Cards:** AX, MC, VI.

SOME UNITS

──────── WHERE TO DINE ────────

NORTHERN LIGHTS RESTAURANT   **Dinner:** $14-$24   **Phone:** 250/956-3263

Canadian

Location: Hwy 19, 2 km e; in Haida-Way Motor Inn. 1817 Campbell Way V0N 2R0. **Hours:** 5 pm-10 pm. Closed: 12/23-1/3. **Reservations:** suggested, 6/15-9/15. **Features:** Popular among the locals for its tasty food, the restaurant offers summer choices that include fresh local seafood as well as some steak, chicken or pasta dishes. Save room for dessert, as there is always a nice selection. During summer, reservations are recommended. Cocktails. **Parking:** on-site. **Cards:** AX, MC, VI.

PORT RENFREW

──────── WHERE TO STAY ────────

ARBUTUS BEACH LODGE   **Phone:** 250/647-5458

Property failed to provide current rates

Bed & Breakfast   **Location:** Klannanith St at Queesto Dr, follow signs to waterfront. 5 Queesto Dr V0S 1K0. **Facility:** Smoke free premises. 5 one-bedroom standard units, some with efficiencies. 2 stories (no elevator), interior corridors. *Bath:* combo or shower only. **Parking:** on-site. **Terms:** office hours 7 am-10 pm, age restrictions may apply. **Leisure Activities:** whirlpool.

──────── WHERE TO DINE ────────

LIGHTHOUSE NEIGHBORHOOD PUB   **Lunch:** $8-$16   **Dinner:** $8-$16   **Phone:** 250/647-5505

Canadian

Location: 2 km w on Parkenson Rd. General Delivery V0S 1K0. **Hours:** 11 am-9 pm; hours vary off season. Closed: 1/1, 12/25. **Features:** One of the best eating spots in town, the restaurant serves good pub food along with a wide selection of beers by the bottle or on tap. Casual dress; cocktails. **Parking:** on-site. **Cards:** MC, VI.

POWELL RIVER pop. 12,983

──────── WHERE TO STAY ────────

POWELL RIVER TOWN CENTRE HOTEL   *Book at aaa.com*   **Phone:** (604)485-3000

5/1-9/30	1P: $125-$155	2P: $135-$165	XP: $10 F16
3/1-4/30 & 10/1-2/28	1P: $125-$145	2P: $135-$155	XP: $10 F16

Small-scale Hotel   **Location:** 0.8 km e on Duncan St (BC ferry terminal), then 1 km n. 4660 Joyce Ave V8A 3B6. Fax: 604/485-3031. **Facility:** 71 one-bedroom standard units, some with whirlpools. 2 stories, interior corridors. **Parking:** on-site. **Terms:** cancellation fee imposed, [BP] & [CP] meal plans available, package plans, small pets only ($10 extra charge). **Amenities:** video games (fee), voice mail, hair dryers. **Leisure Activities:** whirlpool, limited exercise equipment. **Guest Services:** valet laundry, area transportation. **Business Services:** meeting rooms. **Cards:** AX, CB, DC, MC, VI.

SOME UNITS

FEE

HYATT MOTOR LODGE
[fyi]
Phone: 604/483-3113
Not evaluated. **Location:** From Duncan St (BC ferry terminal), 3.5 km n. 6255 Marine Ave V8A 4K6. Facilities, services, and decor characterize a basic property.

———— **WHERE TO DINE** ————

THE SHINGLEMILL PUB & BISTRO
Lunch: $7-$16   **Dinner:** $8-$24   **Phone:** 604/483-2001
♥♥♥♥♥♥
Canadian
Location: From Duncan St (BC ferry terminal), 3.5 km n on Marine Ave, 1.5 km e on Arbutus. 6233 Powell Pl V8A 4S6.
Hours: 11 am-2:30 & 5-9 pm, Sat 11 am-9 pm, Sun 9 am-9 pm; 11 am-9 pm 7/1-9/5. Closed: 12/25.
Reservations: accepted. **Features:** The popular, longstanding pub and bistro sits on the shores of Powell Lake, and large bay windows overlook the marina. The view is best from the second floor. Food is typical bistro fare: burgers, sandwiches and soups. Although it's a bit of a drive to get here, it's worth the trip. Casual dress; cocktails.
Parking: on-site. **Cards:** AX, DC, MC, VI.
🍸 ✕

WESTVIEW RESTAURANT & PIZZA
Lunch: $8-$15   **Dinner:** $8-$20   **Phone:** 604/485-6162
♥♥♥♥
Greek
Location: From Duncan St (BC ferry terminal), just n; between Burton and Courtney sts. 4553 Marine Ave V8A 2K5.
Hours: 11 am-11 pm, Sat & Sun from 4 pm. Closed: 1/1, 12/25, 12/26. **Reservations:** accepted.
Features: The menu blends Greek dishes, such as souvlaki and moussaka, with Italian fare, including baked lasagna and many pizza varieties. Large bay windows overlook the ocean. Casual dress; cocktails.
Parking: on-site. **Cards:** MC, VI.
✕

PRINCE GEORGE pop. 72,406

———— **WHERE TO STAY** ————

BEST WESTERN CITY CENTRE   *Book at aaa.com*
Phone: 250/563-1267
[CAA] [SAVE]
♥♥♥♥♥♥
Motel

5/1-9/30	1P: $120-$130	2P: $130-$140	XP: $10	F12
3/1-4/30 & 10/1-2/28	1P: $110-$120	2P: $120-$130	XP: $10	F12

Location: Just n of Victoria (Hwy 16) and Patricia Blvd; downtown. 910 Victoria St V2L 2K8. Fax: 250/563-9904.
Facility: 53 units. 49 one-bedroom standard units. 4 one-bedroom suites. 2 stories (no elevator), exterior corridors. **Parking:** on-site, winter plug-ins. **Terms:** office hours 5:30 am-11 pm, check-in 4 pm, cancellation fee imposed. **Amenities:** irons, hair dryers. **Dining:** 7 am-3 pm, Sat & Sun from 8 am. **Pool(s):** heated indoor. **Leisure Activities:** saunas, limited exercise equipment. **Guest Services:** valet and coin laundry. **Cards:** AX, CB, DC, DS, JC, MC, VI. **Special Amenities:** early check-in/late check-out and free room upgrade (subject to availability with advance reservations).
SOME UNITS
[SD] [🍴] [➳] [DATA PORT] [🖥] / ✕ 🔒 /

CARMEL MOTOR INN
Phone: 250/564-6339
♥♥♥♥
Motel

5/1-10/31	1P: $57	2P: $68	XP: $10	F12
3/1-4/30 & 11/1-2/28	1P: $55	2P: $65	XP: $10	F12

Location: 1 km s on Hwy 97 from jct Trans-Canada Hwy 16 (Yellowhead Hwy). 1502 Hwy 97 S V2L 5L9.
Fax: 250/562-0597. **Facility:** 90 units. 89 one-bedroom standard units, some with efficiencies (utensils extra charge). 1 one-bedroom suite. 2 stories, exterior corridors. *Bath:* combo or shower only. **Parking:** on-site, winter plug-ins. **Terms:** office hours 7 am-midnight. **Guest Services:** gift shop. **Cards:** AX, DC, MC, VI.
SOME UNITS
[ASK] [🍴] [✻] 🔒 / ✕ [DATA PORT]

DAYS INN   *Book at aaa.com*
Phone: (250)562-7072
♥♥♥
Small-scale Hotel

3/1-10/31	1P: $79-$87	2P: $89-$99	XP: $10	F12
11/1-2/28	1P: $77-$78	2P: $78-$84	XP: $10	F12

Location: From Victoria (Hwy 16), just n on 7th Ave. 600 Quebec St V2L 1W7. Fax: 250/562-1768. **Facility:** 75 units. 74 one-bedroom standard units. 1 one-bedroom suite ($100) with efficiency. 2 stories, interior corridors. **Parking:** on-site. **Terms:** 30 day cancellation notice. **Amenities:** high-speed Internet, voice mail. *Some:* irons, hair dryers. **Leisure Activities:** limited exercise equipment. **Guest Services:** valet laundry. **Business Services:** meeting rooms. **Cards:** AX, MC, VI.
SOME UNITS
[ASK] [SD] [🍴] [🍸] [✻] [DATA PORT] [🖥] / ✕ 🔒 /

P.G. HI-WAY MOTEL
Phone: (250)564-6869
[CAA] [SAVE]
♥♥♥♥♥♥
Motel

All Year	1P: $50-$60	2P: $55-$70	XP: $10	F6

Location: Jct Hwy 97, 1.2 km e on Trans-Canada Hwy 16 (Yellowhead Hwy). 1737 20th Ave V2L 4B9. Fax: 250/562-5687. **Facility:** 45 one-bedroom standard units, some with efficiency. 2 stories (no elevator), exterior corridors. *Bath:* combo or shower only. **Parking:** on-site, winter plug-ins. **Terms:** office hours 7 am-midnight, pets ($5-$10 extra charge). **Cards:** AX, MC, VI. **Special Amenities:** free local telephone calls and early check-in/late check-out.
SOME UNITS
[SD] [🐾] [✻] [🖥] / ✕ 🔒 🍽 /
FEE

———— **WHERE TO DINE** ————

CHINA SAIL RESTAURANT
Lunch: $9-$15   **Dinner:** $9-$15   **Phone:** 250/564-2828
♥♥♥♥♥♥
Chinese
Location: Hwy 97, 1.7 km w on 5th Ave; corner of 5th and Tabor. 4288 5th Ave V2N 7A2. **Hours:** 11:30 am-11 pm, Fri & Sat-midnight, Sun 2 pm-9 pm. Closed: 12/25, 12/26. **Features:** A local favorite for more than 20 years, this restaurant continues to serve delicious Chinese and Canadian dishes. You may select an individual meal, family dinner or combination plate; all are reasonably priced. Good food and good service. Casual dress; cocktails. **Parking:** on-site. **Cards:** AX, MC, VI.

EARLS PRINCE GEORGE

▼▼ ▼▼

Canadian

Lunch: $8-$19   Dinner: $8-$19   Phone: 250/562-1527

Location: Corner of Hwy 97 and 15th Ave. 1440 E Central St V2M 3C1. **Hours:** 11 am-midnight. Closed: 12/25. **Features:** Juicy burgers, fresh salads, chicken wings and beer: What could be better? The food is great and the service friendly. There is plenty of free parking. Casual dress; cocktails. **Parking:** on-site. **Cards:** AX, MC, VI.

⊠

RIC'S GRILL, STEAK SEAFOOD & CHOP HOUSE

(CAA)

▼▼ ▼▼

Steak & Seafood

Lunch: $10-$19   Dinner: $16-$37   Phone: 250/614-9096

Location: Between 5th and 6th aves; downtown. 547 George St V2L 1R8. **Hours:** 11:30 am-10 pm, Fri-11 pm, Sat 4:30 pm-11 pm, Sun 4:30 pm-10 pm. Closed: 12/24, 12/25. **Reservations:** suggested. **Features:** Ric's is located downtown and close to the city's casino. Specializing in steak, this restaurant features Western Canadian beef known as "sterling silver," which is cooked any way you like it. Bustling atmosphere. Try a cozy booth for two. Cocktails. **Parking:** street. **Cards:** AX, MC, VI.

⊠

PRINCE RUPERT pop. 14,643

——— **WHERE TO STAY** ———

ALEEDA MOTEL

(CAA) (SAVE)

▼▼

Motel

			Phone: (250)627-1367
5/16-10/1	1P: $60	2P: $70	XP: $10 F12
3/1-5/15 & 10/2-2/28	1P: $54	2P: $60	XP: $10 F12

Location: Corner of 3rd Ave W and 8th St. 900 3rd Ave W V8J 1M8. Fax: 250/624-3132. **Facility:** 31 one-bedroom standard units, some with efficiencies. 2 stories (no elevator), interior corridors. **Parking:** on-site. **Terms:** weekly rates available, pets ($5 extra charge). **Cards:** AX, MC, VI. **Special Amenities:** free continental breakfast and free local telephone calls.

SOME UNITS

⧖ ⊞ 🛏 ⚟ 🎿 📷 DATA PORT / ⊠ 🗄 🖥 /
FEE

HOWARD JOHNSON HIGHLINER PLAZA HOTEL   *Book at aaa.com*

▼▼ ▼▼

Small-scale Hotel

			Phone: (250)624-9060
6/1-9/30	1P: $115-$125	2P: $115-$125	XP: $10 F16
3/1-5/31 & 10/1-2/28	1P: $85-$105	2P: $85-$105	XP: $10 F16

Location: Corner of 1st Ave W and 7th St; downtown. 815 1st Ave W V8J 1B3. Fax: 250/627-7759. **Facility:** 94 one-bedroom standard units. 17 stories, interior corridors. **Parking:** on-site. **Terms:** small pets only (in smoking units). **Amenities:** dual phone lines, voice mail, irons, hair dryers. **Guest Services:** valet and coin laundry. **Business Services:** meeting rooms. **Cards:** AX, MC, VI.

SOME UNITS

A$K ⧖ 🛏 ⚟ 🎿 DATA PORT 🖥 / ⊠ 🗄 🖥 /

TOTEM LODGE MOTEL

(CAA) (SAVE)

▼▼

Motel

			Phone: 250/624-6761
6/1-9/30	1P: $79-$82	2P: $89-$95	XP: $8 F12
3/1-5/31 & 10/1-2/28	1P: $65-$79	2P: $72-$85	XP: $8 F12

Location: 1.6 km w on Hwy 16 (2nd Ave W) from downtown. 1335 Park Ave V8J 1K3. Fax: 250/624-3831. **Facility:** 31 one-bedroom standard units, some with kitchens. 3 stories (no elevator), interior corridors. **Parking:** on-site. **Terms:** cancellation fee imposed. **Guest Services:** coin laundry. **Cards:** AX, MC, VI.

SOME UNITS

⚟ 🎿 📷 DATA PORT 🖥 / ⊠ 🗄 🖥 /

——— *The following lodgings were either not evaluated or did not* ———
meet AAA rating requirements but are listed for your information only.

CREST HOTEL

(fyi)

Phone: 250/624-6771

Not evaluated. **Location:** Hwy 16, just nw on 2nd St; downtown. 222 1st Ave W V8J 3P6 (PO Box 277). Facilities, services, and decor characterize a mid-range property.

PACIFIC INN

(fyi)

Phone: 250/627-1711

Not evaluated. **Location:** Corner of 3rd Ave and 8th St. 909 3rd Ave W V8J 1M9. Facilities, services, and decor characterize a mid-range property.

——— **WHERE TO DINE** ———

OPA JAPANESE SUSHI STORY

▼▼

Japanese

Lunch: $3-$10   Dinner: $3-$10   Phone: 250/627-4560

Location: From 3rd Ave E, 1 km n; in Cow Bay. 34 Cow Bay Rd V8J 1A5. **Hours:** 11:30 am-2 & 5-9 pm. Closed: Sun & Mon. **Features:** The sushi restaurant occupies an old loft originally used for taking the main conk lines off the nets and putting them into a pot filled with tar that helped preserve the rope from rot and salt damage. The tar pot is still here, as is the tar on the floor. Seating is limited. Prices listed are for individual sushi rolls. Beer only. **Parking:** street. **Cards:** MC, VI.

🎿 ⊠

SMILES SEAFOOD CAFE

▼▼

Seafood

Cards: MC, VI.

Lunch: $6-$16   Dinner: $8-$16   Phone: 250/624-3072

Location: Hwy 16, 1 km nw. 113 Cow Bay Rd V8J 1A4. **Hours:** Open 3/1-12/25 & 2/1-2/28; 11 am-9 pm; 9 am-10 pm 6/1-9/6. Closed: 12/25. **Features:** In business since 1934, the distinctive diner-style restaurant serves locals and tourists alike with a variety of seafood, steaks, chops, sandwiches and salads. Any local can point the way to the cafe, in the city's Cow Bay area. Casual dress; cocktails. **Parking:** street.

⊠

THE WATERFRONT RESTAURANT   **Lunch:** $8-$16   **Dinner:** $9-$34   **Phone:** 250/624-6771

▼▼▼   **Location:** Hwy 16, just nw on 2nd St; in Crest Hotel. 222 1st Ave W V8J 3P6. **Hours:** 6:30 am-10 pm. **Closed:**
12/25. **Features:** This restaurant offers absolutely the best, most incredible view of the harbor and
mountains as the hotel sits atop a cliff overlooking the strait. This all-day restaurant serves traditional dishes
such as pasta, burgers, steak and specializes in seafood. Casual dress; cocktails. **Parking:** on-site.

Canadian

Cards: AX, DC, DS, MC, VI.

PRINCETON pop. 2,610

─────── **WHERE TO STAY** ───────

BEST WESTERN PRINCETON INN   *Book at aaa.com*   **Phone:** (250)295-3537

6/1-9/6 [CP]	1P: $109	2P: $119	XP: $10	F12
3/1-5/31 & 9/7-2/28 [CP]	1P: $79	2P: $89	XP: $10	F12

(CAA) (SAVE)

▼▼▼▼   **Location:** On Hwy 3. 169 Hwy 3 V0X 1W0 (PO Box 1555). Fax: 250/295-3547. **Facility:** 44 one-bedroom
standard units, some with kitchens. 2 stories (no elevator), exterior corridors. **Parking:** on-site, winter plug-
ins. **Terms:** small pets only ($10 fee). **Amenities:** irons, hair dryers. **Pool(s):** heated outdoor. **Leisure
Activities:** sauna, whirlpool. **Cards:** AX, CB, DC, DS, MC, VI. **Special Amenities: free continental
breakfast and free local telephone calls.**

Motel

ECONO LODGE PRINCETON (VILLAGER INN)   *Book at aaa.com*   **Phone:** (250)295-6996

All Year	1P: $79-$129	2P: $79-$129	XP: $10	F12

(CAA) (SAVE)

▼   **Location:** Just off Hwy 3. 244 4th St V0X 1W0 (PO Box 160). Fax: 250/295-3667. **Facility:** 26 one-bedroom
standard units, some with efficiencies. 2 stories (no elevator), exterior corridors. **Parking:** on-site, winter
plug-ins. **Terms:** office hours 6:30 am-midnight, cancellation fee imposed, small pets only ($5 fee).
Amenities: hair dryers. **Pool(s):** small heated outdoor. **Guest Services:** coin laundry. **Cards:** AX, DC,
MC, VI. **Special Amenities: free continental breakfast and free local telephone calls.**

Motel

─────── **WHERE TO DINE** ───────

BELAIRE RESTAURANT   **Lunch:** $5-$8   **Dinner:** $9-$14   **Phone:** 250/295-7711

▼   **Location:** Hwy 3, just w. 161 Vermilion Ave V0X 1W0. **Hours:** 8 am-9 pm; to 7 pm 6/1-10/31. Closed major
holidays; also 12/24-1/2. **Features:** Along one of the main downtown streets just off the highway and next
door to the town museum, this simple diner housed the mine rescue training center, which served the area's

Canadian

nine underground coal mines during the 1930s, 40s and 50s. It's been a restaurant for more than 10 years.
On the menu is good, old-fashioned Canadian food, including sandwiches, burgers and hearty steaks. Cocktails. **Parking:**
street. **Cards:** AX, MC, VI.

QUADRA ISLAND —See Gulf Islands National Park Reserve p. 477.

QUALICUM BAY pop. 19,900

─────── **WHERE TO DINE** ───────

SANDBAR CAFE   **Lunch:** $6-$10   **Dinner:** $7-$11   **Phone:** 250/757-9995

▼   **Location:** Hwy 19, exit 75 (Qualicumbay/Bowser), 3 km e, follow Hwy 19A signs, then 2.5 km n on Hwy 19A. 6087 W
Island Hwy V0R 1G0. **Hours:** 8 am-8 pm. Closed: 12/25, 12/26. **Features:** The Sandbar Cafe is a roadside-
style diner and features a very nice view of the water. The traditional fare of very good food includes a daily

Canadian

selection of tasty sandwiches and homemade soup. The coffee is always fresh! Friendly and prompt
service. Casual dress; beer & wine only. **Parking:** on-site. **Cards:** AX, MC, VI.

QUALICUM BEACH pop. 6,921

─────── **WHERE TO STAY** ───────

BAHARI BED & BREAKFAST   *Book at aaa.com*   **Phone:** (250)752-9278

6/1-9/10 [BP]	1P: $205-$275	2P: $205-$275	XP: $20	
3/1-5/31 & 9/11-10/31 [BP]	1P: $125-$225	2P: $125-$225	XP: $20	

▼▼ ▼▼

Bed & Breakfast   **Location:** Hwy 19, exit 60 (Qualicum Beach/Port Alberni), 4 km e on Memorial Ave, then 11 km n on Hwy 19A. 5101
Island Hwy W V9K 1Z1. Fax: 250/752-9038. **Facility:** Smoke free premises. 4 one-bedroom standard units. 2
stories (no elevator), interior corridors. *Bath:* combo or shower only. **Parking:** on-site. **Terms:** open 3/1-10/31, office hours 8
am-10 pm, 2 night minimum stay - seasonal, age restrictions may apply, 7 day cancellation notice-fee imposed, package plans.
Amenities: fax, hair dryers. **Leisure Activities:** whirlpool. **Cards:** AX, MC, VI.

OCEAN CREST MOTEL   **Phone:** 250/752-5518

7/1-9/14	1P: $89-$99	2P: $89-$99	XP: $10	D18
9/15-2/28	1P: $59-$75	2P: $59-$75	XP: $10	D18
5/1-6/30	1P: $65-$70	2P: $65-$70	XP: $10	D18
3/1-4/30	1P: $59-$65	2P: $59-$65	XP: $10	D18

▼▼ ▼▼

Motel

Location: Hwy 19, exit 60 (Qualicum Beach/Port Alberni), 4 km e on Memorial Ave, then 3 km n on Hwy 19A. 3292 W Island Hwy V9K 2C6.
Fax: 250/752-5798. **Facility:** Smoke free premises. 19 one-bedroom standard units, some with efficiencies. 2 stories (no
elevator), exterior corridors. **Parking:** on-site. **Terms:** office hours 8 am-10 pm, cancellation fee imposed, weekly rates
available. **Amenities:** hair dryers. **Cards:** AX, MC, VI.

OLD DUTCH INN (BY THE SEA)

Small-scale Hotel

Phone: (250)752-6914

	1P: $79-$109	2P: $79-$109	XP: $15	F10
6/2-9/30				
3/1-6/1 & 10/1-2/28	1P: $69-$89	2P: $69-$89	XP: $15	F10

Location: Hwy 19, exit 60 (Qualicum Beach/Port Alberni), 4 km on Memorial Ave at jct Hwy 19A. 2690 Island Hwy W V9K 1G8. Fax: 250/752-6910. **Facility:** 35 one-bedroom standard units. 2 stories, interior corridors. *Bath:* combo or shower only. **Parking:** on-site. **Terms:** package plans, small pets only ($15 extra charge). **Pool(s):** heated indoor. **Leisure Activities:** sauna, whirlpool. **Guest Services:** gift shop. **Business Services:** meeting rooms. **Cards:** AX, DC, DS, MC, VI.

SOME UNITS

(ASK) (S/) (🐾) (🍴) (Y) (🍲) (AC) (📱) (💻) / (✕) /
FEE

QUALICUM HERITAGE INN

Historic
Small-scale Hotel

Phone: (250)752-9262

| All Year | 1P: $89-$119 | 2P: $89-$119 | XP: $10 | F12 |

Location: Hwy 19, exit 60 (Qualicum Beach/Port Alberni), 4 km e on Memorial Ave, then 1 km s on Island Hwy 19A. 427 College Rd V9K 2G4. Fax: 250/752-5144. **Facility:** This Inn was a private boys' boarding school from 1937 to 1970, today the school has been turned into comfortable rooms, and ocenview dining room. 70 one-bedroom standard units. 4 stories (no elevator), interior corridors. **Parking:** on-site. **Terms:** cancellation fee imposed, package plans, small pets only ($10 extra charge, patio level units). **Amenities:** hair dryers. **Business Services:** meeting rooms. **Cards:** AX, MC, VI.

SOME UNITS

(ASK) (S/) (🐾) (🍴) (Y) (AC) (DATA PORT) (💻) / (✕) /
FEE

———— *The following lodging was either not evaluated or did not* ————
meet AAA rating requirements but is listed for your information only.

HOLLYFORD GUEST ROOMS

[fyi]

Phone: 250/752-8101

Not evaluated. **Location:** 1 km e on Memorial Ave. 106 Hoy Lake Rd E V9K 1L7. Facilities, services, and decor characterize a mid-range property.

———— **WHERE TO DINE** ————

OLD DUTCH INN DINING ROOM

Dutch

Lunch: $5-$10   **Dinner:** $11-$25   **Phone:** 250/752-6914

Location: Hwy 19, exit 60 (Qualicum Beach/Port Alberni), 4 km on Memorial Ave at jct Hwy 19A; in Old Dutch Inn (By The Sea). 2690 Island Hwy W V9K 1G8. **Hours:** 7 am-9:30 pm. **Reservations:** suggested, for dinner. **Features:** You'll enjoy the wonderful ocean view at this restaurant, which offers creatively prepared, world-famous pastries as well as early bird specials and Dutch specialties. The servers dressed in Dutch costumes complete the Old Dutch atmosphere and decor. Cocktails. **Parking:** on-site. **Cards:** AX, DC, DS, MC, VI.

(Y) (✕)

SHANGRI-LA RESTAURANT

Chinese

Dinner: $8-$13   **Phone:** 250/752-5522

Location: Hwy 19, exit 60 (Qualicum Beach/Port Alberni), 4 km e on Memorial Ave, then 3 km n on Hwy 19A. 333 Garrett Rd (W Island Hwy) V9K 1H4. **Hours:** 4 pm-9 pm, Fri & Sat-10 pm. Closed: 12/25. **Features:** The combination Chinese and Vietnamese restaurant lays out a smorgasbord daily from 5 to 8 pm. Dishes are free of monosodium glutamate. Combination dinners are available for parties of two, three, four, five or six. The hilltop location affords great views of the ocean. Casual dress; cocktails. **Parking:** on-site. **Cards:** AX, MC, VI.

(✕)

QUESNEL pop. 10,044

———— **WHERE TO STAY** ————

BEST WESTERN TOWER INN

(CAA) (SAVE)

Small-scale Hotel

Book at aaa.com

Phone: (250)992-2201

| All Year | 1P: $65-$75 | 2P: $70-$90 | XP: $5 | F12 |

Location: Hwy 97, just e on Shepherd Ave; downtown. 500 Reid St V2J 2M9. Fax: 250/992-5201. **Facility:** 63 units. 62 one- and 1 two-bedroom standard units, some with whirlpools. 4 stories, interior corridors. **Parking:** on-site. **Terms:** 7 day cancellation notice. **Amenities:** high-speed Internet, irons, hair dryers. **Dining:** 6:30 am-10 pm, Sat & Sun 7 am-9 pm, cocktails. **Leisure Activities:** exercise room. **Guest Services:** valet laundry. **Business Services:** meeting rooms, business center. **Cards:** AX, DC, DS, MC, VI. **Special Amenities:** free local telephone calls and early check-in/late check-out.

SOME UNITS

(S/) (🍴) (Y) (💺) (DATA PORT) (📱) (💻) / (✕) /

TALISMAN INN

(CAA) (SAVE)

Motel

Phone: (250)992-7247

| All Year | 1P: $55-$65 | 2P: $65-$81 | |

Location: Hwy 97, 1 km n of Carson Ave. 753 Front St V2J 2L2. Fax: 250/992-3126. **Facility:** 85 one-bedroom standard units, some with efficiencies, kitchens and/or whirlpools. 2 stories, interior corridors. *Bath:* combo or shower only. **Parking:** on-site, winter plug-ins. **Terms:** cancellation fee imposed, small pets only (on ground floor, in main building). **Amenities:** irons. *Some:* DVD players, high-speed Internet, fax, hair dryers. **Leisure Activities:** whirlpool, limited exercise equipment. **Guest Services:** coin laundry. **Business Services:** meeting rooms, business center. **Cards:** AX, CB, DC, DS, MC, VI.

SOME UNITS

(🐾) (🍴) (💺) (📱) (🖥) (💻) / (✕) / (DATA PORT)

———— **WHERE TO DINE** ————

GRANVILLE'S COFFEE

Canadian

Lunch: $4-$7   **Dinner:** $4-$7   **Phone:** 250/992-3667

Location: Reid St at St Laurent Ave; downtown. 383 Reid St V2J 2M5. **Hours:** 7 am-10 pm, Sun 9 am-5 pm. Closed: 12/25. **Features:** Patrons easily can become too busy viewing the eatery's eclectically decorated walls to finish their coffee. Good choices include jumbo muffins, deli sandwiches and homemade soups. Fluent espresso is spoken here. **Parking:** street. **Cards:** MC, VI.

(✕)

RADIUM HOT SPRINGS pop. 583

WHERE TO STAY

BIG HORN MOTEL

Phone: (250)347-9522

6/16-9/20	1P: $55-$70	2P: $60-$80	XP: $5 F4
12/21-2/28	1P: $50-$70	2P: $60-$75	XP: $5 F4
3/1-6/15 & 9/21-12/20	1P: $45-$65	2P: $50-$65	XP: $5 F4

Motel **Location:** Hwy 93 and 95 (4-way stop), just s, then just w. 4881 St Marys St V0A 1M0 (PO BOX 176). Fax: 250/347-9594. **Facility:** Designated smoking area. 20 units. 13 one- and 6 two-bedroom standard units, some with efficiencies. 1 one-bedroom suite with efficiency. 1 story, exterior corridors. **Parking:** on-site, winter plug-ins. **Terms:** office hours 8 am-11 pm, cancellation fee imposed, weekly rates available, package plans. **Amenities:** video library (fee). *Some:* hair dryers. **Cards:** MC, VI.

SOME UNITS
ASK ⬛ 🍽 ⤬ 📷 DATA PORT 🛏 🖥 / VCR 📷 /
FEE

CEDAR MOTEL

Phone: (250)347-9463

CAA SAVE

6/26-10/15	1P: $67-$80	2P: $67-$85	XP: $10 F4
5/11-6/25	1P: $57-$77	2P: $57-$82	XP: $10 F4
10/16-2/28	1P: $52-$67	2P: $52-$72	XP: $8 F4
3/1-5/10	1P: $47-$65	2P: $47-$70	XP: $5 F4

Motel **Location:** Hwy 93 and 95, just s of jct Hwy 93, on service road (Main St). 7593 Main St W V0A 1M0 (PO Box 157). Fax: 250/347-9303. **Facility:** 17 units. 8 one- and 9 two-bedroom standard units, some with efficiencies. 2 stories (no elevator), exterior corridors. **Parking:** on-site, winter plug-ins. **Terms:** office hours 8 am-11 pm, pets ($5 extra charge, with prior approval). **Cards:** AX, MC, VI.

SOME UNITS
⬛ 🐾 🍽 📷 🛏 🖥 / ⤬ 📷 /
FEE

CHALET EUROPE

Phone: 250/347-9305

5/19-10/15	1P: $109-$159	2P: $109-$159	XP: $10 F7
3/1-5/18 & 10/16-2/28	1P: $79-$129	2P: $79-$129	XP: $10 F7

Motel **Location:** Hwy 93 and 95, just e, 1 km off Hwy 93 up the hill. 5063 Madsen Rd V0A 1M0 (PO Box 94). Fax: 250/347-9316. **Facility:** Smoke free premises. 17 one-bedroom suites. 3 stories (no elevator), exterior corridors. **Parking:** on-site. **Terms:** office hours 7 am-11 pm, 7 day cancellation notice-fee imposed, package plans, pets ($10 extra charge, in limited units). **Amenities:** hair dryers. *Some:* DVD players. **Leisure Activities:** sauna, whirlpool, cross country skiing, hiking trails, jogging, limited exercise equipment, game room. **Guest Services:** coin laundry. **Cards:** DC, MC, VI. *(See ad below)*

ASK ⬛ 🐾 🍽 ⤬ ⤬ 📷 DATA PORT 🛏 📷 🖥
FEE

LIDO MOTEL

Phone: 250/347-9533

6/15-9/30	1P: $50-$60	2P: $65-$75	XP: $10
3/1-6/14 & 10/1-2/28	1P: $40-$48	2P: $48-$60	XP: $10

Motel **Location:** Hwy 93 and 95 S, Stanley St W to Main St W, then s. 4876 McKay St V0A 1M0 (PO Box 36). Fax: 250/347-9533. **Facility:** Smoke free premises. 10 units. 2 one- and 8 two-bedroom standard units, some with efficiencies. 1 story, exterior corridors. *Bath:* combo or shower only. **Parking:** on-site, winter plug-ins. **Terms:** office hours 7:30 am-11 pm, cancellation fee imposed, pets ($5 extra charge). **Cards:** MC, VI.

🐾 ⤬ 📷 🛏 📷 🖥
FEE

MOTEL BAVARIA

Phone: 250/347-9915

CAA SAVE

5/1-9/30	1P: $50-$125	2P: $55-$125	XP: $10 F6
3/1-4/30 & 10/1-2/28	1P: $45-$125	2P: $50-$125	XP: $10 F6

Motel **Location:** Just w off Hwy 95; on Pioneer Ave. Located in a quiet area. 4872 McKay St V0A 1M0 (PO Box 148). Fax: 250/347-9218. **Facility:** Designated smoking area. 26 one-bedroom standard units, some with efficiencies (no utensils) and/or whirlpools. 2 stories (no elevator), exterior corridors. **Parking:** on-site, winter plug-ins. **Terms:** office hours 8 am-11 pm, 3 day cancellation notice, package plans. **Amenities:** *Some:* hair dryers. **Leisure Activities:** barbecue area, gazebo, horseshoes. **Cards:** MC, VI. **Special Amenities:** free local telephone calls and preferred room **(subject to availability with advance reservations).**

SOME UNITS
⬛ ⤬ 📷 🛏 🖥 / AC VCR 📷 /

SUNRISE SUITES MOTEL

▼▼ ▼▼
Condominium

All Year   1P: $60-$175   2P: $70-$175   XP: $10   F10

Phone: (250)347-0008

Location: Hwy 93 and 95, 0.7 km n on Hwy 95, just sw. 7369 Prospector Ave V0A 1M0 (PO Box 581). Fax: 250/347-0038. **Facility:** Designated smoking area. 5 units. 2 one-, 2 two- and 1 three-bedroom suites with kitchens. 1-2 stories (no elevator), exterior corridors. **Parking:** on-site, winter plug-ins. **Terms:** office hours 8 am-10 pm, check-in 4 pm, 7 day cancellation notice-fee imposed, small pets only (with prior approval). **Amenities:** video library (fee), irons, hair dryers. **Leisure Activities:** miniature golf, playground, horseshoes. **Guest Services:** gift shop. **Cards:** MC, VI.

🛏️ 🗙 🗙 🖑 VCR 🖥️ 🖨️ 🖥️

SUNSET MOTEL

▼▼▼▼
Motel

3/1-9/30   1P: $65-$120   2P: $65-$120
10/1-2/28   1P: $55-$105   2P: $55-$105

Phone: 250/347-0021

Location: Hwy 93 and 95 S, w to service road (Main St), just s. 4883 McKay St V0A 1M0 (PO Box 158). Fax: 250/347-0074. **Facility:** Smoke free premises. 20 units. 14 one-bedroom standard units, some with efficiencies. 1 one- and 5 two-bedroom suites ($60-$100), some with efficiencies or kitchens. 1 story, exterior corridors. *Bath:* combo or shower only. **Parking:** on-site, winter plug-ins. **Terms:** office hours 8 am-midnight, weekly rates available, pets (with prior approval, in designated units). **Cards:** MC, VI.

SOME UNITS

🆂🅳 🐾 🗙 🖉 🖥️ 🖨️ / 🖑 🖥️ /

VILLAGE COUNTRY INN & TEA ROOM

CAA SAVE
▼▼ ▼▼ ▼▼
Country Inn

6/15-9/30   1P: $110-$145   2P: $110-$145
4/5-6/14 & 10/1-2/28   1P: $85-$125   2P: $85-$125
3/1-4/4   1P: $75-$115   2P: $75-$115

Phone: (250)347-9392

Location: Hwy 93 and 95, w on St Joseph St, then just w. Located in a residential area, across from playground. 7557 Canyon Ave V0A 1M0 (PO Box 15). Fax: 250/347-9375. **Facility:** From the luxurious duvets to the serene setting, this property is suitable for short- or long-term stays and offers a retreatlike ambience. Smoke free premises. 13 one-bedroom standard units. 2 stories (no elevator), interior corridors. *Bath:* combo or shower only. **Parking:** on-site, winter plug-ins. **Terms:** office hours 7 am-10 pm, check-in 4 pm, age restrictions may apply, 7 day cancellation notice-fee imposed. **Amenities:** video library (fee), hair dryers. **Leisure Activities:** board games, chess and cards available in tea room, local art display. **Cards:** AX, MC, VI. *(See color ad below)*

🖑 🗙 VCR 🖥️

THE OLD SALZBURG RESTAURANT   Lunch: $7-$10   Dinner: $12-$25   Phone: 250/347-6553

CAA

▼▼▼ ▼▼▼

Austrian

Location: Hwy 93 and 95, just w; centre. 4943 Hwy 93 V0A 1M0. **Hours:** 11:30 am-4 & 5-11 pm; to 10 pm off season. Closed: Mon & lunch off season. **Reservations:** suggested, in summer. **Features:** Prepared here are traditional Austrian and Continental dishes, such as schnitzel, hearty spaetzle, pasta, chicken and steak. The atmosphere is warm with a mountain village ambience. In the summer, patio seating is offered. Those who opt for a window seat in the dining room are treated to lovely mountain views. Casual dress; cocktails. **Parking:** on-site. **Cards:** AX, MC, VI.

⊠

REVELSTOKE pop. 7,500

BEST WESTERN WAYSIDE INN   Phone: (250)837-6161

CAA SAVE

▼▼▼ ▼▼▼

Small-scale Hotel

5/15-9/30	1P: $109-$139	2P: $119-$149	XP: $6	F12
3/1-5/14 & 10/1-2/28	1P: $79-$119	2P: $89-$129	XP: $6	F12

Location: North side of Trans-Canada Hwy 1, at intersection nearest east end of Columbia River Bridge. Located in a quiet area. 1901 LaForme Blvd V0E 2S0 (PO Box 59). Fax: 250/837-5460. **Facility:** 88 one-bedroom standard units, some with efficiencies. 2 stories (no elevator), interior/exterior corridors. **Parking:** on-site, winter plug-ins. **Terms:** pets (in designated units). **Amenities:** irons, hair dryers. **Dining:** 6:30 am-2 & 5-9 pm; to 10 pm in season, cocktails. **Pool(s):** heated indoor. **Leisure Activities:** saunas, whirlpool. **Guest Services:** valet laundry. **Business Services:** meeting rooms. **Cards:** AX, CB, DC, DS, JC, MC, VI. **Special Amenities:** free local telephone calls and free room upgrade (subject to availability with advance reservations).

SOME UNITS

[icons]

THE COAST HILLCREST RESORT HOTEL   *Book at aaa.com*   Phone: (250)837-3322

CAA SAVE

▼▼◆▼▼

Large-scale Hotel

6/1-9/30	1P: $130-$180	2P: $130-$180	XP: $15	F17
1/1-2/28	1P: $119-$165	2P: $119-$165	XP: $15	F17
3/1-5/31	1P: $110-$165	2P: $110-$165	XP: $15	F17
10/1-12/31	1P: $110-$145	2P: $110-$145	XP: $15	F17

Location: 4.3 km e on Trans-Canada Hwy 1, 0.9 km sw. 2100 Oak Dr V0E 2S0 (PO Box 1979). Fax: 250/837-3340. **Facility:** Smoke free premises. 75 one-bedroom standard units, some with whirlpools. 3 stories, interior corridors. **Bath:** combo or shower only. **Parking:** on-site, winter plug-ins. **Terms:** pets ($15 fee, 1st floor units). **Amenities:** safes, irons, hair dryers. *Some:* high-speed Internet (fee). **Dining:** 7 am-9:30 pm, cocktails. **Leisure Activities:** sauna, whirlpools, steamroom, helicopter skiing, ATV tours, exercise room. *Fee:* white water rafting, massage, game room. **Guest Services:** gift shop. **Business Services:** meeting rooms, PC (fee). **Cards:** AX, DC, DS, JC, MC, VI. **Special Amenities:** free local telephone calls and free newspaper.

SOME UNITS

[icons] FEE

MONASHEE LODGE   Phone: 250/837-6778

CAA SAVE

▼▼ ▼▼

Motel

6/27-9/2	1P: $67-$75	2P: $75-$86	XP: $5	F8
3/1-6/26	1P: $40-$70	2P: $45-$78	XP: $5	F8
9/3-9/30	1P: $49-$57	2P: $55-$70	XP: $5	F8
10/1-2/28	1P: $40-$45	2P: $46-$66	XP: $5	F8

Location: South side of Trans-Canada Hwy 1, just e of Columbia River Bridge at Victoria Rd, then just se on Wright Ave. 1601 3rd St W V0E 2S0 (PO Box 3299). Fax: 250/837-4842. **Facility:** Smoke free premises. 18 one-bedroom standard units, some with kitchens (utensils extra charge). 2 stories (no elevator), exterior corridors. **Parking:** on-site, winter plug-ins. **Terms:** office hours 7 am-11 pm, package plans, pets ($5 extra charge). **Amenities:** voice mail. **Leisure Activities:** whirlpool. **Business Services:** PC. **Cards:** DC, MC, VI.

SOME UNITS

[icons] FEE

THE REGENT INN   Phone: (250)837-2107

CAA SAVE

▼▼▼ ▼▼▼

Small-scale Hotel

All Year	1P: $109-$129	2P: $119-$149	XP: $10	F12

Location: 2 km s from Trans-Canada Hwy 1 at Victoria Rd; downtown. Located adjacent to Grizzly Plaza. 112 1st St E V0E 2S0 (PO Box 582). Fax: 250/837-9669. **Facility:** 50 one-bedroom standard units, some with whirlpools. 3 stories, interior corridors. **Parking:** on-site, winter plug-ins. **Terms:** package plans, small pets only ($10 fee). **Amenities:** high-speed Internet. **Dining:** The One Twelve Restaurant & Lounge, see separate listing. **Leisure Activities:** sauna, whirlpool, scenic kayaking, whitewater rafting, bicycles, exercise room. *Fee:* helicopter skiing, mountain bike guides in summer, horseback riding. **Guest Services:** area transportation-bus station. **Business Services:** meeting rooms, PC (fee). **Cards:** AX, DC, MC, VI. **Special Amenities:** free expanded continental breakfast and free newspaper.

SOME UNITS

[icons] FEE

SUPER 8 MOTEL REVELSTOKE   *Book at aaa.com*   Phone: 250/837-0888

▼▼ ▼▼

Small-scale Hotel

6/12-9/5	1P: $79-$95	2P: $89-$105	XP: $7	F14
9/6-10/31	1P: $65-$75	2P: $69-$81	XP: $7	F14
3/1-6/11	1P: $62-$70	2P: $67-$76	XP: $7	F14
11/1-2/28	1P: $55-$65	2P: $60-$70	XP: $7	F14

Location: South side of Trans-Canada Hwy 1, just e of Columbia River Bridge at Victoria Rd (town centre exit). 1700 W Victoria Rd V0E 2S0 (Box 2964). Fax: 250/837-0880. **Facility:** 44 units. 35 one-bedroom standard units. 9 one-bedroom suites ($100-$125). 2 stories (no elevator), interior corridors. **Parking:** on-site, winter plug-ins. **Terms:** office hours 7 am-midnight. **Pool(s):** small heated indoor. **Leisure Activities:** whirlpool. **Guest Services:** coin laundry. **Cards:** AX, MC, VI.

SOME UNITS

[icons]

SWISS CHALET MOTEL

AAA **SAVE** | 6/29-9/3 | 1P: $64-$69 | 2P: $69-$82 | XP: $5 | F6
| 9/4-10/31 | 1P: $49-$59 | 2P: $54-$69 | XP: $5 | F6
(diamond) | 3/1-6/28 | 1P: $45-$59 | 2P: $49-$69 | XP: $5 | F6
| 11/1-2/28 | 1P: $43-$49 | 2P: $49-$59 | XP: $5 | F6

Phone: (250)837-4650

Motel **Location:** 1 km s from Trans-Canada Hwy 1. 1101 Victoria Rd V0E 2S0 (PO Box 359). Fax: 250/837-2485. **Facility:** Designated smoking area. 22 units. 20 one- and 2 two-bedroom standard units, some with efficiencies. 1-2 stories (no elevator), exterior corridors. *Bath:* combo or shower only. **Parking:** on-site, winter plug-ins. **Terms:** office hours 7:30 am-11 pm, package plans, small pets only ($10 extra charge, in designated units). **Amenities:** *Some:* hair dryers. **Business Services:** PC (fee). **Cards:** AX, MC, VI. **Special Amenities:** free continental breakfast and free local telephone calls.

SOME UNITS

(icons) FEE ⌧ (icons) DATA PORT ⌨ / (icon) /

── WHERE TO DINE ──

BLACK FOREST RESTAURANT

Menu on aaa.com • **Dinner:** $12-$28 **Phone:** 250/837-3495

(AAA) (diamonds) Continental

Location: 5 km w on Trans-Canada Hwy 1. 3251 Weird Wood Rd V0E 2S0. **Hours:** Open 3/1-11/1 & 12/1-2/28; 5 pm-9 pm. Closed: 12/25; also Tues. **Reservations:** suggested. **Features:** The Bavarian two-story house offers a good selection of dishes cooked in a variety of ways. Diners can choose from traditional German or North American food or Swiss fondues. Homemade Black Forest cake is well worth trying. The owners and staff deliver friendly service. Casual dress; cocktails. **Parking:** on-site. **Cards:** AX, DC, MC, VI.

⌧

THE ONE TWELVE RESTAURANT & LOUNGE

Lunch: $9-$11 **Dinner:** $15-$30 **Phone:** 250/837-2107

(AAA) (diamonds) American

Location: 2 km s from Trans-Canada Hwy 1 at Victoria Rd; downtown; in The Regent Inn. 112 1st St E V0E 2S0. **Hours:** 11:45 am-2 & 5:30-9 pm. Closed major holidays. **Reservations:** suggested. **Features:** This restaurant maintains a cozy but elegant atmosphere with the help of subdued lighting, soft music, an antique fireplace and friendly service. Diners' taste buds are tempted with specialties such as Alberta steak, veal, lamb and seafood. Lunchtime offerings include a soup of the day, as well as quiche Lorraine and several chicken sandwiches. Casual dress; cocktails. **Parking:** on-site. **Cards:** AX, DC, MC, VI. (icons) ⌧

THREE VALLEY LAKE CHATEAU

Lunch: $6-$15 **Dinner:** $7-$17 **Phone:** 250/837-2109

(diamonds) Canadian MC, VI.

Location: 19.2 km w on Trans-Canada Hwy 1, on Three Valley Lake; in Three Valley Gap Lake Chateau. 8903 Trans-Canada Hwy 1 V0E 2S0. **Hours:** Open 4/1-10/15; 7 am-close. **Features:** This easily accessible restaurant is a good place to stop for a rest and let the children browse. Fast, simple food is served in ample portions. A ghost town and antique train are next door. Casual dress; cocktails. **Parking:** on-site. **Cards:** AX, DC, ⌧

TONY'S ROMA

Lunch: $6-$14 **Dinner:** $9-$16 **Phone:** 250/837-4106

(diamonds) Italian Cards: MC, VI.

Location: Downtown. 306 Mackenzie Ave V0E 2S0. **Hours:** 11 am-10 pm. Closed: Sun in winter. **Features:** Italian fare—including popular versions of pasta, pizza, veal and poultry dishes—is prepared with North American influences and matches well with local microbrewery products. The rustic decor is comfortable, appealing and welcoming to families. Casual dress; cocktails. **Parking:** on-site.

⌧

RICHMOND —*See Vancouver p. 589.*

ROGERS PASS

——— WHERE TO STAY ———

BEST WESTERN GLACIER PARK LODGE   *Book at aaa.com*   **Phone:** (250)837-2126

7/1-9/30	1P: $139	2P: $149	XP: $10	F12
5/1-6/30	1P: $119	2P: $129	XP: $10	F12
10/1-2/28	1P: $79	2P: $89	XP: $10	F12
3/1-4/30	1P: $75	2P: $85	XP: $10	F12

Small-scale Hotel **Location:** On Trans-Canada Hwy 1; near Summit of Rogers Pass. Located in remote area, in Glacier National Park. (The Summit). Fax: 250/837-2130. **Facility:** 50 one-bedroom standard units. 2 stories (no elevator), interior corridors. **Parking:** on-site. **Terms:** check-in 4 pm, 3 day cancellation notice-fee imposed, [AP] meal plan available, package plans. **Amenities:** Some: CD players. **Dining:** 2 restaurants, 24 hours, cocktails. **Leisure Activities:** sauna, whirlpool, heated outdoor covered pool, backcountry skiing, hiking trails. **Guest Services:** gift shop, coin laundry. **Business Services:** meeting rooms. **Cards:** AX, DC, DS, MC, VI. **Special Amenities:** early check-in/late check-out and free room upgrade (subject to availability with advance reservations). *(See color ad below)*

SOME UNITS

ROSSLAND pop. 3,646

——— WHERE TO STAY ———

THRIFTLODGE ROSSLAND   *Book at aaa.com*   **Phone:** (250)362-7364

3/1-4/9 & 12/2-2/28 [ECP]	1P: $59-$79	2P: $69-$89
4/10-12/1 [ECP]	1P: $54-$69	2P: $64-$79

Motel   **Location:** 1 km w on Hwy 3B, jct Hwy 22. 1199 Nancy Green Hwy V0G 1Y0 (PO Box 1071). Fax: 250/362-7315. **Facility:** 42 units. 40 one-bedroom standard units, some with efficiencies or kitchens. 2 one-bedroom suites ($89-$159) with kitchens. 2 stories (no elevator), exterior corridors. **Parking:** on-site, winter plug-ins. **Terms:** office hours 6 am-11 pm, 2 night minimum stay - weekends, 3 day cancellation notice-fee imposed, pets ($10 fee, in designated units). **Leisure Activities:** whirlpool. *Fee:* bicycles. **Guest Services:** complimentary laundry, area transportation. **Cards:** AX, MC, VI.

SOME UNITS

——— The following lodging was either not evaluated or did not meet AAA rating requirements but is listed for your information only. ———

UPLANDER HOTEL   **Phone:** 250/362-7375

[fyi]   Not evaluated. **Location:** On Hwy 3B; centre. 1919 Columbia Ave V0G 1Y0 (PO Box 1510). Facilities, services, and decor characterize a mid-range property.

SAANICHTON —See Victoria p. 634.

SALMO pop. 1,120

——— WHERE TO DINE ———

CHARLIE'S PIZZA & SPAGHETTI HOUSE   **Lunch:** $5-$18   **Dinner:** $5-$18   **Phone:** 250/357-9335

Italian   **Location:** Just n of Hwy 6; centre. 205 4th St V0G 1Z0. **Hours:** 5:30 am-7 pm. Closed: 12/25. **Features:** In the small mountain town, the downtown restaurant enjoys great popularity. The food is a mixture of several types, with Italian being the main fare. Vinyl booths and some tables contribute to the "diner-style" feel. The warm greeting makes guests feel the staff is really glad to see them. Casual dress; beer & wine only. **Parking:** on-site. **Cards:** MC, VI.

TRAPPER JOHN'S RESTAURANT **Lunch:** $6-$11 **Dinner:** $11-$21 **Phone:** 250/357-2296
Canadian
Location: Jct Hwy 3 and 6, 0.4 km w on Hwy 3. 103 Motel Ave V0G 1Z0. **Hours:** 10 am-8 pm, Fri-9 pm, Sat 9 am-9 pm, Sun 9 am-8 pm. **Closed:** 12/25, 12/26. **Reservations:** accepted. **Features:** Just outside town on Highway 3, the restaurant presents a menu of North American food to suit most tastes. Friendly service and large portions are the standard. The rustic log construction, with a large rock fireplace at one end of the room and beautiful stained-glass windows, adds to the ambience. Casual dress; cocktails. **Parking:** on-site. **Cards:** MC, VI.

SALMON ARM pop. 15,210

———— **WHERE TO STAY** ————

HOLIDAY INN EXPRESS HOTEL & SUITES SALMON ARM
All Year 1P: $107-$125 2P: $107-$125 **Phone:** (250)832-7711
XP: $10 F18
Small-scale Hotel
Location: 0.5 mi on Trans-Canada Hwy 1. 1090 22nd St NE V1E 2V5. Fax: 250/833-0340. **Facility:** 115 units. 86 one-bedroom standard units, some with whirlpools. 29 one-bedroom suites. 5 stories, interior corridors. **Bath:** combo or shower only. **Parking:** on-site. **Terms:** pets ($10 extra charge). **Amenities:** video games, high-speed Internet, dual phone lines, voice mail, irons, hair dryers. **Pool(s):** heated indoor. **Leisure Activities:** whirlpool, waterslide, limited exercise equipment. **Guest Services:** valet and coin laundry. **Business Services:** meeting rooms, business center. **Cards:** AX, DC, DS, MC, VI. *(See color ad card insert)*

SOME UNITS
(ASK) (SD) (☎) (↑↓) (&M) (🔥) (🦢) (✕) (🎥) (DATA PORT) (☕) / (✕) (🔒) (📶) /
FEE

SUPER 8 MOTEL *Book at aaa.com* **Phone:** 250/832-8812
6/15-9/6 [CP] 1P: $79-$106 2P: $85-$150 XP: $6 F12
4/16-6/14 & 9/7-2/28 [CP] 1P: $63-$100 2P: $69-$120 XP: $6 F12
3/1-4/15 [CP] 1P: $54-$89 2P: $60-$100 XP: $6 F12
Small-scale Hotel
Location: 1 km e on Trans-Canada Hwy 1. 2901 10th Ave NE V1E 2S3. Fax: 250/832-2217. **Facility:** 40 units. 39 one-bedroom standard units, some with kitchens and/or whirlpools. 1 one-bedroom suite ($100-$160). 2 stories (no elevator), interior corridors. **Parking:** on-site. **Terms:** cancellation fee imposed, pets (with prior approval). **Amenities:** video library (fee). **Cards:** AX, MC, VI.

SOME UNITS
(SD) (☎) (↑↓) (&M) (VCR) (🎥) (DATA PORT) / (✕) (🔒) (📶) /

———— *The following lodging was either not evaluated or did not* ————
meet AAA rating requirements but is listed for your information only.

PRESTIGE HARBOURFRONT RESORT & CONVENTION CENTRE **Phone:** 250/833-5800
(fyi)
Large-scale Hotel
Did not meet all AAA rating requirements for some property operations at time of last evaluation on 04/21/2004. **Location:** Trans-Canada Hwy 1, exit 4th St to Lakeshore, just s to Marine Park Dr, then just w. 251 Harbourfront Dr V1E 2W7. Facilities, services, and decor characterize a mid-range property.

———— **WHERE TO DINE** ————

THE HERB GARDEN SMOKEHOUSE GRILL **Lunch:** $6-$12 **Dinner:** $11-$19 **Phone:** 250/833-4983
Canadian
Location: At Alexander St NE; centre. 111 Lakeshore Dr NE V1E 4N9. **Hours:** 11 am-close. **Reservations:** suggested. **Features:** The nostalgia of Mom's cuisine is evoked at the small country restaurant, where the owner proudly prepares wholesome food with an accent on freshness and sensitivity to the season's offerings. Dishes are creative yet comfortable. Weekend dinners feature roast beef with all the trimmings. Casual dress; cocktails. **Parking:** on-site. **Cards:** MC, VI.

POE THONG THAI FOOD RESTAURANT **Lunch:** $9-$15 **Dinner:** $9-$15 **Phone:** 250/832-0699
Thai
Location: From Trans-Canada Hwy 1, just sw at Alexander St to Hudson Ave, just e. 131 Hudson Ave NE V1E 4N7. **Hours:** 11:30 am-2:30 & 5-8:30 pm, Sat & Sun from 5 pm. **Closed:** 12/25. **Features:** Bangkok-trained chefs prepare both spicy and mild dishes for the extensive menu. The entire family manages and staffs the simple dining room, and the chef often comes out to see how guests' meals are. Patrons need look no further for a tasty taste of Thailand in the middle of British Columbia. Casual dress; cocktails. **Parking:** street. **Cards:** MC, VI.

PRIMAVERA RISTORANTE ITALIANO **Lunch:** $7-$10 **Dinner:** $9-$17 **Phone:** 250/833-0065
Italian
Location: Trans-Canada Hwy 1, exit Ross St, just n. 260 Ross St NE V0E 1H1. **Hours:** 11 am-9 pm, Fri & Sat-close. **Closed** major holidays. **Reservations:** suggested, weekends. **Features:** A small, authentic piece of Italy can be found just off the highway. Red-checkered tablecloths, vine-covered walls and Italian music create a cozy environment in which patrons can savor hearty dishes, ranging from veal to seafood fettuccine. The restaurant is busy on weekends and when entertainers perform several nights a week. Casual dress; cocktails; entertainment. **Parking:** street. **Cards:** MC, VI.

SALTSPRING ISLAND —*See Gulf Islands National Park Reserve p. 478.*

SATURNA ISLAND —*See Gulf Islands National Park Reserve p. 479.*

SAVONA

———— WHERE TO STAY ————

LAKESIDE COUNTRY INN
Phone: (250)373-2528

♦♦♦	6/15-9/15	1P: $99-$169	2P: $99-$169	XP: $10
	5/1-6/14 & 9/16-11/30	1P: $79-$149	2P: $79-$149	XP: $10
Motel	3/1-4/30	1P: $69-$129	2P: $69-$129	XP: $10

Location: Trans-Canada Hwy 1, exit Savona; along the Business Frontage Rd. 7001 Savona Access Rd V0K 2J0 (Box 260). Fax: 250/373-2432. **Facility:** Smoke free premises. 9 one-bedroom standard units, some with efficiencies or kitchens. 2 stories (no elevator), exterior corridors. *Bath:* combo or shower only. **Parking:** on-site, winter plug-ins. **Terms:** open 3/1-11/30, office hours 8 am-10 pm, age restrictions may apply, 3 day cancellation notice. **Leisure Activities:** rental canoes, rental paddleboats, boat dock, fishing, bicycles. **Cards:** AX, MC, VI.

SOME UNITS

SCOTCH CREEK pop. 527

———— WHERE TO STAY ————

SCOTCH CREEK COTTAGES RESORT
Phone: 250/675-5355

♦♦♦	6/24-9/10 Wkly	1P: $800-$3000	2P: $800-$3000	
	9/11-10/20 Dly	1P: $150-$375	2P: $150-$375	
Cottage	5/1-6/23 Dly	1P: $150-$375	2P: $150-$375	XP: $25	F16

Location: Trans-Canada Hwy 1, 18 km e on Squilax Rd to Scotch Creek, 1 km s on Scotch Creek Warf Rd, then 1 km e. 4044 Express Point Rd (3549 Eagle Bay Rd, RR 1, BLIND BAY, V0E 1H1). Fax: 250/675-3549. **Facility:** Close to the lake, these self-contained, modern cottages offer many amenities and a family-friendly ambience. Smoke free premises. 20 cottages ($800-$3000). 1 story, exterior corridors. *Bath:* combo or shower only. **Parking:** on-site. **Terms:** open 5/1-10/20, 2 night minimum stay - seasonal and/or weekends, 90 day cancellation notice-fee imposed, weekly rates available. **Amenities:** hair dryers. **Leisure Activities:** rental boats, boat dock, playground, horseshoes, volleyball. **Guest Services:** coin laundry. **Cards:** MC, VI.

SOME UNITS

SECHELT pop. 7,775

———— WHERE TO STAY ————

DRIFTWOOD INN
Phone: (604)885-5811

♦♦	5/1-2/28	1P: $89-$159	2P: $99-$169	XP: $15	F16
Motel	3/1-4/30	1P: $79-$139	2P: $89-$149	XP: $15	F16

Location: Follow Sunshine Coast Hwy 101, just w of city centre. 5454 Trail Ave V0N 3A0 (Box 829). Fax: 604/885-5836. **Facility:** Smoke free premises. 28 one-bedroom standard units, some with efficiencies. 2 stories (no elevator), interior/exterior corridors. **Parking:** on-site. **Terms:** office hours 7 am-11 pm, package plans, small pets only ($10 extra charge). **Business Services:** meeting rooms. **Cards:** AX, DC, MC, VI.

SOME UNITS

———— *The following lodging was either not evaluated or did not* ————
meet AAA rating requirements but is listed for your information only.

BELLA BEACH MOTOR INN
Phone: 604/885-7191

[fyi] Not evaluated. **Location:** On Hwy 101, 5 km s. 4748 Hwy 101 V0N 3A0 (RR 1, C-21). Facilities, services, and decor characterize a basic property.

SICAMOUS pop. 2,720

———— WHERE TO STAY ————

SICAMOUS SUPER 8 MOTEL   *Book at aaa.com*
Phone: 250/836-4988

♦♦♦	All Year	1P: $50-$110	2P: $60-$130	XP: $10	F12

Location: Trans-Canada Hwy 1, s on Hwy 97A, just w on Main St to traffic circle, then just s. 1120 Riverside Ave V0E 2V0 (PO Box 940). Fax: 250/836-2466. **Facility:** 22 units. 18 one-bedroom standard units, 4 one-bedroom suites. 2 stories (no elevator), exterior corridors. **Parking:** on-site, winter plug-ins. **Terms:** office hours 7 am-10 pm, package plans, small pets only ($10 extra charge). **Amenities:** *Some:* high-speed Internet. **Leisure Activities:** whirlpool. **Guest Services:** *Fee:* tanning facility. **Cards:** AX, MC, VI.

SOME UNITS

SIDNEY —*See Victoria p. 634.*

SILVERTON pop. 222

———— WHERE TO STAY ————

WILLIAM HUNTER CABINS
Phone: (250)358-2844

♦♦	6/16-9/20	1P: $108	2P: $108	XP: $10	F8
Cabin	3/1-6/15 & 9/21-2/28	1P: $80	2P: $85	XP: $10	F8

Location: Centre. 303 Lake Ave V0G 2B0 (PO Box 180). Fax: 250/358-2841. **Facility:** Smoke free premises. 6 one-bedroom suites with efficiencies. 1 story, exterior corridors. **Parking:** on-site, winter plug-ins. **Terms:** 10 day cancellation notice, weekly rates available, small pets only. **Amenities:** *Some:* CD players. **Leisure Activities:** canoeing, fishing, bicycles, hiking trails. **Cards:** MC, VI.

SOME UNITS

SMITHERS pop. 5,414

——— WHERE TO STAY ———

ASPEN MOTOR INN

(CAA) (SAVE)

▼▼▼▼▼

Motel

All Year   1P: $80-$85   2P: $85-$95   XP: $5   Phone: (250)847-4551
                 F14
Location: 1.5 km w on Hwy 16 (Yellowhead Hwy). 4628 Yellowhead Hwy V0J 2N0 (PO Box 756). **Fax:** 250/847-4492. **Facility:** 60 units. 55 one-bedroom standard units, some with efficiencies. 5 one-bedroom suites ($114-$121) with efficiencies. 2 stories, exterior corridors. **Parking:** on-site, winter plug-ins. **Terms:** weekly rates available, package plans, small pets only ($7 extra charge, ground floor units). **Amenities:** hair dryers. **Dining:** 6 am-10 pm, cocktails. **Pool(s):** heated indoor. **Leisure Activities:** saunas, whirlpool. **Business Services:** meeting rooms. **Cards:** AX, CB, DC, DS, JC, MC, VI.

SOME UNITS

(S)(D) 🐾 ❙❙ 🏊 📷 ▣ / ⊠ ❙ 📺 /
FEE

——— WHERE TO DINE ———

IRON HORSE CAFE & GALLERY

▼▼▼

Regional
Canadian

Lunch: $6-$12   **Dinner:** $20-$25   **Phone:** 250/877-7870
Location: Downtown; in train station, at Murray St. 3815 Railway Ave V0J 2N0. **Hours:** 8 am-3 pm, also Thurs-Sat 5 pm-9 pm. Closed: Sun. **Features:** Contemporary local art and crafts animate the new-generation cafe with eclecticism and charm. Drop by for fresh Italian coffee and homemade breakfast or to sample the creative Northwest market cuisine offered at dinnertime. Casual dress; beer & wine only. **Parking:** on-site. **Cards:** MC, VI.

🎨 ⊠

SOOKE —See Victoria p. 635.

SORRENTO pop. 1,197

——— WHERE TO DINE ———

HOME RESTAURANT

▼▼▼

Canadian

Lunch: $6-$8   **Dinner:** $8-$12   **Phone:** 250/675-3552
Location: Trans-Canada Hwy 1; in the Petro Canada Gas Station. 1235C Trans-Canada Hwy V0E 2W0. **Hours:** 7 am-9 pm. Closed: 12/25. **Features:** The basic diner is good for delicious home-style cooking and large portions. Reasonable prices make eating here a good value. Scrumptious homemade desserts are the specialty. Servers are friendly. Casual dress; beer & wine only. **Parking:** on-site. **Cards:** MC, VI.

⊠

SQUAMISH pop. 14,247

——— WHERE TO STAY ———

MOUNTAIN RETREAT HOTEL & SUITES *Book at aaa.com*   **Phone:** (604)815-0883
CAA SAVE   All Year   1P: $94-$138   2P: $94-$138   XP: $10   F12
▼▼ ▼▼   **Location:** 1.5 km n on Hwy 99 at Industrial Way. 38922 Progress Way V0N 3G0. Fax: 604/815-0884. **Facility:** 87 one-bedroom standard units, some with efficiencies. 4 stories, interior corridors. **Parking:** on-site. **Terms:** check-in 4 pm, cancellation fee imposed, package plans. **Amenities:** video games (fee), irons, hair Small-scale Hotel dryers. **Dining:** Mountain Retreat Hotel & Suites, see separate listing. **Pool(s):** heated indoor. **Leisure Activities:** whirlpool, waterslide, limited exercise equipment. **Guest Services:** coin laundry. **Business Services:** meeting rooms. **Cards:** AX, DC, DS, JC, MC, VI. *(See color ad below)*   SOME UNITS

SEA TO SKY HOTEL *Book at aaa.com*   **Phone:** (604)898-4874
CAA SAVE   All Year   1P: $89-$159   2P: $89-$159   XP: $10   F17
▼▼ ▼▼   **Location:** 4.5 km n on Hwy 99 at Garibaldi Way. 40330 Tantalus Way V0N 1T0 (PO Box 310, GARIBALDI HIGHLANDS). Fax: 604/898-3692. **Facility:** 52 one-bedroom standard units. 3 stories, interior corridors. **Parking:** on-site. **Terms:** cancellation fee imposed, package plans, small pets only ($15 extra charge). Small-scale Hotel **Amenities:** irons, hair dryers. **Dining:** 6 am-9 pm, cocktails. **Leisure Activities:** sauna, whirlpool, limited exercise equipment. **Guest Services:** valet and coin laundry. **Business Services:** meeting rooms. **Cards:** AX, DC, DS, MC, VI. *(See color ad below)*   SOME UNITS

MOUNTAIN RETREAT HOTEL & SUITES **Lunch:** $5-$10   **Dinner:** $17-$24   **Phone:** 604-892-3733

Canadian
Location: 1.5 km n on Hwy 99 at Industrial Way; in Super 8 Motel of Squamish. 38922 Progress Way V0N 3G0. **Hours:** 6 am-9 pm. **Features:** The restaurant is known for its Texas-style toast and loaves of bread, which are made fresh daily on the premises. Daily specials and an evening salad bar are nice features. Casual dress; cocktails. **Parking:** on-site. **Cards:** AX, MC, VI.

SUMMERLAND pop. 10,713

──── WHERE TO STAY ────

SUMMERLAND MOTEL **Phone:** (250)494-4444

7/1-9/4	1P: $99-$159	2P: $99-$159	XP: $10	D12
3/1-6/30 & 9/5-10/16	1P: $79-$109	2P: $79-$109	XP: $10	D12
10/17-2/28	1P: $59-$89	2P: $69-$89	XP: $10	D12

Motel
Location: 5 km s on Hwy 97. 2107 Tait St V0H 1Z0 (RR 4, Site 91, Comp 5). Fax: 250/494-4448. **Facility:** Smoke free premises. 30 units. 27 one-bedroom standard units. 3 one-bedroom suites ($79-$159) with kitchens, some with whirlpools. 2 stories (no elevator), exterior corridors. **Parking:** on-site. **Terms:** office hours 8 am-10 pm, 2 night minimum stay - seasonal, 7 day cancellation notice-fee imposed, weekly rates available, package plans, small pets only ($10 fee). **Amenities:** voice mail. *Some:* hair dryers. **Pool(s):** heated outdoor. **Leisure Activities:** barbecues. **Guest Services:** sundries, coin laundry. **Business Services:** PC. **Cards:** DC, MC, VI. **Special Amenities:** free expanded continental breakfast and free newspaper.

SOME UNITS

──── WHERE TO DINE ────

CELLAR DOOR BISTRO AT SUMAC RIDGE ESTATE WINERY **Lunch:** $9-$12   **Dinner:** $13-$28   **Phone:** 250/494-0451

Regional Canadian
Location: Hwy 97, follow signs for Sumac Ridge Estate Winery. Hwy 97 V0H 1Z0. **Hours:** Open 3/1-12/31; 11:30 am-2:30 & 5:30-9 pm. **Reservations:** suggested. **Features:** The restaurant at Sumac Ridge is perched atop the ridge. Some tables afford stunning views of the vineyard and valley below. After entering the wine and tasting shop, patrons notice the upscale, bistro-style eatery at the back. Local ingredients go into the marvelous, artistic dishes. The seasonal menu may feature a sandwich of the day, soup and a decadent dessert, and patrons also can opt to try a flight of wine. Cocktails. **Parking:** on-site. **Cards:** AX, MC, VI.

SUN PEAKS

--- **WHERE TO STAY** ---

DELTA SUN PEAKS RESORT
Book at aaa.com

(CAA) (SAVE)   **Phone:** (250)578-6000

12/16-2/28	1P: $179-$269	2P: $179-$269	XP: $30	F18
3/1-4/10	1P: $143-$170	2P: $143-$170	XP: $30	F18
4/11-12/15	1P: $99-$134	2P: $99-$134	XP: $30	F18

Location: Hwy 5, 31 km ne on Todd Mountain Rd, follow signs to village. 3240 Village Way V0E 1Z1.
Large-scale Hotel **Fax:** 250/578-6001. **Facility:** Set within the Sun Peaks Village, this resort hotel strives for superb service and offers ritzy accommodations done up in a Rocky Mountain theme. 220 units. 205 one-bedroom standard units. 15 one-bedroom suites. 5 stories, interior corridors. **Parking:** on-site (fee) and valet. **Terms:** check-in 4 pm, 7 day cancellation notice-fee imposed, pets ($15 extra charge). **Amenities:** video games, high-speed Internet (fee), dual phone lines, voice mail, irons, hair dryers. *Some:* CD players. **Dining:** Mantles Restaurant, see separate listing. **Pool(s):** heated outdoor. **Leisure Activities:** sauna, whirlpools, steamroom, ski valet & storage, recreation programs, children's play area, hiking trails, jogging, exercise room, game room. *Fee:* downhill & cross country skiing, snowmobiling, ice skating, massage. **Guest Services:** valet and coin laundry. **Business Services:** conference facilities, business center. **Cards:** AX, DC, MC, VI.
(See color ad below)

SOME UNITS

[icons]

NANCY GREENE'S CAHILTY LODGE

      Phone: (250)578-7454

12/17-12/31	1P: $189-$199	2P: $189-$199	XP: $20	F16
1/1-2/28	1P: $169-$189	2P: $169-$189	XP: $20	F16
3/1-3/27	1P: $189	2P: $189	XP: $20	F16
3/28-12/16	1P: $109-$139	2P: $109-$139	XP: $20	F16

Condominium

Location: Hwy 5, 31 km ne on Todd Mountain Rd, follow signs to village. 3220 Village Way V0E 1Z1. **Fax:** 250/578-7451.
Facility: Olympic gold and silver medals are displayed in the lobby of this activity-oriented lodge, which offers ski-in/ski-out access to the slopes. Smoke free premises. 192 units. 147 one-bedroom standard units, some with efficiencies or kitchens. 38 one-, 6 two- and 1 three-bedroom suites, some with kitchens. 4 stories, interior corridors. **Parking:** on-site, winter plug-ins. **Terms:** check-in 4 pm, 2 night minimum stay - seasonal, package plans. **Amenities:** video library (fee), voice mail, hair dryers. **Leisure Activities:** whirlpool, hiking trails, exercise room. *Fee:* downhill & cross country skiing, snowmobiling, ice skating. **Guest Services:** coin laundry. **Business Services:** meeting rooms. **Cards:** AX, MC, VI.

SOME UNITS

[icons]

SUNDANCE LODGE AT SUN PEAKS

      Phone: (250)578-0200

2/1-2/28	1P: $170-$285	2P: $170-$285	XP: $20	F16
3/1-4/15 & 11/21-1/31	1P: $150-$200	2P: $150-$200	XP: $20	F16
4/16-10/30	1P: $115-$150	2P: $115-$150	XP: $20	F16

Condominium

Location: Hwy 5, 31 km ne on Todd Mountain Rd, follow signs to village. 3160 Creekside Way V0E 1Z1.
Fax: 250/578-0222. **Facility:** Smoke free premises. 84 units. 64 one-bedroom standard units, some with efficiencies. 15 one- and 5 two-bedroom suites ($300-$500), some with efficiencies or kitchens. 4 stories, interior corridors. **Parking:** on-site.
Terms: open 3/1-10/30 & 11/21-2/28, 2 night minimum stay - weekends, 30 day cancellation notice-fee imposed, package plans. **Amenities:** irons, hair dryers. **Leisure Activities:** whirlpool, hiking trails, exercise room. *Fee:* downhill & cross country skiing, snowmobiling, ice skating. **Guest Services:** gift shop, coin laundry. **Business Services:** meeting rooms. **Cards:** AX, MC, VI.

SOME UNITS

[icons]

MANTLES RESTAURANT **Lunch:** $12-$16 **Dinner:** $16-$30 **Phone:** 250/578-6060

▼▼▼ **Location:** Hwy 5, 31 km ne on Todd Mountain Rd, follow signs to village; in Delta Sun Peaks Resort. 3240 Village Way
V0E 1Z1. **Hours:** 6:30 am-10 pm. **Reservations:** suggested. **Features:** Pacific Northwest fare is made in the
Pacific Rim vibrant family restaurant. The funky, upscale dining room, complete with an open-concept demonstration
kitchen, sets the scene after a day on the ski hills. Among tempting starters are varied distinctive appetizers,
ranging from scallops and portobello mushrooms to Caesar salad. The entrees are a piece of art. Good choices include salmon
woven on a stalk of lemongrass, rack of lamb and oven-fired pizzas. Casual dress; cocktails. **Parking:** on-site and valet.
Cards: AX, DC, DS, JC, MC, VI.

♿ⓂⓎ ✕

SURREY —See Vancouver p. 593.

TERRACE pop. 12,109

──── **WHERE TO STAY** ────

BEST WESTERN TERRACE INN *Book at aaa.com* **Phone:** (250)635-0083

ⒶⒶ ⓈⒶⓋⒺ All Year 1P: $70-$105 2P: $80-$115 XP: $5 F12
Location: Hwy 16, just e on Greig Ave, follow City Centre signs. 4553 Greig Ave V8G 1M7. Fax: 250/635-0092.
▼▼▼ **Facility:** 62 one-bedroom standard units, some with whirlpools. 5 stories, interior corridors. **Parking:** on-
site. **Terms:** package plans, small pets only ($10 extra charge). **Amenities:** high-speed Internet, voice mail,
Small-scale Hotel irons, hair dryers. **Dining:** 6:30 am-10 pm, cocktails. **Leisure Activities:** limited exercise equipment. **Guest**
Services: valet laundry. **Business Services:** meeting rooms. **Cards:** AX, DC, DS, JC, MC, VI.
Special Amenities: free continental breakfast and free local telephone calls.

SOME UNITS

ⓈⒹ 🐾 🍴 Ⓨ ✦ 🖧 📠 / ✕ 🔒 /
FEE

COAST INN OF THE WEST *Book at aaa.com* **Phone:** (250)638-8141

ⒶⒶ ⓈⒶⓋⒺ All Year 1P: $65-$105 2P: $75-$115 XP: $10 F18
Location: Hwy 16 to City Centre, 0.5 km e to Emerson, just n. 4620 Lakelse Ave V8G 1R1. Fax: 250/638-8999.
▼▼▼ **Facility:** 58 one-bedroom standard units. 3 stories, interior corridors. **Parking:** on-site. **Terms:** package
plans, small pets only. **Amenities:** irons, hair dryers. **Dining:** 6:30 am-11 pm, cocktails. **Guest Services:**
Small-scale Hotel valet laundry. **Business Services:** meeting rooms. **Cards:** AX, DC, DS, JC, MC, VI.

SOME UNITS

ⓈⒹ 🐾 🍴 Ⓨ ✦ 🖧 📠 / ✕ /

──── **WHERE TO DINE** ────

THE BAVARIAN INN STEAK & SEAFOOD GRILL **Dinner:** $15-$25 **Phone:** 250/635-9161

▼▼▼ **Location:** Hwy 16 to City Centre, 1 km w. 4332 Lakelse Ave V8G 1N8. **Hours:** 4 pm-10 pm. Closed: 12/25.
Features: Downstairs is The Black Eddy Pub, while the more formal dining room, which offers great views,
Steak & Seafood is upstairs. In addition to the expected German specialties, the menu lists seafood, steaks and pasta. This
place is just east of the downtown mall. Casual dress; cocktails. **Parking:** on-site. **Cards:** MC, VI.

Ⓨ ✕

BISTRO L'AMBIANCE **Lunch:** $9-$20 **Dinner:** $9-$20 **Phone:** 250/615-0486

▼▼ **Location:** Hwy 16 to City Centre, just n on Emerson, just e. 4608 Lakelse Ave V8G 1R1. **Hours:** 11 am-9 pm.
Closed major holidays; also Sun. **Features:** The little French bistro is next to the Coast Inn of the West, and
French parking is anywhere on the street. A French flair punctuates the food offerings, which range from fondues
and appetizers to seafood, lunch sandwiches, children's choices and desserts. Casual dress; cocktails.
Parking: street. **Cards:** MC, VI.

✕

HOT HOUSE FLAVOURFUL FOOD **Lunch:** $6-$16 **Dinner:** $6-$16 **Phone:** 250/615-5800

▼ **Location:** Corner of Spark St and Lakelse Ave; in small shopping complex. #6-4717 Lakelse Ave V8G 1R5.
Hours: 10:30 am-9 pm, Fri & Sat-10 pm. Closed major holidays; also Sun. **Features:** In a small strip mall,
Indian the simple eat-in-or-take-out restaurant presents a menu with worldwide influences, ranging from East
Indian and Mexican to Asian and Cajun. Something extra distinguishes the flavorful food. Ask about the
signature dishes. Casual dress; beer & wine only. **Parking:** on-site. **Cards:** MC, VI.

✕

──── *The following restaurant has not been evaluated by AAA* ────
but is listed for your information only.

BLACKSTONE RESTAURANT **Phone:** 250/635-6667

ⓕⓨⓘ Not evaluated. **Location:** 2 km e on Hwy 16, just s on Hwy 37, just e, follow signs; centre. 4035 Motz Rd.
Features: Continental traditions and contemporary Northwest approaches to cuisine influence the chef's
creations at the intimate alpine restaurant, nestled in the forest just east of town.

TETE JAUNE CACHE

──── **WHERE TO STAY** ────

──── *The following lodging was either not evaluated or did not* ────
meet AAA rating requirements but is listed for your information only.

TERRACANA RANCH RESORT **Phone:** 250/968-4304

ⓕⓨⓘ Did not meet all AAA rating requirements for some property operations at time of last evaluation on
05/23/2003. **Location:** 14 km e of Tete Jaune on Hwy 16 E (McBride Hwy). 12155 McBride Hwy 16 E V0E 2Z0 (Box
Cabin 909, VALEMOUNT). Facilities, services, and decor characterize a mid-range property.

TOFINO pop. 1,466

─── WHERE TO STAY ───

BEST WESTERN TIN WIS RESORT LODGE
Book at aaa.com
Phone: (250)725-4445

CAA SAVE ▼▼▼▼

	1P: $199	2P: $199	XP: $20	F11
6/21-10/20	1P: $199	2P: $199	XP: $20	F11
4/1-6/20	1P: $159	2P: $159	XP: $20	F11
10/21-2/28	1P: $139	2P: $139	XP: $20	F11
3/1-3/31	1P: $119	2P: $119	XP: $20	F11

Small-scale Hotel Location: 3.5 km s on Hwy 4. 1119 Pacific Rim Hwy V0R 2Z0 (Box 389). Fax: 250/725-4447. **Facility:** 85 units. 82 one-bedroom standard units, some with efficiencies. 3 one-bedroom suites ($249-$345) with efficiencies and whirlpools. 2 stories, exterior corridors. **Parking:** on-site. **Terms:** pets ($20 extra charge, in designated units). **Amenities:** irons, hair dryers. **Dining:** 7 am-noon & 5-10 pm, cocktails. **Leisure Activities:** whirlpool, exercise room. **Guest Services:** gift shop, coin laundry. **Business Services:** meeting rooms. **Cards:** AX, CB, DC, DS, JC, MC, VI. **Special Amenities:** free local telephone calls.

SOME UNITS
[S] [D] 🛏 [Ⅱ] [Y] [⌂M] [AC] [🐕] [DATA PORT] 🔌 ▣ / [✕] [▦]
FEE

CABLE COVE INN
Phone: 250/725-4236

▼▼▼

6/1-9/30	1P: $160-$235	2P: $160-$235
3/1-5/31 & 10/1-2/28	1P: $140-$190	2P: $140-$190

Bed & Breakfast Location: From centre, just n to Main St via First St, then just w. 201 Main St V0R 2Z0 (PO Box 339). Fax: 250/725-2857. **Facility:** These upscale rooms have fireplaces, private decks and whirlpools; breakfast is served in guest rooms. Smoke free premises. 7 one-bedroom standard units with whirlpools. 2 stories (no elevator), interior corridors. **Parking:** on-site. **Terms:** office hours 8 am-8 pm, 2 night minimum stay - seasonal, age restrictions may apply, 7 day cancellation notice-fee imposed. **Amenities:** hair dryers. **Guest Services:** complimentary laundry. **Cards:** AX, MC, VI.

[✕] [AC] [W] [☎]

HIMWITSA LODGE
Phone: (250)725-2017

▼▼▼

6/15-9/15	1P: $180	2P: $250	XP: $25

Small-scale Hotel Location: Just n of centre via First St. 300 Main St V0R 2Z0 (PO Box 176). Fax: 250/725-2361. **Facility:** Smoke free premises. 4 one-bedroom standard units. 2 stories (no elevator), interior corridors. **Parking:** on-site. **Terms:** open 6/15-9/15, office hours 8:30 am-9:30 pm, 2 night minimum stay - seasonal, 14 day cancellation notice-fee imposed. **Amenities:** video library, irons, hair dryers. **Guest Services:** gift shop. **Cards:** AX, MC, VI.

[ASK] [S] [Ⅱ] [✕] [AC] [VCR] [🐕] [DATA PORT] 🔌 [▦] ▣

LONG BEACH LODGE RESORT
Phone: (250)725-2442

CAA SAVE ▼▼▼

6/24-9/5 [ECP]	1P: $269-$529	2P: $269-$529	XP: $30
9/6-10/10 [ECP]	1P: $219-$459	2P: $219-$459	XP: $30
3/1-6/23 [ECP]	1P: $199-$429	2P: $199-$429	XP: $30
10/11-2/28 [ECP]	1P: $189-$429	2P: $189-$429	XP: $30

Small-scale Hotel Location: 7.5 km s on Hwy 4. 1441 Pacific Rim Hwy V0R 2Z0 (PO Box 897). Fax: 250/725-2402. **Facility:** Smoke free premises. 51 units. 41 one-bedroom standard units, some with whirlpools. 10 cottages with whirlpools. 3 stories, interior corridors. **Parking:** on-site. **Terms:** 2 night minimum stay - seasonal and/or weekends, 7 day cancellation notice-fee imposed, package plans, pets ($50 extra charge, in ground floor units). **Amenities:** video library, DVD players, voice mail, irons, hair dryers. **Dining:** Restaurant at Long Beach Lodge Resort, see separate listing. **Business Services:** meeting rooms. **Cards:** AX, MC, VI. **Special Amenities:** free expanded continental breakfast and free newspaper.

SOME UNITS
🛏 [Ⅱ] [✕] [AC] [🐕] [DATA PORT] 🔌 ▣ / [▦] /
FEE

MIDDLE BEACH LODGE
Phone: (250)725-2900

CAA SAVE ▼▼▼

6/16-9/30 [ECP]	1P: $115-$395	2P: $115-$395	XP: $25	D16
3/1-6/15 & 10/1-10/31 [ECP]	1P: $115-$325	2P: $115-$325	XP: $25	D16
11/1-2/28 [ECP]	1P: $115	2P: $275	XP: $25	D16

Small-scale Hotel Location: 3.5 km s on Hwy 4. 400 McKenzie Beach Rd V0R 2Z0 (Box 100). Fax: 250/725-2901. **Facility:** Smoke free premises. 64 units. 58 one- and 6 two-bedroom standard units, some with efficiencies, kitchens and/or whirlpools. 2 stories (no elevator), interior/exterior corridors. **Parking:** on-site. **Terms:** office hours 8 am-10 pm, 2 night minimum stay - seasonal, 7 day cancellation notice-fee imposed, package plans. **Amenities:** video library, hair dryers. *Some:* CD players. **Dining:** 6 pm-10 pm; closed 10/1-5/31, cocktails. **Leisure Activities:** limited exercise equipment. **Guest Services:** coin laundry. **Business Services:** meeting rooms. **Cards:** AX, MC, VI. **Special Amenities:** free expanded continental breakfast and free local telephone calls.

SOME UNITS
[Ⅱ] [✕] [AC] [🐕] / [W] [VCR] [☎] 🔌 [▦] /

PACIFIC SANDS BEACH RESORT
Phone: (250)725-3322

CAA SAVE ▼▼▼

All Year	1P: $215-$490	2P: $215-$490	XP: $20	D15

Location: 7.5 km s on Hwy 4. Located next to Pacific Rim National Park. 1421 Pacific Rim Hwy V0R 2Z0 (PO Box 237). Fax: 250/725-3155. **Facility:** Smoke free premises. 77 units. 50 one-bedroom standard units with kitchens, some with whirlpools. 26 two- and 1 three-bedroom units with kitchens, some with whirlpools. 1-3 stories **Small-scale Hotel** (no elevator), exterior corridors. **Parking:** on-site. **Terms:** 3 night minimum stay - seasonal, 7 day cancellation notice-fee imposed, package plans. **Amenities:** video library (fee). *Some:* voice mail, hair dryers. **Leisure Activities:** recreation programs in summer, barbecue, hiking trails. **Guest Services:** coin laundry. **Business Services:** PC (fee). **Cards:** AX, MC, VI.

SOME UNITS
[✕] [✕] [AC] [VCR] [🐕] 🔌 [▦] ▣ / [DATA PORT] [☎] /

SCHOONER MOTEL
Phone: 250/725-3478

CAA SAVE ▼▼

6/1-10/16	1P: $149-$225	2P: $149-$225	XP: $10	F7
3/1-5/31	1P: $85-$185	2P: $95-$185	XP: $10	F7
10/17-2/28	1P: $75-$145	2P: $75-$145	XP: $10	F7

Motel Location: Campbell and 2nd sts; downtown. 311-321 Campbell St V0R 2Z0 (PO Box 202). Fax: 250/725-3499. **Facility:** Designated smoking area. 18 one-bedroom standard units, some with efficiencies. 2 stories, exterior corridors. **Bath:** combo or shower only. **Parking:** on-site. **Terms:** 14 day cancellation notice-fee imposed. **Amenities:** hair dryers. **Guest Services:** coin laundry. **Cards:** DC, MC, VI.

[Ⅱ⁺] [✕] [AC] [🐕] 🔌

TOFINO MOTEL Phone: 250/725-2055

▼▼ ▼▼	7/1-9/30	1P: $145-$180	2P: $145-$180
	4/1-6/30	1P: $110	2P: $110
Motel	10/1-2/28	1P: $85-$105	2P: $85-$105
	3/1-3/31	1P: $85	2P: $85

Location: Campbell and 4th sts; downtown. 542 Campbell St V0R 2Z0 (PO Box 246). Fax: 250/725-2455. **Facility:** Smoke free premises. 13 units. 12 one- and 1 two-bedroom standard units. 2 stories (no elevator), exterior corridors. **Parking:** on-site. **Terms:** office hours 8:30 am-10 pm, 21 day cancellation notice-fee imposed, package plans. **Amenities:** hair dryers. **Cards:** AX, CB, DC, DS, JC, MC, VI.

WICKANINNISH INN   *Book at aaa.com* Phone: (250)725-3100

CAA SAVE	6/1-9/30	1P: $400-$1500	2P: $400-$1500	XP: $40
	10/1-10/31	1P: $280-$1000	2P: $280-$1000	XP: $40
▼▼▼ ▼▼▼	3/1-5/31	1P: $240-$1000	2P: $240-$1000	XP: $40
	11/1-2/28	1P: $220-$1000	2P: $220-$1000	XP: $40

Small-scale Hotel **Location:** 4.3 km e on Hwy 4. Located in a quiet area. Osprey Ln at Chesterman Beach V0R 2Z0 (PO Box 250). Fax: 250/725-3110. **Facility:** The inn is on an oceanfront rock outcropping in an area known for its wild winter storms; rooms feature ocean views, fireplaces and soaker tubs. Smoke free premises. 75 units. 64 one-bedroom standard units, some with whirlpools. 11 one-bedroom suites, some with kitchens. 3 stories, interior corridors. **Parking:** on-site. **Terms:** check-in 4 pm, 2 night minimum stay - seasonal and/or weekends, 7 day cancellation notice-fee imposed, package plans, pets ($40 extra charge, in designated units). **Amenities:** CD players, dual phone lines, voice mail, safes, honor bars, irons, hair dryers. **Dining:** Pointe Restaurant, see separate listing. **Leisure Activities:** steamroom, limited exercise equipment, spa. **Business Services:** meeting rooms, PC. **Cards:** AX, DC, MC, VI. **Special Amenities:** free local telephone calls.

FEE

The following lodging was either not evaluated or did not meet AAA rating requirements but is listed for your information only.

DAYS INN TOFINO WEIGH WEST MARINE ADVENTURE RESORT Phone: 250/725-3277

[fyi] Did not meet all AAA rating requirements for. **Location:** 2 km e on Hwy 4. Located in Inner Harbour Marina. 634 Small-scale Hotel Campbell St V0R 2Z0 (PO Box 69). Facilities, services, and decor characterize a mid-range property.

WHERE TO DINE

LOFT RESTAURANT Lunch: $5-$9 Dinner: $10-$19 Phone: 250/725-4241

▼▼ **Location:** Campbell and 2nd sts; downtown. 346 Campbell St V0R 2Z0. **Hours:** 7 am-10 pm; to 9 pm 10/1-5/31. Closed: 12/25. **Features:** The Loft features West Coast-style casual dining and offers a good selection of Canadian fresh seafood, including Dungeness crab, salmon, halibut and Vancouver Island oysters. Cozy cedar-paneled dining rooms provide a nice display of regional art and photos. Casual dress; cocktails. **Parking:** on-site. **Cards:** AX, MC, VI.

POINTE RESTAURANT Lunch: $11-$22 Dinner: $24-$40 Phone: 250/725-3100

CAA **Location:** 4.3 km e on Hwy 4; in Wickaninnish Inn. Osprey Ln/Chesterman Bch V0R 2Z0. **Hours:** 7:30 am-11, 11:30-▼▼▼ ▼▼▼ 2 & 5-9:30 pm. **Reservations:** required, for dinner. **Features:** Built above the rocks and jutting out into the ocean, this restaurant offers breathtaking scenery of wild waves in the winter. The Canadian West Coast Regional cuisine features fresh seafood and a good selection of wines. Walk-ins welcome for breakfast and lunch. Canadian Casual dress; cocktails. **Parking:** on-site. **Cards:** AX, DC, MC, VI.

RAINCOAST CAFE Dinner: $17-$30 Phone: 250/725-2215

▼▼▼ **Location:** Fourth and Campbell sts; downtown. 101-120 Fourth St V0R 2Z0. **Hours:** 5:30 pm-10 pm; to 9 pm in Pacific Rim winter. Closed: 12/25. **Reservations:** required. **Features:** Located in a shopping complex, this small, intimate bistro features a distinctive Pacific Rim cuisine, fresh ingredients, local seafood, pasta and vegetarian dishes, but no red meat. The decor displays an open kitchen, patio dining and artwork. Casual dress; cocktails. **Parking:** on-site and street. **Cards:** AX, MC, VI.

RESTAURANT AT LONG BEACH LODGE RESORT Lunch: $8-$14 Dinner: $18-$42 Phone: 250/725-2442

▼▼▼ **Location:** 7.5 km s on Hwy 4; in Long Beach Lodge Resort. 1441 Pacific Rim Hwy V0R 2Z0. **Hours:** noon-10 pm. **Reservations:** required, for dinner. **Features:** This restaurant is located in a new lodge situated right along Continental the beach, each table offering wonderful views of the waves and sand. The menu offers a wide range of items, and many ingredients are found locally or are strictly from the province, such as salmon, Salt Spring Island goat cheese, free range chickens and locally grown beef. Cocktails. **Parking:** on-site. **Cards:** AX, MC, VI.

SCHOONER RESTAURANT Lunch: $10-$23 Dinner: $22-$28 Phone: 250/725-3444

▼▼ ▼▼ **Location:** Corner of 2nd St; downtown. 331 Campbell St V0R 2Z0. **Hours:** 9 am-3 & 5-10 pm. Closed: 12/25. **Reservations:** suggested, for dinner. **Features:** Great food has been a part of this building since 1949. Ask Regional about "Morris the Ghost," who lived here in the early 70s and always made the chowder. Open for Canadian breakfast, lunch and dinner, the downtown restaurant prepares "out to sea" and "land ho" entrees. Casual dress; cocktails. **Parking:** on-site. **Cards:** AX, MC, VI.

SHELTER RESTAURANT
Phone: 250/725-3353
[fyi] Not evaluated. **Location:** 0.8 km se on Hwy 4 (Campbell St). 601 Campbell St V0R 2Z0. **Features:** On the edge of town, the tastefully renovated old village house welcomes diners with regional cuisine featuring market produce and local seafood. Seating is offered by the stone fireplace in the lounge or in the candlelit upstairs loft.

TRAIL pop. 7,575

WHERE TO STAY

BEST WESTERN TERRA NOVA HOTEL *Book at aaa.com*
Phone: 250-368-3355
Property failed to provide current rates
◆◆◆ ◆◆◆ **Location:** On Hwy 3B; centre. 1001 Rossland Ave V1R 3N7. **Fax:** 250/368-3930. **Facility:** 58 units. 56 one-
Small-scale Hotel bedroom standard units. 2 one-bedroom suites with whirlpools. 4 stories, interior corridors. *Bath:* combo or shower only. **Parking:** on-site, winter plug-ins. **Amenities:** high-speed Internet, voice mail, irons, hair dryers. **Leisure Activities:** whirlpool, exercise room. **Guest Services:** valet laundry. **Business Services:** meeting rooms.
SOME UNITS

WHERE TO DINE

COLANDER RESTAURANT (1999) LTD *Menu on aaa.com* **Lunch:** $5-$9 **Dinner:** $8-$15 **Phone:** 250/364-1816
(AAA) **Location:** Centre. 1475 Cedar Ave V1R 4C5. **Hours:** 11:30 am-2 & 4:30-8:30 pm, Sat & Sun from 4:30 pm.
◆◆◆ Closed: 12/25. **Reservations:** suggested. **Features:** The Colander offers a nice selection of items at a self-service buffet. Lunch includes items such as pasta, chicken, burgers, subs and sandwiches; dinner is more
Italian extensive. Regional beers are served also. Pleasant atmosphere. Fee for to-go container. Casual dress; cocktails. **Parking:** street. **Cards:** MC, VI.

UCLUELET pop. 1,559

WHERE TO STAY

THORNTON MOTEL
Phone: 250-726-7725
◆◆ All Year 1P: $79-$175 2P: $79-$175 XP: $10 D12
Motel **Location:** E on Peninsula Rd at Bay St. 1861 Peninsula Rd V0R 3A0 (PO Box 490). **Fax:** 250/726-2099.
Facility: 17 units. 13 one- and 4 two-bedroom standard units, some with efficiencies. 2-3 stories (no elevator). **Parking:** on-site. **Terms:** office hours 8 am-9 pm, cancellation fee imposed. **Cards:** AX, MC, VI.
SOME UNITS

A SNUG HARBOUR INN
Phone: 250-726-2686
[fyi] Did not meet all AAA rating requirements for locking devices in some guest rooms at time of last evaluation
Bed & Breakfast on 02/06/2004. **Location:** 1.6 km e on Peninsula Rd, then just s. 460 Marine Dr V0R 3A0 (PO Box 318). Facilities, services, and decor characterize a mid-range property.

CANADIAN PRINCESS RESORT
Phone: 250-726-7771
[fyi] Not evaluated. **Location:** Just e. 1948 Peninsula Rd V0R 3A0 (PO Box 939). Facilities, services, and decor characterize a mid-range property.

TAUCA LEA BY THE SEA
Phone: 250-726-4625
[fyi] Did not meet all AAA rating requirements for some property operations at time of last evaluation on
Condominium 06/02/2003. **Location:** From Peninsula Rd, just n on Sea Plane Base Rd, then just e on Harbour Rd. 1971 Harbour Crescent V0R 3A0 (PO Box 1171). Facilities, services, and decor characterize a mid-range property.

WHERE TO DINE

BLUEBERRIES
Lunch: $8-$10 **Dinner:** $10-$20 **Phone:** 250-726-7707
◆◆ ◆◆ **Location:** Peninsula Rd and Main St, just e. 1627 Peninsula Rd V0R 3A0. **Hours:** 7:30 am-3 & 5-9 pm. Closed:
Canadian 12/25, 12/26. **Features:** Known for eggs Benny, the quaint restaurant serves full breakfast, lunch and dinner. An outdoor patio is open during warmer months. Try the fresh seafood, wraps, fish and chips and burgers. Casual dress; cocktails. **Parking:** on-site. **Cards:** AX, MC, VI.

BOAT BASIN RESTAURANT
Dinner: $20-$40 **Phone:** 250-726-4644
◆◆◆ ◆◆◆ **Location:** From Peninsula Rd, just n on Sea Plane Base Rd, then just e on Harbour Rd; in Tauca Lea by the Sea. 1971
Pacific Rim Harbour Crescent V0R 3A0. **Hours:** 4 pm-9 pm. **Reservations:** required. **Features:** Open for dinner only, this restaurant is located on the marina with both outdoor patio seating or fireside dining available. The menu features fresh Pacific cuisine, and the menu itself changes weekly. Sample locally caught fish and market fresh vegetables. Casual dress; cocktails. **Parking:** on-site. **Cards:** AX, MC, VI.

MATTERSON HOUSE RESTAURANT **Lunch:** $5-$8 **Dinner:** $8-$18 **Phone:** 250/726-2200

▼▼▼

Canadian

Location: E on Peninsula Rd. 1682 Peninsula Rd V0R 3A0. **Hours:** 7:30 am-9 pm. Closed: 12/25, 12/26. **Reservations:** required, for dinner. **Features:** This causal style restaurant is in a converted house located along the main road through town. Open for breakfast, lunch and dinner, the restaurant offers a menu that features regular Canadian type fare, such as soups and sandwiches for lunch, and more complex dinner entrees. Casual dress; beer & wine only. **Parking:** on-site. **Cards:** MC, VI.

🅧 ☒

VALEMOUNT pop. 1,195

—— WHERE TO STAY ——

CANOE MOUNTAIN LODGE *Book at aaa.com* **Phone:** 250-566-9171

(CAA) SAVE				
6/15-9/15	1P: $99	2P: $125	XP: $12	F12
3/1-6/14	1P: $70	2P: $78	XP: $12	F12
▼▼▼ 9/16-2/28	1P: $60	2P: $78	XP: $12	F12

Location: Just e of Hwy 5 (Yellowhead Hwy). 1465 5th Ave V0E 2Z0 (BOX 1029). Fax: 250/566-4198. **Facility:** 47 Small-scale Hotel one-bedroom standard units. 2 stories (no elevator), interior corridors. *Bath:* combo or shower only. **Parking:** on-site, winter plug-ins. **Terms:** office hours 7 am-11 pm, cancellation fee imposed, package plans, pets ($10 fee). **Amenities:** hair dryers. **Leisure Activities:** whirlpool, steamroom. **Guest Services:** gift shop, coin laundry. **Cards:** AX, DS, MC, VI.

SOME UNITS
ⓢⒹ ✈ 🛏 🍽 📷 [DATA PORT] 🖥 🖨 / ☒ 🅧 VCR 🗄 /
FEE

CHALET CONTINENTAL MOTEL **Phone:** (250)566-9787

(CAA) SAVE				
6/15-9/15	1P: $99-$120	2P: $99-$130	XP: $15	F12
▼▼▼ 3/1-6/14 & 9/16-2/28	1P: $70-$85	2P: $75-$95	XP: $10	F12

Motel

Location: Just e, off Hwy 5 (Yellowhead Hwy). 1450 5th Ave V0E 2Z0 (Box 127). Fax: 250/566-9785. **Facility:** 37 units. 35 one-bedroom standard units, some with kitchens and/or whirlpools. 2 one-bedroom suites. 2 stories (no elevator), exterior corridors. **Parking:** on-site. **Terms:** office hours 7 am-11 pm, cancellation fee imposed, pets ($10 fee). **Amenities:** hair dryers. *Some:* DVD players (fee). **Pool(s):** small heated indoor. **Leisure Activities:** sauna, whirlpool, steamroom, sun deck, barbecue area, exercise room, horseshoes. **Guest Services:** *Fee:* beauty salon. **Cards:** AX, DC, DS, MC, VI. **Special Amenities:** free local telephone calls and free room upgrade (subject to availability with advance reservations).

SOME UNITS
ⓢⒹ ✈ 🛏 🍽 🏊 ☒ 📷 [DATA PORT] 🖥 🖨 🖥 / ☒ VCR /
FEE FEE

HOLIDAY INN HOTEL & SUITES VALEMOUNT *Book at aaa.com* **Phone:** (250)566-0086

(CAA) SAVE				
6/16-9/16	1P: $140-$180	2P: $140-$180	XP: $10	F18
9/17-2/28	1P: $90-$150	2P: $90-$150	XP: $10	F18
▼▼▼ 3/1-6/15	1P: $85-$145	2P: $85-$145	XP: $10	F18

Location: 1.5 km s on Hwy 5 (Yellowhead Hwy). Located near wildlife sanctuary. 1950 Hwy 5 S V0E 2Z0 (PO Box Small-scale Hotel 1060). Fax: 250/566-4149. **Facility:** 78 units. 52 one-bedroom standard units, some with whirlpools. 26 one-bedroom suites. 2 stories, interior corridors. *Bath:* combo or shower only. **Parking:** on-site, winter plug-ins. **Terms:** 7 day cancellation notice-fee imposed, pets ($35 extra charge). **Amenities:** dual phone lines, voice mail, irons, hair dryers. *Some:* video games. **Dining:** 6:30 am-1 & 4:30-9 pm, Thurs-Sat to 10 pm, cocktails. **Pool(s):** small heated indoor. **Leisure Activities:** whirlpool, waterslide, cross country skiing, birdwatching, hiking trails, exercise room. *Fee:* bicycles. **Guest Services:** gift shop, coin laundry, area transportation. **Business Services:** meeting rooms. **Cards:** AX, MC, VI. **Special Amenities:** free local telephone calls and preferred room (subject to availability with advance reservations).

SOME UNITS
ⓢⒹ 🛏 🍽 Ⓜ ☕ 📶 🏊 ☒ [DATA PORT] 🖥 / ☒ VCR 🗄 🖨 /
FEE

—— WHERE TO DINE ——

CARIBOU GRILL **Dinner:** $10-$25 **Phone:** 250/566-8244

(CAA)

▼▼▼

Canadian

Location: Hwy 5 (Yellowhead Hwy), 1 km e at 5th Ave. 1002 5th Ave V0C 2Z0. **Hours:** Open 3/1-10/31 & 12/1-2/28; 4:30 pm-10 pm. Closed: 12/25. **Reservations:** not accepted. **Features:** About five blocks off Highway 97 in a beautiful log cabin toward the end of the main street, the restaurant prepares casual fare. The menu centers on Canadian cuisine, from traditional pasta and meat dishes to the namesake caribou. Expect attentive, friendly service and original log house decor. Casual dress; cocktails. **Parking:** on-site. **Cards:** AX, DC, MC, VI.

☒

Destination Vancouver
pop. 545,671

*L*ose yourself in Vancouver. There's much to do, and getting there is half the fun.

*Y*ou can walk to downtown attractions, parks and shops; let SkyTrain whisk you to suburban destinations; or ride a ferry to the outer limits for recreation.

© Richard Cummins / Photophile

Chinatown, Vancouver. Parades usher in the new year for the second-largest area of its kind in North America. (See listing page 159)

Grouse Mountain

Mountain biking, Vancouver. Cyclists will find more than 45 miles of trails in the city, where mountain biking is a school sport. (See mention page 157)

© Gibson Stock Photography

See Downtown map page 531

Vancouver

West Vancouver

North Vancouver

Port Moody

Burnaby

Port Coquitlam

Coquitlam

New Westminster

Maple Ridge

Richmond

Delta

Surrey

Mission

Langley

Aldergrove

Lonsdale Quay, North Vancouver. Fresh vegetables, seafood and flowers are among the offerings at this waterfront market. (See mention page 158)

See Vicinity map page 536

UNITED STATES

CANADA

BRITISH COLUMBIA
WASHINGTON

*P*laces included in this AAA Destination City:

Vancouver Harbour Cruises, Ltd.

Harbour Cruises, Vancouver. Sightseeing trips depart from Stanley Park aboard the paddlewheeler MPV *Constitution*. (See listing page 156)

DOWNTOWN VANCOUVER ACCOMMODATIONS

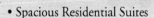

Downtown Vancouver

This index helps you "spot" where approved accommodations and restaurants are located on the corresponding detailed maps. Lodging rate ranges are for comparison only and show the property's high season; rates are per night, unless only weekly (W) rates are available. Restaurant rate range is for dinner, unless only lunch (L) is served. Turn to the listing page for more detailed rate information and consult display ads for special promotions.

Spotter/Map Page Number	OA	DOWNTOWN VANCOUVER - Lodgings	Diamond Rating	Rate Range High Season	Listing Page
1 / p. 531	CAA	The Westin Bayshore Resort & Marina - see color ad p 5, p 560	◆◆◆◆	$215-$460 SAVE	559
3 / p. 531	CAA	Renaissance Vancouver Hotel Harbourside - see color ad p 556	◆◆	$209-$239 SAVE	555
4 / p. 531		Sylvia Hotel	◆◆	$95-$240	558
6 / p. 531	CAA	Best Western Sands - see color ad p 543	◆◆◆	$179-$239 SAVE	545
7 / p. 531		Listel Vancouver	◆◆◆	$240-$320	552
8 / p. 531	CAA	Pacific Palisades Hotel	◆◆◆	$185-$390 SAVE	553
9 / p. 531		Blue Horizon Hotel - see color ad p 546	◆◆◆	$149-$209	546
10 / p. 531		The Fairmont Waterfront	◆◆◆◆	$279-$349	548
11 / p. 531	CAA	Pan Pacific Vancouver - see color ad p 554	◆◆◆◆◆	$490-$540 SAVE	554
12 / p. 531	CAA	Hyatt Regency Vancouver - see color ad p 552	◆◆◆	$195-$295 SAVE	550
13 / p. 531	CAA	Days Inn Downtown - see color ad p 546, p 545	◆◆	$159-$209 SAVE	547
14 / p. 531		'O Canada' House B&B	◆◆◆	$185-$255	553
15 / p. 531	CAA	The Sutton Place Hotel - see color ad p 558	◆◆◆◆	$247-$464 SAVE	558
16 / p. 531	CAA	Metropolitan Hotel	◆◆◆◆	$219-$399 SAVE	553
17 / p. 531	CAA	Delta Vancouver Suites - see color ad p 547	◆◆◆◆	$199-$269 SAVE	548
18 / p. 531		The Fairmont Hotel Vancouver	◆◆◆◆	$279-$379	548
19 / p. 531	CAA	West End Guest House	◆◆◆	$120-$255 SAVE	559
20 / p. 531	CAA	Four Seasons Hotel Vancouver	◆◆◆◆	$320-$1060 SAVE	548
21 / p. 531		Terminal City Tower Hotel	◆◆◆	$200-$375	558
22 / p. 531	CAA	Ramada Limited Downtown Vancouver - see color ad p 555	◆◆◆	$189 SAVE	555
23 / p. 531	CAA	The Wedgewood Hotel - see color ad p 559	◆◆◆◆	$268-$448 SAVE	559
24 / p. 531	CAA	Sunset Inn & Suites - see color ad p 531	◆◆	$169-$259 SAVE	557
25 / p. 531	CAA	Sheraton Vancouver Wall Centre Hotel - see color ad p 557, p 5	◆◆◆◆	$225-$429 SAVE	557
26 / p. 531	CAA	Holiday Inn Hotel & Suites Vancouver-Downtown - see color ad card insert	◆◆◆	$199-$299 SAVE	549
27 / p. 531	CAA	Bosmans Hotel	◆◆	$109-$129 SAVE	547
28 / p. 531	CAA	Howard Johnson Hotel - see color ad p 550	◆◆	$139-$229 SAVE	550
29 / p. 531	CAA	Comfort Inn Downtown	◆◆◆	$129-$229 SAVE	547
30 / p. 531	CAA	Hampton Inn & Suites Downtown Vancouver - see color ad p 544, p 545, p 552	◆◆◆	$225-$289 SAVE	549
31 / p. 531	CAA	Best Western Chateau Granville	◆◆◆	$159-$209 SAVE	543

Spotter/Map Page Number	OA	**DOWNTOWN VANCOUVER -** Lodgings (continued)	Diamond Rating	Rate Range High Season	Listing Page
32 / p. 531		Landis Hotel & Suites - see color ad p 553	▽▽	$289-$329	552
33 / p. 531	CAA	**Residence Inn by Marriott Vancouver** - see color ad p 556	▽▽▽	$179-$233 SAVE	555
34 / p. 531	CAA	**Ramada Inn & Suites Downtown Vancouver** - see color ad p 555	▽▽	$139-$209 SAVE	554
35 / p. 531		The Georgian Court Hotel	▽▽▽	$185-$260	548
36 / p. 531		Quality Hotel Downtown-The Inn at False Creek	▽▽	$179-$209	554
37 / p. 531	CAA	**Best Western Downtown Vancouver** - see color ad p 544, p 545, p 552	▽▽▽	$169-$219 SAVE	543
39 / p. 531	CAA	**Granville Island Hotel** - see color ad p 549	▽▽▽	$190-$230 SAVE	548
40 / p. 531	CAA	**Crowne Plaza Vancouver-Hotel Georgia**	▽▽▽	$209-$239 SAVE	547
41 / p. 531	CAA	**Vancouver Marriott Pinnacle Downtown**	▽▽▽▽	$259-$339 SAVE	559
42 / p. 531		Barclay House in the West End	▽▽▽	$130-$250	543
43 / p. 531	CAA	**Hotel Le Soleil**	▽▽▽▽	$245-$275 SAVE	550
44 / p. 531		Sandman Hotel Downtown Vancouver	▽▽	$139-$189	557
45 / p. 531	CAA	**St Regis Hotel**	▽▽	$145-$165 SAVE	556
46 / p. 531	CAA	**The Westin Grand, Vancouver** - see color ad p 5	▽▽▽▽	$219-$429 SAVE	561
		DOWNTOWN VANCOUVER - Restaurants			
1 / p. 531		Cafe de Paris	▽▽	$19-$26	562
2 / p. 531		Ciao Bella Ristorante	▽▽	$13-$20	562
3 / p. 531		Vistas Revolving Restaurant - see color ad p 556	▽▽▽	$25-$40	567
4 / p. 531		Rex Rotisserie & Grill	▽▽▽	$15-$28	566
5 / p. 531		Imperial Chinese Seafood Restaurant	▽▽▽	$15-$25	564
6 / p. 531		Cafe Presto Panini	▽▽	$9-$14	562
7 / p. 531		Foo Faa Thai Hot Pot Restaurant	▽▽	$10-$20	564
8 / p. 531		Al Porto Ristorante	▽▽▽	$13-$25	561
9 / p. 531		Le Gavroche Restaurant Francais	▽▽▽	$19-$32	565
10 / p. 531	CAA	**Tropika Malaysian & Thai Cuisine**	▽▽	$10-$20	567
11 / p. 531	CAA	**Zin**	▽▽▽	$16-$20	568
12 / p. 531		Ezogiku Noodle Cafe	▽	$6-$9	563
13 / p. 531		The Hermitage	▽▽▽	$20-$29	564
14 / p. 531		Milestone's Restaurant	▽▽	$7-$13	565
15 / p. 531		CINCIN	▽▽▽	$16-$36	562
16 / p. 531		Cactus Club Cafe	▽▽	$9-$27	562
17 / p. 531		Earls On Top	▽▽	$8-$15	563
18 / p. 531		Settebello Ristorante	▽▽▽	$14-$26	566
19 / p. 531		Joe Fortes Seafood & Chop House	▽▽▽	$19-$56	564

Spotter/Map Page Number	OA	DOWNTOWN VANCOUVER - Restaurants (continued)	Diamond Rating	Rate Range High Season	Listing Page
⑳ / p. 531		Cafe de Medici	◆◆◆	$15-$35	562
㉑ / p. 531		Herons Restaurant	◆◆◆	$20-$30	564
㉒ / p. 531		Cardero's Restaurant	◆◆	$18-$25	562
㉓ / p. 531		Thurlow Keg	◆◆◆	$17-$30	567
㉔ / p. 531		Diva at the Met	◆◆◆◆	$22-$35	563
㉕ / p. 531		Chartwell	◆◆◆◆	$19-$37	562
㉖ / p. 531		Kobe Japanese Steak House	◆◆	$25-$49	565
㉗ / p. 531		Delilah's	◆◆◆	$23-$33	563
㉘ / p. 531		Water St. Cafe	◆◆	$10-$20	567
㉙ / p. 531		Mexico Sabroso	◆	$7-$13	565
㉚ / p. 531		Oritalia	◆◆◆	$20-$30	565
㉛ / p. 531		Romano's Macaroni Grill	◆◆	$9-$23	566
㉜ / p. 531		Random	◆◆	$13-$15	566
㉝ / p. 531		Piccolo Mondo Ristorante	◆◆◆	$15-$30	566
㉞ / p. 531		Fleuri Restaurant	◆◆◆◆	$14-$36	564
㉟ / p. 531		Stepho's Souvlaki Greek Taverna	◆◆	$7-$10	567
㊱ / p. 531	CAA	**Bacchus Restaurant**	◆◆◆◆	$20-$35	561
㊲ / p. 531	CAA	**Don Francesco Ristorante**	◆◆◆	$30-$40	563
㊳ / p. 531		Il Giardino	◆◆◆	$16-$37	564
㊴ / p. 531		Kam's Place Singaporean Cuisine	◆◆	$9-$13	565
㊵ / p. 531	CAA	**The William Tell**	◆◆◆	$23-$38	567
㊶ / p. 531		Show Case Restaurant	◆◆◆	$20-$30	567
㊷ / p. 531		Le Crocodile	◆◆◆◆	$24-$34	565
㊸ / p. 531		Lickerish	◆◆◆	$17-$25	565
㊹ / p. 531		Won More Szechuan Cuisine	◆◆	$7-$14	568
㊺ / p. 531		900 West	◆◆◆	$27-$40	561
㊻ / p. 531		Rain City Grill	◆◆◆	$19-$32	566
㊼ / p. 531		The Sandbar Seafood Restaurant	◆◆◆	$11-$30	566
㊽ / p. 531		Just One Thai Bistro	◆◆	$9-$15	564
㊾ / p. 531		Aqua Riva	◆◆◆	$18-$28	561
㊿ / p. 531	CAA	**A Kettle Of Fish**	◆◆	$18-$25	561
(51) / p. 531		Da Pasta Bar on Robson	◆◆	$11-$17	563
(52) / p. 531		Five Sails Restaurant	◆◆◆◆◆	$26-$45	563
(53) / p. 531		Blue Water Cafe	◆◆◆	$10-$21	561
(54) / p. 531		Indigo Bistro - see color ad p 557	◆◆◆	$15-$30	564

Spotter/Map Page Number	OA	DOWNTOWN VANCOUVER - Restaurants (continued)	Diamond Rating	Rate Range High Season	Listing Page
55 / p. 531		Fiddlehead Joe's	◆◆	$14-$24	563
56 / p. 531	ⒶⒶ	**Glowbal Grill & Satay Bar**	◆◆◆	$18-$28	564
57 / p. 531		Villa de Lupo Restaurant	◆◆◆	$18-$30	567
58 / p. 531		Vera's Burger Shack	◆	$5-$9	567
59 / p. 531		Yaletown Brewing Company	◆◆	$13-$21	568
60 / p. 531		C Restaurant	◆◆◆	$27-$35	562
61 / p. 531		La Terrazza	◆◆◆	$25-$30	565
62 / p. 531		Brix Restaurant & Wine Bar	◆◆◆	$19-$26	562
63 / p. 531		Elixir Bar & Restaurant	◆◆◆	$15-$28	563
64 / p. 531		Provence Marinaside	◆◆◆	$15-$35	566
65 / p. 531		Vera's Burger Shack	◆	$5-$9	567
66 / p. 531		Subeez Cafe	◆◆	$8-$20	567
67 / p. 531		Milestone's Grill & Bar	◆◆	$10-$21	565
68 / p. 531		Oysi Oysi Japanese Restaurant	◆◆	$7-$19	566
69 / p. 531		Parkside on Haro Street	◆◆◆	$20-$23	566
70 / p. 531		Dockside Brewing Company	◆◆	$20-$30	563

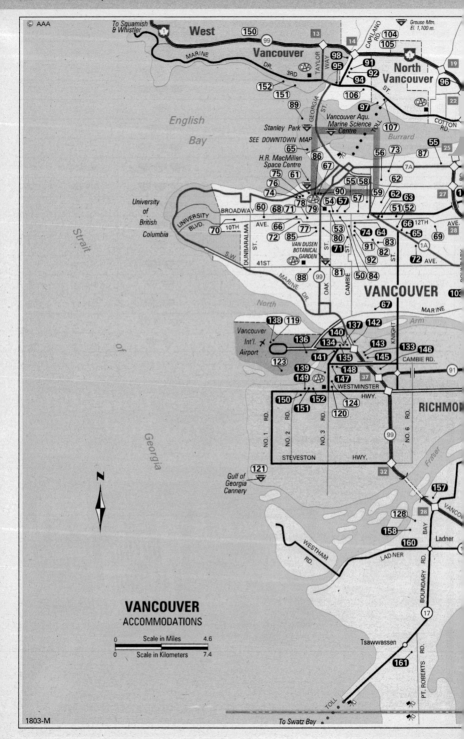

VANCOUVER
ACCOMMODATIONS

Scale in Miles 4.6
Scale in Kilometers 7.4

1803-M

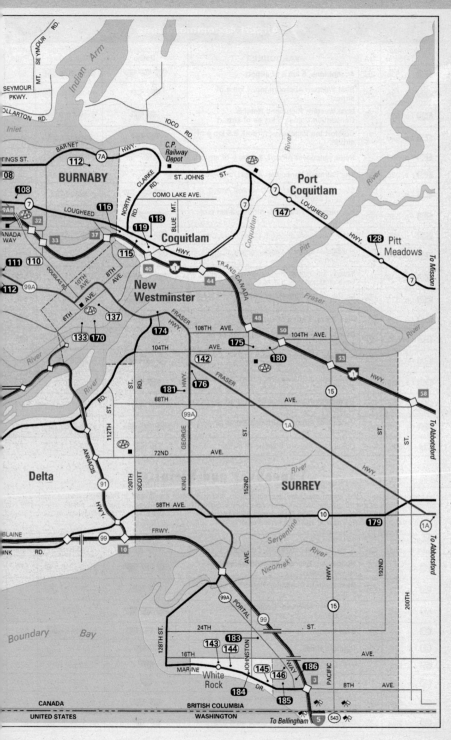

✈ Airport Accommodations

Spotter/Map Page Number	OA	VANCOUVER	Diamond Rating	Rate Range High Season	Listing Page
145 / p. 536	CAA	Accent Inns, 5 km e of airport	◆◆◆	$119-$149 SAVE	589
137 / p. 536	CAA	Best Western Abercorn Inn, 4 km e of airport	◆◆	$109-$159 SAVE	589
149 / p. 536	CAA	Best Western Richmond Hotel & Convention Center, 5 km se of airport	◆◆	$109-$129 SAVE	589
141 / p. 536	CAA	Comfort Inn Vancouver Airport, 2.6 km e of airport	◆◆	$84-$124 SAVE	589
136 / p. 536	CAA	Delta Vancouver Airport, 2.4 km e of airport	◆◆◆	$169-$189 SAVE	590
138 / p. 536	CAA	The Fairmont Vancouver Airport, at airport	◆◆◆◆	$199-$289 SAVE	590
147 / p. 536		Four Points by Sheraton Vancouver Airport, 5 km se of airport	◆◆◆	$230-$250	590
135 / p. 536	CAA	Hampton Inn Vancouver Airport, 3 km e of airport	◆◆◆	$144-$159 SAVE	591
152 / p. 536		Hilton Vancouver Airport, 5 km se of airport	◆◆◆	$129-$169	591
142 / p. 536		Holiday Inn Express Vancouver-Airport, 4 km e of airport	◆◆◆	$119-$159	591
146 / p. 536		Holiday Inn International Vancouver Airport, 5 km e of airport	◆◆◆	$129-$169	592
148 / p. 536	CAA	La Quinta Inn Vancouver Airport - see color ad p 573	◆◆◆	$99-$189 SAVE	592
143 / p. 536	CAA	Park Plaza, 5 km e of airport	◆◆	$109-$129 SAVE	592
150 / p. 536	CAA	Quality Hotel Airport (South), 5 km se of airport	◆◆	$109-$149 SAVE	592
139 / p. 536	CAA	Radisson President Hotel & Suites, 4 km se of airport	◆◆	$139 SAVE	592
134 / p. 536		Sandman Hotel Vancouver Airport, 5 km e of airport	◆◆	$79-$159	592
140 / p. 536	CAA	Travelodge Hotel Vancouver Airport, 5 km e of airport	◆◆	$99-$149 SAVE	593
151 / p. 536	CAA	Vancouver Airport Marriott, 5 km se of airport	◆◆◆	$129-$169 SAVE	593
67 / p. 536	CAA	Quality Inn Airport, 9 km ne of airport	◆◆	$129-$174 SAVE	575

Vancouver and Vicinity

This index helps you "spot" where approved accommodations and restaurants are located on the corresponding detailed maps. Lodging rate ranges are for comparison only and show the property's high season; rates are per night, unless only weekly (W) rates are available. Restaurant rate range is for dinner, unless only lunch (L) is served. Turn to the listing page for more detailed rate information and consult display ads for special promotions.

Spotter/Map Page Number	OA	VANCOUVER - Lodgings	Diamond Rating	Rate Range High Season	Listing Page
55 / p. 536	CAA	Holiday Inn Express Vancouver - see color ad card insert	◆◆◆	$108-$315 SAVE	570
56 / p. 536	CAA	Best Western Exhibition Park - see color ad p 568	◆◆	$129-$199 SAVE	569
57 / p. 536		Holiday Inn Vancouver-Centre (Broadway) - see color ad card insert	◆◆◆	$209	570
62 / p. 536	CAA	Best Western Uptown	◆◆◆	$119-$129 SAVE	569
63 / p. 536	CAA	Biltmore Hotel	◆◆	$89-$129 SAVE	569
64 / p. 536		Windsor Guest House B & B	◆	$75-$145	575
65 / p. 536		The London Guard Motel	◆	$65-$75	571
66 / p. 536	CAA	Days Inn-Vancouver Metro - see color ad p 570	◆◆	$99-$139 SAVE	570
67 / p. 536	CAA	Quality Inn Airport - see color ad p 573	◆◆	$129-$174 SAVE	575

Spotter/Map Page Number	OA	**VANCOUVER** - Lodgings (continued)	Diamond Rating	Rate Range High Season	Listing Page
71 / p. 536	CAA	**Plaza 500 Hotel & Convention Centre - see** color ad p 5	▽▽▽	$159-$179 [SAVE]	574
72 / p. 536		2400 Motel	▽▽	$75-$125	568
74 / p. 536		Columbia Cottage	▽▽	$95-$135	569
		VANCOUVER - Restaurants			
50 / p. 536		Rugby Beach Club Grille	▽▽	$8-$12	578
51 / p. 536		The Green Grape Restaurant	▽▽	$6-$12	576
52 / p. 536		House of Dosas	▽	$8-$15	576
53 / p. 536		Memphis Blues Barbeque House	▽	$7-$19	577
54 / p. 536		Tojo's Restaurant	▽▽	$16-$25	578
55 / p. 536		Dun Huang Seafood Restaurant	▽▽	$13-$25	576
56 / p. 536		Memphis Blues Barbeque House	▽	$7-$19	577
57 / p. 536		Rasputin	▽▽	$12-$25	577
58 / p. 536		Monk McQueen's	▽▽▽	$16-$30	577
59 / p. 536		Typhoon	▽▽	$6-$9	578
60 / p. 536		Calhoun's	▽	$4-$9	575
61 / p. 536		Yew First Restaurant Lounge	▽▽	$14-$20	579
62 / p. 536		Aurora Bistro	▽▽▽	$18-$24	575
65 / p. 536	CAA	**The Fish House at Stanley Park**	▽▽▽	$17-$30	576
66 / p. 536		Gramercy Grill	▽▽▽	$15-$33	576
67 / p. 536		Las Margaritas Restaurante & Cantina	▽▽	$11-$18	576
68 / p. 536		Portobello Ristorante	▽▽▽	$12-$26	577
69 / p. 536		Lombardo's Ristorante Pizzeria	▽	$10-$24	576
70 / p. 536		Provence Mediterranean Grill	▽▽▽	$14-$24	577
71 / p. 536		Lumiere	▽▽▽▽▽	$100-$130	576
72 / p. 536		Trafalgars at Sweet Obsession	▽▽	$12-$25	578
73 / p. 536		Pink Pearl Chinese Restaurant	▽▽	$10-$19	577
74 / p. 536		Quattro on Fourth	▽▽▽	$18-$33	577
75 / p. 536		Sophie's Cosmic Cafe	▽	$6-$10	578
76 / p. 536		Bishop's	▽▽▽	$30-$38	575
77 / p. 536		The Ouisi Bistro	▽▽	$7-$22	577
78 / p. 536		Wild Garlic	▽▽▽	$10-$22	579
79 / p. 536		Maurya Indian Cuisine	▽▽	$13-$16	576
80 / p. 536		Star Anise	▽▽▽	$20-$27	578
81 / p. 536		Shaughnessy Restaurant At VanDusen Garden	▽▽	$19-$28	578
82 / p. 536		Cipriano's Ristorante And Pizzeria	▽	$13-$21	575
83 / p. 536		Sawasdee Thai Restaurant	▽▽	$8-$13	578
84 / p. 536		Tomato Fresh Food Cafe	▽▽	$12-$20	578
85 / p. 536		West Restaurant & Bar	▽▽▽	$20-$35	579
86 / p. 536		New City Restaurant	▽▽	$7-$12	577
87 / p. 536	CAA	**The Cannery**	▽▽▽	$18-$30	575

Spotter/Map Page Number	OA	**VANCOUVER** - Restaurants (continued)	Diamond Rating	Rate Range High Season	Listing Page
(88) / p. 536		Avenue Grill	◆◆	$11-$16	575
(89) / p. 536	CAA	**Sequoia Grill in Stanley Park**	◆◆◆	$17-$28	578
(90) / p. 536		Capers	◆	$5-$8	575
(91) / p. 536		Harlo Gourmet Burger	◆◆	$8-$12	576
(92) / p. 536		Seasons in the Park	◆◆◆	$18-$30	578
		NORTH VANCOUVER - Lodgings			
(91) / p. 536	CAA	**Ramada Inn Vancouver North Shore** - see color ad p 587	◆◆	$131 SAVE	587
(92) / p. 536	CAA	**Comfort Inn and Suites**	◆◆	$139-$259 SAVE	586
(94) / p. 536	CAA	**Best Western Capilano Inn & Suites**	◆◆	$109-$139 SAVE	586
(95) / p. 536		Lionsgate Travelodge	◆	$129-$139	587
(96) / p. 536	CAA	**Holiday Inn Hotel & Suites North Vancouver** - see color ad card insert, p 571, p 587, p 545, p 552	◆◆◆	$149-$179 SAVE	586
(97) / p. 536	CAA	**Lonsdale Quay Hotel**	◆◆	$125-$350 SAVE	587
(98) / p. 536	CAA	**Grouse Inn** - see color ad p 549	◆◆	$119-$148 SAVE	586
		NORTH VANCOUVER - Restaurants			
(104) / p. 536		Azure Mediterranean Bistro	◆◆	$13-$27	588
(105) / p. 536		Kilby's Restaurant	◆◆	$12-$23	588
(106) / p. 536		Moustache Cafe	◆◆◆	$18-$29	588
(107) / p. 536		Gusto di Quattro	◆◆◆	$16-$30	588
		BURNABY - Lodgings			
(103) / p. 536	CAA	**Holiday Inn Express Metrotown**	◆◆◆	$139-$189 SAVE	580
(106) / p. 536	CAA	**Accent Inns** - see color ad p 488, p 608	◆◆◆	$119-$149 SAVE	579
(108) / p. 536		Lake City Motor Inn - see color ad p 572	◆◆	$89-$104	580
(111) / p. 536	CAA	**Best Western Kings Inn and Conference Centre**	◆◆	$97-$127 SAVE	579
(112) / p. 536	CAA	**Hilton Vancouver Metrotown** - see ad p 580	◆◆◆◆	$159-$229 SAVE	580
		BURNABY - Restaurants			
(108) / p. 536		Milestone's Grill & Bar	◆◆	$7-$13	581
(109) / p. 536	CAA	**Crystal Bar and Grille** - see ad p 580	◆◆◆	$12-$24	581
(110) / p. 536	CAA	**Hart House on Deer Lake**	◆◆◆	$17-$30	581
(112) / p. 536		HORIZON'S	◆◆◆	$20-$28	581
		COQUITLAM - Lodgings			
(116) / p. 536	CAA	**Best Western Coquitlam Inn Convention Centre**	◆◆◆	$149-$179 SAVE	581
(118) / p. 536	CAA	**Holiday Inn Vancouver-Coquitlam**	◆◆◆	$109-$159 SAVE	582
(119) / p. 536	CAA	**Best Western Chelsea Inn** - see color ad p 581	◆◆◆	$119-$349 SAVE	581
		COQUITLAM - Restaurant			
(115) / p. 536		Joey Tomato's Mediterranean Grill	◆◆	$12-$24	582
		PITT MEADOWS - Lodgings			
(128) / p. 536		Ramada Inn & Suites Hotel Royale	◆◆◆	$112	588
		RICHMOND - Lodgings			
(133) / p. 536		Ramada Plaza	◆◆	$109-$129	592

Spotter/Map Page Number	OA	**RICHMOND** - Lodgings (continued)	Diamond Rating	Rate Range High Season	Listing Page
134 / p. 536		Sandman Hotel Vancouver Airport	◇◇	$79-$159	592
135 / p. 536	Ⓐ	**Hampton Inn Vancouver Airport** - see color ad p 572	◇◇◇	$144-$159 SAVE	591
136 / p. 536	Ⓐ	**Delta Vancouver Airport** - see color ad p 591	◇◇◇	$169-$189 SAVE	590
137 / p. 536	Ⓐ	**Best Western Abercorn Inn** - see color ad p 589	◇◇	$109-$159 SAVE	589
138 / p. 536	Ⓐ	**The Fairmont Vancouver Airport** - see color ad p 571	◇◇◇◇	$199-$289 SAVE	590
139 / p. 536	Ⓐ	**Radisson President Hotel & Suites** - see color ad p 574, p 573	◇◇◇	$139 SAVE	592
140 / p. 536	Ⓐ	**Travelodge Hotel Vancouver Airport**	◇◇	$99-$149 SAVE	593
141 / p. 536	Ⓐ	**Comfort Inn Vancouver Airport** - see color ad p 590, p 570	◇◇	$84-$124 SAVE	589
142 / p. 536		Holiday Inn Express Vancouver-Airport - see color ad card insert	◇◇◇	$119-$159	591
143 / p. 536	Ⓐ	**Park Plaza** - see color ad p 573, p 574	◇◇	$109-$129 SAVE	592
145 / p. 536	Ⓐ	**Accent Inns** - see color ad p 488, p 608	◇◇◇	$119-$149 SAVE	589
146 / p. 536		Holiday Inn International Vancouver Airport - see color ad card insert	◇◇◇	$129-$169	592
147 / p. 536		Four Points by Sheraton Vancouver Airport - see color ad p 5	◇◇◇	$230-$250	590
148 / p. 536	Ⓐ	**La Quinta Inn Vancouver Airport** - see color ad p 573	◇◇◇	$99-$189 SAVE	592
149 / p. 536		**Best Western Richmond Hotel & Convention Center** - see color ad p 569	◇◇	$109-$129 SAVE	589
150 / p. 536	Ⓐ	**Quality Hotel Airport (South)**	◇◇	$109-$149 SAVE	592
151 / p. 536	Ⓐ	**Vancouver Airport Marriott**	◇◇◇	$129-$169 SAVE	593
152 / p. 536		Hilton Vancouver Airport - see color ad p 572	◇◇◇	$129-$169	591
		RICHMOND - Restaurants			
119 / p. 536		Globe at YVR	◇◇◇	$20-$30	593
120 / p. 536		Cactus Club Cafe	◇◇	$8-$26	593
121 / p. 536	Ⓐ	**Steveston Seafood House**	◇◇◇	$18-$35	593
123 / p. 536		Flying Beaver	◇	$9-$15	593
124 / p. 536		Floata Seafood Restaurant	◇	$15-$30	593
		DELTA - Lodgings			
157 / p. 536	Ⓐ	**Delta Town & Country Inn**	◇◇◇	$99-$129 SAVE	582
158 / p. 536		River Run Cottages	◇◇◇	$150-$210	582
160 / p. 536		Clair's Bed & Breakfast	◇◇	$85-$150	582
161 / p. 536		The Coast Tsawwassen Inn	fyi	$119-$149	582
		DELTA - Restaurant			
128 / p. 536	Ⓐ	**La Belle Auberge**	◇◇◇	$25-$28	582
		NEW WESTMINSTER - Lodgings			
170 / p. 536	Ⓐ	**Inn at Westminster Quay**	◇◇◇	$160-$215 SAVE	585
		NEW WESTMINSTER - Restaurants			
133 / p. 536		Burger Heaven	◇	$5-$10	586
137 / p. 536		La Rustica Ristorante	◇◇	$11-$20	586
		SURREY - Lodgings			
174 / p. 536	Ⓐ	**Howard Johnson Express Inn & Suites**	◇◇	$80-$90 SAVE	594

Spotter/Map Page Number	OA	SURREY - Lodgings (continued)	Diamond Rating	Rate Range High Season	Listing Page
175 / p. 536	CAA	Sheraton Vancouver Guildford Hotel - see ad p 594 & color ad p 5	fyi	$149-$399 SAVE	595
176 / p. 536	CAA	Days Hotel-Surrey - see color ad p 594	◇◇	$125 SAVE	594
179 / p. 536		Ramada Limited Surrey-Langley	◇◇	$119-$139	595
180 / p. 536		Ramada Hotel & Suites Surrey/Guildford	◇◇	$89-$139	595
181 / p. 536	CAA	Best Western King George Inn & Suites	◇◇◇	$109-$135 SAVE	593
183 / p. 536	CAA	Econo Lodge Peace Arch	◇◇	$90-$150 SAVE	594
		SURREY - Restaurant			
(142) / p. 536		Yokohama Japanese Restaurant	◇	$10-$21	596
		WHITE ROCK - Lodgings			
184 / p. 536	CAA	Ocean Promenade Hotel	◇◇◇	$139-$489 SAVE	596
185 / p. 536	CAA	Seacrest Motel & RV Park	◇◇	$87-$96 SAVE	596
186 / p. 536		Aston Pacific Inn Resort & Conference Ctr	◇◇	$129	596
		WHITE ROCK - Restaurants			
(143) / p. 536		Sam's Waterfront Cafe	◇◇◇	$16-$24	597
(144) / p. 536		Giraffe	◇◇◇	$14-$23	597
(145) / p. 536		La Baia Italian Restaurant	◇◇	$10-$20	597
(146) / p. 536		The Turkey House & Deli	◇	$7-$9	597
		PORT COQUITLAM - Restaurant			
(147) / p. 536		Earls	◇◇	$8-$15	588
		WEST VANCOUVER - Restaurants			
(150) / p. 536		Salmon House on the Hill	◇◇	$20-$28	596
(151) / p. 536		La Regalade French Bistro	◇◇	$16-$23	596
(152) / p. 536		The Beach House at Dundarave Pier	◇◇◇	$19-$30	596

DOWNTOWN VANCOUVER   (See map and index starting on p. 531)

──── WHERE TO STAY ────

BARCLAY HOUSE IN THE WEST END   *Book at aaa.com*   Phone: (604)605-1351   **42**

♦♦♦ Historic Bed & Breakfast

6/1-9/30 [BP]	1P: $130-$225	2P: $160-$250	XP: $30
10/1-2/28 [BP]	1P: $115-$195	2P: $130-$225	XP: $30
4/1-5/31 [BP]	1P: $120-$185	2P: $140-$195	XP: $30
3/1-3/31 [BP]	1P: $115-$155	2P: $130-$165	XP: $30

Location: Between Broughton and Jervis sts. Located in a residential area in West End. 1351 Barclay St V6E 1H6. Fax: 604/605-1382. **Facility:** Cast-iron, claw-foot tubs are among the vintage touches featured at this renovated 1904 Victorian home. Smoke free premises. 5 one-bedroom standard units. 3 stories (no elevator), interior/exterior corridors. *Bath:* combo or shower only. **Parking:** on-site. **Terms:** 2 night minimum stay - seasonal and/or weekends, age restrictions may apply, 7 day cancellation notice-fee imposed, [ECP] meal plan available, package plans. **Amenities:** video library, CD players, hair dryers. **Cards:** DC, JC, MC, VI.

SOME UNITS

BEST WESTERN CHATEAU GRANVILLE   *Book at aaa.com*   Phone: (604)669-7070   **31**

CAA SAVE ♦♦♦ Small-scale Hotel

5/1-6/30	1P: $159-$199	2P: $169-$209	XP: $20	F17
3/1-4/30 & 10/1-2/28	1P: $119-$199	2P: $139-$209	XP: $20	F17
7/1-9/30	1P: $199	2P: $209	XP: $20	F17

Location: Between Davie and Helmcken sts. 1100 Granville St V6Z 2B6. Fax: 604/669-4928. **Facility:** 114 units. 19 one-bedroom standard units. 95 one-bedroom suites ($199-$209). 15 stories, interior corridors. **Parking:** on-site (fee). **Terms:** cancellation fee imposed, weekly rates available, [AP] meal plan available, package plans, small pets only ($20 extra charge). **Amenities:** dual phone lines, voice mail, irons, hair dryers. **Dining:** 7 am-1 & 5-9 pm, cocktails. **Guest Services:** valet laundry. **Business Services:** meeting rooms. **Cards:** AX, CB, DC, DS, JC, MC, VI. **Special Amenities:** free local telephone calls and free room upgrade (subject to availability with advance reservations).

SOME UNITS

BEST WESTERN DOWNTOWN VANCOUVER   *Book at aaa.com*   Phone: (604)669-9888   **37**

CAA SAVE ♦♦♦ Small-scale Hotel

5/16-10/15	1P: $169-$219	2P: $169-$219	XP: $20	F12
3/1-5/15	1P: $129-$219	2P: $129-$219	XP: $20	F12
10/16-2/28	1P: $99-$169	2P: $99-$169	XP: $20	F12

Location: Corner of Drake and Granville sts. 718 Drake St V6Z 2W6. Fax: 604/669-3440. **Facility:** 143 one-bedroom standard units, some with efficiencies and/or whirlpools. 12 stories, interior corridors. **Parking:** on-site (fee). **Terms:** cancellation fee imposed, small pets only ($15 extra charge). **Amenities:** high-speed Internet, voice mail, safes, irons, hair dryers. **Leisure Activities:** saunas, whirlpool, exercise room. **Guest Services:** valet and coin laundry, area transportation-within downtown. **Cards:** AX, CB, DC, JC, MC, VI. **Special Amenities:** free local telephone calls and free room upgrade (subject to availability with advance reservations). *(See color ad p 544, p 545 & p 552)*

SOME UNITS

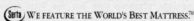

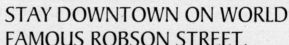

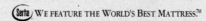 

(See map and index starting on p. 531)

BEST WESTERN SANDS *Book at aaa.com* Phone: (604)682-1831 **6**

CAA SAVE

7/1-9/30	1P: $179-$229	2P: $189-$239	XP: $15	F12
5/1-6/30	1P: $149-$209	2P: $159-$209	XP: $15	F12
3/1-4/30 & 10/1-2/28	1P: $119-$179	2P: $129-$189	XP: $15	F12

Small-scale Hotel **Location:** Between Bidwell and Denman sts. 1755 Davie St V6G 1W5. Fax: 604/682-3546. **Facility:** 121 one-bedroom standard units, some with efficiencies. 6 stories, interior corridors. **Parking:** on-site (fee). **Terms:** check-in 4 pm, [BP] meal plan available, package plans, small pets only ($10 extra charge). **Amenities:** video games (fee), high-speed Internet, voice mail, irons, hair dryers. **Dining:** 7 am-11 pm, cocktails. **Leisure Activities:** sauna, limited exercise equipment. **Guest Services:** valet and coin laundry. **Business Services:** meeting rooms. **Cards:** AX, CB, DC, DS, JC, MC, VI. **Special Amenities:** free expanded continental breakfast and free local telephone calls. *(See color ad p 543)*

SOME UNITS

(See map and index starting on p. 531)

BLUE HORIZON HOTEL *Book at aaa.com*   **Phone: (604)688-1411** 9

	5/14-10/1	1P: $149-$189	2P: $159-$209	XP: $15	F16
Small-scale Hotel	4/29-5/13	1P: $109-$169	2P: $119-$199	XP: $15	F16
	3/1-4/28 & 10/2-2/28	1P: $99-$159	2P: $109-$189	XP: $15	F16

Location: Between Jervis and Bute sts. 1225 Robson St V6E 1C3. Fax: 604/688-4461. **Facility:** 214 one-bedroom standard units. 31 stories, interior corridors. **Parking:** on-site (fee). **Terms:** cancellation fee imposed. **Amenities:** high-speed Internet, voice mail, safes, irons, hair dryers. *Some:* honor bars. **Pool(s):** small heated indoor. **Leisure Activities:** sauna, whirlpool, limited exercise equipment. **Guest Services:** valet laundry. **Business Services:** meeting rooms. **Cards:** AX, DC, MC, VI. *(See color ad below)*

SOME UNITS

(ASK) (S0) (T1) (Y) (≈) (X) (☀) (DATA PORT) (💻) / (X) (🔒) /

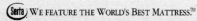

(See map and index starting on p. 531)

BOSMANS HOTEL *Book at aaa.com* — Phone: (604)682-3171 **27**

(CAA) (SAVE)

◆◆◆ ◆◆◆

5/16-9/30	1P: $109-$119	2P: $119-$129	XP: $10	F11
3/1-5/15 & 10/1-2/28	1P: $69	2P: $79	XP: $10	F11

Location: Between Nelson and Helmcken sts. 1060 Howe St V6Z 1P5. Fax: 604/684-4010. **Facility:** 102 one-bedroom standard units. 4 stories, interior corridors. **Parking:** on-site. **Terms:** small pets only. **Small-scale Hotel** **Amenities:** voice mail, hair dryers. **Dining:** 7 am-3 pm, Sat & Sun-2 pm. **Pool(s):** small heated outdoor. **Guest Services:** valet laundry. **Cards:** AX, CB, DC, MC, VI. **Special Amenities:** free newspaper and early check-in/late check-out.

SOME UNITS

[S/D] [🛏] [🍴] [Y] [🏊] [DATA PORT] / [X] /

COMFORT INN DOWNTOWN *Book at aaa.com* — Phone: (604)605-4333 **29**

(CAA) (SAVE)

◆◆◆◆ ◆◆◆◆

6/1-9/30	1P: $129-$229	2P: $129-$229	XP: $15	F12
5/1-5/31	1P: $95-$189	2P: $95-$189	XP: $15	F12
3/1-4/30 & 10/1-2/28	1P: $72-$149	2P: $72-$149	XP: $15	F12

Location: Between Granville and Seymour sts. 654 Nelson St V6B 6K4. Fax: 604/605-4334. **Facility:** 82 one-**Small-scale Hotel** bedroom standard units, some with whirlpools. 7 stories, interior corridors. **Parking:** on-site (fee). **Terms:** small pets only. **Amenities:** high-speed Internet, voice mail, irons, hair dryers. **Dining:** nightclub. **Guest Services:** valet laundry. **Cards:** AX, CB, DC, DS, JC, MC, VI. **Special Amenities:** free expanded continental breakfast and free newspaper.

SOME UNITS

[S/D] [🛏] [Y] [💪] [📷] [DATA PORT] [💻] / [X] /
FEE

CROWNE PLAZA VANCOUVER-HOTEL GEORGIA *Book at aaa.com* — Phone: (604)682-5566 **40**

(CAA) (SAVE)

◆◆◆ ◆◆◆

5/1-10/31	1P: $209-$239	2P: $209-$239	XP: $30	F18
3/1-4/30 & 11/1-2/28	1P: $159-$179	2P: $159-$179	XP: $30	F18

Location: Between Howe and Hornby sts. 801 W Georgia St V6C 1P7. Fax: 604/642-5579. **Facility:** A bygone elegance characterizes this historic 1927 hotel, which has been completely renovated back to its original **Classic Historic** appearance. 313 one-bedroom standard units. 12 stories, interior corridors. *Bath:* combo or shower only. **Small-scale Hotel** **Parking:** on-site (fee) and valet. **Terms:** cancellation fee imposed, [BP] & [CP] meal plans available, package plans, small pets only. **Amenities:** video games (fee), CD players, high-speed Internet, dual phone lines, voice mail, irons, hair dryers. **Dining:** 6:30 am-10 pm, cocktails. **Leisure Activities:** limited exercise equipment. **Guest Services:** gift shop, valet laundry. **Business Services:** meeting rooms, business center. **Cards:** AX, CB, DC, DS, JC, MC, VI. **Special Amenities:** free newspaper.

SOME UNITS

[S/D] [🛏] [🍴] [24] [Y] [♿M] [📷] [DATA PORT] [💻] / [X] /

DAYS INN DOWNTOWN *Book at aaa.com* — Phone: (604)681-4335 **13**

(CAA) (SAVE)

◆◆ ◆◆

5/1-10/14	1P: $159-$209	2P: $159-$209	XP: $15	F12
3/1-4/30 & 10/15-2/28	1P: $115-$160	2P: $115-$160	XP: $15	F12

Location: Between Burrard and Hornby sts. Located in the financial district. 921 W Pender St V6C 1M2. Fax: 604/681-7808. **Facility:** 85 one-bedroom standard units. 6 stories, interior corridors. *Bath:* combo or **Small-scale Hotel** shower only. **Parking:** on-site (fee) and valet. **Terms:** cancellation fee imposed, package plans. **Amenities:** high-speed Internet, voice mail, safes, irons, hair dryers. **Dining:** 7 am-3 pm, Sat & Sun-11 am, cocktails. **Guest Services:** valet and coin laundry. **Cards:** AX, CB, DC, DS, JC, MC, VI. *(See color ad p 546 & p 545)*

SOME UNITS

[S/D] [🍴] [Y] [📷] [DATA PORT] [💻] / [X] [🔋] [🍽] /

(See map and index starting on p. 531)

DELTA VANCOUVER SUITES — *Book at aaa.com* — Phone: (604)689-8188 — **17**

CAA SAVE ▼▼▼

6/1-10/14	1P: $199-$269	2P: $199-$269	XP: $20	F17
5/1-5/31	1P: $179-$219	2P: $179-$219	XP: $20	F17
3/1-4/30 & 10/15-2/28	1P: $159-$199	2P: $159-$199	XP: $20	F17

Location: Between Seymour and Richards sts; entrance in alley way. 550 W Hastings St V6B 1L6.
Large-scale Hotel Fax: 604/605-8881. **Facility:** 225 units. 40 one-bedroom standard units. 185 one-bedroom suites. 23 stories, interior corridors. **Parking:** on-site (fee) and valet. **Terms:** cancellation fee imposed, small pets only. **Amenities:** video games (fee), high-speed Internet, dual phone lines, voice mail, honor bars, irons, hair dryers. *Some:* CD players. **Dining:** 6:30 am-2:30 & 5-11 pm, Sat & Sun from 7 am, cocktails. **Pool(s):** heated indoor. **Leisure Activities:** sauna, whirlpool, exercise room. **Guest Services:** gift shop, valet laundry. **Business Services:** meeting rooms, business center. **Cards:** AX, DC, DS, JC, MC, VI. *(See color ad p 547)*

SOME UNITS

THE FAIRMONT HOTEL VANCOUVER — *Book at aaa.com* — Phone: (604)684-3131 — **18**

▼▼▼▼

5/1-8/31	1P: $279-$379	2P: $279-$379	XP: $30	F18
9/1-10/31	1P: $267-$327	2P: $267-$327	XP: $30	F18
3/1-4/30 & 11/1-2/28	1P: $199-$299	2P: $199-$299	XP: $30	F18

Classic Historic
Large-scale Hotel **Location:** Corner of Burrard at W Georgia St; enter from Hornby St. 900 W Georgia St V6C 2W6. Fax: 604/662-1929. **Facility:** Opened by the Queen Mother in 1938, this historic downtown landmark hotel remains distinguished with elegantly restored rooms and lobby boutiques. 556 units. 527 one-bedroom standard units. 29 one-bedroom suites. 21 stories, interior corridors. **Parking:** on-site (fee) and valet. **Terms:** cancellation fee imposed, small pets only ($25 extra charge). **Amenities:** video games (fee), voice mail, honor bars, irons, hair dryers. *Some:* high-speed Internet, dual phone lines. **Dining:** 900 West, see separate listing. **Pool(s):** heated indoor. **Leisure Activities:** saunas, whirlpool, spa. **Guest Services:** gift shop, valet laundry. **Business Services:** conference facilities, business center. **Cards:** AX, CB, DC, DS, JC, MC, VI.

SOME UNITS

THE FAIRMONT WATERFRONT — *Book at aaa.com* — Phone: (604)691-1991 — **10**

▼▼▼▼

5/1-10/31	1P: $279-$349	2P: $279-$349	XP: $30	F18
1/1-2/28	1P: $219-$289	2P: $219-$289	XP: $30	F18
3/1-4/30 & 11/1-12/31	1P: $209-$279	2P: $209-$279	XP: $30	F18

Large-scale Hotel **Location:** Howe St at Cordova St. Located opposite Canada Place. 900 Canada Place Way V6C 3L5. Fax: 604/691-1999. **Facility:** Conveniently located near downtown and the cruise-ship terminal, this attractive property has rooms with city or water views. 489 units. 478 one-bedroom standard units. 11 one-bedroom suites ($499-$1599). 23 stories, interior corridors. **Parking:** on-site (fee) and valet. **Terms:** cancellation fee imposed, package plans, small pets only ($25 extra charge). **Amenities:** video games (fee), high-speed Internet, dual phone lines, voice mail, honor bars, irons, hair dryers. *Some:* CD players, safes. **Dining:** Herons Restaurant, see separate listing. **Pool(s):** heated outdoor. **Leisure Activities:** whirlpool, steamrooms. *Fee:* massage. **Guest Services:** valet laundry. **Business Services:** conference facilities, business center. **Cards:** AX, DC, MC, VI.

SOME UNITS

FOUR SEASONS HOTEL VANCOUVER — *Book at aaa.com* — Phone: (604)689-9333 — **20**

CAA SAVE

5/1-10/31	1P: $320-$1060	2P: $320-$1060	XP: $30	F18
3/1-4/30 & 11/1-2/28	1P: $230-$780	2P: $230-$780	XP: $30	F18

▼▼▼▼ **Location:** Howe and W Georgia sts. Connected to a shopping complex. 791 W Georgia St V6C 2T4. Fax: 604/684-4555. **Facility:** A luxury downtown hotel featuring impeccable service; a large shopping **Large-scale Hotel** complex is attached. 376 units. 308 one-bedroom standard units. 68 one-bedroom suites ($440-$1060). 28 stories, interior corridors. **Parking:** on-site (fee) and valet. **Terms:** cancellation fee imposed, small pets only. **Amenities:** dual phone lines, voice mail, safes, honor bars, irons, hair dryers. *Fee:* video games, high-speed Internet. *Some:* DVD players, CD players, fax. **Dining:** 2 restaurants, 6:30 am-11 pm, cocktails, also, Chartwell, see separate listing. **Pool(s):** heated indoor/outdoor. **Leisure Activities:** saunas, whirlpool. *Fee:* massage. **Guest Services:** gift shop, valet laundry, area transportation-downtown. **Business Services:** conference facilities, business center. **Cards:** AX, DC, JC, MC, VI. **Special Amenities:** free newspaper and free room upgrade (subject to availability with advance reservations).

SOME UNITS

THE GEORGIAN COURT HOTEL — *Book at aaa.com* — Phone: (604)682-5555 — **35**

▼▼▼

5/1-10/15	1P: $185-$240	2P: $205-$260	XP: $20	F17
3/1-4/30 & 10/16-2/28	1P: $115-$135	2P: $115-$135	XP: $20	F17

Small-scale Hotel **Location:** Between Georgia and Robson sts. Located opposite the stadium. 773 Beatty St V6B 2M4. Fax: 604/682-8830. **Facility:** 180 units. 179 one- and 1 two-bedroom standard units. 12 stories, interior corridors. **Parking:** on-site (fee). **Terms:** package plans, small pets only ($20 extra charge). **Amenities:** high-speed Internet, voice mail, honor bars, irons, hair dryers. **Dining:** The William Tell, see separate listing. **Leisure Activities:** sauna, whirlpool, limited exercise equipment. **Guest Services:** gift shop, valet laundry. **Business Services:** meeting rooms. **Cards:** AX, CB, DC, JC, MC, VI.

SOME UNITS

GRANVILLE ISLAND HOTEL — *Book at aaa.com* — Phone: (604)683-7373 — **39**

CAA SAVE ▼▼▼

5/1-9/30	1P: $190-$220	2P: $200-$230	XP: $10	F16
3/1-4/30 & 10/1-2/28	1P: $140-$150	2P: $150-$160	XP: $10	F16

Location: Granville Island; below the bridge, follow signs. 1253 Johnston St V6H 3R9. Fax: 604/683-3061.
Facility: 82 one-bedroom standard units, some with whirlpools. 3-4 stories, interior corridors. **Parking:** on-**Small-scale Hotel** site (fee). **Terms:** package plans, pets ($25 extra charge). **Amenities:** high-speed Internet, dual phone lines, voice mail, honor bars, irons, hair dryers. **Dining:** Dockside Brewing Company, see separate listing. **Leisure Activities:** sauna, whirlpool, rental bicycles. **Guest Services:** valet laundry. **Business Services:** meeting rooms. **Cards:** AX, DC, DS, JC, MC, VI. *(See color ad p 549)*

SOME UNITS

(See map and index starting on p. 531)

HAMPTON INN & SUITES DOWNTOWN
VANCOUVER   *Book at aaa.com*   Phone: (604)602-1008   **30**

(CAA) (SAVE)   6/15-9/30 [ECP]   1P: $225-$289   2P: $225-$289
WWWW   5/1-6/14 [ECP]   1P: $199-$229   2P: $199-$229
             3/1-4/30 & 10/1-2/28 [ECP]   1P: $145-$180   2P: $145-$180

Location: Between Cambie and Beatty sts. 111 Robson St V6B 2A8. Fax: 604/602-1007. **Facility:** 132 one-bedroom standard units, some with efficiencies, kitchens and/or whirlpools. 16 stories, interior corridors. **Parking:** on-site (fee). **Terms:** cancellation fee imposed. **Amenities:** video games (fee), high-speed Internet, dual phone lines, voice mail, safes, irons, hair dryers. **Dining:** 7 am-10 pm, cocktails. **Leisure Activities:** sauna, whirlpool, limited exercise equipment. **Guest Services:** gift shop, valet and coin laundry, area transportation-downtown. **Business Services:** meeting rooms. **Cards:** AX, CB, DC, DS, JC, MC, VI. **Special Amenities:** free expanded continental breakfast and free local telephone calls. *(See color ad p 544, p 545 & p 552)*

SOME UNITS

HOLIDAY INN HOTEL & SUITES
VANCOUVER-DOWNTOWN   *Book at aaa.com*   Phone: (604)684-2151   **26**

(CAA) (SAVE)   6/1-10/8   1P: $199-$299   2P: $199-$299   XP: $20   F
WWWW   3/1-5/31 & 10/9-10/31   1P: $179-$249   2P: $179-$249   XP: $20   F
             11/1-2/28   1P: $109-$159   2P: $109-$159   XP: $20   F

Location: Between Helmcken and Davie sts. 1110 Howe St V6Z 1R2. Fax: 604/684-4736. **Facility:** 245 one-bedroom standard units, some with efficiencies, kitchens and/or whirlpools. 7 stories, interior corridors. *Bath:* combo or shower only. **Parking:** on-site (fee). **Terms:** cancellation fee imposed, small pets only. **Amenities:** video games (fee), high-speed Internet, voice mail, irons, hair dryers. *Some:* honor bars. **Dining:** 6:30 am-11 pm, cocktails. **Pool(s):** heated indoor. **Leisure Activities:** saunas, unsupervised children's play center, exercise room. **Guest Services:** gift shop, valet and coin laundry. **Business Services:** meeting rooms, PC. **Cards:** AX, MC, VI. **Special Amenities:** free newspaper and early check-in/late check-out. *(See color ad card insert)*

SOME UNITS

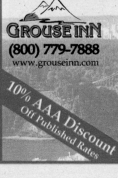

(See map and index starting on p. 531)

HOTEL LE SOLEIL   *Book at aaa.com*   Phone: (604)632-3000   **43**

(CAA) (SAVE)
5/1-10/15	1P: $245-$275	2P: $245-$275	XP: $25 F18
3/1-4/30 & 10/16-2/28	1P: $165-$195	2P: $165-$195	XP: $25 F18

▽▽▽ ▽▽▽ **Location:** Between Dunsmuir and Pender sts. 567 Hornby St V6C 2E8. Fax: 604/632-3001. **Facility:** This service-oriented luxury hotel is decorated with furnishings, fabrics and fine artwork imported from Europe. 119 units.
Small-scale Hotel 9 one-bedroom standard units. 110 one-bedroom suites, some with whirlpools. 16 stories, interior corridors. **Bath:** combo or shower only. **Parking:** valet. **Terms:** package plans, small pets only ($75 fee).
Amenities: high-speed Internet, dual phone lines, voice mail, safes, honor bars, irons, hair dryers. *Some:* fax. **Dining:** 6:30 am-10 pm, cocktails, also, Oritalia, see separate listing. **Guest Services:** valet laundry. **Business Services:** meeting rooms.
Cards: AX, DC, MC, VI. **Special Amenities:** free newspaper and free room upgrade (subject to availability with advance reservations).

SOME UNITS
(S/D) 🐾 🍴 🍸 👤M ♿ 🎥 DATA/PORT 💻 / ✕ /
FEE

HOWARD JOHNSON HOTEL   *Book at aaa.com*   Phone: (604)688-8701   **28**

(CAA) (SAVE)
6/1-9/30 [CP]	1P: $139-$229	2P: $139-$229	XP: $15 F16
5/1-5/31 [CP]	1P: $99-$189	2P: $99-$189	XP: $15 F16
3/1-4/30 & 10/1-2/28 [BP]	1P: $89-$159	2P: $89-$159	XP: $15 F16

▽▽▽ ▽▽▽ **Location:** Between Davie and Helmcken sts. 1176 Granville St V6Z 1L8. Fax: 604/688-8335. **Facility:** 110 units.
Small-scale Hotel 105 one-bedroom standard units. 5 one-bedroom suites ($159-$249). 5 stories, interior corridors. **Parking:** on-site (fee). **Terms:** cancellation fee imposed, package plans, small pets only ($40 extra charge).
Amenities: high-speed Internet, voice mail, hair dryers. *Some:* fax, irons. **Dining:** 7 am-11 pm, cocktails. **Guest Services:** valet and coin laundry. **Cards:** AX, CB, DC, DS, JC, MC, VI. **Special Amenities:** free newspaper and early check-in/late check-out. *(See color ad below)*

SOME UNITS
(S/D) 🛏 🍴 🍸 ♿ 🎥 DATA/PORT 💻 / ✕ 🛗 🖼 /
FEE

HYATT REGENCY VANCOUVER   *Book at aaa.com*   Phone: (604)683-1234   **12**

(CAA) (SAVE)
5/1-10/31	1P: $195-$295	2P: $195-$295
3/1-4/30 & 11/1-2/28	1P: $109-$229	2P: $109-$229

▽▽▽▽ **Location:** Between W Georgia and Melville sts. Connected to shopping centre. 655 Burrard St V6C 2R7.
Large-scale Hotel Fax: 604/689-3707. **Facility:** 645 units. 634 one-bedroom standard units. 10 one- and 1 two-bedroom suites. 34 stories, interior corridors. **Bath:** combo or shower only. **Parking:** on-site (fee) and valet.
Terms: check-in 4 pm, 14 day cancellation notice-fee imposed. **Amenities:** dual phone lines, voice mail, honor bars, irons, hair dryers. *Some:* high-speed Internet, safes. **Dining:** 6:30 am-11 pm, cocktails. **Pool(s):** heated outdoor.
Leisure Activities: whirlpool, exercise room. *Fee:* massage. **Guest Services:** valet laundry. **Business Services:** conference facilities, business center. **Cards:** AX, CB, DC, DS, JC, MC, VI. *(See color ad p 552)*

SOME UNITS
🍴 🍸 👤M ♿ ✈ ✕ 🎥 DATA/PORT 💻 / ✕ /

(See map and index starting on p. 531)

LANDIS HOTEL & SUITES   *Book at aaa.com*   **Phone: (604)681-3555** 32

7/1-9/30 [CP]	1P: $289-$319	2P: $299-$329	XP: $15	F12
3/1-6/30 [CP]	1P: $219-$259	2P: $229-$269	XP: $15	F12
10/1-2/28 [CP]	1P: $199-$219	2P: $209-$229	XP: $15	F12

Small-scale Hotel   **Location:** Between Drake and Davie sts. 1200 Hornby St V6Z 1W2. Fax: 604/681-9222. **Facility:** 50 two-bedroom standard units with kitchens. 18 stories, interior corridors. **Parking:** on-site (fee). **Terms:** weekly rates available, package plans. **Amenities:** high-speed Internet, dual phone lines, voice mail, irons, hair dryers. **Pool(s):** heated indoor. **Leisure Activities:** whirlpool, exercise room. **Guest Services:** valet and coin laundry, area transportation. **Cards:** AX, DC, DS, JC, MC, VI. *(See color ad p 553)*

SOME UNITS

ASK Sⓓ 🍴 🏊 VCR 🔌 🚭 📷 💻 / ⊠ /

LISTEL VANCOUVER   *Book at aaa.com*   **Phone: (604)684-8461** 7

5/1-9/30	1P: $240-$320	2P: $240-$320	XP: $20	F18
3/1-4/30 & 10/1-2/28	1P: $200-$300	2P: $200-$300	XP: $20	F18

Small-scale Hotel   **Location:** Between Broughton and Jervis sts. 1300 Robson St V6E 1C5. Fax: 604/684-7092. **Facility:** Smoke free premises. 130 one-bedroom standard units. 6 stories, interior corridors. **Parking:** on-site (fee) and valet. **Terms:** package plans. **Amenities:** high-speed Internet, dual phone lines, voice mail, honor bars, irons, hair dryers. **Leisure Activities:** whirlpool, limited exercise equipment. **Guest Services:** valet laundry. **Business Services:** meeting rooms. **Cards:** AX, CB, DC, DS, JC, MC, VI.

ASK Sⓓ 🍴 🍷 ⊠ 🎥 🔌 💻

(See map and index starting on p. 531)

METROPOLITAN HOTEL   *Book at aaa.com*   Phone: (604)687-1122   [16]

(CAA) (SAVE)   5/1-9/30   1P: $219-$399   2P: $219-$399

▽▽▽ ▽▽▽   3/1-4/30 & 10/1-2/28   1P: $189-$335   2P: $189-$335

Location: Between Georgia and Dunsmuir sts. Located across from shopping mall. 645 Howe St V6C 2Y9.
Fax: 604/643-7267. **Facility:** The hotel features an understated, oak-dominated decor; all rooms feature a
Large-scale Hotel small balcony. 197 units. 181 one-bedroom standard units. 16 one-bedroom suites, some with whirlpools. 18
stories, interior corridors. **Parking:** on-site (fee) and valet. **Terms:** cancellation fee imposed, package plans,
small pets only. **Amenities:** CD players, dual phone lines, voice mail, safes, honor bars, irons, hair dryers. *Fee:* video games,
high-speed Internet. **Dining:** Diva at the Met, see separate listing. **Pool(s):** small heated indoor. **Leisure Activities:** saunas,
whirlpool, steamroom, exercise room. *Fee:* massage. **Guest Services:** valet laundry, area transportation-downtown. **Business
Services:** meeting rooms, business center. **Cards:** AX, DC, DS, JC, MC, VI.

SOME UNITS

(S/D) 🐾 🍴 24⊤ ⊺ (&M) ⊘ ⇌ ⊠ 🎥 [DATA PORT] ☕ / ⊠ /

'O CANADA' HOUSE B&B   Phone: (604)688-0555   [14]

5/1-10/31 [BP]   2P: $185-$255   XP: $20

▽▽▽   3/1-4/30 & 11/1-2/28 [BP]   2P: $135-$195   XP: $20

Historic Bed   **Location:** Between Thurlow and Bute sts. Located in a residential area in West End. 1114 Barclay St V6E 1H1.
& Breakfast   Fax: 604/488-0556. **Facility:** This restored 1897 Victorian home is in a West End neighborhood within
walking distance of many restaurants and shops. Smoke free premises. 6 one-bedroom standard units. 3
stories (no elevator), interior corridors. *Bath:* combo or shower only. **Parking:** on-site. **Terms:** office hours 7 am-7 pm, 2 night
minimum stay - weekends, age restrictions may apply, 7 day cancellation notice. **Amenities:** video library, hair dryers.
Cards: MC, VI.

(ASK) ⊠ (AC) (VCR) 🍴

PACIFIC PALISADES HOTEL   *Book at aaa.com*   Phone: (604)688-0461   [8]

(CAA) (SAVE)   5/1-10/15   1P: $185-$390   2P: $185-$390   XP: $30   F

▽▽▽   3/1-4/30 & 10/16-2/28   1P: $130-$390   2P: $130-$390   XP: $30   F

Location: Between Jervis and Bute sts. 1277 Robson St V6E 1C4. Fax: 604/688-4374. **Facility:** 233 one-bedroom
standard units, some with kitchens. 20-23 stories, interior corridors. **Parking:** on-site (fee) and valet.
Large-scale Hotel **Terms:** cancellation fee imposed, small pets only. **Amenities:** video games (fee), high-speed Internet, dual
phone lines, voice mail, honor bars, irons, hair dryers. **Dining:** Zin, see separate listing. **Pool(s):** heated
indoor. **Leisure Activities:** whirlpool, steamroom. *Fee:* massage. **Guest Services:** valet and coin laundry. **Business Services:**
meeting rooms. **Cards:** AX, DC, JC, MC, VI. **Special Amenities:** free newspaper and early check-in/late check-out.

SOME UNITS

(S/D) 🐾 🍴 24⊤ ⊺ (&M) ⊘ ⇌ 🏋 ⊠ 🎥 [DATA PORT] 🖥 ☕ / ⊠ 🍴 /

(See map and index starting on p. 531)

PAN PACIFIC VANCOUVER   *Book at aaa.com*   Phone: (604)662-8111 [11]

CAA SAVE

5/1-10/31	1P: $490-$540	2P: $490-$540	XP: $35	F18
3/1-4/30 & 11/1-2/28	1P: $390-$420	2P: $390-$420	XP: $35	F18

Location: Motor entrance off Burrard St. Located at Canada Place. 300-999 Canada Place V6C 3B5.
Large-scale Hotel **Fax:** 604/685-8690. **Facility:** This service-oriented hotel is attached to the convention center as well as a pier where huge cruise ships dock during summer months. 504 units. 473 one-bedroom standard units. 29 one- and 2 two-bedroom suites ($650-$3800), some with kitchens and/or whirlpools. 23 stories, interior corridors. **Parking:** on-site (fee) and valet. **Terms:** check-in 4 pm, 7% service charge, small pets only ($30 extra charge). **Amenities:** CD players, dual phone lines, voice mail, safes, honor bars, irons, hair dryers. *Fee:* video games, high-speed Internet. *Some:* fax. **Dining:** 3 restaurants, 6:30 am-11 pm, cocktails, also, Five Sails Restaurant, see separate listing, entertainment. **Pool(s):** heated outdoor. **Leisure Activities:** saunas, whirlpools, steamrooms, spa. *Fee:* racquetball court, squash. **Guest Services:** gift shop, valet laundry, area transportation-downtown. **Business Services:** conference facilities, business center. **Cards:** AX, MC, VI. **Special Amenities:** free newspaper and early check-in/late check-out. *(See color ad below)*

SOME UNITS

QUALITY HOTEL DOWNTOWN-THE INN AT FALSE
CREEK   *Book at aaa.com*   Phone: (604)682-0229 [36]

6/1-9/30	1P: $179-$209	2P: $179-$209	XP: $20	F18
5/1-5/31	1P: $149-$189	2P: $149-$189	XP: $20	F18
3/1-4/30	1P: $99-$139	2P: $99-$139	XP: $20	F18
10/1-2/28	1P: $89-$139	2P: $89-$139	XP: $20	F18

Small-scale Hotel **Location:** Between Drake and Pacific sts. 1335 Howe St V6Z 1R7. Fax: 604/662-7566. **Facility:** 157 units. 137 one-bedroom standard units. 20 one-bedroom suites ($139-$229), some with kitchens. 7 stories, interior corridors. **Parking:** on-site (fee). **Terms:** cancellation fee imposed, weekly rates available, package plans, small pets only ($15 extra charge). **Amenities:** voice mail, irons, hair dryers. *Some:* high-speed Internet, dual phone lines. **Pool(s):** small heated outdoor. **Guest Services:** valet laundry. **Business Services:** meeting rooms. **Cards:** AX, CB, JC, MC, VI.

SOME UNITS

RAMADA INN & SUITES DOWNTOWN VANCOUVER   *Book at aaa.com*   Phone: (604)685-1111 [34]

CAA SAVE

7/1-10/8	1P: $139-$199	2P: $149-$209	XP: $10	F18
5/1-6/30	1P: $109-$169	2P: $119-$179	XP: $10	F18
10/9-2/28	1P: $99-$139	2P: $109-$169	XP: $10	F18
3/1-4/30	1P: $89-$149	2P: $99-$159	XP: $10	F18

Small-scale Hotel **Location:** Between Davie and Drake sts. Located in Granville Street District. 1221 Granville St V6Z 1M6. **Fax:** 604/685-0707. **Facility:** 116 one-bedroom standard units, some with efficiencies. 6 stories, interior corridors. *Bath:* combo or shower only. **Parking:** on-site (fee) and valet. **Terms:** check-in 4 pm, cancellation fee imposed, [BP] meal plan available, package plans, pets ($20 extra charge). **Amenities:** voice mail, irons, hair dryers. **Dining:** 7 am-10 pm, cocktails. **Guest Services:** valet laundry. **Business Services:** meeting rooms. **Cards:** AX, DC, DS, JC, MC, VI. **Special Amenities:** free local telephone calls and free newspaper. *(See color ad p 555)*

SOME UNITS

(See map and index starting on p. 531)

RAMADA LIMITED DOWNTOWN VANCOUVER   *Book at aaa.com*   Phone: (604)488-1088   22

CAA SAVE

| 5/16-9/30 [ECP] | 1P: $189 | 2P: $189 | XP: $15 | F17 |
| 3/1-5/15 & 10/1-2/28 [ECP] | 1P: $119 | 2P: $119 | XP: $15 | F17 |

Small-scale Hotel **Location:** Between Homer and Richards sts. 435 W Pender St V6B 1V2. Fax: 604/488-1090. **Facility:** 80 one-bedroom standard units. 6 stories, interior corridors. **Parking:** valet. **Amenities:** high-speed Internet, dual phone lines, voice mail, irons, hair dryers. **Guest Services:** valet and coin laundry. **Business Services:** meeting rooms. **Cards:** AX, DC, DS, MC, VI. **Special Amenities: free expanded continental breakfast and free newspaper.** *(See color ad below)*

SOME UNITS

$D 11+ M DATA PORT / X /

RENAISSANCE VANCOUVER HOTEL
HARBOURSIDE   *Book at aaa.com*   Phone: (604)689-9211   3

CAA SAVE

| 5/1-10/14 | 1P: $209-$239 | 2P: $209-$239 | XP: $30 | F18 |
| 3/1-4/30 & 10/15-2/28 | 1P: $129-$159 | 2P: $129-$159 | XP: $30 | F18 |

Large-scale Hotel **Location:** Between Bute and Thurlow sts. 1133 W Hastings St V6E 3T3. Fax: 604/689-4358. **Facility:** 438 units. 426 one-bedroom standard units. 12 one-bedroom suites. 19 stories, interior corridors. **Parking:** on-site (fee) and valet. **Terms:** cancellation fee imposed, pets ($25 extra charge). **Amenities:** video games (fee), high-speed Internet, voice mail, honor bars, irons, hair dryers. *Some:* safes. **Dining:** 2 restaurants, 6:30 am-2 & 5:30-10 pm, cocktails, also, Vistas Revolving Restaurant, see separate listing, entertainment. **Pool(s):** small heated indoor. **Leisure Activities:** sauna, whirlpool. *Fee:* massage. **Guest Services:** gift shop, valet laundry, area transportation-downtown. **Business Services:** meeting rooms, business center. **Cards:** AX, CB, DC, DS, JC, MC, VI. **Special Amenities: free newspaper and preferred room (subject to availability with advance reservations).** *(See color ad p 556)*

SOME UNITS

$D ⊟ 11 Y M ⇌ ⊷ X DATA PORT / X /
FEE

RESIDENCE INN BY MARRIOTT VANCOUVER   *Book at aaa.com*   Phone: (604)688-1234   33

CAA SAVE

6/1-9/30 [BP]	1P: $179-$233	2P: $179-$233	XP: $20	F18
5/1-5/31 [BP]	1P: $152-$197	2P: $152-$197	XP: $20	F18
3/1-4/30 & 10/1-2/28 [BP]	1P: $107-$134	2P: $107-$134	XP: $20	F18

Small-scale Hotel **Location:** Between Drake and Davie sts. 1234 Hornby St V6Z 1W2. Fax: 604/689-1762. **Facility:** 200 one-bedroom standard units, some with efficiencies or kitchens. 22 stories, interior corridors. **Parking:** on-site (fee). **Terms:** check-in 4 pm, cancellation fee imposed, pets ($75 fee, $5 extra charge). **Amenities:** video games (fee), high-speed Internet, voice mail, irons, hair dryers. **Dining:** 3 pm-10 pm, cocktails. **Pool(s):** heated indoor. **Leisure Activities:** whirlpool, exercise room. **Guest Services:** valet and coin laundry. **Business Services:** meeting rooms. **Cards:** AX, DC, DS, JC, MC, VI. **Special Amenities: free full breakfast and free newspaper.** *(See color ad p 556)*

SOME UNITS

$D ⊟ 11 M ⇌ ⊷ DATA PORT ⊟ ⊞ / X /
FEE

(See map and index starting on p. 531)

ST REGIS HOTEL *Book at aaa.com* Phone: (604)681-1135 **45**

(See map and index starting on p. 531)

SANDMAN HOTEL DOWNTOWN VANCOUVER — *Book at aaa.com* — Phone: (604)681-2211 **44**

7/1-10/15	1P: $139-$179	2P: $149-$189	XP: $10
5/1-6/30	1P: $129-$169	2P: $139-$179	XP: $10
3/1-4/30 & 10/16-2/28	1P: $109-$149	2P: $119-$159	XP: $10

Small-scale Hotel **Location:** Between Cambie and Beatty sts. 180 W Georgia St V6B 4P4. Fax: 604/681-8009. **Facility:** 303 one-bedroom standard units. 11-12 stories, interior corridors. **Parking:** on-site (fee). **Terms:** [AP] meal plan available, package plans, small pets only ($10 extra charge). **Amenities:** video games (fee), voice mail, hair dryers. *Some:* irons. **Pool(s):** heated indoor. **Leisure Activities:** whirlpool. **Guest Services:** gift shop, valet laundry. **Business Services:** meeting rooms. **Cards:** AX, CB, DC, DS, JC, MC, VI.

SOME UNITS

ASK SD ⊞ ¶¶ ⬛ ➷ (↔) 📷 DATA PORT 🖥 / ✕ /
FEE   FEE

SHERATON VANCOUVER WALL CENTRE HOTEL — *Book at aaa.com* — Phone: (604)331-1000 **25**

(AAA) (SAVE)

5/16-10/23	1P: $225-$429	2P: $225-$429	XP: $30	F18
3/1-5/15 & 10/24-2/28	1P: $165-$369	2P: $165-$369	XP: $30	F18

Large-scale Hotel **Location:** Between Helmcken and Comox sts. 1088 Burrard St V6Z 2R9. Fax: 604/331-1001. **Facility:** Art deco styling distinguishes this 35-story hotel; rooms feature floor-to-ceiling windows with city views. 735 units. 662 one-bedroom standard units. 39 one-, 30 two- and 4 three-bedroom suites ($225-$469), some with kitchens. 28-35 stories, interior corridors. *Bath:* combo or shower only. **Parking:** on-site (fee) and valet. **Terms:** check-in 4 pm, pets ($60 extra charge). **Amenities:** video games (fee), high-speed Internet, dual phone lines, voice mail, safes, irons, hair dryers. *Some:* fax, honor bars. **Dining:** 6:30 am-11 pm, cocktails, also, Indigo Bistro, see separate listing. **Pool(s):** heated indoor. **Leisure Activities:** sauna, whirlpools, steamroom, spa. **Guest Services:** gift shop, valet laundry, area transportation-downtown. **Business Services:** conference facilities, business center. **Cards:** AX, DC, MC, VI. **Special Amenities:** free newspaper. *(See color ad below & p 5)*

SOME UNITS

SD ☐ ¶¶ 24¶ ⬛ ➷ (&M) ☺ ➷ (↔) ✕ 📷 DATA PORT 🖥 / ✕ 🔒 🖥 /
FEE   FEE

SUNSET INN & SUITES — *Book at aaa.com* — Phone: (604)688-2474 **24**

(AAA) (SAVE)

6/1-9/30	1P: $169-$259	2P: $169-$259	XP: $10	F12
10/1-12/31	1P: $149-$209	2P: $149-$209	XP: $10	F12
3/1-5/31 & 1/1-2/28	1P: $129-$209	2P: $129-$209	XP: $10	F12

Small-scale Hotel **Location:** Between Thurlow and Bute sts. 1111 Burnaby St V6E 1P4. Fax: 604/669-3340. **Facility:** 50 one-bedroom suites with kitchens. 11 stories, interior corridors. **Parking:** on-site. **Terms:** office hours 7 am-11 pm, 3 day cancellation notice, weekly rates available. **Amenities:** voice mail, irons, hair dryers. **Leisure Activities:** limited exercise equipment. **Guest Services:** coin laundry. **Cards:** AX, DC, JC, MC, VI. **Special Amenities:** free local telephone calls and preferred room (subject to availability with advance reservations). *(See color ad p 531)*

SOME UNITS

SD DATA PORT 🔒 🖥 🖥 / ✕ 🔪 /

(See map and index starting on p. 531)

THE SUTTON PLACE HOTEL　*Book at aaa.com*　　　　　　　Phone: (604)682-5511　**15**

(CAA) (SAVE)

5/1-10/31	1P: $247-$464	2P: $247-$464	XP: $30	F18
3/1-4/30 & 11/1-2/28	1P: $185-$308	2P: $185-$308	XP: $30	F18

Location: Between Smythe and Robson sts. 845 Burrard St V6Z 2K6. Fax: 604/682-5513. **Facility:** This service-oriented hotel is convenient to many shops and restaurants and features a spa and health club on site. 397

Large-scale Hotel units. 350 one-bedroom standard units. 47 one-bedroom suites ($257-$1855). 21 stories, interior corridors. **Parking:** on-site (fee) and valet. **Terms:** 3 day cancellation notice-fee imposed, package plans, pets ($150 fee). **Amenities:** DVD players, CD players, dual phone lines, voice mail, safes, honor bars, irons, hair dryers. *Fee:* video games, high-speed Internet. **Dining:** Fleuri Restaurant, see separate listing, entertainment. **Pool(s):** heated indoor. **Leisure Activities:** sauna, whirlpool, steamroom, sauna for women; steam room for men, exercise room, spa. **Guest Services:** gift shop, valet laundry, area transportation-downtown. **Business Services:** meeting rooms, business center. **Cards:** AX, CB, DC, DS, JC, MC, VI. **Special Amenities:** free newspaper. *(See color ad below)*

SOME UNITS

SYLVIA HOTEL　　　　　　　　　　　　　　　　　　Phone: (604)681-9321　**4**

5/1-10/31	1P: $95-$225	2P: $100-$240	XP: $15	F18
3/1-4/30 & 11/1-2/28	1P: $70-$175	2P: $80-$180	XP: $15	F18

Historic **Location:** Beach Ave and Gilford St; across from English Bay. 1154 Gilford St V6G 2P6. Fax: 604/682-3551.
Small-scale Hotel **Facility:** Ivy clings to the walls of the 1912 building which houses this hotel. 119 one-bedroom standard units, some with efficiencies or kitchens. 8 stories, interior corridors. **Parking:** on-site (fee). **Amenities:** hair dryers. **Guest Services:** valet laundry. **Cards:** AX, DC, MC, VI.

SOME UNITS

TERMINAL CITY TOWER HOTEL　*Book at aaa.com*　　　　　　Phone: (604)681-4121　**21**

4/29-10/31	1P: $200-$375	2P: $200-$375	XP: $25	F12
3/1-4/28 & 11/1-2/28	1P: $155-$255	2P: $155-$255	XP: $25	F12

Large-scale Hotel **Location:** W Hastings and Hornby sts. 837 W Hastings St V6C 1B6. Fax: 604/488-8604. **Facility:** Smoke free premises. 60 units. 30 one-bedroom standard units. 30 one-bedroom suites ($305-$375). 30 stories, interior corridors. **Parking:** on-site (fee). **Terms:** 3 day cancellation notice-fee imposed. **Amenities:** high-speed Internet, dual phone lines, voice mail, irons, hair dryers. **Pool(s):** heated indoor. **Leisure Activities:** saunas, whirlpool, steamrooms, racquetball courts. *Fee:* massage. **Guest Services:** valet laundry. **Business Services:** meeting rooms. **Cards:** AX, DC, JC, MC, VI.

(See map and index starting on p. 531)

VANCOUVER MARRIOTT PINNACLE DOWNTOWN   *Book at aaa.com*   **Phone:** (604)684-1128   **41**

| (AAA) (SAVE) | 5/1-10/14 | 1P: $259-$339 | 2P: $259-$339 | XP: $30 | F18 |
| | 3/1-4/30 & 10/15-2/28 | 1P: $199-$279 | 2P: $199-$279 | XP: $30 | F18 |

Location: Between Thurlow and Bute sts. 1128 W Hastings St V6E 4R5. Fax: 604/298-1128. **Facility:** These spacious, elegantly decorated guest rooms offer breathtaking views of the mountains, water and downtown
Large-scale Hotel Vancouver. 434 one-bedroom standard units. 31 stories, interior corridors. **Parking:** on-site (fee) and valet. **Terms:** cancellation fee imposed, package plans. **Amenities:** video games (fee), high-speed Internet, dual phone lines, voice mail, safes, honor bars, irons, hair dryers. *Some:* CD players. **Dining:** Show Case Restaurant, see separate listing. **Pool(s):** heated indoor. **Leisure Activities:** sauna, whirlpool, steamroom, exercise room. **Guest Services:** gift shop, valet laundry. **Business Services:** conference facilities, business center. **Cards:** AX, CB, DC, DS, JC, MC, VI. **Special Amenities:** free newspaper.

SOME UNITS

THE WEDGEWOOD HOTEL   *Book at aaa.com*   **Phone:** 604/689-7777   **23**

(AAA) (SAVE)	5/1-9/30	1P: $268-$448	2P: $268-$448	XP: $30	F14
	10/1-2/28	1P: $188-$438	2P: $188-$438	XP: $30	F14
	3/1-4/30	1P: $228-$408	2P: $228-$408	XP: $30	F14

Location: Between Smythe and Robson sts. 845 Hornby St V6Z 1V1. Fax: 604/608-5348. **Facility:** Afternoon tea
Small-scale Hotel is offered on weekends at this stylish yet intimate boutique hotel where attentive service is the norm. Smoke free premises. 83 units. 45 one-bedroom standard units. 38 one-bedroom suites ($398-$538), some with whirlpools. 13 stories, interior corridors. **Parking:** on-site (fee) and valet. **Terms:** cancellation fee imposed, package plans. **Amenities:** video games (fee), CD players, high-speed Internet, dual phone lines, voice mail, safes, honor bars, irons, hair dryers. **Dining:** Bacchus Restaurant, see separate listing, entertainment. **Leisure Activities:** steamroom, exercise room, spa. **Guest Services:** valet laundry. **Business Services:** meeting rooms, business center. **Cards:** AX, CB, DC, DS, JC, MC, VI. **Special Amenities:** free newspaper. *(See color ad below)*

SOME UNITS

WEST END GUEST HOUSE   **Phone:** (604)681-2889   **19**

| (AAA) (SAVE) | 5/7-9/30 [BP] | 1P: $120-$236 | 2P: $139-$255 | XP: $19 | F12 |
| | 3/1-5/6 & 10/1-2/28 [BP] | 1P: $91-$180 | 2P: $110-$199 | XP: $19 | F12 |

Location: Between Broughton and Jervis sts. Located in a quiet residential area. 1362 Haro St V6E 1G2.
Fax: 604/688-8812. **Facility:** A ghost allegedly lives in this well-preserved Victorian home located in a quiet
Historic Bed residential neighborhood known as the West End. Smoke free premises. 8 one-bedroom standard units. 2
& Breakfast stories (no elevator), interior corridors. *Bath:* combo or shower only. **Parking:** on-site. **Terms:** office hours 8 am-10 pm, 2 night minimum stay - seasonal and/or weekends, 3 day cancellation notice-fee imposed, package plans. **Amenities:** video library, hair dryers. **Leisure Activities:** bicycles. **Cards:** AX, DS, MC, VI. **Special Amenities:** free full breakfast and free local telephone calls.

SOME UNITS

THE WESTIN BAYSHORE RESORT & MARINA   *Book at aaa.com*   **Phone:** (604)682-3377   **1**

(AAA) (SAVE)	5/1-10/31	1P: $215-$460	2P: $215-$460	XP: $30	F17
	11/1-2/28	1P: $175-$360	2P: $175-$360	XP: $30	F17
	3/1-4/30	1P: $170-$350	2P: $170-$350	XP: $30	F17

Location: W Georgia and Cardero sts. 1601 Bayshore Dr V6G 2V4. Fax: 604/687-3102. **Facility:** Manicured
Large-scale Hotel grounds surround this downtown hotel; guest rooms offer good views of the harbor, city and mountains. 510 units. 482 one-bedroom standard units. 28 one-bedroom suites. 9-16 stories, interior corridors. **Parking:** on-site (fee) and valet. **Terms:** check-in 4 pm, cancellation fee imposed, package plans, small pets only. **Amenities:** video games (fee), dual phone lines, voice mail, safes, honor bars, irons, hair dryers. *Some:* high-speed Internet. **Dining:** 2 restaurants, 6:30 am-10 pm, cocktails. **Pool(s):** heated outdoor. **Leisure Activities:** saunas, whirlpool, steamroom, jogging, exercise room. *Fee:* marina, massage. **Guest Services:** gift shop, valet laundry, area transportation-downtown. **Business Services:** conference facilities, business center. **Cards:** AX, DC, DS, JC, MC, VI. *(See color ad p 5 & p 560)*

SOME UNITS

modern

luxury

At Vancouver's only downtown resort, you'll enjoy a scenic waterfront location, complete fitness facility, indoor and outdoor pools, Westin's signature Heavenly Bed® innovative cuisine at Currents Restaurant and Lounge, and the casual atmosphere of the Seawall Bar & Grill's harbourside patio.

Let us reserve your stay.
Call 604-682-3377 or 1-800-WESTIN1.
or visit westin.com/bayshore.

THE WESTIN BAYSHORE
RESORT & MARINA
Vancouver

MEMBER OF ◯ STARWOOD PREFERRED GUEST®

(See map and index starting on p. 531)

THE WESTIN GRAND, VANCOUVER   *Book at aaa.com*   Phone: (604)602-1999   **46**

5/1-10/14	1P: $219-$429	2P: $219-$429	XP: $30 F17
10/15-2/28	1P: $209-$429	2P: $209-$429	XP: $30 F17
3/1-4/30	1P: $199-$429	2P: $199-$429	XP: $30 F17

Location: Between Homer and Richards sts. 433 Robson St V6B 6L9. Fax: 604/647-2502. **Facility:** Shaped like a baby-grand piano, this chic, all-suite hotel on trendy Robson Street has floor-to-ceiling, city-view windows in every unit. 207 units. 23 one-bedroom standard units. 184 one-bedroom suites. 26 stories, interior corridors.
Large-scale Hotel
Parking: on-site (fee) and valet. **Terms:** cancellation fee imposed, small pets only ($50 extra charge). **Amenities:** dual phone lines, voice mail, safes, honor bars, irons, hair dryers. *Fee:* video games, high-speed Internet. *Some:* CD players, fax. **Dining:** 6:30 am-10 pm, cocktails. **Pool(s):** heated outdoor. **Leisure Activities:** sauna, whirlpool, steamrooms, exercise room. **Guest Services:** gift shop, valet laundry. **Business Services:** meeting rooms. **Cards:** AX, DC, DS, JC, MC, VI. **Special Amenities:** preferred room (subject to availability with advance reservations). *(See color ad p 5)*

SOME UNITS

FEE

---------- *The following lodgings were either not evaluated or did not* ----------
meet AAA rating requirements but are listed for your information only.

THE BUCHAN HOTEL   Phone: 604/685-5354

[fyi]   Did not meet all AAA rating requirements for some property operations at time of last evaluation on 10/24/2003. **Location:** Between Denmen and Chilco sts. 1906 Haro St V6G 1H7. Facilities, services, and decor
Small-scale Hotel characterize a basic property.

THE CENTURY PLAZA HOTEL & SPA   Phone: 604/687-0575

[fyi]   Not evaluated. **Location:** Between Nelson and Comox sts. 1015 Burrard St V6Z 1Y5. Facilities, services, and decor characterize a mid-range property.

---------- **WHERE TO DINE** ----------

900 WEST   Dinner: $27-$40   Phone: 604/669-9378   **45**
Location: Corner of Burrard at W Georgia St; enter from Hornby St; in The Fairmont Hotel Vancouver. 900 W Georgia St V6C 2W6. **Hours:** 5:30 pm-10 pm. Closed major holidays; also Sun & Mon. **Reservations:** required.
Steak & Seafood **Features:** In the impressive lobby area of grand old Hotel Vancouver, the restaurant lets guests peruse a wonderful "sea and steak-food" menu. Dishes show a focus on local produce, meats and seafood. The view of the incredible lobby should take into account the wonderful details that went into the restoration just a few short years ago. Included on the extensive wine list is a nice selection of by-the-glass choices. Servers are prompt and attentive. Casual dress; cocktails; entertainment. **Parking:** on-site (fee) and valet. **Cards:** AX, CB, DC, DS, JC, MC, VI.

A KETTLE OF FISH   Dinner: $18-$25   Phone: 604/682-6661   **50**
Location: Corner of Hornby and Pacific sts. 900 Pacific St V6Z 2E3. **Hours:** 5:30 pm-9:30 pm. Closed: 12/25. **Reservations:** suggested. **Features:** You'll enjoy this restaurant's enchanting, casually elegant atmosphere and lush garden setting. They are known for their commitment to fresh seafood, and the "kettle" fish soup is their specialty. Visitors and locals alike dine here. Fun, friendly staff. Cocktails. **Parking:** on-site (fee).
Seafood **Cards:** AX, DC, JC, MC, VI.

AL PORTO RISTORANTE   Lunch: $10-$16   Dinner: $13-$25   Phone: 604/683-8376   **8**
Location: Between Richards and Cambie sts; in Gastown. 321 Water St V6B 1B8. **Hours:** 11:30 am-10:30 pm, Sat & Sun from 5:30 pm. **Reservations:** suggested. **Features:** Located in the heart of Old Gastown, this restaurant is housed in a century-old Hudson Bay Trading Company warehouse. Tables upstairs offer a
Northern Italian great harbor view; the downstairs area is like dining in a Tuscan villa. The prosciutto di parma is excellent. Casual dress; cocktails. **Parking:** on-site (fee). **Cards:** AX, DC, JC, MC, VI.

AQUA RIVA   Lunch: $10-$23   Dinner: $18-$28   Phone: 604/683-5599   **49**
Location: Between Cordova and Howe sts. 200 Granville St V6C 1S4. **Hours:** 11:30 am-2:30 & 5-10 pm. Closed: 12/24, 12/25. **Reservations:** suggested. **Features:** Wood-fired pizza and Pacific tuna stand out on a menu
Peruvian of rotisserie and seafood dishes. Casual dress; cocktails. **Parking:** on-site (fee). **Cards:** AX, DC, JC, MC, VI.

BACCHUS RESTAURANT   Lunch: $9-$17   Dinner: $20-$35   Phone: 604/608-5319   **36**
Location: Between Smythe and Robson sts; in Wedgewood Hotel. 845 Hornby St V6Z 1V1. **Hours:** 6:30 am-11 pm. **Reservations:** suggested. **Features:** The elegant establishment occupies a wonderful, boutique-style downtown hotel. On warm summer evenings, the windows are opened so diners can people-watch. The creative menu reflects a heavy French influence, and each night a special entree is prepared in the classical
French French style along with a la carte menu items. A signature appetizer is the caramelized pan-seared day scallops. The staff is highly attentive. Dressy casual; cocktails; entertainment. **Parking:** on-site and valet. **Cards:** AX, CB, DC, DS, JC, MC, VI.

BLUE WATER CAFE   Lunch: $8-$18   Dinner: $10-$21   Phone: 604/688-8078   **53**
Location: Between Nelson and Helmcken sts. 1095 Hamilton St V6B 5T4. **Hours:** 11 am-11 pm. Closed: 12/25. **Reservations:** suggested. **Features:** In the hip Yaletown district, the cafe has a wonderful oyster bar, fresh fish, live lobster and crab tank, as well as premium steaks and sushi items. During warm weather, the patio
Seafood is a hot spot for people-watching. Casual dress; cocktails. **Parking:** street. **Cards:** AX, DC, JC, MC, VI.

(See map and index starting on p. 531)

BRIX RESTAURANT & WINE BAR **Dinner:** $19-$26 **Phone:** 604/915-9463 (62)
Pacific Rim
cocktails.
Location: Between Helmcken and Davie sts. 1138 Homer St V6B 2X6. **Hours:** 5 pm-1 am. Closed major holidays. **Reservations:** required. **Features:** A nice place to drop in for a glass of wine and a bite, the restaurant is pure Yaletown—a funky old space with wood floors and high ceilings. A wine list with 50-odd by-the-glass choices complements the tapas selections, as well as items on the varied main menu. Casual dress; cocktails. **Parking:** street. **Cards:** AX, DC, MC, VI.

CACTUS CLUB CAFE **Lunch:** $9-$27 **Dinner:** $9-$27 **Phone:** 604/687-3278 (16)
Canadian
overlook the street.
Location: Between Bute and Thurlow sts. 1136 Robson St V6E 1B2. **Hours:** 11 am-midnight, Fri & Sat-1:30 am. Closed: 12/25. **Features:** On trendy Robson Street, the casual restaurant prepares huge beef burgers, sandwiches, a little bit of pasta and heartier entrees, such as steak and chicken dinners. The three thick and creamy milkshakes come highly recommended. Small patio decks, which allow for great people-watching, overlook the street. Casual dress; cocktails. **Parking:** street. **Cards:** AX, MC, VI.

CAFE DE MEDICI **Lunch:** $15-$22 **Dinner:** $15-$35 **Phone:** 604/669-9322 (20)
Italian
Location: Between Burrard and Thurlow sts. 109-1025 Robson St V6E 1A9. **Hours:** noon-2:30 & 5:30-10:30 pm, Sat from 5:30 pm, Sun 5:30 pm-10 pm. Closed: 12/25. **Reservations:** suggested. **Features:** On fashionable Robson Street, the distinctive restaurant is tucked away in a small courtyard. On sunny days, patrons linger on the large patio deck. Included on a menu of primarily traditional fare are antipasto, wonderful pasta preparations, lighter fare and larger main dishes. A nice wine list accents the menu. Casual dress; cocktails. **Parking:** street. **Cards:** AX, DC, MC, VI.

CAFE DE PARIS **Lunch:** $9-$18 **Dinner:** $19-$26 **Phone:** 604/687-1418 (1)
French
Location: Between Robson and Alberni sts. 751 Denman St V6G 2L6. **Hours:** 11:30 am-2 & 5:30-10 pm, Sat & Sun from 5:30 pm. Closed: 1/1, 12/25. **Reservations:** suggested, weekends. **Features:** The long-established bistro-style French restaurant has been a West End staple since 1977. Guests can choose from among longtime menu favorites and daily chef's creations. The wonderful wine list features a nice selection of both French and British Columbia wines. Dressy casual; cocktails. **Parking:** street. **Cards:** AX, MC, VI.

CAFE PRESTO PANINI **Lunch:** $9-$14 **Dinner:** $9-$14 **Phone:** 604/684-4445 (6)
Italian
Parking is at street meters or in nearby lots.
Location: Between Robson and Smythe sts. 895 Hornby St V6Z 1T9. **Hours:** 11:30 am-2 & 5-9 pm, Sat from 5 pm. Closed major holidays; also Sun. **Reservations:** suggested, for lunch. **Features:** The small cafe satisfies cravings for reasonably priced homemade food, from delicious grilled panini sandwiches on focaccia bread to penne or linguine pasta with any of six sauces. Vegetarian choices also are available. Parking is at street meters or in nearby lots. Casual dress; beer & wine only. **Parking:** street. **Cards:** AX, DC, MC, VI.

CARDERO'S RESTAURANT **Lunch:** $9-$18 **Dinner:** $18-$25 **Phone:** 604/669-7666 (22)
Pacific Rim
Location: Between Cardero and Nicola sts. 1583 Coal Harbour Quay V6G 3E7. **Hours:** 11:30 am-11 pm, Sun-10 pm. Closed: 12/25. **Reservations:** suggested. **Features:** The waterfront restaurant presents a selection of fresh grilled fish, juicy rib-eye steaks, wok squid and wood oven pizzas. Casual dress; cocktails. **Parking:** valet. **Cards:** AX, MC, VI.

CHARTWELL **Dinner:** $19-$37 **Phone:** 604/689-9333 (25)
Continental
casual; cocktails.
Location: Howe and W Georgia sts; in Four Seasons Hotel Vancouver. 791 W Georgia St V6C 2T4. **Hours:** 5 pm-10 pm. Closed: 1/1-1/5. **Reservations:** required. **Features:** You'll enjoy this restaurant's understated elegance warmed by the glow of a fireplace. The highest-quality ingredients are used, and meals such as rack of lamb, salmon and lobster are expertly presented. Friendly, attentive service. Validated parking. Dressy casual; cocktails. **Parking:** on-site and valet. **Cards:** AX, CB, DC, DS, JC, MC, VI.

CIAO BELLA RISTORANTE **Lunch:** $8-$13 **Dinner:** $13-$20 **Phone:** 604/688-5771 (2)
Italian
(fee).
Location: Between Robson and Alberni sts. 703 Denman St V6G 2L6. **Hours:** 11:30 am-2:30 & 5-10:30 pm. Closed: 12/25. **Features:** Patrons can taste some excellent Italian food. Convenient parking is at the rear of the building, just off Alberni Street. The menu lists many classics—including pasta dishes with authentic sauces and hearty main courses. This place is well worth the stop. Casual dress; cocktails. **Parking:** on-site (fee). **Cards:** AX, DC, JC, MC, VI.

CINCIN **Lunch:** $13-$17 **Dinner:** $16-$36 **Phone:** 250/688-7338 (15)
Mediterranean
Parking: on-site (fee).
Location: Between Bute and Thurlow sts. 1154 Robson St V6E 1B5. **Hours:** 11:30 am-2:30 & 5-11 pm, Sat & Sun from 5 pm. Closed: 1/1, 12/25. **Reservations:** suggested. **Features:** The menu at this restaurant features homemade sausage, pasta and thin-crust, wood-oven pizza. The bustling atmosphere is known as a trendy place—sometimes film stars dine here. The service is prompt and attentive. Casual dress; cocktails. **Parking:** on-site (fee). **Cards:** AX, DC, DS, JC, MC, VI.

C RESTAURANT **Lunch:** $18-$25 **Dinner:** $27-$35 **Phone:** 604/681-1164 (60)
Seafood
Location: 1 blk below Beach Ave. 2-1600 Howe St V6Z 2L9. **Hours:** 11:30 am-2:30 & 5:30-10 pm, Sat & Sun from 5:30 pm. Closed: 12/25, 12/26. **Reservations:** required. **Features:** Located along the seawall just at the end of Howe St, one of the biggest treats is dining on the outdoor patio during the summer. This restaurant features a wonderful array of fresh fish and seafood along with an extensive wine list that will compliment each of every dish. Recommend using valet parking since parking is limited in this area. Casual dress; cocktails. **Parking:** valet. **Cards:** AX, DC, MC, VI.

(See map and index starting on p. 531)

DA PASTA BAR ON ROBSON Lunch: $7-$14 Dinner: $11-$17 Phone: 604/688-1288 (51)
Italian
Location: Between Jervis and Bute sts. 1232 Robson St V6E 1C1. **Hours:** 11:30 am-10 pm. Closed: 1/1, 12/25.
Features: You'll certainly enjoy this restaurant's fresh pasta with a Canadian West Coast flair. Combine your favorite pasta with one of their 15 creative sauces. The decor is close and cozy, but seating may be limited. Casual dress; cocktails. **Parking:** on-site (fee). **Cards:** AX, MC, VI.

DELILAH'S Dinner: $23-$33 Phone: 604/687-3424 (27)
Pacific Rim
DC, MC, VI.
Location: Between Denman and Bidwell sts. 1789 Comox St V6G 1P5. **Hours:** 5:30 pm-11:30 pm. Closed: 12/25, 12/26. **Reservations:** suggested. **Features:** Just off trendy Denman Street, the tucked-away restaurant is known for its martinis and over-the-top atmosphere. All dinners—from the small, two-course selection to the full, four-course feast—are prix fixe. Casual dress; cocktails. **Parking:** on-site (fee) and street. **Cards:** AX,

DIVA AT THE MET Lunch: $12-$24 Dinner: $22-$35 Phone: 604/602-7788 (24)
Regional
Canadian
Location: Between Georgia and Dunsmuir sts; in Metropolitan Hotel. 645 Howe St V6C 2Y9. **Hours:** 6:30 am-11 pm.
Reservations: required. **Features:** An affluent clientele patronizes the fashionable fine-dining establishment. Creative nouvelle cuisine, which is equal parts health-conscious and delicious, is elevated to an art form. Dressy casual; cocktails. **Parking:** on-site and valet. **Cards:** AX, CB, DC, JC, MC, VI.

DOCKSIDE BREWING COMPANY Lunch: $10-$15 Dinner: $20-$30 Phone: 604/685-7070 (70)
Steak & Seafood
Cards: AX, DC, MC, VI.
Location: Granville Island; below the bridge, follow signs; in Granville Island Hotel. 1253 Johnston St V6H 3R9.
Hours: 7 am-10 pm. **Reservations:** suggested. **Features:** Floor-to-ceiling windows offer views of the marina, and a 50-foot aquarium adds to the restaurant's charm. In the heart of the kitchen is a wood-fired grill where breakfast, lunch and dinner dishes are prepared. Casual dress; cocktails. **Parking:** on-site.

DON FRANCESCO RISTORANTE *Menu on aaa.com* Lunch: $25-$30 Dinner: $30-$40 Phone: 604/685-7770 (37)
(AAA)
Italian
Location: Between Smythe and Robson sts. 860 Burrard St V6Z 1X9. **Hours:** 11:30 am-3 & 5-11 pm, Sun from 5 pm. Closed: 1/1, 12/25. **Reservations:** suggested. **Features:** Located in heart of Vancouver's vibrant downtown area, this wonderful Italian restaurant offers market-fresh specialties prepared with a Mediterranean flare, served in a warm and inviting atmosphere. Dressy casual; cocktails. **Parking:** on-site (fee). **Cards:** AX, DC, MC, VI.

EARLS ON TOP Lunch: $8-$15 Dinner: $8-$15 Phone: 604/669-0020 (17)
Canadian
MC, VI.
Location: Between Bute and Thurlow sts. 1185 Robson St V6E 1B5. **Hours:** 11:30 am-10 pm. Closed: 12/25.
Features: On trendy Robson Street, the second-floor eatery overlooks the busy street, allowing for great people-watching. On the menu are burgers, salads and a large array of appetizers. Monthly specials are popular, and the servers are very friendly. Casual dress; cocktails. **Parking:** street. **Cards:** AX, DC,

ELIXIR BAR & RESTAURANT Lunch: $10-$18 Dinner: $15-$28 Phone: 604/642-0557 (63)
French
Location: Between Hamilton and Mainland sts. 350 Davie St V6B 5Z6. **Hours:** 6:30 am-11 pm.
Reservations: suggested. **Features:** Guests feel as if they have been transported to Paris. The design is pure Parisian, and the funky lounge is known for its martinis. Delightful surprises abound on the classic French brasserie menu. Dressy casual; cocktails. **Parking:** valet and street. **Cards:** AX, DC, MC, VI.

EZOGIKU NOODLE CAFE Lunch: $6-$9 Dinner: $6-$9 Phone: 604/685-8606 (12)
Japanese
acceptable method of payment at the restaurant, which offers mostly counter service. Casual dress. **Parking:** street.
Location: Between Jervis and Broughton. 1329 Robson St V6E 1C6. **Hours:** 11 am-11 pm. Closed: 12/25.
Features: The Japanese noodle shop offers something different from standard restaurants. For less than $10, diners can order a steaming bowl of egg noodles served with a choice of three mouthwatering broths and a choice of such complementary items as teriyaki chicken, wontons or seafood. Cash is the only

FIDDLEHEAD JOE'S Lunch: $9-$12 Dinner: $14-$24 Phone: 604/688-1969 (55)
Continental
personal pizzas are good, but lamb lasagna is a favorite. The view of the marina is breathtaking. Casual dress; cocktails. **Parking:** on-site (fee) and street. **Cards:** MC, VI.
Location: Between Thurlow and Hornby sts; under the Burrard Bridge by the Aquatic Centre. 1A-1012 Beach Ave V6E 1T7. **Hours:** 10 am-10 pm, Sat & Sun 9 am-11 pm. Closed: 12/24, 12/25, 12/26. **Reservations:** accepted, for dinner. **Features:** Tucked away on a seawall curve in a labyrinth of waterfront condominiums, the unassuming little restaurant turns out some delicious food. Panini and gourmet sandwiches and eight-inch

FIVE SAILS RESTAURANT Dinner: $26-$45 Phone: 604/662-8111 (52)
Continental
Jackets suggested. Dressy casual; cocktails. **Parking:** valet. **Cards:** AX, DC, JC, MC, VI.
Location: Motor entrance off Burrard St; in The Pan Pacific Vancouver. 300-999 Canada Pl V6C 3B5. **Hours:** 6 pm-10 pm. Closed: 12/25, 12/26. **Reservations:** suggested. **Features:** Five Sails features extraordinary meals, excellent flavors, artful presentations, and breathtaking views of the harbor. The sophisticated menu includes roasted lobster, pan-seared halibut and a diverse wine list. Professional service. Validated parking.

(See map and index starting on p. 531)

FLEURI RESTAURANT   **Lunch:** $14-$25   **Dinner:** $14-$36   **Phone:** 604/682-5511   (34)
Location: Between Smythe and Robson sts; in The Sutton Place Hotel. 845 Burrard St V6Z 2K6. **Hours:** 6:30 am-11 pm. **Reservations:** suggested. **Features:** In the elegant hotel, the restaurant offers quiet seclusion from the bustling city streets. Diners enjoy consistently professional, personable service and a fine Continental menu, which includes both a la carte choices and a chef's tasting selection. Dressy casual; cocktails. **Parking:** Continental valet. **Cards:** AX, CB, DC, DS, JC, MC, VI.

FOO FAA THAI HOT POT RESTAURANT   **Dinner:** $10-$20   **Phone:** 604/688-3632   (7)
Location: Between Robson and Hard St. 832 Cardero St V6G 2G5. **Hours:** 5 pm-9:30 pm. Closed: 12/25. **Reservations:** accepted. **Features:** Dining is different here. Meals start with a hot pot, which sits inside a heating pad set in the table. When the broth comes to a boil, diners add in food items they've chosen from the conveyor belt that circles past the table. It's fresh, fun and fast. Individual Thai dishes can be ordered instead. Casual dress; cocktails. **Parking:** street. **Cards:** AX, MC, VI.

GLOWBAL GRILL & SATAY BAR   **Lunch:** $9-$12   **Dinner:** $18-$28   **Phone:** 604/602-0835   (56)
Location: Between Helmcken and Nelson sts. 1079 Mainland St V6B 5P9. **Hours:** 11:30 am-midnight, Thurs-Sat to 1 am. Closed: 12/25. **Reservations:** required. **Features:** In the funky Yaletown district, the hip grill might make visitors feel like they've stepped back into the 70s. Lending to the mood are amazing hanging lamps that look like sea anemones and great 70s-like carpet. The satay bar offers a nice selection of individually priced items, as well as a $20 sampler. Some fun wines are not badly priced, as is also the case with the entrees. Dressy casual; cocktails. **Parking:** street. **Cards:** AX, DC, MC, VI.

THE HERMITAGE   **Lunch:** $10-$16   **Dinner:** $20-$29   **Phone:** 604/689-3237   (13)
Location: Between Thurlow and Burrard sts; in courtyard area. 115 1025 Robson St V6E 4A9. **Hours:** 11:30 am-2:30 & 5:30-10:30 pm, Sat from 5:30 pm, Sun 6 pm-10 pm. Closed: 1/1, 12/25, 12/26; also 1/2. **Reservations:** suggested. **Features:** A former chef to King Leopold of Belgium, the chef/owner offers a Traditional French menu that includes delicious rack of lamb, crepes Suzette and many French specialties. Servers are trained to be proper and exact. Patio dining is available in fair weather. The restaurant sits along trendy Robson Street. Casual dress; cocktails. **Parking:** street. **Cards:** AX, DC, JC, MC, VI.

HERONS RESTAURANT   **Lunch:** $12-$20   **Dinner:** $20-$30   **Phone:** 604/691-1991   (21)
Location: Howe St at Cordova St; in The Fairmont Waterfront. 900 Canada Place Way V6C 3L5. **Hours:** 6:30 am-10 pm. **Reservations:** suggested. **Features:** Patrons are treated to panoramic views of the harbor, the mountains and distant Stanley Park. The restaurant's menu is a showcase for the best of seasonal British Columbian cuisine. The open kitchen enables guests to view the chefs as they create magic for breakfast, lunch and dinner. Try the popular Sunday brunch. Dressy casual; cocktails. **Parking:** on-site (fee) and valet. **Cards:** AX, DC, DS, MC, VI.

IL GIARDINO   **Lunch:** $12-$16   **Dinner:** $16-$37   **Phone:** 604/669-2422   (38)
Location: Corner of Pacific and Hornby sts. 1382 Hornby St V6Z 1W5. **Hours:** noon-2:30 & 5:30-11 pm, Sat from 6 pm. Closed major holidays; also Sun. **Reservations:** suggested. **Features:** This very nice restaurant, which specializes in game, fowl and pasta, is designed to look like the Tusca Villa of the owner, Umberto Menghi. The very charming decor has bright colors, open beams and exquisite furniture. Wonderful wine, good service. Casual dress; cocktails. **Parking:** valet. **Cards:** AX, DC, MC, VI.

IMPERIAL CHINESE SEAFOOD RESTAURANT   **Lunch:** $10-$25   **Dinner:** $15-$25   **Phone:** 604/688-8191   (5)
Location: Between W Hastings and Cordova sts. 355 Burrard St V6C 2G8. **Hours:** 11 am-10 pm. **Reservations:** suggested. **Features:** To take advantage of the spectacular views of the harbor and North Shore mountains, diners at this long-established restaurant should request a table next to one of the floor-to-ceiling windows. Dishes include fresh lobster and crab, shark fin and bird's nest soups and preparations of chicken, duck, pork and beef. Barbecue items also are tasty. Casual dress; cocktails. **Parking:** on-site (fee) and valet. **Cards:** DC, MC, VI.

INDIGO BISTRO   **Lunch:** $13-$17   **Dinner:** $15-$30   **Phone:** 604/893-7150   (54)
Location: Between Helmcken and Comox sts; in Sheraton Vancouver Wall Centre Hotel. 1088 Burrard St V6Z 2R9. **Hours:** 6:30 am-10 pm. **Reservations:** suggested. **Features:** A contemporary all day eatery, the Indigo Bistro features a nice blend of French and Italian cuisines. Entrees include fresh seafood, chicken, beef and veal. Distinctive pieces created by local artisans highlight the decor. Servers are knowledgeable. Casual dress; cocktails. **Parking:** on-site (fee) and valet. **Cards:** AX, DC, MC, VI. *(See color ad p 557)*

JOE FORTES SEAFOOD & CHOP HOUSE   **Lunch:** $9-$24   **Dinner:** $19-$56   **Phone:** 604/669-1940   (19)
Location: Between Robson and Alberni sts. 777 Thurlow St V6E 3V5. **Hours:** 11:30 am-11 pm. Closed: 12/25, 12/26. **Reservations:** suggested. **Features:** A San Francisco-style seafood grill along trendy Robson Street, this restaurant features delightful rooftop garden dining in season. They also have a popular oyster bar and fireplace lounge. Be sure to ask about turn-of-the-century legend Joe Fortes. Casual dress; cocktails; entertainment. **Parking:** valet. **Cards:** AX, DS, MC, VI.

JUST ONE THAI BISTRO   **Lunch:** $6-$15   **Dinner:** $9-$15   **Phone:** 604/685-8989   (48)
Location: Between Thurlow and Hornby sts. 1018 Beach Ave V6E 3N9. **Hours:** 11 am-10:30 pm. Closed: 12/25. **Features:** Along trendy Denman Street in the downtown West End neighborhood, the restaurant prepares spicy Thai favorites, including satays, pad Thai noodles and coconut rice. The friendly staff will help guests pick dishes, which can be requested in milder varieties. Casual dress; cocktails. **Parking:** street. **Cards:** AX, MC, VI.

(See map and index starting on p. 531)

KAM'S PLACE SINGAPOREAN CUISINE   **Lunch:** $9-$13   **Dinner:** $9-$13   **Phone:** 604/669-3389   ③⑨
Asian
Location: Between Thurlow and Burrard sts. 1043 Davie St V6E 1M5. **Hours:** 11 am-3 & 5-10 pm. Closed: 12/25. **Features:** In the part of West End known as Davie Village, the restaurant dishes up food in huge portions. Lines are not uncommon, and reservations are taken only for large groups. Don't forget to ask about lunch and dinner specials. Casual dress; cocktails. **Parking:** street. **Cards:** AX, DC, MC, VI.

KOBE JAPANESE STEAK HOUSE   **Dinner:** $25-$49   **Phone:** 604/684-2451   ②⑥
Steak & Seafood
Location: Between Burrard and Thurlow sts. 1042 Alberni St V6E 1A3. **Hours:** 5 pm-10 pm. Closed major holidays. **Reservations:** required. **Features:** Visitors and locals alike enjoy this restaurant's style of dinner, which seats several guests at a teppan table where the chef prepares your meal of steak, chicken, shrimp or lobster on the grill in front of you. Valet parking is available Friday-Saturday only. Casual dress; cocktails. **Parking:** on-site (fee) and street. **Cards:** AX, DC, DS, JC, MC, VI.

LA TERRAZZA   **Dinner:** $25-$30   **Phone:** 604/899-4449   ⑥①
Northern Italian
DS, MC, VI.
Location: By Cambie St Bridge. 1088 Cambie St & Pacific Blvd V6B 6J5. **Hours:** 5 pm-11 pm. Closed: 1/1, 12/24-12/26. **Reservations:** required. **Features:** Near the Cambie Street bridge in Yaletown, the lovely restaurant features an impressive wine list with many bottles displayed in a huge rack against one wall. On the menu is an array of meat dishes—such as grilled venison, rack of lamb and Cornish game hen—along with some seafood and a choice of pasta. Casual dress; cocktails. **Parking:** on-site (fee) and valet. **Cards:** AX, DC,

LE CROCODILE   **Lunch:** $15-$19   **Dinner:** $24-$34   **Phone:** 604/669-4298   ④②
French
keep busy. Dressy casual; cocktails.
Location: Smythe and Burrard sts. 100-909 Burrard St V6Z 2N2. **Hours:** 11:30 am-2 & 5:30-10 pm, Sat from 5:30 pm. Closed major holidays; also Sun. **Reservations:** required. **Features:** The French restaurant's menu shows an emphasis on beef and seafood. The signature dish is Alsatian onion pie; other offerings include grilled lamb chops and pan-fried Dover sole filleted tableside. The atmosphere is bustling, and the servers **Parking:** on-site (fee) and valet. **Cards:** AX, DC, MC, VI.

LE GAVROCHE RESTAURANT FRANCAIS   **Lunch:** $11-$19   **Dinner:** $19-$32   **Phone:** 604/685-3924   ⑨
French
and the ever-popular lobster. Dressy casual; cocktails.
Location: Between Cardero and Bidwell sts. 1616 Alberni St V6G 1A6. **Hours:** 11:30 am-2:30 & 5:30-10:30 pm, Sat & Sun from 5:30 pm. Closed: 1/1, 12/25. **Reservations:** required. **Features:** In a small, character house, the charming French restaurant's second-floor dining room affords views of the harbor and North Shore. Try the lamb, beef tenderloin, veal or veal sweetbread. For seafood lovers, there are salmon, prawns **Parking:** street. **Cards:** AX, DC, MC, VI.

LICKERISH   **Dinner:** $17-$25   **Phone:** 604/696-0725   ④③
Pacific Rim
vegetarian dishes. Casual dress; cocktails.
Location: Between Burrard and Hornby sts. 903 Davie St V62 1B8. **Hours:** 5:30 pm-11 pm, Fri & Sat-midnight. Closed: 12/25. **Reservations:** suggested. **Features:** One of several trendy restaurants on Davie Street, this place sets itself apart by emphasizing food rather than decor. On the menu are reasonably priced entrees, such as grilled venison burger, Mandarin beef and tiger prawns, wild British Columbia salmon and **Parking:** street. **Cards:** AX, DC, MC, VI.

MEXICO SABROSO   **Lunch:** $7-$13   **Dinner:** $7-$13   **Phone:** 604/688-7426   ②⑨
Mexican
$13. Only cash is
Cards: AX, MC.
Location: Between Richards and Homer sts. 440 W Hastings St V6B 1L8. **Hours:** 11:30 am-8 pm. Closed major holidays; also Sun. **Features:** The hole-in-the-wall restaurant is easy to miss, so look for the street sign board that says "Mexico Taco." On the menu are the types of foods typically encountered in small Mexican cafes: tacos, tortas, burritos, enchiladas, tostadas, fajitas and quesadillas, the most pricey of which costs accepted. The only available parking is in metered spots on the street. Casual dress. **Parking:** street.

MILESTONE'S GRILL & BAR   **Lunch:** $7-$18   **Dinner:** $10-$21   **Phone:** 604/684-9111   ⑥⑦
Canadian
Casual dress; cocktails.
Location: Between Helmcken and Davie sts. 1109 Hamilton St V6B 2Y1. **Hours:** 11 am-11 pm, Fri & Sat-midnight, Sun 10 am-10 pm. Closed: 12/25. **Features:** Whether for lunch, brunch, dinner or a drink, the establishment lures guests with globally inspired meals, enticing bar creations, friendly staff and a warm, welcoming atmosphere—and all for a reasonable price. Only metered parking is available at the trendy Yaletown spot. **Parking:** street. **Cards:** AX, DC, MC, VI.

MILESTONE'S RESTAURANT   **Lunch:** $7-$10   **Dinner:** $7-$13   **Phone:** 604/682-4477   ①④
Canadian
dress; cocktails.
Location: Between Bute and Thurlow sts. 1145 Robson St V6E 1B5. **Hours:** 10:30 am-10 pm, Thurs-11 pm, Fri-midnight, Sat 9:30 am-midnight, Sun 9:30 am-10 pm. Closed: 12/25. **Reservations:** suggested, evenings. **Features:** Whether for lunch, brunch, dinner or a drink, the restaurant offers globally inspired meals, enticing bar creations, friendly staff and a warm, welcoming atmosphere. Prices are reasonable. Casual **Parking:** street. **Cards:** AX, DC, MC, VI.

ORITALIA   **Lunch:** $14-$18   **Dinner:** $20-$30   **Phone:** 604/689-8862   ③⓪
Continental
Parking: valet. **Cards:** AX, DC, MC, VI.
Location: Between Dunsmuir and Pender sts; in Le Soleil Hotel & Suites Vancouver. 567 Hornby St V6C 2E8. **Hours:** 6:30 am-10 pm. Closed: 12/25. **Reservations:** suggested. **Features:** Oriental and Italian influences are fused to create a neat blend of beauty and out-of-this-world tastes—hence the name "Oritalia." The bustling atmosphere of the bi-level dining room features a large, open kitchen. Casual dress; cocktails.

(See map and index starting on p. 531)

OYSI OYSI JAPANESE RESTAURANT **Lunch:** $7-$19 **Dinner:** $7-$19 **Phone:** 604/682-0011 68
Japanese
Location: Between Thurlow and Bute sts. 1136 Alberni St V6E 1A5. **Hours:** 11 am-10:30 pm, Fri-11:30 pm, Sat noon-11:30 pm, Sun noon-10 pm. **Features:** The downtown restaurant's menu lists fresh seafood, barbecue and sushi, as well as take-out combination trays. Guests can park in metered street spots or in a limited number of free spaces in underground parking lot stalls 200 through 300. Casual dress; cocktails. **Parking:** on-site and street. **Cards:** AX, DC, MC, VI.

PARKSIDE ON HARO STREET **Dinner:** $20-$23 **Phone:** 604/683-6912 69
Regional
Continental
Location: Between Gilford and Chilco sts. 1906 Haro St V6G 1H7. **Hours:** 6 pm-midnight. Closed major holidays. **Reservations:** suggested. **Features:** In the lower level of the Buccan Hotel, the restaurant is tucked away in the Westend amid many apartment buildings. Described as "New York," the decor includes a lush garden patio that is heated at night. Such menu offerings as baked sea bass, grilled tenderloin of beef, Bombay duck breast and grilled salmon might be termed "luxurious comfort food." This place is well worth a visit. Casual dress; cocktails. **Parking:** valet. **Cards:** MC, VI.

PICCOLO MONDO RISTORANTE **Lunch:** $12-$18 **Dinner:** $15-$30 **Phone:** 604/688-1633 33
Northern
Italian
Location: Between Robson and Haro sts. 850 Thurlow St V6E 1W2. **Hours:** noon-2 & 6-10 pm, Sat from 6 pm. Closed major holidays; also Sun. **Reservations:** suggested. **Features:** Ravioline in brodo ricco soup and squid-ink risotto are examples of menu fare. Casual dress; cocktails. **Parking:** street. **Cards:** AX, DC, JC, MC, VI.

PROVENCE MARINASIDE **Lunch:** $9-$20 **Dinner:** $15-$35 **Phone:** 604/681-4144 64
Continental
Location: End of Davie St, towards the water. 1177 Marinaside Crescent V6Z 2Y3. **Hours:** 8 am-10:30 pm, Fri & Sat-11 pm. Closed: 12/25. **Reservations:** required. **Features:** The delightful restaurant faces the seawall and a small marina in an area known as Falsecreek. The menu spans breakfast, lunch and dinner, so guests can fit this place into any part of their day. In addition to choices from the antipasto display case, selections include wonderful pasta and panini, as well as beef, chicken and fish entrees. Dressy casual; cocktails. **Parking:** street. **Cards:** AX, DC, MC, VI.

RAIN CITY GRILL **Dinner:** $19-$32 **Phone:** 604/685-7337 46
Continental
Location: Just n of jct Denman and Davie sts. 1193 Denman St V6G 2N1. **Hours:** 5 pm-11 pm, Sat & Sun also 10:30 am-2:30 pm. Closed: 12/24, 12/25. **Reservations:** required. **Features:** You'll enjoy the Rain City's Pacific Northwest cuisine with a menu that includes fresh ingredients and weekly changes. The atmosphere is simple yet stately, the server staff is attentive and nicely attired, and the wine list is extensive. Limited seating. Dressy casual; cocktails. **Parking:** valet and street. **Cards:** AX, DC, MC, VI.

RANDOM **Dinner:** $13-$15 **Phone:** 604/696-9996 32
Continental
Location: Between Jervis and Broughton sts. 1326 Davie St V6E 1N6. **Hours:** 6 pm-11 pm, Fri-Sun to midnight. Closed: 1/1, 12/25; also Mon. **Features:** The owners morphed an old dingy restaurant into a funky little place with good, affordable food. The menu is blocked into $6 and $9 for appetizers and $13 and $15 for entrees made with chicken breast, tuna and lamb. Reservations are taken only for groups of six or more; otherwise it's first come, first served. Casual dress; cocktails. **Parking:** street. **Cards:** AX, MC, VI.

REX ROTISSERIE & GRILL **Lunch:** $8-$16 **Dinner:** $15-$28 **Phone:** 604/683-7390 4
Southwestern
Location: Between Thurlow and Burrard sts; plaza level of Bentall Centre. 1055 Dunsmuir St V7X 1G4. **Hours:** 11:30 am-9:30 pm. Closed major holidays; also Sat & Sun. **Reservations:** suggested. **Features:** Featuring hot rotisserie chicken and prime rib, also fresh made sandwiches and some pasta. Patio dining in season. Validated parking after 5 pm. Casual dress; cocktails. **Parking:** on-site (fee). **Cards:** AX, DC, MC, VI.

ROMANO'S MACARONI GRILL **Lunch:** $9-$16 **Dinner:** $9-$23 **Phone:** 604/689-4334 31
Italian
Location: Between Cadero and Nicola sts. 1523 Davie St V6G 3A2. **Hours:** noon-10 pm, Fri & Sat-11 pm, Sun 11 am-10 pm. Closed: 12/25. **Reservations:** suggested. **Features:** A warm, homey atmosphere awaits in the restaurant, which is in the restored Roger's Sugar Family Mansion on tony Davie Street. Representative of the fare are varied pasta dishes, brick-oven pizzas and seafood, veal and pork preparations. Casual dress; cocktails. **Parking:** valet and street. **Cards:** AX, DC, MC, VI.

THE SANDBAR SEAFOOD RESTAURANT **Lunch:** $8-$18 **Dinner:** $11-$30 **Phone:** 604/669-9030 47
Seafood
Location: Below the bridge, follow signs to Granville Island. #9 The Creekhouse, 1535 Johnston St V6H 3R9. **Hours:** 11:30 am-11 pm, Sun-10 pm. Closed: 12/25. **Reservations:** suggested, for dinner. **Features:** More than a century ago, Granville Island was known as "the great sandbar," where native tribes came to fish. Today, the 300-seat fresh seafood restaurant perches on the waterfront and offers great views from every seat. Complimentary parking is available for three hours during the day and all night after 7 p.m. Casual dress; cocktails. **Parking:** on-site. **Cards:** AX, MC, VI.

SETTEBELLO RISTORANTE **Lunch:** $8-$15 **Dinner:** $14-$26 **Phone:** 604/681-7377 18
Northern
Italian
Location: Between Thurlow and Bute sts. 1133 Robson St V6E 1B5. **Hours:** 11:30 am-10 pm, Fri & Sat-11 pm. Closed: 12/25. **Reservations:** suggested. **Features:** Features open concept room, lounge and rooftop terrace serving Mediterranean dishes and west coast inspired tapas and entrees. The open kitchen boasts a wood burning oven which produces gourmet thin curst pizza. Hearty pasta, chops and seafood are all served by friendly staff in a warm vibrant atmosphere in the heart of Vancouver's shopping district- Robson St. Casual dress; cocktails. **Parking:** on-site (fee). **Cards:** AX, JC, MC, VI.

(See map and index starting on p. 531)

SHOW CASE RESTAURANT   Lunch: $15-$20   Dinner: $20-$30   Phone: 604/639-4040   41
Pacific Rim
Location: Between Thurlow and Bute sts; in Vancouver Marriott Pinnacle Downtown. 1128 W Hastings St V6E 4R5. **Hours:** 6:30 am-2 & 5-10 pm. **Reservations:** suggested. **Features:** Natural light shining through floor-to-ceiling windows illuminates the restaurant and adjoining bar. Distinctive presentations characterize offerings of West Coast cuisine. Breakfast, lunch and dinner are available daily. Casual dress; cocktails. **Parking:** on-site (fee) and valet. **Cards:** AX, CB, DC, DS, JC, MC, VI.

STEPHO'S SOUVLAKI GREEK TAVERNA   Lunch: $7-$10   Dinner: $7-$10   Phone: 604/683-2555   35
Greek
Location: Between Bute and Thurlow sts. 1124 Davie St V6E 1N1. **Hours:** 11:30 am-11:30 pm. Closed: 12/25. **Features:** On bustling Davie Street, the longstanding restaurant is a favorite for its generous plates of rice, roasted potatoes, souvlaki, lamb and chicken. There's often a line, so diners are encouraged to arrive early. Casual dress; cocktails. **Parking:** street. **Cards:** AX, MC, VI.

SUBEEZ CAFE   Lunch: $8-$20   Dinner: $8-$20   Phone: 604/687-6107   66
Canadian
Location: Between Smythe and Robson sts. 891 Homer St V6B 2W2. **Hours:** 11:30 am-1 am, Sat from 11 am. Closed: 12/25. **Features:** Around for more than 10 years, the restaurant serves casual fare to the masses. On the menu are sandwiches, all-day breakfast items, pasta, salads and larger entrees for those who are particularly hungry. The patio opens on warmer days. Casual dress; cocktails. **Parking:** street.
Cards: MC, VI.

THURLOW KEG   Lunch: $10-$25   Dinner: $17-$30   Phone: 604/685-4388   23
Steak & Seafood
Location: Between Robson and Alberni sts. 742 Thurlow St V6E 1V8. **Hours:** 11:30 am-1 am, Fri-1:30 am, Sat 3:30 pm-1:30 am, Sun 3:30 pm-midnight. Closed: 12/25. **Features:** Great steaks, a casual atmosphere and friendly, knowledgeable servers are trademarks of the small steakhouse chain, where the specialty is perfectly seasoned slow-roasted prime rib. Guests should arrive early to this popular spot, as seating is on a first-come, first-served basis. Casual dress; cocktails. **Parking:** street. **Cards:** AX, DC, MC, VI.

TROPIKA MALAYSIAN & THAI CUISINE   Lunch: $8-$15   Dinner: $10-$20   Phone: 604/737-6002   10
CAA
Asian
Location: Between Bute and Thurlow sts. 1128 Robson St V6E 1B2. **Hours:** 11:30 am-10:30 pm. **Reservations:** suggested. **Features:** A quick trip through the extensive menu, which combines Malaysian, Thai and Singapore cuisine, turns up Thai curries that are eight hours in preparation, pan-fried roti bread that disappears within seconds of reaching the table and Malaysian chili sauce dishes. The restaurant is on trendy Robson Street. Casual dress; cocktails. **Parking:** on-site (fee). **Cards:** AX, DC, JC, MC, VI.

VERA'S BURGER SHACK   Lunch: $5-$9   Dinner: $5-$9   Phone: 604/228-8372   65
Canadian
Location: Between Walnut and Cypress sts. 1935 Cornwall Ave V6J 1C8. **Hours:** 11 am-11 pm. Closed: 12/25. **Features:** Vera's, as it has come to be known, has received kudos for its burgers for the past few years. The secret to its success is simple, fresh ground beef that's cooked to perfection. In addition to burgers, guests might want to try the dogs, fries, onion rings or daily specials. A children's menu is available. Casual dress. **Parking:** street. **Cards:** VI.

VERA'S BURGER SHACK   Lunch: $5-$9   Dinner: $5-$9   Phone: 604/893-8372   58
Canadian
Location: Between Thurlow and Burrard sts. 1030 Davie St V6E 1M3. **Hours:** 11 am-11 pm. Closed: 1/1, 12/25. **Features:** This Davie Village location, Vera's third and newest, joins others in Kitsilano and Dundarave. The local favorite is known for fresh ground beef burgers, juicy hot dogs, huge onion rings and thick milk shakes. This place is great for something different. Guests can eat in or order for take-out. Casual dress. **Parking:** street. **Cards:** MC, VI.

VILLA DE LUPO RESTAURANT   Dinner: $18-$30   Phone: 604/688-7436   57
Italian
Location: Between Robson and Smythe sts. 869 Hamilton St V6B 2R7. **Hours:** 5:30 pm-10 pm. Closed: 1/1, 12/25. **Reservations:** suggested. **Features:** You'll enjoy the fine cuisine at this restaurant; all meals—such as homemade pasta and the lamb osso bucco—are prepared with fresh, local ingredients. The menu also features a wide range of fine wines, and the lovely atmosphere has a romantic feel. Casual dress; cocktails. **Parking:** on-site and valet. **Cards:** AX, DC, MC, VI.

VISTAS REVOLVING RESTAURANT   Dinner: $25-$40   Phone: 604/691-2777   3
Seafood
Location: Between Bute and Thurlow sts; in Renaissance Vancouver Hotel Harbourside. 1133 W Hastings St V6E 3T3. **Hours:** 5:30 pm-10 pm. **Reservations:** required. **Features:** The revolving restaurant couples an elegant setting with majestic views of the harbor, city and North Shore Mountains. Guests palates are tantalized with delectable seafood, along with some chicken and steak items. Dressy casual; cocktails. **Parking:** on-site and valet. **Cards:** AX, CB, DC, DS, JC, MC, VI. *(See color ad p 556)*

WATER ST. CAFE   Lunch: $10-$16   Dinner: $10-$20   Phone: 604/689-2832   28
Italian
Location: Corner of Cambie and Water sts; in Gastown. 300 Water St V6B 1B6. **Hours:** 11:30 am-10 pm, Fri & Sat-11 pm. Closed: 1/1, 12/25. **Reservations:** suggested. **Features:** Located in a Victorian building across the street from Old Gastown's steam clock landmark, the Water Street Cafe features elegant yet casual dining with a Continental and Italian cuisine inspired with British Columbia and Canadian West Coast touches. Casual dress; cocktails. **Parking:** street. **Cards:** AX, DC, MC, VI.

THE WILLIAM TELL   Dinner: $23-$38   Phone: 604/688-3504   40
CAA
Swiss
Location: Between Georgia and Robson sts; in The Georgian Court Hotel. 765 Beatty St V6B 2M4. **Hours:** 5:30 pm-9 pm, Sun-8 pm. Closed major holidays; also Mon. **Reservations:** suggested. **Features:** Tiger prawns, rainbow trout, rack of lamb and steak tartare are the favorites at the established, popular William Tell's. The restaurant displays an attractive, European-style elegance. Sunday night features a Swiss-style buffet. Casual dress; cocktails. **Parking:** on-site (fee). **Cards:** AX, CB, DC, JC, MC, VI.

(See map and index starting on p. 531)

WON MORE SZECHUAN CUISINE **Dinner:** $7-$14 **Phone:** 604/688-8856 ㊹

Chinese

Location: Between Davie and Pendrell sts. 201-1184 Denman St V6G 2M9. **Hours:** 4 pm-10 pm. Closed: 12/25; also Tues. **Features:** On the corner of Davie and Denmen streets, the second-floor restaurant overlooks English Bay. The wonderful eatery is known for its dry ginger beef and salt and pepper squid. Those who like it hot and spicy should look for the highlighted items on the menu. Casual dress; beer & wine only. **Parking:** street. **Cards:** MC, VI.

YALETOWN BREWING COMPANY **Lunch:** $11-$14 **Dinner:** $13-$21 **Phone:** 604/681-2739 (59)

Canadian

Location: Between Helmcken and Davie sts. 1111 Mainland St V6B 2T9. **Hours:** 11:30 am-10 pm, Thurs-Sat to 11 pm. Closed: 1/1, 12/25. **Reservations:** suggested. **Features:** In the trendy Yaletown area, the distinctive brew pub offers homemade beers to accompany its thin-crust pizzas and wonderful burgers. On warm days, patrons can unwind on the large outdoor patio. Casual dress; cocktails. **Parking:** street. **Cards:** AX, MC, VI.

ZIN **Lunch:** $9-$13 **Dinner:** $16-$20 **Phone:** 604/408-1700 ⑪

CAA

Pacific Rim

Location: Between Jervis and Bute sts; in Pacific Palisades Hotel. 1277 Robson St V6E 1C4. **Hours:** 7:30 am-2 & 4-11 pm. **Reservations:** suggested. **Features:** On trendy Robson Street, the funky restaurant gets its name from zinfandel wines, which servers say pair well with the global cuisine on the wonderful, meant-for-sharing tapas menu. Casual dress; cocktails. **Parking:** on-site (fee). **Cards:** AX, DC, JC, MC, VI.

The following restaurant has not been evaluated by AAA but is listed for your information only.

HY'S ENCORE **Phone:** 604/683-7671

fyi

Not evaluated. **Location:** Between W Georgia and Dunsmuir sts. 637 Hornby St V6C 2G3. **Features:** This long-established steakhouse is located in the heart of the downtown area. The decor might be older but the steaks are the best; watch as your choice of steak is prepared from a glass-enclosed grill and don't forget to ask about their garlic bread.

VANCOUVER pop. 545,671 (See map and index starting on p. 536)

WHERE TO STAY

2400 MOTEL *Book at aaa.com* **Phone:** 604/434-2464 (72)

Motel

5/1-9/30	1P: $75-$100	2P: $75-$125	XP: $10	F14
10/1-11/30	1P: $57-$85	2P: $57-$95	XP: $10	F14
3/1-4/30	1P: $57-$80	2P: $57-$95	XP: $10	F14
12/1-2/28	1P: $55-$70	2P: $55-$85	XP: $10	F14

Location: 7.2 km se on Hwy 1A and 99A (Kingsway). 2400 Kingsway V5R 5G9. Fax: 604/430-1045. **Facility:** 65 units. 32 one- and 33 two-bedroom standard units, some with kitchens. 1 story, exterior corridors. *Bath:* combo or shower only. **Parking:** on-site. **Terms:** cancellation fee imposed, pets ($5 extra charge). **Cards:** AX, MC, VI.

SOME UNITS

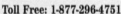

FEE

(See map and index starting on p. 536)

BEST WESTERN EXHIBITION PARK   *Book at aaa.com*

Phone: (604)294-4751   **56**

(CAA) (SAVE)

	1P: $129-$139	2P: $179-$199	XP: $10	F12
7/1-9/30	1P: $129-$139	2P: $179-$199	XP: $10	F12
5/1-6/30	1P: $90-$99	2P: $129-$139	XP: $10	F12
10/1-2/28	1P: $69-$79	2P: $119-$129	XP: $10	F12
3/1-4/30	1P: $69-$79	2P: $109-$119	XP: $10	F12

Small-scale Hotel **Location:** Trans-Canada Hwy 1, exit 26; jct Trans-Canada Hwy 1 and 7A. 3475 E Hastings St V5K 2A5. Fax: 604/294-1269. **Facility:** 58 one-bedroom standard units. 3 stories, interior corridors. **Parking:** on-site. **Terms:** cancellation fee imposed. **Amenities:** irons, hair dryers. **Leisure Activities:** saunas, whirlpool. **Guest Services:** valet and coin laundry. **Cards:** AX, DC, MC, VI. **Special Amenities:** free expanded continental breakfast and free local telephone calls. *(See color ad p 568)*

SOME UNITS

BEST WESTERN UPTOWN

Phone: (604)267-2000   **62**

(CAA) (SAVE)

	1P: $119	2P: $129	XP: $10	F17
7/1-9/15 [CP]	1P: $119	2P: $129	XP: $10	F17
5/1-6/30 [CP]	1P: $104	2P: $115	XP: $10	F17
3/1-4/30 & 9/16-2/28 [CP]	1P: $79-$85	2P: $79-$85	XP: $10	F17

Location: Corner of E 10th St. 205 Kingsway V5J 3J5. Fax: 604/872-6072. **Facility:** 69 one-bedroom standard Small-scale Hotel units, some with whirlpools. 4 stories, interior corridors. **Parking:** on-site. **Amenities:** high-speed Internet, voice mail, irons, hair dryers. *Some:* dual phone lines. **Dining:** 7 am-9 pm, cocktails. **Leisure Activities:** limited exercise equipment. **Guest Services:** valet laundry. **Business Services:** meeting rooms. **Cards:** AX, CB, DC, DS, MC, VI. **Special Amenities:** free continental breakfast and free newspaper.

SOME UNITS

BILTMORE HOTEL   *Book at aaa.com*

Phone: (604)872-5252   **63**

(CAA) (SAVE)

6/1-10/31 [CP]	1P: $89-$109	2P: $99-$129	XP: $10	F12
3/1-5/31 [CP]	1P: $79-$99	2P: $89-$109	XP: $10	F12
11/1-2/28 [CP]	1P: $69-$89	2P: $79-$99	XP: $10	F12

Location: Corner of E 12th Ave and Hwy 99A (Kingsway). 395 Kingsway V5T 3J7. Fax: 604/874-3003. **Facility:** 96 Small-scale Hotel one-bedroom standard units. 7 stories, interior corridors. **Parking:** on-site. **Amenities:** voice mail, safes, hair dryers. **Dining:** 7 am-11 pm, cocktails. **Pool(s):** small outdoor. **Business Services:** meeting rooms. **Cards:** AX, DC, MC, VI. **Special Amenities:** free continental breakfast.

SOME UNITS

COLUMBIA COTTAGE

Phone: (604)874-7787   **74**

All Year [BP]	1P: $95-$135	2P: $95-$135	XP: $20	F14

Bed & Breakfast **Location:** W 14th Ave at Columbia St. Located in a residential area. 205 W 14th Ave V5Y 1X2. **Facility:** Smoke free premises. 4 one-bedroom standard units, some with kitchens. 2 stories (no elevator), interior corridors. *Bath:* combo or shower only. **Parking:** street. **Terms:** cancellation fee imposed. **Cards:** MC, VI.

SOME UNITS

(See map and index starting on p. 536)

DAYS INN-VANCOUVER METRO _Book at aaa.com_ Phone: (604)876-5531 66

(CAA) (SAVE)

Motel

	7/1-9/30 [CP]	1P: $99-$139	2P: $99-$139	XP: $10	F13
	5/1-6/30 [CP]	1P: $79-$99	2P: $79-$99	XP: $10	F13
	3/1-4/30 & 10/1-2/28 [CP]	1P: $59-$89	2P: $59-$89	XP: $10	F13

Location: 6 km se on Hwy 1A and 99A (Kingsway). 2075 Kingsway V5N 2T2. Fax: 604/872-2676. **Facility:** 66 one-bedroom standard units. 2 stories (no elevator), exterior corridors. _Bath:_ combo or shower only. **Parking:** on-site. **Terms:** cancellation fee imposed. **Amenities:** hair dryers. _Some:_ irons. **Cards:** AX, CB, DC, DS, JC, MC, VI. **Special Amenities:** free continental breakfast and free newspaper. _(See color ad below)_

SOME UNITS

HOLIDAY INN EXPRESS VANCOUVER _Book at aaa.com_ Phone: (604)254-1000 55

(CAA) (SAVE)

Small-scale Hotel

| | 6/1-9/30 [ECP] | 1P: $108-$315 | 2P: $108-$315 | XP: $10 | F18 |
| | 3/1-5/31 & 10/1-2/28 [ECP] | 1P: $99-$315 | 2P: $99-$315 | XP: $10 | F18 |

Location: Between Renfrew and Kaslo sts. 2889 E Hastings St V5K 2A1. Fax: 604/253-1234. **Facility:** 100 units. 99 one-bedroom standard units. 1 one-bedroom suite ($249-$350) with whirlpool. 4 stories, interior corridors. **Parking:** on-site. **Terms:** check-in 4 pm, package plans, small pets only ($25 extra charge). **Amenities:** video games (fee), dual phone lines, voice mail, irons, hair dryers. **Leisure Activities:** sauna, exercise room. **Guest Services:** valet and coin laundry. **Business Services:** meeting rooms. **Cards:** AX, DC, DS, MC, VI. **Special Amenities:** free expanded continental breakfast and free local telephone calls. _(See color ad card insert)_

SOME UNITS

FEE

HOLIDAY INN VANCOUVER-CENTRE (BROADWAY) _Book at aaa.com_ Phone: (604)879-0511 57

Small-scale Hotel

	6/1-9/30	1P: $209	2P: $209	XP: $15	F18
	5/1-5/31	1P: $189	2P: $189	XP: $15	F18
	10/1-2/28	1P: $179	2P: $179	XP: $15	F18
	3/1-4/30	1P: $169	2P: $169	XP: $15	F18

Location: Between Heather and Willow sts. 711 W Broadway V5Z 3Y2. Fax: 604/872-7520. **Facility:** 200 one-bedroom standard units. 16 stories, interior corridors. **Parking:** on-site (fee). **Terms:** cancellation fee imposed, small pets only (in smoking units). **Amenities:** high-speed Internet, voice mail, irons, hair dryers. _Some:_ fax. **Pool(s):** heated indoor. **Leisure Activities:** sauna, exercise room. **Guest Services:** gift shop, valet laundry. **Business Services:** meeting rooms. **Cards:** AX, CB, DC, DS, JC, MC, VI. _(See color ad card insert)_

SOME UNITS

(ASK)

(See map and index starting on p. 536)

THE LONDON GUARD MOTEL   **Phone:** 604/430-4646   65

7/1-9/30	1P: $65-$75	2P: $65-$75	XP: $10 D18
3/1-6/30	1P: $49-$59	2P: $49-$65	XP: $10 D18
10/1-2/28	1P: $49-$59	2P: $49-$59	XP: $10 D18

Motel   **Location:** 6.8 km se on Hwy 1A and 99A (Kingsway). 2227 Kingsway. Fax: 604/430-8951. **Facility:** 46 units. 31 one- and 15 two-bedroom standard units, some with efficiencies. 1 story, exterior corridors. *Bath:* combo or shower only. **Parking:** on-site. **Terms:** cancellation fee imposed, small pets only ($4 fee). **Cards:** MC, VI.

SOME UNITS

VACATION. AIRPORT. LUXURY HOTEL.
a seamless connection

Whether your stay here is brief or extended, simply book a room at The Fairmont Vancouver Airport and the resting is easy. You'll spend less time scurrying to connect with your flight, and more time connecting with your loved ones.

Call your travel agent or 1-800-441-1414. www.fairmont.com

THE *Fairmont*
VANCOUVER AIRPORT

NORTH VANCOUVER'S FULL-SERVICE, MULTIPLE AWARD-WINNING HOTEL.

- ♦ Just 20 mins. from downtown Vancouver, 90 mins. to Whistler
- ♦ Easy access off Hwy #1, take exit 22
- ♦ Close to Grouse Mountain and Capilano Suspension Bridge
- ♦ Spa, fitness facility, indoor swimming pool and whirlpool
- ♦ High speed Internet access
- ♦ Restaurant and Lounge - kids 12 and under eat free
- ♦ Ask for your Free Car Wash!

Look for our
Discount Coupons
in this book

(Serta) WE FEATURE THE WORLD'S BEST MATTRESS.™

Call Toll Free 1-877-985-3111 U.S. and Canada

Holiday Inn Hotel & Suites North Vancouver
700 Old Lillooet Road, North Vancouver
Tel: (604) 985-3111 ♦ www.hinorthvancouver.com

Approved

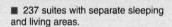
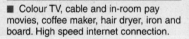
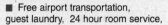

(See map and index starting on p. 536)

PLAZA 500 HOTEL & CONVENTION CENTRE *Book at aaa.com* Phone: (604)873-1811 71

(CAA) (SAVE)

	5/1-10/15	1P: $159-$179	2P: $159-$179	XP: $15	F12
	10/16-2/28	1P: $139-$159	2P: $139-$159	XP: $15	F12
	3/1-4/30	1P: $129-$139	2P: $129-$139	XP: $15	F12

Location: Corner of W 12th Ave at Cambie St. 500 W 12th Ave V5Z 1M2. **Fax:** 604/873-5103. **Facility:** 153 one-
Large-scale Hotel bedroom standard units. 17 stories, interior corridors. **Parking:** on-site (fee). **Terms:** check-in 4 pm, 30 day
cancellation notice-fee imposed, weekly rates available, package plans. **Amenities:** video games (fee),
high-speed Internet, dual phone lines, voice mail, irons, hair dryers. **Dining:** 6:30 am-10 pm, cocktails. **Guest Services:** valet
laundry, area transportation-downtown. **Business Services:** conference facilities. **Cards:** AX, DC, JC, MC, VI.
Special Amenities: free room upgrade and preferred room (each subject to availability with advance reservations).

SOME UNITS

(See map and index starting on p. 536)

QUALITY INN AIRPORT   *Book at aaa.com*   Phone: (604)321-6611   **67**

6/16-9/15 [CP]	1P: $129-$169	2P: $129-$174	XP: $10 F18
4/16-6/15 [CP]	1P: $89-$119	2P: $89-$124	XP: $10 F18
9/16-2/28 [CP]	1P: $74-$99	2P: $74-$99	XP: $10 F18
3/1-4/15 [CP]	1P: $69-$89	2P: $69-$89	XP: $10 F18

Small-scale Hotel Location: Corner of SE Marine Dr and Fraser St. 725 SE Marine Dr V5X 2T9. Fax: 604/327-3570. **Facility:** 100 one-bedroom standard units. 6 stories, interior corridors. **Parking:** on-site. **Terms:** [AP] meal plan available, package plans. **Amenities:** voice mail, irons, hair dryers. **Dining:** 6 am-10 pm, cocktails. **Leisure Activities:** bowling centre. **Guest Services:** gift shop, valet laundry. **Business Services:** meeting rooms. **Cards:** AX, CB, DC, DS, MC, VI.
(See color ad p 573)

SOME UNITS

WINDSOR GUEST HOUSE B & B   Phone: 604/872-3060   **64**

5/16-10/15	1P: $75-$135	2P: $85-$145	XP: $15 D3
3/1-5/15 & 10/16-2/28	1P: $55-$95	2P: $65-$105	XP: $15 D3

Historic Bed & Breakfast   **Location:** Between Alberta and Yukon sts. Located in a historic neighborhood. 325 W 11th Ave V5Y 1T3. Fax: 604/873-1147. **Facility:** This grand Victorian manor is convenient to City Hall and Vancouver General Hospital. Smoke free premises. 11 one-bedroom standard units. 4 stories (no elevator), interior corridors. *Bath:* some shared or private, combo or shower only. **Parking:** on-site. **Terms:** office hours 7:30 am-11 pm, 7 day cancellation notice-fee imposed. **Cards:** AX, MC, VI.

------ **WHERE TO DINE** ------

AURORA BISTRO   **Lunch:** $8-$11   **Dinner:** $18-$24   Phone: 604/873-9944   **62**

Continental   **Location:** Between Broadway and E 8th St. 2420 Main St V5T 3E2. **Hours:** 11:30 am-midnight. Closed: 12/25; also Mon. **Features:** Rising out of the ashes of an old Chinese restaurant, the bistro is the belle of this still-gritty section of Main Street, just north of Broadway. The impressively inventive chef/owner adds a seductive allure to what is essentially comfort food. The owner has opted for all British Columbia choices on the modest wine list. Casual dress; cocktails. **Parking:** street. **Cards:** AX, MC, VI.

AVENUE GRILL   **Lunch:** $8-$10   **Dinner:** $11-$16   Phone: 604/266-8183   **88**

Continental   **Location:** Between Yew St and W Boulevard. 2114 W 41st Ave V6M 1Z1. **Hours:** 8 am-9:30 pm. Closed: 12/25. **Reservations:** required, weekends. **Features:** The long-established Kerrisdale restaurant enables diners to choose from nearly 40 pasta toppings and a huge selection of wines by the glass. Cocktails. **Parking:** street. **Cards:** AX, DC, MC, VI.

BISHOP'S   **Dinner:** $30-$38   Phone: 604/738-2025   **76**

Continental   **Location:** Between Arbutus and Yew sts. 2183 W 4th Ave V6K 1N7. **Hours:** 5:30 pm-11 pm, Sun-10 pm. Closed: 12/24-12/26. **Reservations:** required. **Features:** The long-established restaurant has been serving wonderful contemporary North American cuisine for more than 20 years. The weekly changing menu highlights the season's freshest ingredients, such as British Columbia salmon, which has a short season. Try the signature death by chocolate dessert. Dressy casual; cocktails. **Parking:** street. **Cards:** AX, DC, MC, VI.

CALHOUN'S   **Lunch:** $4-$8   **Dinner:** $4-$9   Phone: 604/737-7062   **60**

Canadian   **Location:** Between Carnarvon and Balaclava sts. 3035 W Broadway V6K 2G9. **Hours:** 24 hours. Closed: 12/25, 12/26. **Features:** In the shopping district along West Broadway, this self-serve eatery features a nice selection of fresh food and desserts. The tandoori chicken, vegetarian cannelloni and chocolate turtle cake are good choices. Sandwiches and coffees too. Limited seating. Beer & wine only. **Parking:** street. **Cards:** MC, VI.

THE CANNERY   **Lunch:** $15-$20   **Dinner:** $18-$30   Phone: 604/254-9606   **87**

Seafood   **Location:** E Hastings St to Renfrew St, just n to McGill, just e to Commissioner St, then 1.5 km n. 2205 Commissioner St V5L 1A4. **Hours:** 11:30 am-2:30 & 5:30-9:30 pm, Sat 5 pm-10 pm, Sun 5 pm-9:30 pm. Closed: 12/24-12/26. **Reservations:** required. **Features:** For 34 years, the seafood restaurant has set the standards for fresh seafood. In an industrial section of town, it's well worth the visit. The setting offers a memorable view of the harbor, mountains and sea lions at play. The many fresh seafood dishes, such as salmon Wellington, and local wines are excellent. Casual dress; cocktails. **Parking:** on-site. **Cards:** AX, DC, DS, JC, MC, VI.

CAPERS   **Lunch:** $5-$8   **Dinner:** $5-$8   Phone: 604/739-6676   **90**

Natural/Organic   **Location:** Between Vine and Yew sts. 2285 W 4th Ave V6K 4S2. **Hours:** 8 am-10 pm. Closed: 12/25, 12/26. **Features:** Cafeteria-style counter service awaits diners who take advantage of the many vegetarian options here, as well as fish, chicken and beef dishes. Sandwiches, salads and soups are made with fresh, organic ingredients. The warm, cozy place is popular with the locals, who hustle in for limited seating on a first-come basis. Casual dress. **Parking:** street. **Cards:** AX, MC, VI.

CIPRIANO'S RISTORANTE AND PIZZERIA   **Dinner:** $13-$21   Phone: 604/879-0020   **82**

Italian   **Location:** Between Prince Edward and 24th Ave. 3995 Main St V5V 3P3. **Hours:** 4 pm-9 pm. Closed major holidays; also Sun & Mon. **Reservations:** suggested. **Features:** In one of the city's older neighborhoods, the family-run restaurant and pizzeria has sparse parking space, so guests should allow time to find a spot if they have reservations. The thick-fingered garlic bread is a fitting starter to a meal of pizza or pasta. Diners won't go home hungry. Casual dress; cocktails. **Parking:** street. **Cards:** VI.

(See map and index starting on p. 536)

DUN HUANG SEAFOOD RESTAURANT   **Lunch:** $13-$16   **Dinner:** $13-$25   **Phone:** 604/876-7855   [55]
Chinese
Location: Between Heather and Willow sts. 705 W Broadway V5Z 3Y2. **Hours:** 10:30 am-10 pm, Sat & Sun from 10 am. **Reservations:** suggested. **Features:** Cantonese cooking uses fresh ingredients, particularly regional seafood. Many excellent a la carte dishes and complete dinners for two, four or six patrons and even tables of 10. Casual dress; cocktails. **Parking:** on-site. **Cards:** DC, MC, VI.

**THE FISH HOUSE AT
STANLEY PARK**   *Menu on aaa.com*   **Lunch:** $10-$17   **Dinner:** $17-$30   **Phone:** 604/681-7275   [65]
Seafood
Location: Beach Ave entrance to Stanley Park; next to tennis courts. 8901 Stanley Park Dr V6G 3E2. **Hours:** 11:30 am-10 pm, Sun from 11 am. **Closed:** 12/24, 12/25, 12/26. **Reservations:** suggested. **Features:** Located in the lush and quiet surroundings of Stanley Park, this restaurant features a wide variety of fresh seafood wonderfully prepared with a Canadian West Coast influence. Its casual atmosphere offers patio dining in season. Pay parking lot in effect at all times. Casual dress; cocktails. **Parking:** on-site (fee). **Cards:** AX, DC, DS, JC, MC, VI.

GRAMERCY GRILL   **Lunch:** $8-$18   **Dinner:** $15-$33   **Phone:** 604/730-5666   [66]
Pacific Rim
Location: Between W 10th and W 11th aves. 2685 Arbutus St V6J 3Y4. **Hours:** 11:30 am-3 & 5-11 pm, Sat & Sun from 10 am. **Closed:** major holidays. **Features:** Named after a New York district, the restaurant offers a dark-wood interior, comfortable booths and tables and a showpiece bar. During warm days and evenings, patrons gather on the pleasant patio. Prices for such dishes as osso buco, roast lamb sirloin, game hen and, of course, West Coast salmon are reasonable. Several wines by the glass are available. Casual dress; cocktails. **Parking:** street. **Cards:** AX, DC, MC, VI.

THE GREEN GRAPE RESTAURANT   **Lunch:** $6-$10   **Dinner:** $6-$12   **Phone:** 604/879-7559   [51]
Continental
Location: Between E 11th and E 12th sts. 2779 Commerical Dr V5N 4C5. **Hours:** 11:30 am-2:30 & 5:30-8:30 pm, Sat & Sun 10 am-3 pm. **Closed:** major holidays; also Mon. **Features:** The charming little restaurant serves up a number of tasty dishes, and everything is as close to homemade as it gets. Burgers are made the old-fashioned way, hand-formed and served sizzling hot. In addition to varied sandwiches, the menu lists organic burgers made from British Columbia-raised buffalo, pork schnitzel and a steak sandwich. Casual dress. **Parking:** street. **Cards:** MC, VI.

HARLO GOURMET BURGER   **Lunch:** $8-$12   **Dinner:** $8-$12   **Phone:** 604/879-2297   [91]
Canadian
Location: Between W 17th and W 18th aves. 3346 Cambie St V5Z 2W6. **Hours:** 11:30 am-9:30 pm. **Closed:** 1/1, 12/25; also Mon. **Features:** Burgers are broiled to perfection and served on rolls prepared exclusively by well-known Vancouver bakery Ecco Il Pane. A choice of crispy fries or a green salad comes with every burger. The warm atmosphere and friendly service lift this place above that fast-food feel. Casual dress. **Parking:** street. **Cards:** AX, MC, VI.

HOUSE OF DOSAS   **Lunch:** $8-$13   **Dinner:** $8-$15   **Phone:** 604/875-1283   [52]
Indonesian
Location: Between Clark and Knight sts. 1391 Kingsway V5V 3E3. **Hours:** noon-3 & 5-10 pm. **Closed:** 12/25, 12/26; also Mon. **Features:** Specializing in Sri Lankan, South Indian, Malaysian and Singaporean cuisine, the restaurant highlights tropical design in its cozy interior. A heady stream of aromas rises from plates of such dishes as garlic chicken, mutton curry, masala calamari, beef kothu and Sri Lankan-style bread, a gentle fried swirl of dough that resembles a danish. Casual dress; cocktails. **Parking:** street. **Cards:** AX, MC, VI.

LAS MARGARITAS RESTAURANTE & CANTINA   **Lunch:** $7-$13   **Dinner:** $11-$18   **Phone:** 604/734-7117   [67]
Mexican
Location: Between Cypress and Maple sts. 1999 W 4th Ave V6J 1M7. **Hours:** 11:30 am-10 pm, Fri & Sat-11 pm. **Closed:** 1/1, 12/25. **Reservations:** suggested. **Features:** Las Margaritas features a bright, festive atmosphere accented with Mexican artifacts. The menu includes healthy choices and offers fajitas, grilled salmon burritos and chipotle chicken. The server staff is prompt and attentive. Reservations are required. Casual dress; cocktails. **Parking:** street. **Cards:** AX, DC, MC, VI.

LOMBARDO'S RISTORANTE PIZZERIA   **Lunch:** $10-$24   **Dinner:** $10-$24   **Phone:** 604/251-2240   [69]
Pizza
Location: Corner of 1st St and Commercial Dr; in Il Mercato Mall. 120 1641 Commercial Dr V5L 3A4. **Hours:** 11 am-11 pm, Sun 4 pm-10 pm. **Closed:** 12/25. **Features:** Located in the Mercata Mall, Lombardo's is known as one of the oldest brick-oven pizza houses in town, and it offers 15 types of pizza. The lasagna is very good also. Locals and visitors alike enjoy the family-style atmosphere. Seating is a bit limited. Casual dress; beer & wine only. **Parking:** street. **Cards:** AX, DC, MC, VI.

LUMIERE   **Dinner:** $100-$130   **Phone:** 604/739-8185   [71]
French
Location: Between Trafalgar and Larch sts. 2551 W Broadway V6K 2E9. **Hours:** 5:30 pm-10 pm. **Closed:** 12/25, 12/26; also Mon. **Reservations:** required. **Features:** The restaurant merges European elegance, North American flair and Asian minimalism. Food critics worldwide have bestowed accolades on this place, a must for visitors to the city. Prices for the chef's tasting menu, which consists of nine or 13 courses, range from $100 to $130; wine pairings are extra. The menu changes monthly. Dressy casual; cocktails. **Parking:** valet and street. **Cards:** AX, DC, MC, VI.

MAURYA INDIAN CUISINE   **Lunch:** $13-$16   **Dinner:** $13-$16   **Phone:** 604/742-0622   [79]
Indian
Location: Between Fir and Pine sts. 1643 W Broadway V6J 1W9. **Hours:** noon-11 pm, Sat & Sun 4 pm-10 pm. **Closed:** 1/1, 12/25, 12/26. **Features:** Representative of the cuisine is moist, flavorful tandoori chicken, vindaloo lamb and a number of vegetarian dishes. Don't forget to order naan bread with three dipping sauces. Lending to the warm, inviting atmosphere are rich wood accents and professional decoration down to the last detail. Parking is at street meters. Casual dress; cocktails. **Parking:** street. **Cards:** AX, MC, VI.

(See map and index starting on p. 536)

MEMPHIS BLUES BARBEQUE HOUSE   Lunch: $7-$19   Dinner: $7-$19   Phone: 604/215-2599   56
♦♦♦   **Location:** Between Kitchener and Charles sts. 1342 Commercial Dr V5L 3X6. **Hours:** 11 am-10 pm, Fri-midnight,
     Sat noon-midnight, Sun noon-10 pm. Closed: 12/25. **Features:** A sure sign that diners are likely to get
Barbecue   messy fingers and faces is the roll of paper towels at each table. Savory favorites include slabs of ribs,
     pulled pork, Cornish game hens and, of course, heaps of barbecue wings. Locations are on Broadway at
Granville Street and on Commercial Drive. Casual dress; beer & wine only. **Parking:** street. **Cards:** AX, JC, MC, VI.   🅰 ✖

MEMPHIS BLUES BARBEQUE HOUSE   Lunch: $7-$19   Dinner: $7-$19   Phone: 604/738-6806   53
♦   **Location:** Between Granville and Hemlock sts. 1465 W Broadway V6H 1H6. **Hours:** 11 am-10 pm, Fri-midnight,
     Sat noon-midnight, Sun noon-10 pm. Closed: 12/25. **Features:** A sure sign that diners are likely to get
Barbecue   messy fingers and faces is the roll of paper towels at each table. Savory favorites include slabs of ribs,
     pulled pork, Cornish game hens and, of course, heaps of barbecue wings. Locations are on Broadway at
Granville Street and on Commercial Drive. Casual dress; beer & wine only. **Parking:** street. **Cards:** AX, JC, MC, VI.   🅰 ✖

MONK MCQUEEN'S   Lunch: $10-$18   Dinner: $16-$30   Phone: 604/877-1351   58
♦♦♦   **Location:** W 6 Ave and Moberly Rd, just w of Cambie St Bridge. 601 Stamps Landing V5Z 3Z1. **Hours:** 11:30 am-
     10:30 pm, Sat & Sun from 11 am. Closed: 12/25. **Reservations:** suggested. **Features:** The restaurant
Seafood   affords great views of the mountains and the south shore of False Creek, with its numerous moored
     sailboats and condominiums. Two moods are sustained: casual in the downstairs area and more upscale
upstairs, where the sounds of live jazz filter out on Wednesday through Sunday evenings in summer and on weekends in
winter. Casual dress; cocktails. **Parking:** valet and street. **Cards:** AX, DC, MC, VI.   🍸 ✖

NEW CITY RESTAURANT   Lunch: $7-$12   Dinner: $7-$12   Phone: 604/737-2889   86
♦♦   **Location:** Between Maple and Cypress sts. 1944 W 4th Ave V6J 1M5. **Hours:** 11:30 am-3 & 4:30-10 pm, Sat &
     Sun from 4 pm. Closed: 1/1, 10/10, 12/25. **Features:** Diners who appreciate hot, spicy and full-flavored
Chinese   cooking should make this place a sure stop. Dishes, several of which are vegetarian, are prepared with
     plenty of ginger and garlic. Servers are friendly and attentive. Casual dress; beer & wine only. **Parking:**
street. **Cards:** AX, DC, MC, VI.   ✖

THE OUISI BISTRO   Lunch: $6-$11   Dinner: $7-$22   Phone: 604/732-7550   77
♦♦   **Location:** Between W 15th and W 14th sts. 3014 Granville St V6H 3J8. **Hours:** 11 am-midnight, Sat & Sun from 9
     am. Closed: 12/25. **Reservations:** suggested. **Features:** Located along trendy Granville Street with its mix
Cajun   of high-end shops and restaurants, this low-key restaurant serves Louisiana Creole and Cajun dishes from
     its open-style kitchen. They also have live jazz Sunday and Tuesday nights. Metered street parking.
Cocktails. **Parking:** street. **Cards:** AX, MC, VI.   ✖

PINK PEARL CHINESE RESTAURANT   Lunch: $4-$10   Dinner: $10-$19   Phone: 604/253-4316   73
♦♦   **Location:** Just w of Clark St. 1123 E Hastings St V6A 1S2. **Hours:** 9 am-9 pm, Fri & Sat-10 pm.
     Reservations: accepted. **Features:** Pink Pearl's focus is on fresh ingredients, local produce and West
Chinese   Coast seafood. An excellent and varied array of dim sum items is offered 9 am-3 pm This restaurant has
     received numerous write-ups in newspapers, magazines and travel guides. Casual dress; cocktails.
Parking: on-site. **Cards:** AX, DC, MC, VI.   ✖

PORTOBELLO RISTORANTE   Dinner: $12-$26   Phone: 604/734-0697   68
♦♦♦   **Location:** Between Trafalgar and Larch sts. 2585 W Broadway V6K 2E9. **Hours:** 5:30 pm-10:30 pm, Fri & Sat-11
     pm. Closed: 12/25. **Reservations:** suggested. **Features:** This is a family-owned restaurant that's quite
Italian   popular with the locals and well-known for its outstanding food and Sicilian flat bread. The restaurant
     features a cuisine representing Italy's north and south regions. Its decor is fun, funky and colorful. Casual
dress; cocktails. **Parking:** street. **Cards:** AX, MC, VI.   ✖

PROVENCE MEDITERRANEAN GRILL   Lunch: $8-$18   Dinner: $14-$24   Phone: 604/222-1980   70
♦♦♦   **Location:** Between Sasamat and Trimble sts. 100-4473 W 10th Ave V6R 2H2. **Hours:** 11:30 am-10 pm, Sat-11 pm,
     Sun 10 am-10 pm. Closed: 12/25, 12/26. **Reservations:** suggested. **Features:** The pleasant restaurant
Continental   offers casual southern French and Italian cuisine in a warm neighborhood atmosphere. At the end of the
     month, the owners have a culinary tasting or chef's sampling at a set price. Casual dress; cocktails.
Parking: street. **Cards:** AX, DC, MC, VI.   ✖

QUATTRO ON FOURTH   Dinner: $18-$33   Phone: 604/734-4444   74
♦♦♦   **Location:** Between MacDonald and Trimble sts. 2611 W 4th Ave V6K 1P8. **Hours:** 5 pm-11 pm, Fri & Sat-
     midnight, Sun-10 pm. Closed: 1/1, 12/25, 12/26. **Reservations:** suggested. **Features:** Quattro on Fourth
Italian   features an airy, fun and lively decor; it makes you feel like you're in Tuscany. This place has a great local
     reputation, as its pasta and other dishes are heartful, full-flavored and created with healthy ingredients.
Good service, too. Casual dress; cocktails. **Parking:** street. **Cards:** AX, DC, MC, VI.   ✖

RASPUTIN   Dinner: $12-$25   Phone: 604/879-6675   57
♦♦♦   **Location:** Between Cambie and Yukon sts. 457 W Broadway V5Y 1R4. **Hours:** 5 pm-11 pm, Fri & Sat-midnight.
     Closed: 1/1, 12/25. **Reservations:** suggested. **Features:** The restaurant's Russian cuisine is as rich and
Russian   varied as the land it comes from. A typical meal usually features several appetizers accompanied by shots
     of vodka. Representative of the fare are Ukrainian borscht, black caviar and pirozhki, Russia's famous
stuffed buns. Dinner entrees include kebabs, chicken Kiev and "the feast," a mixed grill of several items. Casual dress;
cocktails. **Parking:** street. **Cards:** AX, DC, MC, VI.   ✖

(See map and index starting on p. 536)

RUGBY BEACH CLUB GRILLE   **Dinner:** $8-$12   **Phone:** 604/736-2438   50
▼▼ ▼▼   **Location:** Between Oak and Laurel sts. 201-950 W Broadway V5Z 1K7. **Hours:** 4:25 pm-11 pm, Fri & Sat-12:30
Continental   am. **Closed:** 12/25. **Features:** The 250-seat restaurant is spacious and comfortable, but when this place
          gets going, it gets noisy. This energy buzz is a big part of the appeal, as is the food, which is priced a la
          carte. The 4:25 p.m. opening time is not a typo; it's an attempt at humor. Casual dress; cocktails. **Parking:**
street. **Cards:** AX, MC, VI.
☒

SAWASDEE THAI RESTAURANT   **Lunch:** $8-$13   **Dinner:** $8-$13   **Phone:** 604/876-4030   83
▼▼ ▼▼   **Location:** Main St and 27th Ave. 4250 Main St V5V 3P9. **Hours:** noon-2 & 5-10 pm, Sat-Mon from 5 pm. **Closed:**
Thai   1/1, 12/24, 12/25. **Reservations:** suggested, weekends. **Features:** Flavorful food and pleasant service are
          hallmarks of the popular restaurant, which is outside the downtown core. It is closed for lunch Saturday
          through Monday. Cocktails. **Parking:** street. **Cards:** MC, VI.
☒

SEASONS IN THE PARK   **Lunch:** $13-$23   **Dinner:** $18-$30   **Phone:** 604/874-8008   92
▼▼▼▼   **Location:** Cambie St at 33rd Ave: in Queen Elizabeth Park. 33rd Ave & Cambie St V6G 3E7. **Hours:** 11:30 am-2 &
Continental   5-10 pm. **Closed:** 1/1, 12/25. **Reservations:** suggested. **Features:** Atop a small hill in Queen Elizabeth
          Park, the restaurant—a favorite for fish and meat preparations—offers lovely views of the park and its
          flowers. Dressy casual; cocktails. **Parking:** on-site (fee) and valet. **Cards:** AX, DC, MC, VI.
⬛ ☒

SEQUOIA GRILL IN STANLEY PARK   **Lunch:** $12-$18   **Dinner:** $17-$28   **Phone:** 604/669-3281   89
(CAA)   **Location:** Ferguson Point; in Stanley Park. 7501 Stanley Park Dr V6G 3E2. **Hours:** 11:30 am-10 pm, Sun from
▼▼▼▼   10:30 am. **Closed:** 12/25. **Reservations:** required. **Features:** In the charming country-garden setting of
Pacific Rim   Stanley Park, the restaurant affords spectacular views of English Bay and the mountains. The menu
          standout is the fabulous roasted rack of lamb. Couples and visitors especially enjoy the atmosphere of
          casual elegance. Pay parking is in effect. Casual dress; cocktails. **Parking:** on-site (fee). **Cards:** AX,
          MC, VI.
☒

SHAUGHNESSY RESTAURANT AT VANDUSEN
GARDEN   **Lunch:** $11-$15   **Dinner:** $19-$28   **Phone:** 604/261-0011   81
▼▼ ▼▼   **Location:** Between W 33rd and W 37th aves. 5251 Oak St V6M 4H1. **Hours:** 11:30 am-9 pm. **Closed:** 12/25.
Pacific Rim   **Reservations:** suggested. **Features:** Overlooking the wonderful Vandusen Gardens, the quiet haven uses
          fresh ingredients in beautiful lunch and dinner entrees. Among daily specials are homemade soups. Ask
          about the chicken pot pie, a longtime favorite. After the meal, enjoy a stroll through the gardens. Casual
dress; cocktails. **Parking:** on-site. **Cards:** AX, DC, MC, VI.
☒

SOPHIE'S COSMIC CAFE   **Lunch:** $6-$10   **Dinner:** $6-$10   **Phone:** 604/732-6810   75
▼▼   **Location:** Between Arbutus and Maple sts. 2095 W 4th Ave V6J 1N3. **Hours:** 8 am-9:30 pm. **Closed:** 12/25.
Canadian   **Features:** Guests should be prepared to stand in line for this popular restaurant, the walls of which are
          covered with decorations that serve as reminders of a bygone time. Breakfast is the specialty meal, but
          burgers and sandwiches rarely disappoint. Casual dress. **Parking:** street. **Cards:** MC, VI.
☒

STAR ANISE   **Lunch:** $14-$17   **Dinner:** $20-$27   **Phone:** 604/737-1485   80
▼▼▼▼   **Location:** Between Hemlock and Granville sts. 1485 W 12th Ave V6H 1M6. **Hours:** 11:30 am-2:30 & 5:30-11 pm,
Regional   Sun 5:30 pm-10 pm. **Closed:** 12/25. **Reservations:** suggested. **Features:** Superb Pacific Rim cuisine
Canadian   reflects West Coast Canadian touches. Excellent local wines pair with local seafood and such meat dishes
          as Alberta pork chops. Casual dress; cocktails. **Parking:** street. **Cards:** AX, DC, MC, VI.
☒

TOJO'S RESTAURANT   **Dinner:** $16-$25   **Phone:** 604/872-8050   54
▼▼ ▼▼   **Location:** Between Heather and Willow sts. 202-777 W Broadway V5Z 4J7. **Hours:** 5:30 pm-11 pm. **Closed:** 1/1,
Japanese   12/25; also Sun. **Reservations:** required. **Features:** On the second floor is this Japanese restaurant, where
          each item on the menu is prepared using traditional Japanese methods. Dishes are made with only the
          freshest ingredients and no monosodium glutamate. Casual dress; cocktails. **Parking:** on-site (fee) and
street. **Cards:** AX, MC, VI.
☒

TOMATO FRESH FOOD CAFE   **Lunch:** $7-$12   **Dinner:** $12-$20   **Phone:** 604/874-6020   84
▼▼ ▼▼   **Location:** Corner of Cambie St and 17th Ave. 3305 Cambie St V5Z 2W6. **Hours:** 9 am-10 pm. **Closed:** 12/25,
Canadian   12/26. **Features:** Neighborhood bistro; market fresh and innovative, comfort food with a spin. Table spacing
          is close and seating can be limited in peak periods, patio in summer. Cocktails. **Parking:** street. **Cards:** AX,
          MC, VI.
☒

TRAFALGARS AT SWEET OBSESSION   **Lunch:** $8-$12   **Dinner:** $12-$25   **Phone:** 604/739-0555   72
▼▼ ▼▼   **Location:** Between Trafalgar and Stephens sts. 2603 W 16th Ave V6K 3C2. **Hours:** 9 am-11 pm, Fri & Sat-
Pacific Rim   midnight. **Closed:** 12/25, 12/26. **Reservations:** required, evenings. **Features:** In addition to an on-site
          bakery where cakes and pastries tempt browsers, the restaurant nurtures a cozy cafe where brunch is
          served daily from 9 a.m. to 4 p.m. The outdoor patio is a nice spot during warm weather. Casual dress;
cocktails. **Parking:** street. **Cards:** AX, MC, VI.
☒

TYPHOON   **Dinner:** $6-$9   **Phone:** 604/676-3602   59
▼▼   **Location:** Between E 11th and E 10th sts. 2610 Main St V5T 3E6. **Hours:** 5 pm-10 pm, Sat & Sun from noon.
Thai   **Closed:** 12/25. **Features:** Amazing but inexpensive Thai food is prepared in an uncluttered restaurant.
          Starters are $5 to $8, soups and curries $8 to $9 and other main dishes $8. Parking is on the street at
          meters that go until 8 pm. This wonderful spot comes highly recommended. Casual dress; beer & wine only.
Parking: street. **Cards:** MC, VI.
🍸 ☒

(See map and index starting on p. 536)

WEST RESTAURANT & BAR	**Lunch:** $11-$20	**Dinner:** $20-$35	**Phone:** 604-738-8938 [85]

▼▼▼▼▼
International

Location: Between 12th and 13th aves. 2881 Granville St V6H 3J4. **Hours:** 11:30 am-3 & 5:30-11 pm, Sat & Sun from 5:30 pm. Closed: 1/1, 12/25. **Reservations:** suggested. **Features:** The chef, who was trained in Europe, combines traditional French techniques with the best of West Coast ingredients. A magnificent "wall of wine" houses some 3,000 bottles. Dressy casual; cocktails. **Parking:** street. **Cards:** AX, DC, MC, VI.   [✕]

WILD GARLIC	**Lunch:** $8-$17	**Dinner:** $10-$22	**Phone:** 604-730-0880 [78]

▼▼▼▼▼
Asian

Location: Between Arbutus and Yew sts. 2120 W Broadway V6K 2C8. **Hours:** 11 am-2 & 5-10 pm, Sat & Sun from 5 pm. Closed: 12/25, 12/26. **Reservations:** suggested. **Features:** Garlic is strictly supported in spicy dishes that blend Asian and European influences. Cocktails. **Parking:** street. **Cards:** AX, DC, MC, VI.   [✕]

YEW FIRST RESTAURANT LOUNGE	**Lunch:** $7-$12	**Dinner:** $14-$20	**Phone:** 604-738-6515 [61]

▼▼▼▼▼
Italian

Location: Corner of W 1st Ave and Yew St; in Kitsilano District. 2201 W 1st Ave V6K 1E9. **Hours:** 4:30 pm-10 pm, Sat & Sun 9 am-2:30 pm. Closed: 1/1, 12/25; also Tues. **Reservations:** suggested. **Features:** Longtime Italian favorites share menu space with a hint of West Coast cuisine, such as grilled wild salmon, veal and osso buco. Maine lobster is served with a choice of pasta. On weekends, guests take advantage of a wonderful brunch. Casual dress; cocktails. **Parking:** on-site and street. **Cards:** AX, DC, MC, VI.   [✕]

The Vancouver Vicinity

ALDERGROVE pop. 11,910

—————— WHERE TO STAY ——————

BEST WESTERN COUNTRY MEADOWS	*Book at aaa.com*		
			Phone: (604)856-9880
(CAA) (SAVE)	6/22-9/7 [ECP]	1P: $99-$119	2P: $99-$119	XP: $10	F17
	3/1-6/21 & 9/8-2/28 [ECP]	1P: $79-$89	2P: $79-$89	XP: $10	F17

▼▼▼▼▼
Small-scale Hotel

Location: Trans-Canada Hwy 1, exit 73 (264th St/Aldergrove), 5 km s on 264th St (Hwy 13). 3070 264th St V4W 3E1. Fax: 604/856-0086. **Facility:** 78 units. 77 one-bedroom standard units, some with efficiencies and/or whirlpools. 1 two-bedroom suite ($119-$189) with kitchen and whirlpool. 2 stories (no elevator), interior corridors. **Parking:** on-site. **Terms:** check-in 4 pm, small pets only ($10 extra charge, in designated units). **Amenities:** high-speed Internet, voice mail, irons, hair dryers. **Dining:** 7 am-10 pm, wine/beer only. **Pool(s):** heated indoor. **Leisure Activities:** whirlpool, limited exercise equipment. **Guest Services:** valet and coin laundry. **Business Services:** meeting rooms, business center. **Cards:** AX, CB, DC, DS, MC, VI. **Special Amenities:** free expanded continental breakfast and free local telephone calls. *(See color ad p 583)*

SOME UNITS

[S/D] [🐾] [FEE] [🍴] [&M] [🏊] [🎥] [DATA PORT] [💻] / [✕] [🛏] [📷] /

BURNABY pop. 193,954   (See map and index starting on p. 536)

—————— WHERE TO STAY ——————

ACCENT INNS	*Book at aaa.com*		
			Phone: (604)473-5000 [106]
(CAA) (SAVE)	5/1-9/30	1P: $119-$139	2P: $129-$149	XP: $10	F16
	3/1-4/30 & 10/1-2/28	1P: $109-$119	2P: $109-$119	XP: $10	F16

▼▼▼▼▼
Motel

Location: Trans-Canada Hwy 1, exit 28 (Grandview Hwy), just n on Boundary Rd. Located across from a movie studio. 3777 Henning Dr V5C 6N5. Fax: 604/473-5095. **Facility:** 128 one-bedroom standard units, some with efficiencies. 3 stories, exterior corridors. **Parking:** on-site. **Terms:** small pets only ($10 fee). **Amenities:** video games (fee), voice mail, hair dryers. *Some:* high-speed Internet, dual phone lines. **Dining:** 6:30 am-10 pm, wine/beer only. **Leisure Activities:** sauna, whirlpool, limited exercise equipment. **Guest Services:** valet and coin laundry. **Business Services:** meeting rooms, business center. **Cards:** AX, DC, MC, VI. **Special Amenities:** free local telephone calls and free newspaper. *(See color ad p 488 & p 608)*

SOME UNITS

[S/D] [🐾] [FEE] [🍴] [&M] [♿] [✕] [🎥] [DATA PORT] [💻] / [✕] [🛏] [📷] /

BEST WESTERN KINGS INN AND CONFERENCE CENTRE	*Book at aaa.com*	
		Phone: (604)438-1383 [111]
(CAA) (SAVE)	4/1-9/30 [CP]	1P: $97-$127	2P: $97-$127	XP: $10	F17
	3/1-3/31 & 10/1-2/28 [CP]	1P: $76-$102	2P: $76-$102	XP: $10	F17

▼▼▼▼▼
Small-scale Hotel

Location: Trans-Canada Hwy 1, exit 29 (Willingdon Ave S), 3 km s to Kingsway, then 2 km e. 5411 Kingsway V5H 2G1. Fax: 604/438-2954. **Facility:** 132 one-bedroom standard units, some with efficiencies, kitchens and/or whirlpools. 2 stories (no elevator), exterior corridors. **Parking:** on-site. **Terms:** weekly rates available, [AP] & [BP] meal plans available, package plans, small pets only ($10 fee, $25 deposit). **Amenities:** voice mail, irons, hair dryers. **Dining:** 7 am-2 & 5-9 pm, Sat & Sun-11:30 am, cocktails. **Pool(s):** small heated outdoor. **Guest Services:** valet and coin laundry. **Business Services:** meeting rooms. **Cards:** AX, DC, MC, VI. **Special Amenities:** free continental breakfast and free local telephone calls.

SOME UNITS

[🛏] [🍴] [🍷] [🏊] [FEE] [🎥] [DATA PORT] [🛏] [💻] / [✕] [📷] /

(See map and index starting on p. 536)

HILTON VANCOUVER METROTOWN   *Book at aaa.com*   Phone: 604/438-1200   112

CAA SAVE
	6/1-9/30	1P: $159-$229	2P: $159-$229	XP: $20	F18
	10/1-2/28	1P: $145-$216	2P: $145-$216	XP: $20	F18
	3/1-5/31	1P: $135-$206	2P: $135-$206	XP: $20	F18

Large-scale Hotel   **Location:** Trans-Canada Hwy 1, exit 29 (Willingdon Ave S), 3 km S to Kingsway, then just e. Located next to Metrotown Shopping Mall. 6083 McKay Ave V5H 2W7. Fax: 604/431-7782. **Facility:** This service-oriented hotel offers business-friendly accommodations with the latest in computer connections; located by Metrotown shopping center. 283 one-bedroom standard units. 18 stories, interior corridors. **Parking:** on-site and valet. **Terms:** cancellation fee imposed, small pets only ($50 deposit). **Amenities:** video games (fee), high-speed Internet, dual phone lines, voice mail, irons, hair dryers. **Dining:** Crystal Bar and Grille, see separate listing. **Pool(s):** small heated outdoor, wading. **Leisure Activities:** whirlpool, exercise room. **Guest Services:** valet laundry, area transportation-within 10 km. **Business Services:** conference facilities, business center. **Cards:** AX, CB, DC, DS, JC, MC, VI. **Special Amenities:** free newspaper and early check-in/late check-out. *(See ad below)*

SOME UNITS

FEE

HOLIDAY INN EXPRESS METROTOWN   *Book at aaa.com*   Phone: (604)438-1881   103

CAA SAVE
	6/1-9/30 [ECP]	1P: $139-$189	2P: $139-$189	XP: $10	F
	3/1-5/31 [ECP]	1P: $129-$159	2P: $129-$159	XP: $10	F
	10/1-2/28 [ECP]	1P: $129	2P: $129	XP: $10	F

Small-scale Hotel   **Location:** Trans-Canada Hwy 1, exit 29 (Willingdon Ave S), 5 km s to Central Blvd, then just e. Located adjacent to a large shopping centre. 4405 Central Blvd V5H 4M3. Fax: 604/438-1883. **Facility:** 100 one-bedroom standard units. 6 stories, interior corridors. **Parking:** on-site. **Terms:** package plans. **Amenities:** video games (fee), high-speed Internet, voice mail, irons, hair dryers. **Pool(s):** small heated outdoor. **Leisure Activities:** limited exercise equipment. **Guest Services:** gift shop, valet laundry. **Business Services:** meeting rooms. **Cards:** AX, CB, DC, DS, JC, MC, VI. **Special Amenities:** free expanded continental breakfast and free local telephone calls.

SOME UNITS

 / ⊠

LAKE CITY MOTOR INN   Phone: 604-294-5331   108

Motel	5/1-10/15	1P: $89-$94	2P: $99-$104	XP: $5	F12
	10/16-2/28	1P: $75-$79	2P: $79-$99	XP: $5	F12
	3/1-4/30	1P: $75-$79	2P: $79-$89	XP: $5	F12

Location: Boundary Rd, 3 km e on Lougheed Hwy at Holdom Ave; entrance on north side of highway. Located in a residential area. 5415 Lougheed Hwy V5B 2Z7. Fax: 604/294-5629. **Facility:** 48 units. 42 one- and 6 two-bedroom standard units, some with efficiencies. 2 stories (no elevator), exterior corridors. **Parking:** on-site. **Terms:** office hours 6:30 am-midnight, small pets only ($5 extra charge). **Amenities:** irons. **Pool(s):** small heated outdoor. **Leisure Activities:** whirlpool. **Guest Services:** coin laundry. **Business Services:** meeting rooms. **Cards:** AX, DC, MC, VI. *(See color ad p 572)*

SOME UNITS

ASK 🐕 ➤ 🛢 📺 / ⊠

FEE

(See map and index starting on p. 536)

———— WHERE TO DINE ————

CRYSTAL BAR AND GRILLE   Lunch: $9-$12   Dinner: $12-$24   Phone: 604/438-1200   109

Continental

Location: Trans-Canada Hwy 1, exit 29 (Willingdon Ave S), 3 km S to Kingsway, then just e; in Hilton Vancouver Metrotown. 6083 McKay Ave V5H 2W7. **Hours:** 6 am-11 pm. **Reservations:** suggested. **Features:** On the third floor of the Hilton Vancouver Metrotown, the 80-seat restaurant is open for breakfast, lunch and dinner and also serves a fabulous Sunday brunch. Creative dishes center on fish, beef or pasta. Casual dress; cocktails. **Parking:** on-site and valet. **Cards:** AX, DC, DS, JC, MC, VI. *(See ad p 580)*

HART HOUSE ON DEER LAKE   Lunch: $10-$16   Dinner: $17-$30   Phone: 604/298-4278   110

Pacific Rim

Location: Trans-Canada Hwy 1, exit 33 (Kensington S), 1 km e on Canada Way to Sperling Ave, follow signs to Burnaby Village Museum. 6664 Deer Lake Ave V5E 4H3. **Hours:** 11:30 am-2:30 & 5:30-9 pm, Sat-10 pm, Sun 11 am-2 & 5:30-10 pm. Closed: 1/1, 12/26; also Mon & 11/11. **Reservations:** suggested. **Features:** The turn-of-the-20th-century Tudor-style country home has been turned into a lovely setting overlooking Deer Lake and two acres of lush lawn. The menu features rack of lamb, fish and pasta, along with lighter fare for lunch. Casual dress; cocktails. **Parking:** on-site. **Cards:** AX, MC, VI.

HORIZON'S   Lunch: $14-$17   Dinner: $20-$28   Phone: 604/299-1155   112

Pacific Rim

Location: Lougheed Hwy, 5 km n on Gaglardi Way, just n on University Dr, then just n, follow signs. 100 Centennial Way V5A 2X9. **Hours:** 11:30 am-2 & 5-9 pm, Sun from 11 am. Closed: 12/24, 12/25. **Reservations:** suggested. **Features:** Horizon's hilltop location in Burnaby Mountain Park gives you a spectacular view of the city and mountains. Its menu specializes in alderwood-fired fresh seafood and steak as well as rack of lamb and roasted duck. This is a casual, fine-dining experience. Casual dress; cocktails. **Parking:** on-site. **Cards:** AX, DC, MC, VI.

MILESTONE'S GRILL & BAR   Lunch: $7-$10   Dinner: $7-$13   Phone: 604/291-7393   108

Canadian

Location: Between Rosser and Willingdon aves. 4420 Lougheed Hwy V5C 3Z3. **Hours:** 10 am-10 pm, Fri & Sat-11 pm. Closed: 12/25. **Features:** Whether it's lunch, brunch, dinner or a drink, you'll find it here, along with a friendly staff and a warm, welcoming atmosphere, all for a reasonable price. Casual dress; cocktails. **Parking:** on-site. **Cards:** AX, DC, MC, VI.

COQUITLAM pop. 112,890   (See map and index starting on p. 536)

———— WHERE TO STAY ————

BEST WESTERN CHELSEA INN   *Book at aaa.com*   Phone: (604)525-7777   119

Small-scale Hotel

6/1-9/30	1P: $119-$349	2P: $119-$349	XP: $10	F12
3/1-5/31 & 10/1-2/28	1P: $109-$299	2P: $109-$299	XP: $10	F12

Location: Trans-Canada Hwy 1, exit 40B (Brunette Ave N). 725 Brunette Ave V3K 1C3. Fax: 604/525-3051. **Facility:** 61 units. 60 one-bedroom standard units, some with efficiencies and/or whirlpools. 1 one-bedroom suite with kitchen and whirlpool. 3 stories, interior corridors. **Parking:** on-site. **Terms:** small pets only. **Amenities:** high-speed Internet, voice mail, irons, hair dryers. *Some:* DVD players. **Dining:** 7 am-2 & 4:30-10 pm, cocktails. **Pool(s):** small heated outdoor. **Leisure Activities:** sauna, whirlpool, limited exercise equipment. **Guest Services:** valet and coin laundry. **Cards:** AX, CB, DC, DS, JC, VI. **Special Amenities:** free local telephone calls and early check-in/late check-out. *(See color ad below)*

SOME UNITS

BEST WESTERN COQUITLAM INN CONVENTION CENTRE   *Book at aaa.com*   Phone: (604)931-9011   116

Small-scale Hotel

5/1-9/30	1P: $149-$179	2P: $149-$179	XP: $10	F12
3/1-4/30 & 10/1-2/28	1P: $139-$169	2P: $139-$169	XP: $10	F12

Location: Trans-Canada Hwy 1, exit 37 (Cariboo Rd/Gaglardi Way), 2 km on Lougheed Hwy (Hwy 7), then just s. 319 North Rd V3K 3V8. Fax: 604/931-7298. **Facility:** 106 units. 90 one-bedroom standard units, some with whirlpools. 16 two-bedroom suites ($179-$289) with kitchens. 2 stories, interior/exterior corridors. **Parking:** on-site. **Amenities:** voice mail, irons, hair dryers. **Dining:** 2 restaurants, 6:30 am-10 pm, cocktails. **Pool(s):** heated indoor. **Leisure Activities:** sauna, whirlpool, limited exercise equipment. **Guest Services:** valet laundry. **Business Services:** conference facilities. **Cards:** AX, CB, DC, DS, JC, MC, VI. **Special Amenities:** free local telephone calls and free newspaper.

SOME UNITS

(See map and index starting on p. 536)

HOLIDAY INN VANCOUVER-COQUITLAM

Phone: (604)931-4433   **118**

6/16-9/15	1P: $109-$149	2P: $119-$159	XP: $10	F19
3/1-6/15	1P: $89-$109	2P: $99-$119	XP: $10	F19
9/16-2/28	1P: $79-$99	2P: $89-$109	XP: $10	F19

Location: Trans-Canada Hwy 1, exit 37 (Gaglardi Way) eastbound, 3.5 km e on Lougheed Hwy (Hwy 7); exit 44 (Coquitlam) westbound, then 3 km w on Lougheed Hwy (Hwy 7). 631 Lougheed Hwy V3K 3S5. Fax: 604/931-4250.
Small-scale Hotel   **Facility:** 84 one-bedroom standard units, some with whirlpools. 2 stories (no elevator), interior/exterior corridors. **Parking:** on-site. **Terms:** package plans, small pets only ($30 fee). **Amenities:** video games (fee), voice mail, irons, hair dryers. **Dining:** 6:30 am-10 pm, cocktails. **Pool(s):** heated indoor. **Leisure Activities:** whirlpool. **Guest Services:** valet and coin laundry. **Business Services:** meeting rooms. **Cards:** AX, CB, DC, DS, JC, MC, VI. **Special Amenities:** free newspaper and early check-in/late check-out.

SOME UNITS

------ **WHERE TO DINE** ------

JOEY TOMATO'S MEDITERRANEAN GRILL

Lunch: $8-$16   Dinner: $12-$24   Phone: 604/939-3077   **115**

Location: Trans-Canada Hwy 1, exit 37 (Gaglardi Way) eastbound, 3.8 km e on Longhead Hwy (Hwy 7); exit 44 (Coquitlam) westbound, 3.2 km w on Lougheed Hwy. 550 Lougheed Hwy V3K 353. **Hours:** 11:30 am-10 pm.
Mediterranean   Closed: 12/25. **Features:** The tucked-away restaurant is easily missed, so watch for the road sign. Good food, including the signature spit-roasted chicken, is reasonably priced and goes well with selections from the good wine list. Among other choices are Pavarotti-size salads, which are perfect for lunch or a light dinner; "tapatizers" for sharing; and thin-crust pizzas. Servers are attentive. Casual dress; cocktails. **Parking:** on-site. **Cards:** AX, MC, VI.

DELTA pop. 96,950   (See map and index starting on p. 536)

------ **WHERE TO STAY** ------

CLAIR'S BED & BREAKFAST

Phone: 604/940-8867   **160**

5/15-9/30 [BP]	1P: $85-$125	2P: $105-$150	XP: $25	D16
3/1-5/14 & 10/1-2/28 [BP]	1P: $65-$90	2P: $85-$130	XP: $20	D16

Location: Hwy 17, 1.8 km w on Ladner Trunk Rd to Elliott St, just n on 48th Ave. Located in Ladner Village. 4919 48th
Historic Bed Ave V4K 1V4. **Facility:** Built in 1913, this Edwardian-style house served as a family home for its first 60
& Breakfast years. Smoke free premises. 6 one-bedroom standard units, some with whirlpools. 2 stories (no elevator), interior/exterior corridors. *Bath:* combo, shower or tub only. **Parking:** on-site. **Terms:** office hours 8 am-10 pm, check-in 4 pm, 7 day cancellation notice-fee imposed, weekly rates available. **Cards:** MC, VI.

THE COAST TSAWWASSEN INN

Phone: (604)943-8221   **161**

5/1-9/30	1P: $119	2P: $149	XP: $15	F17
10/1-2/28	1P: $99	2P: $115	XP: $15	F17
Small-scale Hotel 3/1-4/30	1P: $99	2P: $109	XP: $15	F17

Under major renovation, scheduled to be completed May 2005. **Last rated:** Location: Hwy 99, exit 28 (Tsawwassen Ferries), 8 km w on Hwy 17; 5 km from the BC ferry terminal. 1665 56th St V4L 2B2. Fax: 604/943-8299. **Facility:** 90 one-bedroom suites, some with efficiencies and/or whirlpools. 3 stories, interior corridors. **Parking:** on-site. **Terms:** package plans, small pets only ($10 extra charge). **Amenities:** video games (fee), voice mail, irons, hair dryers. *Some:* high-speed Internet. **Pool(s):** heated indoor. **Leisure Activities:** sauna, whirlpool, limited exercise equipment. **Guest Services:** valet and coin laundry, area transportation. **Business Services:** conference facilities. **Cards:** AX, DC, DS, MC, VI.

SOME UNITS

DELTA TOWN & COUNTRY INN

Book at aaa.com   Phone: (604)946-4404   **157**

5/1-9/30	1P: $99-$129	2P: $99-$129	XP: $20	D16
3/1-4/30	1P: $90-$119	2P: $90-$119	XP: $15	D16
10/1-2/28	1P: $90-$119	2P: $90-$119	XP: $20	D16

Location: Hwy 99 at jct Hwy 17, exit 28 (Tsawwassen Ferries), 12 km ne on Hwy 17 of Tsawwassen-Victoria ferry
Small-scale Hotel terminal. Located in a quiet rural area. 6005 Hwy 17 at Hwy 99 V4K 5B8. Fax: 604/946-5916. **Facility:** 49 one-bedroom standard units. 2 stories (no elevator), interior corridors. **Parking:** on-site. **Amenities:** voice mail, irons, hair dryers. *Some:* high-speed Internet. **Dining:** 6 am-9:30 pm, Sun from 7 am, cocktails. **Pool(s):** heated outdoor. **Leisure Activities:** whirlpool, 5 tennis courts (4 indoor, 4 lighted), exercise room. **Guest Services:** valet and coin laundry. **Business Services:** meeting rooms, business center. **Cards:** AX, DC, MC, VI. **Special Amenities:** free room upgrade and preferred room (each subject to availability with advance reservations).

SOME UNITS

RIVER RUN COTTAGES

Phone: (604)946-7778   **158**

4/1-9/30 [BP]	2P: $150-$210	XP: $20	D
3/1-3/31 & 10/1-2/28 [BP]	2P: $130-$190	XP: $20	D

Location: Hwy 17, 2.5 km n on Ladner Trunk Rd (which becomes 47A St), then becomes River Rd W. Located in
Bed & Breakfast Ladner Village. 4551 River Rd W V4K 1R9. Fax: 604/940-1970. **Facility:** These three self-contained cottages are built on pillars over tidal mud flats on the Fraser River; one floating accommodation is tied to a dock. Smoke free premises. 4 one-bedroom standard units. 1 story, exterior corridors. *Bath:* combo or shower only. **Parking:** on-site. **Terms:** office hours 7 am-10 pm, check-in 4 pm, 2 night minimum stay - seasonal, age restrictions may apply, 21 day cancellation notice-fee imposed, small pets only (in designated unit). **Amenities:** CD players, hair dryers. **Leisure Activities:** bicycles. **Cards:** MC, VI.

------ **WHERE TO DINE** ------

LA BELLE AUBERGE

Menu on aaa.com   Dinner: $25-$28   Phone: 604/946-7717   **128**

Location: Hwy 17, 1.8 km w on Ladner Trunk Rd to Elliott St, then just n. 4856 48th Ave V4K 1V2. **Hours:** 6 pm-midnight. Closed: Mon. **Reservations:** suggested. **Features:** This charming Ladner home has been
French transformed into a comfortable inn serving fine French cuisine. The restaurant is owned and operated by a chef and Olympic gold medalist on the Canadian culinary team. A six-course meal for $50-$60 per person is offered. Casual dress; cocktails. **Parking:** on-site. **Cards:** AX, DC, MC, VI.

LANGLEY pop. 23,643

──────── **WHERE TO STAY** ────────

BEST VALUE WESTWARD INN   *Book at aaa.com*   **Phone:** (604)534-9238

(CAA) (SAVE)   All Year   1P: $57-$72   2P: $61-$77   XP: $6   F13

Location: Trans-Canada Hwy 1, exit 58 (200th St/Langley City), 5 km s on 200th St, 1 km w on Hwy 10, then just w. 19650 Fraser Hwy V3A 4C7. Fax: 604/534-0629. **Facility:** 55 one-bedroom standard units, some with kitchens. 1 story, exterior corridors. **Parking:** on-site. **Terms:** pets ($4 extra charge). **Guest Services:** coin laundry.

Motel   **Cards:** AX, MC, VI. **Special Amenities:** free local telephone calls.

SOME UNITS

BEST WESTERN LANGLEY INN   *Book at aaa.com*   **Phone:** (604)530-9311

(CAA) (SAVE)

| | 6/1-9/20 | 1P: $109-$119 | 2P: $109-$119 | XP: $6 | F12 |
| | 3/1-5/31 & 9/21-2/28 | 1P: $95-$99 | 2P: $95-$99 | XP: $6 | F12 |

Location: Trans-Canada Hwy 1, exit 66 (232nd St), 6 km s, follow signs. 5978 Glover Rd V3A 4H9.
Small-scale Hotel Fax: 604/530-2438. **Facility:** 78 units. 77 one-bedroom standard units, some with efficiencies. 1 two-
bedroom suite with kitchen. 2 stories (no elevator), interior corridors. **Parking:** on-site. **Terms:** small pets
only ($15 extra charge, in limited units). **Amenities:** video games (fee), voice mail, irons, hair dryers. *Some:*
high-speed Internet. **Dining:** 6:30 am-10:30 pm, wine/beer only. **Pool(s):** heated indoor. **Leisure Activities:** whirlpool, limited
exercise equipment. **Guest Services:** valet and coin laundry. **Business Services:** meeting rooms, business center. **Cards:** AX,
DC, DS, MC, VI. **Special Amenities:** free expanded continental breakfast and free local telephone calls.
(See color ad p 583)

SOME UNITS
🆂🅳 🛏 🍽 🚲 🎥 📠 💻 / ✕ 📶 🖨 /
FEE

HAMPTON INN & SUITES   *Book at aaa.com*   **Phone:** (604)530-6545

| | 6/1-9/15 | 1P: $109-$139 | 2P: $119-$165 | | |
| | 3/1-5/31 & 9/16-2/28 | 1P: $94-$139 | 2P: $99-$149 | | |

Small-scale Hotel **Location:** Trans-Canada Hwy 1, exit 58 (200th St), 5 km s, then 1.2 km w on Hwy 10. 19500 Langley Bypass V3S 7R2.
Fax: 604/530-9192. **Facility:** 96 units. 78 one-bedroom standard units. 18 one-bedroom suites ($109-$165)
with efficiencies. 4 stories, interior corridors. **Parking:** on-site. **Terms:** weekly rates available. **Amenities:** video games (fee),
high-speed Internet, voice mail, irons, hair dryers. *Some:* dual phone lines. **Pool(s):** heated indoor. **Leisure
Activities:** whirlpool, waterslide, limited exercise equipment. **Guest Services:** valet and coin laundry. **Business Services:**
meeting rooms, business center. **Cards:** AX, CB, DC, DS, JC, MC, VI. *(See color ad p 583)*

SOME UNITS
(ASK) 🆂🅳 🍽 📺 ♿🅼 🚲 ✕ 🎥 📠 💻 / ✕ 📶 🖨 /

HOLIDAY INN EXPRESS HOTEL & SUITES
LANGLEY   *Book at aaa.com*   **Phone:** (604)882-2000

(CAA) (SAVE)

	5/16-9/15 [ECP]	1P: $117	XP: $10	F19
	1/1-2/28 [ECP]	1P: $109	XP: $10	F19
	3/1-5/15 & 9/16-12/31 [ECP]	1P: $107	XP: $10	F19

Location: Trans-Canada Hwy 1, exit 58 (200th St), just e on 88th Ave. 8750 204th St V1M 2Y5. Fax: 604/882-2008.
Small-scale Hotel **Facility:** 85 one-bedroom standard units, some with whirlpools. 4 stories, interior corridors. **Parking:** on-
site. **Terms:** small pets only ($10 extra charge). **Amenities:** video games (fee), high-speed Internet, dual
phone lines, voice mail, irons, hair dryers. **Pool(s):** heated indoor. **Leisure Activities:** sauna, whirlpool, steamroom, limited
exercise equipment. **Guest Services:** valet and coin laundry. **Business Services:** meeting rooms. **Cards:** AX, DC, DS, JC,
MC, VI. **Special Amenities:** free expanded continental breakfast and free local telephone calls.

SOME UNITS
🆂🅳 🛏 🍽 ♿🅼 🚲 ✕ 🎥 📠 💻 / ✕ 📶 🖨 /
FEE

SANDMAN HOTEL LANGLEY   *Book at aaa.com*   **Phone:** (604)888-7263

| | 5/1-9/30 | 1P: $129-$149 | XP: $10 | F14 |
| | 3/1-4/30 & 10/1-2/28 | 1P: $119-$139 | XP: $10 | F14 |

Small-scale Hotel **Location:** Trans-Canada Hwy 1, exit 58 (200th St), just e on 88th Ave. 8855 202nd St V1M 2N9. Fax: 604/888-7271.
Facility: 145 units. 129 one-bedroom standard units, some with efficiencies. 16 one-bedroom suites. 4
stories, interior corridors. **Parking:** on-site. **Terms:** [BP], [CP] & [ECP] meal plans available, small pets only ($10 extra charge).
Amenities: voice mail, hair dryers. *Some:* irons. **Leisure Activities:** limited exercise equipment. **Guest Services:** valet laundry.
Business Services: meeting rooms. **Cards:** AX, DC, DS, MC, VI.

SOME UNITS
(ASK) 🆂🅳 🛏 🍽 📺 🎥 📠 💻 / ✕ 📶 🖨 /
FEE

SLEEP INN LANGLEY   *Book at aaa.com*   **Phone:** (604)514-3111

| | 5/1-9/30 | 1P: $80-$100 | 2P: $90-$110 | XP: $10 | F18 |
| | 3/1-4/30 & 10/1-2/28 | 1P: $70-$90 | 2P: $80-$100 | XP: $10 | F18 |

Small-scale Hotel **Location:** Trans-Canada Hwy 1, exit 66 (232nd St), 4 km s on Glover Rd, follow signs. Located close to railroad tracks.
6722 Glover Rd V2Y 1S6. Fax: 604/514-9098. **Facility:** 46 one-bedroom standard units. 2 stories, interior
corridors. *Bath:* combo or shower only. **Parking:** on-site. **Terms:** weekly rates available, small pets only ($10 extra charge).
Amenities: voice mail. **Leisure Activities:** sauna, limited exercise equipment. **Guest Services:** valet laundry. **Business
Services:** meeting rooms. **Cards:** AX, DC, MC, VI.

SOME UNITS
(ASK) 🆂🅳 🛏 📠 / ✕ /
FEE

TRAVELODGE-LANGLEY CITY   *Book at aaa.com*   **Phone:** (604)533-4431

(CAA) (SAVE)

| | All Year | 1P: $69-$99 | 2P: $69-$99 | XP: $8 | F12 |

Location: Trans-Canada Hwy 1, exit 66 (232nd St), 6 km s, 1 km se on Langley Bypass, then 1.5 km e to 216 St.
21653 Fraser Hwy V3A 4H1. Fax: 604/514-7620. **Facility:** 65 one-bedroom standard units, some with kitchens
Motel and/or whirlpools. 2 stories (no elevator), exterior corridors. **Parking:** on-site. **Terms:** small pets only ($10
extra charge). **Amenities:** hair dryers. **Guest Services:** valet and coin laundry. **Business Services:**
meeting rooms. **Cards:** AX, MC, VI. **Special Amenities:** free continental breakfast and free local
telephone calls.

SOME UNITS
🆂🅳 🛏 📶 📠 💻 / ✕ 📶 🖨 /
FEE

MAPLE RIDGE pop. 63,169

—— WHERE TO STAY ——

BEST WESTERN MAPLE RIDGE   *Book at aaa.com*   Phone: (604)463-5111

CAA SAVE

5/15-10/14	1P: $89-$129	2P: $89-$129	XP: $10 F17
3/1-5/14 & 10/15-2/28	1P: $79-$119	2P: $79-$119	XP: $10 F17

Location: 2 km w on Lougheed Hwy (Hwy 7). 21735 Lougheed Hwy V2X 2S2. Fax: 604/463-3113. **Facility:** 61
one-bedroom standard units, some with kitchens and/or whirlpools. 2 stories (no elevator), exterior
Small-scale Hotel corridors. **Parking:** on-site. **Terms:** 7 day cancellation notice-fee imposed. **Amenities:** voice mail, irons, hair
dryers. **Dining:** 6:30 am-9:30 pm, wine/beer only. **Leisure Activities:** whirlpool, limited exercise equipment.
Guest Services: coin laundry. **Business Services:** meeting rooms. **Cards:** AX, DC, DS, MC, VI. **Special Amenities:** free
local telephone calls and free room upgrade (subject to availability with advance reservations).

SOME UNITS

TRAVELODGE MAPLE RIDGE   *Book at aaa.com*   Phone: (604)467-1511

CAA SAVE

6/1-9/30 [CP]	1P: $85-$95	2P: $95-$99	XP: $10 F16
3/1-5/31 & 10/1-2/28 [CP]	1P: $75-$85	2P: $85-$95	XP: $10 F16

Motel

Location: 2 km w on Lougheed Hwy (Hwy 7). 21650 Lougheed Hwy V2X 2S1. Fax: 604/467-1532. **Facility:** 56
one-bedroom standard units, some with efficiencies. 2 stories (no elevator), interior corridors. **Parking:** on-
site. **Terms:** weekly rates available, pets ($50 deposit, $10 extra charge). **Amenities:** video library (fee),
hair dryers. **Leisure Activities:** sauna, whirlpool, limited exercise equipment. **Guest Services:** valet and
coin laundry. **Business Services:** meeting rooms. **Cards:** AX, DC, MC, VI. **Special Amenities:** free continental breakfast
and free local telephone calls.

SOME UNITS

—— WHERE TO DINE ——

ROOSTER'S QUARTERS   **Lunch:** $7-$11   **Dinner:** $8-$21   Phone: 604-463-9691

Location: Lougheed Hwy (Hwy 7), just n on 226th St. 22590 Dewdney Trunk Rd V2X 3J9. **Hours:** 11 am-9 pm, Sat
& Sun 9:30 am-10 pm. **Closed:** 12/25, 12/26. **Features:** You'll like this restaurant decorated in a chicken
Canadian   motif with ceramic hens and pictures of roosters. What do they specialize in? Chicken, of course. The
cordon bleu is excellent. Park behind the building; the entrance is near Canada Safeway on 226th St.
Cocktails. **Parking:** on-site. **Cards:** AX, MC, VI.

MISSION pop. 31,272

—— WHERE TO STAY ——

BEST WESTERN MISSION CITY LODGE   *Book at aaa.com*   Phone: (604)820-5500

CAA SAVE

5/1-9/30	1P: $89-$122	2P: $89-$122	XP: $7 F12
3/1-4/30 & 10/1-2/28	1P: $79-$101	2P: $79-$101	XP: $7 F12

Location: Just w of Hwy 11, corner of Lougheed Hwy (Hwy 7) and Hurd St. 32281 Lougheed Hwy V2V 1A3.
Fax: 604/820-5510. **Facility:** 80 one-bedroom standard units, some with efficiencies and/or whirlpools. 4
Small-scale Hotel stories, interior corridors. **Parking:** on-site. **Terms:** small pets only ($10 extra charge). **Amenities:** voice
mail, irons, hair dryers. **Dining:** 6:30 am-11 pm, cocktails. **Pool(s):** heated indoor. **Leisure
Activities:** sauna, whirlpool, limited exercise equipment. **Guest Services:** coin laundry. **Business Services:** meeting rooms.
Cards: AX, DC, DS, MC, VI. **Special Amenities:** free local telephone calls.

SOME UNITS

NEW WESTMINSTER pop. 54,656   (See map and index starting on p. 536)

—— WHERE TO STAY ——

INN AT WESTMINSTER QUAY   *Book at aaa.com*   Phone: (604)520-1776   **170**

CAA SAVE

5/1-9/30	1P: $160-$215	2P: $170-$215	XP: $10 F16
3/1-4/30 & 10/1-2/28	1P: $150-$205	2P: $160-$205	XP: $10 F16

Location: Along the waterfront, follow signs to Westminster Quay. Located adjacent to public market. 900 Quayside Dr
V3M 6G1. Fax: 604/520-5645. **Facility:** 126 one-bedroom standard units, some with whirlpools. 9 stories,
Large-scale Hotel interior corridors. **Parking:** on-site (fee). **Terms:** package plans. **Amenities:** video games (fee), voice mail,
honor bars, irons, hair dryers. **Dining:** 6:30 am-2 & 5-10 pm, cocktails. **Leisure Activities:** sauna, whirlpool,
exercise room. **Guest Services:** valet laundry. **Business Services:** conference facilities. **Cards:** AX, CB, DC, DS, JC, MC, VI.
Special Amenities: free newspaper and early check-in/late check-out.

SOME UNITS

—— *The following lodging was either not evaluated or did not* ——
meet AAA rating requirements but is listed for your information only.

THE MET HOTEL   Phone: 604/520-3815

fyi   Not evaluated. **Location:** Between 4th and 6th sts. 411 Columbia St V3L 1A9. Facilities, services, and decor
characterize a mid-range property.

(See map and index starting on p. 536)

──────── **WHERE TO DINE** ────────

BURGER HEAVEN   **Lunch:** $5-$10   **Dinner:** $5-$10   **Phone:** 604/522-8339   [133]

American   **Location:** From Royal Ave, just e. 77 10th St V3M 3X4. **Hours:** 11:30 am-9 pm, Fri & Sat-10 pm. Closed: 12/24, 12/25. **Features:** This locally popular dining spot features all kinds of burgers—chicken, veggie, beef—cooked to order and served with many different fresh toppings. They also have a wide variety of sandwiches, a living-room atmosphere, beer, wine and coolers. Casual dress; beer & wine only. **Parking:** street. **Cards:** AX, MC, VI.

LA RUSTICA RISTORANTE   **Lunch:** $6-$9   **Dinner:** $11-$20   **Phone:** 604/525-6355   [137]

Italian   **Location:** Between 3rd and 2nd aves. 228 6th St V3L 3A4. **Hours:** 11:30 am-2 & 5-10 pm, Fri-11 pm, Sat 5 pm-11 pm, Sun 5 pm-10 pm. Closed: 12/25, 12/26. **Reservations:** suggested, weekends. **Features:** This restaurant's traditional homemade cuisine is complemented by French and Continental dishes. The veal piccata and pepper steak are good choices. The setting was converted from two older side-by-side houses. The servers are pleasant and friendly. **Cocktails. Parking:** street. **Cards:** AX, DC, MC, VI.

NORTH VANCOUVER pop. 44,303   (See map and index starting on p. 536)

──────── **WHERE TO STAY** ────────

BEST WESTERN CAPILANO INN & SUITES   *Book at aaa.com*   **Phone:** (604)987-8185   [94]

6/1-9/30	1P: $109-$139	2P: $119-$139
5/1-5/31	1P: $89-$119	2P: $99-$119
3/1-4/30 & 10/1-2/28	1P: $79-$109	2P: $89-$109

Motel   **Location:** Trans-Canada Hwy 1, exit 14 (Capilano Rd), 1.5 km s; from north end of Lions Gate Bridge, 1 km e on Marine Dr, then just n. 1634 Capilano Rd V7P 3B4. Fax: 604/987-5153. **Facility:** 74 units. 73 one- and 1 two-bedroom standard units, some with efficiencies, kitchens and/or whirlpools. 2 stories (no elevator), exterior corridors. **Parking:** on-site. **Terms:** cancellation fee imposed. **Amenities:** voice mail, irons, hair dryers. **Dining:** 7 am-3:30 pm. **Pool(s):** heated outdoor. **Guest Services:** coin laundry. **Business Services:** meeting rooms. **Cards:** AX, DC, DS, MC, VI. **Special Amenities:** free newspaper and preferred room (subject to availability with advance reservations).

SOME UNITS

COMFORT INN AND SUITES   *Book at aaa.com*   **Phone:** (604)988-3181   [92]

6/16-9/15 [CP]	1P: $139-$259	2P: $139-$259	XP: $10	F18
5/1-6/15 [CP]	1P: $99-$199	2P: $99-$199	XP: $10	F18
9/16-2/28 [CP]	1P: $99-$179	2P: $99-$179	XP: $10	F18
3/1-4/30 [CP]	1P: $89-$169	2P: $99-$169	XP: $10	F18

Motel   **Location:** Trans-Canada Hwy 1, exit 14 (Capilano Rd), 1.5 km s; from north end of Lions Gate Bridge, 1 km e on Marine Dr, then just n. 1748 Capilano Rd V7P 3B4. Fax: 604/904-2755. **Facility:** 94 units. 91 one- and 3 two-bedroom standard units, some with kitchens. 2 stories (no elevator), exterior corridors. **Parking:** on-site. **Amenities:** video games (fee), hair dryers. **Pool(s):** heated outdoor. **Leisure Activities:** whirlpool. **Guest Services:** coin laundry. **Cards:** AX, DC, DS, JC, MC, VI. **Special Amenities:** free continental breakfast and free local telephone calls.

SOME UNITS

GROUSE INN   *Book at aaa.com*   **Phone:** (604)988-7101   [98]

7/1-10/9 [CP]	1P: $119-$148	2P: $119-$148
5/1-6/30 [CP]	1P: $99-$119	2P: $99-$119
3/1-4/30 & 10/10-2/28 [CP]	1P: $89-$99	2P: $89-$109

Motel   **Location:** Trans-Canada Hwy 1, exit 14 (Capilano Rd), 1.5 km s; from north end of Lions Gate Bridge, 1 km e on Marine Dr. 1633 Capilano Rd V7P 3B3. Fax: 604/988-7102. **Facility:** 80 units. 73 one- and 7 two-bedroom standard units, some with efficiencies, kitchens and/or whirlpools. 2 stories (no elevator), exterior corridors. **Parking:** on-site. **Terms:** cancellation fee imposed, weekly rates available, package plans. **Amenities:** video library (fee), voice mail, irons, hair dryers. **Pool(s):** heated outdoor. **Guest Services:** coin laundry. **Business Services:** meeting rooms. **Cards:** AX, CB, DC, DS, JC, MC, VI. **Special Amenities:** free continental breakfast and free local telephone calls. *(See color ad p 549)*

SOME UNITS

FEE

HOLIDAY INN HOTEL & SUITES NORTH VANCOUVER   *Book at aaa.com*   **Phone:** (604)985-3111   [96]

7/1-9/30	1P: $149-$179	2P: $149-$179	XP: $10	F18
5/1-6/30	1P: $129-$169	2P: $129-$169	XP: $10	F18
10/1-2/28	1P: $99-$139	2P: $99-$139	XP: $10	F18
3/1-4/30	1P: $99-$129	2P: $99-$129	XP: $10	F18

Large-scale Hotel   **Location:** Trans-Canada Hwy 1, exit 22 (Mt Seymour Pkwy), follow signs. 700 Old Lillooet Rd V7J 2H5. Fax: 604/985-0857. **Facility:** 162 one-bedroom standard units, some with efficiencies and/or whirlpools. 6 stories, interior corridors. **Parking:** on-site. **Terms:** [BP] meal plan available, package plans, pets ($20 extra charge, no cats). **Amenities:** video games (fee), high-speed Internet, dual phone lines, voice mail, safes, irons, hair dryers. **Dining:** 6 am-10 pm, cocktails. **Pool(s):** heated indoor. **Leisure Activities:** sauna, whirlpool, exercise room. **Guest Services:** valet and coin laundry. **Business Services:** meeting rooms. **Cards:** AX, CB, DC, DS, JC, MC, VI. *(See color ad card insert, p 571, p 587, p 545 & p 552)*

SOME UNITS

FEE

(See map and index starting on p. 536)

LIONSGATE TRAVELODGE   *Book at aaa.com*   **Phone:** (604)985-5311   [95]

▽▽   5/1-9/30   1P: $129   2P: $139   XP: $10   F17
         10/1-10/31   1P: $89   2P: $99   XP: $10   F17
Motel   3/1-4/30 & 11/1-2/28   1P: $79   2P: $89   XP: $10   F17
         Location: Trans-Canada Hwy 1, exit 14 (Capilano Rd), 1.5 km s; from n end of Lions Gate Bridge, just e on Marine Dr.
2060 Marine Dr V7P 1V7. Fax: 604/985-5391. **Facility:** 61 one-bedroom standard units. 2 stories (no elevator), exterior corridors.
Bath: combo or shower only. **Parking:** on-site. **Terms:** cancellation fee imposed, package plans, $2 service charge.
Amenities: irons, hair dryers. **Pool(s):** small heated outdoor. **Cards:** AX, DC, DS, MC, VI.

SOME UNITS
(ASK) (S/D) [🛏] [🍽] [☰] [🖥] / [✕] /

LONSDALE QUAY HOTEL   *Book at aaa.com*   **Phone:** (604)986-6111   [97]

(CAA) (SAVE)   5/1-9/30   1P: $125-$350   2P: $125-$350   XP: $25   F18
             10/1-10/31   1P: $125-$210   2P: $125-$210   XP: $25   F18
▽▽▽▽   11/1-2/28   1P: $115-$210   2P: $115-$210   XP: $25   F18
             3/1-4/30   1P: $115-$200   2P: $115-$200   XP: $25   F18
Small-scale Hotel **Location:** Trans-Canada Hwy 1, exit 18 (Lonsdale Ave), 2.5 km s. Located in the Lonsdale Quay Market. 123 Carrie
Gates Ct V7M 3K7. Fax: 604/986-8782. **Facility:** 70 one-bedroom standard units, some with whirlpools. 4
stories, interior corridors. **Parking:** on-site (fee). **Terms:** cancellation fee imposed, [BP] meal plan available, package plans, $2
service charge. **Amenities:** high-speed Internet, voice mail, irons, hair dryers. *Some:* honor bars. **Dining:** 7 am-10 pm,
cocktails. **Leisure Activities:** exercise room. **Guest Services:** gift shop, valet and coin laundry. **Business Services:** meeting
rooms. **Cards:** AX, DC, DS, MC, VI. **Special Amenities:** free newspaper and early check-in/late check-out.

SOME UNITS
(S/D) [🍽] [🍷] [GM] [📽] [DATA PORT] [🔌] [🖥] / [✕] [🖨] /

RAMADA INN VANCOUVER NORTH SHORE   **Phone:** (604)987-4461   [91]

(CAA) (SAVE)   5/1-9/15 [ECP]   1P: $131   2P: $131   XP: $10   F18
             3/1-4/30 & 9/16-2/28 [ECP] 1P: $75   2P: $75   XP: $10   F18
▽▽▽▽   **Location:** Trans-Canada Hwy 1, exit 14 (Capilano Rd), 1.5 km s; from north end of Lions Gate Bridge, 1 km e on
Motel   Marine Dr, then just n. 1800 Capilano Rd V7P 3B6. Fax: 604/984-4244. **Facility:** 72 one-bedroom standard units,
some with kitchens. 2 stories (no elevator), exterior corridors. **Parking:** on-site. **Terms:** cancellation fee
imposed, package plans, pets (in limited units). **Amenities:** voice mail, irons, hair dryers. **Pool(s):** heated
outdoor. **Leisure Activities:** playground. **Guest Services:** valet and coin laundry. **Cards:** AX, DC, DS, MC, VI.
Special Amenities: free expanded continental breakfast and free local telephone calls. *(See color ad below)*

SOME UNITS
[🛏] [🍽] [GM] [☰] [🛁] [📽] [DATA PORT] [🖥] / [✕] [🔌] [🖨] /

(See map and index starting on p. 536)

──────── **WHERE TO DINE** ────────

AZURE MEDITERRANEAN BISTRO   Lunch: $8-$13   Dinner: $13-$27   Phone: 604/985-9125   104

♦♦♦ ♦♦♦

Mediterranean

Location: 1.8 km n on Capilano Rd, 1 km e on Ridgewood Dr, just s; in Edgemont Village. 3135 Edgemont Blvd V7R 2N7. **Hours:** 11:30 am-2 & 5:30-10 pm. Closed: 12/25. **Reservations:** suggested. **Features:** In the quaint Edgemont Shopping Village on the road to Grouse Mountain, the quaint restaurant prepares a large selection of pastas in the $14 range and poultry, meats and seafood in the $20 range. Selections from the primarily Italian wine list are reasonably priced. Don't leave without trying the amazing tiramisu. Casual dress; cocktails. **Parking:** street. **Cards:** MC, VI.

✕

GUSTO DI QUATTRO   Lunch: $10-$15   Dinner: $16-$30   Phone: 604/924-4444   107

♦♦♦ ♦♦♦

Italian

Location: Trans-Canada Hwy 1, exit 18 (Lonsdale Ave), 2.5 km s to Lonsdale Quay Market. 1 Lonsdale Ave V7M 2E4. **Hours:** 11 am-2 & 5-10 pm. Closed: 1/1, 12/25, 12/26. **Reservations:** suggested. **Features:** Translated, Gusto di Quattro means "a taste of Quattro." The North Shore favorite, which has a small dining space, is by Lonsdale Quay Market. Wonderful pastas and freshly made breads await. Patrons likely will have to wait for a table if they didn't make a reservation. A pay parking lot is right across the street. Dressy casual; cocktails. **Parking:** street. **Cards:** AX, DC, MC, VI.

✕

KILBY'S RESTAURANT   Lunch: $9-$14   Dinner: $12-$23   Phone: 604/990-4334   105

♦♦♦ ♦♦♦

Continental

Location: 1.8 km n on Capilano Rd, 1 km e on Ridgewood Dr, just s; in Edgemont Village. 3108 Edgemont Blvd V7R 2N6. **Hours:** 11:30 am-2:30 & 5-9:30 pm. Closed: 12/25, 12/26. **Reservations:** accepted. **Features:** In the quaint Edgemont Shopping Village on the road to Grouse Mountain, the restaurant is cozy and comfortable. The place is known for its "Sunday roasts," which feature different roasts as the selected entree once weekly. The wine list includes a wonderful selection of reasonably priced choices. Cocktails. **Parking:** street. **Cards:** AX, MC, VI.

✕

MOUSTACHE CAFE   Lunch: $12-$15   Dinner: $18-$29   Phone: 604/987-8461   106

♦♦♦ ♦♦♦

Italian

Location: Marine Dr at Pemberton. 1265 Marine Dr V7P 1T3. **Hours:** 11:30 am-2:30 & 5:30-10:30 pm, Sat from 5:30 pm. Closed major holidays; also Sun. **Reservations:** suggested. **Features:** You'll like this restaurants cozy dining setting as it's in a home that was built in 1918, where the decor is bright and colorful. The regular menu items include spice-crusted beef carpaccio, mustard aioli, asiago and capers, homemade potato gnocci with tomato cream and fresh cream. Limited parking in the rear. Casual dress; beer & wine only. **Parking:** on-site. **Cards:** AX, DS, MC, VI.

✕

PITT MEADOWS pop. 14,670   (See map and index starting on p. 536)

──────── **WHERE TO STAY** ────────

RAMADA INN & SUITES HOTEL ROYALE   *Book at aaa.com*   Phone: (604)460-9859   128

♦♦♦ ♦♦♦

Small-scale Hotel

5/1-9/30	1P: $112	2P: $112	XP: $10	F18
3/1-4/30 & 10/1-2/28	1P: $89	2P: $89	XP: $10	F18

Location: Lougheed Hwy (Hwy 7) and Harris Rd. 19267 Lougheed Hwy V3Y 2J5. Fax: 604/460-9857. **Facility:** 80 one-bedroom standard units, some with efficiencies and/or whirlpools. 3 stories, interior corridors. **Parking:** on-site. **Amenities:** voice mail, irons, hair dryers. **Pool(s):** heated outdoor. **Leisure Activities:** whirlpool, limited exercise equipment. **Guest Services:** valet and coin laundry. **Business Services:** meeting rooms. **Cards:** AX, DC, DS, MC, VI.

SOME UNITS

(ASK) (SƎ) (¶) (Y) (ꞨM) (Ꞩ) (Ꞩ) (Ꞩ) (DATA PORT) (Ꞩ) / (✕) (Ꞩ) (Ꞩ) /

PORT COQUITLAM pop. 51,257   (See map and index starting on p. 536)

──────── **WHERE TO STAY** ────────

────── *The following lodging was either not evaluated or did not* ──────
meet AAA rating requirements but is listed for your information only.

BEST WESTERN POCO INN & SUITES   Phone: 604/941-6216

fyi

Not evaluated. **Location:** 3.5 km e of Coquitlam on Lougheed Hwy (Hwy 7). 1545 Lougheed Hwy V3B 1A5. Facilities, services, and decor characterize a mid-range property.

──────── **WHERE TO DINE** ────────

EARLS   Lunch: $8-$12   Dinner: $8-$15   Phone: 604/941-1733   147

♦♦♦ ♦♦♦

Canadian

Location: Corner of Shaughnessy St and Lougheed Hwy. 5100 Lougheed Hwy V3C 6K5. **Hours:** 11:30 am-10:30 pm, Fri & Sat-11 pm. Closed: 12/25. **Features:** Offering an experience that falls between fast food and fine dining, the fun, relaxed restaurant offers great food at a great price. Everything from burgers to sandwiches to made-from-scratch soups makes an appearance on the menu. This place strives to treat customers like honored guests. Casual dress; cocktails. **Parking:** on-site. **Cards:** AX, MC, VI.

✕

RICHMOND pop. 164,345 (See map and index starting on p. 536)

—— WHERE TO STAY ——

ACCENT INNS
Book at aaa.com   Phone: (604)273-3311   145

CAA SAVE

7/1-9/30	1P: $119-$139	2P: $129-$149	XP: $10	F16
5/1-6/30	1P: $89-$119	2P: $99-$129	XP: $10	F16
3/1-4/30 & 10/1-2/28	1P: $89-$109	2P: $99-$119	XP: $10	F16

Location: Hwy 99, exit 39 (Bridgeport/Airport) northbound to St. Edwards Dr; exit 39A (Richmond/Airport) southbound. **Small-scale Hotel** 10551 St. Edwards Dr V6X 3L8. Fax: 604/273-9522. **Facility:** 206 one-bedroom standard units, some with efficiencies. 3 stories, exterior corridors. **Parking:** on-site. **Terms:** small pets only ($10 extra charge, in limited units). **Amenities:** video games (fee), voice mail, irons, hair dryers. *Some:* high-speed Internet. **Dining:** 6:30 am-10 pm, wine/beer only. **Leisure Activities:** whirlpool, limited exercise equipment. **Guest Services:** valet and coin laundry. **Business Services:** meeting rooms. **Cards:** AX, DC, MC, VI. **Special Amenities:** free local telephone calls and free newspaper. *(See color ad p 488 & p 608)*

SOME UNITS

BEST WESTERN ABERCORN INN
Book at aaa.com   Phone: (604)270-7576   137

CAA SAVE

7/1-9/30 [CP]	1P: $109-$159	2P: $109-$159	XP: $15	F17
5/16-6/30 [CP]	1P: $89-$139	2P: $89-$139	XP: $15	F17
3/1-5/15 & 10/1-2/28 [CP]	1P: $79-$139	2P: $79-$139	XP: $15	F17

Location: Hwy 99, exit 39 (Bridgeport/Airport) northbound; exit 39A (Richmond/Airport) southbound. 9260 Bridgeport Rd **Small-scale Hotel** V6X 1S1. Fax: 604/270-0001. **Facility:** 94 one-bedroom standard units, some with whirlpools. 3 stories, interior corridors. **Parking:** on-site. **Terms:** [AP], [BP] & [MAP] meal plans available, package plans, small pets only ($15 extra charge). **Amenities:** voice mail, irons, hair dryers. **Dining:** 6:30 am-10 pm, cocktails. **Leisure Activities:** limited exercise equipment. **Guest Services:** valet laundry. **Business Services:** meeting rooms, business center. **Cards:** AX, DC, DS, MC, VI. **Special Amenities:** free continental breakfast and free local telephone calls. *(See color ad below)*

SOME UNITS

BEST WESTERN RICHMOND HOTEL & CONVENTION CENTER
Book at aaa.com   Phone: (604)273-7878   149

CAA SAVE

5/1-9/30	1P: $109-$129	2P: $109-$129	XP: $15	F18
3/1-4/30 & 10/1-2/28	1P: $89-$109	2P: $89-$109	XP: $15	F18

Location: Corner of Minoru Rd and Westminster Hwy. 7551 Westminster Hwy V6X 1A3. Fax: 604/278-0188. **Facility:** 390 one-bedroom standard units, some with whirlpools. 6-7 stories, interior corridors. **Parking: Large-scale Hotel** on-site (fee). **Terms:** small pets only. **Amenities:** video games (fee), voice mail, irons, hair dryers. **Dining:** 6 am-11 pm, cocktails. **Pool(s):** heated outdoor. **Leisure Activities:** saunas, whirlpool, exercise room. **Guest Services:** gift shop, valet and coin laundry. **Business Services:** conference facilities, business center. **Cards:** AX, CB, DC, DS, JC, MC, VI. **Special Amenities:** free local telephone calls and free newspaper. *(See color ad p 569)*

SOME UNITS

COMFORT INN VANCOUVER AIRPORT
Book at aaa.com   Phone: (604)278-5161   141

CAA SAVE

All Year [CP]	1P: $84-$124	2P: $84-$124	XP: $10	F18

Location: Hwy 99, exit 39 (Bridgeport/Airport) northbound; exit 39A (Richmond/Airport) southbound. 3031 #3 Rd V6X 2B6. Fax: 604/207-2380. **Facility:** 129 one-bedroom standard units. 3 stories, interior corridors. **Parking:** on-site. **Terms:** cancellation fee imposed, package plans, pets ($10 extra charge). **Amenities:** voice mail, **Small-scale Hotel** hair dryers. **Dining:** 6:30 am-10 pm, cocktails. **Pool(s):** heated outdoor. **Guest Services:** valet laundry. **Business Services:** meeting rooms. **Cards:** AX, DC, MC, VI. **Special Amenities:** free local telephone calls. *(See color ad p 590 & p 570)*

SOME UNITS

(See map and index starting on p. 536)

DELTA VANCOUVER AIRPORT   *Book at aaa.com*   Phone: (604)278-1241   [136]

(CAA) (SAVE)   5/1-9/30   1P: $169-$189   2P: $169-$189   XP: $20   F18
▽▽▽▽   3/1-4/30 & 10/1-2/28   1P: $149-$169   2P: $149-$169   XP: $20   F18
Fax: 604/276-1975. **Facility:** 412 one-bedroom standard units. 10 stories, interior corridors. **Parking:** on-
Location: Corner of Russ Baker Way and Cessna Dr; near the Moray Bridge. 3500 Cessna Dr V7B 1C7.
Large-scale Hotel site (fee) and valet. **Terms:** cancellation fee imposed, small pets only ($25 extra charge). **Amenities:** video
games (fee), voice mail, irons, hair dryers. *Some:* high-speed Internet. **Dining:** 2 restaurants, 6 am-
midnight, cocktails. **Pool(s):** heated outdoor. **Leisure Activities:** exercise room. *Fee:* marina. **Guest Services:** gift shop, valet
laundry. **Business Services:** conference facilities, business center. **Cards:** AX, DC, DS, MC, VI. *(See color ad p 591)*

SOME UNITS

⬛ ✈ 🛏 🍴 24 🍷 🔊M 🔧 🏊 📷 DATA PORT 💻 / ✕ /
FEE

THE FAIRMONT VANCOUVER AIRPORT   *Book at aaa.com*   Phone: (604)207-5200   [138]

(CAA) (SAVE)   All Year   1P: $199-$289   2P: $199-$289   XP: $30   F18
▽▽▽ ▽▽▽   **Location:** In Vancouver International Airport. 3111 Grant McConachie Way V7B 1X9 (PO Box 23798).
Fax: 604/248-3205. **Facility:** This hotel features luxurious rooms with sound-insulated windows and high-
tech temperature and lighting controls. 392 one-bedroom standard units, some with whirlpools. 14 stories,
Large-scale Hotel interior corridors. **Parking:** on-site (fee) and valet. **Terms:** cancellation fee imposed, small pets only ($25
extra charge). **Amenities:** video games (fee), high-speed Internet, dual phone lines, voice mail, safes,
honor bars, irons, hair dryers. *Some:* CD players. **Dining:** Globe at YVR, see separate listing, entertainment. **Pool(s):** small
heated indoor, wading. **Leisure Activities:** saunas, whirlpool, spa. **Guest Services:** valet laundry. **Business Services:** meeting
rooms, business center. **Cards:** AX, CB, DC, DS, JC, MC, VI. *(See color ad p 571)*

SOME UNITS

⬛ 🛏 🍴 24 🍷 🔊M 🔧 🏊 🌐 ✕ 📷 DATA PORT 💻 / ✕ /
FEE

FOUR POINTS BY SHERATON VANCOUVER
AIRPORT ·   *Book at aaa.com*   Phone: (604)214-0888   [147]

▽▽▽   5/1-9/30   1P: $230-$250   2P: $230-$250   XP: $10   F16
3/1-4/30 & 10/1-2/28   1P: $210-$230   2P: $210-$230   XP: $10   F16
Small-scale Hotel   **Location:** No. 3 Rd, just e on Alderbridge Way, then just n on Hazelbridge Way. 8368 Alexandra Rd V6X 4A6.
Fax: 604/214-0887. **Facility:** 139 one-bedroom standard units. 6 stories, interior corridors. **Parking:** on-site.
Amenities: video games (fee), high-speed Internet, dual phone lines, voice mail, irons, hair dryers. **Pool(s):** heated indoor.
Leisure Activities: whirlpool, limited exercise equipment. **Guest Services:** valet laundry. **Business Services:** meeting rooms,
business center. **Cards:** AX, CB, DC, DS, JC, MC, VI. *(See color ad p 5)*

SOME UNITS

ASK ⬛ ✈ 🍴 🍷 🔊M 🏊 📷 DATA PORT 💻 / ✕ 📶 /

(See map and index starting on p. 536)

HAMPTON INN VANCOUVER AIRPORT *Book at aaa.com*   Phone: (604)232-5505   **135**

5/16-9/30	1P: $144	2P: $159	XP: $10 F18
3/1-5/15 & 10/1-2/28	1P: $99	2P: $109	XP: $10 F18

Location: Hwy 99, exit 39 (Bridgeport/Airport) northbound; exit 39A (Richmond/Airport) southbound. 8811 Bridgeport Rd V6X 1R9. Fax: 604/232-5508. **Facility:** 112 one-bedroom standard units. 5 stories, interior corridors. **Small-scale Hotel** **Parking:** on-site. **Terms:** 3 day cancellation notice-fee imposed. **Amenities:** video games (fee), voice mail, irons, hair dryers. *Some:* dual phone lines. **Leisure Activities:** limited exercise equipment. **Guest Services:** valet laundry. **Business Services:** business center. **Cards:** AX, CB, DC, DS, MC. **Special Amenities: free expanded continental breakfast and free local telephone calls.** *(See color ad p 572)*

SOME UNITS

HILTON VANCOUVER AIRPORT *Book at aaa.com*   Phone: (604)273-6336   **152**

7/1-9/30	1P: $129-$169	2P: $129-$169	XP: $20 F18
3/1-6/30 & 10/1-2/28	1P: $119-$149	2P: $119-$149	XP: $20 F18

Small-scale Hotel **Location:** Corner of Minoru Rd and Westminster Hwy. 5911 Minoru Blvd V6X 4C7. Fax: 604/273-6337. **Facility:** 237 units. 235 one- and 2 two-bedroom standard units. 15 stories, interior corridors. **Parking:** on-site (fee). **Terms:** cancellation fee imposed. **Amenities:** video games (fee), dual phone lines, voice mail, irons, hair dryers. *Some:* high-speed Internet. **Pool(s):** small heated outdoor. **Leisure Activities:** whirlpool, lighted tennis court, limited exercise equipment. **Guest Services:** gift shop, valet laundry. **Business Services:** meeting rooms, business center. **Cards:** AX, CB, DC, DS, JC, MC, VI. *(See color ad p 572)*

SOME UNITS

HOLIDAY INN EXPRESS VANCOUVER-AIRPORT *Book at aaa.com*   Phone: (604)273-8080   **142**

5/1-9/15 [ECP]	1P: $119-$159	2P: $119-$159	XP: $10 F19
3/1-4/30 & 9/16-2/28 [ECP]	1P: $99-$139	2P: $99-$139	XP: $10 F19

Small-scale Hotel **Location:** Hwy 99, exit 39 (Bridgeport/Airport) northbound; exit 39A (Richmond/Airport) southbound. 9351 Bridgeport Rd V6X 1S3. Fax: 604/214-8488. **Facility:** 107 one-bedroom standard units, some with whirlpools. 8 stories, interior corridors. **Parking:** on-site. **Terms:** package plans, small pets only ($10 extra charge). **Amenities:** dual phone lines, voice mail, irons, hair dryers. **Guest Services:** valet laundry. **Business Services:** meeting rooms. **Cards:** AX, CB, DC, DS, JC, MC, VI. *(See color ad card insert)*

SOME UNITS

FEE

(See map and index starting on p. 536)

HOLIDAY INN INTERNATIONAL VANCOUVER AIRPORT   *Book at aaa.com*

▼▼▼▼

Small-scale Hotel

Phone: (604)821-1818   146

5/1-9/15	1P: $129-$169	2P: $129-$169	XP: $10 F19
3/1-4/30 & 9/16-2/28	1P: $109-$149	2P: $109-$149	XP: $10 F19

Location: Hwy 99, exit 39 (Bridgeport/Airport) northbound to St. Edwards Dr; exit 39A (Richmond/Airport) southbound, then e. 10720 Cambie Rd V6X 1K8. Fax: 604/821-1819. **Facility:** 165 one-bedroom standard units. 6 stories, interior corridors. **Parking:** on-site. **Terms:** check-in 4 pm, package plans. **Amenities:** high-speed Internet, dual phone lines, voice mail, irons, hair dryers. **Leisure Activities:** whirlpool, limited exercise equipment. **Guest Services:** valet laundry. **Business Services:** meeting rooms, business center. **Cards:** AX, CB, DC, DS, JC, MC, VI. *(See color ad card insert)*

SOME UNITS

(ASK) (SD) ⊤⊤ (&M) (✦) (DATA PORT) (▣) / (✕) (⊟) (▣)

LA QUINTA INN VANCOUVER AIRPORT   *Book at aaa.com*

(CAA) (SAVE)

▼▼▼▼

Small-scale Hotel

Phone: (604)276-2711   148

5/1-9/30 [ECP]	1P: $99-$179	2P: $109-$189	XP: $10 F18
3/1-4/30 & 10/1-2/28 [ECP]	1P: $79-$159	2P: $89-$169	XP: $10 F18

Location: N 3rd, just e on Alderbridge Way, just n on Kwantlen St. 8640 Alexandra Rd V6X 1A4. Fax: 604/276-2733. **Facility:** 50 one-bedroom standard units. 5 stories, interior corridors. **Parking:** on-site. **Amenities:** high-speed Internet, dual phone lines, voice mail, irons, hair dryers. **Pool(s):** small heated indoor. **Leisure Activities:** whirlpool, limited exercise equipment. **Guest Services:** valet and coin laundry. **Business Services:** meeting rooms, business center. **Cards:** AX, DC, DS, MC, VI. **Special Amenities:** free expanded continental breakfast and free local telephone calls. *(See color ad p 573)*

SOME UNITS

(SD) (✦) (🐾) (&M) (♿) (🛏) (🦮) (DATA PORT) (▣) / (✕) (⊟)

PARK PLAZA   *Book at aaa.com*

(CAA) (SAVE)

▼▼ ▼▼

Small-scale Hotel

Phone: (604)278-9611   143

5/1-9/30	1P: $109-$129	2P: $109-$129	XP: $20 F18
3/1-4/30 & 10/1-2/28	1P: $89-$99	2P: $89-$99	XP: $20 F18

Location: Hwy 99, exit 39 (Bridgeport/Airport) northbound to St Edwards Dr; exit 39A (Richmond/Airport) southbound. 10251 St Edwards Dr V6X 2M9. Fax: 604/276-1121. **Facility:** 227 units. 224 one-bedroom standard units. 3 one-bedroom suites. 2-15 stories, interior corridors. **Parking:** on-site (fee) and valet. **Terms:** pets ($25 fee). **Amenities:** video games (fee), voice mail, irons, hair dryers. *Some:* CD players. **Dining:** 6:30 am-10 pm, cocktails. **Pool(s):** 2 heated outdoor, heated indoor. **Leisure Activities:** saunas, whirlpool, waterslide, 4 lighted indoor tennis courts, rental bicycles, playground, sports court. *Fee:* tennis & instruction, massage. **Guest Services:** gift shop, valet laundry, area transportation. **Business Services:** conference facilities. **Cards:** AX, DC, DS, MC, VI. **Special Amenities:** free newspaper. *(See color ad p 573 & p 574)*

SOME UNITS

(SD) (✦) (🐾) (⊤⊤) (▽) (&M) (🌀) (🦮) (🐾) (✕) (🐕) (DATA PORT) (▣) / (✕) /
FEE

QUALITY HOTEL AIRPORT (SOUTH)   *Book at aaa.com*

(CAA) (SAVE)

▼▼ ▼▼

Small-scale Hotel

Phone: (604)244-3051   150

6/16-9/15	1P: $109-$149	2P: $119-$149	XP: $10 F18
5/16-6/15 & 9/16-2/28	1P: $99-$114	2P: $109-$114	XP: $10 F18
3/1-5/15	1P: $89-$109	2P: $104-$109	XP: $10 F18

Location: Between Gilbert Rd and Alderbridge Way. 7228 Westminster Hwy V6X 1A1. Fax: 604/244-3081. **Facility:** 70 one-bedroom standard units, some with whirlpools. 4 stories, interior corridors. **Parking:** on-site. **Terms:** cancellation fee imposed, package plans. **Amenities:** high-speed Internet, voice mail, irons, hair dryers. **Guest Services:** valet laundry. **Business Services:** meeting rooms. **Cards:** AX, CB, DC, JC, MC, VI. **Special Amenities:** free local telephone calls and free newspaper.

SOME UNITS

(SD) (⊤⊤) (&M) (DATA PORT) (▣) / (✕) (⊟)

RADISSON PRESIDENT HOTEL & SUITES   *Book at aaa.com*

(CAA) (SAVE)

▼▼▼ ▼▼▼

Small-scale Hotel

Phone: (604)276-8181   139

5/1-9/30 [CP]	1P: $139	2P: $139	XP: $15 F17
3/1-4/30 & 10/1-2/28 [CP]	1P: $109	2P: $109	XP: $15 F17

Location: Corner of No. 3 and Cambie rds. 8181 Cambie Rd V6X 3X9. Fax: 604/276-8381. **Facility:** 184 one-bedroom standard units, some with whirlpools. 12 stories, interior corridors. **Parking:** on-site (fee). **Terms:** cancellation fee imposed, package plans. **Amenities:** video games (fee), high-speed Internet, voice mail, safes, irons, hair dryers. **Dining:** 6:30 am-10 pm, cocktails. **Pool(s):** heated indoor. **Leisure Activities:** whirlpool, limited exercise equipment. **Guest Services:** gift shop, valet laundry. **Business Services:** conference facilities, business center. **Cards:** AX, CB, DC, DS, JC, MC, VI. **Special Amenities:** free continental breakfast and early check-in/late check-out. *(See color ad p 574 & p 573)*

SOME UNITS

(✦) (⊤⊤) (▽) (&M) (🦮) (🐕) (✕) (🐾) (DATA PORT) (▣) / (✕) (⊟) (▣) /

RAMADA PLAZA   *Book at aaa.com*

▼▼ ▼▼

Small-scale Hotel

Phone: (604)278-9611   133

5/1-9/30	1P: $109-$129	2P: $109-$129	XP: $20 F18
3/1-4/30 & 10/1-2/28	1P: $89-$99	2P: $89-$99	XP: $20 F18

Location: Hwy 99, exit 39 (Bridgeport/Airport) northbound to St Edwards Dr; exit 39A (Richmond/Airport) southbound. 10251 St Edwards Dr V6X 2M9. Fax: 604/276-1121. **Facility:** 211 one-bedroom standard units. 21 stories, interior corridors. **Parking:** on-site (fee) and valet. **Terms:** pets ($25 fee). **Amenities:** video games (fee), voice mail, irons, hair dryers. **Pool(s):** 2 heated outdoor, heated indoor. **Leisure Activities:** saunas, whirlpool, waterslide, 4 lighted indoor tennis courts, rental bicycles, playground, sports court. *Fee:* massage. **Guest Services:** gift shop, valet laundry. **Business Services:** conference facilities. **Cards:** AX, DC, DS, MC, VI.

SOME UNITS

(ASK) (SD) (✦) (🐾) (⊤⊤) (▽) (&M) (🌀) (🦮) (✕) (🐕) (DATA PORT) (▣) / (✕) (⊟) (▣) /
FEE

SANDMAN HOTEL VANCOUVER AIRPORT   *Book at aaa.com*

▼▼▼ ▼▼▼

Small-scale Hotel

Phone: (604)303-8888   134

All Year	1P: $79-$159	2P: $79-$159	XP: $10 F16

Location: Hwy 99, exit 39 (Bridgeport/Airport) northbound to St. Edwards Dr; exit 39A (Richmond/Airport) southbound. 3233 St. Edwards Dr V6X 3K4. Fax: 604/303-8877. **Facility:** 172 one-bedroom standard units, some with whirlpools. 5 stories, interior corridors. **Parking:** on-site. **Terms:** weekly rates available, package plans, small pets only ($10 extra charge). **Amenities:** video games (fee), voice mail, irons, hair dryers. **Pool(s):** heated indoor. **Leisure Activities:** whirlpool, limited exercise equipment. **Guest Services:** valet laundry. **Business Services:** meeting rooms, business center. **Cards:** AX, CB, DC, DS, JC, MC, VI.

SOME UNITS

(ASK) (SD) (✦) (🐾) (⊤⊤) (▽) (&M) (🦮) (🐕) (DATA PORT) (▣) / (✕) (⊟) (▣)
FEE

(See map and index starting on p. 536)

TRAVELODGE HOTEL VANCOUVER AIRPORT *Book at aaa.com* Phone: (604)278-5155 **140**

CAA SAVE

Small-scale Hotel

5/1-9/30	1P: $99-$149	2P: $99-$149	XP: $10	F18
3/1-4/30 & 10/1-2/28	1P: $89-$119	2P: $89-$119	XP: $10	F18

Location: Hwy 99, exit 39 (Bridgeport/Airport) northbound to St Edwards Dr; exit 39A (Richmond/Airport) southbound. 3071 St Edwards Dr V6X 3K4. Fax: 604/278-5125. **Facility:** 159 one-bedroom standard units. 10 stories, interior corridors. **Parking:** on-site. **Terms:** [BP] & [CP] meal plans available, package plans. **Amenities:** video games (fee), voice mail, irons, hair dryers. **Dining:** 7 am-10 pm, cocktails. **Pool(s):** heated indoor. **Leisure Activities:** whirlpool. **Guest Services:** valet laundry. **Business Services:** meeting rooms. **Cards:** AX, DC, MC, VI.

SOME UNITS

VANCOUVER AIRPORT MARRIOTT *Book at aaa.com* Phone: (604)276-2112 **151**

CAA SAVE

Small-scale Hotel

7/1-9/30	1P: $129-$169	2P: $129-$169	XP: $20	F18
3/1-6/30 & 10/1-2/28	1P: $119-$149	2P: $119-$149	XP: $20	F18

Location: Corner of Minoru Rd and Westminster Hwy. 7571 Westminster Hwy V6X 1A3. Fax: 604/276-0112. **Facility:** 237 units. 235 one- and 2 two-bedroom standard units. 18 stories, interior corridors. **Parking:** on-site (fee). **Terms:** package plans, small pets only ($30 extra charge). **Amenities:** video games (fee), high-speed Internet, dual phone lines, voice mail, irons, hair dryers. **Dining:** 6 am-10 pm, cocktails. **Pool(s):** small heated outdoor. **Leisure Activities:** whirlpool, exercise room. **Guest Services:** valet and coin laundry. **Business Services:** meeting rooms, business center. **Cards:** AX, DC, DS, JC, MC, VI. **Special Amenities:** free newspaper and preferred room (subject to availability with advance reservations).

SOME UNITS

FEE

------- **WHERE TO DINE** -------

CACTUS CLUB CAFE Lunch: $8-$26 Dinner: $8-$26 Phone: 604/244-9969 **120**

Canadian

DC, MC, VI.

Location: Corner No. 3 and Lansdowne rds. 5500 No 3 Rd V6X 2C8. **Hours:** 11 am-midnight, Fri & Sat-1 am. Closed: 12/25. **Features:** The fun, bustling place has plenty of free parking. The menu lists so many great things that it's hard to know where to start. Offerings include salads, soups, quesadillas, burgers, fajitas, vegetarian dishes, steak, ribs, chicken, fish and pasta. Casual dress; cocktails. **Parking:** on-site. **Cards:** AX,

FLOATA SEAFOOD RESTAURANT Lunch: $4-$6 Dinner: $15-$30 Phone: 604/270-8889 **124**

Chinese

Location: No. 3 Rd at Cambie St. 1425-4380 No. 3 Rd V6X 3V7. **Hours:** 9 am-10 pm. Closed: 12/25. **Reservations:** suggested. **Features:** The restaurant's menu features prix fixe courses that make it easy for diners to sample many dishes without ordering individual selections. Casual dress; cocktails. **Parking:** on-site. **Cards:** AX, DC, MC, VI.

FLYING BEAVER Lunch: $7-$11 Dinner: $9-$15 Phone: 604/273-0278 **123**

Canadian

Location: Russ Baker Way, 1 km w on Inglis Dr towards south terminal. 4760 Inglis Dr V7B 1W4. **Hours:** 11 am-midnight, Sat & Sun from 8 am. Closed: 1/1, 12/25. **Features:** The pub is in the terminal of Harbour Air, a small float plane operation. While chowing down on a good burger or some appetizers, patrons can gaze through large bay windows to watch planes land and take off. Signs to the South Terminal lead to this place, where there's plenty of free parking. Casual dress; cocktails. **Parking:** on-site. **Cards:** AX, MC, VI.

GLOBE AT YVR Lunch: $15-$20 Dinner: $20-$30 Phone: 604/207-5200 **119**

Regional Pacific Rim

DS, JC, MC, VI.

Location: In Vancouver International Airport; in The Fairmont Vancouver Airport. **Hours:** 6 am-11 pm. **Reservations:** suggested. **Features:** This restaurant treats diners to a memorable view of air traffic creeping in and out of the gates as service vehicles buzz around like bees. In addition to complete lunch and dinner service, the restaurant offers a wonderful Sunday brunch. The skilled culinary team keeps up the pace in the open-activity kitchen. Casual dress; cocktails. **Parking:** on-site (fee) and valet. **Cards:** AX, DC,

STEVESTON SEAFOOD HOUSE Dinner: $18-$35 Phone: 604/271-5252 **121**

CAA

Seafood

Location: Jct Moncton St and No. 1 Rd; in Steveston Village. 3951 Moncton St V7E 3A2. **Hours:** 5:30 pm-9 pm. Closed major holidays. **Reservations:** suggested. **Features:** You'll enjoy your fine-dining experience at this restaurant located in the historic village of Steveston. The menu offers ocean-fresh seafood based on availability. The prawns and scallops are delicious, and the warm and friendly decor is quite pleasant. Casual dress; cocktails. **Parking:** street. **Cards:** AX, DC, MC, VI.

SURREY pop. 347,825 (See map and index starting on p. 536)

------- **WHERE TO STAY** -------

BEST WESTERN KING GEORGE INN & SUITES Phone: (604)502-9000 **181**

CAA SAVE

Small-scale Hotel

7/1-9/15 [ECP]	1P: $109-$135	2P: $109-$135	XP: $10	F17
5/1-6/30 [ECP]	1P: $99-$129	2P: $99-$129	XP: $10	F17
3/1-4/30 & 9/16-2/28 [ECP]	1P: $85-$115	2P: $85-$115	XP: $10	F17

Location: Jct Fraser Hwy (Hwy 1A), 4 km s to 80th Ave. 8033 King George Hwy V3W 5B4. Fax: 604/507-4999. **Facility:** 72 one-bedroom standard units, some with efficiencies. 3 stories, interior corridors. **Parking:** on-site. **Amenities:** voice mail, irons, hair dryers. *Some:* dual phone lines. **Pool(s):** small heated indoor. **Leisure Activities:** whirlpool, limited exercise equipment. **Guest Services:** valet and coin laundry. **Business Services:** meeting rooms. **Cards:** AX, CB, DC, DS, MC, VI. **Special Amenities:** free expanded continental breakfast and free local telephone calls.

SOME UNITS

(See map and index starting on p. 536)

DAYS HOTEL-SURREY

Phone: (604)588-9511 **176**

CAA SAVE

7/1-9/15	1P: $125	2P: $125	XP: $10	F18
5/1-6/30	1P: $98	2P: $98	XP: $10	F18
3/1-4/30 & 9/16-2/28	1P: $94	2P: $94	XP: $10	F18

Location: Jct Fraser Hwy (Hwy 1A) and Hwy 99A (King George Hwy). 9850 King George Hwy V3T 4Y3.
Small-scale Hotel Fax: 604/588-7949. **Facility:** 81 one-bedroom standard units. 6 stories, interior corridors. *Bath:* combo or shower only. **Parking:** on-site. **Terms:** weekly rates available, package plans, small pets only ($10 extra charge, in smoking units). **Dining:** 2 restaurants, 6:30 am-10 pm, Sun-9 pm, cocktails. **Pool(s):** small heated indoor. **Leisure Activities:** whirlpool, limited exercise equipment. **Guest Services:** valet and coin laundry. **Business Services:** meeting rooms. **Cards:** AX, CB, DC, DS, JC, MC, VI. **Special Amenities:** free newspaper and early check-in/late check-out.
(See color ad below)

SOME UNITS

ECONO LODGE PEACE ARCH

Phone: (604)541-8100 **183**

CAA SAVE

5/1-9/30	1P: $90-$140	2P: $99-$150	XP: $10	F10
3/1-4/30 & 1/1-2/28	1P: $80-$140	2P: $90-$150	XP: $10	F10
10/1-12/31	1P: $75-$140	2P: $85-$145	XP: $10	F10

Motel **Location:** Hwy 99, exit 10 southbound, 4.5 km s; exit 2 northbound, 3.5 km n. 2293 King George Hwy V4A 5A4. Fax: 604/541-8700. **Facility:** Smoke free premises. 42 one-bedroom standard units, some with whirlpools. 3 stories, interior corridors. **Parking:** on-site. **Terms:** weekly rates available, package plans. **Amenities:** high-speed Internet, voice mail, hair dryers. **Pool(s):** heated indoor. **Leisure Activities:** sauna, whirlpool, limited exercise equipment. **Guest Services:** coin laundry. **Business Services:** meeting rooms. **Cards:** AX, DC, MC, VI. **Special Amenities:** free continental breakfast and free local telephone calls.

HOWARD JOHNSON EXPRESS INN & SUITES

Book at aaa.com

Phone: (604)588-0181 **174**

CAA SAVE

5/16-9/30 [CP]	1P: $80-$85	2P: $85-$90	XP: $10	F17
3/1-5/15 [CP]	1P: $70-$80	2P: $80-$85	XP: $10	F17
10/1-2/28 [CP]	1P: $70-$75	2P: $75-$80	XP: $10	F17

Motel **Location:** Southbound from the Pattullo Bridge to 112th Ave; 5 km n from jct Fraser Hwy (Hwy 1A) and Hwy 99A (King George Hwy). 13245 King George Hwy V3T 2T3. Fax: 604/588-0180. **Facility:** 54 units. 42 one- and 12 two-bedroom standard units, some with efficiencies and/or whirlpools. 2 stories (no elevator), exterior corridors. *Bath:* combo or shower only. **Parking:** on-site. **Terms:** weekly rates available. **Guest Services:** coin laundry. **Cards:** AX, CB, DC, DS, JC, MC, VI. **Special Amenities:** free continental breakfast and free newspaper.

SOME UNITS

(See map and index starting on p. 536)

RAMADA HOTEL & SUITES SURREY/GUILDFORD   *Book at aaa.com*   Phone: (604)930-4700   180
All Year [CP]   1P: $89-$139   2P: $89-$139   XP: $10   F18
Location: Trans-Canada Hwy 1, exit 50 (160th St), just w on 104th Ave. 10410 158th St V4N 5C2.
Small-scale Hotel   Fax: 604/930-4702. Facility: 77 one-bedroom standard units. 3 stories, interior corridors. Parking: on-site.
Terms: cancellation fee imposed, package plans, small pets only ($10 extra charge). Amenities: voice mail,
irons, hair dryers. Pool(s): heated outdoor. Leisure Activities: whirlpool, limited exercise equipment. Guest Services: valet
laundry. Business Services: meeting rooms. Cards: AX, MC, VI.

SOME UNITS

ASK SD 🛏 🍴 &M ⟨ 🏊 🐾 💺 DATA/PORT 💻 / ⊠ 🔌 🖥 /
FEE

RAMADA LIMITED SURREY-LANGLEY   *Book at aaa.com*   Phone: (604)576-8388   179
5/1-9/19 [ECP]   1P: $119-$139   2P: $119-$139   XP: $10   F18
3/1-4/30 [ECP]   1P: $95-$115   2P: $95-$115   XP: $10   F18
9/20-2/28 [ECP]   1P: $97   2P: $97   XP: $10   F18
Small-scale Hotel   Location: Trans-Canada Hwy 1, exit 58, 5 km s on 200th St, then 2 km w on Rt 10; corner of 192nd St and Rt 10.
19225 Hwy 10 V3S 8V9. Fax: 604/576-8332. Facility: 85 one-bedroom standard units, some with efficiencies. 3 stories, interior
corridors. Parking: on-site. Terms: small pets only ($10 extra charge). Amenities: voice mail, irons, hair dryers. Some: high-
speed Internet. Pool(s): heated indoor. Leisure Activities: whirlpool, limited exercise equipment. Guest Services: valet and
coin laundry. Business Services: meeting rooms. Cards: AX, CB, DC, DS, MC, VI.

SOME UNITS

ASK SD 🛏 🍴 &M ⟨ 🏊 🐾 💺 DATA/PORT 💻 / ⊠ 🔌 🖥 /
FEE

SHERATON VANCOUVER GUILDFORD HOTEL   Phone: (604)582-9288   175
All Year   1P: $149-$399   2P: $149-$399   XP: $20   F16
Under major renovation, scheduled to be completed May 2005. Last rated: ♥♥ Location: Trans-Canada
Hwy 1, exit 48 eastbound, 1 km s on 152 St, then just e; exit 50 westbound, just w. 15269 104th Ave V3R 1N5.
Large-scale Hotel   Fax: 604/582-9712. Facility: 278 one-bedroom standard units, some with whirlpools. 20 stories, interior
corridors. Parking: on-site (fee). Terms: check-in 4 pm, package plans, small pets only. Amenities: video
games (fee), high-speed Internet, voice mail, irons, hair dryers. Dining: 6:30 am-10 pm, cocktails. Pool(s): heated outdoor.
Leisure Activities: whirlpool, limited exercise equipment. Guest Services: gift shop, valet laundry. Business Services:
meeting rooms. Cards: AX, CB, DC, MC, VI. Special Amenities: free newspaper and early check-in/late check-out.
(See ad p 594 & color ad p 5)

SOME UNITS

SD 🛏 🍴 24🍴 🍽 🐾 💺 DATA/PORT 💻 / ⊠ /

(See map and index starting on p. 536)

──────── WHERE TO DINE ────────

YOKOHAMA JAPANESE RESTAURANT   **Lunch:** $7-$10   **Dinner:** $10-$21   **Phone:** 604/584-4555   ⌐142¬

▼▼▼   **Location:** Just e off Hwy 99A (King George Hwy) at 104th Ave on Whalley Ring Rd. 10356 137th St V3T 4H4.
Hours: 11:30 am-2:30 & 5-10 pm, Fri & Sat-10:30 pm, Sun 5 pm-10 pm. **Closed:** 1/1, 12/24, 12/25.
Japanese   **Reservations:** suggested, weekends. **Features:** Tatami rooms and a full sushi bar contribute to the cozy
environment. The combination dinner includes beef teriyaki, tempura, noodles, rice and dessert. Another
option is the all-you-can-eat lunch and dinner menu. Service is pleasant. Casual dress; cocktails. **Parking:** on-site. **Cards:** AX,
MC, VI.

⌐⊠¬

──────── *The following restaurant has not been evaluated by AAA* ────────
but is listed for your information only.

HAZELMERE COUNTRY CLUB DINING ROOM   **Phone:** 604/538-1212

⌐fyi¬   Not evaluated. **Location:** Hwy 99, exit 2, 4 km e. 18150 8th Ave V3S 9R9. **Features:** This dining room, at the
Hazelmere Golf Course, is open for lunch and dinner.

WEST VANCOUVER pop. 41,421   (See map and index starting on p. 536)

──────── WHERE TO DINE ────────

THE BEACH HOUSE AT DUNDARAVE PIER   **Lunch:** $13-$18   **Dinner:** $19-$30   **Phone:** 604/922-1414   ⌐152¬

▼▼▼   **Location:** Marine Dr at 25th St, towards ocean. 150 25th St V7V 4H8. **Hours:** 11:30 am-11 pm, Fri & Sat-midnight,
Sun 10:30 am-10 pm. **Closed:** 12/25. **Reservations:** suggested. **Features:** The oceanfront restaurant offers
Seafood   spectacular views of the water and entices guests to walk along the sea wall after a filling meal. Seafood
dishes suit every taste. Those who can't find a parking spot in the limited lot behind this place should park
wherever possible along the street. Casual dress; cocktails. **Parking:** street. **Cards:** AX, DC, DS, MC, VI.

⌐⊠¬

LA REGALADE FRENCH BISTRO   **Lunch:** $12-$17   **Dinner:** $16-$23   ⌐Phone:¬ 604/921-2228   ⌐151¬

▼▼ ▼▼   **Location:** Trans-Canada Hwy 1, exit 10 (22nd St), 1.5 km s, then just w. #103 2232 Marine Dr V7V 1K4. **Hours:** 11:30
am-2 & 5:30-10 pm, Sat from 5:30 pm. Closed major holidays; also Sun. **Reservations:** required.
French   **Features:** The tiny, family-run bistro blends fantastically fresh ingredients in heaping plates of great food.
The chef/owner hails from France and has cooked at fine restaurants both in France and here in the city.
Daily specials are listed on the wall chalkboard. Don't leave without trying one of the many homemade desserts on display.
Casual dress; beer & wine only. **Parking:** street. **Cards:** MC, VI.

⌐⊠¬

SALMON HOUSE ON THE HILL   **Lunch:** $12-$16   **Dinner:** $20-$28   **Phone:** 604/926-3212   ⌐150¬

▼▼ ▼▼   **Location:** Trans-Canada Hwy 1, exit 10 (22nd St), follow signs. 2229 Folkestone Way V7S 2Y6. **Hours:** 11:30 am-
2:30 & 5-9:30 pm, Fri & Sat 5 pm-10 pm. **Closed:** 12/24, 12/25. **Reservations:** suggested, for dinner.
Seafood   **Features:** You'll certainly appreciate the incredible panoramic view of the city and harbor from the Salmon
House's hilltop location. The restaurant's cuisine specializes in Pacific Rim influences, with fresh British
Columbia salmon as the house specialty. Cocktails. **Parking:** on-site. **Cards:** AX, DC, MC, VI.

⌐⊓⊠¬

WHITE ROCK pop. 18,250   (See map and index starting on p. 536)

──────── WHERE TO STAY ────────

ASTON PACIFIC INN RESORT & CONFERENCE CTR   **Phone:** (604)535-1432   ⌐186¬

▼▼ ▼▼	5/1-9/30	1P: $129	2P: $129	XP: $10	F12
	3/1-4/30 & 10/1-2/28	1P: $109	2P: $109	XP: $10	F12

Small-scale Hotel   **Location:** Hwy 99, exit 2B southbound; exit 2 northbound, just n. 1160 King George Hwy V4A 4Z2.
Fax: 604/531-6979. **Facility:** 150 one-bedroom standard units, some with whirlpools. 4 stories, interior
corridors. **Parking:** on-site. **Terms:** package plans. **Amenities:** voice mail, irons, hair dryers. **Pool(s):** heated indoor. **Leisure
Activities:** sauna, whirlpool, exercise room, game room. **Guest Services:** valet and coin laundry, area transportation, beauty
salon. **Business Services:** conference facilities. **Cards:** AX, DS, MC, VI.

SOME UNITS

⌐ASK¬ ⌐S/D¬ ⌐⊓⊔¬ ⌐Y¬ ⌐&M¬ ⌐≈¬ ⌐⊠¬ ⌐DATA PORT¬ ⌐▭¬ /⌐⊠¬/

OCEAN PROMENADE HOTEL   **Phone:** (604)542-0102   ⌐184¬

⌐CAA¬ ⌐SAVE¬   All Year   1P: $139-$489   2P: $139-$489

▼▼ ▼▼   **Location:** Hwy 99, exit 2B southbound; exit 2 (White Rock/8th Ave) northbound, 2 km w. 15611 Marine Dr V4B 1E1.
Fax: 604/542-0338. **Facility:** 51 one-bedroom standard units, some with kitchens and/or whirlpools. 3
stories, interior/exterior corridors. **Parking:** on-site. **Terms:** check-in 4 pm, package plans, small pets only
Small-scale Hotel   ($100 fee). **Amenities:** DVD players, voice mail, safes, irons, hair dryers. *Some:* high-speed Internet. **Guest
Services:** valet and coin laundry. **Business Services:** meeting rooms. **Cards:** AX, MC, VI.
Special Amenities: free local telephone calls and free room upgrade (subject to availability with advance
reservations).

SOME UNITS

⌐S/D¬ ⌐⊓¬ ⌐⊓⊩¬ ⌐DATA PORT¬ ⌐▭¬ /⌐⊠¬ ⌐⊟¬ ⌐⊡¬/
FEE

SEACREST MOTEL & RV PARK   **Phone:** (604)531-4720   ⌐185¬

⌐CAA¬ ⌐SAVE¬	5/1-9/30	1P: $87-$91	2P: $92-$96	XP: $10	F13
	10/1-2/28	1P: $77-$96	2P: $82-$96	XP: $10	F13
▼▼ ▼▼	3/1-4/30	1P: $77-$96	2P: $82-$86	XP: $10	F13

Motel   **Location:** Hwy 99, exit 2B southbound; exit 2 northbound, 1 km w on 8th Ave, follow signs. 864 160th St V4A 4W4.
Fax: 604/531-4735. **Facility:** Smoke free premises. 12 one-bedroom standard units, some with kitchens. 1
story, exterior corridors. *Bath:* combo or shower only. **Parking:** on-site. **Terms:** office hours 8 am-10 pm,
cancellation fee imposed, weekly rates available, package plans. **Guest Services:** coin laundry. **Cards:** MC, VI.
Special Amenities: free local telephone calls and free newspaper.

SOME UNITS

⌐⊠¬ ⌐K¬ /⌐⊟¬/

(See map and index starting on p. 536)

———— **WHERE TO DINE** ————

GIRAFFE   **Lunch:** $8-$12   **Dinner:** $14-$23   **Phone:** 604/538-6878   (144)

Pacific Rim

Location: Hwy 99, exit 2B southbound; exit 2 northbound, 3 km w. 15053 Marine Dr V4B 1C5. **Hours:** 11:30 am-2 & 5:30-10 pm, Sun 10 am-2 pm. Closed: 1/1, 12/24-12/26. **Reservations:** suggested. **Features:** All tables at this lovely, intimate restaurant face the water. The giraffe-centric decor, including the noteworthy napkin holders, suits this place's name. Daily specials, which are printed on a blackboard at the entrance, are can't-miss choices, as are lemon grass steamed salmon filet, roasted free-range chicken and pasta. Casual dress; cocktails. **Parking:** on-site (fee). **Cards:** AX, MC, VI.

LA BAIA ITALIAN RESTAURANT   **Dinner:** $10-$20   **Phone:** 604/531-6261   (145)

Italian

Location: Hwy 99, exit 2B southbound; exit 2 northbound, 1.5 km w. 15791 Marine Dr V4B 1E5. **Hours:** 5 pm-10 pm, Fri & Sat-11 pm. Closed: 1/1, 12/25, 12/26. **Reservations:** suggested. **Features:** The varied cuisine at this restaurant offers delicious rack of lamb and veal marsala. The bright and airy decor displays antiques and a nice view of the park. The atmosphere is cozy and the service is friendly and attentive. Visitors like this place. Casual dress; cocktails. **Parking:** on-site (fee). **Cards:** AX, MC, VI.

SAM'S WATERFRONT CAFE   **Lunch:** $9-$13   **Dinner:** $16-$24   **Phone:** 604/536-7707   (143)

Pacific Rim

Location: Hwy 99, exit 2B southbound; exit 2 northbound, 3.5 km w. 15015 Marine Dr VHB 1C3. **Hours:** 11:30 am-2:30 & 5-10 pm. Closed: 1/1, 12/25. **Reservations:** suggested. **Features:** The bistro-style restaurant is a local favorite for its ocean-view tables and menu. Choices include warm seafood salad, steamed mussels and potato-crusted sea bass. The cuisine and atmosphere are unforgettable. Casual dress; cocktails. **Parking:** on-site (fee). **Cards:** AX, MC, VI.

THE TURKEY HOUSE & DELI   **Lunch:** $7-$9   **Dinner:** $7-$9   **Phone:** 604/531-6222   (146)

Deli/Subs
Sandwiches

Location: Hwy 99, exit 3 southbound; from Canada/US border, exit 2 northbound, then 1 km n. 1433 King George Hwy V4A 4Z5. **Hours:** 9 am-7 pm, Sat-6 pm. Closed major holidays; also Sun & Mon. **Features:** Since 1973, the distinctive combination restaurant and delicatessen has been serving 100 percent turkey products and unforgettable home-cooked meals. On the menu are varied sandwiches and soups, as well as hot items that can be eaten here or taken out. Visitors can purchase turkey deli meats and pre-made dishes that can be warmed at home, including turkey pies, sausage rolls and lasagna. Casual dress. **Parking:** on-site. **Cards:** MC, VI.

This ends listings for the Vancouver Vicinity.
The following page resumes the alphabetical listings of
cities in British Columbia.

VERNON pop. 33,494

──── WHERE TO STAY ────

BEST WESTERN VERNON LODGE & CONFERENCE CENTRE
Book at aaa.com

Phone: (250)545-3385

CAA SAVE

| | 5/16-9/15 | 1P: $114-$160 | 2P: $124-$170 | XP: $10 | F13 |
| | 3/1-5/15 & 9/16-2/28 | 1P: $89-$120 | 2P: $99-$130 | XP: $10 | F13 |

Location: 1.5 km n on Hwy 97 (32nd St). 3914 32nd St V1T 5P1. Fax: 250/545-7156. **Facility:** 127 units. 119 one-bedroom standard units. 8 one-bedroom suites, some with whirlpools. 3 stories (no elevator); interior
Small-scale Hotel corridors. **Parking:** on-site. **Terms:** cancellation fee imposed, pets ($10 extra charge). **Amenities:** video games, voice mail, irons, hair dryers. **Dining:** 6:30 am-11 pm, cocktails. **Pool(s):** heated indoor. **Leisure Activities:** whirlpool. **Guest Services:** gift shop, valet laundry. **Business Services:** conference facilities, business center. **Cards:** AX, DC, DS, JC, MC, VI. **Special Amenities:** free local telephone calls and early check-in/late check-out.

SOME UNITS

BEST WESTERN VILLAGER MOTOR INN
Book at aaa.com

Phone: (250)549-2224

CAA SAVE

| | 5/13-9/17 [ECP] | 1P: $90-$98 | 2P: $90-$98 | XP: $10 | F12 |
| | 3/1-5/12 & 2/28/28 [ECP] | 1P: $73-$89 | 2P: $73-$81 | XP: $10 | F12 |

Location: 2.5 km n on 27th St. Located across from Village Green Mall. 5121 26th St V1T 8G4. Fax: 250/549-2224. **Facility:** 53 one-bedroom standard units, some with efficiencies. 2 stories (no elevator); interior/exterior
Small-scale Hotel corridors. **Parking:** on-site, winter plug-ins. **Terms:** office hours 7 am-11 pm, package plans, small pets only ($10 extra charge, with prior approval). **Amenities:** irons, hair dryers. **Pool(s):** heated indoor. **Leisure Activities:** whirlpool. **Guest Services:** valet laundry. **Cards:** AX, DC, DS, MC, VI. **Special Amenities:** free expanded continental breakfast and free room upgrade (subject to availability with advance reservations).

SOME UNITS

CASTLE ON THE MOUNTAIN B & B

Phone: (250)542-4593

| | All Year | 1P: $75-$250 | 2P: $85-$250 | XP: $35 | D14 |

Location: Hwy 97A, exit 48th Ave (turns into Silver Star Rd), 10 km e. 8227 Silver Star Rd V1B 3M8.
Bed & Breakfast Fax: 250/542-2206. **Facility:** Home to spectacular views and gracious hosts, this comfortable property overlooks the scenic Okanagan Valley. Smoke free premises. 7 units. 5 one-bedroom standard units, some with whirlpools. 1 one-bedroom suite with kitchen. 1 cottage. 3 stories (no elevator); interior corridors. *Bath:* combo or shower only. **Parking:** on-site, winter plug-ins. **Terms:** check-in 4 pm, 3 night minimum stay - seasonal, 10 day cancellation notice. **Amenities:** video library, hair dryers. *Some:* CD players. **Leisure Activities:** whirlpool, hiking trails. *Fee:* massage. **Guest Services:** complimentary laundry. **Business Services:** meeting rooms. **Cards:** AX, MC, VI.

SOME UNITS

HOLIDAY INN EXPRESS HOTEL & SUITES VERNON
Book at aaa.com

Phone: (250)550-7777

| | 3/13-9/15 [CP] | 1P: $134-$164 | 2P: $134-$164 | XP: $10 | F18 |
| | 9/16-2/28 [CP] | 1P: $104-$134 | 2P: $104-$134 | XP: $10 | F18 |

Small-scale Hotel **Location:** Hwy 97 (32nd St) northbound at 48th Ave. 4716 34th St V1T 5Y9. Fax: 250/260-7728. **Facility:** 85 one-bedroom standard units, some with whirlpools. 3 stories, interior corridors. *Bath:* combo or shower only. **Parking:** on-site. **Terms:** cancellation fee imposed, pets ($20 extra charge, in designated units). **Amenities:** high-speed Internet, dual phone lines, voice mail, irons, hair dryers. **Pool(s):** heated indoor. **Leisure Activities:** whirlpool, exercise room. **Guest Services:** valet and coin laundry. **Business Services:** meeting rooms, business center. **Cards:** AX, DC, DS, MC, VI.

SOME UNITS

LAKESIDE ILLAHEE INN

Phone: (250)260-7896

	6/16-9/15	1P: $159-$329	2P: $159-$329	XP: $30	D12
	4/16-6/15	1P: $124-$289	2P: $139-$289	XP: $25	D12
	3/1-4/15 & 9/16-2/28	1P: $99-$289	2P: $109-$289	XP: $25	D12

Country Inn **Location:** Hwy 97 (32nd St), s of Vernon, 2.5 km se on College Way, then 2 km e on Kalamalka Rd, 3 km s on Kidston Rd, follow signs. Located in a quiet residential area. 15010 Tamarack Dr V1B 2E1. Fax: 250/260-7826. **Facility:** Luxurious rooms, all with balconies, and a lake setting give this upscale inn a relaxed atmosphere; a scenic provincial park is nearby. Designated smoking area. 5 one-bedroom standard units, some with whirlpools. 3 stories (no elevator); interior/exterior corridors. *Bath:* combo or shower only. **Parking:** on-site. **Terms:** age restrictions may apply, 7 day cancellation notice-fee imposed, package plans. **Amenities:** video library, irons, hair dryers. **Leisure Activities:** whirlpool, canoeing. *Fee:* massage. **Business Services:** meeting rooms. **Cards:** MC, VI.

SOME UNITS

SCHELL MOTEL

Phone: 250/545-1351

CAA SAVE

| | All Year | 1P: $50-$85 | 2P: $55-$85 | XP: $10 | F13 |

Motel

Location: Corner of 35th St and 30th Ave; centre. 2810 35th St V1T 6B5. Fax: 250/545-2287. **Facility:** 32 units. 14 one- and 1 two-bedroom standard units. 17 one- and 1 two-bedroom suites ($85-$135), some with kitchens. 2 stories (no elevator), exterior corridors. **Parking:** on-site. **Terms:** office hours 7 am-11 pm, package plans, small pets only ($5 extra charge, ground floor units). **Pool(s):** heated outdoor. **Leisure Activities:** sauna, whirlpool. **Cards:** AX, DC, MC, VI. **Special Amenities:** free local telephone calls and free newspaper.

SOME UNITS

TIKI VILLAGE MOTOR INN

Phone: (250)503-5566

CAA SAVE

WWW WW

Motel

5/2-10/1	1P: $99-$155	2P: $99-$155	XP: $10	F10
10/2-2/28	1P: $89-$135	2P: $89-$135	XP: $10	F10
3/1-5/1	1P: $79-$135	2P: $79-$135	XP: $10	F10

Location: Jct Hwy 97 (32nd St) and 6 (25th Ave), just w. 2408 34th St V1T 5W8. **Fax:** 250/503-1818. **Facility:** 30 units. 26 one- and 2 two-bedroom standard units, some with efficiencies. 2 one-bedroom suites. 2 stories (no elevator), exterior corridors. **Parking:** on-site. **Terms:** office hours 7 am-11 pm, 3 day cancellation notice, pets ($10 fee). **Amenities:** hair dryers. **Dining:** 8 am-10, noon-2 & 5-9 pm, cocktails. **Pool(s):** heated outdoor. **Leisure Activities:** sauna, whirlpool, dog walk, playground, limited exercise equipment. **Guest Services:** coin laundry. **Business Services:** meeting rooms, PC. **Cards:** AX, MC, VI. **Special Amenities:** free local telephone calls and preferred room (subject to availability with advance reservations).

SOME UNITS

THE TUCK INN BED & BREAKFAST

Phone: (250)545-3252

WWW WW

Historic Bed & Breakfast

All Year [BP]	1P: $50-$85	2P: $65-$85	XP: $20	F12

Location: On 30th Ave (which becomes Pleasant Valley Rd) at 24th St. Located in a quiet residential area. 3101 Pleasant Valley Rd V1T 4L2. **Fax:** 250/549-3254. **Facility:** The inn, operated as a B&B since 1992, is in a historic home that was expanded using materials salvaged from buildings of the same vintage. Designated smoking area. 5 one-bedroom standard units. 2 stories (no elevator), interior corridors. *Bath:* some shared or private, combo or shower only. **Parking:** on-site. **Terms:** 7 day cancellation notice. **Amenities:** *Some:* hair dryers. **Guest Services:** complimentary laundry. **Cards:** AX, MC, VI.

SOME UNITS

VERNON TRAVELODGE   *Book at aaa.com*

Phone: (250)545-2161

WWW WW

Small-scale Hotel

5/16-9/30	1P: $85-$99	2P: $105-$115	XP: $10	F18
3/1-5/15 & 10/1-2/28	1P: $65-$99	2P: $75-$99	XP: $10	F18

Location: Hwy 97 (32nd St), just e on 28th Ave, near Polson Park. 3000 28th Ave V1T 1W1. **Fax:** 250/545-5536. **Facility:** 39 one-bedroom standard units. 2 stories (no elevator), exterior corridors. *Bath:* combo or shower only. **Parking:** on-site. **Terms:** office hours 7:30 am-11 pm, small pets only ($10 extra charge). **Pool(s):** heated outdoor. **Cards:** AX, MC, VI.

SOME UNITS

———— **WHERE TO DINE** ————

AMARIN THAI RESTAURANT

Lunch: $8-$14   **Dinner:** $9-$14   **Phone:** 250/542-9300

WW WW

Thai

Location: Between 29th and 30th aves. 2903 31st St V1T 5H6. **Hours:** 11:30 am-2:30 & 5-10 pm, Sat & Sun from 5 pm. Closed: Sun. **Reservations:** suggested. **Features:** Lining the extensive menu are many salads, some with meat, as well as beef, seafood, chicken and pork dishes. The stylish decor, including Thai artifacts and art, is warm and appealing. Service is fine. Parking is limited to the street. Cocktails. **Parking:** street. **Cards:** AX, MC, VI.

DIVINO'S ITALIANO RISTORANTE

Lunch: $9-$11   **Dinner:** $8-$20   **Phone:** 250/549-3463

WWW WW

Italian

Location: Corner of 30th Ave and 33rd St; downtown. 3224 30th Ave V1T 2C5. **Hours:** 11 am-2 & 5-10 pm, Sat from 5 pm. Closed major holidays; also Sun & Mon. **Features:** The small, downtown, bistro-style restaurant serves a variety of homemade pastas, all made on the premises. Choices include fresh gnocchi, lasagna and spaghetti. Each table was painted by a local artist, which enables diners to enjoy art with their hearty, delicious meal. Casual dress; cocktails. **Parking:** street. **Cards:** MC, VI.

THE ECLECTIC MED RESTAURANT INC

Lunch: $8-$15   **Dinner:** $9-$20   **Phone:** 250/558-4646

WWW WWW

Mediterranean

Location: Corner of Hwy 97 (32nd St) and 32nd Ave. 100-3117 32nd St V1T 5Z1. **Hours:** 11 am-2 & 5-10 pm, Sat from 5 pm, Sun 5 pm-9 pm. Closed: Sun. **Reservations:** suggested. **Features:** In a word, the restaurant can be summed up as "funky," with a varied and eclectic menu of Mediterranean food. The many tempting food choices entice diners to return repeatedly. Appetizers are big enough to enjoy as a meal, and entrees incorporate everything from seafood to vegetarian staples. Throw in a superb wine list, a warm atmosphere and friendly service, and you've found the recipe for a fantastic evening. Dressy casual; cocktails. **Parking:** on-site. **Cards:** AX, MC, VI.

INTERMEZZO RESTAURANT

Dinner: $10-$17   **Phone:** 250/542-3853

WWW WW

Italian

Location: Hwy 97 (32nd St), just w. 3206 34th Ave V1T 6M1. **Hours:** 5 pm-10 pm, Sun-9 pm. Closed: 12/24, 12/25. **Reservations:** not accepted. **Features:** You'll enjoy the wide variety of pasta, chicken, seafood, barbecue ribs and the specialty veal, prepared in six classic ways, at the Intermezzo, which is located downtown behind a small shopping complex. Meals are delicious and attractively presented. Casual dress; cocktails. **Parking:** street. **Cards:** AX, MC, VI.

THE ITALIAN KITCHEN COMPANY

Lunch: $6-$10   **Dinner:** $9-$17   **Phone:** 250/558-7899

WW WW

Italian

Location: Downtown. 2916 30th Ave V1T 2B7. **Hours:** 11 am-2 & 5-10 pm, Sat & Sun from 5 pm. Closed major holidays. **Features:** Hearty, delicious food awaits at the funky, upbeat restaurant, along the main street downtown. Among offerings are traditional dishes, ranging from pastas to salads to savory soups. Hardwood floors and an exposed-brick wall are accentuated by large local art in a bright and cheery decor. Service is friendly and attentive. Casual dress; cocktails. **Parking:** street. **Cards:** AX, MC, VI.

Destination Victoria
pop. 74,125

*T*he Trans-Canada Highway ends in Victoria, but your journey isn't complete until you've seen the city and its surroundings.

*W*ander down cobblestone streets lined with Victorian lampposts. Tour one glorious English garden after another. Do the town in a double-decker bus. Or cruise to neighboring islands.

Tourism Victoria

Golfing in Victoria.
With its mild climate and coastal location, Victoria offers year-round golf with an ocean view. (See mention page 177)

© bachmann / Photophile

Victoria Harbour.
Passenger and automobile ferries transport visitors to and from this island city. (See mention page 169)

Parliament Buildings, Victoria. Formal gardens, fountains and monuments surround the capital seat overlooking the Inner Harbor. (See listing page 174)

© R. Krubner Robertstock

BRITISH COLUMBIA
WASHINGTON

Sidney

Saanichton

Brentwood Bay

Malahat

(14)

(17)

See Vicinity map page 601

Sooke

Victoria

CANADA
UNITED STATES

Tourism Victoria

Sport fishing off the Saanich Peninsula, Victoria. Anglers can rent a boat or hop aboard a charter to hook salmon, halibut and cod. (See mention page 177)

*P*laces included in this AAA Destination City:

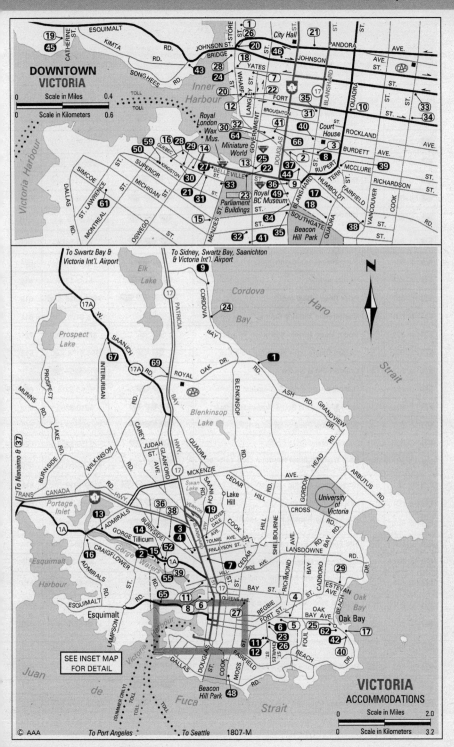

DOWNTOWN VICTORIA

Scale in Miles 0 0.4
Scale in Kilometers 0 0.6

To Swartz Bay & Victoria Int'l. Airport

To Sidney, Swartz Bay, Saanichton & Victoria Int'l. Airport

To Nanaimo & 37

To Port Angeles

To Seattle

1807-M

© AAA

VICTORIA ACCOMMODATIONS

Scale in Miles 0 2.0
Scale in Kilometers 0 3.2

Victoria

This index helps you "spot" where approved accommodations and restaurants are located on the corresponding detailed maps. Lodging rate ranges are for comparison only and show the property's high season; rates are per night, unless only weekly (W) rates are available. Restaurant rate range is for dinner, unless only lunch (L) is served. Turn to the listing page for more detailed rate information and consult display ads for special promotions.

Spotter/Map Page Number	OA	**VICTORIA** - Lodgings	Diamond Rating	Rate Range High Season	Listing Page
1 / p. 601	CAA	**Sea View Inn: A Clarion Collection Hotel** - see color ad p 623	◆◆	$79-$399 SAVE	622
2 / p. 601	CAA	**Days Inn Victoria Waterway** - see color ad starting on p 606	◆◆	$99-$159 SAVE	612
3 / p. 601	CAA	**Mayfair Motel**	◆◆	$59-$89 SAVE	618
4 / p. 601	CAA	**Blue Ridge Inns**	◆◆	$89-$119 SAVE	611
6 / p. 601		Amethyst Inn at Regents Park	◆◆◆	$199-$399	609
7 / p. 601	CAA	**Holiday Inn Victoria** - see color ad card insert	◆◆◆	$99-$179 SAVE	616
8 / p. 601		Chateau Victoria Hotel and Suites - see color ad p 611	◆◆◆	$117-$325	611
9 / p. 601		Sunnymeade House Inn	◆◆	$85-$175	624
11 / p. 601		Fairholme Manor	◆◆◆	$155-$325	614
12 / p. 601	CAA	**Prior House B&B Inn**	◆◆◆◆	$225-$325 SAVE	619
13 / p. 601	CAA	**Cheltenham Motel & Suites**	◆	$75-$100 SAVE	611
14 / p. 601	CAA	**Robin Hood Motel** - see color ad p 620	◆◆	$70-$94 SAVE	621
15 / p. 601	CAA	**Oxford Castle Inn** - see color ad p 619	◆◆	$95-$158 SAVE	619
16 / p. 601	CAA	**Comfort Inn & Suites**	◆◆◆	$119-$259 SAVE	611
17 / p. 601		Humboldt House Bed & Breakfast	◆◆	$245-$315	617
18 / p. 601		Ambrosia Historic Bed & Breakfast Retreat	◆◆◆	$210-$280	609
19 / p. 601	CAA	**Accent Inns** - see color ad p 488, p 608	◆◆◆	$129-$159 SAVE	605
20 / p. 601		Swans Hotel	◆◆◆	$159-$259	624
21 / p. 601	CAA	**Best Western Inner Harbour** - see color ad starting on p 606	◆◆◆	$159-$269 SAVE	610
22 / p. 601	CAA	**Hotel Grand Pacific** - see color ad p 616	◆◆◆◆	$199-$319 SAVE	616
23 / p. 601		Villa Marco Polo Inn	◆◆◆	$285-$325	628
24 / p. 601	CAA	**The Victoria Regent Hotel** - see color ad p 627	◆◆◆	$129-$339 SAVE	627
25 / p. 601	CAA	**The Fairmont Empress** - see color ad p 614	◆◆◆◆	$309-$549 SAVE	614
26 / p. 601		Abbeymoore Manor Bed & Breakfast Inn	◆◆	$169-$249	605
27 / p. 601	CAA	**Days Inn on the Harbour** - see color ad p 612, p 545	◆◆	$183-$223 SAVE	612
28 / p. 601	CAA	**Admiral Inn** - see color ad p 609	◆◆◆	$159-$249 SAVE	608
29 / p. 601	CAA	**Ramada Huntingdon Hotel & Suites** - see color ad p 621	◆◆	$149-$229 SAVE	620
30 / p. 601	CAA	**Harbour Towers Hotel & Suites** - see color ad p 615	◆◆◆	$175-$435 SAVE	615
31 / p. 601	CAA	**Royal Scot Suite Hotel** - see color ad p 622	◆◆◆	$159-$339 SAVE	621
32 / p. 601		Rosewood Victoria Inn	◆◆◆	$145-$250	621
33 / p. 601	CAA	**Embassy Inn** - see color ad p 613	◆◆	$99-$259 SAVE	613
34 / p. 601	CAA	**Helm's Inn** - see color ad p 615	◆◆◆	$135-$210 SAVE	615

Spotter/Map Page Number	OA	VICTORIA - Lodgings (continued)	Diamond Rating	Rate Range High Season	Listing Page
35 / p. 601		Shamrock Suites on the Park - see color ad p 623	◈◈	$145-$185	623
36 / p. 601	CAA	Crystal Court Motel	◈	$98-$125 [SAVE]	611
37 / p. 601	CAA	Executive House Hotel	◈◈◈	$155-$195 [SAVE]	614
38 / p. 601		Beaconsfield Inn	◈◈◈	$219-$295	610
39 / p. 601	CAA	Abigail's Hotel - see color ad p 608	◈◈◈	$259-$409 [SAVE]	605
40 / p. 601	CAA	Quality Inn Downtown - see color ad starting on p 606	◈◈◈	$139-$229 [SAVE]	619
41 / p. 601	CAA	James Bay Inn - see color ad p 617	◈◈	$127-$152 [SAVE]	617
42 / p. 601		Oak Bay Beach Hotel & Marine Resort	◈◈◈	$199-$475	618
43 / p. 601	CAA	Delta Victoria Ocean Pointe Resort & Spa - see color ad p 613	◈◈◈◈	$225-$310 [SAVE]	613
44 / p. 601	CAA	Victoria Marriott Inner Harbour - see color ad p 626	◈◈◈◈	$259-$479 [SAVE]	626
45 / p. 601	CAA	Spinnaker Brewpub and Guesthouse - see color ad p 624	◈◈◈	$149-$249 [SAVE]	624
46 / p. 601	CAA	Best Western Carlton Plaza Hotel - see color ad p 610, p 552	◈◈◈	$159-$249 [SAVE]	610
48 / p. 601	CAA	Dashwood Seaside Manor	◈◈	$165-$255 [SAVE]	612
49 / p. 601	CAA	Queen Victoria Hotel and Suites - see color ad p 620	◈◈◈	$195-$285 [SAVE]	620
50 / p. 601		A Haterleigh Heritage Inn	◈◈◈	$225-$355	608
52 / p. 601	CAA	Howard Johnson Hotel-City Centre	◈◈	$115-$169 [SAVE]	617
55 / p. 601	CAA	Travelodge Victoria - see color ad p 625, p 545	◈◈◈	$125-$175 [SAVE]	624
59 / p. 601		Andersen House Bed & Breakfast	◈◈◈	$175-$275	609
61 / p. 601		Heathergate House Bed & Breakfast	◈◈	$110-$140	615
62 / p. 601		Oak Bay Guest House Bed & Breakfast	◈◈	$140-$195	619
64 / p. 601	CAA	Union Club of British Columbia - see color ad p 626	◈◈◈	$179-$269 [SAVE]	626
65 / p. 601		An Ocean View Bed & Breakfast	◈	$100-$180	609
66 / p. 601	CAA	The Magnolia Hotel & Spa - see color ad p 618	◈◈◈◈	$289-$349 [SAVE]	617
67 / p. 601		Iris Garden Country Manor Bed & Breakfast	◈◈	$145-$175	617
69 / p. 601		Howard Johnson Hotel & Suites	◈◈◈	$169-$219	616
		VICTORIA - Restaurants			
1 / p. 601		Hunan Village	◈	$8-$15	629
2 / p. 601		Barkley's Steak & Seafood	◈◈◈	$19-$38	628
3 / p. 601		Bowman's Rib House	◈◈	$14-$18	628
4 / p. 601		The Blethering Place Tea Room & Restaurant	◈◈	$8-$17	628
5 / p. 601		White Heather Tea Room	◈◈	$8-$11(L)	632
6 / p. 601	CAA	Taj Mahal	◈◈	$12-$22	632
7 / p. 601		Periklis Greek Restaurant	◈◈	$11-$28	630
8 / p. 601		Canoe Brewpub Marina Restaurant	◈◈	$15-$25	628
9 / p. 601		Fire & Water Fish & Chop House - see color ad p 626	◈◈◈	$22-$35	629

Spotter/Map Page Number	OA	**VICTORIA** - Restaurants (continued)	Diamond Rating	Rate Range High Season	Listing Page
⑩ / p. 601	·	The Spice Jammer Restaurant	◈◈	$15-$20	631
⑪ / p. 601		Herald Street Caffe	◈◈◈	$12-$28	629
⑫ / p. 601		Koto Japanese Restaurant	◈◈	$6-$16	630
⑬ / p. 601		The Empress Room	◈◈◈◈	$30-$40	629
⑭ / p. 601	CAA	**Victoria Harbour House Restaurant**	◈◈	$14-$30	632
⑮ / p. 601	CAA	**James Bay Tea Room & Restaurant**	◈	$7-$10(L)	629
⑯ / p. 601		Pablo's Dining Lounge	◈◈◈	$19-$33	630
⑰ / p. 601		The Marina Restaurant	◈◈◈	$16-$30	630
⑱ / p. 601		Restaurant Matisse	◈◈◈	$20-$37	631
⑲ / p. 601		Spinnakers Brew Pub & Restaurant	◈◈	$8-$20	631
⑳ / p. 601		The Keg Steakhouse	◈◈	$19-$30	629
㉑ / p. 601	CAA	**The Black Olive**	◈◈◈	$15-$26	628
㉒ / p. 601		Siam Thai Restaurant	◈◈	$8-$16	631
㉓ / p. 601	CAA	**The Mark**	◈◈◈◈	$26-$36	630
㉔ / p. 601	CAA	**Charter's Restaurant at McMorran's Beach House**	◈◈◈	$12-$24	628
㉕ / p. 601		Penny Farthing Public House	◈◈	$9-$17	630
㉖ / p. 601	CAA	**Wild Saffron Bistro & Wine Bar**	◈◈◈	$15-$34	632
㉗ / p. 601		Haultain's Fish & Chips	◈	$7-$14	629
㉘ / p. 601		Il Terrazzo	◈◈◈	$15-$36	629
㉙ / p. 601		Paprika Bistro	◈◈◈	$17-$29	630
㉚ / p. 601		Milestone's Grill & Bar	◈◈	$7-$13	630
㉛ / p. 601		Pagliacci's	◈	$16-$22	630
㉜ / p. 601		Pescatore's Fish House	◈◈	$18-$25	631
㉝ / p. 601		Passero's Mediterranean Cuisine	◈◈	$11-$19	630
㉞ / p. 601		Pluto's	◈◈	$7-$11	631
㉟ / p. 601		Dilettantes Cafe	◈◈	$10-$20	629
㊱ / p. 601		Superior Chinese Restaurant	◈	$10-$16	631
㊲ / p. 601		Six Mile Pub	◈	$4-$11	631
㊳ / p. 601		Brady's Fish & Chips	◈	$8-$13	628
㊴ / p. 601		South Bay Pub & Restaurant	◈◈	$9-$17	631
㊵ / p. 601		The Snug English Pub	◈◈	$9-$18	631
㊶ / p. 601		Hugo's Grill and Brewhouse	◈◈	$17-$28	629

VICTORIA pop. 74,125 (See map and index starting on p. 601)

──── WHERE TO STAY ────

ABBEYMOORE MANOR BED & BREAKFAST INN   **Phone: 250/370-1470**   [26]

♦♦♦ ♦♦♦

6/17-9/30 [BP]	2P: $169-$249	XP: $20
5/1-6/16 [BP]	2P: $129-$199	XP: $20
3/1-4/30 & 10/1-2/28 [BP]	2P: $109-$179	XP: $20

Bed & Breakfast **Location:** Blanshard St (Hwy 17), 2 km e on Fort St, just s on St. Charles St, then just w. 1470 Rockland Ave V8S 1W2. Fax: 250/370-1470. **Facility:** Smoke free premises. 7 units. 5 one-bedroom standard units. 2 one-bedroom suites with efficiencies and whirlpools. 3 stories (no elevator), interior/exterior corridors. *Bath:* combo or shower only. **Parking:** on-site. **Terms:** office hours 7 am-10 pm, 14 day cancellation notice, weekly rates available, package plans. **Amenities:** CD players, hair dryers. **Cards:** MC, VI.

SOME UNITS

(ASK) ⊠ 🄚 / 🄿 🄩 🄗 🄐 🄜 /

ABIGAIL'S HOTEL   *Book at aaa.com*   **Phone: (250)388-5363**   [39]

(CAA) (SAVE)

7/1-9/30 [BP]	1P: $259-$409	2P: $259-$409	XP: $30 F10
3/1-4/30 [BP]	1P: $199-$339	2P: $199-$399	XP: $30 F10
5/1-6/30 [BP]	1P: $229-$374	2P: $229-$374	XP: $30 F10
10/1-2/28 [BP]	1P: $199-$339	2P: $199-$339	XP: $30 F10

♦♦♦♦ ♦♦♦♦

Bed & Breakfast **Location:** Blanshard St (Hwy 17), just e on Fairfield Rd, then just n on Vancouver St. Located in a quiet residential area. 906 McClure St V8V 3E7. Fax: 250/388-7787. **Facility:** A European-style hotel, Abigail's is distinguished by its elegant public area, hardwood floors, quality furnishings and professional service. Smoke free premises. 23 one-bedroom standard units, some with whirlpools. 2-3 stories (no elevator), interior corridors. *Bath:* combo or shower only. **Parking:** on-site. **Terms:** age restrictions may apply, 14 day cancellation notice-fee imposed, small pets only ($25 extra charge). **Amenities:** voice mail, hair dryers. **Guest Services:** gift shop, valet laundry. **Cards:** AX, MC, VI. **Special Amenities:** free full breakfast and free local telephone calls. *(See color ad p 608)*

SOME UNITS

🄗 🄐⊠ 🄚 🄳🄰🄣🄰🄿🄾🄡🄣 / 🄿 🄐 🄜 /
        FEE

ACCENT INNS   *Book at aaa.com*   **Phone: (250)475-7500**   [19]

(CAA) (SAVE)

7/1-9/30	1P: $129-$149	2P: $139-$159	XP: $10 F16
5/1-6/30	1P: $99-$119	2P: $109-$129	XP: $10 F16
3/1-4/30 & 10/1-2/28	1P: $89-$109	2P: $99-$119	XP: $10 F16

♦♦♦ ♦♦♦

Location: 3 km n on Blanshard St (Hwy 17); corner of Blanchard St and Cloverdale Ave. 3233 Maple St V8X 4Y9. **Small-scale Hotel** Fax: 250/475-7599. **Facility:** 118 one-bedroom standard units, some with efficiencies (utensils extra charge). 3 stories, exterior corridors. **Parking:** on-site. **Terms:** small pets only ($10 extra charge, ground floor units). **Amenities:** video games (fee), voice mail, hair dryers. *Some:* high-speed Internet. **Dining:** 6:30 am-9 pm, wine/beer only. **Guest Services:** valet and coin laundry. **Business Services:** meeting rooms. **Cards:** AX, DC, MC, VI. **Special Amenities:** free local telephone calls and free newspaper. *(See color ad p 488 & p 608)*

SOME UNITS

🅂🄳 🄗 🄮 🄶🄼 🄐🄣 🄳🄰🄣🄰🄿🄾🄡🄣 🄜 / ⊠ 🄐 🄜 /
        FEE

(See map and index starting on p. 601)

ADMIRAL INN
Phone: (250)388-6267   [28]

(CAA) (SAVE)

▼▼▼▼▼

Motel

7/1-9/30 [ECP]	1P: $159-$239	2P: $169-$249	XP: $10 F12
3/1-6/30 [ECP]	1P: $99-$169	2P: $109-$179	XP: $10 F12
12/24-2/28 [ECP]	1P: $89-$149	2P: $99-$159	XP: $10 F12
10/1-12/23 [ECP]	1P: $79-$129	2P: $89-$139	XP: $10 F12

Location: Corner of Belleville and Quebec sts. 257 Belleville St V8V 1X1. Fax: 250/388-6267. **Facility:** Designated smoking area. 32 units. 21 one-bedroom standard units, some with kitchens. 11 one-bedroom suites ($109-$249) with kitchens. 3 stories, exterior corridors. **Parking:** on-site. **Terms:** cancellation fee imposed, weekly rates available, small pets only (main floor). **Amenities:** hair dryers. **Guest Services:** coin laundry. **Cards:** AX, DS, MC, VI. **Special Amenities:** free expanded continental breakfast and free local telephone calls. *(See color ad p 609)*

SOME UNITS

 / FEE

A HATERLEIGH HERITAGE INN   *Book at aaa.com*
Phone: (250)384-9995   [50]

▼▼▼▼

Historic Bed
& Breakfast

5/16-10/15 [BP]	1P: $225-$355	2P: $225-$355
3/1-5/15 & 10/16-2/28 [BP]	1P: $155-$225	2P: $155-$225

Location: Corner of Pendray and Kingston sts. Located in the Inner Harbour. 243 Kingston St V8V 1V5. Fax: 250/384-1935. **Facility:** Distinguishing this Victorian home are a sweeping staircase, semicircular porch and stained-glass and leaded windows. 7 one-bedroom standard units, some with whirlpools. 2 stories (no elevator), interior corridors. **Parking:** on-site. **Terms:** check-in 4 pm, age restrictions may apply, 14 day cancellation notice-fee imposed. **Amenities:** hair dryers. **Business Services:** PC (fee). **Cards:** MC, VI.

(See map and index starting on p. 601)

AMBROSIA HISTORIC BED & BREAKFAST RETREAT

Phone: (250)380-7705   **18**

5/1-9/30 [BP]	1P: $210-$280	2P: $210-$280	XP: $25
3/1-4/30 & 10/1-10/15 [BP]	1P: $175-$235	2P: $175-$235	XP: $25
10/16-2/28 [BP]	1P: $145-$185	2P: $145-$185	XP: $25

Classic Resort Bed & Breakfast

Location: Between Southgate and Humboldt sts. 522 Quadra St V8V 3S3. Fax: 250/381-7739. **Facility:** Located within walking distance of Beacon Hill Park and downtown, the inn offers spacious rooms in a fully restored Victorian style home. Smoke free premises. 4 one-bedroom standard units, some with whirlpools. 2 stories (no elevator), interior corridors. *Bath:* combo or shower only. **Parking:** on-site. **Terms:** office hours 7 am-10 pm, check-in 5 pm, 2 night minimum stay - seasonal, age restrictions may apply, 14 day cancellation notice-fee imposed. **Amenities:** CD players, hair dryers. **Cards:** AX, MC, VI.

AMETHYST INN AT REGENTS PARK

Phone: (250)595-2053   **6**

5/1-10/15	2P: $199-$399	XP: $45
10/16-12/31	2P: $129-$349	XP: $45
3/1-4/30 & 1/1-2/28	2P: $129-$299	XP: $45

Historic Bed & Breakfast

Location: Blanshard St (Hwy 17), 2 km e on Fort St to St. Charles St. Located in a residential area. 1501 Fort St V8S 1Z6. Fax: 250/595-2054. **Facility:** An authentic 1885 Victorian mansion with antiques, stained glass and a magnificent staircase, located in a charming neighborhood of old stately homes. Smoke free premises. 16 one-bedroom standard units, some with whirlpools. 3 stories (no elevator), interior/exterior corridors. **Parking:** on-site. **Terms:** office hours 8 am-9:30 pm, check-in 4 pm, age restrictions may apply, 14 day cancellation notice-fee imposed, package plans. **Amenities:** CD players, hair dryers. **Cards:** MC, VI.

SOME UNITS

ANDERSEN HOUSE BED & BREAKFAST

Phone: 250/388-4565   **59**

6/1-9/30 [BP]	1P: $175-$255	2P: $195-$275	XP: $45
5/1-5/31 [BP]	1P: $125-$230	2P: $145-$250	XP: $45
10/1-2/28 [BP]	1P: $95-$195	2P: $125-$235	XP: $45
3/1-4/30 [BP]	1P: $95-$195	2P: $105-$235	XP: $45

Historic Bed & Breakfast

Location: Between Pendray and Montreal sts. Located in the Inner Harbour. 301 Kingston St V8V 1V5. Fax: 250/721-3938. **Facility:** This charming home built in 1891 blends historic details with contemporary furnishings and artwork. Smoke free premises. 4 one-bedroom standard units, some with whirlpools. 3 stories (no elevator), interior/exterior corridors. *Bath:* combo or shower only. **Parking:** on-site. **Terms:** office hours 8 am-10 pm, 2 night minimum stay - weekends, age restrictions may apply, 14 day cancellation notice-fee imposed, package plans. **Amenities:** CD players, hair dryers. **Cards:** MC, VI.

SOME UNITS

AN OCEAN VIEW BED & BREAKFAST

Book at aaa.com   Phone: (250)386-7330   **65**

5/21-9/15 [BP]	1P: $100-$175	2P: $105-$180	XP: $35
9/16-10/4 [BP]	1P: $85-$150	2P: $100-$150	XP: $25
4/1-5/20 [BP]	1P: $85-$145	2P: $100-$150	XP: $25

Bed & Breakfast

Location: Douglas St, 1.5 km w on Pandora St (which becomes Esquimalt Rd), just n on Dalton St to Suffolk St. Located in a residential area. 715 Suffolk St V9A 3J5. Fax: 250/389-0280. **Facility:** Smoke free premises. 6 one-bedroom standard units. 2 stories (no elevator), interior corridors. *Bath:* combo or shower only. **Parking:** on-site. **Terms:** open 4/1-10/4; office hours 8 am-9 pm, check-in 4 pm, 2 night minimum stay, age restrictions may apply, 7 day cancellation notice-fee imposed, package plans. **Leisure Activities:** whirlpool. **Cards:** MC, VI.

SOME UNITS

(See map and index starting on p. 601)

BEACONSFIELD INN Phone: (250)384-4044 38

7/1-9/19	1P: $219-$295	2P: $219-$295	XP: $35
5/14-6/30 & 9/20-2/28	1P: $169-$229	2P: $169-$229	XP: $35
3/1-5/13	1P: $129-$179	2P: $129-$179	XP: $35

Bed & Breakfast **Location:** Blanshard St (Hwy 17), just e on Fairfield Rd, then just s on Vancouver St. Located in quiet, residential area. 998 Humboldt St V8V 2Z8. Fax: 250/384-4052. **Facility:** Leaded-glass windows and mahogany floors distinguish this restored 1905 Edwardian mansion, part of a stately neighborhood well-suited for strolling. Designated smoking area. 9 one-bedroom standard units, some with whirlpools. 4 stories (no elevator), interior corridors. *Bath:* combo or shower only. **Parking:** on-site. **Terms:** office hours 7 am-10 pm, age restrictions may apply, 14 day cancellation notice-fee imposed, [BP] meal plan available. **Amenities:** CD players, hair dryers. **Guest Services:** complimentary evening beverages. **Cards:** AX, MC, VI.

BEST WESTERN CARLTON PLAZA HOTEL   *Book at aaa.com*   Phone: (250)388-5513 46

5/16-9/30	1P: $159-$249	2P: $159-$249	XP: $20
3/1-5/15 & 10/1-2/28	1P: $89-$169	2P: $89-$169	XP: $20

F17

Small-scale Hotel **Location:** Between Douglas and Broad sts. 642 Johnson St V8W 1M6. Fax: 250/388-5343. **Facility:** 103 units. 97 one-bedroom standard units, some with efficiencies or kitchens. 6 one-bedroom suites with kitchens. 7 stories, interior corridors. **Parking:** on-site (fee) and valet. **Terms:** weekly rates available, package plans. **Amenities:** voice mail, irons, hair dryers. *Some:* high-speed Internet. **Dining:** 6:30 am-3 pm. **Leisure Activities:** exercise room. **Guest Services:** valet and coin laundry. **Cards:** AX, DC, DS, MC, VI. **Special Amenities:** free continental breakfast and free newspaper. *(See color ad below & p 552)*

SOME UNITS

BEST WESTERN INNER HARBOUR   *Book at aaa.com*   Phone: (250)384-5122 21

7/1-10/14 [ECP]	1P: $159-$269	2P: $159-$269	XP: $20
5/20-6/30 [ECP]	1P: $119-$229	2P: $119-$229	XP: $20
3/1-5/19 & 10/15-2/28 [ECP]	1P: $84-$179	2P: $84-$179	XP: $20

F13
F13
F13

Small-scale Hotel **Location:** Between Oswego and Menzies sts. 412 Quebec St V8V 1W5. Fax: 250/384-5113. **Facility:** Smoke free premises. 74 units. 66 one-bedroom standard units, some with efficiencies (utensils extra charge). 7 one- and 1 two-bedroom suites ($159-$799) with whirlpools, some with efficiencies or kitchens (utensils extra charge). 8 stories, interior corridors. **Parking:** on-site. **Terms:** check-in 4 pm. **Amenities:** video library (fee), voice mail, irons, hair dryers. **Pool(s):** small heated outdoor. **Leisure Activities:** sauna, whirlpool, steamroom, limited exercise equipment. **Guest Services:** valet and coin laundry. **Cards:** AX, DC, DS, MC, VI. **Special Amenities:** free expanded continental breakfast and free room upgrade (subject to availability with advance reservations). *(See color ad starting on p 606)*

SOME UNITS

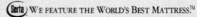

(See map and index starting on p. 601)

BLUE RIDGE INNS   *Book at aaa.com*   Phone: (250)388-4345   **4**

7/1-9/30	1P: $89-$109	2P: $99-$119	XP: $10	F16
5/1-6/30	1P: $69-$79	2P: $79-$89	XP: $10	F16
3/1-4/30 & 10/1-2/28	1P: $59-$69	2P: $69-$79	XP: $10	F16

Location: Between Finlayson St and Speed Ave. 3110 Douglas St V8Z 3K4. Fax: 250/388-7613. **Facility:** 62 units. Small-scale Hotel 61 one- and 1 two-bedroom standard units, some with efficiencies or kitchens. 2 stories (no elevator), exterior corridors. *Bath:* combo or shower only. **Parking:** on-site. **Terms:** small pets only. **Amenities:** *Some:* voice mail. **Dining:** 6:30 am-3 pm. **Pool(s):** heated indoor. **Leisure Activities:** sauna. **Guest Services:** coin laundry. **Cards:** AX, DC, MC, VI. **Special Amenities:** free local telephone calls and free newspaper.

SOME UNITS

CHATEAU VICTORIA HOTEL AND SUITES   *Book at aaa.com*   Phone: (250)382-4221   **8**

5/1-6/15	1P: $117-$325	2P: $117-$325	XP: $15	F18
6/16-10/14	1P: $139-$299	2P: $139-$299	XP: $15	F18
3/1-4/30	1P: $89-$178	2P: $89-$178	XP: $15	F18
10/15-2/28	1P: $82-$159	2P: $82-$159	XP: $15	F18

Large-scale Hotel
Location: Between Douglas St and Fairfield Rd. 740 Burdett Ave V8W 1B2. Fax: 250/380-1950. **Facility:** 177 units. 170 one-bedroom standard units, some with efficiencies or kitchens. 7 two-bedroom suites with kitchens, some with whirlpools. 19 stories, interior corridors. **Parking:** on-site. **Terms:** pets ($15 extra charge, dogs only). **Amenities:** video games (fee), voice mail, irons, hair dryers. **Pool(s):** heated indoor. **Leisure Activities:** whirlpool, limited exercise equipment. **Guest Services:** valet laundry, area transportation. **Business Services:** meeting rooms. **Cards:** AX, CB, DC, DS, JC, MC, VI. *(See color ad below)*

SOME UNITS

FEE

CHELTENHAM MOTEL & SUITES   Phone: (250)385-9559   **13**

6/1-9/15	1P: $75-$85	2P: $85-$100	XP: $10

Motel
Location: Douglas St, 4.5 km w. Located across from a park. 994 Gorge Rd W V9A 1P2. Fax: 250/383-2394. **Facility:** Smoke free premises. 19 units. 7 one-bedroom standard units. 8 one- and 4 two-bedroom suites ($125-$300) with kitchens. 1 story, exterior corridors. **Parking:** on-site. **Terms:** open 6/1-9/15, office hours 8 am-11 pm, 4 day cancellation notice-fee imposed, package plans. **Guest Services:** coin laundry. **Cards:** AX, MC, VI.

SOME UNITS

COMFORT INN & SUITES   *Book at aaa.com*   Phone: (250)388-7861   **16**

7/1-9/30 [ECP]	1P: $119-$259	2P: $119-$259	XP: $15	F17
5/1-6/30 [ECP]	1P: $89-$199	2P: $89-$199	XP: $15	F17
3/1-4/30 & 10/1-2/28 [ECP]	1P: $79-$179	2P: $79-$179	XP: $15	F17

Location: Douglas St, 5 km w on Gorge Rd, then just s on Admirals Rd. 101 Island Hwy V9B 1E8. Small-scale Hotel Fax: 250/388-7862. **Facility:** 106 units. 96 one- and 10 two-bedroom standard units, some with efficiencies or kitchens. 2 stories (no elevator), interior/exterior corridors. **Parking:** on-site. **Terms:** pets ($10 extra charge). **Amenities:** irons, hair dryers. **Pool(s):** heated outdoor. **Leisure Activities:** rental bicycles. *Fee:* kayaks. **Guest Services:** valet and coin laundry. **Business Services:** meeting rooms. **Cards:** AX, DC, MC, VI.

SOME UNITS

FEE

CRYSTAL COURT MOTEL   Phone: 250/384-0551   **36**

6/1-9/30	1P: $98	2P: $104-$125	XP: $10	F16
10/1-2/28	1P: $67	2P: $73-$89	XP: $10	F16
3/1-5/31	1P: $65	2P: $69-$87	XP: $10	F16

Motel
Location: Between Douglas and Blanshard sts. 701 Belleville St V8W 1A2. Fax: 250/384-5125. **Facility:** 56 one-bedroom standard units, some with kitchens. 2 stories, exterior corridors. **Parking:** on-site. **Cards:** DS, MC, VI. **Special Amenities:** free local telephone calls and free newspaper.

SOME UNITS

(See map and index starting on p. 601)

DASHWOOD SEASIDE MANOR   Phone: (250)385-5517   48

CAA SAVE   6/1-9/30 [BP]   2P: $165-$255   XP: $25
             5/1-5/31 [BP]   2P: $125-$195   XP: $25
             3/1-4/30 & 10/1-2/28 [BP]   2P: $95-$145   XP: $25

Location: 1 km e of Douglas St on Dallas Rd. Located in a residential area, across from Beacon Hill Park. 1 Cook St
Bed & Breakfast   V8V 3W6. Fax: 250/383-1760. **Facility:** Smoke free premises. 12 one-bedroom standard units with
efficiencies, some with whirlpools. 3 stories (no elevator), interior corridors. **Parking:** on-site. **Terms:** office
hours 8 am-9 pm, age restrictions may apply, 14 day cancellation notice-fee imposed, weekly rates available, package plans,
small pets only ($25 extra charge, with prior approval). **Amenities:** hair dryers. **Cards:** AX, MC, VI. **Special Amenities: free
full breakfast.**

FEE

DAYS INN ON THE HARBOUR   *Book at aaa.com*   Phone: (250)386-3451   27

CAA SAVE   7/1-10/15   1P: $183-$223   2P: $183-$223   XP: $10   F12
             5/1-6/30   1P: $143-$183   2P: $143-$183   XP: $10   F12
             3/1-4/30 & 10/16-2/28   1P: $99-$143   2P: $99-$143   XP: $10   F12

Location: Entrance on Oswego at Quebec sts. 427 Belleville St V8V 1X3. Fax: 250/386-6999. **Facility:** 71 one-
Small-scale Hotel   bedroom standard units, some with efficiencies (utensils extra charge). 4 stories, interior corridors. **Bath:**
combo or shower only. **Parking:** on-site. **Terms:** [AP], [BP] & [CP] meal plans available, small pets only
($10 extra charge, in smoking units). **Amenities:** video library (fee), voice mail, safes, irons, hair dryers. *Some:* DVD players
(fee). **Dining:** 7 am-10 pm, cocktails. **Pool(s):** heated outdoor. **Leisure Activities:** whirlpool. **Guest Services:** valet laundry.
Cards: AX, DC, DS, JC, MC, VI. **Special Amenities: free newspaper and free room upgrade (subject to availability with
advance reservations).** *(See color ad below & p 545)*

SOME UNITS

FEE

DAYS INN VICTORIA WATERWAY   *Book at aaa.com*   Phone: (250)386-1422   2

CAA SAVE   7/1-9/4   1P: $99-$159   2P: $99-$159   XP: $15.   F12
             5/20-6/30   1P: $69-$139   2P: $69-$139   XP: $10   F12
             3/1-5/19 & 9/5-2/28   1P: $55-$99   2P: $55-$99   XP: $10   F12

Location: Douglas St. 1.4 km w. 123 Gorge Rd E V9A 1L1. Fax: 250/386-1254. **Facility:** 94 one-bedroom
Small-scale Hotel   standard units, some with efficiencies or kitchens. 4 stories, interior corridors. **Parking:** on-site.
Amenities: voice mail, irons, hair dryers. **Dining:** 7 am-10 pm, cocktails. **Pool(s):** heated outdoor. **Guest
Services:** valet and coin laundry. **Business Services:** meeting rooms. **Cards:** AX, DC, DS, JC, MC, VI. **Special Amenities:
early check-in/late check-out and free room upgrade (subject to availability with advance reservations).**
(See color ad starting on p 606)

SOME UNITS

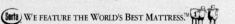

(See map and index starting on p. 601)

DELTA VICTORIA OCEAN POINTE RESORT & SPA   *Book at aaa.com*   Phone: (250)360-2999   **43**

CAA SAVE

	7/1-10/13	1P: $225-$310	2P: $225-$310	XP: $30	F18
	5/1-6/30	1P: $179-$275	2P: $179-$275	XP: $30	F18
	3/1-4/30	1P: $169-$249	2P: $169-$249	XP: $30	F18
	10/14-2/28	1P: $155-$229	2P: $155-$229	XP: $30	F18

Large-scale Hotel **Location:** Just w of Johnson St Bridge, Esquimalt at Tyee rds. 45 Songhees Rd V9A 6T3. Fax: 250/360-5884. **Facility:** Rooms with city and Inner Harbour views are featured at this waterfront hotel; guests may observe sea planes land and take off right from the harbor. 244 units. 239 one-bedroom standard units, some with efficiencies. 5 one-bedroom suites, some with efficiencies and/or whirlpools. 8 stories, interior corridors. **Parking:** on-site (fee) and valet. **Terms:** check-in 4 pm, cancellation fee imposed. **Amenities:** CD players, high-speed Internet (fee), dual phone lines, voice mail, honor bars, irons, hair dryers. **Dining:** 7 am-10 pm, cocktails. **Pool(s):** heated indoor. **Leisure Activities:** sauna, whirlpool, 2 lighted tennis courts, racquetball court, art gallery, squash, spa. **Guest Services:** gift shop, valet laundry, area transportation-downtown/inner harbour. **Business Services:** conference facilities, business center. **Cards:** AX, DC, DS, JC, MC, VI. *(See color ad below)*

SOME UNITS

EMBASSY INN   Phone: (250)382-8161   **33**

CAA SAVE

	7/1-10/14	1P: $99-$259	2P: $99-$259	XP: $20	F16
	5/1-6/30	1P: $99-$195	2P: $99-$195	XP: $15	F16
	3/1-4/30 & 10/15-2/28	1P: $83	2P: $83-$93	XP: $15	F16

Small-scale Hotel **Location:** Corner of Quebec St. Located adjacent to Parliament buildings. 520 Menzies St V8V 2H4. Fax: 250/382-4224. **Facility:** 103 one-bedroom standard units, some with efficiencies or kitchens. 3-4 stories, interior/exterior corridors. **Parking:** on-site. **Terms:** check-in 3:30 pm. **Amenities:** voice mail, hair dryers. *Some:* irons. **Dining:** 7 am-9:30 pm, cocktails. **Pool(s):** heated outdoor. **Leisure Activities:** sauna. **Guest Services:** valet and coin laundry. **Business Services:** meeting rooms. **Cards:** AX, CB, DC, MC, VI. *(See color ad below)*

SOME UNITS

(See map and index starting on p. 601)

EXECUTIVE HOUSE HOTEL   *Book at aaa.com*

Phone: (250)388-5111   **37**

6/15-9/30	1P: $155-$195	2P: $155-$195	XP: $15	F16
5/1-6/14	1P: $125-$195	2P: $125-$195	XP: $15	F16
3/1-4/30 & 10/1-2/28	1P: $85-$195	2P: $85-$195	XP: $15	F16

Location: Between Blanshard and Douglas sts; downtown. 777 Douglas St V8W 2B5. Fax: 250/385-1323.
Large-scale Hotel **Facility:** 181 units. 98 one-bedroom standard units, some with efficiencies and/or whirlpools. 78 one- and 5 two-bedroom suites ($215-$895), some with kitchens and/or whirlpools. 17 stories, interior corridors.
Parking: on-site (fee). **Terms:** weekly rates available, package plans, small pets only ($20 extra charge). **Amenities:** video games (fee), voice mail, irons, hair dryers. *Some:* CD players, high-speed Internet. **Dining:** 7 am-11 pm, cocktails, also, Barkley's Steak & Seafood, see separate listing. **Leisure Activities:** whirlpool, steamroom, exercise room. **Guest Services:** valet and coin laundry, area transportation-Inner Harbour/downtown. **Business Services:** meeting rooms. **Cards:** AX, CB, DC, DS, JC, MC, VI. **Special Amenities:** free newspaper and free room upgrade (subject to availability with advance reservations).

SOME UNITS

FAIRHOLME MANOR

Phone: (250)598-3240   **11**

5/16-10/15	1P: $155-$325	2P: $175-$325	XP: $35	D6
5/1 & 10/16-2/28	1P: $125-$250	2P: $125-$250	XP: $35	D6

Historic Bed **Location:** Blanshard St (Hwy 17), 2 km e on Fort St, then just s on St. Charles St to Rockland Ave, look for Rockland Pl
& Breakfast sign, then down alley. Located in historic Rockland District. 638 Rockland Pl V8S 3R2. Fax: 250/598-3299.
Facility: Built in 1885, this restored Italianate mansion has been converted into luxury suites and is surrounded by an acre of parklike gardens and lawn. Smoke free premises. 6 units. 5 one- and 1 two-bedroom standard units. 2 stories (no elevator), interior/exterior corridors. **Parking:** on-site. **Terms:** office hours 8 am-10 pm, check-in 4 pm, age restrictions may apply, 14 day cancellation notice-fee imposed, [BP] meal plan available. **Amenities:** video library, CD players, irons, hair dryers. **Cards:** AX, MC, VI.

THE FAIRMONT EMPRESS   *Book at aaa.com*

Phone: (250)384-8111   **25**

7/1-10/15	1P: $309-$549	2P: $309-$549	XP: $30	F
5/1-6/30	1P: $209-$459	2P: $209-$459	XP: $30	F
3/1-4/30 & 10/16-2/28	1P: $179-$339	2P: $179-$339	XP: $30	F

Location: Between Belleville and Humboldt sts. Located on the Inner Harbour. 721 Government St V8W 1W5.
Large-scale Hotel Fax: 250/381-4334. **Facility:** Renowned for its tradition of afternoon tea, this landmark Victorian-style property built in 1908 features many rooms with views of the harbor. 476 one-bedroom standard units, some with whirlpools. 8 stories, interior corridors. **Parking:** on-site (fee) and valet. **Terms:** check-in 4 pm, cancellation fee imposed, small pets only ($25 extra charge). **Amenities:** video games (fee), voice mail, honor bars, irons, hair dryers. *Some:* CD players, high-speed Internet, dual phone lines, safes. **Dining:** 2 restaurants, 6:30 am-11 pm, cocktails, also, The Empress Room, see separate listing, entertainment. **Pool(s):** heated indoor, wading. **Leisure Activities:** saunas, whirlpool, exercise room, spa. **Guest Services:** gift shop, valet laundry. **Business Services:** conference facilities, business center. **Cards:** AX, DC, DS, MC, VI. **Special Amenities:** free newspaper and free room upgrade (subject to availability with advance reservations).
(See color ad below)

SOME UNITS

(See map and index starting on p. 601)

HARBOUR TOWERS HOTEL & SUITES   *Book at aaa.com*   Phone: (250)385-2405   **30**
CAA SAVE   7/1-10/11   1P: $175-$435   2P: $175-$435   XP: $15   F16
                5/1-6/30   1P: $131-$326   2P: $131-$326   XP: $15   F16
▼▼▼▼▼   3/1-4/30 & 10/12-2/28 1P: $99-$240   2P: $99-$240   XP: $15   F16
Location: Between Oswego and Pendray sts. 345 Quebec St V8V 1W4. Fax: 250/360-2313. **Facility:** Smoke free
Large-scale Hotel premises. 195 units. 123 one-bedroom standard units, some with efficiencies. 45 one- and 27 two-bedroom
suites ($120-$519), some with efficiencies, kitchens and/or whirlpools. 12 stories, interior corridors. **Parking:**
on-site (fee). **Terms:** cancellation fee imposed, small pets only ($15 fee). **Amenities:** video games (fee), high-speed Internet,
voice mail, irons, hair dryers. *Some:* CD players. **Dining:** 7 am-10 pm, cocktails. **Pool(s):** heated indoor. **Leisure
Activities:** sauna, whirlpool, spa. **Guest Services:** gift shop, valet and coin laundry, area transportation-downtown, salon.
Business Services: meeting rooms, business center. **Cards:** AX, DC, JC, MC, VI. *(See color ad below)*

SOME UNITS

[icons row] FEE

HEATHERGATE HOUSE BED & BREAKFAST   Phone: (250)383-0068   **61**
▼▼▼▼   7/1-9/5 [BP]   1P: $110-$130   2P: $120-$140   XP: $35
                3/1-6/30 [BP]   1P: $85-$115   2P: $95-$125   XP: $25
Bed & Breakfast 9/6-10/11 [BP]   1P: $85-$115   2P: $95-$125   XP: $30
                10/12-2/28 [BP]   1P: $65-$85   2P: $75-$95   XP: $25
Location: Between St. Lawrence and Montreal sts. 122 Simcoe St V8V 1K4. Fax: 250/383-4320. **Facility:** Smoke free premises. 5
units. 4 one- and 1 two-bedroom standard units. 2 stories (no elevator), interior/exterior corridors. *Bath:* combo or shower only.
Parking: on-site. **Terms:** office hours 8 am-11 pm, 2 night minimum stay - seasonal and/or weekends, age restrictions may
apply, 14 day cancellation notice-fee imposed. **Amenities:** hair dryers. **Cards:** AX, DC, DS, JC, MC, VI.

SOME UNITS

[icons row]

HELM'S INN   Phone: (250)385-5767   **34**
CAA SAVE   6/23-10/9 [CP]   1P: $135-$210   2P: $135-$210   XP: $15   F12
                5/13-6/22 [CP]   1P: $110-$190   2P: $110-$190   XP: $15   F12
▼▼▼▼   3/1-5/12 & 10/10-2/28 [CP] 1P: $85-$125   2P: $85-$125   XP: $15   F12
Location: Corner of Douglas and Superior sts. 600 Douglas St V8V 2P8. Fax: 250/385-2221. **Facility:** Designated
Small-scale Hotel smoking area. 42 units. 36 one-bedroom standard units, some with kitchens. 6 one-bedroom suites, some
with kitchens. 3 stories (no elevator), interior corridors. **Parking:** on-site (fee). **Terms:** check-in 4 pm.
Amenities: voice mail, irons, hair dryers. **Guest Services:** coin laundry. **Cards:** AX, DS, MC, VI. **Special Amenities:** free
continental breakfast and free local telephone calls. *(See color ad below)*

[icons row]

(See map and Index starting on p. 601)

HOLIDAY INN VICTORIA   *Book at aaa.com*   **Phone:** (250)382-4400   **7**

CAA SAVE

5/16-9/30	1P: $99-$179	2P: $99-$179	XP: $10
3/1-5/15 & 10/1-10/31	1P: $88-$129	2P: $88-$129	XP: $10
11/1-2/28	1P: $75-$89	2P: $75-$89	XP: $10

F18 / F18 / F18

Location: 2.6 km n on Blanshard St (Hwy 17); just s of Finlayson St. 3020 Blanshard St V8T 5B5.
Small-scale Hotel **Fax:** 250/382-4053. **Facility:** 152 units. 143 one-bedroom standard units, some with efficiencies. 9 one-bedroom suites ($125-$250), some with efficiencies. 3-4 stories, interior/exterior corridors. **Parking:** on-site.
Terms: cancellation fee imposed, package plans. **Amenities:** video games (fee), dual phone lines, voice mail, irons, hair dryers. *Some:* high-speed Internet. **Dining:** 6:30 am-10 pm, cocktails. **Leisure Activities:** sauna, whirlpool, limited exercise equipment. **Guest Services:** gift shop, valet and coin laundry. **Business Services:** meeting rooms. **Cards:** AX, MC, VI.
Special Amenities: free local telephone calls and free newspaper. *(See color ad card insert)*

SOME UNITS

[icons]

HOTEL GRAND PACIFIC   *Book at aaa.com*   **Phone:** (250)386-0450   **22**

CAA SAVE

7/1-10/10	1P: $199-$319	2P: $199-$319	XP: $30
5/1-6/30	1P: $159-$289	2P: $159-$289	XP: $30
3/1-4/30 & 10/11-2/28	1P: $119-$289	2P: $119-$289	XP: $30

F18 / F18 / F18

Location: Belleville at Menzies St; downtown. 463 Belleville St V8V 1X3. Fax: 250/380-4474. **Facility:** The upscale
Large-scale Hotel high-rise building offers a variety of views; modern rooms with private balconies overlook the Olympic Mountains or the Inner Harbour. 304 units. 298 one-bedroom standard units. 6 one-bedroom suites ($329-$1200) with whirlpools. 10 stories, interior corridors. **Parking:** on-site. **Terms:** small pets only ($60 extra charge). **Amenities:** video games (fee), high-speed Internet, dual phone lines, voice mail, safes, honor bars, irons, hair dryers. **Dining:** 2 restaurants, 6:30 am-10 pm, cocktails, also, The Mark, see separate listing. **Pool(s):** heated indoor, wading. **Leisure Activities:** sauna, whirlpool, racquetball court, spa. **Guest Services:** gift shop, valet laundry, area transportation-inner Harbour/Downtown. **Business Services:** conference facilities, business center. **Cards:** AX, DC, DS, JC, MC, VI.
Special Amenities: free local telephone calls and free newspaper. *(See color ad below)*

SOME UNITS

[icons] FEE

HOWARD JOHNSON HOTEL & SUITES   *Book at aaa.com*   **Phone:** (250)704-4656   **69**

5/15-10/2	1P: $169-$219	2P: $169-$219	XP: $10
4/1-5/14	1P: $139-$169	2P: $139-$169	XP: $10
10/3-2/28	1P: $119-$149	2P: $119-$149	XP: $10
3/1-3/31	1P: $109-$139	2P: $109-$139	XP: $10

F18 / F18 / F18 / F18

Small-scale Hotel
Location: Hwy 17, just w on Royal Oak Dr, then just n. 4670 Elk Lake Dr V8Z 5M2. Fax: 250/704-4655. **Facility:** 88 one-bedroom standard units, some with kitchens. 3 stories, interior/exterior corridors. **Bath:** combo or shower only. **Parking:** on-site.
Terms: package plans, pets ($15 extra charge). **Amenities:** high-speed Internet, voice mail, irons, hair dryers. **Pool(s):** heated outdoor. **Leisure Activities:** whirlpool, limited exercise equipment. **Guest Services:** valet and coin laundry. **Business Services:** meeting rooms. **Cards:** AX, DC, DS, MC, VI.

SOME UNITS

[icons] FEE

(See map and index starting on p. 601)

HOWARD JOHNSON HOTEL-CITY CENTRE   *Book at aaa.com*

Phone: (250)382-2151   52

(CAA) (SAVE)

6/16-9/15	1P: $115-$169	2P: $115-$169	XP: $10	D18
3/1-6/15	1P: $69-$129	2P: $69-$129	XP: $10	D18
9/16-2/28	1P: $49-$99	2P: $49-$99	XP: $10	D18

Large-scale Hotel

Location: Douglas St, 1.4 km w. 310 Gorge Rd E V8T 2W2. Fax: 250/382-3856. **Facility:** 80 one-bedroom standard units, some with kitchens (utensils extra charge). 3 stories, interior corridors. **Parking:** on-site. **Terms:** cancellation fee imposed, package plans, small pets only (in designated units, with prior approval). **Amenities:** voice mail, irons, hair dryers. *Some:* high-speed Internet. **Dining:** 7 am-1 & 5-9 pm, cocktails. **Pool(s):** heated indoor. **Leisure Activities:** saunas, limited exercise equipment. **Guest Services:** valet and coin laundry. **Business Services:** meeting rooms, PC (fee). **Cards:** AX, CB, DC, DS, MC, VI. **Special Amenities:** free newspaper and early check-in/late check-out.

SOME UNITS

HUMBOLDT HOUSE BED & BREAKFAST

Phone: (250)383-0152   17

6/16-9/30 [BP]	1P: $245-$315	2P: $245-$315	XP: $40	D12
3/1-6/15 & 10/1-2/28 [BP]	1P: $147-$250	2P: $147-$250	XP: $40	D12

Historic Bed & Breakfast

Location: Humboldt and Quadra sts. Located in a quiet area. 867 Humboldt St V8V 2Z6. Fax: 250/383-6402. **Facility:** A retreat-like ambience makes this B&B well-suited for romantic getaways. Smoke free premises. 6 one-bedroom standard units, some with whirlpools. 2 stories (no elevator), interior corridors. *Bath:* combo or shower only. **Parking:** on-site. **Terms:** office hours 7 am-11 pm, 7 day cancellation notice-fee imposed, package plans. **Amenities:** CD players, hair dryers. **Cards:** AX, JC, MC, VI.

IRIS GARDEN COUNTRY MANOR BED & BREAKFAST

Phone: 250/744-2253   67

5/1-9/30 [BP]	2P: $145-$175	
3/1-4/30 & 10/1-2/28 [BP]	2P: $115-$135	

Bed & Breakfast

Location: Hwy 17, exit Royal Oak Dr, just w, then 4.5 km n on W Saanich Rd (Hwy 17A N), watch for sign. 5360 W Saanich Rd V9E 1J8. **Facility:** Smoke free premises. 4 one-bedroom standard units, some with whirlpools. 2 stories (no elevator), interior corridors. *Bath:* combo or shower only. **Parking:** on-site. **Terms:** office hours 8 am-10 pm, check-in 4 pm, age restrictions may apply, 14 day cancellation notice-fee imposed. **Amenities:** hair dryers. **Cards:** MC, VI.

JAMES BAY INN   *Book at aaa.com*

Phone: (250)384-7151   41

(CAA) (SAVE)

7/1-10/15	1P: $127-$152	2P: $127-$152	XP: $15	F16
5/1-6/30	1P: $99-$122	2P: $99-$122	XP: $15	F16
3/1-4/30 & 10/16-2/28	1P: $70-$80	2P: $70-$80	XP: $15	F16

Small-scale Hotel

Location: Between Toronto and Marifield sts. 270 Government St V8V 2L2. Fax: 250/385-2311. **Facility:** 45 one-bedroom standard units, some with kitchens. 4 stories (no elevator), interior corridors. *Bath:* combo or shower only. **Parking:** on-site. **Dining:** 7:30 am-9 pm, cocktails. **Cards:** AX, MC, VI. *(See color ad below)*

SOME UNITS

THE MAGNOLIA HOTEL & SPA   *Book at aaa.com*

Phone: (250)381-0999   66

(CAA) (SAVE)

6/1-10/15	1P: $289-$349	2P: $289-$349	XP: $30	F12
5/1-5/31	1P: $229-$289	2P: $229-$289	XP: $30	F12
3/1-4/30 & 10/16-2/28	1P: $189-$249	2P: $189-$249	XP: $30	F12

Small-scale Hotel

Location: Corner of Courtney and Gordon sts. Located on the Inner Harbour. 623 Courtney St V8W 1B8. Fax: 250/381-0988. **Facility:** A luxury hotel offering elegant rooms with large bay windows, The Magnolia is in Victoria's Inner Harbour area, convenient for strolling and shopping. 63 one-bedroom standard units. 7 stories, interior corridors. **Parking:** valet. **Terms:** cancellation fee imposed, package plans, small pets only ($60 extra charge). **Amenities:** CD players, high-speed Internet, dual phone lines, voice mail, honor bars, irons, hair dryers. **Dining:** 2 restaurants, 11 am-11 pm, cocktails. **Leisure Activities:** limited exercise equipment, spa. **Guest Services:** valet laundry. **Business Services:** meeting rooms. **Cards:** AX, DC, DS, JC, MC, VI. *(See color ad p 618)*

SOME UNITS

FEE

(See map and index starting on p. 601)

MAYFAIR MOTEL

					Phone: (250)388-7337	**3**
	7/1-9/30	1P: $59-$79		2P: $79-$89	XP: $10	D12
	5/1-6/30	1P: $49-$59		2P: $59-$79	XP: $10	D12
	3/1-4/30 & 10/1-2/28	1P: $39-$49		2P: $49-$59	XP: $10	D12

Motel

Location: From downtown; 3.5 km n on Douglas St. 650 Speed Ave V8Z 1A4. Fax: 250/388-7398. **Facility:** 22 one-bedroom standard units with kitchens (utensils extra charge). 3 stories, interior corridors. **Parking:** on-site. **Terms:** office hours 8 am-11:30 pm. **Guest Services:** coin laundry. **Cards:** AX, MC, VI. **Special Amenities:** free local telephone calls and preferred room (subject to availability with advance reservations).

SOME UNITS

OAK BAY BEACH HOTEL & MARINE RESORT   *Book at aaa.com*

				Phone: (250)598-4556	**42**
6/15-9/15 [ECP]	1P: $199-$475	2P: $199-$475		XP: $25	F12
3/1-6/14 & 9/16-2/28 [ECP]	1P: $129-$425	2P: $129-$425		XP: $25	F12

Historic
Small-scale Hotel

Location: 6.8 km e via Oak Bay Ave, then just s. Located in a quiet residential area. 1175 Beach Dr V8S 2N2. Fax: 250/598-6180. **Facility:** This Tudor-style mansion features fine landscaping and sweeping bay views; room sizes and styles vary. Designated smoking area. 50 one-bedroom standard units. 3 stories, interior corridors. **Parking:** on-site. **Terms:** cancellation fee imposed, [AP], [BP] & [MAP] meal plans available, package plans. **Dining:** The Snug English Pub, see separate listing. **Leisure Activities:** bicycles. **Guest Services:** gift shop, valet laundry, area transportation. **Business Services:** meeting rooms. **Cards:** AX, DC, MC, VI.

SOME UNITS

(See map and index starting on p. 601)

OAK BAY GUEST HOUSE BED & BREAKFAST Phone: (250)598-3812 62

♦♦♦ ♦♦♦

Historic Bed & Breakfast

7/1-9/15 [BP]	1P: $140-$195	2P: $140-$195	XP: $15	F10
4/1-6/30 [BP]	1P: $119-$170	2P: $119-$170	XP: $15	F10
3/1-3/31 & 9/16-2/28 [BP]	1P: $99-$150	2P: $99-$150	XP: $15	F10

Location: 4.8 km e on Oak Bay Ave (which becomes Newport Ave). 1052 Newport Ave V8S 5E3. Fax: 250/598-0369. **Facility:** In keeping with the age of this historic building, the guest rooms are average-size and some bathrooms are compact. Smoke free premises. 11 one-bedroom standard units. 2 stories (no elevator), interior corridors. *Bath:* combo or shower only. **Parking:** on-site. **Terms:** office hours 8 am-11 pm, age restrictions may apply, 7 day cancellation notice, package plans. **Amenities:** hair dryers. **Cards:** AX, MC, VI.

(ASK) (S⌀) ⊠ (Ⓧ) (Ⓦ) (Ⓩ)

OXFORD CASTLE INN   *Book at aaa.com*   Phone: 250/388-6431 15

(CAA) (SAVE)

♦♦♦ ♦♦♦

Small-scale Hotel

6/1-10/15	1P: $95-$138	2P: $108-$158	XP: $10	D8
3/1-5/31	1P: $68-$88	2P: $88-$108	XP: $10	D8
10/16-2/28	1P: $78-$108	2P: $78-$108	XP: $10	D8

Location: Douglas St, 2 km w. 133 Gorge Rd E V9A 1L1. Fax: 250/388-6437. **Facility:** 58 one-bedroom standard units, some with kitchens (utensils extra charge). 4 stories, interior corridors. **Parking:** on-site. **Terms:** office hours 7:30 am-10 pm, cancellation fee imposed, small pets only ($15 extra charge). **Amenities:** voice mail. **Pool(s):** heated indoor. **Leisure Activities:** sauna, whirlpool. **Guest Services:** coin laundry. **Cards:** AX, DC, MC, VI. *(See color ad below)*

SOME UNITS

(S⌀) (🛏) (🍴⁺) (🏊) (Ⓧ) / ⊠ (DATA PORT) (🔌) (🖥) /
FEE

PRIOR HOUSE B&B INN Phone: (250)592-8847 12

(CAA) (SAVE)

♦♦♦ ♦♦♦ ♦♦♦

Historic Bed & Breakfast

5/16-9/25 [BP]	1P: $225-$325	2P: $225-$325	XP: $45
4/1-5/15 & 9/26-2/28 [BP]	1P: $150-$275	2P: $150-$275	XP: $45
3/1-3/31 [BP]	1P: $125-$240	2P: $125-$240	XP: $45

Location: Blanshard St (Hwy 17), 2 km e on Fort St, then just s. Located in a quiet area. 620 St. Charles St V8S 3N7. Fax: 250/592-8223. **Facility:** Antique furniture and a wood-burning fireplace add warmth to this restored 1912 manor set on lush, landscaped grounds in a tree-lined area. Smoke free premises. 6 units. 4 one-bedroom standard units, some with whirlpools. 2 two-bedroom suites with whirlpools. 3 stories (no elevator), interior corridors. *Bath:* combo or shower only. **Parking:** on-site. **Terms:** office hours 7 am-8 pm, check-in 4 pm, age restrictions may apply, 14 day cancellation notice-fee imposed, weekly rates available, package plans. **Amenities:** video library, CD players, irons, hair dryers. **Guest Services:** coin laundry. **Cards:** MC, VI. **Special Amenities:** free full breakfast and free local telephone calls.

SOME UNITS

(S⌀) ⊠ (Ⓧ) (VCR) (Ⓩ) (🖥) / (🔌) /

QUALITY INN DOWNTOWN   *Book at aaa.com*   Phone: (250)385-6787 40

(CAA) (SAVE)

♦♦♦ ♦♦♦

Small-scale Hotel

6/16-9/15	1P: $139-$229	2P: $139-$229	XP: $15	F18
5/1-6/15	1P: $89-$179	2P: $89-$179	XP: $15	F18
3/1-4/30 & 9/16-2/28	1P: $79-$149	2P: $79-$149	XP: $15	F18

Location: Between Courtney St and Burnett Ave; downtown. 850 Blanshard St V8W 2H2. Fax: 250/385-5800. **Facility:** 56 one-bedroom standard units, some with efficiencies and/or whirlpools. 3 stories, interior corridors. **Parking:** on-site. **Amenities:** voice mail, irons, hair dryers. *Some:* high-speed Internet. **Dining:** 7 am-9 pm, cocktails. **Pool(s):** heated indoor. **Leisure Activities:** steamroom, limited exercise equipment. **Guest Services:** valet and coin laundry. **Business Services:** meeting rooms. **Cards:** AX, DC, DS, JC, MC, VI. **Special Amenities:** free local telephone calls and free room upgrade (subject to availability with advance reservations). *(See color ad starting on p 606)*

SOME UNITS

(S⌀) (🍴) (🍸) (🏊) (Ⓧ) (📹) (DATA PORT) (🔌) (🖥) / ⊠ (📷) /

(See map and index starting on p. 601)

QUEEN VICTORIA HOTEL AND SUITES   *Book at aaa.com*   **Phone:** (250)386-1312   **49**

CAA SAVE

	1P: $195-$285	2P: $195-$285	XP: $25	F15
7/1-10/14	1P: $195-$285	2P: $195-$285	XP: $25	F15
5/15-6/30	1P: $135-$230	2P: $135-$230	XP: $25	F15
10/15-2/28	1P: $125-$195	2P: $125-$195	XP: $25	F15
3/1-5/14	1P: $120-$195	2P: $120-$195	XP: $25	F15

Small-scale Hotel **Location:** Between Belleville and Superior sts. 655 Douglas St V8V 2P9. Fax: 250/381-4312. **Facility:** 146 units. 125 one-bedroom standard units, some with efficiencies and/or whirlpools. 14 one- and 7 two-bedroom suites, some with whirlpools. 7 stories, interior corridors. **Parking:** on-site (fee). **Terms:** weekly rates available, package plans. **Amenities:** voice mail, hair dryers. *Some:* high-speed Internet. **Dining:** 6:30 am-9 pm, cocktails. **Pool(s):** heated indoor. **Leisure Activities:** sauna, whirlpool, exercise room. **Guest Services:** valet and coin laundry, area transportation-downtown area. **Cards:** AX, DC, DS, JC, MC, VI. *(See color ad below)*

SOME UNITS

RAMADA HUNTINGDON HOTEL & SUITES   *Book at aaa.com*   **Phone:** 250/381-3456   **29**

CAA SAVE

6/11-9/12	1P: $149-$229	2P: $149-$229	XP: $15	F
3/1-6/10 & 9/13-12/31	1P: $129-$169	2P: $129-$169	XP: $15	F
1/1-2/28	1P: $119-$149	2P: $119-$149	XP: $15	F

Small-scale Hotel **Location:** Between Oswego and Pendray sts. 330 Quebec St V8V 1W3. Fax: 250/382-7666. **Facility:** 116 units. 114 one- and 2 two-bedroom standard units, some with kitchens (utensils extra charge). 3 stories, interior corridors. **Parking:** on-site (fee). **Terms:** cancellation fee imposed, weekly rates available, package plans, 15% service charge, pets ($15 extra charge, in designated units). **Amenities:** video games (fee), voice mail, irons, hair dryers. **Dining:** 7 am-10 pm, cocktails. **Leisure Activities:** sauna, whirlpool. **Guest Services:** gift shop, valet and coin laundry. **Business Services:** meeting rooms. **Cards:** AX, CB, DC, JC, MC, VI. **Special Amenities:** free newspaper and early check-in/late check-out. *(See color ad p 621)*

SOME UNITS

FEE

(See map and index starting on p. 601)

ROBIN HOOD MOTEL   **Phone:** (250)388-4302   **14**

CAA SAVE   6/17-9/30   1P: $70-$79   2P: $79-$94   XP: $6
           5/16-6/16   1P: $67   2P: $73-$78   XP: $6
◆◆◆◆   3/1-5/15 & 10/1-2/28   1P: $46-$56   2P: $51-$61   XP: $6
Motel   **Location:** Douglas St, 2.4 km w. 136 Gorge Rd E V9A 1L4. **Fax:** 250/383-4399. **Facility:** 55 one-bedroom
standard units, some with kitchens. 2 stories (no elevator), exterior corridors. **Parking:** on-site.
Terms: weekly rates available, pets ($5 extra charge, small dogs only). **Guest Services:** coin laundry.
Cards: AX, DC, JC, MC, VI. **Special Amenities:** free local telephone calls and preferred room (subject to availability with
advance reservations). *(See color ad p 620)*

SOME UNITS

FEE

ROSEWOOD VICTORIA INN   **Phone:** 250/384-6644   **32**

◆◆◆   6/1-9/30 [BP]   2P: $145-$250   XP: $35   F9
          3/1-5/31 & 10/1-2/28 [BP]   2P: $125-$175   XP: $35   F9
Bed & Breakfast   **Location:** Between Government and Heather sts. Located by the Parliament buildings. 595 Michigan St V8V 1S7.
Fax: 250/384-6117. **Facility:** Walking distance from downtown Victoria attractions, this elegant inn offers
large, comfortable rooms with luxury appointments. Smoke free premises. 17 one-bedroom standard units. 3 stories (no
elevator), interior corridors. **Parking:** on-site. **Terms:** office hours 7:30 am-8 pm, age restrictions may apply, 14 day cancellation
notice-fee imposed. **Amenities:** voice mail, hair dryers. **Cards:** AX, MC, VI.

ASK ✕ ⚓ ▭

ROYAL SCOT SUITE HOTEL   *Book at aaa.com*   **Phone:** (250)388-5463   **31**

CAA SAVE   6/1-9/30   1P: $159-$339   2P: $159-$339   XP: $25   F16
◆◆◆◆   3/1-5/31 & 10/1-2/28   1P: $109-$339   2P: $109-$339   XP: $25   F16
Large-scale Hotel   **Location:** Between Menzies and Oswego sts. 425 Quebec St V8V 1W7. **Fax:** 250/388-5452. **Facility:** 176 units. 94
one-bedroom standard units, some with kitchens. 78 one- and 4 two-bedroom suites with kitchens. 4
stories, interior corridors. **Parking:** on-site. **Terms:** [BP], [CP] & [ECP] meal plans available.
Amenities: video library (fee), voice mail, irons, hair dryers. **Dining:** 7 am-9 pm, cocktails. **Pool(s):** heated
indoor. **Leisure Activities:** saunas, whirlpool, billiards, limited exercise equipment, game room. **Guest Services:** gift shop, valet
and coin laundry, area transportation-downtown. **Business Services:** meeting rooms. **Cards:** AX, DC, JC, MC, VI.
Special Amenities: free local telephone calls and free newspaper. *(See color ad p 622)*

SOME UNITS

FEE

(See map and index starting on p. 601)

SEA VIEW INN: A CLARION COLLECTION HOTEL *Book at aaa.com* Phone: (250)658-2171 ❶

CAA SAVE All Year [CP] 1P: $79-$399 2P: $79-$399 XP: $20 F18

Location: 10 km n on Hwy 17, exit Royal Oak Dr, 2 km e to Cordova Bay Rd, follow to Mount Douglas Park. Located in a quiet area. 4550 Cordova Bay Rd V8X 3V5. Fax: 250/658-4596. **Facility:** 42 units. 40 one-bedroom standard units, some with efficiencies and/or whirlpools. 2 one-bedroom suites with efficiencies. 4 stories,

Small-scale Hotel interior/exterior corridors. **Parking:** on-site. **Terms:** office hours 7 am-11 pm, 3 day cancellation notice, weekly rates available, package plans. **Leisure Activities:** sauna, steamroom. **Fee:** European skin care studio. **Business Services:** meeting rooms. **Cards:** AX, CB, DC, DS, JC, MC, VI. **Special Amenities:** free continental breakfast and early check-in/late check-out. *(See color ad p 623)*

(See map and index starting on p. 601)

SHAMROCK SUITES ON THE PARK

Phone: (250)385-8768 **35**

6/23-10/9	1P: $145-$185	2P: $149-$185	XP: $15	F12
5/13-6/22	1P: $125-$165	2P: $135-$165	XP: $15	F12
10/10-2/28	1P: $89-$125	2P: $89-$125	XP: $15	F12
3/1-5/12	1P: $89-$115	2P: $89-$115	XP: $15	F12

Small-scale Hotel

Location: Corner of Douglas St. Located across from Beacon Hill Park. 675 Superior St V8V 1V1. Fax: 250/385-1837. **Facility:** Smoke free premises. 16 one-bedroom standard units with kitchens. 3 stories (no elevator), exterior corridors. **Parking:** on-site (fee). **Terms:** office hours 7:30 am-10 pm, weekly rates available. **Cards:** AX, MC, VI. *(See color ad below)*

(See map and index starting on p. 601)

SPINNAKER BREWPUB AND GUESTHOUSE

(CAA) (SAVE)
◆◆◆ ◆◆◆◆

				Phone: (250)386-2739	45
5/20-9/19 [CP]	1P: $149-$249	2P: $149-$249	XP: $15		F5
9/20-10/15 [CP]	1P: $149-$229	2P: $149-$229	XP: $15		F5
3/1-5/19 [BP]	1P: $129-$209	2P: $129-$209	XP: $15		F5
10/16-2/28 [CP]	1P: $129-$209	2P: $129-$209	XP: $15		F5

Small-scale Hotel **Location:** 2 km nw over Johnson St Bridge, just s. 308 Catherine St V9A 3S8. Fax: 250/384-3246. **Facility:** Smoke free premises. 11 one-bedroom standard units, some with efficiencies, kitchens and/or whirlpools. 2 stories (no elevator), interior/exterior corridors. *Bath:* combo or shower only. **Parking:** on-site. **Terms:** office hours 7 am-10 pm, age restrictions may apply, 7 day cancellation notice-fee imposed, weekly rates available, [AP], [CP], [ECP] & [MAP] meal plans available, package plans. **Amenities:** irons, hair dryers. **Dining:** Spinnakers Brew Pub & Restaurant, see separate listing. **Cards:** AX, DC, MC, VI. *(See color ad below)*

SOME UNITS
🖥️🗑️ 🍴 🍸 ✕ 🅰️ 📺 📠 / 🅦 🖥️ /

SUNNYMEADE HOUSE INN

◆◆◆ ◆◆◆◆

				Phone: (250)658-1414	9
5/1-9/30 [BP]	1P: $85-$175	2P: $85-$175	XP: $30		D14
3/1-4/30 [BP]	1P: $75-$145	2P: $79-$145	XP: $30		D14
10/1-2/28 [BP]	1P: $75-$145	2P: $75-$145	XP: $30		D14

Bed & Breakfast **Location:** 12 km n on Hwy 17, exit Cordova Bay, then 3 km e on Sayward/Cordova Bay Rd; across from service station. 1002 Fenn Ave V8Y 1P3. Fax: 250/658-1414. **Facility:** Smoke free premises. 6 one-bedroom standard units, some with whirlpools. 2 stories (no elevator), interior corridors. *Bath:* combo or shower only. **Parking:** on-site. **Terms:** office hours 9 am-10 pm, age restrictions may apply, 7 day cancellation notice-fee imposed. **Cards:** MC, VI.

✕ 🅰️ 🅦 🄩

SWANS HOTEL

◆◆◆ ◆◆◆

				Phone: (250)361-3310	20
6/1-2/28	1P: $159-$259	2P: $159-$259			
4/16-5/31	1P: $129-$219	2P: $129-$219			
3/1-4/15	1P: $109-$189	2P: $109-$189			

Small-scale Hotel **Location:** Corner of Pandora Ave and Store St. 506 Pandora Ave V8W 1N6. Fax: 250/361-3491. **Facility:** Smoke free premises. 30 units. 18 one- and 12 two-bedroom suites with kitchens, some with whirlpools. 2 stories, interior corridors. **Parking:** on-site (fee). **Terms:** office hours 7 am-11 pm, check-in 4 pm, cancellation fee imposed, weekly rates available, package plans. **Amenities:** video library, high-speed Internet, voice mail, irons, hair dryers. **Guest Services:** valet and coin laundry. **Business Services:** meeting rooms. **Cards:** AX, DC, DS, MC, VI.

SOME UNITS
(ASK) 🖥️ 🍴 🍸 ✕ 🅰️ 📠 🖥️ 🖼️ 🖥️ / (VCR) /

TRAVELODGE VICTORIA   *Book at aaa.com*

(CAA) (SAVE)
◆◆◆ ◆◆◆◆

				Phone: (250)388-6611	55
5/1-9/4	1P: $125-$165	2P: $135-$175	XP: $10		F17
9/5-9/30	1P: $89-$130	2P: $99-$140	XP: $10		F17
3/1-4/30	1P: $75-$105	2P: $75-$105	XP: $10		F17
10/1-2/28	1P: $65-$95	2P: $65-$95	XP: $10		F17

Small-scale Hotel **Location:** Douglas St, 2 km w. 229 Gorge Rd E V9A 1L1. Fax: 250/388-4153. **Facility:** 73 one-bedroom standard units, some with efficiencies or kitchens. 3 stories (no elevator), exterior corridors. **Parking:** on-site. **Terms:** small pets only ($10 extra charge, with prior approval). **Amenities:** video library (fee), voice mail, hair dryers. *Some:* DVD players (fee). **Dining:** 7 am-9 pm, cocktails. **Pool(s):** heated indoor. **Leisure Activities:** saunas, limited exercise equipment. **Guest Services:** valet and coin laundry. **Business Services:** meeting rooms. **Cards:** AX, CB, DC, DS, JC, MC, VI. **Special Amenities:** free local telephone calls and free newspaper. *(See color ad p 625 & p 545)*

SOME UNITS
🖥️ 🛏️ 🍴 🍸 🛫 🖥️ / ✕ 📠 🖥️ 🖼️ /
FEE

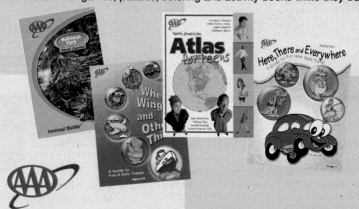

(See map and index starting on p. 601)

UNION CLUB OF BRITISH COLUMBIA   *Book at aaa.com*   Phone: (250)384-1151   **64**

CAA SAVE

WWWW

	7/1-9/30	1P: $179-$269	2P: $179-$269
	5/1-6/30	1P: $169-$259	2P: $169-$259
	3/1-4/30 & 10/1-2/28	1P: $129-$199	2P: $129-$199

Location: Between Courtney and Humboldt sts. 805 Gordon St V8W 1Z6. Fax: 250/384-0538. **Facility:** Smoke free
Large-scale Hotel premises. 23 one-bedroom standard units. 4 stories, interior corridors. **Parking:** street. **Terms:** office hours
7 am-11 pm, age restrictions may apply, 3 day cancellation notice-fee imposed. **Amenities:** irons.
Dining: 7:30-9:30 am, 11:30-2 & 5-10 pm. **Leisure Activities:** steamroom, billiards, exercise room. **Guest Services:** valet
laundry. **Business Services:** meeting rooms. **Cards:** AX, DC, MC, VI. **Special Amenities:** free expanded continental
breakfast and free newspaper. *(See color ad below)*

VICTORIA MARRIOTT INNER HARBOUR   *Book at aaa.com*   Phone: (250)381-8439   **44**

CAA SAVE

WWW WWW

	7/1-9/30	1P: $259-$479	2P: $259-$479	XP: $30	F18
	5/1-6/30	1P: $199-$419	2P: $199-$419	XP: $30	F18
	10/1-2/28	1P: $169-$299	2P: $169-$299	XP: $30	F18
	3/1-4/30	1P: $159-$299	2P: $159-$299	XP: $30	F18

Large-scale Hotel Location: Between Blanshard and Douglas sts. 728 Humboldt St V8W 3Z5. Fax: 250/480-3838. **Facility:** Victoria's
newest full-service hotel is located close to the inner harbour and downtown areas, offering spacious rooms
and wonderful views of downtown. 236 units. 228 one-bedroom standard units. 8 one-bedroom suites ($299-$599). 16 stories,
interior corridors. **Parking:** on-site (fee) and valet. **Terms:** check-in 4 pm, package plans, small pets only ($50 extra charge).
Amenities: CD players, high-speed Internet, dual phone lines, voice mail, safes, honor bars, irons, hair dryers. **Dining:** Fire &
Water Fish & Chop House, see separate listing. **Pool(s):** small heated indoor. **Leisure Activities:** whirlpool, steamroom,
exercise room. **Guest Services:** gift shop, valet laundry. **Business Services:** meeting rooms, business center. **Cards:** AX, DC,
DS, JC, MC, VI. **Special Amenities:** free newspaper and preferred room (subject to availability with advance
reservations).** *(See color ad below)*

SOME UNITS

FEE

◀(See map and index starting on p. 601)

THE VICTORIA REGENT HOTEL   *Book at aaa.com*   Phone: (250)386-2211   **24**

All Year [ECP]   1P: $129-$339   2P: $129-$339   XP: $20   F16

Location: Wharf and Yates sts. Located on the Inner Harbour. 1234 Wharf St V8W 3H9. Fax: 250/386-2622. **Facility:** Spacious, modern, fully equipped condos offer outstanding Inner Harbour views; there are 11 standard, hotel-style rooms without kitchens available. 45 units. 19 one- and 26 two-bedroom standard units, some with kitchens and/or whirlpools. 8 stories, interior corridors. **Parking:** on-site. **Terms:** package plans. **Amenities:** high-speed Internet, voice mail, honor bars, irons, hair dryers. **Guest Services:** valet and coin laundry. **Business Services:** meeting rooms. **Cards:** AX, DC, DS, JC, MC, VI. **Special Amenities:** free expanded continental breakfast and free newspaper. *(See color ad below)*

SOME UNITS

www.victoriaregent.com

Simple elegance

luxurious comfort

open spacious suites

complimentary continental breakfast

scenic harbour views

free underground parking

strolling distance to downtown

10% members discount

off pub. rates

Toll Free 1-800-663-7472

THE VICTORIA

REGENT

HOTEL

tel:(250) 386-2211 fax:(250) 386-2622
e mail: info@victoriaregent.com
1234 Wharf Street, Victoria
British Columbia, Canada V8W 3H9

(See map and index starting on p. 601)

VILLA MARCO POLO INN   **Phone: 250/370-1524**   ㉓

▼▲▼▲▼	5/15-9/15 [BP]	1P: $285-$325	2P: $285-$325	XP: $30
	3/1-5/14 & 9/16-10/15 [BP]	1P: $260-$290	2P: $260-$290	XP: $30
	10/16-2/28 [BP]	1P: $180-$215	2P: $180-$215	XP: $30

Historic Bed & Breakfast   **Location:** Blanshard St (Hwy 17), 2 km e on Fort St, then just s on St. Charles St. Located in a residential area. 1524 Shasta Pl V8S 1X9. Fax: 250/370-1624. **Facility:** This Italian Renaissance-style mansion is set amid classical European gardens and is located in Victoria's elegant Rockland neighborhood. Smoke free premises. 4 one-bedroom standard units, some with whirlpools. 2 stories (no elevator), interior corridors. **Parking:** on-site. **Terms:** check-in 4 pm, 2 night minimum stay - seasonal and/or weekends, age restrictions may apply, 10 day cancellation notice-fee imposed, package plans. **Amenities:** CD players, hair dryers. **Cards:** MC, VI.

[ASK] [S/D] [✕] [K] [TV]

─────── *The following lodging was either not evaluated or did not* ───────
meet AAA rating requirements but is listed for your information only.

SURF MOTEL   **Phone: 250/386-3305**
[fyi]   Not evaluated. **Location:** Jct Oswego St at Dallas Rd. 290 Dallas Rd V8V 1A6. Facilities, services, and decor characterize a basic property.

─────── **WHERE TO DINE** ───────

BARKLEY'S STEAK & SEAFOOD   **Dinner: $19-$38**   **Phone: 250/382-7111**   ②
▼▲▼▲▼   **Location:** Between Blanshard and Douglas sts; downtown; in Executive House Hotel. 777 Douglas St V8W 2B5.
Steak & Seafood   **Hours:** 4:30 pm-10:30 pm, Fri & Sat-11 pm. Closed: 12/26. **Reservations:** suggested. **Features:** Barkley's has an elegant, Victorian atmosphere and an attentive, professional service staff. The restaurant's dishes include steak and seafood, of course, but the menu also offers pasta selections and a choice of Continental dishes. Casual dress; cocktails. **Parking:** on-site (fee). **Cards:** AX, DC, JC, MC, VI.

[Y] [✕]

THE BLACK OLIVE   **Lunch: $8-$16**   **Dinner: $15-$26**   **Phone: 250/384-6060**   ㉑
(CAA)   **Location:** Between Douglas and Blanshard sts. 739 Pandora Ave V8W 1N9. **Hours:** 11:30 am-2:30 & 5-10 pm,
▼▲▼▲▼   Closed: 12/25. **Reservations:** suggested. **Features:** This quaint restaurant is located downtown, serving an
Mediterranean   interesting mix of Mediterranean and Italian influenced west coast food. Parking is available on the street or in nearby pay lots. Casual dress; cocktails. **Parking:** on-site (fee) and street. **Cards:** AX, JC, MC, VI. [✕]

THE BLETHERING PLACE TEA ROOM &
   RESTAURANT   **Lunch: $6-$10**   **Dinner: $8-$17**   **Phone: 250/598-1413**   ④
▼▲▼ ▼▲▼   **Location:** Corner of Monterey and Oak Bay aves; in Oak Bay Village. 2250 Oak Bay Ave V8R 1G5. **Hours:** 8 am-9
Canadian   pm. **Reservations:** accepted. **Features:** Built in 1912, this building is the oldest in the "village." Its English-style decor matches its English-style fare featuring prime rib and Yorkshire pudding and Welsh rarebit. Afternoon tea is served 11 am-7:30 pm. Families are welcomed here. Casual dress; beer & wine only.
Parking: on-site. **Cards:** AX, DC, JC, MC, VI.

[K] [✕]

BOWMAN'S RIB HOUSE   **Dinner: $14-$18**   **Phone: 250/385-5380**   ③
▼▲▼▲ ▼▲▼▲   **Location:** Blanshard St (Hwy 17), just e on Courtney St, then just s on Quadra St. 825 Burdett Ave V8W 1B3.
Continental   **Hours:** 5 pm-9 pm. Closed major holidays. **Features:** Downstairs in the Cherry Bank Hotel, the restaurant has served its famous ribs—smothered in such mouthwatering sauces as hot 'n' spicy, honey garlic or original—since 1964. Every Thursday through Sunday, diners can join a sing-along in a roaring '20s atmosphere with rotating glass ball chandeliers. Casual dress; cocktails. **Parking:** on-site. **Cards:** AX, DC, JC, MC, VI.

[K] [✕]

BRADY'S FISH & CHIPS   **Lunch: $6-$10**   **Dinner: $8-$13**   **Phone: 250/382-3695**   ㊳
▼▲▼   **Location:** Just w of Harriet Rd; in Albion Mall. 1-50 Burnside Rd W V9A 1B5. **Hours:** 11 am-7:30 pm, Fri & Sat-8
Seafood   pm, Sun noon-7:30 pm. Closed: 10/10, 12/25. **Features:** The casual family restaurant serves English-style fish and chips, as well as mouthwatering halibut and cod and fine chowder. Guests can order for dine-in or take-out. Casual dress; beer & wine only. **Parking:** on-site. **Cards:** AX, MC, VI.

[✕]

CANOE BREWPUB MARINA RESTAURANT   **Lunch: $8-$15**   **Dinner: $15-$25**   **Phone: 250/361-1940**   ⑧
▼▲▼▲▼   **Location:** Corner of Stone and Fisgard sts. 450 Swift St V8W 1S3. **Hours:** 11:30 am-10 pm, Fri & Sat-11 pm; 11
Canadian   am-11 pm in summer. Closed: 12/25. **Reservations:** suggested. **Features:** The waterfront brew pub offers freshly brewed beers along with fresh fish, tasty pasta, burgers, sandwiches and pizza. Casual dress; cocktails. **Parking:** on-site. **Cards:** AX, DC, MC, VI.

[Y] [K] [✕]

CHARTER'S RESTAURANT AT
MCMORRAN'S BEACH HOUSE   **Lunch: $7-$12**   **Dinner: $12-$24**   **Phone: 250/658-5527**   ㉔
(CAA)   **Location:** Hwy 17, exit Royal Oak Dr, 2 km e on Royal Oak Dr, then 2.3 km n. 5109 Cordova Bay Rd V8Y 2K1.
▼▲▼▲▼   **Hours:** 11 am-9 pm. Closed: 12/25, 12/26. **Reservations:** accepted. **Features:** If this place were any closer
Steak & Seafood   to the ocean, guests would need a bathing suit. On the city's outskirts, the restaurant has been a local landmark for decades. Although the focus is on fresh seafood, the menu also lines up varied meat dishes and lighter fare for lunch. Patio seating is popular in season. Dressy casual; cocktails. **Parking:** on-site. **Cards:** AX, DC, MC, VI.

[✕]

(See map and index starting on p. 601)

DILETTANTES CAFE
Canadian
Lunch: $6-$10   **Dinner:** $10-$20   **Phone:** 250/381-3327   [35]
Location: Between Douglas and Blanshard sts. 787 Fort St V8W 1G9. **Hours:** 7:30 am-3 pm, Thurs-Sat to 9 pm. Closed: 12/25. **Features:** Inside the simple downtown cafe are bright yellow walls adorned with original artwork for sale. The menu features a mixture of items, including daily specials, homemade soups, freshly made breads, sandwiches, wraps and pasta dishes. Prices are reasonable, with every selection less than $20. Casual dress; cocktails. **Parking:** street. **Cards:** AX, MC, VI.

THE EMPRESS ROOM
Regional Canadian
Dinner: $30-$40   **Phone:** 250/384-8111   [13]
Location: Between Belleville and Humboldt sts; in The Fairmont Empress. 721 Government St V8W 1W5. **Hours:** 6 pm-10 pm. **Reservations:** required. **Features:** Topping the list for fine dining in Victoria, the restaurant enables guests to dine surrounded by tapestry walls and richly carved ceilings that are amazing to see. The menu changes seasonally to showcase the best cuisine the province has to offer, Other aspects that contribute to the experience include the exceptional staff and an outstanding wine list with many flavorful British Columbia vintages. Semi-formal attire; cocktails; entertainment. **Parking:** on-site and valet. **Cards:** AX, CB, DC, DS, JC, MC, VI. **Historic**

FIRE & WATER FISH & CHOP HOUSE
Steak & Seafood
Lunch: $15-$20   **Dinner:** $22-$35   **Phone:** 250/381-8439   [9]
Location: Between Blanshard and Douglas sts; in Victoria Marriott Inner Harbour. 728 Humboldt St V8W 3Z5. **Hours:** 6:30 am-10 pm. **Reservations:** suggested. **Features:** The all-day restaurant offers a comfortable, casual atmosphere. On the menu are premium-quality steaks and seasonal local seafood, such as Pacific rockfish, halibut and wild British Columbia salmon. Dishes are served with a choice of signature sauces and accompaniments, which makes every entree distinctive. Casual dress; cocktails. **Parking:** on-site and valet. **Cards:** AX, DC, DS, JC, MC, VI. *(See color ad p 626)*

HAULTAIN'S FISH & CHIPS
English
Lunch: $7-$14   **Dinner:** $7-$14   **Phone:** 250/383-8332   [27]
Location: From Blanshard St (Hwy 17), 1 km e on Bay St, then just n on Cook St. 1127 Haultain St V8T 1V4. **Hours:** 11:30 am-8 pm, Sun 3:30 pm-7:30 pm. Closed: 12/25, 12/26; also Mon in winter. **Features:** Patrons can dine in or take out an order from this small, neighborhood-favorite restaurant in a quiet residential area. Fish 'n' chips is the specialty, but burgers and specialty dinners also are served. Seating can be limited, but it's well worth the trip. Casual dress; beer & wine only. **Parking:** on-site. **Cards:** MC, VI.

HERALD STREET CAFFE
Regional Canadian
Lunch: $9-$14   **Dinner:** $12-$28   **Phone:** 250/381-1441   [11]
Location: Government and Herald sts. 546 Herald St V8W 1S6. **Hours:** 5 pm-10 pm, Sat & Sun also 11 am-3 pm; Saturday & Sunday brunch. **Reservations:** suggested. **Features:** The Herald Street Cafe features an eclectic offering of West Coast favorites, and the menu displays the chef's skill and imagination. The lamb sandwich, crab cakes and roasted tomato and garlic bisque are well-known. More than 350 International wines. Casual dress; cocktails. **Parking:** street. **Cards:** MC, VI.

HUGO'S GRILL AND BREWHOUSE
Canadian
Lunch: $12-$22   **Dinner:** $17-$28   **Phone:** 250/920-4844   [41]
Location: Between Douglas and Gordon sts. 625 Courtney St V8W 1B8. **Hours:** 11:30 am-11 pm. Closed: 12/25. **Reservations:** suggested. **Features:** With many cold ones on tap, the brewhouse is a great place for a beer. The menu varies from finger foods to burgers to more hearty fare, all served in a fun atmosphere. Casual dress; cocktails. **Parking:** street. **Cards:** AX, DC, JC, MC, VI.

HUNAN VILLAGE
Chinese
Lunch: $8-$15   **Dinner:** $8-$15   **Phone:** 250/382-0661   [1]
Location: Fisgard and Government sts. 546 Fisgard St V8W 1R4. **Hours:** 11 am-11 pm, Sun 5 pm-10 pm. Closed: 12/25. **Features:** Located in Victoria's Chinatown district, this restaurant specializes in Hunan and Cantonese meals. Hot and spicy beef, smoked duck or ham dishes are the local favorites. There's metered street parking or spaces nearby in pay parking lots. Casual dress; cocktails. **Parking:** street. **Cards:** AX, DC, MC, VI.

IL TERRAZZO
Italian
Lunch: $9-$15   **Dinner:** $15-$36   **Phone:** 250/361-0028   [28]
Location: Jct Wharf St near Market Square; main entrance off Waddington Alley. 555 Johnson St V8W 1M2. **Hours:** 11:30 am-3 & 5-10 pm, Sun from 5 pm. Closed: 1/1, 12/25. **Reservations:** required. **Features:** Situated in an old courtyard, Il Terrazzo offers excellent meals such as Australian lamb, ostrich, pasta and seafood, with emphasis on wood-burning oven specialties. Wine choices are extensive, with a nice by-the-glass selection. Fast, friendly service. Casual dress; cocktails. **Parking:** street. **Cards:** AX, DC, MC, VI.

JAMES BAY TEA ROOM & RESTAURANT
Canadian
Menu on aaa.com   **Lunch:** $7-$10   **Phone:** 250/382-8282   [15]
Location: Corner of Superior, just s of the Parliament buildings. 332 Menzies St V8V 2G9. **Hours:** 7 am-5 pm, Sun from 8 am. Closed: 12/24, 12/25, 12/26. **Reservations:** suggested. **Features:** This popular place in a 1907 home has an intimate atmosphere featuring memorabilia and photos of Britain's Royal Family. The menu offers omelets, pot pies, Yorkshire pudding, bangers and kidney pie. Afternoon tea is $7; high tea $10, served all day. Casual dress; beer & wine only. **Parking:** street. **Cards:** AX, MC, VI.

THE KEG STEAKHOUSE
Steak & Seafood
Dinner: $19-$30   **Phone:** 250/386-7789   [20]
Location: Between Wharf and Langley sts. 500 Fort St V8W 1E6. **Hours:** 4:30 pm-11 pm. Closed: 12/25. **Reservations:** suggested. **Features:** Here's the Keg's "steak story": always trimmed, better with age, well marbled, added spice and grilled to perfection. This recipe is why the downtown restaurant is so popular. Parking is in metered spots or in a small pay lot a block away. Casual dress; cocktails. **Parking:** street. **Cards:** AX, DC, MC, VI.

(See map and index starting on p. 601)

KOTO JAPANESE RESTAURANT   Lunch: $6-$16   Dinner: $6-$16   Phone: 250/382-1514   [12]
▼▼▼ ▼▼▼   **Location:** Between Government and Wharf sts. 510 Fort St V8W 1E6. **Hours:** 11:30 am-2 & 5-10 pm. Closed: 1/1,
Japanese   12/25. **Reservations:** suggested. **Features:** Offerings include an extensive array of sushi and sashimi dishes, as well as teriyaki steak, ginger pork and a wide selection of tempura. Casual dress; cocktails. **Parking:** street. **Cards:** AX, MC, VI.   [X]

THE MARINA RESTAURANT   Lunch: $10-$15   Dinner: $16-$30   Phone: 250/598-8555   [17]
▼▼▼▼   **Location:** 6 km e via Oak Bay Ave, just s. 1327 Beach Dr V8S 2N4. **Hours:** 11:30 am-2:30 & 5-10 pm, Fri & Sat-
Seafood   11 pm, Sun 10 am-10 pm. Closed: 12/25. **Reservations:** suggested. **Features:** Located in the Oak Bay Marina, this restaurant provides beautiful sweeping views of the ocean, harbor and mountains. Its menu features a Pacific Northwest cuisine, showcasing fresh local and exotic seafood, sushi bar and cafe deli.
Casual dress; cocktails. **Parking:** on-site. **Cards:** AX, DC, JC, MC, VI.   [X]

THE MARK   Dinner: $26-$36   Phone: 250/386-0450   [23]
(CAA)   **Location:** Belleville at Menzies St; downtown; in Hotel Grand Pacific. 463 Belleville St V8V 1X3. **Hours:** 6 pm-10 pm.
▼▼▼ ▼▼▼   Closed: 12/25. **Reservations:** required. **Features:** With only 28 seats, the restaurant offers the
Regional   discriminating guest a very intimate dining experience. The menu is constantly changing, but it always offers
Canadian   the finest in local ingredients. An excellent selection of wines will complement any meal. Dressy casual; cocktails. **Parking:** on-site and valet. **Cards:** AX, DC, DS, JC, MC, VI.   [Y] [X]

MILESTONE'S GRILL & BAR   Lunch: $7-$10   Dinner: $7-$13   Phone: 250/381-2244   [30]
▼▼▼ ▼▼▼   **Location:** Corner of Government and Humboldt sts. 812 Wharf St V8W 1T3. **Hours:** 11 am-10 pm, Fri & Sat-11
Canadian   pm. Closed: 12/25. **Reservations:** suggested, evenings. **Features:** On the inner harbor directly under the Tourist Information Centre and adjacent to the Empress Hotel, the restaurant affords spectacular views of the Parliament Buildings and Victoria's harbor area. Casual dress; cocktails. **Parking:** street. **Cards:** AX,
DC, MC, VI.   [Y] [X]

PABLO'S DINING LOUNGE   Dinner: $19-$33   Phone: 250/388-4255   [16]
▼▼▼ ▼▼   **Location:** Corner of Pendray and Quebec sts. 225 Quebec St V8V 1W2. **Hours:** 5 pm-11 pm. Closed: 12/25,
French   12/26. **Reservations:** suggested. **Features:** Just one block from the Inner Harbour and steps from downtown, the restaurant has served French specialties for nearly 25 years. Adding to the heritage manor setting are a wood-burning fireplace and intimate tables. Favorite choices include scampi and rack of lamb.
Casual dress; cocktails. **Parking:** street. **Cards:** AX, MC, VI.   [Æ] [X]

PAGLIACCI'S   Lunch: $8-$10   Dinner: $16-$22   Phone: 250/386-1662   [31]
▼▼   **Location:** Between Fort and Broughton sts. 1011 Broad St V8W 2A1. **Hours:** 11:30 am-10 pm, Fri & Sat-11 pm.
Italian   Closed: 12/25. **Features:** A New York style Italian eatery with a bustling Big Apple ambience, and food to match. Enjoy their flavorful pasta dishes. The ravioli is exceptional, or if you're a tomato sauce fan, the Spaghetti Western may be the ticket, made with fresh tomatoes and topped with a couple of large
meatballs, it's as Italian as it gets. Casual dress; cocktails. **Parking:** street. **Cards:** AX, MC, VI.   [Æ] [X]

PAPRIKA BISTRO   Dinner: $17-$29   Phone: 250/592-7424   [29]
▼▼▼   **Location:** Between Dunlevy and Musgrave sts; in the Oak Bay area. 2524 Estevan Ave V8R 2S7. **Hours:** 5 pm-10
Continental   pm. Closed major holidays; also Sun. **Reservations:** suggested. **Features:** In a small neighborhood shopping center, the bistro prepares some wonderful dishes. Among good choices are fresh Digby scallops and bacon tart, beet and fennel salad and the signature duckling. This place makes it well worth the short
drive to Oak Bay. Casual dress; cocktails. **Parking:** street. **Cards:** AX, MC, VI.   [Æ] [X]

PASSERO'S MEDITERRANEAN CUISINE   Lunch: $7-$12   Dinner: $11-$19   Phone: 250/384-6474   [33]
▼▼ ▼▼   **Location:** Corner of Cook St. 1102 Yates St V8V 3M8. **Hours:** 11 am-9 pm, Fri & Sat-10 pm. Closed: 12/25; also
Mediterranean   Sun. **Reservations:** accepted. **Features:** The family-run restaurant serves a fine combination of Greek and Italian cuisine in large portions. Lending to the bistro theme are lots of color and live plants. The patio opens seasonally. Casual dress; cocktails. **Parking:** on-site. **Cards:** AX, DC, MC, VI.   [X]

PENNY FARTHING PUBLIC HOUSE   Lunch: $8-$14   Dinner: $9-$17   Phone: 250/370-9008   [25]
▼▼ ▼▼   **Location:** At Monterey Ave. 2228 Oak Bay Ave V8R 1G5. **Hours:** 11 am-midnight, Sun & Mon-11 pm. Closed:
Canadian   12/25. **Features:** This classic British-style pub is decorated in rich dark wood with brass accents. Sample the fine pub fare or the wide selection of stouts, ales and lagers in the relaxing atmosphere. Casual dress; cocktails. **Parking:** street. **Cards:** AX, DC, MC, VI.   [Y] [X]

PERIKLIS GREEK RESTAURANT   Dinner: $11-$28   Phone: 250/386-3313   [7]
▼▼ ▼▼   **Location:** Between Wharf and Langley sts. 531 Yates St V8W 1K7. **Hours:** 4:30 pm-11:30 pm. Closed: 1/1, 12/25.
Greek   **Reservations:** suggested. **Features:** An open, airy taverna style restaurant, located near the harbour in Victoria's historic area, Periklis Restaurant is a favorite of the locals and tourists alike. A wide variety of Greek dishes, like roast lamb, mousaka, and souvlaki are prepared using authentic recipes from Greece.
Enjoy a tasty meal, followed by their exceptional baklava and coffee for dessert. Casual dress; cocktails. **Parking:** on-site (fee).
Cards: AX, MC, VI.   [Æ] [X]

(See map and index starting on p. 601)

PESCATORE'S FISH HOUSE   **Lunch:** $9-$13   **Dinner:** $18-$25   **Phone:** 250/385-4512   32

Seafood

Location: Between Gordon and Government sts. 614 Humboldt St V8W 1A4. **Hours:** 11:30 am-10 pm. Closed: 1/1, 12/25. **Reservations:** suggested. **Features:** Pescatore's is a chic bistro with excellent fresh seafood such as salmon Wellington and trout stuffed with crab and brie, and great beverage choices such as espresso, cappuccino and martinis. This is hip and funky fine dining, with live jazz on weekends (seasonal). Blue plate specials from 4:30 pm-6:30 pm. Parking at street meters or pay lots. Casual dress; cocktails. **Parking:** on-site (fee). **Cards:** AX, DC, MC, VI.

PLUTO'S   **Lunch:** $7-$11   **Dinner:** $7-$11   **Phone:** 250/385-4747   34

Canadian

Location: Corner of Cook and View sts. 1150 Cook St V8V 3Z9. **Hours:** 8 am-10 pm, Sun & Mon-9 pm. Closed: 12/25. **Features:** The funky-looking, turquoise and pink art deco structure used to be a gas station. In addition to the extensive breakfast menu, which is served until 2 pm, there are also varied wraps and burgers and a few Mexican items. Casual dress; beer & wine only. **Parking:** on-site. **Cards:** AX, MC, VI.

RESTAURANT MATISSE   **Dinner:** $20-$37   **Phone:** 250/480-0883   18

French

Location: Between Government and Wharf sts. 512 Yates St V8W 1K8. **Hours:** 5:30 pm-10 pm. Closed: 12/25; also Mon & Tues. **Reservations:** required. **Features:** This eatery is a wonderful French restaurant located downtown. The first thing you'll notice is the bright sunlight-yellow decor that is warm and inviting. Daily specials along with what they do best include duck, beef and fish. Casual dress; cocktails. **Parking:** street. **Cards:** AX, MC, VI.

SIAM THAI RESTAURANT   **Lunch:** $8-$16   **Dinner:** $8-$16   **Phone:** 250/383-9911   22

Thai

Location: Between Government and Wharf sts. 512 Fort St V8W 1E6. **Hours:** 11:30 am-2 & 5-10 pm, Sun from 5 pm. Closed: 12/25. **Reservations:** required. **Features:** The secret of Thai cooking is to maintain a delicate balance between the spices and main ingredients. The restaurant accomplishes this in its soups, as well as dishes of fried rice, noodles, chicken, beef, pork, seafood and vegetarian items. Lunch specials are available. Casual dress; cocktails. **Parking:** street. **Cards:** AX, DC, MC, VI.

SIX MILE PUB   **Lunch:** $4-$10   **Dinner:** $4-$11   **Phone:** 250/478-3121   37

Canadian

Location: Trans-Canada Hwy 1, exit 10 (Colwood/Sook), 1 km s. 494 Island Hwy V9B 1H5. **Hours:** 11 am-11 pm, Sun-10 pm. Closed: 12/25. **Features:** Built in 1855, this restaurant is known as "British Columbia's oldest working man's pub." They serve burgers, oysters, pot pies, soups, sandwiches, and beer on tap. Pool tables and dartboards are part of the entertainment package. The minimum age to enter pub is 19. Casual dress; cocktails. **Parking:** on-site. **Cards:** AX, DC, MC, VI.

THE SNUG ENGLISH PUB   **Lunch:** $7-$12   **Dinner:** $9-$18   **Phone:** 250/598-4556   40

Canadian

Location: 6.8 km e via Oak Bay Ave, then just s; in Oak Bay Beach Hotel & Marine Resort. 1175 Beach Dr V85 2N2. **Hours:** 11 am-10 pm. **Reservations:** accepted. **Features:** On the shores of Oak Bay, the delightful English pub serves popular pub fare with a full range of beers on tap. Portions are ample. The pleasant patio overlooks the ocean and marina. Casual dress; cocktails. **Parking:** on-site. **Cards:** AX, DC, MC, VI.

SOUTH BAY PUB & RESTAURANT   **Lunch:** $7-$12   **Dinner:** $9-$17   **Phone:** 250/385-5643   39

Canadian

Location: Just w of Gorge Rd. 2940 Jutland Rd V8T 5K6. **Hours:** 11 am-11 pm, Fri & Sat-midnight, Sun 10 am-11 pm. Closed: 10/10, 12/25. **Reservations:** accepted. **Features:** On the Gorge Waterway, the circular pub affords panoramic views through floor-to-ceiling windows. Patio seating is a seasonal option. On the menu is a selection of classic pub fare with a focus on fresh seafood. Casual dress; cocktails. **Parking:** street. **Cards:** AX, MC, VI.

THE SPICE JAMMER RESTAURANT   **Lunch:** $6-$20   **Dinner:** $15-$20   **Phone:** 250/480-1055   10

East Indian

Location: At Quadra St. 852 Fort St V8W 1H8. **Hours:** 11:30 am-2:30 & 5-9 pm, Fri-10 pm, Sat 5 pm-10 pm, Sun 5 pm-9 pm. Closed: 12/25; also Mon. **Reservations:** suggested, Fri & Sat. **Features:** Intimate lighting and warm tones welcome diners to the delights of East Indian cuisine, which is touched by the traditions of Eastern Africa. Fried mogo root and coconut chicken curry are featured alongside fragrant masalas and tandoori dishes. Casual dress; cocktails. **Parking:** street. **Cards:** AX, MC, VI.

SPINNAKERS BREW PUB & RESTAURANT   **Lunch:** $8-$12   **Dinner:** $8-$20   **Phone:** 250/386-2739   19

Canadian

Location: 2 km nw over Johnson St Bridge, then just s; in Spinnaker Brewpub and Guesthouse. 308 Catherine St V9A 3S8. **Hours:** 7 am-10 pm. Closed: 12/25. **Reservations:** suggested. **Features:** Spinnakers is a fun, lively pub/restaurant/bakery featuring terrific breads, a wonderful mile-high apple pie, good Cajun halibut burgers, homemade soup and a stand-up bar area. This is Canada's first in-house brewery, and you can tour the brew house. Take some baking home from their on-site bakery. Cocktails. **Parking:** on-site. **Cards:** AX, DC, DS, MC, VI.

SUPERIOR CHINESE RESTAURANT   **Lunch:** $7-$12   **Dinner:** $10-$16   **Phone:** 250/386-2288   36

Chinese

Location: Corner of Burnside Rd and Harriet. 110 Burnside Rd E V8T 4S1. **Hours:** 11 am-2 & 4-9:30 pm. Closed: 1/1, 12/25, 12/26; also Mon. **Features:** The restaurant's dining room is bright and airy with a casual style. The menu offers a selection of Szechuan, Cantonese and some Canadian dishes. A take-out menu is available, with free delivery. Casual dress; cocktails. **Parking:** on-site. **Cards:** MC, VI.

(See map and index starting on p. 601)

TAJ MAHAL Dinner: $12-$22 Phone: 250/383-4662 ⑥
Location: Between Douglas and Government sts. 679 Herald St V8W 1S8. **Hours:** 5 pm-10 pm. Closed: 12/25. **Reservations:** suggested. **Features:** A traditional East Indian restaurant that is popular with tourists and locals alike, the Taj Mahal Restaurant in Victoria is a good spot to sample the spicy cuisine of the Sub-Continent. You can order your meal mildly spiced, or fiery hot, it's up to you. Casual dress; cocktails.
East Indian **Parking:** street. **Cards:** AX, DC, DS, MC, VI. ☒

VICTORIA HARBOUR HOUSE
RESTAURANT Dinner: $14-$30 Phone: 250/386-1244 ⑭
Location: Corner of Oswego and Quebec sts. 607 Oswego St V8V 4W9. **Hours:** 4:30 pm-11:30 pm. **Reservations:** suggested. **Features:** With a refined, formal elegance and operatic background music, the Victoria Harbour House Restaurant presents an ideal ambience for a fine dining experience. This well-known establishment has long been a favorite of the more well-to-do tourists who are guests at some of the finest nearby hotels. It is also popular with local government and business leaders with their families. Casual
Steak & Seafood dress; cocktails. **Parking:** on-site. **Cards:** AX, MC, VI. Ⓜ ☒

WHITE HEATHER TEA ROOM Lunch: $8-$11 Phone: 250/595-8020 ⑤
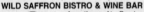 **Location:** Between Fell and Davie sts. 1885 Oak Bay Ave V8R 1C6. **Hours:** 9:30 am-5 pm. Closed major holidays; also Sun & Mon. **Reservations:** suggested. **Features:** On Oak Bay, the wonderful tea room
Bakery/Desserts serves lunch and afternoon tea starting at 1:30 p.m. Among choices are wee tea for $9.75, not-so-wee tea for $14.25 and the big muckle for hearty appetites. Among favorites are the sconewiches, freshly baked scones with varied fillings. Everything is baked on site. Casual dress; beer & wine only. **Parking:** on-site. **Cards:** MC, VI. ☒

WILD SAFFRON BISTRO & WINE BAR Dinner: $15-$34 Phone: 250/361-3150 ㉖
Location: At Pandora St. 1605 Store St V8W 1N6. **Hours:** 5 pm-close. Closed: Sun & Mon. **Reservations:** suggested. **Features:** The warm, contemporary bistro pairs innovative West Coast cuisine with an attractive selection of local and International wines. Seafood, delectable vegetarian preparations and lamb, game and poultry entrees all are presented with artistic flair. A brewery is on site. Casual dress;
Pacific Rim cocktails. **Parking:** street. **Cards:** AX, MC, VI. ☒

The Victoria Vicinity

BRENTWOOD BAY

——— WHERE TO STAY ———

BRENTWOOD BAY LODGE & SPA   *Book at aaa.com*   Phone: (250)544-2079

| | 5/16-10/15 [BP] | 1P: $495-$845 | 2P: $495-$845 | XP: $30 |
| 3/1-5/15 & 10/16-2/28 [BP] | | 1P: $148-$475 | 2P: $148-$475 | XP: $30 |

Small-scale Hotel   **Location:** Hwy 17, exit Brentwood Bay, 3 km w on Keating X Rd, 1.5 km n on W Saanich Rd, then 1 km w (Mill Bay Ferry). 849 Verdier Ave V8M 1C5 (849 Verdier Ave). Fax: 250/544-2069. **Facility:** Smoke free premises. 33 units. 30 one-bedroom standard units with whirlpools. 3 one-bedroom suites with whirlpools. 3 stories, exterior corridors. **Parking:** on-site and valet. **Terms:** age restrictions may apply, 7 day cancellation notice, [AP] meal plan available. **Amenities:** video library, DVD players, CD players, high-speed Internet, voice mail, safes, honor bars, irons, hair dryers. **Pool(s):** heated outdoor. **Leisure Activities:** whirlpool, exercise room, spa. *Fee:* marina. **Guest Services:** valet laundry. **Business Services:** meeting rooms. **Cards:** AX, MC, VI.

——— WHERE TO DINE ———

ARBUTUS GRILLE & WINE BAR   **Lunch:** $10-$20   **Dinner:** $25-$38   **Phone:** 250/544-2079

Pacific Rim   **Location:** Hwy 17 N, exit Brentwood Bay, 3 km w on Keating Rd, 1.5 km n on W Saanich Rd, then 1 km w (Mill Bay Ferry); in Brentwood Bay Lodge & Spa. 849 Verdier Ave V8M 1C5. **Hours:** 7-10 am, 11:30-3 & 6-11 pm. **Reservations:** required. **Features:** In the city's newest luxury oceanfront resort, the restaurant is just minutes from famous Butchart Gardens. Fresh fish, Alberta beef and local produce factor in exquisite, creatively prepared dishes. An extensive wine list features many award-winning British Columbia wines. Dressy casual; cocktails. **Parking:** on-site. **Cards:** AX, MC, VI.

MALAHAT

——— WHERE TO STAY ———

THE AERIE RESORT   Phone: (250)743-7115

	5/23-1/9 & 1/21-2/28 [BP]	1P: $245-$295	2P: $245-$295	XP: $30	F6
	3/28-5/22 [BP]	1P: $245-$275	2P: $245-$275	XP: $30	F6
	3/1-3/27 [BP]	1P: $195-$225	2P: $195-$225	XP: $30	F6

Country Inn   **Location:** 32 km n of Victoria off Trans-Canada Hwy 1, use Spectacle Lake turn off, follow signs. Located in a quiet area. 600 Ebadora Ln V0R 2L0 (PO Box 108). Fax: 250/743-4766. **Facility:** This luxury retreat perched in the mountains offers sweeping ocean views; a helicopter pad is on the grounds. Smoke free premises. 29 units. 10 one-bedroom standard units, some with whirlpools. 19 one-bedroom suites ($395-$995), some with whirlpools. 2-3 stories (no elevator), interior corridors. **Parking:** on-site. **Terms:** open 3/1-1/9 & 1/21-2/28, office hours 7 am-10 pm, 7 day cancellation notice-fee imposed, [MAP] meal plan available, package plans. **Amenities:** CD players, dual phone lines, voice mail, honor bars, irons, hair dryers. **Dining:** 2 restaurants, noon-2 & 6-10 pm, cocktails, also, The Aerie Dining Room, see separate listing, entertainment. **Pool(s):** heated indoor. **Leisure Activities:** sauna, whirlpools, tennis court, yoga, cooking instruction, spa. **Guest Services:** valet laundry. **Business Services:** meeting rooms. **Cards:** AX, DC, MC, VI.

MALAHAT BUNGALOWS MOTEL   Phone: (250)478-3011

| | 6/1-9/30 | 1P: $72-$120 | 2P: $72-$150 | XP: $10 |
| | 3/1-5/31 & 10/1-2/28 | 1P: $62-$100 | 2P: $62-$135 | XP: $10 |

Motel   **Location:** Trans-Canada Hwy 1, 26 km n of Victoria. (PO Box 48). Fax: 250/478-3011. **Facility:** 18 units. 13 one-bedroom standard units, some with kitchens. 5 two-bedroom suites with kitchens. 1 story, exterior corridors. *Bath:* combo or shower only. **Parking:** on-site. **Terms:** office hours 8 am-midnight, 3 day cancellation notice-fee imposed, weekly rates available, pets ($10 extra charge). **Leisure Activities:** whirlpool. **Guest Services:** coin laundry. **Cards:** MC, VI. *(See color ad p 618)*

SOME UNITS

——— WHERE TO DINE ———

THE AERIE DINING ROOM   **Dinner:** $75-$85   Phone: 250/743-7115

Nouvelle French   **Location:** 32 km n of Victoria off Trans-Canada Hwy 1, use Spectacle Lake turn off, follow signs; in The Aerie Resort. 600 Ebadora Ln V0R 2L0. **Hours:** 6 pm-10 pm. **Closed:** 1/6-1/23. **Reservations:** required. **Features:** This restaurant features formal dining and a Northwest-influenced cuisine with fresh local ingredients. A seven-course tasting menu at $65 per person is available for dinner as well as a $36 pre-fixe lunch menu. The unusual location in a mountain resort offers outstanding views from a comfortable setting. Dressy casual; cocktails. **Parking:** on-site. **Cards:** AX, DC, MC, VI.

MALAHAT MOUNTAIN INN   **Lunch:** $8-$15   **Dinner:** $14-$26   **Phone:** 250/478-1944

Regional Canadian   **Location:** Trans-Canada Hwy 1, 26 km n of Victoria. 265 Trans-Canada Hwy 1 V0R 2L0. **Hours:** 11:30 am-9:30 pm. Closed: 12/25. **Reservations:** suggested. **Features:** Gourmet dining is the mode in the relaxed setting. Perched on a hill, the dining room affords a stunning view of the mountains and ocean. The menu displays a Pacific Northwest influence in such seafood dishes as coconut-crusted prawns. Presentation is exceptional. Casual dress; cocktails. **Parking:** on-site. **Cards:** AX, MC, VI.

SAANICHTON

─────── **WHERE TO STAY** ───────

QUALITY INN WADDLING DOG   *Book at aaa.com*   Phone: (250)652-1146

CAA SAVE

	7/1-9/30 [ECP]	1P: $119-$139	2P: $119-$139	XP: $15	F17
	5/1-6/30 & 10/1-2/28 [ECP]	1P: $89-$109	2P: $89-$109	XP: $15	F17
	3/1-4/30 [ECP]	1P: $79-$99	2P: $79-$99	XP: $15	F17

Location: Corner of Hwy 17 and Mt Newton Crossroad. 2476 Mt Newton Crossroad V8M 2B8. Fax: 250/652-4946.
Small-scale Hotel **Facility:** Smoke free premises. 30 one-bedroom standard units. 3 stories, interior corridors. **Parking:** on-site. **Terms:** pets ($10 extra charge). **Amenities:** irons, hair dryers. **Dining:** 11 am-9 pm, cocktails.
Business Services: meeting rooms. **Cards:** AX, DC, JC, MC, VI.

SUPER 8 VICTORIA/SAANICHTON   *Book at aaa.com*   Phone: (250)652-6888

CAA SAVE

	6/30-9/30	1P: $89-$109	2P: $99-$129	XP: $10	F16
	4/16-6/29	1P: $74-$89	2P: $84-$99	XP: $10	F16
	10/1-2/28	1P: $69-$79	2P: $79-$99	XP: $10	F16
	3/1-4/15	1P: $64-$74	2P: $74-$84	XP: $10	F16

Small-scale Hotel **Location:** Just e of Hwy 17. 2477 Mt Newton Crossroad V8M 2B7. Fax: 250/652-6800. **Facility:** 51 one-bedroom standard units, some with whirlpools. 2 stories, interior corridors. **Parking:** on-site. **Terms:** pets ($10 extra charge). **Amenities:** *Fee:* video library, safes. **Cards:** AX, DC, MC, VI. **Special Amenities:** free continental breakfast and free local telephone calls.

SIDNEY pop. 10,929

─────── **WHERE TO STAY** ───────

BEACON INN AT SIDNEY   Phone: (250)655-3288

	5/16-9/30 [BP]	1P: $149-$259	2P: $149-$259	
	10/1-10/31 [BP]	1P: $129-$219	2P: $129-$219	
Bed & Breakfast	3/1-5/15 [BP]	1P: $119-$219	2P: $119-$219	
	11/1-2/28 [BP]	1P: $119-$199	2P: $119-$199	

Location: Hwy 17, exit Sidney, 1 km e on Beacon Ave, then just s. 9724 3rd St V8L 3A2. Fax: 250/655-9118. **Facility:** Royally appointed guest rooms have rich wood furnishings, plush velvet trim and regal feather beds; set on a quiet residential street near the harbor. Smoke free premises. 9 one-bedroom standard units, some with whirlpools. 3 stories (no elevator), interior corridors. **Parking:** on-site. **Terms:** office hours 8 am-8 pm, age restrictions may apply, 7 day cancellation notice, package plans. **Amenities:** hair dryers. **Cards:** MC, VI.

BEST WESTERN EMERALD ISLE MOTOR INN   *Book at aaa.com*   Phone: (250)656-4441

CAA SAVE

	7/1-9/30	1P: $149	2P: $179	XP: $20	F17
	5/1-6/30	1P: $129	2P: $149	XP: $20	F17
	3/1-4/30 & 10/1-2/28	1P: $109	2P: $119	XP: $20	F17

Small-scale Hotel **Location:** Hwy 17, exit Sidney, just e. 2306 Beacon Ave V8L 1X2. Fax: 250/655-1351. **Facility:** 65 one-bedroom standard units, some with efficiencies, kitchens and/or whirlpools. 2 stories, interior corridors. **Parking:** on-site. **Terms:** pets ($20 extra charge). **Amenities:** voice mail, irons, hair dryers. *Some:* high-speed Internet. **Dining:** 7 am-9 pm, cocktails. **Leisure Activities:** sauna, whirlpool. **Guest Services:** valet and coin laundry. **Business Services:** meeting rooms. **Cards:** AX, DC, DS, MC, VI.

THE CEDARWOOD INN & SUITES   Phone: (250)656-5551

	6/15-9/30	1P: $109-$245	2P: $109-$245	XP: $15	F7
	11/1-2/28	1P: $79-$205	2P: $79-$205	XP: $15	F7
Small-scale Hotel	3/1-6/14 & 10/1-10/31	1P: $89-$160	2P: $89-$160	XP: $15	F7

Location: Hwy 17, just e on McTavish Rd, then 1.4 km n. 9522 Lochside Dr V8L 1N8. Fax: 250/656-1551. **Facility:** 46 units. 45 one- and 1 two-bedroom standard units, some with efficiencies, kitchens and/or whirlpools. 2 stories (no elevator), exterior corridors. **Parking:** on-site. **Terms:** office hours 7 am-11 pm, cancellation fee imposed, small pets only ($15 extra charge). **Amenities:** video library (fee), hair dryers. *Some:* irons. **Guest Services:** coin laundry. **Cards:** AX, DS, MC, VI.

SHOAL HARBOUR INN & LATCH DINING ROOM   Phone: (250)656-6622

	7/1-10/31 [ECP]	1P: $139-$339	2P: $139-$339	XP: $30	F12
	5/1-6/30 [ECP]	1P: $139-$279	2P: $139-$279	XP: $30	F12
Small-scale Hotel	3/1-4/30 & 11/1-2/28 [ECP]	1P: $119-$219	2P: $119-$219	XP: $30	F12

Location: Beacon Ave, 2 km n on Resthaven Dr, then 1 km e. 2328 Harbour Rd V8L 2P8. Fax: 250/656-6212. **Facility:** Smoke free premises. 26 units. 15 one-bedroom standard units. 8 one- and 3 two-bedroom suites with efficiencies, some with whirlpools. 2-3 stories, interior corridors. **Bath:** combo or shower only. **Parking:** on-site. **Terms:** office hours 8 am-midnight, 7 day cancellation notice-fee imposed, weekly rates available, package plans, pets ($30 extra charge). **Amenities:** voice mail, irons, hair dryers. *Some:* CD players. **Leisure Activities:** sauna, limited exercise equipment. **Business Services:** meeting rooms. **Cards:** AX, MC, VI.

VICTORIA AIRPORT TRAVELODGE SIDNEY   *Book at aaa.com*   Phone: (250)656-1176

CAA SAVE

| | 5/1-9/30 | 1P: $89-$199 | 2P: $99-$200 | XP: $10 | F16 |
| | 3/1-4/30 & 10/1-2/28 | 1P: $69-$125 | 2P: $79-$135 | XP: $10 | F16 |

Location: Just e of Hwy 17, exit Sidney. 2280 Beacon Ave V8L 1X1. Fax: 250/656-7344. **Facility:** 90 one-bedroom standard units, some with efficiencies. 2-4 stories, interior corridors. **Parking:** on-site. **Terms:** weekly rates available, [CP] meal plan available, package plans, pets ($50 deposit). **Amenities:** voice mail, hair dryers. *Some:* high-speed Internet. **Pool(s):** small heated outdoor. **Guest Services:** valet laundry. **Business Services:** meeting rooms. **Cards:** AX, DC, MC, VI. **Special Amenities:** free continental breakfast and free room upgrade (subject to availability with advance reservations).

222222222222

——— **WHERE TO DINE** ———

BLUE PETER PUB & RESTAURANT **Lunch:** $7-$17   **Dinner:** $7-$17   **Phone:** 250/656-4551

Canadian

Location: Beacon Ave, 2 km n on Resthaven Dr to Harbour Rd, then just e. 2270 Harbour Rd V8L 2P6. **Hours:** 11:30 am-10 pm, Fri & Sat-11 pm. **Features:** This pub located along the wharf has a great view of the harbor. Fresh seafood, steak and pasta are featured, and the laid-back environment offers two sections: one for families with kids and one pub side with a fireplace. Outdoor patio dining in warm weather. Cocktails. **Parking:** on-site. **Cards:** MC, VI.

DEEP COVE CHALET **Lunch:** $15-$25   **Dinner:** $25-$45   **Phone:** 250/656-3541

French

Location: Hwy 17, exit Wain Rd/Deep Cove, 1 km w on Wain Rd, 3 km nw on Tatlow Rd. 11190 Chalet Rd V8L 4R4. **Hours:** 5:30 pm-10 pm, Wed-Sun noon-2:30 pm. **Closed:** 12/24 & Mon. **Reservations:** suggested. **Features:** Visitors and locals alike enjoy this delightful restaurant hidden away in a setting that offers a spectacular view of the inlet. The menu features country French cuisine plus fresh seafood, lamb, ostrich, caribou, wild boar, and a nice variety of wines. Casual dress; cocktails. **Parking:** on-site. **Cards:** AX, MC, VI.

DOCK 503 WATERFRONT CAFE **Lunch:** $7-$10   **Dinner:** $16-$22   **Phone:** 250/656-0828

Canadian

Location: Beacon Ave, 2 km n on Resthaven Dr, then just e. 2320 Harbour Rd V8L 2P6. **Hours:** 11:30 am-2:30 & 5-9 pm. **Closed:** 12/25, 12/26. **Reservations:** suggested. **Features:** In the Van Isle Marina, this quaint restaurant offers great views of the harbor and water. Fresh, local ingredients flavor preparations of Pacific Northwest cuisine, including the signature grilled oysters. The menu changes seasonally, so there's something different for every taste. During the off-season, a coffee service and fresh baked goods replace the morning breakfast. Brunch is served from 8:30 am to 2:30 pm on the weekends. Cocktails. **Parking:** on-site. **Cards:** AX, DC, MC, VI.

SOOKE pop. 8,735

——— **WHERE TO STAY** ———

MARKHAM HOUSE BED & BREAKFAST   *Book at aaa.com*   **Phone:** (250)642-7542

6/16-9/30 [BP]	1P: $95-$215	2P: $115-$215
12/16-2/28 [BP]	1P: $85-$175	2P: $105-$195
3/1-6/15 & 10/1-12/15 [BP]	1P: $85-$175	2P: $95-$185

Bed & Breakfast

Location: 10 km e on Hwy 14. Located in a quiet rural area. 1853 Connie Rd V9C 4C2. Fax: 250/642-7538. **Facility:** This warm Tudor home in a rain forest setting offers golf, hiking and a trout pond for entertainment. Smoke free premises. 4 one-bedroom standard units, some with whirlpools. 2 stories (no elevator), interior corridors. *Bath:* combo or shower only. **Parking:** on-site. **Terms:** 2 night minimum stay - weekends, age restrictions may apply, 7 day cancellation notice-fee imposed, package plans. **Amenities:** video library, CD players, hair dryers. **Leisure Activities:** whirlpool, putting green. **Guest Services:** complimentary laundry. **Cards:** AX, CB, DC, DS, JC, MC, VI. **Special Amenities:** free full breakfast and free local telephone calls.

SOME UNITS

OCEAN WILDERNESS INN & SPA   *Book at aaa.com*   **Phone:** (250)646-2116

5/16-10/15 [BP]	1P: $115-$165	2P: $125-$175	XP: $15
3/1-5/15 & 10/16-2/28 [BP]	1P: $89-$140	2P: $95-$150	XP: $15

Bed & Breakfast

Location: 14 km w on Hwy 14. Located in a secluded area. 109 W Coast Rd V0S 1N0. Fax: 250/646-2317. **Facility:** Smoke free premises. 9 one-bedroom standard units. 2 stories (no elevator), interior/exterior corridors. **Parking:** on-site. **Terms:** office hours 8 am-9 pm, 7 day cancellation notice-fee imposed, package plans, pets ($15 extra charge). **Amenities:** hair dryers. **Leisure Activities:** whirlpool. *Fee:* massage. **Cards:** AX, JC, MC, VI.

FEE

SOOKE HARBOUR HOUSE   **Phone:** (250)642-3421

5/1-10/31	1P: $335-$575	2P: $335-$575	XP: $55	F12
3/1-4/30 & 11/1-2/28	1P: $250-$455	2P: $250-$455	XP: $35	F12

Small-scale Hotel

Location: 2 km w on Hwy 14. 1528 Whiffen Spit Rd V0S 1N0. Fax: 250/642-6988. **Facility:** Smoke free premises. 28 one-bedroom standard units, some with whirlpools. 4 stories, interior/exterior corridors. *Bath:* combo or shower only. **Parking:** on-site. **Terms:** office hours 8 am-1 am, 14 day cancellation notice-fee imposed, package plans, pets ($30 extra charge). **Amenities:** CD players, voice mail, irons, hair dryers. **Dining:** 5:30 pm-9:30 pm, cocktails. **Leisure Activities:** *Fee:* massage. **Guest Services:** gift shop. **Business Services:** meeting rooms. **Cards:** MC, VI.

FEE

This ends listings for the Victoria Vicinity.
The following page resumes the alphabetical listings of
cities in British Columbia.

WESTBANK pop. 15,700

―――――― WHERE TO STAY ――――――

HOLIDAY INN WESTBANK *Book at aaa.com*   Phone: (250)768-8879

6/16-9/30	1P: $122-$155	2P: $122-$155	XP: $10	F18
4/1-6/15	1P: $95-$125	2P: $95-$125	XP: $10	F18
3/1-3/31 & 10/1-2/28	1P: $77-$125	2P: $77-$125	XP: $10	F18

Small-scale Hotel **Location:** Hwy 97 (Dobbin Rd) and Herbert Rd. 2569 Dobbin Rd V4T 2J6. Fax: 250/768-8891. **Facility:** 77 units. 75 one-bedroom standard units, some with whirlpools. 2 two-bedroom suites with kitchens and whirlpools. 3 stories, interior corridors. **Parking:** on-site. **Terms:** pets ($10 fee). **Amenities:** voice mail, irons, hair dryers. **Pool(s):** heated indoor/outdoor. **Leisure Activities:** whirlpool, limited exercise equipment. **Guest Services:** valet laundry. **Business Services:** conference facilities, fax (fee). **Cards:** AX, CB, DC, DS, JC, MC, VI. *(See color ad card insert)*

SOME UNITS
(ASK) (S/D) (🛏) (🕇🕈) (Y) (&M) (≈) (🎥) (DATA PORT) (💻) / (✕) (🔒) (📶)
FEE   FEE   FEE

WICKLOW BY THE LAKE B & B   Phone: (250)768-1330

5/1-11/1 [BP]	1P: $100-$150	2P: $100-$150

Location: Hwy 97, exit Gellantly Rd. 1 km s, 6 km e on Boucherie Rd, then just e. 1454 Green Bay Rd V4T 2B8. Bed & Breakfast Fax: 250/768-1335. **Facility:** Smoke free premises. 4 one-bedroom standard units. 2 stories (no elevator), interior/exterior corridors. *Bath:* some shared or private, combo or shower only. **Parking:** on-site. **Terms:** open 5/1-11/1, 14 day cancellation notice-fee imposed. **Amenities:** hair dryers. *Some:* irons. **Leisure Activities:** boat dock. **Cards:** AX, MC, VI.

SOME UNITS
(ASK) (S/D) (✕) (☎) / (VCR) (💻) /

WEST VANCOUVER —*See Vancouver p. 596.*

WHISTLER pop. 8,896

―――――― WHERE TO STAY ――――――

ALPENGLOW LODGE *Book at aaa.com*   Phone: (604)905-7078

11/25-1/2	1P: $325-$449	2P: $325-$449	XP: $20	F12
3/1-4/30 & 1/3-2/28	1P: $259-$359	2P: $259-$359	XP: $20	F12
5/1-11/24	1P: $149-$209	2P: $149-$209	XP: $20	F12

Small-scale Hotel **Location:** Hwy 99, just n on Village Gate Blvd, just w on Northland Blvd. 4369 Main St V0N 1B4. Fax: 604/905-7053. **Facility:** 84 units. 64 one-bedroom standard units with efficiencies, some with whirlpools. 17 one- and 3 two-bedroom suites with kitchens and whirlpools. 5 stories, interior corridors. **Parking:** on-site (fee). **Terms:** check-in 4 pm, 1-7 night minimum stay - seasonal, 30 day cancellation notice, in winter-fee imposed. **Amenities:** video library (fee), voice mail, irons, hair dryers. **Dining:** Bavaria Restaurant, see separate listing. **Pool(s):** heated outdoor. **Leisure Activities:** sauna, whirlpool, steamroom, limited exercise equipment. **Guest Services:** coin laundry. **Business Services:** meeting rooms. **Cards:** AX, DC, DS, MC, VI.

SOME UNITS
(ASK) (🕇🕈) (≈) (✕) (VCR) (🔒) (🍽) (💻) / (✕) /

BEST WESTERN LISTEL WHISTLER HOTEL *Book at aaa.com*   Phone: (604)932-1133

(CAA) (SAVE)

12/23-1/3	1P: $149-$449	2P: $149-$449	XP: $30	F18
3/1-4/15	1P: $199-$329	2P: $199-$329	XP: $30	F18
1/4-2/28	1P: $129-$329	2P: $129-$329	XP: $30	F18
4/16-12/22	1P: $99-$169	2P: $99-$169	XP: $30	F18

Small-scale Hotel **Location:** Hwy 99, just e on Village Gate Blvd, then follow Whistler Way. 4121 Village Green V0N 1B4. Fax: 604/932-8383. **Facility:** 98 units. 96 one-bedroom standard units. 2 one-bedroom suites ($199-$599) with whirlpools. 3 stories, interior corridors. **Parking:** on-site (fee). **Terms:** check-in 4 pm, cancellation fee imposed, [AP], [BP], [CP] & [MAP] meal plans available, package plans, small pets only ($15 fee, 1st floor units). **Amenities:** video games (fee), voice mail, safes, irons, hair dryers. *Some:* high-speed Internet. **Dining:** Bear Foot Bistro, see separate listing. **Pool(s):** small heated outdoor. **Leisure Activities:** saunas, whirlpool. **Guest Services:** valet and coin laundry. **Business Services:** meeting rooms. **Cards:** AX, CB, DC, DS, JC, MC, VI. **Special Amenities:** free room upgrade and preferred room (each subject to availability with advance reservations).

SOME UNITS
(S/D) (🛏) (🕇🕈) (Y) (≈) (🎥) (DATA PORT) (🔒) (💻) / (✕) (🔒) /
FEE

BLACKCOMB LODGE & SPA *Book at aaa.com*   Phone: (604)932-4155

(CAA) (SAVE)

3/1-3/28 & 2/5-2/28	1P: $197-$260	2P: $197-$260	XP: $20	F18
5/1-2/4	1P: $99-$188	2P: $99-$188	XP: $20	F18
3/29-4/30	1P: $125-$152	2P: $125-$152	XP: $20	F18

Location: Hwy 99, just e on Village Gate Blvd, then just s. 4220 Gateway Dr V0N 1B4. Fax: 604/932-6826. Small-scale Hotel **Facility:** Smoke free premises. 72 one-bedroom units, some with efficiencies. 3 stories, interior corridors. **Parking:** on-site (fee). **Terms:** check-in 4 pm, 30 day cancellation notice-fee imposed, package plans. **Amenities:** DVD players, voice mail, safes, irons, hair dryers. **Pool(s):** heated indoor. **Leisure Activities:** sauna, whirlpool, spa. **Guest Services:** coin laundry. **Business Services:** meeting rooms. **Cards:** AX, MC, VI. **Special Amenities:** free local telephone calls and free room upgrade (subject to availability with advance reservations).

SOME UNITS
(S/D) (🕇🕈) (≈) (✕) (✕) (DATA PORT) (💻) / (🔒) /

CHALET LUISE   Phone: (604)932-4187

6/16-9/15 [BP]	1P: $99-$135	2P: $119-$149	XP: $25	D12
5/1-6/15 & 9/16-11/30 [BP]	1P: $99-$125	2P: $109-$135	XP: $25	D12

Bed & Breakfast **Location:** Hwy 99, exit Nancy Green Dr, follow to Ambassador Crescent. Located in a residential area. 7461 Ambassador Crescent V0N 1B0 (PO Box 352). Fax: 604/938-1531. **Facility:** Smoke free premises. 8 one-bedroom standard units. 2 stories (no elevator), interior corridors. *Bath:* combo or shower only. **Parking:** on-site. **Terms:** open 5/1-11/30, office hours 8 am-10 pm, 2 night minimum stay - weekends, age restrictions may apply, 14 day cancellation notice, in summer-fee imposed, package plans. **Amenities:** hair dryers. **Leisure Activities:** sauna, whirlpool. **Guest Services:** coin laundry. **Cards:** MC, VI.

SOME UNITS
(S/D) (✕) (🍴) (📺) (☎) / (🔒) /

CRYSTAL LODGE *Book at aaa.com*　　　　　　　　　　　　**Phone:** (604)932-2221

	11/19-2/28	1P: $153-$1215	2P: $153-$1215	XP: $25	F12
	3/1-4/2	1P: $260-$1025	2P: $260-$1025	XP: $25	F12
Small-scale Hotel	4/3-11/18	1P: $106-$399	2P: $106-$399	XP: $25	F12

Location: Hwy 99, just e on Village Gate Blvd, then follow Whistler Way. 4154 Village Green V0N 1B0 (PO Box 280). Fax: 604/932-2635. **Facility:** Smoke free premises. 159 units. 145 one-bedroom standard units, some with efficiencies and/or whirlpools. 3 one-, 8 two- and 3 three-bedroom suites, some with whirlpools. 5 stories, interior corridors. **Parking:** on-site (fee). **Terms:** check-in 4 pm, 5 night minimum stay - seasonal, 30 day cancellation notice-fee imposed, pets ($20 extra charge, small dogs only). **Amenities:** video games (fee), voice mail, hair dryers. *Some:* high-speed Internet, safes, irons. **Pool(s):** heated outdoor. **Leisure Activities:** sauna, whirlpool, exercise room. **Guest Services:** valet and coin laundry. **Business Services:** meeting rooms, business center. **Cards:** AX, DC, DS, JC, MC, VI. *(See color ad below)*

SOME UNITS

[🛏 🍴 🍸 🔒M ♿ 🐕 ✕ ✕ 🎬 🖥 📶 / DATA PORT 📠 /]
FEE

DELTA WHISTLER VILLAGE SUITES *Book at aaa.com*　　　　　　**Phone:** (604)905-3987

	11/25-12/31	1P: $209-$1119	2P: $209-$1119	XP: $30	F18
	1/1-2/28	1P: $279-$739	2P: $279-$739	XP: $30	F18
	3/1-4/30	1P: $259-$739	2P: $259-$739	XP: $30	F18
Small-scale Hotel	5/1-11/24	1P: $139-$289	2P: $139-$289	XP: $30	F18

Location: Hwy 99, just e on Village Gate Blvd, just n on Northlands Blvd, then just e. 4308 Main St V0N 1B4. Fax: 604/938-6335. **Facility:** Smoke free premises. 207 units. 135 one- and 72 two-bedroom suites, some with kitchens. 6 stories, interior corridors. **Parking:** on-site (fee) and valet. **Terms:** check-in 4 pm, 5 night minimum stay - seasonal, 30 day cancellation notice, package plans. **Amenities:** video games (fee), voice mail, irons, hair dryers. **Dining:** 10 am-11 pm, cocktails. **Pool(s):** heated outdoor. **Leisure Activities:** sauna, whirlpools, steamrooms, rental bicycles, exercise room. *Fee:* ski equipment. **Business Services:** meeting rooms. **Cards:** AX, CB, DC, DS, JC, MC, VI. *(See color ad below)*

[S/D 🛏 🍴 🍸 🔒M 🐕 ✕ ✕ 🎬 DATA PORT 📠 🖥 📺]
FEE

THE DURLACHER HOF ALPINE INN　　　　　　　　　　　　**Phone:** (604)932-1924

	3/1-3/31 & 12/16-2/28 [BP]	1P: $109-$199	2P: $179-$339	XP: $35	F5
	7/1-12/15 [BP]	1P: $89-$129	2P: $149-$279	XP: $35	F5
Bed & Breakfast	4/1-6/30 [BP]	1P: $89-$109	2P: $129-$249	XP: $35	F5

Location: 1.5 km n on Hwy 99. 7055 Nesters Rd V0N 1B7. Fax: 604/938-1980. **Facility:** Goose-down duvets and hand-carved pine furniture are featured in guest rooms at this service-oriented inn. Smoke free premises. 8 one-bedroom standard units, some with whirlpools. 3 stories (no elevator), interior corridors. **Bath:** combo or shower only. **Parking:** on-site. **Terms:** office hours 9 am-10 pm, age restrictions may apply, 14 day cancellation notice, in summer, 30 day in winter-fee imposed, [AP] & [MAP] meal plans available, package plans. **Amenities:** hair dryers. **Leisure Activities:** sauna, whirlpool. **Cards:** MC, VI.

SOME UNITS

[ASK 🔒M ♿ ✕ 🎿 📺 🅿 / 📠 /]

EDGEWATER LODGE

Motel

Phone: (604)932-0688

All Year [ECP]   1P: $125-$320   2P: $125-$320   XP: $25   F8

Location: 4 km n of Whistler Village via Hwy 99, e on Alpine Way. 8030 Alpine Way V0N 1B0 (PO Box 369). Fax: 604/932-0686. **Facility:** Smoke free premises. 12 one-bedroom standard units. 1 story, exterior corridors. *Bath:* combo or shower only. **Parking:** on-site. **Terms:** office hours 8 am-10 pm, 2 night minimum stay - weekends, age restrictions may apply, 14 day cancellation notice-fee imposed, small pets only ($20 extra charge). **Dining:** 5:30 pm-9 pm for guests & public, reservations recommended, cocktails. **Leisure Activities:** whirlpool. **Cards:** AX, MC, VI. **Special Amenities: free expanded continental breakfast and free newspaper.**

(See color ad below)

FEE

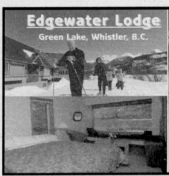

THE FAIRMONT CHATEAU WHISTLER   *Book at aaa.com*   Phone: (604)938-8000

(CAA) (SAVE)

12/17-2/28	1P: $359-$899	2P: $359-$899	XP: $30 F18
3/1-4/22	1P: $269-$548	2P: $269-$548	XP: $30 F18
4/23-12/16	1P: $165-$359	2P: $165-$359	XP: $30 F18

Location: Hwy 99, 1 km e on Lorimer Rd (Upper Village), then just w on Blackcomb Way. 4599 Chateau Blvd V0N 1B4.
Large-scale Hotel Fax: 604/938-2055. **Facility:** Added amenities are featured at this property, which is in a prime skiing area; a spa and a golf course are on site. 550 units. 490 one-bedroom standard units, some with whirlpools. 55 one- and 5 two-bedroom suites, some with whirlpools. 12 stories, interior corridors. **Parking:** on-site (fee) and valet. **Terms:** check-in 4 pm, 2 night minimum stay - seasonal, 30 day cancellation notice-fee imposed, small pets only ($25 extra charge). **Amenities:** video games (fee), voice mail, safes, honor bars, irons, hair dryers. *Some:* CD players, high-speed Internet. **Dining:** 2 restaurants, 7 am-11 pm, cocktails, also, The Wildflower, see separate listing, entertainment. **Pool(s):** 2 heated outdoor. **Leisure Activities:** sauna, whirlpools, steamrooms, 3 tennis courts, jogging, spa. *Fee:* golf-18 holes, tennis instruction, ski & sports equipment. **Guest Services:** gift shop, valet and coin laundry. **Business Services:** conference facilities, business center. **Cards:** AX, DC, DS, MC, VI. *(See color ad p 638)*

SOME UNITS

FOUR SEASONS RESORT WHISTLER   *Book at aaa.com*   Phone: (604)935-3400

12/17-2/28	1P: $570-$690	2P: $570-$690	XP: $30 F17
3/1-4/15	1P: $545-$665	2P: $545-$665	XP: $30 F17
9/13-12/16	1P: $275-$375	2P: $275-$375	XP: $30 F17
4/16-9/12	1P: $245-$375	2P: $245-$375	XP: $30 F17

Large-scale Hotel **Location:** Hwy 99, 1 km e on Lorimer Rd (Upper Village). 4591 Blackcomb Way V0N 1B4. Fax: 604/966-2683. **Facility:** This new lodging near Blackcomb Mountain offers handsome guest rooms warmly decorated in rich wood accents. 242 units. 147 one-bedroom standard units, 63 one-, 30 two- and 2 three-bedroom suites, some with kitchens and/or whirlpools. 6-9 stories, interior corridors. **Parking:** on-site (fee) and valet. **Terms:** 7 night minimum stay - seasonal, cancellation fee imposed, package plans, small pets only. **Amenities:** video library, DVD players, video games (fee), CD players, high-speed Internet, dual phone lines, voice mail, safes, honor bars, irons, hair dryers. **Dining:** Fifty Two 80 Bistro & Bar, see separate listing. **Pool(s):** heated outdoor. **Leisure Activities:** whirlpools, steamrooms, rental bicycles, jogging, spa. **Guest Services:** gift shop, valet laundry, area transportation. **Business Services:** meeting rooms, business center. **Cards:** AX, DC, JC, MC, VI.

SOME UNITS

HOLIDAY INN SUNSPREE RESORT WHISTLER
VILLAGE CENTRE   Phone: (604)938-0878

(CAA) (SAVE)

3/1-4/30	1P: $199-$499	2P: $199-$499	XP: $25 F19
11/22-2/28	1P: $159-$499	2P: $159-$499	XP: $25 F19
5/1-11/21	1P: $119-$229	2P: $119-$229	XP: $25 F19

Location: Hwy 99, just e on Village Gate Blvd. 4295 Blackcomb Way V0N 1B4. Fax: 604/938-9943. **Facility:** 115
Small-scale Hotel units. 105 one- and 10 two-bedroom standard units with whirlpools, some with efficiencies or kitchens. 6 stories, interior corridors. **Parking:** on-site (fee). **Terms:** check-in 4 pm, 2-7 night minimum stay - seasonal, 30 day cancellation notice, 11/16-2/28-fee imposed. **Amenities:** video games (fee), high-speed Internet, voice mail, irons, hair dryers. **Leisure Activities:** whirlpool, limited exercise equipment. **Guest Services:** valet laundry. **Cards:** AX, DC, DS, MC, VI. **Special Amenities:** free local telephone calls. *(See color ad card insert & below)*

SOME UNITS

LE CHAMOIS   *Book at aaa.com*   Phone: (604)932-8700

11/24-2/28		2P: $219-$559	XP: $20 F12
3/1-4/2		2P: $359-$479	XP: $20 F12
4/3-11/23		2P: $139-$299	XP: $20 F12

Small-scale Hotel **Location:** Hwy 99, 1 km e on Lorimer Rd (Upper Village), then just w. 4557 Blackcomb Way V0N 1B0. Fax: 604/905-2576. **Facility:** Smoke free premises. 50 units. 46 one-bedroom standard units, some with whirlpools. 4 three-bedroom suites with kitchens, some with whirlpools. 6 stories, interior corridors. **Parking:** on-site (fee). **Terms:** check-in 4 pm, 2 night minimum stay - seasonal, 30 day cancellation notice-fee imposed, $8 service charge. **Amenities:** video library (fee), voice mail, irons, hair dryers. **Pool(s):** small heated outdoor. **Leisure Activities:** whirlpool. **Guest Services:** coin laundry. **Business Services:** meeting rooms. **Cards:** AX, MC, VI.

LOST LAKE LODGE   *Book at aaa.com*

▼▼◇◇◇   **Phone:** (604)905-7631

	11/25-1/2	1P: $309-$409	2P: $309-$409	XP: $20	F12
	3/1-4/30 & 1/3-2/28	1P: $249-$329	2P: $249-$329	XP: $20	F12
Condominium	5/1-11/24	1P: $149-$209	2P: $149-$209	XP: $20	F12

Location: Hwy 99, 1 km e on Lorimer Rd (Upper Village), 1 km ne. 4660 Blackcomb Way V0N 1B4. Fax: 604-905-0365. **Facility:** Situated in a quiet residential area closer to Blackcomb Mountain, these are very modern and wonderfully decorated condos. Smoke free premises. 75 units. 57 one- and 18 two-bedroom suites with kitchens. 5 stories, interior corridors. **Parking:** on-site (fee). **Terms:** office hours 8 am-8 pm, check-in 4 pm, 1-7 night minimum stay - seasonal, 30 day cancellation notice, in winter-fee imposed. **Amenities:** video library (fee), voice mail, irons, hair dryers. **Pool(s):** heated outdoor. **Leisure Activities:** whirlpool, limited exercise equipment. **Business Services:** meeting rooms. **Cards:** AX, DC, DS, JC, MC, VI.

(ASK) 🛏 ✕ (AC) (VCR) 🎥 (DATA PORT) 🖥 🖨 🖵

PAN PACIFIC WHISTLER MOUNTAINSIDE

(CAA) (SAVE)   **Phone:** (604)905-2999

▼▼◇◇◇

	11/25-1/2	1P: $749-$1209	2P: $749-$1209	XP: $30	F17
	3/1-4/30 & 1/3-2/28	1P: $559-$1059	2P: $559-$1059	XP: $30	F17
Large-scale Hotel	5/1-11/24	1P: $289-$389	2P: $289-$389	XP: $30	F17

Location: Hwy 99, just e on Village Gate Blvd, then just s on Blackcomb Way. 4320 Sundial Cresent V0N 1B4. Fax: 604-905-2995. **Facility:** Smoke free premises. 121 units. 96 one- and 25 two-bedroom suites with kitchens. 8 stories, interior corridors. **Parking:** on-site (fee) and valet. **Terms:** 30 day cancellation notice, 7 day in summer-fee imposed. **Amenities:** video games (fee), high-speed Internet, dual phone lines, voice mail, safes, irons, hair dryers. **Dining:** 7 am-11 pm, cocktails. **Pool(s):** heated outdoor. **Leisure Activities:** whirlpools, steamroom, limited exercise equipment. **Guest Services:** valet and coin laundry, area transportation-within Whistler Village. **Business Services:** meeting rooms. **Cards:** AX, DC, MC, VI. **Special Amenities:** free local telephone calls and free newspaper.

🍴 (&M) 🛏 (✕) ✕ 🎥 (DATA PORT) 🖥 🖨 🖵

PAN PACIFIC WHISTLER VILLAGE CENTRE

(fyi)   **Phone:** 604/905-2999

	11/25-1/2 [AP]	1P: $749-$1999	2P: $749-$1999	XP: $30	F17
	3/1-4/30 & 1/3-2/28 [AP]	1P: $559-$1999	2P: $559-$1999	XP: $30	F17
Small-scale Hotel	5/1-11/24 [AP]	1P: $289-$649	2P: $289-$649	XP: $30	F17

Too new to rate, opening scheduled for December 2004. **Location:** Hwy 99, just e on Village Gate Blvd. 4295 Blackcomb Way V0N 1B4. Fax: 604-905-2995. **Amenities:** 83 units, restaurant, coffeemakers, microwaves, refrigerators, pool. **Terms:** 30 day cancellation notice-fee imposed. **Cards:** AX, DC, MC, VI.

RESIDENCE INN BY MARRIOTT   *Book at aaa.com*

▼▼◇◇◇   **Phone:** (604)905-3400

	11/25-1/2 [ECP]	1P: $499-$559	2P: $499-$559	XP: $20	F12
	3/1-4/30 & 1/3-2/28 [ECP]	1P: $399-$529	2P: $399-$529	XP: $20	F12
Condominium	5/1-11/24 [ECP]	1P: $159-$189	2P: $159-$189	XP: $20	F12

Location: Hwy 99, 1 km e on Lorimer Rd (Upper Village), just se on Blackcomb Way, then just w, follow road all the way to the end. 4899 Painted Cliff Rd V0N 1B4. Fax: 604-905-3432. **Facility:** Fully self-contained condo units on Blackcomb Mountain include studios and one- or two-bedroom units, all with gas fireplaces. Smoke free premises. 186 units. 141 one- and 45 two-bedroom suites with kitchens. 6 stories, interior corridors. **Parking:** on-site (fee). **Terms:** check-in 4 pm, 1-7 night minimum stay - seasonal, 30 day cancellation notice, in winter-fee imposed, pets ($25 extra charge). **Amenities:** video library (fee), voice mail, irons, hair dryers. **Pool(s):** heated outdoor. **Leisure Activities:** whirlpools, limited exercise equipment. **Guest Services:** coin laundry. **Business Services:** meeting rooms. **Cards:** AX, DC, DS, MC, VI.

(ASK) 🛏 🛏 ✕ (AC) (VCR) (DATA PORT) 🖥 🖨 🖵
FEE

SUMMIT LODGE & SPA   *Book at aaa.com*

(CAA) (SAVE)   **Phone:** (604)932-2778

▼▼◇◇◇

	3/1-3/31	1P: $275-$725	2P: $275-$725	XP: $30	F17
	11/21-2/28	1P: $169-$725	2P: $169-$725	XP: $30	F17
Small-scale Hotel	4/1-11/20	1P: $139-$345	2P: $139-$345	XP: $30	F17

Location: Hwy 99, just n on Village Gate Blvd, just w on Northlands Blvd. 4359 Main St V0N 1B4. Fax: 604-932-2716. **Facility:** 81 units. 75 one-bedroom standard units with efficiencies. 6 one-bedroom suites with efficiencies. 5 stories, interior corridors. **Parking:** on-site (fee). **Terms:** check-in 4 pm, 3 night minimum stay - seasonal and/or weekends, 30 day cancellation notice-fee imposed, package plans, small pets only ($15 extra charge). **Amenities:** high-speed Internet, voice mail, irons, hair dryers. **Pool(s):** small heated outdoor. **Leisure Activities:** sauna, whirlpool, spa. **Guest Services:** valet and coin laundry. **Business Services:** meeting rooms. **Cards:** AX, DC, DS, MC, VI. **Special Amenities:** free newspaper and early check-in/late check-out.

(S/D) 🛏 🛏 ✕ 🎥 (DATA PORT) 🖥 🖨 🖵   SOME UNITS
FEE   /(✕)/

SUNDIAL BOUTIQUE HOTEL   *Book at aaa.com*

▼▼◇◇◇   **Phone:** (604)932-2321

	12/24-2/28	1P: $449-$949	2P: $449-$949	XP: $20	F18
	3/1-3/26	1P: $599-$849	2P: $599-$849	XP: $20	F18
	3/27-4/30	1P: $249-$499	2P: $249-$499	XP: $20	F18
Small-scale Hotel	5/1-12/23	1P: $199-$499	2P: $199-$499	XP: $20	F18

Location: Hwy 99, just e on Village Gate Blvd, then just s on Blackcomb Way. 4340 Sundial Cir V0N 1B4. Fax: 604-935-0554. **Facility:** Smoke free premises. 49 units. 27 one- and 22 two-bedroom suites with kitchens, some with whirlpools. 6 stories, interior corridors. **Parking:** on-site (fee). **Terms:** 2 night minimum stay, 45 day cancellation notice-fee imposed, package plans, pets ($30 extra charge). **Amenities:** high-speed Internet, voice mail, safes, irons, hair dryers. **Leisure Activities:** whirlpool. **Guest Services:** coin laundry. **Cards:** AX, MC, VI.

(ASK) (S/D) 🛏 🍴 (&M) ✕ 🎥 (DATA PORT) 🖥 🖨 🖵
FEE

TANTALUS RESORT LODGE   *Book at aaa.com*

(CAA) (SAVE)   **Phone:** (604)932-4146

▼▼◇◇◇

	11/23-2/28	1P: $199-$799	2P: $199-$799	XP: $20	F17
	3/1-4/30	1P: $199-$649	2P: $199-$649	XP: $20	F17
Condominium	5/1-11/22	1P: $119-$299	2P: $119-$299	XP: $20	F17

Location: Hwy 99, just e on Village Gate Blvd, then follow Whistler Way to the end. 4200 Whistler Way V0N 1B4. Fax: 604/932-2405. **Facility:** Smoke free premises. 76 two-bedroom suites with kitchens. 5 stories, interior corridors. **Parking:** on-site (fee). **Terms:** check-in 4 pm, cancellation fee imposed, pets ($15 extra charge). **Amenities:** video games (fee), voice mail, hair dryers. **Pool(s):** heated outdoor. **Leisure Activities:** whirlpools, 2 tennis courts, barbecue area, playground, volleyball. **Guest Services:** coin laundry, area transportation-ski shuttle, in winter. **Business Services:** meeting rooms, PC (fee). **Cards:** AX, DC, MC, VI.

(S/D) 🛏 🛏 ✕ ✕ (AC) 🎥 🖥 🖨 🖵
FEE

TOWN PLAZA SUITES *Book at aaa.com*　　　　　　　　　　　　　　　　　Phone: (604)905-0116

	11/25-1/2	1P: $325-$449	2P: $325-$449	XP: $20	F12
	3/1-4/30 & 1/3-2/28	1P: $259-$359	2P: $259-$359	XP: $20	F12
Condominium	5/1-11/24	1P: $149-$209	2P: $149-$209	XP: $20	F12

Location: Hwy 99, just e on Village Gate Blvd, just n on Northlands Blvd, then just e. 4314 Main St V0N 1B0. Fax: 604/905-0117. **Facility:** Smoke free premises. 51 units. 7 one-bedroom standard units with kitchens. 26 one- and 18 two-bedroom suites with kitchens. 3 stories, interior corridors. **Parking:** on-site (fee). **Terms:** check-in 4 pm, 1-7 night minimum stay - seasonal, 30 day cancellation notice, in winter-fee imposed. **Amenities:** video library (fee), voice mail, irons, hair dryers. **Leisure Activities:** whirlpool, limited exercise equipment. **Guest Services:** complimentary laundry. **Cards:** AX, DC, DS, MC, VI.

SOME UNITS

(ASK) (TI+) (X) (VCR) (DATA PORT) 🖥 🖨 🖵 / (AC) /

THE WESTIN RESORT & SPA *Book at aaa.com*　　　　　　　　　　　　　Phone: (604)905-5000

(CAA) (SAVE)

	12/26-2/28	1P: $199-$799	2P: $199-$799	XP: $30	F18
	3/1-3/28	1P: $199-$499	2P: $199-$499	XP: $30	F18
	11/25-12/25	1P: $199-$399	2P: $199-$399	XP: $30	F18
	3/29-11/24	1P: $149-$199	2P: $149-$199	XP: $30	F18

Large-scale Hotel **Location:** Hwy 99, just e on Village Gate Blvd, then s on Whistler Way. 4090 Whistler Way V0N 1B4. Fax: 604/905-5640. **Facility:** Whistler's upscale hotel is both rustic and chic, and includes shops, meeting rooms, a spa and a health club, all close to Whistler Mountain. Smoke free premises. 419 units. 401 one-, 14 two- and 4 three-bedroom suites, some with efficiencies, kitchens and/or whirlpools. 11 stories, interior corridors. **Parking:** on-site (fee) and valet. **Terms:** check-in 4 pm, 3-7 night minimum stay - seasonal, 7 day cancellation notice-fee imposed, package plans. **Amenities:** video games (fee), high-speed Internet, dual phone lines, voice mail, safes, honor bars, irons, hair dryers. **Dining:** The Aubergine Grille, see separate listing. **Pool(s):** heated outdoor. **Leisure Activities:** sauna, whirlpools, steamrooms, spa. **Business Services:** conference facilities. **Cards:** AX, DC, MC, VI. *(See color ad p 5)*

(S D) (TI) (24TI) (Y) (fi) (&M) (≈) (wm) (X) (X) (⌖) (DATA PORT) 🖥 🖨 🖵
FEE

WHISTLER CASCADE LODGE　　　　　　　　　　　　　　　　　　　　Phone: (604)905-4875

	11/25-1/2	1P: $349-$485	2P: $349-$485	XP: $20	F12
	3/1-4/30 & 1/3-2/28	1P: $279-$389	2P: $279-$389	XP: $20	F12
Condominium	5/1-11/24	1P: $159-$209	2P: $159-$209	XP: $20	F12

Location: Hwy 99, just e on Village Gate Blvd, then just n. 4315 Northlands Blvd V0N 1B0. Fax: 604/905-4089. **Facility:** Smoke free premises. 112 units. 65 one-bedroom standard units with efficiencies. 45 one- and 2 two-bedroom suites with kitchens. 6 stories, interior corridors. **Parking:** on-site (fee). **Terms:** check-in 4 pm, 1-7 night minimum stay - seasonal, 30 day cancellation notice, in winter-fee imposed. **Amenities:** video library (fee), voice mail, irons, hair dryers. **Pool(s):** heated outdoor. **Leisure Activities:** saunas, whirlpools, limited exercise equipment. **Guest Services:** coin laundry. **Business Services:** meeting rooms. **Cards:** AX, DC, DS, JC, MC, VI.

(ASK) (TI+) (≈) (X) (X) (VCR) (DATA PORT) 🖥 🖨 🖵

WHISTLER VILLAGE INN & SUITES *Book at aaa.com*　　　　　　　　Phone: (604)932-4004

(CAA) (SAVE)

	11/16-2/28 [ECP]	1P: $269-$329	2P: $269-$329	XP: $20	F12
	3/1-3/31 [ECP]	1P: $239-$289	2P: $239-$289	XP: $20	F12
	4/1-4/30 [ECP]	1P: $199-$249	2P: $199-$249	XP: $20	F12
	5/1-11/15 [ECP]	1P: $129-$179	2P: $129-$179	XP: $20	F12

Small-scale Hotel **Location:** Hwy 99, just e on Village Gate Blvd, then just s on Blackcomb Way to Sundial Pl. 4429 Sundial Pl V0N 1B4. Fax: 604/932-3487. **Facility:** 87 units. 83 one-bedroom standard units, some with efficiencies. 4 one-bedroom suites with efficiencies. 3 stories, interior corridors. **Parking:** on-site (fee). **Terms:** check-in 4 pm, 2 night minimum stay - weekends, 30 day cancellation notice, 14 day notice in summer-fee imposed. **Amenities:** voice mail, hair dryers. **Pool(s):** heated outdoor. **Leisure Activities:** saunas, whirlpools, limited exercise equipment. **Guest Services:** valet and coin laundry. **Business Services:** meeting rooms. **Cards:** AX, DC, DS, MC, VI. **Special Amenities:** free expanded continental breakfast and free newspaper. *(See color ad below)*

SOME UNITS

(S D) (TI+) (&M) (≈) (X) (VCR) (DATA PORT) 🖵 / (X) 🖥 🖨 /

WHISTLER VILLAGE RESORT
Phone: (604)932-1982

[fyi]	12/16-1/1	1P: $399-$999	2P: $399-$999	XP: $50 F18
	3/1-4/25 & 1/2-2/28	1P: $299-$799	2P: $299-$799	XP: $30 F18
Large-scale Hotel	4/26-12/15	1P: $139-$399	2P: $139-$399	XP: $30 F18

Under major renovation, scheduled to be completed December 2005. **Last rated:** ▼▼▼ **Location:** Hwy 99, just e on Village Gate Blvd, then follow Whistler Way. 4050 Whistler Way V0N 1B4. Fax: 604/932-7332. **Facility:** 288 units. 264 one-bedroom standard units, some with efficiencies and/or whirlpools. 24 one-bedroom suites with whirlpools, some with efficiencies. 8 stories, interior corridors. **Parking:** on-site (fee) and valet. **Terms:** check-in 4 pm; package plans, pets ($20 extra charge). **Amenities:** video games (fee), voice mail, safes, irons, hair dryers. **Pool(s):** heated outdoor. **Leisure Activities:** sauna, whirlpools, rental bicycles, exercise room. **Guest Services:** gift shop, valet and coin laundry. **Business Services:** conference facilities, business center. **Cards:** AX, DC, JC, MC, VI.

SOME UNITS

[ASK] [S/D] [FEE] [🐾] [🍴] [🍸] [&M] [🛢] [🔁] [🗙] [🎦] [DATA PORT] [💻] / [🗙] /

WOODRUN LODGE
Phone: (604)932-6699

▼▼▼	12/1-1/5	1P: $245-$990
	1/6-2/28	1P: $285-$885
	3/1-4/30	1P: $325-$785
Condominium	5/1-11/30	1P: $158-$399

Location: Hwy 99, 1 km e on Lorimer Rd (Upper Village), just se on Blackcomb Way, then just w. 4910 Spearhead Dr V0N 1B0 (PO Box 1383). Fax: 604/932-6622. **Facility:** The property offers self-contained condo units on Blackcomb Mountain, all with washer/dryer; some of the two-bedroom units feature an extra den. Smoke free premises. 40 units. 13 one-, 25 two- and 2 three-bedroom suites with kitchens. 6 stories, interior corridors. **Parking:** on-site. **Terms:** office hours 8 am-8 pm, check-in 4 pm, 2-7 night minimum stay - seasonal, cancellation fee imposed, package plans. **Amenities:** video library (fee), CD players, safes, irons, hair dryers. **Pool(s):** heated outdoor. **Leisure Activities:** whirlpool, limited exercise equipment. **Cards:** AX, DS, MC, VI.

[ASK] [&M] [🔁] [🗙] [🎦] [VCR] [🛢] [📠] [💻]

─────── WHERE TO DINE ───────

ARAXI
Lunch: $10-$15   Dinner: $20-$35   Phone: 604/932-4540

▼▲▼▲▼

Italian

Location: Whistler Village Square, by the Blackcomb Lodge. 4222 Village Square V0N 1B4. **Hours:** 11 am-3 & 5-11 pm; from 5 pm 9/30-5/31. **Reservations:** suggested. **Features:** You'll enjoy Araxi's exceptionally diverse and creative menu that includes tuna tartare, tofino salmon filet and smoked pork loin. They also have an impressive wine list and enticing desserts. The vibrant and theatrical atmosphere has summer patio dining.
Casual dress; cocktails. **Parking:** on-site (fee). **Cards:** AX, DC, JC, MC, VI.

[🎦] [🗙]

THE AUBERGINE GRILLE
Lunch: $10-$18   Dinner: $20-$32   Phone: 604/905-5000

▼▲▼▲▼

Steak & Seafood

Location: Hwy 99, just e on Village Gate Blvd, then s on Whistler Way; in The Westin Resort & Spa. 4090 Whistler Way V0N 1B4. **Hours:** 7 am-10 pm. **Reservations:** suggested, dinner, winter. **Features:** French for "eggplant," Aubergine houses a show kitchen where guests can watch chefs assemble breakfast, lunch and dinner selections. The eclectic menu centers on West Coast seafood, including British Columbia salmon, but it also lists such comfort foods as steak, pizza and pasta. Casual dress; cocktails. **Parking:** on-site (fee) and valet. **Cards:** AX, DC, DS, JC, MC, VI.

[🗙]

BAVARIA RESTAURANT
Dinner: $22-$35   Phone: 604/932-7518

▼▲▼▲▼ ▼

German

Location: Hwy 99, just n on Village Gate Blvd, just w on Northland Blvd; in Alpenglow Lodge. 4369 Main St V0N 1B4. **Hours:** 5:30 pm-10 pm. **Reservations:** suggested. **Features:** Enjoy true German cuisine featuring German beers and schnapps, pork or veal schnitzels and fondues. Try their three course dinner which includes appetizer, choice of schnitzel and dessert. Casual dress; cocktails. **Parking:** on-site (fee). **Cards:** AX, MC, VI.

[🗙]

BEAR FOOT BISTRO
Dinner: $85-$135   Phone: 604/932-3433

(CAA)

▼▲▼▲▼

Continental

Location: Hwy 99, just e on Village Gate Blvd, then follow Whistler Way; in Best Western Listel Whistler Hotel. 4121 Village Green V0N 1B4. **Hours:** 5:30 pm-10 pm. **Reservations:** suggested. **Features:** The bistro features what is reputed to be the city's largest wine cellar, with more than 1,100 bottles. The dining room's strictly table d'hote menu lists a three-course meal at $40 summer and $85 winter and a five-course meal at $75 summer and $125 winter. Those not inclined to eat in the dining room can visit the wine bar, where meals often are served with by-the-glass wines, or the cigar room, which features cigars from around the world.
Casual dress; cocktails. **Parking:** valet. **Cards:** AX, DC, MC, VI.

[🍸] [🗙]

BREW HOUSE
Lunch: $8-$12   Dinner: $12-$30   Phone: 604/905-2739

▼▲▼▲▼

Canadian

Location: Hwy 99, 1 km e on Lorimer Rd (Upper Village), then just w. 4355 Blackcomb Way V0N 1B4. **Hours:** 11:30 am-midnight, Thurs-Sat to 1 am. **Reservations:** suggested. **Features:** This "brewpub" brews beer solely for consumption on the premises. There are six flagship brews which are always available, their menu features a fine selection of pizza, pasta and rotisserie foods chosen to go with their fine selection of beers. Casual dress; cocktails. **Parking:** on-site (fee). **Cards:** AX, MC, VI.

[🍸] [🗙]

FIFTY TWO 80 BISTRO & BAR
Lunch: $12-$22   Dinner: $18-$40   Phone: 604/966-5280

▼▲▼▲▼

Seafood

Location: Hwy 99, 1 km e on Lorimer Rd (Upper Village); in Four Seasons Resort Whistler. 4591 Blackcomb Way V0N 1B4. **Hours:** 6:30 am-10 pm. **Reservations:** suggested. **Features:** The restaurant is named for the number of feet in the vertical mile that can be skied on Blackcomb Mountain. The casual bistro welcomes guests for breakfast, lunch and dinner. British Columbia wines match with items from the seafood bar, including freshly shucked oysters, crab, lobster and prawns. Stylish, casual resort wear is recommended for evenings. Casual dress; cocktails. **Parking:** on-site and valet. **Cards:** AX, CB, DC, DS, JC, MC, VI.

[🍸] [🗙]

LABOCCA RESTAURANT & BAR
◆◇◇ ◆◇◇
Continental

Lunch: $7-$11   **Dinner:** $15-$25   **Phone:** 604/932-2112
Location: In Whistler Village Square. Whistler Village Square V0N 1B0. **Hours:** 10 am-11 pm. **Reservations:** suggested, ski season. **Features:** This restaurant is busy and popular with both the young and mature. The menu features fondue, rack of lamb, pizza, pasta and wok cooking—a real mix of different items to suit almost every taste. The huge outdoor patio is open during the summer. Casual dress; cocktails. **Parking:** no self-parking. **Cards:** MC, VI.
🗙

LA RUA RESTAURANTE
◆◇◇ ◆◇◇
Continental

Dinner: $28-$42   **Phone:** 604/932-5011
Location: Hwy 99, 1 km e on Lorimer Rd (Upper Village), then just w; in Le Chamois Hotel. 4557 Blackcomb Way V0N 1B0. **Hours:** 6 pm-10 pm. **Reservations:** required. **Features:** In the Upper Village, the wonderful restaurant affords wonderful views of Blackcomb Mountain. This place is known for its wild game and fish. Complimentary parking is available in Le Chamois Hotel. Casual dress; cocktails. **Parking:** on-site. **Cards:** AX, DC, MC, VI.
🍴 🗙

QUATTRO AT WHISTLER
◆◇◇ ◆◇◇
Italian

Dinner: $20-$34   **Phone:** 604/905-4844
Location: Hwy 99, just e on Village Gate Blvd, then just n on Northlands Blvd. 4319 Main St V0N 1B4. **Hours:** 5:30 pm-10 pm. **Reservations:** suggested. **Features:** Next to Pinnacle International Resort, the restaurant offers a cozy atmosphere and a wonderful wine list that represents several regions and includes some reasonably priced selections. Adventurous diners might try Fraser Valley duck, rack of lamb, pan-seared beef tenderloin, baked salmon wrapped in phyllo pastry or pazza a pezzi—a combination of five pastas. Two-hour free parking is available in the lot next to Whistler Public Library. Cocktails. **Parking:** on-site. **Cards:** AX, DC, MC, VI.
🍸 🗙

RIMROCK CAFE
◆◇◇ ◆◇◇
Seafood

Dinner: $28-$45   **Phone:** 604/932-5565
Location: From Whistler Village (Village Gate Blvd), 3.5 km s on Hwy 99, just e on Whistler Rd; in The Highland Lodge. 2117 Whistler Rd V0N 1B0. **Hours:** Open 3/1-10/20 & 11/21-2/28; 6 pm-9:30 pm. **Reservations:** required. **Features:** The hidden gem may be hard to find, but the locals know and love this place. Open for dinner, the restaurant serves many seafood items, including swordfish, salmon and halibut, in addition to an interesting selection of such wild game as buffalo and grilled caribou. Reservations are a must at this spot, which is well worth the jog outside of Whistler township. Casual dress; cocktails. **Parking:** on-site. **Cards:** AX, DC, MC, VI.
🍴 🗙

SUSHI VILLAGE JAPANESE CUISINE
ⓐ
◆◇◇ ◆◇◇
Japanese

Lunch: $7-$15   **Dinner:** $12-$35   **Phone:** 604/932-3330
Location: In Westbrook Whistler Hotel, Whistler Village. 4272 Mountain Sq V0N 1B4. **Hours:** 5:30 pm-10 pm, Thurs-Sun noon-2:30 pm; 5:30 pm-10 pm, Wed-Sun from 5 pm 12/1-4/30. **Features:** Located opposite the Blackcomb Gondola, this restaurant specializes in fresh, tasty sushi and sashimi. They also have tatami rooms for small or large groups. The relaxed and friendly setting was one of the original six restaurants in Whistler. Features green salad, steamed rice, steamed vegatables and ice cream. Casual dress; cocktails. **Parking:** on-site (fee). **Cards:** AX, DC, JC, MC, VI.
🗙

VAL D'ISERE
◆◇◇ ◆◇◇
French

Dinner: $15-$25   **Phone:** 604/932-4666
Location: In Whistler Village North, Bear Lodge, Town Plaza. #8-4314 Main St V0N 1B0. **Hours:** 2 pm-10 pm; from 5 pm 11/15-5/1. **Reservations:** suggested. **Features:** The French brasserie is a must-stop. West Coast touches punctuate the wonderfully creative European menu. Casual comfort food is "simply French." Guests should ask about the daily specials and remarkable wine list. Patio seating is a great option in summer. Cocktails. **Parking:** on-site (fee). **Cards:** AX, DC, JC, MC, VI.
🍴 🗙

THE WILDFLOWER
ⓐ
◆◇◇ ◆◇◇
Pacific Rim

Dinner: $25-$42   **Phone:** 604/938-2033
Location: Hwy 99, 1 km e on Lorimer Rd (Upper Village), then just w on Blackcomb Way; in The Fairmont Chateau Whistler. 4599 Chateau Blvd V0N 1B4. **Hours:** 6 pm-10 pm. **Reservations:** required. **Features:** Adjacent to the Great Hall, the restaurant boasts views of both Blackcomb and Whistler mountains. Combinations of fresh, organic and local produce re-create the flavors of the Pacific Northwest. This place is open only for dinner and Sunday brunch, for which reservations are highly recommended. Dressy casual; cocktails. **Parking:** on-site (fee) and valet. **Cards:** AX, DC, DS, JC, MC, VI.
🍸 🗙

ZEUSKI'S MEDITERRANEAN CUISINE
◆◇◇ ◆◇◇
Mediterranean

Lunch: $9-$12   **Dinner:** $13-$30   **Phone:** 604/932-6009
Location: In Whistler Village North; just n of Village Gate Blvd. 40 4314 Main St V0N 1B4. **Hours:** 11:30 am-11 pm. Closed: 12/25. **Reservations:** suggested. **Features:** The fun, cozy restaurant prepares an extensive selection of Mediterranean dishes, including roasted breast of chicken, salmon exohiko and baklava, plus good cheesecake. Patrons can park for two hours at no cost in the nearby public library/Whistler museum lot; otherwise, pay parking is on the street. Casual dress; cocktails. **Parking:** on-site (fee). **Cards:** AX, DC, MC, VI.
🍸 🍴 🗙

WHITE ROCK —See Vancouver p. 596.

WILLIAMS LAKE pop. 11,153

———— **WHERE TO STAY** ————

DRUMMOND LODGE MOTEL
◆◇◇ ◆◇◇
Motel

Phone: 250/392-5334

	1P:	2P:	XP:
5/1-10/31 [CP]	$74-$95	$80-$114	$5
3/1-4/30 [CP]	$69-$89	$75-$109	$5
11/1-2/28 [CP]	$64-$80	$69-$101	$5

Location: 1 km s on Hwy 97. 1405 Cariboo Hwy V2G 2W3. Fax: 250/392-1117. **Facility:** 24 units. 23 one-bedroom standard units, some with efficiencies or kitchens (utensils extra charge). 1 one-bedroom suite ($85-$126) with kitchen. 1-2 stories (no elevator), exterior corridors. **Parking:** on-site, winter plug-ins. **Terms:** office hours 7:30 am-11 pm, small pets only ($6 extra charge). **Amenities:** *Some:* high-speed Internet. **Leisure Activities:** hiking trails. **Guest Services:** coin laundry. **Cards:** AX, DC, DS, MC, VI.
SOME UNITS
🛏 🍴 📷 💻 / 🗙 📞 /
FEE

WILLIAMS LAKE SUPER 8 MOTEL   *Book at aaa.com*   Phone: (250)398-8884

(CAA) (SAVE)	5/1-10/31	1P: $76	2P: $81	XP: $10	F12
◆◆ ◆◆	3/1-4/30	1P: $70	2P: $75	XP: $10	F12
Motel	11/1-2/28	1P: $70	2P: $70	XP: $10	F12

Location: 2 km s on Hwy 97. 1712 Broadway Ave S V2G 2W4. Fax: 250/398-8270. **Facility:** 54 one-bedroom standard units, some with whirlpools. 3 stories (no elevator), interior corridors. **Parking:** on-site, winter plug-ins. **Terms:** package plans, small pets only ($7 extra charge). **Guest Services:** coin laundry. **Cards:** AX, DC, DS, MC, VI. **Special Amenities:** free continental breakfast and free local telephone calls.

SOME UNITS

🆓 🛏️ 🍴 ♿ 📷 DATA PORT ▦ / ⊠ 🯄 🖨️ /
FEE

WINDERMERE pop. 1,060

——— **WHERE TO STAY** ———

WINDERMERE CREEK BED AND BREAKFAST
  CABINS   Phone: (250)342-0356

◆◆◆◆	All Year [BP]	1P: $100-$129	2P: $105-$134	XP: $20
Cabin			

Location: Hwy 95, 8.2 km ne on Kootenay 3 Rd, keep left at fork to Windermere Loop Rd. Located in a quiet area. 1658 Windermere Loop Rd V0B 2L0 (PO Box 409). Fax: 250/342-0356. **Facility:** Set in a mountain valley, the B&B offers four modern cabins with kitchenettes as well as one rustic yet well-appointed 1887 cabin. Smoke free premises. 5 cabins with whirlpools. 1 story, interior/exterior corridors. **Parking:** on-site, winter plug-ins. **Terms:** age restrictions may apply, 14 day cancellation notice. **Amenities:** CD players, hair dryers. **Leisure Activities:** cross country skiing, hiking trails. **Cards:** MC, VI.

SOME UNITS

⊠ 🄰 📺 ☎️ 🯄 ▦ / 📶 VCR 🖨️ /

Manitoba

Whiteshell Provincial
Park, Falcon Lake
© Terrance Klassen
Alamy Images

BRANDON pop. 39,716

―――― WHERE TO STAY ――――

CANAD INNS-BRANDON
[fyi]
All Year   1P: $129   2P: $139   XP: $10   F17
Too new to rate, opening scheduled for February 2005. **Location:** 1125 18th St R7A 7C5. **Amenities:** 159 units, coffeemakers, refrigerators, pool. **Cards:** AX, DC, DS, MC, VI.

COMFORT INN   *Book at aaa.com*   Phone: (204)727-6232

5/1-9/30	1P: $74-$88	2P: $82-$96	XP: $4	F18
1/1-2/28	1P: $70-$84	2P: $78-$90	XP: $4	F18
3/1-4/30 & 10/1-12/31	1P: $68-$82	2P: $76-$90	XP: $4	F18

Small-scale Hotel   **Location:** Northside Trans-Canada Hwy 1 service road; between Hwy 10 N and 10 S, just e of McDonald's Restaurant. Located in a commercial area. 925 Middleton Ave R7C 1A8. Fax: 204/727-2246. **Facility:** 81 one-bedroom standard units. 2 stories (no elevator), interior corridors. **Parking:** on-site, winter plug-ins. **Terms:** cancellation fee imposed, weekly rates available, [ECP] meal plan available, pets (in designated units). **Amenities:** irons, hair dryers. **Guest Services:** valet laundry. **Business Services:** meeting rooms. **Cards:** AX, CB, DC, DS, JC, MC, VI.

SOME UNITS
(ASK) (SD) [icons] / [icon] FEE /

DAYS INN   *Book at aaa.com*   Phone: (204)727-3600
(CAA) (SAVE)
All Year   1P: $94-$104   2P: $94-$104   XP: $5   F17
Location: Jct Trans-Canada Hwy 1, 8 km s on Hwy 10 (Currie Blvd). Located in a commercial area. 2130 Currie Blvd R7B 4E7. Fax: 204/725-1457. **Facility:** 61 units. 58 one-bedroom standard units. 3 one-bedroom suites ($133). 3 stories, interior corridors. **Parking:** on-site, winter plug-ins. **Terms:** check-in 4 pm, pets ($10 extra charge; in smoking units). **Amenities:** high-speed Internet (fee), voice mail, hair dryers. *Some:* irons. **Pool(s):** small heated indoor, wading. **Leisure Activities:** whirlpool, limited exercise equipment. **Guest Services:** valet and coin laundry. **Business Services:** meeting rooms. **Cards:** AX, DC, MC, VI. **Special Amenities:** free continental breakfast and free local telephone calls.

SOME UNITS
(SD) [icons] FEE / [icon] (VCR) [DATA PORT] FEE [icons] FEE

LAKEVIEW INN & SUITES-BRANDON   *Book at aaa.com*   Phone: (204)728-1880
All Year   1P: $96-$120   2P: $96-$120   XP: $10   F17
Location: Just s of jct Trans-Canada Hwy 1 and Hwy 10. Located in a commercial area. 1880 18th St N R7C 1A5. Small-scale Hotel   Fax: 204/727-3924. **Facility:** 66 units. 50 one-bedroom standard units, some with whirlpools. 16 one-bedroom suites. 3 stories, interior corridors. **Parking:** on-site, winter plug-ins. **Terms:** cancellation fee imposed. **Amenities:** video library, high-speed Internet, voice mail, irons, hair dryers. *Some:* video games (fee), dual phone lines. **Pool(s):** small heated indoor. **Leisure Activities:** exercise room. **Guest Services:** valet and coin laundry. **Business Services:** meeting rooms. **Cards:** AX, CB, DC, DS, JC, MC, VI.

SOME UNITS
(ASK) (SD) [icons] (VCR) [DATA PORT] [icons] / [icon]

RODEWAY INN MOTEL   Phone: (204)728-7230
(CAA) (SAVE)
All Year   1P: $56-$59   2P: $58-$63   XP: $4   F6
Location: On Hwy 10 S, 3.2 km s of Trans-Canada Hwy 1. 300 18th St N R7A 7P3. Fax: 204/725-4465. **Facility:** 26 one-bedroom standard units, some with kitchens. 1 story, interior/exterior corridors. **Parking:** on-site, winter plug-ins. **Terms:** office hours 7 am-11 pm, pets ($3 extra charge). **Leisure Activities:** whirlpool. **Guest Services:** valet laundry. **Cards:** AX, DC, DS, MC, VI. **Special Amenities:** free continental breakfast and free local telephone calls.

SOME UNITS
[icons] FEE [icons] / [icon]

ROYAL OAK INN & SUITES   Phone: 204-728-5775
All Year   1P: $84-$114
Location: 5 km s of Trans-Canada Hwy 1; 1.4 km w of jct Hwy 10 (18th St) and 1A (Victoria Ave). Located in a commercial area. 3130 Victoria Ave R7B ON2. Fax: 204/726-5828. **Facility:** 156 units. 96 one-bedroom standard units, some with whirlpools. 60 one-bedroom suites, some with whirlpools. 2-5 stories, interior corridors. **Parking:** on-site, winter plug-ins. **Terms:** package plans, 14% service charge, pets ($10 extra charge, in smoking units). **Amenities:** video games (fee), high-speed Internet, voice mail, irons, hair dryers. **Pool(s):** heated indoor, wading. **Leisure Activities:** whirlpool, waterslide, exercise room. **Guest Services:** valet and coin laundry. **Business Services:** conference facilities. **Cards:** AX, MC, VI.

SOME UNITS
(ASK) (SD) [icons] FEE [icons] / [icons]

SUPER 8 MOTEL BRANDON   *Book at aaa.com*   Phone: (204)729-8024
All Year [ECP]   1P: $81-$101   2P: $87-$107   XP: $6   F16
Location: On Trans-Canada Hwy 1, south service road, just e of Hwy 10 (18th St). Located in a commercial area. 1570 Highland Ave R7C 1A7. Fax: 204/728-3024. **Facility:** 80 units. 78 one-bedroom standard units. 2 one-bedroom suites. 2 stories (no elevator), interior corridors. **Parking:** on-site, winter plug-ins. **Terms:** package plans, pets (in smoking units). **Amenities:** high-speed Internet, voice mail, hair dryers. **Pool(s):** small heated indoor. **Leisure Activities:** whirlpool. **Guest Services:** valet and coin laundry. **Business Services:** meeting rooms. **Cards:** AX, DC, DS, MC, VI.

SOME UNITS
(ASK) (SD) [icons] / [icons] FEE FEE

VICTORIA INN   *Book at aaa.com*   Phone: (204)725-1532
All Year   1P: $92-$110   2P: $92-$110
Location: 5 km s of Trans-Canada Hwy 1; 1.8 km w of jct Hwy 10 (18th St) and 1A (Victoria Ave). Located in a residential/commercial area. 3550 Victoria Ave R7B 2R4. Fax: 204/727-8282. **Facility:** 131 one-bedroom standard units, some with whirlpools. 2 stories (no elevator), interior corridors. **Parking:** on-site, winter plug-ins. **Terms:** pets ($5 extra charge). **Amenities:** video games (fee), high-speed Internet, voice mail, irons, hair dryers. **Pool(s):** heated indoor. **Leisure Activities:** sauna, whirlpool, exercise room. **Guest Services:** valet laundry. **Business Services:** conference facilities. **Cards:** AX, DC, MC, VI.

SOME UNITS
(ASK) [icons] FEE / [icons]

—— WHERE TO DINE ——

DOUBLE HAPPINESS RESTAURANT   **Lunch:** $6-$12   **Dinner:** $6-$12   **Phone:** 204/728-6388
♦♦♦♦ ♦♦♦♦
Chinese
Location: Between 7th and 6th sts. 608 Rosser Ave R7A 0K7. **Hours:** 10 am-10 pm, Fri & Sat-11 pm, Sun 4 pm-10 pm. **Closed:** 12/25. **Reservations:** accepted. **Features:** Bright and clean, the little spot is where locals head when they get a craving for Chinese food. Casual dress; cocktails. **Parking:** street. **Cards:** MC, VI.

⊠

CHURCHILL pop. 1,100

—— WHERE TO STAY ——

POLAR INN & SUITES   **Phone:** (204)675-8878
♦♦♦♦ ♦♦♦♦
Motel

	1P: $195	2P: $195	XP: $20	F12
10/1-2/28	1P: $98	2P: $135	XP: $20	F12
3/1-9/30				

Location: Centre. 153 Kelsey Blvd R0B 0E0 (PO Box 1031). Fax: 204/675-2647. **Facility:** 26 units. 23 one-bedroom standard units, some with kitchens. 3 one-bedroom suites ($150-$175) with kitchens. 1 story, interior corridors. **Parking:** on-site, winter plug-ins. **Terms:** office hours 8 am-8 pm. **Amenities:** video library, hair dryers. *Some:* irons. **Guest Services:** valet laundry. **Cards:** AX, DC, MC, VI.

SOME UNITS
(ASK) 🛏 🍴▶ (AC) 🎦 🔲 🖥 / ⊠ (VCR) (DATA PORT) 📠 /

THE TUNDRA INN   **Phone:** 204/675-8831
♦♦♦♦ ♦♦♦♦
Small-scale Hotel

3/1-12/31	1P: $95-$175	2P: $105-$195	XP: $20
2/1-2/28	1P: $95	2P: $105	XP: $10
1/1-1/31	1P: $95	2P: $105	XP: $20

Location: Centre. Located in a commercial area. 34 Franklin St R0B 0E0 (PO Box 999). Fax: 204/675-2764. **Facility:** 31 one-bedroom standard units. 2 stories (no elevator), interior corridors. **Parking:** on-site, winter plug-ins. **Terms:** office hours 8 am-noon, small pets only. **Amenities:** high-speed Internet, hair dryers. **Guest Services:** valet laundry. **Cards:** AX, DS, MC, VI.

SOME UNITS
🛏 (AC) 🎦 🔲 🖥 / ⊠ (VCR) /

The following lodgings were either not evaluated or did not meet AAA rating requirements but are listed for your information only.

BEAR COUNTRY INN   **Phone:** 204/675-8299
[fyi]
Not evaluated. **Location:** Just w of train station. Located in a commercial area. 126 Kelsey Blvd R0B 0E0 (PO Box 788). Facilities, services, and decor characterize a basic property.

CHURCHILL MOTEL   **Phone:** 204/675-8853
[fyi]
Not evaluated. **Location:** Centre. Located in a commercial area. 152 Kelsey Blvd R0B 0E0 (PO Box 218). Facilities, services, and decor characterize a basic property.

SEAPORT HOTEL   **Phone:** 204/675-8807
[fyi]
Not evaluated. **Location:** Centre. Located in a commercial area. 215 Kelsey Blvd R0B 0E0 (PO Box 339). Facilities, services, and decor characterize a mid-range property.

—— WHERE TO DINE ——

GYPSY BAKERY & COFFEE SHOP   **Lunch:** $4-$8   **Dinner:** $5-$19   **Phone:** 204/675-2322
♦♦♦
American
Location: Centre. 253 Kelsey Blvd R0B 0E0. **Hours:** 7 am-midnight. Closed major holidays. **Features:** This incredibly popular eatery features an extensive selection of fresh baked goods, steak, shrimp, fish, chicken, sandwiches, soup, salad, pizza and pirogies. It is THE place for to-go lunches. Fine wines and cigars are also available. Polite service. Casual dress; cocktails. **Parking:** on-site. **Cards:** AX, DC, MC, VI.

⊠

DAUPHIN pop. 8,085

—— WHERE TO STAY ——

CANWAY INN & SUITES   **Phone:** 204/638-5102
♦♦♦
Small-scale Hotel

| All Year | 1P: $73 | 2P: $79 | XP: $5 | D |

Location: 2.4 km s on Hwy 5A and 10A (Main St). Located in a commercial area. 1601 Main St S R7N 2V4 (PO Box 602). Fax: 204/638-7475. **Facility:** 67 units. 57 one-bedroom standard units, some with whirlpools. 10 one-bedroom suites ($110-$135), some with whirlpools. 2 stories (no elevator), interior/exterior corridors. *Bath:* combo or shower only. **Parking:** on-site, winter plug-ins. **Terms:** office hours 7 am-midnight, small pets only (in ground floor smoking units). **Amenities:** voice mail, hair dryers. **Pool(s):** small heated indoor. **Leisure Activities:** sauna, whirlpool. **Guest Services:** coin laundry. **Business Services:** meeting rooms, fax (fee). **Cards:** AX, DC, MC, VI.

SOME UNITS
🛏 🍴 🍸 🏊 (DATA PORT) 🖥 / ⊠ (VCR) 🔲 /
FEE

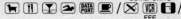

FLIN FLON pop. 6,267

-------- WHERE TO STAY --------

VICTORIA INN NORTH   Phone: (204)687-7555
[CAA] [SAVE]   All Year   1P: $75   2P: $75
◆◆◆ ◆◆◆   **Location:** Jct Hwy 10 and 10A, 1 km nw (eastern approach to city). Located in a commercial area. 160 Hwy 10A N R8A
Small-scale Hotel OC6. Fax: 204/687-5233. **Facility:** 93 one-bedroom standard units, some with whirlpools. 3 stories (no
elevator), interior corridors. **Parking:** on-site, winter plug-ins. **Terms:** package plans, pets ($5 fee).
Amenities: video games (fee), irons, hair dryers. *Some:* high-speed Internet, voice mail. **Dining:** The
Kelsey Dining Room, see separate listing, nightclub. **Pool(s):** heated indoor. **Leisure Activities:** whirlpool,
exercise room. **Guest Services:** valet and coin laundry. **Business Services:** meeting rooms. **Cards:** AX, DC, VI.

SOME UNITS
[icons] FEE FEE

-------- WHERE TO DINE --------

THE KELSEY DINING ROOM   **Lunch:** $6-$8   **Dinner:** $12-$21   Phone: 204/687-7555
◆◆◆ ◆◆◆   **Location:** Jct Hwy 10 and 10A, 1 km nw (eastern approach to city); in Victoria Inn North. 160 Hwy 10A N R8A OC6.
Canadian   **Hours:** 6:30 am-10 pm, Sat & Sun from 8 am. Closed: 12/25. **Reservations:** accepted. **Features:** Friendly,
efficient service and generous portions keep locals and visitors returning to this restaurant. The menu is
varied and offers selections such as steak, chicken, fish and pasta. Booth and table seating are available.
Casual dress; cocktails. **Parking:** on-site. **Cards:** AX, DC, MC, VI.

[icons]

GIMLI pop. 1,657

-------- WHERE TO STAY --------

LAKEVIEW RESORT   *Book at aaa.com*   Phone: (204)642-8565
◆◆◆ ◆◆◆   4/1-9/7   1P: $114-$224   2P: $114-$224   XP: $15   F18
         9/8-2/28   1P: $89-$209   2P: $89-$209   XP: $15   F18
Small-scale Hotel 3/1-3/31   1P: $79-$199   2P: $79-$199   XP: $15   F18
Location: Centre. Located on the beach. 10 Centre St R0C 1B0. Fax: 204/642-4400. **Facility:** 99 units. 42 one-
bedroom standard units. 52 one- and 5 two-bedroom suites, some with efficiencies, kitchens and/or whirlpools. 3 stories, interior
corridors. **Parking:** on-site, winter plug-ins. **Terms:** 7 day cancellation notice-fee imposed, package plans. **Amenities:** voice
mail, irons, hair dryers. **Pool(s):** heated outdoor, heated indoor. **Leisure Activities:** sauna, whirlpool, limited exercise
equipment. **Guest Services:** gift shop, coin laundry. **Business Services:** meeting rooms. **Cards:** AX, DC, DS, MC, VI.

SOME UNITS
[icons]

GULL HARBOUR

-------- WHERE TO STAY --------

GULL HARBOUR RESORT & CONFERENCE
CENTRE   Phone: (204)279-2041
◆◆◆ ◆◆◆   3/1-10/18   1P: $99-$109   2P: $99-$109   XP: $15   F18
Resort   10/19-2/28   1P: $75-$95   2P: $75-$95   XP: $15   F18
Small-scale Hotel **Location:** On Hwy 8; at top of Hecla Island. Located in Hecla Provincial Park. (Box 1000, RIVERTON, R0C 2R0).
Fax: 204/279-2000. **Facility:** Recreation facilities are featured at this resort. 93 units. 89 one-bedroom
standard units, some with whirlpools. 4 one-bedroom suites, some with whirlpools. 2 stories (no elevator), interior
corridors. **Parking:** on-site, winter plug-ins. **Terms:** check-in 4 pm, 14 day cancellation notice-fee imposed, package plans.
Amenities: voice mail, irons, hair dryers. *Some:* DVD players. **Pool(s):** heated indoor, wading. **Leisure Activities:** sauna,
whirlpool, fishing, 2 tennis courts, ice skating, recreation programs, hiking trails, jogging, playground, basketball, volleyball. *Fee:*
golf-18 holes, miniature golf, cross country skiing, tobogganing, bicycles. **Guest Services:** gift shop, valet laundry. **Business
Services:** conference facilities, business center. **Cards:** AX, CB, DC, MC, VI.

SOME UNITS
[icons]

HECLA

-------- WHERE TO STAY --------

SOLMUNDSON GESTA HUS   Phone: (204)279-2088
◆◆◆ ◆◆◆   5/16-1/2 [BP]   1P: $60-$75   2P: $65-$80   XP: $25   F5
         3/1-5/15 & 1/3-2/28 [BP] 1P: $50-$60   2P: $55-$65   XP: $25   F5
Bed & Breakfast **Location:** On Hwy 8; in Hecla Village. Located in Hecla Provincial Park. (Box 76, RIVERTON, R0C 2R0).
Fax: 204/279-2088. **Facility:** Smoke free premises. 4 one-bedroom standard units. 2 stories (no elevator),
interior corridors. *Bath:* some shared or private, combo or shower only. **Parking:** on-site, winter plug-ins. **Terms:** office hours 8
am-9 pm, package plans, small pets only (with prior approval). **Amenities:** video library, hair dryers. **Leisure
Activities:** bicycles, hiking trails. **Cards:** AX, MC, VI.

SOME UNITS
[icons]

NEEPAWA pop. 3,325

-------- WHERE TO STAY --------

BAY HILL INNS & SUITES   Phone: 204/476-8888
◆◆◆ ◆◆◆   All Year   1P: $75-$80   2P: $80-$85   XP: $5   F17
Motel   **Location:** Hwy 16, just w of jct Rt 5. 160 Main St W R0J 1H0 (PO Box 2250). Fax: 204/476-8889. **Facility:** 34 units.
32 one-bedroom standard units. 2 one-bedroom suites ($105-$120), some with whirlpools. 2 stories (no
elevator), interior corridors. **Parking:** on-site, winter plug-ins. **Terms:** pets (in smoking units). **Pool(s):**
heated indoor. **Leisure Activities:** whirlpool. **Cards:** AX, DC, MC, VI.

SOME UNITS
[icons] FEE

PORTAGE LA PRAIRIE pop. 12,976

———— WHERE TO STAY ————

CANAD INNS-PORTAGE LA PRAIRIE
(CAA) (SAVE)
▼▼▼▼
Small-scale Hotel

All Year	1P: $95	2P: $105	XP: $10	F17

Phone: (204)857-9745

Location: Jct Hwy 1A and 24th St W. Located in a commerical area. 2401 Saskatchewan Ave R1N 3L5 (PO Box 1290). **Fax:** 204/239-6245. **Facility:** 93 units. 72 one-bedroom standard units. 21 one-bedroom suites ($110-$120), some with whirlpools. 2 stories, interior corridors. **Bath:** combo or shower only. **Parking:** on-site, winter plugins. **Terms:** [BP] meal plan available. **Amenities:** hair dryers. *Some:* high-speed Internet, irons. **Dining:** 6 am-10 pm, cocktails. **Pool(s):** heated indoor. **Leisure Activities:** sauna, whirlpool, exercise room. *Fee:* game room. **Guest Services:** valet laundry. **Business Services:** conference facilities. **Cards:** AX, DC, DS, MC, VI. **Special Amenities:** free newspaper. *(See color ad p 661)*

SOME UNITS

SUPER 8
▼▼▼
Motel

6/2-2/28	1P: $72	2P: $76	XP: $4	F14
3/1-6/1	1P: $70	2P: $74	XP: $4	F14

Phone: 204/857-8883

Location: 1.5 km w on Trans-Canada Hwy 1A. Located in a commercial area. (PO Box 488, Hwy 1A W). **Fax:** 204/857-9097. **Facility:** 58 units. 56 one-bedroom standard units. 2 one-bedroom suites ($84-$88). 2 stories (no elevator), interior corridors. **Parking:** on-site, winter plug-ins. **Terms:** 7 day cancellation notice. **Amenities:** voice mail, hair dryers. *Some:* high-speed Internet. **Pool(s):** small heated indoor. **Leisure Activities:** whirlpool, waterslide. **Guest Services:** valet and coin laundry. **Business Services:** meeting rooms. **Cards:** AX, DC, MC, VI.

SOME UNITS

WESTGATE INN MOTEL
▼▼
Motel

1/1-2/28	1P: $50-$69	2P: $56-$69	XP: $6	F12
3/1-12/31	1P: $49-$68	2P: $55-$68	XP: $6	F12

Phone: (204)239-5200

Location: 1 km e on Trans-Canada Hwy 1A. Located in a commercial area. 1010 Saskatchewan Ave R1N 0K1 (100 One Evergreen Pl, WINNIPEG, R3L 0E9). **Fax:** 204/239-0588. **Facility:** 25 units. 22 one- and 3 two-bedroom standard units, some with efficiencies. 2 stories (no elevator), exterior corridors. **Parking:** on-site, winter plug-ins. **Terms:** office hours 7 am-1 am, pets (in smoking units). **Cards:** AX, MC, VI.

SOME UNITS

———— WHERE TO DINE ————

BILL'S STICKY FINGERS
▼▼▼
Canadian

Lunch: $3-$19   **Dinner:** $7-$23   **Phone:** 204/857-9999

Location: Just w of Main St. 210 Saskatchewan Ave E R1N 0K9. **Hours:** 11 am-midnight, Sat & Sun from 4 pm. Closed: 1/1, 12/25. **Reservations:** accepted. **Features:** The comfortable, casual, older restaurant offers a wide-ranging menu that includes ribs, chicken, steak, lasagna, gyros and pizza, as well as daily specials. The service is friendly and prompt. Casual dress; cocktails. **Parking:** on-site. **Cards:** AX, DC, MC, VI.

RUSSELL pop. 1,587

———— WHERE TO STAY ————

THE RUSSELL INN HOTEL & CONFERENCE CENTRE
▼▼▼ ▼▼▼
Small-scale Hotel

12/2-2/28	1P: $96	2P: $96	XP: $3	F17
3/1-4/2	1P: $94	2P: $94	XP: $3	F17
4/3-12/1	1P: $87	2P: $90	XP: $3	F17

Phone: (204)773-2186

Location: 1.2 km se on Hwy 16 and 83. Located in a commercial area. Hwy 16 Russell R0J 1W0 (PO Box 578). **Fax:** 204/773-2175. **Facility:** Designated smoking area. 70 units. 47 one-bedroom standard units, some with whirlpools. 23 one-bedroom suites ($129-$175), some with efficiencies. 1 story, interior/exterior corridors. **Parking:** on-site, winter plug-ins. **Terms:** cancellation fee imposed, small pets only. **Amenities:** voice mail. *Some:* high-speed Internet, irons, hair dryers. **Dining:** Russell Inn Dining Room, see separate listing. **Pool(s):** small heated indoor, wading. **Leisure Activities:** whirlpool, waterslide, playground, exercise room. *Fee:* game room. **Business Services:** conference facilities. **Cards:** AX, DC, MC, VI.

SOME UNITS

———— WHERE TO DINE ————

RUSSELL INN DINING ROOM
▼▼▼ ▼▼▼
Canadian

Lunch: $7-$13   **Dinner:** $10-$22   **Phone:** 204/773-2186

Location: 1.2 km se on Hwy 16 and 83; in The Russell Inn Hotel & Conference Centre. **Hours:** 7 am-10 pm, Sun-9 pm. Closed: 12/25. **Reservations:** accepted. **Features:** This popular local dining room offers generous portions and efficient service in a family atmosphere. The varied menu includes such items as pasta, seafood, chicken and ribs, as well as veal, steaks and quesadillas. Some light meals are also available. Casual dress; cocktails. **Parking:** on-site. **Cards:** AX, DC, MC, VI.

STEINBACH pop. 9,227

———— WHERE TO STAY ————

DAYS INN
▼▼▼ ▼▼▼
Small-scale Hotel

6/16-9/1	1P: $81	2P: $81	XP: $5	F18
3/1-6/15 & 9/2-2/28	1P: $76	2P: $76	XP: $5	F18

Phone: (204)320-9200

Location: Jct Trans-Canada Hwy 1 and 12, 20 km s. Located in a commercial area. 75 Hwy 12 N R5G 1T3 (Box 669). **Fax:** 204/320-9222. **Facility:** 49 one-bedroom standard units. 3 stories, interior corridors. **Bath:** combo or shower only. **Parking:** on-site, winter plug-ins. **Terms:** small pets only ($10 extra charge, in smoking units). **Amenities:** voice mail, hair dryers. *Some:* dual phone lines, irons. **Pool(s):** small heated indoor. **Leisure Activities:** whirlpool, waterslide. **Guest Services:** coin laundry. **Business Services:** meeting rooms. **Cards:** AX, DC, MC, VI.

SOME UNITS

FEE

THE PAS pop. 5,795

─── WHERE TO STAY ───

KIKIWAK INN　　　　　　　　　　　　　　　　　　　　　　**Phone:** 204/623-1800

▼▼ ▼▼　　　　　　　　　　　　Property failed to provide current rates
　　　　　　Location: On Hwy 10, 0.6 km n. Located in a commercial area. Hwy 10 N R0B 2J0 (PO Box 10040).
Small-scale Hotel　Fax: 204/623-1812. **Facility:** 60 one-bedroom standard units, some with whirlpools. 3 stories, interior
corridors. **Parking:** on-site, winter plug-ins. **Terms:** small pets only (with prior approval). **Amenities:** voice
mail, irons, hair dryers. **Dining:** Niska Dining Room, see separate listing. **Pool(s):** small heated indoor. **Leisure
Activities:** whirlpool, exercise room. **Guest Services:** valet laundry. **Business Services:** conference facilities, fax (fee).

SOME UNITS

➤+ 🐾 ❙1 ⓨ ⊇ ᴰᴬᵀᴬᴾᴼᴿᵀ ▣ / ⊠ ⱽᶜᴿ 🛢 ▦ ▣ /
FEE

SUPER 8　　*Book at aaa.com*　　　　　　　　　　　　　**Phone:** 204/623-1888

▼▼▼ ▼▼▼　All Year　　　　　　1P: $80-$110　　　2P: $80-$110　　　XP: $5　　　F12
　　　　　　Location: At southern approach to town. Located in a commercial area. 1717 Gordon Ave R9A 1K3 (PO Box 90).
Small-scale Hotel　Fax: 204/623-4488. **Facility:** 70 units. 53 one-bedroom standard units. 17 one-bedroom suites. 2 stories (no
elevator), interior corridors. **Parking:** on-site, winter plug-ins. **Amenities:** voice mail, hair dryers. **Pool(s):**
small heated indoor. **Leisure Activities:** whirlpool, waterslide. **Guest Services:** valet and coin laundry. **Business Services:**
meeting rooms. **Cards:** AX, DC, MC, VI.

SOME UNITS

🐾 ⊇ 🎥 ᴰᴬᵀᴬᴾᴼᴿᵀ / ⊠ ⱽᶜᴿ 🛢 ▦ ▣ /
FEE

WESCANA INN　　　　　　　　　　　　　　　　　　　　　**Phone:** (204)623-5446

ⒸⒶⒶ Ⓢ𝐀𝐕𝐄　All Year　　　　　1P: $89　　　　　　2P: $95　　　　XP: $5　　　F12
　　　　　　Location: On Hwy 10, just s. Located in a commercial area. 439 Fischer Ave R9A 1M3 (PO Box 2519).
▼▼　Fax: 204/623-3383. **Facility:** 76 units. 75 one-bedroom standard units. 1 one-bedroom suite. 2 stories (no
elevator), interior/exterior corridors. **Parking:** on-site, winter plug-ins. **Terms:** small pets only (in smoking
Small-scale Hotel　units). **Amenities:** video library (fee). **Dining:** dining room, see separate listing. **Guest Services:** coin
laundry. **Business Services:** meeting rooms. **Cards:** AX, DC, MC, VI. **Special Amenities:** free local
telephone calls.

SOME UNITS

Ⓢⅅ ➤+ 🐾 ❙1 ⱽᶜᴿ 🛢 ▣ / ⊠ ▦ /
FEE

─── WHERE TO DINE ───

NISKA DINING ROOM　　　　**Lunch:** $8-$23　　　**Dinner:** $8-$23　　　**Phone:** 204/623-1800

▼▼▼ ▼▼▼　　**Location:** On Hwy 10, 0.6 km n; in Kikiwak Inn. Hwy 10 N R0B 2J0. **Hours:** 6 am-10 pm, Sun-8 pm; from 7 am
　　　　　　10/1-4/30. Closed: 12/25. **Reservations:** accepted. **Features:** The menu lists such choices as pickerel, stir-
Canadian　fried beef, steak, chicken, ribs, pasta and salads. Also offered are heart-healthy choices and dishes
recommended for diabetics. Native art is displayed in the dining room. Casual dress; cocktails. **Parking:** on-
site. **Cards:** AX, DC, MC, VI.

ⓨ ⊠

WESCANA DINING ROOM　　　**Lunch:** $7-$10　　　**Dinner:** $10-$18　　　**Phone:** 204/623-5446

▼▼ ▼▼　　**Location:** Just s on Hwy 10; in Wescana Inn. 439 Fischer Ave R9A 1M3. **Hours:** 6:30 am-10 pm, Sun 7 am-2 & 5-
　　　　　　7 pm; Sun hours may vary in winter. Closed: 12/25. **Features:** Unpretentious dining in a casual setting is
American　found at this restaurant, which features an extensive menu with a good selection of prime rib, steak,
chicken, fish and pasta combinations. The lunch menu includes sandwiches, burgers and salads. Casual
dress; cocktails. **Parking:** on-site. **Cards:** AX, DC, MC, VI.

ⓨ ⊠

THOMPSON pop. 13,256

─── WHERE TO STAY ───

COUNTRY INN & SUITES BY CARLSON　　*Book at aaa.com*　　　　　　　**Phone:** (204)778-8879

▼▼▼ ▼▼▼　All Year　　　　　　1P: $98　　　　2P: $108
　　　　　　Location: Just w of Hwy 6. Located in a commercial area. 70 Thompson Dr N R8N 1Y8. Fax: 204/677-3225.
Small-scale Hotel　**Facility:** 60 units. 23 one-bedroom standard units. 37 one-bedroom suites ($108-$118). 2 stories (no
elevator), interior corridors. **Parking:** on-site, winter plug-ins. **Terms:** small pets only ($10 extra charge).
Amenities: video library, irons, hair dryers. **Pool(s):** heated indoor. **Leisure Activities:** sauna, whirlpool, exercise room. **Guest
Services:** coin laundry. **Business Services:** meeting rooms. **Cards:** AX, DC, MC, VI. *(See color ad p 657)*

SOME UNITS

ⒶⓈⓀ Ⓢⅅ 🐾 ❙1+ ⊇ ⊠ ⱽᶜᴿ 🎥 ᴰᴬᵀᴬᴾᴼᴿᵀ 🛢 ▣ / ⊠ ▦ /
FEE

─── *The following lodgings were either not evaluated or did not* ───
meet AAA rating requirements but are listed for your information only.

INTERIOR INN　　　　　　　　　　　　　　　　　　　　　**Phone:** 204/778-5535

ⓕⓨⓘ　Not evaluated. **Location:** Thompson Dr at jct Riverside St. 180 Thompson Dr R8N 1Y8. Facilities, services, and decor
characterize a mid-range property.

RAMADA INN BURNTWOOD　　　　　　　　　　　　　　　**Phone:** 204/677-4551

ⓕⓨⓘ　Not evaluated. **Location:** Jct Cree Rd. 146 Selkirk Ave R8N ON1. Facilities, services, and decor characterize a mid-
range property.

---------- **WHERE TO DINE** ----------

THE HUB

Canadian

Lunch: $7-$15   **Dinner:** $9-$27   **Phone:** 204/778-5630
Location: Centre. 111 Churchill Dr R8N 1M9. **Hours:** 11 am-10 pm. Closed major holidays.
Reservations: accepted. **Features:** The restaurant is a meeting spot for local folks. Fish and chips,
burgers, sandwiches, salads and pizza are served in generous portions. Casual dress; cocktails. **Parking:**
street. **Cards:** AX, MC, VI.

WINKLER pop. 7,943

---------- **WHERE TO STAY** ----------

DAYS INN & SUITES   *Book at aaa.com*   **Phone:** (204)325-8888

Small-scale Hotel

All Year [ECP]   1P: $89-$113   2P: $95-$119   XP: $6   F17
Location: Main St and Hwy 14; centre. Located in a commercial area. 395 Boundary Tr R6W 4B1.
Fax: 204/325-5488. **Facility:** 52 units. 40 one-bedroom standard units, some with whirlpools. 12 one-
bedroom suites ($109-$149). 3 stories, interior corridors. **Parking:** on-site, winter plug-ins. **Terms:** check-in
4 pm. **Amenities:** high-speed Internet (fee), voice mail, hair dryers. *Some:* irons. **Pool(s):** small heated indoor. **Leisure
Activities:** whirlpool, waterslide, limited exercise equipment. **Guest Services:** coin laundry. **Business Services:** meeting
rooms. **Cards:** AX, DC, DS, MC, VI.

SOME UNITS

                                               FEE   FEE   FEE

HEARTLAND RESORT & CONFERENCE CENTRE   **Phone:** (204)325-4381

Small-scale Hotel

All Year   1P: $79-$139   2P: $89-$149
Location: Main St and Hwy 14; centre. Located in a commercial area. 851 Main St N R6W 4A4 (Box 30).
Fax: 204/325-9656. **Facility:** 34 one-bedroom standard units, some with efficiencies and/or whirlpools. 1
story, interior corridors. *Bath:* combo or shower only. **Parking:** on-site, winter plug-ins. **Terms:** package
plans, small pets only ($6 extra charge, in smoking units). **Amenities:** voice mail, hair dryers. **Dining:** Getaways Restaurant,
see separate listing. **Leisure Activities:** whirlpool, exercise room. **Guest Services:** coin laundry. **Business Services:** meeting
rooms. **Cards:** AX, DC, DS, MC, VI.

SOME UNITS

---------- **WHERE TO DINE** ----------

GETAWAYS RESTAURANT   **Lunch:** $7-$11   **Dinner:** $10-$20   **Phone:** 204/325-4381

Canadian

Location: Main St and Hwy 14; centre; in Heartland Resort & Conference Centre. 851 Main St N R6W 4A4. **Hours:** 7
am-11 pm. Closed: 12/25, 12/26. **Reservations:** accepted. **Features:** In addition to Canadian cuisine, the
menu lists some Mennonite dishes, including butter soup, kielke (egg noodles with gravy) and verenikje
(pierogies with white gravy and farmer's sausage). Booth and table seating are available. Casual dress.
Parking: on-site. **Cards:** AX, DC, MC, VI.

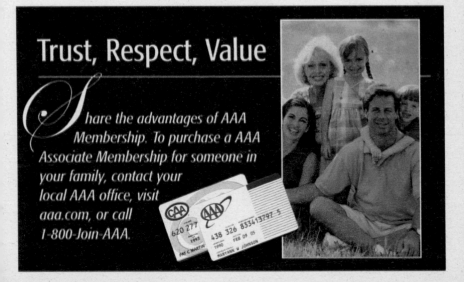

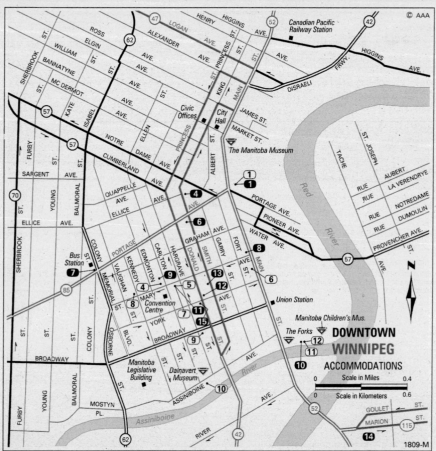

DOWNTOWN WINNIPEG ACCOMMODATIONS

Downtown Winnipeg

This index helps you "spot" where approved accommodations and restaurants are located on the corresponding detailed maps. Lodging rate ranges are for comparison only and show the property's high season; rates are per night, unless only weekly (W) rates are available. Restaurant rate range is for dinner, unless only lunch (L) is served. Turn to the listing page for more detailed rate information and consult display ads for special promotions.

Spotter/Map Page Number	OA	DOWNTOWN WINNIPEG - Lodgings	Diamond Rating	Rate Range High Season	Listing Page
1 / p. 652		The Fairmont Winnipeg	◆◆◆	$109-$359	658
4 / p. 652		Ramada Marlborough Hotel	◆◆	$120-$150	659
6 / p. 652		Radisson Hotel Winnipeg Downtown - see color ad p 657	◆◆◆	$109-$149	659
7 / p. 652	CAA	**Holiday Inn Hotel & Suites Winnipeg-Downtown** - see color ad card insert	◆◆◆	$99-$139 [SAVE]	658
8 / p. 652		Hampton Inn & Suites	◆◆◆	$109-$119	658
9 / p. 652	CAA	**Carlton Inn**	◆◆	$72-$93 [SAVE]	657
10 / p. 652		Inn at the Forks	◆◆◆	$114-$179	658
11 / p. 652	CAA	**Delta Winnipeg** - see color ad p 658	◆◆◆	$89-$159 [SAVE]	657
12 / p. 652	CAA	**Sheraton Hotel** - see color ad p 5	◆◆◆	$95-$159 [SAVE]	659
13 / p. 652	CAA	**Place Louis Riel All-Suite Hotel**	◆◆◆	$90-$150 [SAVE]	659
14 / p. 652	CAA	**Norwood Hotel**	◆◆	$99-$123 [SAVE]	659
15 / p. 652		Best Western Charterhouse Hotel Downtown Winnipeg	◆◆	$92-$139	657
		DOWNTOWN WINNIPEG - Restaurants			
①/ p. 652		The Velvet Glove	◆◆◆◆	$19-$46	660
④/ p. 652		Ichiban Japanese Steak House & Sushi Bar	◆◆◆	$13-$33	660
⑤/ p. 652		Blaze Bistro & Lounge	◆◆◆	$14-$32	659
⑥/ p. 652		Ivory	◆◆	$10-$20	660
⑦/ p. 652		Elephant & Castle	◆◆	$10-$15	660
⑧/ p. 652		Hy's Steak Loft	◆◆	$22-$45	660
⑨/ p. 652		Amici	◆◆◆	$17-$38	659
⑩/ p. 652		Restaurant Dubrovnik	◆◆◆	$20-$44	660
⑪/ p. 652		Branigan's	◆◆	$10-$22	660
⑫/ p. 652		Brio Restaurant & Catering	◆◆	$7-$14(L)	660

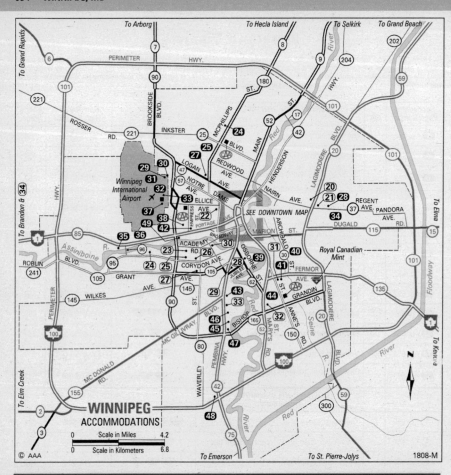

WINNIPEG
ACCOMMODATIONS

Scale in Miles 4.2
Scale in Kilometers 6.8

© AAA

1808-M

✈ Airport Accommodations

Spotter/Map Page Number	OA	WINNIPEG INTERNATIONAL AIRPORT	Diamond Rating	Rate Range High Season	Listing Page
33 / p. 654		Comfort Inn, 2.3 km e of airport	◆◆	$85-$106	662
32 / p. 654		Country Inn & Suites By Carlson, 1.9 km e of airport	◆◆◆	$89-$109	662
37 / p. 654		Four Points Sheraton Winnipeg International Airport, at airport	◆◆◆	$115	663
30 / p. 654	CAA	Greenwood Inn, 1.5 km e of airport	◆◆◆	$99-$139 SAVE	663
29 / p. 654	CAA	Hilton Suites Winnipeg Airport, 1.6 km e of airport	◆◆◆	$139-$189 SAVE	663
31 / p. 654	CAA	Victoria Inn Hotel & Convention Centre, 1.4 km e of airport	◆◆	$89-$99 SAVE	664

Winnipeg

This index helps you "spot" where approved accommodations and restaurants are located on the corresponding detailed maps. Lodging rate ranges are for comparison only and show the property's high season; rates are per night, unless only weekly (W) rates are available. Restaurant rate range is for dinner, unless only lunch (L) is served. Turn to the listing page for more detailed rate information and consult display ads for special promotions.

Spotter/Map Page Number	OA	WINNIPEG - Lodgings	Diamond Rating	Rate Range High Season	Listing Page
24 / p. 654	CAA	**Canad Inns Garden City** - see color ad p 661	◆◆	$97-$107 SAVE	661
25 / p. 654	CAA	**Lincoln Motor Hotel**	◆	$50-$56 SAVE	663
27 / p. 654	CAA	**Days Inn**	◆◆	$109-$139 SAVE	662
28 / p. 654	CAA	**Canad Inns Club Regent Casino** - see color ad p 661	◆◆◆	$129-$139 SAVE	661
29 / p. 654	CAA	**Hilton Suites Winnipeg Airport** - see color ad p 657	◆◆◆	$139-$189 SAVE	663
30 / p. 654	CAA	**Greenwood Inn**	◆◆◆	$99-$139 SAVE	663
31 / p. 654	CAA	**Victoria Inn Hotel & Convention Centre**	◆◆	$89-$99 SAVE	664
32 / p. 654		Country Inn & Suites By Carlson - see color ad p 657	◆◆◆	$89-$109	662
33 / p. 654		Comfort Inn	◆◆	$85-$106	662
34 / p. 654	CAA	**Canad Inns-Transcona** - see color ad p 661	◆◆	$87-$97 SAVE	662
35 / p. 654	CAA	**Holiday Inn Winnipeg Airport/West** - see color ad card insert	◆◆◆	$125-$159 SAVE	663
36 / p. 654		Assiniboine Gordon Inn on the Park	◆	$72-$84	660
37 / p. 654		Four Points Sheraton Winnipeg International Airport - see color ad p 5	◆◆◆	$115	663
38 / p. 654	CAA	**Canad Inns Polo Park** - see color ad p 661	◆◆◆	$109-$119 SAVE	661
39 / p. 654		Twin Pillars Bed & Breakfast	◆	$50-$70	664
40 / p. 654	CAA	**Canad Inns Windsor Park** - see color ad p 661	◆◆	$67-$77 SAVE	662
41 / p. 654	CAA	**Travelodge**	◆◆	$76-$96 SAVE	664
42 / p. 654		Clarion Hotel & Suites	◆◆◆	$129-$269	662
43 / p. 654	CAA	**Holiday Inn Winnipeg-South** - see color ad card insert	◆◆◆	$120-$140 SAVE	663

Spotter/Map Page Number	OA	WINNIPEG - Lodgings (continued)	Diamond Rating	Rate Range High Season	Listing Page
44 / p. 654	CAA	Dakota Village Motor Hotel	◈	$69-$79 SAVE	662
45 / p. 654	CAA	Canad Inns Express Fort Garry - see color ad p 661	◈◈	$60-$70 SAVE	661
46 / p. 654		Super 8	◈◈◈	$88-$158	663
47 / p. 654	CAA	Canad Inns Fort Garry - see color ad p 661	◈◈◈	$129-$139 SAVE	661
48 / p. 654	CAA	Comfort Inn	◈◈	$79-$125 SAVE	662
49 / p. 654	CAA	Viscount Gort Hotel	◈◈	$82 SAVE	664
		WINNIPEG - Restaurants			
20 / p. 654		Royal Fork Buffet Restaurant	◈	$12-$13	665
21 / p. 654		Branigan's	◈◈	$11-$30	664
22 / p. 654		India Palace	◈◈	$8-$20	665
23 / p. 654		Fusion Grill	◈◈◈	$20-$30	665
24 / p. 654		Tavern In The Park	◈◈◈	$16-$40	665
25 / p. 654		Mona Lisa Ristorante	◈◈	$14-$22	665
26 / p. 654	CAA	Bonfire Bistro	◈◈	$12-$20	664
27 / p. 654		Spuntino Cafe	◈◈	$10-$18	665
28 / p. 654		Lux Sole	◈◈	$12-$23	665
29 / p. 654		The Round Table Steak House & Pub	◈◈	$20-$33	665
30 / p. 654		529 Wellington	◈◈◈	$32-$49	664
31 / p. 654		Tiffani's Restaurant	◈◈	$17-$29	665
32 / p. 654		Maxime	◈◈	$10-$22	665
33 / p. 654		Cork & Dock	◈◈	$9-$28	664
34 / p. 654	CAA	Medicine Rock Cafe	◈◈	$14-$23	665

DOWNTOWN WINNIPEG　(See map and index starting on p. 652)

──── WHERE TO STAY ────

BEST WESTERN CHARTERHOUSE HOTEL DOWNTOWN WINNIPEG 〔15〕

Phone: (204)942-0101 F18

◆◆◆ All Year　　1P: $92-$139　　2P: $92-$139　　XP: $10

Location: Between Hargrave and Donald sts. Located in the business district. 330 York Ave R3C ON9. Small-scale Hotel Fax: 204/956-0665. **Facility:** 86 one-bedroom standard units. 5 stories, interior corridors. **Parking:** on-site (fee), winter plug-ins. **Amenities:** high-speed Internet (fee), voice mail, irons, hair dryers. **Leisure Activities:** exercise room. **Guest Services:** valet laundry. **Business Services:** meeting rooms, PC. **Cards:** AX, DC, DS, MC, VI.

SOME UNITS
〔ASK〕〔S⊘〕〔✈〕〔†1〕〔▽〕〔⌖〕〔⊛〕〔DATA PORT〕〔💻〕/〔✕〕〔VCR〕〔▤〕〔▦〕/
FEE　　　　　　　　　　　　　　　　　　　　　FEE FEE FEE

CARLTON INN　*Book at aaa.com* 〔9〕

〔CAA〕〔SAVE〕 Phone: (204)942-0881

◆◆◆ All Year　　1P: $72-$82　　2P: $83-$93　　XP: $6 F17

Location: Just s off Metro Rt 85 (Portage Ave). Located opposite convention centre. 220 Carlton St R3C 1P5. Fax: 204/943-9312. **Facility:** 107 one-bedroom standard units. 3 stories, interior corridors. **Parking:** on-site, winter plug-ins. **Terms:** small pets only. **Amenities:** voice mail. **Dining:** 7:30 am-11:30 pm, Fri & Sat 8 am-Small-scale Hotel 1:30 am, Sun 8 am-11 pm, cocktails. **Pool(s):** small heated outdoor. **Leisure Activities:** sauna. **Guest Services:** valet laundry. **Business Services:** meeting rooms. **Cards:** AX, CB, DC, DS, JC, MC, VI.

SOME UNITS
〔S⊘〕〔🛏〕〔†1〕〔▽〕〔⤢〕〔💻〕/〔✕〕〔VCR〕〔DATA PORT〕〔▤〕/
FEE　　　　　　　　　　　　　　　　　　　FEE

DELTA WINNIPEG　*Book at aaa.com* 〔11〕

〔CAA〕〔SAVE〕 Phone: (204)942-0551

◆◆◆◆ All Year　　1P: $89-$159　　2P: $89-$159　　XP: $15 F18

Location: At Hargrave St. Located adjacent to convention centre. 350 St. Mary Ave R3C 3J2. Fax: 204/943-8702. **Facility:** 393 units. 377 one- and 6 two-bedroom standard units. 10 one-bedroom suites ($189-$349), some Large-scale Hotel with whirlpools. 18 stories, interior corridors. **Bath:** combo or shower only. **Parking:** on-site (fee) and valet. **Terms:** small pets only ($25 fee). **Amenities:** video games (fee), high-speed Internet, voice mail, irons, hair dryers. *Some:* CD players, honor bars. **Dining:** Blaze Bistro & Lounge, Elephant & Castle, see separate listings. **Pool(s):** outdoor, heated indoor, wading. **Leisure Activities:** sauna, whirlpool. **Guest Services:** gift shop, valet and coin laundry. *Fee:* fitness testing. **Business Services:** conference facilities, business center. **Cards:** AX, CB, DC, DS, JC, MC, VI. *(See color ad p 658)*

SOME UNITS
〔🛏〕〔†1〕〔▽〕〔⚙M〕〔⤢〕〔✦〕〔⊛〕〔DATA PORT〕〔💻〕/〔✕〕〔VCR〕〔▤〕〔▦〕/
FEE　　　　　　　　　　　　　　　　　　　　　　　FEE FEE FEE

(See map and index starting on p. 652)

THE FAIRMONT WINNIPEG *Book at aaa.com*
Phone: (204)957-1350 **1**

All Year 1P: $109-$359 2P: $109-$359 XP: $20 F18
Location: Just e of corner Portage Ave and Main St. Located in a commerical area. 2 Lombard Pl R3B 0Y3.
Large-scale Hotel Fax: 204/949-1486. **Facility:** 340 units. 334 one-bedroom standard units, some with whirlpools. 6 one-bedroom suites ($186-$1300), some with whirlpools. 21 stories, interior corridors. **Parking:** on-site (fee) and valet, winter plug-ins. **Terms:** cancellation fee imposed, package plans, small pets only ($25 extra charge). **Amenities:** video games (fee), voice mail, honor bars, irons, hair dryers. *Some:* CD players. *Fee:* DVD players, high-speed Internet. **Dining:** The Velvet Glove, see separate listing. **Pool(s):** heated indoor. **Leisure Activities:** whirlpool, steamroom, exercise room. *Fee:* massage. **Guest Services:** gift shop, valet laundry. **Business Services:** conference facilities, business center. **Cards:** AX, DC, DS, JC, MC, VI.

(ASK) (S/D) (pet/FEE) (restaurant) (Y) (activity) (coffee) (pool) (X) (exercise) (DATA PORT) (icon) / (X) (VCR/FEE) (icon) (icon) /

HAMPTON INN & SUITES *Book at aaa.com*
Phone: 204/942-4222 **8**

All Year [ECP] 1P: $109 2P: $119
Location: Corner of St. Mary Ave. Located in a business district. 260 Main St R3C 1A9. Fax: 204/480-4612.
Small-scale Hotel **Facility:** 128 one-bedroom standard units, some with whirlpools. 6 stories, interior corridors. *Bath:* combo or shower only. **Parking:** on-site, winter plug-ins. **Amenities:** high-speed Internet, dual phone lines, voice mail, irons, hair dryers. *Some: Fee:* high-speed Internet. **Pool(s):** heated indoor. **Leisure Activities:** whirlpool, steamroom, exercise room. **Guest Services:** sundries, valet and coin laundry. **Business Services:** meeting rooms, business center. **Cards:** AX, DC, DS, MC, VI.

SOME UNITS
(ASK) (S/D) (restaurant) (icon) (pool) (X) (exercise) (DATA PORT) (icon) / (X) (icon) (icon) /
FEE FEE

HOLIDAY INN HOTEL & SUITES
WINNIPEG-DOWNTOWN *Book at aaa.com*
Phone: (204)786-7011 **7**

(AAA) (SAVE) All Year 1P: $99-$139 2P: $99-$139 XP: $15 F18
Location: Corner of Portage Ave and Colony St. 360 Colony St R3B 2P3. Fax: 204/772-1443. **Facility:** 140 units.
120 one-bedroom standard units. 20 one-bedroom suites. 11 stories, interior corridors. *Bath:* combo or shower only. **Parking:** on-site (fee), winter plug-ins. **Terms:** [BP], [CP] & [ECP] meal plans available.
Small-scale Hotel **Amenities:** video games (fee), dual phone lines, voice mail, irons, hair dryers. *Some:* high-speed Internet. **Dining:** 7 am-11 pm, Fri & Sat-midnight, Sun 7:30 am-2 & 5-11 pm, cocktails. **Pool(s):** small heated indoor.
Leisure Activities: whirlpool, exercise room. **Guest Services:** valet and coin laundry. **Business Services:** meeting rooms.
Cards: AX, DC, DS, JC, MC, VI. *(See color ad card insert)*

SOME UNITS
(S/D) (restaurant) (Y) (icon) (pool) (X) (DATA PORT) (icon) / (X) (icon) (icon) /
FEE FEE

INN AT THE FORKS *Book at aaa.com*
Phone: (204)942-5656 **10**

All Year 1P: $114-$179 2P: $114-$179 XP: $10 F17
Location: At the Forks. Located in a park and entertainment area. 75 Forks Market Rd R3C 0A2. Fax: 204/942-6979.
Small-scale Hotel **Facility:** 116 units. 107 one-bedroom standard units. 9 one-bedroom suites, some with whirlpools. 5 stories, interior corridors. **Parking:** on-site and valet, winter plug-ins. **Terms:** cancellation fee imposed.
Amenities: dual phone lines, voice mail, safes, irons, hair dryers. *Fee:* video games, high-speed Internet. **Leisure Activities:** exercise room, spa. **Guest Services:** valet laundry. **Business Services:** conference facilities. **Cards:** AX, CB, DC, DS, JC, MC, VI.

SOME UNITS
(ASK) (S/D) (restaurant) (Y) (icon) (exercise) (DATA PORT) (icon) / (X) (VCR) (icon) (icon) /

(See map and index starting on p. 652)

NORWOOD HOTEL   *Book at aaa.com*   Phone: (204)233-4475   **14**
CAA SAVE   All Year   1P: $99-$123   2P: $99-$123   XP: $10   F18
▼▼▼   **Location:** On Metro Rt 115, just e of St. Mary Ave. Located in a commercial area. 112 Marion St R2H 0T1.
               Fax: 204/231-1910. **Facility:** 52 one-bedroom standard units. 5 stories, interior corridors. **Parking:** on-site,
               winter plug-ins. **Amenities:** video library (fee), voice mail, irons, hair dryers. **Dining:** 7 am-9 pm, cocktails.
Small-scale Hotel **Guest Services:** valet laundry. **Business Services:** meeting rooms. **Cards:** AX, CB, DC, JC, MC, VI.

SOME UNITS
〔YI〕〔Y〕〔⊞〕〔DATA PORT〕〔▱〕/〔X〕〔VCR〕〔▤〕〔▨〕/
       FEE   FEE

PLACE LOUIS RIEL ALL-SUITE HOTEL   *Book at aaa.com*   Phone: (204)947-6961   **13**
CAA SAVE   All Year   1P: $90-$150   2P: $90-$150   XP: $10   F17
▼▼▼   **Location:** At St. Mary's Ave. 190 Smith St R3C 1J8. Fax: 204/947-3029. **Facility:** 292 units. 105 one-bedroom
               standard units with kitchens. 170 one- and 17 two-bedroom suites with kitchens. 24 stories, interior
               corridors. **Parking:** on-site (fee), winter plug-ins. **Terms:** pets ($10 extra charge, with prior approval).
Large-scale Hotel **Amenities:** video games (fee), voice mail, irons, hair dryers. **Dining:** 6:30 am-11 pm, Sat from 7:30 am,
Sun 7:30 am-9 pm, cocktails. *Fee:* game room. **Guest Services:** gift
shop, valet and coin laundry. **Business Services:** meeting rooms, business center. **Cards:** AX, DC, MC, VI.
Special Amenities: free newspaper and free room upgrade (subject to availability with advance reservations).

SOME UNITS
〔S/D〕〔▱〕〔YI〕〔Y〕〔&M〕〔✦〕〔DATA PORT〕〔▤〕〔▨〕〔▱〕/〔X〕/
       FEE

RADISSON HOTEL WINNIPEG DOWNTOWN   *Book at aaa.com*   Phone: (204)956-0410   **6**
▼▼▼   3/1-6/30 & 9/12-2/28   1P: $109-$149   2P: $109-$149   XP: $15   F18
               7/1-9/11   1P: $92-$132   2P: $92-$132   XP: $15   F18
Large-scale Hotel **Location:** At Smith St. Located in a commercial area. 288 Portage Ave R3C 0B8. Fax: 204/947-1129. **Facility:** 272
units. 271 one-bedroom standard units. 1 one-bedroom suite ($149). 29 stories, interior corridors. **Parking:**
on-site (fee) and valet, winter plug-ins. **Terms:** small pets only. **Amenities:** video games (fee), voice mail, irons, hair dryers.
Some: high-speed Internet. **Pool(s):** heated indoor. **Leisure Activities:** saunas, whirlpool, exercise room. **Guest Services:** gift
shop, valet laundry, area transportation. **Business Services:** conference facilities, business center. **Cards:** AX, DC, DS,
MC, VI. *(See color ad p 657)*

SOME UNITS
〔ASK〕〔S/D〕〔▱〕〔YI〕〔Y〕〔≋〕〔X〕〔✦〕〔DATA PORT〕〔▤〕/〔X〕〔VCR〕〔▤〕〔▨〕/
                                                            FEE

RAMADA MARLBOROUGH HOTEL   *Book at aaa.com*   Phone: (204)942-6411   **4**
▼▼▼   All Year   1P: $120-$150   2P: $120-$150   XP: $10   F18
               Location: Just n off Metro Rt 85 (Portage Ave). Located in a commercial area. 331 Smith St R3B 2G9.
Small-scale Hotel Fax: 204/942-2017. **Facility:** 148 units. 140 one-bedroom standard units. 8 one-bedroom suites ($150-
               $200). 9 stories, interior corridors. **Parking:** on-site (fee), winter plug-ins. **Terms:** small pets only ($50
deposit, in kennels). **Amenities:** video games (fee), voice mail, irons, hair dryers. *Some:* high-speed Internet. **Pool(s):** small
heated indoor. **Leisure Activities:** whirlpool, waterslide, exercise room. *Fee:* game room. **Guest Services:** gift shop, valet and
coin laundry. **Business Services:** conference facilities. **Cards:** AX, DC, MC, VI.

SOME UNITS
〔ASK〕〔S/D〕〔✈〕〔▱〕〔YI〕〔Y〕〔≋〕〔X〕〔✦〕〔DATA PORT〕〔▤〕/〔X〕〔VCR〕〔▤〕/
               FEE   FEE

SHERATON HOTEL   *Book at aaa.com*   Phone: (204)942-5300   **12**
CAA SAVE   3/1-6/30 & 9/1-2/28   1P: $95-$159   2P: $95-$159   XP: $15   F18
▼▼▼   7/1-8/31   1P: $89-$149   2P: $89-$149   XP: $15   F18
               Location: At York Ave. Located in the business district. 161 Donald St R3C 1M3. Fax: 204/943-7975. **Facility:** 271
               one-bedroom standard units, some with whirlpools. 21 stories, interior corridors. **Parking:** on-site (fee) and
Large-scale Hotel valet, winter plug-ins. **Terms:** [BP], [CP] & [ECP] meal plans available, package plans, small pets only ($15
               extra charge). **Amenities:** dual phone lines, voice mail, irons, hair dryers. *Some:* video games, high-speed
Internet. *Some:* fax. **Dining:** 6:30 am-10 pm, Sat & Sun from 7 am, cocktails. **Pool(s):** heated indoor. **Leisure
Activities:** sauna, whirlpool, exercise room. **Guest Services:** gift shop, valet laundry. **Business Services:** conference facilities.
Cards: AX, DC, DS, JC, MC, VI. *(See color ad p 5)*

SOME UNITS
〔S/D〕〔▱〕〔YI〕〔Y〕〔≋〕〔X〕〔✦〕〔DATA PORT〕〔▤〕/〔X〕〔VCR〕〔▤〕〔▨〕/
       FEE   FEE

――――― *The following lodging was either not evaluated or did not* ―――――
meet AAA rating requirements but is listed for your information only.

THE FORT GARRY   Phone: 204/942-8251
[fyi]   Not evaluated. **Location:** Just w of jct Main St and Broadway Ave. 222 Broadway Ave R3C 0R3. Facilities, services,
               and decor characterize a mid-range property.

――――― **WHERE TO DINE** ―――――

AMICI   Lunch: $9-$18   Dinner: $17-$38   Phone: 204/943-4997   **9**
▼▼▼   **Location:** At Hargrave St. 326 Broadway R3C 0S5. **Hours:** 11:30 am-2 & 5-10 pm, Sat from 5 pm. Closed major
Italian   holidays; also Sun. **Reservations:** suggested. **Features:** You'll find this restaurant offers fine dining in
               contemporary surroundings upstairs, and casual dining and more moderate pricing at the Bombolini Wine
Dressy casual; cocktails. **Parking:** street. **Cards:** AX, DC, MC, VI. Bar downstairs. The innovative menu features dishes with complex preparation and creative presentation.

〔Y〕〔X〕

BLAZE BISTRO & LOUNGE   Lunch: $8-$15   Dinner: $14-$32   Phone: 204/944-7259   **5**
▼▼▼   **Location:** At Hargrave St; in Delta Winnipeg. 350 St. Mary Ave R3C 3J2. **Hours:** 6:30 am-2 & 5-10 pm, Sat 7 am-
               noon & 5-10 pm, Sun 7 am-noon. **Reservations:** accepted. **Features:** This bistro offers an inviting
Canadian   atmosphere with oil paintings that truly depict the prairies. The menu is also regionally inspired and draws
               on local products for dishes such as Manitoba pickerel bruschetta and corn crusted turkey medallions.
Casual dress; cocktails. **Parking:** on-site (fee) and valet. **Cards:** AX, DC, JC, MC, VI.

〔Y〕〔X〕

(See map and index starting on p. 652)

BRANIGAN'S
◆◆◆ ◆◆◆
Canadian

Lunch: $7-$10   **Dinner:** $10-$22   **Phone:** 204/948-0020 ⑪
Location: Behind Union Station. 162-1 Forks Market Rd R3C 4L8. **Hours:** 11 am-midnight, Fri & Sat-1 am. Closed: 12/25. **Reservations:** accepted. **Features:** You'll enjoy the very good menu at this restaurant; it offers daily made soups and breads, fresh salad, classic and unique sandwiches, creative pasta, tender chicken and veal dishes, mouthwatering ribs, sizzling steaks and succulent seafood. Located in a bustling market, it also has outdoor seating. Casual dress; cocktails. **Parking:** on-site. **Cards:** AX, DC, MC, VI.

⧝ ✕

BRIO RESTAURANT & CATERING
◆◆◆ ◆◆◆
Canadian

Lunch: $7-$14   **Phone:** 204/948-0085 ⑫
Location: Just s of Portage Ave; top floor in the Winnipeg Art Gallery. 300 Memorial Blvd R3C 1V1. **Hours:** 11:30 am-2:30 pm, Sat & Sun from 10 am. Closed: 12/25; also Mon. **Reservations:** This restaurant features a progressive menu with some Pacific Rim influences. The Caesar salad and barbecue chicken wrap with salsa are delightful choices, with attractive presentations. The decor is funky, with an open kitchen and outdoor patio. Casual dress; cocktails. **Parking:** street. **Cards:** AX, DC, MC, VI.

♿ ✕

ELEPHANT & CASTLE
◆◆◆ ◆◆◆
English

Lunch: $10-$15   **Dinner:** $10-$15   **Phone:** 204/942-5555 ⑦
Location: At Hargrave St; in Delta Winnipeg. 350 St Mary Ave R3C 3J2. **Hours:** 11 am-2 am. **Reservations:** accepted. **Features:** Exposed beams, brick and decorative accents that suggest jolly old England surround patrons at the comfortable pub. The menu lists traditional dishes, such as shepherd's pie, steak and kidney pie and roast beef. Casual dress; cocktails. **Parking:** on-site (fee). **Cards:** AX, CB, DC, MC, VI.

⧝ ✕

HY'S STEAK LOFT
◆◆ ◆◆
Steak House

Dinner: $22-$45   **Phone:** 204/942-1000 ⑧
Location: 2 blks s of Metro Rt 85 (Portage Ave). 216 Kennedy St R3C 1T1. **Hours:** 4 pm-11 pm, Fri & Sat-midnight, Sun 5 pm-9 pm. Closed major holidays. **Reservations:** accepted. **Features:** Hy's Steak Loft is a popular and established restaurant. In addition to a nice selection of steaks, they offer rack of lamb, as well as a number of seafood and fish dishes and chicken. Great wine list. The atmosphere is friendly and warm. Locals and visitors alike enjoy the private, romantic setting. Dressy casual; cocktails. **Parking:** on-site. **Cards:** AX, DC, MC, VI.

⧝ ✕

ICHIBAN JAPANESE STEAK HOUSE & SUSHI BAR
◆◆◆ ◆◆◆
Japanese

Dinner: $13-$33   **Phone:** 204/925-7400 ④
Location: Corner of St. Mary Ave and Carlton sts. 189 Carlton St R3C 3F1. **Hours:** 4:30 pm-10 pm, Fri & Sat-10:30 pm. Closed major holidays. **Reservations:** accepted. **Features:** Ichiban features a sushi bar and teppan-style cooking, where your meal is prepared in an entertaining manner at your table. Offerings also include North American dishes of steak, chicken and seafood. The server staff is pleasant, cordial and attentive. Casual dress; cocktails. **Parking:** on-site. **Cards:** AX, DC, MC, VI.

⧝ ✕

IVORY
◆◆◆ ◆◆◆
Indian

Lunch: $10-$20   **Dinner:** $10-$20   **Phone:** 204/944-1600 ⑥
Location: Between St. Mary and York aves. 200 Main St R3C 4V9. **Hours:** 11 am-11 pm, Sat from 5 pm, Sun 5 pm-10 pm. Closed: 12/25. **Reservations:** accepted. **Features:** An East Indian treat, the restaurant offers diners the option of choices from a nicely developed menu or from the buffet line, which is a showcase for high-quality, well-presented, hot and cold dishes. Food is delightfully seasoned and reflects the diner's preference for spiciness. The decor blends "art gallery" and "bistro.". Casual dress; cocktails. **Parking:** on-site. **Cards:** AX, DC, MC, VI.

⧝ ✕

RESTAURANT DUBROVNIK
◆◆◆ ◆◆◆
Continental

Lunch: $12-$18   **Dinner:** $20-$44   **Phone:** 204/944-0594 ⑩
Location: Between Carlton and Hargrave sts. 390 Assiniboine Ave R3C 0Y1. **Hours:** 11:30 am-2:30 & 5-10:30 pm. Closed: 12/25; also Sun. **Reservations:** suggested. **Features:** Located in a beautifully restored mansion near the Assiniboine River, this restaurant provides a warm and inviting dining room and an excellent menu with 20 artfully presented entrees such as pork tenderloin, chicken goyko with shrimp, beef and seafood. Dressy casual; cocktails. **Parking:** on-site. **Cards:** AX, DC, MC, VI. **Historic**

✕

THE VELVET GLOVE
◆◆◆ ◆◆◆◆
Continental

Lunch: $12-$16   **Dinner:** $19-$46   **Phone:** 204/957-1350 ①
Location: Just e of corner Portage Ave and Main St; in The Fairmont Winnipeg. 2 Lombard Pl R3B 0Y3. **Hours:** 6:30 am-2 & 5:30-10 pm, Sat 7 am-11 & 6-10 pm, Sun 7 am-2 & 6-10 pm. **Reservations:** suggested. **Features:** The dining room has a warm finish of wood, large chandeliers and a fireplace. Unpretentious servers are attentive, professional and keen to share their knowledge of the well-developed wine list. Guests can order from the main menu, which lists favorite steak and fish dishes, or the seasonal menu, which centers on creative and artistically presented alternatives. Dressy casual; cocktails. **Parking:** on-site (fee) and valet. **Cards:** AX, DC, DS, MC, VI.

⧝ ✕

WINNIPEG pop. 619,544 (See map and index starting on p. 654)

──────── **WHERE TO STAY** ────────

ASSINIBOINE GORDON INN ON THE PARK   **Phone:** (204)888-4806 ㊱
◆◆

	1P: $72-$84	2P: $72-$84	XP: $8	F16
5/1-10/31				
3/1-4/30 & 11/1-2/28	1P: $46-$56	2P: $46-$56	XP: $8	F16

Small-scale Hotel **Location:** At Lyle St. Located opposite large park. 1975 Portage Ave R3J 0J9. Fax: 204/897-9870. **Facility:** 47 one-bedroom standard units. 2 stories (no elevator), interior/exterior corridors. **Parking:** on-site, winter plug-ins. **Business Services:** meeting rooms. **Cards:** AX, CB, DC, MC, VI.

ⒶⓈⓀ ⓈⒹ ⑪ ⧝ ▭ / ✕ 🛈 /   SOME UNITS

(See map and index starting on p. 654)

CANAD INNS CLUB REGENT CASINO   *Book at aaa.com*   Phone: (204)667-5560   **28**
CAA SAVE   All Year   1P: $129   2P: $139   XP: $10   F17
Location: Just w of Plessis Rd. 1415 Regent Ave W R2C 3B2. Fax: 204/667-5913. **Facility:** 146 units. 142 one-bedroom standard units. 4 one-bedroom suites ($229-$249) with whirlpools. 6 stories, interior corridors. *Bath:* combo or shower only. **Parking:** on-site, winter plug-ins. **Amenities:** video games (fee), high-speed Internet, dual phone lines, voice mail, irons, hair dryers. **Dining:** 7 am-10 pm, cocktails, nightclub. **Pool(s):** small heated indoor. **Leisure Activities:** whirlpool, exercise room. **Guest Services:** gift shop, valet laundry. **Business Services:** meeting rooms. **Cards:** AX, DC, DS, MC, VI. **Special Amenities:** free newspaper.
Small-scale Hotel
(See color ad below)

SOME UNITS

CANAD INNS EXPRESS FORT GARRY   Phone: (204)269-6955   **45**
CAA SAVE   All Year   1P: $60   2P: $70   XP: $10   F17
Location: Just n of Bishop Grandin Blvd. 1792 Pembina Hwy R3T 2G2. Fax: 204/261-4543. **Facility:** 36 one-bedroom standard units. 2 stories (no elevator), interior/exterior corridors. **Parking:** on-site, winter plug-ins. **Terms:** cancellation fee imposed, [ECP] meal plan available. **Amenities:** voice mail. **Dining:** 11 am-11 pm, Fri & Sat-midnight, Sun-10 pm, cocktails, nightclub. **Guest Services:** valet laundry. **Business Services:** meeting rooms. **Cards:** AX, DC, DS, MC, VI. **Special Amenities:** free expanded continental breakfast and free newspaper. *(See color ad below)*
Small-scale Hotel

SOME UNITS

CANAD INNS FORT GARRY   *Book at aaa.com*   Phone: (204)261-7450   **47**
CAA SAVE   All Year   1P: $129   2P: $139   XP: $10   F17
Location: Just n of Bishop Grandin Blvd. 1824 Pembina Hwy R3T 2G2. Fax: 204/275-2187. **Facility:** 107 units. 64 one-bedroom standard units, some with whirlpools. 39 one- and 4 two-bedroom suites ($115-$229). 2 stories, interior corridors. *Bath:* combo or shower only. **Parking:** on-site, winter plug-ins. **Terms:** [BP] meal plan available. **Amenities:** high-speed Internet (fee), voice mail, irons, hair dryers. *Some:* video games, CD players. **Dining:** 7 am-1 am, cocktails, nightclub. **Pool(s):** heated indoor, wading. **Leisure Activities:** whirlpool, waterslide. **Guest Services:** valet laundry. **Business Services:** meeting rooms. **Cards:** AX, DC, DS, MC, VI. **Special Amenities:** free newspaper. *(See color ad below)*
Small-scale Hotel

SOME UNITS

CANAD INNS GARDEN CITY   Phone: (204)633-0024   **24**
CAA SAVE   All Year   1P: $97   2P: $107   XP: $10   F17
Location: McPhillips St at Jefferson Ave. Located in a residential, commercial area. 2100 McPhillips St R2V 3T9. Fax: 204/697-3377. **Facility:** 55 units. 46 one-bedroom standard units. 7 one- and 2 two-bedroom suites ($115-$125). 2 stories (no elevator), interior corridors. **Parking:** on-site, winter plug-ins. **Terms:** [BP] meal plan available. **Amenities:** voice mail, irons, hair dryers. *Some:* DVD players, video games, CD players. **Dining:** 6 am-11 pm, cocktails, nightclub. **Pool(s):** small heated indoor, wading. **Leisure Activities:** whirlpool, waterslide. **Business Services:** meeting rooms, fax (fee). **Cards:** AX, DC, DS, MC, VI. **Special Amenities:** free newspaper. *(See color ad below)*
Small-scale Hotel

SOME UNITS

CANAD INNS POLO PARK   *Book at aaa.com*   Phone: (204)775-8791   **38**
CAA SAVE   All Year   1P: $109   2P: $119   XP: $10   F17
Location: Just e of St James St. Located opposite Blue Bomber football stadium. 1405 St. Matthews Ave R3G 0K5. Fax: 204/783-4039. **Facility:** 111 units. 108 one-bedroom standard units, some with whirlpools. 3 one-bedroom suites ($159-$239). 6 stories, interior corridors. *Bath:* combo or shower only. **Parking:** on-site, winter plug-ins. **Terms:** [BP] meal plan available, package plans, small pets only. **Amenities:** video games (fee), high-speed Internet, voice mail, irons, hair dryers. **Dining:** 8 am-10 pm, cocktails, entertainment. **Pool(s):** heated indoor. **Leisure Activities:** whirlpool, waterslide, exercise room. **Guest Services:** gift shop, valet laundry, area transportation. **Business Services:** conference facilities. **Cards:** AX, DC, DS, MC, VI. **Special Amenities:** free newspaper.
Small-scale Hotel
(See color ad below)

SOME UNITS

(See map and index starting on p. 654)

CANAD INNS-TRANSCONA

CAA SAVE ◆◆◆◆ ◆◆◆◆ **Phone: (204)224-1681** 🔟34

Small-scale Hotel

All Year 1P: $87 2P: $97 XP: $10 F17
Location: Regent Ave at Plessis Rd. 826 Regent Ave W R2C 3A8. Fax: 204/222-3216. **Facility:** 50 units. 47 one-bedroom standard units. 3 two-bedroom suites ($115-$120). 2 stories, interior corridors. **Parking:** on-site, winter plug-ins. **Terms:** [BP] meal plan available. **Amenities:** voice mail, irons, hair dryers. **Dining:** 6 am-10 pm, Sun from 7 am, cocktails, nightclub. **Pool(s):** small heated indoor, wading. **Leisure Activities:** whirlpool, waterslide. **Guest Services:** valet laundry. **Business Services:** conference facilities. **Cards:** AX, DC, DS, MC, VI. **Special Amenities:** free newspaper. *(See color ad p 661)*

SOME UNITS
[S⊘] [📶] [Y] [🏊] [📽] [🖥] [🗙]

CANAD INNS WINDSOR PARK

CAA SAVE ◆◆◆◆ ◆◆◆◆ **Phone: (204)253-2641** 🔟40

Small-scale Hotel

All Year 1P: $67-$77 2P: $77 XP: $10 F17
Location: At Lagimodiere Blvd. Located in a residential/commercial area. 1034 Elizabeth Rd R2J 1B3. Fax: 204/254-0689. **Facility:** 54 units. 52 one-bedroom standard units. 2 two-bedroom suites ($95-$185). 2 stories (no elevator), interior corridors. **Parking:** on-site, winter plug-ins. **Terms:** cancellation fee imposed, package plans. **Amenities:** voice mail, irons, hair dryers. **Dining:** 6:30 am-10 pm, Sat from 7 am, Sun 8 am-9 pm, cocktails, nightclub. **Pool(s):** small heated indoor, wading. **Leisure Activities:** whirlpool, waterslide. **Guest Services:** valet laundry. **Business Services:** meeting rooms. **Cards:** AX, DC, DS, MC, VI. **Special Amenities:** free newspaper. *(See color ad p 661)*

SOME UNITS
[S⊘] [📶] [Y] [🏊] [📽] [DATA PORT] [🖥] [🗙]

CLARION HOTEL & SUITES *Book at aaa.com*

◆◆◆◆ **Phone: (204)774-5110** 🔟42

Small-scale Hotel

All Year 1P: $129-$269 2P: $139-$269 XP: $10 F15
Location: Jct Empress St. Located in a commercial area. 1445 Portage Ave R3G 3P4. Fax: 204/783-6858. **Facility:** 139 units. 89 one-bedroom standard units, some with whirlpools. 50 one-bedroom suites ($159-$269). 4 stories, interior corridors. **Parking:** on-site, winter plug-ins. **Terms:** package plans, pets ($10 extra charge, in smoking units). **Amenities:** dual phone lines, voice mail, irons, hair dryers. *Fee:* video games, high-speed Internet. **Pool(s):** heated indoor, wading. **Leisure Activities:** whirlpool, steamroom, waterslide, exercise room, spa. **Guest Services:** valet laundry. **Business Services:** conference facilities, business center. **Cards:** AX, DC, DS, MC, VI.

SOME UNITS
[A$K] [S⊘] [✈] [🛏] [📶] [Y] [🏊] [✕] [📽] [DATA PORT] [🖥] [🗙] [VCR] [🖥] [🖨]
FEE   FEE   FEE FEE FEE

COMFORT INN *Book at aaa.com*

◆◆◆◆ **Phone: (204)783-5627** 🔟33

Small-scale Hotel

6/1-9/30 1P: $85-$96 2P: $95-$106 XP: $10 F18
10/1-2/28 1P: $80-$92 2P: $90-$102 XP: $10 F18
3/1-5/31 1P: $75-$87 2P: $85-$97 XP: $10 F18
Location: At Sargent Ave and King Edward St. Located in a commercial area. 1770 Sargent Ave R3H 0C8. Fax: 204/783-5661. **Facility:** 81 one-bedroom standard units. 2 stories (no elevator), interior corridors. **Parking:** on-site, winter plug-ins. **Terms:** [ECP] meal plan available, pets ($5 extra charge, in smoking units). **Amenities:** irons, hair dryers. **Guest Services:** valet laundry. **Cards:** AX, DC, DS, JC, MC, VI.

SOME UNITS
[A$K] [S⊘] [🛏] [📶] [🍴] [&M] [📽] [DATA PORT] [🖥] [🗙] [VCR] [🖥] [🖨]
FEE   FEE FEE

COMFORT INN *Book at aaa.com*

CAA SAVE ◆◆◆◆ **Phone: (204)269-7390** 🔟48

Small-scale Hotel

6/1-9/30 1P: $79-$115 2P: $89-$125 XP: $8 F18
3/1-5/31 & 10/1-2/28 1P: $75-$110 2P: $85-$120 XP: $8 F18
Location: Just n of jct Perimeter Hwy 100 and 75. Located in a residential, commercial area. 3109 Pembina Hwy R3T 4R6. Fax: 204/261-7565. **Facility:** 85 one-bedroom standard units, some with whirlpools. 2 stories (no elevator), interior corridors. **Parking:** on-site, winter plug-ins. **Terms:** small pets only ($6 extra charge,1st floor smoking units). **Amenities:** irons, hair dryers. **Guest Services:** valet laundry. **Cards:** AX, DC, DS, JC, MC, VI.

SOME UNITS
[S⊘] [🛏] [📽] [DATA PORT] [🖥] [🗙] [🖥] [🖨]
FEE   FEE FEE

COUNTRY INN & SUITES BY CARLSON *Book at aaa.com*

◆◆◆◆ **Phone: (204)783-6900** 🔟32

Small-scale Hotel

All Year 1P: $89-$99 2P: $99-$109 XP: $10 F
Location: Just s of jct Wellington Ave. Located in a commercial area. 730 King Edward St R3H 1B4. Fax: 204/775-7197. **Facility:** 76 units. 39 one-bedroom standard units. 37 one-bedroom suites ($99-$109). 3 stories, interior corridors. **Parking:** on-site, winter plug-ins. **Terms:** package plans, small pets only. **Amenities:** video library, irons, hair dryers. **Leisure Activities:** exercise room. **Guest Services:** valet and coin laundry. **Cards:** AX, DC, MC, VI. *(See color ad p 657)*

SOME UNITS
[A$K] [S⊘] [🛏] [🍴] [&M] [VCR] [DATA PORT] [🖥] [🖥] [🗙] [🖨]

DAKOTA VILLAGE MOTOR HOTEL

CAA SAVE ◆◆◆ **Phone: (204)256-4315** 🔟44

Small-scale Hotel

All Year 1P: $69-$79 2P: $69-$79 XP: $10 F17
Location: At Dunkirk Dr; jct Metro Rt 52 and 62. Located opposite small shopping plaza. 1105 St. Mary's Rd R2M 3T6. Fax: 204/255-1851. **Facility:** 22 one-bedroom standard units. 2 stories (no elevator), interior corridors. **Parking:** on-site, winter plug-ins. **Terms:** 3 day cancellation notice. **Amenities:** voice mail. **Dining:** 7 am-9 pm, Sun 8 am-8 pm, cocktails, nightclub. **Business Services:** meeting rooms. **Cards:** AX, DC, MC, VI. **Special Amenities:** free local telephone calls.

SOME UNITS
[S⊘] [📶] [Y] [📽] [DATA PORT] [🗙] [🖥] [🖥]

DAYS INN *Book at aaa.com*

CAA SAVE ◆◆◆ **Phone: 204/586-8525** 🔟27

Small-scale Hotel

All Year 1P: $109-$119 2P: $129-$139 XP: $10
Location: Just n of Logan Ave. Located in a commercial area. 550 McPhillips St R2X 2H2. Fax: 204/582-5035. **Facility:** 66 one-bedroom standard units. 2 stories (no elevator), interior corridors. **Parking:** on-site, winter plug-ins. **Terms:** cancellation fee imposed, small pets only ($10 extra charge, in smoking units). **Amenities:** voice mail, irons, hair dryers. **Dining:** 7 am-9 pm, Sat 8 am-7 pm, Sun 8 am-2 pm, cocktails. **Pool(s):** small heated indoor. **Leisure Activities:** sauna, whirlpool, waterslide. **Business Services:** meeting rooms. **Cards:** AX, MC, VI. **Special Amenities:** free local telephone calls and free newspaper.

SOME UNITS
[S⊘] [🛏] [📶] [🍴] [Y] [🏊] [✕] [📽] [DATA PORT] [🖥] [🗙] [🖥] [🖨]
FEE

(See map and index starting on p. 654)

FOUR POINTS SHERATON WINNIPEG INTERNATIONAL AIRPORT   *Book at aaa.com*
Phone: (204)775-5222   **37**
All Year   1P: $115   2P: $115   XP: $15   F18
Location: At Winnipeg International Airport. 1999 Wellington Ave R3H 1H5. Fax: 204/775-5333. **Facility:** 132 units.
Small-scale Hotel   114 one-bedroom standard units. 18 one-bedroom suites ($139-$159), some with whirlpools. 7 stories, interior corridors. *Bath:* combo or shower only. **Parking:** on-site (fee), winter plug-ins. **Terms:** cancellation fee imposed, weekly rates available. **Amenities:** high-speed Internet (fee), voice mail, irons, hair dryers. **Leisure Activities:** sauna, exercise room. **Guest Services:** valet laundry. **Business Services:** meeting rooms, business center. **Cards:** AX, DC, DS, MC, VI. *(See color ad p 5)*

SOME UNITS
ASK   ⍼   ▼   ⛱   🛗   VCR   ▦   DATAPORT   ▮   ▭   ▱   /✕/

GREENWOOD INN   *Book at aaa.com*
Phone: (204)775-9889   **30**
All Year   1P: $99-$139   2P: $99-$139   XP: $10   F18
Location: Wellington Ave at Century St. Located in a commercial area. 1715 Wellington Ave R3H 0G1. Fax: 204/775-4576. **Facility:** 213 units. 203 one-bedroom standard units. 10 one-bedroom suites ($249-$279), some with whirlpools. 6 stories, interior corridors. *Bath:* combo or shower only. **Parking:** on-site, winter plug-ins. **Terms:** cancellation fee imposed, small pets only ($10 extra charge, in designated units). **Amenities:** video games (fee), high-speed Internet, voice mail, irons, hair dryers. **Dining:** 6:30 am-11 pm, cocktails. **Pool(s):** heated indoor. **Leisure Activities:** whirlpool, steamroom, exercise room. **Guest Services:** valet laundry. **Business Services:** conference facilities. **Cards:** AX, CB, DC, MC, VI. **Special Amenities:** free local telephone calls and free newspaper.

SOME UNITS
✈   ▤   FEE   ▦   ▼   🛗   ⛱   ✕   ⛎   DATAPORT   ▮   ▭   /✕   ▱/

HILTON SUITES WINNIPEG AIRPORT   *Book at aaa.com*
Phone: (204)783-1700   **29**
All Year   1P: $139-$189   2P: $139-$189   XP: $15   F18
Location: At Berry St. Located in a commercial area. 1800 Wellington Ave R3H 1B2. Fax: 204/786-6588. **Facility:** 160 units. 11 one-bedroom standard units. 149 one-bedroom suites, some with whirlpools. 6 stories, interior corridors. **Parking:** on-site, winter plug-ins. **Terms:** package plans, small pets only (in designated units). **Amenities:** video games (fee), voice mail, irons, hair dryers. **Dining:** 7-10 pm, cocktails. **Pool(s):** heated outdoor, heated indoor. **Leisure Activities:** sauna, whirlpool, exercise room. **Guest Services:** gift shop, valet laundry. **Business Services:** conference facilities. **Cards:** AX, DC, DS, MC, VI.

SOME UNITS
SD   ✈   ▤   ▦   ▼   ⛎M   ⛱   ✕   ⛎   DATAPORT   ▭   /✕   ▮   ▱/

HOLIDAY INN WINNIPEG AIRPORT/WEST   *Book at aaa.com*
Phone: (204)885-4478   **35**
All Year   1P: $125-$159   2P: $125-$159   XP: $20   F19
Location: Just e of Moray St. Located in a residential, commercial area. 2520 Portage Ave W R3J 3T6. Fax: 204/832-7424. **Facility:** 226 units. 208 one-bedroom standard units. 18 one-bedroom suites ($235-$250), some with kitchens and/or whirlpools. 15 stories, interior corridors. *Bath:* combo or shower only. **Parking:** on-site, winter plug-ins. **Amenities:** video games (fee), dual phone lines, voice mail, irons, hair dryers. *Some:* CD players. **Dining:** 6:30 am-11 pm, Sat & Sun from 7:30 am, cocktails. **Pool(s):** heated indoor, wading. **Leisure Activities:** saunas, whirlpool, childrens activity centre, exercise room. *Fee:* game room. **Guest Services:** gift shop, valet and coin laundry, area transportation-Polo Park. **Business Services:** conference facilities, business center. **Cards:** AX, CB, DC, DS, JC, MC, VI. *(See color ad card insert)*

SOME UNITS
SD   ✈   ▤   ▦   ▼   ⛱   ✕   ⛎   DATAPORT   ▮   ▭   /✕   VCR   ▱/

HOLIDAY INN WINNIPEG-SOUTH   *Book at aaa.com*
Phone: (204)452-4747   **43**
All Year   1P: $120-$140   XP: $15   F19
Location: At McGillivray Blvd. Located in a residential, commercial area. 1330 Pembina Hwy R3T 2B4. Fax: 204/284-2751. **Facility:** 170 units. 169 one-bedroom standard units. 1 one-bedroom suite with whirlpool. 11 stories, interior corridors. **Parking:** on-site, winter plug-ins. **Terms:** [AP], [BP], [CP], [ECP] & [MAP] meal plans available, package plans, pets (in designated units). **Amenities:** dual phone lines, voice mail, irons, hair dryers. **Dining:** 6:30 am-10 pm, Sat & Sun from 7 am, cocktails. **Pool(s):** heated indoor, wading. **Leisure Activities:** whirlpool, exercise room. *Fee:* game room. **Guest Services:** valet and coin laundry. **Business Services:** conference facilities. **Cards:** AX, CB, DC, DS, JC, MC, VI. **Special Amenities:** free local telephone calls and free newspaper. *(See color ad card insert)*

SOME UNITS
SD   ✈   ▤   ▦   ▼   ⛱   ✕   ⛎   DATAPORT   ▭   /✕   ▮   ▱/
FEE   FEE

LINCOLN MOTOR HOTEL
Phone: 204/589-7314   **25**
All Year   1P: $50-$52   2P: $54-$56   XP: $6
Location: McPhillips St at Troy Ave. Located in a residential, commercial area. 1030 McPhillips St R2X 2K7. Fax: 204/589-8241. **Facility:** 23 one-bedroom standard units. 2 stories (no elevator), interior corridors. **Parking:** on-site, winter plug-ins. **Terms:** 5 day cancellation notice-fee imposed. **Dining:** 7 am-10 pm; closed Sun, cocktails, nightclub. **Business Services:** meeting rooms. **Cards:** AX, MC, VI.

SOME UNITS
SD   ▤   ▼   DATAPORT   ▭   /✕/

SUPER 8   *Book at aaa.com*
Phone: 204/269-8888   **46**
All Year [ECP]   1P: $88-$148   2P: $98-$158   XP: $10   F12
Location: 1 km n of jct Bishop Grandin Blvd. Located in a commercial area. 1714 Pembina Hwy R3T 2G2. Fax: 204/269-8889. **Facility:** 104 units. 91 one-bedroom standard units. 13 one-bedroom suites, some with whirlpools. 4 stories, interior corridors. **Parking:** on-site, winter plug-ins. **Terms:** cancellation fee imposed, pets (with prior approval). **Amenities:** high-speed Internet, voice mail, safes, irons, hair dryers. *Some:* dual phone lines. **Pool(s):** small heated indoor. **Leisure Activities:** whirlpool, waterslide, exercise room. **Guest Services:** valet and coin laundry. **Business Services:** meeting rooms, business center. **Cards:** AX, DC, DS, MC, VI.

SOME UNITS
ASK   SD   ▤   ▦+   ⛱   ✕   ⛎   DATAPORT   ▭   /✕   VCR   ▮   ▱/

(See map and index starting on p. 654)

TRAVELODGE — *Book at aaa.com* — Phone: (204)255-6000 [41]
CAA SAVE — All Year — 1P: $76-$90 — 2P: $82-$96 — XP: $6 — F17
Location: Just e of jct Fermor Ave and St. Anne's Rd. Located in a residential, commercial area. 20 Alpine Ave R2M 0Y5. Fax: 204/253-1563. **Facility:** 75 units. 71 one-bedroom standard units. 4 one-bedroom suites, some with whirlpools. 2 stories (no elevator), interior corridors. **Parking:** on-site, winter plug-ins. **Small-scale Hotel Terms:** cancellation fee imposed, weekly rates available, package plans, small pets only ($5 extra charge, in smoking units). **Amenities:** video library (fee), voice mail, hair dryers. *Some:* irons. **Dining:** 7 am-10 pm, Sun 8 am-9 pm, cocktails, nightclub. **Pool(s):** small heated indoor, wading. **Leisure Activities:** sauna, whirlpool. *Fee:* 12 bowling lanes, game room. **Guest Services:** valet laundry. **Business Services:** meeting rooms. **Cards:** AX, DC, MC, VI. **Special Amenities:** free local telephone calls and free newspaper.
SOME UNITS

TWIN PILLARS BED & BREAKFAST — Phone: 204/284-7590 [39]
— All Year [ECP] — 1P: $50-$60 — 2P: $60-$70 — XP: $10 — F7
Location: 0.6 km e of Osborne St. Located in a residential area across from park. 235 Oakwood Ave R3L 1E5. Fax: 204/284-1913. **Facility:** Smoke free premises. 4 one-bedroom standard units. 3 stories (no elevator), **Bed & Breakfast** interior corridors. *Bath:* some shared, combo or shower only. **Parking:** on-site, winter plug-ins. **Terms:** office hours 8 am-10 pm, pets ($50 deposit, with prior approval). **Leisure Activities:** bicycles. **Guest Services:** complimentary laundry. **Cards:** AX, DC, MC, VI.
SOME UNITS

VICTORIA INN HOTEL & CONVENTION CENTRE — *Book at aaa.com* — Phone: (204)786-4801 [31]
CAA SAVE — All Year — 1P: $89 — 2P: $99 — XP: $10 — F17
Location: At Berry St. Located in a commercial area. 1808 Wellington Ave R3H 0G3. Fax: 204/786-1329. **Facility:** 275 units. 273 one- and 2 two-bedroom standard units. 5 stories, interior corridors. *Bath:* combo or shower only. **Parking:** on-site, winter plug-ins. **Terms:** cancellation fee imposed, pets ($10 extra charge). **Small-scale Hotel Amenities:** video games (fee), voice mail, irons, hair dryers. **Dining:** 6:30 am-10 pm, Sat & Sun from 7 am, cocktails. **Pool(s):** small heated indoor. **Leisure Activities:** whirlpool, waterslide, exercise room. *Fee:* massage. **Guest Services:** gift shop, valet and coin laundry. **Business Services:** conference facilities. **Cards:** AX, DC, DS, MC, VI.
SOME UNITS

VISCOUNT GORT HOTEL — *Book at aaa.com* — Phone: (204)775-0451 [49]
CAA SAVE — All Year [BP] — 1P: $82 — 2P: $82 — F17
Location: Portage Ave at Rt 90. Located in a commercial area. 1670 Portage Ave R3J 0C9. Fax: 204/772-2161. **Facility:** 135 units. 129 one-bedroom standard units. 6 one-bedroom suites, some with whirlpools. 4-6 stories, interior corridors. **Parking:** on-site, winter plug-ins. **Terms:** 10 day cancellation notice, weekly rates **Small-scale Hotel** available, package plans, small pets only ($10 fee, in smoking units). **Amenities:** video games (fee), voice mail. *Some:* high-speed Internet (fee), irons, hair dryers. **Dining:** 2 restaurants, 7 am-10 pm, Sun-9 pm, cocktails. **Pool(s):** heated indoor, wading. **Leisure Activities:** sauna, whirlpool, limited exercise equipment. **Guest Services:** valet laundry, area transportation-bus & train station. **Business Services:** conference facilities. **Cards:** AX, CB, DC, DS, JC, MC, VI. **Special Amenities:** free full breakfast and free local telephone calls.
SOME UNITS

——— **WHERE TO DINE** ———

529 WELLINGTON — Lunch: $12-$24 — Dinner: $32-$49 — Phone: 204/487-8325 [30]
Location: Jct Acadamy Ave, just s. 529 Wellington Cres R3M 0A5. **Hours:** 11:30 am-2 & 5-11 pm, Sat from 5 pm, Sun 5 pm-10 pm. Closed: 1/1, 12/25. **Reservations:** accepted. **Features:** The restaurant encourages **Steak & Seafood** patrons to think big: big steaks, that is. Also huge on quality are lobster and jumbo prawns. Only Canadian Prime certified Alberta beef is served. Service matches the detailed old dining rooms, which are paneled in rich wood and fitting of a grand old mansion. Dressy casual; cocktails. **Parking:** on-site. **Cards:** AX, DC, MC, VI.

BONFIRE BISTRO — *Menu on aaa.com* — Lunch: $7-$14 — Dinner: $12-$20 — Phone: 204/487-4440 [26]
CAA — **Location:** Jct Waterloo St. 1433 Corydon Ave R3N 0J2. **Hours:** 11:30 am-2:30 & 5-10 pm, Fri & Sat-11 pm. Closed major holidays; also Sun. **Features:** Diners can expect comfortable, simple decor and a friendly atmosphere. Management and staff are focused on creating well-prepared dishes. Among choices are **Italian** wonderful thin-crust gourmet pizzas baked in a wood-fired oven, assorted pasta creations and varied daily specials posted on a blackboard. Casual dress; beer & wine only. **Parking:** on-site. **Cards:** MC, VI.

BRANIGAN'S — Lunch: $5-$9 — Dinner: $11-$30 — Phone: 204/948-0040 [21]
Location: Just e of Lagimodiere Blvd (Metro Rt 20); in Kildonan Place Mall. 1555 Regent Ave R2C 4J2. **Hours:** 11 am-10 pm, Thurs-Sat to 11 pm, Sun-8 pm. Closed: 12/25. **Reservations:** accepted. **Features:** The family **Canadian** restaurant's menu offers a wide variety to cater to varied tastes. The convenient shopping center location has lots of parking. Casual dress; cocktails. **Parking:** on-site. **Cards:** AX, DC, MC, VI.

CORK & DOCK — Lunch: $7-$11 — Dinner: $9-$28 — Phone: 204/275-8822 [33]
Location: 1 km n of jct Bishop Grandin Blvd. 1700 Pembina Hwy R3T 2T2. **Hours:** 11 am-midnight. Closed: 12/25. **Reservations:** accepted. **Features:** At times bustling, this popular restaurant offers a variety of **Continental** Mediterranean-influenced dishes. The dining room has booth and table seating, and many seats offer river views. There is patio seating in season. Casual dress; cocktails. **Parking:** on-site. **Cards:** AX, DC, MC, VI.

(See map and index starting on p. 654)

FUSION GRILL
Canadian
Lunch: $8-$14   **Dinner:** $20-$30   **Phone:** 204/489-6963   ㉓
Location: Just e of jct Kenaston Blvd. 550 Academy Rd R3N 0E3. **Hours:** 11:30 am-2:30 & 5:30-10 pm. Closed major holidays; also Sun & Mon. **Reservations:** suggested. **Features:** This comfortable little restaurant affords a wonderful opportunity to experience fine Canadian food. Manitoba produce is often used and the list of Canadian wines is notable. Casual dress; cocktails. **Parking:** street. **Cards:** AX, DC, MC, VI.

INDIA PALACE
Indian
Lunch: $8   **Dinner:** $8-$20   **Phone:** 204/774-6061   ㉒
Location: Corner of Simcoe St. 770 Ellice Ave R3G 0B8. **Hours:** 11 am-3 & 5-9 pm, Fri & Sat-10 pm. Closed: 12/25. **Reservations:** suggested. **Features:** You'll enjoy the fresh, flavorful cuisine at this restaurant, where the tandoori chicken is exceptional. The menu is so extensive that it will satisfy the most discerning tastes. It has a softly lit decor, and warm, caring and friendly service. Casual dress; cocktails. **Parking:** street. **Cards:** AX, DC, MC, VI.

LUX SOLE
International
Lunch: $7-$13   **Dinner:** $12-$23   **Phone:** 204/453-0222   ㉘
Location: Jct Beresford Ave. 726 Osborne St S R3L 2C2. **Hours:** 11:30 am-10 pm, Thurs-Sat to midnight. Closed major holidays. **Reservations:** accepted. **Features:** Hallmarks of this cafe include a friendly staff and a menu that demonstrates International inspiration and imagination. Casual dress; cocktails. **Parking:** street. **Cards:** MC, VI.

MAXIME
Continental
Lunch: $7-$8   **Dinner:** $10-$22   **Phone:** 204/257-1521   ㉜
Location: Corner of St. Mary's Rd and Bishop Grandin Blvd. 1131 St. Mary's Rd R2M 3T9. **Hours:** 11 am-midnight, Sun 10:30 am-10 pm. Closed: 1/1, 12/25, 12/26. **Reservations:** accepted. **Features:** This restaurant is a favorite with locals. Its menu features pasta, pizza, Greek specialties, steak, chicken and seafood entrees, which are served in large portions. The service is polite, professional and efficient, and the decor is upscale. Casual dress; cocktails. **Parking:** on-site. **Cards:** AX, DC, MC, VI.

MEDICINE ROCK CAFE
Canadian
Lunch: $6-$11   **Dinner:** $14-$23   **Phone:** 204/864-2451   ㉞
Location: 13 km w on Hwy 1 from city limits, then 4 km n. 990 Hwy 26 R0H 1J0. **Hours:** 11 am-10 pm, Sun 10 am-9 pm. Closed: 12/25, 12/26. **Reservations:** suggested. **Features:** The Medicine Rock Cafe offers a beautiful, rustic ambience in a charming log home in a rural area outside Winnipeg. Entrees include chicken piccata, fresh walleye, baked salmon and steak. Old rifles, sabers and a stone fireplace add to the decor. Casual dress; cocktails. **Parking:** on-site. **Cards:** AX, MC, VI.

MONA LISA RISTORANTE
Italian
Lunch: $7-$11   **Dinner:** $14-$22   **Phone:** 204/488-3687   ㉕
Location: Corner of Renfrew St. 1697 Corydon Ave R3N 0J9. **Hours:** 11:30 am-2:30 & 4:30-11:30 pm, Fri-midnight, Sat 4:30 pm-midnight, Sun 4:30 pm-10 pm. Closed: 12/25. **Reservations:** suggested. **Features:** This popular neighborhood restaurant features an extensive cuisine of Northern Italian fare, including mezza lune, melengane alla parmigiana, veal and jumbo prawns. Local hockey hero memorabilia adorn the walls in the lounge, and there's a sidewalk patio. Casual dress; cocktails. **Parking:** street. **Cards:** AX, DC, MC, VI.

THE ROUND TABLE STEAK HOUSE & PUB
Steak House
Lunch: $7-$13   **Dinner:** $20-$33   **Phone:** 204/453-3631   ㉙
Location: Just s of Taylor St. 800 Pembina Hwy R3M 2M7. **Hours:** 11 am-1 am. Closed: 1/1, 9/5, 12/25; also 5/19. **Reservations:** accepted. **Features:** You'll enjoy the casual atmosphere at this restaurant, which has an English-manor decor that includes glowing fireplaces. The house specialty is prime rib, and the menu also offers a very good variety of steak, seafood, chicken and pasta dishes. Casual dress; cocktails. **Parking:** on-site. **Cards:** AX, DC, MC, VI.

ROYAL FORK BUFFET RESTAURANT
American
Lunch: $9-$10   **Dinner:** $12-$13   **Phone:** 204/668-1960   ⑳
Location: Jct Lagimodiere Blvd (Metro Rt 20) and Regent Ave W; in Kildonan Crossing Shopping Centre. 900-1615 Regent Ave W R2C 5C6. **Hours:** 11 am-8:30 pm, Fri & Sat-9 pm, Sun 10 am-8 pm. Closed: 12/25. **Features:** This restaurant features family-oriented dining and a menu with excellent variety. Dinner prices are in effect at 4 pm and all day on Sunday. If you have a big appetite and a limited budget, you'll do well here. Service is friendly and efficient. Casual dress. **Parking:** on-site. **Cards:** MC, VI.

SPUNTINO CAFE
Italian
Lunch: $9-$10   **Dinner:** $10-$18   **Phone:** 204/475-4447   ㉗
Location: Jct Stafford St. 926 Grosvenor Ave R3M 0N4. **Hours:** 11 am-10 pm, Fri-11 pm, Sat noon-11 pm, Sun 5 pm-10 pm. Closed major holidays; also Mon & 3 weeks in Aug. **Reservations:** accepted. **Features:** The delightful little cafe features wonderful pasta dishes, veal and some seafood, which are accompanied by fresh bread that's prepared in-house. Desserts are not to be ignored. Casual dress; cocktails. **Parking:** street. **Cards:** AX, MC, VI.

TAVERN IN THE PARK
Continental
Lunch: $9-$16   **Dinner:** $16-$40   **Phone:** 204/896-7275   ㉔
Location: In Assiniboine Park. 55 Pavilion Cres R3P 2N6. **Hours:** 11:30 am-2:30 & 5-10 pm, Sun 10 am-2 & 5-9 pm. Closed: Mon. **Reservations:** required. **Features:** Set in the city's most famous park, this restaurant's dining room is bright, airy and upscale. Be ready to savor its meals, which are delectable, progressive Continental fare. Its server staff is charming and knowledgeable. One of the city's better spots. Dressy casual; cocktails. **Parking:** on-site. **Cards:** AX, DC, MC, VI.

TIFFANI'S RESTAURANT
Continental
Lunch: $6-$11   **Dinner:** $17-$29   **Phone:** 204/256-7324   ㉛
Location: Just e of jct Fermor Ave and St. Annes Rd; in Appleton Estates Apt Bldg. 133 Niakwa Rd R2M 5J5. **Hours:** 11:30 am-2 & 5-10 pm, Fri & Sat-11 pm. Closed major holidays. **Reservations:** suggested. **Features:** You'll enjoy Tiffani's, an elegant dining room offering a breathtaking view of the city from the 17th floor. The restaurant specializes in veal preparations, but the menu also includes beef, pasta and fish entrees. The serving staff is friendly and polite. Dressy casual; cocktails. **Parking:** on-site. **Cards:** AX, MC, VI.

Northwest Territories and Nunavut

Near Baffin Island,
Nunavut
© SuperStock

YELLOWKNIFE pop. 16,541

——— WHERE TO STAY ———

CHATEAU NOVA
CAA SAVE
▼▼▼
Small-scale Hotel

Phone: 867/873-9700
All Year   1P: $146-$156   2P: $146-$156   XP: $15   F12
Location: Downtown. 4401 50th Ave X1A 2N2 (PO Box 250). Fax: 867/873-9702. **Facility:** 60 one-bedroom standard units, some with efficiencies and/or whirlpools. 4 stories, interior corridors. **Parking:** on-site, winter plug-ins. **Amenities:** high-speed Internet, voice mail, irons, hair dryers. **Dining:** 7 am-2 & 5-9:30 pm, Sat from 8 am, Sun 10 am-2 pm, cocktails. **Leisure Activities:** whirlpool, steamroom, exercise room, spa. **Guest Services:** valet laundry. **Business Services:** meeting rooms, business center. **Cards:** AX, DC, DS, JC, MC, VI. **Special Amenities:** free local telephone calls and early check-in/late check-out.

SOME UNITS

[🛫] [🍴] [🍸] [✕] [📶] [DATA PORT] [💻] / [✕] [🔒] [🖨] /

THE EXPLORER HOTEL   *Book at aaa.com*
▼▼
Large-scale Hotel

Phone: (867)873-3531
All Year   2P: $145-$200   XP: $20   F12
Location: Downtown. 4825 49th Ave X1A 2R3 (PS 7000, 4825 49th Ave). Fax: 867/873-2789. **Facility:** 128 units. 126 one-bedroom standard units. 2 one-bedroom suites. 8 stories, interior corridors. **Parking:** on-site, winter plug-ins. **Amenities:** high-speed Internet, voice mail, hair dryers. **Leisure Activities:** exercise room. **Guest Services:** gift shop, valet laundry. **Business Services:** conference facilities. **Cards:** AX, DC, MC, VI.

SOME UNITS

[ASK] [S📶] [🛫] [🍴] [🍸] [📶] [DATA PORT] [💻] / [✕]

FRASER TOWER SUITE HOTEL   *Book at aaa.com*
▼▼▼
Large-scale Hotel

Phone: (867)873-8700
All Year   1P: $139-$165   2P: $139-$165   XP: $15   F16
Location: Corner of 52nd St and 53rd Ave. 5303 52nd St X1A 1V1. Fax: 867/873-8708. **Facility:** 58 units. 40 one- and 18 two-bedroom standard units with kitchens. 10 stories, interior corridors. **Parking:** on-site, winter plug-ins. **Terms:** cancellation fee imposed, package plans, pets ($200 deposit, $10 extra charge). **Amenities:** dual phone lines, voice mail, irons, hair dryers. *Some:* high-speed Internet. **Leisure Activities:** steamroom, exercise room. **Guest Services:** valet and coin laundry. **Business Services:** meeting rooms. **Cards:** AX, DC, MC, VI.

SOME UNITS

[ASK] [S📶] [🐾] [🎾] [📶] [DATA PORT] [🔒] [🖨] [💻] / [✕] /
FEE

YELLOWKNIFE SUPER 8 MOTEL   *Book at aaa.com*
▼▼
Motel

Phone: (867)669-8888
All Year [CP]   1P: $129-$169   2P: $129-$169   XP: $10   F18
Location: 2 km s on Franklin, 1 km w; in Walmart Plaza. 308 Old Airport Rd X1A 3G3. Fax: 867/669-8801. **Facility:** Smoke free premises. 66 units. 41 one- and 25 two-bedroom standard units. 4 stories, interior corridors. **Parking:** on-site, winter plug-ins. **Terms:** pets ($25 fee, 1st floor units). **Amenities:** high-speed Internet, voice mail, irons, hair dryers. **Leisure Activities:** exercise room. **Guest Services:** valet and coin laundry. **Cards:** AX, DC, MC, VI.

SOME UNITS

[ASK] [S📶] [🛫] [🐾] [🍴+] [✕] [📶] [DATA PORT] [💻] / [🔒] /
FEE

——— *The following lodging was either not evaluated or did not meet AAA rating requirements but is listed for your information only.* ———

THE BAYSIDE B&B
[fyi]

Phone: 867/920-4686
Not evaluated. **Location:** In Old Town. 3505 McDonald Dr X1A 2H2. Facilities, services, and decor characterize a basic property.

——— WHERE TO DINE ———

BULLOCK'S BISTRO
▼▼
▼
Regional Canadian

Lunch: $18-$30   **Dinner: $18-$30**   **Phone: 867/873-3474**
Location: In Old Town. 3534 Weaver Dr X1A 2H2. **Hours:** Open 4/15-10/15; 11 am-10 pm. Closed major holidays. **Reservations:** suggested. **Features:** Ask any local for a place to eat, and the seafood joint is usually one of the first names mentioned. They also are likely to point out the unusual service, which includes some self-service aspects. Patrons get their own beverages and may clear their own plates. Although what service is provided can be slow, a visit here is well worth it. The distinctive decor provides ample things to view while waiting. Casual dress; beer & wine only. **Parking:** on-site. **Cards:** MC, VI.

[🎾] [✕]

LE FROLIC BISTRO/BAR
CAA
▼▼
French

Lunch: $10-$20   **Dinner: $18-$30**   **Phone: 867/669-9852**
Location: Downtown; underneath L'Heritage. 5019 49th St X1A 2N6. **Hours:** 11 am-1 am. Closed major holidays; also Sun. **Features:** Creative, colorful and regionally inspired cuisine is on the menu at the bustling bistro, beneath L'Heritage Restaurant. Locals frequent the restaurant after work and on weekends for its casual, relaxed environment. Guests can mingle with the locals and sample entrees ranging from venison to Arctic char. Casual dress; cocktails. **Parking:** street. **Cards:** AX, DC, JC, MC, VI.

[🍸]

L'HERITAGE RESTAURANT FRANCAIS
CAA
▼▼▼
French

Dinner: $20-$37   **Phone: 867/873-9561**
Location: Downtown. 5019 49th St X1A 2N6. **Hours:** 5 pm-10 pm. Closed: Sun. **Reservations:** suggested. **Features:** One of the city's best-kept downtown secrets, the quaint French restaurant is a pleasant surprise. Small touches of France are incorporated into the decor. Each dish is a delight, with creativity and color, and the menu is heavily influenced with regional ingredients. This spot shouldn't be missed for a fine, elegant meal in lovely surroundings. Casual dress; cocktails. **Parking:** street. **Cards:** AX, DC, JC, MC, VI.

[✕]

WILDCAT CAFE
▼▼
Regional Canadian

Lunch: $6-$12   **Dinner: $10-$15**   **Phone: 867/873-8850**
Location: In Old Town. 3904 Wiley Rd X1A 2N2. **Hours:** Open 6/1-9/15; 11 am-10 pm, Sat & Sun from 10 am. **Features:** In the heart of Old Town, the historic cafe is a popular spot at meal times, both with locals and tourists. One of the city's original buildings, the small log cabin has large picnic tables inside, and guests who can't find their own are invited to partake in a city tradition and join another party's table. Among offerings of regional cuisine are musk-ox stew and awesome milkshakes. Casual dress; cocktails. **Parking:** on-site. **Cards:** VI. **Historic**

[🎾] [✕]

Saskatchewan

© SuperStock

CARONPORT pop. 1,040

―――――― WHERE TO STAY ――――――

THE PILGRIM INN

▼▼▼ ▼▼▼ Small-scale Hotel

Phone: 306/756-5002

All Year [CP]　　1P: $77　　2P: $77

Location: Jct Main Access; on Trans-Canada Hwy 1. Located adjacent to a truck stop. Hwy 1 W SOH 0S0 (510 College Dr). Fax: 306/756-5005. **Facility:** Smoke free premises. 40 units. 39 one-bedroom standard units. 1 one-bedroom suite ($99) with efficiency. 2 stories (no elevator), interior corridors. **Parking:** on-site, winter plug-ins. **Terms:** office hours 7 am-11 pm, pets (in designated units, with prior approval). **Leisure Activities:** 4 tennis courts. **Guest Services:** coin laundry. **Business Services:** meeting rooms. **Cards:** AX, DC, MC, VI.

(ASK) (S/D) [🐕] [✕] [DATA PORT] [💻] / [🖨] /　SOME UNITS

DAVIDSON pop. 1,035

―――――― WHERE TO DINE ――――――

KEEPER'S RESTAURANT & LOUNGE　　**Lunch:** $6-$10　　**Dinner:** $6-$17　　**Phone:** 306/567-4225

▼▼▼ ▼▼▼ American

Location: Shell Station Hwy 11, south approach to town. Hwy 11, Davidson S0G 1A0. **Hours:** 6 am-10 pm; 6:30 am-10 pm 9/1-3/31. **Reservations:** accepted. **Features:** This popular local eatery and truck stop offers hearty fare, served up in generous portions, in an atmosphere of collectibles, bric-a-brac and antiques. Casual dress; cocktails. **Parking:** on-site. **Cards:** MC, VI.

[✕]

ELBOW pop. 298

―――――― WHERE TO DINE ――――――

BACK HOME BAKERY & DELI　　　　　　**Lunch:** $5-$8　　　　　　**Phone:** 306/854-2244

◆ Bakery/Desserts

Location: Jct Pfeffer Ave. 445 Saskatchewan St S0H 1J0. **Hours:** 6 am-4 pm; from 8 am, Sat & Sun-2 pm in winter. Closed: 12/24-1/2. **Features:** Locals sample fresh bread, buns and other sweets that are prepared daily. In addition, there are delicatessen goods, soups and sandwiches. Casual dress. **Parking:** on-site. **Cards:** MC, VI.

[✕]

ESTEVAN pop. 10,242

―――――― WHERE TO STAY ――――――

BEEFEATER INN

(CAA) (SAVE)
▼▼▼ ▼▼▼ ▼▼▼
Small-scale Hotel

Phone: (306)634-6456

All Year [CP]　　1P: $75-$125

Location: Centre. Located in a commercial area. 1305 9th St S4A 2H7 (PO Box 1099). Fax: 306/634-8733. **Facility:** 75 units. 68 one-bedroom standard units, some with whirlpools. 7 one-bedroom suites ($99-$149), some with whirlpools. 3 stories, interior corridors. **Parking:** on-site, winter plug-ins. **Terms:** 7 day cancellation notice, small pets only (with prior approval). **Amenities:** high-speed Internet (fee), voice mail, irons, hair dryers. **Dining:** 2 restaurants, 5:30 am-10 pm, cocktails. **Leisure Activities:** exercise room. **Business Services:** meeting rooms. **Cards:** AX, DC, MC, VI. **Special Amenities:** free continental breakfast and free local telephone calls.

[🐕] [🍽] [✕] [DATA PORT] [📞] [💻] / [✕] [VCR] [📷]　SOME UNITS

PERFECT INNS & SUITES

(CAA) (SAVE)
▼▼▼ ▼▼▼ ▼▼▼
Small-scale Hotel

Phone: (306)634-8585

All Year [ECP]　　1P: $75-$90　　2P: $89-$99　　XP: $5　　F18

Location: Just n of jct Hwy 39 E and 2nd Ave. Located next to Tim Horton's. 134 2nd Ave S4A 2W6. Fax: 306/634-9040. **Facility:** 70 units. 65 one-bedroom standard units. 5 one-bedroom suites, some with whirlpools. 3 stories, interior corridors. **Parking:** on-site, winter plug-ins. **Terms:** small pets only ($8 extra charge, with prior approval). **Amenities:** voice mail, irons, hair dryers. *Some:* dual phone lines. **Fee:** high-speed Internet. **Leisure Activities:** whirlpool, exercise room. **Guest Services:** coin laundry. **Business Services:** meeting rooms. **Cards:** AX, DC, DS, MC, VI. **Special Amenities:** free expanded continental breakfast and free newspaper.

[🐕] [🍽] [✕] [DATA PORT] [📞] [💻] / [✕] [VCR] [📷]　SOME UNITS
FEE　　　　　　　　　　　　　　　　　　　　　　FEE FEE

―――――― WHERE TO DINE ――――――

EDDIE WEBSTER'S GRILL & BAR　　**Lunch:** $6-$13　　**Dinner:** $7-$22　　**Phone:** 306/634-5656

▼▼▼ ▼▼▼ Canadian

Location: Just e of jct Hwy 39 E and 2nd Ave. 2015 Mayfair Bay S4A 1X7. **Hours:** 11 am-11 pm. Closed: 12/25. **Reservations:** accepted. **Features:** The popular, casual restaurant provides efficient, friendly service in a pleasant atmosphere. The menu offers good variety. Patio seating can be requested in season. Casual dress; cocktails. **Parking:** on-site. **Cards:** AX, MC, VI.

[▼] [✕]

FOAM LAKE pop. 1,218

―――――― WHERE TO STAY ――――――

LA VISTA MOTEL

▼▼▼ Motel

Phone: 306/272-3341
D12

All Year　　1P: $50　　2P: $60

Location: On Hwy 16. Located in a commercial area. Jct Hwy 16 & 310 S0A 1A0. Fax: 306/272-4345. **Facility:** 16 one-bedroom standard units, some with efficiencies. 1 story, interior corridors. **Parking:** on-site, winter plug-ins. **Terms:** office hours 7 am-11 pm, 30 day cancellation notice-fee imposed, [ECP] meal plan available, pets ($5 extra charge, in designated units). **Cards:** MC, VI.

[🐕] [✕] [DATA PORT] [📞] [💻] / [📷] /　SOME UNITS
FEE

KINDERSLEY pop. 4,548

———— **WHERE TO STAY** ————

BEST WESTERN WESTRIDGE INN   *Book at aaa.com*   Phone: (306)463-4687
(CAA) (SAVE)   All Year   1P: $85   2P: $90
▼▼▼   **Location:** Jct of Hwy 7 and 21. Located in a commercial area. 100 12 Ave NW S0L 1S0 (PO Box 1657).
Small-scale Hotel   Fax: 306/463-3030. **Facility:** 43 one-bedroom standard units, some with kitchens and/or whirlpools. 2 stories (no elevator), interior/exterior corridors. **Parking:** on-site, winter plug-ins. **Terms:** 7 day cancellation notice, small pets only. **Amenities:** irons, hair dryers. **Dining:** 6 am-11 pm, Sun from 8 am, cocktails. **Leisure Activities:** sauna, exercise room. **Guest Services:** valet laundry. **Business Services:** meeting rooms. **Cards:** AX, CB, DC, DS, MC, VI. **Special Amenities:** free local telephone calls and early check-in/late check-out.

SOME UNITS
[S/D] [🛏] [🍴] [Y] [📷] [DATA PORT] [📶] [📺] / [✕] [📠] /

LANGENBURG pop. 1,107

———— **WHERE TO STAY** ————

LANGENBURG COUNTRY INN   Phone: 306/743-2638
▼   All Year   1P: $45   2P: $59
Motel   **Location:** On Hwy 16, 1 km e. Located in a rural area. 1041 Kaiser William Ave E S0A 2A0 (PO Box 279). Fax: 306/743-5506. **Facility:** 14 one-bedroom standard units. 1 story, exterior corridors. **Parking:** on-site, winter plug-ins. **Terms:** office hours 7:30 am-10 pm, weekly rates available. **Cards:** AX, MC, VI.

SOME UNITS
[ASK] [📷] [DATA PORT] [📺] / [✕] [📶] [📠] /

LLOYDMINSTER —*See also LLOYDMINSTER, AB.*

———— **WHERE TO DINE** ————

SPIRO'S STEAK & PIZZA   **Lunch:** $7-$14   **Dinner:** $10-$16   Phone: 306/825-9787
▼▼ ▼▼   **Location:** Hwy 16 (Yellowhead Hwy), 3425 50th Ave S9V 0N9. **Hours:** 10 am-10 pm. Closed: 1/1, 12/25, 12/26; also Mon. **Features:** A great place to take a family for a meal, the steak and pizza house has
Steak House   something for everyone on its menu. In addition to the requisites, this place serves sandwiches and some Greek dishes. Casual dress; cocktails. **Parking:** on-site. **Cards:** AX, MC, VI.

[✕]

MOOSE JAW pop. 32,131

———— **WHERE TO STAY** ————

CAPONE'S HIDEAWAY MOTEL   Phone: 306/692-6422
(CAA) (SAVE)   All Year   1P: $56-$60   2P: $63-$78   XP: $5   F12
▼▼▼   **Location:** Jct Manitoba St E. Located in a commerical area. 1 Main St N S6H 0V8. Fax: 306/692-8494. **Facility:** 23
Motel   one-bedroom standard units, some with kitchens. 2 stories (no elevator), exterior corridors. **Parking:** on-site. **Terms:** office hours 8 am-11 pm, weekly rates available, pets (with prior approval). **Cards:** AX, JC, MC, VI. **Special Amenities:** free continental breakfast and free local telephone calls.

SOME UNITS
[S/D] [🛏] [📷] [DATA PORT] / [✕] [VCR] [📶] [📠] [📺] /

COMFORT INN   *Book at aaa.com*   Phone: (306)692-2100
▼▼ ▼▼   All Year   1P: $92-$150   2P: $92-$150   XP: $5   F18
   Location: Just w of jct Main St. Located in a commercial area. 155 Thatcher Dr W S6J 1M1. Fax: 306/693-6266.
Small-scale Hotel   **Facility:** 60 units. 58 one-bedroom standard units, some with whirlpools. 2 one-bedroom suites ($150-$175) with whirlpools. 3 stories, interior corridors. **Parking:** on-site, winter plug-ins. **Terms:** weekly rates available, pets ($15 fee, in smoking units). **Amenities:** voice mail. *Some:* high-speed Internet, irons, hair dryers. **Leisure Activities:** limited exercise equipment. **Guest Services:** valet and coin laundry. **Cards:** AX, DC, DS, MC, VI.

SOME UNITS
[ASK] [S/D] [🛏] [DATA PORT] [📺] / [✕] [📶] [📠]
    FEE   FEE FEE

DAYS INN   *Book at aaa.com*   Phone: 306/691-5777
▼▼ ▼▼   All Year [ECP]   1P: $90   2P: $100   XP: $10   F17
   Location: From jct Trans-Canada Hwy 1, just s. Located in a commercial area. 1720 Main St N S6J 1L4.
Small-scale Hotel   Fax: 306/692-0907. **Facility:** 80 units. 69 one- and 11 two-bedroom standard units, some with whirlpools. 4 stories, interior corridors. **Parking:** on-site, winter plug-ins. **Terms:** weekly rates available, pets ($10 extra charge). **Amenities:** high-speed Internet, voice mail, irons, hair dryers. **Pool(s):** small heated indoor. **Leisure Activities:** whirlpool, waterslide, exercise room. **Guest Services:** coin laundry. **Cards:** AX, MC, VI.

SOME UNITS
[ASK] [S/D] [🛏] [🏊] [✕] [📷] [DATA PORT] [📺] / [✕] [📶] [📠]
       FEE

HERITAGE INN   *Book at aaa.com*   Phone: (306)693-7550
▼▼ ▼▼   6/1-2/28   1P: $92   2P: $100   XP: $5   F16
   3/1-5/31   1P: $86   2P: $99   XP: $5   F16
Small-scale Hotel   **Location:** 1.5 km s of jct Trans-Canada Hwy 1 and 2; access from Hwy 2 via Thatcher Dr. Located in a commercial area. 1590 Main St N S6J 1L3. Fax: 306/692-5660. **Facility:** 104 units. 100 one-bedroom standard units. 4 one-bedroom suites ($125-$175) with whirlpools. 2 stories (no elevator), interior corridors. **Parking:** on-site, winter plug-ins. **Terms:** package plans, pets ($10 fee, in smoking units). **Amenities:** voice mail. **Pool(s):** heated indoor. **Leisure Activities:** whirlpool. **Guest Services:** valet laundry. **Business Services:** conference facilities. **Cards:** AX, DC, DS, MC, VI.

SOME UNITS
[ASK] [S/D] [🛏] [🍴] [Y] [🏊] [📷] [DATA PORT] [📺] / [✕] [📶] [📠] /
       FEE

PRAIRIE OASIS MOTEL

CAA SAVE

♦♦♦♦

Motel

All Year   1P: $64   2P: $72-$75   XP: $5   D18
Location: Just s of jct Trans-Canada Hwy 1 and Thatcher Dr E. Located in a rural area. 955 Thatcher Dr E S6H 4N9 (PO Box 250). Fax: 306/692-0041. **Facility:** 40 units. 36 one-bedroom standard units, some with efficiencies. 4 one-bedroom suites ($110-$154) with efficiencies. 1 story, exterior corridors. **Parking:** on-site, winter plug-ins. **Terms:** check-in 4 pm, pets (in designated units). **Amenities:** high-speed Internet (fee). **Pool(s):** heated indoor, wading. **Leisure Activities:** whirlpool, waterslide, playground. Fee: miniature golf. **Guest Services:** sundries, coin laundry. **Business Services:** meeting rooms. **Cards:** AX, DC, DS, MC, VI. **Special Amenities:** free local telephone calls.

SOME UNITS

🐕 🍴 🏊 ✕ 💻 / ✕ 🔒 📷 /

SUPER 8 MOTEL-MOOSE JAW   *Book at aaa.com*   **Phone:** (306)692-8888

♦♦ ♦♦

Motel

All Year   1P: $66-$80   2P: $72-$92   XP: $5   F12
Location: 1.5 km s of jct Trans-Canada Hwy 1; access from Hwy 2 via Thatcher Dr. Located in a commercial area. 1706 Main St N S6J 1L4. Fax: 306/693-7255. **Facility:** 60 units. 58 one-bedroom standard units, some with whirlpools. 2 one-bedroom suites ($103-$108). 3 stories, interior corridors. **Parking:** on-site, winter plug-ins. **Terms:** [ECP] meal plan available, pets ($30 fee, in smoking units, with prior approval). **Guest Services:** coin laundry. **Cards:** AX, DC, DS, MC, VI.

SOME UNITS

ASK 🅢🅓 🐕 🍴 🔥M / ✕ 🔒 📷 /
FEE

TEMPLE GARDENS MINERAL SPA RESORT HOTEL   **Phone:** 306/694-5055

CAA SAVE

♦♦♦♦

Small-scale Hotel

All Year   1P: $99-$399   2P: $99-$399   XP: $10   F
Location: Main St, next to Crescent Park; 3.2 km s of Trans-Canada Hwy 1. Located in a commercial area. 24 Fairford St E S6H 0C7. Fax: 306/694-8310. **Facility:** 181 units. 168 one-bedroom standard units, some with whirlpools. 13 one-bedroom suites, some with whirlpools. 5 stories, interior corridors. **Parking:** on-site, winter plug-ins. **Terms:** cancellation fee imposed. **Amenities:** voice mail, hair dryers. Fee: video games, high-speed Internet. Some: dual phone lines, irons. **Dining:** Harwood's, see separate listing. **Pool(s):** heated indoor/outdoor. **Leisure Activities:** steamroom, mineral spa pool, exercise room, spa. Fee: bicycles. **Guest Services:** gift shop, valet laundry. **Business Services:** conference facilities. **Cards:** AX, DC, MC, VI.

SOME UNITS

🍴 🍸 🏊 ✕ ✕ 🎥 📠 💻 / 🔒 /

———— **WHERE TO DINE** ————

HARWOOD'S   **Lunch:** $7-$15   **Dinner:** $12-$30   **Phone:** 306/693-7778

♦♦

Steak & Seafood

Location: Main St, next to Crescent Park; 3.2 km s of Trans-Canada Hwy 1; in Temple Gardens Mineral Spa Resort Hotel. 24 Fairford St E S6H 0C7. **Hours:** 7 am-11 pm. **Reservations:** suggested. **Features:** Known for its high-quality cuts of beef, the restaurant is a popular spot with locals. Casual dress; cocktails. **Parking:** street. **Cards:** AX, DC, MC, VI.

🍸 ✕

HOUSTON PIZZA   **Lunch:** $6-$10   **Dinner:** $8-$20   **Phone:** 306/693-3934

♦♦

American

Location: Just s of High St; 3.5 km s of Trans-Canada Hwy 1. 117 Main St N S6H 0V9. **Hours:** 11 am-11 pm, Fri & Sat-midnight. **Closed:** 12/25. **Features:** A nice spot for couples or families, the restaurant presents a menu of steaks, spaghetti, lasagna, ribs, barbecue chicken, seafood, stir-fry and salads, as well as yummy pizza. Servers are prompt. Casual dress; cocktails. **Parking:** street. **Cards:** AX, DC, MC, VI.

✕

WAYNE & LAVERNE'S PIZZA & STEAK HOUSE   **Lunch:** $5-$9   **Dinner:** $8-$16   **Phone:** 306/694-1777

♦♦

American

Location: Just s of Hochelaga St; centre. 622 Main St N S6H 3K4. **Hours:** 11 am-9 pm, Fri & Sat-10 pm, Sun 4 pm-9 pm. **Closed:** 12/25. **Reservations:** accepted. **Features:** The family-oriented eatery offers good value and features an Italian buffet, buffalo burgers and heart-smart entrees. The menu includes dishes for small appetites and children's meals. The decor is inviting, and the service staff is cordial and prompt. Casual dress; cocktails. **Parking:** street. **Cards:** AX, MC, VI.

✕

NORTH BATTLEFORD pop. 13,692

———— **WHERE TO STAY** ————

SUPER 8 MOTEL   *Book at aaa.com*   **Phone:** (306)446-8888

♦♦

Small-scale Hotel

7/1-8/31   1P: $72   2P: $78
3/1-6/30 & 9/1-2/28   1P: $66   2P: $72
Location: 0.5 km nw of jct Hwy 16. Located in a commercial area. 1006 Hwy 16 Bypass S9A 3W2 (PO Box 1690). Fax: 306/445-4191. **Facility:** 39 one-bedroom standard units. 2 stories (no elevator), interior corridors. **Parking:** on-site, winter plug-ins. **Terms:** package plans, pets ($10 extra charge). **Cards:** AX, CB, DC, DS, MC, VI.

SOME UNITS

🅢🅓 🐕 📠 / ✕ VCR 🔒 /
FEE   FEE

TROPICAL INN   **Phone:** 306/446-4700

♦♦♦

Small-scale Hotel

All Year   1P: $71-$76   2P: $90-$95   XP: $5   F17
Location: Corner of Battleford Rd and Hwy 16 Bypass. Located in a commercial area. 1001 Hwy 16 Bypass S9A 3W2. Fax: 306/446-2299. **Facility:** 119 units. 115 one-bedroom standard units, some with whirlpools. 4 one-bedroom suites ($99-$129) with whirlpools. 2 stories, interior corridors. **Parking:** on-site, winter plug-ins. **Terms:** small pets only (with prior approval). **Amenities:** voice mail, hair dryers. Fee: video games, high-speed Internet. **Pool(s):** small heated indoor. **Leisure Activities:** sauna, whirlpool, waterslide. **Guest Services:** valet laundry. **Business Services:** meeting rooms. **Cards:** AX, DC, MC, VI.

SOME UNITS

ASK 🐕 🍴 🍸 🏊 ✕ 🎥 📠 💻 / ✕ 🔒 /

PRINCE ALBERT pop. 34,291

———— WHERE TO STAY ————

COMFORT INN
▼▼▼ ▼▼▼
Small-scale Hotel
Book at aaa.com
All Year   1P: $85-$100   2P: $90-$100   **Phone: (306)763-4466**
Location: 2.3 km s at jct Hwy 2 and Marquis Rd. Located in a commercial area. 3863 2nd Ave W S6W 1A1.
Fax: 306/764-2210. **Facility:** 62 one-bedroom standard units. 2 stories (no elevator), interior corridors.
Parking: on-site, winter plug-ins. **Terms:** weekly rates available, package plans, small pets only.
Amenities: irons, hair dryers. **Guest Services:** valet laundry. **Cards:** AX, DC, DS, MC, VI.
SOME UNITS
(ASK) (S☐) (🛏) (🎮) (📷) (DATA PORT) (🖥) / (✕) (🛁) (🍴) /

SUPER 8
▼▼ ▼▼
Small-scale Hotel
Book at aaa.com
All Year   1P: $74-$79   2P: $74-$79   **Phone: (306)953-0088**
Location: Just s of jct Hwy 2 and Marquis Rd. Located in a commercial area. 4444 2nd Ave W S6V 5R5 (PO Box 429).
Fax: 306/763-8388. **Facility:** 60 one-bedroom standard units. 3 stories, interior corridors. **Parking:** on-site,
winter plug-ins. **Terms:** small pets only (in smoking units, with prior approval). **Amenities:** high-speed
Internet, voice mail. **Guest Services:** valet and coin laundry. **Cards:** AX, MC, VI.
SOME UNITS
(ASK) (S☐) (🛏) (🎮) (DATA PORT) / (✕) (VCR) /

TRAVELODGE PRINCE ALBERT   *Book at aaa.com*
▼▼▼ ▼▼▼
Small-scale Hotel
All Year   1P: $68-$87   2P: $68-$87   XP: $10   **Phone: (306)764-6441**
Location: 2.2 km s at jct Hwy 2 and Marquis Rd. Located in a commercial area. 3551 2nd Ave W S6V 5G1.
Fax: 306/763-8250. **Facility:** 80 units. 57 one-bedroom standard units. 23 one-bedroom suites ($75-$135),
some with whirlpools. 2 stories (no elevator), interior/exterior corridors. **Parking:** on-site, winter plug-ins.
Terms: pets (in designated units). **Amenities:** high-speed Internet (fee). *Some:* DVD players, irons, hair dryers. **Guest
Services:** valet laundry. **Business Services:** meeting rooms. **Cards:** AX, CB, DC, MC, VI.
SOME UNITS
(ASK) (S☐) (🛏) (🍴) (🍷) (📷) (DATA PORT) (🖥) / (✕) (VCR) (🛁) /

———— WHERE TO DINE ————

AMY'S ON SECOND RESTAURANT   **Lunch:** $6-$14   **Dinner:** $11-$24   **Phone:** 306/763-1515
▼▼ ▼▼
Continental
Location: 1.5 km s on 2nd Ave W, at 30th St W. 2990 2nd Ave W S6V 7E9. **Hours:** 11:30 am-9 pm. Closed major
holidays; also Sun. **Reservations:** accepted. **Features:** You'll discover a warm and intimate setting here.
Amy's menu specializes in the freshest ingredients for the homemade food and many regional specialties
including wild rice soup, rack of lamb, excellent Saskatchewan pickerel, and cheesecake. Casual dress;
cocktails. **Parking:** on-site. **Cards:** AX, DC, MC, VI.
(✕)

VENICE HOUSE   **Lunch:** $6-$12   **Dinner:** $7-$45   **Phone:** 306/764-6555
▼▼ ▼▼
Greek
Location: 15th St and Central Ave. 1498 Central Ave S6V 4W5. **Hours:** 11 am-midnight, Fri & Sat-1 am, Sun 4
pm-midnight. Closed: 12/25; also for dinner holidays. **Reservations:** accepted. **Features:** A casual, family-
dining experience awaits you at the Venice House. The menu offers steak, pizza, spaghetti and seafood
dishes, but their house specialty is Greek-style ribs. The very relaxed atmosphere is quite comfortable and
appealing. Lightside senior menu offered. Casual dress; cocktails. **Parking:** on-site. **Cards:** AX, MC, VI.
(✕)

REGINA pop. 178,225

———— WHERE TO STAY ————

COMFORT INN
(CAA) (SAVE)
▼▼▼ ▼▼▼
Small-scale Hotel
Book at aaa.com

12/1-2/28	1P: $85-$98	2P: $93-$106	XP: $4	F18	
3/1-11/30	1P: $83-$96	2P: $91-$104	XP: $4	F18	

Phone: (306)789-5522
Location: Trans-Canada Hwy 1, 2 km e of Ring Rd, at eastern approach to Regina. Located in a commercial area.
3221 E Eastgate Dr S4Z 1A4. **Fax:** 306/789-9964. **Facility:** 99 one-bedroom standard units. 2 stories (no
elevator), interior corridors. **Parking:** on-site, winter plug-ins. **Terms:** package plans, pets ($5 extra charge,
1st floor units). **Amenities:** irons, hair dryers. **Guest Services:** valet laundry. **Cards:** AX, CB, DC, DS, JC,
MC, VI.
SOME UNITS
(S☐) (🛏) (🎮) (📷) (DATA PORT) (🖥) / (✕) (🛁) (🍴) /
FEE

COUNTRY INN & SUITES BY CARLSON   *Book at aaa.com*
▼▼▼ ▼▼▼
Small-scale Hotel
All Year [ECP]   1P: $101-$114   2P: $111-$124   XP: $10   F18   **Phone: (306)789-9117**
Location: Trans-Canada Hwy 1, 2 km e of Ring Rd, at eastern approach to city. Located in a commercial area. 3321
Eastgate Bay S4Z 1A4. **Fax:** 306/789-3010. **Facility:** 76 units. 39 one-bedroom standard units. 37 one-
bedroom suites ($114-$124). 3 stories, interior corridors. **Parking:** on-site, winter plug-ins. **Terms:** 3 day
cancellation notice, small pets only (in smoking units). **Amenities:** video library, irons, hair dryers. *Some:* dual phone lines.
Leisure Activities: exercise room. **Guest Services:** coin laundry. **Cards:** AX, DC, DS, MC, VI. *(See color ad p 674)*
SOME UNITS
(ASK) (S☐) (🛏) (🍴) (⚙M) (VCR) (DATA PORT) (🛁) (🖥) / (✕) (🍴) /

DAYS INN
▼▼ ▼▼
Small-scale Hotel
Book at aaa.com
All Year   1P: $99-$135   2P: $99-$135   XP: $5   F12   **Phone:** 306/522-3297
Location: Trans-Canada Hwy 1, exit Prince of Wales Dr, at eastern approach to city. Located in a commercial area.
3875 Eastgate Dr S4Z 1A4. **Fax:** 306/522-0807. **Facility:** 96 one-bedroom standard units, some with
whirlpools. 3 stories, interior corridors. **Parking:** on-site, winter plug-ins. **Terms:** check-in 4 pm, 30 day
cancellation notice, small pets only ($10 extra charge; in designated units). **Amenities:** voice mail, irons, hair dryers. *Some:*
high-speed Internet. **Pool(s):** heated indoor. **Leisure Activities:** whirlpool, waterslide. **Guest Services:** valet and coin laundry.
Cards: AX, DC, DS, MC, VI.
SOME UNITS
(ASK) (S☐) (🛏) (🍴) (🏊) (📷) (DATA PORT) (🛁) (🖥) / (✕) (VCR) /
FEE

DELTA REGINA *Book at aaa.com*   **Phone:** (306)525-5255
▼▼▼▼ All Year   1P: $115   2P: $115   XP: $15   F18
Location: At Rose St; centre. Located opposite Casino Regina. 1919 Saskatchewan Dr S4P 4H2. Fax: 306/781-7188.
Large-scale Hotel   **Facility:** 274 units. 251 one-bedroom standard units. 23 one-bedroom suites ($210-$275), some with
whirlpools. 25 stories, interior corridors. **Parking:** on-site (fee), winter plug-ins. **Terms:** pets ($35 fee).
Amenities: video games (fee), voice mail, irons, hair dryers. *Some:* CD players, high-speed Internet. **Pool(s):** heated indoor,
wading. **Leisure Activities:** whirlpool, waterslide, exercise room. **Guest Services:** gift shop, valet laundry. **Business Services:**
conference facilities, business center. **Cards:** AX, MC, VI.

SOME UNITS
🛏 🍴 🍷 🛥 ✕ 🎬 🔌 💻 / ✕ 📠
FEE

HOLIDAY INN EXPRESS HOTEL & SUITES REGINA   *Book at aaa.com*   **Phone:** (306)569-4600
▼▼▼ All Year   1P: $89-$110   2P: $89-$110   XP: $10   F
Location: Corner of Rose St; centre of downtown. Located in a commercial area. 1907 11th Ave S4P 0J2.
Small-scale Hotel   Fax: 306/569-3531. **Facility:** 78 units. 71 one-bedroom standard units. 7 one-bedroom suites ($110-$120),
some with whirlpools. 5 stories, interior corridors. **Parking:** on-site, winter plug-ins. **Terms:** package plans.
Amenities: high-speed Internet, dual phone lines, voice mail, irons, hair dryers. **Leisure Activities:** exercise room. **Guest
Services:** valet laundry. **Business Services:** meeting rooms, business center. **Cards:** AX, DC, DS, MC, VI.

SOME UNITS
ASK 🆂 🍴 🍷 🎬 🔌 💻 / ✕ 📠 🖨 /

HOLIDAY INN HOTEL & SUITES   *Book at aaa.com*   **Phone:** (306)789-3883
▼▼▼ All Year   1P: $99-$140   2P: $99-$140
Location: From jct Trans-Canada Hwy 1, just n. Located in a commercial area. 1800 Prince of Wales Dr S4Z 1A4.
Small-scale Hotel   Fax: 306/522-0141. **Facility:** 120 one-bedroom standard units, some with whirlpools. 4 stories, interior
corridors. *Bath:* shower only. **Parking:** on-site, winter plug-ins. **Amenities:** high-speed Internet, voice mail,
irons, hair dryers. **Pool(s):** small heated indoor. **Leisure Activities:** whirlpool, waterslide, exercise room. **Guest Services:** valet
and coin laundry. **Business Services:** meeting rooms. **Cards:** AX, DC, DS, MC, VI.

SOME UNITS
ASK 🆂 🍴 🍷 🛥 ✕ 🔌 💻 / ✕ 📠
FEE

HOWARD JOHNSON   *Book at aaa.com*   **Phone:** (306)584-8800
Ⓐ ⓢ(SAVE) All Year   1P: $115-$136   2P: $120-$141   XP: $5   F12
Location: 1.25 km n of jct Trans-Canada Hwy 1 and Albert St (Hwy 6). Located in a commercial area. 4255 Albert St S
▼▼▼ S4S 3R6. Fax: 306/584-0204. **Facility:** 156 units. 155 one-bedroom standard units. 1 one-bedroom suite. 2
stories (no elevator), interior/exterior corridors. **Parking:** on-site, winter plug-ins. **Terms:** check-in 4 pm,
Small-scale Hotel   cancellation fee imposed, weekly rates available, [AP], [BP], [CP], [ECP] & [MAP] meal plans available,
package plans, pets (in smoking units). **Amenities:** voice mail, irons, hair dryers. **Dining:** 7 am-9 pm,
cocktails. **Pool(s):** heated indoor. **Leisure Activities:** whirlpool, waterslide. **Guest Services:** valet and coin laundry. **Cards:** AX,
MC, VI. **Special Amenities:** free newspaper and free room upgrade (subject to availability with advance reservations).

SOME UNITS
🆂 🛏 🍴 🛥 🎬 🔌 💻 / ✕ 📼 📠 🖨 /
FEE FEE FEE

QUALITY HOTEL *Book at aaa.com*   **Phone:** (306)569-4656
▽▽◆▽▽   All Year   1P: $89-$105   2P: $89-$105   XP: $10   F17
Small-scale Hotel   **Location:** Just e of Broad St; downtown. Located in a commercial area. 1717 Victoria Ave S4P 0P9. Fax: 306/569-0010. **Facility:** 126 one-bedroom standard units. 7 stories, interior corridors. **Parking:** on-site, winter plug-ins. **Amenities:** video games (fee), voice mail, irons, hair dryers. **Leisure Activities:** sauna, exercise room. **Guest Services:** coin laundry. **Business Services:** meeting rooms. **Cards:** AX, DC, MC, VI.

SOME UNITS
(ASK) (S/D) (¶¶) (✦) (DATA PORT) (□) / (✕) (∎) /
FEE

RADISSON PLAZA HOTEL SASKATCHEWAN   *Book at aaa.com*   **Phone:** (306)522-7691
(CAA) (SAVE)   All Year   1P: $118-$138   2P: $128-$148   XP: $15   F17
▽▽◆▽▽ ▽▽◆▽▽   **Location:** Victoria Ave at Scarth St; centre. Located adjacent to the business district. 2125 Victoria Ave S4P 0S3. Fax: 306/522-8988. **Facility:** This elegantly restored, 1927 hotel has an impressive lobby. Guest rooms are decorated in Victorian style. 224 units. 198 one-bedroom standard units. 26 one-bedroom suites ($279-
Large-scale Hotel $329), some with whirlpools. 10 stories, interior corridors. **Parking:** on-site and valet, winter plug-ins. **Terms:** package plans, small pets only ($50 fee). **Amenities:** high-speed Internet, dual phone lines, voice mail, honor bars, irons, hair dryers. *Some:* CD players. **Dining:** Cortland Hall Dining Room, see separate listing. **Leisure Activities:** whirlpool, steamroom. *Fee:* massage. **Guest Services:** gift shop, valet laundry. *Fee:* airport transportation-Regina International Airport, area transportation-within city limits. **Business Services:** conference facilities, business center. **Cards:** AX, DC, MC, VI. **Special Amenities:** free local telephone calls and free newspaper. *(See color ad p 674)*

SOME UNITS
(✈) (🛏) (¶¶) (Y) (&M) (🛎) (✕) (✦) (DATA PORT) (□) / (✕) (VCR) (∎) (🖼) /
FEE FEE   FEE

RAMADA HOTEL & CONVENTION CENTRE   *Book at aaa.com*   **Phone:** (306)569-1666
▽▽◆▽▽ ▽▽◆▽▽   All Year [BP]   1P: $96-$190   2P: $96-$190   XP: $12   F18
Location: Victoria Ave and Broad St; centre of downtown. Located in a commercial area. 1818 Victoria Ave S4P 0R1.
Large-scale Hotel Fax: 306/352-6339. **Facility:** 232 units. 226 one-bedroom standard units. 6 one-bedroom suites ($131-$350), some with whirlpools. 15 stories, interior corridors. **Terms:** package plans, small pets only ($12 fee). **Amenities:** voice mail, irons, hair dryers. **Pool(s):** small heated indoor, wading. **Leisure Activities:** sauna, whirlpool, exercise room. **Guest Services:** gift shop, valet and coin laundry, beauty salon. **Business Services:** conference facilities. **Cards:** AX, DC, MC, VI.

SOME UNITS
(ASK) (S/D) (🛏) (¶¶) (Y) (🛥) (✕) (✦) (DATA PORT) (□) / (✕) (VCR) (∎) (🖼) /
FEE   FEE FEE FEE

REGINA INN HOTEL & CONFERENCE CENTRE   *Book at aaa.com*   **Phone:** (306)525-6767
(CAA) (SAVE)   All Year   1P: $99-$109   2P: $99-$109   XP: $10   F18
▽▽◆▽▽ ▽▽◆▽▽   **Location:** Jct Victoria Ave; centre of downtown. Located in a commercial area. 1975 Broad St S4P 1Y2. Fax: 306/525-3630. **Facility:** 235 units. 230 one-bedroom standard units. 5 one-bedroom suites, some with whirlpools. 15 stories, interior corridors. **Terms:** cancellation fee imposed, pets
Large-scale Hotel (in designated units). **Amenities:** voice mail, irons, hair dryers. *Some:* CD players, high-speed Internet. **Dining:** Vic's Steakhouse, see separate listing. **Leisure Activities:** exercise room. **Guest Services:** sundries, valet laundry. **Business Services:** meeting rooms, business center. **Cards:** AX, DC, MC, VI. **Special Amenities:** free local telephone calls and free newspaper.

SOME UNITS
(🛏) (¶¶) (Y) (✦) (DATA PORT) (□) / (✕) (∎) (🖼) /

REGINA SUPER 8   *Book at aaa.com*   **Phone:** (306)789-8833
▽▽◆▽▽   All Year   1P: $66   2P: $66-$80   XP: $4   F12
Location: Trans-Canada Hwy 1, 1.6 km e of Ring Rd, at eastern approach to Regina. Located in a commercial area.
Small-scale Hotel 2730 Victoria Ave E S4N 6M5. Fax: 306/789-9711. **Facility:** 59 units. 58 one-bedroom standard units. 1 one-bedroom suite ($81-$120). 3 stories (no elevator), interior corridors. **Parking:** on-site, winter plug-ins.
Cards: AX, DC, DS, MC, VI.

SOME UNITS
(ASK) (&M) (✦) (DATA PORT) (□) / (✕) (∎) /

REGINA TRAVELODGE HOTEL   *Book at aaa.com*   **Phone:** (306)586-3443
(CAA) (SAVE)   All Year   1P: $85-$125   2P: $95-$135   XP: $10   F18
▽▽◆▽▽ ▽▽◆▽▽   **Location:** 1.5 km n of jct Trans-Canada Hwy 1 and Albert St (Hwy 6). Located in a commercial area. 4177 Albert St S S4S 3R6. Fax: 306/586-9311. **Facility:** 200 one-bedroom standard units. 4 stories, interior corridors. **Parking:** on-site, winter plug-ins. **Terms:** [AP], [BP], [CP] & [MAP] meal plans available.
Small-scale Hotel **Amenities:** voice mail, irons, hair dryers. *Some:* dual phone lines, fax. *Fee:* high-speed Internet. **Dining:** 6:30 am-11 pm, Sat from 7 am, Sun 7:30 am-10:30 pm, cocktails. **Pool(s):** small heated indoor. **Leisure Activities:** whirlpool, waterslide, children's play cave, exercise room. **Guest Services:** valet laundry. **Business Services:** conference facilities. **Cards:** AX, DC, MC, VI. **Special Amenities:** free local telephone calls and free room upgrade (subject to availability with advance reservations).

SOME UNITS
(S/D) (¶¶) (Y) (&M) (🛥) (✕) (✦) (DATA PORT) (□) / (✕) (∎) /
FEE

SANDMAN HOTEL SUITES AND SPA   *Book at aaa.com*   **Phone:** (306)757-2444
▽▽◆▽▽   All Year   2P: $119-$199   XP: $10   F
Location: Just e of jct Ring Rd. Located in a commercial area. 1800 Victoria Ave E S4N 6E6. Fax: 306/757-2445.
Small-scale Hotel **Facility:** 132 units. 49 one-bedroom standard units. 83 one-bedroom suites, some with whirlpools. 4 stories, interior corridors. *Bath:* combo or shower only. **Parking:** on-site, winter plug-ins. **Terms:** check-in 4 pm, cancellation fee imposed, small pets only ($10 extra charge). **Amenities:** video games (fee), voice mail, irons, hair dryers. **Pool(s):** small heated indoor. **Leisure Activities:** whirlpool, exercise room. **Business Services:** business center. **Cards:** AX, DC, DS, MC, VI.

SOME UNITS
(ASK) (S/D) (🛏) (¶¶) (&) (🛥) (✕) (✦) (DATA PORT) (□) / (✕) (∎) (🖼) /
FEE

SHERWOOD HOUSE MOTEL

◆◆ Motel

5/1-11/30	1P: $59-$64	2P: $64-$69	XP: $5	F12
12/1-2/28	1P: $54-$59	2P: $64-$69	XP: $5	F12
3/1-4/30	1P: $54-$59	2P: $59-$64	XP: $5	F12

Phone: 306-586-3131

Location: 1.7 km n of jct Trans-Canada Hwy 1. Located in a commercial area. 3915 Albert St S4S 3R4. Fax: 306/584-7490. **Facility:** 61 units. 50 one- and 11 two-bedroom standard units, some with kitchens. 2 stories (no elevator), exterior corridors. **Parking:** on-site, winter plug-ins. **Pool(s):** heated outdoor. **Guest Services:** valet laundry. **Cards:** AX, JC, MC, VI.

SOME UNITS

(ASK) (†1) (📺) (🛏) / (✕) (VCR) (🔌) (🖥) /
FEE

TRAVELODGE REGINA EAST *Book at aaa.com*

(CAA) (SAVE)
◆◆◆ Small-scale Hotel

All Year 1P: $80-$109 2P: $80-$109 XP: $10 F18

Phone: (306)565-0455

Location: Trans-Canada Hwy 1, just w of Ring Rd, at eastern approach to city. Located in a commercial area. 1110 Victoria Ave E S4N 7A9. Fax: 306/569-0012. **Facility:** 181 one-bedroom standard units. 3 stories, interior corridors. **Parking:** on-site, winter plug-ins. **Terms:** [BP], [CP] & [ECP] meal plans available, package plans, small pets only (in smoking units). **Amenities:** video games (fee), voice mail, irons, hair dryers. **Pool(s):** heated indoor. **Leisure Activities:** whirlpool. **Guest Services:** valet laundry. **Business Services:** meeting rooms. **Cards:** AX, DC, JC, MC, VI. **Special Amenities:** free local telephone calls and free newspaper. *(See color ad p 367)*

SOME UNITS

(S🔒) (🐾) (†1+) (🛏) (📽) (DATA PORT) (🖥) / (✕) (VCR) (🔌) (🖥) /
FEE

WEST HARVEST INN *Book at aaa.com*

◆◆◆ Small-scale Hotel

All Year 1P: $89 2P: $89

Phone: (306)586-6755

Location: 1.6 km n of jct Trans-Canada Hwy 1. Located in a commercial area. 4025 Albert St S S4S 3R6. Fax: 306/584-1345. **Facility:** 105 one-bedroom standard units, some with whirlpools. 5 stories, interior corridors. **Parking:** on-site, winter plug-ins. **Terms:** 7 day cancellation notice. **Amenities:** voice mail, hair dryers. *Some: Fee:* high-speed Internet. **Leisure Activities:** whirlpools, steamrooms, exercise room. **Guest Services:** valet laundry. **Business Services:** meeting rooms. **Cards:** AX, DC, DS, MC, VI.

SOME UNITS

(ASK) (S🔒) (†1) (📺) (✕) (📽) (DATA PORT) (🖥) / (✕) (🔌) (🖥) /
FEE

—— WHERE TO DINE ——

ALFREDO'S ON SCARTH Lunch: $5-$10 Dinner: $10-$20 Phone: 306/522-3366

◆◆◆ Italian

Location: Corner of 11th Ave; centre. 1801 Scarth St S4P 2G9. **Hours:** 11 am-midnight. Closed major holidays; also Sun. **Reservations:** accepted. **Features:** The extremely popular Alfredo's features a trendy-looking dining room and a separate wine bar. The restaurant's extensive menu offers an endless number of fresh pasta dishes. Good service. The downtown location is close to theatres and boutiques. Casual dress; cocktails. **Parking:** street. **Cards:** AX, DC, MC, VI.

(📺) (✕)

CATHEDRAL VILLAGE FREE HOUSE Lunch: $6-$10 Dinner: $10-$21 Phone: 306/359-1661

◆◆◆ Canadian

Location: Jct 13th Ave. 2062 Albert St S4P 2T7. **Hours:** 11 am-midnight, Wed-Sat to 1 am. Closed: 12/25. **Features:** The young and young at heart appreciate the sometimes boisterous atmosphere at the upscale tavern. Servers are friendly. The menu lists an interesting mix of dishes, such as ribs, steak, burritos, tandoori chicken stir fry, soups, salads, sandwiches and pizzas cooked in a wood-fired oven. The patio is open seasonally. Casual dress; cocktails. **Parking:** street. **Cards:** AX, MC, VI.

(📺) (✕)

CORTLAND HALL DINING ROOM Lunch: $8-$15 Dinner: $26-$38 Phone: 306/522-7691

◆◆◆ Canadian

Location: At Scarth St; centre; in Hotel Saskatchewan Radisson Plaza. 2125 Victoria Ave S4P 0S3. **Hours:** 6:30 am-10 pm, Sun-9 pm. **Reservations:** accepted. **Features:** The award-winning chefs at this restaurant prepare a wide-ranging menu of delicious meals served with pleasing presentation and a good selection of in-house dessert and pastries. The attractive Victorian decor provides for intimate dining. Casual dress; cocktails. **Parking:** on-site (fee). **Cards:** AX, DC, MC, VI.

(📺) (✕)

THE CREEK IN CATHEDRAL BISTRO Lunch: $6-$10 Dinner: $16-$25 Phone: 306/352-4448

◆◆◆ Continental

Location: Just e of Elphinstone St. 3414 13th Ave S4T 1P7. **Hours:** 11 am-4 & 5-11 pm, Sat from 10 am. Closed: 1/1, 3/28, 12/25, 12/26; also Sun. **Reservations:** suggested. **Features:** The charming bistro has a tasteful decor and friendly, capable servers. Creatively prepared and artfully presented food keeps the locals returning. Casual dress; cocktails. **Parking:** street. **Cards:** AX, DC, MC, VI.

(✕)

DANBRY'S Lunch: $7-$13 Dinner: $16-$30 Phone: 306/525-8777

◆◆◆ Continental

Location: Corner of Hamilton St; centre. 1925 Victoria Ave S4P 0R3. **Hours:** 11 am-11 pm, Fri-midnight, Sat 4 pm-midnight. Closed: 12/25; also Sun. **Reservations:** suggested. **Features:** This dining room is located in the former, private Assiniboine Club. High ceilings & fine wood paneled walls lend a refined air to the dining room. The items range from fish to red meat to a good selection of pasta. Dressy casual; cocktails. **Parking:** on-site (fee). **Cards:** AX, DC, MC, VI.

(📺) (✕)

THE DIPLOMAT Lunch: $6-$13 Dinner: $14-$34 Phone: 306/359-3366

◆◆◆ Steak & Seafood

Location: Just s of jct Broad St and Victoria Ave. 2032 Broad St S4P 1Y3. **Hours:** 11 am-2 & 4-midnight, Sat from 4 pm, Sun 4 pm-9 pm. Closed: 7/1, 12/25. **Reservations:** suggested, weekends. **Features:** You're sure to appreciate the excellent treatment you'll receive at this restaurant, which offers wonderful steak, filet mignon, coq au vin and seafood, as well as an impressive choice of wine and cognac. Elegant surroundings and knowledgeable servers. Dressy casual; cocktails. **Parking:** on-site. **Cards:** AX, DC, MC, VI.

(📺) (✕)

FIRESIDE BISTRO

▼▼▼▼

Canadian

Lunch: $8-$10 **Dinner:** $10-$25 **Phone:** 306/761-2305
Location: 3 blks s of Victoria Ave. 2305 Smith St S4P 2P6. **Hours:** 11 am-10 pm, Sat from 4 pm. Closed major holidays; also Sun. **Reservations:** accepted. **Features:** The menu lists creative choices alongside such favorites as pasta, chicken, fish and steak. The bistro's dining areas are in the rooms of a large old house. The patio opens seasonally. Casual dress; cocktails. **Parking:** street. **Cards:** AX, MC, VI.

ⓨ ⓧ

GOLF'S STEAK HOUSE

▼▼▼

Steak & Seafood

Lunch: $8-$18 **Dinner:** $14-$40 **Phone:** 306/525-5808
Location: Corner of Victoria Ave and Hamilton St. 1945 Victoria Ave S4P 0R3. **Hours:** 11 am-midnight, Sat from 4 pm, Sun 4 pm-10 pm. **Closed:** 12/25. **Reservations:** accepted. **Features:** This restaurant features hearty portions of very good steak, seafood and rack of lamb dishes that are quite tasty and served in large portions. There's a good variety to the menu. The restaurant has traditional formal decor and professional service. When the torch in front of the restaurant is burning, they are open for business. Casual dress; cocktails. **Parking:** on-site. **Cards:** AX, DC, MC, VI.

ⓨ ⓧ

LA BODEGA

▼▼▼

Mediterranean

Lunch: $7-$10 **Dinner:** $10-$20 **Phone:** 306/546-3660
Location: Just n of jct 15th Ave. 2228 Albert St S4P 2V3. **Hours:** 11 am-10 pm, Fri-11 pm, Sat 10 am-11 pm, Sun 10 am-10 pm. **Closed:** 12/25, 12/26. **Reservations:** accepted. **Features:** Those who enjoy a variety of taste sensations surely will be pleased with the varied tapas menu. The atmosphere is cozy in the dining room and on the seasonal patio. Casual dress; cocktails. **Parking:** street. **Cards:** AX, MC, VI.

ⓧ

THE LAST SPIKE

▼▼

American

Lunch: $5-$20 **Dinner:** $5-$20 **Phone:** 306/781-7000
Location: Centre; in Casino Regina. 1880 Saskatchewan Dr S4P 0B2. **Hours:** 9 am-10:30 pm, Fri & Sat-midnight. **Closed:** 12/24, 12/25. **Reservations:** accepted. **Features:** In the old Regina train station, the restaurant has one dining room section in a rail passenger car. Reservations are required to dine in the car. The menu centers on simple, filling fare along the lines of ribs, chicken and fish 'n' chips. Casual dress; cocktails. **Parking:** on-site (fee). **Cards:** AX, DC, MC, VI.

ⓨ ⓧ

LUIGGI'S PASTA HOUSE

▼▼▼▼

Italian

Lunch: $6-$10 **Dinner:** $8-$17 **Phone:** 306/949-7427
Location: Corner of 9th Ave. 470 Albert St N S4R 3C1. **Hours:** 11 am-10 pm, Fri & Sat-11 pm, Sun 4 pm-9 pm. **Closed:** 12/25. **Reservations:** accepted. **Features:** The family-oriented eatery serves traditional Italian food in a fun and lively atmosphere. Casual dress; cocktails. **Parking:** on-site. **Cards:** AX, DC, MC, VI.

ⓧ

MEDITERRANEAN BISTRO

▼▼▼▼

Continental

Lunch: $6-$10 **Dinner:** $12-$25 **Phone:** 306/757-1666
Location: Trans-Canada Hwy 1, just se of jct Fleet St, at eastern approach to Regina. 2589 Quance St E S4V 2Y7. **Hours:** 11 am-3 & 5-11 pm, Sun from 5 pm. **Closed:** 12/25. **Reservations:** suggested. **Features:** At this casual yet upscale bistro market, fresh products are used to offer a good varity of fish, chicken, red meat and pasta dishes which are all carefully prepared and creatively presented. Casual dress; cocktails. **Parking:** on-site. **Cards:** AX, MC, VI.

ⓧ

PASSIONATE PIZZA & SENSUOUS SUSHI

▼▼▼ ▼▼▼

Sushi

Lunch: $6-$11 **Dinner:** $6-$11 **Phone:** 306/569-5555
Location: Just s of jct 15th Ave. 2330 Albert St S4P 2V7. **Hours:** 11 am-10 pm, Sat noon-11 pm, Sun 5 pm-10 pm. Closed major holidays. **Reservations:** suggested, Fri & Sat. **Features:** The fun little restaurant brings together a surprising combination—gourmet pizza and creative sushi—under one roof. Other menu items include calzones and pasta dishes. Consideration has been given to offering gluten-free, organic, vegetarian and vegan items on the menu. Table seating and a sushi bar are available. Casual dress; cocktails. **Parking:** street. **Cards:** MC, VI.

ⓧ

VIC'S STEAKHOUSE

▼▼▼

Steak & Seafood

Dinner: $25-$45 **Phone:** 306/525-6767
Location: Jct Victoria Ave; centre; in Regina Inn Hotel & Conference Centre. 1975 Broad St S4P 1Y2. **Hours:** 5 pm-11 pm. **Closed:** 12/25; also Sun & Mon. **Reservations:** accepted. **Features:** Diners can sample the highest quality Alberta beef, which is served in large portions in a refined, relaxed atmosphere. Casual dress; cocktails. **Parking:** on-site (fee). **Cards:** AX, DC, JC, MC, VI.

ⓨ ⓧ

SASKATOON pop. 196,811

----------- **WHERE TO STAY** -----------

BEST WESTERN INN & SUITES _Book at aaa.com_

ⓒ ⓐ ⓐ SAVE ▼▼ ▼▼

Small-scale Hotel

Phone: (306)244-5552
All Year 1P: $80-$125 2P: $80-$125 XP: $5 F17
Location: 2.6 km n on Hwy 11 (Idylwyld Dr). Located in a strip mall. 1715 Idylwyld Dr N S7L 1B4. **Fax:** 306/934-5171. **Facility:** 91 units. 82 one-bedroom standard units. 9 one-bedroom suites. 2 stories, interior/exterior corridors. **Parking:** on-site, winter plug-ins. **Terms:** 14 day cancellation notice. **Amenities:** voice mail, irons, hair dryers. **Dining:** Ricky's All Day Grill, see separate listing. **Leisure Activities:** whirlpool, exercise room. Fee: massage. **Guest Services:** valet laundry. **Business Services:** meeting rooms. **Cards:** AX, DC, DS, MC, VI.

SOME UNITS
Ⓢ🄳 ⊷ 🛏 🍴 ⓨ ⓧ 📷 DATA PORT 💻 / ⓧ 🗋 📠 /

COLONIAL SQUARE MOTEL & SUITES

ⓒ ⓐ ⓐ SAVE ▼▼ ▼▼

Small-scale Hotel

Phone: (306)343-1676
All Year 1P: $74-$84 2P: $79-$89 XP: $5 F13
Location: Just w of Cumberland St. Located in a commercial area. 1301 8th St E S7H 0S7. **Fax:** 306/956-1313. **Facility:** 80 one-bedroom standard units. 2 stories (no elevator), interior/exterior corridors. **Parking:** on-site, winter plug-ins. **Terms:** weekly rates available, pets ($5 extra charge). **Amenities:** voice mail, hair dryers. Some: irons. **Business Services:** meeting rooms. **Cards:** AX, DC, MC, VI. **Special Amenities:** free local telephone calls.

SOME UNITS
Ⓢ🄳 🛏 🍴 📷 💻 / ⓧ 🗋 /
FEE

COMFORT INN   *Book at aaa.com*   Phone: (306)934-1122

(AAA) [SAVE]

Small-scale Hotel

All Year   1P: $65-$125   2P: $75-$135   XP: $10   F17
Location: 3 km n; just ne of jct Hwy 11 (Idylwyld Dr) and Circle Dr. Located in a commercial area. 2155 Northridge Dr S7L 6X6. Fax: 306/934-6539. **Facility:** 80 one-bedroom standard units. 2 stories (no elevator), interior corridors. **Parking:** on-site, winter plug-ins. **Terms:** small pets only (in smoking units). **Amenities:** irons, hair dryers. *Some:* honor bars. **Guest Services:** valet laundry. **Business Services:** meeting rooms. **Cards:** AX, DC, DS, MC, VI.

SOME UNITS

COUNTRY INN & SUITES BY CARLSON   *Book at aaa.com*   Phone: (306)934-3900

Small-scale Hotel

All Year [CP]   1P: $88   2P: $88   XP: $8   F18
Location: Just w of jct Hwy 11 (Idylwyld Dr) and Circle Dr. Located in a commercial area. 617 Cynthia St S7L 6B7. Fax: 306/652-3100. **Facility:** 77 units. 37 one-bedroom standard units. 40 one-bedroom suites. 3 stories, interior corridors. **Parking:** on-site, winter plug-ins. **Terms:** small pets only ($10 extra charge). **Amenities:** video library, irons, hair dryers. **Guest Services:** coin laundry. **Business Services:** meeting rooms. **Cards:** AX, DC, MC, VI. *(See color ad p 674)*

SOME UNITS
FEE

DAYS INN   *Book at aaa.com*   Phone: (306)242-3297

(AAA) [SAVE]

Small-scale Hotel

All Year [ECP]   1P: $99-$135   2P: $99-$135   XP: $10   F12
Location: Just nw of jct Hwy 11 (Idylwyld Dr) and Circle Dr. Located in a commercial area. 2000 Idylwyld Dr N S7L 7M7. Fax: 306/955-5115. **Facility:** 102 units. 96 one-bedroom standard units, some with whirlpools. 6 one-bedroom suites ($145-$175), some with whirlpools. 4 stories, interior corridors. *Bath:* combo or shower only. **Parking:** on-site, winter plug-ins. **Amenities:** high-speed Internet, voice mail, irons, hair dryers. *Some:* safes (fee). **Pool(s):** small heated indoor. **Leisure Activities:** whirlpool, waterslide, exercise room. **Guest Services:** valet and coin laundry. **Cards:** AX, DC, DS, MC, VI. **Special Amenities: free expanded continental breakfast and free local telephone calls.**

SOME UNITS
FEE

DELTA BESSBOROUGH   *Book at aaa.com*   Phone: (306)244-5521

Large-scale Hotel

All Year   1P: $99-$189   2P: $109-$199   XP: $10   F18
Location: At 21st St E; centre of downtown. Located beside park and river. 601 Spadina Crescent E S7K 3G8. Fax: 306/665-7262. **Facility:** 225 units. 216 one-bedroom standard units, some with whirlpools. 9 one-bedroom suites ($174-$574). 6 stories, interior corridors. **Parking:** on-site (fee), winter plug-ins. **Amenities:** video games (fee), voice mail, irons, hair dryers. *Some:* CD players, high-speed Internet, dual phone lines, honor bars. **Pool(s):** heated indoor, wading. **Leisure Activities:** sauna, whirlpool, steamroom, recreation programs, jogging, exercise room, spa. **Guest Services:** sundries, valet laundry, beauty salon. **Business Services:** conference facilities, business center. **Cards:** AX, DC, MC, VI.

SOME UNITS

HERITAGE INN   Phone: (306)665-8121

Small-scale Hotel

1/1-2/28   1P: $76   2P: $89   XP: $5   F16
3/1-12/31   1P: $74   2P: $87   XP: $5   F16
Location: Jct Circle and Airport drs. Located in a commercial area. 102 Cardinal Crescent S7L 6H6. Fax: 306/665-0064. **Facility:** 167 units. 159 one-bedroom standard units, some with efficiencies. 8 one-bedroom suites ($92-$115) with efficiencies. 6 stories, interior corridors. **Parking:** on-site, winter plug-ins. **Terms:** package plans, small pets only ($10 extra charge, in designated units). **Amenities:** *Some:* hair dryers. **Pool(s):** small heated indoor. **Leisure Activities:** whirlpool. **Guest Services:** valet laundry. **Business Services:** conference facilities. **Cards:** AX, DC, DS, MC, VI.

SOME UNITS
FEE   FEE

HOLIDAY INN EXPRESS HOTEL & SUITES SASKATOON   *Book at aaa.com*   Phone: (306)384-8844

Small-scale Hotel

All Year [ECP]   1P: $94-$159   2P: $94-$159   XP: $5   F16
Location: Jct 25th St W. Located in a commercial area. 315 Idylwyld Dr N S7L 0Z1. Fax: 306/384-8830. **Facility:** 119 units. 110 one-bedroom standard units. 5 one- and 4 two-bedroom suites ($104-$159). 4 stories, interior corridors. **Parking:** on-site, winter plug-ins. **Terms:** small pets only ($10 extra charge). **Amenities:** high-speed Internet, dual phone lines, voice mail, irons, hair dryers. **Pool(s):** heated indoor. **Leisure Activities:** whirlpool, exercise room. **Guest Services:** valet laundry. **Business Services:** meeting rooms, business center. **Cards:** AX, CB, DC, DS, JC, MC, VI.

SOME UNITS
FEE

QUALITY HOTEL   *Book at aaa.com*   Phone: (306)244-2311

Small-scale Hotel

All Year   1P: $99-$119   2P: $99-$119   XP: $10   F17
Location: Just e of jct Hwy 11 (Idylwyld Dr), 1st and 22nd sts. Located in the downtown business district. 90 22nd St E S7K 3X6. Fax: 306/664-2234. **Facility:** 179 units. 179 one-bedroom standard units. 16 stories, interior corridors. **Parking:** on-site (fee). **Terms:** pets (in smoking units). **Amenities:** *Some:* voice mail, irons, hair dryers. **Dining:** RJ Willoughby's, see separate listing. **Pool(s):** heated indoor. **Leisure Activities:** sauna, whirlpool, exercise room. **Guest Services:** valet laundry. **Business Services:** conference facilities. **Cards:** AX, DC, MC, VI.

SOME UNITS

RADISSON HOTEL SASKATOON *Book at aaa.com*

Phone: (306)665-3322

CAA SAVE — All Year — 1P: $125-$160 — 2P: $125-$160 — XP: $15 — F18
Location: At 4th Ave S; centre. Located close to a river-side park. 405 20th St E S7K 6X6. Fax: 306/665-5531. **Facility:** 291 units. 283 one-bedroom standard units. 8 one-bedroom suites with whirlpools. 19 stories, interior corridors. **Parking:** on-site (fee). **Terms:** package plans, small pets only ($25 fee). **Amenities:** video games (fee), dual phone lines, voice mail, irons, hair dryers. *Some:* high-speed Internet. **Dining:** 6:30 am-10 pm, Sat from 7 am, Sun 7 am-9 pm, cocktails. **Pool(s):** heated indoor. **Leisure Activities:** sauna, whirlpool, waterslide, jogging, exercise room. **Guest Services:** gift shop, valet laundry. **Business Services:** conference facilities, business center. **Cards:** AX, CB, DC, DS, JC, MC, VI. **Special Amenities:** free local telephone calls and free newspaper. *(See color ad p 674)*

SOME UNITS
[icons] FEE

RAMADA HOTEL & GOLF DOME *Book at aaa.com*

Phone: (306)665-6500

All Year — 1P: $91 — 2P: $95 — XP: $4 — F16
Location: 4 km s of jct Circle Dr. Located in a commercial area. 806 Idylwyld Dr N S7L 0Z6. Fax: 306/665-1973. Large-scale Hotel **Facility:** 144 units. 140 one-bedroom standard units, some with whirlpools. 4 one-bedroom suites ($124-$179). 5 stories, interior corridors. **Parking:** on-site, winter plug-ins. **Terms:** 3 day cancellation notice, package plans, small pets only (with prior approval). **Amenities:** voice mail, irons, hair dryers. **Pool(s):** heated indoor. **Leisure Activities:** whirlpool. *Fee:* miniature golf. **Guest Services:** gift shop, valet and coin laundry, beauty salon. **Business Services:** meeting rooms. **Cards:** AX, DC, DS, MC, VI.

SOME UNITS
[icons] FEE FEE

SANDMAN HOTEL *Book at aaa.com*

Phone: (306)477-4844

All Year — 1P: $119-$129 — 2P: $129-$139 — XP: $10 — F
Location: Jct Ave C N. Located in a commercial area. 310 Circle Dr W S7L 2Y5. Fax: 306/477-4944. **Facility:** 190 Large-scale Hotel units. 178 one-bedroom standard units, some with whirlpools. 12 one-bedroom suites. 4 stories, interior corridors. **Parking:** on-site, winter plug-ins. **Terms:** package plans, small pets only ($5 extra charge). **Amenities:** video games (fee), voice mail, irons, hair dryers. **Pool(s):** small heated indoor. **Leisure Activities:** whirlpool, exercise room. **Guest Services:** sundries, valet laundry. **Business Services:** meeting rooms. **Cards:** AX, CB, DC, DS, JC, MC, VI.

SOME UNITS
[icons] FEE FEE FEE

SASKATOON INN HOTEL & CONFERENCE CENTRE *Book at aaa.com*

Phone: (306)242-1440

CAA SAVE — 1/1-2/28 — 1P: $110 — 2P: $120 — XP: $10 — F16
3/1-12/31 — 1P: $105 — 2P: $115 — XP: $10 — F16
Location: Jct Circle and Airport drs. Located in a commercial area. 2002 Airport Dr S7L 6M4. Fax: 306/244-2779. **Facility:** 250 units. 237 one-bedroom standard units, some with whirlpools. 13 one-bedroom suites ($170). Large-scale Hotel 7 stories, interior corridors. **Parking:** on-site, winter plug-ins. **Terms:** [AP], [BP], [CP], & [MAP] meal plans available, package plans. **Amenities:** video games (fee), voice mail, irons, hair dryers. *Some:* CD players, high-speed Internet. **Dining:** 6:30 am-10 pm, cocktails. **Pool(s):** small heated indoor. **Leisure Activities:** whirlpool, exercise room. **Guest Services:** gift shop, valet laundry. **Business Services:** conference facilities. **Cards:** AX, DC, MC, VI. **Special Amenities:** free local telephone calls and free newspaper.

SOME UNITS
[icons]

SASKATOON TRAVELODGE HOTEL *Book at aaa.com*

Phone: (306)242-8881

CAA SAVE — All Year — 1P: $99-$169 — 2P: $109-$179 — XP: $10 — F18
Location: 3 km n, then just w of jct Hwy 11 (Idylwyld Dr). Located in a commercial area. 106 Circle Dr W S7L 4L6. Fax: 306/665-7378. **Facility:** 268 one-bedroom standard units, some with whirlpools. 2-6 stories, interior corridors. **Parking:** on-site, winter plug-ins. **Terms:** small pets only ($10 fee). **Amenities:** high-speed Internet, voice mail, irons, hair dryers. *Some:* fax. **Dining:** 6:30 am-10 pm, cocktails, nightclub. **Pool(s):** heated indoor, small heated indoor, wading. **Leisure Activities:** sauna, whirlpools, waterslide, exercise room. *Fee:* game room. **Guest Services:** gift shop, valet and coin laundry. **Business Services:** conference facilities. **Cards:** AX, DC, DS, MC, VI. **Special Amenities:** free local telephone calls and free newspaper.

SOME UNITS
[icons] FEE

SHERATON CAVALIER *Book at aaa.com*

Phone: (306)652-6770

All Year [ECP] — 1P: $119-$159 — 2P: $135-$174 — XP: $15 — F18
Location: At 21st St E; centre of downtown. Located opposite park and river. 612 Spadina Crescent E S7K 3G9. Fax: 306/244-1739. **Facility:** 249 units. 242 one-bedroom standard units, some with whirlpools. 7 one-Small-scale Hotel bedroom suites with whirlpools. 8 stories, interior corridors. **Parking:** on-site (fee) and valet, winter plug-ins. **Terms:** package plans. **Amenities:** dual phone lines, voice mail, honor bars, irons, hair dryers. *Fee:* video games, high-speed Internet. *Some:* fax. **Dining:** Carver's Steak House, see separate listing. **Pool(s):** small heated indoor. **Leisure Activities:** whirlpools, waterslide, exercise room. **Guest Services:** gift shop, valet laundry. **Business Services:** conference facilities, business center. **Cards:** AX, CB, DC, MC, VI. *(See color ad p 5)*

SOME UNITS
[icons]

SUPER 8 *Book at aaa.com*

Phone: (306)384-8989

All Year — 1P: $82-$114 — 2P: $85-$119 — XP: $6 — F12
Location: 2 km e of jct Hwy 11 (Idylwyld Dr). Located in a commercial area. 706 Circle Dr E S7K 3T7. Fax: 306/384-8955. **Facility:** 69 one-bedroom standard units, some with whirlpools. 3 stories, interior/exterior corridors. *Bath:* combo or shower only. **Parking:** on-site, winter plug-ins. **Terms:** pets ($5 fee). **Amenities:** voice mail, hair dryers. *Some:* irons. **Guest Services:** valet laundry. **Cards:** AX, MC, VI.

SOME UNITS
[icons] FEE

THRIFTLODGE

CAA SAVE

◇◇◇

.Motel

All Year   1P: $67-$99   2P: $77-$99   XP: $5   **Phone:** (306)244-2191   F

Location: Just s of Cirlce Dr N. Located in a commercial area. 1825 Idylwyld Dr N S7L 1B6. **Fax:** 306/978-1230.
Facility: 56 units. 49 one- and 1 two-bedroom standard units. 6 one-bedroom suites. 2 stories (no elevator),
exterior corridors. *Bath:* combo or shower only. **Parking:** on-site, winter plug-ins. **Terms:** small pets only (in
smoking units, with prior approval). **Guest Services:** valet laundry. **Cards:** AX, DC, MC, VI.
**Special Amenities: free local telephone calls and free room upgrade (subject to availability with
advance reservations).**

SOME UNITS

Ⓢ🐕🎥💻/❎ ᴅᴀᴛᴀᴘᴏʀᴛ 🔌

──── WHERE TO DINE ────

2ND AVE GRILL

◇◇ ◇◇

American

MC, VI.

Lunch: $7-$11   **Dinner:** $9-$22   **Phone:** 306/244-9899
Location: Just w of jct 22nd St; centre. 123 2nd Ave S S7K 7E6. **Hours:** 11 am-10 pm, Fri & Sat-11 pm. Closed:
12/25, 12/26; also Sun. **Reservations:** accepted. **Features:** In the heart of the downtown business district,
the upscale grill offers an inviting atmosphere and attentive service. The varied menu features items that
range from soups and salads to jambalaya. Casual dress; cocktails. **Parking:** street. **Cards:** AX, DC,

🍸❎

CARVER'S STEAK HOUSE

◇◇◇

Steak & Seafood

Dinner: $23-$44   **Phone:** 306-652-8292
Location: At 21st St E; centre of downtown; in Sheraton Cavalier. 612 Spadina Crescent E S7K 3G9. **Hours:** 5:30
pm-11 pm, Sun 5 pm-9 pm. **Reservations:** suggested. **Features:** This popular restaurant serves Caesar
salads that are prepared at the table to your taste, and top quality steaks are delivered sizzling on a skillet.
Dressy casual; cocktails. **Parking:** on-site (fee). **Cards:** AX, CB, DC, DS, MC, VI.

❎

CHIANTI

◇◇ ◇◇

Italian

Lunch: $5-$16   **Dinner:** $6-$16   **Phone:** 306/665-8466
Location: Corner 22nd St E; centre. 102 Idylwyld Dr N S7L 0Y7. **Hours:** 11 am-11 pm, Sun-10 pm. Closed: 12/24,
12/25. **Reservations:** suggested. **Features:** Lining the menu is a good selection of fresh pasta creations,
as well as veal, seafood and chicken dishes. Personable servers circulate in an atmosphere that suits
families and couples. Casual dress; cocktails. **Parking:** on-site. **Cards:** AX, DC, MC, VI.

❎

GENESIS FAMILY RESTAURANT

◇◇ ◇◇

Chinese

Lunch: $6-$10   **Dinner:** $9-$12   **Phone:** 306/244-5516
Location: 1 km w of Hwy 11 (Idylwyld Dr). 901 D 22nd St W S7M 0R9. **Hours:** 11 am-10 pm. Closed major
holidays; also 7/1-7/14. **Reservations:** accepted. **Features:** The Genesis features a progressive Chinese
menu offering many healthy choices—all made with fresh ingredients. Portions are large, and the diverse
and creative menu includes Western dishes. Dim sum is served 11 am-2:30 pm each day. Friendly service.
Casual dress; cocktails. **Parking:** on-site. **Cards:** AX, MC, VI.

❎

JOHN'S PRIME RIB HOUSE
♦♦♦ **Lunch:** $7-$20 **Dinner:** $20-$42 **Phone:** 306/244-6384
Steak & Seafood
Location: Just s of 4th Ave S; centre. 401 21st St E S7K 0C5. **Hours:** 11:30 am-11:30 pm, Sat from 4:30 pm. Closed: 7/1; also Sun. **Reservations:** accepted. **Features:** A longstanding city favorite, the restaurant is known for top-quality prime rib and steak. Service is professional, and the rich wood paneling in the dining room creates a pleasant atmosphere. Casual dress; cocktails. **Parking:** street. **Cards:** AX, DC, MC, VI.
⊠

POVERINO'S PASTA GRILL
♦♦♦ ♦♦♦ **Lunch:** $6-$12 **Dinner:** $6-$12 **Phone:** 306/955-7319
Italian
Location: 3 km n of Trans-Canada Hwy 16; corner of Louise Ave. 1625 8th St E S7H 0T2. **Hours:** 11 am-11 pm, Sun noon-10 pm. Closed: 1/1, 3/28, 12/25. **Reservations:** suggested. **Features:** The menu combines a great selection of fresh pasta dishes and pizzas baked in a wood-burning oven. Veal, chicken, steak and burgers round out the choices. A bright, airy decor punctuates the fun and friendly place. Casual dress; cocktails. **Parking:** on-site. **Cards:** AX, DC, MC, VI.
⊠

RICKY'S ALL DAY GRILL
♦♦ ♦♦ **Lunch:** $7-$13 **Dinner:** $7-$20 **Phone:** 306/652-3222
Canadian
Location: 2.6 km n on Hwy 16 and 11 (Idylwyld Dr); adjacent to Best Western Inn & Suites. 1715 Idylwyld Dr N S7L 1B4. **Hours:** 6 am-11 pm, Sun 7 am-10 pm. **Reservations:** accepted. **Features:** The comfortable eatery, which employs friendly servers, presents a varied menu that includes pasta dishes, wraps, omelets, stir-fry preparations and burgers. Portions are generous. Children's and senior selections are offered. Guests can request seating in a booth or at a table. Casual dress; cocktails. **Parking:** on-site. **Cards:** AX, MC, VI.
⊤ ⊠

RJ WILLOUGHBY'S
♦♦ ♦♦ **Lunch:** $6-$13 **Dinner:** $10-$20 **Phone:** 306/665-7576
American
Location: Just e of jct Hwy 11 (Idylwyld Dr), 1st and 22nd sts; downtown; in Quality Hotel. 90 22nd St E S7K 3X6. **Hours:** 6:30 am-9 pm, Fri & Sat-10 pm; hours vary seasonally. **Reservations:** accepted. **Features:** You'll enjoy a fine-dining experience here on Friday and Saturday nights. An excellent lunch buffet is offered Monday-Friday. The atmosphere is semi-casual and colorful, and servers are prompt and attentive. Casual dress; cocktails. **Parking:** on-site (fee). **Cards:** AX, CB, DC, DS, MC, VI.
⊤ ⊠

SAMURAI JAPANESE RESTAURANT
♦♦♦ ♦♦♦ **Dinner:** $17-$36 **Phone:** 306/244-5521
Japanese
Location: At 21st St E; centre; in Delta Bessborough Hotel. 601 Spadina Cres E S7K 3G8. **Hours:** 5 pm-11 pm. Closed: 7/1, 12/25. **Reservations:** accepted. **Features:** Finely crafted sushi and authentic tableside Teppanyaki cuisine are featured at this dining room. Casual dress; cocktails. **Parking:** on-site (fee). **Cards:** AX, DC, MC, VI.
⊤ ⊠

SHAUNAVON pop. 1,775

──── WHERE TO STAY ────

HIDDEN HILTEN MOTEL
♦ **Phone:** (306)297-4166
Motel
All Year **1P:** $50-$70 **2P:** $50-$70
Location: 0.5 km e from jct Hwy 13 and 37, just n. Located in a quiet area. 352 5th St W S0N 2M0 (PO Box 1002). Fax: 306/297-3017. **Facility:** 13 one-bedroom standard units, some with whirlpools. 1 story, exterior corridors. **Parking:** on-site, winter plug-ins. **Terms:** office hours 7 am-11 pm, small pets only. **Cards:** MC, VI.
SOME UNITS
(ASK) (S̄D) 🐾 🛏 🖵 🖳 / ⊠ /

SWIFT CURRENT pop. 14,821

──── WHERE TO STAY ────

BEST WESTERN INN & SUITES *Book at aaa.com*
♦♦ ♦♦ Property failed to provide current rates **Phone:** 306/773-4660
Small-scale Hotel
Location: Jct Trans-Canada Hwy 1 and 4. Located in a commercial area. 105 George St W S9H 0K4. Fax: 306/773-3430. **Facility:** 59 one-bedroom standard units. 2 stories (no elevator), interior corridors. *Bath:* combo or shower only. **Parking:** on-site, winter plug-ins. **Amenities:** voice mail, irons, hair dryers. *Pool(s):* heated indoor. **Leisure Activities:** sauna, whirlpools, exercise room. **Guest Services:** valet laundry. **Business Services:** meeting rooms.
SOME UNITS
🍴 🏊 ⊠ 🎥 (DATA PORT) 🖳 / ⊠ (VCR) 🛏 🖵

CARAVEL MOTEL
(CAA) (SAVE)
♦ Motel
Phone: (306)773-8385

6/1-8/31	1P: $50-$56	2P: $54-$60	XP: $5 F
4/1-5/31	1P: $42-$50	2P: $46-$54	XP: $5 F
3/1-3/31 & 9/1-2/28	1P: $40-$46	2P: $42-$52	XP: $5 F

Location: Just e of Central Ave. Located in a commercial area. 705 N Service Rd E S9H 3X6. Fax: 306/773-5060. **Facility:** 28 units. 26 one-bedroom standard units, some with kitchens. 2 one-bedroom suites with kitchens. 1 story, exterior corridors. **Parking:** on-site, winter plug-ins. **Terms:** office hours 7:30 am-midnight, weekly rates available, small pets only ($5 extra charge, in smoking units, with prior approval). **Cards:** AX, DC, MC, VI. **Special Amenities:** free local telephone calls and preferred room (subject to availability with advance reservations).
SOME UNITS
(S̄D) 🛏 🍴 🎥 🛏 🖳 / ⊠ 🖵 /
FEE

COMFORT INN *Book at aaa.com*
♦♦ ♦♦
Small-scale Hotel
Phone: (306)778-3994
All Year **1P:** $90-$106 **2P:** $90-$112 **XP:** $8 F18
Location: Trans-Canada Hwy 1, just w of 22nd Ave NE. Located in a commercial area. 1510 S Service Rd E S9H 3X6. Fax: 306/773-9312. **Facility:** 74 one-bedroom standard units. 2 stories (no elevator), interior corridors. **Parking:** on-site, winter plug-ins. **Terms:** package plans, pets (in smoking units). **Amenities:** irons. *Some:* hair dryers. **Guest Services:** valet laundry. **Cards:** AX, DC, DS, MC, VI.
SOME UNITS
(ASK) (S̄D) 🐾 🍴 🎥 (DATA PORT) 🖳 / ⊠ 🛏 /
FEE

GREEN HECTARES RANCH/BED & BREAKFAST

Phone: 306/773-7632

▼▼▼ ▼▼▼

Bed & Breakfast

All Year [BP] 1P: $55-$65 2P: $65-$75 XP: $15 D12

Location: Trans-Canada Hwy 1, exit 22nd Ave NE, just n to Waker Rd, 0.5 km e, follow signs. Located in a rural area. Waker Rd S9H 4M7 (PO Box 2039). Fax: 306/773-7635. **Facility:** Smoke free premises. 6 one-bedroom standard units. 1 story, interior/exterior corridors. *Bath:* some shared or private, combo, shower or tub only. **Parking:** on-site, winter plug-ins. **Terms:** office hours 7 am-10 pm, weekly rates available. **Leisure Activities:** whirlpool, canoeing, fishing. **Guest Services:** coin laundry. **Business Services:** meeting rooms.

SOME UNITS

[S/D] [🛏] [✕] [✕] / [✕] [W] [VCR] [☎] [🔲]

RODEWAY INN MOTEL

Phone: (306)773-4664

CAA SAVE
▼▼▼

Small-scale Hotel

All Year 1P: $49-$56 2P: $52-$59

Location: Trans-Canada Hwy 1, just w of 22nd Ave NE. Located in a commercial area. 1200 S Service Rd E S9H 3X6. Fax: 306/773-8117. **Facility:** 28 one-bedroom standard units. 1 story, interior/exterior corridors. **Parking:** on-site, winter plug-ins. **Terms:** office hours 7 am-1 am, weekly rates available, package plans, small pets only ($5 fee, in smoking units). **Dining:** 6 am-9 pm, Sun 9 am-8 pm, cocktails. **Guest Services:** valet laundry. **Business Services:** meeting rooms. **Cards:** AX, MC, VI. **Special Amenities:** free local telephone calls and free newspaper.

SOME UNITS

[🛏] [🍽] [📺] [🔲] / [✕] [🔲] /

FEE

SAFARI MOTEL

Phone: (306)773-4608

CAA SAVE
▼▼▼

Motel

All Year 1P: $40-$50 2P: $48-$60 XP: $5 F3

Location: 1 km w of jct Hwy 1 and 4. Located in a commercial area. 810 S Service Rd E S9H 3T9. Fax: 306/773-0835. **Facility:** 18 units. 16 one-bedroom standard units. 2 one-bedroom suites with efficiencies. 1 story, exterior corridors. **Parking:** on-site, winter plug-ins. **Terms:** office hours 7 am-11 pm, 3 day cancellation notice, weekly rates available, package plans, pets ($5 extra charge). **Cards:** AX, DC, MC, VI.

SOME UNITS

[S/D] [🛏] [🍴] [📺] [🔲] [🔲] [🔲] / [✕]

FEE

SUPER 8 MOTEL *Book at aaa.com*

Phone: (306)778-6088

▼▼▼ ◆

Small-scale Hotel

5/1-10/31	1P: $84-$94	2P: $89-$94	XP: $5
11/1-2/28	1P: $74-$84	2P: $79-$84	XP: $5
3/1-4/30	1P: $73-$82	2P: $78-$82	XP: $5

Location: Just e of Central Ave. Located in a commercial area. 405 N Service Rd E S9H 3X6. Fax: 306/778-0603. **Facility:** 63 one-bedroom standard units, some with whirlpools. 2 stories (no elevator), interior corridors. **Parking:** on-site, winter plug-ins. **Terms:** 30 day cancellation notice, pets ($5 extra charge, in smoking units). **Amenities:** voice mail. **Pool(s):** heated indoor. **Leisure Activities:** whirlpool, exercise room. **Guest Services:** coin laundry. **Cards:** AX, CB, DC, DS, MC, VI.

SOME UNITS

[ASK] [S/D] [🛏] [🍴] [🔌] [DATA PORT] [🔲] [🔲] [🔲] / [✕] [VCR]

FEE

SWIFT CURRENT TRAVELODGE *Book at aaa.com*

Phone: (306)773-3101

▼▼▼ ▼▼▼

Motel

6/1-8/31	1P: $80-$90	2P: $85-$95	XP: $5 F18
3/1-5/31 & 9/1-2/28	1P: $70-$80	2P: $75-$85	XP: $5 F18

Location: Just e of Central Ave, on North Service Rd. Located in a commercial area. Trans-Canada Hwy 1 E S9H 3X6 (N Service Rd, Hwy 1). Fax: 306/773-7399. **Facility:** 49 one-bedroom standard units. 1-2 stories (no elevator), exterior corridors. **Parking:** on-site, winter plug-ins. **Terms:** small pets only ($10 extra charge, in smoking units). **Amenities:** high-speed Internet (fee). **Pool(s):** heated outdoor, heated indoor. **Leisure Activities:** saunas, whirlpool. **Business Services:** meeting rooms. **Cards:** AX, MC, VI.

SOME UNITS

[ASK] [S/D] [🛏] [🍴] [🔌] [📺] [🔲] / [✕] [🔲] /

FEE

WESTWIND MOTEL

Phone: 306/773-1441

CAA SAVE
▼▼▼

Motel

All Year 1P: $48-$56 2P: $52-$64 XP: $5 F12

Location: Trans-Canada Hwy 1, 0.5 km w of Central Ave. Located in a commercial area. 155 N Service Rd W S9H 3X6 (83 Begg St W, S9H 3S8). Fax: 306/778-4085. **Facility:** 20 one-bedroom standard units, some with kitchens. 1 story, exterior corridors. **Parking:** on-site, winter plug-ins. **Terms:** office hours 8 am-midnight, weekly rates available, pets (with prior approval, in smoking units). **Dining:** 8 am-11 pm, Sun 9 am-9 pm, cocktails. **Pool(s):** heated outdoor. **Guest Services:** coin laundry. **Cards:** AX, MC, VI. **Special Amenities:** free local telephone calls and free newspaper.

SOME UNITS

[S/D] [🛏] [🍴] [🔌] [📺] / [✕] [🔲] /

—— WHERE TO DINE ——

SPRINGS GARDEN RESTAURANT

Lunch: $5-$16 **Dinner: $5-$17** **Phone: 306/773-2021**

▼▼ ▼▼

American

Location: Trans-Canada Hwy 1, on north service road; in Swift Current shopping mall. 323 1 Springs Dr S9H 3X6. **Hours:** 8:30 am-9 pm, Fri & Sat-10 pm, Sun 9 am-9 pm. Closed major holidays. **Reservations:** suggested, Thurs-Sun. **Features:** The Springs Garden's decor is casual, contemporary, bright and cheerful. The menu includes a variety of popular dishes: soup, steak, chicken, seafood, pizza, ribs and Greek specialties. The server staff is friendly, efficient and prompt. Casual dress; cocktails. **Parking:** on-site. **Cards:** AX, DC, MC, VI.

[🍸] [✕]

WONG'S KITCHEN

Lunch: $6-$20 **Dinner: $6-$20** **Phone: 306/773-4636**

▼▼▼ ▼▼

Chinese

Location: Trans-Canada Hwy 1, just w of 22nd Ave NE. 320 S Service Rd E S9H 3X8. **Hours:** noon-11 pm, Sun-9 pm. Closed: 12/25. **Reservations:** accepted. **Features:** Wong's Kitchen is one of the best spots in town to visit. The locally popular restaurant features Cantonese-style preparation of its dishes. The menu also offers steak and seafood selections. A smorgasbord is served noon-2 pm each day. Helpful staff. Casual dress; cocktails. **Parking:** on-site. **Cards:** AX, DC, MC, VI.

[✕]

WEYBURN pop. 9,534

—— WHERE TO STAY ——

PERFECT INNS & SUITES
Phone: (306)842-2691

CAA SAVE — Motel
All Year [ECP]   1P: $55-$80   2P: $57-$82   XP: $3   F
Location: 0.5 km w of jct Hwy 35 and 39. Located next to McDonalds. 238 Sims Ave S4H 2J8 (PO Box 69). Fax: 306/842-2121. **Facility:** 59 units. 55 one-bedroom standard units. 4 one-bedroom suites with kitchens. 1 story, interior/exterior corridors. **Parking:** on-site, winter plug-ins. **Amenities:** *Some:* high-speed Internet, hair dryers. **Guest Services:** valet laundry. **Cards:** AX, DC, DS, MC, VI. **Special Amenities: free expanded continental breakfast and free newspaper.**

SOME UNITS

WEYBURN INN
Phone: 306/842-6543

Small-scale Hotel
All Year   1P: $70-$125   2P: $80-$145   XP: $10   F
Location: Centre. Located in a commercial area. 5 Government Rd S4H 0N8. Fax: 306/842-2210. **Facility:** 69 units. 68 one-bedroom standard units. 1 one-bedroom suite ($125-$175) with whirlpool. 2 stories (no elevator), interior/exterior corridors. **Parking:** on-site, winter plug-ins. **Terms:** pets (in smoking units). **Pool(s):** heated indoor. **Leisure Activities:** sauna, whirlpool, exercise room. **Guest Services:** coin laundry. **Business Services:** meeting rooms. **Cards:** AX, DC, MC, VI.

SOME UNITS

—— WHERE TO DINE ——

T & C FAMILY RESTAURANT/DALLAS PIZZA   **Lunch:** $4-$9   **Dinner:** $5-$29   **Phone:** 306/842-2933

American
Location: Just n of Hwy 39; centre. 72 3rd St NE S4H 0V9. **Hours:** 10 am-11 pm. Closed: 12/25. **Features:** This restaurant offers family dining in contemporary and friendly surroundings. The menu features a wide variety of sandwiches, stir-fry, steak, seafood, pizza, souvlakia and Greek ribs. Families, couples and business people alike enjoy this eatery. Casual dress; cocktails. **Parking:** street. **Cards:** AX, MC, VI.

YORKTON pop. 15,107

——— WHERE TO STAY ———

COMFORT INN & SUITES — *Book at aaa.com*
Phone: (306)783-0333

6/1-9/30	1P: $74-$84	2P: $79-$89	XP: $5	F18
10/1-2/28	1P: $79-$84	2P: $89	XP: $5	F18
3/1-5/31	1P: $69-$79	2P: $74-$84	XP: $5	F18

Small-scale Hotel
Location: Just w of jct Hwy 9, 10 and 16 (Yellowhead Hwy). Located in a commercial area. 22 Dracup Ave S3N 3W1. Fax: 306/783-1239. **Facility:** 80 units. 64 one-bedroom standard units. 16 one-bedroom suites ($144-$149), some with whirlpools. 4 stories, interior corridors. **Parking:** on-site, winter plug-ins. **Terms:** small pets only ($5 extra charge). **Amenities:** voice mail, irons, hair dryers. *Some:* high-speed Internet. **Pool(s):** heated indoor. **Leisure Activities:** whirlpool, exercise room. **Guest Services:** coin laundry. **Business Services:** meeting rooms. **Cards:** AX, CB, DC, DS, JC, MC, VI.

SOME UNITS

DAYS INN — *Book at aaa.com*
Phone: (306)783-3297

All Year	1P: $86	2P: $86	XP: $5	F18

Small-scale Hotel
Location: Just e of Hwy 9, 10 and 16 (Yellowhead Hwy). Located in a commercial area. 2 Kelsey Bay S3N 3Z4. Fax: 306/783-3338. **Facility:** 74 one-bedroom standard units, some with whirlpools. 3 stories, interior corridors. **Parking:** on-site, winter plug-ins. **Terms:** check-in 4 pm, [ECP] meal plan available. **Amenities:** voice mail, hair dryers. *Some:* high-speed Internet, irons. **Pool(s):** small heated indoor. **Leisure Activities:** whirlpool, waterslide. **Cards:** AX, CB, DC, DS, JC, MC, VI.

SOME UNITS

HOWARD JOHNSON INN — *Book at aaa.com*
Phone: (306)783-6581

6/1-9/15	1P: $75-$90	2P: $75-$90	XP: $5	F16
9/16-2/28	1P: $69-$79	2P: $69-$79	XP: $5	F16
3/1-5/31	1P: $68-$78	2P: $68-$78	XP: $5	F16

Small-scale Hotel
Location: Jct Hwy 9, 10 and 16 (Yellowhead Hwy). Located in a commercial area. 207 Broadway St E S3N 3K7. Fax: 306/786-6399. **Facility:** 148 one-bedroom standard units. 2 stories (no elevator), interior/exterior corridors. **Parking:** on-site, winter plug-ins. **Terms:** [AP] meal plan available, pets (in smoking units). **Amenities:** voice mail. **Pool(s):** small heated indoor. **Leisure Activities:** whirlpool, waterslide. **Guest Services:** valet and coin laundry. **Business Services:** meeting rooms. **Cards:** AX, DC, MC, VI.

SOME UNITS

TRAVELODGE YORKTON — *Book at aaa.com*
Phone: (306)783-6571

All Year	1P: $99-$169	2P: $109-$179	XP: $10	F17

Small-scale Hotel
Location: West end of town, just e of Agriplex (Hwy 10A). Located in a commercial area. 345 Broadway W S3N 0N8. Fax: 306/786-3311. **Facility:** 71 units. 58 one-bedroom standard units. 13 one-bedroom suites, some with whirlpools. 2 stories (no elevator), interior/exterior corridors. **Parking:** on-site, winter plug-ins. **Terms:** package plans, pets ($50 deposit). **Amenities:** *Some:* high-speed Internet, irons, hair dryers. **Pool(s):** heated indoor. **Leisure Activities:** steamroom. **Guest Services:** valet laundry. **Business Services:** conference facilities. **Cards:** AX, CB, DC, MC, VI.

SOME UNITS

Yukon Territory

Bennett Lake,
near Carcross
© Natural Moments
Photography
PictureQuest

CARCROSS pop. 152

——— WHERE TO DINE ———

CINNAMON CACHE BAKERY & COFFEE SHOP **Lunch: $3-$10** Phone: 867/821-4331

Regional American

Location: 115.5 km on Hwy 2 (Klondike Hwy). KM 115.5 S Klondike Hwy Y0B 1B0. **Hours:** Open 3/15-9/15; 8 am-4 pm. **Features:** You'll enjoy this mom and pop restaurant conveniently located just off the highway in the town with the "smallest dessert on earth." Gail is the baker and BoBo is the chef, and while they are well known for their cinnamon buns, all of their cooking and baking is done using the freshest veggies, meats and fruits, and service is always with a smile. "Come on and get 'yer buns in here!". **Parking:** on-site.

DAWSON CITY pop. 1,251

——— WHERE TO STAY ———

DAWSON CITY BED & BREAKFAST Phone: 867/993-5649

| | 5/1-9/30 [BP] | 1P: $85-$110 | 2P: $95-$135 | XP: $20 |
| | 3/1-4/30 & 10/1-2/28 [BP] | 1P: $75-$100 | 2P: $85-$125 | XP: $20 |

Bed & Breakfast

Location: Just off 7th Ave. 451 Craig St Y0B 1G0 (Box 954). Fax: 867/993-5648. **Facility:** Smoke free premises. 7 one-bedroom standard units. 2 stories (no elevator), interior corridors. *Bath:* some shared or private, combo or shower only. **Parking:** on-site, winter plug-ins. **Amenities:** video library. *Some:* CD players, hair dryers. **Leisure Activities:** library. **Guest Services:** area transportation-bus station & town dock. **Cards:** DC, MC, VI. **Special Amenities: free full breakfast and preferred room (subject to availability with advance reservations).**

SOME UNITS

THE ELDORADO HOTEL Phone: (867)993-5451

| | 5/19-9/19 | 1P: $118-$160 | 2P: $128-$160 | XP: $10 | F12 |
| | 3/1-5/18 & 9/20-2/28 | 1P: $88-$130 | 2P: $93-$150 | XP: $10 | F12 |

Motel

Location: Downtown. 3rd Ave & Princess St Y0B 1G0 (PO Box 338). Fax: 867/993-5256. **Facility:** 52 one-bedroom standard units, some with kitchens. 2 stories (no elevator), interior/exterior corridors. **Parking:** on-site, winter plug-ins. **Terms:** [AP], [BP], [CP] & [ECP] meal plans available. **Amenities:** voice mail. *Some:* honor bars, irons, hair dryers. **Dining:** 6:30 am-10 pm; 7 am-9 pm 10/1-4/30, cocktails. **Guest Services:** coin laundry. **Business Services:** PC. **Cards:** AX, DC, DS, JC, MC, VI. **Special Amenities: free local telephone calls and free room upgrade (subject to availability with advance reservations).**

SOME UNITS

KLONDIKE KATES CABINS & RESTAURANT Phone: (867)993-6527

| | 5/14-9/15 | 1P: $95-$135 | 2P: $95-$135 | XP: $10 | F |
| | 4/8-5/13 & 9/16-9/30 | 1P: $85-$115 | 2P: $85-$115 | XP: $10 | F |

Motel

Location: Downtown. 1103 3rd Ave & King St Y0B 1G0 (Box 417). Fax: 867/993-6044. **Facility:** 15 one-bedroom standard units. 1 story. *Bath:* combo or shower only. **Parking:** on-site. **Terms:** open 4/8-9/30, pets ($10 extra charge). **Amenities:** voice mail. **Guest Services:** gift shop, valet laundry. **Cards:** MC, VI.

SOME UNITS
FEE

WESTMARK INN DAWSON CITY Phone: (867)993-5542

| | 5/20-9/12 | 1P: $149 | 2P: $149 | XP: $15 | F12 |

Motel

Location: At 5th and Harper sts; downtown. 5th St & Harper Y0B 1G0 (PO Box 420). Fax: 867/993-5623. **Facility:** 133 one-bedroom standard units. 2 stories (no elevator), interior/exterior corridors. *Bath:* combo or shower only. **Parking:** on-site. **Terms:** open 5/20-9/12, cancellation fee imposed, pets ($50 deposit, in smoking units, with prior approval). **Amenities:** hair dryers. **Dining:** 6:30 am-9 pm, cocktails. **Guest Services:** gift shop, coin laundry. **Cards:** AX, DC, DS, MC, VI.

SOME UNITS
FEE

The following lodgings were either not evaluated or did not meet AAA rating requirements but are listed for your information only.

AURORA INN Phone: 867/993-6860

[fyi]   Not evaluated. **Location:** 5th Ave Y0B 1G0. Facilities, services, and decor characterize a mid-range property.

BOMBAY PEGGY'S Phone: 867/993-6969

[fyi]   Not evaluated. **Location:** Downtown. (PO Box 411). Facilities, services, and decor characterize a mid-range property.

BONANZA GOLD MOTEL Phone: 867/993-6789

[fyi]   Did not meet all AAA rating requirements for some guest rooms at time of last evaluation on 07/14/2004.
Motel   **Location:** 2.4 km s on Hwy 2. (Bag 5000). Facilities, services, and decor characterize a basic property.

——— WHERE TO DINE ———

AMICA'S RISTORANTE **Lunch: $8-$17** **Dinner: $13-$29** Phone: 867/993-6800

Italian

Location: Corner of 5th Ave. 401 Craig St Y0B 1G0. **Hours:** 11 am-11 pm. Closed major holidays. **Features:** After working up an appetite panning in the gold fields, you'll enjoy the hearty portions of Greek and Italian cuisines at this friendly restaurant. Specialty pizzas boast the freshest of ingredients, as do the pastas and seafood. Casual dress; cocktails. **Parking:** on-site. **Cards:** MC, VI.

KLONDIKE KATE'S *Menu on aaa.com* **Lunch:** $5-$9 **Dinner:** $9-$20 **Phone:** 867/993-6527

Location: Corner of 3rd Ave and King St. 3rd & King Y0B 1G0. **Hours:** Open 4/15-9/15; 6:30 am-11 pm.
Reservations: suggested. **Features:** Along the city's main drag and just a few blocks from the theater, the restaurant captures a sense of history and the gold rush era. During summer, guests can choose to eat inside or on the heated patio. The menu features an array of sandwiches, wraps and seafood and meat dishes. Casual dress; cocktails. **Parking:** on-site. **Cards:** MC, VI. **Historic**

American

HAINES JUNCTION pop. 531

─────── **WHERE TO STAY** ───────

ALCAN MOTOR INN **Phone:** (867)634-2371

	1P: $100-$120	2P: $110-$130	XP: $10
5/1-9/30	1P: $100-$120	2P: $110-$130	XP: $10
3/1-4/30 & 10/1-2/28	1P: $85-$95	2P: $95-$105	XP: $10

Location: Jct of Alaska and Haines hwys (1 and 3). (PO Box 5460, Y0B 1L0). Fax: 867/634-2833. **Facility:** 22 units. 19 one-bedroom standard units. 3 one-bedroom suites, some with efficiencies. 2 stories (no elevator), exterior corridors. **Parking:** on-site, winter plug-ins. **Terms:** cancellation fee imposed, pets ($7.50 deposit).
Amenities: irons, hair dryers. **Guest Services:** gift shop, coin laundry. **Cards:** AX, MC, VI.
Special Amenities: free local telephone calls.

Motel

SOME UNITS

WHITEHORSE pop. 19,058

─────── **WHERE TO STAY** ───────

EDGEWATER HOTEL **Phone:** (867)667-2572

5/1-9/30	1P: $129-$149	2P: $129-$149	XP: $10
3/1-4/30 & 10/1-2/28	1P: $109-$129	2P: $109-$129	XP: $10

Location: Opposite White Pass Rail Depot. 101 Main St Y1A 2A7. Fax: 867/668-3014. **Facility:** 30 units. 27 one-bedroom standard units. 3 one-bedroom suites ($179-$249) with kitchens. 3 stories (no elevator), interior corridors. **Parking:** on-site, winter plug-ins. **Amenities:** high-speed Internet (fee), irons, hair dryers. **Dining:** 7 am-10 pm, cocktails, also, The Cellar Steakhouse and Wine Bar, see separate listing.
Guest Services: valet laundry. **Business Services:** meeting rooms. **Cards:** AX, DC, MC, VI. **Special Amenities:** free local telephone calls.

Small-scale Hotel

SOME UNITS

HAWKINS HOUSE BED & BREAKFAST **Phone:** 867/668-7638

6/15-8/31 [BP]	1P: $136	2P: $163	XP: $15	F12
5/1-6/14 & 9/1-2/28 [BP]	1P: $119	2P: $133	XP: $15	F12
3/1-4/30 [BP]	1P: $104	2P: $124	XP: $15	F12

Bed & Breakfast **Location:** At 3rd Ave; downtown. Located in a residential area. 303 Hawkins St Y1A 1X5. Fax: 867/668-7632.
Facility: Soft-yellow walls and highly polished floors bring a hint of Victorian ambience to this bright, airy B&B; themed guest rooms are featured. Smoke free premises. 4 one-bedroom standard units, some with whirlpools. 2 stories (no elevator), interior corridors. **Parking:** on-site, winter plug-ins. **Terms:** check-in 4 pm, age restrictions may apply, 3 day cancellation notice, no pets allowed (owner's dog on premises). **Amenities:** video library, voice mail, hair dryers. **Guest Services:** complimentary laundry.
Cards: AX, DC, JC, MC, VI.

HIGH COUNTRY INN *Book at aaa.com* **Phone:** (867)667-4471

5/15-9/15	1P: $99-$199	2P: $109-$199	XP: $15	F12
3/1-5/14 & 9/16-2/28	1P: $89-$169	2P: $99-$169	XP: $15	F12

Location: 0.6 km e of Main St. 4051 4th Ave Y1A 1H1. Fax: 867/667-6457. **Facility:** 84 one-bedroom standard units, some with efficiencies, kitchens and/or whirlpools. 4 stories, interior corridors. **Bath:** combo or shower
Small-scale Hotel only. **Parking:** on-site, winter plug-ins. **Terms:** 3 day cancellation notice, pets ($15 extra charge).
Amenities: voice mail, irons, hair dryers. **Dining:** high-speed Internet. **Dining:** 6 am-10 pm; hours may vary seasonally, cocktails. **Leisure Activities:** exercise room. **Guest Services:** valet and coin laundry. **Business Services:** conference facilities, PC. **Cards:** AX, CB, DC, DS, JC, MC, VI. **Special Amenities:** free newspaper and free room upgrade **(subject to availability with advance reservations).** *(See color ad below)*

SOME UNITS

MIDNIGHT SUN INN/BED & BREAKFAST

Phone: (867)667-2255

CAA SAVE

Bed & Breakfast

All Year [BP]　　　　1P: $85-$110　　　2P: $95-$125　　　XP: $20　　　F10
Location: Corner of Cook St. Located in a residential area. 6188 6th Ave Y1A 1N8. Fax: 867/668-4376. **Facility:** In a residential area just outside of the downtown core, this modern B&B is walking distance from shops and offers guest rooms with themed decor. Smoke free premises. 4 one-bedroom standard units. 3 stories (no elevator), interior corridors. **Parking:** on-site, winter plug-ins. **Terms:** check-in 4 pm, 5 day cancellation notice-fee imposed. **Amenities:** hair dryers. *Some:* high-speed Internet, voice mail. **Guest Services:** coin laundry. **Business Services:** meeting rooms. **Cards:** AX, DC, JC, MC, VI. **Special Amenities: free full breakfast and free newspaper.**

THE TOWN AND MOUNTAIN HOTEL

Phone: (867)668-7644

CAA SAVE

Small-scale Hotel

3/1-9/30　　　　　1P: $79-$89　　　2P: $79-$89　　　XP: $10　　　F12
10/1-2/28　　　　　1P: $69-$89　　　2P: $69-$89　　　XP: $10　　　F12
Location: Downtown. 401 Main St Y1A 2B6. Fax: 867/668-5822. **Facility:** 30 one-bedroom standard units, some with kitchens. 3 stories (no elevator), interior corridors. **Parking:** on-site, winter plug-ins. **Terms:** cancellation fee imposed, 7% service charge, pets ($10 extra charge, in smoking units). **Amenities:** *Some:* high-speed Internet, irons. **Dining:** 2 restaurants, noon-11 pm; adults only, cocktails. **Guest Services:** valet laundry. **Cards:** AX, DC, DS, MC, VI. **Special Amenities: free local telephone calls.**

WESTMARK WHITEHORSE HOTEL & CONFERENCE CENTRE　*Book at aaa.com*

Phone: (867)393-9700

CAA SAVE

Small-scale Hotel

5/1-9/30　　　　　　　1P: $159　　　2P: $159　　　XP: $15　　　F12
3/1-4/30 & 10/1-2/28　　1P: $129　　　2P: $129　　　XP: $15　　　F12
Location: At 2nd Ave; centre. 201 Wood St Y1A 2E4. Fax: 867/668-2789. **Facility:** 180 units. 178 one-bedroom standard units. 2 one-bedroom suites, some with whirlpools. 3 stories, interior corridors. *Bath:* combo or shower only. **Parking:** on-site, winter plug-ins. **Terms:** cancellation fee imposed, package plans. **Amenities:** voice mail, irons, hair dryers. *Some:* high-speed Internet. **Dining:** 6 am-9 pm; from 7 am 9/16-5/15, cocktails. **Leisure Activities:** Fee: Frantic Follies Vaudeville Revue. **Guest Services:** gift shop, valet and coin laundry, barber shop. **Business Services:** conference facilities, PC. **Cards:** AX, DC, DS, JC, MC, VI.

──── WHERE TO DINE ────

THE CELLAR STEAKHOUSE AND WINE BAR

Dinner: $19-$44　　　**Phone:** 867/667-2572

Steak & Seafood

Location: Opposite White Pass Rail Depot; in Edgewater Hotel. 101 Main St Y1A 2A7. **Hours:** 5 pm-10 pm. Closed: 1/1, 12/25, 12/26; also Sun & Mon. **Reservations:** accepted. **Features:** You'll enjoy the Cellar Dining Room's offerings of prime rib, halibut, Alaskan king crab, steak, salmon, baby back ribs, chicken, as well as a good selection of wine by the glass. Its well-appointed dining room is one of the hot spots in town. Casual dress; cocktails. **Parking:** on-site. **Cards:** AX, DC, MC, VI.

GIORGIO'S CUCCINA

Dinner: $18-$45　　　**Phone:** 867/668-4050

Italian

Location: Between 2nd and 3rd aves; downtown. 206 Jarvis St Y1A 2Hi. **Hours:** 4:30 pm-10:30 pm, Fri & Sat-11 pm, Sun-10 pm. Closed: 12/25. **Reservations:** accepted. **Features:** The attractive dining room serves up Italian food, including thin crust pizza, fish, seafood, pasta and steaks. Many dishes are prepared on a mesquite-flavoring charbroiler. Fresh fruit smoothies and a wide selection of wines round out the menu. Casual dress; cocktails. **Parking:** on-site. **Cards:** MC, VI.

KLONDIKE RIB & SALMON BBQ

Lunch: $10-$13　　　**Dinner:** $15-$25　　　**Phone:** 867/667-7554

Seafood

Location: Jct Main St; downtown. 2116 2nd Ave Y1A 2B9. **Hours:** Open 5/8-9/17; 11 am-9 pm. **Reservations:** suggested. **Features:** The popular restaurant opens seasonally each year to serve regional cuisine prepared in memorable and creative manners. On the menu are Arctic char, halibut and salmon, as well as entree-size salads and pasta. Guests can eat inside, where they might share a table with other diners, or enjoy the midnight sun on the patio. Beer & wine only. **Parking:** street. **Cards:** MC, VI.

MIDNIGHT SUN COFFEE ROASTERS

Lunch: $4-$6　　　**Dinner:** $4-$6　　　**Phone:** 867/633-4563

Coffee/Espresso

Location: 4th Ave and Black St. 4168C 4th Ave Y1A 5K3. **Hours:** 8 am-10 pm; hours vary seasonally. Closed: 12/25, 12/26. **Reservations:** not accepted. **Features:** Distributing all over the Yukon and even in northeastern Alaska, the funky, casual coffeehouse roasts outstanding coffee beans. This is a great place to catch up with local happenings and enjoy a panini, salad or tasty dessert from the display case. In season, patrons can sit outside and enjoy the midnight sun. Internet access is available, and the staff is exceedingly friendly. **Parking:** on-site. **Cards:** VI.

SANCHEZ CANTINA

Lunch: $12-$20　　　**Dinner:** $12-$20　　　**Phone:** 867/668-5858

Mexican

Location: Corner of 3rd Ave; downtown. 211 Hanson St Y1A 1W3. **Hours:** 11:30 am-3 & 5-9 pm, Sat from 5 pm. Closed: Sun. **Reservations:** suggested. **Features:** This casual restaurant with a seasonal terrace offers a variety of house-prepared authentic Mexican dishes, including tacos and enchiladas. Casual dress; cocktails. **Parking:** street. **Cards:** AX, MC, VI.

TALISMAN CAFE AT THE RIVERVIEW HOTEL

Lunch: $8-$15　　　**Dinner:** $9-$19　　　**Phone:** 867/667-2736

International

Location: Jct 2nd Ave and Wood St; downtown. 102 Wood St Y1A 1B9. **Hours:** 7 am-8 pm, Sun 8 am-2 pm. Closed major holidays. **Features:** While Talisman was voted in the top ten favorites of all vegetarian restaurants in Canada, there's also something for meat eaters, especially the buffalo burgers. Vegetarian offerings are simply the best around, creatively prepared using legumes, veggies, fruits and wonderful spices. The menu is as eclectic as the decor, and service is extremely friendly. Casual dress; beer & wine only. **Parking:** street. **Cards:** AX, MC, VI.

Alaska

Lake Park National
Park and Preserve
© Kennan Ward
imagestate

ANCHORAGE pop. 260,283

✈ Airport Accommodations

Spotter/Map Page Number	OA	ANCHORAGE INTERNATIONAL	Diamond Rating	Rate Range High Season	Listing Page
N/A		Anchorage Airport Courtyard by Marriott, 1.7 mi e of airport	◆◆◆	$189-$229	690
N/A	◆◆◆	Best Western Barratt Inn, 1.8 mi e of airport	◆◆	$112-$180 SAVE	691
N/A	◆◆◆	Coast International Inn, 1.8 mi e of airport	◆◆◆	$149-$229 SAVE	692
N/A	◆◆◆	Holiday Inn Express Anchorage Airport, 1.9 mi e of airport	◆◆	$189-$199 SAVE	694
N/A	◆◆◆	Long House Alaskan Hotel, 2 mi ne of airport	◆	$119-$139 SAVE	695
N/A	◆◆◆	Microtel Inn & Suites, 1.7 mi e of airport	◆◆	$139-$149 SAVE	695
N/A	◆◆◆	Millennium Alaskan Hotel Anchorage, 1.8 mi e of airport	◆◆◆	$260-$290 SAVE	696

——— WHERE TO STAY ———

15 CHANDELIERS ALASKA B & B
◆◆◆ SAVE
◆◆◆◆
Bed & Breakfast

5/15-9/15 [BP]   1P: $125-$220   2P: $125-$220   XP: $20   F12
3/1-5/14 & 9/16-2/28 [BP]   1P: $90-$150   2P: $90-$150   XP: $20   F12

Phone: (907)345-3032

Location: S of Anchorage on US 1 (New Seward Hwy), exit e on DeArmoun, then just s. 14020 Sabine St 99516. **Fax:** 907/345-3990. **Facility:** True to this upscale B&B's name, ornate chandeliers light the common areas and guest rooms; a gourmet breakfast is offered. Smoke free premises. 5 units. 4 one-bedroom standard units. 1 two-bedroom suite. 3 stories (no elevator), interior corridors. *Bath:* shower only. **Parking:** on-site, winter plug-ins. **Terms:** age restrictions may apply, 30 day cancellation notice, no pets allowed (owner's pets on premises). **Amenities:** irons, hair dryers. **Cards:** MC, VI. **Special Amenities:** free full breakfast.

ANCHORAGE AIRPORT COURTYARD BY MARRIOTT   *Book at aaa.com*
◆◆◆
Small-scale Hotel

Phone: (907)245-0322

5/15-9/14   1P: $189-$229
3/1-5/14 & 9/15-2/28   1P: $89-$137

Location: Just w of Jewell Lake and International Airport rds. 4901 Spenard Rd 99517. **Fax:** 907/248-1886. **Facility:** 154 units. 150 one-bedroom standard units, some with whirlpools. 4 one-bedroom suites. 3 stories, interior corridors. *Bath:* combo or shower only. **Parking:** on-site. **Terms:** cancellation fee imposed, [AP] meal plan available. **Amenities:** high-speed Internet, dual phone lines, voice mail, irons, hair dryers. **Pool(s):** small heated indoor. **Leisure Activities:** sauna, whirlpool, exercise room. **Guest Services:** sundries, valet and coin laundry. **Business Services:** meeting rooms, business center. **Cards:** AX, CB, DC, DS, JC, MC, VI.

SOME UNITS

ANCHORAGE CLARION SUITES   *Book at aaa.com*
◆◆◆ SAVE
◆◆◆
Small-scale Hotel

Phone: (907)274-1000

6/1-8/31 [ECP]   1P: $159-$169   2P: $159-$169   XP: $10   F17
9/1-9/30 [ECP]   1P: $89-$99   2P: $89-$99   XP: $10   F17
3/1-5/31 [ECP]   1P: $79-$89   2P: $79-$89   XP: $10   F17
10/1-2/28 [ECP]   1P: $75-$85   2P: $75-$85   XP: $10   F17

Location: Corner of C St and W 8th Ave. 325 W 8th Ave 99501. **Fax:** 907/274-3016. **Facility:** 111 one-bedroom suites. 3 stories, interior corridors. *Bath:* combo or shower only. **Parking:** on-site, winter plug-ins. **Terms:** cancellation fee imposed. **Amenities:** video games, high-speed Internet, dual phone lines, voice mail, irons, hair dryers. **Pool(s):** heated indoor. **Leisure Activities:** whirlpool, exercise room. **Guest Services:** valet and coin laundry, airport transportation-Ted Stevens Airport, area transportation-train depot. **Business Services:** meeting rooms, business center. **Cards:** AX, DC, DS, MC, VI. **Special Amenities:** free expanded continental breakfast and free newspaper.

SOME UNITS

ANCHORAGE GRAND HOTEL   *Book at aaa.com*   Phone: (907)929-8888

AAA SAVE | 5/15-9/15 [CP] | 1P: $159 | 2P: $159 | XP: $10 | F12
| 3/1-5/14 & 9/16-2/28 [CP] | 1P: $89 | 2P: $89 | XP: $10 | F12

Condominium   **Location:** Corner of 2nd Ave and E St; downtown. Located across from Anchorage Market. 505 W 2nd Ave 99501. Fax: 907/929-8899. **Facility:** Smoke free premises. 31 units. 6 one-bedroom standard units with kitchens. 25 one-bedroom suites with kitchens. 5 stories, interior corridors. **Parking:** on-site and street. **Terms:** weekly rates available. **Amenities:** high-speed Internet, voice mail, irons, hair dryers. **Guest Services:** valet laundry. **Business Services:** PC. **Cards:** AX, DS, MC, VI. **Special Amenities:** free continental breakfast and free newspaper. *(See color ad below)*

ANCHORAGE MARRIOTT DOWNTOWN   *Book at aaa.com*   Phone: (907)279-8000

| 5/16-9/15 | 1P: $269-$289 | 2P: $269-$289 | XP: $10 | F12
| 9/2-2/28 | 1P: $129-$149 | 2P: $129-$149 | XP: $10 | F12
Large-scale Hotel | 3/1-5/15 | 1P: $149 | 2P: $149 | XP: $10 | F12

Location: Between I and H sts. 820 W 7th Ave 99501. Fax: 907/279-8005. **Facility:** 392 one-bedroom standard units. 20 stories, interior corridors. *Bath:* combo or shower only. **Parking:** on-site (fee) and valet. **Terms:** cancellation fee imposed, package plans. **Amenities:** high-speed Internet (fee), dual phone lines, voice mail, irons, hair dryers. **Pool(s):** indoor. **Leisure Activities:** whirlpool, exercise room. **Guest Services:** gift shop, valet and coin laundry. **Business Services:** conference facilities, business center. **Cards:** AX, CB, DC, DS, JC, MC, VI.

SOME UNITS

ASPEN HOTELS ANCHORAGE   *Book at aaa.com*   Phone: (907)868-1605

| 5/16-9/15 [ECP] | 1P: $189-$209 | 2P: $189-$209 | XP: $10 | F18
| 5/1-5/15 [ECP] | 1P: $139-$169 | 2P: $139-$169 | XP: $10 | F18
Small-scale Hotel | 3/1-4/30 & 9/16-2/28 [ECP] | 1P: $109-$139 | 2P: $109-$139 | XP: $10 | F18

Location: Corner of 8th Ave and A St; downtown. 108 E 8th Ave 99501. Fax: 907/868-3520. **Facility:** 90 units. 78 one-bedroom standard units, some with whirlpools. 12 one-bedroom suites with efficiencies. 4 stories, interior corridors. *Bath:* combo or shower only. **Parking:** on-site. **Terms:** cancellation fee imposed. **Amenities:** DVD players, high-speed Internet, voice mail, irons, hair dryers. *Some:* video games. **Pool(s):** small heated indoor. **Leisure Activities:** whirlpool, limited exercise equipment. **Guest Services:** valet and coin laundry, area transportation. **Business Services:** meeting rooms, business center. **Cards:** AX, DC, DS, MC, VI.

SOME UNITS

BEST WESTERN BARRATT INN   *Book at aaa.com*   Phone: (907)243-3131

AAA SAVE | 6/1-8/31 | 1P: $112-$170 | 2P: $122-$180 | XP: $10 | F17
| 3/1-5/31 & 9/1-2/28 | 1P: $89-$99 | 2P: $69-$95 | XP: $10 | F17

Location: International Airport Rd, just ne of jct Jewel Lake and Spenard rds. 4616 Spenard Rd 99517-3299. Fax: 907/249-4917. **Facility:** 217 units. 213 one-bedroom standard units, some with efficiencies. 4 one-bedroom suites. 2-5 stories, interior/exterior corridors. **Parking:** on-site, winter plug-ins. **Terms:** small pets only ($50 deposit, $10 extra charge). **Amenities:** video games, high-speed Internet, voice mail, irons, hair dryers. *Some:* dual phone lines. **Dining:** 6 am-10 pm; hours may vary in winter, cocktails. **Leisure Activities:** exercise room. **Guest Services:** valet and coin laundry, area transportation-train station. **Business Services:** meeting rooms, PC. **Cards:** AX, CB, DC, MC, VI. **Special Amenities:** early check-in/late check-out.

SOME UNITS

BEST WESTERN GOLDEN LION HOTEL   *Book at aaa.com*   Phone: (907)561-1522

AAA SAVE | 5/16-9/15 | 1P: $179-$199 | 2P: $179-$199 | XP: $10 | F12
| 3/1-5/15 & 9/16-2/28 | 1P: $89-$99 | 2P: $89-$99 | XP: $10 | F12

Location: US 1 (New Seward Hwy) and 36th Ave. 1000 E 36th Ave 99508. Fax: 907/743-4814. **Facility:** 83 one-bedroom standard units. 3 stories, interior corridors. *Bath:* combo or shower only. **Parking:** on-site. Small-scale Hotel   **Terms:** [AP] meal plan available. **Amenities:** voice mail, irons, hair dryers. *Some:* high-speed Internet, dual phone lines. **Dining:** 7 am-2 & 5-10 pm, Sun-1 pm, cocktails. **Leisure Activities:** sauna, exercise room. **Guest Services:** valet and coin laundry. **Business Services:** meeting rooms, fax (fee). **Cards:** AX, CB, DC, DS, MC, VI. **Special Amenities:** free local telephone calls and early check-in/late check-out. *(See color ad p 692)*

SOME UNITS

CAMAI BED & BREAKFAST

Phone: (907)333-2219

5/16-9/15 [BP]	1P: $95-$125	2P: $95-$125	XP: $20	D10
3/1-5/15 & 9/16-2/28 [ECP]	1P: $50-$80	2P: $50-$80	XP: $15	D10

Bed & Breakfast   **Location:** US 1 (New Seward Hwy), 2.8 mi e on Benson/Northern Lights Blvd, 0.6 mi s on Wesleyn Ave to Queen Ct, then just e. Located in a residential area. 3838 Westminster Way 99508-4834. Fax: 907/337-3959. **Facility:** Well-tended gardens surround this B&B, which features cozy, comfortable rooms; two rooms have private entrances. Smoke free premises. 3 one-bedroom suites, some with efficiencies. 2 stories (no elevator), interior/exterior corridors. **Parking:** on-site, winter plug-ins. **Terms:** 14 day cancellation notice-fee imposed, weekly rates available. **Amenities:** video library, DVD players, high-speed Internet, voice mail, hair dryers. **Business Services:** PC.

CHUGACH BED & BREAKFAST

Phone: (907)333-4615

5/16-9/15 [BP]	1P: $85-$105	2P: $95-$120	XP: $35	D12
3/1-5/14 & 9/16-2/28 [ECP]	1P: $60	2P: $60	XP: $15	D12

Bed & Breakfast   **Location:** US 1 (New Seward Hwy), exit Tudor Rd, 5 mi e to Patterson Rd, just n to Madelynne, then just e on Madellyne to Laron Ln. 3901 Laron Ln 99504. Fax: 907/337-6095. **Facility:** Smoke free premises. 4 units. 3 one-and 1 two-bedroom standard units, some with whirlpools. 2 stories (no elevator), interior corridors. **Bath:** some shared or private. **Parking:** on-site. **Terms:** check-in 4 pm, 7 day cancellation notice, no pets allowed (owner's cat on premises). **Amenities:** video library, CD players, high-speed Internet, irons, hair dryers. **Leisure Activities:** sauna, exercise room. **Guest Services:** complimentary laundry. **Cards:** AX, DS, MC, VI.

SOME UNITS

COAST INTERNATIONAL INN   *Book at aaa.com*

Phone: (907)243-2233

5/11-9/17	1P: $149-$229	2P: $149-$229	XP: $15	F17
3/1-5/10 & 9/18-2/28	1P: $71-$121	2P: $71-$121	XP: $15	F17

Small-scale Hotel   **Location:** Just ne of jct International Airport and Spenard rds, then just w. 3333 W International Airport Rd 99502. Fax: 907/248-3796. **Facility:** 141 one-bedroom standard units. 3 stories (no elevator), interior corridors. **Bath:** combo or shower only. **Parking:** on-site, winter plug-ins. **Terms:** package plans. **Amenities:** video games, high-speed Internet, dual phone lines, voice mail, irons, hair dryers. **Dining:** 6 am-2 & 5-10 pm; to 9 pm off season, cocktails. **Leisure Activities:** sauna, exercise room. **Guest Services:** valet and coin laundry. **Business Services:** meeting rooms, PC. **Cards:** AX, DC, DS, MC, VI.

SOME UNITS

COMFORT INN SHIP CREEK   *Book at aaa.com*

Phone: (907)277-6887

5/15-8/31 [ECP]	1P: $169-$239	2P: $169-$239	XP: $10	F18
9/1-2/28 [ECP]	1P: $79-$139	2P: $79-$139	XP: $10	F18
3/1-5/14 [ECP]	1P: $79-$129	2P: $79-$129	XP: $10	F18

Small-scale Hotel   **Location:** At 3rd and E sts, 0.3 mi n on E St, across the railway, just e on Ship Creek Ave (formerly Warehouse Ave) downtown. 111 W Ship Creek Ave 99501. Fax: 907/274-9830. **Facility:** 100 units. 98 one-bedroom standard units, some with whirlpools. 2 two-bedroom suites with kitchens and whirlpools. 3 stories, interior corridors. **Bath:** combo or shower only. **Parking:** on-site. **Terms:** check-in 4 pm, pets ($10 fee, in smoking units). **Amenities:** video games, dual phone lines, voice mail, irons, hair dryers. **Pool(s):** small heated indoor. **Leisure Activities:** whirlpool, fishing, exercise room. **Guest Services:** valet and coin laundry, airport transportation-Ted Stevens Airport, area transportation-Egan Center & train depot. **Business Services:** business center. **Cards:** AX, DC, DS, MC, VI. **Special Amenities:** free local telephone calls and free newspaper.

FEE

SOME UNITS

DAYS INN DOWNTOWN   *Book at aaa.com*

Phone: (907)276-7226

5/15-9/15	1P: $79-$250	2P: $79-$250	XP: $10	F17
3/1-5/14 & 9/16-2/28	1P: $69-$125	2P: $69-$125	XP: $10	F17

Small-scale Hotel   **Location:** At Cordova and E 5th Ave; downtown. 321 E 5th Ave 99501. Fax: 907/265-5145. **Facility:** 130 units. 129 one-bedroom standard units. 1 one-bedroom suite with efficiency. 4 stories, interior/exterior corridors. **Bath:** combo or shower only. **Parking:** on-site. **Terms:** cancellation fee imposed, weekly rates available, package plans, 8% service charge, pets ($25 deposit, in smoking units). **Amenities:** video games, voice mail, hair dryers. **Fee:** high-speed Internet, safes. **Some:** dual phone lines, irons. **Guest Services:** coin laundry, airport transportation-Ted Stevens Airport, area transportation-Lake Hood, Merrill field, train station. **Business Services:** meeting rooms, business center. **Cards:** AX, DC, DS, JC, MC, VI. **Special Amenities:** free local telephone calls.

FEE

SOME UNITS

DIMOND CENTER HOTEL Book at aaa.com   Phone: (907)770-5000

AAA SAVE   5/16-9/15 [ECP]   1P: $229   2P: $229   XP: $20   F17
WWW   3/1-5/15 & 9/16-2/28 [ECP] 1P: $119   2P: $119   XP: $10   F17

Small-scale Hotel   **Location:** New Seward Hwy 1, exit Dimond Blvd, just w to E Dimond Blvd, then s. 700 E Dimond Blvd 99515. Fax: 907/770-5001. **Facility:** 109 one-bedroom standard units, some with whirlpools. 3 stories, interior corridors. **Parking:** on-site. **Terms:** 7 day cancellation notice, package plans. **Amenities:** CD players, high-speed Internet, dual phone lines, voice mail, irons, hair dryers. **Leisure Activities:** barbecue, chess, limited exercise equipment. **Guest Services:** gift shop, valet and coin laundry, area transportation-downtown. **Business Services:** meeting rooms, PC. **Cards:** AX, CB, DC, DS, MC, VI. **Special Amenities: free expanded continental breakfast and preferred room (subject to availability with advance reservations).** (See color ad below)

SOME UNITS

(S/D) (+) (Y) (M) (hammer) (pencil) (video) (DATA PORT) (refrigerator) (microwave) (iron) / (X) /

FAIRFIELD INN AND SUITES BY MARRIOTT   Phone: 907/222-9000

fyi   5/16-9/15 [CP]   1P: $159-$199   2P: $159-$199
        3/1-5/15 & 9/16-2/28 [CP] 1P: $89-$109   2P: $89-$109
        Too new to rate. **Location:** Jct C St and International Airport Rd. 5060 A St 99503. Fax: 907/222-7611. **Amenities:** 106 units, coffeemakers, microwaves, refrigerators, pool. **Terms:** check-in 4 pm, cancellation fee imposed. **Cards:** AX, DC, DS, MC, VI.

HAMPTON INN-ANCHORAGE Book at aaa.com   Phone: (907)550-7000

WWW   5/16-9/15   1P: $179-$219   2P: $189-$229
        3/1-5/15 & 9/16-10/31   1P: $89-$129   2P: $99-$139
        11/1-2/28   1P: $89-$109   2P: $99-$119

Small-scale Hotel   **Location:** Corner of Tudor Rd and C St. 4301 Credit Union Dr 99503. Fax: 907/561-7330. **Facility:** 101 one-bedroom standard units, some with whirlpools. 3 stories, interior corridors. Bath: combo or shower only. **Parking:** on-site. **Terms:** package plans. **Amenities:** video games, dual phone lines, voice mail, irons, hair dryers. **Pool(s):** small heated indoor. **Leisure Activities:** whirlpool, exercise room. **Guest Services:** gift shop, valet and coin laundry, area transportation. **Business Services:** meeting rooms, business center. **Cards:** AX, CB, DC, DS, JC, MC, VI.

SOME UNITS

(ASK) (S/D) (+) (fork) (M) (pencil) (video) (boat) (TV) (DATA PORT) (refrigerator) (microwave) (iron) / (X) /

Extraordinary! Exceptional!

* Large, comfortable loft style rooms with extra desk space
* Refrigerators, microwaves & coffee makers in every room
* 36-inch television
* Free high-speed internet access

* Luxurious soaking tub
* AVEDA® aromatherapy amenities
* Complimentary breakfast including Belgian waffles

Call 1-866-770-5002 or visit www.DimondCenterHotel.com to make your reservations.

Dimond Center H O T E L

Complimentary 24-hour airport transportation.

700 E. Dimond Blvd ◆ Anchorage, AK 99515 ◆ Reservations 907-770-5000   Approved

Eagle River Motel
Only 15 minutes from Anchorage

11111 Old Eagle River Rd
Eagle River, AK
Fax (907) 694-5000
Toll Free Reservations
866-256-6835

* Cable TV with HBO
* Free local calls and internet
* Data ports and voice mail
* Microwaves, coffeemakers, refrigerators in every room
* Kitchenettes
* Suite, deluxe & standard rooms

Rates

$49*
3/1-5/13/05
9/6/05-2/28/06

$69*
5/14-5/31/05

$89*
6/1-9/5/05

*Based on single occupancy

1-866-AK-MOTEL or www.eaglerivermotel.com

HAWTHORN SUITES LTD *Book at aaa.com* Phone: (907)222-5005

6/1-8/31 [BP]	1P: $159-$169	2P: $159-$169	XP: $10 F17
9/1-9/30 [BP]	1P: $89-$99	2P: $89-$99	XP: $10 F17
3/1-5/31 & 10/1-2/28 [BP]	1P: $79-$89	2P: $79-$89	XP: $10 F17

Location: Corner of L St and W 8th Ave. 1110 W 8th Ave 99501. Fax: 907/222-5215. **Facility:** 111 one-bedroom suites. 3 stories, interior corridors. *Bath:* combo or shower only. **Parking:** on-site. **Terms:** cancellation fee imposed. **Amenities:** video games, high-speed Internet, dual phone lines, voice mail, irons, hair dryers. **Pool(s):** small heated indoor. **Leisure Activities:** whirlpool, limited exercise equipment. **Guest Services:** valet and coin laundry, airport transportation-Ted Stevens Airport, area transportation-train depot. **Business Services:** meeting rooms, business center. **Cards:** AX, DC, DS, MC, VI. **Special Amenities:** free full breakfast and free newspaper.

Small-scale Hotel

SOME UNITS

HILTON ANCHORAGE *Book at aaa.com* Phone: (907)272-7411

5/16-9/30	1P: $169-$289	2P: $189-$309	XP: $20 F18
3/1-5/15 & 10/1-2/28	1P: $79-$179	2P: $99-$199	XP: $20 F18

Location: At E St; downtown. 500 W 3rd Ave 99501. Fax: 907/265-7044. **Facility:** 607 units. 597 one-bedroom standard units. 10 one-bedroom suites. 15-21 stories, interior corridors. *Bath:* combo or shower only. **Parking:** on-site (fee) and valet. **Terms:** cancellation fee imposed, [AP] meal plan available, package plans. **Amenities:** video games, high-speed Internet (fee), dual phone lines, voice mail, irons, hair dryers. **Dining:** 2 restaurants, 6 am-1 am, cocktails, also, The Top of the World, see separate listing. **Pool(s):** small heated indoor. **Leisure Activities:** whirlpool, steamrooms. **Guest Services:** gift shop, valet laundry. **Business Services:** conference facilities, business center. **Cards:** AX, CB, DC, DS, JC, MC, VI. *(See color ad below)*

Large-scale Hotel

SOME UNITS

HILTON GARDEN INN *Book at aaa.com* Phone: (907)729-7000

5/1-9/30	1P: $209-$299	2P: $219-$309	XP: $10 F18
10/1-2/28	1P: $139-$179	2P: $179-$189	XP: $10 F18
3/1-4/30	1P: $139-$179	2P: $149-$189	XP: $10 F18

Location: Corner of Tudor Rd and A St. 100 W Tudor Rd 99503. Fax: 907/729-8000. **Facility:** 125 one-bedroom standard units, some with whirlpools. 4 stories, interior corridors. *Bath:* combo or shower only. **Parking:** on-site. **Terms:** package plans. **Amenities:** video games (fee), high-speed Internet, dual phone lines, voice mail, irons, hair dryers. **Pool(s):** heated indoor. **Leisure Activities:** whirlpool, exercise room. **Guest Services:** sundries, valet and coin laundry, area transportation. **Business Services:** meeting rooms, business center. **Cards:** AX, DC, DS, MC, VI.

Small-scale Hotel

SOME UNITS

HOLIDAY INN EXPRESS ANCHORAGE AIRPORT *Book at aaa.com* Phone: (907)248-8848

5/16-9/15 [CP]	1P: $189-$199	2P: $189-$199	
9/16-10/15 [CP]	1P: $129-$139	2P: $129-$139	
3/1-5/15 & 10/16-2/28 [CP]	1P: $109-$119	2P: $109-$119	

Location: 0.5 mi ne of Jewell Lake and International Airport rds. 4411 Spenard Rd 99517. Fax: 907/248-8847. **Facility:** 128 one-bedroom standard units, some with whirlpools. 3 stories, interior corridors. *Bath:* combo or shower only. **Parking:** on-site. **Terms:** cancellation fee imposed. **Amenities:** video games, high-speed Internet, dual phone lines, voice mail, irons, hair dryers. **Pool(s):** heated indoor. **Leisure Activities:** whirlpool. **Guest Services:** sundries, valet and coin laundry, airport transportation-Ted Stevens Airport. **Business Services:** meeting rooms, business center. **Cards:** AX, DC, DS, MC, VI.

Small-scale Hotel

SOME UNITS

HOMEWOOD SUITES-ANCHORAGE *Book at aaa.com* Phone: (907)762-7000

5/16-9/15 [BP]	1P: $229		XP: $10 F18
3/1-5/15 & 9/16-2/28 [BP]	1P: $129		XP: $10 F18

Location: New Seward Hwy, exit Tudor Rd W, turn on C St. 140 W Tudor Rd 99503. Fax: 907/762-8000. **Facility:** 122 units. 47 one-bedroom standard units with kitchens. 71 one- and 4 two-bedroom suites with kitchens. 4 stories, interior corridors. *Bath:* combo or shower only. **Parking:** on-site. **Terms:** package plans. **Amenities:** video games (fee), high-speed Internet, dual phone lines, voice mail, irons, hair dryers. *Some:* DVD players (fee). **Pool(s):** heated indoor. **Leisure Activities:** whirlpool, exercise room, basketball. **Guest Services:** sundries, complimentary evening beverages: Mon-Thurs, valet and coin laundry, area transportation. **Business Services:** meeting rooms, business center. **Cards:** AX, CB, DC, DS, MC, VI.

Small-scale Hotel

SOME UNITS
FEE

HOWARD JOHNSON PLAZA HOTEL　　　　　　　　　　　　　　　Phone: (907)793-5500

AAA SAVE 6/2-9/28 　　　　　　1P: $159　　　　2P: $159　　　XP: $20　　　F
　　　　　 5/16-6/1 　　　　　　 1P: $99　　　　 2P: $99　　　 XP: $20　　　F
◆◆ ◆◆ 3/1-5/15 & 9/29-2/28 　1P: $69　　　　 2P: $69　　　 XP: $20　　　F

Location: At 3rd Ave and C St; downtown. 239 W 4th Ave 99501. Fax: 907/258-4733. **Facility:** 247 one-bedroom
Small-scale Hotel standard units. 3 stories, interior corridors. *Bath:* combo or shower only. **Parking:** on-site. **Amenities:** video
games, voice mail, irons, hair dryers. **Dining:** 5:30 am-11 & 5:30-10 pm, cocktails. **Pool(s):** heated indoor.
Leisure Activities: exercise room. **Guest Services:** valet and coin laundry. **Business Services:** meeting rooms. **Cards:** AX,
CB, DC, DS, MC, VI. **Special Amenities:** free continental breakfast and free newspaper.

LONG HOUSE ALASKAN HOTEL　*Book at aaa.com*　　　　　Phone: (907)243-2133

AAA SAVE 6/1-9/10 [ECP]　　　1P: $119-$139　　2P: $119-$139　XP: $10　　F16
　　　　　 5/15-5/31 [ECP]　　　 1P: $89-$104　　 2P: $89-$104　 XP: $10　　F16
◆◆ ◆◆ 3/1-5/14 & 9/11-2/28 [ECP] 1P: $62-$71　 2P: $62-$71　　 XP: $10　　F16

Location: International Airport Rd, 1.5 mi ne on Spenard Rd, nw on Wisconsin St at 43rd Ave, then just e. 4335
Small-scale Hotel Wisconsin St 99517. Fax: 907/243-6060. **Facility:** 54 one-bedroom standard units. 2 stories (no elevator),
interior corridors. *Bath:* combo or shower only. **Terms:** check-in 4 pm, pets
($50 deposit, $10 extra charge; in smoking units). **Amenities:** voice mail, hair dryers. **Leisure Activities:** walk-in fish freezer.
Guest Services: valet and coin laundry, airport transportation-Ted Stevens Airport, area transportation. *Fee:* beauty salon.
Cards: AX, DS, MC, VI. **Special Amenities:** free expanded continental breakfast.

MERRILL FIELD INN　　　　　　　　　　　　　　　　　　Phone: (907)276-4547

AAA SAVE 5/15-9/15　　　　　　1P: $108-$118　　2P: $124-$136
◆◆ ◆◆ 3/1-5/14 & 9/16-2/28 　1P: $55-$60　　　2P: $65-$70

Location: 1 mi e via US 1 (Glenn Hwy). Located opposite from Merrill Field Airstrip. 420 Sitka St 99501.
Motel Fax: 907/276-5064. **Facility:** 39 one-bedroom standard units, some with whirlpools. 2 stories (no elevator),
exterior corridors. **Parking:** on-site, winter plug-ins. **Terms:** cancellation fee imposed, weekly rates
available, pets ($7 extra charge). **Amenities:** video library (fee), high-speed Internet, hair dryers. **Guest
Services:** coin laundry. **Cards:** AX, DC, DS, MC, VI. **Special Amenities:** free continental breakfast and free local telephone
calls. *(See color ad below)*

MICROTEL INN & SUITES　*Book at aaa.com*　　　　　　　Phone: (907)245-5002

AAA SAVE 5/16-9/15　　　　　　1P: $139-$149　　2P: $139-$149　XP: $5　　　F16
◆◆ ◆◆ 3/1-5/15 & 9/16-2/28 　1P: $69-$79　　　 2P: $69-$79　　 XP: $5　　　F16

Location: 1.7 mi e of airport. 5205 Northwood Dr 99517. Fax: 907/245-5030. **Facility:** 79 one-bedroom standard
units, some with whirlpools. 3 stories, interior corridors. *Bath:* combo or shower only. **Parking:** on-site.
Small-scale Hotel **Terms:** pets ($10 extra charge, in smoking units). **Amenities:** video games. *Some:* irons, hair dryers.
Leisure Activities: whirlpools. **Guest Services:** valet and coin laundry. **Business Services:** meeting
rooms, PC. **Cards:** AX, DC, DS, MC, VI. **Special Amenities:** free expanded continental breakfast and free local telephone
calls.

MILLENNIUM ALASKAN HOTEL ANCHORAGE

Book at aaa.com   **Phone:** (907)243-2300

AAA [SAVE]

5/16-9/22	1P: $260-$280	2P: $270-$290	XP: $20	F17
9/23-2/28	1P: $150-$175	2P: $160-$190	XP: $15	F17
3/1-5/15	1P: $150-$170	2P: $160-$180	XP: $15	F17

Location: International Airport Rd, just ne from jct Jewel Lake and Spenard rds. 4800 Spenard Rd 99517.

Large-scale Hotel   **Fax:** 907/243-8815. **Facility:** 247 units. 245 one-bedroom standard units. 2 one-bedroom suites ($199-$800) with whirlpools. 4 stories, interior corridors. *Bath:* combo or shower only. **Parking:** on-site. **Terms:** package plans, pets ($50 deposit). **Amenities:** video games, dual phone lines, voice mail, irons, hair dryers. *Some:* high-speed Internet (fee). **Dining:** 6 am-2 & 5-10:30 pm, cocktails. **Leisure Activities:** sauna, whirlpool, steamroom, seaplane dock on adjacent Lake Spenard, exercise room. **Guest Services:** gift shop, valet and coin laundry, airport transportation-Ted Stevens Airport, area transportation-Diamond Mall and downtown. **Business Services:** conference facilities, business center. **Cards:** AX, CB, DC, DS, JC, MC, VI. *(See color ad p 690)*

SOME UNITS

MOTEL 6-4216

Book at aaa.com   **Phone:** 907/677-8000

AAA [SAVE]

5/16-9/15	1P: $139	2P: $149
3/1-5/15 & 9/16-2/28	1P: $59	2P: $64

Motel   **Location:** Jct C St and International Airport Rd. 5000 A St 99503. Fax: 907/677-8640. **Facility:** 85 one-bedroom standard units. 3 stories, interior corridors. *Bath:* combo or shower only. **Parking:** on-site. **Terms:** cancellation fee imposed. **Amenities:** voice mail. **Guest Services:** coin laundry. **Cards:** AX, DC, DS, MC, VI. **Special Amenities:** free local telephone calls.

SOME UNITS

RAMADA INN ANCHORAGE DOWNTOWN

Book at aaa.com   **Phone:** (907)272-7561

6/1-8/31 [ECP]	1P: $169-$239	2P: $169-$239	XP: $10	F18
9/1-9/15 [ECP]	1P: $99-$239	2P: $99-$239	XP: $10	F18
3/1-5/31 [ECP]	1P: $79-$239	2P: $79-$239	XP: $10	F18
9/16-2/28 [ECP]	1P: $79-$189	2P: $79-$189	XP: $10	F18

Small-scale Hotel   **Location:** Jct Barrow St; downtown. 115 E 3rd Ave 99501. Fax: 907/272-3879. **Facility:** 90 one-bedroom standard units, some with whirlpools. 3 stories, interior/exterior corridors. *Bath:* combo or shower only. **Parking:** on-site. **Terms:** [MAP] meal plan available, pets ($10 extra charge, in designated units). **Amenities:** voice mail, irons, hair dryers. **Leisure Activities:** limited exercise equipment. **Guest Services:** valet and coin laundry. **Business Services:** meeting rooms, PC. **Cards:** AX, CB, DC, DS, JC, MC, VI.

SOME UNITS

RAMADA LIMITED HOTEL OF ANCHORAGE

Book at aaa.com   **Phone:** (907)929-7000

AAA [SAVE]

5/16-9/15	1P: $149-$199	2P: $149-$199	XP: $10	F16
3/1-5/15 & 9/16-2/28	1P: $79-$159	2P: $79-$159	XP: $10	F16

Small-scale Hotel   **Location:** 5 mi ne on US 1 (Glenn Hwy), just s. 207 Muldoon Rd 99504. Fax: 907/929-7070. **Facility:** 50 one-bedroom standard units, some with whirlpools. 3 stories, interior corridors. **Parking:** on-site. **Amenities:** voice mail, irons, hair dryers. *Some:* dual phone lines. **Dining:** How How Chinese Restaurant, see separate listing. **Guest Services:** valet and coin laundry, airport transportation-Ted Stevens Airport, area transportation-within 5 mi. **Business Services:** meeting rooms, PC. **Cards:** AX, CB, DC, DS, JC, MC, VI. **Special Amenities:** free full breakfast and free local telephone calls. *(See color ad below)*

SOME UNITS

RESIDENCE INN BY MARRIOTT

Book at aaa.com   **Phone:** (907)563-9844

5/15-9/14	1P: $230-$344
3/1-5/14 & 9/15-2/28	1P: $129-$159

Small-scale Hotel   **Location:** Corner of US 1 (New Seward Hwy) and 36th Ave. 1025 E 35th Ave 99508. Fax: 907/563-9636. **Facility:** 148 units. 56 one-bedroom standard units with kitchens. 56 one- and 36 two-bedroom suites with kitchens. 2 stories, interior corridors. *Bath:* combo or shower only. **Parking:** on-site. **Terms:** cancellation fee imposed, [ECP] meal plan available, pets ($85 fee, $10 extra charge). **Amenities:** video games, high-speed Internet, voice mail, irons, hair dryers. *Some:* dual phone lines. **Pool(s):** heated indoor. **Leisure Activities:** sauna, whirlpool, bicycles, exercise room, sports court. **Guest Services:** complimentary evening beverages: Mon-Thurs, valet and coin laundry, area transportation. **Business Services:** meeting rooms, business center. **Cards:** AX, CB, DC, DS, JC, MC, VI.

SOME UNITS

SHERATON ANCHORAGE HOTEL   *Book at aaa.com*   **Phone:** (907)276-8700

5/1-9/30	1P: $279	2P: $279 XP: $10 F18
3/1-4/30 & 10/1-2/28	1P: $169	2P: $169 XP: $10 F18

Large-scale Hotel   **Location:** 6th Ave and Denali St. 401 E 6th Ave 99501. Fax: 907/276-7561. **Facility:** 375 units. 370 one-bedroom standard units. 5 one-bedroom suites ($400-$1200), some with whirlpools. 16 stories, interior corridors. *Bath:* combo or shower only. **Parking:** on-site and valet. **Terms:** cancellation fee imposed. **Amenities:** video games, high-speed Internet (fee), voice mail, irons, hair dryers. *Some:* fax. **Leisure Activities:** saunas, whirlpool, steamrooms, exercise room. *Fee:* massage. **Guest Services:** gift shop, valet laundry, area transportation. **Business Services:** conference facilities, business center. **Cards:** AX, CB, DC, DS, JC, MC, VI. *(See color ad below)*

SOME UNITS

SPRINGHILL SUITES BY MARRIOTT   *Book at aaa.com*   **Phone:** (907)562-3247

5/15-9/14	1P: $179-$199
3/1-5/14 & 9/15-2/28	1P: $89

Small-scale Hotel   **Location:** Corner of 36th Ave and A St. 3401 A St 99503. Fax: 907/562-3250. **Facility:** 102 one-bedroom standard units. 3 stories, interior corridors. *Bath:* combo or shower only. **Parking:** on-site. **Terms:** cancellation fee imposed, [CP] meal plan available. **Amenities:** high-speed Internet, dual phone lines, voice mail, irons, hair dryers. **Pool(s):** small heated indoor. **Leisure Activities:** whirlpool, limited exercise equipment. **Guest Services:** valet and coin laundry. **Business Services:** business center. **Cards:** AX, CB, DC, DS, JC, MC, VI.

SOME UNITS

SUPER 8 MOTEL-ANCHORAGE   *Book at aaa.com*   **Phone:** (907)276-8884

6/9-9/8	1P: $130	2P: $150	XP: $10 F12
3/1-6/8	1P: $60-$80	2P: $70-$90	XP: $10 F12
9/9-10/30	1P: $80	2P: $90	XP: $10 F12
10/31-2/28	1P: $60	2P: $70	XP: $10 F12

Small-scale Hotel   **Location:** At 36th Ave, just n of Spenard Rd. 3501 Minnesota Dr 99503. Fax: 907/279-8194. **Facility:** 85 one-bedroom standard units. 4 stories, interior corridors. **Parking:** on-site. **Terms:** pets ($25 deposit). **Amenities:** safes (fee). **Guest Services:** valet and coin laundry, area transportation. **Business Services:** meeting rooms. **Cards:** AX, CB, DC, DS, JC, MC, VI.

SOME UNITS

FEE

THE VOYAGER HOTEL   *Book at aaa.com*   **Phone:** (907)277-9501

AAA SAVE   6/1-8/31 [CP]   1P: $169   2P: $169   XP: $10
                9/1-2/28 [CP]   1P: $89-$129   2P: $89-$129   XP: $10
WWW WWW   5/16-5/31 [CP]   1P: $129   2P: $129   XP: $10
                3/1-5/15 [CP]   1P: $89   2P: $89   XP: $10

Small-scale Hotel **Location:** At K St and 5th Ave; downtown. 501 K St 99501. Fax: 907/274-0333. **Facility:** Smoke free premises. 40 units. 37 one-bedroom standard units. 3 one-bedroom suites. 4 stories, interior corridors. **Parking:** on-site (fee). **Amenities:** high-speed Internet, dual phone lines, voice mail, hair dryers. **Dining:** Corsair Restaurant, see separate listing. **Guest Services:** valet laundry. **Cards:** AX, CB, DC, DS, JC, MC, VI. **Special Amenities:** free **continental breakfast** and free **local telephone calls.** *(See color ad p 697)*

 Do you know the facts?

$\mathscr{AAA}$ publishes the Digest of Motor Laws to assist traveling motorists. Filled with facts and information, this one-of-a-kind compilation includes a comprehensive description of the laws that govern motor vehicle registration and operation in the United States and Canada. This guide has a new, easy-to-read format with graphics, state-by-state tax summary tables and detailed information on occupant protection laws, driver licensing laws, automated enforcement laws and motor vehicle fees and taxes.

You can easily locate various licensing and motor laws governing the states in which you are traveling. In addition to vehicle registration and operation laws, the Digest contains information and facts about alcohol laws, traffic safety laws and more.

Call your local club to obtain a copy of the Digest.

The book retails for $13.95.

Digest of Motor Laws

WESTMARK ANCHORAGE HOTEL *Book at aaa.com* Phone: (907)276-7676

	6/1-9/15	1P: $219	2P: $219	XP: $15	F12
	5/16-5/31	1P: $129	2P: $129	XP: $15	F12
	3/1-5/15 & 9/16-2/28	1P: $109	2P: $109	XP: $15	F12

Location: At G St and W 5th Ave; downtown. 720 W 5th Ave 99501. **Fax:** 907/276-3615. **Facility:** 200 one-bedroom standard units. 14 stories, interior corridors. *Bath:* combo or shower only. **Parking:** on-site. **Large-scale Hotel** **Terms:** cancellation fee imposed, package plans, pets (with prior approval). **Amenities:** video games, high-speed Internet (fee), dual phone lines, voice mail, irons, hair dryers. **Dining:** 2 restaurants, 5:30 am-10 pm; 6:30 am-2:30 & 5-9 pm off season, cocktails. **Leisure Activities:** exercise equipment available for in-room use. **Guest Services:** gift shop, valet laundry. **Business Services:** meeting rooms, PC. **Cards:** AX, DC, DS, MC, VI.

SOME UNITS

The following lodgings were either not evaluated or did not meet AAA rating requirements but are listed for your information only.

THE HOTEL CAPTAIN COOK Phone: 907-276-6000

(fyi) Not evaluated. **Location:** Just w of centre at K St. 4th Ave at K St 99510 (PO Box 102280). Facilities, services, and decor characterize a mid-range property.

MAHOGANY MANOR Phone: 907-278-1111

(fyi) Not evaluated. **Location:** Between A and Cordova sts; just e of downtown. 204 E 15th Ave 99501. Facilities, services, and decor characterize a mid-range property.

WHERE TO DINE

CAMPOBELLO BISTRO **Lunch:** $11-$14 **Dinner:** $16-$24 Phone: 907-563-2040

Location: Just w at Arctic Blvd. 601 W 36th Ave 99503. **Hours:** 11 am-2:30 & 5-close, Mon-2:30 pm, Sat from 5 pm. Closed major holidays; also Sun. **Reservations:** suggested. **Features:** A true gem is hidden in the Midtown roadside mall. The elegantly simple dining room is a perfect place for a casual yet romantic meal. **Italian** Italian cooking, including various preparations of pasta and seafood, reflects an Alaskan flair. Casual dress; beer & wine only. **Parking:** on-site. **Cards:** DC, MC, VI.

CLUB PARIS **Lunch:** $5-$15 **Dinner:** $18-$42 Phone: 907/277-6332

Location: Between D and E sts; downtown. 417 W 5th Ave 99501. **Hours:** 11:30 am-2:30 & 5-11 pm, Sun 5 pm-10 pm. Closed: 11/24, 12/25. **Features:** Home to the locally renowned four-inch filet mignon, the **Steak House** longstanding downtown restaurant—said to be the oldest steakhouse in the city—is a favorite of visitors and locals alike. The dimly lit dining room, with its dark upholstery and padded booths, has a loungelike feel. In addition to a good selection of steaks, the menu also lists Alaskan seafood options. Casual dress; cocktails. **Parking:** street. **Cards:** AX, CB, DC, DS, MC, VI.

CORSAIR RESTAURANT **Dinner:** $22-$41 Phone: 907/278-4502

Location: At K St and 5th Ave; downtown; in The Voyager Hotel. 944 W 5th Ave 99501. **Hours:** 5 pm-10 pm, Fri & Sat-11 pm. Closed major holidays; also Sun. **Reservations:** suggested. **Features:** The restaurant provides **Continental** its guests a fine dining experience featuring fresh Alaskan seafood, veal, steak and rack of lamb. The dining room decor is nautical but romantic, with impressive, fabric-upholstered booths acting as a focal point. Sweeping curves resemble ocean waves. The award-winning wine list offers an excellent selection of domestic and imported vintages. This eatery opens for lunch the last Friday of each month. Casual dress; cocktails. **Parking:** street. **Cards:** AX, DC, DS, MC, VI.

CROW'S NEST RESTAURANT **Dinner:** $28-$40 Phone: 907-276-6000

Location: Just w of centre at K St; in The Hotel Captain Cook. **Hours:** 6 pm-9:30 pm. Closed major holidays; also Sun. **Reservations:** suggested. **Features:** Perched high on the 20th floor of The Hotel Captain Cook, the restaurant affords panoramic mountain and Cook Inlet views, especially on long summer days. Service is **Continental** attentive and formal but unstuffy. The menu's accent is on seafood although it also offers an excellent variety of meats and exotic foods, such as Caspian Sea caviar, truffles, foie gras and seaweed. The excellent wine cellar houses more than 10,000 bottles. Casual dress; cocktails. **Parking:** on-site and valet. **Cards:** AX, DC, DS, JC, MC, VI.

DOWNTOWN DELI & CAFE **Lunch:** $5-$8 **Dinner:** $5-$8 Phone: 907-276-7116

Location: Downtown; across from Log Cabin Visitors Centre. 525 W 4th Ave 99501-2211. **Hours:** 6 am-10 pm; 7 am-9 pm 10/1-4/30. Closed major holidays. **Reservations:** not accepted. **Features:** Across from the log **Deli/Subs** cabin visitor center downtown, the popular eatery is known for its huge portions and all-day breakfast items. **Sandwiches** Such offerings as the quiche of the day, eggs with reindeer sausage and fish and chips will satisfy any appetite. Casual dress; cocktails. **Parking:** street. **Cards:** AX, DC, DS, MC, VI.

FU DO CHINESE RESTAURANT **Lunch:** $5-$7 **Dinner:** $8-$15 Phone: 907-561-6611

Location: Jct Old Seward Hwy, 1 mi e. 2600 E Tudor Rd 99507. **Hours:** 11 am-10 pm, Fri & Sat-11 pm. **Reservations:** suggested. **Features:** A good mix of Mandarin, Cantonese and Szechuan selections is offered at this restaurant. The crispy duck, orange beef and sesame chicken are good choices. The **Chinese** attractive dining room is situated in a brightly decorated building in a commercial area. Casual dress; cocktails. **Parking:** on-site. **Cards:** AX, DC, DS, MC, VI.

GLACIER BREWHOUSE

Lunch: $8-$16   **Dinner:** $10-$34   **Phone:** 907-274-2739

American

Location: At H St; downtown. 737 W 5th Ave, Suite 110 99501. **Hours:** 11 am-11 pm. Closed: 7/4, 11/24, 12/25. **Reservations:** suggested. **Features:** Characterized by a large stone fireplace as its focal point, the decor blends contemporary, industrial and rustic themes. Large beer-brewing vats, which produce a number of tasty brews, loom behind glass walls. Varied seafood and roasted meat dishes, pizzas, sandwiches, salads and pastas are served in generous portions. Seasonal salmon is the standout, but other preparations—including dinner prime rib, tangy barbecue pork ribs, bread pudding and peanut butter pie—are plenty tempting. Casual dress; cocktails. **Parking:** street. **Cards:** AX, DC, DS, MC, VI.

THE GREEK CORNER

Lunch: $6-$9   **Dinner:** $10-$15   **Phone:** 907-276-2820

Greek

Location: Corner of W Fireweed Ln and C St. 302 W Fireweed Ln 99503. **Hours:** 11 am-10 pm, Sat from noon, Sun from 4 pm. Closed major holidays. **Features:** Folks might miss the small, family-run restaurant, one of the city's best-kept secrets. The menu lists both Greek and Italian cuisine, and there is something for everyone. Guests are greeted warmly, whether they are there all the time or for their first visit, and the service is friendly. Portions are hearty. The casual, traditional atmosphere is family-friendly. Beer & wine only. **Parking:** on-site. **Cards:** MC, VI.

GWENNIE'S OLD ALASKA RESTAURANT

Lunch: $6-$23   **Dinner:** $6-$23   **Phone:** 907-243-2090

American

Location: International Airport Rd, just ne of jct Jewel Lake and Spenard rds. 4333 Spenard Rd 99517. **Hours:** 6 am-10 pm, Sun-8 pm. Closed: 12/25. **Reservations:** not accepted. **Features:** For a taste of the Alaskan experience, the popular family restaurant serves huge portions in a dining room bedecked with authentic Alaskan paraphernalia, including black and white photographs, dog sleds and even snowshoes. Service is attentive, and patrons get great value for the dollar. Casual dress; cocktails. **Parking:** on-site. **Cards:** AX, CB, DC, DS, MC, VI.

HARRY'S BAR & GRILL

Lunch: $8-$12   **Dinner:** $16-$24   **Phone:** 907-561-5317

American

Location: 1.5 mi s at C St and Benson Blvd; in Key Bank Building. 101 W Benson Blvd 99503. **Hours:** 11 am-10 pm, Sun 10 am-9 pm; to 11 pm, Sun-9 pm in summer. Closed: 5/30, 7/4, 12/25. **Reservations:** accepted, evenings. **Features:** The cheerful, casual ambience lends to the restaurant's popularity as both a lunch and dinner spot. Greatly varied dishes are prepared in a fresh, contemporary way. There is an excellent selection of microbrewed beers and heavenly pies made on the premises. Casual dress; cocktails. **Cards:** AX, DC, DS, MC, VI.

HOW HOW CHINESE RESTAURANT

Lunch: $7   **Dinner:** $7-$18   **Phone:** 907/337-2116

Chinese

Location: 5 mi ne on US 1 (Glenn Hwy), just s; in Ramada Limited Hotel of Anchorage. 207 Muldoon Rd 99504. **Hours:** 7 am-9 & 11-10 pm. Closed: 1/1, 11/24, 12/25. **Features:** Attached to the Howard Johnson at the east end of town, the popular restaurant is one of the oldest in Anchorage. This place bustles during lunch, when an all-you-can-eat buffet is featured. Dinner guests can expect traditional a la carte menu items, as well as some Western fare. Glance overhead to admire the traditional Chinese panels. Cocktails. **Parking:** on-site. **Cards:** AX, DC, DS, JC, MC, VI.

HUMPY'S GREAT ALASKAN ALE HOUSE

Lunch: $7-$16   **Dinner:** $7-$16   **Phone:** 907/276-2337

American

Location: Between F and G sts; downtown. 610 W 6th Ave 99501. **Hours:** 11 am-2 am, Fri & Sat-3 am, Sun noon-2 am. Closed: 1/1, 3/27, 12/25. **Reservations:** not accepted. **Features:** With an impressive selection of Alaskan microbrewed beers, the casual ale house is a favorite among locals. Guests can choose from a variety of sandwiches, burgers and pastas. Patio seating can be requested in season, and often local bands perform to an enthusiastic crowd. Cocktails; entertainment. **Parking:** street. **Cards:** AX, CB, DC, DS, JC, MC, VI.

JENS' RESTAURANT

Lunch: $7-$26   **Dinner:** $7-$33   **Phone:** 907/561-5367

Continental

Location: Just e of Arctic Blvd and W 36th Ave. 701 W 36th Ave 99503. **Hours:** Open 3/1-12/31 & 2/1-2/28; 11:30 am-2 & 6-11 pm, Mon-2 pm. Closed: 12/25; also Sun. **Reservations:** suggested. **Features:** Danish by day and French by night, the cozy, bistro-style restaurant, which includes a casual tapas bar, is one of the city's finest. Local artists are featured, and the casual side has a stool bar where guests can enjoy a glass of wine from the extensive wine list. The eclectic, monthly changing menu relies heavily on local ingredients and flavors, which the talented chef prepares with a Danish and French twist. Casual dress; cocktails. **Parking:** on-site. **Cards:** AX, DC, DS, MC, VI.

LAS MARGARITAS

Lunch: $7-$14   **Dinner:** $9-$16   **Phone:** 907/349-4922

Mexican

Location: Between Artic Blvd and C St. 541 W Dimond 99515. **Hours:** 11:30 am-10:30 pm, Sat & Sun 4 pm-10 pm. Closed major holidays. **Reservations:** suggested. **Features:** This restaurant is a little out of the way, but it's worth the drive. The restaurant has a charming and casual country-style ambience, and its cuisine features popular Mexican and Italian specialties including burritos, spaghetti, pizza, steak and shrimp. Casual dress; cocktails. **Parking:** on-site. **Cards:** AX, MC, VI.

MARX BROS. CAFE

Dinner: $25-$42   **Phone:** 907/278-2133

Nouvelle American

Location: At F St; downtown. 627 3rd Ave W 99501. **Hours:** 6 pm-9:30 pm, Fri & Sat 5:30 pm-10 pm; 5:30 pm-10 pm 5/31-9/6. Closed major holidays; also Sun & Mon. **Reservations:** suggested. **Features:** For a truly exquisite meal, look no further than the dining rooms of this renovated 1916 home. Innovative and colorful selections of Alaskan seafood highlight the menu, and the locally renowned Caesar salad is prepared tableside. Choices include not only a wide selection of seafood, such as oysters, salmon and halibut, but also lamb and other meats. Save room for one of the divine desserts. The atmosphere is delightful, and the service friendly and genuine. Dressy casual; beer & wine only. **Parking:** street. **Cards:** AX, DC, MC, VI. **Historic**

MIDDLE WAY CAFE   **Lunch:** $5-$8   **Dinner:** $5-$8   **Phone:** 907/272-6433
▼▼▼
Vegetarian
Location: Jct Arctic and Northern Lights blvds; in shopping plaza. 1200 W Northern Lights Blvd 99503. **Hours:** 7 am-6:30 pm, Sat from 8 am, Sun 9 am-5 pm. Closed major holidays. **Reservations:** not accepted. **Features:** Considered one of the city's best vegetarian restaurants, the casual coffeehouse is tucked away from crowds in a small shopping plaza. Patrons can look to the blackboard for a choice of sandwiches, smoothies and homemade soups, most of which are organic. The funky, upbeat atmosphere draws on a variety of characters. It's not unusual to stumble upon musicians playing an impromptu concert out front. Casual dress. **Parking:** on-site. **Cards:** MC, VI.

MOOSE'S TOOTH PUB & PIZZERIA   **Lunch:** $6-$10   **Dinner:** $6-$10   **Phone:** 907/258-2537
▼▼▼
American
Location: Old Seward Hwy at 34th St. 3300 Old Seward Hwy 99503. **Hours:** 11 am-midnight, Sun noon-11 pm, Mon 11 am-11 pm. Closed: 3/27, 11/24, 12/25. **Features:** This rustic hangout with a bustling, casual atmosphere is popular with locals and tourists alike, so expect a long wait as no reservations are accepted. The specialty is gourmet pizzas, and they come with regular or thick crust; red sauce, green sauce or sauceless; assorted meats, steak, chicken, seafood or vegetable toppings; cheeses ranging from mozzarella and provolone to gorgonzola, parmesan, cheddar and feta. Also featured are sodas and beers brewed in their own brewery. Casual dress; beer & wine only. **Parking:** on-site. **Cards:** AX, DC, DS, MC, VI.

RISTORANTE ORSO   **Lunch:** $8-$15   **Dinner:** $12-$34   **Phone:** 907/222-3232
ⒶⒶⒶ
▼▼▼▼
Regional
Italian
Location: Centre. 737 W 5th Ave 99501. **Hours:** 11:30 am-2 & 5-10 pm, Fri & Sat-11 pm. Closed: 7/4, 11/24, 12/25. **Reservations:** suggested. **Features:** You'll enjoy the regional Italian cuisine in this newest addition to the downtown Anchorage restaurant scene. The chef's creativity shines with dishes such as prosciutto-wrapped halibut with carmelized onion relish. Pasta lovers would enjoy the wild mushroom ravioli. Please save room for the in-house prepared desserts, especially the marscapone chocolate cheesecake. Casual dress; cocktails. **Parking:** on-site (fee) and street. **Cards:** AX, DC, DS, MC, VI.

SACK'S CAFE & RESTAURANT   **Lunch:** $5-$15   **Dinner:** $18-$30   **Phone:** 907/274-4022
▼▼▼
International
Location: Between 3rd and 4th aves; downtown. 328 G St 99501. **Hours:** 11 am-2:30 & 5-9:30 pm, Fri-10:30 pm, Sat 11 am-3 & 5-10:30 pm, Sun 11 am-3 & 5-9:30 pm; Sun-Thurs to 9 pm 10/1-5/31. Closed major holidays; also 12/24. **Reservations:** suggested. **Features:** In a word, the restaurant is delightful. The chic choice's menu draws largely on area ingredients, including fresh salmon, scallops and halibut. Thai and Asian influences are abundant. At lunch, sandwiches and casual fare are at the heart of the offerings; dinner is a bit more complex, with several entrees that change nightly as the season changes. Casual dress; cocktails. **Cards:** AX, DC, MC, VI.

SIMON & SEAFORTS   **Lunch:** $10-$20   **Dinner:** $20-$40   **Phone:** 907/274-3502
▼▼▼
Regional American
Location: Between 4th and 5th aves, overlooking Cook Inlet; downtown. 420 L St 99501. **Hours:** 11 am-2:30 & 4:30-11:30 pm; 11 am-2:30 & 5-10 pm in winter. Closed: 11/24, 12/25. **Reservations:** suggested. **Features:** This local favorite specializes in fresh, creatively prepared seafood flown in daily from Homer. Angus beef from Nebraska, pasta and chicken and are also good. The dining room has a scenic inlet view. Try their world-famous sipping dessert, brandy ice! Casual dress; cocktails. **Parking:** valet. **Cards:** AX, DC, MC, VI.

SKYFIRE CAFE   **Lunch:** $8-$10   **Phone:** 907/561-2969
▼
American
Location: Old Seward Hwy, exit 36th Ave, 2 mi, then 2 mi s. 5701 Lake Otis Pkwy, Suite 600 99507. **Hours:** 7 am-4 pm; Sunday brunch. Closed major holidays; also Sat. **Reservations:** not accepted. **Features:** In a small roadside mall, the simple cafe and bakery serves fantastic breakfasts and great sandwiches for lunch. Patrons find great value for the dollar. The menu offers a choice of various omelets and hearty sandwiches. Those in a hurry can grab one of the massive cinnamon buns or muffins. **Parking:** on-site. **Cards:** MC, VI.

SNOW CITY CAFE   **Lunch:** $4-$10   **Phone:** 907/272-2489
▼▼ ▼▼
American
Location: Downtown. 1034 W 4th Ave 99501. **Hours:** 7 am-4 pm. Closed major holidays. **Reservations:** not accepted. **Features:** It's all but guaranteed that a line will form on Saturday morning at the popular spot, and it is definitely worth the wait. Home to an all-day breakfast, this one has been ranked highly by city residents. The cafe bustles with energy during the breakfast and lunch hours and provides an upbeat atmosphere in which to enjoy hearty, delicious food. Casual dress; beer & wine only. **Parking:** street. **Cards:** AX, MC, VI.

SNOW GOOSE RESTAURANT   **Lunch:** $9-$15   **Dinner:** $12-$30   **Phone:** 907/277-7727
▼▼▼ ▼▼▼
American
Location: Corner of 3rd Ave and G St; downtown. 717 W 3rd Ave 99501. **Hours:** 11:30 am-midnight; to 11 pm, Sat & Sun from 5 pm 10/1-5/1. Closed: 11/24, 12/25. **Reservations:** suggested. **Features:** Those looking for a pint of locally brewed beer might visit this great stop, which also offers views of the Cook Inlet and shipyard. Upstairs is a casual pub-type atmosphere, and downstairs, though still casual, is more of a restaurant. Service can be unpredictable, but the food and view make a visit worthwhile. Casual dress; cocktails. **Parking:** street. **Cards:** AX, DC, DS, MC, VI.

SOUTHSIDE BISTRO   **Lunch:** $8-$16   **Dinner:** $13-$25   **Phone:** 907/348-0088
ⒶⒶⒶ
▼▼▼▼
American
Location: 0.6 mi nw of US 1 (New Seward Hwy), exit Huffman Rd. 1320 Huffman Park Dr 99515. **Hours:** 11:30 am-10 pm. Closed major holidays; also Sun & Mon. **Reservations:** suggested. **Features:** Located in the heart of a southside Anchorage business park is this little strip mall eatery with an upbeat and contemporay decor. The menu offers a wide variety of items to suit all tastes with cooking styles that defy classification. Fresh seafood, assorted meat dishes, pastas and thin crust pizzas are offered, all oozing with flavor and a creative bent. Lunch menus offer an additional selection of sandwiches. The wine list focuses mainly on western U.S. product. Casual dress; beer & wine only. **Parking:** on-site. **Cards:** AX, DS, MC, VI.

SULLIVAN'S STEAKHOUSE

Steak House

Dinner: $17-$29

Location: 5th Ave at C St. 320 W 5th Ave 99501. **Hours:** 5:30 pm-11 pm, Fri-Sun from 5 pm. **Reservations:** suggested. **Features:** The steak and chops menu and decor reflect a masculine attitude built around notorious bare-knuckle fighter, John L. Sullivan. Casual dress; cocktails. **Parking:** street. **Cards:** AX, DC, DS, MC, VI.

Phone: 907/258-2882

SWEET BASIL CAFE

Coffee/Espresso

Cards: MC, VI.

Lunch: $6-$10

Location: Downtown; across from Hilton. 335 E St 99501. **Hours:** 7:45 am-3 pm, Sat 9 am-4 pm. Closed major holidays; also Sun. **Reservations:** not accepted. **Features:** Diners who enjoy homemade soups, freshly squeezed juices, large sandwiches and salads, and sumptuous desserts might find the casual, cozy cafe an appealing spot. Locals and visitors alike frequent this place. Casual dress; cocktails. **Parking:** street.

Phone: 907/274-0070

THE TOP OF THE WORLD

American

Dinner: $21-$29

Location: At E St; downtown; in Hilton Anchorage. 500 W 3rd Ave 99501. **Hours:** 6 pm-10 pm. Closed: 1/1, 11/24, 12/25. **Reservations:** suggested. **Features:** On the 15th floor of Westward Tower, the tiered dining room offers an excellent view of Anchorage Harbor and Ship Creek. The elegant yet casual atmosphere enables diners to enjoy a relaxing dinner after an active day of touring or shopping. On the menu are selections of seafood, beef and game with cooking twists that touch on an eclectic variety of International influences. If driving to the Hilton, inquire about validated valet parking. Dressy casual; cocktails. **Parking:** on-site (fee) and valet. **Cards:** AX, DC, DS, JC, MC, VI.

Phone: 907/265-7111

TURNAGAIN HOUSE

Steak & Seafood

Dinner: $25-$30

Location: 30 mi s on US 1 (Seward Hwy). Milepost 103 Seward Hwy 99511. **Hours:** Open 3/1-10/31 & 2/1-2/28; 5 pm-10 pm. **Reservations:** suggested. **Features:** The top reason to visit the restaurant is its coastal location. Although a bit of a drive from Anchorage, this place is well worth it for the steak and seafood, as well as the view. Guests who time their visit right might catch the tide coming in, which is a sight to see. Casual dress; cocktails. **Parking:** on-site. **Cards:** AX, DC, DS, MC, VI.

Phone: 907/653-7500

CANTWELL pop. 222—See also DENALI NATIONAL PARK AND PRESERVE.

——— **WHERE TO STAY** ———

BACKWOODS LODGE

Motel

6/12-8/31	1P: $120-$130	2P: $120-$130	XP: $10
5/1-6/11	1P: $100-$110	2P: $100-$110	XP: $10
9/1-2/28	1P: $95-$105	2P: $95-$105	XP: $10
3/1-4/30	1P: $90-$100	2P: $90-$100	XP: $10

Phone: 907/768-2232

Location: Parks Hwy, (Milepost 210), just e on Denali Hwy. Located in a quiet area. Denali Hwy MM 133.8 99729 (Box 90). Fax: 907/768-2472. **Facility:** Smoke free premises. 10 units. 9 one-bedroom standard units. 1 one-bedroom suite ($120-$150) with kitchen. 1 story, exterior corridors. **Bath:** combo or shower only. **Parking:** on-site, winter plug-ins. **Terms:** 10 day cancellation notice-fee imposed. **Amenities:** hair dryers. **Leisure Activities:** pond with campfire area, shared barbecue on exterior walkway, hiking trails. **Guest Services:** gift shop. **Cards:** AX, DS, MC, VI. **Special Amenities:** free local telephone calls and preferred room (subject to availability with advance reservations). *(See color ad below)*

COOPER LANDING pop. 369

——— **WHERE TO STAY** ———

KENAI PRINCESS WILDERNESS LODGE

Small-scale Hotel

6/4-9/5		2P: $239-$269	XP: $10	F12
5/14-6/3 & 9/6-9/11		2P: $159-$189	XP: $10	F12

Phone: (907)595-1425

Location: SR 1 (Sterling Hwy) at milepost 47.8, just n of bridge, then 2.1 mi w. Mile 2 Bean Creek Rd 99572 (PO Box 676). Fax: 907/595-1424. **Facility:** Smoke free premises. 86 one-bedroom standard units. 1 story, exterior corridors. **Bath:** combo or shower only. **Terms:** open 5/14-9/11, check-in 3:30 pm, 8 day cancellation notice-fee imposed. **Amenities:** hair dryers. **Leisure Activities:** whirlpools, fishing, cross country skiing, hiking trails, limited exercise equipment, horseshoes, shuffleboard. **Fee:** charter fishing. **Guest Services:** gift shop, coin laundry. **Business Services:** meeting rooms. **Cards:** AX, DS, MC, VI.

DENALI NATIONAL PARK AND PRESERVE —See also *CANTWELL & HEALY.*

──────── WHERE TO STAY ────────

DENALI BACKCOUNTRY LODGE   **Phone:** (907)932-8801

AAA [SAVE]   6/16-8/31   1P: $560   2P: $750   XP: $300
               6/3-6/15 & 9/1-9/10   1P: $475   2P: $640   XP: $260

◆◆◆ ◆◆◆ **Location:** End of the 90 mi Denali National Park Rd. Located in Denali National Park. MM 95 Denali Park Rd 99755
Cabin   (410 Denali St, ANCHORAGE, 99501). Fax: 907/932-8701. **Facility:** Smoke free premises. 30 one-bedroom
         standard units. 1 story, exterior corridors. *Bath:* shower only. **Parking:** on-site. **Terms:** open 6/3-9/10, check-
         out 6:15 am, 60 day cancellation notice-fee imposed, [AP] meal plan available, package plans. **Leisure**
Activities: fishing, fishing equipment, Denali wildlife drive, recreation programs, gold panning, bicycles, hiking trails. *Fee:* flight
seeing. **Guest Services:** gift shop, area transportation-park entrance & lodge. **Cards:** MC, VI. *(See color ad below & p 304)*

[SD] [Y] [X] [X] [X] [W] [Z]

DENALI BLUFFS HOTEL   *Book at aaa.com*   Phone: (907)683-700
[AAA] [SAVE]   5/28-9/7   1P: $199-$219   2P: $199-$219   XP: $20   F1
◆◆◆◆ ◆◆◆◆   5/15-5/27 & 9/8-9/15   1P: $135-$155   2P: $135-$155   XP: $20   F1
          Location: 1 mi n of park entrance. Milepost 238.4 Parks Hwy 99755 (416 7th Ave, FAIRBANKS, 99701
Small-scale Hotel   Fax: 907/683-7500. **Facility:** Smoke free premises. 112 one-bedroom standard units. 2 stories (no elevator
          exterior corridors. **Parking:** on-site. **Terms:** open 5/15-9/15, 30 day cancellation notice-fee imposec
          Amenities: voice mail, hair dryers. **Dining:** Mountaineer Bar & Grill, see separate listing. **Guest Services**
gift shop, coin laundry, area transportation. **Cards:** AX, DS, MC, VI. *(See color ad below & p 305)* 📶 ⊠ 🎟 🔌 ⊡

DENALI CABINS   Phone: (907)683-264
[AAA] [SAVE]   5/25-9/12   1P: $99-$219   2P: $99-$219   XP: $20   F1
◆◆◆◆   **Location:** 9 mi s of park entrance. Milepost 229 Parks Hwy 99755. Fax: 907/683-2595. **Facility:** Smoke fre
          premises. 43 cabins. 1 story, exterior corridors. *Bath:* shower only. **Parking:** on-site. **Terms:** open 5/25-9/12
Cabin   office hours 6 am-10 pm, 10 day cancellation notice-fee imposed, package plans. **Amenities:** voice mai
          Dining: 6 pm & 7:30 pm seatings; reservations required; set menu family style dinners. **Leisur**
          Activities: whirlpools, picnic tables, hiking trails. *Fee:* Denali Backcountry Adenture Tours. **Guest Services**
area transportation. **Cards:** MC, VI. **Special Amenities: free expanded continental breakfast and free local telephon
calls.**
                                                                                      SOME UNITS
                                         🅂⒟ 🍴 🔥M ⊠ ⊠ 🎟 📠 ⊡ / 🔌 ⊡

DENALI PRINCESS LODGE   Phone: (907)683-2282
◆◆◆◆ ◆◆◆◆   6/4-9/5   1P: $219-$279   2P: $219-$279   XP: $10   F1
          5/11-6/3 & 9/6-9/13   1P: $139-$249   2P: $139-$249   XP: $10   F1
Large-scale Hotel   **Location:** SR 3 (Parks Hwy), 1.5 mi n of park entrance. Milepost 238.5 99755 (PO Box 110). Fax: 907/683-2808
          Facility: Smoke free premises. 440 units. 437 one-bedroom standard units, some with whirlpools. 3 one
bedroom suites ($249-$279) with whirlpools..2 stories (no elevator), exterior corridors. *Bath:* combo or shower only. **Parking**
on-site. **Terms:** open 5/11-9/13, check-in 3:30 pm, cancellation fee imposed, package plans. **Amenities:** voice mail, hair dryers
Dining: The Summit, see separate listing. **Leisure Activities:** whirlpools, exercise room. *Fee:* massage. **Guest Services:** gif
shop, coin laundry, area transportation, beauty salon. *Fee:* tanning facilities. **Business Services:** meeting rooms. **Cards:** AX
DC, DS, MC, VI.
                                         🍴 🍸 🔥 🚭 ⊠ ⊠ 🎟 📠

NALI RIVERVIEW INN
Phone: (907)683-2663

| | 6/7-8/31 | 1P: $144 | 2P: $144 | XP: $5 | F5 |
| | 5/20-6/6 & 9/1-9/12 | 1P: $89 | 2P: $89 | XP: $5 | F5 |

Motel
Location: 1 mi n of park entrance. Milepost 238.4 Parks Hwy 99755 (PO Box 49). Fax: 907/683-7433. **Facility:** Smoke free premises. 12 one-bedroom standard units. 2 stories (no elevator), exterior corridors. rking: on-site. **Terms:** open 5/20-9/12, office hours 7 am-10 pm, 7 day cancellation notice-fee imposed. **Guest Services:** gift p. **Cards:** DS, MC, VI.

ANDE DENALI LODGE
Phone: (907)13650700

| | 5/28-9/7 | 1P: $219-$269 | 2P: $219-$269 | XP: $20 | F12 |
| | 5/15-5/27 & 9/8-9/15 | 1P: $155-$205 | 2P: $155-$205 | XP: $20 | F12 |

hall-scale Hotel
Location: SR 3, at Milepost 238.2 (Parks Hwy), on east side of road. Located in a rustic area. Milepost 238.2 George Parks Hwy 99707 (416 7th St, FAIRBANKS, 99701). Fax: 907/683-5101. **Facility:** 160 units. 154 one-bedroom standard units. 6 cabins ($245-$395). 4 stories, interior/exterior corridors. *Bath:* combo or shower only. **Parking:** on-site. **Terms:** open 5/15-9/15, 30 day cancellation notice-fee imposed. **Amenities:** voice mail, r dryers. **Dining:** Alpenglow, see separate listing. **Leisure Activities:** hiking trails. *Fee:* dinner theater "peak experience". est Services: gift shop, coin laundry, area transportation-within 5 mi. **Business Services:** meeting rooms, PC. **Cards:** AX, , MC, VI. *(See color ad p 305 & p 704)*

SOME UNITS

KINLEY CHALET RESORT   **Book at aaa.com**
Phone: (907)683-8200

	9/5-9/14	1P: $239	2P: $3-$239	XP: $20	F12
	6/2-9/4	1P: $239	2P: $239	XP: $20	F12
	5/16-6/1	1P: $179	2P: $179	XP: $20	F12

rge-scale Hotel
Location: Milepost 238.5 SR 3 (Parks Hwy). Milepost 238 (Parks Hwy) 99755 (PO Box 87). Fax: 907/258-3668. **Facility:** 345 units. 55 one-bedroom standard units. 290 one-bedroom suites. 2 stories (no elevator), exterior corridors. *Bath:* combo or shower only. **Parking:** on-site, winter plug-ins. **Terms:** open 5/16-9/14, 7 y cancellation notice. **Amenities:** voice mail, hair dryers. **Dining:** Nenana View Grille, see separate listing. **Leisure tivities:** recreation programs, hiking trails, basketball, horseshoes, volleyball. *Fee:* rafting, massage. **Guest Services:** gift p, area transportation. **Cards:** AX, DC, DS, MC, VI. **Special Amenities:** free local telephone calls.

SOME UNITS

KINLEY CREEKSIDE CABINS   **Book at aaa.com**
Phone: (907)683-2277

| | 5/15-9/15 | 1P: $79-$129 | 2P: $109-$179 | | |

Location: 13 mi s; MM 224 Parks Hwy. Milepost 224 Parks Hwy 99755 (PO Box 89, DENALI NATIONAL PARK). Fax: 907/683-1558. **Facility:** Smoke free premises. 25 cabins. 1 story, exterior corridors. *Bath:* shower only. **Parking:** on-site. **Terms:** open 5/15-9/15, office hours 6 am-11 pm, 14 day cancellation notice. **Dining:** Creekside Cafe, see separate listing. **Leisure Activities:** picnic and barbecue facilities, hiking trails, playground. **Guest Services:** gift shop. **Business Services:** fax (fee). **Cards:** DS, MC, VI.

Cabin

SOME UNITS

ORTH FACE LODGE
Phone: (907)683-2290

| | 6/6-9/9 [AP] | 1P: $500 | 2P: $800 | | |

Motel
Location: Milepost 89 Denali National Park Rd. Mile 89 Denali National Park Rd 99755 (PO Box 67). Fax: 907/683-1568. **Facility:** Smoke free premises. 15 units. 14 one- and 1 two-bedroom standard units. 1 story, exterior corridors. **Parking:** no self-parking. **Terms:** open 6/6-9/9, office hours 8 am-4 pm, check-out 45 am, 3 night minimum stay, 60 day cancellation notice-fee imposed, package plans. **Leisure Activities:** canoeing, boat ck, fishing, recreation programs, bicycles, hiking trails, jogging. **Guest Services:** gift shop, area transportation.

The following lodging was either not evaluated or did not meet AAA rating requirements but is listed for your information only.

CAMP DENALI
[fyi]
Not evaluated. **Location:** Milepost 89 Denali National Pk Rd 99755 (PO Box 67). Facilities, services, and de characterize a basic property.
Phone: 907/683-22

WHERE TO DINE

ALPENGLOW
Regional American
Lunch: $7-$15   **Dinner:** $9-$32   **Phone: 907/683-87**
Location: SR 3, at Milepost 238.2 (Parks Hwy), on east side of road; in Grande Denali Lodge. Milepost 238.2 Pa Hwy. **Hours:** Open 5/15-9/14; 4:30 am-10 pm. **Reservations:** accepted. **Features:** Take the drive one r up to enjoy this restaurant perched on the side of a mountain, featuring a full windowed dining room w spectacular panoramic views of Denali. Grilled fresh Alaskan Salmon is a favorite of many diners. Cas dress; cocktails. **Parking:** on-site. **Cards:** AX, CB, DC, DS, MC, VI. *(See color ad p 305 & p 704)*

CREEKSIDE CAFE
Regional American
Lunch: $7-$10   **Dinner:** $10-$18   **Phone: 907/683-22**
Location: 13 mi s; MM 224 Parks Hwy; in McKinley Creekside Cabins. Milepost 224 Parks Hwy 99755. **Hours:** Op 5/15-9/15; 6 am-10 pm. **Features:** Though the decor and service is simple, the cafe's food is hearty a delicious. You'll find a wide selection of sandwiches and salads, as well as one of the best breakfasts in park. At the front of the restaurant is a large dessert case featuring selections such as cookies, squar cinnamon buns and cakes. Casual dress; beer & wine only. **Parking:** on-site. **Cards:** DS, MC, VI.

MOUNTAINEER BAR & GRILL
Italian
Lunch: $6-$15   **Dinner:** $15-$24   **Phone: 907/683-88**
Location: 1 mi n of park entrance; in Denali Bluffs Hotel. Milepost 238.4 George Parks Hwy 99755. **Hours:** Op 5/15-9/15; 4:30 am-10 pm. **Reservations:** accepted. **Features:** The restaurant offers a nice change of pa with Italian selections. Items are freshly prepared and flavorful. The dining room has an early 1900s the with log walls, antique outdoor decorative items and windows for viewing the mountains. Casual dre cocktails. **Parking:** on-site. **Cards:** AX, DC, DS, MC, VI.

NENANA VIEW GRILLE
American
Lunch: $10-$20   **Dinner:** $10-$28   **Phone: 907/683-82**
Location: Milepost 238.5 SR 3 (Parks Hwy); in McKinley Chalet Resort. Milepost 238 Parks Hwy 99755. **Hours:** Op 5/15-9/15; 6 am-10:30 pm. **Reservations:** suggested. **Features:** This contemporary restaurant, one of newest in Denali, features a wide variety of Alaskan fare, ranging from salmon to chowder and delectal desserts; the lounge is a great place to relax and unwind. Casual dress; cocktails. **Parking:** on-s **Cards:** AX, DC, DS, MC, VI.

THE PERCH
Regional American
Lunch: $7-$22   **Dinner:** $18-$31   **Phone: 907/683-25**
Location: Milepost 224 (George Parks Hwy) 99755. **Hours:** 6 am-10 pm, Fri & Sat from 5 pm 5/1-9/15; Sun am-3 pm 9/16-4/30. **Features:** As the name suggests, The Perch sits nestled on a side of a mounta offering incredible views of the Denali Mountain Range. The fragrance of freshly baked bread envelops y as you approach the dining room, and again as a loaf is placed on your table. The planked Salmon a halibut with herbed butter melting on top is the specialty of the house. Casual dress; cocktails. **Cards:** D MC, VI.

THE SUMMIT
Regional American
Lunch: $5-$13   **Dinner:** $13-$30   **Phone: 907/683-22**
Location: SR 3 (Parks Hwy), 1.5 mi n of park entrance; in Denali Princess Lodge. Milepost 238.5 997 **Hours:** Open 5/16-9/16; 5 am-10 pm. **Reservations:** accepted. **Features:** This spacious restaura adjacent to the Princess Lodge satisfies those looking to feast on tasty Alaskan seafood dishes wh enjoying a view that is spectacular. Sure to be a favorite at your table, the seafood sampler consists tempura prawns, pan seared halibut and Alaskan crab cake. Casual dress; cocktails; entertainment. **Parking:** on-s **Cards:** AX, DC, DS, MC, VI.

The following restaurant has not been evaluated by AAA but is listed for your information only.

BUB'S SUBS
[fyi]
Not evaluated. **Location:** Milepost 238.5 Parks Hwy; next to Denali Riverview Inn. Mile 238.5 Parks Hv **Features:** There are no tables at this little hut located just off the Parks Highway, but the lineups indic this is one of the most popular places to get a freshly made sub or wrap. The portions are absolutely huge, and you definite won't leave hungry.
Phone: 907/683-78

DENALI STATE PARK

WHERE TO STAY

MT. MCKINLEY PRINCESS WILDERNESS LODGE   *Book at aaa.com*
Resort
Large-scale Hotel

6/11-8/31	1P: $179-$279	XP: $10
5/11-6/10 & 9/1-9/13	1P: $139-$239	XP: $10

Phone: 907/733-29

Location: SR 3 (George Parks Hwy), milepost 133.1, 1 mi e on Mt McKinley View Rd. Milepost 133.1 99683 (PO 13550, TRAPPER CREEK, 99683-0550). Fax: 907/733-2922. **Facility:** The hotel's guest rooms feature contemporary, mountain-wilderness motif; public areas are extensive. Smoke free premises. 334 units. 3 one-bedroom standard units. 4 one-bedroom suites with whirlpools. 2 stories (no elevator), interior/exterior corridors. Ba combo or shower only. **Parking:** on-site. **Terms:** open 5/11-9/13, check-in 3:30 pm, cancellation fee imposed, package plan **Amenities:** voice mail, hair dryers. **Leisure Activities:** whirlpools, recreation programs, hiking trails, playground, limit exercise equipment. **Fee:** horseback riding. **Guest Services:** gift shop, coin laundry. **Cards:** AX, DC, DS, MC, VI.

SOME UNIT

EAGLE RIVER

──────── WHERE TO STAY ────────

EAGLE RIVER INN & SUITES   *Book at aaa.com*   **Phone:** (907)622-3232
All Year   1P: $59-$139   2P: $59-$139   XP: $10   F18
Small-scale Hotel   **Location:** Jct Glenn Hwy (SR 1), Eagle River exit, just e, just s. 13049 Old Glenn Hwy 99577. **Fax:** 907/622-3233. **Facility:** 60 one-bedroom standard units. 3 stories, interior corridors. *Bath:* combo or shower only. **Parking:** on-site. **Terms:** weekly rates available, pets ($10 extra charge). **Amenities:** high-speed Internet, voice mail. **Leisure Activities:** exercise room. **Guest Services:** sundries, coin laundry. **Business Services:** meeting rooms. **Cards:** AX, DS, MC, VI.

SOME UNITS

(ASK) (S/D) 🐾 🎛 📺 [DATA PORT] / ✕ 🔟 🖥 💻 /
FEE

EAGLE RIVER MOTEL   **Phone:** (907)694-5000
(AAA) [SAVE]   6/1-9/5 [CP]   1P: $89   2P: $94   XP: $5   F12
                 5/14-5/31 [CP]   1P: $69   2P: $74   XP: $5   F12
▼   3/1-5/13 & 9/6-2/28   1P: $49   2P: $54   XP: $5   F12
Motel   **Location:** Glenn Hwy, exit Eagle River, just e; center. Located in a residential area. 11111 Old Eagle River Rd 99577. **Fax:** 907/694-1713. **Facility:** 14 one-bedroom standard units, some with efficiencies or kitchens. 3 stories (no elevator), exterior corridors. **Parking:** on-site, winter plug-ins. **Terms:** 3 day cancellation notice, pets ($7 extra charge, with prior approval). **Amenities:** video library (fee), voice mail. *Some:* DVD players (fee). **Guest Services:** complimentary laundry. **Business Services:** PC. **Cards:** AX, DS, MC, VI. **Special Amenities:** free local telephone calls and early check-in/late check-out. *(See color ad p 693)*

SOME UNITS

🔟 🎛 📺 [DATA PORT] 🔟 🖥 💻 / ✕ /
FEE

──────── WHERE TO DINE ────────

HAUTE QUARTER GRILL   **Lunch:** $8-$13   **Dinner:** $17-$23   **Phone:** 907/622-4745
American   **Location:** Jct Glenn Hwy (SR 1), exit Eagle River, just e. 11221 Old Glenn Hwy 99577. **Hours:** Open 3/1-1/9 & 2/4-2/28; 11 am-2 & 5-10 pm, Sat from 5 pm. Closed major holidays; also Sun & Mon. **Reservations:** accepted. **Features:** This locally-popular restaurant offers upscale cuisine in a relaxed, casual atmosphere. Food is well prepared using fresh ingredients and the kitchen shows its creative and innovative talent in many of the preparations. The flavorful creations and attentive staff combine to make this an enjoyable experience. Casual dress; cocktails. **Parking:** on-site. **Cards:** AX, DS, MC, VI.

✕

PACHAMAMA CAFE   **Lunch:** $7-$9   **Dinner:** $13-$19   **Phone:** 907/694-8414
American   **Location:** Jct Glenn Hwy (SR 1), exit Eagle River, just e. 16535 Artillery Rd 99577. **Hours:** 10 am-8 pm, Thurs & Fri-9 pm, Sat 9 am-9 pm, Sun 11:30 am-2:30 pm. Closed: 11/24, 12/25; also Mon. **Features:** Enjoy leisurely dining in this little bistro. Although the atmosphere is relaxed and casual, the kitchen makes delightful preparations that add special touches to more traditional selections. Dinner entrees such as an untraditional lasagna, Parisian crepes and stuffed pork chops are examples of the diversity and the creativity offered on the menu, as are appetizers such as bacon-wrapped halibut with dill sauce and Asian shrimp twists in ginger garlic sauce. Casual dress; beer & wine only. **Parking:** on-site. **Cards:** MC, VI.

(K) ✕

FAIRBANKS pop. 30,224

──────── WHERE TO STAY ────────

A BED AND BREAKFAST INN ON MINNIE STREET   *Book at aaa.com*   **Phone:** (907)456-1802
(AAA) [SAVE]   3/1-5/14 [BP]   1P: $85-$155   2P: $85-$155   XP: $25   F5
                 6/1-9/15 [BP]   1P: $115-$145   2P: $115-$145   XP: $25   F5
▼▼▼   5/15-5/31 [BP]   1P: $100-$125   2P: $100-$125   XP: $25   F5
                 9/16-2/28 [BP]   1P: $75-$100   2P: $75-$100   XP: $25   F5
Bed & Breakfast   **Location:** Just n of downtown, follow Cushman St over Bridge to Illinois St, then just e. Located in a residential area. 345 Minnie St 99701. **Fax:** 907/451-1751. **Facility:** Simple rooms that vary in size and style are offered at this B&B, which is made up of two detached houses connected by a garden and deck. Smoke free premises. 9 units. 6 one- and 1 two-bedroom standard units, some with whirlpools. 1 one- and 1 two-bedroom suites ($100-$210) with kitchens. 2 stories (no elevator), interior/exterior corridors. *Bath:* some shared or private, combo or shower only. **Parking:** on-site, winter plug-ins. **Terms:** 14 day cancellation notice-fee imposed. **Amenities:** video library, hair dryers. *Some:* CD players, irons. **Guest Services:** gift shop, coin laundry. **Business Services:** PC. **Cards:** AX, DS, MC, VI. **Special Amenities:** free full breakfast and free local telephone calls.

SOME UNITS

✕ 📺 [DATA PORT] / (K) (VCR) 🔟 🖥 💻 /

ALL SEASONS INN   *Book at aaa.com*   **Phone:** (907)451-6649
(AAA) [SAVE]   6/1-8/31   1P: $135-$185   2P: $135-$185   XP: $25
                 3/1-5/31 & 9/1-9/15   1P: $75-$130   2P: $75-$130   XP: $25
▼▼▼   9/16-2/28   1P: $75-$110   2P: $75-$110   XP: $25
Bed & Breakfast   **Location:** Just w of Barnette St; downtown. Located in a residential area. 763 7th Ave 99701. **Fax:** 907/474-8448. **Facility:** This well-tended, European-style property features an attractive lobby and is within walking distance of shopping and restaurants. Smoke free premises. 8 one-bedroom standard units. 2 stories (no elevator), interior corridors. **Parking:** on-site, winter plug-ins. **Terms:** check-in 4 pm, 14 day cancellation notice-fee imposed, package plans. **Amenities:** video library. **Leisure Activities:** board games in sun room, library. **Guest Services:** coin laundry, area transportation-train station. **Business Services:** meeting rooms, PC. **Cards:** CB, DC, DS, JC, MC, VI. **Special Amenities:** free full breakfast and free local telephone calls.

SOME UNITS

✈ (&M) ✕ (K) 📺 [DATA PORT] / (VCR) /

ASPEN HOTEL
Book at aaa.com

▼▼▼ ▼▼▼
Small-scale Hotel

5/16-9/15 [ECP]	1P: $179-$209	2P: $179-$209	XP: $10
5/1-5/15 & 9/16-2/28 [ECP]	1P: $119-$149	2P: $119-$149	XP: $10
3/1-4/30 [ECP]	1P: $99-$129	2P: $99-$129	XP: $10

Phone: (907)457-2281

Location: Near jct Parks Hwy and Airport Rd. 4580 Old Airport Rd 99709. Fax: 907/457-2297. **Facility:** 97 units. 9 one- and 2 two-bedroom standard units, some with whirlpools. 1 one-bedroom suite with efficiency (no utensils). 2 stories interior corridors. *Bath:* combo or shower only. **Parking:** on-site. **Terms:** cancellation fee imposed. **Amenities:** voice mail, irons hair dryers. *Fee:* video library, high-speed Internet. *Some:* video games. **Pool(s):** small heated indoor. **Leisure Activities:** whirlpool, limited exercise equipment. **Guest Services:** valet and coin laundry, area transportation. **Business Services:** meeting rooms, business center. **Cards:** AX, DC, DS, MC, VI.

SOME UNITS

(ASK) (S) (✈) (†↑) (&M) (&) (◎) (➢) (VCR) (🎥) (DATA PORT) (■) (➡) (▭) / (✗) /

A TASTE OF ALASKA LODGE
Book at aaa.com

(AAA) (SAVE)
▼▼▼ ▼▼▼
Bed & Breakfast

All Year   1P: $175   2P: $175   XP: $25

Phone: (907)488-7855

Location: 4.5 mi ne on US 2 (Steese Hwy), 5.3 mi e on Chena Hot Springs Rd, then 0.5 mi s, follow signs. Located in a quiet, secluded area. 551 Eberhardt Rd 99712. Fax: 907/488-3772. **Facility:** Tucked away in the woods on the outskirts of town, this secluded B&B offers sweeping views and a rustic ambience. Smoke free premises. 1 units. 8 one-bedroom standard units. 2 cabins ($200-$250), some with whirlpools. 2 stories (no elevator) interior/exterior corridors. *Bath:* combo or shower only. **Parking:** on-site, winter plug-ins. **Terms:** 45 da cancellation notice-fee imposed. **Amenities:** video library, voice mail, hair dryers. *Some:* irons. **Leisure Activities:** sauna whirlpool, cross country skiing, hiking trails, limited exercise equipment, horseshoes. *Fee:* dog mushing, gold panning. **Guest Services:** gift shop. **Business Services:** meeting rooms. **Cards:** AX, MC, VI. **Special Amenities:** free full breakfast and free local telephone calls.

SOME UNITS

(&M) (&) (✗) (✗) (✗) / (VCR) (■) (➡) (▭) /

BEST WESTERN FAIRBANKS INN
Book at aaa.com

▼▼▼ ▼▼▼
Small-scale Hotel

5/16-8/31	1P: $139-$179	2P: $139-$179	XP: $10
9/1-9/15	1P: $79-$139	2P: $89-$139	XP: $10
3/1-5/15 & 9/16-2/28	1P: $59-$110	2P: $59-$110	XP: $10

Phone: (907)456-6602

Location: Just s of Airport Way. 1521 S Cushman St 99701. Fax: 907/452-2724. **Facility:** 102 one-bedroom standard units, some with whirlpools. 2 stories (no elevator), interior corridors. **Parking:** on-site, winter plug-ins. **Terms:** cancellation fee imposed, small pets only ($10 extra charge). **Amenities:** voice mail, irons, hair dryers. **Guest Services:** valet and coin laundry, area transportation. *(See color ad below)*

SOME UNITS

(ASK) (S) (✈) (🐾) (†↑) (🍴) (&M) (🛏) (🎥) (DATA PORT) (➡) / (✗) (■) /
FEE

BRIDGEWATER HOTEL
Book at aaa.com

▼▼▼ ▼▼▼
Small-scale Hotel

5/15-9/15   1P: $134-$150   2P: $134-$150   XP: $10

Phone: (907)452-6661

Location: Just w of Cushman St; downtown. 723 1st Ave 99701. Fax: 907/452-6126. **Facility:** Smoke free premises. 94 one-bedroom standard units. 5 stories, interior corridors. *Bath:* combo or shower only. **Parking:** on-site, winter plug-ins. **Terms:** open 5/15-9/15. **Amenities:** hair dryers. **Guest Services:** valet laundry, area transportation. **Cards:** AX, CB, DC, DS, JC, MC, VI.

(ASK) (S) (✈) (†↑) (◎) (🛏) (✗) (🎥) (DATA PORT) (➡)
FEE

COMFORT INN-CHENA RIVER
Book at aaa.com

(AAA) (SAVE)
▼▼▼ ▼▼▼
Small-scale Hotel

6/1-9/15 [ECP]	1P: $159-$169	2P: $159-$169	
5/16-5/31 [ECP]	1P: $99-$109	2P: $99-$109	
3/1-5/15 & 9/16-2/28 [ECP]	1P: $79-$89	2P: $79-$89	

Phone: (907)479-8080

Location: Airport Way, just n on Peger Rd, then just e on Phillips Field Rd, follow signs in wooded area south of road. Located in a quiet area. 1908 Chena Landings Loop 99701. Fax: 907/479-8063. **Facility:** 74 one-bedroom standard units, some with whirlpools. 3 stories, interior corridors. *Bath:* combo or shower only. **Parking:** on-site, winter plug-ins. **Terms:** check-in 4 pm, cancellation fee imposed, pets ($10 fee, in smoking units). **Amenities:** video games (fee), irons, hair dryers. **Pool(s):** heated indoor. **Leisure Activities:** whirlpool. **Guest Services:** valet and coin laundry, area transportation-train station. **Business Services:** meeting rooms, PC. **Cards:** AX, DC, DS, MC, VI. **Special Amenities:** free expanded continental breakfast and free local telephone calls.

SOME UNITS

(✈) (&M) (&) (➢) (🎥) (DATA PORT) (➡) / (✗) (■) (▭) /
FEE

CRESTMONT MANOR BED & BREAKFAST

Phone: 907/456-3831

6/1-9/6 [BP]	1P: $85-$100	2P: $85-$100	XP: $25
3/1-5/31 [CP]	1P: $65-$85	2P: $65-$85	XP: $25
9/7-2/28 [CP]	1P: $55-$75	2P: $55-$75	

F12
F12

Bed & Breakfast   **Location:** SR 3 (Parks Hwy), exit Chena Pump Rd, just w to Chena Ridge Rd, 0.7 mi n, then just e. 510 Crestmont Dr 99709. Fax: 907/456-3841. **Facility:** Original artwork is displayed in common areas and handmade quilts adorn guest beds at his B&B near the university. Smoke free premises. 5 one-bedroom standard units. 2 stories (no elevator), interior corridors. Bath: combo or shower only. **Parking:** on-site. **Terms:** check-in 5 pm, 14 day cancellation notice. **Amenities:** hair dryers. Some: irons. **Guest Services:** coin laundry. **Cards:** AX, DS, MC, VI.

SOME UNITS
(A$K) (X) (K) / (W) (VCR) (Z) /

FAIRBANKS DOWNTOWN BED & BREAKFAST   *Book at aaa.com*

Phone: (907)452-7700

(AAA) (SAVE)

5/15-9/1	1P: $100	2P: $100	XP: $20

Location: Jct Airport Way and Gillam Way, just s. Located in a residential area. 1461 Gillam Way 99701. Fax: 907/456-1116. **Facility:** Smoke free premises. 5 one-bedroom standard units. 2 stories (no elevator), interior corridors. Bath: combo or shower only. **Parking:** on-site, winter plug-ins. **Terms:** open 5/15-9/1, 14 day cancellation notice. **Cards:** AX, DS, MC, VI.

Bed & Breakfast

SOME UNITS
(X) (K) (CTV) (Z) / (🖨) /

FAIRBANKS PRINCESS RIVERSIDE LODGE   *Book at aaa.com*

Phone: (907)455-4477

5/6-9/15	2P: $199-$239	XP: $10
3/1-5/5 & 9/16-2/28	2P: $99-$149	XP: $10

F12
F12

Large-scale Hotel   **Location:** Jct Airport and Pikes Landing rds, just nw. 4477 Pikes Landing Rd 99709. Fax: 907/455-4476. **Facility:** 325 units. 322 one-bedroom standard units, some with whirlpools. 3 one-bedroom suites ($199-$499), some with efficiencies and/or whirlpools. 3 stories, interior corridors. Bath: combo or shower only. **Parking:** on-site, winter plug-ins. **Terms:** check-in 3:30 pm, cancellation fee imposed, package plans. **Amenities:** voice mail, irons, hair dryers. Some: fax. **Leisure Activities:** steamrooms, hiking trails, exercise room, horseshoes. **Guest Services:** gift shop, valet and coin laundry, area transportation. **Business Services:** conference facilities, business center. **Cards:** AX, DC, DS, MC, VI.

SOME UNITS
(✈) (🍴) (Y) (🚹) (M) (🚻) (🅿) (X) (📹) (DATA PORT) (💻) / (X) (VCR) (🖨) (📠)
FEE

MIDGE'S BIRCH LANE BED & BREAKFAST

Phone: 907/388-8084

Property failed to provide current rates

Location: Airport Rd W, 0.6 mi n on George Parks Hwy, 1 mi e on Geist Rd, 0.4 mi s on Fairbanks St, then 0.3 mi w. Located in a quiet, residential area. 4335 Birch Ln 99709 (PO Box 81013, 99708). Fax: 907/479-4894. **Facility:** Smoke free premises. 4 one-bedroom standard units. 2 stories (no elevator), interior corridors. Bath: some shared or private, combo or shower only. **Parking:** on-site, winter plug-ins. **Terms:** check-in 4 pm. **Amenities:** video library. **Leisure Activities:** bicycles.

Bed & Breakfast

SOME UNITS
(X) (K) / (W) (VCR) (Z) /

PIKE'S WATERFRONT LODGE   *Book at aaa.com*   Phone: (907)456-4500

(AAA) (SAVE)

5/26-8/31	1P: $210-$235	2P: $210-$235	XP: $10	F1
5/9-5/25	1P: $119-$139	2P: $119-$139	XP: $10	F1
9/1-2/28	1P: $99-$129	2P: $99-$129	XP: $10	F1
3/1-5/8	1P: $99-$119	2P: $99-$119	XP: $10	F1

Small-scale Hotel Location: Jct Airport and Hoselton rds. 1850 Hoselton Rd 99709. **Fax:** 907/456-4515. **Facility:** 208 units. 179 one-bedroom standard units, some with whirlpools. 1 one-bedroom suite ($229-$460). 28 cabins ($245). 1-stories, interior/exterior corridors. **Bath:** combo or shower only. **Parking:** on-site, winter plug-ins. **Terms:** [BP] & [CP] meal plan available, small pets only ($10 extra charge). **Amenities:** voice mail, irons, hair dryers. *Some:* video games. **Dining:** 6 am-2 & 5-9 pm, cocktails. **Leisure Activities:** sauna, steamroom, exercise room. *Fee:* game room. **Guest Services:** gift shop, vale and coin laundry, area transportation-train station. **Business Services:** meeting rooms, business center. **Cards:** AX, MC, VI **Special Amenities:** free local telephone calls and free newspaper. *(See color ad p 709)*

SOME UNITS

[icons]

REGENCY FAIRBANKS HOTEL   *Book at aaa.com*   Phone: (907)452-3200

5/15-9/14	1P: $149-$159	2P: $159-$169	XP: $10	F1
3/1-5/14 & 9/15-2/28	1P: $89-$99	2P: $99-$109	XP: $10	F1

Small-scale Hotel Location: Just w of SR 2 (Steese Expwy); center. 95 10th Ave 99701. **Fax:** 907/452-2720. **Facility:** 128 units. 116 one-bedroom standard units with efficiencies, some with whirlpools. 9 one- and 3 two-bedroom suites ($149-$225) with kitchens, some with whirlpools. 3 stories, interior corridors. **Parking:** on-site, winter plug-ins. **Terms:** cancellation fee imposed, weekly rates available, [AP] & [ECP] meal plans available, package plans, pets ($50 fee, $50 deposit). **Amenities:** voice mail, hair dryers. **Leisure Activities:** exercise room. **Guest Services:** valet and coin laundry, area transportation. **Business Services:** meeting rooms, business center. **Cards:** AX, MC, VI.

SOME UNITS

[icons]

RIVER'S EDGE RESORT   *Book at aaa.com*   Phone: (907)474-0286

(AAA) (SAVE)

6/1-8/31	1P: $175-$200	2P: $175-$200	XP: $10	F1
5/1-5/31 & 9/1-9/30	1P: $95-$115	2P: $95-$115	XP: $10	F1

Cabin **Location:** Airport Way, just n on Sportsman Way, 0.5 mi w. 4200 Boat St 99709. **Fax:** 907/474-3665. **Facility:** 94 units. 8 one-bedroom standard units. 86 cabins. 2 stories (no elevator), interior/exterior corridors. **Parking:** on-site, winter plug-ins. **Terms:** open 5/1-9/30. **Amenities:** voice mail, hair dryers. **Dining:** Chena's Fine Dining & Deck, see separate listing. **Leisure Activities:** rental bicycles. **Guest Services:** gift shop, coin laundry, area transportation-train station & tour sites. **Business Services:** meeting rooms, business center. **Cards:** AX, DS, MC, VI. *(See color ad below)*

SOME UNITS

[icons]

SOPHIE STATION HOTEL   *Book at aaa.com*   Phone: (907)479-3650

5/15-9/15	1P: $179-$245	2P: $179-$245	XP: $10	
3/1-5/14 & 9/16-2/28	1P: $89-$175	2P: $89-$175	XP: $10	

Condominium **Location:** Airport Way, just s. 1717 University Ave S 99709. **Fax:** 907/479-7951. **Facility:** 148 units. 8 one-bedroom standard units with efficiencies, some with whirlpools. 140 one-bedroom suites with kitchens. 3 stories, interior corridors. **Parking:** on-site, winter plug-ins. **Terms:** [AP], [BP], [CP] & [ECP] meal plans available. **Amenities:** voice mail, irons, hair dryers. *Some:* high-speed Internet (fee). **Guest Services:** gift shop, valet and coin laundry, area transportation. **Business Services:** meeting rooms, PC. **Cards:** AX, CB, DC, DS, MC, VI.

SOME UNITS

[icons]

PRINGHILL SUITES BY MARRIOTT   *Book at aaa.com*   **Phone:** (907)451-6552
▼▼▼▼
small-scale Hotel

5/15-9/14	1P: $189
3/1-5/14 & 9/15-2/28	1P: $94

Location: Downtown. Located across from Visitors Center. 575 1st Ave 99701. Fax: 907/451-6553. **Facility:** 140 one-bedroom standard units. 6 stories, interior corridors. *Bath:* combo or shower only. **Parking:** on-site, inter plug-ins. **Terms:** cancellation fee imposed, [CP] meal plan available. **Amenities:** video games (fee), high-speed Internet, oice mail, irons, hair dryers. **Dining:** Lavelle's Bistro, see separate listing. **Pool(s):** small heated indoor. **Leisure ctivities:** whirlpool, exercise room. **Guest Services:** valet and coin laundry. **Business Services:** meeting rooms, PC, fax. ards: AX, CB, DC, DS, JC, MC, VI.

SOME UNITS

(ASK) 🅢🅓 ✈ 🍴 🔥M 🚭 📷 🛥 ⚟ [DATA PORT] 🔌 📠 📺 / ⊠ /

UPER 8 MOTEL   *Book at aaa.com*   **Phone:** (907)451-8888
▼
Motel

5/16-9/15	1P: $129-$134	2P: $134-$139
3/1-5/15 & 9/16-2/28	1P: $75-$89	2P: $79-$93

Location: Airport Way at Wilbur St. Located near Pioneer Park. 1909 Airport Way 99701. Fax: 907/451-6690. **Facility:** 77 one-bedroom standard units. 3 stories (no elevator), interior corridors. **Parking:** on-site, winter ug-ins. **Terms:** 8% service charge, pets ($25 deposit, 1st floor units). **Guest Services:** coin laundry, area ansportation. **Business Services:** meeting rooms, fax (fee). **Cards:** AX, CB, DC, DS, MC, VI.

SOME UNITS

(ASK) 🅢🅓 ✈ 🐾 🍴 📺 [DATA PORT] / ⊠ 🔌 📠 /
FEE

EDGEWOOD RESORT   *Book at aaa.com*   **Phone:** (907)452-1442
▼▼ ▼▼
Condominium

5/15-9/15	1P: $157-$245	2P: $157-$245	XP: $10
3/1-5/14 & 9/16-2/28	1P: $75-$175	2P: $75-$175	XP: $10

Location: Johanson Expwy. 1 mi w on College Rd to Margaret Dr, then just s. 212 Wedgewood Dr 99701. Fax: 907/451-8184. **Facility:** 460 units. 155 one-bedroom standard units. 233 one- and 72 two-bedroom uites with kitchens. 3 stories (no elevator), interior/exterior corridors. *Bath:* combo or shower only. **Parking:** on-site, winter ug-ins. **Terms:** check-in 4 pm. **Amenities:** voice mail, irons, hair dryers. *Some:* DVD players, high-speed Internet (fee). eisure **Activities:** cross country skiing. **Guest Services:** gift shop, valet and coin laundry, area transportation. **Business ervices:** conference facilities, PC. **Cards:** AX, CB, DC, DS, MC, VI.

SOME UNITS

(ASK) ✈ 🍴 🍷 🔥M 🚭 📷 🏃 ⚟ [DATA PORT] / ⊠ 🔌 📠 📺 /
FEE

WESTMARK FAIRBANKS HOTEL & CONFERENCE CENTER   Book at aaa.com

Phone: (907)456-772

AAA SAVE

5/16-9/15	1P: $200	2P: $200	XP: $15
3/1-5/15 & 9/16-2/28	1P: $159	2P: $159	XP: $15

Location: Just n of Airport Way at 10th Ave; just w of SR 2; downtown. 813 Noble St 99701. **Fax:** 907/451-747

Small-scale Hotel

Facility: 400 units. 391 one-bedroom standard units. 9 one-bedroom suites. 4-8 stories, interior corridor *Bath:* combo or shower only. **Parking:** on-site, winter plug-ins. **Terms:** cancellation fee imposed, packag plans. **Amenities:** voice mail, irons, hair dryers. *Some:* dual phone lines. **Dining:** 6 am-midnight, cocktail

Leisure Activities: exercise room. *Fee:* massage. **Guest Services:** gift shop, valet and coin laundry, area transportation-tra station. **Business Services:** conference facilities, PC. **Cards:** AX, DC, DS, MC, VI.

SOME UNITS

The following lodging was either not evaluated or did not meet AAA rating requirements but is listed for your information only.

FORGET ME NOT/AURORA EXPRESS

Phone: 907/474-094

fyi

Not evaluated. **Location:** SR 3, exit Chena Pump, 6.5 mi s; 5.2 mi s of the Pump House. Located in a quiet, seclude area. 1540 Chena Ridge 99707 (PO Box 80128, 99708). Facilities, services, and decor characterize a mid-rang property.

WHERE TO DINE

ALASKA COFFEE ROASTING CO

Lunch: $4-$6   **Dinner:** $4-$6   **Phone:** 907/457-528

Coffee/Espresso

Location: Just w of University Ave; in West Valley Plaza. 4001 Geist Rd, Suite 2 99709. **Hours:** 7 am-10 pm, Sa from 8 am, Sun from 9 am. **Features:** Known for its huge selection of coffee roasted on the premises, th funky, upbeat and contemporary coffeehouse also serves a variety of light lunches. You can enjoy vegetab empanadas, wraps and pizzas, and there is a large dessert case to tempt your sweet tooth. You order at th counter and can either get your food to go or linger in the cafe at this locally popular spot. Casual dress. **Parking:** on-site **Cards:** MC, VI.

ALASKA SALMON BAKE

Dinner: $23-$26   **Phone:** 907/452-727

American

Location: Airport Way; in Pioneer Park. **Hours:** Open 5/15-9/10; 5 pm-9 pm; show offered at 8:15 pm **Features:** This traditional salmon bake has an excellent salad bar and the option of the salmon dinner or prime rib dinner. Pay for your ticket at the counter and serve yourself at the salad bar, fish barbecue an dessert cabin. You can either eat at the picnic tables outside or inside the covered area; either way, you ca satisfy any appetite. Casual dress; beer & wine only. **Parking:** on-site. **Cards:** AX, DS, MC, VI.

CHENA'S FINE DINING & DECK

Lunch: $10   **Dinner:** $19-$28   **Phone:** 907/474-364

American

Location: Airport Way, just n on Sportsman Way, 0.5 mi w; in River's Edge Resort. 4200 Boat St 99709. **Hours:** Ope 5/15-10/15; 6 am-9, noon-2 & 5-10 pm; hours vary off season. **Reservations:** suggested, for dinne **Features:** Antiques and upscale appointments are used in creating a decor that suggests early 1900 Alaska. The menu emphasizes steaks and seafood and items are very well prepared and nicely presented Dining is casual and leisurely, with outside deck dining available in season. Casual dress; cocktails. **Parking:** on-site **Cards:** AX, DS, MC, VI.

THE COOKIE JAR

Lunch: $7-$10   **Dinner:** $10-$20   **Phone:** 907/479-831

American

Location: Jct Johanson Expwy, just n on Danby St. 1006 Cadillac Ct 99701. **Hours:** 6:30 am-9 pm, Mon-8:30 pm Sun 8 am-7 pm. Closed: 11/24, 12/25. **Features:** Enjoy leisurely dining in a casual and relaxed atmosphere The kitchen turns out a variety of selections prepared using fresh ingredients. Much is made on-site an when ordered. Save room for indulging in the restaurant's homemade cookies and pastries. Casual dress **Parking:** on-site. **Cards:** AX, DS, MC, VI.

GAMBARDELLA'S PASTA BELLA

Lunch: $7-$10   **Dinner:** $10-$20   **Phone:** 907/456-341

AAA

Italian

Location: Downtown. 706 2nd Ave 99701. **Hours:** 11 am-10 pm, Sun from 4 pm. Closed major holidays **Reservations:** suggested, for dinner. **Features:** Business travelers and couples enjoy the excellent lasagna and tiramisu at the warm, comfortable restaurant. Among other good choices are homemade pizza, bread pie, cheesecake, espresso and cappuccino. Seating is available on the covered patio in season. Casua dress; beer & wine only. **Parking:** on-site. **Cards:** AX, MC, VI.

LAVELLE'S BISTRO

Dinner: $19-$28   **Phone:** 907/450-055

Regional American

Location: Downtown; in SpringHill Suites by Marriott. 575 1st Ave 99701. **Hours:** 4:30 pm-10 pm. Closed majo holidays. **Features:** This upscale trendy restaurant is one of the best in the city. Featuring an impressive and extensive wine list, a funky modern interior and a varied menu, this is a great place for a reunion with a friend and a good meal. The menu can range from halibut to salmon, from lamb to pasta, but they are a tasty, artistic and creative. Casual dress; cocktails. **Parking:** on-site. **Cards:** AX, CB, DS, JC, MC, VI.

PIKE'S LANDING RESTAURANT & LOUNGE

Lunch: $9-$12   **Dinner:** $20-$30   **Phone:** 907/479-650

Regional American

Location: Jct Airport Way and Hoselton; next to Pike's Waterfront Lodge. 4438 Airport Way 99709. **Hours:** 11 am-10 pm; hours vary in winter. Closed: 12/25. **Features:** One nice thing about Alaska in the summer is endless nights under the midnight sun, and one of the city's best places to enjoy this is on the patio of the restaurant, which is set along the riverbank. Patrons find an extensive selection of Alaskan seafood and car eat inside or out. Because it is such a popular place, prepare yourself for a lingering meal. Service is exceptionally friendly Casual dress; cocktails. **Parking:** on-site. **Cards:** AX, DC, DS, MC, VI.

THE PUMP HOUSE RESTAURANT & SALOON

Lunch: $7-$13   **Dinner:** $17-$40   **Phone:** 907/479-8452

(AAA) ▼▼▼ ▼▼▼

American

Location: Jct Parks Hwy and Geist Rd (Chena Rd), just e to Chena Pump Rd, 1.3 mi s. 796 Chena Pump Rd 99709. **Hours:** 11:30 am-10 pm, Sun from 10 am; 4 pm-10 pm, Sat from noon, Sun from 10 am 9/16-05/14. Closed: 1/1; also 12/24. **Reservations:** suggested, dinner. **Features:** An authentic former tin pumphouse used in gold-mining operations, the restaurant is listed on the National Register of Historic Places. The deck affords a great view of the Chena River. The decor exudes a warm Victorian charm. Casual dress; cocktails. **Parking:** on-site. **Cards:** AX, DS, MC, VI. **Historic**

(Y) (X)

THAI HOUSE RESTAURANT

Lunch: $7-$9   **Dinner:** $8-$14   **Phone:** 907/452-6123

▼▼▼ ▼▼▼

Thai

Location: Downtown. 526 5th Ave 99701. **Hours:** Open 3/1-12/31 & 1/15-2/28; 11 am-4 & 5-10 pm. Closed major holidays; also Sun. **Reservations:** accepted. **Features:** The popular restaurant is a cozy, unassuming spot. Yellow curry powder, onion, egg, fresh ginger, chili and garlic are a few of the ingredients that bring the cuisine to life. Servers are friendly. Casual dress; beer & wine only. **Parking:** street. **Cards:** MC, VI.

(AC) (X)

THE TURTLE CLUB

Dinner: $19-$30   **Phone:** 907/457-3883

▼▼▼ ▼▼▼

Steak & Seafood

Location: 10 mi n on SR 2 (Steese Expwy), 0.6 mi w on SR 6 (Old Steese Hwy). 10 Mile Old Steese Hwy 99712. **Hours:** 6 pm-10 pm, Sun 5 pm-9 pm. Closed: 1/1, 11/24, 12/25; also 11/22 & 11/23. **Reservations:** suggested. **Features:** Although menu selections are limited, the restaurant uses quality products. While specializing in prime rib and seafood, one of the restaurant's signature items is giant prawns. Throughout the restaurant are curio cabinets filled with turtle knick-knacks. Casual dress; cocktails. **Parking:** on-site. **Cards:** AX, DS, MC, VI.

(&M) (Y) (X)

WOLF RUN RESTAURANT

Lunch: $5-$8   **Dinner:** $8-$25   **Phone:** 907/458-0636

▼▼▼ ▼▼▼

American

Location: Jct of Johanssen Expwy and University Ave. 3360 Wolf Run 99709. **Hours:** 11 am-9 pm, Fri & Sat-11 pm, Sun noon-8:30 pm, Mon-3 pm. Closed: 11/24, 12/25. **Reservations:** suggested. **Features:** Known for its sinful and decadent desserts, this cozy and comfortable dessert house also features a good selection of homemade soups, sandwiches and salads. You may not want to come in for anything but dessert, as you'll have to choose from a list of 20 creations! Originally designed as a private home, the restaurant still maintains the coziness with its simple decor. A very popular spot with the locals, this is a great place to sit and lounge over a cup of coffee and dessert. Casual dress; beer & wine only. **Parking:** on-site. **Cards:** AX, CB, DC, DS, JC, MC, VI.

(&M) (AC) (X)

GIRDWOOD

——— WHERE TO STAY ———

ALYESKA PRINCE HOTEL

Book at aaa.com   **Phone:** (907)754-1111

(AAA) (SAVE)
▼▼▼ ▼▼▼ ▼▼▼

Resort
Large-scale Hotel

	1P:	2P:	XP:	
5/16-9/15	$249-$1600	$249-$1600	$25	F18
3/1-5/15 & 9/16-2/28	$160-$1200	$160-$1200	$25	F18

Location: 2 mi n on Alyeska Blvd from SR 1 (Seward Hwy), then 0.9 mi e. Located in a quiet area. 1000 Arlberg Ave 99587 (PO Box 249). Fax: 907/754-2200. **Facility:** Fine dining, upscale rooms and attention to service are featured at this resort-style hotel set in a valley next to ski hills. 307 units. 303 one-bedroom standard units. 4 one-bedroom suites. 8 stories, interior corridors. *Bath:* combo or shower only. **Parking:** on-site and valet. **Terms:** check-in 4 pm, package plans, 8% service charge. **Amenities:** video games, voice mail, safes, irons, hair dryers. **Dining:** 5 restaurants, 6 am-11 pm, cocktails, also, Seven Glaciers Restaurant, see separate listing. **Pool(s):** heated indoor. **Leisure Activities:** sauna, whirlpool, cross country skiing, snowmobiling, ice skating, hiking trails, exercise room. **Fee:** downhill skiing, heliskiing, aerial tram rides dogsledding, bicycles, massage. **Guest Services:** gift shop, valet laundry, area transportation-within Girdwood. **Business Services:** conference facilities, PC (fee), fax. **Cards:** AX, CB, DC, DS, JC, MC, VI.

SOME UNITS

(S)(D) (↑↓) (Y) (♦) (&M) (⊡) (≋) (X) (AC) (★) (DATA PORT) (◘) (▣) / (X) (VCR) (▦) /

——— WHERE TO DINE ———

DOUBLE MUSKY INN

Dinner: $22-$30   **Phone:** 907/783-2822

▼▼▼ ▼▼▼

Regional Cajun

Location: 1.9 mi n on Alyeska Blvd from SR 1 (Seward Hwy), 0.3 mi w. Milepost 0.3 (Crow Creek Rd) 99587. **Hours:** 5 pm-10 pm, Fri & Sat from 4:30 pm. Closed: Mon. **Features:** You're sure to enjoy the twist on New Orleans dishes prepared with fresh Alaskan seafood. Many savory delights such as crab meat dressing stuffed halibut served with Creole burre blanc or shrimp etouffee are among the favorites of the local crowds. Unique decor of Mardi Gras beads and masks surrounding locally made framed stained glass create a festive atmosphere for you to dine in. Casual dress; cocktails. **Parking:** on-site. **Cards:** MC, VI.

(AC) (X)

SEVEN GLACIERS RESTAURANT

Dinner: $24-$42   **Phone:** 907/754-2249

(AAA)
▼▼▼ ▼▼▼

Regional American

Location: 2 mi n on Alyeska Blvd from SR 1 (Seward Hwy), then 0.9 mi e; in Alyeska Prince Hotel. 1000 Arlberg Ave 99587. **Hours:** Open 3/1-4/14 & 5/6-2/28; 5:30 pm-9:30 pm. Closed: 10/1-11/15, Tues-Wed 5/1-5/31 & 9/1-9/30. **Reservations:** suggested. **Features:** The unusual mountaintop location is a spectacular setting, accessible only by an aerial tram from the hotel. The menu centers on creative Alaskan and West Coast preparations of seafood, beef and more exotic game. Seasonal salmon and halibut are always popular. Although the ambience is elegant, diners are at home either dressed up or in more casual resort attire. A reservation will ensure a free tram ride to the dining room. Casual dress; cocktails. **Parking:** on-site and valet. **Cards:** AX, CB, DC, DS, JC, MC, VI.

(Y) (AC) (X)

GLENNALLEN pop. 554

———— WHERE TO STAY ————

LAKE LOUISE LODGE

▽▽▽

Small-scale Hotel

All Year [BP]   1P: $70-$95   2P: $80-$105   XP: $15   D16

Phone: 907/822-3311

Location: 27.7 mi w on US 1, 16.1 mi n on dirt road. Mile 16.1 Lake Louise Rd 99588 (HC01 Box 1716). **Fax:** 907/822-3311. **Facility:** Designated smoking area. 6 one-bedroom standard units. 2 stories (no elevator), interior/exterior corridors. *Bath:* shower only. **Parking:** on-site, winter plug-ins. **Terms:** check-in 4 pm, 14 day cancellation notice-fee imposed, weekly rates available, [AP] meal plan available. **Amenities:** hair dryers. **Leisure Activities:** rental boats, boat dock, fishing, hiking trails. *Fee:* charter fishing. **Guest Services:** TV in common area. **Cards:** AX, DC, DS, MC, VI.

SOME UNITS

GUSTAVUS pop. 429

———— WHERE TO STAY ————

ANNIE MAE LODGE

▽▽▽ ▽▽▽

Country Inn

5/1-9/17 [AP]   1P: $150-$170   2P: $235-$280   XP: $95   D12
3/1-4/30 & 9/18-2/28 [AP]   1P: $150   2P: $235   XP: $95   D12

Phone: (907)697-2346

Location: From airport, 3 mi w to Good River Rd, 0.5 mi to Grandpa's Farm Rd. Located in a quiet area. #2 Grandpa's Farm Rd 99826 (PO Box 55). **Fax:** 907/697-2211. **Facility:** Smoke free premises. 11 one-bedroom standard units. 2 stories (no elevator), interior/exterior corridors. *Bath:* some shared or private, combo or shower only. **Parking:** on-site. **Terms:** office hours 5:30 am-10:30 pm, 30 day cancellation notice-fee imposed, package plans. **Leisure Activities:** fishing, recreation programs, bicycles. **Guest Services:** gift shop, valet laundry, area transportation. **Cards:** AX, DS, MC, VI.

GLACIER BAY LODGE

▲▲▲ SAVE
▽▽▽ ▽▽▽

Motel

5/18-9/10   2P: $189

Phone: (907)697-2225

Location: 9 mi w of airport. 199 Bartlett Cove 99826 (PO Box 199). **Fax:** 907/697-2419. **Facility:** Smoke free premises. 54 one-bedroom standard units. 2 stories (no elevator), exterior corridors. **Parking:** on-site. **Terms:** open 5/18-9/10, office hours 5 am-11 pm, 7 day cancellation notice, package plans. **Dining:** 6-9 am, 11:30-2 & 5:30-10 pm; patio dining at dinner in season, cocktails. **Leisure Activities:** marina, hiking trails. *Fee:* fishing, kayaking, bicycles. **Guest Services:** gift shop, coin laundry. **Cards:** AX, DC, DS, JC, MC, VI.

Special Amenities: free local telephone calls.

FEE

GLACIER BAY'S BEAR TRACK INN

▽▽▽ ▽▽▽

Motel

5/20-9/14 [AP]   1P: $352   2P: $704   XP: $150   D3

Phone: (907)697-3017

Location: 7 mi e of airport; at the end of Rink Creek Rd. Located in a quiet area. 255 Rink Creek Rd 99826. **Fax:** 907/697-2284. **Facility:** Designated smoking area. 14 one-bedroom standard units. 2 stories (no elevator), interior corridors. **Parking:** on-site. **Terms:** open 5/20-9/14, office hours 5 am-11 pm, 60 day cancellation notice-fee imposed, weekly rates available, package plans, pets ($50 deposit). **Amenities:** hair dryers. **Leisure Activities:** hiking trails. **Guest Services:** gift shop, valet laundry, area transportation. **Business Services:** meeting rooms. **Cards:** DC, MC, VI.

FEE

———— WHERE TO DINE ————

FAIRWEATHER DINING ROOM

▽▽▽

American

Lunch: $10-$18   **Dinner:** $20-$30   **Phone:** 907/697-2226

Location: 9 mi w of airport; inside Glacier Bay Lodge. 199 Bartlett Cove 99826. **Hours:** Open 5/15-9/30; 6 am-9, 11:30-2 & 5:30-10 pm. **Features:** The hotel dining room offers both a wonderful view of the inlet and creatively prepared, locally caught seafood, as well as a variety of standards ranging from sandwiches to steaks. Casual dress. **Parking:** on-site. **Cards:** AX, DS, MC, VI.

HAINES pop. 1,811

———— WHERE TO STAY ————

CAPTAIN'S CHOICE INC MOTEL

▲▲▲ SAVE
▽▽▽

Motel

4/15-10/14   1P: $107   2P: $117   XP: $5   F12
10/15-2/28   1P: $81   2P: $86   XP: $5   F12
3/1-4/14   1P: $77   2P: $82   XP: $5   F12

Phone: (907)766-3111

Location: Jct 2nd Ave and Dalton St. 108 2nd Ave N 99827 (PO Box 392). **Fax:** 907/766-3332. **Facility:** 39 units. 37 one-bedroom standard units, some with whirlpools. 2 one-bedroom suites ($132-$172). 2 stories (no elevator), exterior corridors. **Parking:** on-site. **Terms:** package plans, pets ($10 extra charge). **Amenities:** voice mail, hair dryers. **Leisure Activities:** sun deck. **Guest Services:** coin laundry, area transportation-ferry. **Cards:** AX, CB, DC, DS, MC, VI.

SOME UNITS

FEE   FEE

———— WHERE TO DINE ————

CHILKAT RESTAURANT & BAKERY

▲▲▲
▽▽▽

American

Lunch: $10-$15   **Phone:** 907/766-3653

Location: Jct 5th Ave and Dalton St. 25 5th Ave 99827. **Hours:** 7 am-3 pm. Closed major holidays. **Features:** A few steps away from downtown, this local favorite offers a variety of well prepared and hearty dishes and features in-house bakery items. Casual dress. **Parking:** on-site. **Cards:** MC, VI.

ORT SEWARD LODGE RESTAURANT & SALOON   **Dinner:** $10-$25   **Phone:** 907/766-2009
▼▼▼   **Location:** In Fort William H Seward. 39 Mud Bay Rd 99827. **Hours:** Open 5/15-9/20; 5 pm-10 pm.
Reservations: accepted. **Features:** The casual dining room has been restored to reflect its former gold
American   rush saloon days and offers a variety of bar favorites including hamburgers and locally caught seafood.
Casual dress; cocktails. **Parking:** on-site. **Cards:** DS, MC, VI.   ⊤ 𝕂 ⊠

HEALY pop. 1,000—*See also DENALI NATIONAL PARK AND PRESERVE.*

─────── **WHERE TO STAY** ───────

DENALI DOME HOME BED & BREAKFAST   **Phone:** (907)683-1239
AAA [SAVE]   6/8-9/4 [BP]   1P: $125   2P: $135   XP: $25   D5
5/15-6/7 [BP]   1P: $85-$95   2P: $100-$110   XP: $25   D5
▼▼▼   9/5-2/28 [BP]   1P: $75-$100   2P: $85-$110   XP: $25   D5
3/1-5/14 [BP]   1P: $75   2P: $85   XP: $25   D5
Bed & Breakfast   **Location:** Jct SR 3 and Healy Spur Rd, 0.5 mi e. Located in a quiet area. 137 Healy Spur 99743 (PO Box 151,
DENALI NATIONAL PARK, 99755). **Facility:** In a scenic area, this unusual dome-shaped B&B offers cozy,
comfortable rooms and spacious living areas. Smoke free premises. 7 one-bedroom standard units, some with whirlpools. 3
stories (no elevator), interior/exterior corridors. *Bath:* combo or shower only. **Parking:** on-site, winter plug-ins. **Terms:** check-in 4
pm, cancellation fee imposed, package plans, no pets allowed (owner's pets on premises). **Amenities:** video library, hair dryers.
Some: DVD players. **Leisure Activities:** hiking trails, jogging. **Business Services:** business center. **Cards:** AX, DS, MC, VI.
SOME UNITS
[S][D] [🚿M] ⊠ [VCR] [DATA PORT] / [𝕂] [📞]

DENALI LAKESIDE LODGING   **Phone:** (907)683-2511
▼▼▼   6/1-8/31 [ECP]   1P: $120-$130   2P: $120-$130   XP: $15
5/1-5/31 & 9/1-9/30 [ECP]   1P: $90   2P: $90   XP: $15
Small-scale Hotel   **Location:** SR 3, 1.4 mi w at Milepost 247, follow signs. Mile 1.4 Otto Lake Rd 99743 (PO Box 323).
Fax: 907/683-2511. **Facility:** Smoke free premises. 4 units. 2 one- and 1 two-bedroom standard units, some
with kitchens. 1 cabin ($120). 2 stories, interior/exterior corridors. *Bath:* combo or shower only. **Parking:** on-site, winter plug-ins.
Terms: open 5/1-9/30, check-in 4 pm, 21 day cancellation notice-fee imposed. **Amenities:** video library, hair dryers. **Leisure
Activities:** canoeing, boat dock, fishing, hiking trails, jogging. **Guest Services:** coin laundry. **Cards:** MC, VI.
SOME UNITS
⊠ ⊠ [𝕂] [CTV] [VCR] [DATA PORT] / [📞] [🖥] [💻] /

DENALI LAKEVIEW INN   **Phone:** (907)683-4035
AAA [SAVE]   6/6-8/31   1P: $130-$175   2P: $130-$175   XP: $15   F5
9/1-9/30   1P: $89-$129   2P: $89-$129   XP: $15   F5
▼▼▼   3/1-6/5   1P: $69-$129   2P: $69-$129   XP: $10   F5
10/1-2/28   1P: $69-$99   2P: $69-$99   XP: $10   F5
Bed & Breakfast   **Location:** SR 3, milepost 247, 1.2 mi w. Mile 1.2 Otto Lake Rd 99743 (PO Box 14). Fax: 907/683-4038.
Facility: Guest rooms at this modern inn, which fronts on a tranquil lake, all feature cheery decor and have
decks. Smoke free premises. 18 one-bedroom standard units, some with kitchens and/or whirlpools. 2-3 stories (no elevator),
interior/exterior corridors. **Parking:** on-site, winter plug-ins. **Terms:** check-in 4 pm, 14 day cancellation notice-fee imposed.
Amenities: hair dryers. **Leisure Activities:** fishing, hiking trails, jogging. *Fee:* canoes. **Guest Services:** coin laundry.
Cards: MC, VI.
SOME UNITS
⊠ ⊠ [𝕂] [CTV] [DATA PORT] [📞] [🖥] [💻] / [VCR] /

HEALY HEIGHTS FAMILY CABINS   **Phone:** (907)683-2639
▼▼▼   6/1-8/31   1P: $115-$200   2P: $115-$200   XP: $10   F6
5/1-5/31 & 9/1-9/20   1P: $95-$180   2P: $95-$180   XP: $10   F6
Cabin   **Location:** SR 3, milepost 247; 0.9 mi w on Otto Lake Rd, 1.5 mi n, follow signs. Hill Top Rd 99743 (PO Box 277).
Fax: 907/683-2640. **Facility:** Smoke free premises. 6 cabins. 1 story, exterior corridors. *Bath:* combo or
shower only. **Parking:** on-site, winter plug-ins. **Terms:** open 5/1-9/20, check-in 4 pm, 15 day cancellation notice-fee imposed.
Leisure Activities: hiking trails, jogging. **Cards:** MC, VI.
SOME UNITS
⊠ [𝕂] [📞] [🖥] [💻] / [PW] [VCR] [ℤ] /

HOMER pop. 3,946

─────── **WHERE TO STAY** ───────

BEST WESTERN BIDARKA INN   *Book at aaa.com*   **Phone:** (907)235-8148
AAA [SAVE]   5/16-9/15   1P: $125-$143   2P: $134-$143
3/1-5/15 & 9/16-2/28   1P: $71-$98   2P: $89-$98
▼▼▼   **Location:** 0.3 mi n on Sterling Hwy (SR 1): 575 Sterling Hwy 99603. Fax: 907/235-8140. **Facility:** 74 one-bedroom
Motel   standard units, some with whirlpools. 2 stories (no elevator), interior/exterior corridors. **Parking:** on-site.
Terms: check-in 4 pm, pets ($10 extra charge). **Amenities:** high-speed Internet, irons, hair dryers.
Dining: 2 restaurants, 5 am-10 pm, cocktails. **Leisure Activities:** exercise room. **Guest Services:** gift
shop, coin laundry, area transportation-ferry. **Business Services:** meeting rooms, PC. **Cards:** AX, DC, DS, MC, VI.
Special Amenities: early check-in/late check-out and preferred room (subject to availability with advance
reservations).
SOME UNITS
[S][D] [🚏] [🍴] [⊤] [𝕂] [CTV] [DATA PORT] [📞] [🖥] [💻] / [⊠] /
FEE

PIONEER INN   *Book at aaa.com*   **Phone:** (907)235-5670
▼▼   5/15-9/14 [CP]   1P: $79-$119   2P: $79-$119   XP: $13   D12
3/1-5/14 & 9/15-2/28   1P: $45   2P: $59   XP: $13   D12
Motel   **Location:** Just e off Sterling Hwy (SR 1); at entrance of town. 244 W Pioneer Ave 99603 (PO Box 1430, 99603-1430).
Facility: Smoke free premises. 7 units. 2 one-bedroom standard units. 5 one-bedroom suites ($109-$119)
with kitchens. 2 stories (no elevator), exterior corridors. **Parking:** on-site. **Terms:** 7 day cancellation notice-fee imposed.
Cards: AX, DS, MC, VI.
SOME UNITS
[🚏] ⊠ [𝕂] [ℤ] [💻] / [📞] /

VICTORIAN HEIGHTS BED AND BREAKFAST

Phone: (907)235-635?

(AAA) (SAVE)	5/15-9/15 [BP]	1P: $95-$135	2P: $95-$135	XP: $15	F1?
▼▼▼▼	3/1-5/14 & 9/16-2/28 [BP]	1P: $65-$95	2P: $65-$95	XP: $15	F1.

Location: Sterling Hwy (SR 1), 1.8 mi ne on Pioneer Ave (turns into East End Rd), 2.1 mi nw on East Hill Rd, 0.3 mi on Cottonwood, follow signs. 1585 Race Rd 99603 (PO Box 1706). Fax: 907/235-6357. **Facility:** This tasteful?
Bed & Breakfast decorated, spacious B&B offers two rooms with private balconies overlooking the bay and mountains? Smoke free premises. 4 one-bedroom standard units, some with whirlpools. 2 stories (no elevator), interior corridors. *Bath:* combo or shower only. **Parking:** on-site, winter plug-ins. **Terms:** check-in 4 pm, 2 night minimum stay, 14 da? cancellation notice. **Leisure Activities:** whirlpool, cross country skiing, snowmobile trails. **Guest Services:** TV in common area? coin laundry. **Business Services:** PC. **Cards:** MC, VI. **Special Amenities:** free full breakfast and free local telephone? calls.

SOME UNITS?

———— WHERE TO DINE ————

CAFE CUPS

Lunch: $7-$13　　**Dinner:** $16-$23　　**Phone:** 907/235-833?

▼▼▼
American

Location: Center. 162 W Pioneer Ave 99603. **Hours:** 11 am-10 pm. Closed: 12/25; also Sun? **Reservations:** suggested. **Features:** Considered to be one of the best places in town, this eclectic, funky restaurant serves up a variety of homemade goods, and is well-known for its seafood options. There are only about fifteen tables at this funky place, which features a unique mosaic wall around the door. You can choose from salmon, shrimp and other seafood dishes, or try the feature of the day. The servers are efficient and personable? Casual dress; beer & wine only. **Parking:** on-site. **Cards:** MC, VI.

CAPTAIN PATTIE'S FISH HOUSE

Lunch: $10-$15　　**Dinner:** $12-$25　　**Phone:** 907/235-513?

▼▼▼
Regional Seafood

Location: 5 mi along Homer Spit Rd. 4241 Homer Spit Rd 99603. **Hours:** Open 5/1-9/30; 11 am-10 pm? **Reservations:** accepted. **Features:** Those who spent the day fishing and can't wait to eat their catch can bring it in to the restaurant for preparation and cooking. Alaskan art contributes to the simple decor. The ever-changing menu boasts freshly caught fish dishes, along the lines of halibut, scallops and salmon. Early birds can take advantage of specials from 5 pm to 6 pm. On the famous Homer Spit, this spot is distinctive and casual. Casual dress; beer & wine only. **Parking:** on-site. **Cards:** DS, MC, VI.

THE HOMESTEAD

Dinner: $9-$27　　**Phone:** 907/235-872?

▼▼▼
American

Location: 8.2 mi s. Mile 8.2 East End Rd 99603. **Hours:** Open 4/1-10/1 & 12/1-1/1; 5 pm-9 pm. **Reservations:** suggested. **Features:** Diners can enjoy views of the Homer Spit in this lively restaurant which centers its menu on innovative preparations of fresh seafood. Casual dress; cocktails. **Parking:** on-site. **Cards:** AX, MC, VI.

SOURDOUGH EXPRESS BAKERY & CAFE

Lunch: $7-$12　　**Dinner:** $16-$20　　**Phone:** 907/235-7571

▼▼▼
Bakery/Desserts

Location: 3 mi sw on Sterling Hwy (SR 1). 1316 Ocean Dr 99603. **Hours:** Open 3/1-10/1; 7 am-9 pm. **Features:** A popular spot with the locals, the Sourdough Express is a warm, inviting place serving up locally produced and some organic fare. Whether you're stopping in for a big breakfast, a sandwich for lunch or an evening bite to eat, you might also be tempted by the display case in the bakery, which features a wide array of delicious desserts. In the summer, outdoor patio dining is available, complete with a small play area for the kids. Beer & wine only. **Parking:** on-site. **Cards:** MC, VI.

TWO SISTERS BAKERY

Lunch: $3-$8　　**Dinner:** $3-$8　　**Phone:** 907/235-228?

▼▼▼
Bakery/Desserts

Location: Sterling Hwy (SR 1), just s at Main St, then just e. 233 E Bunnell 99603. **Hours:** 7 am-8 pm, Sun 9 am-4 pm; hours vary in winter. Closed: 1/1, 1/23. **Reservations:** not accepted. **Features:** For healthy, organic baked goods and light lunches, the three sisters at the Two Sisters Bakery have what it takes. Located in a big house just on the outskirts of downtown, and near several galleries, the eatery offers giant cinnamon buns, scones, quiches, breakfast granola and, of course, a fine selection of fresh breads. Lounge for a few hours, or take your baked goods to go. Either way, you'll receive service with a smile. Casual dress. **Parking:** on-site. **Cards:** MC, VI.

JUNEAU pop. 30,711

———— WHERE TO STAY ————

AK FIREWEED HOUSE BED & BREAKFAST

Phone: 907/586-3885

▼▼▼	5/1-9/30 [BP]	1P: $129-$299	2P: $139-$329	XP: $50
	3/1-4/30 & 10/1-2/28 [BP]	1P: $99-$199	2P: $99-$199	XP: $50

Bed & Breakfast
Location: From airport, 12 mi s on Egan Dr to Juneau/Douglas bridge; across bridge, 5.1 mi n. Located in a secluded area on Douglas Island. 8530 N Douglas Hwy 99801. Fax: 907/586-3385. **Facility:** A two-story home and a cedar-beamed guest house are featured at this B&B on four acres of rain forest wetlands. Smoke free premises. 4 units. 3 one-bedroom standard units, some with whirlpools. 1 vacation home ($199-$369) with whirlpool. 1-2 stories (no elevator), interior/exterior corridors. *Bath:* combo or shower only. **Parking:** on-site. **Terms:** 3 night minimum stay - seasonal, 30 day cancellation notice-fee imposed, weekly rates available, package plans, no pets allowed (owner's dog on premises). **Amenities:** video library, high-speed Internet, irons, hair dryers. *Some:* CD players, voice mail. **Leisure Activities:** hiking trails, playground. **Guest Services:** coin laundry. **Business Services:** PC. **Cards:** AX, DS, MC, VI.

SOME UNITS

ALASKA WOLF HOUSE

Phone: (907)586-2422

▼▼▼	3/1-10/15 [BP]	1P: $115-$305	2P: $115-$305	XP: $35	F12
	10/16-2/28 [BP]	1P: $95-$155	2P: $95-$155	XP: $35	F12

Bed & Breakfast
Location: 2 mi n of downtown; from Highland Ave, 0.9 mi n on Glacier Ave, just e. Located in a quiet residential area. 1900 Wickersham Dr 99801 (PO Box 21321, 99802). Fax: 907/586-9053. **Facility:** Smoke free premises. 5 one-bedroom standard units, some with kitchens and/or whirlpools. 2 stories (no elevator), interior corridors. *Bath:* some shared or private, combo or shower only. **Parking:** on-site. **Terms:** 2 night minimum stay - seasonal, 30 day cancellation notice-fee imposed, no pets allowed (owner's pet on premises). **Amenities:** video library. *Some:* hair dryers. **Cards:** MC, VI.

SOME UNITS

ASPEN HOTELS **Book at aaa.com** Phone: (907)790-6435

5/16-9/15 [ECP]	1P: $159-$189	2P: $159-$189	XP: $10 F18
5/1-5/15 [ECP]	1P: $119-$149	2P: $119-$149	XP: $10 F18
3/1-4/30 & 9/16-2/28 [ECP]	1P: $99-$129	2P: $99-$129	XP: $10 F18

Small-scale Hotel **Location:** At Juneau International Airport. 1800 Shell Simmons Dr 99801. Fax: 907/790-6621. **Facility:** 94 units. 91 one-bedroom standard units, some with whirlpools. 3 one-bedroom suites with efficiencies. 2 stories, interior corridors. *Bath:* combo or shower only. **Parking:** on-site. **Terms:** cancellation fee imposed. **Amenities:** voice mail, irons, hair dryers. *Fee:* video library, high-speed Internet. **Pool(s):** small heated indoor. **Leisure Activities:** whirlpool, exercise room. **Guest Services:** valet and coin laundry, area transportation. **Business Services:** meeting rooms, PC. **Cards:** AX, DC, DS, MC, VI.

SOME UNITS

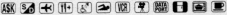

BEST WESTERN COUNTRY LANE INN **Book at aaa.com** Phone: (907)789-5005

5/1-9/30 [CP]	1P: $118	2P: $130	XP: $10
3/1-4/30 & 10/1-2/28 [CP]	1P: $90	2P: $100	

Motel **Location:** Just e off Egan Dr. 9300 Glacier Hwy 99801. Fax: 907/789-2818. **Facility:** 55 units. 54 one-bedroom standard units, some with efficiencies and/or whirlpools. 1 one-bedroom suite ($110-$130) with efficiency. 2 stories (no elevator), exterior corridors. **Parking:** on-site. **Terms:** pets ($50 deposit, $10 extra charge, in limited units). **Amenities:** irons, hair dryers. *Some:* high-speed Internet (fee). **Guest Services:** valet and coin laundry, area transportation. **Business Services:** PC. **Cards:** AX, DC, DS, MC, VI.

SOME UNITS

FEE

BEST WESTERN GRANDMA'S FEATHER BED Phone: (907)789-5566

[fyi]

5/1-9/30 [BP]	1P: $160	2P: $160	XP: $10 F17
3/1-4/30 & 10/1-2/28 [BP]	1P: $120	2P: $120	

Small-scale Hotel Under major renovation, scheduled to be completed July 2005. **Location:** Just e off Egan Dr. 2358 Mendenhall Loop Rd 99801 (9300 Glacier Hwy). Fax: 907/789-2818. **Facility:** 14 one-bedroom standard units with whirlpools. 2 stories, interior corridors. **Parking:** on-site. **Terms:** off-site registration. **Amenities:** high-speed Internet (fee), voice mail, irons, hair dryers. **Guest Services:** valet laundry, area transportation. **Cards:** AX, CB, DC, DS, MC, VI.

FRONTIER SUITES AIRPORT HOTEL

Book at aaa.com

Phone: (907)790-6600

5/16-9/15	1P: $117-$144	2P: $117-$144	XP: $10	F11
3/1-5/15 & 9/16-2/28	1P: $90-$135	2P: $90-$135	XP: $10	F11

Location: At Juneau International Airport. 9400 Glacier Hwy 99801. Fax: 907/790-6612. **Facility:** 104 units. 74 one-bedroom standard units, some with efficiencies, kitchens and/or whirlpools. 30 one-bedroom suites with kitchens, some with whirlpools. 2-4 stories, interior/exterior corridors. **Parking:** on-site. **Terms:** pets (small dogs only). **Amenities:** high-speed Internet (fee), dual phone lines, voice mail, safes, irons, hair dryers. **Dining:** 6:30 am-9 pm, cocktails. **Leisure Activities:** playground, exercise room, basketball. **Guest Services:** coin laundry, area transportation-Marine Ferry Terminal. **Business Services:** meeting rooms. **Cards:** AX, CB, DC, DS, MC, VI. **Special Amenities:** free local telephone calls.

SOME UNITS

GOLDBELT HOTEL JUNEAU

Book at aaa.com

Phone: (907)586-6900

5/16-9/15	1P: $169-$179	2P: $169-$179	XP: $15	F12
3/1-5/15 & 9/16-2/28	1P: $139-$149	2P: $139-$149	XP: $15	F12

Location: Just n of Main St; downtown. 51 Egan Dr 99801. Fax: 907/463-3567. **Facility:** 105 one-bedroom standard units. 7 stories, interior corridors. **Parking:** on-site. **Terms:** cancellation fee imposed. **Amenities:** high-speed Internet (fee), voice mail, irons, hair dryers. **Dining:** 7 am-2 & 5-10 pm, cocktails. **Guest Services:** valet laundry. **Business Services:** meeting rooms, PC. **Cards:** AX, DC, DS, MC, VI.

SOME UNITS

JUNEAU SUPER 8

Book at aaa.com

Phone: (907)789-4858

5/16-10/16	1P: $99-$109	2P: $104-$114	XP: $5	F14
3/1-5/15 & 10/17-2/28	1P: $70-$85	2P: $80-$95	XP: $5	F14

Location: At airport, just nw to Glacier Hwy, just e. 2295 Trout St 99801. Fax: 907/789-5819. **Facility:** 75 one-bedroom standard units. 3 stories, interior corridors. **Parking:** on-site. **Terms:** pets ($25 deposit). **Amenities:** safes (fee). **Guest Services:** coin laundry, area transportation. **Business Services:** meeting rooms. **Cards:** AX, DC, DS, MC, VI.

SOME UNITS

FEE

PEARSON'S POND LUXURY INN & ADVENTURE SPA

Book at aaa.com

Phone: (907)789-3772

5/15-9/15 [ECP]	1P: $219-$269	2P: $269-$319	XP: $50	D5
9/16-2/28 [ECP]	1P: $119-$179	2P: $169-$229	XP: $50	D5
3/1-5/14 [ECP]	1P: $119-$169	2P: $169-$219	XP: $50	D5

Location: From Egan Dr, 2.2 mi n on Mendenhall Loop Rd, 1.2 mi w on Mendenhall Loop Rd, 0.3 mi s on River Rd, just w on Kelly Ct, then just s. Located in a quiet residential area. 4541 Sawa Cir 99801-8723. Fax: 907/789-6722. **Facility:** A placid pond beautifies the property's grounds, while guest rooms offer luxurious amenities; hosts can assist with activity planning. Smoke free premises. 5 one-bedroom standard units with efficiencies, some with whirlpools. 2 stories (no elevator), interior/exterior corridors. **Bath:** combo or shower only. **Parking:** on-site. **Terms:** 2 night minimum stay - seasonal, age restrictions may apply, 21 day cancellation notice, in summer, 3 days in winter-fee imposed, package plans. **Amenities:** video library, CD players, high-speed Internet, dual phone lines, voice mail, irons, hair dryers. *Some:* DVD players, fax. **Leisure Activities:** whirlpools, boating, paddleboats, boat dock, fishing, fishing equipment, cross country skiing, ice skating, barbecue facility, yoga instruction, bicycles, hiking trails, exercise room. *Fee:* massage. **Guest Services:** gift shop, complimentary evening beverages, complimentary laundry. **Business Services:** PC. **Cards:** AX, CB, DC, DS, MC, VI. **Special Amenities:** free expanded continental breakfast and free local telephone calls.

THE SILVERBOW INN BAKERY & RESTAURANT   *Book at aaa.com*   Phone: (907)586-4146

	7/1-8/31	1P: $138-$148	2P: $138-$148	XP: $20
	5/16-6/30	1P: $108-$128	2P: $118-$138	XP: $20
	3/1-5/15	1P: $88-$98	2P: $98-$108	XP: $20
	9/1-2/28	1P: $78-$88	2P: $88-$98	XP: $20

Historic Bed & Breakfast

Location: Downtown. 120 2nd St 99801. **Fax:** 907/586-4242. **Facility:** This restored 1914 building has quaint guest rooms with cheery, bright decor. Smoke free premises. 6 one-bedroom standard units. 3 stories (no elevator), interior corridors. **Parking:** on-site. **Terms:** 2 night minimum stay - seasonal, 3 day cancellation notice-fee imposed. **Amenities:** video library, voice mail, hair dryers. **Guest Services:** valet laundry. **Cards:** AX, DS, MC, VI.

SOME UNITS

`ASK` `[11+]` `X` `K` `🐾` `/VCR/`

WESTMARK BARANOF   *Book at aaa.com*   Phone: (907)586-2660

(AAA) (SAVE)

| | 5/16-9/15 | 1P: $159 | 2P: $159 | XP: $15 | F12 |
| | 3/1-5/15 & 9/16-2/28 | 1P: $139 | 2P: $139 | XP: $15 | F12 |

Small-scale Hotel

Location: At 2nd and Franklin sts; downtown. 127 N. Franklin St 99801. **Fax:** 907/586-8315. **Facility:** 196 units. 174 one-bedroom standard units, some with kitchens. 22 one-bedroom suites ($199-$229), some with efficiencies. 9 stories, interior corridors. **Bath:** combo or shower only. **Parking:** on-site. **Terms:** pets (with prior approval). **Amenities:** voice mail, irons. **Dining:** 2 restaurants, 6:30 am-2 & 5-10 pm, cocktails. **Guest Services:** gift shop, valet laundry. **Business Services:** conference facilities. **Cards:** AX, DC, DS, MC, VI.

SOME UNITS

`🐕` `11` `Y` `∅` `K` `*` `DATA PORT` `🖥` `/X` `🔌`

—— WHERE TO DINE ——

BACAR'S   Lunch: $6-$12   Phone: 907/463-4202

(AAA)

American

Location: Center. 230 Seward St 99801. **Hours:** 6 am-3 pm. Closed: 7/4, 11/24; also 2 weeks after Christmas. **Reservations:** accepted. **Features:** The restaurant is the place to go to get away from the hustle and bustle of the cruise ships. Many locals mention the popular family diner when asked about a place to eat. On the menu are hearty all-day breakfast dishes, as well as sandwiches, soups and salmon. The simple, yet cozy, dining room is tucked away from the crowds, and service is friendly and attentive. Casual dress. **Parking:** street. **Cards:** AX, DS, MC, VI.

`K` `X`

BREAKWATER INN RESTAURANT   Lunch: $15-$20   Dinner: $20-$30   Phone: 907/586-6303

(AAA)

Steak & Seafood

Location: Jct Highland Dr; in Breakwater Inn Hotel. 1711 Glacier Ave 99801. **Hours:** 7 am-10 pm, Fri & Sat-midnight. **Reservations:** accepted. **Features:** Located on the second floor, this nautical-themed restaurant commands an impressive view of the harbor where the chef purchases the daily specials such as fresh salmon, king crabs and clams as they are brought in by fishermen. Casual dress; cocktails. **Parking:** on-site. **Cards:** AX, DC, DS, MC, VI.

`Y` `X`

CHAN'S THAI KITCHEN   Lunch: $8-$12   Dinner: $8-$15   Phone: 907/789-9777

Thai

Location: 12 mi nw on Glacier Hwy; at Auke Bay; across from Auke Bay harbor. 11820 Glacier Hwy 99801. **Hours:** 11:30 am-2 & 4:30-8:30 pm, Sat from 4:30 pm, Sun 4:30 pm-8 pm. Closed: 7/4, 11/24; also 12/15-1/15. **Reservations:** not accepted. **Features:** This nondescript eatery tucked away in a small strip mall across from Auke Bay Marina will be worth finding. Authentic Thai cooking is served up hot and spicy. The spring rolls are some of the best to be had. This extremely popular restaurant does not take reservations and the seating is limited, so expect a wait for a table in the evening. Casual dress. **Parking:** on-site. **Cards:** MC, VI.

`K` `X`

DI SOPRA   Dinner: $16-$29   Phone: 907/586-3150

Italian

Location: At Whittier St; downtown; upstairs from the Fiddlehead Restaurant. 429 W Willoughby Ave 99801. **Hours:** 5 pm-9:30 pm. Closed: 11/24, 12/25. **Reservations:** suggested. **Features:** "Di sopra" literally translates to "upstairs," and so guests find the restaurant located upstairs from the Fiddlehead. Up a notch in decor, food and service, this place unites chic decor with both Alaskan and Italian cuisine. Fine dining remains friendly and welcoming. Casual dress; cocktails. **Parking:** on-site. **Cards:** AX, DS, MC, VI.

`X`

FERNANDO'S   Lunch: $4-$9   Dinner: $8-$13   Phone: 907/463-3992

Traditional Mexican

Location: Downtown; across from Westmark Baronoff Hotel. 116 N Franklin St 99801. **Hours:** 11 am-9 pm. Closed major holidays; also Sun. **Reservations:** accepted. **Features:** Mexican food is artfully served in the small eatery in the historic district. The overhead trellis with its trailing plants helps transport diners to old Mexico. The selection of foods prepared with all fresh ingredients delights the palate. Casual dress; wine only. **Parking:** street. **Cards:** AX, DC, DS, MC, VI.

`K` `X`

FIDDLEHEAD RESTAURANT & BAKERY   Lunch: $7-$15   Dinner: $15-$25   Phone: 907/586-3150

American

Location: At Whittier St; downtown. 429 W Willoughby Ave 99801. **Hours:** 7 am-10 pm; 8 am-9 pm in winter. Closed: 1/1, 11/24, 12/25. **Reservations:** suggested. **Features:** In the heart of downtown Juneau, in an unpretentious building, two restaurants are housed. Both are Fiddlehead but one is on the ground floor and is more casual, trendy and informal. Up a notch in decor, food and service, is the second floor dining room known as Di Sopra (meaning "upstairs"). There, classic decor unites with both Alaskan and Italian cuisine to offer you the option of fine dining which is still friendly and welcoming. Casual dress; beer & wine only. **Parking:** on-site. **Cards:** AX, DS, MC, VI.

`X`

GOLD CREEK SALMON BAKE   Lunch: $29   Dinner: $29   Phone: 907/789-0052

American

Location: Jct Glacier Hwy and Hospital Dr, just n. 1061 Salmon Creek Ln 99801. **Hours:** Open 5/15-9/21; 11 am-2 & 5-8 pm. **Features:** Catering to cruise ship customers, this outdoor buffet offers all-you-can-eat wood-grilled salmon filets in a forest mining camp setting. Casual dress; cocktails. **Parking:** on-site. **Cards:** AX, DS, MC, VI.

`🅼` `K` `X`

THE HANGAR ON THE WHARF

Lunch: $7-$16　　**Dinner:** $12-$27　　**Phone:** 907/586-5018

American

Location: On the wharf at the Sea Plane runway; downtown. #2 Marine Way, Suite 106 99801. **Hours:** 11 am-10 pm; hours may vary in winter. Closed: 11/24, 12/25. **Features:** Located on the wharf and popular with locals, the vibrant eatery offers no-frills dining. Guests can watch seaplanes take off and land while munching on fried halibut fingers and sipping an Alaskan Brewing Company amber ale. Casual dress; cocktails. **Parking:** on-site. **Cards:** AX, DS, MC, VI.

SILVERBOW BAGELS

Lunch: $7-$15　　**Phone:** 907/586-4146

Deli/Subs
Sandwiches

Location: Jct Main and 2nd sts; downtown. 120 2nd St 99801. **Hours:** 7 am-6 pm, Sat & Sun 9 am-4 pm; Sat 7 am-6 pm 6/1-9/15. Closed: 1/1, 12/25. **Features:** You'll have fun at the Silverbow, a restored historical structure, with its funky decor and classic and golden oldies films shown two nights a week. Kids can color on the table covers too. A New York-style bakery is adjacent and offers sinful desserts. Casual dress; beer & wine only. **Parking:** on-site. **Cards:** DS, MC, VI.

THE SUMMIT RESTAURANT

Dinner: $16-$25　　**Phone:** 907/586-2050

Regional American

Location: Downtown; across the street from Tram. 455 S Franklin St 99801. **Hours:** 5 pm-10 pm. **Reservations:** suggested. **Features:** The chef prepares not only regional seafoods with a creative flair, but you will also find some French cuisine offered. Located on the main street in an historic inn, the restaurant allows you to enjoy people watching through the windows or holding hands over candlelight in this intimate setting. Casual dress; beer & wine only. **Parking:** street. **Cards:** AX, MC, VI.

TIMBERLINE BAR & GRILL

Lunch: $8-$11　　**Dinner:** $13-$29　　**Phone:** 907/463-3412

American

Location: Downtown, then to the top of the Mount Roberts Tramway. 490 S Franklin 99801. **Hours:** Open 5/10-9/25; 11 am-9 pm. **Features:** Take a six-minute cable car ride to the top of Mount Roberts—$21.95 for adults and $10.95 for children—from which you'll be treated to stunning views of Juneau and the Gastineau Channel below. It also takes you to this restaurant, which would be equally worthy at sea level. The Alaskan Alpine experience is sure to be memorable. Casual dress; cocktails; entertainment. **Parking:** on-site. **Cards:** AX, CB, DC, DS, MC, VI.

TWISTED FISH COMPANY

Lunch: $6-$11　　**Dinner:** $9-$29　　**Phone:** 907/463-5033

Seafood

Location: Downtown. 455 S Franklin St 99801. **Hours:** Open 5/1-9/30; 11 am-10 pm. **Features:** Alaskan seafood is the specialty at this restaurant, located on the pier near the cruise ship landing areas. Service is quick and friendly, and on those sunny days enjoy dining al fresco. Casual dress; beer & wine only. **Parking:** on-site. **Cards:** AX, DS, MC, VI.

KENAI pop. 6,942

——— **WHERE TO STAY** ———

HARBORSIDE COTTAGES

Phone: (907)283-6162

Cottage

Location: Just s on Main St, then just e; center. 813 Riverview Dr 99611 (PO Box 942). Fax: 907/283-0906. 5/1-10/1 [CP]　　1P: $125-$165　　2P: $125-$165. **Facility:** Smoke free premises. 5 cottages ($125-$165). 1 story, exterior corridors. *Bath:* shower only. **Parking:** on-site. **Terms:** open 5/1-10/1, check-in 4 pm, 3 night minimum stay - seasonal, 30 day cancellation notice. **Amenities:** irons. **Leisure Activities:** barbecue deck with picnic table, breakfast basket. **Cards:** AX, DS, MC, VI. **Special Amenities:** free continental breakfast and free local telephone calls.

——— **WHERE TO DINE** ———

PARADISOS RESTAURANT

Lunch: $5-$15　　**Dinner:** $10-$29　　**Phone:** 907/283-2222

Italian

Location: Downtown. Main St & Frontage Rd 99611. **Hours:** 11 am-11 pm, Fri & Sat-midnight. Closed: 11/24, 12/25. **Reservations:** suggested. **Features:** Greek, Mexican and Italian selections round out this restaurant's extensive menu, which also offers steak and fresh local seafood such as halibut and Alaskan king crab legs. Expect to be served good-size portions in a bustling, welcoming ambience. Casual dress; cocktails. **Parking:** on-site. **Cards:** AX, DS, MC, VI.

VERONICA'S

American

Lunch: $6-$11   **Dinner:** $6-$11   **Phone:** 907/283-2725

Location: In historic district. 604 Peterson Way 99611. **Hours:** Open 5/1-12/31; 9 am-7 pm. **Features:** This charming bistro is the perfect spot to savor a homemade pastry with an aromatic cup of coffee or tea. Available until the early evening, delicious specialty lunch dishes—such as salmon in puff pastry, creative soups and pecan chicken salad—are made in-house. Casual dress. **Parking:** on-site. **Historic** [image]

KETCHIKAN pop. 7,922

-------- **WHERE TO STAY** --------

BEST WESTERN LANDING   *Book at aaa.com*   **Phone:** (907)225-5166

5/1-9/30	1P: $155-$175	2P: $165-$185	XP: $10	F12
10/1-2/28	1P: $125-$149	2P: $135-$159	XP: $10	F12
3/1-4/30	1P: $119-$145	2P: $129-$155	XP: $10	F12

Location: Across from the Alaska Marine Hwy ferry terminal. 3434 Tongass Ave 99901. Fax: 907/225-6900. **Small-scale Hotel Facility:** 76 units. 60 one-bedroom standard units. 15 one- and 1 two-bedroom suites, some with kitchens. 2-3 stories, interior/exterior corridors. **Parking:** on-site. **Terms:** pets ($50 deposit, $10 extra charge). **Amenities:** irons, hair dryers. **Dining:** 2 restaurants, 6 am-11 pm; to 10 pm 11/1-4/30, cocktails. **Leisure Activities:** exercise room. **Guest Services:** sundries, valet laundry, area transportation-within city limits. **Business Services:** meeting rooms. **Cards:** AX, DC, DS, MC, VI. **Special Amenities: early check-in/late check-out and preferred room (subject to availability with advance reservations).**

SOME UNITS

[icons] FEE

KETCHIKAN SUPER 8 MOTEL   *Book at aaa.com*   **Phone:** (907)225-9088

5/1-2/28	1P: $100-$105	2P: $120-$135	XP: $10	F12
3/1-4/30	1P: $82-$92	2P: $97-$107	XP: $10	F12

Small-scale Hotel Location: From Alaska Marine Hwy ferry terminal, 0.9 mi se to Washington St, then just s; from airport ferry terminal, 1.3 mi se. 2151 Sea Level Dr 99901. Fax: 907/225-1072. **Facility:** 82 one-bedroom standard units. 4 stories, interior corridors. **Parking:** on-site. **Terms:** weekly rates available, small pets only. **Amenities:** safes (fee). **Guest Services:** coin laundry, area transportation. **Business Services:** meeting rooms. **Cards:** AX, CB, DC, DS, MC, VI.

SOME UNITS

[icons] FEE

WESTCOAST CAPE FOX LODGE   *Book at aaa.com*   **Phone:** (907)225-8001

5/1-9/30	1P: $189-$199	2P: $189-$199	XP: $30	F12
3/1-4/30 & 10/1-2/28	1P: $139-$149	2P: $139-$149	XP: $30	F12

Location: Above Creek St (Tramway from Creek St). 800 Venetia Way 99901. Fax: 907/225-8286. **Facility:** 72 units. 70 one-bedroom standard units. 2 one-bedroom suites with whirlpools. 3 stories, interior/exterior **Large-scale Hotel** corridors. **Bath:** combo or shower only. **Parking:** on-site. **Terms:** [AP] & [BP] meal plans available, package plans, $2 service charge. **Amenities:** voice mail, irons, hair dryers. **Fee:** video games, high-speed Internet. **Dining:** Heen Kahidi Dining Room & Lounge, see separate listing. **Guest Services:** gift shop, valet laundry. **Business Services:** meeting rooms. **Cards:** AX, DC, DS, MC, VI. **Special Amenities: free local telephone calls and preferred room (subject to availability with advance reservations).**

SOME UNITS

[icons]

-------- **WHERE TO DINE** --------

ANNABELLE'S FAMOUS KEG & CHOWDER HOUSE   **Lunch:** $13-$34   **Dinner:** $13-$34   **Phone:** 907/225-9423

Seafood

Location: Center; across from cruise ship docks; in Gilmour Hotel. 326 Front St 99901. **Hours:** 10 am-10 pm; 11 am-9 pm off season. Closed: 1/1, 11/24, 12/25; also Sun. **Features:** Located directly across from the cruise ship docks, diners can enjoy freshly caught seasonal seafood such as fresh salmon, clam chowder or halibut cheeks in either an attractive bar or classy dining room. Casual dress; cocktails. **Parking:** street. **Cards:** AX, DS, MC, VI. [icons]

HEEN KAHIDI DINING ROOM & LOUNGE   **Lunch:** $8-$15   **Dinner:** $16-$40   **Phone:** 907/225-8001

American

Location: Above Creek St (Tramway from Creek St); in Westcoast Cape Fox Lodge. 800 Venetia Way 99901. **Hours:** 7 am-3 & 5:30-9 pm; to 10 pm in summer. Closed: 11/24, 12/25. **Reservations:** accepted. **Features:** Perched 130 feet above Creek Street and high above the busy cruise ship harbor is the Westcoast Cape Fox Lodge and its reputable dining room, Heen Kahidi—meaning "house by the creek." This place is legendary for celebrating special events. Local seafood anchors the menu, which also includes aged beef, chicken and pasta. Spectacular views of the harbor are framed by pine boughs just outside the windows. Casual dress; cocktails. **Parking:** on-site. **Cards:** AX, CB, DC, DS, MC, VI. [icons]

THE NARROWS RESTAURANT   **Lunch:** $7-$12   **Dinner:** $15-$25   **Phone:** 907/247-2600

American

Location: 1.6 mi n from Alaska Marine Hwy ferry terminal; 1.2 mi n from Airport ferry terminal. 4871 N Tongass Hwy 99901. **Hours:** 9 am-2 & 5-9 pm, Sun-2 pm; seasonal hours may vary. Closed: Sun 10/1-5/1. **Reservations:** accepted. **Features:** Named for the Tongass Narrows on whose shores it is located, the restaurant offers casual dining about 1.5 miles north of town. The quiet rain-forest setting is adjacent to The Narrows Inn. The menu features fresh local seafood as well as pasta, steaks and chops. Casual dress; cocktails. **Parking:** on-site. **Cards:** AX, CB, DC, DS, MC, VI. [icons]

NEW YORK CAFE   **Lunch:** $8-$12   **Phone:** 907/225-0246

American

Location: Adjacent to Creek St; center. 211 Stedman St 99901. **Hours:** 7 am-3 pm, Sun-2 pm. Closed major holidays. **Features:** Popular with the local crowd, this casual storefront restaurant is located steps away from the historic town. While not wide ranging, the menu offers a variety of creatively prepared dishes including fresh, locally caught seafood. Casual dress. **Parking:** street. **Cards:** AX, MC, VI. [icon]

SALMON FALLS RESORT
▼▼▼▼ ▼▼▼▼
Steak & Seafood
Dinner: $22-$36
Phone: 907/225-2752
Location: 14.5 mi n from Alaska Marine Hwy ferry terminal; 14.1 mi n from Airport ferry terminal. 16707 Tongass Hwy 99901. **Hours:** Open 5/25-9/15; 5 pm-10:30 pm. **Reservations:** accepted. **Features:** Overlooking the Clarence Straits and Behm Canal of the Inland Passageway, the restaurant serves fresh northern water seafood and grilled steaks. Casual dress; cocktails. **Parking:** on-site. **Cards:** AX, MC, VI.

STEAMERS ON THE DOCK
▼▼▼▼ ▼▼▼▼
Seafood
Lunch: $13-$34
Dinner: $13-$34
Phone: 907/225-1600
Location: Across from cruise ship dock; on 3rd floor of Commercial Building; center. 76 Front St 99901. **Hours:** 10 am-10 pm; 11 am-9 pm off season. Closed major holidays; also Sun. **Features:** The casual third floor restaurant commands a magnificent view of Ketchikan harbor and features a variety of locally caught seafood including salmon and clams. Casual dress; cocktails. **Parking:** street. **Cards:** AX, DS, MC, VI.

KLAWOCK pop. 854

——— **WHERE TO STAY** ———

——— *The following lodging was either not evaluated or did not* ———
meet AAA rating requirements but is listed for your information only.

FIREWEED LODGE
[fyi]
Phone: 907/775-2930
Not evaluated. **Location:** 4.5 mi w of Hollis ferry terminal. 6863 Klawock/Hollis Hwy 99925 (PO Box 116). Facilities, services, and decor characterize a mid-range property.

KODIAK pop. 6,334

——— **WHERE TO STAY** ———

BEST WESTERN KODIAK INN   *Book at aaa.com*
AAA [SAVE]
▼▼▼▼ ▼▼▼▼
Small-scale Hotel
Phone: (907)486-5712

	5/16-9/15	1P: $109-$129	2P: $109-$129	XP: $15	F17
	9/16-10/31	1P: $99-$119	2P: $99-$119	XP: $15	F17
	3/1-5/15 & 11/1-2/28	1P: $89-$109	2P: $89-$109	XP: $15	F17

Location: 0.3 mi w of ferry terminal; center. 236 W Rezanof Dr 99615. Fax: 907/486-3430. **Facility:** 80 units. 78 one-bedroom standard units. 2 one-bedroom suites ($209-$229). 3 stories, interior/exterior corridors. **Parking:** on-site. **Terms:** 30 day cancellation notice-fee imposed, weekly rates available, [AP] & [BP] meal plans available, package plans, pets ($25 fee, $50 deposit). **Amenities:** voice mail, irons, hair dryers. *Some:* high-speed Internet. **Dining:** 6:30 am-10 pm; 7 am-9 pm off season, cocktails. **Leisure Activities:** whirlpool, fish and game freezer. **Guest Services:** gift shop, coin laundry, area transportation-ferry. **Business Services:** meeting rooms, fax (fee). **Cards:** AX, DC, DS, MC, VI. **Special Amenities:** free local telephone calls and free newspaper.

SOME UNITS

MOOSE PASS pop. 206

——— **WHERE TO STAY** ———

TRAIL LAKE LODGE
AAA [SAVE]
▼▼▼▼
Motel
Phone: (907)288-3101

| | 6/1-8/31 | 1P: $89-$105 | 2P: $89-$105 | XP: $10 | F12 |
| | 3/1-5/31, 9/1-9/30 & 11/1-2/28 | 1P: $59-$89 | 2P: $59-$89 | XP: $10 | F12 |

Location: US 9 (Seward Hwy) at MM 29.5. MM 29.5 Seward Hwy 99631 (PO Box 5). Fax: 907/288-3106. **Facility:** Designated smoking area. 22 one-bedroom standard units. 1-2 stories (no elevator), exterior corridors. *Bath:* shower only. **Parking:** on-site. **Terms:** open 3/1-9/30 & 11/1-2/28, office hours 7 am-10 pm, 7 day cancellation notice, pets ($50 deposit). **Dining:** 7 am-9 pm, Fri & Sat-10 pm, cocktails. **Guest Services:** gift shop. **Cards:** AX, DS, MC, VI.

SOME UNITS

PETERSBURG pop. 3,224

——— **WHERE TO STAY** ———

——— *The following lodging was either not evaluated or did not* ———
meet AAA rating requirements but is listed for your information only.

SCANDIA HOUSE
[fyi]
Phone: 907/772-4281
Not evaluated. **Location:** Downtown. 110 Nordic Dr 99833 (PO Box 689). Facilities, services, and decor characterize a mid-range property.

SELDOVIA pop. 286

——— **WHERE TO STAY** ———

——— *The following lodging was either not evaluated or did not* ———
meet AAA rating requirements but is listed for your information only.

SWAN HOUSE SOUTH B & B
[fyi]
Phone: 907/234-8888
Not evaluated. **Location:** E on Main St, ne on Airport Rd, just s on North Rd after the Seldovia Slough bridge, look for double swans sign; center. 175 N Augustine 99663 (6840 Crooked Tree Dr, ANCHORAGE, 99516). Facilities, services, and decor characterize a mid-range property.

——— WHERE TO DINE ———

THE MAD FISH RESTAURANT **Lunch:** $8-$17 **Dinner:** $15-$28 **Phone:** 907/234-7676
◈◈ ◈◈ **Location:** Center. 221 Main St 99663. **Hours:** Open 5/1-9/5; noon-3 & 5:30-8:30 pm, Fri & Sat-9 pm.
American **Reservations:** suggested. **Features:** A fun and vibrant eatery serving creative fare ranging from seafood to vegetarian dishes and homemade gourmet desserts. Casual dress; beer & wine only. **Parking:** on-site.
Cards: MC, VI.

SEWARD pop. 2,830

——— WHERE TO STAY ———

BOX CANYON CABINS **Phone:** (907)224-5046
◈◈ ◈◈ All Year [CP] 1P: $130-$230 2P: $130-$230 XP: $15
Cabin **Location:** 3.5 mi n on SR 9, just w on Herman Leirer Rd; 1 mi n on Old Exit Glacier Rd, just e. 31515 Lois Way 99664 (PO Box 1662). Fax: 907/694-5074. **Facility:** Smoke free premises. 5 cabins. 1 story, exterior corridors. *Bath:* shower only. **Parking:** on-site, winter plug-ins. **Terms:** check-in 4 pm, 30 day cancellation notice-fee imposed. **Amenities:** hair dryers. **Leisure Activities:** hiking trails. *Fee:* charter fishing. **Cards:** MC, VI.

(ASK) ⊠ (Ⓚ) 🎥 🔒 ☎ 🖥

HARBORVIEW INN *Book at aaa.com* **Phone:** (907)224-3217
(AAA) (SAVE) 5/1-9/30 1P: $79-$139 2P: $79-$139 XP: $10
◈◈ ◈◈ 3/1-4/30 & 10/1-2/28 1P: $59 2P: $59 XP: $10
Motel **Location:** Just n of the Alaska Sealife Center. 804 Third Ave 99664 (PO Box 1305). Fax: 907/224-3218. **Facility:** Smoke free premises. 39 units. 36 one-bedroom standard units. 2 two- and 1 three-bedroom suites ($149-$189) with kitchens. 2 stories (no elevator), exterior corridors. *Bath:* combo or shower only. **Parking:** on-site, winter plug-ins. **Terms:** office hours 8 am-10 pm, check-in 4 pm, 3 day cancellation notice. **Amenities:** hair dryers. **Cards:** AX, DS, MC, VI. **Special Amenities:** free local telephone calls. *(See color ad below)*

SOME UNITS
⊠ (Ⓚ) (DATA PORT) 🖥 / 🔒 ☎

HOTEL EDGEWATER *Book at aaa.com* **Phone:** (907)224-2700
(AAA) (SAVE) 5/15-9/15 [CP] 1P: $110-$245 2P: $110-$245 XP: $10 F18
◈◈ ◈◈ 3/1-5/14 & 9/16-2/28 [CP] 1P: $69-$89 2P: $69-$89 XP: $10 F18
Small-scale Hotel **Location:** Just n of Alaska Sealife Center. 200 5th Ave 99664 (PO Box 1570). Fax: 907/224-2701. **Facility:** 76 one-bedroom standard units. 3 stories, interior corridors. *Bath:* combo or shower only. **Parking:** on-site and valet. **Terms:** 3 day cancellation notice. **Amenities:** video library, dual phone lines, hair dryers. **Leisure Activities:** sauna, whirlpool, limited exercise equipment. **Guest Services:** gift shop, valet laundry, airport transportation-Seward Airport, area transportation-within 5 mi & train depot. **Business Services:** meeting rooms, PC. **Cards:** AX, DS, MC, VI. **Special Amenities:** free continental breakfast and free local telephone calls. *(See color ad p 724)*

SOME UNITS
(S/D) ✈ 🍴 (♿) ⊠ (Ⓚ) (VCR) 🎥 (DATA PORT) 🖥 / ⊠ 🔒 ☎

RIVER VALLEY CABINS **Phone:** (907)224-5740
(AAA) (SAVE) 6/1-9/7 2P: $135-$225 XP: $15 D14
◈◈ ◈◈ **Location:** 3.5 mi n on SR 9, just w on Herman Leirer Rd, 1 mi n on Old Exit Glacier Rd (gravel), follow signs. Located in a quiet area. 12672 Old Exit Glacier Rd 99664 (PO Box 1910). Fax: 907/224-2333. **Facility:** Smoke free premises.
Cabin 8 cabins. 1 story, exterior corridors. *Bath:* combo or shower only. **Parking:** on-site. **Terms:** open 6/1-9/7, check-in 4 pm, 14 day cancellation notice. **Amenities:** hair dryers. **Leisure Activities:** hiking trails. **Cards:** DC, MC, VI. **Special Amenities:** free local telephone calls and early check-in/late check-out.

SOME UNITS
⊠ (Ⓚ) 🔒 🖥 / (W) (Z) ☎ /

SEWARD WINDSONG LODGE

 [AAA] **[SAVE]**

6/1-8/31　　　　　　　　1P: $199-$239　　2P: $199-$239　　XP: $15　　　　F11
5/14-5/31 & 9/1-9/18　　1P: $129-$179　　2P: $129-$179　　XP: $15　　　　F11

Phone: (907)224-7116

◆◆◆ **Location:** 3.5 mi n on SR 9, 0.5 mi w on Herman Leirer Rd (former exit Glacier Rd). Milepost 0.5 Herman Leirer Rd 99664 (PO Box 2301). Fax: 907/224-7118. **Facility:** Smoke free premises. 108 one-bedroom standard units,
Small-scale Hotel　some with whirlpools. 2 stories (no elevator), exterior corridors. *Bath:* combo or shower only. **Parking:** on-site. **Terms:** open 5/14-9/18, 15 day cancellation notice-fee imposed, [AP] meal plan available.
Amenities: video library, voice mail, hair dryers. **Dining:** Resurrection Roadhouse, see separate listing. **Guest Services:** gift shop, airport transportation-Seward Airport, area transportation-downtown & harbor. **Business Services:** conference facilities.
Cards: AX, DS, MC, VI. **Special Amenities:** free local telephone calls. *(See color ad below)*

SOME UNITS

——— WHERE TO DINE ———

CHRISTO'S PALACE **Lunch:** $8-$16 **Dinner:** $15-$25 **Phone:** 907/224-5255
▼▼ ▼▼ **Location:** Across from Alaska Sealife Center; downtown. 133 Fourth Ave 99664. **Hours:** 11 am-11 pm; hours may
vary in winter. Closed: 3/27, 11/24, 12/25. **Reservations:** accepted. **Features:** Locals are quick to
Continental recommend the restaurant for its plush, open dining room; friendly, attentive service; and varied menu.
Among selections are preparations of pasta, sandwiches, hamburgers and fresh seafood. Cocktails.
Parking: street. **Cards:** AX, DS, MC, VI.

PEKING RESTAURANT **Lunch:** $7 **Dinner:** $9-$15 **Phone:** 907/224-5444
▼▼ ▼▼ **Location:** Downtown. 338 4th Ave 99664. **Hours:** 10 am-11 pm. Closed major holidays.
Reservations: accepted. **Features:** The traditional restaurant serves a variety of dishes, including chicken
Chinese balls and lemon chicken and rice, as well as dishes inspired by the area. For a new twist, try the kung pao
halibut, a tasty dish that is sure to please. At lunch you satisfy any hunger at the all-you-can-eat buffet, or
order a la carte off the menu. Casual dress; cocktails. **Parking:** street. **Cards:** AX, CB, DC, DS, JC, MC, VI.

RESURRECTION ROADHOUSE **Lunch:** $5-$15 **Dinner:** $11-$26 **Phone:** 907/224-7116
▼▼ ▼▼ **Location:** 3.5 mi n on SR 9, 0.5 mi w on Herman Leirer Rd (formerly exit Glacier Rd); in Seward Windsong Lodge.
Milepost 0.6 (Herman Leirer Rd) 99664. **Hours:** Open 5/1-9/15; 5:30 am-10:30 pm. **Reservations:** accepted.
Regional American **Features:** Continuing the theme of the adjacent lodge, you'll be seated in a dining room with a natural wood
decor while enjoying the views of the wooded setting overlooking a glacial stream. Heaping portions of tasty
Alaskan seafood is the standout here. Casual dress; cocktails. **Parking:** on-site. **Cards:** AX, DS, MC, VI.
(See color ad p 724)

SITKA pop. 8,835

——— WHERE TO STAY ———

ALASKA OCEAN VIEW BED AND BREAKFAST INN *Book at aaa.com* **Phone:** (907)747-8310
▼▼▼▼▼ 5/15-9/15 [BP] 1P: $109-$169 2P: $129-$199 XP: $20 D15
3/1-5/14 [ECP] 1P: $89-$119 2P: $89-$159 XP: $15 D15
9/16-12/31 [BP] 1P: $80-$119 2P: $89-$159 XP: $20 D15
Bed & Breakfast 1/1-2/28 [ECP] 1P: $79-$119 2P: $89-$139 XP: $10 D15
Location: 1 mi n on Halibut Point Rd; 5.7 mi s of Alaska Marine Hwy ferry terminal, just e on Kashevarof St, then just s. Located in a
residential area. 1101 Edgecumbe Dr 99835. Fax: 907/747-3440. **Facility:** Attractively decorated rooms with excellent amenities are
offered at this ocean-view B&B; a garden pond enhances the setting. Smoke free premises. 3 one-bedroom standard units,
some with whirlpools. 2 stories (no elevator), interior corridors. **Parking:** on-site. **Terms:** 2 night minimum stay - seasonal, 60
day cancellation notice, peak season-fee imposed. **Amenities:** video library, DVD players, CD players, high-speed Internet,
irons, hair dryers. **Leisure Activities:** whirlpool, horseshoes. **Cards:** AX, CB, DC, DS, MC, VI.

HELGA'S BED & BREAKFAST BY THE SEA **Phone:** 907/747-5497
▼▼ ▼▼ All Year 1P: $75 2P: $85 XP: $20
Location: 3 mi n on Halibut Point Rd; or 3.4 mi s of Alaska Marine Hwy ferry terminal. 2827 Halibut Point Rd 99835 (PO
Box 1885). **Facility:** Smoke free premises. 4 units. 3 one-bedroom standard units. 1 two-bedroom suite
Bed & Breakfast ($170). 2 stories (no elevator), interior corridors. *Bath:* combo or shower only. **Parking:** on-site. **Terms:** age
restrictions may apply, 30 day cancellation notice-fee imposed. **Guest Services:** coin laundry. **Cards:** AX, MC, VI.

SUPER 8 MOTEL-SITKA *Book at aaa.com* **Phone:** 907/747-8804
▼▼ ▼▼ 6/1-9/30 1P: $112-$122 2P: $119-$129 XP: $6 F12
3/1-5/31 & 10/1-2/28 1P: $94-$104 2P: $100-$110 XP: $6 F12
Small-scale Hotel **Location:** Just e from corner of Lake St and Halibut Point/Sawmill Creek rds; center. 404 Sawmill Creek Rd 99835.
Fax: 907/747-6101. **Facility:** 35 one-bedroom standard units. 2 stories (no elevator), interior corridors.
Parking: on-site. **Terms:** pets (with prior approval). **Leisure Activities:** whirlpool. **Guest Services:** coin laundry. **Cards:** AX,
CB, DC, DS, JC, MC, VI.
SOME UNITS

TOTEM SQUARE INN   *Book at aaa.com*

▼▼▼▼   6/1-8/31   1P: $119   Phone: (907)747-6302
              XP: $15
Location: Center; in Totem Square Complex (near Municipal Office). 201 Katlian 99835. Fax: 907/747-6307.
Small-scale Hotel **Facility:** Smoke free premises. 66 one-bedroom standard units. 4 stories, interior corridors. **Parking:** on-site. **Terms:** open 6/1-8/31. **Amenities:** voice mail, hair dryers. **Guest Services:** coin laundry. **Business Services:** meeting rooms. **Cards:** AX, DC, MC, VI.

[ASK] [†↑→] [✕] [✗] [DATA PORT]

WESTMARK SITKA   *Book at aaa.com*

(AAA) [SAVE]   5/15-9/15   1P: $159   Phone: (907)747-6241
              XP: $15   F18
▼▼ ▼▼   3/1-5/14 & 9/16-2/28   1P: $149   XP: $15   F18
Location: Center. 330 Seward St 99835. Fax: 907/747-5486. **Facility:** 101 one-bedroom standard units, some with kitchens. 4 stories, interior corridors. *Bath:* combo or shower only. **Parking:** on-site. **Amenities:** video
Small-scale Hotel library (fee), voice mail, irons, hair dryers. *Some:* high-speed Internet. **Dining:** 6:30 am-2 & 5-10 pm, Sun & off season-9 pm, cocktails. **Guest Services:** valet laundry. **Business Services:** meeting rooms. **Cards:** AX, CB, DC, DS, JC, MC, VI.

SOME UNITS

[S/D] [†↑] [Y] [⌒] [✗] [DATA PORT] [▤] / [✕] [VCR] [▯] [☎]
                                    FEE   FEE

WILD STRAWBERRY LODGE FISHING RESORT   Phone: 907/747-8883

▼▼   5/1-8/31 [BP]   1P: $95-$105   2P: $95-$105   XP: $25   D12
Resort Motel 3/1-4/30 & 9/1-2/28 [CP]   1P: $50-$65   2P: $65-$75   XP: $25   D12
Location: 1 mi n on Halibut Point Rd, just w on Katlian (only traffic light on island). Located at Thomsen Harbor. 724 Siginaka Way 99835 (PO Box 2300). Fax: 907/747-3646. **Facility:** This is not your typical "fishing lodge," as the owners encourage males and females of all ages to try their hand at catching "the big one". Smoke free premises. 10 units. 8 one-bedroom standard units. 1 two-bedroom suite with kitchen. 1 vacation home. 1 story, interior/exterior corridors. *Bath:* combo or shower only. **Parking:** on-site. **Terms:** 60 day cancellation notice-fee imposed, weekly rates available. **Leisure Activities:** Fee: charter fishing. **Guest Services:** complimentary laundry, area transportation. **Business Services:** PC. **Cards:** AX, DC, MC, VI.

SOME UNITS

[↦] [✕] [✗] / [W] [VCR] [☎] [▯] [▭] [▤] /

———— WHERE TO DINE ————

BAYVIEW RESTAURANT   Lunch: $8-$15   Dinner: $12-$25   Phone: 907/747-5440

▼▼   **Location:** Center; on 2nd floor of Mac Donald Trading Company building. 407 Lincoln St 99835. **Hours:** 5 am-10 pm, Sun-3 pm; 7 am-3 pm off season. **Reservations:** accepted. **Features:** The second floor location can be
American difficult to find, but this casual restaurant offers an extensive menu ranging from sandwiches to fresh seafood and steak as well as a large variety of daily made desserts. Casual dress; cocktails. **Parking:** street. **Cards:** AX, DS, MC, VI.

[✗] [✕]

LUDVIG'S BISTRO   Lunch: $15-$18   Dinner: $20-$30   Phone: 907/747-5080

▼▼▼▼   **Location:** 0.3 mi n of Totem Square; center. 256 Katlian St 99835. **Hours:** 11:30 am-10 pm. Closed major holidays; also Sun & Mon. **Reservations:** suggested. **Features:** A popular choice with locals and visitors
Mediterranean alike, the restaurant serves a variety of Mediterranean fare prepared with a regional influence. Dressy casual; wine only. **Parking:** street. **Cards:** AX, DS, MC, VI.

[✕]

RAVEN DINING ROOM   Lunch: $8-$12   Dinner: $15-$22   Phone: 907/747-6241

▼▼ ▼▼   **Location:** Center; in Westmark Sitka. 330 Seward St 99835. **Hours:** 6:30 am-2 & 5-10 pm, Sun-9 pm; hours may vary off season. **Features:** This casual restaurant has long served as the training kitchen for chefs who later
American go on to work on the cruise ships that the restaurant overlooks. Diners can expect standard items ranging from sandwiches to steak as well as creative touches to locally caught and seasonal seafood. Casual dress; cocktails. **Parking:** on-site. **Cards:** AX, DS, MC, VI.

[&M] [Y] [✗] [✕]

TEA-LICIOUS TEA HOUSE & BAKERY   Lunch: $5-$7   Dinner: $5-$7   Phone: 907/747-4535

▼▼ ▼▼   **Location:** Center. 315 Lincoln St, Suite 110 99835. **Hours:** 10 am-6 pm. Closed major holidays; also Sun.
Deli/Subs **Features:** Not surprisingly, this casually upscale restaurant is the scene of many afternoon tea parties. As well as offering an extensive selection of both hot and iced teas, the restaurant features a variety of delicate
Sandwiches deli sandwiches and bakery items. Casual dress. **Parking:** street. **Cards:** AX, DS, MC, VI.

[✕]

VAN WINKLE & SONS RESTAURANT   Lunch: $7-$12   Dinner: $9-$26   Phone: 907/747-7652

▼▼ ▼▼   **Location:** Downtown; across from Crescent Harbor, just before O'Connell Bridge. 225 Harbor Dr 99835. **Hours:** 11:30 am-1:45 pm, Sat from 5 pm. Closed: 12/25; also Sun. **Reservations:** suggested, in summer.
American **Features:** Tasty regional cuisine awaits you at this popular eatery. Alaskan art adorns the walls, and you can gaze at the water while dining. Located upstairs of a small shopping mall near the bridge, the restaurant's view of the bay is spectacular and the food well prepared. Casual dress; cocktails. **Parking:** on-site. **Cards:** AX, MC, VI.

[&M] [✗] [✕]

SKAGWAY pop. 862

———— WHERE TO STAY ————

WESTMARK INN SKAGWAY   *Book at aaa.com*

▼▼▼▼   5/24-9/10   1P: $121   2P: $121   XP: $15   F12
Location: Downtown. 3rd & Spring St 99840 (PO Box 515). Fax: 907/983-6100. **Facility:** 151 one-bedroom
Small-scale Hotel standard units. 2 stories (no elevator), interior/exterior corridors. **Parking:** on-site. **Terms:** open 5/24-9/10, cancellation fee imposed, package plans, pets ($30 deposit). **Amenities:** irons, hair dryers. **Guest Services:** coin laundry, area transportation. **Business Services:** meeting rooms, PC. **Cards:** AX, DC, DS, MC, VI.

SOME UNITS

[ASK] [↦] [☂] [†↑] [&M] [✗] [▦] [DATA PORT] [▤] / [✕] [▯]
              FEE

——— WHERE TO DINE ———

BONANZA BAR & GRILL   **Lunch:** $6-$10   **Dinner:** $12-$15   **Phone:** 907/983-2420
American
Location: Jct 3rd and Broadway sts; downtown. 3rd & Spring St 99840. **Hours:** Open 5/15-9/15; 6 am-midnight. **Features:** Open seasonally, this sports bar can be loud and boisterous and is a popular spot for those looking for a wide selection of bar favorites. Casual dress; cocktails. **Parking:** street. **Cards:** AX, DS, MC, VI.

HAVEN CAFE   **Lunch:** $3-$8   **Dinner:** $3-$8   **Phone:** 907/983-3553
Coffee/Espresso
Location: 9th St and State. **Hours:** 6 am-10 pm; hours vary seasonally. Closed major holidays. **Reservations:** not accepted. **Features:** Off the beaten track from downtown, the upscale coffeehouse brews a great cup of coffee, which patrons often sip with one of the varied breakfast options, salads, panini sandwiches, shakes or desserts. The cozy refuge is attached to a health-food store. A few coveted tables are outside. Casual dress. **Parking:** street. **Cards:** MC, VI.

SWEET TOOTH CAFE   **Lunch:** $11-$20   **Phone:** 907/983-2405
American
Location: Jct 3rd St; downtown. 315 Broadway St 99840. **Hours:** 6 am-2 pm. Closed major holidays. **Features:** A local favorite, this casual Victorian-style restaurant offers few surprises but is well regarded for its well-prepared breakfasts and lunches. Casual dress. **Parking:** street. **Cards:** MC, VI.

SOLDOTNA pop. 3,759

——— WHERE TO STAY ———

ALASKAN SERENITY BED AND BREAKFAST   _Book at aaa.com_   **Phone:** (907)262-6648

Bed & Breakfast

5/1-9/30 [BP]	1P: $100-$175	2P: $100-$175	XP: $20
3/1-4/30 & 10/1-2/28 [BP]	1P: $75-$125	2P: $75-$125	XP: $10

Location: Sterling Hwy (SR 1), 1.5 mi e, 1.6 mi n on Mackey Lake Rd, then 0.5 mi e on Denise Lake Rd. 41598 Aksala Ln 99669 (Box 2734). Fax: 907/260-6609. **Facility:** Smoke free premises. 5 units. 2 one- and 1 two-bedroom standard units. 2 cabins. 2 stories (no elevator), interior/exterior corridors. _Bath:_ combo or shower only. **Parking:** on-site, winter plug-ins. **Terms:** check-in 4 pm, 2 night minimum stay - seasonal and/or weekends, 30 day cancellation notice-fee imposed, 5% service charge. **Amenities:** video library. **Leisure Activities:** whirlpool. **Cards:** AX, DS, MC, VI. **Special Amenities:** free full breakfast and free local telephone calls.
SOME UNITS

ASPEN HOTEL-SOLDOTNA   _Book at aaa.com_   **Phone:** (907)260-7736

Small-scale Hotel

5/16-9/15 [ECP]	1P: $159-$189	2P: $159-$189	XP: $10	F18
5/1-5/15 [ECP]	1P: $119-$149	2P: $119-$149	XP: $10	F18
3/1-4/30 & 9/16-2/28 [ECP]	1P: $99-$129	2P: $99-$129	XP: $10	F18

Location: Sterling Hwy (SR 1) at Binkley Cir; centre. 326 Binkley Cir 99669. Fax: 907/260-7786. **Facility:** 63 units. 58 one- and 2 two-bedroom standard units, some with whirlpools. 3 one-bedroom suites with efficiencies. 2 stories, interior corridors. _Bath:_ combo or shower only. **Parking:** on-site, winter plug-ins. **Terms:** cancellation fee imposed. **Amenities:** video library (fee), DVD players, high-speed Internet, dual phone lines, voice mail, irons, hair dryers. _Some:_ video games. **Pool(s):** small heated indoor. **Leisure Activities:** whirlpool, limited exercise equipment. **Guest Services:** valet and coin laundry. **Business Services:** meeting rooms, PC. **Cards:** AX, DC, DS, MC, VI.
SOME UNITS

BEST WESTERN KING SALMON MOTEL   _Book at aaa.com_   **Phone:** (907)262-5857

Motel

5/16-7/31	1P: $149-$159	2P: $159-$169	XP: $10	F12
8/1-8/31	1P: $109-$119	2P: $119-$129	XP: $10	F12
3/1-5/15 & 9/1-2/28	1P: $89-$99	2P: $99-$109	XP: $10	F12

Location: 1 mi nw on Kenai Spur Hwy. 35546 A Kenai Spur Hwy 99669 (PO Box 430). Fax: 907/262-9441. **Facility:** 48 one-bedroom standard units, some with efficiencies (no utensils). 2 stories (no elevator), exterior corridors. **Parking:** on-site, winter plug-ins. **Terms:** office hours 7 am-11 pm, check-in 4 pm, 14 day cancellation notice. **Amenities:** dual phone lines, voice mail, irons, hair dryers. _Some:_ high-speed Internet. **Dining:** 6 am-10 pm, cocktails. **Guest Services:** coin laundry. **Business Services:** meeting rooms, fax. **Cards:** AX, CB, DC, DS, MC, VI. **Special Amenities:** free local telephone calls and free room upgrade (subject to availability with advance reservations).
SOME UNITS
FEE

KENAI JIM'S LODGE & GUIDE SERVICE   **Phone:** (907)262-1324

Condominium

7/1-7/31	1P: $125	2P: $145	XP: $30	F5
5/1-6/30 & 8/1-9/30	1P: $95	2P: $125	XP: $30	F5

Location: Sterling Hwy (SR 1), 0.3 mi w on Kalifornsky Beach Rd, s on Polar St. Located in a quiet area. Polar St, Bldg A 99669 (PO Box 3675). **Facility:** Smoke free premises. 3 two-bedroom suites with kitchens. 2 stories (no elevator), interior corridors. **Parking:** on-site, winter plug-ins. **Terms:** open 5/1-9/30, package plans. **Leisure Activities:** Fee: charter fishing. **Guest Services:** coin laundry. **Cards:** MC, VI. **(See color ad p 332)**

KENAI RIVER RAVEN BED & BREAKFAST LODGE   **Phone:** (907)262-5818

Bed & Breakfast

7/1-7/31 [ECP]	1P: $200-$285	2P: $200-$285	XP: $50	D18
4/1-6/30 & 8/1-9/30 [ECP]	1P: $185-$250	2P: $185-$250	XP: $50	D18
10/1-10/31 [ECP]	1P: $160-$220	2P: $160-$220	XP: $50	D18

Location: Sterling Hwy (SR 1) at Milepost 96.5, just e. Mile 0.2 Funny River Rd 99669 (PO Box 3447). Fax: 907/260-3972. **Facility:** A modern log home in a secluded wooded area near the river, this B&B offers bright guest rooms; the breakfast room has a stone fireplace. Smoke free premises. 7 one-bedroom standard units, some with efficiencies and/or whirlpools. 3 stories (no elevator), interior corridors. **Parking:** on-site, winter plug-ins. **Terms:** open 4/1-10/31, check-in 4 pm, 2 night minimum stay - seasonal and/or weekends, age restrictions may apply, 45 day cancellation notice-fee imposed, package plans. **Leisure Activities:** fishing, river access. _Fee:_ fishing guides. **Cards:** AX, DS, MC, VI. **Special Amenities:** free expanded continental breakfast and free local telephone calls.
SOME UNITS

LONGMERE LAKE LODGE B & B

Phone: (907)262-9799

AAA [SAVE]

5/15-9/1 [BP]	1P: $98-$250	2P: $105-$255	XP: $25	D12
3/1-5/14 & 9/2-2/28 [BP]	1P: $75-$125	2P: $85-$150	XP: $15	D12

Bed & Breakfast

Location: 5 mi e of town at Milepost 88, on Sterling Hwy (SR 1); 1 mi s on St. Theresa Rd, then just w. Located in a quiet, secluded area. 35955 Ryan Ln 99669 (PO Box 2492). Fax: 907/262-7115. **Facility:** Smoke free premises. 6 units. 5 one-bedroom standard units, some with whirlpools. 1 one-bedroom suite with kitchen. 2 stories (no elevator), interior corridors. *Bath:* combo or shower only. **Parking:** on-site, winter plug-ins. **Terms:** check-in 4 pm, 14 day cancellation notice, no pets allowed (owner's dog on premises). **Amenities:** video library. **Leisure Activities:** canoeing, paddleboats, boat dock, fishing, freezer for fish, barbecue, croquet, horseshoes, volleyball. **Guest Services:** coin laundry. **Cards:** AX, MC, VI. **Special Amenities:** free local telephone calls and preferred room (subject to availability with advance reservations).

SOME UNITS

NORTH STAR BED & BREAKFAST

Phone: 907/262-6004

Property failed to provide current rates

Bed & Breakfast

Location: Sterling Hwy (SR 1) at Milepost 96.5, 0.5 mi e. 48494 Funny River Rd 99669 (PO Box 3292). Fax: 907/262-6004. **Facility:** Smoke free premises. 5 one-bedroom standard units. 2 stories (no elevator), interior corridors. *Bath:* shared. **Parking:** on-site, winter plug-ins. **Terms:** open 5/1-9/1. **Amenities:** video library. **Guest Services:** TV in common area.

ORCA LODGE

Phone: (907)262-5649

Cottage

5/1-9/30	1P: $150-$175	XP: $20	F12

Location: Sterling Hwy (SR 1) at Milepost 96.5, 0.8 mi e on Funny River Rd, just n. 44250 Oehler Dr 99669 (PO Box 4653). Fax: 907/262-9516. **Facility:** Smoke free premises. 6 cottages. 1 story, exterior corridors. **Parking:** on-site. **Terms:** open 5/1-9/30, 60 day cancellation notice, weekly rates available, package plans. **Leisure Activities:** whirlpool. *Fee:* charter fishing. **Cards:** AX, MC, VI.

PATRICK'S ALASKA FISHING & LODGING

Phone: (907)262-6468

Condominium

5/10-9/20	1P: $85	2P: $125-$195	XP: $30	D6

Location: Just s on Sterling Hwy (SR 1), 1.5 mi w on S Kubak, just s on So Hi Ln, then just w. 390 Starlight 99669 (382 S Kobuk). Fax: 907/262-6468. **Facility:** Smoke free premises. 4 two-bedroom suites with kitchens. 2 stories (no elevator), interior corridors. **Parking:** on-site, winter plug-ins. **Terms:** open 5/10-9/20, 15 day cancellation notice, weekly rates available, package plans. **Guest Services:** complimentary laundry. **Cards:** MC, VI.

—————— WHERE TO DINE ——————

CHARLOTTE'S RESTAURANT

Lunch: $6-$10   **Phone:** 907/283-2777

American

Location: Jct Sterling Hwy (SR 1) and Kenai Spur; attached to bookstore. 115 S Willow St, Suite 102 99611. **Hours:** 7 am-4 pm. Closed major holidays. **Reservations:** accepted. **Features:** Tucked in the back of a bookstore, the restaurant is one of the city's best-kept secrets. Healthy, hearty fare cooked by Charlotte is sure to please. The limited menu lists a choice of sandwiches, wraps, soups and often a quiche of the day. Guests might linger over dessert, then browse the bookstore. Casual dress. **Parking:** on-site. **Cards:** AX, MC, VI.

STERLING pop. 4,705

—————— WHERE TO STAY ——————

RED FISH LODGE

Phone: 907/260-3537

Cabin

Property failed to provide current rates

Location: Sterling Hwy (SR 1) at MM 81/Anna St, just s, then just w, follow signs. MM 81 99672 (11941 Avion St, ANCHORAGE, 99516). **Facility:** Smoke free premises. 15 cabins. 1 story, exterior corridors. *Bath:* shower only. **Parking:** on-site. **Terms:** open 5/1-9/15. **Leisure Activities:** hiking trails. *Fee:* charter fishing. **Guest Services:** coin laundry.

—————— WHERE TO DINE ——————

SUZIE'S PLACE

Lunch: $7-$9   **Dinner:** $9-$14   **Phone:** 907/260-5751

American

Location: Milepost 83, Sterling Hwy (SR 1). Milepost 82.7, Sterling Hwy 99672. **Hours:** 11:30 am-9 pm, Sat & Sun from 8 am. Closed: 12/25. **Reservations:** not accepted. **Features:** Ask anyone in Sterling for a great, inexpensive place to eat, and this eatery will be mentioned again and again. This diner-style eatery is conveniently located on the highway, so whether you're passing through town or staying a few days, you can stop and enjoy huge burgers, fish and chips, sandwiches and salads. Breakfast is available on weekends, and the service is prompt and attentive. Casual dress; beer & wine only. **Parking:** on-site. **Cards:** AX, MC, VI.

TALKEETNA pop. 772

—————— WHERE TO STAY ——————

TALKEETNA ALASKAN LODGE

Phone: (907)733-9500

AAA [SAVE]

6/1-8/31	1P: $249-$539	2P: $249-$539	XP: $15	F11
5/15-5/31 & 9/1-9/18	1P: $149-$329	2P: $149-$329	XP: $15	F11

Small-scale Hotel

Location: 3.5 mi s of Talkeetna. Mile 12.5 Talkeetna Spur Rd 99676 (2525 C St, Suite 405, ANCHORAGE, 99503). Fax: 907/733-9545. **Facility:** Smoke free premises. 200 units. 198 one-bedroom standard units, some with whirlpools. 2 one-bedroom suites ($229-$539) with whirlpools. 3 stories, interior/exterior corridors. *Bath:* combo or shower only. **Parking:** on-site, winter plug-ins. **Terms:** open 5/15-9/18, 15 day cancellation notice-fee imposed, [AP] meal plan available, package plans. **Amenities:** voice mail, hair dryers. **Dining:** 2 restaurants, 6 am-midnight, cocktails. **Leisure Activities:** outdoor viewing deck, hiking trails. **Guest Services:** gift shop, airport transportation-Talkeetna Airport, area transportation-train depot. **Business Services:** meeting rooms. **Cards:** AX, DS, MC, VI. **Special Amenities:** free local telephone calls. *(See color ad p 705)*

SOME UNITS

——— **WHERE TO DINE** ———

CAFE' MICHELE   **Lunch:** $9-$17   **Dinner:** $11-$27   **Phone:** 907/733-5300
▼▼ ▼▼   **Location:** Milepost 13.5 (Talkeetna Spur Rd) and Second St. 13.75 Talkeetna Spur Rd 99676. **Hours:** Open 5/1-10/1;
                11 am-4 & 5:30-10 pm. **Reservations:** accepted. **Features:** A meal at Michele's is a must when traveling to
Regional American Talkeetna. The atmosphere is casual and fitting for this "Northern Exposure" town. You may have a difficult
                time choosing between the yummy fresh Alaskan seafood on pasta and the king crab legs served with the
freshest vegetables this side of Anchorage! Your basket of freshly baked bread will be refilled often, but save room for one of
the homemade desserts, such as the delicious and light chocolate ricotta cheesecake. Casual dress; beer & wine only.
Parking: on-site. **Cards:** MC, VI.   ⓀⒸ ☒

TALKEETNA ROADHOUSE   **Lunch:** $4-$9   **Dinner:** $7-$12   **Phone:** 907/733-1351
▼▼   **Location:** Downtown; in historic district. **Hours:** 6:30 am-3 & 5-9 pm; Sat & Sun 8 am-2 pm in winter. Closed
                major holidays. **Reservations:** not accepted. **Features:** The food is simple and the decor basic, but the
Coffee/Espresso atmosphere and desserts are unforgettable. A city stop is not complete without a stop to the historic
                roadhouse. The dessert case is stocked with fresh, homemade goodies, ranging from huge hiker cookies to
pies to the ultimate cinnamon bun. Guests seat themselves as they walk in the door and are entertained by the banter of the
staff. Casual dress; beer & wine only. **Parking:** on-site. **Cards:** MC, VI. **Historic**   ⓀⒸ ☒

TOK pop. 1,393

——— **WHERE TO STAY** ———

CLEFT OF THE ROCK BED & BREAKFAST   **Phone:** (907)883-4219
ⒶⒶⒶ [SAVE]   5/2-9/30 [BP]   1P: $80-$130   2P: $85-$135   XP: $15   F12
                10/1-2/28 [BP]   1P: $65-$85   2P: $70-$90   XP: $20   F12
▼▼ ▼▼   3/1-5/1 [BP]   1P: $60-$80   2P: $65-$85   XP: $15   F12
                Location: Jct SR 1 and 2 (Alaskan Hwy), 3 mi w on SR 2 (Alaskan Hwy) to Sundog Tr, then 0.5 mi n. MM 0.5 Sundog
Cabin   Tr 99780 (PO Box 122). **Facility:** Smoke free premises. 8 units. 3 one-bedroom standard
units, some with whirlpools. 5 cabins ($105-$135). 2 stories (no elevator), interior/exterior corridors. *Bath:*
some shared or private, combo or shower only. **Parking:** on-site, winter plug-ins. **Terms:** check-in 5 pm, 3 day cancellation
notice-fee imposed, pets ($25 deposit, $5 extra charge, owner's pet on premises). **Amenities:** video library. **Leisure
Activities:** rental canoes, cross country skiing, play area, hiking trails, basketball. *Fee:* bicycles. **Business Services:** business
center. **Cards:** AX, DS, JC, MC.   SOME UNITS
                                    🛏 ☒ ☒ Ⓚ [VCR] 🖥 🖨 / 🖨 ☎ 🖨 /
                                    FEE

WESTMARK INN TOK   *Book at aaa.com*   **Phone:** (907)883-5174
ⒶⒶⒶ [SAVE]   5/20-9/13   1P: $129   2P: $129   XP: $15   F12
▼▼ ▼▼   **Location:** On SR 1; jct SR 2 (Alaskan Hwy). Jct Alaska Hwy & Glenn Hwy 99780 (PO Box 130). **Fax:** 907/883-5178.
                Facility: 93 one-bedroom standard units. 2 stories (no elevator), exterior corridors. **Parking:** on-site.
Motel   **Terms:** open 5/20-9/13, cancellation fee imposed, package plans, small pets only (in limited units).
Amenities: voice mail, irons, hair dryers. **Dining:** 5:30-9 am & 5-9:30 pm, cocktails. **Guest Services:** gift
shop, coin laundry. **Business Services:** PC. **Cards:** AX, DC, DS, MC, VI.   SOME UNITS
                                    🛏 🍴 Ⓨ Ⓚ 🐾 [DATA PORT] 🖨 / ☒ /

——— **WHERE TO DINE** ———

FAST EDDY'S RESTAURANT   **Lunch:** $6-$12   **Dinner:** $6-$28   **Phone:** 907/883-4411
▼▼ ▼▼   **Location:** Jct SR 1 and 2 (Alaskan Hwy) , 1 mi e on SR 2 (Alaska Hwy). 1313 Alaska Hwy 99780. **Hours:** 6 am-11
                pm; to 10 pm in winter. Closed: 1/1, 11/24, 12/25. **Features:** Decorated in contemporary appointments, the
American   comfortable, family-oriented restaurant specializes in hoagies, steaks, halibut and handmade pizzas. The
                key word is "fast"—meals are served with remarkable speed. Also on the diverse menu are gourmet
burgers, sandwiches and pasta. Casual dress; beer & wine only. **Parking:** on-site. **Cards:** AX, DS, MC, VI. ⓀⒸ ☒

GATEWAY SALMON BAKE   **Lunch:** $7-$10   **Dinner:** $12-$19   **Phone:** 907/883-5555
▼▼ ▼▼   **Location:** Jct SR 1 and 2 (Alaska Hwy), 1 mi e on SR 2 (Alaska Hwy). Mile 1313.1 Alaska Hwy 99780. **Hours:** Open
                5/15-9/1; 11 am-9 pm, Sun from 2 pm. **Features:** A trip to Tok would not be complete without a stop at
American   Gateway Salmon Bake, an Alaskan treat. Guests order a choice of reindeer, buffalo, salmon or halibut at the
                office, then unwind on the outdoor patio or in the cabin while their selection is being barbecued. Seafood
chowder and a salad bar round out the meal. The restaurant offers great value for the dollar. **Parking:** on-site. **Cards:** AX, DS,
MC, VI.   ⓀⒸ ☒

TRAPPER CREEK pop. 423

——— **WHERE TO STAY** ———

GATE CREEK CABINS   **Phone:** (907)733-1393
▼▼ ▼▼   6/1-9/15   2P: $125   XP: $45   F6
                3/1-5/31 & 9/16-2/28   2P: $90   XP: $45   F6
Cottage   **Location:** From MM 114 (Parks Hwy), 10.5 mi w at Petersville Rd. Mile 10.5 Petersville Rd 99683 (PO Box 13390).
                Fax: 907/733-1393. **Facility:** Smoke free premises. 8 cottages. 2 stories (no elevator), exterior corridors.
Bath: combo or shower only. **Parking:** on-site, winter plug-ins. **Terms:** check-in 4 pm, 2 night minimum stay - seasonal and/or
weekends, 7 day cancellation notice, weekly rates available, pets ($10 fee, in selected cottages). **Amenities:** video library (fee).
Leisure Activities: sauna, canoeing, paddleboats, bicycles, playground. *Fee:* snowmobiling. **Cards:** AX, MC, VI.
                            [ASK] 🛏 ☒ ☒ Ⓚ [VCR] 🐾 ☎ 🖨 🖨
                                 FEE

VALDEZ pop. 4,036

——— WHERE TO STAY ———

ASPEN HOTEL   *Book at aaa.com*   **Phone: (907)835-4445**

♦♦♦ ♦♦♦

5/16-9/15 [ECP]	1P: $159-$189	2P: $159-$189	XP: $10	F18
5/1-5/15 [ECP]	1P: $119-$149	2P: $119-$149	XP: $10	F18
3/1-4/30 & 9/16-2/28 [ECP]	1P: $109-$139	2P: $109-$139	XP: $10	F18

Small-scale Hotel   **Location:** Richardson Hwy to Egan Dr; center. 100 Meals Ave 99686. Fax: 907/835-2437. **Facility:** 103 units. 96 one- and 2 two-bedroom standard units, some with whirlpools. 5 one-bedroom suites with efficiencies. 3 stories (no elevator), interior corridors. *Bath:* combo or shower only. **Parking:** on-site. **Terms:** cancellation fee imposed. **Amenities:** video library (fee), voice mail, irons, hair dryers. *Some:* video games. **Pool(s):** small heated indoor. **Leisure Activities:** whirlpool, limited exercise equipment. **Guest Services:** coin laundry. **Business Services:** meeting rooms, PC. **Cards:** AX, DC, DS, MC, VI.

SOME UNITS

(ASK) (S/D) (†¶→) (∅) (⚲) (X) (VCR) (✈) (DATA PORT) (🛏) (🖼) (☕) / (✕) /

BEST WESTERN VALDEZ HARBOR INN   *Book at aaa.com*   **Phone: (907)835-3434**

(AAA) (SAVE)
♦♦♦ ♦♦♦

5/16-9/15	1P: $129-$139	2P: $139-$179	XP: $15	F12
3/1-5/15 & 9/16-2/28	1P: $79-$89	2P: $89-$99	XP: $15	F12

Location: Just s at Meals Dr. 100 Harbor Dr 99686 (PO Box 468). Fax: 907/835-2308. **Facility:** 88 one-bedroom standard units. 2 stories (no elevator), interior corridors. *Bath:* combo or shower only. **Parking:** on-site.
Small-scale Hotel   **Terms:** pets ($25 fee, $50 deposit). **Amenities:** video library (fee), DVD players, voice mail, irons, hair dryers. *Some:* high-speed Internet. **Dining:** Alaska's Bistro, see separate listing. **Leisure Activities:** exercise room. *Fee:* massage. **Guest Services:** coin laundry, area transportation-ferry. **Business Services:** meeting rooms. **Cards:** AX, DC, DS, MC, VI. **Special Amenities:** free local telephone calls and free room upgrade (subject to availability with advance reservations).

SOME UNITS

(S/D) (FEE) (🐾) (⌨) (†¶) (♿) (X) (✈) (DATA PORT) (🛏) (🖼) (☕) / (✕) /

——— WHERE TO DINE ———

ALASKA'S BISTRO   **Lunch:** $9-$20   **Dinner:** $14-$28   **Phone:** 907/835-5688

(AAA)
♦♦ ♦♦
Italian

Location: Just s at Meals Dr; in Best Western Valdez Harbor Inn. 100 Harbor Dr 99686. **Hours:** 7-10 am, 11-2 & 5-9 pm; 7 am-10, noon-2 & 5-11 pm 6/10-9/10. **Closed:** 12/25. **Reservations:** suggested. **Features:** The nice restaurant offers fine service, a casually upscale atmosphere and a menu that centers on local seafood prepared with Italian influences. Casual dress; cocktails. **Parking:** on-site. **Cards:** AX, MC, VI.

(Y) (X) (✕)

MIKE'S PALACE RISTORANTE   **Lunch:** $6-$8   **Dinner:** $10-$20   **Phone:** 907/835-2365

♦♦ ♦♦
Italian

Location: On the harbor. 201 N Harbor Dr 99686. **Hours:** 11 am-11 pm. **Closed:** 11/24. **Features:** This eatery offers a menu of Italian, Greek and Mexican selections, as well as some sandwiches, steaks and seafood. Dining is casual and the service informal. Casual dress; beer & wine only. **Parking:** street. **Cards:** DS, MC, VI.

(X) (✕)

WASILLA pop. 5,469

——— WHERE TO STAY ———

AGATE INN   *Book at aaa.com*   **Phone: (907)373-2290**

♦♦♦ ♦♦♦
Condominium

All Year [CP]	1P: $99-$125	2P: $99-$125

Location: 2.7 mi e of George Parks Hwy (SR 3) on Palmer-Wasilla Hwy, just s on Begich, then just e. 4725 Begich Cir 99654. **Facility:** Smoke free premises. 9 units. 4 one-bedroom standard units, some with whirlpools. 3 two- and 1 three-bedroom suites ($145-$225) with kitchens. 1 cottage with whirlpool. 2 stories (no elevator), interior corridors. *Bath:* combo or shower only. **Parking:** on-site, winter plug-ins. **Terms:** check-in 5 pm, 14 day cancellation notice-fee imposed. **Amenities:** video library, high-speed Internet (fee), voice mail, hair dryers. *Some:* irons. **Leisure Activities:** horseshoes. **Guest Services:** coin laundry. **Business Services:** meeting rooms, PC (fee). **Cards:** AX, DS, MC, VI.

SOME UNITS

(ASK) (X) (X) (✈) (DATA PORT) / (VCR) (🛏) (🖼) (☕) /

BEST WESTERN LAKE LUCILLE INN   *Book at aaa.com*   **Phone: (907)373-1776**

(AAA) (SAVE)
♦♦♦ ♦♦♦

5/16-9/15	1P: $134-$209	2P: $152-$219	XP: $10	F12
3/1-5/15 & 9/16-2/28	1P: $79-$109	2P: $89-$119	XP: $10	F12

Location: George Parks Hwy (SR 3), just w on Hallea Ln; center. 1300 W Lake Lucille Dr 99654. Fax: 907/376-6199. **Facility:** 54 units. 50 one-bedroom standard units. 4 one-bedroom suites ($145-$209) with whirlpools. 2 stories (no elevator), interior corridors. **Parking:** on-site. **Terms:** pets ($10 extra charge, in smoking units).
Small-scale Hotel   **Amenities:** high-speed Internet, voice mail, irons, hair dryers. **Dining:** 11 am-3:30 & 4-10 pm; seasonal hours may vary, cocktails. **Leisure Activities:** sauna, whirlpool, fishing, hiking trails, exercise room. *Fee:* boat dock. **Guest Services:** coin laundry. **Business Services:** meeting rooms. **Cards:** AX, CB, DC, DS, JC, MC, VI. **Special Amenities:** free continental breakfast and free newspaper. *(See color ad p 295)*

SOME UNITS

(S/D) (FEE) (⌨) (†¶) (Y) (∅) (X) (X) (DATA PORT) (☕) / (✕) (VCR) (FEE) (🛏)

GRANDVIEW INN & SUITES   **Phone:** 907/357-7666

(fyi)
Small-scale Hotel

6/1-9/6	1P: $140	2P: $160	XP: $10	F16
3/1-5/31 & 9/7-2/28	1P: $70	2P: $80	XP: $10	F16

Too new to rate. **Location:** 1 mi n of jct Parks Hwy and Fairview Loop exit. 2900 E Parks Hwy 99654. Fax: 907/357-6776. **Amenities:** 79 units, pets, restaurant, coffeemakers, microwaves, refrigerators, pool. **Cards:** AX, DC, MC, VI.

PIONEER RIDGE B & B INN

Phone: (907)376-7472

5/15-9/15   1P: $79-$155   2P: $79-$155   XP: $10   F12

Location: Jct George Parks Hwy (SR 3), 1.5 mi s on Fairview Loop Rd, follow signs onto Lin-Lu Rd and onto Yukon. 2221 Yukon Cir 99654 (HC 31, Box 50 83K). Fax: 907/376-7470. **Facility:** Smoke free premises. 7 units. 5 one-bedroom standard units. 1 one-bedroom suite with kitchen. 1 cabin. 1 story, interior corridors. *Bath:* combo or shower only. **Parking:** on-site, winter plug-ins. **Terms:** open 5/15-9/15, check-in 4 pm, 7 day cancellation notice-fee imposed, weekly rates available, pets ($10 fee, with prior approval). **Leisure Activities:** sauna, limited exercise equipment, game room. **Guest Services:** TV in common area. **Business Services:** PC, fax. **Cards:** AX, DS, MC, VI.

Bed & Breakfast

SOME UNITS

FEE

WILLOW pop. 201

——— WHERE TO STAY ———

ALASKAN HOST BED & BREAKFAST

Phone: (907)495-6800

All Year [BP]   1P: $70-$75   2P: $90-$115   XP: $15   F8

Location: Parks Hwy, Milepost 66, 1 mi e at Old Parks Hwy. Milepost 66.5 Old Parks Hwy 99688 (PO Box 38). Fax: 907/495-6802. **Facility:** Smoke free premises. 4 one-bedroom standard units, some with whirlpools. 3 stories (no elevator), interior/exterior corridors. *Bath:* combo or shower only. **Parking:** on-site. **Terms:** 14 day cancellation notice, small pets only. **Leisure Activities:** canoeing, paddleboats, fishing, bicycles, hiking trails. **Business Services:** PC. **Cards:** MC, VI.

Bed & Breakfast

SOME UNITS

Offices

Cities with main offices are listed in **BOLD TYPE** and toll-free member service numbers in *ITALIC TYPE*.
All are closed Saturdays, Sundays and holidays unless otherwise indicated.

The type of service provided is designated below the name of the city where the office is located:

✛ Auto travel services, including books/maps, marked maps and on-demand Triptik maps

● Auto travel services, including books/maps, marked maps, but no on-demand Triptik maps

■ Provides books/maps only. No marked maps or on-demand Triptik maps available

▲ Travel agency services

NATIONAL OFFICE: 1000 AAA DRIVE, HEATHROW, FLORIDA 32746-5063, (407) 444-7000

ALASKA

ANCHORAGE—AAA MOUNTAINWEST, 9191 OLD SEWARD HWY #20, 99515. MON-FRI 8:30-5:30. (907) 344-4310, *(800) 391-4222.*✛▲

FAIRBANKS—AAA MOUNTAINWEST, 3409 AIRPORT WAY, 99709. MON-FRI 8:30-5:30. (907) 479-4442.●▲

PROVINCE OF ALBERTA

CALGARY—ALBERTA MOTOR ASSOCIATION, #100 530 8TH AVE SW, T2P 3S8. MON-FRI 8-5. (403) 262-2345, *(800) 642-3810.*●▲

CALGARY—ALBERTA MOTOR ASSOCIATION, 3650 20 AVE NE, T1Y 6E8. MON-FRI 9-5, SAT 9-5. (403) 590-0001, *(800) 642-3810.*●▲

CALGARY—ALBERTA MOTOR ASSOCIATION, 10816 MACLEOD TRAIL SE, T2J 5N8. MON-FRI 9-5, SAT 9-5. (403) 278-3530, *(800) 642-3810.*●▲

CALGARY—ALBERTA MOTOR ASSOCIATION, 220 CROWFOOT CRES NW, T3G 3N5. MON-FRI 9-5, SAT 9-5. (403) 239-6644, *(800) 642-3810.*●▲

CALGARY—ALBERTA MOTOR ASSOCIATION, #600 85 SHAWVILLE BLVD SE, T2Y 3W5. MON-FRI 9-5, SAT 9-5. (403) 254-2447.●▲

CALGARY—ALBERTA MOTOR ASSOCIATION, 4700 17TH AVE SW, T3E 0E3. MON-FRI 9-5, SAT 9-5. (403) 240-5300, *(800) 642-3810.*✛▲

CAMROSE—ALBERTA MOTOR ASSOCIATION, 6702 48 AVE, T4V 4S3. MON-FRI 9-5, SAT 10-3. (780) 672-3391, *(800) 642-3810.*●▲

EDMONTON—**ALBERTA MOTOR ASSOCIATION,** 10310 GA MCDONALD AVE, T6J 6R7. MON-FRI 9-5:30, SAT 9-5. (780) 430-5555, *(800) 642-3810.*●▲

EDMONTON—ALBERTA MOTOR ASSOCIATION, 9780 170 ST, T5T 5L9. MON-FRI 9:30-5:30, SAT 9-5. (780) 484-1221, *(800) 642-3810.*●▲

EDMONTON—ALBERTA MOTOR ASSOCIATION, 5040 MANNING DR NW, T5A 5B4. MON-FRI 9-5, SAT 9-5. (780) 473-3112, *(800) 642-3810.*●▲

EDMONTON—ALBERTA MOTOR ASSOCIATION, 11220 109 ST, T5G 2T6. MON-FRI 9-5, SAT 9-5. (780) 474-8601, *(800) 642-3810.*✛▲

FORT MCMURRAY—ALBERTA MOTOR ASSOCIATION, #4 HOSPITAL ST, T9H 5E4. MON-FRI 9-5, SAT 9-5. (780) 743-2433, *(800) 642-3810.*●▲

GRANDE PRAIRIE—ALBERTA MOTOR ASSOCIATION, 11401 99 ST, T8V 2H6. MON-FRI 8-5, SAT 9-2. (780) 532-3819, *(800) 642-3810.*●▲

LETHBRIDGE—ALBERTA MOTOR ASSOCIATION, 120 SCENIC DR S, T1J 4R4. MON-FRI 8:30-5, THU 8:30-7, SAT 9-12:30. (403) 328-1181, *(800) 642-3810.*●▲

MEDICINE HAT—ALBERTA MOTOR ASSOCIATION, 2710 13 AVE SE, T1A 3P8. MON-FRI 9-5, SAT 9-12:30. (403) 527-1166, *(800) 642-3810.*●▲

RED DEER—ALBERTA MOTOR ASSOCIATION, 2965 BREMNER AVE, T4R 1S2. MON-FRI 9-5, SAT 9-12:30. (403) 342-6633, *(800) 642-3810.*●▲

PROVINCE OF BRITISH COLUMBIA

ABBOTSFORD—CAA BRITISH COLUMBIA, 33310 S FRASER WAY, V2S 2B4. MON-FRI 9-5:30, SAT 9-5. (604) 855-0530, *(800) 663-1956.*●▲

BURNABY—**CAA BRITISH COLUMBIA,** 4567 CANADA WAY, V5G 4T1. MON-FRI 9-5:30, SAT 9-5. (604) 268-5000, *(800) 663-1956.*✛▲

CHILLIWACK—CAA BRITISH COLUMBIA, #190-45428 LUCKAKUCK WAY, V2R 3S9. MON-FRI 9-5:30, SAT 9-5. (604) 858-2222, *(800) 663-1956.*●▲

COQUITLAM—CAA BRITISH COLUMBIA, 50-2773 BARNET HWY, V3B 1C2. MON-FRI 9-6, SAT 9-5. (604) 268-5750, *(800) 663-1956.*●▲

COURTENAY—CAA BRITISH COLUMBIA, 17-1599 CLIFFE AVE, V9N 2K6. MON-FRI 9-5:30, SAT 9-5. (250) 338-5313.●▲

DELTA—CAA BRITISH COLUMBIA, SCOTT 72 CTR 7343-120 ST, V4C 6P5. MON-FRI 9-6, THU 9-8, SAT 9-5. (604) 268-5900, *(800) 663-1956.*●▲

KAMLOOPS—CAA BRITISH COLUMBIA, 400-500 NOTRE DAME DR, V2C 6T6. MON-FRI 9-6, SAT 9-5. (250) 372-9577, *(800) 663-1956.*●▲

KELOWNA—CAA BRITISH COLUMBIA, #18-1470 HARVEY AVE, V1Y 9K8. MON-FRI 9-6, SAT 9-5. (250) 861-4554, *(800) 663-1956.*●▲

LANGLEY—CAA BRITISH COLUMBIA, 10 - 20190 LANGLEY BYPASS, V3A 9J9. MON-FRI 9-6, THU 9-8, SAT 9-5. (604) 268-5950, *(800) 663-1956.*●▲

NANAIMO—CAA BRITISH COLUMBIA, METRAL PL 6581 AULDS RD, V9T 6J6. MON-FRI 9-6, SAT 9-5. (250) 390-3533, *(800) 663-1956.*●▲

NELSON—CAA BRITISH COLUMBIA, 596 BAKER ST, V1L 4H9. MON-FRI 9-5, SAT 9-5. (250) 352-3535, *(800) 663-1956.*●▲

NEW WESTMINSTER—CAA BRITISH COLUMBIA, 501 6TH ST, V3L 3B9. MON-FRI 9-5:30, SAT 9-5. (604) 268-5700, *(800) 663-1956.*●▲

NORTH VANCOUVER—CAA BRITISH COLUMBIA, 333 BROOKSBANK AVE, V7J 3S8. MON-FRI 9-6, SAT 9-5, SUN 10-5. (604) 990-1546, *(800) 663-1956.*●▲

PENTICTON—CAA BRITISH COLUMBIA, 100-2100 MAIN ST, V2A 5H7. MON-FRI 9-5:30, SAT 9-5. (250) 492-7016, *(800) 663-1956.*●▲

PRINCE GEORGE—CAA BRITISH COLUMBIA, 492 VICTORIA ST, V2L 2J7. MON-FRI 9-5, SAT 9-5. (250) 563-0417, *(800) 663-1956.*●▲

RICHMOND—CAA BRITISH COLUMBIA, 180-5951 NO 3 RD, V6X 2E3. MON-FRI 9-5:30, SAT 9-5. (604) 268-5850, *(800) 663-1956.*●▲

SURREY—CAA BRITISH COLUMBIA, #C4-15285 101 AVE, V3R 9V8. MON-FRI 9-6, SAT 9-5. (604) 205-1000, *(800) 663-1956.*●▲

VANCOUVER—CAA BRITISH COLUMBIA, 2347 W 41ST AVE, V6M 2A3. MON-FRI 9-5:30, SAT 9-5. (604) 268-5800, *(800) 663-1956.*●▲

VANCOUVER—CAA BRITISH COLUMBIA, 999 W BROADWAY, V5Z 1K5. MON-FRI 9-5:30, SAT 9-5. (604) 268-5600, *(800) 663-1956.*●▲

VERNON—CAA BRITISH COLUMBIA, 4400 32ND ST #520, V1T 9H2. MON-FRI 9-6, SAT 9-5. (250) 542-1022, *(800) 663-1956.*●▲

VICTORIA—CAA BRITISH COLUMBIA, 1075 PANDORA AVE, V8V 3P7. MON-FRI 9-5, SAT 9-5. (250) 389-6700, *(800) 663-1956.*●▲

VICTORIA—CAA BRITISH COLUMBIA, #120-777 ROYAL OAK DR, V8X 4V1. MON-FRI 8:30-5:30, FRI 8:30-6:30, SAT 9-5. (250) 744-2202, *(800) 663-1956.*●▲

WEST VANCOUVER—CAA BRITISH COLUMBIA, 608 PARK ROYAL N, V7T 1H9. MON-FRI 9-6, SAT 9-5. (604) 268-5650, *(800) 663-1956.*●▲

PROVINCE OF MANITOBA

ALTONA—CAA MANITOBA, 61 2ND AVE NE, R0G 0B0, MON-FRI 9-5, SAT 9-1. (204) 324-8474.●▲

BRANDON—CAA MANITOBA, 20 - 1300 18TH ST, R7A 6X7. MON-FRI 9-5, MAY-SEP THU 9-8, SAT 10-2. (204) 571-4111, *(877) 222-1321.*+▲

WINNIPEG—CAA MANITOBA, 870 EMPRESS ST, R3C 2Z3. MON-FRI 9-6, SAT 10-4. (204) 262-6161.+▲

WINNIPEG—CAA MANITOBA, 2211 MCPHILLIPS ST UNIT C, R2V 3M5. MON-FRI 9-6, SAT 10-4. (204) 262-6223.●▲

WINNIPEG—CAA MANITOBA, 501 ST ANNES RD, R2M 3E5. MON-FRI 9-6, SAT 10-4. (204) 262-6201.●▲

PROVINCE OF SASKATCHEWAN

ESTEVAN—CAA SASKATCHEWAN, 1340-400 KING ST, S4A 2B4. MON-FRI 9-5:30, SAT 9-5:30. (306) 637-2185, *(800) 564-6222.*+▲

MOOSE JAW—CAA SASKATCHEWAN, 80 CARIBOU ST W, S6H 2J6. MON-FRI 9-5:30, SAT 9-5:30. (306) 693-5195, *(800) 564-6222.*+▲

NORTH BATTLEFORD—CAA SASKATCHEWAN, 2002-100TH ST, S9A 0X5. MON-FRI 9-5:30, SAT 9-5:30. (306) 445-9451, *(800) 564-6222.*+▲

PRINCE ALBERT—CAA SASKATCHEWAN, #29 2995 2ND AVE W, S6V 5V5. MON-FRI 9-5:30, SAT 9-5:30. (306) 764-6818, *(800) 564-6222.*+▲

REGINA—CAA SASKATCHEWAN, 200 ALBERT ST N, S4R 5E2. MON-FRI 9-5:30. (306) 791-4321, *(800) 564-6222.*+▲

REGINA—CAA SASKATCHEWAN, 2510 E QUANCE ST, S4V 2X5. MON-FRI 9-5:30, SAT 9-5:30. (306) 791-4323, *(800) 564-6222.*●▲

REGINA—CAA SASKATCHEWAN, 3806 ALBERT ST, S4S 3R2. MON-FRI 9-5:30, SAT 9-5:30. (306) 791-4322, *(800) 564-6222.*+▲

SASKATOON—CAA SASKATCHEWAN, 150 - 1ST AVE S, S7K 2L9. MON-FRI 9-5:30, SAT 9-5:30. (306) 668-3737, *(800) 564-6222.*+▲

SASKATOON—CAA SASKATCHEWAN, 3110-8TH ST E/#1 BEDFD SQ, S7H 0W2. MON-FRI 9-5:30, SAT 9-5:30. (306) 668-3770, *(800) 564-6222.*●▲

SWIFT CURRENT—CAA SASKATCHEWAN, 15 DUFFERIN ST W, S9H 5A1. MON-FRI 9-5:30, SAT 9-5:30. (306) 773-3193, *(800) 564-6222.*+▲

WEYBURN—CAA SASKATCHEWAN, 110 SOURIS AVE, S4H 2Z8. MON-FRI 9-5:30, SAT 9-5:30. (306) 842-6651, *(800) 564-6222.*+▲

YORKTON—CAA SASKATCHEWAN, 159 BROADWAY ST E, S3N 3K6. MON-FRI 9-5:30, SAT 9-5:30. (306) 783-6536, *(800) 564-6222.*+▲

Population

Canadian population figures—Statistics Canada's 2001 GeoSuite, by permission of Canadian Minister of Industry.

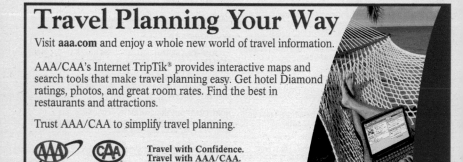

GOLDEN PASSPORTS

Golden Passports, available in three types, offer benefits and significant savings to individuals who plan to visit federal recreation sites.

The *Golden Eagle Passport*, available for a **$65** annual fee, is valid for entrance only to all federal recreation areas that have an entrance fee. Sites include those operated by the National Forest Service, National Park Service, Bureau of Land Management and the U.S. Fish and Wildlife Service. The passport admits all occupants of a private vehicle at locations where entrance is on a per vehicle basis. At locations where a per person fee is charged, the pass covers the pass holder, spouse, parents and children.

Citizens or permanent residents of the United States who are 62 and older can obtain *Golden Age Passports* for a one-time **$10** fee. Proof of age is required.

Golden Access Passports are free to citizens or permanent residents of the United States (regardless of age) who are medically blind or permanently disabled. Medical documention is required.

Both *Golden Age* and *Golden Access Passports* cover entrance fees for the holder and accompanying private party to all national parks and sites managed by the U.S. Fish and Wildlife Service, the U.S. Forest Service and the Bureau of Land Management, plus a 50% discount on federal recreation use fees. When a per person fee is imposed, the pass covers the pass holder, spouse and children. Apply in person at a federally operated area where an entrance fee is charged.

NATIONAL PARKS PASS

The *National Parks Pass*, valid for 1 year from its first use in a park, allows unlimited admissions to all U.S. national parks. The **$50** pass covers all occupants of a private vehicle at parks where the entrance fee is per vehicle. At parks with individual entry fees, the pass covers the pass holder, spouse, parents and children.

As a result of a partnership with the National Park Foundation, AAA members may purchase the pass for **$48**, either through AAA's internet site (www.aaa.com) or by visiting a participating AAA office. Members may also phone the National Park Foundation at **(888) 467-2757** or purchase the pass online at www.nationalparks.org. Non-members may purchase the pass through participating AAA offices for the full **$50** price or online at www.nationalparks.org.

For an upgrade fee of **$15**, a Golden Eagle Hologram sticker can be added to a *National Parks Pass*. The hologram covers entrance fees not just at national parks, but at any federal recreation area that has an admission fee. Valid for the duration of the *National Parks Pass* to which it is affixed, the Golden Eagle hologram is available at National Park Service, Fish and Wildlife Service and Bureau of Land Management fee stations.

Metric Equivalents Chart

TEMPERATURE

To convert Fahrenheit to Celsius, subtract 32 from the Fahrenheit temperature, multiply by 5 and divide by 9.
To convert Celsius to Fahrenheit, multipy by 9, divide by 5 and add 32.

ACRES

1 acre = 0.4 hectare (ha)	1 hectare = 2.47 acres

MILES AND KILOMETRES

Note: A kilometre is approximately 5/8 or 0.6 of a mile.
To convert kilometres to miles multiply by 0.6.

Miles/Kilometres		Kilometres/Miles	
15	24.1	30	18.6
20	32.2	35	21.7
25	40.2	40	24.8
30	48.3	45	27.9
35	56.3	50	31.0
40	64.4	55	34.1
45	72.4	60	37.2
50	80.5	65	40.3
55	88.5	70	43.4
60	96.6	75	46.6
65	104.6	80	49.7
70	112.7	85	52.8
75	120.7	90	55.9
80	128.7	95	59.0
85	136.8	100	62.1
90	144.8	105	65.2
95	152.9	110	68.3
100	160.9	115	71.4

Celsius °		Fahrenheit °
100	BOILING	212
37		100
35		95
32		90
29		85
27		80
24		75
21		70
18		65
16		60
13		55
10		50
7		45
4		40
2		35
0	FREEZING	32
-4		25
-7		20
-9		15
-12		10
-15		5
-18		0
-21		-5
-24		-10
-27		-15

LINEAR MEASURE

Customary	Metric
1 inch = 2.54 centimetres	1 centimetre = 0.4 inches
1 foot = 30 centimetres	1 metre = 3.3 feet
1 yard = 0.91 metres	1 metre = 1.09 yards
1 mile = 1.6 kilometres	1 kilometre = .62 miles

LIQUID MEASURE

Customary	Metric
1 fluid ounce = 30 millilitres	1 millilitre = .03 fluid ounces
1 cup = .24 litres	1 litre = 2.1 pints
1 pint = .47 litres	1 litre = 1.06 quarts
1 quart = .95 litres	1 litre = .26 gallons
1 gallon = 3.8 litres	

WEIGHT

If You Know:	Multiply By:	To Find:
Ounces	28.000	Grams
Pounds	0.450	Kilograms
Grams	0.035	Ounces
Kilograms	2.200	Pounds

PRESSURE

Air pressure in automobile tires is expressed in kilopascals. Multiply pound-force per square inch (psi) by 6.89 to find kilopascals (kPa).

24 psi = 165 kPa	28 psi = 193 kPa
26 psi = 179 kPa	30 psi = 207 kPa

GALLON AND LITRES

Gallons/Litres				Litres/Gallons			
5	19.0	12	45.6	10	2.6	40	10.4
6	22.8	14	53.2	15	3.9	50	13.0
7	26.6	16	60.8	20	5.2	60	15.6
8	30.4	18	68.4	25	6.5	70	18.2
9	34.2	20	76.0	30	7.8	80	20.8
10	38.0	25	95.0	35	9.1	90	23.4

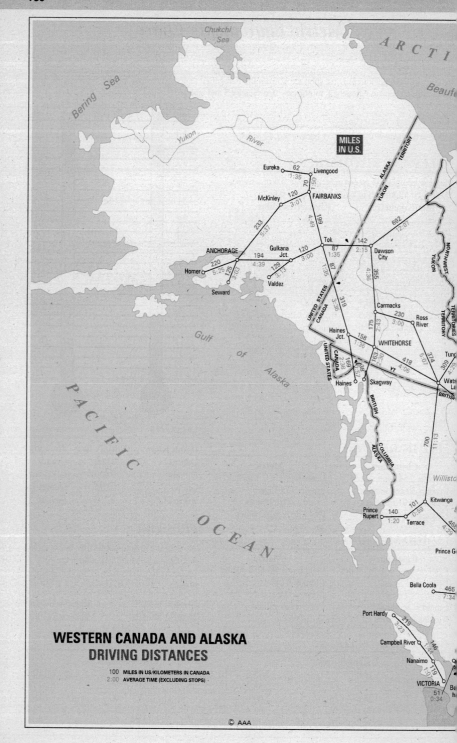

MILES
IN U.S.

Eureka — 62 — Livengood
1:35

70
1:05

McKinley — 120 — FAIRBANKS
3:01

ANCHORAGE

233
5:37

199
4:49

Tok — 142 — Dawson City
87
1:35

692
12:07

ALASKA
YUKON TERRITORY

Gulkana Jct. — 120 — 3:00

194
4:39

Homer — 220 — 6:25

129
3:13

125
3:03

Valdez

Seward

UNITED STATES
CANADA

319
3:36

87
1:35

355
4:36

Carmacks — 230 — Ross River
3:00

175
2:43

NORTHWEST
YUKON

Haines Jct. — 158 — WHITEHORSE
1:36

163

418
4:06

374
5:01

TERRITORIES

YT

269
2:38

Haines — Skagway

Wats
La

BRITISH

700
11:13

BRITISH
COLUMBIA
ALASKA

Willisto

Kitwanga

Prince Rupert — 140 — 1:20

101
0:59

Terrace

460
4:29

Prince G

Bella Coola — 465
7:34

Port Hardy

219
3:23

Campbell River

146

Nanaimo

119
1:01

VICTORIA

51
0:34

WESTERN CANADA AND ALASKA
DRIVING DISTANCES

100   MILES IN US/KILOMETERS IN CANADA
2:00 AVERAGE TIME (EXCLUDING STOPS)

© AAA

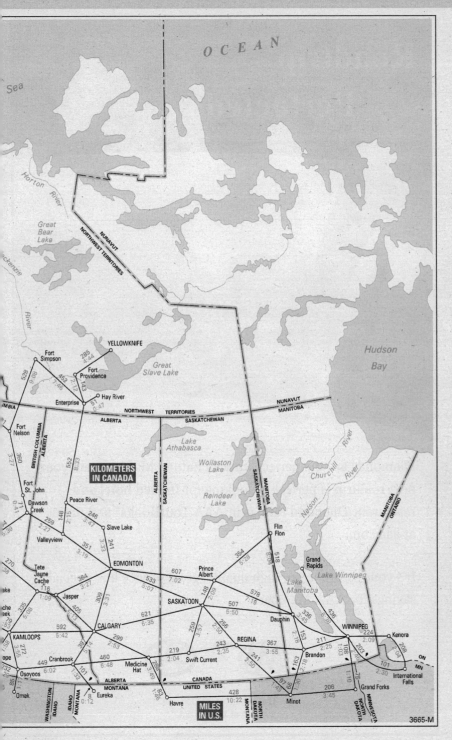

O C E A N

Sea

Great
Bear
Lake

Horton River

NORTHWEST TERRITORIES

NUNAVUT

Mackenzie

River

Hudson
Bay

YELLOWKNIFE

Fort
Simpson

285
4:44

Fort
Providence

Great
Slave Lake

452
7:46

528

2:17
143

Enterprise

Hay River

51
0:47

NUNAVUT

NORTHWEST TERRITORIES

MANITOBA

IMBIA

Fort
Nelson

ALBERTA

SASKATCHEWAN

Lake
Athabasca

Wollaston
Lake

360
3:27

552
8:33

BRITISH COLUMBIA
ALBERTA

KILOMETERS
IN CANADA

Churchill River

Reindeer
Lake

Nelson River

MANITOBA
ONTARIO

ALBERTA
SASKATCHEWAN

Fort
St. John

0:41

Dawson
Creek

Peace River

246
8:47

SASKATCHEWAN
MANITOBA

259
2:27

148
2:15

Slave Lake

Flin
Flon

Valleyview

351
3:33

241

354
6:28

518

Grand
Rapids

270

Tete
Jaune
Cache

364
3:27

607
7:02

EDMONTON

Prince
Albert

Lake
Manitoba

Lake Winnipeg

ake

116
1:09

Jasper

608

533
5:07

578
7:19

336
3:45

436

255
5:08

405

148
2:09

SASKATOON

507
5:50

Dauphin

WINNIPEG

224

Kenora

che
eek

179

592
5:42

621
6:35

259
3:57

256
2:30

153
2:18

211
2:25

208

KAMLOOPS

CALGARY

299
2:53

REGINA

367
3:55

Brandon

1:03

203
2:09

101

ON
MN

219
2:04

243
2:35

241

163

2:30

International
Falls

ope

449
6:02

Cranbrook

460
6:48

Medicine
Hat

Swift Current

87
1:45

66

206

75

Grand Forks

732

Osoyoos

ALBERTA

CANADA

101

85

Omak

WASHINGTON
IDAHO

8
0:12

Eureka

IDAHO
MONTANA

MONTANA

UNITED   STATES

428
10:22

Havre

MILES
IN U.S.

Minot

NORTH
DAKOTA

MINNESOTA

3:45

NORTH DAKOTA

3665-M

Border Information

ENTERING CANADA AND RETURNING TO THE UNITED STATES

PASSPORTS to enter Canada or return to the United States are NOT required for native-born citizens of either country. However, proof of citizenship must be carried; a certified birth certificate accompanied by a photo ID usually will suffice. Proof of residence also may be required. Naturalized citizens should carry their naturalization certificate, and U.S. resident aliens must have an Alien Registration Receipt Card (Green Card). **A passport is the best proof of citizenship and its use is strongly suggested.**

Due to concerns over child abduction, single parents, grandparents or guardians traveling abroad with a minor should be prepared to document their legal custody and provide proof of citizenship for each child. Most common carriers, such as airlines, trains and buses, will demand proof and accept only the minor's passport or the parents' passport that includes the child. When the child is with only one parent, that parent should have a notarized letter of consent from the other parent or have legal custody documents. In other cases, the minor (if traveling alone) or the individual with the minor, should have a notarized letter of consent from both parents (including a telephone number) or a custody document.

THE CANADIAN GST: A 7 percent Goods and Services Tax (GST) is levied on most items sold and most services rendered in Canada. In Nova Scotia, New Brunswick and Newfoundland, a Harmonized Sales Tax (HST) of 15 percent (7 percent GST and 8 percent provincial) is charged on most goods and services. Visitors may apply for a GST/HST rebate on many items, including short-term accommodations (less than 1 month in one location). A rebate may be claimed on a minimum of $200 of eligible purchases prior to taxes, provided the goods are exported 60 days from date of purchase. Purchased items on which the GST/HST is not refundable include alcohol, food and beverages, tobacco, transportation, entertainment, automobile fuel and such services as dry cleaning. Original receipts must be submitted; each receipt must be for $50 or more before tax.

Free brochures explaining the GST and containing a rebate form are available in Canada at participating land border Duty Free shops, Tourist Information Centers, Customs Offices and at hotels. Allow 4 to 6 weeks for processing. For more information write: Visitor Rebate Program, Summerside Tax Centre, Canada Customs and Revenue Agency, 275 Pope Rd., Suite 104, Summerside, P.E., Canada C1N 6C6; phone (902) 432-5608 outside Can., or (800) 668-4748 in Can.

CANADIAN CUSTOMS REGULATIONS

EMPLOYMENT OF VISITORS and other non-immigrants is not permitted without employment authorization, usually obtained prior to entry into Canada. Permits authorizing paid employment at a specified job for a specified period of time must be obtained from the Human Resources Canada Centre. You will be denied entry if you intend to finance your visit by seeking a paying job.

FIREARMS are regulated by classification. All firearms must be declared and registered upon entry into Canada. The fee for a Firearms Declaration is $50. Visitors who borrow a firearm must obtain in advance a Non-Resident's Sixty-Day Possession License ($30); phone (800) 731-4000. It is advised that U.S. residents register weapons with U.S. Customs before departure. Upon return, U.S. residents may be asked to show proof that they had the weapon before departure. Under certain circumstances individuals and businesses may import firearms.

Prohibited (may not enter Canada): weapons with no legitimate sporting or recreational use, including weapons that discharge bullets in rapid succession during one pull of the trigger, such as a fully automatic rifle or machine gun (regardless of conversion); and rifles or shotguns designed or adapted so the barrel is less than 470 mm (18.5 in.) long or the overall length is less than 660 mm (26 in.); handguns with a barrel length of 105 mm (4.14 in.) or less, or using 25 or 32 calibre cartridges; and any other firearm prohibited by an Order in Council.

Other prohibited items include any large capacity cartridge magazines (limited to five rounds for semiautomatic rifles or shotguns and 10 rounds for handguns); tasers; any device designed to stop the sound of a firearm; any knife with a blade that opens by spring pressure, such as a switchblade; and any other weapons declared prohibited by an Order in Council, such as mace, tear gas (if designed for use against humans), throwing stars,

When You Travel In Canada

AAA-affiliated motor clubs form the Canadian Automobile Association, with its national office at 1145 Hunt Club Rd., Suite 200, Ottawa, ON, Canada K1V 0Y3. CAA clubs provide the same services for AAA members as do the AAA clubs in the United States. Establishments displaying the Official Appointment sign have met the rigid inspection requirements of the two associations.

SEAT BELTS: The use of seat belts by vehicle drivers and all passengers is required in Canada.

RADAR DETECTORS: The possession of radar detection devices is illegal in Manitoba, New Brunswick and Yukon Territory. The use of radar detectors is illegal in Newfoundland, Northwest Territories and Nunavut, Nova Scotia, Ontario, Prince Edward Island and Québec.

INSURANCE: In the event of an accident, if proper proof is not presented, a substantial fine may be imposed. If renting a vehicle, check with the rental car company regarding insurance.

CURRENCY: All prices and admission fees quoted are in Canadian dollars. Private establishments are under no obligation to accept, convert or pay a premium on the currencies of other countries. It is to your financial advantage to use Canadian currency when traveling in Canada. The only means of obtaining the official exchange rate is to change U.S. funds at a bank or purchase travelers checks in Canadian currency. If you plan to carry cash instead of travelers checks, be aware that some Canadian banks will not accept U.S. bills in large denominations for exchange.

PROVINCIAL REGULATIONS: Check the Fast Facts page for any additional regulations imposed by individual provinces or territories.

LEGAL ISSUES: Persons with felony convictions, driving while intoxicated records or other offenses may be denied admittance into Canada. Contact the Canadian Embassy or nearest Canadian Consulate before travel.

Nunchaku sticks, belt-buckle knives, spiked wristbands, blowguns, stun guns, finger rings with blades, brass knuckles, armor-piercing handgun cartridges, explosive projectiles for small arms cartridges, shotgun cartridges containing "flechettes," a "bull pup" stock for rifles and carbines, and trigger enhancement devices.

Restricted (admitted only for approved shooting competitions at which time an Authorization to Transport is required from the provincial chief firearms officer—phone (800) 731-4000 for addresses and phone numbers) semiautomatic firearms that have a barrel less than 470 mm (18.5 in.) and that discharge center-fire ammunition; and those that can be fired when reduced to less than 660 mm (26 in.) in length. Other restricted weapons include any firearm designed, altered or intended to be aimed and fired by the action of one hand, such as pistols and revolvers; and any firearm that is declared to be a restricted firearm by an Order in Council.

Non-restricted (regular hunting rifles or shotguns): You must be at least 18 to import and they may be imported only for legitimate purposes such as hunting or use during hunting season; use in approved competitions; protection against wildlife in Canadian wilderness areas; or in-transit movement through Canada.

Hunters may bring in, duty-free, 200 rounds of ammunition; participants in a competition, 1,500 rounds. **A valid license or declaration must be shown to purchase ammunition.** If you hunt in Canada's parks or game reserves, you may have to get a hunting license from each province or territory in which you plan to hunt.

For more information about parks and hunting regulations, contact the appropriate provincial or territorial tourism information office: Alberta, (800) 661-8888 or (780) 427-4321; British Columbia, (800) 663-6000 or (250) 387-1642; Manitoba, (800) 665-0040 or (204) 945-3777; New Brunswick, (800) 561-0123 or (506) 789-4982; Newfoundland and Labrador, (800) 563-6353 or (709) 729-2830; Northwest Territories (Western NWT), (800) 661-0788 or (867) 873-7200; Nova Scotia, (800) 565-0000 or (902) 425-5781; Nunavut (Eastern NWT), (800) 491-7910 or (867) 979-6551; Ontario, (800) 668-2746 or (416) 314-0944; Prince Edward Island, (888) 734-7529 or (902) 368-4444; Québec (800) 363-7777 or (514) 873-2015; Saskatchewan (877) 237-2273 or (306) 787-2300; Yukon, (867) 667-5340.

Most provinces and territories also have their own laws regulating the transportation of firearms through their area. Contact the provincial or territorial tourism information office listed above. For further information on the entry of firearms, contact Canada Customs and Revenue Agency at (506) 636-5064, or (800) 461-9999 inside Can.

PERSONAL BAGGAGE is admissible into Canada on a temporary basis without payment of duty and taxes; however, a refundable security deposit may be required by Customs at the time of entry. Deposits normally are not required when visits are made for health or pleasure, provided all items are exported at the end of your trip.

Personal baggage that may be taken into Canada on a duty- and tax-free basis includes clothing and personal effects, sporting goods, automobiles, vessels, aircraft, snowmobiles, cameras, personal computers, food products and other items appropriate for the purpose and duration of your visit. Tobacco products are limited per person to 50 cigars, 200 cigarettes, 200 grams (7 oz.) of tobacco, and 200 tobacco sticks. Alcoholic beverages are limited to 1.14 liters (40 oz.) of liquor, *or* 1.5 liters (1.6 qts.) of wine *or* 8.5 liters (9 qts.) of beer or ale (equivalent to 24 twelve-ounce bottles/cans). Generally, a minimum stay of 24 hours is required to transport any liquor or tobacco into Canada.

All articles above allowable quantities are subject to federal duty and taxes, as well as provincial liquor fees. Provincial fees can be paid at Customs at the time of entry in all provinces and the Yukon Territory. In the Northwest Territories and Nunavut, it is illegal to bring in more alcohol than specified above. The minimum legal age for the importation of alcoholic beverages or tobacco products is 18 or 19 years, depending on the province or territory; check the Fast Facts page.

Articles purchased at Canadian duty-free shops are subject to U.S. Customs exemptions and restrictions; those purchased at U.S. duty-free shops before entering Canada are subject to duty if brought back into the United States.

Persons who may require prescription drugs while visiting Canada are permitted to bring medication for their own use. Prescription drugs should be clearly identified and should be carried in the original packaging with the label listing the drug and its intended use. It also is good to bring a copy of the prescription and the contact number of the doctor.

GIFTS, excluding tobacco, alcoholic beverages and advertising matter, taken into or mailed to Canada are allowed free entry if the value of each gift does not exceed $60 (Canadian currency).

Gifts valued at more than $60 are subject to the regular duty and taxes on the excess amount.

PETS AND PLANTS: Dogs and cats 3 months of age and older must be accompanied by a certificate

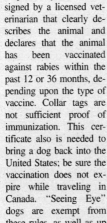

signed by a licensed veterinarian that clearly describes the animal and declares that the animal has been vaccinated against rabies within the past 12 or 36 months, depending upon the type of vaccine. Collar tags are not sufficient proof of immunization. This certificate also is needed to bring a dog back into the United States; be sure the vaccination does not expire while traveling in Canada. "Seeing Eye" dogs are exempt from these rules, as well as up to two healthy puppies and kittens under 3 months old; it is recommended that the owner obtain a certificate of health from a veterinarian indicating that an animal is too young to vaccinate. Puppies under 4 months will not be admitted into the U.S. before 30 days after their rabies vaccination.

Plants or plant material must be declared. For additional information about pets and plants, contact one of the following Canadian Food Inspection Agency (CFIA) Import Service Centres: eastern Canada (877) 493-0468; central Canada (800) 835-4486; or western Canada (888) 732-6222.

RADIO COMMUNICATION EQUIPMENT: You may bring your cellular or PCS phone or citizens band (CB) or Family Radio Service (FRS) radio into Canada without any prior registration. You may use your aircraft, marine or amateur radio in Canada without prior authorization. All other types of radio transmitting stations may only be used in Canada if accompanied by a letter of authorization from Industry Canada's Radiocommunication and Broadcasting Regulatory Branch. For additional information contact Industry Canada at (613) 990-4737.

SPECIAL PERMITS: A CITIES (Convention on International Trade in Endangered Species) permit is required for any endangered species brought into Canada, including those kept as pets and for any items made from them, such as coats, handbags or shoes. For further information contact Environment Canada, Canadian Wildlife Service; phone (819) 997-1840.

Canada has restrictions to keep objects that are of historical, cultural or scientific signification inside Canada. If you wish to take objects more than 50 years old, such as fossils, archeological artifacts,

National Park Entrance Fees

At Canada's national parks, the basic per person or per family entry fee gives visitors access to the park, scenic outlooks, picnic areas and a variety of facilities. Additional fees are charged for visitors who choose to use other recreational services such as campgrounds, special interpretation programs and golf courses

To receive a free Parks Canada vacation planner, phone (888) 773-8888. Detailed information on the services, benefits, entry fees and discounts at all national parks and historic sites is available by calling the following numbers:

(800) 748-7275 for Alberta;

(902) 426-3436 for the Atlantic provinces (Newfoundland and Labrador, New Brunswick, Nova Scotia and Prince Edward Island);

(604) 513-4777 for British Columbia;

(888) 748-2928 for Manitoba;

(800) 748-7275 for Northwest Territories and Nunavut;

(800) 839-8221 for Ontario;

(800) 748-7275 for Saskatchewan;

(800) 463-6769 for Québec;

(800) 661-0486 for Yukon Territory.

fine and decorative art, technological objects or books and archival material, out of the country, you may need an export permit to do so. Contact the Moveable Cultural Property Program of Canadian Heritage, 15 Eddy St., 3rd floor, Hull, Québec, Canada K1A 0M5; phone (819) 997-7761.

Importation of clothing, textiles, steel and certain agricultural products in excess of minimum quantities may be subject to import permit requirements under the Export and Import Permits Act. For further information, write the Department of Foreign Affairs and International Trade, Export and Import Control Bureau, P.O. Box 481, Station A, Ottawa, ON Canada K1N 9K6. Goods originating in Iraq are not admissible.

VEHICLES, including trailers not exceeding 2.6 metres (8 ft., 6 in.) in width, entering Canada for touring are generally subject to quick and routine entry procedures. You may not leave or store a car, trailer or other goods in Canada while you leave the country without either paying import duty and taxes or presenting the necessary permit to leave the items in Canada. This and any other required permits are issued by Canadian Customs officials at the point of entry. Vacation trailers may not be stored in Canada during the off-season.

Vehicle registration cards are necessary for Canadian travel. If you are driving a car other than your own, you must get written permission from the owner for use of the car in Canada. A copy of the contract is required for rented cars. A valid U.S. driver's license is valid in Canada for varying periods of time as ruled by the individual provinces and territories.

Some provinces and territories have made it a statutory requirement that motorists drive with vehicle headlights on for extended periods after dawn and before dusk. In Alberta, British Columbia, New Brunswick and Prince Edward Island lights must be turned on when light conditions restrict visibility to 150 metres (500 ft.); in Manitoba, the restriction is 60 metres (200 ft.). Headlights must remain on at all times in the Yukon Territory and Northwest Territories and Nunavut.

In cases of accident involving death, injury or property damage, the Canadian provinces and territories require evidence of financial responsibility. In some provinces, you may be asked to show this evidence at any time. The penalties for not producing such evidence vary by province and territory and can result in costly and time-consuming problems if you are unprepared.

The minimum liability insurance requirement is $200,000 in all provinces and territories except Québec, which requires $50,000, and Northwest Territories and Nunavut, which requires $100,000. Should the courts' judgments exceed these figures, motorists held accountable are responsible for paying the full amount.

U.S. CUSTOMS REGULATIONS

EXEMPTIONS granted to returning U.S. residents include an $800 exemption, if not used within the past 30 days, for residents who have been in Canada **no less than 48 hours.** Any amount over the $800 exemption is subject to duty. The exemptions are based on fair retail value and apply to articles acquired for personal or household use or as gifts, but **not intended for sale.**

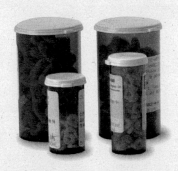

Exemptions for a family (related persons living in the same house) may be combined; thus, a family of 5 would be entitled to a duty-free $4,000 exemption on one declaration, even if the articles declared by one member of the family exceeded that individual's $800 exemption. **Sales slips should be kept; they are proof of fair retail value.** All articles for which the $800 exemption is claimed must accompany you at the time of return.

You may send *bona fide* gifts to friends and relatives in the United States free of duty and taxes provided the recipient does not receive more than $100 worth of gifts per day. Tobacco products, alcoholic beverages and perfume containing alcohol and valued at more than $5 retail are excluded from this provision. The package containing the gift must be marked "Unsolicited Gift," with the contents and retail value indicated on the outside. These gifts are not included in your $800 exemption and are not to be declared upon your return.

If you are entitled to the $800 exemption, you may include 100 cigars and 200 cigarettes duty free. Cigarettes may be subject to state or local tax. Persons 21 years of age or older may include liquor to the amount of 1 litre (33.8 fl. oz.) per person in their $800 resident's exemption from duty and tax. In all cases, state liquor laws are enforced by Customs.

If you have been in Canada for **less than 48 hours,** you may bring back merchandise valued at $200 or less, duty and tax free. Such an exemption must not include more than 10 cigars, 50 cigarettes, 150 milliliters (5 fl. oz.) of alcoholic beverage *or* 150 milliliters (5 fl. oz.) of perfume containing alcohol. If any article brought back is subject to duty or tax or if the total value of all articles exceeds $200, no article may be exempted from duty or tax. Members of a family unit may not combine the value of their purchases under this exemption. All goods must be declared.

CERTAIN ARTICLES considered injurious or detrimental to the general welfare of the United States are *prohibited* entry by law. Among these are such items as narcotics and dangerous drugs; drug paraphernalia; hazardous articles (e.g., fireworks, dangerous toys and toxic or poisonous substances), obscene articles and publications; lottery tickets; switchblade knives; seditious or treasonable matter; and merchandise originating in Afghanistan, Cuba, Iran, Iraq, Libya, Serbia and Sudan.

Prohibited also are endangered species of plants and wildlife, or products made of any part of such species. If you are considering the purchase or import of fur, animal skins other than cowhide or any product manufactured wholly or in part from wildlife, write to the U.S. Fish and Wildlife Service, Department of the Interior, Washington, DC 20240 for additional information.

RESTRICTED ITEMS often require special licenses or controls. While some agricultural products of Canadian origin (fruit, plants with phytosanitary certificates, meats, etc.) may be brought into the United States, many are restricted to prevent the introduction of plant and animal pests and diseases into the country. All must be declared to customs officials at the U.S. border. For specific information, write for the free booklet "Traveler's Tips," available in English, Spanish, Italian or Japanese from USDA-APHIS Public Affairs, 4700 River Road Unit 51, Riverdale, MD 20737, ATTN: AQI Publications.

If you require medicines containing narcotics or habit-forming drugs, including cough and headache remedies, you should have them properly identified and carry only such quantities as might normally be needed for a health problem. You should carry proof, either in prescription form or as a written statement from your physician, that the medicines are being used under a doctor's direction and are necessary for your well-being.

Other restricted items include imported automobiles; biological materials (disease organisms and vectors for research); cultural treasures; firearms and ammunition; articles bearing marks or names copying or simulating trademarked articles or trade names (e.g., watches, cameras, perfumes); pirated copies of copyrighted articles (e.g., books, CDs, DVDs, computer programs); and pets, wildlife and fish.

Additional helpful booklets such as "Visiting the U.S.: Requirements for Non-Residents," "Importing or Exporting a Car," "Know Before You Go" and "Pets, Wildlife and U.S. Customs," are available online and by writing Customs Service Center, 1300 Pennsylvania Ave. N.W., Room 3.4A, Washington, DC 20229; phone (202) 354-1000.

Choose Well.
AAA/CAA Approved.

Discover the secret to choosing well, every time ...
AAA/CAA Approved.

From simple motels to rustic ranches to luxury resorts, rest assured you've chosen well. **AAA/CAA's professional evaluators** have tested the locks and peeked under the beds, checking for qualities like cleanliness, service, and value — assigning a rating from one to five Diamonds.

Choose your Diamond rated accommodations from the TourBook® listings, in print and on aaa.com, and look for the bold red AAA/CAA logo on signage and billboards. Choose AAA/CAA Approved.

For more information on **AAA/CAA Lodging Diamond Ratings,** turn to page 16.

Show Your Card
Approved Lodging

Points of Interest Index

AIRPORTS

AMUSEMENTS & THEME PARKS

AMPHITHEATERS

ANTIQUES

AQUARIUMS

ARBORETUMS

ARCHEOLOGICAL SITES

ART GALLERIES

Index Legend

⏚ GEM: Points of Interest Offering a *Great Experience for Members*®

HISTORIC DOCUMENTS, MANUSCRIPTS & RARE BOOKS

HISTORIC SITES

INDIAN MOUNDS, REMAINS & RUINS

INDIAN PICTOGRAPHS & PETROGLYPHS

MUSIC HALLS & OPERA HOUSES

MYTHICAL PERSONS & ANIMALS

NATIONALITIES & ETHNIC AREAS

NATURAL PHENOMENA

NATURE CENTERS

NATURE TRAILS

OBSERVATORIES

PAINTINGS

PARKS, CITY; STATE; PROVINCIAL

PARKS, NATIONAL

PIERS

PLANETARIUMS

RACETRACKS-AUTO

RACETRACKS-HORSE

RAILROADS

RAILROADS-LOCOMOTIVES & CARS

RAILROADS & SKI LIFTS, CABLE; COG; INCLINE; NARROW GAUGE

RANCHES

RECREATION-SUMMER ACTIVITIES

RECREATION-WINTER ACTIVITIES

SAVE *Attraction Admission Discount Index*

Bed & Breakfast Lodgings Index

Some bed and breakfasts listed below might have historical significance. Those properties are also referenced in the Historical index. The indication that continental [CP] or full breakfast [BP] is included in the room rate reflects whether a property is a Bed-and-Breakfast facility.

Country Inns Index

Some of the following country inns can also be considered as bed-and-breakfast operations. The indication that continental [CP] or full breakfast [BP] is included in the room rate reflects whether a property is a Bed-and-Breakfast facility.

Historical Lodgings & Restaurants Index

Some of the following historical lodgings can also be considered as bed-and-breakfast operations. The indication that continental [CP] or full breakfast [BP] is included in the room rate reflects whether a property is a Bed-and-Breakfast facility.

Resorts Index

Many establishments are located in resort areas; however, the following places have extensive on-premises recreational facilities:

Comprehensive City Index

Here is an alphabetical list of all cities appearing in this TourBook® guide. Cities are presented by state/province. Page numbers under the POI column indicate where points of interest text begins. Page numbers under the L&R column indicate where lodging and restaurant listings begin.

COMPREHENSIVE CITY INDEX (CONT'D)

COMPREHENSIVE CITY INDEX (CONT'D)

COMPREHENSIVE CITY INDEX (CONT'D)

Help Towty™ get to the car and fix the flat tire

Connect The Dots
& Word Scrambler

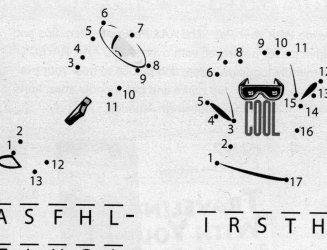

A S F H L -   I R S T H

T L H G I

L N A P E